The SAGE
Handbook of

Education for Citizenship
and Democracy

The SAGE
Handbook of

Education for Citizenship and Democracy

Edited by
James Arthur
Ian Davies
and Carole Hahn

Los Angeles • London • New Delhi • Singapore

SAGE Publications Ltd
1 Oliver's Yard
55 City Road
London EC1Y 1SP

SAGE Publications Inc.
2455 Teller Road
Thousand Oaks, California 91320

SAGE Publications India Pvt Ltd
B 1/I 1 Mohan Cooperative Industrial Area
Mathura Road
New Delhi 110 044

SAGE Publications Asia-Pacific Pte Ltd
33 Pekin Street #02-01
Far East Square
Singapore 048763

Library of Congress Control Number: 2007938260

British Library Cataloguing in Publication data

A catalogue record for this book is available from the British Library

ISBN 978-1-4129-3620-0
ISBN 978-1-4129-3621-7 (pbk)

Typeset by CEPHA Imaging Pvt. Ltd., Bangalore, India
Printed in Great Britain by The Cromwell Press, Trowbridge, Wiltshire
Printed on paper from sustainable resources

Contents

Notes on Contributors

Wolfgang Althof is the Teresa M. Fischer Professor of Citizenship Education at the University of Missouri, St. Louis. He was at the University of Fribourg, Switzerland, 1984–2004, a Visiting Scholar at Harvard University 1995–1996. Dr. Althof taught university courses and workshops in Germany, Switzerland, Austria, and the US, and lectured in many other countries. Dr. Althof's research includes studies in professional morality; democracy and education in schools; changes in individual conceptions of personal and societal values and morality in East and West Germany after the liquidation of the German Democratic Republic; intergenerational values transmission; and prevention of right-wing extremism and ethnic violence in schools. His recent focus has been on moral/character development and citizenship education.

John Annette is Professor of Citizenship and Lifelong Learning and Pro Vice Master at Birkbeck College, University of London. He has published articles on citizenship and service learning, community development and community leadership and his publications include *Education for Democratic Citizenship* co-edited with Sir Bernard Crick and Professor Andrew Lockyer published by Ashgate in December 2003. He has been an advisor to the British government on citizenship education in schools and also adult learning for citizenship through civic engagement.

James Arthur is Professor of Education at Canterbury Christ Church University and has written on the relationship between theory and practice in education, particularly the links between communitarianism, social virtues, citizenship, religion and education. He was involved as a member of the National Forum for Values in Education and the Community and has subsequently participated in various curriculum consultations with the QCA. He was a member of the History Task Group in 1999 to revise the History National Curriculum and has since been a member of a sub-group of the Citizenship Working Party as well as a member of various committees on citizenship in the Department for Education and Skills and the Teacher Development Agency. Professor Arthur is also Director of CitizED (www.citized.info).

Patricia G. Avery is a Professor in the Department of Curriculum and Instruction at the University of Minnesota in the US. She has studied political education and socialization for over 25 years, with a particular emphasis on the development of political tolerance among adolescents. Currently she is the lead evaluator for the Deliberating in a Democracy Project, a five-year study in which models for discussing controversial public issues are implemented in secondary classrooms in five post-Communist countries (Azerbaijan, Czech Republic, Estonia, Lithuania, Russia) and the US. Professor Avery teaches graduate courses in social studies education and research methodology.

James A. Banks is Kerry and Linda Killinger Professor of Diversity Studies and Director of the Center for Multicultural Education at the University of Washington, Seattle. He is a past President of both the American Educational Research Association (AERA) and the National Council for the Social Studies (NCSS). Professor Banks is a member of the National Academy of Education and was a fellow at the Center for Advanced Study in the Behavioral Sciences at Stanford during the 2005–2006 academic year. His books include *Diversity and Citizenship Education: Global Perspectives*; *Educating Citizens in a Multicultural Society*; *Teaching Strategies for Ethnic Studies; Cultural Diversity and Education: Foundations, Curriculum and Teaching; and Race, Culture, and Education*.

Keith C. Barton is a Professor in the Division of Teacher Education at the University of Cincinnati and has served as a visiting professor at the UNESCO Centre for Education in Pluralism, Human Rights and Democracy at the University of Ulster. His work focuses on the teaching and learning of history and social studies, and he has conducted several studies of students' historical understanding in the US and Northern Ireland. He is co-author, with Linda S. Levstik, of *Doing History: Investigating with Children in Elementary and Middle Schools and Teaching History for the Common Good*.

Marvin W. Berkowitz is a developmental psychologist and the Sanford N. McDonnell Professor of Character Education and co-director of the Center for Character and Citizenship at the University of Missouri-St. Louis.He is co-editor of the *Journal of Research in Character Education* and recipient of the 2006 lifetime achievement award from the Character Education Partnership.

Jane Bernard-Powers is Professor of Elementary Education at San Francisco State University.

Kathy Bickmore is Associate Professor in Curriculum Studies and Teacher Development at the Ontario Institute for Studies in Education, University of Toronto, Canada. She teaches (graduate and pre-service teacher education) and conducts research in education for constructive conflict, peace building, conflict resolution, equity, and citizenship/ democratization in public school contexts.

David Carr is Professor of Philosophy of Education at the University of Edinburgh. He is author of *Educating the Virtues* (1991), *Professionalism and Ethics in Teaching* (2000) and *Making Sense of Education* (2003), as well as of many philosophical and educational papers. He is also editor of *Education, Knowledge and Truth* (1998), co-editor (with Jan Steutel) of *Virtue Ethics and Moral Education* (1999), and (with John Haldane) of *Spirituality, Philosophy and Education* (2003).

Sir Bernard Crick is Emeritus Professor of Politics at Birkbeck College, London. He was knighted in 2001 for 'services to citizenship and political studies'. He is author of *In Defence of Politics*, and *George Orwell: a Life*, and recently *Essays on Citizenship*. He is the chair of the advisory group that reported as *The Teaching of Citizenship and Democracy in Schools* (QCA, 1998). Citizenship adviser to the Department for Education (England), 1998 to 2001 and to the Home Office 2002–2005. He is chair of the advisory group on citizenship and language learning for immigrants, reporting in 2004 as *The New and the Old*.

Ian Davies is Reader in Educational Studies at the University of York, UK. He is a deputy director of citizED (www.citized.info), the editor of the journal *Citizenship, Teaching and*

Learning and the author of books and articles about citizenship education. He has collaborated on many international projects. He is a past fellow of the Japan Society for the Promotion of Science and has been appointed by the Council of Europe as an expert on education for democratic citizenship.

Bernadette L. Dean is an Associate Professor, head academic and student affairs and team leader of the citizenship rights and responsibilities Pakistan Programme at the Aga Khan University, Institute for Educational Development, Karachi, Pakistan. She gained her PhD from the University of Alberta, Canada, in 2000. Her teaching and research interests are in education and development, social studies education, citizenship education and action research. She has taught at all educational levels, from kindergarten to graduate level and is interested in identifying ways to improve the quality of education in Pakistan. She has presented her research at many national and international conferences and has published widely in academic journals and books. In addition, she has written social studies textbooks and a teaching learning resource entitled *Creating a Better World: Education for citizenship, human rights and conflict resolution.*

Joseph Jinja Divala is a tutor in the Department of Education Policy Studies at the University of Stellenbosch, South Africa, and he previously lectured in Philosophy and Philosophy of Education at Chancellor College in the University of Malawi. His research interests are in democracy and citizenship education, education and justice, and educational autonomy. His current research is centred on higher education autonomy, with particular reference to governance arrangements of higher education systems in Africa.

Lisa Duty is a policy advisor in the areas of high school transformation and college access and success with KnowledgeWorks Foundation. Lisa helps provide leadership in the areas of policy development, state relations and legislative advocacy. Prior to KnowledgeWorks, she was a consultant at the Ohio Department of Education in the areas of middle and high school reform. She participated in exchanges and served as a citizenship education consultant in Poland, Ukraine and South Africa.

Penny Enslin is Professor of Education in the Department of Educational Studies at the University of Glasgow and Professor Emeritus at the University of the Witwatersrand, Johannesburg. She teaches philosophy of education and her research interests lie in the area of political philosophy and education. She has published widely on citizenship and democracy education, gender and the education of girls, higher education, peace education, nationalism, and liberalism.

Mark Evans is Senior Lecturer in the Department of Curriculum, Teaching and Learning at the Ontario Institute for Studies in Education, University of Toronto and has held different administrative positions (Director of the Secondary Teacher Education Program; Acting Associate Dean, Teacher Education). Mark teaches a variety of courses and has been involved in a variety of curriculum reform initiatives locally and internationally in the areas of citizenship and teacher education. He has written and contributed to numerous articles, books, and learning resources.

Elizabeth Frazer is Official Fellow and Tutor in Politics, New College, Oxford, and University Lecturer in Politics, Department of Politics and International Relations, University of Oxford.

Stephen Gorard is Professor of Education at the University of Birmingham. His research is focused on issues of equity (*Pupils' Views of Equity in Education*, 2005, Compare), especially in educational opportunities and outcomes ('Value-added is of little value', 2006, *Journal of Educational Policy*), and on the effectiveness of educational systems. Recent project topics include widening participation in learning (*Overcoming the Barriers to HE*, 2007, Trentham), the role of technology in lifelong learning (*Adult Learning in the Digital Age*, 2006, Routledge), informal learning, 14–19 provision, the role of targets, the impact of market forces on schools, underachievement, teacher supply and retention (*Teacher Supply: the Key Issues*, 2006, Continuum), and developing international indicators of inequality.

Carole L. Hahn is the Charles Howard Candler Professor of Educational Studies at Emory University in Atlanta, USA. She is a past president of the National Council for the Social Studies (NCSS) and was the US national research coordinator for the Civic Education Study of the International Association for the Evaluation of Educational Achievement. She is an Advisory Professor at the Hong Kong Institute of Education, author of the book *Becoming Political: Comparative Perspectives on Citizenship Education*, and recipient of the Jean Dresden Grambs Distinguished Career Research Award from NCSS.

Diana Hess is Associate Professor of Curriculum and Instruction at the University of Wisconsin-Madison in the US. Since 1998 she has been researching what young people learn from deliberating highly controversial political and legal issues in schools. Currently, she is the lead investigator of a five-year study that seeks to understand the relationship between various approaches to issues discussions in secondary schools and the actual political engagement of young people after they leave high school. She teaches undergraduate and graduate courses in social studies and democratic education. Professor Hess holds a PhD from the University of Washington, Seattle, WA.

Chi-Hang Ho is a Lecturer in the Department of Chinese at the Hong Kong Institute of Education, People's Republic of China.

John Huckle is an ESD consultant and visiting fellow at the University of York. He is the co-editor with Stephen Sterling of *Education for Sustainability* (Earthscan, 1996) and co-author with Adrian Martin of *Environments in a Changing World* (Prentice Hall, 2001). John has written curriculum and teacher training materials for WWF-UK; facilitated workshops for WWF-China's Environmental Education Initiative; and prepared materials on ESD for the citizED website. He has a particular interest in socially critical approaches to ESD.

Andrew S. Hughes is a university teaching professor, a title recognizing contributions to excellence in university teaching, at the University of New Brunswick, Canada. He is the author of some 75 articles and an equal number of commissioned reports. His particular interest lies in the application of evidenced based teaching to citizenship education. His recent work has involved collaboration with the Russian Association of Civic Education, culminating in the Spirit of Democracy Project.

Orit Ichilov is a professor and sociologist whose research has focused on the political socialization of young people, and on citizenship and human rights education. Ichilov was the Israeli National Representative and chief investigator in the Civic Education International Study of the IEA. She chaired the Department of Educational Sciences at Tel-Aviv University and was vice-president of the International Society of Political Psychology. Ichilov chaired a sub-committee on education advising the Ministry of Justice on the implementation in legislation of the UN Convention on the Rights of the Child. In 2007, she was Visiting Scholar at Oxford University in the UK.

Lee Jerome is the Secondary PGCE Programme Director at London Metropolitan University and has been involved in initial and continuing citizenship teacher education since 2000, at the Institute for Citizenship, where he co-authored *The Citizenship Co-ordinator's Handbook* (2003), and in H.E. posts. He has published a variety of teaching resources to support citizenship teachers and acted as consultant for a range of organisations focusing on history, identity and citizenship. He served on a government working group developing assessment guidance and is a trustee of the Association for Citizenship Teaching and School Councils UK. Lee is currently researching the implementation of citizenship education policy in schools.

Scott Jones is a social studies teacher at Hazelwood West High School (Hazelwood, MO) and a doctoral student in Educational Psychology at the Center for Character and Citizenship at the University of Missouri-St.Louis.

Kerry J. Kennedy is a professor and Dean of the Faculty of Professional and Early Childhood Education at the Hong Kong Institute of Education. He has played an active role in teacher professional associations and public policy forums and is a Fellow of the Australian College of Education and a Life Member of the Australian Curriculum Studies Association.

David Kerr is Principal Research Officer at NFER (National Foundation for Educational Research in England and Wales) and Visiting Professor in Citizenship at Birkbeck College, University of London. He is currently the Director of the eight-year Citizenship Education Longitudinal Study in England and Associate Director of the new IEA International Civic and Citizenship Education Study (ICCS). He has worked closely with the Council of Europe on its Education for Democratic Citizenship and Human Rights Education Project (EDC/HRE), carried out consultancies in Europe and internationally and published widely in the field.

Martina Klicperová-Baker is senior research scholar at the Institute of Psychology, Academy of Sciences of the Czech Republic in Prague and adjunct professor at San Diego State University in the US. Born in Prague, Czechoslovakia, she received her education in social and educational psychology from the Universita Karlova. A specialist in political psychology, she has done extensive international research in psychological preconditions for democracy, post-totalitarian syndrome, transitions to democracy, political culture and civility. She is an author and editor of a number of books including *Democratic citizenship in comparative perspective, Ready for Democracy? Civic Culture and Civility and Democratic culture in the Czech Republic.*

Wing On Lee is Professor and Vice President (Academic) at The Hong Kong Institute of Education (HKIEd) and is a world renowned scholar in the fields of comparative education, citizenship education, and moral and values education.

Linda S. Levstik is Professor in the Department of Curriculum and Instruction at the University of Kentucky. She is co-author with Keith C. Barton of *Doing History and Teaching History for the Common Good* (Erlbaum). She is also co-editor with Cynthia Tyson of *Handbook on Research in Social Education* (Routledge, Taylor and Francis). Her research on childrens' and adolescents' historical thinking in national and cross-national settings appears in a number of journals including *Theory and Research in Social Education, Teachers College Record, The American Educational Research Journal*, and *The International Review of History Education*. Professor Levstik currently works with several grants to improve history teaching in rural schools.

Katherine Madjidi is a doctoral student at the University of Outario, Canada, whose areas of interest include international development, transformative and experiential learning, and indigenous knowledge.

Bethan Marshall worked as an English teacher in London for nine years before taking up her post at King's College. Currently a senior lecturer in education she specializes in issues relating to the teaching of English and assessment. She was part of the King's Medway Formative Assessment Project (KMOFAP) team and, for two years, the director at King's of the Learning How to Learn project, funded by the Economic and Social research Council. She has written extensively on the subject of English and assessment including her book *English Teachers: An unofficial Guide and as a co-author of Assessment for Learning: Putting it into practice*.

Merry M. Merryfield is Professor of Social Studies and Global Education at the Ohio State University, USA. Her research has focused on the teaching and learning of global perspectives, cross-cultural experiential education, the role of social studies in the development of African nations, and online pedagogy for diversity and equity. Her most recent book is *Social Studies and the World: Teaching Global Perspectives*, co-authored with Angene Wilson. Last year she was a visiting scholar at the Hong Kong Institute of Education. She has won awards from SITE for her research on online intercultural communication and from AACTE for her teacher education program in international and global education.

Mitsuharu Mizuyama is a professor at Kyoto University of Education, Japan, where he has been employed since 1998, after teaching in junior high schools in Kyoto. He has been head of the Kyoto University's Education Center for Educational Research and Training since 2005. He also serves as a committee member of the Kyoto Environmental Education Center and the Kyoto Environment Council, working on measures against global warming. He has published books in Japanese on environmental education and on social studies in junior high school.

Fouad Moughrabi is Professor and head of the Department of Political Science at the University of Tennessee at Chattanooga and director of the Qattan Center for Educational Research and Development in Ramallah, Palestine.

Audrey Osler is Professor of Education and Director of the Centre for Citizenship and Human Rights Education at the University of Leeds, UK. Her publications include *Changing Citizenship: Democracy and Inclusion in Education* (Open University Press, 2005) co-written with Hugh Starkey. In 2007 she was a visiting scholar at the University of Washington in Seattle.

Farid Panjwani is Senior Instructor at the Institute for the Study of Muslim Civilisations of the Aga Khan University in London.

Marianna Papastephanou is Assistant Professor in the Department of Education, University of Cyprus. She completed her undergraduate studies at the University of Crete (Department of Philosophy and Social Studies 1992); graduate studies at the University of Cardiff, UK (PhD in Philosophy, 1996) and at Humboldt University, Berlin, Germany (1994). She has worked as a part-time Lecturer (1995–1996) and Associate Lecturer (1996–1997) at the University of Cardiff. Her research interests are: Modernism, Postmodernism and Philosophy of Education, Cognitive interests, Theories of Subjectivity, Language, Culture and the ensuing educational implications, and Social and Critical Theory of the Frankfurt School.

Lynne Parmenter works as a professor in the School of Culture, Media and Society of Waseda University, Tokyo, Japan. She has lived and worked in Japan for the past 14 years, teaching at high school and university levels. Her main research interest is in global citizenship education, and she also carries out research in the areas of foreign language education and comparative education policy.

Graham Pike is Professor and Dean of Education at the University of Prince Edward Island, Canada where he teaches global and international education. He has directed many projects in environmental education, global education and human rights education, in partnership with government and non-governmental organizations. As a consultant he has visited more than 20 countries, including substantial work for UNICEF on school improvement projects in the Middle East and Eastern Europe. He has written extensively on global education, including ten co-authored books for teachers. He is the 2006 winner of the *Award for Innovation in International Education*, given by the Canadian Bureau for International Education.

Murray Print is Director of the Centre for Research and Teaching in Civics and Professor of Education, University of Sydney. He is a recognized leader in Civic Education and Curriculum Development within Australia and internationally. He has directed many projects in civics including Values, Policy and Civics Education in the Asia-Pacific Region; Civics Education Assessment and Benchmarking; the Consortium Project in Civics and Citizenship Education; the first phase of the IEA International Civics Study; and most recently a major ARC-funded project on youth participation in democracy. He is Vice President of Civitas International, an international civic education organization.

Alan Reid is Professor of Education at the University of South Australia, and Director of the Concentration for Research in Education, Equity and Work (CREEW) in the Hawke Research Institute for Sustainable Societies. His research interests include educational policy, curriculum change, social justice and education, citizenship education and the history and politics of public education.

Alistair Ross is Professor of Education at London Metropolitan University, where he directs the Institute for Policy Studies in Education. He co-ordinates the Children's Identity and Citizenship in Europe Erasmus Thematic network. His research interests are in social justice and equity in education, children's social and political learning, teachers and their careers, and access to higher education.

Alan Sears is Professor of Social Studies Education and a member of the Citizenship Education Research and Development Group at the University of New Brunswick, Canada. He has been a social studies teacher for more than 25 years working at all levels from primary to graduate school. Professor Sears teaches undergraduate courses in social studies education and graduate courses in research methods and educational policy and regularly supervise PhD and MEd students. He has published widely in social studies and citizenship education and is the Chief Regional Editor for Canada for the journal, *Citizenship Teaching and Learning*.

Daniel Schugurensky is Associate Professor in the Department of Adult Education and Counselling Psychology, University of Ontario, Canada.

Alan Smith is the UNESCO Chair in Education at University of Ulster (Coleraine) in Northern Ireland. He is currently the Director of the ESRC Values and Teacher Education Policy in Northern Ireland Project and leading the evaluation of the Introduction of Citizenship to the Curriculum in Northern Ireland for CCEA. He has undertaken numerous consultancies in the UK, Europe and internationally and published and lectured widely in the field of citizenship and human rights education.

Hugh Starkey is Reader of Education at the University of London Institute of Education. He has published widely on human rights education and intercultural education. He has acted as expert to and undertaken research for the Council of Europe, European Commission and UNESCO.

Vanita Sundaram is Lecturer in Education at the University of York. Her current area of research is students' perceptions of fairness (equity). This includes how students 'learn' and experience justice in different educational contexts, how these notions and experiences may differ between and within groups of students, and the link to perceptions of justice in a wider, societal context. Also of interest is the formation of gender and sexual identities in school and young peoples' understanding of sexual rights as taught through the Citizenship curriculum.

Kazuya Taniguchi is a professor at Tohoku University, Japan.

Bernard Trafford has been Head of Wolverhampton Grammar School, UK, since 1990. From September 2008 he takes up the Headship of the Royal Grammar School, Newcastle upon Tyne. He is 2007/2008 Chairman of the Headmasters' and Headmistresses' Conference also Chair of Trustees of School Councils UK. He writes and speaks widely on school/student councils and children's rights in education. He has recently been advising the UK government on Citizenship and Participation and has co-written a manual on the democratic governance of schools for the Council of Europe. His doctoral research charted the changes within his school as it adopted a democratic, power-sharing ethos.

Christine Twine has recently retired from her post as Education for Citizenship Development Officer for Learning and Teaching Scotland (LT Scotland) based in Glasgow. She has been closely involved in education for citizenship developments in Scotland over the past decade. She has overseen the production of numerous guidance and resources for all sectors of education and has been instrumental in bringing the Scottish Framework for Education for Citizenship to life. She has also contributed to a number of European collaborative projects concerning citizenship and human rights education.

Cynthia A. Tyson is an associate professor at Ohio State University, USA. Her research interests focus on the development of culturally relevant teaching and the use of children's literature in early childhood social studies/civic education. She has worked as an educational consultant both nationally and internationally exploring frameworks for teaching for social justice. She has presented numerous papers at national and international meetings including NCSS and the affiliate College University Faculty Assembly (CUFA). Dr. Tyson is the Chair of the NCSS Social Justice Committee. She has scholarly work in Theory and Research in Social Education,

Social Education, Social Studies and the Young Learner, Educational Researcher and other books and journals.

Lew Zipin lectures in sociology and policy of education at the University of South Australia, where he is key researcher in the Centre for Studies of Literacy, Policy and Learning Culture within the Hawke Research Institute for Sustainable Societies. His research interests include critical theories of power in education; issues of policy, governance, work and ethics in schools and higher education, and education for social justice.

Acknowledgements

The editors would like to thank Helen Fairlie at Sage for all her support. We would especially like to thank warmly Roma Woodward and Elizabeth Melville who have helped us manage this project through all the stages of production. Their assistance and expertise have been invaluable and we are most grateful and appreciative of their significant contribution.

James Banks would like to thank the publishers Kappa Delta Pi, International Honor Society in Education, for allowing him to reproduce material that appeared in *The Educational Forum* journal, Volume 68, Summer 2004.

Penny Enslin and Joseph Divala would like to thank Nicki Hedge for her advice in the preparation of their chapter.

Carole Hahn would like to thank the following people who reviewed her chapter and offered helpful suggestions: Diana Hess, University of Wisconsin; Peter Levine, Director of CIRCLE (Center for Information and Research on Civic Learning and Education); Walter Parker, University of Washington; and Judith Torney-Purta, University of Maryland.

Lee Jerome would like to thank Bhavini Algarra for helpful comments on a draft of his chapter and Terry Pickeral for drawing his attention to the assessment work being developed by the National Center for Learning and Citizenship.

Martina Klicperova-Baker would like to thank the Grant Agency of the Academy of Sciences of the Czech Republic for supporting her research project # IAA7025303 'Democratic ethos: Social Psychological Analysis and Intercultural Empirical Probes', and the following expert reviewers: Antonìn Stank, Univerzita PalackÈho, Czech Republic; Ivo K. Feierabend, San Diego State University, USA.

Audrey Osler's contribution draws on material first published as Osler, A. (2008) 'Human rights education and education for democratic citizenship', in: C. Mahler., A. Mihr and R. Toivanen (eds.) *The United Nations Decade for Human Rights Education and the Inclusion of National Minorities*. Frankfurt: Peter Lang Verlag. She would like to thank the editors for allowing her to re-use this material.

Marianna Papastephanou wishes to thank the editors of the *Journal of Philosophy of Education* for permission to use material that first appeared in Volume 39, Number 3 of that journal.

Graham Pike would like to acknowledge Maryam Wagner's assistance in preparing his chapter and to thank Deborah Hutton and Merry Merryfield for their insights into recent developments in the US.

Alan Sears and Andy Hughes would like to thank the following people for their contribution in reviewing their chapter on Canada: William Hatley, MA. Student, Faculty of Education, University of Calgary; Barbara Hillman, University of New Brunswick; Emery Hyslop-Margison, University of New Brunswick; Yvonne Hébert, University of Calgary; Jennifer Tupper, University of Regina.

Foreword

Judith Torney-Purta

Thirty years ago a handbook reviewing political socialization research through the mid-1970s was issued. The authors of the chapters were almost all political scientists from the US, and they were preoccupied with debating which agent of socialization was the most important. Was it the family, the peer group, the school, or the mass media? Little attention was given to learning processes or developmental processes that might characterize these contexts or to influential people in them. Psychological approaches received some attention. Empirical findings from the multi-method study of a large US sample of elementary school students, conducted in the 1960s at the University of Chicago by Robert Hess and myself, were referenced. The other psychologists mentioned, such as Piaget and Kohlberg, were recognized for their broad theories that could be applied to the political or civic domain. Only one of the 15 authors of this handbook suggested ways to improve education for citizenship. The concept of democracy was implicit rather than explicit, appearing just once in the index.

The mid-seventies was the last time for nearly two decades that substantial research attention was given to political socialization or citizenship education in the US (or other countries). For example, the release of results from the first IEA Civic Education Study reporting on 30,000 students tested in 1972 in 9 countries received little attention. Its most interesting finding was that students whose classes encouraged discussion of issues had higher scores on civic knowledge and were less authoritarian than other students, even after a variety of other factors were controlled. Perhaps because political scientists were not comfortable working in schools or with young people who couldn't be expected to make rational choices, these scholars turned their attention to other age groups and issues. The field of political psychology developed during this period, but it has remained largely the province of social and personality psychologists, most of whom are more interested in studying university students rather than younger subjects.

It took the fall of the Soviet Empire in one part of Europe and distressing levels of political disengagement in other parts of Europe and North America in the early 1990s to bring political socialization and education for citizenship back to the forefront of concern. Young people in post-Communist Europe represented a new generation needing preparation for democracy, and their parents and teachers were not well-equipped to undertake this task. Educators from North America and Scandinavia enthusiastically proposed citizenship education programs, sometimes with and sometimes without opportunities to reflect on assumptions or evaluate results.

The IEA Civic Education Study (also called the second IEA study or the CIVED Study) was begun at about this time. IEA is a consortium of educational research institutes established in 1957, with headquarters in Amsterdam. In 1993 members of the IEA General Assembly requested a study to examine the role of schools in preparing young people for democracy. I served as the International Steering Committee Chair for this study working with the

International Coordinating Center at the Humboldt University of Berlin. I will not review the findings here; they are available in reports and articles on the web, and are referred to in chapters in this book. Some features of the design of this study are relevant, however.

First, 11 of the 29 countries participating in the study were from Central or Eastern Europe. Because so little was known about how these newly democratic countries would approach a renewal of citizenship education, the CIVED study was conducted in two phases. The first phase was an exploration of what was expected of 14-year-old people in this domain. This was accomplished through chapter-length case studies assessing the content, context and processes of citizenship education in 24 countries, published by IEA in 1999.

Second, the study was conducted as an international collaborative effort in which participating national research co-ordinators provided input to the conceptual framework for the test and survey. The items and scales included in the testing of 140,000 adolescents in 29 countries during the study's second phase were also vetted by these national co-ordinators. These results were published in 2001 and 2002. A recent survey of the process of international collaboration in 26 social and behavioral science projects found that the IEA's structures, honed through decades of experience, were effective in ensuring rigor while incorporating countries' views.

Third, because it is the IEA's policy to release the original data from students, teachers, and schools, considerable secondary analysis has been undertaken by teams in different countries, ranging from studies of active citizenship in Europe to analysis of civic knowledge and attitudes of disenfranchised groups in North America and Scandinavia. A number of chapters in this volume include primary or secondary analyses of these data.

Fourth, the IEA study began during a period of enhanced interest in education for citizenship among policy makers and the public in many countries of the world. This meant that emerging scholars who participated in the study in their own country could find support for continuing work in this area, and several are authors of chapters in this volume.

I have traced this context in some detail because it suggests that this is a propitious moment for an assessment of the state of the art in citizenship education in relation to democracy and thus for the publication of this handbook. The volume is unique in a number of ways in comparison to those of the past. Among its authors are specialists in political studies, sociologists, philosophers, and curriculum specialists, as well as individuals familiar with learning and psychological processes and with the preparation of teachers. There is material for those interested in furthering research, in debating policy, in improving programs' design or materials, and in enhancing educators' pedagogical skill.

In contrast to earlier handbooks where US scholars predominated, authors from three other English speaking countries,(Australia, Canada, and the UK) are well represented here. In addition to providing information about their own country's trajectory of political socialization and citizenship education for the past decade, these authors grapple with the conceptual foundations of civic education in relation to democracy, with approaches that draw on several disciplines, with research conducted using qualitative as well as quantitative methods, and with a diversity of perspectives (from marginalized groups as well as political elites). In describing country-level programs and concrete challenges, scholars from a number of other countries have contributed their insights. Thus the work has the character of an international collaboration focused on concepts and issues rather than a collection of unrelated descriptions of national programs.

In addition to the representation of different perspectives, a distinct strength of this volume is that the authors go beyond slogans or accepted truisms to grapple with issues that are contested but benefit from being addressed from different viewpoints. It is notable, for example, that themes related to equity are discussed not only in the chapter with that title in the foundational section but are also elaborated in other chapters in that section, in several of the chapters in the section dealing with specific countries, and in the section on pedagogy when the focus is on the discussion of controversial issues. The chapter on globalization as a foundational concept relates in several ways to the chapter on global education as a form of citizenship education, and both hold up the issue to consider its different facets. A critique of ideological assumptions is central in a chapter focused on this topic, and is also echoed elsewhere in the volume.

The chapters on specific countries call attention to the role of national and local context, suggesting caveats on the general prescriptive statements that so often characterize this field. The voices and perspectives of students are taken into account on topics such as the meaning of equity and of political discussion, rather than assuming that there is a barrier-free channel between elaborate statements of goals in a curriculum and the realities of students' understanding. The authors expand our grasp of the important issues without becoming vague and insubstantial. The chapters are constructive without becoming a detailed manual for classroom activities.

In short, I recommend the volume to a wide range of readers for its breadth of vision and success in moving the field forward. I hope we will not wait another 30 years to refine and test these ideas in the real world of political and educational controversy and in the actions of teachers and their students.

Judith Torney-Purta, PhD,
Professor of Human Development,
University of Maryland (College Park), USA

Judith Torney-Purta PhD, is a developmental and educational psychologist who is Professor of Human Development in the College of Education at the University of Maryland, College Park, Maryland, 20742, US. In 2005 she won the national Decade of Behavior Research Award in Democracy and the University of Maryland's Landmark International Research Award.

Introduction to the Sage Handbook of Education for Citizenship and Democracy

James Arthur, Ian Davies and Carole Hahn

Democracy, citizenship and citizenship education are complex, dynamic and controversial. They are highly significant international phenomena through which fundamentally important ideas and practices are characterized and by which individuals and groups work. The alignment of democracy, citizenship and citizenship education is deliberate in that this Handbook contains discussions in the context of an appreciation that legitimacy emanates from the people. The international experts who have contributed to this handbook explore and support active participation in a democracy by means of an analysis of the nature and purposes (actual and possible) of citizenship education. In this introduction the editors sketch the rationale for this publication and the means by which these chapters were brought together; comment on the meaning of citizenship and citizenship education; provide an overview of the pedagogical issues in citizenship education; and, sketch some conclusions and recommendations.

KEY THEMES IN THE HANDBOOK

In the handbook the team of authors have undertaken and provided the following.

- Explorations of fundamental ideas underlying citizenship education – chapters in section one include themes such as globalization, equity and democracy. These key ideas illustrate our bias in this handbook to explore forms of education that are relevant to an acceptance and celebration of a diverse inclusive democratic society while not being complacent about the academic and practical challenges in ensuring that education can help achieve justice.
- Insights into the comparative expression of citizenship education – there may be an increasing international consensus about the significance of citizenship education but this does not mean that programs of citizenship education are uniform throughout the world. Indeed one of the purposes of choosing such a broad range of in-country illustrations of citizenship education that appear in section 2 is to reflect on the very different traditions that exist.
- Considerations of different perspectives about citizenship education – broadly, the chapters in

section 3 have been chosen to encompass three overlapping themes: traditions that are related to belief systems or what might broadly be described as political or cultural positions; ideas and movements that relate to specific groups that may be related to ethnicity, social class or gender; and, disciplinary perspectives that affect the teaching of citizenship.

- Reflections on frameworks for and forms of citizenship education – this means that in section 4 of the handbook we have included discussions about types of citizenship education. These types share a great deal but there are also significant differences in origin, purpose and in the approaches recommended and actually adopted to teaching and learning.
- Discussions about the specific forms of teaching and learning that are appropriate for citizenship education – this involves chapters in section 5 that focus on the construction of curricula for citizenship education and the nature of intended and achieved practice in classrooms and elsewhere. There are discussions about the ways in which understandings are shaped, styles of teaching and learning in a range of contexts and the key issues in the theory and practice of assessment.
- Descriptions of available research and identification of avenues of research that needs to be undertaken in the future – all sections of the Handbook are based on research and development work that has already been done but the authors hope that these chapters provide – explicitly and implicitly – signposts to what could and perhaps should be done in the future.

THE PROCESS THAT LED TO THE PRODUCTION OF THE HANDBOOK

The themes outlined above were put together after much work with colleagues across the globe. Part of the discussions that led to this book emerged through the citizED network (www.citized.info). Face-to-face discussions at conferences on citizenship education involving leading figures in the field were held at the University of Toronto (2005) and the University of Oxford (2006). These discussions and further advice gathered through

correspondence were informed by other networks. The citizED journal *Citizenship Teaching and Learning* (www.citized.info/ ejournal) is served by an international editorial board that spans the globe. We were fortunate to benefit from the experience of colleagues who were very closely connected with the Civic Education Study of the International Association for the Evaluation of Educational Achievement (IEA Civic Education Study – (Torney-Purta et al., 2001)) and the US-based National Council for the Social Studies. Canadian colleagues brought experience gained through the Citizenship Education Research Network as well as provincial initiatives. The experience of Australian colleagues was essential with insights gained through the Discovering Democracy initiative. Work by the European Union (EU) and Council of Europe including that undertaken through the 2005 *European Year of Education for Democratic Citizenship through Education* and the EU Thematic Network *Children's Identity and Citizenship in Europe* was important. We also learned much from in-country analyses with individuals being able to advise us, for example, about the work of the National Foundation for Educational Research's nine-year longitudinal evaluation of England's National Curriculum for citizenship. Close collaboration with colleagues based in Asia was essential and we drew from the work of colleagues in Hong Kong, China, Japan, Pakistan and elsewhere. We were determined to include voices from the Middle East and actively recruited experts in citizenship education from that region. We were also aware of significant developments in citizenship education across South America. Finally, and importantly, we were very keen to ensure that African perspectives were included in the handbook. We attempted to be as inclusive as possible. Our work for this handbook in which new work would be specifically commissioned was also informed by the development of the four-volume reader of already published key articles about citizenship education (Arthur and Davies, 2008). The production of that work allowed us to see the range of perspectives that would need to be covered or at least referred to here. However, we are acutely aware that our networks have been restricted to English language journals and conferences. We have not been able to draw on the work of scholars whose work has been published solely in other languages. We hope that in the future multilingual scholars will be able to bridge that divide.

The proposal was revised on several occasions. Once an initial proposal for the handbook had been written we were pleased to learn a great deal from the detailed feedback of 13 anonymous reviewers. Individual authors were encouraged to seek guidance and feedback on their chapters. As editors, we engaged in dialogue with all authors about their work and all chapters were revised at least once. This process of revision was assisted in some cases by sharing of chapters between authors so that unhelpful overlaps could be identified and work revised.

We could not possibly aim to cover all aspects of citizenship education. The nature of the field is far too diverse to allow for that. We recognize that there are gaps in what we have produced. There is, for example, extensive implicit consideration of what could broadly be referred to as virtues and citizenship education but we have not included a separate chapter to deal with those issues exclusively. There is nothing here that deals in detail with economic aspects of citizenship education (both in the relationship between levels of economic prosperity in societies and the consequent development of particular forms of citizenship education nor in the precise elaboration of the teaching and learning of economic matters). We have not, of course, been able to include separate country analyses for each nation that has introduced citizenship education. We have included a chapter for only two religions and have not shown the links between all faiths and beliefs and types of citizenship education. We have not included a chapter on media although we realize that media are important venues for citizenship education. In the next section of

this introduction we describe some of the key issues that characterize citizenship and citizenship education and which have influenced the decision to include the chapters published here.

KEY ISSUES IN CITIZENSHIP AND CITIZENSHIP EDUCATION

In a politically relevant pursuit of the highest academic standards that frame the chapters included here we have to take account of the different meanings of citizenship (Heater, 1999). It is possible to characterize citizenship in relation to legal and political status. This is connected usually with citizenship of a nation state although there are forms of transnational legal status (e.g. in the EU) that are developing and some formal political status that exist below the level of a state (e.g. in the states of the US). Citizenship also involves identity (Isin and Wood, 1999). This can relate to an individual as well as to a group. There are at times connections between these identities and legal and political status but often less tangible matters are more obviously significant. Citizenship is often perceived as being closely connected to issues of practical engagement (Marinetto 2003). These matters are not necessarily without problems. The legal status of citizenship can be used to exclude as well as to guarantee rights; a concentration on identity can be used to divide as well as unite societies; an emphasis on participation can be misused by those who wish to use teachers and others to convince learners of the appropriateness of particular forms of action.

The challenges of understanding citizenship education are simultaneously enhanced and restricted by its relative immaturity as an academic field. Although the roots of citizenship itself are extremely long, citizenship is not (yet) regarded as an academic discipline in its own right (although academic posts are increasingly advertised using 'citizenship' in the job title and SAGE has also published an

International Handbook on Citizenship Studies (Isin and Turner, 2002)). Longer established disciplines such as History, Political Studies, Political Science, Psychology and Sociology may be used in order to bring understanding to the field. Social Studies in the US, civic and moral education in much of East Asia and other educational frameworks are relevant to the academic focus of citizenship education. Issues about the economy, child development, racism, and feminism are all relevant to specific academic disciplines. Citizenship may also be explored in a cross disciplinary manner. The chapters in this handbook make use of a variety of insights.

Citizenship can be explored and practised locally, regionally, nationally and globally. The meaning of these terms will shift depending on one's perspective (would 'the Amazon' and 'South America' each be described as an example of a 'region'?) The use of the word 'global' may in an age of perceived globalization deliberately signify an attachment to something that goes further than 'internationalism' (i.e. relations *between* and not across the nations) but should this be used instead of, for example, 'cosmopolitan'? The nature of the citizenship that exists in these different contexts is varied although not necessarily mutually exclusive. Consideration of these matters raises questions about the extent to which citizenship is dependent upon a polity and we have included chapters that relate directly to separate nation states as well as to broader geographical areas and wider conceptual fields.

The civic republican and liberal traditions of citizenship overlap but are also possibly distinct. Simply, the former emphasizes the performance of duties in public contexts, while the latter stresses the exercise of rights by private individuals. The liberal emphasizes a limited role for the state as a night watchman, while the civic republican looks for some sort of Rousseau-like social contract in which the 'will' exercised by the people cannot be separated from the priorities adopted by the state. To these perhaps

largely western-oriented traditions may be added Confucian-based ideas of reciprocity in relationships. It would be rare to see these traditions translating simply into statements and actions by individuals – human beings are too complicated to expect simple performance in relation to an ideal. However, we can use the lenses of those traditions in order to understand the different issues that might be contained within the statements of people who will view citizenship very differently.

Citizenship is built upon understandings of individuals and society. As such there is a need to reflect upon the extent to which political, economic, moral and other ways of understanding the world are relevant. This connects closely to what is taught and learned and the authors show the ways in which ideas about pedagogy and curriculum are considered. This is not a handbook that could be used for detailed practical planning by teachers but it will be of use in clarifying the parameters for teaching and for stimulating educational action.

THE EMERGENCE OF CITIZENSHIP EDUCATION IN ITS CURRENT FORM

Citizenship education is not new. Plato, Aristotle, Confucius, Rousseau, and Thomas Jefferson preceded current scholars in proposing particular approaches to education for citizenship. In the 18th and 19th centuries concern for citizenship education accompanied the growth of nation states and the expansion of public or state education in many parts of the world. Following World War II and the period of decolonialization, newly independent nations, particularly in Africa, Asia, and the Middle East included education for citizenship in their plans for nation building. And as formerly authoritarian regimes – from Germany and Japan after World War II to former dictatorships in South America – transitioned to democracy, plans for democratization included not only creating democratic institutions, such as an independent judiciary and protection for freedom of speech, but also education for democratic citizenship.

Most recently, with the fall of the Soviet empire, nations in Central and Eastern Europe have undertaken numerous initiatives in democratic citizenship education. In recent years, there have also been new initiatives in citizenship education in older democracies, such as Australia, the UK, the US and nations of the EU. These initiatives have developed out of concern for perceived trends such as declining voter turnout, decreased participation in civil society organizations and an increase in youth criminal activity in some areas. Globalization, migration and research on youth political socialization have further raised concerns about the need to revitalize education for citizenship and democracy in diverse parts of the world.

All of these forces have combined to create exponential growth in scholarship on citizenship education both within and across nations. When the International Association for the Evaluation of Educational Achievement (IEA) undertook their first Civic Education Study in 1975, only nine countries participated. By the time of the second IEA Civic Education Study in 1999, some 30 nations participated and at the time of this writing it is likely that more will participate in the forthcoming assessment.

There are other signs of growing international dialogue about education for citizenship and democracy. CIVITAS International has been holding annual conferences on citizenship education since 1996, with attendees coming from countries as diverse as Argentina, the Netherlands, Lebanon and Malaysia. In Asia since the 1990s there have been numerous transnational conferences on civic and moral education and national education, as well as a series of conferences sponsored by the Asian Consortium for Citizenship Education in the Schools (ACCES) that brought together civic education scholars from the Asia-Pacific region. In Europe, the Council of Europe and European Union sponsored a European Year of Education for Democratic Citizenship through Education and the network on Children's Identity and Citizenship stimulated dialogue through conferences and publications. In 2005, the Comparative and International Education Society established a special interest group on Citizenship and Democratic Education that brings together comparative education scholars who study non-formal, as well as formal, settings for citizenship education in economically developing and developed nations.

CITIZENSHIP EDUCATION IN COMPARATIVE PERSPECTIVE

From the country chapters, we see that there is no one way – or single best practice – for doing citizenship education. Culture and context matter. The forms that civic education takes and the emphases in goals and practices clearly reflect differing social and political histories, as well as cultural values. As different societies face particular challenges, those are reflected in their priorities for citizenship education. For example, we read about the implications of a divided society in Israel, of an occupied society in the Palestinian territories, and an Islamic society in Pakistan. In the chapter on China's experience, we learn of changes in political or ideological education as a consequence of becoming a more open, market-oriented society than it was in the past. We learn about localized projects in Brazil that seek to empower citizens living in poverty, about new national curricula in England and Japan, and of varied initiatives in decentralized countries like Canada and the US. These and other country chapters show us that it would not be appropriate to take a 'one size fits all' approach to education for citizenship.

Yet, despite this great variety, we see that educators and policy makers in many countries share a common concern: they want to instil in young people the knowledge, skills and attitudes that will enable them to participate in the communities of which they are a part, locally, nationally, and globally. Authors emphasize the challenges in moving from didactic, teacher-centered approaches to more student-centered approaches in which students experience participatory citizenship. Many also note the challenges in creating an inclusive sense of 'we-ness' in pluralistic societies and across national borders in a global society. We turn now more explicitly to some of the pedagogical issues that must be addressed if citizenship education is to be achieved in all its variant richness.

TEACHING, LEARNING AND KNOWLEDGE

Teaching, learning and knowledge are huge concepts in citizenship education. A number of authors in this handbook discuss what content should be included in citizenship education as well as how it should be taught. All express the basic concern that how we teach children will influence what kind of citizens they become. But this does not necessarily mean that *how* we teach is more important than *what* we teach. Citizenship education is a multidisciplinary subject with a contested and extremely varied curricular content. The content of citizenship classes vary considerably and can be found under the name of civics, social studies, personal and moral · education. Such classes may be timetabled or integrated into other subjects such as history and geography. Teaching strategies also vary from country to country and range from progressive e-learning, role play, drama, discussion, self-study and interactive learning to a whole range of more traditional methods including rote-learning. Each country is different in terms of what is recognized as citizenship education, how – and what – content is selected and how it is taught. The field of citizenship education is extremely eclectic.

A systematic review of citizenship education undertaken in England (Deakin-Crick, 2005) concluded that citizenship education

'requires a focus on higher order critical and creative thinking skills and the processes of learning itself'. The challenge the review set was to develop an appropriate pedagogy so that teachers operated with a critical perspective. Crick (1999: 337) wrote that students should not only be taught to understand the general concepts in citizenship but they should also engage in practical activity, as he said 'an education that creates a disposition to active citizenship is a necessary condition of free societies'. This also means a life-long approach that considers a wider range of learning experiences than offered in formal institutions: in communities, workplaces and families. Citizenship education is not restricted to schools and universities, but ought to be integrated into every community. In this handbook, we focus primarily on citizenship education as it occurs in schools, while recognizing that there is much that occurs in families, religious and community associations and adult education. Authors of chapters in this book describe citizenship education that is delivered in focused courses in civics, citizenship or government; many note, however, that most civic instruction occurs in social studies, moral education or history lessons, and to a lesser degree in other subjects. Several authors describe ways in which students learn participatory or active citizenship through decision-making in class or tutor groups, student or school councils and in extra-curricular programs. A few authors refer to programs in which students participate in community action projects. While arguing that civic education should help young people to understand issues and identify with communities at local, national and global levels, most of the authors acknowledge that the dominant focus has been on national citizenship, with some attention to local communities, particularly for younger children. What our authors collectively seek is a pedagogy and citizenship content that promotes the knowledge, skills, attitudes, dispositions and values necessary for citizens to participate meaningfully in society.

School teachers, by their teaching and example, help students see the world in particular ways. This 'seeing the world in particular ways' can be a by-product of teaching, it can be accidental, but it can also be deliberately intended, explicit or implicit. Teaching is not simply about the direct transmission of knowledge and skills, it is also about discovery and inquiry and within citizenship education many believe that teaching needs a critical pedagogy. Therefore, in citizenship classes, they would argue, we should be teaching students to embrace the qualities of co-operation, independence and generosity, as these qualities influence how people participate in political and social life. As a consequence, teaching ought to involve pedagogical approaches that emphasize thinking for yourself, which necessarily demands critical reflective inquiry: after all, you do not send your child to school to be taught what the teacher thinks. This philosophy of pedagogy is not neutral in intention as it implies or promotes the teaching of egalitarianism and places a large value on social difference for it does not simply teach that diversity is a social fact, but that diversity is a social good. It is also linked to a concern for participation in the affairs of society in order to achieve the ideals of freedom and justice – to build a new and fairer society through active citizenship. It will involve teaching content that is controversial. Therefore it is inevitable that the underlying political and social beliefs among those who teach citizenship differ.

Any teacher would no doubt agree that students ought to be encouraged to inquire for themselves, to engage with others, to learn to trust and respect each other and to ultimately become active participants and shapers of their own learning. They may also agree that we ought to examine the pedagogical possibilities in citizenship education and consider how schools involve students in decision-making. Most teachers will agree that citizenship education ought to contribute to helping students become independent learners. Consequently the teacher's role is to guide their students, to facilitate open and democratic classrooms that empower students to question their relationship with the social, cultural and political structures of society. This would require a pedagogy that transforms the learner from the passive to the active, but this is a pedagogy that remains the exception in schools. The question that arises is how teachers can operate with this kind of critical pedagogy when they need to deliver a pre-specified curriculum? How can they operate with a flexible curriculum that starts from the students' interests when the teachers may have issues with classroom management? The kind of teaching and learning that supports independent thinking and respect for difference is often more of a myth than a reality in schools.

Citizenship education is not therefore simply about the transmission of knowledge or about information and facts, it must be about understanding and awareness. Citizens need to know their rights, but they also need to know how these rights operate within a democracy. What students learn does not necessarily make them active citizens. However, learning through participation and developing skills such as how to negotiate, to compromise, to collaborate, to exercise leadership, to communicate and to listen is essential and often involves designing out-of-school learning opportunities. This necessarily will involve the student voice and the promotion of certain values and dispositions such as a commitment to voluntary service, a concern for the environment and a concern for justice. There are those who argue that the child should be allowed to 'develop freely' and that the teacher simply facilitates an atmosphere for learning. The reason given is often that it is authoritarian to impose any view on a child, but in that case why have a school or citizenship education? The same could be said about the idea of an 'atmosphere' – what atmosphere? Choices about content and teaching strategies are unavoidable and citizenship education, however contested, has to stand for something.

Ross (2002: 53f) argues that there are three distinct approaches to constructing a curriculum each with a different pedagogic style. The content-driven approach views knowledge as a distinct body of data which needs to be acquired. The process-driven approach views education as a process; rather than knowing *what*, one should know *how* because learning how to learn about knowledge is more important than acquiring knowledge itself. The third model is an objectives-driven approach in which knowledge simply becomes a commodity. Ross believes that citizenship education borrows from all three models and that none of these models are neutral as they are permeated with objectives and intentions. Nevertheless, citizenship teachers tend to select one of these models as desirable and reject the others. We need to ask what is possible in teaching and learning in citizenship in the context that the minority of the world lives in advanced liberal democracies and have a degree of freedom to determine or at least discuss what kind of citizens they wish to be. Active and participatory learning, often seen as a major aim of citizenship education, is not widespread, even in some parts of the advanced liberal democracies. It is also the case that in most countries there is no specific initial training of teachers for citizenship education and few in-service courses for practising teachers. Kerr (1999) in his international comparison of citizenship education claimed that the challenges of citizenship education are to achieve an increase in the range of teaching and learning approaches, improve the quality and range of resources and disseminate more widely effective practice.

CONCLUSIONS AND TOWARDS RECOMMENDATIONS

What then needs to be done if we are to promote citizenship education? Given the challenges that we have referred to above we are painfully aware that it is certainly not a simple task to move things forward. Nevertheless we wish to provide a few comments that indicate the areas that we feel are important and the direction in which we would hope things would develop.

Policy

Given our comments above about the significance of context we are wary of providing a series of imperatives that would appear inappropriately all-encompassing. We are also wary of seeming to suggest that policy is necessarily simplistically connected with practice or that central bodies are better placed than others to develop guidance for teachers and learners. The burden of bureaucracy and the restrictions on professional and other autonomy are dangers that we recognize as we seek to encourage policy makers to focus their attention on citizenship education. Policy can take many forms and have many purposes: as a reflection of what is happening, a set of aspirations, or a statement of requirements insisted upon by those who judge professionals and others. Perhaps we need policy as a framework engendered by dialogue and understanding as opposed to a set of directives. This would mean that citizenship education is recognized formally as something that is important and which occurs in many different ways as people learn. It is something that applies for all learners whatever their age and place. It is something that is related to wider societal reform and should be seen as a key part of the creation and development of a diverse democracy and can only be achieved through many inputs including those to do with teacher education. It is, in short, related to the issues outlined above in this Introduction and in more detail in many of the chapters included in this handbook.

School practice

Citizenship education is about the knowledge, understanding, skills and dispositions that are connected with public life. The nature of that knowledge and understanding cannot be set in stone as a list of information or topics. The skills of citizenship education should be those that are cognitive as well as affective and can be developed by individuals as well as groups. Dispositions are those which can be explored and promoted as part of a democratic society. This needs to be done in learning communities that are open to a range of inputs including those that cross institutional boundaries and challenge pre-conceptions. The learning that takes place will need to be reviewed and evaluated although a rigidly objectives-driven system seems inappropriate when considered against the aims of citizenship education.

Teacher education

Teachers need to be prepared for the diverse, challenging and changing learning contexts that are in evidence when successful citizenship education occurs. Newly qualified teachers must have practical experience that is informed by deep understanding; be able to work with learners of all abilities and a wide range of ages; be able to operate in many different contexts including those in the communities – virtual and real – within and beyond their own national settings. It is likely that teachers and schools will rediscover (if they ever lost it) their roles as academic experts who are simultaneously community facilitators collaborating with others from a wide range of backgrounds. Citizenship education teachers and learners have very specific roles to play: they also have a duty to work expansively and creatively in order to develop democratic diversity.

Research

Much of the scholarship to date has been advocating particular approaches or descriptions of policies and programs in particular

countries. Political socialization researchers have gathered descriptive data about student knowledge, experiences, and attitudes in some countries. The IEA Civic Education studies are the only ones so far to gather such information from representative samples of students in many countries. There is a growing body of ethnographic case study research on civic education in particular schools and out-of-school settings. There are both quantitative and qualitative studies of teachers that use non-representative samples. Increasing numbers of researchers are doing 'mixed methods' studies in particular settings, for example when they survey large numbers of students, conduct focus group interviews with some students, interview individual teachers, and observe classes and school wide programs over an extended period of time. A few researchers are beginning to conduct longitudinal studies and a few others are using sophisticated analytic techniques doing secondary analysis of large data sets. We hope that scholars will continue to use quantitative and qualitative studies in a complementary fashion. We would like to see more research with younger students, with students who can be followed longitudinally, and with representative samples of teachers. We would like to see more research that focuses on the unique experiences and meanings of students and teachers from varied demographic groups to provide a more nuanced understanding of the connections between teaching and learning for individuals from different points of positionality, such as various ethnic, economic, and regional groups within and across nations.

Wider societal reform

All the above suggests that citizenship education is part of a wider agenda: one that has the capacity to engage people in the creation of a better world. We recognize that this is a daunting challenge. Schools, cannot compensate for society. What, then, is the scale of the challenge if we expect much more than a school-focused approach from the citizenship educator? There must be a multi-dimensional approach to the achievement of justice: recognition and celebration of diversity, commitment to human rights and an intention to maximize the potential (learning and other) of individuals and groups. This handbook – whatever the level of erudition achieved by the invited experts – will not solve problems or provide solutions. But we hope that it helps to clarify understandings and stimulates action to promote the necessity of citizenship education.

REFERENCES

Arthur, J. and Davies, I. (eds) (2008) *Citizenship Education* (4 volumes). London: Sage.

Crick, B. (1999) The Presuppositions of Citizenship Education, *Journal of Philosophy of Education* 33 (3): 337–352.

Deakin Crick, R. (2005) 'Citizenship education and the provision of schooling: a systematic review of evidence'. *International Journal of Citizenship and Teacher Education*, 1 (1): 55–75.

Heater, D. (1999) *What is Citizenship?* Cambridge: Polity Press.

Isin, E. F. and Turner, B. S. (eds) (2002) *Handbook of Citizenship Studies*. London: Sage.

Isin, E. F. and Wood, P. K. (1999) *Citizenship and Identity*. London: Sage.

Kerr, (1999) Citizenship Education: An International Comparison. http://www.inca.org.uk/pdf/citizenship_no_intro.pdf (accessed 4 September 2007).

Marinetto, M. (2003) Who wants to be an active citizen? The politics and practice of community involvement. *Sociology*, 37 (1): 103–120.

Ross, A. (2002) Citizenship Education and Curriculum Theory, in David Scott and Helen Lawson (eds) *Citizenship Education and the Curriculum*. Westport, CT: Ablex Publishing. pp. 45–62.

Torney-Purta, J., Lehmann, R., Oswald, H., and Schulz, W. (2001). *Citizenship and Education in Twenty-eight Countries: Civic Knowledge and Engagement at Age Fourteen*. Amsterdam: IEA.

Key Ideas Underlying Citizenship Education

Democracy

Bernard Crick

Democracy is both a sacred and a promiscuous word. We all love her but we see her differently. She is hard to pin down. Everyone claims her but no one can possess or even name her fully. To give any definition for a class to learn would not be particularly democratic. To have any open-ended discussion about possible meanings could be reasonably democratic. Like 'Britishness' it is more a matter of recognizable behaviour over time than of definitive definition for a precise curricular moment. Besides, definitions don't settle arguments. 'Democracy' can suggest certain institutional arrangements or it can suggest authorities or individuals behaving in a democratic manner. To some it means that the will of the majority must prevail; but to many others it is simply a synonym for good or just government – which may some have to contradict and restrain majority opinion. Not every decision can be judged by whether it is reached democratically or not. BBC news programmes, in the UK, ask listeners to send in their opinion on road-pricing for motor vehicles or on the provision of a super-expensive new drug in the National Health Service, but this is an illusion of democracy, perhaps better called populism. Representative government is best conducted as dialogue and

mediation between opinion and knowledge, popular majorities and elected minorities.

A moment's thought or reading a short book could remind us why the concept, while so important, is yet so often so confusing, even sometimes dangerously misleading (Crick, 2002). Some world leaders recently assumed that if an oppressive and intolerant autocracy was destroyed, democracy would automatically follow. But the concept that we take so much for granted has had, at its best, an essential historical and logical precondition: the idea of politics itself, practised in what we would regard as pre-democratic societies; politics as a willingness both to offer and to accept compromises binding on both governments and majorities.

Historically 'democracy' has had four broad usages, each of which can be invoked as the *real* meaning even today. History is not a dead past but conditions how we understand the present and the future. There are no real meanings, only different usages of concepts; some more acceptable than others, some less self-contradictory or more compatible with others. The report that led to citizenship becoming a compulsory part of the national curriculum in England was titled *Education for Citizenship and the*

Teaching of Democracy in Schools (Advisory Group, 1998); but noticeably offered no explicit definition or even extended discussion of 'democracy'; rather it chose to concentrate on 'citizenship', especially *active* not just *good* citizenship, 'participation', 'rights and responsibilities'.

The first historical usage is found in Plato's attack on democracy and in Aristotle's highly qualified defence: democracy is simply, in the Greek, *demos* (the many, or more often invidiously 'the mob') and *cracy*, meaning rule. Plato attacked democracy as being the rule of the poor and ignorant over the educated and the knowledgeable, ideally philosophers. His fundamental distinction was between knowledge and opinion: democracy is rule, or rather the anarchy, of mere opinion. Even in modern times this view has some resonance. Beatrice Webb, a democratic socialist, once said 'democracy is not the multiplication of ignorant opinions'. Aristotle modified Plato's view rather than rejecting it utterly: good government was a mixture of elements, the educated few ruling with the consent of the many. The few should have *'aristoi'* or the principle of excellence from which the highly idealized concept of aristocracy derives. But many more can qualify for citizenship by virtue of some education and some property (both of which he thought necessary conditions for citizenship), and so must be consulted and can, indeed, on occasion be promoted to office. He did not call his 'best possible' state democracy, rather *politea* or polity, a political or civic community of citizens deciding on common action by public debate. But democracy could be the next best thing in practice if it observed 'ruling and being ruled in turn'. As a principle unchecked, by aristocratic experience and knowledge democracy was a fallacy: 'that because men are equal in some things, they are equal in all'. The citizen class in Athens in the 5th century BC excluded women, the propertyless, foreigners and there were slaves. Citizens were a minority but they made decisions by public debate, chose officials by vote or by lot, and had forcibly resisted and overthrown rule by tyrants or narrow oligarchies (Farrar, 1988).

The second usage is found in the Roman Republic, in Machiavelli's great republican Discourses, in 17th century English and Dutch republicans, and in the early American republic: that good government is mixed government, just as in Aristotle's theory, but under constitutional law – laws that could only be made and changed by a special procedure not a simple majority vote. But a democratic popular element could actually give greater power to a state. The plebeians, the common people of Rome, elected tribunes to represent them in the aristocratic Senate. Good laws to protect all were not good enough unless subjects became active citizens making their own laws collectively. When Oliver Cromwell at the end of the English Civil War argued in the Putney Debates for a property franchise, one of his colonels, a Leveler, famously hurled back in his face: 'The poorest he that is in England has life to live as the greatest he' (but beneath the rhetoric even Colonel Rainborough believed that servants, debtors and tenants could not have the vote because they would lack 'independency', would be in the power of another). The republican argument was both moral and military. The moral argument is the more famous: both Roman paganism and later Protestantism had in common a view of man as an active individual, a maker and shaper of things, not just a law-abiding well-behaved subject of a traditional rule-bound monarchical or religious order. But also it was believed that free citizens would defend their state from aggressors more strongly and reliably than professional soldiers or mercenaries.

The third usage of democracy is found in the rhetoric and events of the French Revolution and in the writings of Jean Jacques Rousseau – that everyone, regardless of education or property, has a right to make his or her will felt in matters of state; and indeed the 'general will' or common good is better understood by any well-meaning, simple, unselfish and natural ordinary person from their own experience and conscience than by the over-educated living amid the artificiality of high society. Now this view can have a lot to do with the liberation of a class or a nation, whether from oppression or ignorance and superstition, but it is not necessarily connected with individual liberty. (In the European 18th and 19th centuries most people who cared for liberty did not call themselves democrats at all – rather constitutionalists or civic republicans, or, in the Anglo-American discourse, 'Whigs'). In the French Revolution the Jacobins turned Rousseau's ideas into the slogan 'the sovereignty of the people' they spoke of 'Our Sovereign Masters, the People'. The difficulty was that they exercised sovereignty on behalf of whom they took to be 'the people' with no clear representative institutions to check them. The general will could have more to do with popularity than with representative institutions, the rule of law, reasoned debate or individual rights. Napoleon was a genuine heir of the French Revolution when he said that 'the politics of the future will be the art of stirring the masses'. His popularity was such, playing on both revolutionary and nationalist sentiments, that he was able for the very first time to introduce mass conscription – that is to trust the common people with arms. The autocratic Hapsburg's and Romanovs had to be most careful to whom and where they applied selective conscription.

The fourth usage of democracy is found in the American constitution and in many of the new constitutions in Europe in the 19th century and in the new West German and Japanese constitutions following the Second World War, also in the writings of John Stuart Mill and Alexis de Tocqueville: that all can be active citizens if they care, but must mutually respect the equal rights of fellow citizens within a regulatory legal order that defines, protects and limits those rights. So what is generally meant by 'democracy' today, especially in the US, Europe and countries influenced by their political ideas, is the fusion of the idea of the power of the people and the idea of legally guaranteed individual rights. Sometimes this fusion can be confusion. The two should, indeed, be combined, but they are distinct ideas, and can in practice contradict each other. There can be intolerant democracies and reasonably tolerant autocracies. It may not always be helpful to call the system of government under which we live

'democratic' without qualification or pause for thought. To do so begs the question. It can close the door on discussion of how the actual system could be made *more* democratic, just as others once feared – and some still do so – that the democratic element can become too powerful. For many years the Reverend Ian Paisley, in Northern Ireland, proclaimed it undemocratic to stop the majority in an elected parliament from ruling over the Catholic minority. It took him a long time to accept such an artificial and imposed political device as power-sharing; and any system of proportional representation is a deliberate check on majoritarian democracy.

Sociologically and socially England is still in many ways a profoundly undemocratic society (Scotland and Wales are perhaps somewhat more democratic), certainly when compared to the US – but even in the US there is now very little active citizenship or positive participation in politics in the republican style of the early American Republic. There are some interesting but very localized experiments in direct democracy, local referenda and 'citizenship panels' etc, and of course people vote (albeit in disappointing numbers); but between elections any talking about and active participation in politics rates far lower as the most favoured national activity, apart from work, than shopping. (Lipset, 1996). But institutionally we know what we mean by calling Britain and the US democracies: institutional procedures protected by law and custom allow public debate, freedom of the press and free and fair elections so that presidents, governments and representatives can be changed peaceably. But that is a different matter to behaving democratically: treating everyone one as worthy of equal respect even when unequal in talent or status. All opinions are to be respected (to a varying degree) but not all can be judged of equal worth.

Aristotle said that as part of the good life, to fulfill our humanity, we must enter into the *polis* as citizens, into political relationships with other citizens. 'To be political, to live in a *polis* meant that everything was decided through words and persuasion and not through violence. In Greek self-understanding to force people by violence, to command rather than persuade, were prepolitical ways … characteristic of life outside the *polis'*. (Arendt, 1958: 26–27). What we mean by politics and citizenship has been shaped by the Aristotelian tradition of thought. Politics is an activity among free citizens living in a state or *polis,* how they govern themselves by public debate. To him the special sense of *polis* or civic state was that of a conditional teleological ideal: both a standard and a goal to which all states would naturally move if not impeded, as well they might be impeded, by folly, unrestrained greed, power-hunger by leaders lacking civic sense or by conquest. Aristotle brings out the intense specificity of the political relationship when, in the second book of *The Politics,* he examines and criticizes schemes for ideal states. He says that his teacher Plato made the mistake in *The Republic* of trying to reduce everything in the *polis* to an ideal unity; rather, it is the case that:

> … there is a point at which a polis, by advancing in unity, will cease to be a polis: there is another point, short of that at which it may still remain a polis, but will none the less come near to losing its essence, and will thus be a worse polis. It is as if you were to turn harmony into mere unison, or to reduce a theme to a single beat. The truth is that the polis is an aggregate of many members (Barker, 1958: 51).

So politics arises in organized societies that recognize themselves to be an aggregate of many members, not a single tribe, religion, interest or even tradition. It can be defined as the activity by which the differing interests and values that exist in any complex society are conciliated (Crick, 2005: 3–5). Democratic politics are a device for such conciliation needed in modern industrial and post-industrial society. Politics only arises when there is a perception of diversities as natural and a tolerant democratic politics when that perception is widely shared. But historically and logically politics preceded what in the modern world is usually called democracy. Ruling elites in 5th century Greece and in republican Rome did act politically among themselves (democratically, if you like), even while the majority of inhabitants were shut out of political activity – just like in 18th and 19th century Britain.

Not all regimes that style themselves democratic are democratic in any sense other than that a majority of the people accept the regime and may, indeed, be proud of it – as when the 'peoples' democracies of the former Communist world had survived war and were in working order, or in many African, South-East Asian and South American regimes today inspired (if sometimes deceived by) intense nationalism. It is bad mistake to assume that all dictatorships were and are unpopular, even if in our eyes their leaders subvert political compromises and individual liberties by appealing to the masses against traditional institutions and restraints.

Consider by way of contrast to even the best democratic practices of today a passage from an ancient author that in the 19th and early 20th centuries 'every school boy knew', or so it was said; certainly all those who thought seriously about politics – the Periclean oration.

> Our constitution is called a democracy because power is in the hands not of a minority but of the whole people. When it is a question of settling private disputes, every one is equal before the law; when it is a question of putting one person before another in positions of public responsibility, what counts is not membership of a particular class, but the actual ability which the man possesses. No one, so long as he has it in him to be of service to the state, is kept in political obscurity because of poverty. …

> Here each individual is interested not only in his own affairs but in the affairs of the state as well: even those who are mostly occupied with their own business are extremely well-informed on general politics – this is a peculiarity of ours: we do not say that a man who takes no interest in politics is a man who minds his own business; we say that he has no business here at all. We Athenians, in our own persons, take our decisions on policy or submit them to proper discussions: for we do not think that there is an incompatibility between words and deeds; the worst thing is to rush into action before the consequences have been properly debated … (Rieu: 1954, 117–119).

But historians now tell us that Pericles was a populist demagogue, a kind of democratic dictator. And today to say 'a man who minds his own business … has no business here at all' would be seen as a dangerous denial of individual rights. But, that point apart, the ideal is eternally impressive that Pericles had to invoke to persuade and deceive his fellow citizens.

There is little need to search further if we want to find the moral and practical basis for an inclusive, just society: Alexis de Tocqueville wrote his great book *Democracy in America* to convince conservative, autocratic Europeans that following the ideas and forces released by the French Revolution, the future lay with democracy whether they liked it or not. It held a great capacity for human betterment, but it could, if there were no internal checks and balances, degenerate into 'a tyranny of the majority' or a 'democratic despotism'. His argument was balanced. The famous chapter on 'The Unlimited Power of the Majority ...', which could lead to intolerance, conformity and mediocrity, was thankfully followed by a chapter on 'Causes Which Mitigate the Tyranny of the Majority ...' (Bradley, 1945: 254–280). The main causes were the dispersal of power: the federal system itself and the strength of democratic local institutions. A whole theory of political sociology emerged stressing the importance of intermediary institutions between the individual and the state, what Adam Smith and his contemporary Adam Ferguson in the Scottish enlightenment had earlier called 'civil society'. If Rousseau had been right to search for some justification why everyone should be a citizen regardless of rank or education, yet he was wrong to suggest in his theory of the General Will to argue that all intermediary groups and institutions between the individual and 'the Legislator' (his selfless and benign state) are divisive of the general interest. Jeremy Bentham had called intermediary groups 'sinister interests'; he was so concerned with sweeping away corrupt feudal and municipal relics that he seemed not to notice the abundance in Britain of more benign voluntary groups which others still see as the school of democracy.

de Tocqueville, however, saw another danger to liberty that could arise from the very success of a democratic franchise and a contented people. He pictured democracy as:

> ... an innumerable multitude of men, all equal and alike, incessantly endeavoring to procure the petty and paltry pleasures with which they glut their lives. Each of them, living apart, is a stranger to the fate of all the rest; his children and his private friend constitute to him the whole of mankind.

> Above this race of men stands an immense and tutelary power, which takes upon itself alone to secure their gratifications and to watch over their fate. That power is absolute, minute, regular, provident and mild. It would be like the authority of a parent if, like that authority, its object was to prepare men for manhood; but it seeks, on the contrary, to keep them in perpetual childhood ... For their happiness such a government willingly labours, but it chooses to be the sole agent and the only arbiter of that happiness; it provides for their security, foresees and supplies their necessities, facilitates their pleasures ...: what remains but to spare them all the care of thinking and all the trouble of thinking (Bradley, 1945: 318).

An ideologically conservative view of the future welfare state? But it could remind us that the downside of one type of democracy, what we now call the consumer society and dumbing down, could be imagined by a political thinker long before its contemporary form and force.

Benjamin Constant in a once famous essay of 1820. 'The Liberty of the Ancients Compared to that of the Moderns', drew less rhetorically a distinction for a democratic age between two ideas of liberty:

> The aim of the ancients was the sharing of social power among citizens of the same fatherland: this is what they called liberty. The aim of the moderns is the enjoyment of liberty in private pleasures; and they call liberty the guarantees accorded by institutions to these pleasures (Gauchet, 1997).

So if we see democracy as simply majority will and opinion, we must also see that to result in good government constrains, whether cultural or legal, have to be considered. Morality is the most general such limitation. Just as Adam Smith saw ordinary morality and trustworthiness in observing contracts as essential underpinnings of a market economy, so a well functioning democracy needs such common virtues. And beliefs in 'the rule' of law, human rights and working through established procedures to change laws (rather than a president or prime minister simply appealing to public opinion) are parts of any sophisticated definition of democracy or necessary limitations on any simplistic definition.

In a modern democracy the politician must, of course, always be aware of the dangers of trying to ignore strong public opinion. But they must also be aware of the dangers of simply trying to flatter and follow public opinion at a given moment if it appears to be against the long term public interest or common good. The democratic politician must have the courage to stand up and argue back when the public is being urged by populist leaders (whether other politicians, preachers or press lords) to break laws or conventions democratically legitimated and designed to mediate compromises between the different interests and values that are characteristic of a modern state and a complex society. Pericles had said in his praise of democracy, 'the secret of liberty is courage'. The great American jurist, Oliver Wendell Holmes, a Justice of the Supreme Court, once said ironically, 'Democracy is what the crowd wants'. He was defending his view of constitutional guarantees of freedom of speech under the Bill of Rights against some repressive but highly popular anti-socialist legislation by a State legislature.

Sometimes democracy is 'what the crowd wants', but more often not. Populism can arise from the failure of intermediate institutions and experts to consider ordinary opinion at all; or when a political party, president or prime minister appears to treat the government machine and the institutions of state as their own property, rather than as a public trust. Populism is when it can be thought plausible to treat the diverse citizens of a state as if they were 'the people', a single entity with a common will or moral consensus (Crick, 2007). Both the broadcast media and the press are then tempted to present almost any ordinary sounding individual (the more ordinary the better) as if their opinions are typical of everyone. Populism is the simplification of democracy. Populism can be stirred – perhaps even should be stirred, on occasion – when

a purely pragmatic, purely compromising practice of politics lacks any sense of vision or moral purpose. '[When] too great a gap opens between haloed democracy and the grubby business of politics, populists tend to move onto the vacant territory, promising instead of the dirty world of party manoeuvring the shiny ideal of democracy renewed' (Canovan, 1999: 2–16). The practices of politics in a democracy can be as difficult as understanding in the classroom or seminar the different meanings of the concept; but as important and compellingly interesting to do so.

Nevertheless perhaps the shrewdest contemporary student of government, the American Robert Dahl, has suggested the following characteristics of the institutions of modern democracy: elected representatives with free, fair and frequent elections; freedom of expression and access to alternative, independent sources of information; autonomous associations, that is citizens must be free to combine together for a wide variety of purposes – including religion, interest groups and political parties; and inclusive citizenship – that no one permanently resident in a country should be denied rights available to citizens (Dahl, 1991, 1999). Perhaps one only needs to add as institutions the independence of the judiciary and respect for a professional and politically neutral bureaucracy. But it is men and women acting as citizens who work institutions and who try to participate. Democracy depends on all of us: the price of liberty is not just 'eternal vigilance', as Abraham Lincoln said, but eternal activity.

REFERENCES

Advisory Group on Citizenship (1998) *Education for Citizenship and the Teaching of Democracy in Schools.* London: Qualifications and Curriculum Authority.

Arendt, H. (1958) *The Human Condition.* London: Cambridge University Press.

Barker, E. (ed.) (1958) *The Politics of Aristotle.* Oxford: Clarendon Press.

Bradley, P. (ed.) (1945) *Democracy in America by Alexis de Tocqueville*, Vol. I.

New York: Knopf. (There have been several later translations but this still reads best).

Canovan, M. (1999) 'Trust the People! Populism and the Two Faces of Democracy', *Political Studies*, 47 (1): 2–16.

Crick, B. (2002) *Democracy: A Very Short Introduction*. Oxford: Oxford University Press.

Crick, B. (2005) *In Defence of Politics* 5th edn. London: Continuum

Crick, B. (2007) 'Politics, Populism and Democracy' in Julio Faundez (ed.) *On the State of Democracy*. Abingdon: Routledge.

Dahl, R.A. (1991) *Democracy and Its Critics*. New Haven and London: Yale University Press.

Dahl, R.A. (1999) *On Democracy*. New Haven and London: Yale University Press.

Farrar, C. (1988) *The Origins of Democratic Thinking: The Invention of Politics in Classical Athens*. Cambridge: Cambridge University Press.

Gauchet, M. (ed.) (1997) 'De La Libert des Anciens Comparee a celle des Modernes' in *Benjamin Constant Ecrits Politiques*. Paris: Gallimard.

Lipset, S.M. (1996) *American Exceptionalism: A Double-Edged Sword*. New York and London: W.W. Norton.

Rieu, R.V. (ed.) (1954) *Thucydides, The Peloponnesian War* (tr. Rex Warner) London: Penguin.

2

Rights, Duties and Responsibilities

David Carr

One can hardly avoid talk of rights and duties in any contemporary discussion of issues of personal and public concern – at all events, in developed liberal democracies. Such talk is certainly embedded in debates about education, schooling and childcare with regard to which any and all acceptable policy-making needs to be mindful of and sensitive to the rights as well as the responsibilities of such diverse stakeholders as children, parents, teachers, social workers and officers of the law. However, it should also not be hard to see that the prospects of any legislation that aspires to do full justice to the rights and claims of all interested parties are likely to be dim in (the not uncommon) circumstances where rights claims are at some odds with one another. Thus, for example, one can see how a professional proposal to promote religious or sex education in the school curriculum – on the grounds that children have a right to such provision – may well be resisted by some parents, precisely on the grounds that such instruction violates their rights to protect their offspring from what they regard as dubious influences. Again, a *prima facie* parental right to custody over their natural offspring may well come into conflict with what social workers are likely to regard as the rights of the child (not to be harmed) in

circumstances of apparent parental neglect or abuse.

Hence, even if we can make sense of the attribution of educational or other rights to human (or other) agencies, it is evident that rights claims or attributions seldom form consistent or mutually agreeable sets – and it is far from clear, in the face of evident conflicts between competing rights, on what principled grounds such tensions might be resolved (see, on rights in general, Waldron 1984). In this light, it will be the aim of this brief chapter, not to focus upon any particular issues or questions of educational rights, but more generally to explore some influential concepts of rights and responsibilities in the works of a number of key past and social and political philosophers.

It is commonly claimed (see, for example, Almond 1991) that the idea of rights hails from so-called natural law theory that is also usually traced back to classical antiquity – perhaps primarily to the Stoics, but also (a little more controversially) to themes in Plato and Aristotle. Concepts of natural law turn basically on the idea that just as the world of empirical experience derives its order and coherence from rationally discernible laws of nature, so there are rationally discernible and divinely, or otherwise, ordained moral laws by reference to which human wellbeing or flourishing may be comprehended. From this viewpoint, a good or flourishing human life would be one that is lived in the light of (perhaps rationally principled) observance of the imperatives or prescriptions of natural law – specifically in recognition of the human rights that such law identifies and the duties that it enjoins with respect to those rights. The more difficult question now is that of what such rights and corresponding responsibilities could be, and of how such rights might be rationally grounded?

In this regard, though the rights of natural law theory have their principal roots in ancient and medieval philosophy, modern and contemporary notions of moral, social and political rights and duties are implicated more in the post-scholastic contract theories of the ages of reason and enlightenment. Here, it is helpful to start with the British political theorist Thomas Hobbes who – in his epic work *Leviathan* (1968) – is precisely exercised by the question of the grounds and justification of social order in an age of scientific reason and method in which it no longer seems rational to appeal to traditional religious or other authority. Indeed, from the dogma-free and rationally disinterested standpoint of scientific enquiry, Hobbes starts with the question of how any kind of social order or co-operation might be possible in the face of what he takes to be the undisputed fact of individual human self-interest. Since human agents are psycho-biologically disposed to be concerned only with their own survival (or perhaps also with that of their progeny), it is to be wondered how they have ever entered into states of social co-operation at all. Thus, in the state of nature into which humans have been cast by physical nature, existence is a 'war of all against all' and life is 'nasty, poor, solitary, brutish and short' (Hobbes, 1968: 186). Moreover, in circumstances of inevitable competition for scarce resources in which survival is the main concern, freedom to act in any manner that conduces to self-preservation – including murder of, or theft from,

rivals or competitors – becomes an imperative if not also something like a right. Indeed, how in such a world could peaceful co-operation appear advisable, wise or virtuous?

Hobbes' short answer is that while life in the state of nature is free, it is not secure: human agents soon recognize that the very same liberty that they have to kill and dispossess rivals leaves them vulnerable to a similar fate. To be sure, they quickly realize that one way to resist the predation of the stronger is to combine with others who are weaker – so that the weak may jointly overmaster the individually stronger. Eventually, however, individual agents come to recognize that it lies in the common interest to accept a general rule of restraint on any and all pre-civil liberty to do violence to others: for whilst such a rule may curb the freedom of individuals to do violence to others, it also restricts the freedom of others to do violence to them. In short, the loss of individual liberty that such social contract entails is justified rationally as the price to be paid for individual and common security. But the upshot of Hobbes' argument is that the civil order bought by social contract is not ultimately compatible with individual liberty: human agents are not inherently co-operative, they are driven by anti-social impulses and tendencies and they may only be 'civilized' by the rule of law. Moreover, Hobbes explicitly held that any such law would need to be guaranteed and enforced by some sovereign power (such as absolute monarchy) whose dissolution or overthrow could never be rationally justified – since even tyranny could not be worse than the dog-eat-dog anarchy of civil breakdown and disorder.

One can see both of the other key early modern contract theorists – Locke and Rousseau – as responding critically to Hobbes' view that individual liberty and social order are not mutually sustainable. However, the sharp contrast between their views on the place of rights and duties in political theory and public policy also serves well to highlight some of the main conceptual and normative questions to which these notions give rise. To begin with, John Locke (1966) – who may well be regarded as the founding father of political liberalism – is primarily concerned to uphold the cause of individual liberty against what he takes to be the overly repressive sovereignty of Hobbes' civil law. Departing from Hobbes' apparently dim view of the anti-social character of natural human impulse and inclination, Locke reinterprets the state of nature more normatively than descriptively – arguing that it is the state in which the law of nature (something close to the ideal of natural law) would be acknowledged and respected by human beings. In turn, the law of nature is defined as that which is generally conducive to positive and beneficial human association and which therefore requires respect for the moral rights of human beings as determined by that law. For Locke, the most basic of these are the rights to life, liberty and personal property or estate – and for him all these basic rights are connected. First, whilst it goes without saying that life is a pre-condition of any human fulfilment at all, a rationally fulfilling or fulfilled human life could also only be one in which agents are able to think or act with some measure of freedom: the life of an indoctrinated slave would hardly be a fully flourishing life. But, perhaps more controversially, Locke also takes the right to property as a key condition of freedom.

In line with his liberal credentials, Locke holds that there are two key – negative and positive – dimensions to freedom. His view of positive freedom – which he again shares with other liberal theorists – is that it is basically entrepreneurial: in order to express or realize their freedom, human agents need scope to engage in enterprises and develop projects over which they can claim some ownership. For liberals, any genuine freedom – the positive freedom upon which the sense of individual self so dear to liberals depends – turns crucially on being able to say at the close of one's efforts: 'I have done this' or 'this is mine'. In this connection, the reason why liberals are generally opposed to notions of common or state ownership of property

(as in communism, socialism or fascism) is that such arrangements greatly undermine the individual (sense of) self and its forward development and by so doing also tend to sap any and all drive and initiative. From this viewpoint, liberals are also inclined to support those social, political and economic arrangements that promote negative freedom through the reduction of state restraint of personal initiative and enterprise: thus, for example, liberals will generally favour free market over command economies. That said these views engender some tensions in Locke's thought. For one thing, although Locke wishes to rebut Hobbes' view that it is never appropriate to oppose the rule of sovereign law even if that rule is unjust or tyrannical, it is not clear upon what legitimate Lockian grounds such refutation might be constructed.

Such opposition could hardly be mounted on the grounds that injustice permits inequality, since Locke's defence of private ownership is ultimately consistent with wide disparities of inherited or otherwise accumulated wealth – and in fact the rulers of unjust societies invariably justify such inequalities on grounds of their divinely ordained or other entitlement (for example, the 'Divine right of kings') to inherited or otherwise appropriated wealth. In short, Locke needs an argument against tyranny and injustice that: (i) is not based on any simple opposition to unequal property distribution; and (ii) shows how there may be legitimate inequalities of wealth. Locke famously finds this argument in the idea that human agents have a right to whatever they 'have mixed with their labour' (Locke, 1966: 130). On this view, the difference between the legitimate wealth and property of industrious entrepreneurs and the more suspect inherited wealth and estate of tyrannical monarchs or aristocrats is that whereas the former are entitled to what they have earned by the sweat of their brows, the latter will have invariably come by what they have through more dubious routes of extortionate taxation or violent seizure. Hence, for Locke, injustice consists ultimately in any and all attempts to take away from individuals what they may be said to have legitimately earned: this, we should note, would apply no less to radical egalitarian (socialist or communist) attempts to redistribute wealth – to take from the rich and give to the poor – than to the robber baron operations of much traditional sovereignty.

The trouble is, however, that Locke's distinction seems far from clear cut: where, one might ask, is one to find clear examples of ownership – albeit mixed with labour – that do not involve some dubious appropriation? When, for example, the colonial pioneers of the American continent (of whom Locke doubtless approved) hewed wealth and estate from the backwoods wilderness, they invariably did this by taking over land that was not theirs, and on which there were indeed prior claims. Likewise, the global entrepreneurs of Western industrial Europe who grew wealthy through the transatlantic shipment of resources and materials for the cotton-trade, clearly did so on the back of appalling exploitation of black slave labour. In general, indeed, the basic Lockian liberal political and economic principles which were to inspire the American revolutionary vision of a social order dedicated to the protection of life, liberty and the pursuit of happiness seems to have produced a society that is hard to characterize in terms of justice as fairness or equality. From this perspective, indeed, it also seems worth asking – as we shall now see that Rousseau does effectively ask – what might be the precise status or grounds of Locke's claim that property (or anything else for that matter) is a *right*?

Like Locke, Jean-Jacques Rousseau can also be regarded as attempting to refute Hobbes' view that the ideas of human freedom and civil society are not compatible. On the face of it, Rousseau's famous opening sentence in the *Social Contract* that 'man is born free and everywhere he is in chains' (Rousseau 1973: 181) may seem to endorse – under this or that interpretation – Hobbes' rather pessimistic understanding of the human condition. However, Rousseau completely overturns Hobbes' account of the causes of human suffering and injustice. First, although he appears to follow Hobbes in offering a quasi-descriptive account of the state of nature, he thinks that Hobbes has greatly misdescribed it. Drawing upon available anthropological evidence (from the new world and elsewhere) of pre-civil modes of tribal association of aboriginal peoples, he argues that they are not characterized by Hobbes' 'war of all against all' but by a high degree of social solidarity, cohesion and mutual assistance. From this viewpoint, if property is a right, it does not seem to be 'natural' in an innate sense – since primitive pre-civil societies are precisely not possessive in any such way. On the contrary, Rousseau traces injustice to the inequality consequent upon transition from the economically simple and socially cohesive states of pre-civil association to the economic diversity and division of labour of complex civil societies. When Rousseau writes that 'the first man who, after fencing off a piece of land, took it upon himself to say 'This belongs to me' and found people simple enough to believe him, was the true founder of civil society' (Rousseau, 1973: 84), it is clear that any alleged right to property is not in his view an unmixed blessing.

On the contrary, Rousseau sees the possessive individualism of civil societies as the origin of social class divisions and the prime source of the exploitation and enslavement of some by others: it is with the emergence of economically differentiated classes that distinctions between 'haves' and 'have nots' emerge – in which those that 'have' become filled with a false pride (*amour propre*) and those that 'have not' are branded as inferior. Moreover, Rousseau clearly thinks that any such *de haut en bas* contempt for others is not just misplaced or mistaken, but that it is based on moral and spiritual delusion. In the *Social Contract*, he writes – in much the spirit of natural law theory – that 'there is a universal justice emanating from reason alone' (Rousseau, 1974: 210). But what could be the basis of this moral law: does it consist in some set of rights to freedom and so on with which all men have been endowed by God or nature – and which the master has somehow failed to recognize in the servant or slave? Rousseau's answer seems to be yes and no. His key point is that there are no natural rights in the sense that these might form part of some complete description of human nature (of the form: humans have one head, two arms, two legs, they are sexually reproductive, mortal and have rights to life, liberty and property). From this viewpoint, the unjust master has not failed to recognize some natural (empirical) characteristic of the slave that he has not noticed before: it is rather that he has failed to grasp that there is a rational *imperative* to respect the liberty of others upon which his own claim to freedom is morally dependent (see, on this point, Benn and Peters, 1957).

The point is that rights attributions are not descriptions but *prescriptions* – albeit prescriptions of a peculiarly general or universal sort. The trouble with the slave owner is that he denies to others that (liberty) which he nevertheless evidently claims for himself – which leaves him in a rationally and morally compromised position. From this viewpoint, any and all intelligible claims to rights require an appreciation that the respect for ourselves and our own wellbeing that we might claim in this or that regard is logically inseparable from readiness to return that same respect to others. In short, on this view, rights are not just correlative to or inter-definable with duties (so that a right might be defined in terms of no duty not to do something, and a duty as no right not to do it), but rights claims are logistically dependent upon the acknowledgement of obligations to respect them. It is not just that rights claims may only be honoured where agents appreciate the logical dependence of their own claims to liberties or entitlements on universal obligations to respect the liberties or entitlements of others, but that rights claims are apt to be empty or impotent in the absence of supporting and/or publicly supported legislation. At all events, Rousseau holds that this insight into the relationship of rights to

responsibilities has been the major moral casualty of the transition from pre-civil to civil association. Hence, while he thinks that no return to the pre-lapsarian state of nature is possible for citizens of economically advanced modern polities, he holds that what is required is a new conception of moral and political education (or re-education) that might reclaim this vision for corrupted post-civil sensibilities.

It is this re-education of sensibility – with regard, precisely, to an impartial or 'disinterested' appreciation that our own interests are bound up with a concern for the common good – that Rousseau attempts to outline in his educational work *Emile* (1974). It is also expressed, however, in the account that Rousseau gives in his *Social Contract* of the difference between appropriate and inappropriate democratic participation focused on the distinction between the 'will of all' and the 'general will'. Whilst one certainly has a democratic right in an open society to vote for whatever party one likes – which includes the right to support those that would promote one's own interests, liberties and entitlements, Rousseau clearly regards it as the democratic duty of responsible citizens to support policies that conduce to the common good – even where this might reduce one's own social advantage. Thus, for example, while it might be to my personal advantage as a citizen of wealth to oppose a policy that raises taxes to provide for the less well-off (say, for a system of common schooling from which my own privately educated children would not benefit), I may yet recognize it as the duty of a rationally responsible citizen to raise the general level of wellbeing and welfare of the less well advantaged. In short, while policies based on the will of all simply reflect the prevailing state of self-interest in a given social context, those expressing the general will are or should be the result of rationally responsible reflection on what best conduces to the common good.

The Rousseauian claim that rights are more accurately conceived as derivative of duties than vice versa is basically the view of so-called *deontology*, and the chief apostle of deontology – who explicitly acknowledged his own profound debt to Rousseau – is undoubtedly the great enlightenment philosopher Immanuel Kant. For Kant, whose work has had an enormous influence on latter day moral and social theory, what mainly distinguishes the logic of normative discourse from that of empirical science is that the judgements of the former are prescriptive rather than descriptive; and what distinguishes moral prescriptions – for example, those that recognize duties to respect the rights of others – is their absolute law-like character. In his *Groundwork of the Metaphysic of Morals* and other works, Kant (1948) distinguishes moral prescriptions as categorical imperatives from hypothetical imperatives on the grounds that whereas the latter are merely concerned with the satisfaction of particular empirically conditioned desires, the former express moral duties that no rational agent could possibly regard as other than inherently compelling. The key test of a moral duty is that it can be regarded as universally authoritative – which Kant expresses in so many words in his famous formula: 'act only on that maxim through which you can at the same time will that it should become a universal law' (Kant, 1948: 80). More substantially, however, the moral law rests on the idea of respect for persons (ourselves no less than others) as members of what Kant calls 'the kingdom of ends'. However, Kant holds that the special status owed to human agents as persons is due to their possession of an empirically transcendent rational-moral self, and that it is this 'noumenal' self that demands unqualified respect.

True to their (British) empiricist heritage, the key 19th century apostles of liberalism had little time for the metaphysical baggage of Kant's account of moral duty – but they were generally no less sympathetic to any Lockian or other talk of natural rights (which Bentham described as 'nonsense on stilts'). Nevertheless, in his key works of moral, social and political theory, the high priest of modern liberalism John Stuart Mill (1970) regarded the idea of individual freedom as a cornerstone of civil association and the idea of universal benevolence (utility) as a basic moral obligation. For utilitarian liberals, however, neither of these notions has or requires any metaphysical or non-empirical support. First, respect for individual liberty is to be valued not because it is a natural right but rather because it is an indispensable precondition of positive moral and political association. For Mill, any and all forward moral and social progress depends upon the possibility of the free and open expression and/or exchange of views and ideas – which is only possible in an open democratic society in which freedom of belief and speech is respected or at the very least tolerated. That said, the fundamental utilitarian obligation to promote the greatest happiness of the greatest number – arguably defensible on the straightforwardly empirical grounds that given the general human value of happiness a larger quantity of such happiness must be preferable to a smaller quantity – it seems that any individual claim to freedom as a right may be overridden where it might impede greater general happiness. Since, for utilitarians, the moral rightness, or otherwise, of actions is to be measured by reference to the amounts of happiness over unhappiness they might be expected to engender, it would be clearly be wrong from the utilitarian perspective to condemn millions to death in a nuclear strike, if this could be averted by the brutal torture and death of a single (innocent) individual.

The status in classic Millian liberalism of what many would see as the basic human entitlement to freedom is therefore variously problematic. On the one hand, (positive) freedom is granted a high profile as something that is apt for wide and largely unrestricted promotion – the only restriction being that the individual pursuit of projects should not impede or violently intrude upon the liberties of others. While this would certainly rule out colonial genocide or slavery, it certainly does not rule out – and is mostly taken by many liberals to be actually supportive of – the kind of free enterprise that opens up and/or endorses wide disparities between the haves and have-nots of contemporary market economies. The whole point of such liberalism is to give those who have the wit, will and/or initiative to make something of themselves in the world, the freedom and scope to do so: it offers little consolation to those who are not so well placed to make the best of such freedom. Indeed, as we have seen, the utilitarian rejection of (even negative) freedom as a right offers little to safeguard the welfare of those born losers on the inevitably uneven playing field of liberal enterprise. Moreover, while it was (and is) part of the traditional rhetoric of liberal economic theory that the benefits of free enterprise are likely to have a 'trickle-down' effect on the general welfare, it has been no less plausibly maintained by Marxist and other critics of liberalism that the gap between the enterprising rich and the (exploited) poor has shown no indication of lessening and every sign of widening in post-industrial 19th and 20th century liberal economies.

In this light, one of the key problems of modern social and political theory is that classical liberal theory generally promotes a fairly unrestricted conception of liberty which – barring actual violent intrusion into the affairs of others – is nevertheless compatible with a diverse range of economic and other deprivation and exploitation of the vulnerable, and that is actually wedded to a moral theory (utilitarianism) which attaches little sense to rights and is consequently prepared to overrule individual claims to life, security and freedom in some (albeit extreme) circumstances. On the other hand, while the deontological tradition of Rousseau and Kant offers to give a higher social theoretical profile to rights – via a normative understanding of rights as derivative from universal duties – it seems wedded to a highly questionable metaphysical view of human freedom as the effect of some mysterious non-empirical rational will (as well as, in at least some Rousseauian and post-Kantian versions, to

potentially oppressive redistributive social policies). From this viewpoint, one might see the holy grail of modern Western social theory as the development of a liberal democratic account of social justice which could precisely reconcile a substantial (i.e., not unduly restrictive) conception of individual freedom with a proper regard for basic human rights – the fundamental conditions of flourishing – of especially vulnerable people. This is more or less what the great modern American social theorist John Rawls set out to do in the middle of the last century in his celebrated work *A Theory of Justice* (1985).

Basically, the philosophy of John Rawls can be understood as an attempt to reinterpret liberal theory in Kantian terms, but entirely shorn of the metaphysical baggage and associations of Kant's deontology. To this end, Rawls generally endorses Kant's normative analysis of the idea of a right. Far from being natural properties of agents, rights are attributed or ascribed on the basis of the duties recognized by Kant's categorical imperatives: people are entitled to freedom, true testimony and honoured promises on the grounds that slavery, lies and promise-breaking could not be rationally willed as universal laws. Like the classical contract theorists, however, Rawls is more interested in the question of social order and cohesion than in that of individual moral conscience: in particular, he is interested in the issue of how the laws that enable liberal democratic citizens to co-exist co-operatively – not least in the face of those individual differences of interest and value that often threaten to divide them – might be rationally grounded (on this, see also Rawls, 1993). To this end, he gives a largely *contractualist* interpretation to the Kantian categorical imperative: the rules that any and all rational individuals are likely to accept as a common basis for civil legislation are those that one might will to be universal laws: such rules should reflect what Rawls calls an 'overlapping consensus' of general agreement that transcends local cultural differences. It is also a virtue of such rules that while they are sufficiently substantial to secure social solidarity and cohesion, they are also 'thin' enough to avoid undue state constraint on individual liberty. In so far as such universal rules prescribe freedom, tolerance and respect for all regardless of race, creed, colour, gender or sexuality, however, they precisely reflect the Kantian impartiality that Rawls takes to be at the heart of justice as fairness. In short, Rawls' use of Kantian deontology enables him to place individual rights to respect and fair treatment at the very heart of liberal theory. Still, the problem remains that such theoretical equal regard in the real social world of wide disparities of personal means, status and needs may yet involve treating some unjustly: the freedom of the already well placed to advance their interests yet further could well lead to further disadvantage of the not so well favoured.

It is in response to this problem that Rawls offers the thought experiment of the 'original position' for which he is particularly well known. We are asked to imagine ourselves (behind a 'veil of ignorance') as not yet knowing what the circumstances of our birth and life might be – whether we are going to be intellectually able or challenged, rich or poor, black or white, male or female. In such circumstances, what balance of legislation might we think best reflects just social and public policy? Rawls argues that it would be most rational to aim for policies that precisely avoid undue curtailment of the developmental prospects of the advantaged on the one hand and further disadvantaging the already disadvantaged on the other. If I am rich and intelligent, I may expect through my efforts to make some contribution (through taxes or other public service) to helping the less well-off – if, that is, the initiatives upon which my effective contribution to the common good depends are not subject to undue sate control or interference. On the other hand, however, if already disadvantaged by social status, disability or poverty, I would hope to be shielded from further disadvantage and/or oppression – not least that which might follow from exploitation by already better placed others. In short, as both

Rousseau and Kant effectively argued, the best possible political arrangement we might hope for is one that encourages the reasonably unfettered pursuit of individual talent and initiative – but always with a view to the common good and appropriate concern for the less well favoured. On the face of it, this would seem to be an intellectually, politically and economically open society – a liberal democracy – that also recognizes and respects the rights of all citizens to a certain state funded minimum of welfare with regard to such basic conditions of flourishing as healthcare, education and legal aid.

While these ideas of Rawls' have been highly influential and are (in essentials) widely endorsed by latter day theorists of liberal democracy, they have also not lacked for criticisms – either internal or external to liberal theory. Since space is short, I shall not spend much time here on the objections to Rawls of other liberal theorists, but concentrate on criticisms of his views – and of liberal analyses of rights and duties in general – from non-liberal perspectives. Many of these have hailed from what are generally labelled 'communitarian' perspectives. The term 'communitarian' has diverse senses in modern social and political theory (see Carr, 2003, Chapter 11) and so-called communitarians come in many stripes and colours: many communitarian critiques of liberalism draw their inspiration from religious perspectives and commitments, but others acknowledge direct debts to various forms of post-Kantian philosophical (mainly German) idealism – particularly to Hegel and Marx. Broadly, however, communitarians are inclined to hold that individual or personal human values are conditioned by social or cultural context rather than vice versa: that, in the famous words of Marx, 'it is not the consciousness of man that determines society, but society that determines the consciousness of man' (Marx and Engels, 1968: 181). In this light, the moral values and principles that underpin or shape the social and political rights and obligations of individual human agents are not the product of some rationally detached philosophical thought experiment but a matter of social and cultural – including as often as not religious – inheritance. Indeed, since such values and principles also have affective and sentimental as well as cognitive dimensions (if these can even be separated), it may make no more sense to ask why we are attached to our values than a ask parents why they feel love for or obligation towards their children (see, for thinking broadly along these lines, MacIntyre, 1981, 1987; Sandel, 1982).

At all events, the communitarian view of the provenance of moral values and principles has significant implications for questions of rights and responsibilities. The first is that many communitarians question the claim or assumption of Rawls and many other liberals that there are and even can be cross-culturally or universally agreed moral values or beliefs: there is, in short, a strong vein of cultural and moral relativism in much (though not all) communitarianism which insists that moral values are socially constructed and liable to local variation and conflict that cannot be resolved from any neutral rational standpoint or 'view from nowhere'. But secondly, whereas the universalism of liberals seems to regard rights as attaching primarily to individual citizens, communitarians attach great significance to the idea of communal or group rights – which, they will claim, individuals enjoy by virtue of cultural (including religious) tradition or inheritance. The trouble is, however, that such cultural or communal rights often seem to conflict with the universal rights of liberals. Thus, for example, while liberals would regard freedom from discrimination on grounds of sexuality as a universal right of all citizens, some groups would claim a religiously sanctioned right to discriminate against non-heterosexuals in at least some circumstances (for example, in priesthood or ministry). Similarly, whereas a liberal viewpoint would generally favour monogamy on the grounds of gender equality, polygamy might well be defended from some non-liberal perspectives as a religious right. Again, although liberal legislation may be inclined to place a universal ban on

whaling in the ecological interests of any and all contemporary global citizens, some indigenous people have claimed the right to whale hunting as an important part of their cultural as well as economic heritage. In sum, these and other issues between liberals and communitarians (as well as within these two camps) are sufficient to show that the most basic moral questions concerning rights, duties and responsibilities are as yet some way from satisfactory resolution.

REFERENCES

Almond, B. (1991) 'Rights', in P. Singer (ed.) *A Companion to Ethics*. Oxford: Blackwell.

Benn, S.I. and Peters, R.S. (1957) *Social Principles and the Democratic State*. London: George Allen and Unwin.

Carr, D. (2003) *Making Sense of Education: An Introduction to the Philosophy and Theory of Education and Teaching*. London: Routledge/Falmer.

Hobbes, T. (1968) *Leviathan*. Harmondsworth: Penguin.

Kant, I. (1948) *Groundwork of the Metaphysic of Morals*, translated by H.J. Paton under the title, *The Moral Law*. London: Hutchinson.

Locke. J. (1966) *Two Treatises of Civil Government*. London: Dent Everyman.

MacIntyre, A.C. (1981) *After Virtue*. Notre Dame: Notre Dame Press.

MacIntyre, A.C. (1987) *Whose Justice, Which Rationality?* Notre Dame: Notre Dame Press.

Marx, K. and Engels, F. (1968) *Selected Writings*. London: Lawrence and Wishart.

Mill, J.S. (1970) 'On Liberty' and 'Utilitarianism', in M. Warnock (ed.) *Utilitarianism*. London: Collins, The Fontana Library.

Rawls, J. (1985) *A Theory of Justice*. Cambridge: Harvard University Press.

Rawls, J. (1993) *Political Liberalism*. New York: Columbia University Press.

Rousseau, J-J. (1973) *The Social Contract and Other Discourses*. London: Dent.

Rousseau, J-J. (1974) *Emile*. London: Dent.

Sandel, M. (1982) *Liberalism and the Limits of Justice*. New York: Cambridge University Press.

Waldron, J. (ed.) (1984) *Theories of Rights*. Oxford: Oxford University Press.

3

Civic Education, Social Justice and Critical Race Theory

Cynthia A. Tyson and Sung Choon Park

INTRODUCTION

Social studies educators often acknowledge the history of social injustices rooted in our nationhood. Two distinct paradigms in contemporary civic education and multicultural education have highlighted the issues often marginalized in American society related to race, ethnicity and class. Each of these areas theoretically and in classroom practice have marginally theorized race in the social studies and delineated strategies for societal transformation (Dewy, 1916; Banks, 1990, 1991, 1990; Bickmore, 1993; Goodman, 1992; Lynch, 1992).

At the core of both multicultural and civic education are the essential concepts of democracy, equality and civic participation. Although their tenets support an examination of social justice, the placement of social justice and race at the center as a unit of analysis and critique of the promises and rights of democracy has not been done until contemporary times. Specific areas of teaching and research have included (but are not limited to) the development of political, or civic identity, the relationship between engagement and opportunity related to social justice, consequences of civic engagement for individuals or institution, political participation across the influence of technology and/or the media on civic engagement, civic engagement in the context of schools, the role of culture in shaping civic engagement.

Social justice as a theoretical perspective can facilitate that critique providing a lens to critique civic education in an attempt to move beyond the traditional boundaries of traditional civic and social education. Such a critique proposes how we have standardized the concepts of civic participation and responsibilities in a racialized society, and moves discussions of social justice and race in civic education from the margins to the core of citizenship education in the social studies teaching and research. In addition to social justice theory (SJT), critical race theory (CRT) places race as a unit of analysis becoming instrumental in discussing the roles of race, racism and power in civic education.

Social studies educators have traditionally and conservatively focused on civic competencies (Torney-Purta et al., 2000) in curriculum standards and pedagogy. With a broader view that explores beyond a list of proposed civic competencies, we define being what it means to be engaged as a citizen, a concept that must include addressing the inequities that are the byproduct of endemic racism.

In this chapter I using suggest SJT and CRT as frameworks for critiquing education for citizenship – civic education. After a brief review of the literature related to SJT and CRT, I will highlight three exemplars of education for citizenship and race: Literacy acquisition during African enslavement, activist civic educator Septima Clark and the Mississippi Freedom Schools.

SOCIAL JUSTICE EDUCATION: A REVIEW OF THE LITERATURE

Lived experiences ignite the conditions and activate the potentials. For this reason, realistic narratives are commonly used in scholarly works in order to challenge the world of oppression and struggle for social justice (Collins, 1991, 1998; Nieto, 2000; Sleeter, 1995; Krieger, 1983; Bell, 1992; Ladson-Billings, 2001; Ayers et al., 1998; Finn, 1999; Mabokela and Green, 2001).

With its root in Greek philosophy, conventional theories begin with an overarching concept of social justice. It is an ideal and universal concept that applies equally to everyone in a normatively and culturally neutral world. The principle of justice has been explained through different concepts such as 'the common good' (Bobhouse, 1922), 'equality' (Frankena, 1962), 'fairness' (Rawls, 1971, 1993), and 'impartiality, choice, and reciprocity' (Barry, 1989). In this approach, the meaning of social justice is only legitimate within the 'hegemony of autonomous individualism' (Fine et al., 2000: 116). It provides the procedural and distributive theory of social justice (Young, 1990, North, 2006).

It is John Rawls (1971, 1993) who theorizes the logocentric approach to social justice as fairness. In his theory there are two principles of justice, which are:

a. 'Each person has an equal right to a fully adequate scheme of equal basic liberties which is compatible with a similar scheme of all'.

b. 'Social and economic inequalities are to satisfy two conditions. First, they must be attached to offices and positions open to all under conditions of fair equality of opportunity; and second, they must be to the greatest benefit of the least advantaged members of society' (Rawls, 1993: 291).

Rawls (1971) strongly believes that the two principles are 'perfectly credible' (183). However, it is notable that he has to fabricate the concept of the original position in order to 'set up a fair procedure so that any principles agreed to will be just' and to 'use the notion of pure procedural justice as a basis of justice' (136). In addition, as he clearly points out, it is 'a purely hypothetical situation characterized so as to lead to a certain conception of justice' (Rawls, 1971: 12).

Consequently, the logocentric theory of justice has an intrinsic inadequacy in addressing socially, culturally and institutionally unjust relationships because it reduces social justice as something measurable based on his contrived situations. For example, Alexander (2005) investigates racial issues in the US by considering justice as 'the allocation of resources and burdens fairly' (120). He finds that African Americans receive less justice compared with other racial groups. However, the concept of justice should not be confined within the distributive concept of material justice because it prevents people in social and cultural margins from confronting structural violence. When the logocentric approach is applied to the field of education, school becomes 'an institution with a basic function of maintaining and transmitting ... the consensual values of society' (Kohlberg, 1967: 165) and justice becomes 'the basic valuing process that underlies each person's capacity for moral judgment' (Power, Higgins, and Kohlberg, 1989: 15).

On the contrary to inferring the procedural concept of justice, Young (1990) develops a different theory of justice aiming to eliminate oppression, which are 'the vast and deep injustices some groups suffer as a consequence of often unconscious assumptions

Table 3.1 **Two approaches to social justice**

	Logocentric Theories	Grounded Theories
Approach	Deductive	Inductive
Starting point	Ideal concept of justice	Concrete examples of injustice
Main concept	Fairness and impartiality	Oppression and domination
Emphasis	Redistribution/Procedure	Resistance/Recognition
Context	Universal and culturally neutral	Historically and culturally specific
Perspective	Everyone's perspective	Perspectives of the oppressed
Representative Theorists	Rawls (1971)	Young (1990)
	Barry (1989)	Collins (1991, 1998)
	Kohlberg (1981)	Adams et al. (1997, 2000)
Theoretical background	Political liberalism	Postmodern critical theories

and reactions of well-meaning people in … the normal processes of everyday life' (41). Unlike the logocentric theorists, grounded theorists deal with concrete examples of social injustices without wearing 'the veil of ignorance'. Instead of theorizing social justice, grounded theorists focus on social injustice either by constructing an account of separate system of oppression for each oppressed group such as racism, sexism, heterosexism, anti-semitism, ableism, classism and multiple issues (Adams et al., 1997, 2000), or by describing criteria for determining whether individuals and groups are oppressed (Young, 1990; Bell, 1997).

A grounded approach to social justice begins with socially unjust realities per se. It moves people to struggle 'not just because they either think justice is logical or see pragmatic reasons for pursuing it, but because they believe that achieving it is the right thing to do' (Collins, 1998: 244). It is to 'first focus on what is wrong before embarking upon a program based on what is right' (Simon, 1995: 24). Social injustice takes priority over social justice and it is not abnormality or breakdown of social justice (Shklar, 1990; Simon, 1995). Necessity of social justice does not come from aberration of social justice but from clear presence of social injustice.

The unjust reality of the world has been explained with the concepts such as hegemony (Gramsci, 1975), structural violence (Galtung, 1975), culture of power (Delpit, 1988), etc. A critical theorist Henry Giroux (1999) shows how political, economic

and cultural inequalities are interrelated in cultural politics. Unequal diversity and diverse inequalities have been revealed through cultural incongruities among different racial, ethnic, gender, and language groups. According to Gay (2000), the greatest of all obstacles to diversity is mainstream ethnocentrism. The imposition of Eurocentric values and orientation is 'morally suspect and pedagogically unsound' (208). Young (1990) calls ethnocentrism cultural imperialism that 'involves the universalization of a dominant group's experience and culture, and its establishments as the norm' (59).

The above table shows differences between conventional theories of justice and grounded theories of justice.

Unlike logocentric theorists whose focus is heavily on social justice focusing on redistribution from everyone's perspective in a normatively and culturally neutral stance, grounded theorists deal with social injustice as well as social justice from the oppressed perspectives in culturally specific contexts. Social justice is considered both as goal and process (Bell, 1997).

WHAT IS SOCIAL JUSTICE IN CURRENT LITERATURE?

Definitions of social justice range from very simple to very complicated. For example, in her tribute to Bill Ayers, Therese Quinn defines social justice as

[L]ove-infused and hopeful vision of teaching that is grounded, against the grain of governmental push and current trend, not at all in the interests of the market but rather in the specific lives of particular children. It is all about ... teaching in the hope of making the world a better place. (Quinn, 2003: 2003)

Jamie B. Lewis, on the other hand, defines social justice as something that 'involves exploring the social construction of unequal hierarchies, which result in a social group's differential access to power and privilege', and '[e]xploring issues of social justice also involves the deconstruction of unjust and oppressive structures' (Lewis, 2001: 189).

Whatever their particular intricacies and nuances may be, most definitions and conceptions of social justice contain key distinctive components. Respect for diversity; coalition building; intercultural dialogue; experiential learning; cross-cultural communication and interaction; individual agency (Adams et al., 1997; Applebaum, 2001; Lewis, 2001; McCall, 2004; Nagda et al., 2003; Smith, 1999; Wade, 2003) all fit within the continuum of social justice education in the US. Understanding, criticizing and confronting racism, sexism, ableism, classism, homophobia and such others that thrive in the 'domination–subordination' (Nagda et al.,: 167) structure of the contemporary American society causing broad systemic oppression (Adams et al., 1997; Applebaum, 2001; Lewis, 2001; McCall, 2004; Nagda et al., 2003; Sapon-Shevin, 2003; Wade, 2003) are also distinctive components of the same continuum.

An important goal of social justice education is to prepare students and teachers alike to understand, accept, and even embrace 'cultural pluralism' (Lewis, 2001: 189) in their classrooms, and also in their communities, their society, and ultimately the world. To use Rabima C. Wade's words, social justice education is successful when,

[A]ll people have their basic needs met, are physically and psychologically safe, are able to develop their full capacities, and are capable of interacting with others in the democratic sphere ... In a socially just society, every person is treated

according to their need toward the goal of becoming capable and contributing members of society. (Wade, 2003: 25)

We would add that a socially just society is composed of citizens whose mind and character constantly seek social justice and are not at rest until social justice is served. A powerful long-term indicator of a successful social justice education is the kind citizen, in whose hands there lies the responsibility of a just social-democratic actor. We wish for social justice education to insure that when our children take our place of world leaders and safe-keepers, they are, as Nagda et al. (2003: 166–167) poignantly state, '[A]ctive in the public sphere of the community and can deliberate with a diversity of perspectives and people; they have 'the ability to keep an open mind, to stand in another person's shoes, to change and to make decisions with others'.

Given this consideration of social justice, an examination of it theoretical underpinnings used in concert with Critical Race theory, leads to broader understandings of education for civic engagement.

CIVIC EDUCATION, SOCIAL JUSTICE AND CRITICAL RACE THEORY: A (RE)VISIONING

Using CRT as a framework in the critical examination of social studies civic education allows the existing gaps in the teaching and researching, to become more visible and can lead to a re-visioning of the mission for civic education. To that end the National Council of Social Studies (NCSS) announced a position statement prepared by the NCSS Task Force on Revitalizing Citizenship Education, a position approved by the NCSS Board of Directors in May 2001. This position revealed a commitment to the revitalization of citizenship education in our schools and provides a perfect 'site' to challenge the exclusion of racialized hegemony as a fundamental component of education for civic participation (Parker, 1996). NCSS has taken the position that the basic objective of public education is to 'prepare students to be engaged and effective citizens' (NCSS, 2001). This preparation will help students acquire the knowledge, skills and attitudes requisite to assume the 'office of citizen' in our democracy.

NCSS believes an effective citizen:

- Embraces core democratic values and strive to live by them.
- Accepts responsibility for the well being of one-self, one's family and the community.
- Has knowledge of the people, history, and traditions that have shaped our local communities, our nation and the world.
- Has knowledge of our nations founding documents, civic institutions and political processes.
- Is aware of issues and events that have an impact on people at local, state, national and global levels.
- Seeks information from varied sources and perspectives to develop informed opinions and creative solutions.
- Asks meaningful questions and is able to analyze and evaluate information and ideas.
- Uses effective decision-making and problem-solving skills in public and private life.
- Has the ability to collaborate effectively as a member of a group.
- Actively participates in civic and community life.

(NCSS, 2001: 319)

The recommendation that citizenship education become a part of the core in social studies (NAEP, 1999) also leads to the delineation of the characteristics of effective citizenship education programs. That is, a civic education program should ensure that:

- Civic knowledge, skill and values are taught explicitly and a systematically at every grade level.
- School and classroom management and culture exemplify and demonstrate core democratic values.
- Citizenship education is integrated throughout and cross the curriculum.
- Students have meaningful opportunities to participate in class and school governance.
- All students at every grade level are provided with opportunities to participate in the civic life of their school and community.
- Learning activities extend beyond the school and invite parents and the community to participate and work with students.
- Student are provided with opportunities to participate in simulation, service learning projects, conflict resolution programs, and other activities that encourage the application of civic knowledge, skills and values.
- All students are provided with instruction on out nations' founding documents, civic institution ad political processes.
- All students are provided with instruction on the people history and traditions that have shaped our local communities, our nation and the world.
- Preparing students to be effective citizens is explicitly recognized as an important part of the school mission.

(NCSS, 2001: 319)

Before every student at every grade level is able to take the 'office of citizen', attention must be given to the cultural and legal foundations that underpin what it historically been taught. This facilitates a departure from the traditional ways we may impart citizenship knowledge with respect to what it means to be patriotic.

How we set up the terms for a conversation of social justice issues in civics education can shape student perceptions and responses to the issues. The use of principles found in critical race theory can assist. One fundamental principle of critical race theory is that racism is pervasive and endemic in all aspects of our society. While critical race theory is an outgrowth of the critical legal studies movement, the attempt to demonstrate how legal ideology has helped to create, support and legitimatize, civic values that later translated in to what it means to be an effective citizen, often while simultaneous oppressing others is important. As critical race theory departed from traditional legal scholarship, it created a particular space for storytelling to describe the racial and social realities of American society (Ladson-Billings, 1995). Ladson-Billings notes that the narratives (counter stories) add 'necessary contextual contours' (11). Critical race theory also maintains that the limitations of American jurisprudence to bring about social change is found in the hegemonic power structures of society that were legally in place to act as beneficiary for some and oppressive for others. When it is not explicitly stated, the context of citizenship (the legal rights and privileges of being a citizen) is left as a social construction that can reify an ideology that maintains hegemony (Omi and Winant, 1993).

Each of the tenets of what it means to be an effective citizen speaks to embracing democratic values. These values when juxtaposed with explicitly challenging injustices can become the cornerstone of an examination of privilege and power.

How can the use of critical race theory in an examination of civic education historically, begin to re (vision) becoming an effective decision-maker and active participant in civic and community life? The personal stories of these lived experiences analyzed from a CRT perspective would include more than a study of the historical timeline of events. The use of CRT would lead us to ask, what are the stories and counter stories of the educational endeavors of those considered to be outside the mainstream educationally venues?

Social Justice Theory and CRT can facilitate a retooling of what it means to be an effective citizen in the face of injustices, highlight with explicit critique the racialized barriers to full civic participation. Notably, this would add social activism, a tenet of CRT, definitively to the knowledge, skills and values of civic education.

Civic education with a strong social justice component would include lessons about power, about intellectual frameworks that are analytical, critical and action oriented. Critical race theory can operate as a tool to fill in the gaps in the collective memory of civic knowledge. This is not a new concept. A look at the critical race narratives from enslaved Africans acquisition of literacy, the Mississippi Freedom Schools, and educator Septima Clark, can highlight how pivoting the lens in civic education to race and social justice, adds to the notions of what it means to educate a citizenry for full participation in this constitutional democracy.

CIVIC EDUCATION AN EXEMPLAR: ENSLAVEMENT AND LITERACY ACQUISITION

'Many are aware of the dangers to those enslaved in the Antebellum South if they learned to read and write. While there are few traces of how they learned it has been documented that they indeed did learn' (Cornelius,). It is further documented that those who learned to read and write often taught others and gained positions of leadership after slavery was abolished. A document analysis of the 3,428 responses of ex-slaves questioned by the Federal Writers Project reveals that 'over 5 percent (179) who mentioned having learned to read and write' were slaves. Many of those enslaved that learned to read and write were urban and house slaves. The accounts of teaching slaves to read and write are most interesting. While many masters and mistresses of the day were interested in religious reading – the Bible, the accounts support that teaching was an acceptable female function and many of women taught slaves to read and write. Many of the teachers were children. The connections to civic education can be found in what happened immediately after slavery ended, Literate slaves opened schools immediately after the war, including Sally Johnson, taught by her owners – some of these became community leaders. It was apparent that the connect between literacy and their later public leadership careers suggest that the belief by slaves in the liberating aspects of literacy as a bridge to civic participation is not unfounded.

After slavery, many of the black who learned reading and writing skills as slaves used their learning in public leadership positions, including famous 'men of mar' like Frederic Douglas and 'women of mark' like Susie King Taylor; founders and presidents of black colleges such as Isaac Lane and Isaac Burgan; scholars and writers like W.S. Scarborough and N. W. Harlee; and businessmen like Edward Walker of Windsor, Ontario. Government office holders included Blance K. Bruce, U.S. Senator from Mississippi and Isaiah Montgomery, who with his family founded the black colony of Mound Bayou, Mississippi. (Cornelius, 1983: 183)

A connection to further civic engagement was the by-product of this 'underground literacy education' effort. The goal was to rise above the entrapments of enslavement to liberatory participation in this new democracy.

CIVIC EDUCATION AN EXEMPLAR: SEPTIMA POINSETTIA CLARK

Septima Clark was called the 'Mother of the Civil Rights Movement' since she used civic education as a means to liberate and empower black people to fight against segregation and racial discrimination. But even before she began working for civil rights, Septima Clark had helped organize for equal rights for black teachers in the 1920s.

Septima Clark's courage, faith, patience, skill and intellect were a motivating force behind the civil rights movement. Her work as an educator was fundamental to black people's literacy and access to political life in the US.

Septima Clark was an activist educator. She was born to an enslaved African and a native Haitian. She became a teacher in South Carolina public schools at the age of 18. She believed in the connections of civic engagement and full participation and education.

After a successful 40-year teaching career, she was fired because she refused to give up her membership in the National Association for the Advancement of Colored People (NAACP). Although she could have retired (at age 58) Ms. Clark moved to Tennessee where she worked as director of professional development at the Highlander Folk School in Tennessee. This school's mission was that of civic education and action. It was a training ground for people desiring change in their communities. Ms. Rosa Park was a student at Highlander.

Ms. Clark was the founder of the Citizenship Schools that were part of the civil

rights movement. These schools were set up all over the South. Working with the Southern Christian Leadership Conference (SCLC) she engaged in civic education with a particular goal, to teach black people to read and write so they could pass the 'literacy tests' that blocked may black Americans from becoming registered voters. Thousands of black people registered to vote because of Septima Clark's work either directly with them, or through one of the local people she had trained as a teacher. The most unique as aspect of her work lay in the fact that Ms. Clark developed a pedagogical model that prepared people not to just become teachers. She trained people explicitly to become Citizenship teachers so that they could go back into their communities to teach others (Branch, 1990). Citizenship schools taught black people basic literacy, including how to write their names (instead of signing with an 'x'), balance their checkbooks and read road signs, but the schools also taught democratic principles using the US constitution as the curriculum content, teaching the intricate way that the executive, judicial and legislative branches of government worked in concert with or in direct opposition to the right and privileges promised in a Constitutional democracy (Brown, 1993). The Septima Clark initiated Citizenship schools, re-visioned citizen conceptualization of politics in the South.

CIVIC EDUCATION AN EXEMPLAR: THE FREEDOM SCHOOLS OF MISSISSIPPI 1964

Mr. Charlie Cobb could no longer be silent. The conditions of Mississippi were likened to a 'rotting shack'. He believes this was an analogue to a 'rotting America'. Charlie Cobb's mission was to make sure that all black Americans over the age of 21, living in Mississippi would have the right to vote. This was the original plan for the Freedom Schools in Mississippi. This civic ideal, would transform Mississippi. It was more than a passing political initiative. The decision to have Freedom Schools in Mississippi was a decision to free the people for political engagement, the right he, and other organizers, believed was due all American citizens.

The curriculum for the Freedom Schools was set in the pedagogical commitment and understanding that the curriculum for the proposed schools were to be rooted in realities of Mississippi. The levels of introspection in the curricular development were reported to be, 'torment', as those involved confronted the lived realities of life for men, women and especially the children of Mississippi. The development of this model of civic education involved taking a hard look at multifaceted concerns of the community on an individual and communal level. The Mississippi Freedom Summer initiatives were rooted in the critical theoretical constructs, critiquing – asking questions, about voter registration, and other civil right actives all over the South with a view to change.

This model of civic education challenged and questioned from a social justice perspective. The 'Citizenship Curriculum' set up two sets of questions. The primary set was:

1. Why are we (teachers and students) in Freedom Schools?
2. What is the Freedom Movement?
3. What alternatives does the Freedom Movement offer us?

What was called the secondary set of questions, but what seemed to me the more important, because they are the more personal, set was:

1. What does the majority culture have that we want?
2. What does the majority culture have that we don't want?
3. What do we have that we want to keep?
   (....)

Many of the students that participated in the Freedom Summer School had aspirations to leave the state as soon as they were old enough to do so. They saw change connected

to the physical removal of them to the North. It is reported that by the end of the summer many of the students planned to stay in Mississippi. They had an understanding that change could come though the social, political action of the people living there. Simultaneously, they began to discover that they themselves could take action against the injustices – the specific injustices and the condition of injustice.

The pedagogical choice to include in the curriculum the history of African and African American people who had against all odds fought for and won freedom created culturally relevant (Ladson-Billings, 1995) connections between the students and the curriculum. The skillful use of questions in this model for civic education became the corner stone for the connections from historical to contemporary times. One teacher reports,

Connections between then and now kept being made – at first by the teachers, very soon by the students: who do you know that is like Joseph Cinque? How is Bob Moses like Moses in the Bible? How is he different? Why did Harriet Tubman go back into the South after she had gotten herself free into the North – and why so many times? And why doesn't Mrs. Hamer stay in the North once she gets there to speak, since she doesn't have a job on that man's plantation any more, and since her life is in so much danger? And what do you think about Fredrick Douglass's talking so straight to the President of the United States? And how does the picture of Jim Forman in the Emancipation Proclamation issue of *Ebony* suggest that same kind of straight talking? And who do you think the Movement is proving right – Booker T. Washington or W. E. B. DuBois? And why are the changes of gospel songs into Freedom Songs significant? What does 'We Shall Overcome' really mean in terms of what we are doing, and what we can do?

The Freedom School's social justice and civic education focused curriculum taught the students that the concerns they had about their schools, were legitimate grievances that could be redressed through petition. The understanding of the First Amendment Constitutional Redress of Grievances, that 'Congress shall make no law ... abridging the freedom of … or the right of the people' began to be real to them. The act of 'becoming a citizen' was at the core of their enquiry. The students were able to ask and clearly interrogate through this well-crafted civic education curriculum the seriousness of their concerns. The students created a list of grievances and submitted them to school officials, senators, city officials, newspapers and the President of the United States. The students were taken seriously. They redressed their grievances and their voices were heard. The school civic mission was a success. The summer Mississippi project continued into the fall, winter, spring, and plans for the following summer. The summer projects transforming influence reached nearly 3,000, from preschool to adults.

This curricular effort placed the social injustices reflected in the lack of political capital for the black and poor people of Mississippi. It was a special analysis, the use of a critical race theory perspective that uncovers the particular ways that the right to vote would redress the grievance of those living in the segregated South in general and Mississippi in particular. Civic education critiqued from the intersections of race and social justice yielded for this particular initiative the critical questioning of privilege and power that leads to social change. Many civic educators have ignored how race continues to shape the American story in ways that are expressly racist in our nation's schools and curriculum.

Critical race theory acknowledges racialzed structures that are limited by a dominant construction of reality that perpetuates racial oppression. Social justice theoretical approach acknowledges that any approach is unjust unless it filters through the perspectives of the people who experience social injustice. These structures create a reality and relationship to what it means to be a citizen and participate in American democracy. Educators' approaches to the teachings of civic education using similar models should be with an intention to: transform civic education; revitalize citizenship

participation and answer the call of a democratic imperative.

CONCLUSION

The adage, the apple does not fall far from the tree, can be apropos here. Our efforts for civic education have not fallen far from the racism, sexism, homophobia, classism (and the list continues) reflected in our society. The failure to recognize that the ideals of justice and equity for all cannot be achieved without fundamental change to our conceptualizations of social justice is ill considered. The failure to recognize that the historical influence of endemic racism in American and the vestiges of it globally from a civic education perspective is irresponsible.

To that end, civic educators and researchers must engage in deeper explorations of the relationship of becoming an effective citizen, social justice and race. The development of critical pedagogies for classroom praxis continues to be a worthwhile mission for education. The moral project is social construction of a socially just world. It is an 'unending project of democratic social transformation' (Giroux, 2002: 1157).

Understanding with it means to be a citizenry in a Constitution democracy – in a racialized society – challenges us all. Looking to exemplars of those effective initiatives children and adults alike must be allowed under the sometimes contradictory duality of contemporary America, where the 'ideal' and the 'real' are within a grasp of some and almost entirely out of reach for others. Civic education with a view to social justices helps to uncover and confront the inconsistencies between the ideals of equality and pluralism, and lived experiences of many of its citizens (Pang and Gibson, 2001). Change is imperative if America will live up to its promise for all of her citizens – the promises of the American dream – freedom. The change can be facilitated through models of education for citizenship – let us begin again.

REFERENCES

Barber, R.B. (1989) 'Public talk and civic action: Education for participation in a strong democracy', *Social Education*, 53: 355–356, 370.

Bell, D. (1995). Racial realism after we're gone: Prudent speculations on America in a post-racial epoch. In R. Delgado (Ed.), *Critical Race Theory: The Cutting Edge*. Philadelphia: Temple University Press. pp. 2–8.

Bennett, L. (1962) *Before the Mayflower: A history of Black America*. Chicago: Johnson Publishing Co.

Brown, C. (1993) Ready from within: Septima Clark and the Civil Rights Movement. In, Darlene Clark Hine, (Ed.), *Black Women in America: An Historical Encyclopedia, Vol. 1*.

Crenshaw, K. (1995) Race, reform and retrenchment: Transformation and legitimization in anti-discrimination law. In K. Crenshaw, N. Gotanda, Peller, B. and Thomas, K. (Eds), *Critical Race Theory: Key Writing that Formed the Movement*. New York: The New Press. pp. 103–122.

Delgado, R. (1995) *Critical Race Theory: The Cutting Edge*. Philadelphia: Temple University Press.

Delgado, R. (1995). The imperial scholar. In K. Crenshaw, N. Gotanda, Peller, B. and Thomas, K. (Eds), *Critical Race Theory: Key Writing that Formed the Movement*. New York: The New Press. pp. 46–57.

Delgado Bernal, D. (1998). 'Using a Chicana feminist epistemology in educational research', *Harvard Educational Review*, 68 (4): 555–582.

Ellison, R. (1935) *The invisible man*. New York: Grove Press.

Goodman, J. and Adler, S. (1985) 'Becoming an elementary social studies teacher: A study of perspective', *Theory and Research in Social Education*, 13 (2): 1–20.

Hahn, C.L. (1991) Controversial issues in social studies. In Shaver, J. (Ed.) *Handbook of Research on Social Studies Teaching Learning*. pp. 470–480.

Hahn, C. (1996) Research on issues-centered social studies. In R.W. Evan and D. W. Sace. (Eds.) *Handbook on Teaching Social Issues*. pp. 26–39.

Hahn, C. (1998) *Becoming Political: Comparative Perspective on Citizenship Education*. New York: State University of New York Press.

Irvine, J. (1997) *Critical Knowledge for Diverse Teachers and Learners*. Washington, D.C.: AACTE.

Krug, M.M. (1970) 'Primary sources in teaching history', *The History Teacher*, 3 (3): 401–411.

Ladson-Billings, G. (1995) 'Just what is critical race theory and what is it doing in a nice field like education?' *International Journal of Qualitative Studies in Education*, 11 (1): 7–24.

Ladson-Billings, G. and Tate, W. (1995) 'Toward a critical race theory of education', *Teachers College Record*, 97: 47–68.

Ladson-Billings, G. (2001) *Crossing over Canaan: The Journey of New Teachers in Diverse Classrooms*. San Francisco: Jossey-Bass.

Miller, B. and Singleton, L. (1977) *Preparing Citizens: Linking Authentic Assessment and Instruction in Civic/Law Related Education*. Boulder: Social Science Education Consortium.

National Council for the Social Studies (1994) *Expectations of Excellence: Curriculum Standards for Social Studies Teaching*. Washington, D.C. National council for the Social Studies.

National Center for Education Statistics (1999) *NAEP 1998 Civics Report Card for the Nation*. Washington, DC: U.S. Department of Education.

Omi, M. and Winant, H. (1993). On the theoretical status of the concept of race. In C. McCarthy and W. Crinchlow (Eds), *Race, Identity, and Representation in Education*. New York: Routledge. pp. 3–10.

Parker, L. (1998) 'Race is race ain't it: An exploration of the utility of critical race theory in qualitative research in education', *International Journal of Qualitative Studies in Education*, 11: 43–55.

Parker, W.C. (2002)Education for democracy: Contexts, curricula, assessments.

Parker, W.C. (1996) Curriculum for democracy. In R. Soder (Ed.), *Democracy Education and the Schools*. San Francisco: Jossey-Bass Publishers. pp. 182–210.

Parker, W. (1989) 'Participatory citizenship: Civics in the strong sense', *Social Education*, 53: 353–354.

Sansone, S.C. (1999) 'Get your students involved in civics', *Social Education*, 63 (4): 228–232.

SNCC, The Student Nonviolent Coordinating Committee Papers, 1959–1972 (Sanford, NC: Microfilming Corporation of America, 1982) Reel 68, File 346, Page 0224.

Taylor, I. (1999) *I Was Born a Slave: An Anthology of Classic Slave Narratives*. Lawrence Hill Books: Illinois.

Taylor Branch, T. (1990) *Parting the Waters: America in the King Years, 1954–63*. New York: Simon and Schuster.

Torney-Purta, J., Hahn, C. and Amadeo, J. (2000) Principles of subject specific instruction in education for citizenship. In J. Brophy (Ed.), *Subject Specific Instructional Methods and Activities*. Stamford, CT: JAI Press. pp. 271–408.

Tyson, C. and Kenreich, T. (2001) 'Social studies, social action, and realistic fiction', *Social Studies and the Young Learner*, (September–October): 22–26.

Tyson, C (2002) 'Get up off that thing: African American middle school students respond to literature to develop a framework for understanding social action', *Theory in Social Studies Education* 30 (1): 42–65.

Tyson, C. (1999) 'Shut my mouth wide open: Realistic fiction and social action', *Theory into Practice*, 38 (3): 155–159.

U.S. Commission on Civil Rights (1964) *Law Enforcement*. Washington, D.C.: Government Printing Office. pp. 12–13.

Zinn, H. (1999) A people's history of the United States: 1492-present (20th anniversary Ed.)

4

Philosophical Presuppositions of Citizenship Education and Political Liberalism

Marianna Papastephanou

ABSTRACT

Much contemporary discourse of citizenship education relies on, or draws from, a new philosophical conception of liberalism that declares itself 'political'. Political liberalism purports to be independent from any controversial philosophical presuppositions, and its basic principles and features are often presented as the most accommodating of difference and heterogeneity, so long as the latter is not illiberal, oppressive and fanatic. In this essay I argue that the often receptive and arguably uncritical way in which educational theory utilizes this view in citizenship curriculum debates works against a more encompassing idea of citizenship for justice and equality. I shall critique the above view, then, by unveiling the contestable epistemological and anthropological theses underlying Rawls' liberalism and by discussing the conception of education that they ground. The reason why I focus on Rawls is that he offered the strongest defense of political liberalism up

to now. I shall draw especially on sociology of education and its questioning of the 'racism of intelligence' in order to show that political liberalism mistakes its self- and world-understanding as a reflection of general and undisputed facts. Further, I shall explain how a more critical perspective would give educational theory a more active role by challenging the so-called 'reproductive' conception of education. I shall conclude by assessing the significance of such a critique for teaching citizenship, putting forward some suggestions for a reorientation of political education.

INTRODUCTION AND PRELIMINARY REMARKS

As the present handbook (part of which is this essay) asserts, education for citizenship is, among other things, education committed to justice. But, as citizenship is not yet institutionally established as an academic field in its own right, it is dependent on inter-disciplinary research, both regarding its general premises as well as regarding its particular concern with justice. Therefore, education for citizenship emerges through theoretical decisions and choices that are demarcated by particular ways of relating education and the fields of endeavour that inform it on this subject matter. Philosophy is one of the fundamental sources of material that is significant for citizenship and, in turn, educational philosophy aspires to be the terrain where education for citizenship finds theoretical support and justification. This invites some comments on the relation of philosophy and education, prior to any discussion of the philosophical presuppositions of citizenship.

In educational discourse relating to fashionable philosophical trends, a very simple model predominates: Here is the philosophy, there is the education. Philosophy is applied to education. The tendency of much educational theoretical work is to explore the educational implications of influential philosophical theories – and Rawls' theory of justice has been no exception. In spite of their merits, such moves often limit education to a passive and receptive role. A concomitant demerit is that in this way the major stakes, dilemmas and debates surrounding the particular philosophical theory are bequeathed to educational theory almost unaltered. In this essay, I shall allocate education a more active part, arguing that, in its theoretical dimension, it can operate as a corrective to Rawls' epistemological and anthropological justifications of political liberalism and, in its more practical and applied dimension, as transformative of liberal society through a reformulated conception of the province of teaching citizenship.

One of the issues that general philosophy hands down to education regarding Rawls' recent theory of justice, one that I find narrow and problematic, is whether political liberalism succeeds in handling radical otherness justly and effectively without conceding too much to it or expecting too much from it.

As Geraint Parry puts this, the prime limitation on teaching political neutrality,

> ... which profoundly affects education, is that the liberal state cannot be neutral about its own neutrality. It must seek to instil respect for its fundamental principle in its future citizenry. The problem posed by this requirement is that neutralist liberalism may, in its educational programme, be less accommodating than it claims towards those who wish to bring their children up to share their own non-liberal doctrines and consequently to adopt more negative attitudes to what they variously see to be the spread of the contagion of secularism, anti-traditionalism or laxity of manners (Parry, 1999: 33).

Whereas such criticisms or reservations regarding the treatment of radical otherness seem at first sight to be quite sharp, I believe that, in fact, they are condescending or even patronizing for 'otherness' and that they make things too easy for liberalism. The problem is pictured in such a manner that liberalism appears truly to have achieved neutrality or, as a theory, truly to have been political in the Rawlsian sense of being 'free-standing'. Hence, now, its major difficulty appears to be how to deal with the non-liberal segment of the population. Within this account, the other becomes the obtrusive and cumbersome case that crops up and disrupts the otherwise solid and strong prospect for a just society.[1] In this way, the discourse on citizenship that derives from such an account ends up suffering from a conventionalist and self-congratulatory ethnocentrism, where the 'we' is placed in a privileged political position and the 'others' are the ones to make all the effort to 'catch up with' the supposedly morally advanced liberal elite.

Rawlsian justice as fairness has, in its evolution, come to be understood as part of a political liberalism that 'can be formulated independently of any particular comprehensive doctrine, religious, philosophical or moral. [I]t is not presented as depending upon, or as *presupposing* any such view' (emphasis added) (Rawls, 1995: 135). Unmanageable others will be attracted to this kind of liberalism because, after all, they are only human: as such they possess two moral powers, the capacity for an effective sense of justice and the capacity to form, revise and rationally pursue a conception of the good (Rawls, 1999: 312). To help them adjust themselves to political liberalism, we liberals recommend a conversational restraint – that is, a bracketing of disputable ultimate questions about the self, life and the world. We are able to do so because our own conception of the political relies solely on the 'undisputed facts' of natural science and social theory.

I shall argue that the principles of justice and more recent developments in Rawlsian theory rely in one way or other on many currently or potentially *contestable* epistemological and anthropological cultural assumptions of Western societies. In the end, epistemological and anthropological assumptions will emerge as key issues of pivotal importance for citizenship education, contrary to the received view that restricts the scope or relevance of philosophy regarding citizenship to legal or, at most, to socio-ethical discourse. Elsewhere (Papastephanou, 2004), I have argued from a general philosophical perspective that political liberalism cannot avoid comprehensiveness, but here I shall examine a similar claim from a more hybrid point of view, the educational one. In that work, emphasis was placed not on epistemology but on anthropology. Here, in order to avoid covering the ground of the previous work, my emphasis will be on the former. This explains the uneven space these two issues will be given here. Thus, the problems of political liberalism go beyond the simple accommodation of radical alterity and touch upon its own self-understanding as political and independent from, that is, as not presupposing, comprehensive liberalism. I see this topic as a case where educational theory can offer much corrective work to general philosophy by showing why some general philosophical tenets might plausibly be questionable from an educational point of view. Such corrective work has been occluded by the fact that the search for the implications for teaching political attitudes and values has so far

limited education to the role of passive recipient of some fashionable theories.

To conclude my preliminary remarks, I claim that my approach does not aim to diminish the import of Rawls' theory and the quality of its architectonic, but to point to problems that I view as inherent in liberalism and transferable to citizenship discourse. Thus, I am not saying that there can be a liberalism that is more political than the Rawlsian – that is, that Rawls has, inadvertently perhaps, let some non-political elements slip into his notion of liberalism. Instead, I am saying that any sharp duality insulating the political and granting it priority over the comprehensive overlooks the former's inescapable dependence on some form of the latter (Papastephanou, 2004). In what follows, I demonstrate that the epistemological and anthropological assumptions implied in political liberalism play a subterranean, crucial role in justice as fairness and its principles. Then I discuss how these principles assume a particular conception of education, its confines and potentialities. Further, I explore the possibility and perhaps necessity for a different conception of education functioning as a corrective to political liberalism, showing at the same time the limits of liberalism in general. In this way, citizenship education may direct its efforts to objectives that may partly go further than, or against, the Rawlsian vision of a just society.

PHILOSOPHICAL ASSUMPTIONS IN POLITICAL LIBERALISM

In Rawls' most recent work, the principles of justice that are constitutive of his justice as fairness are couched in an idiom that purports to be political and not metaphysical. It is political not only because it is divorced from religious legitimation but also because it demands the exercise of public rather than secular reason (Rawls, 1999: 583). Secular reason is reasoning in terms of comprehensive non-religious worldviews; the latter resonate with various contestable assumptions about the self and social life. But, as I shall argue, upon closer inspection, the principles of justice themselves presuppose particular and by now already disputed views, the defense of which extends far beyond public reason, drawing from the secular – and secularized (Papastephanou, 2004) – cultural reservoir of Occidental significations.

Rawls holds that the principles of justice can be viewed 'as an understanding between moral persons not to exploit for one's own advantage the contingencies of their world, but to regulate the accidental distributions of nature and social chance in ways that are mutually beneficial for all' (Rawls, 1999: 175). An initial suspicion of philosophical comprehensiveness is raised by the very first part of Rawls' statement. An agreement to avoid exploitation of contingencies for one's own advantage presupposes that before the agreement there must have been such an intention or inclination to self-interest, or – more weakly – a strong possibility of this. Granted that Rawls does not share Hobbes' conception of human nature, we should opt for the latter, weaker interpretation (Papastephanou, 2004). A possibility for self-interestedness is endemic in humanity according to Kantian anthropological views of human motivation, which maintain that the human being is characterized by unsocial sociability. Rawls may have remained faithful to Kant in other respects of his thought, but there is no guarantee that the above statement reflects a commitment to Kant's anthropology. A Rawlsian might respond that the fact that the principles of justice hinder exploitation of contingency for one's advantage reveals only an empirical and not a logically necessary effect. This suspicion, then, requires further textual evidence and elaboration.

Another suspicion of comprehensiveness, an equally vague one at this stage, arises when we consider the second part of the remark, the regulation of accidental distributions of nature and social chance in mutually beneficial ways. I believe that the idea of accidental distributions of nature reveals

epistemological presuppositions about giftedness of an essentialist character that are quite far from being undisputed facts. I shall tackle the latter suspicion first and then move to anthropology because, in Rawls, as will be shown later on, the epistemological self-understanding of the moral person seems to affect significantly the way the ego is motivated to think of justice and equality.

Epistemological self-understanding

When Rawls analyzes his maximin or difference principle,[2] he employs metaphors that pertain to a biologistic essentialist interpretation of good performance – metaphors such as 'natural assets', 'native talents', 'giftedness', 'natural endowment' and so on. Consider the following, for instance:

> If the two principles of justice are acknowledged, the understanding is, in effect, that those favored in the natural lottery (that is, the lottery of native talents and abilities) and who *know that they have been favored* undertake to gain from their good fortune only on terms that improve the condition of those who have lost out. They are not to win advantages simply because *they are more gifted*, but only to cover the costs of the necessary efforts of training and cultivating their endowments and for putting them to use in a way which benefits the losers. [...] Accepting a society in which the two principles are satisfied is, then, the best way for the less gifted to overcome their *misfortune in the natural lottery*. The offer of the more gifted man to acknowledge the second principle would probably be accepted, since doing so would strike the ungifted as a fair way to take advantage of the *natural fact of differing native endowments* (Rawls, 1999: 82, emphasis added).

The strong epistemological assumptions we have here are not limited to the obvious essentialist accounts of talent: along with them there is a self-conception (i.e. they 'know that they have been favored') on the axis of natural fortune and misfortune that ushers the social actors to their proper social space. This self-knowledge secures a feeling of justice for all, since the social actor who recognizes herself as ungifted accepts the advantages of the gifted as means for long-term benefits. She even knows that such benefits would never be expected if society were politically to read talent along lines of desert (as in some libertarian views, compared to which Rawls' position is far more radical). Likewise, the social actor who knows he is gifted – how does one know that really? – acknowledges that he cannot be thought to 'deserve his greater natural capacity' (p. 165). Therefore, all advantages to which he is entitled derive only from their being motivationally efficacious in leading him to promoting social wealth and progress.

Even in his 'Kantian Constructivism', which is a text of the middle period, Rawls takes such epistemological assumptions for granted.

> An essential distinction is between the *unequal distribution of natural assets, which is simply a natural fact and neither just nor unjust*, and the way the basic structure of society makes use of these *natural differences* and permits them to affect the social fortune of citizens, their opportunities in life, and the actual terms of cooperation between them (p. 337, emphasis added).

Here, Rawls interprets differences in performance in a naturalist and morally neutral way and assumes that there is no alternative construal (I extrapolate that from his term 'natural fact'). An alternative way to view such a difference would be to treat it as a result of existential dissimilarity, and with this term I describe the complex set of conditions of existence that are unique for each individual (Papastephanou, 2003). Social origin, family, language, narrativity, identification, the relational position of one's race or nation in the wider social context, culture and worldviews are some constitutive factors of existential dissimilarity that condition performance and success at what society cherishes. In this context nature is minimally or not at all informative and the unequal possession or development of abilities can be explained through some initial social injustices, discrimination and exclusion or even through some axiologically neutral relational terms.[3] Unlike Rawls' commitment to innateness, an account of existential dissimilarity

does not require a robust and encompassing notion of natural difference. Thus, the passage from natural difference to political inequality, which sustains an analogy that justifies the latter through the former, is not allowed within the alternative account that I provide.

As to the distinction between naturalness and its social treatment that Rawls has drawn in the previous passage, it shows, or so it seems to me, his intention to avoid the libertarian leap from existential dissimilarity to political inequality (that is, to connect naturalness and desert). Overall, however, this distinction is not elaborated in such a way as to break free from naturalistic essentialism and so to avoid the charge of a similar kind of naturalistic fallacy.

The difference principle can be regarded as an agreement to consider the distribution of natural assets as common property and to share in the benefits of this distribution, whatever it turns out to be. Those who have been favored by nature, whoever they are, may gain from their good fortune only on terms that improve the situation of those who have done less well. The naturally advantaged are not to gain merely because they are more gifted, but rather in order to cover the costs of training and cultivating their endowments and for putting them to use in a way that helps the less fortunate as well. No one is thought to deserve his greater natural capacity or to merit a more favorable starting place in society (Rawls, 1999: 165).

By seeing existential dissimilarity as a natural fact rather than a social construction and qualitative appraisal of difference, Rawls ends up in justifying inequality on naturalistic grounds (in a way deriving the Ought from the Is) even when he tethers this to moral final purposes. For, ultimately, he argues that those who are naturally endowed may enjoy some kind of favorable inequality in order to be motivated to make their talents available to all for the common good.

A crucial question here, of course, is how or why all this matters in Rawls' original position. In his words, 'we assume that in the original position the parties have the general information provided by natural science and social theory' (p. 236). As Johnston puts it, 'going into the original position, we know only a few facts of moral psychology/sociology … and nothing about our particular selves, communities, or societies' (Johnston, 2005: 210).[4] This means, amongst other things, that the parties do not know their own personal luck in the natural lottery but they know generally that, inevitably, in their society, some people will be naturally more gifted than the rest. That this is a natural fact is corroborated, in Rawls' mind, I assume, by science or common sense, but, with hindsight, this paradigmatic conviction of the Rawls of the 1970s can be explained as the myth of a society that employed science as a tool for specific ideological purposes. If we recall the numerous tests by which the American immigration policy tried to sift the incoming population, the well-known arguments by Jensen about a supposedly intrinsic intellectual inferiority of black people, and more general efforts based on streaming to separate the wheat from the chaff (often keeping the chaff!), we realize that when Rawls committed himself to this kind of innateness he was led astray by the spirit of the times. By this I do not mean that he subscribed to any of the above mentioned blatant forms of exclusion and discrimination but rather that those were more extreme articulations of a general and popular innateness conviction.

The Rawlsian kind of innateness breaks with any speculative or theological metaphysical worldview, but its foundations share something with those of biologism and scientism. Thus, when Rawls contrasts the metaphysical with the political and opts for the latter, he means, more or less, that there is no *psychic* kernel in the idealist metaphysical sense. He does not wish to imply that the self is 'ontologically prior to the facts about persons that the parties are excluded from knowing' (Johnston, 2005: 211) in the original position. Nor, however, does he realize that the description of those facts as natural,

according to a particular, and by now disputed, set of scientific theories, might equally be metaphysical. In any case, the reliance on natural science and social theory is hardly political as such, but the fact that this reliance is on controversial questions that different ideological camps answer in different ways proves that here we have a clear case of liberalist dependence on comprehensiveness (Papastephanou, 2004).

All the same, one may notice in Rawls' texts occasional shifts in his accounts of natural assets, for example, of intelligence. True, these shifts may prove that he does not have a crude or naive notion of intelligence, but they also unveil the extent to which polemics intervene in the shaping of a theory that purports to be political and in a certain sense impervious to comprehensive (for example, ideological) influence. Rawls exaggerates the supposed naturalness of intelligence when he feels compelled to justify the accommodation of some inequalities that he finds inevitable, and he downplays it only when he sees it as leading away from his theoretical priorities and becoming a conceptual weapon for the opponent. Here is a telling example. In rejecting the idea of a lump sum tax on natural abilities (an idea that derives from the Marxist precept 'from each according to his abilities, to each according to his needs'), Rawls emphasizes the non-measurable and unfixed character of natural assets and their precarious and changing social use:

> Intelligence, for example, is hardly any one such fixed native ability. It must have indefinitely many dimensions that are shaped and nurtured by different social conditions; even as a potential, as opposed to a realized, capacity it is bound to vary significantly in little understood and complex ways … Thus potential earnings capacity is not something independent from the social forms and the particular contingencies over the course of life, and the idea of a lump sum tax does not apply (Rawls, 1999: 253).

But one may reverse this argument and turn it against Rawls' theory too. Why should intelligence then be informative at all for political theory if it is so elusive and dependent on contingency? How does a person know if she is gifted or ungifted? Why should intelligence be classified as a natural given and be taken for granted, thus setting an ontological limit to educationally formative or reformative effects on people? Rawls himself has, as we have seen in some previous citations too, fallen elsewhere[5] into the positivist trap of the measurable and the locatable. Therefore, the concession here appears to serve only polemical purposes instead of being a consistent shift of perspective.

Education assists us in unmasking the concealed comprehensive character of political liberalism as well as the mistaken epistemological framework that informs the self-understanding of the Rawlsian moral subject. Current sociology of education, influenced by Pierre Bourdieu's research, not only questions ideas of giftedness and natural talent but also exposes their ideological functioning as mechanisms for the reproduction of consolidated social power structures and inequalities. Good school performance is not explained as a sign of innate intelligence but as a product of the concurrence and coordination of cultural capital and teaching expectations. More explicitly, children from educated strata enter education already equipped with an informal and subtle cultivation that is called cultural capital. Such capital is not directly measured in schools, but it is nevertheless a non-thematized advantage. This is so because children's attempts to decipher the communication code of the teacher and the transmitted knowledge depend on the extent to which their own vocabulary and cultural experience match the upper-middle class origin of the taught material and the teaching method. Educators mistake that initial success for a token of charisma and natural giftedness, and interpret failures as signs of inherent inability thus imposing on the 'bad' pupils the self-image of the ungifted (Bourdieu and Passeron, 1985). This often produces a self-fulfilling prophecy. At a later stage of education, cultural capital is accompanied by symbolic capital, which is the intellectual aura that the 'charismatic' enjoy due to the academic titles they have obtained

from prestigious institutions, and by social capital, which denotes the social affiliations and acquaintances that open ways to power. Thus, using apparently egalitarian and meritocratic methods, education selects and supports those pupils whose social origin has endowed them with the capital of hegemonic discourse. By declaring this success an indication of natural giftedness, it produces in them that elitist self-understanding that is necessary for the justification of their social position. But more importantly, it ensures that those who have not succeeded in the selection process will internalize the failure as a personal inadequacy, remaining thus unsuspecting of the hidden character of the selection mechanism itself. In this way, the natural disguise of social privilege guarantees compliance and legitimates inequality and its ancillary procedures by giving them ontological citizenship, that is, by accounting for performance in physiologist or geneticist essentialist terms. The route to wealth and enjoyment of culture is largely predetermined for the possessors of cultural capital by their initial social positioning. Successful progress to higher education and political power is not obstructed by cultural ignorance along the way; it poses, however, as a deserving and inevitable personal development of natural individual excellence. Such legitimation of privilege is almost invulnerable, and Rawls' theory is a good example of that. Arbitrary inequality on the grounds of property must be ousted, but inequality on the grounds of merit and talent is not only tolerated but also made good for society. Bourdieu considers the racism of intelligence as the worst of all racisms (Bourdieu, 1984).

Additionally, the natural endowment conviction has also been questioned and its undesirable pedagogical implications exposed by educational theorists of persuasions that share very little in common with Bourdieu and Passeron. Charles Jencks has shown that any egalitarian school reform is doomed to fail so long as there is no further and more drastic change at the level of societal and economic conditions. Thus, he has attributed differences of performance to the latter conditions rather than genetic endowment. Even before Jencks, James Coleman (Coleman et al., 1996) had explored social factors intervening in learning outcomes and fought against the racism of intelligence. Along with other theorists, they attacked Jensen's assumptions about genetic racial differences and argued that the only way to check whether – and to what extent – heredity of intellect plays some role would be through first ensuring that all social variables are equal for many generations. More recently, sociologists of education such as Michael Young, Geoffrey Esland and Nell Keddie converge in the problematization of categorizations based on such notions as 'talent' and 'competence' and the exposition of the social construction of knowledge (Blackledge and Hunt, 1989).

True, there are problems in Bourdieu and Passeron's conception of education as reproduction and several difficulties with what is now called 'new sociology of education', and those cannot be dealt with in this essay. However, what is crucial here is that this whole discourse shows that there is no unanimity regarding those epistemological issues that Rawls takes for granted. Consequently, their supposed generality can no longer ground the claim that liberalism's reliance on them is political rather than comprehensive. As Parry puts it, 'the once clear liberal notion of education preparing for the career open to the talents has become obscured as the central ideas of merit and talent have joined the ranks of contested concepts' (Parry, 1999: 24). What is perhaps more important is that even within the innateness hypothesis there is a variety of positions, some of which assume *universal* competences and attack the *individualist* theoretical differentiation of them as elitist and racist. Noam Chomsky's (1975) work in his *Reflections of Language* is a significant example. Jacques Maritain's conception of natural intelligence (D'Souza, 1996) as universal is another case that proves that the assumptions of winners and losers in the natural lottery are not taken for granted even within more traditional educational theories.

Thus, for my argument here, it suffices that these assumptions are contested. Controversial substantive positions belong to the sphere of the comprehensive rather than the political (Papastephanou, 2004), and this demonstrates that such positions operate within – and sometimes through – the principles of justice. Showing this constitutes an immanent critique. The challenge to the established epistemological admissions about who the moral subject is and who she believes herself to be as a knower in relation to existential variety and difference exposes liberalism's unavoidable dependence on comprehensiveness. This challenge is immanent because it does not draw from a supposedly incommensurable language game of illiberal radical otherness, inferior, fanatic and burdensome, but from sources upon which liberalism itself has bestowed authority.

A further issue is, evidently, whether this immanent critique drastically affects Rawls' conclusions about the necessity of a dose of inequality in the basic structure of society. We may indirectly reach some answer to this question after the examination of the second set of assumptions, that is, the anthropological. By the end of that discussion we shall also be able to move to the active role of education. I now proceed with a discussion of those tacit accounts of human nature underpinning justice as fairness that will prove once again that political liberalism is not as antiseptically devoid of comprehensiveness as Rawls would expect it to be.

Anthropological implicit assumptions

For my anthropological argument and the way it connects to the aforementioned cognitive dimensions, the following quotation is revealing: in his 1969 text 'The Justification of Civil Disobedience', Rawls says about the original position:

> The parties do not know their position in society, past, present, or future; nor do they know which institutions exist. Again, they do not know their

own place in the distribution of natural talents and abilities, whether they are intelligent or strong, man or woman, and so on. [...] What the parties do know (or assume) is that Hume's circumstances of justice obtain: namely, that the bounty of nature is not so generous as to render cooperative schemes superfluous nor so harsh as to make them impossible. Moreover, they assume that the extent of their altruism is limited and that, in general, they do not take an interest in one another's interests (Rawls, 1999: 178).

In this passage, a very specific conception of human nature appears to hold for the actors themselves whose self-image is that of the rational egoist – perhaps not in the anthropologically stronger libertarian sense but in the more mitigated one of Humean and Continental liberalism (Papastephanou, 2004).

For liberalism to be convincing in claiming that its assumption is political – that is, it does not rest on controversial grounds[6] – what is necessary is to show not only that it is shared by all but that such universality is not the outcome of mere conformity or hegemonic enforcement. It is true that the liberal notion of the self as interest-seeking enjoys much empirical and theoretical support; however, it is especially from a deontological cognitivist ethics such as Rawls' that one expects a distinction between validity and social currency. Even within Occidental thought itself, there have been alternative scenarios about the self (for example, the Stoic, the Rousseauist, to some extent the Marxist, and some anarchist conceptions) most of which have operated as undercurrents and counterfactual theoretical possibilities. Whether those or other contemporary or future accounts of the self are more justified than the liberalist and might have better implications for a radical politics is a matter of external critique of Rawls. For the purposes of this essay, it suffices that the sheer existence of such alternative views problematizes the supposedly uncontroversial character of political liberalism and offers a springboard for an internal critique.

The political implication of the Rawlsian coupling of epistemological and anthropological self-depiction is that all should agree that the 'gifted' of society will be motivated to make their talents available to society, not out of altruism but out of egoism. This is so because the difference principle exists precisely in order to provide to them that kind of satisfaction that stems from recognition of their superiority – a recognition that is vouchsafed by accommodation to inequality. Proof of that is the following passage from Rawls' 'Justice as Reciprocity', written in 1971:

If there are inequalities which satisfy the conditions of the second principle, the immediate gain which equality would allow can be considered as intelligently invested in view of its future return. If, as is quite likely, these inequalities work as incentives to draw out better efforts, the members of this society may look upon them as concessions to human nature: they, like us, may think that people ideally should want to serve one another. But as they are mutually self-interested, their acceptance of these inequalities is merely the acceptance of the relations in which they actually stand, and a recognition of the motives which lead them to engage in their common practices. Being themselves self-interested, they have no title to complain of one another (Rawls, 1999: 203).

The way by which a theory of human nature demarcates ideals is another example of the Is-Ought fallacy, one that illustrates the dependence of political liberalism on anthropological views of comprehensive liberalism. By declaring themselves facts, these anthropological views don the guise of the political. This becomes clearer in a passage that explains how, in justice as fairness, the conception of the moral person is a companion ideal of that of a well-ordered society.

Like any other ideal, it must be possible for people to honor it sufficiently closely; and hence the feasible ideals of the person are limited by the capacities of human nature and the requirements of social life. To this extent such an ideal presupposes a theory of human nature, and social theory generally, but the task of a moral doctrine is to specify an appropriate conception of the person that *general facts about human nature and society allow* (p. 321, emphasis added).

A crucial political implication is that the transformation of society is thereby determined.[7] For Rawls, certain social and economic inequalities exist either as 'requirements for maintaining social arrangements or as incentives satisfying the relevant standard of justice' (p. 245). Why do we need such an incentive if it is possible for people not to be motivated by inequality? Thus, in a negative way, we see that there is an implicit account of human motivation delineating impossibilities, one of them being the other-oriented stance. The anthropological limits of ideality along with the epistemologically assisted transition from existential dissimilarity to political inequality shape the liberalist conception of a desirable society and the positioning of education in it.

THE ROLE OF EDUCATION

Rawls' ideas about education and its role in connection with his aforementioned epistemological and anthropological assumptions emerge first and foremost in his dismissive discussion of the principle of redress. This is:

> ... the principle that undeserved inequalities call for redress; and since inequalities of birth and natural endowment are undeserved, these inequalities are to be somehow compensated for. Thus the principle of redress holds that in order to treat all persons equally, to provide genuine equality of opportunity, society must give more attention to those with fewer native assets and to those born into the less favorable social positions. ... In pursuit of this principle greater resources might be spent on the education of the less rather than the more intelligent, at least over a certain time of life, say, the earlier years of school (p. 165).

This principle shares the dominant interpretation of variant performance of cognitive tasks but treats it in a more charitable manner and subjugates it to a more egalitarian political ideal. Education within its context is more interventionist than in the Rawlsian framework. It is expected to work less in favor of societal reproduction and more in favor of a perfectionist ideal of human individuality and collectivity. Still, this kind of redress leaves the physiologist or geneticist essentialism untouched, and, therefore, the kind of off-setting education it suggests is

problematic. The real causes of the translation of dissimilarity into inequality may be obscured, resulting in an educational inability to address the social and cultural origins of the categorization of people into the advanced and those 'lagging behind' them. Thus, without considering the principle of redress a preferable alternative to the Rawlsian maximin, I have discussed it here nevertheless in order to facilitate the exposition of Rawls' conception of education. Rawls contrasts the two principles, that is, the difference and the redress, as follows:

> The difference principle is not, of course, the principle of redress. It does not require society to move in the direction of an equality of natural assets. We are not to try to even out handicaps as if all were expected to compete on a fair basis in the same race. But the difference principle would allocate resources in education, say, so as to improve the long-term expectation of the least favored. If this end is attained by giving more attention to the better endowed, it is permissible; otherwise not. And in making this decision, the value of education should not be assessed only in terms of its productivity effects, that is, its realising a person's capacity to acquire wealth. Equally important, if not more so, is the role of education in enabling a person to enjoy the culture of his society and to take part in its affairs, and in this way to provide each man with a secure sense of his own worth (p. 166).

Let us comment on the conception of education that Rawls' epistemological assumptions allow, as displayed in the above citation. Education appears to be an institution that does not aim to even out something that precedes it: differences in performance are not the outcome of education itself. They emerge from differences in natural endowment that pre-exist enculturation. Far from being responsible for their existence, education, therefore, stands in a subject-object relation to them. It takes them as given and has the function of channeling them in such a way that collective profit will emerge from them. It is even legitimate for education, according to Rawls, to concentrate on the better 'endowed', if that would promote the long-term end of improving the life of the least favored. It is obvious here that the cogency of Rawls' difference principle not only presupposes a comprehensive genetic account of talent but even stands or falls by the latter's validity. For, if the debatable assumption about natural giftedness proves wrong and social theory is right in claiming that qualitative difference of intellect is exclusively the outcome of social asymmetry and often injustice, the difference principle will be nothing but a further legitimation of inequality. Likewise, the Rawlsian conception of education would produce an institutional apparatus for the perpetuation of inequality, unconscious of its role in social reproduction and unable to address the problem of the initial artificial separation of the 'sheep and the goats', judged in terms of knowledge. Justice as fairness would block interventionist efforts and off-setting educational treatment of cultural capital. It would be incompatible with a political teaching for reforming purposes. So the educational dilemma is either to cling to liberalism or to contribute to its reformulation.

Also, since the anthropological assumptions underlying justice as fairness reflect the individualist tenets of liberalism, it is predictable that education will serve the accommodation of competitiveness as a constant of interested selfhood in the social context rather than change it. On dealing with the arrangements of the institutions of a constitutional democracy in a way that justifies the two principles of justice, Rawls explains that approximations are possible,

> ... provided the government regulates a free economy in a certain way. More fully, if law and government act effectively to keep markets competitive, resources fully employed, property and wealth widely distributed over time, and to maintain the appropriate social minimum, then if there is equality of opportunity underwritten by education for all, the resulting distribution will be just (p. 140).

Below we shall discuss whether the goal of equal opportunities exhausts the significance of education for justice. To summarize what we have explored so far, Rawls' theory not only is more comprehensive than it admits, but, in the wake of this comprehensiveness, holds a particular conception of education

that is unaware of its own complicities and reproductive function. Couched in a framework that understands difference in natural qualitative terms and assumes a concomitant motivational ground of social/moral action, education would be compelled to undertake only a very limited and long-term reforming task regarding social justice.

As I mentioned previously, another point where Rawls' account of education emerges concerns equal opportunity.[8] The egalitarian formalism underlying the role given to education becomes clearer in the following formulation: 'we suppose that, in addition to maintaining the usual social overhead capital, government provides for equal educational opportunities for all either by subsidizing private schools or by operating a public school system' (p. 141). Egalitarian educational formalism signifies the idea that schools must have a standard formal approach to all students – didactically and with regard to the course material – in order to secure meritocracy and equal opportunity to achieve distinction. We encounter this idea in Talcott Parsons' sociology of education, which has attracted criticisms to the effect that he loses sight of the fact that equal standards of teaching and assessment cannot neutralize uneven performances that derive from social inequalities (Blackledge and Hunt, 1989). Rawls' view that 'equality of opportunity is a certain set of institutions which assures equally good education and chances of culture for all and which keeps open the competition for positions on the basis of qualities reasonably related to performance' (Rawls, 1999: 143) echoes Parsonian social theory.[9] Rawls understands equal educational opportunities only as the eradication of discrimination and favoritism in classrooms because his epistemological assumptions commit him to a naturalist interpretation of talent, ability and effort:

> Assuming that there is a distribution of natural assets, those at the same level of talent and ability and who have the same willingness to use them, should have the same prospects of success regardless of their initial place in the social system, that

is, irrespective of the class into which they were born. In all sectors of society there should be roughly equal prospects of culture and achievement for everyone similarly endowed and motivated (p. 161).

Had Rawls questioned the naturalist account of endowment, he would have been compelled to reconsider the functionalist socio-theoretical basis of the difference principle and perceive its complicity in the symbolic and practical reproduction of inequality.

Overall, Rawls overlooks the active involvement of education in the shaping of subjectivity (including aspects of it such as ability and motivation) and this leads him to a vision of education that is more reproductive of social inequality than transformative. The reforming effect of education can be better served through a vigilance that uncovers the ways in which some interpretations of existential dissimilarity, on the one hand, and political inequality, on the other, become secret accomplices. To summarize, I have so far argued that:

1. Rawls promotes a political liberalism, one that does not, he claims, presuppose any contestable metaphysical accounts of the self and the world.
2. To explain why some inequalities are allowed within his second principle of justice, he assumes, epistemologically, that there is such a thing as natural intelligence and, anthropologically, that human beings are rational egoists. He considers these assumptions intuitive as well as undisputable facts of science and social theory.
3. Yet, despite their *intuitive* force in the Western worldview, those epistemological and anthropological assumptions have been contested, precisely as ideological – that is, metaphysical after all – justifications of the status quo.
4. Regardless of whether these assumptions prove right or wrong in future, that they are by now contestable renders them ill-placed in Rawlsian political liberalism. The justification they provide for inequality has negative political implications.
5. Educational theory can expose some of the problems in these Rawlsian assumptions and contrast them with new interpretations of the human self.
6. Thus, my aim has not been to refute Rawls' assumptions empirically but to show, first, that

their place in his theory of justice betrays the fact that his liberalism is not political (in the Rawlsian sense) and, second, that they are not as enabling as they are usually taken to be. Exploring the counterintuitive – that is, those assumptions that go against the Rawlsian intuitive ones – may point to a new springboard for organizing political education and reforming the political system, and to an ethic that would offer no legitimation to inequality.

TEACHING CITIZENSHIP

Let us pull together the main arguments. Rawls' principles of justice depend on comprehensive liberalist assumptions about the knowing and ethical self that are so deeply entrenched in hegemonic discourse about subjectivity as to give the impression that they map indisputable natural facts. Educational theory in its hybrid drawing from diverse disciplines such as sociology and philosophy could play a more active part than is usual and provide alternative accounts of the self, thereby exposing the comprehensive character of Rawls' political liberalism. Educational theory also demonstrates that, regrettably, as an institution, education has a more serious and consistent involvement in shaping subjectivities along the divisive lines that the dominant epistemology of giftedness and inherent self-centeredness establishes. In this way, education has a political responsibility for existing inequalities. From this, it follows that educationalists also have a moral duty to reconsider its reproductive role and to contribute to social change instead of accommodating and serving unequal enculturation. Such a conception of education presupposes a sense of inequality redress that puts it at odds with Rawls' account of education for equality. Organizing citizenship education in a political liberalist fashion, either as a separate curricular provision or as a general pedagogical attitude-orientation, enervates the critical and social-reforming potential of pedagogy. It becomes ethnocentric in presenting liberalist convictions as true descriptions of the human condition. When such education faces the neutralist predicament – that is, the robust demand on all cultures to commit themselves to neutralism[10] – this subtle ethnocentrism becomes manifest, since the management of non-liberal otherness conveniently appears to be the only challenge to liberalism's apotheosis.

What kind of citizenship education does this critique of Rawls point to? Using the above summary as a background, I shall move to my suggestions. First, a more interventionist and transformative education can be approached both theoretically and practically through a rejection of liberalist epistemological and anthropological essentialism. Teaching citizenship should not comprise only the transmission of values, substantive or otherwise, nor simply familiarization with civic virtues or acquisition of political scientific knowledge. A more expressive, active and participative practice (Mills, 2004: 260 and 276) may effect more involvement in decision-making but it cannot change, by itself, a politically suspect self-image. Consider, for instance, the following passage in Rawls' *Political Liberalism* (1993). Political liberalism

> will ask that children's education include such things as knowledge of their constitutional and civic rights so that, for example, they know that liberty of conscience exists in their society and that apostasy is not a legal crime, all this to insure that their continued membership when they come of age is not based simply on ignorance of their basic rights or fear of punishment for offences that do not exist. Moreover, their education should also prepare them to be fully cooperating members of society and enable them to be self-supporting; it should also encourage the political virtues so that they want to honor the fair terms of social cooperation in their relations with the rest of society (p. 199).

Teaching and practicing tolerance and respect may contribute to the cultivation of refined and sensitive political attitudes. If, however, a person's political conception of herself as intellectually superior and interest-driven remains unaltered, her attitudes will lapse into condescension and competitiveness. Likewise, the feeling of intellectual

inferiority of the 'losers' in the natural lottery will effect an internalization of social failure. This will never let them question established Occidental divisions such as the mentalist privileging of the intellectual over the manual or the performative over the non-measurable, and it will never allow the inequalities to be revealed and more radical social change to be pursued. Political education then should give priority to the de-schooling of those presuppositions that influence the affective and the imaginary, that is, our feelings about ourselves and others and our visions about what is possible for humanity. When political thinking is determined by such presuppositions, it accommodates inequality at a deeper level; it gives it ontological citizenship, so to speak. It renounces inequality politically, only to reintroduce a version of it – the Rawlsian principle of difference has served as an example of this – as a motivating force for 'naturally gifted' people to make their 'talents' available to the 'less gifted', for the benefit of all. The Rawlsian justification for economic inequalities, even where this is found in mitigated forms, is not independent of political inequalities, in my view, and it must be combated both theoretically and in practice.

To combat such political implications, citizenship education must enlarge its perspective by turning to the connection of the public sphere with the way in which pupils understand themselves and their positioning in society. It must use the negating of essentialism as a springboard from which to explore the possibility of alternative, more daring and more just political and social bonds in the future.

In more concrete educational terms, teaching citizenship for critique and social change rather than adaptation and social maintenance should involve an open questioning of the way the self is pictured epistemologically and anthropologically. Such questioning can be carried out theoretically as a part of a (meta)-critical thinking approach within a citizenship course where students will be directed towards examining, or questioning, the political implications of their self-image for issues of justice and equality. Students could also be invited to consider possible worlds and utopias in which our assumptions about the human condition would be different. A strategy of exchange of positions and narrative imagination regarding one's perception of one's performance and its social significance as well as an attempt to explain non-essentialistically one's progress would be helpful. A very early and simple example of this is Heraclitus' statement (another Pre-Socratic, Thales, had a similar idea too) that he would not have had the intellectual quality that characterized his life if he had been born a slave, or a poor citizen, or a woman. Even if not taken at face value, since the aspects that affect one's life history are more multiple and complex than such categories of social differentiation, this example has a political pertinence for citizenship education. It points to a contemplation of one's own existential position and a capacity to imagine oneself in an alternative, less favorable condition that are often missing today, even in discourses belonging to the politics of difference. For, arguably, such discourses seem more frequently to shift the attention of citizenship education to participatory, inclusive, even 'charitable' models of treating otherness to the neglect of the theoretical perception and construction of otherness in hegemonic discourse that lies behind these.

CONCLUSION

The liberal paradigm of citizenship is dominant in modern Western political thought, often challenged only by the civic republican tradition. The former gives priority to individual rights, negative duties and the coordination of conflicting private interests. The latter's emphasis is placed on active participation in the public sphere and the protection of the communal bond. Despite their differences, they share a conventional understanding of citizenship as a domain of thinking that is distinct from considerations about current or alternative depictions of the self. As a result, they disconnect citizenship discourse and thought experiments about the good in a utopian sense (i.e. as radically different from existing conceptions). Such political 'realism' renders citizenship a discipline of the here and now of hegemonic human understanding. Ultimately, a citizenship discourse that exhausts itself by this foreshortened perspective, works for the future reproduction and perpetuation of the political actuality.

Thinking about epistemological and anthropological issues has important implications for teaching citizenship in a way that is critical to the existing major traditions for the following reasons. First, the scope of political education depends on how we understand the role of education in general. For instance, a fatalist indictment of education as inescapably reproductive of existing structures of inequality, ultimately attributable to human nature, is bound to elicit less radical expectations from citizenship education than a more interventionist conception. How much we concede to education's capacity to redirect interests and shape better subjectivities is a crucial determining factor of what citizenship should mean today. Second, the aims of political education vary according to the way we comprehend the reforming effect of schooling. In spite of the importance of the fact that, as Johnston (2005) convincingly argues, a Rawlsian educational theory encourages pluralistic dialogue and debate, a political education modeled on Rawls' liberalism would promote social integration and socialization, but to a lesser degree social change. In fact, the demands of a neutralist political education are greater in reconstructive terms on those who espouse non-liberal doctrines than they are on liberals themselves, where they are likely to have a reinforcing effect that extends to the comprehensive dimensions of liberalism (Parry, 1999: 34). Finally, answers to ultimate questions about the self and the world, far from being circumventible, determine political education both in content and purpose. If abilities and dispositions are to a large degree natural and pre-given, political education preparing future citizens for justice and equality will consist in imparting the political attitudes that favour the unobstructed deployment of individual talents for the sake of the public weal. If one questions the innateness assumption and the liberalist account of human motivation, however, one is likely to become an advocate for a political education that prepares future citizens for more critical conceptions of justice and redistribution of wealth. Ultimately, what is at stake is the positioning of citizenship education between the Is and the Ought: in other words, what should citizenship education aim to achieve? Should it be closer to a morally-disposed management of existing realities or to a commitment to change those realities for the sake of a more profound ethical worldview? I have argued that, if thought through to its end, this positioning relies on, or, perhaps, is conditioned by, implicit comprehensive depictions of the knowing and moral self. The widely-held idea that citizenship is built upon understandings of individuals and society is thus not only confirmed but also radicalized and refined so as to go beyond narrow considerations of political, economic and moral world perspectives and to encompass epistemological and anthropological accounts. The philosophical presuppositions of citizenship must then be enlarged and more profoundly scrutinized.

As a final illustration of how this applies to Rawls' theory, consider his notion of what a realistic utopia might be in one of his last works, *The Law of Peoples*. The vision of a reasonably just constitutional democratic society is a realistic utopia on two conditions, the first of which is relevant here. To be realistic, a liberal conception of justice 'must rely on the actual laws of nature and achieve the kind of stability those laws allow, that is, stability for the right reasons. It takes people as they are (by the laws of nature), and constitutional and civil laws as they might be, that is, as they would be in a reasonably just and well-ordered democratic society' (Rawls, 2002: 12–13). What does it mean to 'take

people as they are (by the laws of nature)'? I hope to have shown that, for Rawls, this means to hold the epistemological and anthropological ideas that he takes as general facts of natural science and social theory, and to allow 'science' (natural and social) to decipher for us the constraints that reality imposes on the imagination. As I have argued, however, ideas that are taken as facts by some trends in some sciences are questioned by other trends within those sciences or by other sciences. By contrasting those ideas to alternative views and exposing their contestable status, I hope also to have shown that the only sense in which the myth of 'realism' they offer is 'realistic' is that it blocks the imaginative reach of normativity. By this I mean that these ideas are employed by liberalism in order to demarcate what is feasible and worth pursuing; in this sense they appear as realistic, that is, sensitive to 'how things actually are'. Yet, ironically, they are realistic only in another sense: in their unwitting reinforcement of reality as it is. In other words, a theory that takes accounts of 'how people are' for granted serves the affirmation and conservation of the actual – the status quo – as against the possible. It seeks the best feasible vision within the naturalized confines of existing reality. Education might rather want those confines shattered.

NOTES

1 As Kenneth Strike remarks, Rawls holds that comprehensive doctrines are necessary for people having a conception of the good but at the same time he regards them as 'the problem' (Strike, 1998: 222).

2 The difference principle: 'all differences in wealth and income, all social and economic inequalities, should work for the good of the least favored' (Rawls, 1999: 163). The difference principle is also 'a reciprocity principle expressing a natural condition of mutual advantage' (Ibid.).

3 The difference principle: 'all differences in wealth and income, all social and economic inequalities, should work for the good of the least favored' (Rawls, 1999: 163). The difference principle is also

'a reciprocity principle expressing a natural condition of mutual advantage' (Ibid.).

4 Hence, the fact that the principles of justice are not founded on the social position or natural endowments of the particular social agent does not entail, as one might think, that they are independent from the very assumption of natural endowments. On the contrary, as we have seen, the content of the difference principle relies on a naturalist essentialist conception of talent.

5 'It is perfectly true, as some have said [with reference to Hayek – M.P.], that unequal inheritance of wealth is no more inherently unjust than unequal inheritance of intelligence' (Rawls, 1999: 143).

6 In 'Kantian Constructivism' Rawls admits in passing (while arguing for something else) the following: 'in justice as fairness the first principles of justice depend upon those general beliefs about human nature and how society works which are allowed to the parties in the original position' (Rawls, 1999: 351). Thus he admits a dependence on philosophical assumptions, but the crucial point for him is their generality.

7 In justice as fairness, 'the main ideals of the conception of justice are embedded in the two model-conceptions of the person and of a well-ordered society. And, granting that these ideals are allowed by the theory of human nature and so in that sense feasible, the first principles of justice to which they lead, via the constructivist procedure of the original position, determine the long-term aim of social change' (Rawls, 1999: 352).

8 In his words, it is necessary 'that the various offices to which special benefits or burdens attach are open to all. It may be, for example, to the common advantage, as just defined, to attach special benefits to certain offices. Perhaps by doing so the requisite talent can be attracted to them and encouraged to give its best efforts. But any offices having special benefits must be won in a fair competition in which contestants are judged on their merits. If some offices were not open, those excluded would normally be justified in feeling unjustly treated, even if they benefited from the greater efforts of those who were allowed to compete for them' (Rawls, 1999: 51).

9 In his words, it is necessary 'that the various offices to which special benefits or burdens attach are open to all. It may be, for example, to the common advantage, as just defined, to attach special benefits to certain offices. Perhaps by doing so the requisite talent can be attracted to them and encouraged to give its best efforts. But any offices having special benefits must be won in a fair competition in which contestants are judged on their merits. If some offices were not open, those excluded would normally be justified in feeling unjustly treated, even if they benefited from the greater efforts of those who were allowed to compete for them' (Rawls, 1999: 51).

10 As Parry puts it, contemporary political liberals hope to produce 'an education which will encourage future citizens to sustain a form of politics which is limited in its scope and neutral in its dealings with the diversity of conceptions of the good life which exist within modern pluralist societies' (Parry, 1999: 23).

REFERENCES

Blackledge, D. and Hunt, B. (1989) *Sociological Interpretations of Education*. London and New York: Routledge.

Bourdieu, P. (1984) Le Racisme de l'Intelligence, in: Pierre Bourdieu, *Questions de Sociologie*. Paris: Les Editions de Minuit.

Bourdieu, P. and Passeron, J.-C. (1985) *Les Héritiers: Les Étudiants et La Culture*. Paris: Les Editions de Minuit.

Chomsky, N. (1975) *Reflections on Language*. New York: Pantheon Books.

Coleman, J., Campbell, E., Hobson, C., McPartland, J., Mood, A., Weinfeld, F.D. and York, R. (1966) *Equality of Educational Opportunity*. Washington: Department of Health, Education and Welfare.

D'Souza, M. (1996) Educational Pastiche Versus the Education of Natural Intelligence and the Intellectual Virtues According to Jacques Maritain, *Educational Theory*, 46 (4): 501–510.

Gearon, L. (2003) *Learning to Teach Citizenship in the Secondary School*. London and New York: Routledge Falmer.

Jencks, C. (1972) *Inequality: A Reassessment of the Effect of Family and Schooling in America*. New York: Harper and Row.

Jensen, A. (1969) How Much Can We Boost IQ and Scholastic Achievement, *Harvard Educational Review*, 39 (1): 1–123.

Johnston, J.S. (2005) Rawls's Kantian Educational Theory, *Educational Theory*, 55 (2): 201–218.

Mills, I. (2004) Citizenship: Pupil Involvement in Scottish Schools, *Pedagogy, Culture and Society*, 12 (2): 259–277.

Papastephanou, M. (2003) Subjectivity, Community and Education, *Educational Philosophy and Education*, 35 (4): 395–406.

Papastephanou, M. (2004) The Implicit Assumptions of Dividing a Cake: Political or Comprehensive?, *Human Studies*, 27 (1): 307–334.

Parry, G. (1999) Constructive and Reconstructive Political Education, *Oxford Review of Education*, 25 (1–2): 23–38.

Rawls, J. (1992) *A Theory of Justice*. Oxford: Oxford University Press.

Rawls, J. (1993) *Political Liberalism*. New York: Columbia University Press.

Rawls, J. (1995) Reply to Habermas, *The Journal of Philosophy*, XCII (3): 132–180.

Rawls, J. (1999) *John Rawls: Collected Papers*, Samuel Freeman (ed.). Cambridge, MA.: Harvard University Press.

Rawls, J. (2002) *The Law of Peoples*. Cambridge, MA.: Harvard University Press.

Strike, K.A. (1998) Liberalism, Citizenship, and the Private Interest in Schooling, *Studies in Philosophy and Education*, 17 (4): 221–229.

5

Diversity and Citizenship Education in Global Times

James A. Banks

The increasing recognition and visibility of ethnic, cultural, language, and religious diversity in nation-states around the world have raised new questions and possibilities about educating students for effective citizenship. Immigrant nations such as Australia, Canada, and the US have been diverse since their founding. Although immigration has a long history in Western Europe that dates back to the middle of the nineteenth century (Lucassen, 2005), Western European nations have not traditionally viewed themselves as immigration countries. Ethnic, cultural, racial, and religious diversity in Western European nations such as the UK, France, Germany, and the Netherlands increased greatly after World War II when groups from the former colonies of these nations in Asia, Africa, and the West Indies immigrated to Europe to satisfy labor needs and to improve their economic status (Banks, 2004; Banks and Lynch, 1986; Luchtenberg, 2004). The races, cultures, languages, and religions of these groups differ significantly from earlier groups of immigrants to Europe and have challenged established notions of national identity and citizenship within Western European nation-states (Hargreaves, 1995; Modood, 2007; Parekh, 2006).

The increase in international migration, the tightening of national borders, the quest for rights by ethnic minority groups that intensified in the 1960s and 1970s, and the growth in the number of nation-states make a new conception of citizenship education essential in this global age. The number of recognized nation-states increased from 43 in 1900 to approximately 190 in 2000. The number of people living outside their country of birth or citizenship grew from 120 million in 1990 to 160 million in 2000 (Martin and Widgren, 2002). The growth in international migration, the increasing recognition of structural inequality within democratic nation-states, and the growing recognition and legitimacy of international human rights have problematized issues related to citizenship and citizenship education in nation-states throughout the world, and especially in the Western democracies (Castles, 2004; Osler, 2000).

CHALLENGES TO THE ASSIMILATIONIST NOTION OF CITIZENSHIP

An assimilationist conception of citizenship education existed in most of the Western democratic nation-states prior to the rise of the ethnic revitalization movements of the 1960s and 1970s (Banks, 2004). A major goal of citizenship education in these nations was to create nation-states in which all groups shared one dominant mainstream culture. It was assumed that ethnic and immigrant groups had to forsake their original cultures in order to fully participate in the nation-state (Patterson, 1977).

The ethnic revitalization movements of the 1960s and 1970s strongly challenged the assimilationist conception of citizenship education. These movements, triggered by the Civil Rights Movement in the US, echoed throughout the world. French and Indians in Canada, West Indians and Asians in Britain, Indonesians and Surinamese in the Netherlands, and Aborigines in Australia joined the series of ethnic movements, expressed their feelings of marginalization, and worked to make the institutions within their nation-states responsive to their economic, political, and cultural needs.

Indigenous peoples and ethnic groups within the various Western nations – such as American Indians in the US, Aborigines in Australia, Maori in New Zealand, African Caribbeans in the UK, and Moluccans in the Netherlands – want their histories and cultures to be reflected in their national cultures and in the school, college, and university curriculum (Eldering and Kloprogge, 1989; Gillborn, 1990; Mitchell and Salsbury, 1996; Smith, 1999). Multicultural education was developed, in part, to respond to the concerns of ethnic, racial, cultural, and language groups that feel marginalized within their

societies and nation-states (Banks and Banks, 2004).

The right of ethnic and cultural minorities to maintain important aspects of their cultures and languages has been supported by philosophers and educators in the US since the first decades of the 1900s (Drachsler, 1920; Kallen, 1924; Banks, 2005). Kymlicka (1995) – the Canadian political theorist – maintains that ethnic and immigrant groups should have the right to maintain their ethnic cultures and languages as well as participate fully in the civic cultures of democratic nation-states. He argues that because of the increasing diversity within modernized democratic nations and the needs of marginalized racial, ethnic, and language groups for inclusion and recognition, that traditional human rights that focus on individuals should be supplemented with a theory of minority rights. This theory of justice will include 'both universal rights, assigned to individuals regardless of group membership, and certain group-differentiated rights of "special status" for minority cultures' (p. 6).

Young (1989) also argues for differentiated citizenship that recognizes group rights. She maintains that a conception of universal citizenship within a stratified society results in some groups being treated as second-class citizens if group rights are not recognized and represented. Oppression and inequality are perpetuated within an unequal and stratified society if the principle of equal treatment is strictly applied. When group differences are not included in a conception of universal citizenship, homogeneity is imposed that suppresses the differences of groups that have experienced oppression, such as women, Canadian Indians, Australian aborigines, and Muslims in France.

BALANCING UNITY AND DIVERSITY

Cultural, ethnic, racial, language, and religious diversity exist in nations around the world (Banks, 2004; Luchtenberg, 2004; Mitchell and Salsbury, 1996). However, diversity is more publicly recognized, sanctioned, and legitimate in some nations than in others. Diversity has become increasingly recognized and sanctioned in the Western democratic nations since the ethnic revitalization movements of the 1960s and 1970s (Banks and Lynch, 1986), although it is still contested and to some extend marginalized (Modood, 2007).

One of the challenges to diverse democratic nation-states is to provide opportunities for different groups to maintain aspects of their community cultures while building a nation in which these groups are structurally included and to which they feel allegiance. A delicate balance of diversity and unity should be an essential goal of democratic nation-states and of teaching and learning in democratic societies (Banks et al., 2001). Unity must be an important aim when nation-states are responding to diversity within their populations. They can protect the rights of minorities and enable diverse groups to participate only when they are unified around a set of democratic values such as justice and equality (Gutmann, 2004). Citizenship education must be transformed in the twenty-first century because of the deepening racial, ethnic, cultural, language, and religious diversity in nation-states around the world. Citizens in a diverse democratic society should be able to maintain attachments to their cultural communities as well as participate effectively in the shared national culture.

Unity without diversity results in cultural repression and hegemony, as was the case in the former Soviet Union and during the Cultural Revolution in China that was launched in 1966. Diversity without unity leads to Balkanization and the fracturing of the nation-state, as occurred during the Iraq war when sectarian conflict and violence threatened a fragile nation in the late 2000s. Diversity and unity should co-exist in a delicate balance in democratic multicultural nation-states (Banks, 2006b).

LITERACY, SOCIAL JUSTICE, AND CITIZENSHIP EDUCATION

In the US (Sleeter, 2007), the UK (S. Tomlinson, 2007) and other Western nations, the focus on the teaching and assessment of basic skills has caused teachers to devote increasingly less time to citizenship education and to issues related to race, ethnicity, and social justice (Meier and Wood, 2004; Sleeter, 2005). Literate citizens in a diverse democratic society need knowledge, skills, and values in addition to basic skills. They should be reflective, moral, and active citizens in an interconnected global world who have the knowledge, skills, and commitment needed to act to change the world to make it more just and democratic (Banks, 2006b). The world's greatest problems do not result from people being unable to read and write. They result from people in the world – from different cultures, ethnic groups, races, religious, and nations – being unable to get along and to work together to solve the world's intractable problems such as global warming (Gore, 2006), the HIV/AIDS epidemic, poverty, racism, sexism, genocide, and war (Cheadle and Prendergast, 2007). Examples are the genocide in Darfur and the conflicts between the US and Iraq, North Korea and its neighbors, and the Israelis and Palestinians.

In addition to mastering basic reading and writing skills, literate citizens in democratic multicultural societies such as Australia, Canada, France, Japan, and the UK should develop *multicultural literacy*. Multicultural literacy consists of the skills and ability to identify the creators of knowledge and their interests, to uncover the assumptions of knowledge, to view knowledge critically and from diverse ethnic and cultural perspectives, and to use knowledge to guide action that will help create a humane and just world (Banks, 1996, 2006a). When we teach students how to critique the injustice in the world we should help them to formulate possibilities for action to change the world to make it more democratic and just. Critique without hope may leave students disillusioned and without agency (Freire, 1970/1997).

THE BELLAGIO DIVERSITY AND CITIZENSHIP EDUCATION PROJECT

Citizenship education needs to be reconceptualized and transformed in significant ways because of the increasing recognition and legitimacy of diversity within nation-states throughout the world and the quests by racial, ethnic, cultural, language, and religious groups for cultural recognition and rights (Banks, 2004; Castles, 2004; Mitchell and Salsbury, 1996). The Center for Multicultural Education at the University of Washington has implemented a project to reform citizenship education so that it will advance democracy as well as respond to the needs of the diverse groups within multicultural nation-states. The first part of this project consisted of a conference, 'Ethnic Diversity and Citizenship Education in Multicultural Nation-States,' held at the Rockefeller Foundation's Study and Conference Center in Bellagio, Italy, June 17–21, 2002 (hereafter 'Bellagio Conference'). The conference, which was supported by the Spencer and Rockefeller Foundations, included participants from 12 nations: Brazil, Canada, China, Germany, India, Israel, Japan, Palestine, Russia, South Africa, the UK, and the US. The papers from this conference are published in *Diversity and Citizenship Education: Global Perspectives* (Banks, 2004).

One of the conclusions of the Bellagio Conference was that world migration and the political and economic aspects of globalization are challenging nation-states and national borders. At the same time, national borders remain tenacious; the number of nations in the world is increasing rather than decreasing. The number of UN member states increased from 80 in 1950 to 191 in 2002 (Castles, 2004). Globalization and nationalism are contradictory but co-existing trends and forces in the world today (Calhoun, 2007).

Table 5.1 Principles and concepts for educating citizens in a global age

PRINCIPLES

Section I Diversity, Unity, Global Interconnectedness, and Human Rights

1. Students should learn about the complex relationships between unity and diversity in their local communities, the nation, and the world.
2. Students should learn about the ways in which people in their community, nation, and region are increasingly interdependent with other people around the world and are connected to the economic, political, cultural, environmental, and technological changes taking place across the planet.
3. The teaching of human rights should underpin citizenship education courses and programs in multicultural nation-states.

Section II Experience and Participation

1. Students should be taught knowledge about democracy and democratic institutions, and they should be provided opportunities to practice democracy.

CONCEPTS

- Democracy
- Diversity
- Globalization
- Sustainable Development
- Empire, Imperialism, Power
- Prejudice, Discrimination, Racism
- Migration
- Identity/Diversity
- Multiple Perspectives
- Patriotism and Cosmopolitanism

Reprinted with permission from Banks, J.A., Banks, C.A. M., Cortés, C.E., Merryfield, M.M., Moodley, K.A., Murphy-Shigematsu, S., Osler, A., Park, C. and Parker, W.C. (2005). *Democracy and diversity: Principles and concepts for educating citizens in a global age.* Seattle: University of Washington, Center for Multicultural Education.

Consequently, educators throughout the world should rethink and redesign citizenship education courses and programs. Citizenship education should help students acquire the knowledge, attitudes, and skills needed to function in their nation-states as well as in a diverse world society that is experiencing rapid globalization and quests by ethnic, cultural, language, and religious groups for recognition and inclusion. It should also help them to develop a commitment to act to change the world to make it more democratic and just. The Bellagio Conference also concluded that citizenship and citizenship education are defined and implemented differently in various nations and in diverse social, economic, and political contexts. It is also a contested idea in nation-states around the world. However, there are shared problems, concepts, and issues, such as the need to prepare students in various nations to function within as well as across national borders. The Bellagio Conference recommended that these shared issues and problems be identified by an international group of educators and scholars that would formulate guidelines for dealing with them. In response to this recommendation, the Center for Multicultural Education at the University of Washington created an international consensus panel that wrote a report that identified principles and concepts for educating citizens for democracy and diversity in a global age (Banks et al., 2005). Table 5.1 contains the principles and concepts identified and described in the consensus panel report. The complete report can be downloaded as a pdf at the Center for Multicultural Education website: http://depts.washington.edu/centerme/home.htm

INCREASING DIVERSITY AND GLOBAL CITIZENSHIP EDUCATION

Citizens in this century need the knowledge, attitudes, and skills required to function in their cultural communities and beyond their cultural borders. They should also be able and willing to participate in the construction of a national civic culture that is a moral and just community. The national community should embody democratic ideals and values, such as those articulated in the Universal Declaration of Human Rights. Students also need to acquire the knowledge and skills required to become effective citizens in the global community.

The community cultures and languages of students from diverse groups were to be eradicated in the assimilationist conception of citizenship education that existed in the US and most other Western nations prior to the Civil Rights Movement of the 1960s and 1970s (Alba and Nee, 2003; Lucassen, 2005). One consequence of assimilationist citizenship education was that many students lost their first cultures, languages, and ethnic identities (Wong Fillmore, 2005). Some students also became alienated from family and community. Another consequence was that many students became socially and politically alienated within the national civic culture.

Members of identifiable racial, ethnic, and language groups often became marginalized in both their community cultures and in the national civic culture because they could function effectively in neither. When they acquired the language and culture of the mainstream dominant culture, they were often denied structural inclusion and full participation into the civic culture because of their characteristics that differed from those of the mainstream population (Alba and Nee, 2003; Gordon, 1964).

THE DEVELOPMENT OF CULTURAL, NATIONAL, AND GLOBAL IDENTIFICATIONS

Assimilationist notions of citizenship are ineffective in this century because of the increasing recognition and legitimacy of diversity throughout the world and the quests by marginalized groups for cultural recognition and rights. *Multicultural citizenship* is essential for today's global age (Kymlicka, 1995; Young, 1989). It recognizes and legitimizes the right and need of citizens to maintain commitments both to their cultural communities and to the national civic culture. Only when the national civic culture is transformed in ways that reflect and give voice to the diverse ethnic, racial, language, and religious communities that constitute it will it be viewed as legitimate by all of its citizens. Only then can they develop clarified commitments to the nation-state and its ideals.

Citizenship education should help students to develop thoughtful and clarified identifications with their cultural communities and their nation-states. It should also help them to develop clarified global identifications and deep understandings of their roles in the world community. Students need to understand how life in their cultural communities and nation influences other nations and the cogent influence that international events have on their daily lives. Global education should have as major goals helping students to develop understandings of the interdependence among nations in the world today, clarified attitudes toward other nations, and reflective identifications with the world community.

Non-reflective and unexamined cultural attachments may prevent the development of a cohesive nation with clearly defined national goals and policies (Calhoun, 2007). Although we need to help students develop reflective and clarified cultural identifications, they must also be helped to clarify their identifications with their nations. Despite the criticisms they justly and frequently receive (Appadurai, 1996), nation-states and nationalism provide a 'form of social solidarity' and is 'one of the background conditions on which modern democracy has been based.' Nation-states have also 'helped secure domestic inclusion and redistributive policies even while [they have] inhibited cosmopolitan attention to the needs of non-nationals' (Calhoun, 2007: 1).

It is important for students to develop *reflective* nationalism because blind nationalism will prevent them from developing thoughtful and positive global identifications (Westheimer, 2007). Nationalism and national attachments in most nations are strong and tenacious. An important aim of citizenship education should be to help students develop global identifications. They also need to develop a deep understanding of the need to take action as citizens of the global community to help solve the world's difficult global problems, such as war, genocide, and global warming. Cultural, national, and global experiences and identifications are interactive and interrelated in a dynamic way.

Students should develop a delicate balance of cultural, national, and global identifications (see Figure 5.1). A nation-state that alienates and does not structurally include all cultural

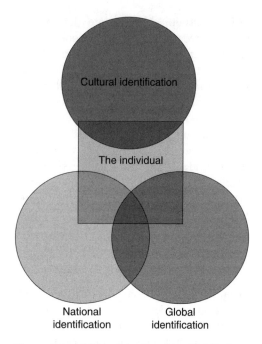

Figure 5.1   Cultural, national, and global identifications. Copyright © 2007 by James A. Banks. Reprinted with permission of the author.

groups into the national culture runs the risk of creating alienation and causing groups to focus on specific concerns and issues rather than on the overarching goals and policies of the nation-state. To develop reflective cultural, national, and global identifications, students must acquire the knowledge, attitudes, and skills needed to function within and across diverse racial, ethnic, cultural, language, and religious groups.

Cultural, national, and global identifications and attachments are complex, interactive, and contextual. The ways in which they influence an individual's behavior is determined by many factors.

THE CONTINUING IMPORTANCE OF CULTURAL IDENTIFICATIONS

I have argued that students should develop a delicate balance of cultural, national, and global identifications and allegiances. I conceptualize global identification similar to the way in which Nussbaum (2002) defines *cosmopolitanism*. She defines cosmopolitans as people 'whose allegiance is to the worldwide community of human beings' (p. 4). She points out, however, that 'to be a citizen of the world one does not need to give up local identifications, which can be a source of great richness in life' (p. 9).

Strong, positive, and clarified cultural identifications and attachments are a prerequisite to cosmopolitan beliefs, attitudes, and behaviors. It is not realistic to expect Puerto Rican students in New York City to have a strong allegiance to US national values or deep feelings for dying people in Darfur if they feel marginalized and rejected within their community, their school, and in their nation-state. Educators must nurture, support, and affirm the identities of students from marginalized cultural, ethnic, and language groups if we expect them to endorse national values, become cosmopolitans, and work to make their local communities, the nation, and the world more just and humane.

I believe that cultural, national, and global identifications are interrelated in a developmental way. Students cannot develop thoughtful and clarified national identifications until they have reflective and clarified cultural identifications. They cannot develop a global or cosmopolitan identification until they have acquired a reflective national identification. Mexican American students who do not value their own cultural identity and who have negative attitudes toward Mexican American culture will find it difficult to interact positively with outside groups, such as African American and Jewish Americans.

THE STAGES OF CULTURAL IDENTITY

Self-acceptance is a prerequisite to the acceptance and valuing of others. Students from racial, cultural, and language minority groups that have historically experienced institutionalized discrimination, racism, or other forms of marginalization often have a difficult time accepting and valuing their own ethnic and cultural heritages. Teachers should be aware of and sensitive to the stages of cultural development that all of their students – including mainstream students, ethnic minority students, and other marginalized groups of students – may be experiencing and facilitate their identity development.

I have developed a *Stages of Cultural Identity Typology* which teachers can use when trying to help students attain higher stages of cultural development and to develop clarified cultural, national, and global identifications (see Figure 5.2) (Banks, 2006a). I believe that students need to reach stage 3 of this typology, *Cultural Identity Clarification*, before we can expect them to embrace other cultural groups or attain thoughtful and clarified national or global identifications. The typology is an ideal-type concept. Consequently, it does not describe the actual identity development of any particular individual. Rather, it is a framework for thinking about and facilitating the identity development of students who approximate one of the stages.

During stage 1 – *Cultural psychology captivity* – individuals internalize the negative stereotypes and beliefs about their cultural groups that are institutionalized within the larger society and may exemplify cultural self-rejection and low self-esteem. Cultural encapsulation and cultural exclusiveness, and the belief that their ethnic group is superior to others, characterize stage 2 – *Cultural encapsulation*. Often individuals within this stage have newly discovered their cultural consciousness and try to limit participation to their cultural group. They have ambivalent feelings about their cultural group and try to confirm, for themselves, that they are proud of it. In stage 3 – *Cultural identity clarification* – individuals are able to clarify their personal attitudes and cultural identity and to develop clarified positive attitudes toward their cultural group. In this stage, cultural pride is genuine rather than contrived. Individuals within stage 4 – *Biculturalism* – have a healthy

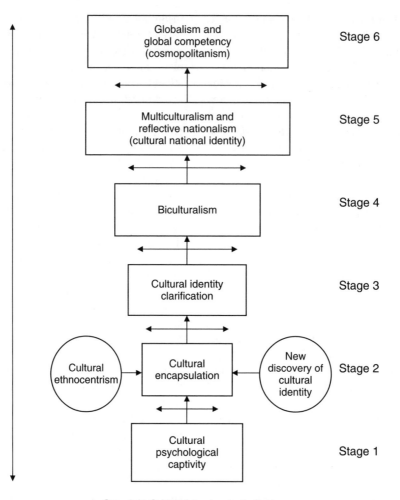

Figure 5.2   The stages of cultural identity: a typology

sense of cultural identity and the psychological characteristics to participate successfully in their own cultural community as well as in another cultural community. They also have a strong desire to function effectively in two cultures.

Stage 5 individuals (*Multiculturalism and reflective nationalism*) have clarified, reflective, and positive personal, cultural, and national identifications and positive attitudes toward other racial, cultural, and ethnic groups. At stage 6 – *Globalism and global competency* – individuals have reflective and

clarified national and global identifications. They have the knowledge, skills, and attitudes needed to function effectively within their own cultural communities, within other cultures within their nation-state, in the civic culture of their nation, as well as in the global community. Individuals within stage 6 exemplify cosmopolitanism and have a commitment to all human beings in the world community (Nussbaum, 2002). Gutmann (2004) states that the primary commitment of these individuals is to justice and not to any human community.

RESEARCH AND THE STAGES OF CULTURAL IDENTITY TYPOLOGY

Researchers and practitioners have found the Stages of Cultural Identity Typology helpful in their work and an effective vehicle for stimulating classroom discussion, which is an essential component of a democratic classroom (Parker, 2003). The typology has been used in a number of research studies on race and ethnicity and as a teaching tool in classrooms. Ford (1979) developed an instrument to measure the first five of the stages. Her study demonstrated that teachers are spread into the five stages that I had hypothesized. The sixth stage of the typology was developed after Ford completed her study. Tomlinson (1995, 1996) used the typology in several studies of reading instruction to determine how curriculum goals are related to it and to help teachers with instruction. She concluded that the typology helped 'teachers with the delicate maneuvering in addressing critical issues of ethnic identity that often remain overlooked when units of multicultural literacy instruction are attempted (1996: 18). Mallette et al. (1998) used the typology to guide discussions of multiethnic literature and concluded that it 'produced vibrant and lengthy discussions' (p. 197).

CREATING DEMOCRATIC CLASSROOMS AND SCHOOLS

Democratic classrooms and schools are needed to help students develop reflective cultural, national, and global identifications and the knowledge, attitudes, and skills needed to function across groups. Dewey (1959) believed that 'all genuine education comes about through experience' (p. 13). Students not only need knowledge about democracy in order to internalize democratic attitudes and beliefs, they also need to experience it in democratic classrooms and schools (Banks, 2007; Parker, 2003).

During the 1970s Kohlberg and his colleagues created models of democratic schools called 'just community schools,' one of which was established in Cambridge, Massachusetts (Kohlberg et al., 1975). The just community school was characterized by 'participatory democracy with teachers and students having equal rights, emphasis on conflict resolution through consideration of fairness and morality, and inclusion of developmental moral discussion in the curriculum' (Kohlberg et al.). Kohlberg and the school leaders tried to make the school a microcosm of a democratic community in which students and teaches could practice democracy and develop high levels of moral reasoning. Kohlberg developed a theory of moral development and moral dilemmas derived from the theory to help students learn to reason morally at increasingly higher levels. Kohlberg (1981) hypothesized that an individual's ability to reason morally develops sequentially in a series of stages. He also hypothesized that the use of moral dilemmas and democratic experiences can facilitate and accelerate an individual's stage of moral reasoning.

THE IMPLICATIONS OF SOCIAL IDENTITY THEORY FOR DEMOCRATIC SCHOOLS

In order for students to experience democracy, educators must design and implement strategies to improve intergroup relations in schools and classrooms because whenever students from different racial, ethnic, cultural, religious, language, and social-class groups interact in schools and classrooms, *ingroups* and *outgroups* develop as well as stereotypes, prejudice, and discrimination (Stephan, 1999).

Social psychological theory and research – known as the *minimal group paradigm or social identity theory* – indicate that when mere categorization develops, individuals favor the ingroup over the outgroup and discriminate against the outgroup (Tajfel, 1970; Smith and Mackie, 1995). This can occur in situations without prior historical conflict and animosity, competition, physical differences, or any kind of important difference. One important cause and perpetuator of group distinctions is *categorization* itself. When one group is viewed as similar to us and another as different or 'the other,' the basis for distinctions and discrimination is created.

One implication of social identity theory is that to increase positive intergroup contact the salience of group characteristics should be minimized and a superordinate group to which students from different cultural and language groups can become identified should be constructed. For example, in a classroom characterized by language diversity, group salience is likely to be reduced to the extent that all students become competent in the same languages. In a classroom with both European Americans and Mexican Americans, group salience is increased if only the Mexican American students speak Spanish. However, if both Mexican and European Americans student become competent in English and Spanish, bilingual competency can be the basis for the formation of a superordinate group to which all of the students belong.

THE CONTACT HYPOTHESIS

Most of the work in intergroup relations has been guided by the contact hypothesis and related research that emerged as responses to the Nazi anti-Semitism that developed during the Second World War. Allport's (1954/1979) intergroup contact theory was one of the most important intergroup theories formulated in the post-war period. Teachers can create democratic classrooms by using teaching strategies guided by Allport's theory and related research (Cohen, 1994; Cohen and Lotan, 1995). Allport stated that contact between groups will improve intergroup relations when contract is characterized by these conditions:

(1) equal-status;
(2) common goals;
(3) intergroup cooperation; and
(4) support of authorities, law and custom.

Pettigrew (2004) provides new perspectives and an informative review of Allport's theory.

COOPERATIVE LEARNING AND INTERRACIAL CONTACT

During the last 40 years, investigators in the US (Dovidio and Gaertner, 1986), Canada (Zanna and Olson, 1994), Israel (Horenczyk and Bekerman, 1997) – as well as in other nations – have accumulated an impressive body of research on the effects of cooperative learning groups and activities on students' racial attitudes, friendship choices, and achievement. Much of this research has been conducted as well as reviewed by investigators such as Aronson and his colleagues (Aronson and Bridgeman, 1979; Aronson and Gonzalez, 1988), Cohen and her colleagues (Cohen, 1972, 1984; Cohen and Roper, 1972; Cohen and Lotan, 1995), Johnson and Johnson (1981, 1991), Slavin (1979, 1983, 1985), and Slavin and Madden (1979).

The research on cooperative learning and interracial contact – most of which is grounded in Allport's (1954) contact hypothesis – lends considerable support to the postulate that cooperative interracial contact situations in schools, if the conditions stated by Allport are present in the contact situations, have positive effects on student interracial behavior, student academic achievement (Aronson and Gonzalez, 1988; Slavin, 1979, 1983), and on cross-racial friendships, racial attitudes, and behavior (Slavin, 2001). Most of this research indicates that minority group students and white mainstream students have a greater tendency to make cross-racial friendship choices after they have participated in interracial learning teams such as the jigsaw (Aronson and Bridgeman, 1979) and the Student Teams-Achievement Divisions (STAD) (Slavin, 1979). Investigators have also found that cooperative learning methods have increased student motivation and self-esteem (Slavin, 1985) and helped students to develop empathy (Aronson and Bridgeman, 1979).

An essential characteristic of effective cooperative learning groups and methods is that the students experience *equal-status* in the contact situation (Allport, 1954). Cohen (1972) has pointed out that both African American and white students may expect and attribute higher status to whites in an initial interracial contact situation that may perpetuate white dominance. Cohen and Roper (1972) designed an intervention to change this expectation. They increased the status of African American students by teaching them to build transistor radios and to teach this skill to white students. The African American children taught the white children to build transistor radios after the children watched a videotape showing the African American children building them. When interracial work groups were structured, equal status was achieved only in those groups in which the African American children taught the white students to build transistor radios. The white children dominated in the other groups. The research by Cohen and Roper (1972) indicates that equal-status between groups in interracial situations has to be constructed by teachers rather than assumed. If students from diverse racial, ethnic, and language groups are mixed without structured interventions that create equal-status conditions in the contact situation, racial and ethnic conflict and categorization are likely to increase.

CONCLUSION

The quests by marginalized racial, ethnic, cultural, language, and religious groups require educators around the world to reconceptualize and transform citizenship education so that it will enable students from diverse groups to participate in the public civic culture while maintaining commitments to their family and community cultures and languages. Students should not have to deny and reject important aspects of their cultures and languages in order to participate fully in the national civic culture. This was a price that many ethnic and language minorities had to pay for civic participation in the past (Wong Fillmore, 2005).

Multicultural citizenship allows citizens to fully participate in the national civic culture while retaining important identities and commitments to their community cultures and languages (Kymlicka, 1995; Young, 1989). Cultural, national, and global identities are interactive, overlapping, and contextual. Having a commitment to community cultures and languages does not make people less committed to their national civic community or less cosmopolitan. Appiah (2006), a proponent of cosmopolitanism, does not see a conflict between 'local partialities and universal morality – between being a part of the place you were and a part of a broader human community' (p. xviii).

Experiencing democracy in classrooms and schools enables students to acquire the knowledge, skills, and abilities needed to function cross-culturally and to develop a commitment to act to make their communities, nation, and the world more just and humane. Martin Luther King (1963/1994) eloquently expressed why it is essential for all individuals in our highly interdependent global world to develop cosmopolitan commitments, values, and action when he said, 'Injustice anywhere is a threat to justice everywhere. We are caught in an inescapable network of mutuality, tied in a single garment of destiny. Whatever affects one directly affects all indirectly' (pp. 2–3).

NOTE

Parts of this chapter are adapted from the author's article, 'Teaching for social justice, diversity, and citizenship in a global world,' *The Educational Forum*, 68 (Summer, 2004): 296–305 and is used with the permission of Kappa Delta Pi.

REFERENCES

Alba, R. and Nee, V. (2003) *Remaking the American Mainstream: Assimilation and Contemporary Immigration*. Cambridge: Harvard University Press.

Allport, G.W. (1954/1979) *The Nature of Prejudice*. (25th anniversary edn). Reading, MA: Addison-Wesley. (original work published 1954).

Appadurai, A. (1996) *Modernity at Large: Cultural Dimensions of Globalization*. Minneapolis: University of Minnesota Press.

Appiah, K.A. (2006) *Cosmopolitanism: Ethnics in a World of Strangers*. New York: Norton.

Aronson, E. and Bridgeman, D. (1979) Jigsaw Groups and the Desegregated Classroom: In Pursuit of Common Goals. *Personality and Social Psychology Bulletin*, 5. 438–446.

Aronson, E. and Gonzalez, A. (1988) Desegregation, Jigsaw, and the Mexican-American Experience. In P. A. Katz and D. A. Taylor (Eds), *Eliminating racism: Profiles in controversy*. New York: Plenum Press. pp. 301–314.

Banks, C.A.M. (2005) *Improving Multicultural Education: Lessons from the Intergroup Education Movement*. New York: Teachers College Press.

Banks, J.A. (1996) *Multicultural Education, Transformative Knowledge and Action: Historical and Contemporary Perspectives*. New York: Teachers College Press.

Banks, J.A. (ed.) (2004) *Diversity and Citizenship Education: Global Perspectives*. San Francisco: Jossey-Bass.

Banks, J.A. (2006a) *Cultural Diversity and Education: Foundations, Curriculum, and Teaching* (5th edn). Boston: Allyn and Bacon.

Banks, J.A. (2006b) *Race, Culture, and Education: The Selected Works of James A. Banks*. London and New York: Routledge.

Banks, J.A. (2007) *Educating Citizens in a multicultural Society* (2nd edn). New York: Teachers College Press.

Banks, J.A. and Banks, C.A.M. (eds) (2004) *Handbook of Research on Multicultural Education* (2nd edn). San Francisco: Jossey-Bass.

Banks, J.A. and Lynch, J. (eds) (1986) *Multicultural Education in Western Societies*. London: Holt.

Banks, J.A., Cookson, P., Gay, G., Hawley, W.D., Irvine, J.J., Nieto, S., Schofield, J.W., and Stephan, W.G. (2001) *Diversity Within Unity: Essential Principles for Teaching and Learning in a Multicultural Society*. Seattle: Center for Multicultural Education, University of Washington.

Banks, J.A., Banks, C.A.M., Cortés, C.E., Hahn, C., Merryfield, M., Moodley, K., Osler, A., Murphy-Shigematsu, S., and Parker, W.C. (2005) *Democracy and Diversity: Principles and Concepts for Educating Citizens in a Global Age*. Seattle: Center for Multicultural Education, University of Washington.

Calhoun, C. (2007) *Nations Matter: Culture, History, and the Cosmopolitan Dream*. London and New York: Routledge.

Castles, S. (2004) Migration, Citizenship, and education. In J.A. Banks (ed.), *Diversity and citizenship education: Global perspectives*. San Francisco: Jossey-Bass. pp. 17–48.

Cheadle, D. and Prendergast, J. (2007) *Not on Our Watch: The Mission to End Genocide in Darfur and Beyond*. New York: Hyperion.

Cohen, E. (1972) Interracial Interaction Disability. *Human Relations*, 25 (6): 9–24.

Cohen, E.G. (1984) Talking and working together: Status, Interaction, and Learning. In P. Peterson, L.C. Wilkinson, and M. Hallinan (eds), *The social context of instruction*. New York: Academic Press. pp. 171–186.

Cohen, E.G. (1994) *Designing Groupwork: Strategies for the Heterogeneous* Classroom (2nd edn) New York: Teachers College Press.

Cohen, E.G. and Lotan, R.A. (1995) Producing Equal-status Interaction in the Heterogeneous Classroom. *American Educational Research Journal*, 32 (1): 99–120.

Cohen, E.G. and Roper, S.S. (1972) Modification of Interracial Interaction Disability: An Application of Status Characteristic Theory. *American Sociological Review*, 37 (6): 643–657.

Dewey, J. (1959) *Experience and Education*. New York: Macmillan.

Dovidio, J.F. and Gaertner, S.L. (Eds) (1986) *Prejudice, Discrimination, and Racism*. San Diego: Academic Press.

Drachsler, J. (1920) *Democracy and Assimilation*. New York: Macmillan.

Eldering, L. and Kloprogge, J. (1989) *Different Cultures, Same School: Ethnic Minority Children in Europe*. Amsterdam: Swets & Seitlinger.

Ford, M. (1979) *The Development of an Instrument for Assessing Levels of Ethnicity in Public School Teachers*. Unpublished doctoral dissertation, University of Houston.

Freire, P. (1970/1997) *Pedagogy of the Oppressed* (20th anniversary edn) New York: Continuum.

Gillborn, D. (1990) *Race, Ethnicity, and Education*. London: Unwin Hyman.

Gore, A. (2006) *An Inconvenient Truth: The Planetary Emergency of Global Warming and What We can Do about It*. Emmaus, PA: Rodale.

Gordon, M.M. (1964) *Assimilation in American Life*. New York: Oxford University Press.

Gutmann, A. (2004) Unity and Diversity in Democratic Multicultural Education: Creative and Destructive Tensions. In J. A. Banks (Ed.), *Diversity and Citizenship Education: Global Perspectives*. San Francisco: Jossey-Bass. pp. 71–96.

Hargreaves, A.G. (1995) *Immigration, 'Race' and Ethnicity in Contemporary France*. London and New York: Routledge.

Horenczyk, G. and Bekerman, Z. (1997) 'The Effects of Intercultural Acquaintance and Structured Intergroup Interaction on Ingroup, Outgroup, and Reflected Ingroup Stereotypes.' *International Journal of Intercultural Relations*, 21 (1): 71–83.

Johnson, D.W. and Johnson, R.T. (1981) Effects of Cooperative and Individualistic Learning Experiences on Interethnic Interaction. *Journal of Educational Psychology*, 73 (3): 444–449.

Johnson, D.W. and Johnson, R.T. (1991) *Learning Together and Alone* (3rd edn) Eaglewood Cliffs, NJ: Prentice-Hall.

Kallen, H.M. (1924) *Culture and Democracy in the United States*. New York: Boni and Liveright.

King, M.L. Jr. (1963/1994) *Letter from a Birmingham Jail*. New York/SanFrancisco: Harper (original work published 1963).

Kohlberg, L. (1981) *The Philosophy of Moral Development: Moral Stages and the Idea of Justice*. San Francisco: Harper & Row.

Kohlberg, L. et al. (1975) *The Just Community school: The theory and the Cambridge Cluster School Experiment*. Cambridge: Harvard University, Graduate School of Education. Retrieved August 15, 2007 from http://www.eric.ed.gov:80/ERICWebPortal/custom/portlets/recordDetails/detailmini.jsp?_nfpb=true&_&ERICExtSearch_SearchValue_0=ED223511&ERICExtSearch_SearchType_0=eric_accno&accno=ED22351

Kymlicka, W. (1995) *Multicultural citizenship: A Liberal Theory of Minority Rights*. New York: Oxford University Press.

Lucassen, L. (2005) *The Immigrant Threat: The Integration of Old and New Migrants in Western Europe since 1850*. Urbana and Chicago: University of Illinois Press.

Luchtenberg, S. (Ed.) (2004) *Migration, Education and Change*. London and New York: Routledge.

Mallette, M.H., Bean, T.W., and Readence, J. E. (1998) Using Banks' Typology in the Discussion of Young Adult, Multiethnic Literature: A Multicase Study. *Journal of Reseach and Development in Education*, 31 (4): 193–204.

Martin, P. and Widgren, J. (2002) International Migration: Facing the Challenge. *Population Reference Bulletin*, 57, No. 1. Washington, DC: Population Reference Bureau.

Meier, D. and Wood, G. (eds) (2004) *Many Children Left Behind: How the No Child Left Behind Act is Damaging Our Children and Our Schools*. Boston: Beacon.

Mitchell, B.M. and Salsbury, R.E. (eds) (1996) *Multicultural Education: An International Guide to Research, Policies, and Programs*. Westport, CT: Greenwood Press.

Modood, T. (2007) *Multiculturalism: A Civic Idea*. Cambridge, UK: Polity Press.

Nussbaum, M. (2002) Patriotism and Cosmopolitansim. In J. Cohen (Ed.), *For love of country*. Boston: Beacon Press. pp. 2–17.

Osler, A. (ed.) (2000) *Citizenship and Democracy in School: Diversity, Identity, and Equality*. Stoke-on-Trent, UK: Trentham.

Parekh, B. (2006) *Rethinking Multiculturalism: Cultural Diversity and Political Theory*. New York: Palgrave Macmillan.

Parker, W.C. (2003) *Teaching Democracy: Unity and Diversity in Public Life*. New York: Teachers College Press.

Patterson, O. (1977) *Ethnic Chauvinism: The Reactionary Impulse*. New York: Stein & Day.

Pettigrew, T.F. (2004) Intergroup Contact: Theory, Research, and New Perspectives. In J.A. Banks and C.A.M. Banks, *Handbook of Research on Multicultural Education* (2nd edn). San Francisco: Jossey-Bass. pp. 770–781.

Slavin, R.E. (1979) Effects of Biracial Learning Teams on Cross-racial Friendships. *Journal of Educational Psychology,* 71 (3): 381–387.

Slavin, R.E. (1983) *Cooperative Learning.* New York: Longman.

Slavin, R.E. (1985) Cooperative Learning: Applying Contact Theory in Desegregated Schools. *Journal of Social Issues,* 41 (1): 45–62.

Slavin, R.E. (2001) Cooperative learning and intergroup relations. In J.A. Banks and C.A.M. Banks (Eds) *Handbook of Research on Multicultural Education.* San Francisco: Jossey-Bass. pp. 628–634.

Slavin, R.E. and Madden, N.A. (1979) School Practices that Improve Race Relations. *American Educational Research Journal,* 16 (2): 169–180.

Sleeter, C.A. (2005) *Un-Standardizing Curriculum: Multicultural Teaching in the Standards-Based Classroom.* New York: Teachers College Press.

Sleeter, C.A. (Ed.) (2007) *Facing Accountability in Education: Democracy and Equity at Risk.* New York: Teachers College Press.

Smith, E.R. and Mackie, D.M. (1995) *Social Psychology.* New York: Worth Publishers.

Smith, L.T. (1999) *Decolonizing Methodologies: Research and Indigenous Peoples.* New York: Zed Books.

Stephan, W. (1999) *Reducing Prejudice and Stereotyping in Schools.* New York: Teachers College Press.

Tajfel, H. (1970) Experiments in Intergroup Discrimination. *Scientific American,* 223 (5): 96–102.

Tomlinson, L.M. (1995) *The Effects of Instructional Interaction Guided by a Typology of Ethnic Identity Development: Phase One.* Athens: National Reading Center, University of Georgia.

Tomlinson, L. M. (1996) *Teachers' Application of Banks' Typology of Ethnic Identity Development and Curriculum Goals to Story Content and Classroom Discussion: Phase Two.* Athens: National Reading Center, University of Georgia.

Tomlinson, S. (2007) Ruthless Assessment in a Post-Welfare U. K. Society. In C.A. Sleeter (Ed.), *Facing Accountability in Education: Democracy and Equity at Risk.* New York: Teachers College Press. pp. 172–187.

Westheimer, J. (Ed.) (2007) *Pledging Allegiance: The Politics of Patriotism in America's Schools.* New York: Teachers College Press.

Wong Fillmore, L. (2005) When Learning a Second Language Means Losing the First. In M. Suárez-Orozco, C. Suárez-Orozco, and D. B. Quin (Eds) *The New Immigration: An Interdisciplinary Readers.* New York: Routledge. pp. 289–307.

Young, I.M. (1989) Polity and Group Difference: A Critique of the Ideal of Universal Citizenship. *Ethics,* 99 (2): 250–274.

Zanna, M.P. and Olson, J.M. (Eds) (1994) *The Psychology of Prejudice: The Ontario Symposium* (vol. 7) Hillside, NJ: Erlbaum.

6

Equity and its Relationship to Citizenship Education

Stephen Gorard and Vanita Sundaram

In this chapter, we will argue that greater attention to equity in educational systems is important, and suggest ways in which equity can be enhanced – particularly from the perspective of pupils in schools. We start by outlining some ideas about what equity entails, then why equity is important in education, why we might wish to listen more carefully to the views of pupils, and conclude with some examples of the views of pupils about equity, and their implications for school systems.

WHAT IS EQUITY?

'Equity' in the sense used in this chapter can represent two related ideas. First, equity is used as a synonym for the terms 'fair' and 'fairness'. It simply means the state, quality, or ideal of being impartial, just, and fair. Second, and more importantly, it refers to an attempt to understand how and why we can judge something to be fair or unfair. Of course, there are well-known principles, such as equality of treatment or equal access to opportunities that purport to lay down what

is fair. But as we shall illustrate in this chapter, there is no single principle or set of criteria that adheres in all situations. What underlies our sense of whether a principle, such as equality of treatment, should be applied in a specific situation? Whatever that is, it is what we mean by equity in this second sense. The same situation applies in law, especially in a common-law system such as that in the UK, where the application of previous case law or strict adherence to legislation might give the plaintiff inadequate redress under certain conditions. So equity is like the underlying system of jurisprudence used to supplement and modify common law, where needed, to try and ensure that any outcome is fair.

Without wishing to labour the point, it is important to be clear from the outset that any given criterion intended to enhance justice will be flawed in the sense that it will tend to lead to injustice in some situations. For example, should schools and teachers discriminate between pupils? We would probably not want schools to use more funds to educate boys than girls, or offer different curriculum subjects to different ethnic groups. But we might want schools to use more funds for pupils with learning difficulties, or to respect the right of each pupil to study their first language. Should a teacher be allowed to punish a pupil who misbehaves, or reward a pupil who has shown talent or effort? If so, then the teacher is being discriminating. If we adhere inflexibly to a principle of equality of opportunity, then the likely result in education will be marked inequality of outcomes. Is this acceptable? Those who start with greater talent, who can marshall greater resources at home, are the most interested in education, or who put the most effort into their study will tend to be the most successful. If, on the other hand, we seek greater equality of educational outcomes then we may need to treat individuals unequally from the outset, identifying the most disadvantaged and given them enhanced (and so unequal) opportunities.

Principles of justice, such as equality of treatment, work only in limited contexts, from specific perspectives, and on some occasions. This makes any transparent judgement of fairness a confusing task yet our own work with pupil perspectives (see Sundaram et al., 2006, for example) has suggested that individuals show a high level of agreement about whether any situation or treatment is fair, and from this near-consensus we might begin to establish a better idea of what equity means for those participating in education.

Table 6.1 provides a summary of six possible principles of justice, orthogonal to six possible domains in which pupils might wish to apply these principles. The point made here is that people apply different principles in different settings. For example, a pupil might agree that final outcomes such as public examination results could recognise merit and so differentiate between pupils (A in the table). However, the organisation of school procedures such as parent evenings should not be based on merit but should be open to all equally (B in the table). In education, some assets are, or should be, distributed evenly regardless of background differences – such as setting an equal teacher:pupil ratio for schools in different regions (C in the table), or equal respect shown to pupils by teachers (D). Other assets are, or might be, distributed in proportion between contribution and reward (E, F) – such as formal qualifications or punishments (Trannoy, 1999). Further assets may be deliberately distributed unequally without consideration of contribution, such as greater attention given to disadvantaged pupils (G). All of these actions could be defended as equitable by the same person, apparently consistently, as they strive to remain fair while respecting differences between individuals or groups of pupils. Our research with pupils shows that individuals do hold these differing views at the same time, varying their use between discourse and practice, in different domains (EGREES, 2005). Views even vary according to pupils' recent experience. For example, when pupils are made to work on an individual basis in school they tend to favour the principle of recognising merit. But pupils asked to work co-operatively in classrooms tend to favour equality (Lerner, 1980).

Each row in Table 6.1 could be further sub-divided, so that respect for the individual encompasses respect for personal autonomy,

Table 6.1   Some principles of justice and the domains in which they might be applied

Principles	School procedures	Classroom interaction	Regular assessments	Final outcomes	Family and home	Wider society
Equal outcome	C					
Equal opportunity	B					
Recognise merit				A		
Respect individual		D				
Fair procedures		F		E		
Appropriate treatment	G					

respect for differences between individuals, and the protection of a pupil's self-esteem. Equality of outcome could refer to the outcomes for all or, more narrowly, equality of outcomes for individuals of equivalent talent (Rawls, 1971), or equality between socio-economic groups. It could refer to equal achievement for equivalent work. Fairness of procedures could include equality before the 'law', either consistent or flexible interpretation of rules, or transparency, or the level of pupil participation in procedures. Similarly, appropriateness of treatment could involve no discrimination or positive discrimination, unequal resources between advantaged and disadvantaged but equal resources for equal talent (Trannoy, 1999), proportionate punishment for transgression, proportionate reward for performance, effort, or improvement, and proportionate final outcomes for performance, effort, or improvement. All of these could be considered 'fair', but many of them would be contradictory if applied together in the same domains (Dubet, 2006).

Some of the principles lead to disputed concepts, even in isolation. For example, respect for the autonomy of the individual has been proposed as just (Jansen et al., 2006), but can be considered anti-educational if the purpose of education is to open minds to new ideas. To encourage autonomy in the sense of making people ignore expert advice might be considered ill-judged, for example, if it poses a risk to health, or safety (Hand, 2006). Each column in Table 6.1 could also be further sub-divided, so that final outcomes might include minimum educational thresholds, such as basic literacy, which it would be fair for everyone to attain, and also graded examination results which it might be fair to allocate on merit.

Of course, there will also be other important dimensions behind the table – such as the origin and victim of any injustice. The former might include authorities, schools, teachers, other pupils, and family members. The latter could be the individual, others such as peers or friends, a category of pupils, or all pupils. The combination of actors involved might affect our judgement about whether any principle should apply in a particular domain. We might be concerned about sub-groups of pupils, and wish to offer an advantage to those from a disadvantaged group from which the individual cannot 'escape.' Thus, geographic, institutional, and linguistic differences may be less important than family background, sex, or innate disability. However, there is also a view that any difference, in itself, is not unjust and so an inequality is only unjust precisely insofar as it can be avoided (Whitehead, 1991). Responsibility theory (Roemer, 1996; Fleurbaey, 1996) suggests a fair allocation of resources between individuals defined by their 'talent' – for which they are not responsible – and their 'effort' – for which they are. However, even this falls down if effort is the product of motivation, which is itself a product of socio-economic background for which individuals are not responsible.

WHY EQUITY MATTERS

From 1996, the Council of Europe expressed concern over the dangers of intolerance within each country towards elements of society deemed different, such as recent immigrants and local ethnic minorities. This concern was one part of the drive towards the establishment of the Crick committee in the UK that would, in turn, lead to the compulsory National Curriculum for citizenship in England (Davies et al., 2005). Citizenship education has been presented by government as the means by which societal problems can be ameliorated, because it has important implications for developing students' perceptions about what it is to be part of an equitable and democratic society. The teaching of citizenship and democracy is, purportedly, needed to counter 'worrying levels of apathy, ignorance and cynicism about public life' (QCA, 1998: 8). The model for citizenship teaching has, at its foundation, a curriculum based around the key concepts of 'fairness, rights and responsibilities' (p. 20), which seeks to encourage in pupils 'self-confidence and socially and morally responsible behaviour both in and beyond the classroom, towards those in authority and towards each other' (DfES, 2002), to such an extent as to cause 'no less than a change in the political culture of this country both nationally and locally' (QCA, 1998: 7). Close to the heart of developing a model of democractic citizenship among students is the need to encourage children to develop their own concepts of fairness, and probably the fundamental influence on pupils in developing their perceptions of what constitutes a fair and equitable society is their experience of school (Wilson, 1959; Howard and Gill, 2000).

The problems here are two-fold. Schools in England, as elsewhere, are not structured, nor pupil places allocated, on the basis of fairness alone. Thus, pupils can experience dissonance between what they are being told and the way they live their lives in school. Second, and inevitably perhaps, some pupils report being treated unfairly – including being despised and humiliated by their teachers (Dubet, 1999; Merle, 2005). Across school systems, we know that some pupils are treated unfairly by some teachers, and that this has been the case for some time (Sirota, 1988; Spender, 1982).

In a series of previous publications, sometimes with colleagues, we have illustrated clear differences between varying national systems of allocating pupils to secondary schools and the ensuing clustered nature of the intake to each school (EGREES, 2005). The OECD-funded Programme for International Student Assessment (PISA) studies were conducted in 2000 and 2003 (OECD, 2007). In general, countries with selective school systems, whether by academic ability, ability to pay, or religious belief, have the most clustered schools in terms of reading scores. Austria, for example, had a tracked system in which 62 per cent of the weakest readers would have to exchange schools for these to be evenly distributed between schools. Sweden, on the other hand, had a local comprehensive system of allocating school places,

in which only 29 per cent of the weakest readers would have to exchange schools for these to be evenly distributed between schools (Gorard and Smith, 2004). In addition, the figures for both 2000 and 2003 show there is a strong link between clustering by ability/attainment and clustering by social and ethnic background of the pupils. For example, Sweden has one of the lowest scores for clustering by reading score, and also by parental occupation. Luxembourg has a low score for clustering on all three measures, including non-native students. Austria has high scores for clustering on both measures and also the clustering of students born outside the country. All other things being equal, systems without tiering or selection by the schools have lower intake segregation (Gorard, 2007).

The same thing applies to regions and local areas. In the UK, for example, local areas that retain selection to grammar schools have higher levels of pupil segregation by poverty than areas using non-selective systems (Gorard et al., 2003). The same also applies to the clustering of pupils in specific schools by ethnicity, country of origin, first language, and specific learning difficulties. There is no evidence here of a sustained advantage from having a segregated system, in terms of test scores, and these findings are confirmed by a number of other analyses (Haahr et al., 2005; Gorard, 2006).

In terms of creating students' awareness of equity, tolerance, and democracy, the mixture of pupils in a school does appear to matter however (Halstead and Taylor, 2000). Inclusive schools are generally more tolerant (Slee, 2001), and exhibit that tolerance in racial, social, and religious terms, and this is also associated with greater civic awareness (Schagen, 2002). The level of ethnic, and other, segregation between schools can affect racial attitudes, subsequent social and economic outcomes, and patterns of residential segregation (Clotfelter, 2001). The experience of Northern Ireland shows that, if true, this school outcome can be a force for even greater societal segregation (Smith, 2003), and that teachers become unwilling even to discuss issues of sectarianism with their (segregated) students (Mansell, 2005). So, in divided societies, citizenship education can generate negative results, including the ghettoisation of minority communities, perhaps culminating in greater social unrest as it has in some central European countries (Print and Coleman, 2003). Tracking from an early age can also have a dispiriting effect on the lifelong aspirations of the majority (Gorard and Rees, 2002; Casey et al., 2006).

One of the purposes of compulsory education in developed countries is to try and compensate for early disadvantage. Integrated, rather than selective or tracked, school systems seem to lead to the desirable outcome that a pupil's achievement depends less on their social and cultural background (Dupriez and Dumray, 2006). Although most egalitarian school systems are also set in countries with egalitarian structures and income equality anyway, these systems are designed to delay for as long as possible the separation of pupils by attainment (Boudon, 1973). This allows most time for schools to counteract resource differences.

Whatever the school system, we know that disadvantaged pupils tend to make less progress than other pupils during any given school phase, especially where they are clustered together (Duru-Bellat and Mingat, 1997), perhaps because they have poorer learning conditions than other pupils (Grisay, 1997). Thus, pupils' experiences of justice and, especially, injustice could undermine their interpersonal and institutional trust, promote passive attitudes towards political and civic participation, generate intolerance towards others who are clearly 'different', and even lead them to doubt whether an equitable existence is possible.

PUPILS' VIEWS OF EQUITY

To understand more about equity in education, it is important to ask the participants themselves. The views of pupils are still surprisingly scarce in education research, despite their clear competence as commentators (Wood, 2003). This absence is perhaps particularly marked for pupils in already marginalised groups (Rose and Shevlin, 2004; Hamill and Boyd, 2002). The skewed representation of pupils in the literature towards those already possessing advantages (Reay, 2006) may lead to the 'uncritical adoption' of their partial view as an accurate reflection of all pupils' experiences and views of schooling and justice in school (Noyes, 2005: 537). Thus, it is important in understanding more about equity to seek out the views of all, including the most disadvantaged and least likely to speak out. This is what we are doing in a series of EU-funded studies (http://www.york.ac.uk/depts/educ/equity/Socrates2005/Socrates%20home.htm).

The 1989 United Nations Convention on the Rights of the Child asserts that children and young people have the right to express their opinions on all matters affecting them. The Convention calls upon governments and agencies working with young people to acknowledge and act upon the views expressed in relation to decisions which directly affect their lives. Therefore, as education concerns its pupils, so they should be consulted seriously about its conduct and reform (Fielding and Bragg, 2003), and treated with respect in its implementation (Osler, 2000). The introduction of citizenship education into the National Curriculum for England in 2002 brought attention to the potential of pupil voice in contributing to learning processes, and stimulated debate about the links between pupils' experiences of fairness, democracy, and participation in school and their views and expectations as citizens in society (DfES, 2002).

This is not something that is worth doing half-heartedly. In health studies, by way of analogy, it has been found that talking and teaching about healthy eating for pupils is largely ineffective unless the school also adopts a health-promoting whole-school approach, most obviously in its catering, but also by listening to and incorporating pupils' opinions/views on food, bodies, and health (Christensen, 2004). In the same way, pupil participation in citizenship may be best 'taught' by engaging pupils as active partners in school processes and not merely by its inclusion in the curriculum. This means moving away from a situation in which pupils largely experience schooling as something that is done to them, and in which they simply learn to perform in order to succeed (Duffield et al., 2000). If citizenship studies is to promote a climate of tolerance, democratic dialogue, respect for human rights and cultural diversity (Osler and Starkey, 2006), then these characteristics must be made manifest in the structure and organisation of the school. Schools that model democratic values by promoting an open climate for discussion are more likely to be effective in promoting both civic knowledge and civic engagement among their students (Civic Education Study, 2001; Torney-Purta et al., 2001).

Despite increasing prominence being given to pupil voice in official circles (such as the inspection system in England) and by schools, the extent to which pupils' views are listened to and used in genuinely democratic processes over which students can claim ownership are often 'compromised by political structures determined by adults' (Wyness, 2006: 209). And, in many cases, the clear purpose of engaging with pupils like this is to increase student performance and attainment in academic terms (Noyes, 2005), or to improve pupil self-confidence (Rose et al., 1999). There is little sense that pupils might actually have sound views on equity and fairness in school processes, and that listening to them should be an aspect of democratic schooling that seeks to shape well-informed and critical citizens. Further, that engaging with pupil views could not only lead to real educational reform (Pomeroy, 1999), but may have longer-term implications for young people's self-perceived capabilities, resources and values as citizens. The actual impact of suggestions or decisions made by student groups is often very limited (TES, 2006). While participatory and democratic

initiatives such as school councils are now widespread in England, a limited and highly selected proportion of students actually tend to be involved (Wyness, 2006). There is little progress in terms of actually giving pupils a democratic say in the way their schools are run, or in facilitating their participation in, and contribution to, their local community.

In general, based on our re-analysis of the PISA 2003 data, pupils' attitudes to school and their 'senses of belonging' are somewhat worse in countries with segregated systems of schools (Gorard, 2007). In the Netherlands, for example, with a relatively segregated system, there is a very large difference in the attitudes of native-born and other pupils. The non-native pupils are much less enthusiastic about school. In a separate survey of 6,000 school students in five EU countries, pupils in countries with more segregated systems tend to report greater favouritism for one or more groups of pupils. Often, it was the girls, the brighter children, and those from richer families, who were thought to benefit from more favourable treatment. Pupils generally reported favouring an egalitarian system where all students were treated in the same way. In most countries a considerable number of pupils thought that the least able should receive more support and attention in class (Smith and Gorard, 2006). This view was particularly marked among students who reported achieving low marks. In the UK, the overwhelming majority believed that all pupils should receive the same attention. There was almost no support in any of the countries for the notion that able students should receive the most attention.

The clear opinion among pupils across all countries and groups is that many schools do generally provide the same quality of education for all students (around 75 per cent reported this in all countries). There is also some limited support, especially in France and Spain, for the idea that schools actually provide a better education for the most able. There is almost no support for the idea that schools are providing a better education for the least able. Therefore, all systems are seen to be failing to meet one specific demand for equity. Other than in the UK, there is considerable disparity between the proportion of students wanting a system in which less able students receive more attention (around 40 per cent) and the proportion who experience this in their school. For example, in Italy, 46 per cent of students felt that secondary schools should provide more attention to the least able students, whereas only 10 per cent report that this was actually the case in their country. Conversely, only around 2 per cent of students had reported wanting a system which gave more attention to the most able, whereas around 20 per cent reported experiencing such a system.

There is enough evidence from these and other studies to suggest that segregated school systems could endanger pupils' attitudes to schools and sense of belonging. It could be thought that pupils' experiences of equity and citizenship in an educational context may impact upon their perceived and actual trajectories in education. This link may be particularly pertinent in an era when purportedly disaffected and alienated (ethnic minority) youth are presented as a threat to social cohesion within and across communities, in many European countries.

CONCLUSION

If the argument so far is accepted, we may conclude that equity is difficult to define but that it represents that sense of fairness which underlies our decisions about the principles of justice to apply in different domains for a given set of actors. In specific situations there is considerable agreement, among pupils, about what is fair and what is unfair. Equity is an important ideal for education, in terms of school as a lived experience as well as its longer-term outcomes for citizens and society. Pupils have quite clear views on what is fair, and are generally willing and able to express those views.

Most available evidence suggests that pupils with differing characteristics should be mixed in schools, rather than clustered by ability, sex, faith, finance, or country of origin. Pupils in more segregated school systems report experiencing more unfairness. It seems that fairness for individuals, a sense of justice, and social cohesion and belonging are as much a product of experiences in schools, as lived in, as they are of the formal educational process. The mix of students in a school therefore matters more for social cohesion than school improvement (Gorard et al., 2003). An interesting finding to emerge from these considerations, and one which has implications for implementing an effective curriculum for citizenship in schools, is that teachers were not always perceived to be treating students fairly and consistently. There is a difference here between the personal experience of the pupils, and their perception of the treatment of a minority of others. A common view was that teachers had pupils who were their favourites, that rewards and punishments were not always applied fairly, and that certain groups of students were treated less fairly than others.

Citizenship is about developing social and moral responsibility, and 'entails treating young people with respect and giving them meaningful fora in which their views can be aired' (Kerr, 2003: 28). How can a curriculum for citizenship, which embraces issues of fairness and democracy, be effectively implemented if the students themselves do not mostly believe that their teachers are generally capable of such behaviour? In one sense, it does not really matter what the curriculum states about citizenship compared to the importance for students of experiencing mixed ethnic, sex, and religious groups in non-racist and non-sexist settings, and of genuine participation in the decision-making of the schools. Schools, in their structure and organisation, can do more than simply reflect the society we have; they can try to be the precursor of the kind of society that we wish to have.

REFERENCES

Boudon, R. (1973) *Education, Opportunity and Social Inequality*. New York: Praeger Publishers.

Casey, L., Davies, P., Kalambouka, A., Nelson, N. and Boyle, B. (2006) 'The Influence of Schooling on the Aspirations of Young People with Special Educational Needs', *British Educational Research Journal*, 32 (2): 273–290.

Christensen, P. (2004) 'The Health-Promoting Family: A Conceptual Framework for Future Research Social Science and Medicine', *Social Science And Medicine*, 59 (2): 377–387.

Civic Education Study (2001) *IEA Civic Education Study*, http://www2.hu-berlin.de/empir_bf/iea_e.html, accessed January 2005

Clotfelter, C. (2001) 'Are Whites Still Fleeing? Racial patterns and enrolment sifts in urban public schools', *Journal of Policy Analysis and Management*, 20 (2): 199–221.

Davies, I., Gorard, S. and McGuinn, N. (2005) 'Citizenship Studies and Character Studies: Similarities and Contrasts', *British Journal of Educational Studies*, 53 (3): 341–358.

DfES (2002) *Citizenship: The National Curriculum for England*, http://www.dfes.gov.uk/citizenship, Accessed August 2003.

Dubet, F. (1999) Sentiments et Jugements de Justice dans l'expérience Scolaire, in Meuret, D. (ed.) *La justice du système éducatif*. Paris: de Boeck.

Dubet, F. (2006) *Injustices*. Paris: Seuil.

Duffield, J., Allan, J., Turner, E. and Morris, B. (2000) 'Pupils' Voices on Achievement: An Alternative to the Standards Agenda', *Cambridge Journal of Education*, 30 (2): 263–274.

Dupriez, V. and Dumray, X. (2006) 'Inequalities in School Systems: Effect of School Structure or of Society Structure?', *Comparative Education*, 42 (2): 243–260.

Duru-Bellat, M. and Mingat, A. (1997) 'La Constitution de Classes de Niveau dans les Colleges', *Revue Francais de Sociologie*, 38: 759–789.

European Group for Research on Equity in Educational Systems, (2005) 'Equity in European Educational Systems: a set of indicators', *European Educational Research Journal*, 4 (2): 1–151.

Fielding, M. and Bragg, S. (2003) *Students as Researchers: Making a Difference*. Cambridge: Pearson.

Fleurbaey, M. (1996) *Theories Economiques de la Justice*. Paris: Economica.

Gorard, S. (2006) 'Is There a School Mix Effect?', *Educational Review*, 58 (1): 87–94.

Gorard, S. (2007) 'Justice et Equite a l'Ecole: Ce qu'en Dissent les Eleves Dans les Etudes Internationales', *Revue Internationale d'Education Sevres*, 44 (April): 79–84.

Gorard, S. and Rees, G. (2002) *Creating a Learning Society?* Bristol: Policy Press.

Gorard, S. and Smith, E. (2004) 'An International Comparison of Equity in Education Systems?' *Comparative Education*, 40 (1): 16–28.

Gorard, S., Taylor, C. and Fitz, J. (2003) *Schools, Markets and Choice Policies*. London: RoutledgeFalmer.

Grisay, A. (1997) *Evolution des Acquis Cognitifs et Socio-affectifs Des Élèves au Cours des Années de Collège*. MEN-Direction de l'Evaluation et de la Prospective, Dossiers Education et formations, 88.

Haahr, J., with Nielsen, T, Hansen, E. and Jakobsen, S. (2005) *Explaining Student Performance: Evidence from the International PISA, TIMSS and PIRLS Surveys*, Danish Technological Institute, www.danishtechnology.dk, accessed August 2005.

Halstead, J. and Taylor, M. (2000) 'Learning and Teaching about Values: a review of recent research', *Cambridge Journal of Education*, 30 (2): 169–202.

Hamill, P. and Boyd, B. (2002) 'Equality, Fairness and Rights – The Young Person's Voice', *British Journal of Special Education* 29 (3): 111–117.

Hand, M. (2006) 'Against Autonomy as an Educational Aim', *Oxford Review of Education*, 32 (4): 535–550.

Howard, S. and Gill, J. (2000) 'The Pebble in the Pond: Children's Constructions of Power, Politics and Democratic Citizenship', *Cambridge Journal of Education*, 30 (3): 357–378.

Jansen, T., Chioncel, N. and Dekkers, H. (2006) 'Social Cohesion and Integration: Learning Active Citizenship', *British Journal of Sociology of Education*, 27 (2): 189–205.

Kerr, D. (2003) Citizenship Education in England: The Making of a New Subject. *Online Journal for Social Science Education* (http://www.sowi-onlinejournal.de/2003-2/england_kerr.htm).

Lerner, J. (1980) *The Belief in a Just World: A Fundamental Delusion*. New York: Plenum Press.

Mansell, W. (2005) Don't Mention the Troubles, *Times Educational Supplement*, 18/2/05, p. 16.

Merle, P. (2005) *L'élève Humilié*. Paris: PUF.

Noyes, A. (2005) 'Pupil Voice: Purpose, Power and the Possibilities for Democratic Schooling', *British Educational Research Journal* 31 (4): 533–540.

OECD (2007) *The Programme for International Student Assessment* (PISA), http://www.pisa.oecd.org/pages/0,2987,en_32252351_32235731_1_1_1_1_1,00.html, [Accessed January 2007].

Osler, A. (2000) 'Children's Rights, Responsibilities and Understandings of School Discipline', *Research Papers in Education*, 15 (1): 49–67.

Osler, A. and Starkey, H. (2006) 'Education for Democratic Citizenship: A Review of Research, Policy and Practice 1995–2005', *Research Papers in Education*, 21 (4): 433–466.

Pomeroy, E. (1999) 'The Teacher-Student Relationship in Secondary School: Insights from Excluded Students', *British Journal of Sociology of Education,* 20 (4): 465–482.

Print, M. and Coleman, D. (2003) 'Towards Understanding of Social Capital and Citizenship Education', *Cambridge Journal of Education*, 33 (1): 123–149.

QCA (1998) *Education for Citizenship and the Teaching of Democracy in Schools, Final Report of the Advisory Group on Citizenship*. London: QCA.

Rawls, J. (1971) *A Theory of Justice*. Oxford: Oxford University Press.

Reay, D. (2006) '"I'm Not Seen as One of the Clever Children": Consulting Primary School Pupils About the Social Conditions of Learning', *Educational Review,* 58 (2): 171–181.

Roemer, J. (1996) *Theories of Distributive Justice*. Cambridge MA.: Harvard University Press.

Rose, R. and Shevlin, M. (2004) 'Encouraging Voices: Listening to Young People Who Have Been Marginalised', *Support for Learning,* 19 (4): 155–161.

Rose, R., Fletcher, W. and Goodwin, G. (1999) 'Pupils With Severe Learning Difficulties as Personal Target Setters', *British Journal of Special Education,* 26 (4): 206–212.

Schagen, I. (2002) 'Attitudes to Citizenship in England: Multilevel Statistical Analysis of the IEA Civics Data', *Research Papers in Education*, 17 (3): 229–259.

Sirota, R. (1988) *L'ecole Primaire au Quotidien*. Paris: Presses Universitaires de France.

Slee, R. (2001) 'Driven to the Margins: Disabled Students, Inclusive Schooling and the Politics of Possibility', *Cambridge Journal of Education*, 31 (3): 385–397.

Smith, A. (2003) 'Citizenship Education in Northern Ireland: Beyond National Identity', *Cambridge Journal of Education*, 33 (1): 15–31.

Smith, E. and Gorard, S. (2006) 'Pupils' Views of Equity in Education', *Compare*, 36 (1): 41–56.

Spender, D. (1982) *Invisible Women: The Schooling Scandal*. London: Women's Press.

Sundaram, V., Gorard, S. and Smith, E. (2006) *Why Does the School Mix Matter?: Equity From the Students' Perspective*, BERA Annual Conference, Warwick, September 2006, also available on Education-line, http://www.leeds.ac.uk/educol/documents/157555.htm

Trannoy, A. (1999) 'Social Dominance Egalitarianism and Utilitariaris', *Revue Economique*, 50 (4): 733–755.

TES (2006) 'Why Some Schools Still Need 'A bit of a Kicking', *Times Educational Supplement*, 23/06/06, p. 18.

Torney-Purta, J., Lehmann, R., Oswald, H., and Schulz, W. (2001) *Citizenship and Education in Twenty-eight Countries: Civic Knowledge and Engagement at Age 14*, Amsterdam: IEA.

Whitehead, M. (1991) 'The Concepts and Principles of Equity and Health', *Health Promotion International*, 6 (3): 217–228.

Wilson, A. (1959) 'Residential Segregation of Social Classes and Aspirations of High School Boys', *American Sociological Review*, 24: 836–845.

Wood, E. (2003) 'The Power of Pupil Perspectives in Evidence-based Practice: The Case of Gender and Underachievement', *Research Papers in Education,* 18 (4): 365–383.

Wyness, M. (2006) 'Children, Young People and Civic Participation: Regulation and Local Diversity', *Educational Review,* 58 (2): 209–218.

7

Globalization

Merry M. Merryfield with Lisa Duty

Humankind is experiencing one of the greatest periods of rapid change in its long history. Accelerated by new communication, transportation, and information technologies, today's world is characterized by the outcomes of globalization – the growing integration of local, national, and global economic, environmental, cultural, technological, and political systems. Increased connectivity over time and space is the essence of our global age (Tomlinson, 1999).

This chapter examines how some outcomes of globalization are changing what young people need to know and be able to do in order to be effective, engaged citizens. It is our underlying assumption that students must be prepared to be active participants in the world community as they live in a globally interconnected world, interact with people of diverse cultures and make decisions that impact the future of the planet. We begin by identifying outcomes of globalization that are most relevant for citizenship education and suggest knowledge, skills, and habits of the mind that students should develop in order to understand those outcomes and make decisions as informed citizens within a global community.

Although schools will continue to prepare students for citizenship within their nation-states, we argue that the realities of global interconnections extend many citizenship roles beyond national borders (Noddings, 2005). When young people affect and are affected by issues, changes, and actions across the world, they need to be given the tools to participate in global discourse and decision-making. In a global age, civic responsibility is complemented by worldmindedness. Civil society is strengthened when more members of a political community take their responsibility seriously and enter public deliberation about the common good. That they have different views about the public good is neither here nor there. It is the perspective or attitude of civil responsibility that is important. The same is true with citizenship in a global age. Although players on the world scene have conflicting worldviews, it is their participation in public deliberation that is important. This global perspective is not at odds with ordinary civic responsibility at all; indeed, they generally complement each other and share a common opposition to what is really inimical to our maintaining what is good about the world and opposing what is bad – namely selfishness and indifference (Dower and Williams, 2002: 255).

GLOBAL INTERCONNECTEDNESS

The processes of globalization are not new. They were in place hundreds of years ago as local borrowing and adapting of ideas, language, foods, textiles, technologies, and other products gradually gave way to regional interconnectedness through trade, conquest and cultural diffusion (Raskin et al., 2002). The integration of economic, social, and political systems has historical antecedents going back to Phoenician sailors in the Mediterranean, the reach of the Pax Romana, the spread of Islam from Arabia to North Africa and Asia, the Silk Road across Asia and Europe, and the Triangular Trade connecting West Africa with the Americas and Europe. A forerunner of today's transnationals, The Dutch East India Company (founded in 1602) exploited world markets and developed innovations, such as the issuing of shares, that other transnational organizations have adopted and improved upon up to the present day (Scheuerman, 2006). New technologies aided exploration and trade and expanded the reach of imperialism and the effects of colonialism on the creation of knowledge and new disciplines. Contemporary issues of cultural imperialism, human rights, loss of sovereignty, movement of people, and environmental exploitation have historical antecedents (Cooper, 2005).

History teaches us that time and distance are critical components of globalization. When it took years or months for information, people or products to move across a region, change came slowly and events happening across the world or even across the same continent were usually unknown or unimportant in people's daily lives. But as time to connect diverse cultures and regions has been reduced, distance has become compressed. This temporal and geographic compression alters people's perceptions of space, in effect making the world seem smaller (Scheuerman, 2006). When we compare how our grandparents perceived communication with, travel to or news from another continent when they were young with how such interaction is perceived by our children, we

can see how time and distance have been compressed over three generations. How has the meaning of 'far away' changed in the last 50 years? What will it mean in the lifetime of the students we teach? When events, decisions, and issues in one place immediately enter into and affect people's lives thousands of miles away, global connections merge with local and national contexts and the old dichotomies of us and them lose meaning in a deterritorialization of culture and place (Tomlinson, 1999).

Today the world's communities are increasingly enmeshed in a web of global connections (Appiah, 2006). Our hometowns are integrated into the global political economy, although not always in ways we understand or desire. Local shops, banks, industries, and stock markets are influenced by international standards, treaties and agreements on trade, finance, and production. With some exceptions (usually due to tariffs, subsidies, or domestic taxes), global markets and agreements greatly influence the prices we pay for food, petrol, loans, services, and manufactured products. More and more the kinds of jobs that will be available in our hometowns and the education that will be required to attain them are influenced by global competition and infrastructure, technological change, and the reach of multinational companies. Events happening thousands of miles away – a decision made by a transnational organization, a terrorist act, a financial crisis, a new invention, or ethnic conflict – may expand jobs, play havoc with our insurance rates, bring refugees into our neighbourhood, or create new domestic political issues (Held et al., 1999).

Interconnectedness also means that what happens in our hometowns affects others and the state of the planet (Stromquist, 2002). Decisions made by consumers, companies, workers, governance, and investors may have a profound effect on people's lives and places around the world. When people with strong purchasing power increase demand for petroleum, fresh flowers, inexpensive textiles, illegal drugs, arms, seafood, or tropical hardwoods, the market responds and somewhere across the planet there are changes in the use of natural resources, the development of new products, transfer of capital, and the lives of people. The history of the world demonstrates that consumer demand and the search for profits often leads to environmental change (deforestation, pollution, lost of habitat and biodiversity, over-fishing), innovation, increased crime (as some consumer demand is usually for illegal products), the expansion of job opportunities, exploitation of the poor and uneducated, political change, labor organizing, and profits for people, organizations and their investors who can meet those private and public sector demands (Stiglitz, 2002; Stromquist, 2002). Continuing cycles of increased demand for particular goods and services often lead to regional and global movement of people (such as migrant labor in the Middle East, the US, South Africa), increased urbanization, conflicts over land and natural resources, and societal problems.

There are international actors contributing to or benefiting from global interconnectedness. International financial institutions such as the International Monetary Fund (IMF) and the World Trade Organization (WTO), international political entities (the World Court), organizations of regional integration (the European Union), and multinational and transnational organizations (corporations and non-governmental organizations) are more powerful than many nation-states. Civil society organizations (CSOs), trade unions, faith-based organizations, indigenous peoples movements, environmental organization work to improve forest conservation, health care, micro-credit, and Internet development (Kriegman et al., 2006; also see http://web. worldbank.org/WBSITE/EXTERNAL/TOPIC S/CSO/0,,contentMDK:20127718~menuPK: 288622~pagePK:220503~piPK:220476~ theSitePK:228717,00.html for a list of CSOs working to monitor World Bank projects). 'The same forces that power the world technological system onward seem to awaken new forms of global citizenship in a global civil society' (Strijbos, 2002: 230).

Global interconnectedness (and this chapter is barely skimming the surface of this topic) constrains a single nation-state's ability to solve major problems unilaterally. Water crises, air pollution, global warming, weapons of mass destruction, the spread of pandemics, food security, terrorism, international trade in women, and many other issues cannot be effectively addressed unless nations work together (Held et al., 1999). In an interconnected world, citizens must work across borders to manage many issues affecting their quality of life (Axtmann, 2002).

At the same time global interconnectedness can empower ordinary citizens (Axford, 2005; Strijbos, 2002). A growing number of people are working together through regional or international organizations to promote social justice, protect the environment, or reduce conflicts. There are organizations working for fair trade coffee, dolphin-free tuna, AIDS education, human rights, and regulations to protect working children and adults in export-oriented industries. Religious groups from Evangelical Christians to Islamic fundamentalists are working across regions and the planet to spread their religious faith, political ideology or hold onto cherished traditions and ways of living in the face of change. New technologies have led to interactive web-based networks for citizen action (Axford, 2005). Regional and global organizations have developed to strengthen programs giving small loans to women, improve AIDS education, counter totalitarian propaganda, or create new political movements. From protests against the WTO to global conferences on the rights of women and indigenous peoples, people are connecting across borders in new civil societies and seeking cosmopolitan justice (Kriegman et al., 2006; Stromquist, 2002; Tan, 2004).

When people work across borders to effect political goals – regulate labor practices, protect the environment, even preserve national sovereignty – they are expanding their responsibilities as citizens. As outcomes of globalization engage citizens, new knowledge and competencies are needed. Students need to recognize and understand the effects of global connections in their lives. As part of their citizenship education they can research how people and organizations across the planet affect their own community and other communities across the world and then identify ways in which their actions and those of people in their region affect others and the planet. Students also need to develop expertise in working with others to address felt needs, problems, or challenges that are outcomes of global interconnectedness. As they work with others on economic, political, and environmental issues, students develop skills within regional and global networks and come to envision alternative futures.

MULTICULTURAL SOCIETIES AND GLOBAL CULTURES

Global movements of people are changing cultures and patterns of interaction within and across regions. The flattening effect of global transportation and porous borders has accelerated regional and global movements of peoples who seek better economic opportunities next door or across the ocean. Others move seeking freedom from religious persecution, ethnic strife, or political repression. The old ties of colonialism have created new global highways. From Algerians in France to Pakistanis in Britain to Koreans in Japan, people from former empires are now 'colonizing' the mother country. New diasporas are transforming regions (Rizvi, 2000).

Demographic changes have created new multicultural communities within most nations that have economic opportunities or provide political asylum, although some nations, such as Saudi Arabia, do not allow economic migrants to become citizens. The growing multiculturalism of nations and regions is significant socially, economically, and politically as it raises issues of national identity, competition for jobs, and a clash of cultures (Tomlinson, 1999). People's cultural identities can become much more important when suddenly surrounded by people of different religions, languages, or ethnicities. The changing demographics that are often seen as an outcome of globalization may 'implode' communities, changing their politics and creating uncertainty about not only The Other within, but about one's own identity (Appadurai, 1999: 321–322).

Paradoxically, this increase in diversity within communities and nations is happening at the same time as a global trend towards increased cultural homogeneity, which some perceive as Westernization, Americanization, or cultural imperialism (Meyer and Geschiere, 1999; Said, 1993; Tomlinson, 1999). Today many of the more affluent and connected young people on the planet participate in shared aspects of a global popular culture from films (Hollywood, Bollywood, Hong Kong), sports stars (Beckham), music (reggae, salsa), games (Sudoku), television (Pokemon is viewed in over 60 countries), fashions, and modes of entertainment (Karaoke). The British talent series 'Pop Idol' has led to Idol shows in over 30 countries, and websites with social networking (YouTube, ArabSpace) have millions of participants. Teenagers in many countries share the twenty-first century affinity for mobile phones and text-messaging. Yet these shared experiences do not necessarily contradict the deep culture of beliefs, values, and norms of behavior taught at home and school that are at the heart of local and national cultures. The long-term effects of global pop culture are hotly contested (Rothkopf, 1997; Stromquist, 2002).

Some professions are becoming global sub-cultures as practitioners across the world become more alike (Berger, 1997; Sassen, 1998). As national professional organizations adopt more international norms for training and accreditation, practice becomes more standardized across the world. Pilots, journalists, bankers, accountants, engineers, nurses, even teachers can move from London to Singapore to Cairo to Mexico City and in many ways feel at home within their profession and its institutions. Banks, stock markets, hospitals, airports, postal services, and universities are becoming more and more similar across the world. Perhaps it is successful businessmen and women who are most alike. No matter whether they are from Los Angeles, Tokyo, Abu Dhabi, or Shanghai, they drive the same cars, wear the same brands of clothes, and share an understanding of how to adapt to the culture of the marketplace (Rothkopf, 1997).

There are other cultural outcomes of globalization. The intersections of culture and power have long played out in the contexts of hybridity, the complex and layered identities generated by cross-cultural interaction, mingling, and blending (Mudimbe-Boyi, 2002). Today hybridity has taken on new meanings that differ markedly from the colonial era categorizations of people (such as creoles, mestizas, mulattoes) that sprang from European and American obsession with ethnic and racial purity (Daniel, 2005). In today's global milieu, hybridity comes from people making connections across multiple cultures to meet the challenges of conflicting situations and changing realities. It has become less about race or ethnicity and more about the 'changing repertory of cultural modalities' (Williams and Chrisman, 1994, as referenced in Daniel, 2005: 263). Unlike essentialist or dichotomous thinking (black/white, civilized/uncivilized) of past eras, hybridity in a global age is based on egalitarian pluralism that rejects broad divisions and blurs distinctions. It also represents marginalities that are common to the human condition within and across all groups (Dirlik, 2002).

As communities and regions become more multicultural and global, people who have the knowledge and skills to work across different cultures and languages are needed in all professions. In a global age people with culturally complicated backgrounds are more likely to have the cosmopolitan mindsets and cross-cultural skills that make it easier to interact on the world stage. The new cosmopolitan citizen recognizes that 'no local loyalty can ever justify forgetting that each human being has responsibilities to every other' (Appiah, 2006: xvi). As more and more people collaborate with others across the planet, it follows that they will come to identify with and care about those people as fellow human beings. As intercultural and international associations grow and people develop more complex identities from multiethnic or multinational contexts and multiple loyalties, those who chose to live segregated lives (based on ethnic, linguistic, or religious purity) will be increasingly isolated.

Globalization affects the knowledge, skills, and experiences young people need in order to engage in discourse and decision-making in culturally diverse settings and global cultures. As they acquire substantive knowledge of their own and other cultures, students develop insights into how culture shapes their own and others' interpretation of events. Intercultural skills, substantive culture learning, and cross-cultural experiences prepare young people to live, work, and mediate cultural conflicts and misunderstandings in culturally diverse world.

VOICE AND REPRESENTATION WITHIN AN INFORMATION REVOLUTION

The voices of the status quo – be they political, economic, scientific, religious, medical, business, or other – continue to shape mainstream academic knowledge taught across the world. Media giants influence global audiences through their control of outlets for news and entertainment (Stromquist, 2002). Although the scope of corporate media and publishing has expanded greatly in past decades due to satellite technology, the Internet, and DVDs, there is a growing challenge to their hegemony over knowledge production (Apple and Buras, 2006).

Contrapuntal knowledge is being developed and disseminated by people outside the mainstream across all world regions (Stromquist, 2002). Cable television, Fax machines, the web, cellular phones and alternative radio, and newspapers are circulating the messages, programs, and experiences of young people, religious and environmental organizations, and cultural and political groups. From blogs to Wikipedia (with articles in 261 languages), new voices are being heard and information is being authored and disseminated in new ways with often unpredictable consequences. What some people perceive as freedom of expression and community, others perceive as chaos or worse (Burbules and Torres, 2000).

Information is critical to citizenship in a democracy (Strijbos, 2002). In an interconnected world, citizens need to be informed not only about their own nation-state, but they also need to understand the ideas, voices, knowledge, and experiences of people across their region and the planet. In many countries today people have access to points of view and information that was unheard of in previous generations. Where once North Americans only learned about China through the eyes of western journalists, tourists, scholars, or politicians, they now have access to Chinese sources in print, film, television, the web or through Chinese visitors, students, or immigrants in their communities. People in many nations regularly listen to politicians, authors, journalists, and others from other parts of the world – a speech by a South Africa political leader, reports from Lebanese and Israeli journalists, a documentary created by a Brazilian. As websites proliferate, students can read today's editorials in online newspapers in Accra, Sydney, or Jakarta or view via webcam a protest taking place in New York City. Primary sources from around the world inform a global audience in ways secondary sources (filtering content through political or cultural lenses) can never do.

There are problems, of course, with the information explosion. Much information that is available promotes hate, propaganda, or sexual content. Pornography flourishes in many new formats. Being in print, on the web or on the airways is no guarantee of truth or taste. Money and education often determine access, which multiplies the advantages of the privileged within and across regions in a digital divide (Compaine, 2001). As the trend towards globally accepted mainstream academic knowledge grows, the world's information will likely become more global and less nation-centric. Cultures and nations with less global power are likely to suffer a new digital divide as their knowledge and information may be valued less as people feel compelled to learn mainstream global knowledge that becomes the currency of the knowledge economy in a global age (Stromquist, 2002).

Changes in the generation and outflow of knowledge and information affect civil society and citizenship education. Students need to understand knowledge construction: the politics of mainstream academic knowledge, post-colonial efforts to rewrite or resist master narratives, and the inheritance of imperial worldviews (Apple and Buras, 2006; Willinsky, 1998). Students can examine the underlying assumptions of knowledge in other cultures in order to appreciate different world views and the need to seek out multiple perspectives. If they are to meet the challenges of our information age, students must develop skills in research and evaluation of conflicting sources of information.

GLOBAL POWER AND INEQUITIES

International actors have increasing power in a global age. International financial institutions, transnational companies, economic and political alliances, and other global players influence the debt, social safety nets, economic stratification, environmental problems, human rights, and basic human needs of people across the planet (Rodrik, 1997). Debates rage on whether the forces of globalization have effected new global economic inequities or simply rearranged old ones.

There is general agreement that global systems in place today benefit those individuals, corporations, organizations, and governments who have the education and capital to take advantage of changing technologies, economic integration, global markets, and global financial institutions and procedures (Rodrik, 1997; Stiglitz, 2002). Unfortunately billions living in poverty have not benefited from globalization and feel trapped by the hegemony of multinational companies and international institutions such as the International Monetary Fund, the World Trade Organization, and the World Bank (Shiva, 2005; Stiglitz, 2002). Loss of control and national sovereignty is a major issue as transnational corporations, the World Bank, and agreements such as the Uruguay Round of the WTO decide what many farmers will be paid and even which farmers can export what (Shiva, 2005).

While many value the actions of these international entities, others see them as authoritarian bodies that have exerted extreme power over the lives of billions through structural adjustment policies and trade liberalization policies (Stiglitz, 2002). The Intellectual Property Rights Agreement (TRIPS), drafted by Monsanto for the WTO, has forced India 'to dismantle its democratically designed patent laws, creating monopolies on seeds and medicines, pushing farmers to suicide, and denying victims of AIDs, Cancer, TB and Malaria access to life saving drugs' (Shiva, 2005: 3). In what has been called the race to the bottom, multinational corporations have nations competing to be the cheapest and most malleable labor force with the least restrictive environmental regulations.

Globalization has unequal effects (Sassen, 1998; Stiglitz, 2002). Across the world there is a continuum from communities where many people benefit greatly from global interconnectedness with investments in infrastructure, more jobs, more amenities, a building boom, and a higher standard of living to communities that are dying out as young people leave to find economic opportunities, local schools, and health care dwindle, roads and water systems suffer cut-backs, and those remaining often depend upon remittances as the larger society ignores their plight or lacks the resources to counter global forces (Foreign Policy, 2006; Sachs, 1998). The unequal effects can be seen within nations that are benefiting from global trends as even in the most globally-oriented nation-states there are places with declining populations, capital, and quality of life. In some cases it is not only towns disappearing, but whole cultures and languages that are being lost as the forces of globalization appear to reward those who acquire cultural, economic and linguistic attributes of a larger, more powerful society (Fishman, 1998/99).

The information age, knowledge economy and digital technologies have added new layers of inequities within and across communities, nation-states, and regions (Burbules and Torres, 2000; Campaine, 2001). The expansion of the world wide web is one of many factors leading to the demise of less commonly spoken languages and the dominance of English as the language of business and finance. Technological innovation and technology transfer, whether in health, agriculture, education, or business, most often benefit those who have the capital to exploit and market them (Stromquist, 2002).

If we want students to create a more just and equitable world, citizenship education must address the realities of global power and methods for overcoming poverty and oppression. Students need to understand how power is exerted globally, the effects of global actors on social, economic, cultural, environmental, and political inequities and injustice, and the ways in which people have resisted oppression and worked to gain rights and self-determination. Citizenship education is not just about the ideas, experiences, and goals of those who are well educated, privileged, or affluent. If students are to be responsible citizens in multicultural and globally connected societies, they must understand why inequities and injustices exist and how people have made a difference in overcoming poverty, oppression, prejudice, and injustice. Ethics, inclusion, and concerns for the common good should be central to citizenship education.

IMPLICATIONS FOR CITIZENSHIP EDUCATION

Globalization has expanded the engagement and political efficacy of citizens in the twenty-first century. As they interact within global economic, political, and environmental systems, today's citizens enter new civil societies and contribute to emerging global discourse on issues facing the planet. The acceleration of knowledge creation and the contributions of contrapuntal voices are changing the nature of public discourse (Stromquist, 2002). As more and more people gain access to new forms of information, new communities, and new tools to organize, debate, learn, and create, their participation changes the scope of civic action, consciousness, and responsibility. Such global engagement is likely to expand people's identities as they develop loyalties to people and issues beyond their borders. Hybrid identities and multiple loyalties may lead to cosmopolitan world views and actions (Appiah, 2006). Engagement across borders increases knowledge of global inequities and the ways in which power is wielded on the planet. These developments provide opportunities for civic engagement in human rights, peace, fair trade, and environmental justice (Tan, 2004).

Globalization is changing what citizens need to know and be able to do by interrupting the assumption that the actions of citizens only take place within national borders. If our neighborhoods and nations are affecting and being affected by the world, then our political consciousness must be world-minded. Across the outcomes of globalization discussed above are several implications for civic educators, their curriculum, resources, and pedagogy.

First, students need to study the outcomes of globalization through both mainstream academic knowledge and the transformative, contrapuntal knowledge that gives voice and agency to people and issues largely ignored by those in power (Marri, 2005; Merryfield and Wilson, 2005; Willinsky, 1998). Whether learning about global systems, their own multicultural democracy, or ways in which people in their region make decisions on water, students must learn from the diverse experiences and ideas of relevant stakeholders if they are to develop a global perspective. Young people cannot understand their world without learning from people with differing degrees of power – including children, women, religious or ethnic minorities, refugees, immigrants or guest workers, or those with the least economic wealth (Apple and Buras, 2006; Pike, in press). Understanding the points of view of people different from themselves requires that students develop skills in perspective consciousness. Perspective consciousness is:

> the recognition or awareness on the part of the individual that he or she has a view of the world that is not universally shared, that this view of the world has been and continues to be shaped by influences that often escape conscious detection, and that others have views of the world that are profoundly different from one's own (Hanvey, 1976, n.p.).

Perspective consciousness creates an appreciation of how culture affects perception and an understanding of how and why people in their local community or across the planet often perceive events or issues quite differently. These skills provoke reflections needed to examine cultural patterns of thinking and have profound applications in students' analyses of their lived realities and the conflicts that surround them (Dam and Volman, 2004; Knight-Abowitz and Harnish, 2006; Osler and Starkey, 2003; Parmenter, 2006). Study of the intersections of knowledge creation and power and skills in perspective consciousness are essential if students are to work across cultures, participate in global discourse and engage in global issues.

Second, students need to develop intercultural competence to participate effectively in today's multicultural societies. Culture study needs to focus on internal culture (norms of behaviour, beliefs and values, patterns of thinking, communication styles) and interaction patterns. Experiential pedagogy creates activities in which students apply their knowledge and skills to deal with real-life situations, issues, and problem-solving (Merryfield and Wilson, 2005). Intercultural competence can be authentically assessed as students use their knowledge to work cooperatively across diverse cultures face to face or online. Citizenship education must combat cultural and religious stereotypes, challenge media's exotic images and overcome prejudice and racism. These skills and dispositions are necessary for shared visions and global citizen movements (Kriegman et al., 2006).

Third, critical thinking skills, especially the ability to evaluate conflicting information, are vital for today's citizens (Dam and Volman, 2004, ALA, 1989). Societies committed to freedom must guarantee access to information and nurture citizens' capacities to interrogate that information in order to effectively preserve personal liberties (ALA, 1989). Students need to be equipped to investigate knowledge, construct information and use it to influence public policy and address global issues (Hermes, 2006; Pithers, 2000). Students must learn to unpack the prepackaged information prevalent in the media and schools and seek out and evaluate information from diverse sources. In a world of six billion people, conflicting points of view are the norm. Without skills in locating and evaluating the merit and worth of conflicting information, students cannot make informed decisions. There are no easy answers to the major problems of our time. Students need to appreciate complexity, recognize ambiguity, and abandon the search for one correct answer (ALA, 1989; Vysoka, 2003). Multiple perspectives and critical thinking are central to the complex problem solving required in the real world (Dam and Volman, 2004).

Finally there are habits of the mind that go hand in hand with civic responsibilities in a global age. Students need to approach judgments and decisions with open-mindedness, anticipation of complexity, and resistance to stereotyping (Case, 1993). As they consider alternatives, students should develop the habit of asking: is this in the common good? Will this protect the rights of all people? Will these actions harm the environment or its biodiversity (Merryfield and Wilson, 2005)? Worldmindedness is critical if students are to become accustomed to making decisions that are cognizant of global ramifications.

What are today's K-12 students learning about globalization? In this volume see Graham Pike's chapter on global education. Although there have been studies of K-12 instruction related to global issues (Gaudelli, 2003; Merryfield and White, 1995), global conflicts (Merryfield, 1993; Shapiro and Merryfield, 1995), global interconnectedness (Levak et al., 1993; Lo et al., 2006; Merryfield, 2001) most have not focused on citizenship education outcomes. There need to be studies of how students and teachers in many contexts are making connections between their understanding of globalization (the changing world, global issues, and systems, cross-cultural interaction) and their roles as citizens.

Globalization will continue to change life on the planet. Citizenship education will meet these challenges by fostering civic responsibility and engagement without borders. Global perspectives will be infused into education of citizens because we cannot isolate our nation's well-being and that of future generations from that of others across the planet. As William Scheuermann (2006) has suggested:

> ... the disintegration of the domestic-foreign divide probably calls for us to consider, to a greater extent than ever before, how our fundamental normative commitments about political life can be effectively achieved on a global scale. If we take the principles of justice or democracy seriously, for example, it is no longer self-evident that the domestic arena is the main site for their pursuit, since domestic and foreign affairs are now deeply

and irrevocably intermeshed. In a globalizing world, the lack of democracy or justice in the global setting necessarily impacts deeply on the pursuit of justice or democracy at home. Indeed, it may no longer be possible to achieve our normative ideals at home without undertaking to do so transnationally as well (Scheuermann, 2006, n.p.).

REFERENCES

Appiah, K.A. (2006) *Cosmopolitanism: Ethics in a World of Strangers*. New York: W.W. Norton.

American Library Association (ALA) (1989) Presidential Committee on Information Literacy. Retrieved from http://www.ala.org/acrl/legalis.html (11 April 2007).

Appadurai, A. (1999) 'Dead Certainty: Ethnic Violence in an Era of Globalization,' in Birgit Meyer and Peter Geschiere (eds) *Globalization and Identity*. Oxford: Blackwell Publishers. pp. 305–324.

Apple, M.W. and Buras, K.L. (eds) (2006) *The Subaltern Speaks*. New York: Routledge.

Axford, B. (2005) 'Critical Globalization Studies and a Network Perspective on Global Civil Society,' in Richard P. Appelbaum and William I. Robinson (eds) *Critical Globalization Studies*. New York: Routledge. pp. 187–196.

Axtmann, R. (2002). 'What's Wrong with Cosmopolitan Democracy?' in N. Dower and J. Williams (eds) *Global Citizenship: A Critical Introduction*. New York: Routledge. pp 101–113.

Berger, P. L. (1997) 'Four Faces of Global Culture'. *The National Interest*, 49 (Fall): 23–29.

Burbules, N.C. and Torres, C.A. (eds) (2000) *Globalization and Education: Critical Perspectives*. New York: Routledge.

Case, R. (1993) 'Key Elements of a Global Perspective'. *Social Education*, 57 (6): 318–325.

Compaine, B.M. (2001) *The Digital Divide: Facing a Crisis Or Creating a Myth?* Cambridge, MA: MIT Press.

Cooper, F. (2005) *Colonialism in Question*. Berkeley, CA: University of California Press.

Dam, G. and Volman, M. (2004) 'Critical Thinking as a Citizenship Competence: Teaching Strategies'. *Learning and Instruction*, 14 (4): 359–379.

Daniel, C.R. (2005) 'Beyond Eurocentrism and Afrocentrism: Globalization, Critical Hybridity and Postcolonial Blackness,' in Richard P. Appelbaum and William I. Robinson (eds) *Critical Globalization Studies*. New York: Routledge. pp. 259–268.

Dirlik, A. (2002) 'Bringing History Back in: Of Diasporas, Hybridities, Places and Histories,' in Elisabeth Mudimbe-Boyi (ed.). *Beyond Dichotomies: Histories, Identities, Cultures and the Challenge of Globalization*. Albany, NY: SUNY Press. pp. 93–128.

Dower, N. and Williams, J. (2002) *Global Citizenship: A Critical Introduction*. New York: Routledge.

Fishman, J.A. (Winter 1998/1999) 'The New Linguistic Order'. *Foreign Policy 113*. Carnegie Endowment for International Peace.

Foreign Policy (May/June 2006*) The Failed States Index*. The Fund for Peace and the Carnegie Endowment for International Pace. Retrieved at http://www.foreignpolicy.com/story/cms.php?story_id=3420 (4 April 2007).

Foster, S.J. and Rosch, R. (1997) 'Teaching World War I from Multiple Perspectives'. *Social Education* 61: 429–434.

Hanvey, R. (1976) 'An Attainable Global Perspective'. Denver, CO: Center for War/Peace Studies. Retrieved from http://www.globaled.org/An_Att_Glob_Persp_04_11_29.pdf (4 February 2007).

Gaudelli, W. (2003) *World Class: Teaching and Learning in Global Times*. Mahwah, NJ: Lawrence Erlbaum Associates.

Held, D., McGrew, A., Goldblatt, D., and Perraton, J. (1999) *Global Transformations: Politics, Economics and Culture*. Stanford, CA: Stanford University Press. Retrieved from http://www.polity.co.uk/global/research.asp#political (3 January 2007).

Hermes, J. (2006) 'Citizenship in the Age of the Internet'. *European Journal of Communication*, 21 (3): 295–309.

Knight A.K. and Harnish, J. (2006) 'Contemporary Discourses of Citizenship'. *Review of Educational Research*, 76 (4): 653–690.

Kriegman, O. with Amalric, F. and Wood, J. (2006) *Dawn of the Cosmopolitan: The Hope of a Global Citizens Movement*. GTO Paper Series 15. Retrieved from http://www.gtinitiative.org/documents/PDFFINALS/15Movements.pdf (2 April 2007).

Levak, B., Merryfield, M., and Wilson, R. (1993) 'Global Connections'. *Educational Leadership,* 51 (1): 73–75.

Lo, J., Merryfield, M.M. and Po, S. (2006) 'Teaching about the World: Two Case Studies,' *Research in Comparative and International Education*, 1 (3): 286–300.

Marri, A. (2005) 'Building a Framework for Classroom Based Democratic Multicultural Education (CMDE): Learning from Three Skilled Teachers'. *Teachers College Record*, 104 (5): 1036–1059.

Merryfield, M.M. (1993) 'Responding to the Gulf War: A Case Study of Instructional Decision-Making'. *Social Education,* 57 (1): 33–41.

Merryfield, M.M. (2001) 'Pedagogy for Global Perspectives in Education,' in Patrick O'Meara, Howard Mehlinger and Roxana Ma Newman (eds) *Changing Perspectives on International Education*. Bloomington, IN: Indiana University Press. pp. 244–280.

Merryfield, M. and White, C. (1996) 'Issues-Centered Global Education,' in Ronald Evans and David Warren Saxe (eds) *The Handbook on Teaching Social Issues*. Washington DC: The National Council for the Social Studies.

Merryfield, M.M. and Wilson, A. (2005) *Social Studies and the World*. Silver Spring, MD: National Council for the Social Studies.

Meyer, B. and Geschiere, P. (eds) (1999) *Globalization and Identity*. Oxford: Blackwell Publishers.

Mudimbe-Boyi, E. (2002) *Beyond Dichotomies: Histories, Identities, Cultures and the Challenge of Globalization*. Albany, NY: SUNY Press.

Noddings, N. (ed.) (2005) *Educating Citizens for Global Awareness*. New York: Teachers College Press.

Osler, A. and Starkey, H. (2003) 'Learning for Cosmopolitan Citizenship: Theoretical Debates and Young People's Experiences'. *Educational Review,* 55 (3): 243–254.

Parmenter, L. (2006) 'Asian (?) Citizenship Education and Identity in Japanese Education'. *Citizenship Teaching and Learning,* 2 (2): 9–20.

Pike, G. (in press) 'Reconstructing the Legend: Educating for Global Citizenship,' in A. Abdi and L. Schultz (eds) *Educating for Human Rights and Global Citizenship*. Albany: SUNY Press.

Pithers, R.T. (2000) 'Critical Thinking in Education: A Review'. *Educational Research,* 42 (3): 237–249.

Raskin, P., Banuri, T., Gallopin, G., Gutman, P., Hammond, A., Kates, R., and Swart, R. (2002) *Great Transition: The Promise and Lure of the Times Ahead*. SEI PoleStar Series Report no. 10. Boston: Stockholm Environment Institute, Tellus Institute. Retrieved from http://www.gtinitiative.org/documents/Great_Transitions.pdf (1 February 2007).

Rizvi, F. (2000) 'International Education and the Production of Global Imagination,' in Nicholas C. Burbules and Carlos Alberto Torres, (eds) *Globalization and Education: Critical Perspectives*. New York: Routledge. pp. 205–225.

Rodrik, D. (Summer, 1997) 'Sense and Nonsense in the Globalization Debate'. *Foreign Policy 107*. Carnegie Endowment for International Peace.

Rothkopf, D. (Summer, 1997) 'In Praise of Cultural Imperialism'. *Foreign Policy 107*. Carnegie Endowment for International Peace. pp. 443–453.

Sachs, J. (Spring, 1998) 'International Economics: Unlocking the Mysteries of Globalization'. *Foreign Policy 110*. Carnegie Endowment for International Peace.

Said, E.W. (1993) *Culture and Imperialism*. New York: Alfred A. Knopf.

Sassen, S. (1998) *Globalization and Its Discontents*. New York: The New Press.

Scheuerman, W.E. (2006) 'Globalization'. Stanford Encyclopedia of Philosophy. Stanford, CA: The Center for the Study of Language and Information. Retrieved from http://plato.stanford.edu/entries/globalization/ (14 February 2007).

Shapiro, S. and Merryfield, M. (1995) 'A Case Study of Unit Planning in the Context of School Reform,' in Merry M. Merryfield and Richard Remy (eds) *Teaching About International Conflict and Peace*. Albany, NY: The State University of New York Press.

Shiva, V. (2005) 'The Polarized World of Globalisation (A Response to Friedman's Flat Earth Hypothesis)'. Global Policy Forum. Retrieved from http://www.globalpolicy.org/globaliz/define/2005/0510polar.htm (1 March 2007).

Stiglitz, J.E. (2002) *Globalization and its Discontents*. New York: W.W. Norton and Company.

Strijbos, S. (2002) 'Citizenship in Our Globalising World of Technology,' in Nigel Dower and John Williams (eds) *Global citizenship*. New York: Routledge. pp. 222–230.

Stromquist, N.P. (2002) *Education in a Globalized World*. Oxford: Rowman & Littlefield.

Tan, K.C. (2004) *Justice without Borders: Cosmopolitanism, Nationalism and Patriotism*. Cambridge: Cambridge University Press.

Tomlinson, J. (1999) *Globalization and Culture*. Cambridge: Polity Press.

Vysoka, A. (2003) 'Educational Democracy in the Czech Republic'. *Social Education*, 67 (4): 231–234.

Willinsky, J. (1998) *Learning to Divide the World*. Minneapolis: University of Minnesota Press.

Geographically Based Overviews – Comparative Research

8

Education for Democratic Citizenship in Australia

Murray Print

Despite an enduring belief that the Australian system of government created by the constitution makers has functioned effectively as a robust, stable and successful constitutional democracy, the need for learning about democratic citizenship in schools achieved remarkable consensus in the 1990s (CEG, 1994; Kemp, 1997; Kennedy, 1997; Erebus, 1999; Print, 1999). The research evidence indicates that need remains today.

Concern at the lack of provision for education for democratic citizenship, and a commensurate dearth of civic and democratic understanding by young citizens, has been evident for some time in Australia (CEG, 1994). There is also a clear problem in Australia, particularly within democratic education that links the educative endeavour to the practice of democracy. Relative to other groups, research has found young Australians care little for the body politic, political parties, politicians and government (Print et al., 2004; MCEETYA, 2006). A recent national inquiry by the Australian Parliament confirmed these findings (JSCEM, 2007), while in international studies such as the IEA Civic Study (Torney-Purta, et al., 2001), Australian data show the young know relatively little about politics and democracy and believe that the body

politic does not adequately care for them (Mellor et al., 2001).

That this situation exists after a decade of education for democratic citizenship (EDC) through the vehicle of *Discovering Democracy*, a promising programme designed specifically to develop student understanding of Australian democracy, is all the more confounding. In 1997 the federal government introduced *Discovering Democracy* after an earlier national inquiry (CEG, 1994) concluded a civic deficit existed in Australian schools. The outcome was a major curriculum initiative, designed to meet a widely held view, particularly by the government of the day (Kemp, 1997), that young Australians knew little, and understood less, about their system of democratic government.

That civics and citizenship education promotes political knowledge and active citizenship is widely assumed, though the relationship is less clear. Research shows it should and can contribute to the democratic goal of engagement (Nicmi and Junn, 1998), though the particular educational variables which predict engagement have yet to be clarified. For example, in Australia McAllister (1998) noted that education produced higher levels of political knowledge that, in turn, made people a 'better demo-cratic citizen.' But what form of education and for whom? Citizenship education, which encourages students to acquire civic knowl-edge, civic skills and civic values, is more likely to produce engaged citizens (Niemi and Junn, 1998; Saha, 2000) as well as to assist with formation of social capital (Print and Coleman, 2003).

Yet, nearly a decade after *Discovering Democracy* was introduced a national study (MCEETYA, 2006) shows Years 6 and 10 students appear to know relatively little about Australian government, democracy, parliamentary systems and citizenship edu-cation more generally, suggesting that the *Discovering Democracy* programme has made limited impact in schools in terms of building student outcomes. How did we get to this situation? Before this question is addressed it is essential to ask what educa-tion for democratic citizenship means in an Australian context.

EDUCATIONAL APPROACHES TO DEMOCRATIC CITIZENSHIP

That students and the young generation need to be educated about democratic citizenship in order to sustain democracy has become a common call internationally in recent years (Kemp, 1997; Kennedy, 1997; Niemi and Junn, 1998; Crick, 1998; Hahn, 1998; Torney-Purta et al., 1999, 2001; Parker, 1996; Macedo, 2005). But what is a demo-cratic citizen? And how should they be educated?

Citizenship is a contested concept and not surprisingly education for democratic citizen-ship is similarly contested. One view argues that education for democratic citizenship (EDC) is divided between traditional, demo-cratic approaches while more recent attempts have been dominated by neo-conservative perspectives forced by neo-conservative governments (Howard and Patten, 2006). Approaches in schools which educate for

democratic citizens, however, may be syn-thesised into three categories – personally responsible citizens through a minimalist, traditional approach; active, participatory cit-izens through engagement and third, values-based, justice-oriented citizens through a change approach (Parker, 1996; Kerr, 2003; Westheimer and Kahne, 2004).

The first approach utilises citizenship theory that argues citizenship is a legal status of rights and responsibilities in a democratic system. Consequently democratic citizenship education should prepare people to under-stand and act on these rights and responsibil-ities. This is a more traditional, conservative view, which draws heavily upon a thorough understanding of a nation's history and gov-ernment. This may be categorised as a mini-malist view to prepare what Westheimer and Kahne (2004) called the personally responsi-ble citizen.

A second approach contends that citizen-ship is about active participation within soci-etal structures and processes, such as voting and engaging in civic activities in the context of a democracy. Consequently education for this type of citizenship requires active partic-ipation in both government and community issues (Print and Coleman, 2003; Print and Saha, 2006), for what Westheimer and Kahne (2004) call participatory citizenship. This type of citizenship education includes the acquisition of knowledge and skills from a variety of school experiences, including tra-ditional school subjects as well as cross-cur-ricular studies such as the environmental sciences and globalisation as well as the informal curriculum (Print, 2007).

Third, some advocate that citizenship is more about supporting participation of all people in a democracy, where the citizen is one who pursues social justice, purposively attends to matters of injustice and attempts to change people's values and attitudes towards their fellow citizens (Osler, 2000; Westheimer and Kahne, 2004). Education for this type of democratic citizenship would address issues of discrimination and oppres-sion, and aim to help students become agents of social change (Osler, 2000). For Westheimer and Kahne (2004) this approach is designed to produce the justice-oriented citizen, the ultimate goal of democratic citizenship education.

In Australia, EDC, or civics and citizenship education as it is known, may be defined as the opportunity to learn in schools about one's system of government, democracy, rule of law, rights and responsibilities, democratic values and political issues in order to become an active, participating citizen in that democracy (CEG, 1994; Kemp, 1997; Curriculum Corporation, 1998). In terms of the above categories, this definition is more consistent with a combination of the first and second approaches (personally responsible and active, participatory citizens), than the third (Kemp, 1997; Howard and Patten, 2006). Indeed, David Kemp, as the federal minister who initiated the *Discovering Democracy* programme, argued that students should be able to '... distinguish between opinion and fact ... evaluate an argument ... recognise different points of view .... [and] use democratic processes and structure to manage conflicts' (Kemp, 1997).

Given that healthy democracies are those where citizens participate, and despite the declared need for education about democratic citizenship which would enhance voting and build social capital (Print and Coleman, 2003), many established democracies have become curiously complacent about educating their future citizens. Other competing forces in society have impacted on the school curriculum and been more successful in gaining resources and curriculum time within schools. Until recently Australia was one of these countries. It relied upon some vague, benign expectation that young Australians would learn about their democracy through exposure to schooling. The reality is quite different. As the evaluators of the DD programme found,

... without the direct funding and support of the federal government, and despite the high levels of interest in CCE within the various Australian educational bureaucracies in the 1990s, CCE would have been but a pale imitation of the current programme. There is little evidence that the eight jurisdictions would have committed the resources to developing independent or cooperative programmes in CCE. The proof will be found when federal funding ceases in mid-2004 – what level of resources will the jurisdictions provide to ensure CCE continues in schools? (Erebus, 2003)

AUSTRALIAN EDUCATION FOR DEMOCRATIC CITIZENSHIP

Despite the theoretical, historical and empirical bonds between education and democracy, the presence of education for democratic citizenship in the Australian school curriculum has been problematic. In the early years of the Australian federation civic education was an important component of the school curriculum with its mandate for nation building, political cohesiveness, national identity and democracy building (CEG, 1994; Print et al., 1999; Print, 1999; Howard and Patten, 2006). In the decades following WWII, however, civic education received scant attention by education systems, and what existed was diffused and difficult to identify in the school curriculum despite a period of massive migration (CEG, 1994; McAllister, 1998; Print, 2000). In a country where voting has been compulsory for national government elections for eighty years, this is more than a little ironic.

The Australian Constitution presents another complication for engaging schools with EDC. The Australian government's involvement in education is severely limited by the constitution, though in reality its fiscal powers allow it to achieve most of its educational goals. Ostensibly the Australian government's role is not to direct schools or education systems, nor does it have a direct responsibility for achieving student learning outcomes. Over the past four decades, however, it has wielded enormous influence through its budgetary strategies of financial inducements, and in the process refining the pre-conditions necessary to facilitate successful implementation of its 'consensus' driven policies across educational systems and sectors (Painter, 1998).

In the 1990s, civics and citizenship education re-emerged in the curriculum, with the support of several Commonwealth initiatives (Kemp, 1997; Print et al., 1999; Print, 2000). This civics and citizenship initiative attempted to include more critical and diverse elements of citizenship, though the extent to which this has been achieved is contentious (Gill and Reid, 1999). The reports and initiatives that led to the development of this new civics and citizenship education are detailed elsewhere (Print et al., 1999) and summarised in Table 8.1.

The initial attempts to address the fundamental concerns for democratic citizenship education were, as Print (1999) shows, noteworthy only by their lack of success. The first serious overtures were made in the 1980s which led to two Senate reviews (Table 8.1), though neither made significant impact on the various governments of the day. However, sensing a change in the Australian people and desirous to lay the foundations for a future republic, the Labour Prime Minister Paul Keating formed the Civics Expert Group (CEG) early in 1994 to inquire into the condition of civics and citizenship education in Australian education. Late that year the CEG report *Whereas the People ... Civics and Citizenship Education in Australia* (1994), identified a national chronic deficit of civic knowledge as well as grossly inadequate school education for democratic citizenship. The report recommended an extensive programme for schools to educate young Australians in democratic citizenship.

The Labour government commenced policy development in 1995, but early the next year was defeated in the general elections and replaced by a Liberal-National Coalition. In May 1997, the Howard government released its own policy on education for democratic citizenship called *Discovering Democracy* (Kemp, 1997), in part to counter the educational directions of the former

government, but more to forge a new, conservative sense of democratic citizenship under a neo-conservative government (Howard and Patten, 2006). And, as seen in Table 8.1, it was not until the implementation of *Discovering Democracy* that there is any evidence of a real sense of a viable, supported and funded programme in education for democratic citizenship in Australia.

Over this past decade a conundrum has also emerged for the state education authorities in terms of EDC and national assessment. In recent years MCEETYA authorised the development of *A Measurement Framework for National Key Performance Measures* (MCEETYA, 2003). In a groundbreaking development one of the first subject areas to be approved was EDC with national assessment conducted in 2004 and reported two years later (MCEETYA, 2006). Ironically, the review of *Discovering Democracy* had recommended its termination (Erebus, 2003) and, in 2004, the new Minister abandoned EDC while introducing a new values education strategy, as seen in Table 8.1. Not surprisingly schools, teachers and the states are perplexed.

THE *DISCOVERING DEMOCRACY* PROGRAMME

For the past decade what counts as education for democratic citizenship in Australian schools has been the federally initiated and funded programme *Discovering Democracy*. From its origins in 1997 the programme was accepted and implemented by the states and territories with little controversy as the principal direction of education for democracy. Its primary purpose was to build Australian students' understanding of their democracy through the provision of curriculum resources and support for schools and teachers (Kemp, 1997), and its centrality to EDC cannot be underestimated. Indeed, the Australian government injected some $32 million directly into the project with further resources from

Table 8.1   Major developments and responses in Civics and Citizenship Education in Australia, 1989–2006

Year	Development	Response
1989	*Education for Active Citizenship* Senate report assessed schools' roles in preparing young citizens.	Senate Standing Committee on Employment, Education, and Training
	Recommended strengthening civics and citizenship education.	(Ignored by governments)
1989	*Hobart Declaration: Common and Agreed National Goals for Schooling in Australia*	Australian Education Council (AEC)
	Goal 7: To develop knowledge, skills, attitudes and values which will enable students to participate as active and informed citizens in our democratic Australian society within an international context.	(Despite the rhetoric, largely ignored by governments in terms of policy and funding priorities)
1991	*Active Citizenship Revisited* Senate report renewed pressure for preparing young citizens though civics and citizenship education.	Senate Standing Committee on Employment, Education, and Training
		(Ignored by governments)
1994	*Whereas the People: Civics and Citizenship Education Report* Review of, and plan for, education in civics and citizenship, including the integration of civics and citizenship education (CCE) into school curricula.	Civics Expert Group (CEG) (Accepted by states and education systems as a serious concern to address)
1994	*National Statements and National Profiles, Studies of Society and Environment, SOSE*	Australian Education Council (AEC)
	New learning area statements; includes (CCE) goals and content in SOSE.	(Dropped by states after considerable political wrangling)
1997	*Discovering Democracy: Civics and Citizenship Education*	Department of Education, Science and Training (DEST)
	Materials for primary, lower and upper secondary levels developed. Later distributed nationally to all teachers.	(Developed and accepted by states, driven by federal funding)
1999	*Adelaide Declaration: National Goals for Schooling in the 21st Century* '… assist young people to contribute to Australia's social, cultural and economic development in local and global contexts … assist young people to develop a disposition towards learning throughout their lives so that they can exercise their rights and responsibilities as citizens of Australia.'	Ministerial Council (MCEETYA) (Supported by the states and Commonwealth, though limited connection with action in systems and schools. Less effective version of Hobart Declaration)
1999	*Review of Discovering Democracy* Conducted early in the Programme. Showed few schools had adopted and implemented materials nationally.	Erebus for DEST (Provided formative feedback to systems and educators; recommended continuation)
2003	*Discovering Democracy Final Review* Conducted late in the second funding phase. Many schools had implemented materials nationally, but no extensive adoption. Recommended termination.	Erebus for DEST (Evidence of teacher resistance in secondary schools and less than expected adoption. Recommended termination)
2004	*Values Education Strategy* New Commonwealth Minister of Education initiative. Linked with civic and democratic values, but more generic, and broadbased.	Minister for Education, Science and Training. (Limited success despite funding; lacked support from systems and schools)

Continued

Table 8.1   Major developments and responses in Civics and Citizenship Education in Australia, 1989–2006—Cont'd

Year	Development	Response
2006	Australian Parliament JSCEM Review of Civics and Electoral Education NSW Parliament JSCEM Inquiry into Voter Enrolment National Assessment Program – Civics and Citizenship Years 6 &10 Report All demonstrate the lack of effectiveness of educating young Australians in civics and citizenship as well as engaging them in participating in democracy.	Commonwealth Parliament – Joint Standing Committee on Electoral Matters NSW Parliament – Joint Standing Committee on Electoral Matters MCEETYA report (More direct government involvement and funding needed. All recommend greater education in CCE)

the states over the period 1997–2003 (MCEETYA, 2006). Centrally devised curriculum resources were produced over the period 1997–2003 and distributed free, in hard copy and electronically, to all of Australia's 10,000 schools. Substantial teacher professional development was funded by the programme, but managed by the states, to familiarise teachers with the programme and the materials.

As such, *Discovering Democracy* is an example of what Painter (1998) called collaborative federalism. A highlight of the programme was the close cooperation evidenced between the states and Australian governments as they developed and implemented the programme. And while each of the six states and two territories (which constitute the Australian federation) interpreted and applied the non-compulsory programme slightly differently, most of this difference, at system level, is marginal. Significantly, they mostly chose to rewrite or strengthen their existing systemic curricula to incorporate elements of education for democratic citizenship. In NSW, for example, where a third of Australia's students reside, the K-6 Human Society and Its Environment Syllabus was revised for primary schools, as were History and Geography Years 7–10 syllabuses, to include opportunities to utilise *Discovering Democracy* resources.

Although schools and teachers have the option to select what to teach from within the programme's offerings, and they do, (Erebus, 1999, 2003; Gore, 2007), there are similar options within all subjects that constitute the social education curriculum. The outcome of such choice is that it is difficult to determine exactly what is being taught about education for democratic citizenship in schools nationally.

Conceptually, the central feature of the *Discovering Democracy* programme was the enhancement of democratic concepts, principles, procedures, dispositions and values in Australian schools. Furthermore, the programme was intended to assist Australian students to understand their political and legal systems as well as to develop capacities to participate as informed, reflective and active citizens in their multiple civic communities. More specifically the outcomes were for students to:

- gain knowledge and understanding of Australia's democratic processes, government and judicial system and of the nation's place in the international community;
- understand how participation and decision-making operate in contemporary Australia and how the nation's civic life might change in the future;
- develop personal character traits such as respecting individual worth and human dignity, empathy, respect for the law, being informed about public issues, critical mindedness and willingness to express points of view, listen, negotiate and compromise;

- understand how our system of government works in practice and how it affects citizens; and
- understand the rights and responsibilities of citizens, and the opportunities for exercising them at local, state and federal levels. (Curriculum Corporation, 1998).

What is also clearly present in *Discovering Democracy* is an explicit statement of the importance of a set of values, particularly those underpinning democracy. These values are encouraged within *Discovering Democracy* in order to reflect and enhance the cohesive, pluralistic nature of Australian society. Those values which are recognised include democratic processes and freedoms (such as speech, association, religion), government accountability, civility and respect for the law, tolerance and respect for others, social justice and acceptance of cultural diversity. These were seen as highly important to how young Australians would come to understand their democracy. In launching the programme the Federal Minister argued:

> Such values should be explicit and public within the programme. Students should learn about the importance of principles such as popular sovereignty, the principle of government accountability, and the rule of law. The programme will articulate values such as tolerance, respect for others, and freedom of speech, religion and association (Kemp, 1997: 4).

What then has been the impact of *Discovering Democracy* on EDC in Australia nationally and state/territory education systems? How have schools and how have teachers utilised these programmes? And what has been the impact on student outcomes?

DISCOVERING DEMOCRACY AND EDUCATION FOR DEMOCRATIC CITIZENSHIP

Over recent years numerous reviews and research studies (Print et al., 2001; DeJaeghere, 2002; Print et al., 2004; NSW JSCEM, 2006; Howard and Patten, 2006; Print and Saha, 2006; JSCEM, 2007), evaluations

(Erebus, 1999, 2003) and assessments of student achievement (MCEETYA, 2006) have addressed EDC generally and *Discovering Democracy* specifically. What then has happened in the decade since the programme, and EDC more generally, were initiated?

National initiative

Although the Australian Constitution limits the federal government's involvement in the states' domain, in reality its fiscal power enables extensive involvement in areas such as education. In the case of *Discovering Democracy* and EDC the Commonwealth created a 'national' policy (Kemp, 1997) based upon fiscal inducements, curriculum materials for schools (Curriculum Corporation, 1998), together with funding for teacher professional development (Gore, 2007; Print, 2007), which effectively controlled the nature and form of EDC in Australian schools. It has also pursued a policy of national assessment, as seen above, based upon nationally agreed performance measures (Print and Hughes, 2001), to measure student knowledge and understanding (MCEETYA, 2006) and subsequently to hold educational systems accountable.

From the Australian Government's perspective, *Discovering Democracy* may be construed as a federal success story, though it was not, as Gore (2007) notes, a simple matter nor was it uncontested (Gill and Reid, 1999; DeJaghere, 2002; Howard and Patten, 2006). As a funded offering to the states it was accepted and implemented, and, to a considerable extent, the federal government's policy goals for *Discovering Democracy* were achieved. These included a high level of commitment and engagement of the eight-state and territory educational systems to develop an agreed curriculum framework, provision of abundant quality curriculum resources and support for teacher professional development. Nationally EDC has a clear place among the National Goals for Schooling, and an identifiable, if not strong, presence in the school curriculum in all states and territories. A national assessment framework has been implemented that subsequently measured student outcomes in EDC (MCEETYA, 2006).

States and territories

The states and territories that form the Australian federation jealously guard their limited political power in education. While the federal government has policy initiatives in education, they do not always correspond to those of the states. *Discovering Democracy* was one programme where consensus existed between the jurisdictions from the beginning, supplemented by federal funding. Nevertheless, the states and territories devised independent curricula frameworks which addressed EDC and how the resources of *Discovering Democracy* could be applied in their jurisdiction. Consequently, no state adopted the programme as its sole response to teaching EDC (Gore, 2007).

Despite the initial financial incentives associated with participation in *Discovering Democracy*, for the state and territory education jurisdictions federal initiatives over the past few years (Table 8.1) has meant a problematic outlook for EDC. Although substantial achievements have been made, significant use of the *Discovering Democracy* materials within a well-structured, whole school programme demonstrating improved student learning outcomes has been achieved in no more than half the schools nationally (Erebus, 2003). State and territory education officials would agree that this is an unsatisfactory outcome, and as Erebus noted,

Without further funding input, it is doubtful whether use of the materials by schools or teachers would be sustained for more than a few years. In this case, and without explicit direction, the quality and intensity of civics and citizenship education is not likely to improve' (2003).

Further, as Gore noted, '... like many such programmes, the lack of sustainability meant that since 2004 there has been little support

nationally for citizenship education.' (2007: 2). These prophetic statements have indeed become reality as manifest in the demise of federal funding and national student outcome data (MCEETYA, 2006; JSCEM, 2007).

Additionally, in implementing EDC the states have also been faced with a classical curriculum 'stand-off.' If more needs to be added to the curriculum, what should be removed? As EDC is but one of many initiatives, how much space within an already overcrowded curriculum should it be accorded? The states have addressed this question by choosing to integrate civics within existing school subjects such as Studies of Society and Environment (SOSE), History and also Geography (Gore, 2007). In turn this has produced substantial identity problems for both existing subjects as well as for EDC. The most common outcomes have been the often less than harmonious adoption and utilisation of EDC within existing curricula in a way that enables teachers and schools to largely avoid teaching it. Ironically, indications are that *Discovering Democracy*'s narrower perception of civics, and its emphasis on history as a curricular vehicle, have not been widey adopted by the states (Erebus, 2003; Gore, 2007).

Schools

What has become clear over the past decade is that schools have utilised the *Discovering Democracy* resources as appropriate to their interpretation of, and implementation of, education for democratic citizenship within their curriculum. The effect has been substantial variability in school application of EDC. In a national study of schools conducted as part of a national evaluation of *Discovering Democracy*, three principal areas of variance were found (Erebus, 2003) – school policy, the formal school curriculum and third, the informal curriculum.

Few schools demonstrated clearly articulated policies on EDC, though about a quarter identified a specific programme related to civics and citizenship (Erebus, 2003). Most schools identified EDC as part of their formal curriculum, largely because educational systems had incorporated elements within their curricular requirements. They did not, however, link these learning opportunities with similar opportunities for students in the informal curriculum, such as elections for student council, school debating, fund raising for charity and student civic participation through volunteering or service learning.

A significant reason for this proportion was that many schools also had an identifiable leader for the civics and citizenship programme. In secondary schools this was usually the Head Teacher of the subject department or Coordinator for SOSE. For schools, having a strong advocate for the programme was a significant factor in facilitating the success of EDC or the *Discovering Democracy* programme (Erebus, 2003).

In the national evaluation, schools were asked to rate factors which had impacted negatively on their implementation of *Discovering Democracy*. Competing school priorities was consistently reported as the most significant constraint, with difficulties encountered in implementing the programme had little to do with access to, costs of, or the quality of, the materials themselves. While access to professional development is an inhibitor in some schools, as would be expected, for others it is not an issue. Similarly, access to the internet and computers impacted negatively in about forty percent of schools in the study. This is particularly the case for those schools with limited funding for IT, including many government schools.

If the primary intention of the *Discovering Democracy* programme was to build student knowledge of democracy (Kemp, 1997), based upon the CEG report (1994) and the *National Goals for Schooling in the Twenty-First Century* (1999) which all sought to encourage students to become knowledgeable, participating citizens in the future, then there is cause for grave concern. Reviewing the research and evaluations it is clear that

the approach to EDC found in Australian schools is one that, if not taught very well, encourages superficial understanding and fails to address the principal objective of providing depth and breadth of civic understanding. By way of confirmation, the national assessment of students (MCEETYA, 2006) identified performance levels of students in Australian schools as low, given that

> ... many of the Year 10 students clearly did not have the knowledge outlined in the assessment domain as being designated for year 6. ... Ignorance of such fundamental information indicates a lack of knowledge of the history of our democratic tradition, and this ignorance will permeate and restrict the capacity of students to make sense of many other aspects of Australian democratic forms and processes. Without the basic understandings, they will be unable to engage in a meaningful way in many other levels of action or discourse. (MCEETYA, 2006: 91).

TEACHER PRACTICE OF EDC AND *DISCOVERING DEMOCRACY*

If schools experienced difficulties implementing *Discovering Democracy* and building an EDC programme, what effect did this have upon classroom teaching? Real curriculum control as practised in Australian schools lies with the individual teacher who decides, within broad curricular constraints, what will be taught, when and how. Consequently in reviewing the research it was not surprising to find considerable variability amongst teachers in terms of interest in, adoption of and participation in, EDC.

At the basic level of teacher awareness it was surprising how many teachers were only a little aware of the *Discovering Democracy* programme. By 2003 nearly a third of relevant teachers had minimal awareness, while half were moderately aware of the curriculum materials and professional development opportunities (Erebus, 2003). After many year's exposure to the materials, it was somewhat surprising that most teachers used the materials minimally, with one in eight not using them at all, and a greater proportion of primary school teachers making use of them than secondary teachers (Erebus, 2003). After a decade of the programme in schools, Gore (2007) summarised the level of use as 'unexciting' and clearly not a burning passion for the majority of teachers in Australian schools.

Teaching EDC, particularly through the use of *Discovering Democracy*, tends to be very traditional. By the final evaluation there was greater evidence of group work and inquiry strategies, though the emphasis remained on traditional expository strategies such as teacher talk and worksheets (Erebus, 2003). As found in the IEA Civics Study (Torney-Purta et al., 2001), teachers around the world are still trying to teach participative democratic citizenship using traditional expository methods.

If few schools teach EDC comprehensively, particularly if based upon the *Discovering Democracy* programme, how *is* teaching conducted? It was clear from the final evaluation that primary schools make frequent use of isolated teaching activities related to specific events, such as Anzac Day – the national remembrance day – and more than half of teachers utilised the units of work across and within particular learning areas (Erebus, 2003). A similar, but less robust, pattern is evident at the secondary level. However, more than three quarters of secondary schools claim to have taught some of the units of work within a specific learning area (SOSE or equivalent).

Teacher professional development was conducted through specifically formed committees in the states and territories to address curriculum resources specifically, and more broadly, in education for democratic citizenship (Gore, 2007). This was credited with improving teacher understanding and confidence, moderately impacting on curriculum planning and teaching practices, with least impact in the area of assessment practices (Erebus, 2003; Gore, 2007).

STUDENT OUTCOMES

Independently, all states and territories developed some form of educational programme for democratic citizenship that, by 2000, employed, to varying degrees, the resources of *Discovering Democracy*. By the time of national testing in 2004, therefore, it could reasonably be expected that young Australians would understand their system of government and democracy. Given that the programme sought to build student knowledge and understanding of democracy, government and the rights and responsibilities of citizens, this is a reasonable expectation.

In 2001, in part to address the National Goals for Schooling, which included educating students to understand Australian democracy, as well as a changing emphasis towards more systemic and national assessment, Key Performance Measures (KPMs) in EDC were researched and developed (Print and Hughes, 2001). These were accepted by MCEETYA for implementation and in 2004 a national sample of students was tested on the KPMs (MCEETYA, 2006).

Australia had already participated in the IEA Civic Study (1996–2001) though it came late to the study. The first phase case study showed a country desperately in need of EDC as both the federal and state governments had all but ignored this area in school curricula (Print et al., 1999). This neglect was all the more significant given that Australia has become a highly multicultural country over recent decades and mandates compulsory voting in elections. Unsurprisingly students displayed relatively low levels of civic knowledge compared with similarly advanced countries, though their generic skills raised their scores to average levels (Mellor et al., 2001). As the main assessment was conducted in 1999 the outcomes of that exercise had minimal relevance to *Discovering Democracy* and state programmes. By 2004 students should have been well prepared in EDC at least through exposure to the *Discovering Democracy* materials.

Test data (MCEETYA, 2006), however, reveal this has not occurred. Nearly a decade after *Discovering Democracy* was introduced, students in Years 6 and 10 know relatively little about Australian government, democracy, parliamentary systems and EDC more generally. While many schools have done an excellent job in engaging students, the national pattern is weak and problematic in terms of student outcomes in schools. Indeed, the report continued,

> Student achievement at both year levels was below that expected by the experts who participated in the proficient standards setting exercise, by the State and Territory officers who participated in the marker training and by the experts who marked the open-ended responses. ... Formal, consistent instruction has not been the experience of Australian students in civics and citizenship. (2006: 93)

For New South Wales, the most populous Australian state, the results were surprisingly good, given that the state usually performs below or around the mean in national assessments. The reason lies with NSW consciously integrating EDC into its school curriculum over the past several years. In the MCEETYA (2006) assessments it outperformed all other states and territories at Year 10 level and was equally highest with two other states and territories at Year 6 level. But as Gore noted,

> The reason for this success is very simple: students tend to do better on tests if you teach them the material to be tested on. Explicit curriculum, high compliance by teachers and relevant professional development paid off. Some states and territories are yet to understand this point. (2007: 3).

A few years earlier it became increasingly clear that a significant problem existed with young people in regard to democratic engagement. Relative to other groups, research has found the young appear to care little for the body politic and Australian government (Saha, 2000; Print et al., 2004). Given the mandate of *Discovering Democracy*, have young people become more engaged with Australian democracy? As the CEG reported a 'civics deficit in the early 1990s, has EDC addressed this

successfully? If engagement is measured by participation in democracy, the answer is probably not. This has been reiterated by the number of recent inquiries into youth engagement in Queensland, NSW and nationally (JSCEM, 2007) as well as national research in the form of the Youth Electoral Study (Print et al., 2004).

CONCLUSIONS

The past decade has been problematic for EDC in Australia. After a successful implementation *Discovering Democracy* achieved a sense of national presence and a consensual set of national educational directions (Erebus, 1999; Print, 2000; Print et al., 2001; JSCEM, 2007). Though modestly financed by the Australian Government, without the infusion of direct government funding, any form of EDC would have struggled to gain recognition (Table 8.1). Other funding sources are simply inadequate or non-existent. Yet, as is often the case with curriculum innovations in Australia, *Discovering Democracy* received insufficient financial support to institutionalise it within schools. The accumulated evidence shows that a decade after the programme was launched, much remains to be achieved as despite initial government support, reinforced by state-level curriculum requirements, the position of EDC in most schools remains tenuous. At this stage EDC is found in schools within the fifteen to twenty percent of early adopters and the thirty to forty percent of moderate adopters. As yet it has to win over the thirty percent of slow, resistant adopters who wait and see and the fifteen percent or so of 'recalcitrants.'

This situation was exacerbated by the review of *Discovering Democracy* which recommended termination of the programme (Erebus, 2003). The federal government soon ceased funding programmes for teachers and schools which was the death knell for both the programme and education for democratic citizenship more broadly for, as Gore (2007) notes, the states had neither the resources nor the political will to ensure the continuance of EDC. Subsequently EDC, and particularly *Discovering Democracy*, has withered from lack of funding and political leadership (Gore, 2007) unlike England (Crick, 2007).

There are several areas of EDC which need support, though little in the way of promising directions until either the federal government changes or its educational policies change. Evidence-based policy is needed to identify successful programmes that enhance student knowledge, skills and dispositions to democratic citizenship (MCEETYA, 2006). Second, like many countries, we need to identify and engage teachers in appropriate pedagogy that works in enhancing student knowledge and participation (JSCEM, 2007; Gore, 2007). One promising line of research is that exploring links between citizenship education, civic and democratic behaviour as in the YES research (Print and Saha, 2006; JSCEM, 2007). This research has revealed strong links between forms of EDC and subsequent engagement (Print and Saha, 2006; Print, 2007).

As a significant curriculum innovation, *Discovering Democracy* displayed many signs of success at the adoption and implementation phases. The innovation was characterised by high levels of political and bureaucratic cooperation between jurisdictions, sectors and schools. In the process of development, some excellent curriculum resources were produced and these have been appreciated and applied by teachers in classrooms (Erebus, 1999, 2003). Extensive, successful teacher professional development programmes, organised through state educational authorities, also characterised the programme. Once federal funding ceased, however, so did the professional development.

Yet, if judged by student performance, *Discovering Democracy* and EDC have been less than successful. If student civic knowledge is the yardstick, as it often is, the MCEETYA report concluded that 'Although young Australians appear to accept and appreciate their democracy, their level of knowledge and understanding of civics and citizenship is less than was expected by a range of experts in the field.' (2006: 93).

Several factors may account for this situation with lessons for future innovations. The lack of curriculum consolidation in schools has meant that many students have simply not studied EDC or have done so minimally. Second, the lack of a high profile for EDC has meant it is too often not taken seriously by teachers. Third, widespread teacher engagement is lacking largely because EDC is not represented as a full academic subject or a substantial subject presence in the school curriculum. Fourth, schools display a lack of consolidation of the informal curriculum components of EDC, (such as school elections, student councils and student volunteering) with the formal curriculum so as to provide a comprehensive approach to learning about and participating in education for democratic citizenship. Until these issues are addressed seriously the future for democratic citizenship in Australian schools will remain problematic.

REFERENCES

Australian Council for Education (1989) *National Goals for Schooling in Australia*. Hobart: AEC.

Civics Expert Group (CEG) (S. Macintyre, chair) (1994*) Whereas the People ... Civics and Citizenship Education*. Canberra: Australian Government Printing Service.

Crick, B. (1998) (Chair) *Education for Citizenship and the Teaching of Democracy in Schools*. London: Qualifications and Curriculum Authority.

Crick, B. (2007) Citizenship, the Political and the Democratic. Keynote Address, 3rd International Citized Conference, University of Sydney, Sydney.

Curriculum Corporation (1998) *Discovering Democracy Schools Material Project*. Melbourne: Curriculum Corporation.

DeJaeghere, J. (2002) Citizenship and Citizenship Education in Australia: New

Meaning in an Era of Globalization. PhD Thesis, University of Minnesota.

Erebus Consulting Group (1999) *Evaluation of the Discovering Democracy Program*. Canberra: Department of Education, Training and Youth Affairs.

Erebus Consulting Group (2003) *Evaluation of the Discovering Democracy Program, 2000–2003*. Canberra: Department of Education, Training and Youth Affairs.

Gill, J. and Reid, A. (1999) Civics Education: The State of Play or the Play of the State. *Curriculum Perspectives*, 19 (3): 31–40.

Gore, J. (2007) Keeping Citizenship Education Afloat in a Sea of Apathy. Keynote address International CitizEd Conference, University of Sydney, Sydney, April.

Hallet, B. (in press) Legislation on youth enrolment and voting. In L. Saha, M. Print and K. Edwards (Eds) *Youth and Political Participation*. Amsterdam: Sense Publishers.

Hahn, C. (1998) *Becoming Political: Comparative Perspectives on Citizenship Education*. Albany, NY: SUNY Press.

Howard, C. and Patten, S. (2006) Valuing Civics: Political Commitment and the New Citizenship Education in Australia. *Canadian Journal of Education*, 29 (2): 454–475.

Joint Standing Committee on Electoral Matters (2007) *Report of the Inquiry into Civic and Electoral Education*. Canberra: Parliament of Australia.

Kemp, D. (1997) *Discovering Democracy: Civics and Citizenship Education*. Ministerial Statement. Canberra: Minister for Schools, Vocational Education and Training.

Kennedy, K. (ed.) *Citizenship Education and the Modern State*. London: Falmer Press.

Kerr, D. (2003) Citizenship: Local, National and International Contexts. In L.Gearon (Ed) *Learning to Teach Citizenship in the Secondary School*. London: Routledge Farmer.

McAllister, I (1998) Civic Education and Political Knowledge in Australia. *Australian Journal of Political Science*, 33 (2): 7–23.

Macedo, S. et al. (2005) *Democracy at Risk*. Washington, DC: Brookings Institute

Mellor, S., Kennedy, K. and Greenwood, L. (2001) *Citizenship and Democracy: Students' Knowledge and Beliefs. Australian Fourteen Year Olds & the IEA Civic Education Study*. Canberra: Commonwealth of Australia.

Ministerial Council for Employment, Education, Training and Youth Affairs (MCEETYA) (1999) *National Goals for Schooling in the Twenty-first Century*. Adelaide: MCEETYA.

Ministerial Council for Employment, Education, Training and Youth Affairs (MCEETYA (2003) *A Measurement Framework for National Key Performance Measures*, Canberra: MCEETYA

Ministerial Council for Employment, Education, Training and Youth Affairs (MCEETYA (2006) *National Assessment Program – Civics and Citizenship Years 6 and 10 Report*, Canberra: MCEETYA

New South Wales Joint Standing Committee on Electoral Matters (2006) *Report of the Inquiry into Civic and Electoral Education*. Canberra: Parliament of Australia.

Niemi, R. and Junn, J. (1996) What Knowledge for a Reinforced Citizenship in the United States of America. *Prospects*, 26 (4): 663–672.

Niemi, R. and Junn, J. (1998) *Civic Education: What Makes Students Learn*. New Haven, CT.: Yale University Press.

Norris, P. (ed.) *Critical Citizens: Global Support for Democratic Government*. Oxford: Oxford University Press.

Osler, A. (ed.) (2000) *Citizenship and Democracy in Schools: Diversity, Identity, Equality*. Stoke-on-Trent: Trentham.

Painter, M. (1998) *Collaborative Federalism: Economic Reform in Australia in the 1990s*. Cambridge: Cambridge University Press.

Parker, W. (ed.) (1996) *Educating the Democratic Mind*. Albany, New York: State University of New York Press.

Patrick, J. (1999) Education for Constructive Engagement of Citizens in Democratic Civil Society. In C. Bahmueller and J. Patrick (eds) *Principles and Practices of Education for Democratic Citizenship*. Bloomington, Indiana: ERIC Clearinghouse.

Print, M. (1999) Building Democracy for the Twenty-First Century: Rediscovering Civics and Citizenship Education in Australia. In C. Bahmueller and J. Patrick (eds) *Principles and Practices of Education for Democratic Citizenship*. Bloomington, Indiana: ERIC Clearinghouse

Print, M., Kennedy, K. and Hughes, J. (1999) Reconstructing Civic and Citizenship Education in Australia. In J. Torney-Purta, J. Schwille and J. Amadeo (eds) (1999) *Civic*

Education Across Countries: Twenty-four Case Studies from the IEA Civic Education Project. Amsterdam: International Association for the Evaluation of Educational Achievement.

Print, M. (2000) Discovering Democracy: The Confirmation of Civics and Citizenship Education in Australia. *International Journal of Social Education*, 15 (1): 65–79.

Print, M. and Hughes, J. (2001) *National Key Performance Measures in Civics and Citizenship Education*. Report to the National Key Performance Measures Taskforce, Ministerial Council for Education, Training and Youth Affairs, Canberra.

Print, M., Moroz, W. and Reynolds, P. (eds) (2001*) Discovering Democracy in Civics and Citizenship Education*. Sydney: Social Science Press.

Print, M., Ornstrom, S. and Nielsen, H. (2002) Education for Democratic Processes in Schools and Classrooms. *European Journal of Education*, 37 (2): 193–210.

Print, M. and Coleman, D. (2003) Towards Understanding Social Capital and Citizenship Education. *Cambridge Journal of Education*, 33 (1): 123–149.

Print, M., Saha, L. and Edwards, K. (2004) *Youth Electoral Study: Report 1*. Canberra: Australian Electoral Commission

Print, M. and Saha, L. (2006) *Adequacy of Civics and Electoral Education in Australia*. Invited submission to the Joint Standing Committee on Electoral Matters. Canberra: Parliament of Australia.

Print, M. (2007) Citizenship Education and Youth Participation in Democracy. *British Journal of Educational Studies*, 55 (3): 325–345.

Putnam, R. (2000) *Bowling Alone: The Collapse and Revival of American Community*. New York: Simon & Schuster.

Saha, L. (2000) Political Activism and Civic Education Among Australian Secondary School Students. *Australian Journal of Education*, 44 (2): 155–174.

Senate Select Committee on Employment, Education and Training (SSCEET) (1989). *Education for Active Citizenship Education in Australian Schools and Youth Organisations*. Canberra: Parliament of Australia.

Torney-Purta, J., Schwille, J. and Amadeo, J. (eds) (1999) *Civic Education Across Countries: Twenty-four Case Studies from the IEA Civic Education Project*. Amsterdam: International Association for the Evaluation of Educational Achievement (IEA).

Torney-Purta, J., Lehaman, R., Oswald, H. and Schulz, W. (2001) *Citizenship and Education in Twenty-eight Countries: Civic Knowledge and Engagement at Age Fourteen*. Amsterdam: International Association for the Evaluation of Educational Achievement.

Westheimer, J. and Kahne, J. (2004) What kind of citizen? The politics of educating for democracy. *American Educational Research Journal*, 41(2): 237–269.

9

Reinventing Freire: Exceptional Cases of Citizenship Education in Brazil

Daniel Schugurensky and Katherine Madjidi

INTRODUCTION

Like most Latin American countries, Brazil is characterized by severe economic and social inequalities that result in exclusion and extreme poverty for large segments of the population. Without access to basic human rights such as sufficient food and clean water, gainful employment, land ownership, or meaningful social and political participation, the basic preconditions for full citizenship are negated for millions of Brazilians. Educational opportunities are particularly affected in this segmented and hierarchical system, which tends to reproduce inequalities rather than diminish them.

Brazilian schools are mandated with promoting education for citizenship, but many public schools – largely due to the state withdrawal and funding cuts that occurred during the last two decades – are not even able to provide a decent basic education to their students. In addition to the harsh material conditions that inhibit the activation of full citizenship among large sectors of the population, schools do not cultivate many of the subjective conditions, especially the development of autonomy, basic academic competencies, and critical thinking.

At the same time, the Brazilian context, perhaps because of its extreme disparities, offers fertile ground for the development of radical social and educational alternatives. Inspired in part by the ideas of Paulo Freire and traditions of popular education, these efforts are aimed at the expansion and deepening of popular engagement for democratic citizenship. This chapter examines two such efforts, one at the level of municipal governments (Citizen Schools) and the other in the context of social movements (Landless Movement, or *Movimento Sem Terra*), as examples of innovative educational strategies for a new kind of citizenship.

HISTORICAL AND SOCIAL CONTEXT

Covering nearly half of South America, Brazil ranks fifth in the world in area and population, and ninth in economic power, with geographic diversity ranging from the mouth of the Amazon to the majestic Igacú Falls. Such vast wealth is contrasted by sharp poverty: 59 million of Brazil's 190 million inhabitants live below the poverty line, and 38 million barely survive on less than one dollar a day (UNDP, 2006). Moreover, Brazil has been haunted for years by the paradox of being one of the world's main exporters of agricultural commodities and having millions of its citizens go hungry.[1] Internationally, this country has one of the highest concentrations of land in the fewest number of hands (1 per cent of the population owns nearly 50 per cent of the country's arable land) and one of the greatest inequalities in income distribution (scoring 54 in the Gini coefficient index of inequality assessment) (World Bank, 2004; Samman, 2005). These factors have led to Brazil's being given the dubious title of 'world champion in social inequality' (Bethell, 2000: 15).

The root of this inequality can be traced back to the division of land following Portuguese colonization in 1494. In an attempt to secure the territory, land grants were offered averaging around 250,000 acres per person (5,000 times the 50 acres/person offered in the US). These areas evolved into large plantations, worked by African slaves (it is estimated that around 37 per cent of all slave traffic between Africa and the Americas had Brazil as the destination) as well as by Amerindians and poor European immigrants.[2] During the last decades, despite the rhetoric of successive governments supporting land reform, no significant redistribution has been carried out, and income inequalities still persist.

DEMOCRACY, CITIZENSHIP RIGHTS, AND IDENTITY

Brazil's political history can be summarized as a transit from elections without democracy to democracy without citizenship (Bethell, 2000). Interestingly, Brazil has consistently held elections since 1821, even under military dictatorships (1964–1985). However, few of these elections have offered real democratic power, often taking place under threat of intimidation, with extremely limited suffrage, or without the ability to elect executives in significant positions of power.

Citizenship status has varied widely throughout Brazil's history, but has often excluded vast sectors of the population (including poor, rural, black, slave, female) from decision-making processes. For instance, a law passed in the 1880s required all voters to pass a literacy test, thereby excluding 85 per cent of the population. Brazil made little effort to promote literacy amongst the general populace, effectively prohibiting the majority from democratic involvement. It was not until 1985, with the military dictatorship fading and transition towards civilian rule, that universal suffrage was finally extended and indirect elections were held. In 1989, Fernando Collor de Mello became president by direct popular vote, only to be impeached in 1992 for corruption. Since then, electoral democracy has strengthened and widened, with lively municipal and state elections. In the twenty-first century a new era opened when Lula da Silva, a leftist union leader born to a poor and illiterate peasant family, was elected president in 2002 and again in 2006.

Citizenship identity in Brazil is a controversial topic. Brazil is known for the diversity of its peoples (primarily from European, African, Amerindian, and Asian descent), and prides itself on the fact that there is one 'Brazilian race', with multiracial identities more often mixed in one individual than separated into different communities. This 'myth of the racial democracy' has been heavily critiqued for concealing Brazil's history of oppression and encouraged miscegenation, as well as for supporting structural racism in Brazil (Cleary, 1999). Nevertheless, despite continuing inequalities (often based directly on colour of skin), there is consensus that most Brazilians do generally 'feel' Brazilian and are proud of their national identity, and that sub-categories of race, ethnicity or family background factor *less* into concepts of citizenship identity than they might in other countries (Langur, 2006).

EDUCATION AND CITIZENSHIP LEARNING IN BRAZIL

According to the Brazilian Constitution, basic education is free and compulsory and ensures equal conditions of access and permanence in school. However, formal democracy should not be equated with substantive democracy. Although work under the age of 16 is forbidden, child labour is common in Brazil. Moreover, despite the fact that 97.2 per cent of children aged 7–14 enrol in elementary schools, less than 70 per cent complete their studies, and only just over half of them enter secondary schools. Repetition rates are high, as less than 50 per cent of first grade students pass to the second grade in their first attempt (Gandin and Apple, 2004).

As Brazilian education tends to be segmented along class lines, this predominantly affects children from low-income families: children whose mothers have low levels of schooling are seven times more likely to be poor, eleven times more likely to abandon school, and 23 times more likely to be illiterate (IPEA, 2005: 11). Regional inequalities also abound – wealthier jurisdictions provide more funding and better paid teachers than poorer ones. Unfortunately, the Brazilian public school has become a '*coisa pobre para o pobre*', that is, a poor thing for poor people (Demo, 2006). The upper classes attend elite private schools and are more likely to be accepted in highly subsidized, good quality public universities. Paradoxically, poorer students who graduate from public schools have to enrol in lower quality but more costly private universities.

This segmented education system, then, is nurturing two types of citizens. With fewer resources, lower quality of instruction, and high dropout rates, public schools are stratifying students into lower socio-economic classes and at the same time are less likely to nurture critical thinking and autonomy,

basic conditions for the activation of full citizenship.

The practice of citizenship education in Brazil has changed as frequently as its political structures and concurrently shifting social and political objectives. In the early days of the republic, as discussed above, education was provided only to the elite and used effectively as a barrier to the exercise of citizenship rights. During the military dictatorship, 'citizenship education' focused on inculcating patriotism and allegiance to the military state, and included measures to silence critical thought or dissent. A liberal sense of citizenship education has only recently been included with the turn towards democracy in the 1980s and with the new Brazilian Constitution of 1988 that incorporated statements on human rights, citizenship rights and the related role of education (Siss et al., 1999, Romão, 2004).

According to the National Curricular Guidelines, based on the 1988 Constitution's Basic Educational Law (Article 2), the themes of citizenship and preparation for work are the foundation for the social sciences area of 'Human Sciences and its Technologies' (Ministério da Educação e Cultura, 1999). The guidelines specify that

> secondary Education, as the final stage of Basic Education, must count the exercise of citizenship among its indispensable elements and not just in the political sense of formal citizenship, but also in the perspective of social citizenship, extending to work relations, among other social relations ... One should not lose sight that citizenship must not be faced ... as an abstract concept but as a lived experience that includes all aspects of life in society. (Ministério da Educaçao e Cultura, 1999: 12)

The Ministry of Education also states that citizenship learning should be incorporated as an interdisciplinary subject across school curriculum.

However, public school teachers lack pedagogical tools for teaching about citizenship. In a recent study involving 69 elementary school teachers, Iosif (2007) reports that when asked about the main function of schools, the great majority replied that it is to educate for citizenship. But when asked about their conceptual and methodological approaches to accomplish this goal, most of them seemed lost. Citizenship education, then, for many teachers, became a cliché, a superficial statement of political correctness without much substance or pedagogical practice. Further, when faced with extreme pressure to use the minimal resources available to educate children in basic reading, writing, and mathematics, 'supplementary' topics such as citizenship education tend to be relegated to the side (Bertan, 2002). Municipal and regional control of primary and secondary education also leads to varying curricular content, including for citizenship education.

Given the lack of a consistent national citizenship education framework, it is difficult to assess the overall state of citizenship education in Brazil. However, we propose that in the context of Brazil, it may in fact be more interesting to examine more unique and radical alternatives which have developed in parallel to mainstream curricula.

PAULO FREIRE AND POPULAR EDUCATION

Five hundred years of inequality and injustice in Brazil has offered fertile ground for a long legacy of social resistance and the birth of numerous grassroots social movements, including those for educational change and new forms of citizenship learning (Goncalves e Silva, 2004). Isolated public schools are implementing innovative and inspiring citizenship education programmes that involve school democracy, curricular connections to local realities, community participation, action research, and so on. It is also possible to identify collective efforts that have gone beyond the confines of individual institutional initiatives, aiming precisely at advancing an agenda of social justice and participatory democracy. Frequently, these efforts are guided by principles of popular education and inspired by the pedagogical contributions of Paulo Freire.

Paulo Freire began his literacy work in 1962 as Director of Education in Northeast Brazil. It was in this role that Freire realized the critical relationship between literacy, citizenship, and democracy, famously teaching 300 sugar cane workers to read and write in only 45 days. In 1963, the model was expanded to 20,000 literacy circles aimed at teaching two million people to read and write (Branford and Rocha, 2002). This programme, which was raising both the knowledge and the potential mass political participation of the poor, was a cause for serious concern for elite classes. Together with other rising socialist movements and the leftist politics of President João Goulart, the literacy circles are considered part of the impetus for the 1964 military coup and dictatorship, by which Freire was considered an 'enemy of the state' and was immediately imprisoned and exiled.

During Freire's exile, he wrote several books reflecting on education as a means to achieve personal and societal transformation. In his most well-known work, *Pedagogy of the Oppressed*, he criticized 'banking education' (in which teachers 'deposit' knowledge in the minds of students), and proposed instead a problem-posing, dialogical pedagogy that respects learners' knowledge and encourages them to reflect critically on social reality. In Freire's theory of conscientization, the oppressed must be made aware of their own state of dehumanization and arise as 'historical subjects' to liberate both themselves and their oppressors, becoming 'human in the process of achieving freedom' (Freire 1970: 31).

Freire's work is connected to the rise of liberation theology in Brazil in the 1960s, which promoted the image of Christ as liberator of the oppressed, called for a preferential option of the poor, and supported local centres for political activism and mobilization for social rights. The simultaneous deepening and expansion of popular education traditions promoted education as a means for achieving social justice.[3] Freirean pedagogy and popular education principles have since been employed by Brazilian social movements and more recently by local education authorities. They have also been studied and adopted around the world, including in countries such as South Africa, Korea, the US, and Germany.

Critics question whether Freire's model, specific to the context of Northeast Brazil, is in fact applicable in other countries and social contexts. Even in Brazil, Freire's efforts to implement his pedagogical theories were twice interrupted, first in 1969 and then again in 1992 (as we will discuss in the following section), so it is difficult to determine what the results might have been if carried to fruition. Like many great thinkers, Freire has become something of an icon, whereas it is unquestionable that his work was also significantly supported and influenced by the simultaneous development of vibrant social movements, the strengthening of political groups such as the Worker's Party in Brazil, and the collaborative work of individuals such as Moacir Gadotti. Nevertheless, Freire has influenced educational thought around the world, particularly in connection with popular education, and he is cited as one of the strongest influencers in the South-North flow of ideas since the 1970s.

The remainder of our chapter will present two cases, both based on Freirean pedagogy, which have emerged as strong alternatives for citizenship learning in Brazil. The first describes a series of projects which are part of the *Citizen School movement*, aimed at transforming schools into sites for democratic participation and learning. The second section, on the *Landless Movement*, presents an example from organized civil society.

CITIZENSHIP, DEMOCRACY, AND FORMAL EDUCATION: THE CITIZEN SCHOOL MOVEMENT

The citizen school movement in Brazil, which started in the 1980s, is comprised of a broad, loosely affiliated collective of initiatives aimed at transforming educational spaces into democratic spaces, at connecting the curriculum to issues affecting the community, and at nurturing new practices of citizenship engagement. Since its beginnings, the citizen school movement called for the democratization of access, re-investments in public education, quality improvements in public schools, and relating school effectiveness to the educational and social realities of learners. It also sought an expansion and democratization of adult literacy and adult basic education programmes (O'Cadiz et al., 1998).

The citizen schools movement became formally incorporated into the formal education system in 1989, when Paulo Freire was appointed as Secretary of Education of São Paulo, the most populated Brazilian city and the one with the largest number of illiterates. Freire envisioned the citizen school as one that promotes the exercise of citizenship by all those who participate in it: 'It is a school of community and camaraderie for collective production of knowledge and freedom, a space that articulates rights and obligations and lives the tense experience of democracy' (Freire, cited in Gadotti, 2000: 2).[4]

From the position of Secretary of Education, Freire undertook reforms to replace the prevailing authoritarian model of education with more democratic forms of management, including partnerships with local groups for participatory decision-making processes regarding planning, implementation, and resource allocations.[5] This open system was intended to create more school autonomy and community responsibility, ensure more transparency, accountability, and sustainability of educational reforms, and allow schools and government the opportunity to elaborate education policies together (Bordignon et al., 1989; Gadotti 1997, 2000, 2006; Freire, 1996, 1998). The citizen school project of São Paulo made some accomplishments, but the process was interrupted in 1992 when the progressive coalition lost the municipal elections.[6] However, the more important contribution was to open the path for other citizen school projects to emerge and gain momentum, not only in São Paulo but also throughout Brazil.

Among them were the second generation of the citizen school project in São Paulo and the citizen school project of Porto Alegre, which deepened the original project and generated interesting innovative practices that have inspired educators around the world.

REBIRTH OF THE CITIZEN SCHOOLS IN SÃO PAULO: CEUS AND THE PARTICIPATORY BUDGET

The citizen schools movement was re-ignited in São Paulo during the municipal administration of Marta Suplicy (2001–2004), whose government spearheaded a variety of educational initiatives. Two initiatives worthy of note are the Unified Educational Centres (CEUs) and the Children's Participatory Budget (PB).

The Unified Educational Centres are large educational, cultural, and recreational centres built in the poorest neighbourhoods of São Paulo. The mandate of the CEU is not only to provide educational services but also to promote social interactions, participatory democracy and community development.[7] Each one of the 21 centres built during the Suplicy administration has classrooms, a community library, a community radio, sport facilities, a computer lab, a science lab, spaces for workshops and meetings, kitchens, cafeterias, art gallery, and a theatre. Each CEU is open seven days/week, and involves the local community in management, maintenance, and the hiring and firing of staff. The model of governance is based on participatory principles and includes participatory budgeting.[8]

The CEUs have succeeded in providing significant infrastructure and services to communities that have historically being denied them. In some CEUs, people have access to theatres, orchestras, second language courses, and swimming lessons for the first time. An evaluation conducted by the University of São Paulo also reported

that satisfaction among parents increases to 90 per cent among parents of children participate in the CEU's activities. The evaluation concluded that the CEUs contributed to innovative practices for the democratization of the use of public spaces and the allocation of public resources (Antunes and Gadotti, 2005; Gadotti, 2004; FIA, 2004).

The second programme, the Children's Participatory Budget, was launched in São Paulo in 2003 in 447 elementary schools and 21 CEUs. This initiative was inspired by the Convention of the Rights of the Child and by several municipal participatory budgeting experiments that matured during the 1990s throughout Brazil. The Children's PB aimed at increasing learners' opportunities to become historical subjects by encouraging them to express themselves freely, ask questions, dream collectively about the school they want, and exercise their citizenship to follow those dreams by making decisions about budget allocations in their schools and their communities. The Children's PB was not conceived as an extracurricular pedagogical project. Rather, it was incorporated into the instruction and evaluation of all subject areas.

The Children's PB model includes two phases. The first deals with school issues, and starts with familiarizing students with basic concepts related to democratic participation and decision-making processes. Children develop research methodologies competencies appropriate to their level, and start collecting data on their school. In the classroom, they discuss issues that require urgent solutions (e.g. infrastructure or the daily life of school), collect and analyze data, prepare reports outlining their top priorities for the school, and elect delegates to take those proposals to a forum of delegates. Delegates present to a general assembly at which the top ten school priorities are selected. A student committee is formed to mobilize resources to address the chosen priorities, to follow up on the implementation of decisions, and to keep students informed throughout the process.

The second phase – conceptualized as expanded participation – deals with neighbourhood and citywide issues. The process is similar to the first phase, but the field research deals with issues (environmental, social, infrastructural, etc.) that affect their region. Each school presents their priorities at a large gathering with delegates from all schools, and develops proposals with the main demands of children and adolescents for the São Paulo. These demands are presented in a public forum at City Hall to the mayor and city council, with the intention that they will be seriously considered in municipal planning, policies, and actions.

Although there are not yet thorough evaluations of the Children's PB in São Paulo, the team that coordinated the project was invited by the city of Fortaleza to develop a similar project, and Spaniard educator César Muñoz (2004) argues that it constitutes one of the most innovative school experiments of participatory democracy and citizenship learning.

CITIZEN SCHOOLS IN PORTO ALEGRE

In Porto Alegre, the citizen schools took a different form, starting with an ambitious open process to define collectively the guiding principles that would orient the democratization of public schools. This deliberative forum, known as the Constituent Congress of Education, took 18 months and involved four constituencies: students, parents, educators, and administrators. The debates of the Congress revolved around two questions: What school do we have, and what school do we want? The first led to a participatory diagnosis of the educational system, and the second to the collective production of normative guidelines.

The Congress approved 94 guidelines and principles, which became the philosophical and organizational foundations of the Citizen School project in Porto Alegre. Its final document stated that a democratic and high-quality public education is both a citizens'

right and a state's obligation. Democratic principles should be enacted through stakeholders' participation in school management and in access to knowledge. The Constituent Congress reaffirmed the humanist character of public education, and its consolidation as a public space in which knowledge and values are collectively created and participants become masters of their own destinies. The Congress concluded that its main task was the radical democratization of schools. This was operationalized in three main dimensions: democratization of management, democratization of access to the school, and democratization of access to knowledge.

The democratization of management included the institutionalization of direct elections for school principals, vice-principals, and school council representatives (which must include the four constituencies of students, parents, teachers, and administrators). These direct elections generated unprecedented levels of participation in the community: In the 1998 elections for principals, for instance, almost 30,000 people voted. Another tool for the democratization of management in Porto Alegre has been the school participatory budget, modelled after Porto Alegre's renowned municipal participatory democracy model. The Porto Alegre school PB aims at democratizing decision-making and information sharing, at facilitating participatory planning, and at increasing schools' financial autonomy. The Porto Alegre school PB differs from the São Paulo Children's PB in three ways: it includes the four constituencies and not only students, it operates within the budget cycle of the municipal board of education, and resources to implement the chosen proposals are already contemplated in the allocations of each budget cycle.

Additionally, the municipal educational system undertook a deep political and administrative reform that dismantled the traditional hierarchy. This vertical model – with the Secretary of Education on top and students at the bottom – was replaced by units linked through horizontal relations, and by a new logic that conceived administrative activities as means rather than as ends in themselves, and put them at the service of pedagogical activities rather than the other way around. As part of this model, an interdisciplinary action team was established in each region of the city to provide regular advice to schools on pedagogical and institutional matters, and more fluid school-community channels were developed and nurtured (Heron da Silva, 1999; Clovis, 2000; Gandin, 2007). The democratization of management was also nurtured with the creation of a municipal council of education, in which the majority of representatives belong to civil society organizations that are linked to the education sector. Moreover, there was a legal obligation to hold a municipal congress of education every four years with participation of all sectors of the educational community.

In sum, the Porto Alegre's Citizen School project was a collective political-pedagogical project based on principles of humanism, democracy, inclusion, and social justice. These principles were not imposed by a group of experts; they were discussed by the educational community throughout the city and adopted after 18 months of democratic deliberation and decision-making. The Congress believed that the role of public education is not only to prepare skilled workers for the market but also to develop happy human beings and autonomous, critical, active, caring, and creative citizens who can participate in the governance of their societies and promote social transformation. In this sense, the Porto Alegre's citizen schools became part of a larger project of radical democracy.

THE CITIZEN SCHOOL AS AN INCLUSIONARY AND DEMOCRATIC EDUCATIONAL MOVEMENT

The Citizen School movement, though still in its infancy, has made an important contribution to collective efforts towards educational and societal democratization. The projects carried out in São Paulo and Porto Alegre in the last 15 years represent a bold attempt by local educational authorities to reinvent the educational ideas and pedagogical principles of popular education to meet the challenges of the twenty-first century. For the Citizen School movement, public education is not only a social right, but also a space for the construction of democracy and active citizenship. The citizen school thus puts great emphasis in addressing the needs of those students who are socially and economically disadvantaged. Its curriculum is organized around the economic, social, cultural, and political life of the surrounding communities. In so doing, the citizen school not only attempts to promote a critical analysis of reality, but also to empower students and school communities to change that reality.

Despite significant achievements by the Citizen School project in both cities, some challenges still persist. Teacher training programmes offered in universities often do not support working with alternative curricula and pedagogical models. Indeed, a central challenge encountered by the staff coordinating the Citizen School project related to difficulties in reconciling teachers' established preconceptions of what constitutes essential content matter to be transmitted to students and the project's insistence on linking all curriculum areas to generative themes relevant to students (O'Cadiz et al., 2000; Clovis, 2000). Similarly, in both cities there was a small but vocal minority of teachers who resisted inclusion policies and democratic school practices. More significantly, the progressive coalitions that implemented the Citizen School projects in São Paulo and Porto Alegre are no longer in government, which means that some aspects of the project have been discontinued.

However, other aspects – particularly some democratic initiatives that have been rooted in practice – still continue in both cities. Some innovative projects of the Citizen School movement like the CEUs, the Children Participatory Budget, the Constituent

Congress and the School Participatory Budget are being studied by scholars and educational practitioners inside and outside Brazil, and noted as inspirations for educational systems that aim to transform schools into more democratic, inclusive, relevant, and social justice-oriented institutions (Gandin and Apple, 2004; Fischman and McLaren, 2000; Clovis, 2000; Muñoz, 2004; Clovis and Schugurensky, 2005). Furthermore, the Citizen School movement is now expanding to other Brazilian cities that are currently adopting several of its projects.

CITIZENSHIP LEARNING IN SOCIAL MOVEMENTS: *MOVIMENTO SEM TERRA*

The *Movimento Sem Terra* (MST), or the Landless Rural Workers movement, was founded upon the belief that as social and economic inequality in Brazil relates directly to unequal land distribution, the first step towards achieving equality and justice should be widespread agrarian reform. The newest manifestation in a history of Brazilian land reform movements, MST was born during the rise of liberation theology in the south of Brazil.

Today, MST is established in all 21 Brazilian states, and claims to have settled more than 500,000 families on 17 million hectares of land. The process has not been smooth, and has entailed varying degrees of contestation. However, MST has enjoyed relative freedom of action compared to prior land reform movements which were violently oppressed. It is no coincidence that MST's emergence mirrors the end of the military dictatorship: Brazil's move towards democracy has clearly created an opening for increased freedom of social action and citizen agency.

The MST platform closely follows a Freirean pedagogical model. Freire's theory of conscientization is central to the MST's vision of education for the transformation of society and construction of a new social order. Vilsom Santim, of the MST leadership,

states, 'The MST educates for life, educates in the sense of liberty, in the sense of exercising citizenship, ... for these values that point towards a new type of society' (cited in Dalmago, 2003: 11). João Pedro Stédile confirms this connection between education and citizenship:

> Solely the struggle for land will not transform subjects into citizens .... Agrarian Reform is the junction of these two things: having access to land, and having access to schooling ... If we do not democratize education, we will not be able to construct a society that is more just and more egalitarian (preface in Caldart, 1997: 25–26).

Thus, for the MST, agrarian reform is not only redistribution of land, but having the resources to sustain a decent life. The MST has built an extensive infrastructure, with sectors addressing education, health, production, the environment, gender, communications, international relations, and culture, at local, regional, and national levels. These sectors help the MST to play a dual function of supporting individuals to acquire land and to build a productive life, as well as of working strategically to generate action towards social transformation (Stédile and Gorgen, 1991; Betto, 2002; Dalmagro, 2003).

MST: A MODEL OF ACTIVE CITIZENSHIP LEARNING[9]

MST defines education as a process of human and societal transformation, not limited to schooling. In the movement, education itself is understood as inherently political, and all activities are conceived as connected to citizenship learning and community engagement (Madjidi, 2000). The first example of this is the process by which Landless People (*Sem Terra*) occupy and fight for their future land. For the MST, this is the ultimate act of conscientization, as individuals become historical subjects in the process of achieving their own freedom. Once land is won, the new community must organize its production, housing, health, schooling, and overall life in the settlements. In this way, the *Sem Terra* are practicing 'real utopia' (Fung and Wright, 2003), co-creating their own civic reality.

While MST views education as ubiquitous to its efforts, it also has pioneered direct pedagogical approaches on many levels. Education in the MST includes at least the following: primary schools in the settlements, itinerant schools in the encampments (occupation sites), literacy programmes, early childhood education, adult education, training of teachers, and special courses in areas such as women's rights, primary health care, micro-finance, and rural development (MST, 1996). In the patriarchal context of rural Brazil, it is relevant to note that 50 per cent of those attending all courses should be women and at least one term of the course should be used for discussing gender-related issues (Knijnik, 2001).

Citizenship learning in these varied educational contexts is practised in engaged ways. For children in itinerant schools (during a land occupation or march), they are participating in direct political activism while in school:

> Under trees, in a rented room, in soccer fields, in the middle of the road, in pavilions of parks where protests were happening, the classes continue; classes on citizenship, on reality, that create knowledge about life and about how to make it more beautiful, more just, more humane (MST, 1998a).

Teachers are forced to use their surroundings as their curriculum; for example, during a march the students count participants, or learn vocabulary for places and objects they pass by.

An adult literacy course in an MST settlement presents an equally active pedagogical format. Entering into the classroom, one would notice the benches and chairs set up in circular fashion, physically creating space for a 'co-intentional' learning process (Freire, 1997). Inspirational quotations, images of the land, and flags of Brazil and the MST would help create a contextual learning environment. The students would be instructed to cut out words from magazines to make an alphabet. However, they are not constructing just any alphabet—it is the 'ABC's of Land Reform.' The words they select must be related to this topic, such as 'Agrarian, Brazil, Citizenship, Democracy.' In this vein, curricula for each subject are based on students' reality and aimed to develop a sense of agency.

The MST also has a national, residential school to train its own educators. Consistent with MST democratic principles, this school is organized as a large cooperative, and students are expected to take collective responsibility for running it, including making decisions on timetables and curriculum (Caldart, 2000).

For the MST, framing its citizenship education within the context of Brazil means encouraging the *Sem Terra* to think critically about what it means to be Brazilian. For example, in 2000, the year of the 500th anniversary celebration of Brazil, MST held a contest asking *Sem Terra* children to respond through essay, poetry or art to the question: *Brazil, How Old are You?* The children's submissions demonstrated critical analysis, questioning the date Brazil was 'discovered' and depicting how the colonizers had treated the indigenous inhabitants of the land and the African slaves who fed its economic development. In another contest, children were asked to respond to the topic: *The Brazil We Want* (MST, 1998b). Pedagogically, this demonstrates an important aspect of citizenship education: envisioning the future. The children's responses are moving testaments to the vision of the 'Little Landless' for a better Brazil:

> The Brazil we want is a Brazil where everyone has social and economic equality ...
>
> The Brazil we want is a Brazil where I can wish you a good morning even without knowing you, even if you wear an earring and chains round your neck, even if you have dyed or bleached hair, if you are white, brown, Indian, or black ... This is why we are in this struggle: for a better country and better world.
>
> – Hernandes da Silva (16 years old) (Viera, 2002)

MST: CITIZENSHIP LEARNING FOR BRAZIL

Despite this hopeful vision, there are many challenges to be addressed. As a national movement, there can be inconsistency in application and implementation. Varying quality of leadership, combined with the willingness of local governments to work with the *Sem Terra*, can profoundly impact the process. Cases of violent occupations (or violent responses from landowners) have given the MST a bad reputation in some regions. Once families are settled there can be disenchantment/disengagement, as settlers continue to look to the MST leadership to provide services, demonstrating a still undeveloped sense of agency (Dalmagro, 2003). Related to this is the risk of indoctrination which is present in all processes of political education, including in social movements aiming at democratization. The application of critical thought (central to Freirean pedagogy) is thus particularly important in this context. Further challenges relate to globalization, such as whether agricultural life is still viable for the small farmer in the current world economy, and increasing rural-urban migration, particularly of youth, meaning that even with land, many will still move to the cities where they are likely to end up in *favelas* (urban slums) in poverty.

Nevertheless, the MST constitutes an enormous school of citizenship that provides crash courses in political awareness, collective values, and participatory democracy (Bogo, 1998; Kane, 2001). For Kane, the MST 'makes genuine efforts to promote democracy and participation, not feed people a 'party line' from above (as has happened in other left-wing organizations). This combination of open-ended educational enquiry ... makes it a case study of worldwide significance' (Kane, 2001: 107). Likewise, Miguel Carter, of the Oxford-based Centre for Brazilian Studies, notes that 'by improving the material conditions and cultural resources of its members, the landless movement has

fortified the social foundations for democracy in Brazil' (Martinez, 2007).

The final objective of the MST and its pedagogy is to develop conscious, historical subjects who are committed to building a new Brazil. The MST sees its work as intimately connected to citizenship: 'It is for love of this country Brazil that we keep marching ...!' (MST, 1998b: 10) The greatest challenge will be to translate the engaged citizenship learning practices of the MST that are so powerful while in 'the struggle' to a more permanent context of sustained action in building the Brazil the *Sem Terra* have envisioned.

CITIZENSHIP EDUCATION FOR THE TWENTY-FIRST CENTURY: REINVENTING FREIRE

In these pages, we have presented two exceptional, somewhat radical examples of Freirian-inspired citizenship education initiatives in Brazil. These examples – one in the context of municipal governments, the other in the context of social movements – are still peripheral within the national landscape, to the extent that many Brazilian educators know little about these models. However, we propose that they may in fact provide some of the most promising and workable ideas for an emancipatory citizenship education that have emanated from the Latin American region in the last decades.

From a pedagogical standpoint, Freirean ideas have fundamentally influenced the development of popular education movements and pedagogy inside and outside Brazil. The examples of the Citizen Schools and the *Movimento Sem Terra* show that this pedagogy holds exciting potential for the development of engaged, participatory models of citizenship education. Further, these frameworks ground citizenship learning as deeply motivated by values of justice, equality, and a belief in the inherent potential of every human being to co-create and define their civic reality.

These models are offered, not so that they may be replicated, but rather to be 'reinvented', as encouraged by Freire, in ways appropriate to local contexts. Perhaps, as Freire's educational principles once informed pedagogy around the world, these ideas can be creatively applied to citizenship education, as we search for models that promote new democratic potential in a global context.

NOTES

1 Two decades ago around 50 per cent of Brazilians were going hungry, and more recently 16.7 million are still undernourished (Burns, 1993; FAO, 2003).

2 Brazil was the last country in the Americas to officially abolish slavery in 1888, even though Portugal had already abolished slavery in 1761. Also, slavery in Brazil was not confined to the colonial mode of production. Today, the number of people working under conditions analogous to slavery ranges from 25,000 to 50,000. Most of these contemporary slaves are located in the Eastern Amazon region.

3 A key element of popular education is its commitment to promoting social justice. Although it includes a range of practices and ideological approaches, it often includes four features:

a) a rejection of the neutrality of adult education, which implies a recognition of the relations between knowledge and power and between structure and agency, and the acknowledgment that adult education can play a role to reinforce but also to challenge oppressive social relations;

b) an explicit political commitment to work with the poor and the marginalized, and to assist social movements in fostering progressive social and economic change;

c) a participatory pedagogy that focuses on the collective, departs from people's daily lived experiences and promotes a dialogue between popular knowledge and systematized (scientific) knowledge; and

d) an attempt to constantly relate education and social action, linking critical reflection with research, mobilization and organization strategies (Schugurensky, 2000).

4 'A Escola Cidadã é aquela que se assume como um centro de direitos e de deveres. O que a caracteriza é a formação para a cidadania. A Escola Cidadã, então, é a escola que viabiliza a cidadania de quem está· nela e de quem vem a ela. Ela não pode ser uma escola cidadã em si e para si. Ela é cidadã na medida mesma em que se exercita na construção da cidadania de quem usa o seu espaço. A Escola Cidadã é uma escola coerente com a liberdade. É coerente com o seu discurso formador, libertador. É toda escola que, brigando para ser ela mesma, luta para que os educandos-educadores também sejam eles mesmos. E como ninguém pode ser só, a Escola Cidadã é uma escola de comunidade, de companheirismo. É uma escola de produção comum do saber e da liberdade. É uma escola que vive a experiência tensa da democracia' (Escola Cidada. Interview with Paulo Freire by TV Educativa do Rio de Janeiro, March 19, 1997. Cited in Gadotti, 2000: 2)'

5 They argued since in a closed managerial system parents and students are seen only as users, and teachers and staff are only perceived as employees, they are are unlikely to participate because they do not feel responsible for the direction of education or entitled to take decisions.

6 Freire resigned as Secretary of Education in May 1991 to return to his academic duties at the university. One of his closest collaborators (Mário Sérgio Cortella) replaced him as Secretary of Education, but the initiative was interrupted when the Workers Party lost the municipal elections in 1992.

7 The educational philosophy of the CEUs was inspired by the pedagogical principles proposed by Freire, the Charter of the Earth and the learning communities movement. A learning community is conceptualized as an organized human community that creates and implements its own intergenerational educational and cultural projects to educate its members within the framework of endogenous development, cooperation, solidarity, and participatory democracy (Torres, 2001).

8 Participatory budgeting is a model of local democracy that includes citizen engagement in deliberation and decision-making processes around municipal expenditures. Since its beginnings in Porto Alegre in 1989, it has been implemented in hundreds of cities in all continents. In the last decade, several Children's Participatory Budgeting initiatives have been implemented in Brazil and in Spain.

For the purposes of this analysis, citizenship is understood as a multidimensional concept that connotes four dimensions: status, identity, civic virtues and agency. The first relates to issues of membership, the second to feelings of identity and belonging, the third to dispositions, values and behaviors, and the last to issues of engagement and political efficacy (Schugurensky, 2006).

REFERENCES

Antunes, A. and M. Gadotti (2005) *A ecopedagogia como pedagogia apropriada ao processo da Carta da Terra*. São Paulo: Instituto Paulo Freire.

Bertan, Levino (ed.) (2002) *Educacao, Sociedade e Cidadania*. Londrina, Brasil: Universidade do Oeste Paulista.

Bethell, Leslie (2000) 'Politics in Brazil: From Elections Without Democracy to Democracy without citizenship', [Electronic version] *Daedalus*, 129 (2).

Betto, Frei (2002) 'The Church and Social Movements', in Else R.P. Vieira (ed.), *The Sights and Voices of Dispossession: The Fight for the Land and the Emerging Culture of the MST (The Movement of the Landless Rural Workers of Brazil)*. Project hosted by the School of Modern Languages, University of Nottingham, UK; web site produced and designed by John Walsh. Retrieved online December 10, 2006, from http://www.landless-voices.org/vieira.

Bordignon, Genuino and Luiz S. Macedo de Oliveira (1989) 'A Escola Cidadã: Uma Utopia Municipalista' União Nacional de Dirigentes Municipais de Educação (UNDIME), *Cortez/Undime/Cead*, no. 4, May 1989, pp. 5–13.

Branford, Sue and Rocha, Jan (2002) *Cutting the Wire: The Story of the Landless Movement in Brazil*. London: Latin America Bureau.

Bogo, Ademar (1998) *A Vez dos Valores*. Sao Paulo, Brazil: Grafica e Editora Peres Ltda.

Burns, E. Bradford (1993) *A History of Brazil*. New York: Columbia University Press.

Caldart, Roseli Salete (2002) Movement of the Landless Rural Workers (MST): Pedagogical Lessons. In Vieira, E. (ed.) 2006. *The Sights and Voices of Dispossession: The Fight for the Land and the Emerging Culture of the MST (The Movement of the Landless Rural Workers of Brazil)*. Project hosted by the School of Modern Languages, University of Nottingham, UK; web site produced and designed by John Walsh. Retrieved online December 10, 2006, from http://www.land-less-voices.org/vieira.

Caldart, Roseli Salete (2000) *Pedagogia do Movimento Sem Terra:Eescola e Mais do que Escola*. Petropolis, Brasil: Editora Vozes Ltda.

Caldart, Roseli Salete (1997) *Educacao em Movimento: Formacao de Educadoras e Educadores no MST*. Petropolis, Brasil: Editora Vozes Ltda.

Cleary, David (1999) 'Race, Nationalism and Social Theory in Brazil: Rethinking Gilberto Freyre', working paper for the David Rockefeller Centre for Latin American Studies, Harvard University. Retrieved December 10, 2006, from http://www.transcomm.ox.ac.uk/working%20papers/cleary.pdf.

Clovis, José (2000) *Escola Cidadã: Desafios, Diálogos e Travessias*. Vozes, Petrópolis, 2000.

Clovis, J. and Schugurensky, D. (2005) 'Three Dimensions of Educational Democratization: The Citizen School project of Porto Alegre', *Our Schools/Our Selves,* 15 (1–81): 41–58.

Dalmagro, Sandra (2003) *The Pedagogical Significance of the Landless Movement: The Formation of Historical Subjects*. Paper presented at the Lifelong Citizenship Learning, Participatory Democracy and Social Change Conference, Transformative Learning Centre, Ontario Institute of Studies in Education/University of Toronto.

Demo, P. (2006) 'Avaliação: Para Cuidar que o Aluno Aprenda'. Criarp, São Paulo.

Fundação Instituto de Administração(FIA)/USP (2004) *Avaliação dos Centros Educacionais Unificados – CEUs*. São Paulo: FIA.

Fischman G. and McLaren P. (2000) 'Expanding Democratic Choices: Schooling for Democracy: Toward a Critical Utopianism', *Contem-porary Sociology*, 29 (1): 168–180.

Food and Agriculture Organization (FAO) (2003). Brazil: The Hunger of the Missed Meal. www.fao.org/english/newsroom/news/2003/13320-en.html.

Freire, Paulo (1998) *Pedagogy of Freedom: Ethics, Democracy and Civic Courage*. Rowman and Littlefield: Maryland.

Freire, Paulo (1996) *Pedagogy of Hope*. New York: Continuum.

Freire, Paulo (1970) *Pedagogy of the Oppressed*. New York: Continuum.

Fung, Archon and Wright, Erik Olin (2003) *Deepening Democracy: Institutional Innovations in Empowered Participatory Governance*. New York: Verso.

Gadotti, Moacir (2006) Decálogo da Escola Cidadã: Pacto por uma Nova Qualidade de Educacão. São Paulo: Instituto Paulo Freire.

Gadotti, Moacir (2004) Educação com quali-dade social: Projeto, implantação e desafios dos Centros Educacionais Unificados (CEUs). São Paulo: Instituto Paulo Freire.

Gadotti, Moacir (2000) *Escola Cidadã: Educacão para e pela Cidadania*. São Paulo: Instituto Paulo Freire.

Gadotti, Moacir (1997) 'Contemporary Brazilian Education: Challenges of Basic Education', in Adriana Puiggrós and Carlos Alberto Torres (eds), *Latin American Education: Comparative Perspectives*. Boulder, CO: Westview Press. pp. 123–148.

Gadotti, Moacir (1992) Escola Cidadã: Uma Aula sobre a Autonomia da Escola. São Paulo: Cortez.

Gandin, L. (2007) 'The Construction of the Citizen School Project as an Alternative to Neoliberal Educational Policies', *Policy Futures in Education*, 5 (2): 179–193.

Gandin, L. and M. Apple (2004) 'New Schools, New Knowledge, New Teachers: Creating the Citizen School in Porto Alegre, Brazil', *Teacher Education Quarterly*, 31 (1) (Winter): 173–198.

Goncalves e Silva, Petronilha (2004) 'Citizenship and Education in Brazil: The Contribution of Indian Peoples and Blacks in the Struggle for Citizenship and Recognition', In J. Banks (ed.), *Diversity and Citizenship Education: Global Perspectives*. San Francisco: Jossey-Bass.

Heron da Silva, Luiz (1999). *Escola Cidadã: Teoria e Prática*. Petropolis: Vozes.

Instituto Paulo Freire (1994) Projeto de Escola Cidadã: A Hora da Sociedade. São Paulo: Instituto Paulo Freire.

Iosif Guimaraes, Ranilce (2007) 'A Aprendizagem na Escola Pública Fundamental e o Comprometimento da Cidadania', PhD Dissertation, Universidade de Brasília.

IPEA (Instituto de Pesquisa Econômica Aplicada) (2005). Radar Social. Brasília: IPEA.

Kane, Liam (2001) *Popular Education and Social Change in Latin America*. UK: Latin American Bureau.

Knijnik, Gelsa (2001) 'Review of Chapter 4: Popular Education and the Landless People's Movement in Brazil', in Liam Kane (2001), *Popular Education and Social Change in Latin America*. UK: Latin American Bureau, pp. 108–110.

Langur, Hal (2006) 'Could this be Heaven or could this be Hell? Reconsidering the Myth of Racial Democracy in Brazil', *Ethnohistory*, 53 (3): 603–613.

Madjidi (Wiatt), K. (2000) 'Revolucão Humana: Stories of Struggle and Human Transformation within the Movimento Sem Terra'. Thesis, Stanford University, Stanford, CA.

Martinez, Nadia (2007) 'Latin America Rising, Democracy Rising: Grassroots Movements Change the Face of Power,' *YES! Magazine*, Summer 2007. http://yesmagazine.org/article.asp?ID=1730

Ministério da Educação e Cultura (1999). Parâmetros Curriculares Nacionais do Ensino Médio: bases legais. Brasília: Ministério da Educação/Secretaria de Educação Médio e Tecnológica.

Movimento dos Trabalhadores Rurais Sem Terra (1998a). *Escola Itinerante em Acampamentos do MST*. São Paulo: Grafica e Editora Peres Ltda.

Movimento dos Trabalhadores Rurais Sem Terra (1998b). *O Brasil que Queremos*. São Paulo: Grafica e Editora Peres Ltda.

Movimento dos Trabalhadores Rurais Sem Terra (1996). *Principios da Educacão no MST:Caderno de Educacão no. 8*. São Paulo: Grafica e Editora Peres Ltda.

Muñoz, César (2004) Pedagogia da Vida Cotidiana e Participação Cidadã. Cortez/IPF, Cortez, São Paulo.

Nunes, Michelle (2007) *Orcamento Participativo Crianca: Projeto Pedagógico Para a Cidadania*. Belo Horizonte, MG: Instituto Cultiva.

O'Cadiz, Maria, Lindquist Wong, Pia and Torres, Carlos A. (1998) *Education and Democracy. Paulo Freire, Social Movement and Educational Reform in Sao Paulo*. Boulder, CO: Westview Press.

Romão, J. (2004) 'Educacão e Cidadania', in J. Pinsk (ed.), *Práticas de Cidadania*. São Paulo: Contexto.

Samman, Emma (2005) 'Gini Coefficients for Subsidy Distribution in Agriculture,' Human Development Report Office: UNDP.

Sampaio, Plínio Arruda (2002). 'The Mìstica of the MST,' in Viera Else R P (ed.), *The Sights and Voices of Dispossession: The Fight for the Land and the Emerging Culture of the MST (The Movement of the Landless Rural Workers of Brazil)*. Resource ID: MSTICAOF657. http://www.landless-voices.org/vieira/ (accessed Jan. 4, 2008).

Schugurensky, Daniel (2000). 'Adult Education and Social Transformation: On Gramsci, Freire and the Challenge of Comparing Comparisons', *Comparative Education Review* 44 (4): 515–522.

Schugurensky, Daniel (2006). 'Adult Citizenship Education: An Overview of the Field,' in Tara Fenwick, Tom Nesbit and Bruce Spencer (eds.), *Contexts of Adult Education: Canadian Perspectives*. Toronto: Thompson Educational Publishing, Inc. pp. 68–80.

Siss, A., Silveira, C., Silva, M., Goncalves, M., Tura, M. and Maccariello, M. (1999) *Educacão e Cultura: Pensando em Cidadania*. Rio de Janeiro, Brasil: Quartet.

Stédile, J.P. and Gorgen, F.S.A. (1991) *Assentamentos: A Reposta Economica da Reforma Agraria*. Petropolis, Brasil: Editora Vozes Ltda.

Takahashi, Fábio (2007). 'Ensino público piorou mais que o privado', *Jornal Folha de São Paulo/ Folha Online, Caderno de Educação*, February 09, 2007, http://www1.folha.uol.com.br/folha/educacao/ult305u19359.shtml

Torres, Rosa Maria (2001) 'Learning communities: Re-thinking education through local development and learning', paper presented at the International Symposium on Learning Communities, Barcelona, 5–6 October.

United Nations Development Program (2006) Human Development Index Report, http://hdr.undp.org/hdr2006/statistics/.

Vieira, E. (ed.) (2006) *The Sights and Voices of Dispossession: The fight for the land and the emerging culture of the MST (The Movement of the Landless Rural Workers of Brazil)*. Project hosted by the School of Modern Languages, University of Nottingham, UK; web site produced and designed by John Walsh. Retrieved online December 10, 2006, from http://www.landless-voices.org/vieira.

World Bank (2004). *World Development Report*. Washington.

10

The Struggle for Citizenship Education in Canada: The Centre Cannot Hold

Andrew S. Hughes and Alan Sears

In August 2005 the Ministers of Education from member countries of the Organization of American States (OAS) met in Trinidad and Tobago on the theme 'Quality Education for a Democratic Citizenry' (OAS, 2005). The summit culminated with a commitment to a hemisphere-wide programme of education for democratic values and practices comprising 'a broad range of activities undertaken within the framework of the OAS to strengthen democracy through education' (OAS, 2006). The programme included a presentation by Judith Torney-Purta, Chair of the International Steering Committee for the Civic Education study of the International Association for the Evaluation of Educational Achievement (IEA) and a co-author of the OAS report, 'Strengthening Democracy in the Americas Through Civic Education: An Empirical Analysis Highlighting the Views of Students and Teachers' (Torney-Purta and Amadeo, 2004) that had been a focus for discussions at the summit. Dr. Torney-Purta had worked diligently to secure Canadian involvement at various stages of the IEA's and OAS's work on civic education so she took the opportunity afforded by the meeting to talk with the Canadian delegation. She found them largely unaware of the citizenship education research work of the IEA, Canada's involvement in Phase 1 and its absence from Phase 2 of the Civic Education Study; nor were they much aware of the state of citizenship education in Canada generally and certainly no one in the delegation was in a position to speak for Canada.

We relate this vignette not by way of criticism of the individuals in the Canadian delegation but to illustrate the central fact of public education in Canada. Quite simply, it is impossible to speak of Canadian education in any legal or formal sense. To be sure, there is education and schooling in Canada but it falls under the direction and governance of each of the 13 provinces and territories; there is no federal ministry of education. Coordination and collaboration is minimal, particularly in citizenship education, with a nod toward pan-Canadian interests provided by the Council of Ministers of Education

Canada (CMEC) (Note that in Canada we dare not speak of national interests; rather convention dictates that they are pan-Canadian). The Canadian delegation's response to Dr. Torney-Purta reinforced her view that compared with many other jurisdictions, civic education in Canada is simply not a priority (Hughes and Sears, 2006).

CANADA AS PART OF THE INTERNATIONAL CONSENSUS IN CITIZENSHIP EDUCATION

Over the past 15 years a pervasive consensus about citizenship education has been growing across the democratic world. That consensus consists of four central elements: a sense of crisis about the state of democratic citizenship; a belief that the crisis can and should be addressed by effective citizenship education; a commitment to a largely civic republican conception of citizenship and a move toward constructivist approaches to teaching and learning as best practice in citizenship education. Canada shares in all aspects of this consensus.

The crises of citizenship

There has been a sense of crisis or, more accurately, overlapping crises in democracies around the world about the disengagement of citizens from participation in even the most basic elements of civic life. This concern is commonly expressed in both academic literature and popular media and often called a 'democratic deficit' (Cook and Westheimer, 2006: 349). We will not discuss it in detail here but Table 10.1 provides an overview of the overlapping crises of ignorance, alienation and agnosticism underlying this widespread concern particularly as regards young people. A number of critics have questioned the degree to which these crises accurately reflect the nature of young citizens' knowledge about and engagement in civic processes in Canada and elsewhere but, nevertheless, they permeate literature and policy statements in the area of civic education (For a fuller discussion see, Sears and Hyslop-Margison, 2006, 2007; Chareka and Sears, 2006).

In Canada the sense of crisis around young citizens' lack of knowledge has been well illustrated in books over many years with provocative titles such as *So Little for the Mind* (Neatby, 1953), *What Culture?*

Table 10.1 Perceived crises of citizenship

Crises	Manifested by	Signs of Health
Ignorance of civic institutions and processes	Widespread disengagement from the political process (e.g. not voting or joining political parties).	Re-engagement with the political process at both the formal and non-formal levels.
Alienation from politics and civil society	Widespread disengagement from nonformal civil associations (e.g., volunteer or charitable associations; any form of community activism).	Active participation in the affairs of civil society.
Lack of interest in and commitment to the values of democracy and democratic citizenship. (Agnosticism)	Rise in political and social extremism (e.g., neo-nazi and skin-head groups).	Willingness to pursue non-violent and respectful political protest (e.g., peaceful protest and political action).
	Rise in violent/destructive destructive forms of political engagement (e.g., violent protests linked to meetings of the World Trade Organization).	

What Heritage? (Hodgetts, 1968), and *Who Killed Canadian History?* (Granatstein, 1998). In the introduction of a recent special issue of the *Canadian Journal of Education* on the theme of democratic citizenship education, Cook and Westheimer (2006: 349) write, 'Canadians' knowledge about public issues and, perhaps more importantly their ability to connect particular perspectives on these issues to political parties and candidates is disturbingly low.' A series of books and reports have lamented various manifestations of youth disengagement, particularly record low voter turnouts among 18–22 year-olds. One of these was provocatively sub-titled, 'Is Canadian Democracy in Crisis?' (CRIC, 2001, 2004; Milner, 2002; Gidengil et al., 2004). Finally, concerns about citizens' lack of commitment to democratic values, particularly those of acceptance and accommodation of diversity, is evident in the ubiquitous concern for promoting 'social cohesion' which shows up in policy discourse in Canada (Russell, 2002; Joshee, 2004; Bickmore, 2006).

Faith in citizenship education

As other chapters in this volume make clear, across the democratic world jurisdictions have largely chosen to address the crises of citizenship through renewed commitment to citizenship education. While Canada has not seen nearly the same level of engagement in reform of citizenship education, a tacit commitment to it as central to public schooling is evident in curriculum and policy documents across the country.

The Province of British Columbia (BC Ministry of Education, 2004: 3–4), for example, identifies citizenship as a key goal of public schooling. In outlining the qualities of high school graduates the Ministry of Education writes:

In their human and social development, graduates should achieve:

The knowledge and skills required to be socially responsible citizens who act in caring and principled ways, respecting the diversity of all people

and the rights of others to hold different ideas and beliefs.

The knowledge and understanding they need to participate in democracy as Canadians and global citizens, acting in accordance with the laws, rights and responsibilities of democracy.

Similarly, the Province of Saskatchewan, for example, describes 'the ultimate aim' of social studies education as graduating 'students who have a sense of themselves as active participants in and citizens of an interdependent world' (Saskatchewan Learning, 1999).

At the other end of the country the Atlantic Provinces Education Foundation (n.d.) identifies citizenship as one of six 'Essential Graduation Learnings' for public schooling across the region. In its recently released vision statement for the future of Education in New Brunswick the Provincial Government (Province of New Brunswick, Education, 2007: 14) states that 'one of the prime responsibilities of public education is ... to engage students in understanding citizenship and their role as active citizens in society.' Lest we think this focus on citizenship as a central goal for public education is exclusive to English Canada, Quebec's Ministry of Education (Gouvernment du Quebec, 2005: 10) contends, 'Quebec's elementary and secondary schools are being encouraged to emphasize citizenship and intercultural education based on the great diversity of their students' geographical origins, mother tongues and cultural roots.'

Ministries of education in Canada are not alone in identifying education for citizenship as central to the educational enterprise. The Canadian Teachers' Federation (Wall et al., 2000: 5) claims that 75 per cent of teachers support the idea 'that the role of public education is to provide a well-balanced general education to prepare children for life and to assume the responsibilities of good citizenship.' More recently, a series of public opinion surveys in Canada demonstrate support for a wide range of purposes for public schooling, 'but the two dominant goals emerging from such polls are preparing students for the world of work and preparing them for citizenship' (Leithwood et al., 2003: 5; see also, Ungerleider, 2003).

The civic republican ideal

International consensus exists not only at the level of deciding that citizenship education should be a priority, but also in regard to the kind of citizenship that ought to be the focus of that education. Although declining youth voting rates is a key empirical factor often cited as a reason for concern about citizenship, most jurisdictions expect citizens to be engaged in much broader ways than simply through voting (Hughes and Sears, 2006). In McLaughlin's (2000: 550) terms, for example, initiatives in England call for a 'maximal' rather than 'minimal' approach to citizenship; that is, citizens are expected to go far beyond minimal requirements of voting and obeying the law to be actively engaged in both the formal mechanisms of the political system and the grassroots community involvement of civil society. Cunningham (2002) demonstrates that several contemporary approaches to democratic citizenship including participatory and deliberative democracy are consistent with more ancient civic republican approaches in focusing on active engagement focused on seeking common goods and building a sense of community or social cohesion. This civic republican (Barber, 1992; Abowitz and Harnish, 2006) approach to citizenship with its emphasis on the obligation to participate actively in shaping society at all levels is endemic to definitions of citizenship and citizenship education across the democratic world.

For the past several decades an active approach to citizenship education including the fostering of a sense of agency has been core in curriculum policy across Canada (Sears and Hughes, 1996; Sears et al., 1999). This is well illustrated in British Columbia where active citizenship is mandated at every level of the curriculum. In the elementary

social studies curriculum (British Columbia Ministry of Education, 1998), for example, students are expected each year to identify relevant issues and take some action to address them; from kindergarten where teachers are to 'challenge students to plan a course of action that leads to an improvement in the school environment' (p. 20), through grades two and three where students might 'contact a representative of a local environmental group or of the provincial or federal environment ministry and discuss ways in which the class could practice global citizenship' (p. 32), to grade five where working in the context of studying their region:

> it is expected that students will: identify and clarify a problem, issue, or inquiry; gather and record a body of information from a variety of primary and secondary sources; develop alternative interpretation from varied sources [and] design, implement, and assess strategies to address community problems or projects' (p. 44).

This trend of engaging students in civic action in ever wider contexts is present throughout the elementary curriculum culminating in attention to global issues at grades six and seven. BC also mandates a substantial project in civic action as the heart of the new high school Civics Studies 11 curriculum (British Columbia Ministry of Education, 2005).

Alberta is similar in focusing curricular attention on civic agency from elementary school onward with specific curricular outcomes related to this idea appearing at virtually every grade level (Alberta Education, 2005) and Manitoba has implemented a programme of grants to schools for innovative projects that engage students in civic action (Manitoba Education Citizenship and Youth, 2006). The goals of the grade eight curriculum in Saskatchewan are saturated with language related to civic agency calling for students who are able to: 'make reflective decisions and participate in society as responsible citizens;' 'take action' consistent with democratic values, and 'recognize that they have the opportunity to shape their future' (Saskatchewan Learning, 1999). Other jurisdictions recognize agency as central to citizenship but often in a much more general sense. In the Atlantic Provinces, for example, commitment to active civic engagement is expressed more generically with phases such as, 'students will be expected to take age appropriate actions to demonstrate their responsibilities as citizens' (APEF, n.d: 16).

Constructivism as best practice

In addition to this wide agreement regarding the civic republican nature of good citizenship, there is consensus across Canada and around the world that best practice in citizenship education is broadly constructivist in character and must engage students in meaningful activities designed to help them make sense of, and develop competence with, civic ideas and practices (See, for example, Carnegie Corporation of New York and CIRCLE: Center for Information & Research, on Civic Learning & Engagement, 2003; Deakin Crick et al., 2005). Active approaches to citizenship education advocated as best practice around the world generally flow from constructivist theories of teaching and learning and call for students to be engaged in substantive study of authentic and important issues related to citizenship. While the terms are often loose and not clearly defined, contemporary curricula across Canada, including those in social studies, where citizenship most commonly finds its place, are infused with the language of constructivism. Quebec is most overt about this, arguing that 'the development of competencies and the mastery of complex knowledges, call for practices that are based on the constructivist approach to learning' (Gouvernment du Quebec, 2001: 5). Even where the term is not used explicitly, constructivism informs discussions of teaching and learning in curriculum documents across the country. Good teaching and learning are described as, among other things, 'collaborative, issues-based, interactive and participatory' and students are described as being engaged in an 'active process of constructing meaning' (APEF, n.d..: 29–30) all hallmarks of what is broadly referred to as constructivist teaching (Windschitl, 2002).

A growing body of international research demonstrates a strong association between classrooms, schools and communities that encourage active engagement of young people around critical social and civic issues and positive citizenship outcomes. Evidence from the IEA study of 90,000 students in 28 countries confirms this indicating that 'schools that operate in a participatory democratic way, foster an open climate for discussion within the classroom and invite students to take part in shaping school life are effective in promoting both civic knowledge and engagement' (Torney-Purta et al., 2001: 176).

CANADIAN NUANCES

Hébert and Wilkinson (2002: 3) point out that Canada's unique history and mix of peoples has meant that 'Canadian citizenship exists today within multi-layered belongings and complex understandings.' Therefore, while Canadian educational jurisdictions are clearly in sync with recent developments and policy directions in citizenship education across the democratic world, there are nuances in Canadian policy and practice that deserve comment. Two of those are Canada's emphasis on and particular approaches to diversity and social cohesion.

Several recent publications document the considerable shift in Canadian society generally, and in Canadian education in particular, since 1960 with regard to diversity (Bruno-Jofré and Aponiuk, 2001; Hébert, 2002; Kymlicka, 2007). Troper (2002), for example, describes the substantial change in Canadian social policy over the years, particularly in the area of immigration, and the corresponding growth and recognition of diversity in the country. Until after the Second World War, he argues, Canadian public policy was designed to keep out immigrants who did not fit the dominant White, British culture, and to assimilate any people already in the country who did not fit that mould. With the Citizenship Act of 1947, Troper contends, policy began to shift and today multiculturalism is presented 'as the true and only basis of Canadian Identity' (p. 159). This move to a liberal pluralist (Castles, 2004) approach to diversity policy is not unique to Canada but, as Kymlicka (2003: 374) points out, Canada is unique both in the range of diversity present in the country, and 'in the extent to which it has not only legislated but also constitutionalized practices of accommodation.'

Concurrent with this shift in public policy generally has been a shift in policy and practice in education. Until at least the end of the second World War, 'the aim of public schools in Canada was to create a homogenous nation built on a common English language, a common culture, a common identification with the British Empire and an acceptance of British institutions and practices' (Bruno-Jofré, 2002: 113). Battiste and Semaganis (2002: 93) describe something of this 'cognitive imperialism' as it applied to Aboriginal peoples, arguing it was, and for them largely still is, an attempt to extinguish 'Aboriginal conceptions of society.' Most would argue, however, that policy and practice in education have changed significantly to the point where 'during the past thirty years, public schools have been the primary area where multiculturalism has been implemented as the new conception of identity formation' (Bruno-Jofré and Henley, 2001: 51).

Joshee (2004) traces shifts in educational policy from the 'ideal of assimilation' (p. 138), through 'cultural diversity and citizenship' (p. 140) and 'focus on identity' (p. 141), to 'social justice and education' (p. 144), and, more recently, 'social cohesion' (p. 146). Although she describes the latter as somewhat of a retreat from a more activist promotion of diversity, it is clear that schools which were once mandated to eliminate diversity have become, officially at least, 'more concerned with the concept of inclusion – how to teach for tolerance, develop respect for diversity, and entrench anti-racism and equality programs in school curricula' (Shields and Ramsay, 2004: 43).

One of the most overt manifestations of this focus on developing understanding and acceptance of diversity in citizenship education is the pervasive focus on perspective taking in the Alberta social studies curriculum. In laying out the rationale for the programme the curriculum document states, 'Central to the vision of the Alberta social studies program is the recognition of the diversity of experiences and perspectives and the pluralistic nature of Canadian society' (Alberta Education, 2005: 1–4). While the Alberta curriculum mandates teaching about a wide diversity of perspectives 'for historical and constitutional reasons' (p. 4) there is a particularly strong focus on Aboriginal and Francophone perspectives and experiences. Other Canadian jurisdictions also identify the development of understanding of and respect for multiple perspectives as central to social studies.

Recent events around the world and particularly in Europe have caused many countries to rethink diversity and multiculturalism policies and focus on social cohesion. One of the most obvious of these has been proposals to teach 'Britishness' in schools in the UK (Garner, 2007). Canada too has a significant policy focus on social cohesion (Russell, 2002; Joshee, 2004) but the difference is that this is just the latest manifestation of a ubiquitous concern for developing a sense of national identity that has permeated citizenship education in Canada from at least the mid-1940s (Sears, 1996; Osborne, 2001). The search for a single sense of national identity has largely been abandoned but the focus on developing a deep commitment to social cohesion has not.

This commitment is demonstrated in social studies curriculum documents across the country. One of the most explicit expressions of this concern is found in Quebec. The introduction to the primary-elementary curriculum in that province states, 'In a plu-ralistic society such as ours, schools must act as agents of social cohesion by fostering a feeling of belonging to the community and teaching students how to live together' (Gouvernment du Quebec, 2001: 3). A sim-ilar focus on promoting social cohesion is central to social studies curriculum docu-ments from coast to coast. The front matter for the new Alberta curriculum has a section titled 'Pluralism: Diversity and Cohesion' (Alberta Education, 2005: 8) and the Ontario Civics curriculum expresses similar sentiments, if in different language, when it proposes challenging questions that Canadian citizens must be equipped to tackle including: 'As our population becomes more diverse, how do we ensure that all voices are heard? How do we resolve important societal and community issues in the face of so many diverse and divergent views influenced by differing values?' (Ontario Ministry of Education, 2005: 63).

Neither the focus on developing under-standing of and respect for diverse perspec-tives nor a commitment to social cohesion are unique to citizenship education in Canada. Because of its particular history and mix of peoples, however, Canada has overtly wrestled with these issues for longer than most jurisdictions and has developed a sig-nificant body of scholarship dealing with both (see, for example, Taylor and Laforest 1993; Cairns, 2000; Bruno-Jofré and Aponiuk, 2001; Hébert, 2002; Kymlicka, 1998, 2003, 2007; Banting et al., 2007).

CANADA DABBLES AS THE WORLD MOVES ON

With some nuances then, Canada is largely in step with the widespread international con-sensus around citizenship education. Looking beyond the rhetoric, however, exposes the extraordinarily weak commit-ment of educational jurisdictions in Canada

to implementing strong programmes in the area. In Canada, we simply do not have the capacity to provide a national response and there seems to be no stomach for the struggle that would be required to create such a capacity. There are a number of ways this lack of commitment shows up but it is partic-ularly evident when comparing what others have done to build capacity to support citi-zenship education to the largely 'unfunded mandates' (Howard et al., 2004: 207) of Canadian provinces. We will examine this capacity building in four areas:

- the development of clear, consistent and widely accepted goals or outcomes for establishing directions and formulating standards;
- the provision and/or the development of curricu-lum materials to support both teaching and learning in citizenship education;
- the provision of substantive programmes for teacher development at both pre- and in-service levels; and
- the funding of research and development to sup-port policy and programme development as well as teaching and learning in citizenship education.

Many international jurisdictions have built capacity in some of these areas; some have built capacity in all. Canada has built sub-stantial capacity in none.

Clear, consistent and widely accepted goals

In our work with undergraduate teacher edu-cation students we spend some time examin-ing research related to goal setting as it relates to teaching. The evidence is clear. Students do much better when teachers set specific but flexible goals and take steps to encourage students to personalize those goals (Marzano et al., 2001). What works for stu-dents in classrooms can also work for educa-tors in the field. They will have a much better chance of attaining goals that are clear to them, that they can work toward in a variety of ways, and which they have personalized or made their own. Our experience is that in Canada educational goal setting is largely an obscure activity that excludes practitioners and the public more generally and, consequently, school district personnel and teachers are often not clear on what it is that is expected of them (Shields and Ramsay, 2004).

Around the world, national jurisdictions such as Australia (Civic Experts Group, 1994), England (Advisory Group on Citizenship, 1998) and the US (Carnegie Corporation of New York, and CIRCLE, 2003; Torney-Purta and Vermeer, 2004) as well as pan-national organizations such as the Council of Europe (2005) have fostered extensive public and professional discussions of citizenship and citizenship education. In some jurisdictions (Australia and England) these began with government commissions and in others (US) private sector groups took the lead but in all the discussions were substantive and provided the groundwork for moving forward in other areas.

No such broad, open consultations have taken place around the development of standards for citizenship education in Canada. In fact, as a number of commentators point out, curriculum goals in social studies (the subject where citizenship education is most explicitly addressed) are often borrowed almost unchanged from the United States (Clark, 2004; Shields and Ramsay, 2004;). In writing about difficulties implementing democracy in many former communist states in Eastern Europe, Tsilevich (2001: 156) contends that a key issue is the importation of democratic ideas developed over many years in the West. He writes, 'Post-Communist countries [are] consumers, rather than co-authors, of this modern and generally accepted liberal democratic political philosophy.' We believe the same difficulty plagues educational goals and objectives in Canada. The educators expected to implement them are treated as consumers of the ideas and not co-authors. This results in a lack of understanding of and commitment to the goals and often hinders effective implementation.

The production and dissemination of curriculum materials

A key enterprise in the successful introduction of new programmes is the production and dissemination of curriculum materials. We mean this in two ways: first, the production of quality curriculum guidelines oriented toward teachers, with clear and flexible standards and ideas of how to implement those standards; and, second, the production and dissemination of quality materials oriented toward pupils to support the teaching and learning of the intended curriculum. In the case of the former, the Canadian experience is mixed. The move to outcomes or standards-based curricula over the past ten years has been rooted in the idea of developing clear and attainable expectations for student achievement expressed in performance terms. In the area of cultural understanding, for example, students in Atlantic Canada are expected before the end of grade six to be able to, among other things: 'Use examples of material and non-material elements of culture to explain the concept of culture' (Atlantic Provinces Education Foundation, n.d.:18).

This kind of broad key stage outcome is then broken down to more specific expectations at particular grade levels. So, for example, at grade five students focus their learning about culture on Aboriginal Peoples in Canada and are expected to be able to 'explain the importance of oral tradition in early Aboriginal societies' or 'describe traditions from early Aboriginal Societies that are part of contemporary Canada' (Council of Atlantic Ministers of Education and Training, 2005).

These kinds of outcomes or standards are consistent with promising practices in that they are clear and flexible expressions of goals as discussed above. They state what is expected but allow for significant variation in the content and activities that might be used to attain them. This flexibility indicates a high degree of respect for teacher professionalism.

A key concern, however, is that many teachers, particularly elementary teachers, have very limited backgrounds in citizenship education and moving from standards to actual lesson and unit plans proves difficult (Shields and Ramsay, 2004). Our experience with new teachers indicates they often do not know where to begin and curriculum guidelines often provide very little guidance. The new social studies curriculum in Alberta, for example, includes clear outcome expectations at both general and specific levels but offers virtually no help for teachers in how to attain them (Alberta Education, 2005). This lack of direction and support is common across Canada.

Some new curricula, however, are beginning to extend a helping hand. A new grade seven curriculum in Atlantic Canada, for example, uses a multiple column format to include suggested activities for teaching to outcomes (New Brunswick Department of Education Educational Programs and Services Branch, 2004). The document also includes specific ideas for developing and employing this instrument to assess students' progress toward the standards. These ideas are presented as suggestions and are not intended to be compulsory or comprehensive. In this sense, they do not violate the principle of flexibility outlined above but they do provide teachers with a starting point for effective practice. Curriculum guides that build capacity to implement effective citizenship education need to include clear, specific and flexible outcome statements as well as accessible teaching and assessment ideas to help teachers effectively plan and monitor instruction.

Shields and Ramsay (2004) point out that a key challenge facing elementary school teachers across Canada is accessing quality materials for teaching social studies generally and citizenship education in particular. For the most part, Canadian teachers depend on resources from their provincial ministries of education, often in the form of approved textbooks. There is no equivalent of the Curriculum Corporation in Australia providing materials on a national scale. While NGOs and businesses in Canada do produce a range of materials for citizenship education there is not the same level of collaboration and coordination that can be seen between NGOs such as the Citizenship Foundation and Community Service Volunteers and the associated governmental departments in England.

Teacher development

In education, as in other professions, we are fully aware that the best policies and materials will come to naught without well-educated and skilful professionals to implement them. In his history of the Canada Studies Foundation (CSF), Grant (1986) argues that the lasting impact of the organization can largely be attributed to the creation of a significant cadre of expert teachers which ensured the organization's reforms would have wide and ongoing impact. Some 30,000 Canadian teachers had some form of in-service training related to CSF projects. In addition, 1,300 teachers were intimately involved in the development of the materials and the provision of workshops for their colleagues. The latter, Grant contends, built on this professional experience to become leaders in schools, districts and ministries of education.

The importance of teacher development is widely recognized in citizenship education initiatives in many parts of the world. There is nothing in Canada to compare with the breadth and depth of the professional development components of Australia's Discovering Democracy programme or the Citized initiative in England. The preparation of teachers who might have some citizenship education responsibility is subsumed within larger subject areas such as history or social studies teaching. And furthermore, when teachers are assigned their school responsibilities, there is no particular requirement that their academic and professional qualifications match their teaching assignment. It would sometimes appear that being a citizen is often viewed as adequate qualification for being a teacher of citizenship. Any attention to citizenship education at the pre-service and in-service levels is sporadic, episodic and dependant upon individual initiative rather than system-wide commitments.

Research and development to support policy and practice

When the Citizenship Order took effect in England in 2002, policy and programme developers realized full well that 'the evidence base concerning citizenship education was weak' (Cleaver et al., 2005: 1) but they moved forward to implement the citizenship curriculum order using the evidence that was available. They were not, however, satisfied to leave the research base where it was. With extensive support from the DfES, a multi-layered system of research, monitoring and assessment was put into place. In the US the Department of Education has supported research on citizenship through the National Assessment of Educational Progress (NAEP) as well as funding participation in the IEA study.

In comparison the research base for citizenship education in Canada is weak and fragmented. The Federal Government, through the Department of Secretary of State/Canadian Heritage, has sponsored some work with the Council of Ministers of Education over the years including a review of policy and practice in Canada (Sears and Hughes, 1996) and Canadian participation in Phase 1 of the IEA civic education study which constituted the development of a national case study of the intended curriculum (Sears et al., 1999). While the CMEC cooperated with that phase of the IEA study, it declined to participate in Phase 2. The result was that Canada did not have the opportunity to collect important base-line information on student knowledge, skills and attitudes with regard to citizenship as well as on teaching practices in the field. That information was collected in 28 countries and has been important in fostering informed discussion of citizenship education in them.

In the late 1990s the CMEC and Statistics Canada did include citizenship education in its first round of commissioned papers for the Pan-Canadian Educational Research Initiative (Sears et al., 2000). That paper set out a series of proposed research questions designed to develop a national consensus around definitions of citizenship, appropriate pedagogical approaches for citizenship education and the academic and professional education necessary for teachers in the field. A similar proposal for a national research agenda in citizenship education had been made in 1998 by the Citizenship Research Education Network (CERN), a collaboration of university-based researchers and policy makers, but neither of these ever received coordinated attention or funding. There are a number of strong individual and collaborative research programmes in citizenship education in Canada as is evidenced by two recent special editions of journals focused on citizenship education (Hébert et al., 2005; Cook and Westheimer, 2006), but beyond the largely voluntary efforts of members of CERN little has been done to provide capacity to link these or mechanisms to disseminate the results of the research to policy makers and practitioners.

CONCLUSION

In 1994 one of the participants in a Delphi study designed to garner consensus among 100 prominent Canadians about the key features of democratic citizenship argued strongly that traditional skills in reading, writing, speaking and other forms of communication were absolutely essential for effective citizenship. What is the use of the right to free speech, he contended, if a person has no ability to express himself or herself effectively? Such a person has the right but no remedy – no way to access or operationalize it – and rights without remedy are meaningless (Hughes, 1994).

We see a clear connection between this analysis and the findings outlined here. All the jurisdictions reviewed mandate a civic republican approach to citizenship education and agree on the broad parameters of what constitutes best practice. Further, all agree that classroom, school and community structures need to be consistent with the democratic principles being learned in that they provide opportunity for students, teachers and community members to work together to shape school practice and procedures and foster civic engagement among students.

These kinds of educational policies and mandates without the capacity to carry them out provided by clear goals, accessible materials, appropriate training and access to reliable research and policy information, however, put practitioners at all levels in the position of the citizen with the right to speak but no capacity to do so. They have the right, in fact the obligation, to pursue the policies of the state but without access to the human and material resources necessary they find it impossible to infuse life into the inert requirements of public policy and programme directives. This, we would argue, is exactly the position in which Canada has placed its educators in the area of citizenship education. Other nations, and even international groups with common interests, that face similar challenges to those we find in Canada, have moved forward to build capacity to support quality teaching and learning related to democratic citizenship; Canada has not. The building of capacity is best practice in any professional field and all other good practice depends on it.

It seems to us that a key component in moving forward in Canada will be leadership at the national level and that the Federal Government needs to be involved. The myth that education is purely a provincial concern in Canada is belied by years of substantial federal involvement in areas including technical and vocational education, second language education and information technology – just to name a few. A key part of federal involvement in those areas, and in citizenship education in the past, has been in building

just the kinds of capacities other jurisdictions have more recently built for citizenship education (See, for example, Hodgson, 1976, 1988; Sears, 1997). Whether that national leadership comes from the Council of Ministers of Education in consultation with the Federal Government or through some other mechanism it is crucial, in our view. Few of the separate provinces, if any, have the capacity to create the kind of support structures we see in the other jurisdictions examined here. Surely, if federal nation states with strong commitments to local control of education like Australia and the US and trans-national bodies like the European Community can work together to create common purposes and approaches in citizenship education, Canada can as well. Without some sort of wider national – or pan-national – leadership in the field citizenship education in Canada will continue to languish in comparison to other jurisdictions. To borrow from Yeats, in the current system, 'things fall apart; the centre cannot hold.'

REFERENCES

Abowitz, K.K. and Harnish, J. (2006) 'Contemporary Discourses of Citizenship,' *American Educational Research Journal*, 37 (4): 877–907.

Advisory Group on Citizenship (1998) *Education for Citizenship and the Teaching of Democracy in Schools: Final Report of the Advisory Group on Citizenship*. London: Qualifications and Curriculum Authority.

Alberta Education (2005). *Social Studies K–12*. Retrieved August 29, 2005, from http://www.education.gov.ab.ca/k_12/curriculum/bySubject/social/sockto3.pdf

Atlantic Provinces Education Foundation (n.d.) *Foundation for the Atlantic Canada Social Studies Curriculum*. Halifax: Atlantic Provinces Education Foundation.

Banting, K., Courchene, T.J., and Seidle, L. (eds) (2007) *The Art of the State Volume III: Belonging? Diversity, Recognition and Shared Citizenship in Canada*. Montreal: The Institute for Research on Public Policy.

Barber, B.R. (1992) *An Aristocracy of Everyone: The Politics of Education and the Future of America*. New York: Ballantine Books.

Battiste, M. and Semaganis, H. (2002). 'First Thoughts on First Nations Citizenship Issues in Education,' in Y. Hébert (ed.), *Citizenship in Transformation in Canada*. Toronto: University of Toronto Press. pp. 93–111.

Bickmore, K. (2006) 'Democratic Social Cohesion (assimilation)? Representations of Social Conflict in Canadian Public School Curriculum,' *Canadian Journal of Education*, 26 (2): 359–386.

British Columbia Ministry of Education (1998) *Social Studies K to 7: Integrated Resource Package 1998*. Victoria: British Columbia Ministry of Education.

British Columbia Ministry of Education (2004) *The Graduation Program 2004*. Victoria: Author.

British Columbia Ministry of Education (2005) *Civic Studies 11(Final Draft: April 2005): Intergrated Resource Package 2005*. Victoria: Ministry of Education, Province of British Columbia.

Bruno-Jofré, R. (2002) 'Citizenship and Schooling in Manitoba Between the End of the First World War and the End of the Second World War,' in Y. Hébert (ed.), *Citizenship in Transformation in Canada*. Toronto: University of Toronto Press. pp. 112–133.

Bruno-Jofré, R. and Aponiuk, N. (eds) (2001) *Educating Citizens for a Pluralistic Society*. Calgary: Canadian Ethnic Studies.

Bruno-Jofré, R. and Henley, D. (2001) 'Public Schooling in English Canada: Addressing Difference in the Context of Globalization,' in R. Bruno-Jofré and N. Aponiuk (eds), *Educating Citizens for a Pluralistic Society*. Calgary: Canadian Ethnic Studies. pp. 49–70.

Cairns, A. (2000) *Citizens Plus: Aboriginal Peoples and the Canadian State*. Vancouver: UBC Press.

Carnegie Corporation of New York, and CIRCLE: Center for Information & Research on Civic Learning & Engagement (2003) *The Civic Mission of Schools*. New York: Carnegie Corporation of New York and CIRCLE: Center for Information & Research on Civic Learning & Engagement.

Castles, S. (2004) 'Migration, Citizenship and Education,' in J.A. Banks (ed.), *Diversity and Citizenship Education: Global Perspectives*. San Francisco: Jossey-Bass. pp. 17–48.

Centre for Research and Information on Canada (2001) *Voter Participation in Canada: Is Canadian Democracy in Crisis?* Ottawa: author.

Centre for Research and Information on Canada, (2004) *Canadian Democracy: Bringing Youth Back into the Political Process*. Ottawa: author.

Chareka, O. and Sears, A. (2006) 'Civic Duty: Young People's Conceptions of Voting as a Means of Political Participation,' *Canadian Journal of Education*, 29 (2): 521–540.

citzED (2005) *About citizED*. Retrieved November 15, 2005, from http://www.citized.info/index.php?l_menu=about

Civics Expert Group (1994) *Whereas the People ... Civics and Citizenship Education* Canberra: Australian Government Publishing Services.

Clark, P. (2004) 'Social Studies in English Canada: Trends and Issues in Historical Context,' in A. Sears and I. Wright (eds), *Challenges and Prospects for Canadian Social Studies*. Vancouver: Pacific Educational Press. pp. 17–37.

Cleaver, E., Ireland, E., Kerr, D., and Lopes, J. (2005) *Citizenship Education Longitudinal Study: Second Cross-Sectional Survey 2004 – Listening to Young People: Citizenship Education in England* (No. RR626). Berkshire: National Foundation for Educational Research.

Cook, S.A., and Westheimer, J. (2006) 'Introduction: Democracy and Education,' *Canadian Journal of Education*, 29 (2): 347–358.

Council of Atlantic Ministers of Education and Training (2005) *Social Studies Outcomes Framework K-8: Draft*. Halifax: CAMET.

Council of Europe (2005) *The European Year of CitizenshipThrough Education*. Retrieved February 9, 2005, from http://www.coe.Int/T/E/Cultural_Co-operation/education/E.D.C/Documents_and_publications/By_subject/Year_2005/

Cunningham, F. (2002) *Theories of Democracy: A Critical Introduction*. London; New York: Routledge.

Curriculum Corporation (2005) *Discovering Democracy: Civics and Citizenship Education, Curriculum Resources*. Retrieved August 1, 2005, from http://www.curriculum.edu.au/democracy/aboutdd/materials.htm

Deakin Crick, R., Taylor, M., Tew, M., Samuel, E., Durant, K., and Ritchie, S. (2005) *A Systematic Review of the Impact of Citizenship Education on Student Learning and Achievement*. London: EPPI Centre, Institute of Education.

Garner, R. (2007) *Pupils to Learn 'Britishness' in History*. Retrieved January 28, 2007, from http://education.independent.co.uk/news/article2186513.ece

Gidengil, E., Blais, A., Nevitte, N., and Nadeau, R. (2004) *Citizens*. Vancouver: UBC Press.

Gouvernment du Quebec (2001) *Quebec Education Program, Approved Version: Preschool Education, Elementary Education*. Quebec: Gouvernment du Quebec, Ministere de l'Education.

Gouvernment du Quebec (2005) *Education in Quebec: An Overview*. Quebec: Gouvernment du Quebec, Ministere de l'Education, du Loisir, et du Sport.

Grant, J.N. (1986) 'The Canada Studies Foundation: An Historical Overview,' in J.N. Grant, R.M. Anderson and P.L. McCreath (eds), *The Canada Studies Foundation*. Toronto: The Canada Studies Foundation.

Granatstein, J. (1998) *Who Killed Canadian History?* Toronto: Harper-Collins.

Hébert, Y. (ed.) (2002) *Citizenship in Transformation in Canada*. Toronto: University of Toronto Press.

Hébert, Y., Eyford, G., and Jutras, F. (2005) 'The Values Debate at the Nexus of Transnational Perspectives on Human Rights and Citizenship Education,' *Canadian and International Education*, 34 (1): 1–11.

Hébert, Y., and Wilkinson, L. (2002) 'The Citizenship Debates: Conceptual, Policy, Experiential, and Educational Issues,' in Y. Hébert (ed.), *Citizenship in Transformation in Canada*. Toronto: University of Toronto Press. pp. 3–36.

Hodgetts, A. (1968) *What Culture? What Heritage? A Study of Civic Education in Canada*. Toronto: OISE Press.

Hodgson, E.D. (1976) *Federal Intervention in Public Education*. Toronto: Canadian Education Association.

Hodgson, E.D. (1988) *Federal Involvement in Public Education*. Toronto: Canadian Education Association.

Howard, R.W., Berkowitz, M.W., and Schaeffer, E.F. (2004) 'Politics of Character Education,' *Educational Policy*, 18 (1): 188–215.

Hughes, A.S. (1994) 'Under Standing Citizenship: A Delphi Study,' *Canadian and International Education*, 23 (2): 13–26.

Hughes, A.S. (1994) 'Understanding Citizenship: A Delphi Study,' *Canadian and International Education*, 23 (2):13–26.

Hughes, A.S. and Sears, A.M. (2006) 'Citizenship Education: Canada Dabbles While the World Plays On,' *Education Canada*, 46 (4): 6–9.

Joshee, R. (2004) 'Citizenship and Multicultural Education in Canada: From Assimilation to Social Cohesion,' in J.A. Banks (ed.), *Diversity and Citizenship Education: Global Perspectives*. San Francisco: Jossey-Bass.

Kymlicka, W. (1998) *Finding Our Way: Rethinking Ethnocultural Relations in Canada*. Toronto: Oxford University Press.

Kymlicka, W. (2003) 'Being Canadian,' *Government and Opposition*, 38(3), 357–385.

Kymlicka, W. (2007) 'Ethnocultural Diversity in a Liberal State: Making Sense of the Canadian Model(s),' in K. Banting, T.J. Courchene and L. Seidle (eds), *The Art of the State Volume III: Belonging? Diversity, Recognition and Shared Citizenship in Canada*. Montreal: The Institute for Research on Public Policy. pp. 39–86.

Leithwood, K.A., Fullan, M., and Watson, N. (2003) *The Schools We Need: A New Blueprint for Ontario Final Report*. Toronto: OISE/UT.

Manitoba Education Citizenship and Youth (2006) *Celebrating Citizenship Education Kindergarten to Grade 12*. Retrieved April 1, 2007, from http://www.edu.gov.mb.ca/k12/citizenship/c_grant/index.html.

Marzano, R.J., Pickering, D.J., and Pollock, J.E. (2001) *Classroom Instruction That Works: Research-Based Strategies For Increasing Student Achievement*. Alexandria, Virginia: Association for Supervision and Curriculum Development.

McLaughlin, T.H. (2000) 'Citizenship Education in England: The Crick Report and Beyond,' *Journal of Philosophy of Education*, 34 (4): 541–570.

Milner, H. (2002) *Civic literacy: How Informed Citizens Make Democracy Work*. Handover: University press of New England.

Neatby, H. (1953) *So Little for the Mind*. Toronto: Clarke, Irwin.

New Brunswick Department of Education Educational Programs & Services Branch. (2004) *Atlantic Canada Social Studies Curriculum: Social Studies 7 Empowerment, Draft June 2004*. Fredericton: New Brunswick Department of Education.

Ontario Ministry of Education (2005) *The Ontario Curriculum Grades 9 and 10: Canadian and World Studies*. Toronto: Ministry of Education.

Organization of American States (2005) 'Meeting of Ministers of Education: Education for Democratic Citizenship in the Americas: An Agenda for Action.' Available from http://www.oest.oas.org/ivministerial/ingles/cpo_bienvenida.asp.)

Organization of American States, Inter-American Council for Integral Development (2006) 'Progress Report 2005-2006 – Inter-American Program on Education for Democratic Values and Practices.' Washington: OAS.

Osborne, K. (2001) 'Public Schooling and Citizenship Education in Canada,' in R. Bruno-Jofré and N. Aponiuk (eds), *Educating Citizens for a Pluralistic Society*. Calgary: Canadian Ethnic Studies. pp. 11–48.

Province of New Brunswick Education (2007) *When Kids Come First*. Fredericton: Government of New Brunswick.

Russell, R.J. (2002) 'Bridging the Boundaries for a More Inclusive Citizenship Education,' in Hébert, Y. (ed.), *Citizenship in Transformation in Canada*. Toronto: University of Toronto Press.

Saskatchewan Learning (1999) *Grade 8 Social Studies Curriculum Guide*. Retrieved July 19, 2007, from http://www.sasked.gov.sk.ca/docs/midlsoc/gr8/index.html

Sears, A. (1996) 'Something Different to Everyone: Conceptions of Citizenship and Citizenship Education,' *Canadian and International Education*, 25 (2): 1–16.

Sears, A., Clarke, G.M., and Hughes, A.S. (1999) 'Canadian Citizenship Education: The Pluralist Ideal and Citizenship Education for a Post-Modern State,' in J. Torney-Purta, J. Schwille and J.-A. Amadeo (eds), *Civic Education across Countries: Twenty-four National Case Studies from the IEA Education Project*. Amsterdam: IEA. pp. 111–135.

Sears, A., Clarke, G.M., and Hughes, A.S. (2000) 'Learning Democracy in a Pluralist Society: Building a Research Base for Citizenship Education,' in Y. Lenoir, W. Hunter, D. Hodgkinson, P.de Broucker and A. Dolbec (eds), *A Pan-Canadian Education Research Agenda*. Ottawa: Canadian Society for Studies in Education. pp. 151–166.

Sears, A. and Hughes, A.S. (1996) 'Citizenship Education and Current Educational Reform,' *Canadian Journal of Education*, 21 (2): 123–142.

Sears, A. and Hyslop-Margison, E. (2006) 'The Cult of Citizenship Education,' in G. Richardson and D. Blades (eds), *Troubling the Canon of Citizenship Education*. New York: Peter Lang. pp. 13–24.

Sears, A. and Hyslop-Margison, E. (2007) 'Crisis as a Vehicle for Educational Reform: The Case of Citizenship Education,' *Journal of Educational Thought*, 41 (1): 43–62.

Shields, P. and Ramsay, D. (2004) 'Social Studies Across English Canada', in A. Sears and I. Wright (eds), *Challenges and Prospects for Canadian Social Studies*. Vancouver: Pacific Educational Press. pp. 38–54.

Taylor, C. and Laforest, G. (1993) *Reconciling the Solitudes: Essays on Canadian Federalism and Nationalism*. Montreal: McGill-Queen's University Press.

Tsilevich, B. (2001) 'New Democracies in the Old World: Remarks on Will Kymlicka's Approach to Nation-building in Post-Communist Europe,' in W. Kymlicka and M. Opalski (eds), *Can Liberalism be Exported? Western Political Theory and Ethnic Relations in Eastern Europe*. Oxford: Oxford University Press. pp. 154–170.

Torney-Purta, J.J. and Amadeo, J-A. (2004) 'Strengthening Democracy in the Americas through Civic Education: An Empirical Analysis Highlighting the Views of Students and Teachers.' Washington: Organization of American States, Unit for Social Development and Education.

Torney-Purta, J.J., Lehmann, R., Oswald, H. and Schulz, W. (2001) *Citizenship and Education in Twenty-Eight Countries: Civic Knowledge and Engagement at Age Fourteen*. Amsterdam: IEA.

Torney-Purta, J. and Vermeer, S. (2004) *Developing Citizenship Competencies from Kindergarten through Grade 12: A Background Paper for Policy Makers and*

Educators. Denver: Education Commission of the States.

Troper, H. (2002) 'The Historical Context for Citizenship Education in Urban Canada,' in Y. Hébert (ed.), *Citizenship in Transformation in Canada*. Toronto: University of Toronto Press. pp. 150–161.

Ungerleider, C. (2003) *Failing Our Kids: How We Are Ruining Our Public Schools*. Toronto: McClelland & Stewart.

Wall, D., Moll, M., and Frose-Germain, B. (2000) *Living Democracy: Renewing Our Vision of Citizenship Education*. Ottawa: Canadian Teachers' Federation.

Windschitl, M. (2002) 'Framing Constructivism in Practice as the Negotiation of Dilemmas: An Analysis of the Conceptual, Pedagogical, Cultural, and Political Challenges Facing Teachers,' *Review of Educational Research,* 72 (2): 131–175.

11

Citizenship Education in China: Changing Concepts, Approaches and Policies in the Changing Political, Economic and Social Context

Wing On Lee and Ho Chi-hang

INTRODUCTION

In China, the notion 'citizenship' has been seen as a western construct, perceived by the government as that as such term is imported into China, it is equivalent to opening up the country to being susceptible of western influences an important concept that has seen to be such an integral part of the Chinese tradition as well as an integral part of social cohesion in modern China. The government even feels a need to protect the locally developed terms and ideas, as well as ideologies that would all affect the 'Chinese characteristics of citizenship'. The closest terms to citizenship or citizenship education in China would include political education, ideological education and moral education. A Chinese dictionary of moral education suggests that the

three terms are actually three-in-one in connotation, and can be used interchangeably (Liu, 1998: 120). These concepts are so interrelated that they merge variably into ideopolitical education (*sixiang zhengzhi jiaoyu*) and ideomoral education (*sixiang pinde jiaoyu*) (Lee, 2005).

Recently the term 'citizenship (or civic) education' has surfaced in public (Liu, 2005: A6). Not surprisingly, whether the term should be used, and how this term is to be used has been a sensitive issue, and it has triggered diverse responses. For example, Liu (2005), Director of the 21st Century Education Development Research Academy points out, 'citizenship education' is in its infancy in mainland China and 'the terminology only surfaced in public in the past couple of years. It was very sensitive and could not be mentioned before' (Liu, 2005). On the other hand, there were others who welcomed the adoption of this new terminology into the dictionary of civic, moral and ideopolitical education. Being sensitive and controversial notwithstanding, the proponents for adopting this term argue for the introduction of 'citizenship education' in China. For example, Zhou Hongling, Director of the Beijing New Era Citizen Education Centre, argues that the promotion of civic education could eventually establish a civil society and bring about a peaceful and gradual transition of China from a traditional autocratic society into a modern democratic nation (cited in Liu, 2005). It is obvious that those supporting the status quo would like to see civic/moral/ideopolitical education to continue in China in its prototype. However, being aware of global changes and trends, China is not short of supporters for the introduction of the terminology 'citizenship' in the school curriculum, government policy and academic discourse, with an aspiration to see the emergence of a civil society, which could represent the political aspirations of young people today in China, and also the increased call for adopting a citizenship concept that can be served as a base for international exchanges and dialogues.

Since 1978, China has experienced dramatic multi-faceted changes in the society, both in economical and political terms. The adoption of the open-door and the modernization policy has led to significant changes in the social and economic fabric. One remarkable change was the shift from a planned economy to a market-oriented economy which is called a 'socialist market economy'. The rise of a socialist market economy has led to new demands for citizenship qualities, such as a global perspective, an orientation towards achievement, open-mindedness and democratic awareness, for example. Such changes in political circumstances and social and economic circumstances underscore the recent directions of citizenship curriculum development in China (Lee and Zhong, 2007).

This paper attempts to examine the change of the concept and role of citizenship education in the Chinese society, in light of the changes in political, social and economic circumstances during this period.

ECONOMICAL, POLITICAL AND SOCIETAL CHANGES AND THEIR IMPLICATIONS FOR CHANGES IN MORAL VALUES

China has adopted economic reform and opening up of policy since 1978. The overall goal of the reform was to achieve the four modernizations (modernizations in the fields of agriculture, industry, science and technology, and the military). To attract foreign investment and advanced technology into the country, four Special Economic Zones (SEZs) were established in southern Guangdong (Shenzhen, Zhuhai, and Shantou) and Fujian province (Xiamen), where overseas connections were extensive and the tradition of international links was strong. In 1984, 14 port cities along the East coast were opened up. In 1988 the policy was further extended to cover all coastal provinces (Lin, 2003: 81–2).

Official statistics show that the Chinese economy soared after the implementation of the economic reform programme, and particularly after Deng's 1992 southern tour. The GNP in 1993 (3,447.7 billion *yuan*) was nearly double the GNP in 1990 (1,854.5 billion *yuan*). In 1994, the GNP rose to 4,491.8 billion *yuan* (Prime, 1997: 52).

The growth of private business was also remarkable. In 1978, its share of the gross value of Chinese industrial output was less than 1 per cent; by 1992, it had grown to 7 per cent (Wong and Mok, 1995: 6). Economic reform also increased personal income and savings. In 1994, total national savings rose to 21,519 billion *yuan* from 210.6 billion *yuan* in 1978. Average population savings also rose to 1795.49 *yuan* from 21.88 *yuan* in 1978 (Zheng, 1996: 296–7).

Economic growth brought about massive social change in China. Material living standards of the public have significantly improved. Television sets and refrigerators have become common consumer goods in many households. There was a notable rise of consumerism in post-reform China following the advancement of material living standards. With more cash in their pockets, people were purchasing brand names and luxury products. In the 1990s, commercialization flourished in the economy.

Income inequality between individuals, geographical regions, and rural and urban areas was increasingly wide with economic reform. Zhang and Zhang (2003) report that the regional Gini coefficient rose from 0.19 in 1985 to 0.24 in 1994, 0.26 in 1998, and further to above 0.4 in 2005 (UNDP, 2005). Regional economic inequality also became obvious. Coastal provinces have generated more trade volume (85.96 per cent of the total in 1986–1991 period and 88.08 per cent of the total in 1992–1998 period) and attracted far more foreign direct investment (FDI) (91.93 per cent in 1986–1991 period and 87.42 per cent in 1992–1998 period) than inland provinces. Guangdong ranked top in coastal province with both measurements in both periods (Zhang and Zhang, 2003: 51–3).

In the late 1990s, there was an influx of computers and access to the internet in China. Statistics provided by the ChinaNet Information Centre at the end of 1997 showed that there were more than 49,000 host computers and 250,000 personal computers in China, with about 620,000 browsers connected to the internet (Yu, 1998: 172–3).

Post-reform China has also been plagued with environmental degradation such as air pollution, shortage of water supplies, decreased cultivated areas because of population growth and economic modernization (such as industrial, urban, and residential expansion and so forth) and natural degradative process (such as desertification) accompanied by improper land management (Smil, 1993).

In post-reform China, crime has become an increasing point of concern for the Chinese society. According to the State Statistics Bureau, criminal cases rose alarmingly after the Cultural Revolution. By 1988, there were 830,000 reported criminal cases, averaging 7.7 cases per 100,000 of the population nationwide. In 1994, however, the rate had almost doubled to 14.3 cases per 100,000 of the population. The problem of juvenile delinquency has become notably serious since the 1980s, especially along the coastal areas, where the juvenile crimes have been consistently maintained at around 60 per cent of all crime and have been increasing at 5 per cent annually (Chen, 1998: 157–9). However, the most serious problem perceived by the people in opinion polls in the late 1980s was neither juvenile crime nor drug trafficking and addiction but corruption. Official corruption involving party members was fiercely criticized in the 1989 Tiananmen demonstrations (Wong and Mok, 1995: 11).

'Moral decline' was a general perception among the public in post-reform China. Chen Lai, Professor at Beijing University, described such 'moral decline' (*daode huapo*) as the weakening of individual character, family ethics, occupational ethics (the society filled with fake goods), collectivism, social ethics, patriotism, and sense of national dignity (Nan, 1995: 36). Chinese society had been plagued with pirated handbags, music CDs, movie DVDs, and even food. Statistics showed that people were becoming increasingly dissatisfied with the pirates by the 1990s. According to consumer councils, there were 411,706 complaints in various provinces with regard to fake goods in 1994, a rise of 11.4 per cent from 1993 (Zheng, 1996: 301).

Some surveys revealed changes in the value orientations of the Chinese. In echoing Deng's slogan 'getting rich is glorious,' more people aspired to get rich through individual efforts. There was a popular saying 'either rich or poor, you are on your own' in the reforming China (Wong and Mok, 1995: 12). A study conducted in Shanghai revealed a rise of individualism and the weakening of collectivism. When asked what was the most important thing in one's life, more respondents chose 'to live happily' rather than 'to make a contribution to society'. There was also more agreement with the statement 'life is short, enjoy it while you can' than 'treasure your time, work as hard as possible' when asked about the meaning of life (Chu and Ju, 1993: 185).

Numerous surveys also suggest that Chinese youths were becoming more 'pragmatic' than before. Chinese youths tend to pursue material benefits rather than ideological-political goals. They valued their career more than their political progress, and strived towards 'professional improvement' rather than 'socialist morality'. On the subject of party membership, many youths admit that they joined the party as a means to obtain a good job assignment rather than out of belief in communism. Furthermore, a study of over 1,500 youths in Guangzhou identified the 'concern with concrete matters related to work' as the respondents' most important concern (Wong and Mok, 1995: 13–4). At the same time, some traditional concepts were indeed challenged during the economic reform. Lu (1998: 104) observed that the value of *yi* (in Lu's terms, *yi* includes benevolence, righteousness, morality, faithfulness) was on the verge of decline while the value of *li* (benefits, utilitarianism, profit) had become more prevalent.

On the other hand, spoiled only children have become a potential social problem in post-reform China. As China had a population of 1.3 billion, with a growth rate of around 1 per cent per year in the late 1990s, the government regarded population pressure as a cause of poverty and social crisis and thus introduced the 'one-child policy' in 1979, one year after the start of economic reform. In 1990, 49.4 per cent of new born babies were only children. In urban areas, more than 90 per cent of new born babies were only children (Zheng, 1996: 314). The policy, though to a certain extent helped reduce the population pressure, led to some negative side-effects because of the persistent traditional preference for sons even though post-reform China had passed through a decade of socialist education (Arnold and Liu, 1986: 221–46).

China's education has also undergone a process of marketization in the post-Mao reform period, characterized by the emergence of private educational institutions, the shift of state responsibility for educational provision towards families and individuals and the prominence of fee-charging, as well as the introduction of internal competition among educational institutions. The CCP initiated a decentralization policy in education to allow local government, local communities, individuals and other non-state actors to create more educational opportunities. Education in post-reform China has shifted to the quest for meritocracy rather than the quest for virtuocracy. Education provides a step for students to climb to higher social strata and achieve higher incomes. Since the 1980s, educational credentials have become more important to students for securing the best jobs (Tang and Parish, 2000: 55, 70–7).

IDEOLOGICAL SHIFTS SINCE ECONOMIC LIBERALIZATION

The 1990s witnessed an overall denunciation of Communism in East European countries. China has remained one of the very few countries in the world that still upholds Communism as the state ideology. However, this is far from implying ideological stagnation. On the contrary, over the last 20 years, there were substantial and vibrant internal ideological debates under the brand name of Communism, and as a result, new *ideologies* emerged within the ideology. To cite a few examples: 'reform and open-door policy',[1] 'four cardinal principles',[2] 'four modernizations', 'primary stage of socialism', 'socialist market economy', 'responsibility system', 'three represents', and so on.

WAVES OF IDEOLOGICAL DEBATES SINCE 1978

The Third Plenum of the Eleventh CCP Central Committee held in 1978 marked the beginning of a new age of ideological development. The adoption of the reform and open policy has been accompanied by debates not only on policy issues, but also on moral issues, which are inherently related to ideological issues. The frequency of review, discussion and debate was so high that identifiable new issues emerged almost every other year. Analysing the government's changing perception towards the intellectuals, for example, Franklin (1989) observes a series of waves of debates between 1978 and 1989: The Rehabilitation of the intellectuals (1978–89); The emergence of guidelines for intellectual expressions (1980–82); From expansion of academic freedom to anti-spiritual pollution (1983–84); From liberalization of intellectual expressions to anti-bourgeois liberalization (1985–87); and From further extension of market mechanisms to further student demonstrations (1988–89). Lee and Ho (2005) also identified continued ideological debates after 1989. Ideological consolidation from the aftermath of the June 4 incident (1989–91); Further economic liberalization marked by Deng's Visit to South China (1992–95); The revival of nationalism in association with the handover of Hong Kong and Macau (1996–99); and the recognition of entrepreneurs and further opening up to the world from 2000 onwards.

IDEOLOGICAL SHIFTS IN DIFFERENT TIME PERIODS

The ideological debates during 1978–89 are fully elaborated in Franklin's paper. In the main, during 1978–79, with the adoption of the open policy, Deng Xiaoping revitalized the significance of the intellectuals, so that that they could play a dual role of criticizing both ultra-leftist (such as 'bureaucratic conservatism') and ultra-rightist tendencies (such as 'individualism'), which could hinder the realization of socialist modernization. However, the tide changed during 1980–82. The CCP began to launch campaigns against the 'critical realist' writers who were too negative towards party leaders and produced destructive social and political effects. The CCP required artists and writers to support the Four Cardinal Principles and provide a balanced view of CCP history.

The period 1983–84 was marked by a combination of renewed public campaigns against leftist efforts to hinder the social and political participation of the intellectuals, on the one hand, and critique towards the ultra-rightist intellectuals on the other. The hallmark of ideological debate in this period was the campaign against the pollution of spiritual civilization. Part of the campaign was an ideological debate on the definition and meaning of 'Marxist humanism'. The proponents of Marxist humanism saw Marxism as a progressive science that needed to be constantly updated in the light of new conditions and information. However, its critique saw it as spiritual pollution, inviting Western influences and individualism (Liao, 1989: 7).

The period 1985–87 witnessed another phase of ideological struggle. The CCP Central Committee issued *Decision on Guiding Principles for the Building of a Socialist Society* in September 1986. The *Guiding Principles* put forward the notion of the primary stage of socialism, which acknowledged that China was still backward in productivity and had not yet fulfilled industrialization and commercialization of production, thus requiring continuation of the reform and opening up policy (Wu, 1990: 384). This led to another climax of liberalization, marked by mass student movements. The anti-bourgeois liberalization campaign thus broke out in 1987, leading to the stepping down of Hu Yaobang.[3] The stepping down of Hu led to the proposal for new authoritarianism, which argued that present reform required strong authority, not democracy, and that China could not implement a Western style multi-party system (Nathan, 1990: 113).

The period 1988–89 was characterized by further demand for press freedom and political democracy, with increased public discontent towards inflation and corruption, and increased independent intellectual activities led to further appeals for press freedom and political democracy. In April 1989, another series of student demonstrations took place, leading to the June 4 incident,[4] and the consequential stepping down of Zhao Ziyang[5] (Dassu and Saich, 1992: 234–7).

During 1989–91, right after the June 4 incident, maintaining stability became the top agenda of the CCP leadership. The government launched campaigns against anti-peaceful evolution (*fan heping yanbian*), which was seen as a cause for the collapse of the social regimes in Eastern Europe by gradual introduction of Western democratic ideologies (Dittmer, 2003: 905). Deng reiterated the significance of adhering to the Four Cardinal Principles. Moreover, all Beijing University freshmen were required to undertake ten months of military training, starting from the Fall of 1989 (Vohra, 2000: 278–9). The Propaganda Department reiterated the spirit of Lei Feng (an official portrait of a self-sacrificing patriot), and emphasized the significance of patriotism. However, in order to enhance legitimacy of the government, the State began to focus overwhelmingly on economic development. In this way, in this guise of an apparent reinstatement of political control, maintaining an open market economy environment continued to be a significant government agenda during this period. Moreover, to address concerns raised in the 1989 student demonstration, the government also launched campaigns against official speculation and corruption (Baum, 1996: 3).

During 1992–95, economically, the CCP adopted the policy of economic austerity with the intention of restoring the centrally planned economy after the student demonstration. However, the programme led to economic recession, with a number of factories becoming idle and 1.5 million urban residents losing their jobs. Attempts were made to prevent economic distress from turning into social instability. One major action taken was that in January 1992 Deng paid a visit to South China. This was a symbolic announcement of reviving the policy of economic liberalization, through reinstating the practice of the market economy. Deng's call for further economic reform was supported in the Fourteenth Party Congress, being credited as a contribution to the development of the 'theory of building socialism with Chinese characteristics' (Saich, 2004: 73–8).

The notion 'Socialist Market Economy' was introduced in 1992, officially endorsed by the 14th National Congress of the Chinese Communist Party. By 1992, the State Council had designated 300 open cities. In the year 1992 alone, China opened 28 harbour cities, eight regions along the Yangtze River and 13 border towns. Many open development zones were also established. These zones enjoy preferential policies of expanded rights for foreign-investment projects and foreign trade rights (Wu, 1993: 16).

When the liberalization green light was on, intellectual debates began to flourish again. A new group of intellectual force, known as 'neo-conservatives' began to emerge, publishing their views in dozens of privately funded periodicals appearing during this period. The neo-conservatives, such as Xiao Gongqing,[6] expressed their basic concerns about the emergence of an ideological vacuum and the moral decline in the process of modernization and marketization. They called for reinstating nationalism and Chinese cultural identity as a solution. They held that the Confucian tradition, particularly its moral code and its sense of social responsibility, could be the best foundation upon which to rebuild Chinese cultural identity (Chen, 1997: 595–6, 607–8). This emergence of neo-conservative views had significant ideological implications, as Confucianism was officially denounced during the Cultural Revolution.

During 1996–99, the handover of Hong Kong and Macau to Chinese sovereignty had significant political implications. The notion 'one country, two systems' properly captured the political tensions in this period. To show China's openness to the world, and particularly to Taiwan, the Chinese government did everything to demonstrate open-mindedness and flexibility in allowing for different political systems to exist within the country. However, on the other hand, worrying that the 'two systems' would dominate the political scene and would jeopardise 'one country', the Chinese government made deliberate efforts to show the power and determination of the State to maintain political control. The tension between openness and tightening reached its peak during this period.

On the side of opening up, the National People's Congress (NPC) amended the Criminal Law such that 'counter-revolutionary' political crimes were replaced by a less political designation of offences, namely 'national security' in March 1997. In September, the 15th Party Congress stressed the need to govern the country by law, and for the first time made reference to human rights. In this more relaxed atmosphere, the CCP showed relative tolerance towards political opposition (Wright, 2002: 908). However, the relaxation of control was soon tightened up following a debate about whether open political activism could be allowed in China under the banner of 'socialist spiritual civilization' which was called again in the resolution of the Sixth Plenum of the Fourteenth Central Committee (Chen, 1998: 34). As a result, large numbers of liberal political activists, including key members of the China Democracy Party, were arrested in November 1998 (Mackerras, 2001: 68).

A new ideological move took place in 2000. In a speech in February of that year, Jiang Zemin put forward the notion of 'three represents', namely that the CCP would represent the advanced social productive forces, the most advanced culture and the fundamental interests of all people. By putting forward this new notion, the CCP wanted to welcome

new constituencies into its ideological framework, but also exerted leadership over the new burgeoning sectors of the economy. The notion also took advantage of the close historical connection between the economy and the party-state, as many cadres had 'plunged into the sea' (*xiahai*) of commerce while retaining their foothold in the Party (Saich, 2004: 85).

The various party plenums and NPC meetings from 1999 to 2001 showed struggles between the acceptance of the shake-up of the state sector and the support for further privatization. Nevertheless, with entry into the World Trade Organization (WTO) in December 2001, China could only opt for further marketization and privatization (*ibid.*). Fewsmith (2001: 575–6) claimed that the entry into the WTO triggered restructuring of the state's management of the economy, and fostered the growth of professionalism within the government through the increase in competition stimulated by the WTO.

With Jiang's stepping down as General Secretary at the 16th Party Congress in November 2002, China entered into a new political scene led by Hu Jintao. While there are still many unknowns about the political orientations of the new leadership, the general comments were that Hu would support a more open and professional political system.

CHANGES IN IDEOPOLITICAL-MORAL EDUCATION POLICIES AND SCHOOL CURRICULA

In accordance with the changing economic and social circumstances and ideological shifts, there were corresponding changes in policies regarding ideopolitical-moral education. Analysis of government directives issued by the CCP Central Committee, Ministry of Education (MOE), or State Education Commission (SEC) from 1990 to 2002 revealed changing policies in ideopolitical-moral education in China.

'Moral education' in China comprised basically ideology, politics and morality. However, 'psychological qualities' were officially included in government documents in ideopolitical-moral education in the mid-1990s (SEC, 1995a: 891, 1998: 963). The inclusion of 'psychological qualities' in ideologically-oriented moral education is a significant marker of the broadening content of ideopolitical-moral education and the relative decline of ideological and political contents in ideopolitical-moral education, which is a sign of depoliticization.

The government observed some implementation problems in ideopolitical-moral education. One major problem was the negligence of moral education by school authorities. SEC (1990) reminded the school authorities not to misuse lesson hours allocated to Ideology and Moral Character for other purposes (p. 871). SEC (1997) clearly criticized the over emphasis on knowledge transmission and ignorance of moral education by school authorities (para. 2, p. 2545).

The government stressed that ideopolitical-moral education should meet children's needs, and be based on their age and psychological characteristics. SEC (1993a) criticized rigid or adult-centred moral education and emphasized that teaching should be based on the mental and psychological characteristics of students (p. 104). The call for student-centred moral education became more explicit as the economic reform deepened. SEC (1998) urged that moral education be implemented according to students' moral development (para. 4). MOE (2001) demanded student-centred teaching and criticized current moral education work as "arduous (*fan*), difficult (*nan*), one-sided (*pian*), outdated (*jiu*) (para.1).

It is noteworthy that apart from traditional stresses on 'patriotism', 'socialism', and 'collectivism', there were also stresses on such values as 'national situations (*guoqing*)' and 'Chinese history' in moral education policy documents from 1991 to 1996. 'Traditional ethics' were given particular emphasis from 1993 to 1996 (SEC, 1993b, 1993c, 1994, 1995c; MOE, 1994; CCP, 1996). 'National cohesion' was a particular preoccupation of the government documents from 1994 to 1996 (SEC, 1994, 1995c; CCP, 1996, 1999). 'Labour' was found to be popular before 1997 (SEC, 1992, 1993a, 1995a, 1997; MOE, 1994; CCP, 1996;).

However, after the mid-1990s, moral values tended to out-weigh the above-mentioned national-political values in moral education policy documents. These values included 'moral quality' (SEC, 1995a, 1995b, 1995c, 1997, 1998; CCP, 1996; 2000, 2001; MOE, 1998, 2001) and 'psychological qualities'(SEC, 1995a, 1995c, 1997; CCP, 2000; MOE, 2001). 'Law education' was particularly emphasized in government papers issued from 1994 to 2000 (SEC, 1993a, 1994, 1995a, 1995c; 1997, 1998; MOE, 1994, 1998; CCP, 1996, 1999, 2000). In addition, 'Democracy', concerning the basic rights and obligations of citizens (SEC, 1995a: 893), was stressed together with the concept of 'legal education'.

Moreover, social values, vis-a-vis political values also became increasingly apparent since the mid-1990s, such as stresses on 'social ethics' (MOE, 1994, 1998; SEC, 1995c, 1998; CCP, 1996, 2000, 2001), 'occupational ethics' (MOE, 1994; SEC, 1995c; CCP, 1996, 2000, 2001) (1994–2001), and 'family ethics' (CCP, 1996, 2001).

In the late 1990s, there was a clear rise in the mention of 'global outlook', with China joining the World Trade Organization (SEC, 1998; MOE, 2001). In 2006, the government organised the Beijing 2006 International Forum on Citizenship Education for Children and Youths. Unlike other conferences of this kind, this specific forum was specifically designed for the promotion of global citizenship qualities among the Chinese populace, as a part of preparation for the upcoming Olympics in 2008 (Lo and Shi, 2007). The rise of moral, social and global themes in moral education policy documents from the mid-1990s indicates adjustments of moral education towards economic reform, and the government's attempts to integrate China with the international world.

CHANGES IN IMPLEMENTATION STRATEGIES AND SCHOOL PRACTICES

Impact upon the implementation and school practices in civic and moral education can also be seen, with the changes in ideopolitical-moral policies that correspond to the social, economic and political changes in China. For example, The Third Plenum of the CCP Central Committee in 1978 decided to adopt an open door policy and this marked off the modernization period in China. In the same year, the government reinstated the *Behavioural Code for Primary and Secondary Students* (Ministry of Education, 1979). According to the code, the task of moral education was to cultivate students' ideals, morality, culture, and discipline; affectivity towards the socialist motherland and the socialist enterprise; dedication to the country's development; thirst for new knowledge; willingness to think and the courage to be creative.

Ideopolitical-moral education continued through school education. Independent timetabled courses of Ideology and Moral Character (*sixiang pinde ke*) (once a week in each grade) for primary schools and Ideology and Politics (*sixiang zhengzhi ke*) (twice a week in each grade) for secondary schools were officially implemented in 1981 and 1992 respectively. The course on Ideology and Moral Character emphasized the education of 'five lovings' ('loving motherland', 'loving people', 'loving labour', 'loving sciences', and 'loving public assets') and behaviour such as honesty, bravery, and working hard (Liu, 1995: 3–6). For the course of Ideology and Politics, content areas included Marxism-Leninism-Mao Zedong's thought, political knowledge and legal education (Zhao, 1998: 29–30).

In 1988, a radical revision of the political education curriculum took place. At junior secondary level, 'Civics' was introduced in Year 7, 'Social History' in Year 8, and 'Construction of Chinese Socialism' in Year 9. At senior secondary level, 'Scientific View of Life' was introduced in Year 10, 'Economics' in Year 11, and 'Politics' in Year 12. Although politics was still very much an emphasis of citizenship education in school, 'Civics' began to be introduced as a separate subject, focusing on students' behaviour. In the same year, the government issued the *Outline of Moral Education in Secondary School* (China Education Yearbook, Various Years), which was fully implemented in 1991. The significance of this document is that 'moral education' was used independently, without being prefixed by 'ideology'. Moral education began to emerge as a single focus in the citizenship curriculum (Lee and Zhong, 2007).

As illustrated from the above, the implementation of civic and moral education in China has been characterized influenced by top-down directives issued by the government. As aforementioned, many of those directives were issued in order to cope with many of the moral issues arising out of social, economic and political changes. However, it is notworthy that many of the government policy documents and guidelines issued over the years have increased advocacy for the adoption of diaological, interactive approaches in the implementation of civic and moral education, as well as guarding as indoctrination approaches (Lee, 2002). Beyond school, the government has also encouraged the youths to participate in various youth activities, in order to engage more young people to citizenship activities and to help them become active citizens. An example of such efforts is the Young Pioneer activities for students between the ages of 14 and 28. In addition to develop loyalty to the party, the league has a mandate to engage the young people to be closely linked with the masses, be humble and learn from the people, and in particular develop themselves as critical and self-critical citizens (Lawrence, 2000: 275).

THE NEW THREE CHARACTER CLASSIC MOVEMENT: AN ILLUSTRATIVE CASE OF CHANGING MORAL EDUCATION POLICIES

We have noted the emergence of a new kind of moral education text developed in the mid-1990s. In 1995, three years after Deng's visit to South China, a new wave of moral education text development took place in Guangdong. The *New Three Character Classic (Xin sanjijing)* (Editorial Committee, 1995), an adaptation of the traditional *Three Character Classic* used as literary text 500 years ago, was published by Guangdong Education Press. Since then, various versions of the *New Three Character Classic* have appeared in Beijing and Shanghai. Among the different versions published, the Guangdong version recorded the highest turnover, with about 40 million copies sold throughout China, and it became one of the 'top ten news items' in Guangdong province in 1995.

The Guangdong government developed the Guangdong version of the *New Three Character Classic* with the assistance of a group of university professors and school teachers. Its publication had undergone a series of consultations with various stakeholders, such as teachers, students, and parents. The Classic consists of 424 sentences, and 1,272 characters. Our content analysis of the text in terms of value types finds that the text was orientated towards traditional values (76 occurrences), personal values (51 occurrences) and social values (48 occurrences), rather than political values (21 occurrences). The *New Three Character Classic* placed a lot of emphasis on such personal values as 'righteousness', 'civilized behaviour' and 'enthusiasm for learning', and social values such as 'filial piety', 'unity' and 'concern for society'. Values related to politics were

relatively unmentioned. With respect to political figures, those most frequently mentioned were recent CCP party members with notable scientific achievements (8 occurrences). Previous CCP leaders Mao Zedong, Deng Xiaoping and Zhou Enlai, and the CCP model Lei Feng, were each only mentioned once in the text. As a moral education text, the Classic is basically disassociated from politics.

Comparing the Beijing and Shanghai versions of the *New Three Character Classics*, which were published shortly after the publication of the Guangdong version of the *New Three Character Classic* in 1995, we have found some common emphasis among the three versions of the classics. First they all emphasized the significance of Chinese traditions. 'Historical figures' were used by all the three versions as moral models, followed by 'historical achievements' which glorified the Chinese history and fostered nationalist sentiment among readers. Second, they all regarded personal values as important, in particular emphaiszing such virtues as 'righteousness', 'enthusiasm for learning', 'civilized behaviour', and 'self', though their priorities in different versions of the classics varied. In regard to social values, the three versions of the classics stressed on the traditional virtue of 'filial piety', and called for 'unity', 'devotion', and 'concern for society'. Fourth, politics were under-emphasized in all the three versions of the classics.

The emergence of the three versions of the *New Three Character Classics* shows that para-governmental documents published in Guangdong (a special economic zone on the southern coast), Shanghai (a commercial centre with long history and the political base of the then CCP leaders Jiang Zemin and Zhu Rongji), and Beijing (capital and a political centre of China) in the mid-1990s unanimously place great emphasis on traditional themes, social values, and personal values rather than politics. Obviously, politics had lost their importance in para-governmental moral texts published in the mid-1990s, a period of rapid economic reform.

Three major ideopolitical-moral education documents were issued by the government in the late 1990s, namely *Guangdong Provincial Maxims on ethic building for citizens* (the *Guangdong Maxims*) (Guangdong Provincial Propaganda Department, 2002), the *Curriculum Outline for Primary Moral Character and Junior Secondary Ideopolitical Studies* (MOE, 1997) and the *Curriculum Outline for Moral Character and Society* (MOE, 2002). These policy documents showed an even greater de-politicization in ideopolitical-moral education in the late 1990s. In particular, *Guangdong Maxims*, which was a provincial document, focused on basically personal values and social values, Chinese tradition and global values, with no mention of politics. It shows a clear shift in the direction of moral education in the twenties. There was a revival of traditional themes and downplay of politics.

Moreover, there was very clear attention towards personal and social values in moral education. This is particularly illustrated in the two curriculum outlines published in the late 1990s. In the 1997 document (MOE, 1997), nearly half of the values mentioned were personal values (45 occurrences). Social values ranked second (38 occurrences). In the 2002 document (MOE, 2002), the relative weighting of personal values and social values are reversed. However, political themes and traditional themes comprised less than 10 per cent in both curriculum documents. Depoliticization in ideopolitical and moral education thus became a clear trend as shown in the moral education documents published after the appearance of the various versions of the *New Three Character Classics*.

We have conducted interviews with three authors of the Guangdong version of the *New Three Character Classic*, two school teachers, and three government officials who were responsible for the implementation of ideopolitical-moral education in schools. All of our interviewees expressed the view that the publication of the classic was necessary in view of moral deregulation arising from rapid

social changes, such as the younger generation being spoiled in only child families and consumerism generated from marketization. The government officials saw a need to uphold traditional Chinese ethics when the orthodox socialist values were having decreased market value in society. Moreover, the publication of the classic reflects government recognition of the failure of orthodox socialist moral education which they frankly described as 'false, grand and void' and unattractive to the students. The influence of the *New Three Character Classic* lasted for some years since its publication, and it has been treated as a supplementary moral reader in moral education lessons on a voluntary basis by schools. This influence has been waned in recent years, with the increase in rhyming moral literature published.[i] Our teacher informants gave positive comments on the texts, claiming that the content of the text was attractive to students and could arouse students' interests in moral education lessons.

Moral qualities over taking political qualities

Our analysis of the moral education policy and curriculum documents shows a shift of emphases in ideopolitical-moral education. 'Nationalistic education' was replaced by 'moral qualities' since 1997. In the late 1990s, major emphases of ideopolitical-moral education included 'psychological health', 'individual well-being', 'democracy and legal education', and 'international outlook'. Hence, the *New Three Character Classic* was no longer emphasized in official discourse.

The government also called for 'innovative teaching' and 'diversity of method' in the late 1990s. In addition, the *New Three Character Classic* relied heavily on heroic models. However, the role model strategy was less mentioned in the government directives in the late 1990s. There was even no role model mentioned in the more recently published *Guangdong Maxims*.

The emergence of the *New Three Character Classic* marked the turn to nationalistic education from previously revolutionary education in the first half of the 1990s. The high percentage of traditional themes and the introduction of the morality of Chinese historical figures can be traced to the Ministry of Education which called for the integration of 'Chinese moral tradition into the ethics developing from socialist revolution and socialist construction' (MOE, 1994: para. 8, p. 74). The shift in relative content weighting of the *New Three Character Classic* and its subsequent literature reflects a changing emphasis 'nationalistic education' to 'psychological qualities' (SEC, 1995a, 1995b), and 'social ethics' (MOE, 1994; SEC, 1995c) in citizenship education.

Changing towards individual-oriented pedagogical approaches: the growth of 'I'dentity in moral education

The *New Three Character Classic* and its subsequent literature also indicated changing approaches to ideopolitical-moral education in China in the recent decade. The *New Three Character Classic* emerged at a time when the government called for "innovative" teaching in ideopolitical-moral education (SEC, 1992, 1995c), 'diversity in teaching method' (SEC, 1993a, 1993c, 1994, 1995b), 'relevance' (SEC, 1991b, 1992, 1993a, 1993c, 1994, 1995a, 1995b, 1995c; MOE, 1994), and 'student-centred' methods (SEC, 1991b, 1992, 1993a, 1993c, 1994, 1995a, 1995b, 1995c; MOE, 1994).

The *New Three Character Classic* was 'innovative' for it

(1) employed a previously denounced Confucian genre of *Three Character Classic*;
(2) advocated high percentage of traditional and national values instead of political values; and
(3) quoted historical models with excellent morality instead of revolutionary models to cultivate moral values in readers.

As mentioned, the content of the *New Three Character Classic* was 'relevant' to current social transformation. The writing of the *New Three Character Classic* was also 'student (recipient)-centred'. As an author of the *Classic* pointed out, the *New Three Character Classic* was written in a 'comprehensive' (*xiaochang*) and 'understandable' (*mingbai*) way. Interesting stories and pictures were preferred to ideological jargon and political slogans to avoid boring the young children.

The *Guangdong Maxims* (2002), a subsequent moral text published by Guangdong provincial government also demonstrated official efforts to produce 'student (recipient)-centred' and 'relevant' moral texts. Firstly, the text focused on the cultivation of moral qualities of readers indicated by high percentage of personal and social values. The *Guangdong Maxims* consisted of five chapters, all starting with 'Me' (*wo*), for example, 'Me and my family', 'Me and others'. Besides, the *Guangdong Maxims* was 'innovative' in collecting folklore Chinese maxims instead of rewriting them into a new text, signalling the lessening government intervention. Surprisingly, heroic models were absent from the *Guangdong Maxims*. Suffice to say the *Guangdong Maxims* illustrated the official calls for 'relevance', 'student-centred' and 'diversity of method'(CCP, 2000; CCP, 2001; MOE, 2001) in ideopolitical-moral education. According to Cheung and Pan (2006), this witnessed the growth of 'I'dentity in moral education and signified the growth of individualism in the Chinese society, which they called 'regulated individualism'.

Regionalization and localization in moral education

The publication of the *New Three Character Classic* to a certain extent reflected 'regional flexibility'. According to the government officials, the Guangdong propaganda department was free to organize the publication work, including the invitation of experts and teachers to the editorial board and consultation committee. The authors themselves found that they were free to discuss the publication. They did not feel any government pressure during the process of publication. Close inspection of the materials in different versions of the *New Three Character Classic* further indicates that regional government/publishers enjoyed a lot of flexibility and a high level of autonomy in producing moral education materials.

The production of the *New Three Character Classic* revealed regional autonomy in developing moral education materials. Localization of education enabled the provincial policy makers to make a prompt response to local needs led by economic reform and inadequate socialist ideopolitical-moral education by producing the *New Three Character Classic*.

The professionalization of moral education

The production of the *New Three Character Classic* was a project initiated by the Guangdong provincial government. A group of academic experts (in language or ethics) from universities or research institutions were invited to join the editorial work by the provincial government. The invitation revealed the government's concern for professional knowledge rather than ideology in the publication.

Experienced teachers were also invited for their professional teaching experience. This showed the government's concern for teaching effectiveness and its determination to produce a moral education text in accordance with learning and psychological characteristics of students, and the professional knowledge of teachers.

During the interviews, the authors told us that their opinions were respected by the provincial government throughout the editorial process. One author of the *Classic* commented that the professor responsible for rewriting the draft of the *New Three*

Character Classic enjoyed great autonomy and even felt that the draft reflected to a certain extent the professor's personal opinions. These all showed the increased respect for field experts and the professional knowledge in the development of new moral education texts.

Public participation in defining moral qualities

As the government official informants put it, the *New Three Character Classic* was a product of the cooperation of officials (*guan*) and the people (*min*); the government was no longer the sole author of moral texts but cooperated closely with the masses. Engagement of knowledgeable scholars in the publication actually marked the professionalism of ideopolitical-moral education in China in order to fill the needs of the teachers, the students, the parents, and the society. This was reasonable as education in China was turning towards meritocracy instead of ideocracy as marketization deepened. Moral education was no longer a matter of political slogan or models. Characteristics of its targets (for example, the students) had to be duly considered.

As an author of the *Classic* pointed out, the *New Three Character Classic* was written in accordance with the principle of 'avoiding the use of political terminology'. Thus, the low frequency of political themes in the literature might be due to the avoidance of overloaded young children with too many political elements. Public support was sought in the production of the *New Three Character Classic*. Teachers and parents were invited into consultation panels and their opinions were taken seriously by the government. Several drafts were abandoned because of the criticism received from the panels. Engagement of parents and teachers in the consultation reduced the discrepancy between the government (producer) and the public (final users) and helped reduce resistance from practising teachers or parents but strengthened public support for the reform. The emergence of the *New Three Character Classic* marked the moving down from 'heaven' (*tianshang*) to 'the earth' (*renjian*), and a 'secularization' of ideopolitical-moral education.

CONCLUSIONS

This paper shows a clear change in the concepts, approaches and policies of citizenship education in the changing political, economic and social context over the last twenty years in China, since the adoption of the reform and opening up policy in 1978. This policy has far-reaching social and political impacts in the country. With the launch of the modernization policy, which is associated with the emergence of the market economy, society has become increasingly open.

The impacts of these political, social and economic changes have been obvious in education. Our historical review suggests that the historical development of the citizenship curriculum can be classified into three major periods, from political orientation, to both political and moral orientations in parallel, to moral orientation. Examining the emphases in the government directives, we have found increased elements of globalization with increased advocacy for education for democracy and law education, in the process of modernization and marketization and entrance to the WTO, and increased emphasis on psychological health education, which focuses on the significance of individual well being in the society.

Our case study of the *New Three Character Classic* suggests that the development of the moral education text generated from Guangdong further illustrates the impact of marketization on moral education development in China, in terms of regionalization and decentralization. It shows an increased role played by regions in developing their moral education policy. It shows the openness of the regional government in addressing issues encountered, such

as moral problems in social change and limitations of the traditional mode of moral education. It shows the possibility of increased public participation in developing moral education texts. What is more, it unusually shows the possibility of influence from the South in the development of moral education. All this illustrates an obvious trend to flexibility, openness, decentralization and depoliticization of moral education in China.

The growing emphasis on democratization and psychological health education in the moral curriculum has paved way for the emerging independent status of moral education. It also shows the depoliticization of moral education curriculum as characterized by its disassociation from politics, and an emphasis on personal moral quality and psychological health, which were associated with modernization and the development of the market economy. The recent emphasis on developing global awareness in moral character development further exemplifies the wishes of the Chinese government to prepare the country to become a more integrated member of the globalized world, with increased openness towards global values.

NOTES

1 The Reform and Opening Up policy was formally adopted in The Third Plenary Session of the Eleventh CPC Central Committee in December 1978, whereby the central government made the strategic decision of shifting the focus of work to socialist modernization and defined the guiding policy of revitalizing the domestic economy and opening up to the outside world (see http://china.tyfo.com/int/literature/impression/i991129literature-right.htm. Access date: 12 October 2005).

2 The Four Cardinal Principles were stated by Deng Xiaoping in 1979 and were the four issues for which debate was not allowed within PRC. These are:
  (1) the principle of upholding the socialist path;
  (2) the principle of upholding the people's democratic dictatorship;
  (3) the principle of upholding the leadership of the Communist Party of China; and

(4) the principle of upholding Marxist-Leninist-Mao Zedong thought. The Four Cardinal Principles actually marked a relaxation of control over ideology. In stating the Four Cardinal Principles, the implication was that they could not be questioned, but political ideas other than those in the list could be debated (http://en.wikipedia.org/wiki/Four_Cardinal_Principles. Access date: 12 October 2005).

3 Hu Yaobang served as CCP General Secretary from 1980 to 1987.

4 On June 4, 1989, thousands of pro-democracy demonstrators, including students and workers, were killed in a crackdown by the People's Liberation Army at Tiananmen Square in Beijing, China.

5 Zhao Ziyang served as the CCP General Secretary from 1987, until being removed from the position on 24 June 1989.

6 Xiao Gongqing is a historian at Shanghai Teacher's University and a key figure in the 1980s' neo-authoritarianism debates.

REFERENCES

Arnold, F and Liu, Z. X. (1986) Sex preferences, fertility and family planning in China, *Population and Development Review*, 12: 221–46.

Baum, R. (1996) *Burying Mao: Chinese politics in the age of Deng Xiaoping*. Princeton: Princeton University Press.

Chen, F. (1997) Order and stability in social transition: neoconservative political thought in post-1989 China, *The China Quarterly*, (191): 595–613.

Chen, F. (1998) Rebuilding the Party's normative authority: China's socialist spiritual authority, *Problems of Post-Communism*, 45 (6): 33–41.

Chen, J.F. (1998) Crime in China's Modernization, in J. Zhang and X. B. Li (eds) *Social Transition in China*. Lanham: University Press of America. pp. 157–159.

Cheung, K.W. and Pan, S. (2006) Transition Of Moral Education In China: Towards Regulated Individualism, *Citizenship Teaching and Learning*, 2 (2): 37–50.

Chinese Communist Party (CCP) Central Committee (1996) Zhonggong zhongyang guanyu jiaqiang shehui zhuyi jingshen wenming jianshe ruogan zhongyao wenti di jueyi [*Resolution on Some Important Issues related to Strengthening the Construction of Socialist Spiritual Civilization*], 10 October (ratified in the sixth plenum of the 14th Central Committee) http://big5.xinhuanet.com/gate/big5/news.xinhuanet.com/video/2004-11/29/content_2273313.htm [Accessed 16 January 2006].

Chinese Communist Party (CCP) Central Committee (1999) Zhonggong zhongyang guanyu jiaqiang he gaijin sixiang zhengzhi gongzuo di ruogan yijian [*Some Opinions on Strengthening and Improving Ideopolitical Work*], 29 September, http://202.115.32.34/dangban/zzwx/zzdz.asp [Accessed 16 January 2006].

Chinese Communist Party (CCP) Central Committee (2000) Guanyu shiying xinxingshi jinyibu jiaqiang he gaijin zhongxiaoxue deyu gongzuo di yijian [Opinion on Further Strengthening and Improv-ing Moral Education Work in the Primary and Secondary Schools under the new Circumstances], 14 December, in China Education Yearbook Editorial Board (ed.) *Zhongguo jiaoyu nianjian 2001[China education yearbook 2001]*. Beijing: People's Education Press. pp. 815–820.

Chinese Communist Party (CCP) Central Committee (2001) *Gongmin daode jiansheshishi gangyao [Implementation Outline on Ethic Building for Citizens]*, 24 October, http://www1.people.com.cn/GB/shizheng/16/20011024/589496.html, [Accessed 16 January 2006].

Chu, G. and Ju, Y.A. (1993) *The Great Wall in ruins: Communication and Cultural Changes in China*. Albany, NY.: State University of New York Press. p.185.

Dassu, M. and Saich, T. (eds) (1992) *The reform decade in China: from hope to dismay*. London: Kegan Paul International/Rome: Centro Studi Di Politica Internazionale.

Dittmer, L. (2003) Leadership changes and Chinese political development, *China Quarterly*, 176: 903–925.

Editorial Committee of the *New Three Character Classic* (Ed.) (1995) *Xin Sanzijing*. [The *New Three Character Classic*]. Guangdong: Guangdong Education Press.

Fewsmith, J. (2001) The political and social implications of China's accession to the WTO, *The China Quarterly*, 167: 573–591.

Franklin, R. (1989) Intellectuals and the CCP in the post-Mao period: a study in perceptual role conflict, *Journal of Developing Societies*, 5: 203–217.

Guangdong Provincial Propaganda Department (2002) *Guangdongsheng gongmin daode geyan [Guangdong Provincial Maxims on Ethic Building for Citizens]*, in *Nanfang Ribao*, 23 April, 2002, p. A03; Le, Zheng and Duan, Yabing (eds) (2002) *Gongmin daode jianshe tongsu duben [The Ethic Building for Citizens: A Secular Version]*. Shenzhen: Haitian Press. pp. 32–37.

Ho, C.H. (2007) *The 3,4,5 Literature: Ideopolitical-moral education in Mainland China as a barometer of Political and Economic Changes*, PhD. dissertation, Durham University.

Lee, W.O. (2002) 'Moral education policy in China: The struggle between liberal and traditional approaches', *Perspectives in Education*, 18 (1): 5–22.

Lee W.O. (2005) Teachers' perceptions of citizenship in China. In W.O. Lee and J.T. Fouts (eds) *Education and Social Citizenship: Perception of Teachers in USA, Australia, England, Russia and China*. Hong Kong: Hong Kong University Press. pp. 209–246.

Lee, W.O. and Ho, C.H. (2005) Ideopolitical shifts and changes in moral education policy in China, *Journal of Moral Education*, 34 (4): 417–435.

Lee, W.O. and Zhong, M.H. (2007) Citizenship Curriculum in China: A Shifting Discourse towards Chinese Democracy, Law Education and Psychological Health, in D.L. Grossman, W.O. Lee, K.J. Kennedy (eds), *Citizenship Curriculum in Asia and the Pacific*. Hong Kong: Comparative Education Research Centre, University of Hong Kong/New York: Springer Press.

Luo, J. and Shi, L. (eds) *Explorations and Innovations on Moral Education for Today's Children and Youths – Proceedings of 2006 Beijing International Forum on Citizenship Education for Children and Youths*. Beijing: Capital Normal University Press.

Liao, G.S. (1989) Kaifang zhengce yu zhenya minzhuyundong di maodun [Contradictions between the open policy and suppression of democratic movements], *Ming Pao Monthly*, July, 11–13.

Lin, G.C.S. (2003) An Emerging Global City Region? Economic and Social Integration between Hong Kong and the Pearl River Delta, in A.Y. So, (ed.) *China's Developmental miracle: Origins, Transformations, and Challenges*. Armonk, NY: M. E. Sharpe. pp. 81–2.

Liu, J.S. (1998). *Zhongxue Deyu Cidian [Dictionary of moral education for secondary school]*. Beijing: Chinese People Public Security University Press.

Liu, J. (2005) 'Education key to "transition crisis": Academic calls for teaching to smooth way for social change', *South China Morning Post*, 12 December.

Lu, X. (1998) An Interface Between Individualistic and Collectivistic Orientations in Chinese Cultural Values and Social Relations, *The Howard Journal of Communications*, 9: 104.

Mackerras, C. (2001) *The new Cambridge handbook of contemporary China*. Cambridge: Cambridge University Press.

Nan, S.Y. (1995) Zhongnanhai fachu hongtouwenjian JiangZemin tuidong aiguojiaoyu [Zhongnanhai document: Jiang Zemin's initiation of Patriotic Education], *Guangjiaojing [Wide Angle Monthly]*, 272 (May): 36.

Nathan, A.J. (1990) *China's crisis: dilemmas of reform and prospects for democracy*. New York: Columbia University Press.

PRC Ministry of Education (MOE) (1994) *Zhonggong zhongyang guanyu jinyibu jiaqiang he gaijin xuexiao deyu de ruogan yijian [Opinions on further strengthening and improving moral education work in schools]*, 31 August, in China Education Yearbook Editorial Board (ed.) *Zhongguo jiaoyu nianjian 1995 [China education yearbook 1995]*. Beijing: People's Education Press. pp. 72–77.

PRC Ministry of Education (MOE) (1997) Jiunian yiwujiaoyu xiaoxue sipinke ji zhongxue sixiangzhengzhi kecheng biaozhun [The Revised Nine-year Compulsory Primary Ideomoral and Secondary Ideopolitical Curriculum Standards], *Chinese Education Yearbook 2002*. Beijing: People's Education Press.

PRC Ministry of Education (MOE) (1998) *Guanyu putong gaodeng xuexiao 'liangke' kecheng shezhi de guiding jiqi shishi gongzuo de yijian [Notice of Opinions in*

Relation to Two Lessons Curriculum Regulations and Implementation], http://www.moe.edu.cn/edoas/website18/info4278.htm, [Accessed 12 October 2005].

PRC Ministry of Education (MOE) (2001) Jiunian yiwujiaoyu xiaoxue sipinke ji zhongxue sixiangzhengzhi kecheng biaozhun di tongzhi [Curriculum guidelines for nine-year compulsory ideomoral education in primary school and ideopolitical education in junior secondary school], 17 October, *http://www.edu.cn/20041118/3120755.shtml* [Accessed16 January 2006].

PRC Ministry of Education (MOE) (2002) *Pinde yu shehui kecheng biaozhun (shixing) [Morality and Society Curriculum Standards (Experimental Version)]*. Beijing: Beijing Normal University Press.

PRC State Education Commission (PRCSEC) (1990) Guojia jiaowei guanyu jinyibu jiaqiang zhongxiaoxue deyugongzuo di jidian yijian [Opinions on further strengthening moral education work in primary and secondary schools], 13 April, in China Education Yearbook Editorial Board (ed.) *Zhongguo jiaoyu nianjian 1991 [China education yearbook 1991]*. Beijing: People's Education Press. pp. 869–873.

PRC State Education Commission (PRCSEC) (1991a) Guojia jiaowei guanyu banfa xiaoxuesheng richang xingwei guifan di tongzhi [Notice on the promulgation of *Daily Codes of Behaviour for Primary School Students*], 20 August, in Department of Educational Foundation, State Education Commission (eds) *The Essential Document Information of Moral Education in Primary and Secondary Schools [zhongxiaoxue deyugongzuo wenjianziliao bidu]*. Shanghai: Shanghai Education Press. pp. 114–7.

PRC State Education Commission (PRCSEC) (1991b) Guojia jiaowei guanyu banfa zhongxiaoxue jiaqiang jindai xiandaishi ji guoqing jiaoyu di zongti gangyao (chugao) di tongzhi [Notice on the promulgation of the overall outline of strengthening education of history of contemporary China, modern China, and China condition], 27 August, in Department of Educational Foundation, State Education Commission (eds) *The Essential Document Information of Moral Education in Primary and Secondary Schools [zhongxiaoxue deyugongzuo wenjianziliao bidu]*. Shanghai: Shanghai Education Press. pp. 124–126.

PRC State Education Commission (PRCSEC) (1992) Guojia jiaowei gongqingtuan zhongyang guanyu zai quanguo zhongxiaoxue shenru kaizhan xue Lei Feng huodong di yijian [Opinions on deepening implementation of Learning Lei Feng activities in primary and secondary schools], 7, April, in Li, Ming Yi et al. (eds.) (2001) *The Guidance Book on the Strengthening and Improving Moral Education Work in Primary and Secondary Schools under the new conditions [xinxingshixia jiaqianghegaijin zhongxiaoxue deyugongzuo zhidao quanshu]* (Vol.3). Yanji; Yanbian's People Press. pp. 2494–2496.

PRC State Education Commission (PRCSEC) (1993a) Guojia jiaowei guanyu banfa xiaoxue deyu gangyao di tongzhi [Notice on the promulgation of Outline of moral education in primary school], 26 March, in Department of Educational Foundation, State Education Commission (Eds) *The Essential Document Information of Moral Education in Primary and Secondary Schools [zhongxiaoxue deyugongzuo wenjianziliao bidu]*. Shanghai: Shanghai Education Press. pp. 96–107.

PRC State Education Commission (PRCSEC) (1993b) *Guanyu xinxingshixia jiachang he gaijin gaodeng xuexiao dangdi jianshe he sixiang zhengzhi gongzuo di ruogan yijian [Opinions on strengthening and improving the Party and ideopolitical works in higher institutes in new circumstances]*, 13 August, http://www.ipo.gansu.gov.cn/zlzx/images/ZZQFJXGFG/1942.htm [Accessed: 16 January 2006].

PRC State Education Commission (PRCSEC) (1993c) *Guanyu yunyong youxiu yingshipian zai quanguo zhongxioaxue kaizhan aiguo zhuyi jiaoyu di tongzhi[Notice on the Making Use of Excellent Films for the National Patriotic Education in Primary and Secondary Schools]*, 12 September, in Department of Educational Foundation, State Education Commission (Eds.) *The Essential Document Information of Moral Education in Primary and Secondary Schools [zhongxiaoxue deyugongzuo wenjianziliao bidu]*. Shanghai, Shanghai Education Press. pp. 159–166.

PRC State Education Commission (PRCSEC) (1994) Guojia jiaowei guanyu guanche aiguo zhuyi jiaoyu shishi gangyao di tongzhi [*Notice on the Promulgation of the Outline* on the *Implementation of Education in Patriotism]*, 23 August, in Department of Educational Foundation, State Education Commission (Eds) *The Essential Document Information of Moral Education in Primary and Secondary Schools [zhongxiaoxue deyugongzuo wenjianziliao bidu]*. Shanghai: Shanghai Education Press. pp. 140–151.

PRC State Education Commission (PRCSEC) (1995a) Zhongxue deyu dagang [Outline of moral education in secondary school] (Revised edn.), 27 February, in China Education Yearbook Editorial Board (ed.) *Zhongguo jiaoyu nianjian 1996 [China education yearbook 1996]*. Beijing: People's Education Press. pp. 891–898.

PRC State Education Commission (PRCSEC) (1995b) *Guanyu* xiang quanguo zhongxioaxue tuijian baizhong aiguo zhuyi jiaoyu tushu di tongzhi [Notice on the Recommendation of Hundred Patriotic Education Readers for Primary and Secondary Schools], 22 May, in Li, Ming Yi et al. (Eds) (2001) *The Guidance Book on the Strengthening and Improving Moral Education Work in Primary and Secondary Schools under the new conditions [xinxingshixia jiaqianghegaijin zhongxiaoxue deyugongzuo zhidao quanshu]* (Vol.3). Yanji: Yanbian's People Press. pp. 2521–2526.

PRC State Education Commission (PRCSEC) (1995c) Zhongguo putong gaodeng xuexiao deyu dagang (shixing) [The *Outline of Moral Education in Chinese Higher Schools (Draft)*, November 23, in China Education Yearbook Editorial Board (ed.) *Zhongguo jiaoyu nianjian 1996 [China education yearbook 1996]*. Beijing, People's Education Press. pp. 930–6.

PRC State Education Commission (PRCSEC) (1997) Guanyu dangqian jiji tuijin zhongxiaoxue shishi sushi jiaoyu di ruogan yijian [*Some Opinions on the Current Active Promulgation of Quality Education in Primary and Secondary Schools]*, 29 October, in Li, Ming Yi et al. (Eds.) (2001) *The Guidance Book on the Strengthening and Improving Moral Education Work in Primary and Secondary Schools under the new conditions [xinxingshixia jiaqianghegaijin zhongxiaoxue deyugongzuo zhidao quanshu]* (Vol.3). Yanji: Yanbian's People Press. pp. 2544–2549.

PRC State Education Commission (PRCSEC) (1998) Zhongxiaoxue deyu gongzuo guicheng [The Rule of Moral Education Work in Primary and Secondary Schools], 16 March, in China Education Yearbook Editorial Board (ed) *Zhongguo jiaoyu nianjian 1999 [China education yearbook 1999]*. Beijing: People's Education Press. pp. 963–6.

Prime, P.B. (1997) China's Economic Progress: Is it sustainable? in W.A. Joseph (Ed.) (1997) *China Briefing: the Contradictions of Change*. Armonk, NY: M. E. Sharpe. p. 52.

Reed, G.G. (1996) The Multiple Dimensions of a Unidimensional Role Model: Lei Feng, in L.N.K. Lo, and S.W. Man, (eds) *Moral and Civic Education*, Hong Kong: Hong Kong Institute of Educational Research. p. 248

Saich, T. (2004) *Governance and politics of China*. New York: Palgrave Macmillan.

Smil, V. (1993) *China's Environmental Crisis: An Inquiry into the Limits of National Development*. Armonk, NY: M. E. Sharpe.

Tang, W.F. and Parish, W.L. (2000) *Chinese Urban Life under Reform: the changing social contract*. Cambridge: Cambridge University Press. pp. 55, 70–77.

UNDP (United Nations Devleopment Program) (2005) *Launch of the China Human Development Report 2005*, www.undp. org.cn/modules.php. [Accessed 1 September 2007].

Vohra, R. (2000) *China's path to modernization: a historical review from 1800 to the present*. New Jersey: Prentice Hall.

Wong, L. and Mok, K.H. (1995) The reform and the changing social context, in L. Wong, and S. MacPherson, (eds) (1995) *Social Change and Social Policy in Contemporary China*. Hong Kong: Avebury.

Wright, T. (2002) The China Democracy Party and the politics of protest in the 1980s – 1990s, *The China Quarterly*, (172): 906–926.

Wu, J. (1990) *Guoqing jiaoyu shouce [Handbook of national conditions education]*. Beijing: Huaxia Press.

Wu, N. T. (1993) From planned to market economy, *Beijing Review*, 11–17 January, 13–18.

Yu, Y.M. (1998) The Development of Communication Information Infrastructure: A Revolution in Networking, in J. Zhang and X.B. Li (eds) *Social Transition in China*. Lanham: University Press of America. pp. 172–3.

Zhang, X.B. and Zhang, K.H. (2003) How does Globalization affect Regional Inequality within a Developing Country?: Evidence from China, *Journal of Development Studies*, 39 (4): pp. 51–3.

Zheng, H.S. (ed.) (1996) *Congchuantong xiangxiandai kuaisu zhuanxing guochengzhong di zhongguo shehui: zhongguo renmin daxue shehui fazhan baogao 1994–1995 [Chinese society in fast transformation from traditional to modern modes: a report on social development by People's University of China, 1994–1995]*. Beijing: People's University of China.

12

Education for Citizenship and Democracy: The Case of the Czech Republic

Martina Klicperová-Baker

INTRODUCTION

The Czech Republic, a country of 10 million inhabitants, makes an intriguing case for the study of democratic citizenship. Positioned in the center of Europe, the Czechs repeatedly found themselves involved at the very beginning of significant world conflicts. Still, their most cherished heroes personify valors of humanism and education and they have, even under adverse circumstances, strived for nonviolence and democracy (recent achievements include a democratic Velvet Revolution of 1989 and the Velvet Divorce from the Slovaks in 1992).

The lives of most Czech citizens were rather turbulent. Their socialization reflected dramatic times. The oldest generation had to adapt and almost permanently resocialize to changing political and economic conditions. Those born into the Austro-Hungarian Empire came of age in the democratic First Czechoslovak Republic, experienced Nazi German occupation, a short period of freedom following

May 1945, only to spend most of their lives under Communist dictatorship. The long oppression was eased by the hopeful 1960s but the Prague Spring democratization (1968) was soon crushed by Soviet tanks. Freedom finally prevailed in 1989 yet in 1993 Czechoslovakia split into two separate states. What a socialization rollercoaster for one human life!

The reader does not need arguments for teaching democracy, the problem lies elsewhere. There are no easy guidelines as they tend to be for authoritarian societies. Democracy does not provide individuals or nations with clear procedures to be applied or obeyed. To the contrary, democracy is based on the pursuit of mutually exclusive (!) principles which, by definition, are difficult to follow at the same time. These mutually exclusive democratic principles (listed by a Czech-American political scientist, Ivo K. Feierabend, 2007) include:

- freedom versus equality;
- rights of the majority versus individual or minority rights;

- government limited by constitution (rule of law) versus sovereign will of the people; and
- general interests of the community versus special interests.

Hence, democracy is a challenge to a discourse and good will is needed for the system to stay in a desired equilibrium, satisfying citizens who have opposing demands. No wonder that the path to democracy has no end, or, as Václav Havel put it:

> As long as people are people, democracy in the full sense of the word will always be no more than an ideal; one may approach it as one would a horizon, in ways that may be better or worse, but it can never be fully attained (Havel, 1990).

Since the democratic goal is so elusive, education for democracy has to focus on democratic personality, flexible and tolerant both socially and cognitively (ability to tolerate ambiguity and lack of cognitive closure, to correct cognitive schemata and ideologies). Traits related to authoritarianism (Adorno et al., 1950), dogmatism and ideological rationalization (e.g., Jost et al., 2003) create an obstacle.

What should be of utmost interest to pedagogues and politicians, are pro-democratic social psychological predispositions which may be cultivated by education and encouraged by favorable policies. Based on the analyses of democratic transitions and the Czech case in particular, social scientists argue that these preconditions are three – the 'Feierabend triad': Civic political culture, civility and civic nationalism (Klicperová-Baker et al., 1999: 10). As a tripod, this social psychological base sustains stable democracies. Research in political psychology suggests that the Czechs achieved satisfactory results along these indicators, explaining Czech inclination to democracy.

Roots of the Czech pro-democratic spirit can be traced to the early Reformist Hussite era at the beginning of fifteenth century. A mixed experience of both pride and deep disappointment with democracy in the twentieth century provided the Czechs with realism; a rational awareness that democracy has

both a potential as well as its limits. Surveys confirm that citizens of the Czech Republic tend to be less excited or alienated of democracy than inhabitants of other countries in the region (Klicperová-Baker et al., 2003 and in press). Their view resonates with the Churchillean (1947) quote about democracy being 'the worst form of government except all those other forms that have been tried from time to time'. This experience may constitute a solid head start for national civic education.

HISTORICAL CONTEXTS

Civics has to be perceived in a historical context of national history. Why was the world surprised by the vividness of Kosovo battle or the significance of the ancient partition of Sunni and Shia Muslims? And why amazed over the 'Velvet Divorce' of Czechs and Slovaks who have never fought each other? Whoever wants to comprehend or cultivate a nation needs to take into account its ethnic memories.

The main sources of Czech national pride happen to be closely related to democracy and so are Czech national tragedies. The First Czechoslovak Republic (1918–1938) was established at the end of WWI after the collapse of Austria-Hungary. It was a modern multi-ethnic state, an experiment in civic coexistence (it provided democratic rights to all its citizens – Czechs, Slovaks, Germans, Hungarians, Ruthenians and Roma). It was founded with the diplomatic help of the US, its first president was Professor Thomas G. Masaryk, a believer in humanitarian ideals and democracy (Masaryk, 1938; V. L. Beneš, 1973). Despite political turmoil and economic crisis in 1930s, Czechoslovakia remained democratic even when all its neighbors became authoritarian. The pride of the First Czechoslovak Republic and love for President Masaryk survived almost half a century of Nazi and Communist propaganda. The collective memory of it is for the Czechs a reference point of a golden age, a role model of a progressive, prosperous liberal democracy.

The Velvet Revolution – the strikingly nonviolent manner in which freedom and democracy were reclaimed in November 1989 – is another source of pride. An exemplar of civility (not even flowerbeds were stepped on by the demonstrating crowds), the mass of hundreds of thousands of people behaved itself, it was rational and morally elevated, and led a cogent and witty political dialogue with speakers of various political creeds (unlike a typical crowd described by Le Bon). The revolution resembled more a cultural event than a political struggle. Yet, competition of ideologies was there, even within the umbrella organization Civic Forum. And not just the name 'Forum' but the open confrontation of ideas resembled of the direct Athenian democracy. With no time for elections, a quick national referendum was executed by means of a short general strike. As the peaceful struggle of Gandhi, the Velvet Revolution became a model for future nonviolent struggles.

Disappointment by democracy: Munich. As Hitler rose to power, he demanded annexation of one third of the Czechoslovak territory – the mountainous border region Sudetenland, mostly inhabited by German immigrants. Czechoslovakia could not survive without it for strategic and economic reasons. (The mountains formed the borders and were well defended, the region produced 70 per cent of electricity and steel.) Czechoslovakia had an efficient army, patriotic spirit and a defense treaty with France. Determined to resist, it mobilized. On September 29, 1938, Hitler, Mussolini, the French Prime Minister Daladier and British Prime Minister Chamberlain, without inviting Czechoslovak representatives, made a decision: the infamous Munich Agreement also known as the Munich Dictate. The French repudiated the defense treaty and left Czechoslovakia with a dilemma either give up Sudetenland and be left vulnerable or fight Hitler alone, carrying responsibility for

a new war in Europe and risk annihilation. The morale of the nation during the crisis remained high – President Beneš witnessed: 'The commanding generals asked me not to capitulate, to give the order to advance against the German army (...), they threatened, they begged me, some cried' (L. K. Feierabend, 1994: 99). Still, President Beneš and the Cabinet decided to give up. People who earlier that week demonstrated and resolutely demanded arms, wept; soldiers at the borders were unwilling to hand over bunkers to the enemy, some fled to exile, some committed suicide.

Munich and the subsequent decision to yield without a fight crushed Czechoslovakia psychologically. The substance of the tragedy was not in the loss of Sudetenland, although it meant the loss of freedom in a near future. More importantly, Munich meant a failure of democracy, both Western and domestic. This failure is the reason why the Czechs fell so easily victim to the Eastern, Communist takeover of their country in 1948. Hence Munich had a political impact not just of 7 but of 60 years. And the psychological trauma has never been forgotten. Giving up ideals of Masaryk. Not being able to stand up for truth as Czech Hussites did in their struggle 'against all' in the 1400s.

The high and low points described above are deeply coined to the Czech psychology.

CZECH EDUCATIONAL TRADITIONS

Education has a rich tradition and enjoys high respect in the Czech lands. The most esteemed Czechs are connected to education, whether the top list was assessed by an official opinion poll agency (CVVM) or by a popular TV show 'The Greatest Czech' (Česká televize, 2005). The most respected Czech of all times – the Emperor Charles IV (1316–1378) was a multilingual, highly educated man of letters who led no wars but founded in Prague the first Central European university. The second in popularity was

Professor Masaryk (1850–1937), the founder of Czechoslovakia, and the third, Václav Havel (*1936), writer and philosopher who was deprived of higher education by the Communists yet received some 50 honorary doctorates. The next in popularity (CVVM 2006) was a university president and an early Protestant reformer Jan Hus (1370–1415), tried by a papal court and burnt at the stake because he refused to repent his teaching; and fifth – a pedagogue and proponent of universal education, Comenius – Jan Ámos Komenský (1592–1670), a.k.a. 'teacher of nations' (fourth by the TV poll).

Comenius compiled an educational encyclopedia, *Didactica Magna* (1638). It comprised a system of revolutionary humanistic teaching principles: education should be universal (available without discrimination by gender, wealth or talent), free of charge and compulsory until the age of 12; teaching should respect child psychology (progress from simple to complicated elements, playfully, with examples, pictures and relevance to practical use). His *Schola Pansophica* (1651), recommended a regular reading of newspapers. Comenius was a pioneer of progressive reforms yet he could not improve education in his home country. Bohemia was incorporated into the Austro-Hungarian Empire by the Hapsburgs, recatholicized, germanized and Comenius, being a Protestant bishop, was driven out to exile.

Educational reforms had to wait until the next century, the era of Enlightenment and the open-minded Empress Maria Theresa. She introduced a magnanimous school reform, the Universal School Order (1774), she took schooling away from the clergy and established it as the responsibility of public policies ('Die Schule ist ein Politikum'). Many of Comenius's recommendations came to life although the Catholic reformers would not admit it (Morkes, 2004). Universal education till the age of 12 was finally introduced. The reforms continued also under the reign of Maria Theresa's son, Joseph II. The school attendance was extended to the age of 14 (1869) and strictly enforced (with punishment by jail sentence for parents who failed to send their children to school). This policy led to universal literacy in the Czech lands by the end of the nineteeth century, which was an impressive result in comparison to other countries at that time.

LEARNING TO BE CITIZENS – FORMAL AND INFORMAL EDUCATION

The Enlightenment and general education sparked a wave of Czech emancipation – the *Czech National Awakening* in the eighteenth and nineteenth centuries. Although primarily motivated by cultural sentiments (love of language, literature, theater), this movement soon acquired civic features and created Czech civil society.

Czech intellectuals – 'awakeners' strived to rescue the Czech language and keep up the Czech/Slavic spirit against the Austrian oppression. A patriotic organization Sokol (Falcon) organized by enthusiastic democrats Tyrš and Fügner spread from Prague all over the Czech lands to teach the ancient Greek ideal of *kalokagathia* – the philosophy of harmony of mind and body. It also fostered civic virtues, democratic values and ideals of French revolution – (Sokol, 2007). Sokol provided civic education to the future Czechoslovak citizens and a resource for Czechoslovak legions who fought on the Allied side during WWI and helped to create the forthcoming independent state.

Czechoslovakia was founded in 1918. Its leaders knew the importance of civic education. After all, the Founding Father Masaryk was a Professor of Sociology and inspired the nation (Holý, 1996). He also kept himself educated by reading the work of the other great minds of his time. One of the organizers of regular intellectual meetings, the writer Karel Čapek, documented Masaryk's democratic thinking in his *Conversations*: 'Democracy is made by democrats and better democracy is made by better democrats. Democracy is not only the system but also the mentality of the citizens' (Čapek, 1938: 195).

No time was wasted to better the educational system of the young republic, in particular the civic education. As soon as on January 15, 1919 the Ministry of Education and National Enlightenment issued a ruling 'On educational significance of our times' outlining the new subject of civic education (Staněk, 2007). Great political events as well as everyday life played a role in it. Since 1923 'Civic Education' and 'Manual Skills' were introduced as compulsory subjects, replacing till then compulsory 'Catechism'.

The educational system reflected the character of the Czechoslovak Republic. Its 'democratism', the equality of opportunity (women were equal to men, aristocratic privileges and titles were abolished), secularism, focus on science, respect for work, humanism, civility. Egalitarianism was reflected also in the non-elitist approach to schooling (Válková and Kalous, 1991: 186).

The rising Nazi threat called for patriotism and was reflected in civic education as well as in popular culture. As often before and after, Czech theater helped to foster patriotic spirit. Particularly notable was the intelligent satire of *Liberated Theater* by Voskovec and Werich (Burian, 1977).

Masaryk wished that Czechoslovakia would be allowed at least 50 years of undisturbed development for democracy to settle in. Czechoslovakia was hardly allowed 20 years. Shattered by Munich, it faced 50 years of totalitarian dictatorship instead.

CIVICS UNDER TOTALITARIAN REGIMES

First the Nazi invasion, then the Communist dictatorship and the Soviet occupation prevented the Czechs from full citizenship. The best citizens perished in concentration camps, they were paraded in show trials, executed. Education, a natural enemy of totalitarianism, claimed the bravest university students as martyrs: Jan Opletal died of wounds inflicted on him during the demonstration against Nazis (his funeral day November 17, has become since 1941 an International Students' Day). Student Jan Palach immolated himself in protest against the Soviet invasion and growing complacency with it.

Civic education under the totalitarian regimes either hardly existed (Nazis replaced Civics by classes of German language following assassination of Protector Heydrich by Czech partisans) or it morphed into party propaganda (Civics under the Communists). Nazis also closed Czech universities, executed student leaders and put 1,200 students to concentration camps. And although school education was extended till the age of 15 in 1948, the Communists closely controlled the instruction and admission process to higher levels of schooling, based Civics on Marxism-Leninism, justified with it the leading role of the Communist Party and dictatorship of 'proletariat', and subjugation to the Soviet Union.

Civic education is never limited to formal schooling. That is especially true under violent regimes where natural situations have a particularly intense formative impact. There a child has to learn not only to integrate clashing information but also to understand without a luxury of a mistake the difference between the private and the public spheres. Errors or standing up for one's conscience may be paid by the highest price. The variety of interlocked levels engaged in socialization and their inconsistency can be illustrated by an adapted Behavioral ecological model (Hovell et al., 2002) – Figure 12.1.

Totalitarian regimes have monopolies over all important aspects of society, that includes punishments of civic heroes. Instead of fostering civic virtues, the regimes suppress the notion of citizenship, provoke sense of learned helplessness, suppress individuality, etc. In its entirety, the symptoms constitute what can be labeled a post-totalitarian, or post-communist syndrome (Klicperová et al., 1997) – see Table 12.1.

Sources of interlocked contingencies

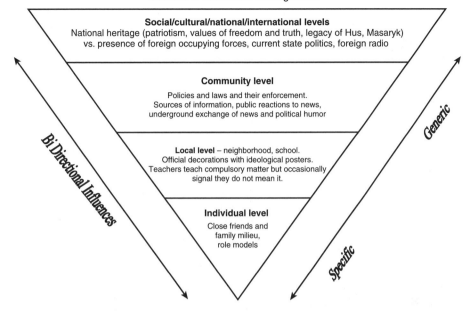

Figure 12.1   Behavioral Ecological Model – An individual is being influenced by multiple and often incongruent social levels. Schema adapted from Hovell et al. (2002).

Life under the Nazi or Communist totalitarianism meant moral dilemmas. Some are documented in literature: A classic example is a short story by Jan Drda (1955/1978) *The Higher* (moral) *Principle*. The hero, a high school teacher, not only taught classical ethics but at the decisive moment following assassination of Heydrich, proved his moral integrity. At the reign of terror this teacher decided to reveal his true feelings about the assassination of the tyrant to his students at the price of death penalty.

Another, real civic lesson of moral struggle, was provided by Václav Havel – then a dissident playwright, when he wrote a *Letter to Dr. Gustáv Husák* (1975), the communist President of Czechoslovakia. Havel presented his President with a detailed analysis of why people conformed to the dreaded regime. He paid for it by serving over four years in prison.

While the free post-WWII world progressed from civil to political liberties and social entitlements (Marshall, 1949), inhabitants of the Communist countries went in the other direction. They traded freedom and rights for social welfare and ended up in what was later nicknamed as 'goulash communism'.

Still, whenever there was an opportunity, the Czechs tried to lift the oppression (most notably in 1968, in an attempt for 'socialism with a human face'). Finally, in 1989, after the Big Soviet Brother had stopped intervening Czechoslovakia liberated itself. The Velvet Revolution was a great civic lesson. Its enlightenment was of such a magnitude that the philosopher Janát (1993) labeled it as the Velvet Revelation! It reconnected the modern generation with the democratic heritage of the First Republic. Again, the 'President Liberator' – this time Václav Havel – became a civic inspiration. He stressed democratic principles, responsibility, the importance of civil society and so called 'non-political politics – a selfless service to one's fellow human beings, morality in practice, based on conscience and truth and backed up by morality' (Havel, 1991).

Revolution brought euphoria and restored pride yet its principle 'The truth and love

Table 12.1 Post-Totalitarian syndrome: main symptoms

	Individual level	Interpersonal level	Community level	Institutional level (Offices, work, law)	Social strata level (ethnic, economic)	State politics level	International politics level	World view level
Identity	Suppressed individuality and aspirations; degraded self-esteem.	Familism, bubmissiveness; conformity; inferiority complex.	Familism, lack of identification with neighbourhood and community.	Absence of concept of citizen; system seen as a) obscure, alien and 'Kafkaesque' or b) corruptible.	Privileged view of 'in-group' (nationalism, class consciousness, racial and religious intolerance).	Government = 'Them' Dependence on paternalistic state.	Hubris, arrogance Confusion Opportunism.	Particular vision, not global view; limited capacity for transcendence.
Emotions	Fear and anxiety, uncertainty, pessimism, nostalgia, depression.	Distrust outside family, envy as a result of vulgar egalitarianism.	Disinterest; apathy.	System viewed with a) distrust, fear or b) ridicule.	Hate, contempt and fear (xenophobia), extreme hate/love attitudes.	Frustration, insecurity, bitterness, anger, hate.	Nostalgia for old orders; distrust; suspicion.	Authoritarianism, Hopelessness, loneliness.
Cognitions	Rigid schemata; external locus of control; orientation to the past.	Dishonesty and smart cheating. Habitual use of defensive mechanisms.	Lack of recognition of neighbourhood and community.	Knowledge of the system and rights is a) poor or b) shrewd, exploitive.	Rationalized prejudice. Intolerance based on out-group categorization, responsiveness to populist propaganda.	B and W thinking, incapacity to deal with dissonance, make choices, face challenge.	Traditional view of hostile pacts. Inability to compromise confusion.	Contempt for global thinking and transcendence.
Actions	Learned helplessness, powerlessness, low self-efficacy.	Low self-assertion, conformity, Irresponsibility.	Non-participation on community level.	Poor citizenship due to a) incapacity, fear b) antisocial exploitiveness.	Authoritarian (fascist) readiness, Discrimination and scapegoating. Nostalgic claims.	Dependence, helplessness, voicing claims.	Demands for old orders.	Apathy, paternalism.
Morals	Mediocrity as a virtue, satisfying lower rather than higher needs.	Moral relativism, incivility, rudeness, dishonesty, no integrity.	Absence of civic virtues (associating, activism, volunteering).	Alienation and anomie, work ethics ridiculed, cime viewed as legitimate, rationalized.	Egotism, injustice toward helpless, minorities.	Parasitism.	Longing for traditional order.	Indifference, fatalism paternalism.

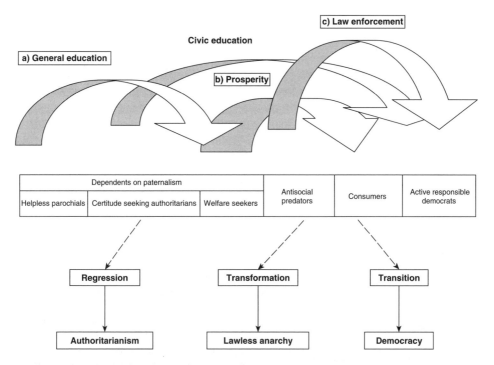

Figure 12.2 Transition to democracy. Hypothetical relationship between types of citizenship (central part of the diagram), socializing agents (upper part) and political regimes (lower part). Civic education is presented in a context with several other socialization processes: a) general education which can raise people from helpless dependence to at least become welfare-seekers b) economic prosperity which can employ welfare-seekers and turn them at least into consumers and c) law enforcement which can influence antisocial predators. The highest objective, the responsible citizenship, guarantees democratic path; other types of citizenship may lead the society to anarchy or authoritarianism.

will win over lie and hatred' was not sufficient alone for a successful transition to democracy. The country also needed the rule of law and prosperity to stay on the path to democracy – see Figure 12.2.

Havel's philosophical appeal competed with a concurrent economic vision for the new society of his finance minister, later a Prime Minister and successor as President, a Thatcherite, Václav Klaus. Klaus publicized a different educational campaign: hands-on lessons in market economy, a populist voucher privatization distributing state enterprises with little concern for morality and ecology.

Coming to terms with the old regime also turned out to be difficult. Initial euphoric and benevolent attempts to forgive Communist misdeeds were not adequately reciprocated.

Abuse instead of repentance from the side of the Communists provoked the 'lustration law' to prevent officials of the former regime from management of public affairs of the new society.

Sudden freedom released a great potential but also exposed imperfections which until then had been pent up by the totalitarian oppression. Once the constraints of the ever-present police state disappeared and prisoners were released by a rather naïve presidential gesture, crime skyrocketed by over 300 per cent. And since almost anything could suddenly be bought in the free market, new types of unscrupulous criminal activities mushroomed as well.

And then there was nationalism. The Czechs were surprised when they learned that many Slovaks longed not just for freedom but for their national sovereignty. The Czecho-Slovak negotiations for federation reforms failed and Czechoslovakia had divided into the Czech and Slovak Republics in 1993. The calm, parliamentary division earned the process a nickname 'Velvet Divorce'. Most likely, it was the democratic heritage of civility, civic culture and civic patriotism which contributed to the peacefulness. But how fared the formal civic education?

INSTITUTIONAL EDUCATION FOR CITIZENSHIP

Democratization was soon to be reflected in education: curricula were liberated from ideology, educational pluralism was restored by the reintroduction of private, religious schools and home schooling. The need for education for citizenship was obvious, yet Civics was discredited – almost synonymous with the totalitarian propaganda. Teachers were getting surprised queries: 'You are teaching Civics? Excuse me, that is still being taught?' (Tesař, 2007).

The rapid victory of democracy brought urgent challenges: *What* to teach and *how*? Civics needed new curricula and textbooks. Hausenblas (2003) and Polechová et al. (1997) describe the new situation well. There was also another question, *who* should teach? Many old instructors were loyal Communists. Should they just turn 180 degrees? According to CERMAT – Center for Assessment of Educational Results (2002) over 20 per cent of high school Civics instructors taught the subject against their will – they had it assigned; and about 28 pre cent were not fully qualified. In-service training was desperately needed. The respected IEA study (Torney-Purta et al., 2001: 161) revealed that only 41 per cent from 379 surveyed Czech Civics teachers took part in some form of continuous training during that important period.

Resources were scarce and needs many: in-service training, preparing new instructors

and new teaching materials. As the Czech pedagogues rushed to develop new curricula and textbooks, generous help came from abroad – from the US, the European Union and non-governmental organizations.

- Among others, Civitas (www.cived.org) – a center for civic education and its International Civic Education Exchange Program (funded by the US Department of Education in cooperation with the US Information Agency and American Embassy) organized a world congress in Prague in 1995, it launched there its website CIVNET http://www.civnet.org to assist civic education practitioners. Civitas also started a curriculum development project for the post-communist countries 'Comparative Lessons for Democracy' (Shinew and Fischer, 1997).
- The Open Society Fund and Research Support Scheme of the Soros foundation came with funding, seminars, support for research, established in Prague a US-licensed Central European University.
- The Open Society Institute provided educational programs in Civics, 'Street Law' project http://www.streetlaw.org/osiinfo.html.
- Institute for Educational Development (IED) from the College of Education of University of Iowa joined its Charles University partner, the Institute for Research and Development in Education at the School of Education. They developed a collaborative curriculum project Civic Education for the Czech Republic (CECR). This collaboration yielded workshops, summer schools and textbooks (Hamot, 1997).
- The Center of Civic Education – Calabasas, USA brought 'Project Citizen'. Dr. Polechová (1998) adapted it for Czech conditions. Hundreds of teachers and students identified problems in their communities (usually environmental or social issues such as recycling, bullying, coexistence with the Roma minority, substance abuse) collected data, networked with civic institutions and suggested solutions.
- American Council of Learned Societies organized a successful Constitutionalism Teacher-Training Project (Dvořáková, 2002)
- IEARN (International Education and Resource Network) connected and empowered civic educators, students and non-profit organizations, over 20,000 schools and youth organizations in more than 115 countries; over a million students were engaged daily in collaborative projects http://www.iearn.cz/

- Constitutional Rights Foundation (CRFC) of Los Angeles and its Chicago branch reached out to Czech teachers with an exchange program, Democracy Educational Exchange program (DEEP) focused on critical thinking and responsible civic actions.
- The European Commission inspired many teachers and students with programs like Phare (for educators in aspiring member states of EU), Socrates (encouraging educational cooperation) and Erasmus (devoted to facilitation of student exchange).
- Last but not least, innumerable national, bilateral, regional and faith-based partnerships achieved intensive and concrete impact with little publicity. This was in particular true of projects developed in border regions and many projects with German partners.

Some projects helped in the initial phase of acute need, some grew into long-lasting programs, others survived as an inspiration for future. Yet, there were also disappointments. The greatest was probably when political pressure of Václav Klaus caused the Central European University to leave Prague for Budapest.

Freedomhouse has given the Czech Republic the highest marks both for political rights and civil liberties since 2005. The state of Czech democracy was further monitored by surveys of Barometer, Eurobarometer and Transparency International. Multiple research teams scrutinized Czech democracy. The 'Feierabend triad' of social psychological preconditions for democracy suggested promising indicators for democratic development.

Civic political culture

Studies of Czech political culture demonstrated civic propensities (Almond, 1983), civic enthusiasm (Dryzek and Holmes, 2000), robust civic culture characterized by relative sophistication, loyalty without blind devotion (Klicperová-Baker et al., 2003; Hofstetter et al., 2000) and realistic levels of trust in democratic institutions (Mishler and Rose, 1997; Macek and Marková, 2004). The manifestations of post-communist syndrome,

alienation or disaffected egalitarianism were less prominent (Dryzek and Holmes, 2000) than in other countries in the region.

Civility (morality of civil society manifested by tolerance, civic virtues, respect for law, honesty and interpersonal trust)

A representative survey of Czech citizens indicated relatively high scores on items related to tolerance, especially tolerance to alternative lifestyles, gender roles, social and ethnic differences; a significant proportion of Czech respondents approved of a liberal 'live and let live' philosophy, while alternative lifestyles of post-communist negativistic amoralism and conservative Christian virtuousness were less pronounced (Klicperová-Baker, 2003). Admittedly, limited tolerance was manifested toward the Roma minority (also Fawn, 2001).

Civic patriotism

The analysis of 'Czechness' revealed a blend of cultural and civic nationalism; this type of liberal patriotism may be better suited for peaceful coexistence than other types of nationalism (Feierabend et al., 1999; Klicperová-Baker et al., 2007).

The most representative inquiry of civic education was performed by the above mentioned IEA study. Torney-Purta et al. (2001) compared civic knowledge and engagement of 14-year olds across 28 countries and proved an overall good standing of the traditional Czech education but also pointed out challenges in fostering active, participant citizens. Czech students scored above the international average in their 'civic knowledge' index (p. 55) consisting of 'content knowledge' (that is where the Czechs achieved particularly good results) and 'interpretative skills' (p. 63). The Czech results in the willingness to take civic or political action were less satisfactory, their gap between civic knowledge and engagement was more pronounced than in other samples. Czech students reported that they seldom belonged to civic-related organizations (p. 142); they were reserved in their trust to government and media; their projected future political participation was also rather low. Czech teens scored below the international average in conventional participation (intentions to join a political party, write to a newspaper or be a candidate for a public office), they were low in volunteering such as collecting money for social causes or signatures for a petition, participating in political marches and taking part in illegal political activities (p. 118–122). These reservations were confirmed also in older, 17–18-year old Czech students (Torney-Purta and Amadeo, 2003).

These IEA youth findings turned out to be consistent with results relevant to the school climate and skepticism of their teachers: the Czech 14-year olds in 1999 rated their classroom climate as less open than the international average and they also expressed low self-efficacy in engagement in school matters (Torney-Purta et al., 2001: 133). On top of that, IEA data show that a mere 53 per cent of Czech civic teachers agreed with a statement that 'teaching civic education makes a difference for students' political and civic development' (p. 170). Although Czechs are generally realists rather than naïve enthusiasts (Klicperová et al., 2007) and also renowned for black humor, such a result raises eyebrows and deserves further analysis. Importantly, these teachers also voiced dissatisfaction with the present teaching process and intensive hope for a change. Torney-Purta et al. (2001) documented their desire to obtain more training and better teaching materials. These instructors voiced intense discrepancies between the current reality and an ideal instruction: 51 per cent reported that most emphasis is placed on the 'transfer of knowledge' and only 3 per cent wished this to continue; conversely, only 18 per cent viewed 'critical thinking' as a center of interest of civic education while many more – 42 per cent wanted to focus

on it; similarly, mere 2 per cent thought that Civics as they knew it was focused on 'participation' and again, many more – 17 per cent thought that 'participation' should be in the foreground of the subject. In sum, the IEA study showed very well what was left to be desired in Czech democratic educational process.

The need for a substantial educational reform had been obvious since the 1989 revolution. Education has been recognized as a value of utmost importance and the public was engaged in a general discussion about it; yet there has always been a struggle with financing and bureaucracy. Several waves or reforms unfolded (as described below) and many new educational facilities (including non-governmental organizations and new universities) were founded.

Civic teachers are now trained at the universities, typically at a school of education (pedagogická fakulta), at the department of civic education (katedra občanské výchovy) or at a department of social sciences (katedra společenských věd); often also at a school of arts, school of economics or school of law. The most important centers in the Czech Republic include:

- Department of Civic Education and Philosophy of School of Education at Charles University in Prague;
- Department of Social Sciences of School of Education at Palacký University in Olomouc;
- Department of Civic Education of School of Education at Masaryk University in Brno;
- Department of Social Sciences of School of Education at South Bohemian University in České Budějovice
- Institute of Philosophy and Social Sciences of School of Humanities at University in Hradec Králové; and
- Department of Social Sciences of School of Education at Ostrava, University in Ostrava.

University education may be supplemented by in-service training by non-governmental organizations or non-traditional university initiatives. For example, in 1993 the Dean of School of Education in Olomouc, Prof. Mezihorák, founded a summer school which became a very popular center of continuous education. It earned international recognition and has been publishing regular proceedings (see for example, Hrachovcová et al., 2000; Dopita and Staněk, 2006). Another kind of initiative is SVOD – Association for Civic Education and Democracy (the acronym in Czech happens to mean 'temptation'). SVOD is an officially accredited apolitical association of volunteers offering training in project 'I-citizen' with a full methodological service at http://www.svod-cz.info/.

The highest institution responsible for Czech education is the Ministry of Education, Youth and Physical Education of the Czech Republic (Ministerstvo školství, mládeže a tělovýchovy České republiky http://www.msmt.cz/). The ministry started the most recent wave of reforms by a directive issued in 1995 called the *Standard of Basic Education*. It is a set of very broad educational objectives which include cognitive aims, skills, values and attitudes along with specific educational targets and 'stem subject matter' for each subject:

> The objectives for Civics include: understanding democratic country and basics of economy; comprehension of basic human rights and elements of law; development of responsible active citizenship; learning to judge domestic, European and global phenomena; acquiring the capacity to solve problems; learning adequate conduct and problem solving in accord with one's conscience. (Since the inventory is quite extensive, we bring only this abridged list.)

The 'stem areas' contain a plethora of themes, as home (city, region, homeland); state (symbols, national memory, heritage, constitution, state organs), European legacy, justice, freedom, authority; market economy, responsibility at work, welfare, free time; human being – body and spirituality, health care, communication, love, marriage, family, sexuality; morality, meaning of life, truth, tolerance; responsibility for the Earth and humankind; democracy, dignity, equality, freedom; human rights, political and economic interests of the Czech Republic, international institutions (also abridged).

Progress in democratic transition and acceptance to the EU prompted the Ministry

to further reforms. It issued the *National Program of Development of Education in the Czech Republic* http://www.msmt.cz/files/pdf/bilakniha.pdf) nicknamed the *White Book* (in English sometimes referred to as the *White Page*). The *White Book* represents a strategic outline. This act coordinates civic education with the European Commission and points out that Civic Competencies are a part of its six Key Educational Competencies. At the same time, Civics has been promoted among subjects for the standardized exit exams ('Matriculation Examinations'). The *White Book* was a starting point for the *New Education Act* (Nový školský zákon) – a basis for the 2007 educational reform.

The *New Education Act* intentionally links education with real life. It also requests the students to be given an opportunity to exert their rights in self-governing bodies at school parliaments or councils involving their community. The highest of the youth parliaments is the National Parliament of Children and Youth, established in 1997 (www.participace.cz). More detailed information on the *Act* and documents of European Commission can be found at the website of the Council of Europe www.coe.int on the page Education for Citizenship and Human Rights, under the profile of the Czech Republic and at the information network on education in Europe at http://www.eurydice.org/portal/page/portal/Eurydice.

The heart of the reform lies in *Framework Educational Programs* (Rámcové vzdělávací programy) which were issued for all main types of schools. They are basic curricular documents which provide more detailed guidelines and education outcomes than the Standards of Basic Education did. The substantial change is not just in the subject matter but in the approach. The traditional Czech curricula (including those introduced in the early years of democratic transition in 1992), suffered from the traditional focus on facts and knowledge. This traditionalism, a well known ailment of Czech education, has also been pointed out by the IEA study. Framework Educational Program enables a revolution for schools willing to accept the challenge. Instead of a list of requirements and necessary knowledge, the Framework Educational Program sets key competencies, values and attitudes which should be fostered. The schools then have a considerable freedom in choice of their own curricula, textbooks, allotment of hours, distribution of themes to subjects, even the liberty to name the subjects. The trend is to use 'Education for Citizenship' or opt for the good old 'Civic Education'.

EDUCATION FOR CITIZENSHIP AT CZECH BASIC SCHOOLS

Since 1948 school attendance is compulsory between the ages of 6 and 15-years, at two levels, at each level there is some form of compulsory civic education. Readers interested in Czech education system will find excellent resources both in English and Czech at Eurydice (information network on European Education), at http://www.eurydice.org/portal/page/portal/Eurydice/DB_Eurybase_Home. Those who like the challenge of Czech language may find a good use of the Czech-English educational dictionary by Průcha (2005).

The first level includes grades 1 to 5. The youngest pupils in grade 1 and 2 traditionally received the civic information within the Elementary Learning (prvouka) and later, in grades 4 and 5 within National Geography and History (vlastivěda = 'patriology') and Natural History (přírodopis).

The new *Framework Educational Program* changes the perspective. A complex educational area 'Man (i.e., human being) and his World' spans over all five years of the first level. It covers five thematic fields: The place where we live, people around us, people and time, variability of nature and human health. Each school can design their own *School Educational Program* within this framework. It is possible to default to the traditional outlines of 'National Geography and History' and 'Natural History" or to be creative and

merge the subject matter of grades 4 and 5 together or fuse the subject matter of all the first five grades and create a brand new subject. See Table 12.2.

The second level of basic schools includes grades 6–9. The civic matter used to be traditionally taught in Civic Education ('občanská výchova' – the Czech term stressed character upbringing). Again, the new *Framework Educational Program* brings a novel approach. The complex educational area for this level is 'Man and Society' and relates to two subjects: 'Education for Citizenship' and 'History'.

'Education for Citizenship' (and let us not forget, it can also be named differently if the school so chooses) became a complex, integrative multidisciplinary field. It consists of seven components:

- National History and Geography;
- Political Science;
- Personality;
- Society;
- Law;
- Economics; and
- Environment.

In addition, *the Framework Educational Program* lists 'cross-sectional themes':

- Personality and Social Education;
- Education of a Democratic Citizen;
- Multicultural Education;
- Education for Thinking in European and Global Contexts;
- Environmental Education; and
- Media Literacy.

These add yet another dimension to the curricula. And some fields, like Ethics do not have any designated category but are supposed to diffuse through the whole subject. See Table 12.3.

The above-mentioned components and cross-sectional themes can be creatively combined. Hence, traditional components such as 'National History and Geography' when taken into account with cross-sectional themes such as 'European and Global Contexts' or 'Multicultural Education' generate

Table 12.2   Education for citizenship at the first level of Czech basic schools

School level	Traditional model (2 hours a week)	New alternatives (min. 2 hours a week – average 2.4 a week)	
Grades 1–3	Elementary learning	'Man and his World'	
Grades 4–5	National Geography and History	Themes: *where we live, people around us, people and time* can be taught traditionally within National Geography and History	'Man and his World' all thematic fields can be merged into a single subject
	Natural History	Themes *Variability of nature* and *Human health* can be taught traditionally within Natural History	

new meanings. So does the legal component in conjunction with 'Media Literacy'; 'Economy' with 'Environmental Education'. Political Science has a particularly strong standing in the outline (it includes such segments as 'State and Law' and 'International Relations and Global World'), they, too, can be combined with various cross-sectional themes.

Finally, there is a 'Social Component'. Staněk in his comprehensive monograph (2007: 40–41) points out the novelty and importance of the inclusion of 'Social Component' to the curricula and its role in strengthening social cohesion, sense for social justice and common good in students. Stěnek also points out the relationship with the *Declaration and Programme on Education for Democratic Citizenship by the Council of Europe* (1999).

Social themes are still rather new in the Czech society, which has only recently been confronted with rising social inequality and immigration. Social issues tend to interact with ethnicity. Children of Roma minority (estimated at 3 per cent of the population) often grow up under lower socio-economical conditions, they fail in culture-biased intelligence tests and they are approximately 15 times more likely than the national average to end up in remedial schools. By some estimates as many as 75 per cent of Roma children are excluded

from mainstream schools (Nedelsky, 2003). Growing up with limited working qualifications, they get trapped in substandard social conditions.

CIVIC EDUCATION AT THE SECONDARY LEVEL/ HIGH SCHOOLS

Civics at secondary technical and vocational schools has been traditionally taught in the third and fourth year, within the subject of 'Civic Education' ('občanská nauka' – the Czech term stressed transfer of knowledge).

The educational standard is higher at academically oriented schools which prepare students for university studies (these schools are often called gymnasia and approach educational standard of colleges). There, Civics has a character of introduction to social sciences. Each semester is devoted to another discipline – see Table 12.4. The *Framework Educational Programs* for this school level are presently being tested and are not yet officially approved – See Table 12.4.

The Czech Republic is a liberal, secular country with a good standard of education. In comparison to other OECD countries, there is a very high secondary educational attainment,

Table 12.3   Education for citizenship at the second level of Czech basic schools

School level	Traditional model (min. 2 hours a week)	New model (min. average 2 hours a week)
Grades 6–9 of basic school	'Civic (Character) Education'	'Man and society' can be taught within Education for Citizenship and History or other subjects

Table 12.4   Civic education at the secondary level/ high schools

School level	Traditional model	New model
Vocational schools and Secondary technical schools	'Civic (knowledge) Education' 0 – 0 – 1 – 2 hours a week	Framework educational programs are not yet available
Grammar schools	'Foundations of Social Sciences' 1 – 1 – 2 – 2 hours a week 1st year – Foundations of Theory of Science and Psychology 2nd year – Foundations of Sociology, Law, Political Science 3rd year – International relations, Planetary problems, Foundations of economy 4th year – Foundations of ethics, History of philosophy	

yet a need to increase the tertiary education and to raise the educational budget. (The Czech Republic allots less than 5 per cent of GDP and less than 10 per cent of total public spending to education – OECD, 2006: 105).

The reforms have elevated the significance of Education to Citizenship. The *Framework Educational Program* provides a progressive reform which increases the autonomy of schools as well as of students. It follows up the successful Czech transition to democracy, it reunites the country with Europe (the Czech Republic has been a member state of the EU since 2004), it also attempts to overcome educational traditionalism. It remains to be seen how well it will be applied in practice. While some conditions for its implementation have improved (freedom of students, technology including web assisted expert supervision at www.rvp.cz), other limiting factors remain, especially the lack of funding, bureaucracy and conservatism. Hopefully, it will be possible to replicate the IEA survey to witness the educational progress of the reforms.

More than ever, the teachers and the schools have the freedom and opportunity to prepare young people for life in a free society. In addition to it, the students themselves are free now to participate more than ever in social life in their communities or to complete their schooling abroad tuition-free within the EU countries. The gate of knowledge is wide open again.

REFERENCES

Adorno, T.W. Frenkel-Brunswik, E., Levinson, D.J. and Sanford, R.N. (1950) *The Authoritarian Personality*. New York: Harper.

Almond, Gabriel A. and Verba, Sidney (1989). *The Civic Culture: Political Attitudes and Democracy in Five Nations*. Princeton, NJ: Princeton University Press.

Almond, G.A. (1983) Communism and Political Culture Theory, *Comparative Politics*, 15 (2): 127–138.

Benes, V. (1973) 'Czechoslovak Democracy and its Problems, 1918–1920', in Victor S. Mamatey and Radomir Luža (eds), *A history of the Czechoslovak Republic 1918–1948*. Princeton, NJ.: Princeton University Press., pp. 39–99.

Burian J.M. (1977) The Liberated Theatre of Voskovec and Werich, *Educational Theatre Journal*, 29 (2): 153–177.

CERMAT (2002) *Centrum pro zjišťování výsledků vzdělávání* [Center for Assessment of Educational Results http://www.cermat.cz/novamaturita/vyzkumneprojekty/mikroso nda/mikrosonda_03.php#vzdelani retrieved on Aug 20, 2007.

Čapek, K. (1938) *Masaryk on Thought and Life, Conversations with Karel Čapek*; translated from the Czech by M. and R. Weatherall London: G. Allen & Unwin.

Česká televize (2005) www.ceskatelevize.cz/specialy/nejvetsicech/ – as retrieved on May 21, 2007 00:51:08 GMT.

Churchill, W. (1947) *Hansard* [House of Commons Daily Debates] Speech, Nov 11, col. 206, quoted from The Concise Oxford Dictionary of Quotations. Oxford / New York: Oxford University Press, 1993.

Council of Europe (1999) Declaration and Programme on Education for Democratic Citizenship, Based on the Rights and Responsibilities of the Citizens. http://www.coe.int/t/dg4/education/edc/Documents_Publications/Adopted_texts/098_DeclarationProgrammeEDCMay97_en.asp

CVVM – Červenka, J. (2006) Osobnosti a události českých dějin očima veřejného mínění. [Public opinion of personalities and events of Czech history]. *CVVM reports* Praha.

Dopita, M. and Staněk, A. (2006) (eds) *Výchova k občanství v rámci školního vzdělávacího programu se zaměřením na potírání rasové a národnostní nesnášenlivosti.* [Education to citizenship within a School Education Program focused on prevention of racial and ethnic intolerance] Olomouc: Univerzita Palackého v Olomouci.

Drda, J. (1978) 'The Higher Principle', in: *The Silent Barricade.* Praha: Academia.

Dryzek, J.S and Holmes, L. (2000) The Real World of Civic Republicanism: Making Democracy Work in Poland and the Czech Republic, *Europe-Asia Studies*, 52 (6): 1043–1068.

Dvořáková, V. (2002) Some reflections on Democracy and the ACLS Constitutionalism Project. In: *East European Constitutionalism Teacher-Training Project.* ACLS Occasional Paper, No. 51, pp. 49–55.

Fawn, R. (2001) Czech Attitudes toward the Roma: 'Expecting More of Havel's Country?', *Europe-Asia Studies*, 53 (8): 1193–1219.

Feierabend, I.K., Hofstetter, C.R. and Klicperová-Baker, M. (1999) Styles of Nationalism. In: Klicperová-Baker (ed.) *Ready for Democracy?* Prague: Institute of Psychology, Academy of Sciences of the Czech Republic. pp. 217–240.

Feierabend, I.K. (2007) Personal communication.

Feierabend, Ladislav K. (1994) *Politické vzpomínky, Díl II.* [Political memories, Volume II. – in Czech] Brno: Atlantis.

Hamot, G.E. (1997) Civic Education in the Czech Republic: Curriculum Reform for Democratic Citizenship. *ERIC Digest.* ERIC Identifier: ED410178.

Hausenblas, O. (2003) Civic Education in the Czech Republic: Citizenship after the Fall of Communism, *Basic Education*, 47 (4): 3–11.

Havel, V. (1975) 'Dear Dr. Husák' in: Václav Havel *Open Letters. Selected Writings 1965–1970.* Selected and edited by Paul Wilson. New York: Vintage Books. Random House. pp. 50–83.

Havel, V. (1990) 'Help the Soviet Union on its Road to Democracy. Consciousness Precedes Being.' Delivered to the Joint Session of Congress February 21, 1990. Vital Speeches of the Day (March 15), p. 330.

Havel, V. (1991) *Speech at New York University,* New York City, October 27, http://old.hrad.cz/president/Havel/speeches/1991/2710_uk.html as retrieved on Apr 7, 2007 02:34:59 GMT.

Hofstetter, C.R., Feierabend, I.K., Synak, B. and Klicperová-Baker, M. (2000) Two Nations or One? Political Culture among Czech Students during the 1990s, *Bulletin Psú*, 6 (2): 1–33.

Holy, L. (1996) *The Little Czech and the Great Czech Nation.* Cambridge: Cambridge University Press.

Hovell M.F., Wahlgren, D.R. and Gehrman, C. (2002) 'The Behavioral Ecological Model: Integrating Public Health and Behavioral Science' in R.J. Di Clemente, R. Crosby, M. Kegler, (eds) *New and Emerging Theories in Health Promotion Practice & Research.* San Francisco: Jossey-Bass Inc.

Hrachovcová, M., Zívalík, P. and Dopita, M. (2000) (eds.) *Multikulturalita, tolerance a odpovědnost.* [Multiculturalism, tolerance and responsibility] Olomouc: Univerzita Palackého, 2000.

Janát, B. (1993) Myslet proti duchu doby [Thinking against the spirit of the times]. *Listy*, 33 (3): 75–81.

Jost, J.T., Glaser, J., Kruglanski, A.W. and Sulloway, F. (2003) Political Conservatism as Motivated Social Cognition, *Psychological Bulletin*, 129 (3): 339–375.

Klicperová-Baker, M., Kovacheva, S, Titarenko, L. Feierabend, L. and Hofstetter, C.R. (2003) *Democratic Citizenship in Comparative Perspective. Psychological Theory and Empirical Study in Four Nations.* San Diego: San Diego State University, Montezuma Publishing.

Klicperová-Baker, M., Feierabend, I.K., Kovacheva, S., Titarenko, L, Košťál, J., Hofstetter, C.R. (2007) *Demokratická kultura v České republice: Občanská kultura, éthos a vlastenectví ze srovnávacího pohledu.*

[Democratic culture in the Czech Republic: Civic culture, ethos and patriotism from a comparative perspective] Academia: Praha.

Klicperová, M. Feierabend, I.K., and Hofstetter, C.R. (1997) In the Search for a Post-communist Syndrome. A Theoretical Framework and Empirical Assessment, *Journal of Community and Applied Social Psychology* 7 (1): 39–52.

Klicperová-Baker, M. et al. (1999) *Ready for Democracy? Civic Culture and Civility with a Focus on Czech Society.*

Klicperová-Baker, M. (2003) Civility and Democratic Spirit: Results of a Representative Research in the Czech Republic and Slovakia, [in Czech]. *Československá psychologie,* 47 (4): 301–318.

Macek, P. and Marková, I. (2004) 'Trust and Distrust in Old and New Democracies', in I. Marková (ed.) *Trust and Democratic Transition in Post-Communist Europe.* Oxford: Oxford University Press. pp. 173–194.

Marshall T.H. (1949) 'Citizenship and Social Class', in: *Class, Citizenship and Social Development.* Chicago: Chicago University Press.

Masaryk, T.G. (1938) *The Ideals of Humanity.* London: George Allen & Unwin.

Mishler, W. and Rose, R. (1997) Trust, Distrust and Skepticism: Popular Evaluations of Civil and Political Institutions in Post-Communist Societies, *The Journal of Politics,* 59 (2): 418–451.

Morkes, F. (2004) Největs¡í reforma s¡kolství v dějinách [The greatest educational reform in history – in Czech] http://www.ucitelskenoviny.cz/obsah_clanku.php?vydani=33&rok=04&odkaz=nejvetsi.htm as retrieved on May 25, 2007 03:57:46 GMT.

Nedelsky, N. (2003) Civic Nationhood and the Challenges of Minority Inclusion: The Case of the Post-Communist Czech Republic, *Ethnicities,* 3 (1): 85–114.

OECD (2006) *OECD Economic Surveys: Czech Republic.* Paris: OECD.

Polechová, P. (1998) 'Projekt "Občan" *Výchova k demokracii, konstitucionalismu a občanství* [Project "Citizen"'. Education to democracy, constitutionalism and citizenship.] Proceedings from a Summer School for Civics teachers. August 24–26, University of Palacký. Czech Republic. pp. 135–137.

Polechova, P., Valkova, J., Dostalova, R., Bahmueller, Ch. F. and Farnbach, B. (1997) Civic Education for Democracy in the Czech Republic, *International Journal of Social Education* 12 (2): 73–83.

Prucha, J. (2005) *Česko-anglický pedagogický slovník.* Praha: Nakladatelství ARSCI.

Shinew, D.M. and Fischer, J.M. (1997) Comparative Lessons for Democracy: An International Curriculum Development Project, *International Journal of Social Education,* 12 (2): 113–125.

Sokol (2007) http://www.sokol-cos.cz/COS/sokol_en.nsf

Staněk, A. (2007) *Výchova k občanství a evropanství.* Olomouc: Nakladatelství Olomouc.

Tesař, P. (2007) official website of Gymnázium Plzeň http://www.mgplzen.cz/index.=php?option=com_content&task=view&id=67&Itemid=107 as retrieved on Apr 17, 2007.

Torney-Purta, J. and Amadeo, J. (2003) A cross-national analysis of political and civic involvement among adolescents. *Political Science and Politics,* April 2003 http://www.apsanet.org/imgtest/CrossAnalysisPoliticalCivicAdolescents.pdf

Torney-Purta, J., Lehman, R., Oswald, H. and Schulz, W. (2001) *Citizenship and Education in Twenty-eight Countries. Civic Knowledge and Engagement at Age Fourteen.* IEA The international Association for the Evaluation of Educational Achievement, Amsterdam, Netherlands.

Válková, J. and Kalous, J. (1991) The changing face of civic education in the Czech Republic. In J. Torney-Purta, J. Schwille, and J. Amadeo. (eds) *Civic Education Across Countries: Twenty-four National Case Studies from the IEA Civic Education Project.* IEA The international Association for the Evaluation of Educational Achievement. Amsterdam, Netherlands. pp.179–202.

13

Citizenship Education in India: From Colonial Subjugation to Radical Possibilities

Reva Joshee

Indian society includes deeply rooted traditions of education but citizenship education as we currently understand it was not part of the Indian tradition until the British colonial period. The British aimed to transmit a sense of loyalty and deference to Britain and the Empire and Indians were taught to be subjects rather than citizens. When the freedom struggle resulted in independence in 1947, Indians worked to replace teaching for subjugation with new curricula that would instill a sense of belonging and loyalty to independent India. The 'new' India was democratic, secular, and socialist and its leaders sought to create an informed nation who could also transform India into an economically successful, modern state. The trajectory of citizenship education remained largely unchanged until the Hindu nationalist Bharatiya Janata Party (BJP) came to power in the late 1990s. The BJP began a process that would see the social science curriculum, particularly history and civics, used to recast India in the image of a Hindu nation. Following the defeat of the BJP in 2004, one of the first acts of the new Congress-led government was to call for a review of the national curriculum. The result was a democratic process that has led to the development of new syllabi and publication of new textbooks that hold a promise of creating a new generation of active and engaged citizens.

DEMOGRAPHIC AND POLICY CONTEXT

India is the seventh largest country in terms of area and is the second most populous (1.1 billion people). In the 2001 national census about 82 per cent of the population identified themselves as Hindu, 13 per cent Muslim, 2.3 per cent Christian, 1.9 per cent Sikh, 0.76 per cent Buddhist, 0.4 per cent Jain, and 0.01 per cent Zoroastrian. Thus India has the second largest national Muslim population in the world and the largest Sikh, Jain, and Zoroastrian populations. There are currently 22 languages recognized as official languages including Hindi and English, which are designated as 'national' or 'link' languages. Two categories that are central to diversity in India are the dalits or 'Scheduled Castes' and adivasi or 'Scheduled Tribes' which make up 16.2 per cent and 8.2 per cent of the population, respectively (Registrar General and Census Commissioner, 2001). The terms 'Scheduled Castes' and 'Scheduled Tribes' are administrative categories, the former used to designate those groups previously know as 'untouchables' and the latter, various indigenous groups that for centuries have resisted assimilation into first agrarian and then industrial societies. The members of these two groups themselves use the terms 'dalit' (literally translated as 'downtrodden') and 'adivasi' (literally translated as 'original dwellers'). These categories are often grouped with a third category, 'Other Backward Classes' (OBC), which is used to encompass a range of groups that have been and continue to be marginalized. This category, which includes lower caste Hindus as well as certain other groups identified on the basis of low economic, social, or educational status, accounts for about 50 per cent of the total population of the country (Government of India, n.d., c).

Administratively, India is divided into 28 states and 7 union territories, each with primary responsibility for education within its own jurisdiction. Until 1975 the states had exclusive responsibility for education. In 1975 the central government adopted an amendment to the constitution that made education part of the concurrent list of responsibilities, meaning that the national government was to have a key role in that area. Specifically, that role was defined in terms of ensuring

'the national and integrative character of education' and 'the international dimensions of education and culture and human resource development' (Patel, 1996: 82). The Indian government has a Department of Education that is currently part of the Ministry of Human Resources Development. The Department works closely with two federal agencies, the National Institute of Educational Planning and Administration (NIEPA) and the National Council of Educational Research and Training (NCERT). NCERT is primarily responsible for establishing national curriculum guidelines as well as supporting research into various aspects of educational practice while NIEPA is tasked with providing advice and support in the areas of policy and administration. In addition, the Central Advisory Board on Education (CABE), which was first established in 1935, has held an important position more in terms of vetting policy and curricula.

A key challenge for India in the area of citizenship has been incorporating the vast diversity of cultures, languages, and religions while trying to dismantle traditional hierarchies and animosities. India's policies in this general area began before it gained independence from Britain. By the 1920s policies for what we might now call affirmative action were in place to ensure that minority religious groups were included in the administration of government. While ostensibly these policies were meant to ensure harmony among all groups in the colony, it is widely accepted today that the policies were part of the larger British policy of 'divide and rule' that created new divisions or exploited existing divisions within the indigenous community (Rodrigues, 1999). This legacy continues to taint some of the current policies, especially those for the dalit, adivasi, and OBC communities.

Current Indian policies addressing citizenship quite clearly encompass objectives related to national unity, equality, and the development of a national identity that includes support for diversity. These commitments were enunciated in the Indian Constitution, which was adopted in 1951. As Bharat Bhusan Gupta (1977) has noted:

> The Preamble although it does not form part of the [Indian] Constitution provided for Justice [sic], social, economic, and political; liberty of thought, expression, belief, faith and worship; Equality of status and of opportunity. The Directive Principles of State Policy enjoined upon future Governments (a) that the citizens, men and women equally, shall have the right to an adequate means of livelihood, (b) that the ownership and control of the material resources of the community are so distributed as best to serve the common good; (c) that the operation of the economic system does not result in the concentration of wealth and means of production to the common detriment; and (d) that there is equal pay for equal work for both men and women. (p. 102).

The Constitution was cast in the mould of the classical liberal democracy (see for example, Beteille, 1998; Hardgrave, 1997) but with what has been called an Indian inflection (Bajpai, 2002). It contains a strong commitment to equality and it seeks to develop an overarching national identity while protecting minority identities

> [y]et minority interests are typically expressed in terms of group identity and political demands may call for the protection and promotion of language, religion, and culture, or the 'group' more generally, in ways that conflict not only with 'the will of the majority', but with the constitutional guarantees of individual rights and equal protection' (Hardgrave, 1997: 333).

Three important principles upon which the Indian Constitution is based have shaped post-independence approaches to education: social justice, secularism, and the need to create a unified national identity.

At the time of independence social justice was defined largely in terms of groups that had long suffered economic and social exclusion, namely lower caste groups, 'outcastes', and women. Policies and programmes were devised to address what had effectively been centuries of oppression and exclusion based on caste and gender hierarchies. A key policy instrument for addressing social justice has been the Indian version of affirmative action known as the system of reservations. Specific articles of the Constitution mandate the achievement of equality for dalit and adivasi communities through a system of reservations. This means that a certain number of positions in the public service and in higher education institutions would be held for persons from the dalit and adivasi groups. While this was initially envisioned as a temporary measure, it continues today. Moreover, in the years since independence the system of reservations has been extended to include OBC communities and women in limited ways. Reservations for OBC groups exist only in government employment although there is currently a lively debate on whether this should be extended to cover institutions of higher education. In the case of women, reservations exist for elected positions at the local levels. In addition to reservations, a bureaucratic infrastructure has been created to safeguard the rights of minority groups. Included in the complex of agencies is the National Commission for Scheduled Castes, the National Commission for Backward Classes, the National Commission for Women, the National Commission for Minorities, the National Human Rights Commission, the Ministry of Social Justice and Empowerment and a host of departments and commissions at the state level.

Secularism in India, unlike the Western versions of this ideal, has meant both that there is no official state religion and that all religions are, at least in theory, equally recognized and valued. In practice this has been translated into several policies and practices including recognition of a variety of religious holidays as official holidays for everyone, flexible dress codes in schools and other public institutions, and parallel systems of family law based on religious principles. While some of these measures, for example, the parallel systems of family law, have been criticized as violating the fundamental principle of gender equality by and large the recognition of multiple religions has been seen as an important component of Indian society as well as a contribution India can make to international discussions about interfaith understanding (Bhargava, 2004).

Finally, the focus on national identity came out of the acknowledgement that at the time of independence there was no single unified sense of what it meant to be Indian. Instead, people were more attached to ethnic, linguistic, religious, or caste-based identities. The Constitution thus gave due recognition to these identities and, rather than trying to eradicate them, sought to use them as building blocks for a unified identity. In part this was accomplished by dividing states along linguistic lines and by recognizing several regional languages as official languages. This same value for diversity was evident in Prime Minister Nehru's approach to governing minority cultural groups which was based on five fundamental principles, the first of which states: 'People should develop along the lines of their own genius and we should avoid imposing anything on them. We should try to encourage in every way their traditional arts and culture.' (Elwin in Bhattacharyya, 2003: 157).

Addressing inequality, incorporating diversity, and building a cohesive national identity have been central themes in citizenship education over the last century and a half.

THE COLONIAL ERA: LOYALTY AND SUBJECTHOOD

Although the British presence in India dates back to the seventeenth century, it was not until the nineteenth century that they became involved in education. As Yvette Rosser (2003) has documented, the interest in education was linked to the passage of the Charter Act of 1833 which allowed Indians to join the civil service. British interest in Indian education was directly related to a desire to ensure the Indians who came to the civil service were properly educated. Such an education would result in the creation of what Thomas Babbington Macaulay famously called 'a class who may be interpreters between us and the millions whom we govern – a class of persons Indian in blood and colour, but English in tastes, in opinions, in morals and in intellect' (Macaulay, 1835).

Macaulay believed that the British should only educate a small elite who would then be responsible for spreading knowledge to their compatriots. After Macaulay's Minute there was some discussion of the need to prepare the Indian elite for eventual self rule and some thought that the masses should be educated (Rosser, 2003). Both of these positions were abandoned in the face of Indian uprisings against the British and the argument that Indians were inherently unsuited for representative government, advanced by such notables as James Mill and John Stuart Mill, became accepted as fact (Palshikar, 2006). In this context education for civilizing rather than for citizenship took centre stage.

The civilizing mission of education included three key components. The first was to ensure English was the language of instruction as it was already the language of government and was envisioned as the language of commerce (Macaulay, 1835). The second was to teach the history of England and Europe with lesser attention to the history of India. What was taught about India generally focused on the inferiority of Indians and the barbarism of the past from which the society had been saved by the British (Panikkar, 2004). Indian society was presented as so deeply divided, especially along religious lines, that it would never have become unified had it not been for the British. The third component was to put forward official knowledge as unassailable facts that needed to be memorized and repeated in many exams (Kumar, 1998). Some argued that a fourth component ought to be conversion to Christianity: this was never the official position of the state but it was generally believed that education would 'remove the obstinate strictures of paganism, ignorance (rendered often as illiteracy), and civilizational decline that many in Britain thought India was mired in' (Glover, 2004: 542). In sum, this curriculum was meant to create the brown Englishmen that Macaulay had envisioned.

The colonial version of civics, which began as a separate subject in the late nineteenth century, emphasized the duties of citizens and constructed good citizens as those who were loyal to the crown (Saigol, 2000). It appeared against a backdrop of increasing unrest among Indians and as part of a larger initiative to promote loyalty within the Empire (NCERT, 2005; Sadler, 1907). The key message was that loyalty, obedience, and doing one's duty would be rewarded by the protection of the state. The civics curriculum also stressed orderliness and discipline as a way of ensuring social order and minimizing violence. The new curriculum also reinforced an older dichotomy that juxtaposed the clean, rational, and disciplined citizen with the dirty, emotional, and unruly native who was prone to lawlessness and degeneration (Saigol, 2000). The overall goal of civics then was to convince the elite to trust the colonial rulers and to see themselves as superior to their "native" compatriots who had not had the benefit of British education.

POST-INDEPENDENCE: NATIONAL INTEGRATION

When India gained independence in 1947 it was evident to its leaders that a key to the success of the 'new' nation had to be creating a sense of unity among its peoples. To this end, as I have noted above, the Constitution was written as a document that would demonstrate that India would be a secular, inclusive, and socially just society. Dr. S. Radhakrishnan said at the start of the first conference on National Integration,

National integration cannot be built by brick and mortar, by chisel and hammer. It has to grow silently in the minds and hearts of men. *The only process is the process of education*. This may be a slow process, but it is a steady and permanent one' (cited in Yadav, 1974: 202, emphasis original).

The image of India that had been created by the British to justify and sustain colonial rule had to be dismantled and replaced. Jawaharlal Nehru asserted that, contrary to the colonial account, India was historically a single civilization where diversity groups had co-existed in relative harmony and it was on this historical basis that post-independence unity ought to be built (Ganguly, 1999). Education was central to supporting this new vision: 'Following Independence, school curricula were thus imbued with the twin themes of inclusiveness and national pride, placing emphasis on the fact that India's different communities could live peacefully side by side as one nation' (Lall, 2005: 2).

The first major commission on school education, the Secondary Education Commission, 1952, noted that a main aim of school education ought to be 'to train our youth for intermediate leadership and for democratic citizenship' (Government of India, n.d., a) but, initially, less attention was given to direct instruction in this area than to three key policies designed to address national integration. The three policies – the three language formula, the common school policy, and a policy to promote national service – were designed to address linguistic, class, and regional differences. The three language formula was meant to ensure that all students would learn their own regional language, which would support the aims of inclusion, as well as Hindi, for national unity and pride, and English for technological advancement (NCERT National Focus Group on Indian Languages, 2005). The philosophy behind the common school policy was that publicly funded neighbourhood schools ought to be established where children could come to know others of different classes, castes and religious backgrounds. The common school proposal was both a critique of private schools and a measure for national integration (Education Commission, 1966). Finally, the national service proposal was originally meant to be obligatory for all students. Such a scheme would bring together people from all parts of the country to work together and learn the spirit of selfless service (Education Commission, 1966).

Each of these policies had varying degrees of success. The three language formula continues to exist today but 'it has been observed more in its violation than adherence'

(NCERT National Focus Group on Indian Languages, 2005: 21). The common school policy was proposed in the Report of the Education Commission 1964–66 and reaffirmed in the National Policy on Education, 1968, but it was never implemented. While a National Service Scheme still exists as part of the Ministry of Youth Affairs and Sports, national service has never been obligatory and many of the current activities tend to provide opportunities for students from relatively privileged families to volunteer with members of disadvantaged communities. The limited success of two of the three policies was not enough to create what Nehru and others called 'emotional integration', in other words, a sense of belonging to the nation.

In 1960 a national meeting of ministers of education suggested more needed to be done. The Union Ministry of Education established an Emotional integration Committee in 1961. This committee recommended that in addition to learning the national anthem and the significance of the flag, which had been mandated by a Union Ministry of Education memorandum in 1954, students should also participate in special assemblies twice each school year where the headmaster would speak to the students about 'any topic dealing with the unity and oneness of the country. On that day, children take a pledge of loyalty to India' (Government of India, n.d., b). While there is no evidence that such assemblies ever took place, the suggested text of the pledge gave keen insight into the evolving meaning of citizenship:

> India is my country, all Indians are my brothers and sisters. I love my country, and I am proud of its rich and varied heritage. I shall always strive to be worthy of it.
> I shall give my parents, teachers and all elders respect, and treat every one with courtesy. I shall be kind to animals.
> To my country and my people, I pledge my devotion. In their well-being and prosperity alone lies my happiness. (Government of India, n.d., b)

A good citizen was one who was accepting of all Indians regardless of social characteristics, proud of India's diverse cultures, respectful of elders, and devoted to the nation.

By 1968 there was concern that there was not enough direct instruction in the area of citizenship. In that year the National Integration Council suggested that a National Board of Textbooks be established to ensure that textbooks were being used to support the cause of national integration. The Council's committee on education took the stand that education at all levels ought to be reoriented to achieve three goals: '(a) to serve the purpose of creating a sense of Indianness, unity and solidarity, (b) to inculcate faith in the basic postulates of Indian democracy, and (c) to help the nation to create a modern society out of the present traditional one' (Yadav, 1974: 203). Also in 1968, a new National Policy on Education was adopted. The new policy made specific mention of the need to develop courses in citizenship. As a result of both the new national policy and the recommendations of the National Integration Council, NCERT developed what would become its first set of mandated social studies textbooks. The history texts in particular were meant to respond to the concerns about national integration (Panikkar, 2004). These texts were written by prominent Indian historians and emphasized harmony and national unity (Wahi, 2003).

The themes of unity and harmony were elaborated in the next iteration of the National Policy on Education that was issued in 1986. The 1986 policy established that there should be a common core curriculum across the country. Among other things this core would include:

> the history of India's freedom movement; constitutional obligations and other content essential to nurture national identity. These core elements are intended to cut across subject areas and were designed to promote a number of values (such as India's cultural heritage, egalitarianism, democracy, and secularism, equality of the sexes, protection of the environment, removal of social barriers, observance of the small-family norm and inculcation of the scientific approach) (NCERT, 1999).

Here we see that citizenship education was linked with the teaching of particular values that supported the post-independence political vision of the nation as well as values that supported other national development goals (i.e. small family norm; development of scientific temper).

Both the 1968 and 1986 policies led to the establishment of national curriculum frameworks (1975 and 1988, respectively). In terms of citizenship education the two frameworks were very similar. Both talked of education as a tool for social transformation, in particular as a way to achieve greater equality and social justice in India. Both continued to emphasize the need to focus on national unity and social harmony. And both talked of citizenship education as a way to build international understanding and cooperation (Subramaniam, n.d.). For the most part, civics and history curricula from independence until the late 1990s were relatively consistent. They focused on nation building through inculcation of pride in the history of India. Although the curricula have been criticized for their continuity with the colonial versions of civics, both in terms of the emphasis on memorizing and repeating factual knowledge and in terms of continuing the myth of the deep Hindu- Muslim divide (Panikkar, 2004), with one notable exception, the post-independence version of civics received very little public critique until the 1990s.

In 1977 following the end of Indira Gandhi's period of emergency rule, the first non-Congress government was elected. The Jan Sangh party, which headed that particular coalition government, was the precursor to the BJP. The Jan Sangh-led government, in a foreshadowing of things to come, criticized history text books for their inaccuracy and Eurocentric perspective. The issue was debated in parliament but the coalition government fell before any action could be taken (Rosser, 2003).

In 1992 a prominent educational researcher, Yash Pal, was asked to head a commission to examine the concerns of parents and students related to an unwieldy curriculum. The commission reported in 1993 and among other things suggested that the teaching of civics was so weak that it could easily be taken out of the curriculum with little consequence. The commission also suggested the teaching of history be revisited so as to make it more relevant to students (Subramaniam, n.d.). These recommendations were significant because, for the first time, a major commission was openly stating that there was a gulf between intent and reality in the area of citizenship education. While citizenship was an important goal of education, in practice civics was a relatively devalued subject to which unenthusiastic and ill-prepared teachers were often assigned (Banaji, 2005). While the Yash Pal recommendations regarding civics and history were not widely discussed in the immediate aftermath of the report, by the end of the decade they would become part of the basis for a major overhaul of the civics curriculum.

THE BJP YEARS: HINDU NATIONALISM

In 1998 the Hindu Nationalist political party, the BJP, came to power. The BJP is part of a large group of Hindu Nationalist organizations known as the Sangh Parivar (literally 'family of organizations'). The Sangh Parivar is based in a philosophy of Hindutva. The major premise is that the only people who have a right to claim Indian citizenship are those whose ancestors and religious roots originate in India (for a fuller discussion see Thapar, 2004). Effectively, then, Muslims and Christians, regardless of their ethnic ancestry are excluded from citizenship. It was this vision of citizenship that would guide the development of the National Curriculum Framework on School Education (NCFSE, 2000).

Shortly after the BJP came to power, the Minister of Human Resources Development presented a curriculum in use in schools run by the Sangh Parivar and announced his intention to 'Indianise, nationalize, and spiritualise' the national curriculum of the country (Panikkar, 1999: 72–73). Several of the state ministers walked out in protest yet the national government went forward with its plan. It undertook a review of the National Curriculum ostensibly because it was time; the framework had not been changed since 1988, the Yash Pal Commission had made various recommendations related to curriculum overload, and the Ministry of Human Resources Development had appointed a committee to report on values-based education.

The review was done in relative secrecy and in 2000 the new Curriculum Framework was released. Not surprisingly the framework took aim at the existing civics and history curricula. A press release issued to announce the new curriculum noted that for the first time in Indian education there would be a subject called citizenship education and this would help students to 'develop a proper understanding of their roles and responsibilities as citizens in a modern democracy' (Press Information Bureau, 2001). It noted that the new history curriculum would

> help promote a deeper understanding of the core values that has kept Indian civilisation ticking through the ages. A route to instill pride in India's background as a great contributor to human progress. It will be a history free of rhetoric, stereotypes and objectionable attributes to any one stream of Indian culture (Press Information Bureau, 2001).

While a separate citizenship education program did not materialize, the new approach to citizenship was meant to rest on the development of a set of values seen as crucial to Indian citizens. The key values were 'regularity and punctuality, cleanliness, self-control, industriousness, sense of duty, desire to serve, responsibility, enterprise, creativity, sensitivity to greater equality, fraternity, democratic attitude and sense of obligation to environmental protection.' (NCERT cited in Subramaniam, n.d.). The Committee's list included five personal values (truth, righteous conduct, peace, love and nonviolence), three 'social values' (concern for the whole community, dignity of labour, and self-dependence), and 'national values' (not clearly enunciated but linked to the freedom struggle, India's cultural heritage, and constitutional obligations)

(Parliamentary Committee on Human Resources Development, 1999). Compared to the Committee's list, the NCERT values focused almost entirely on the individual and, as C.N. Subramaniam has suggested, would create a docile and loyal citizen who was neither assertive nor socially-minded.

The greatest controversy surrounding the NCFSE, 2000 came in relation to the content of history textbooks. All of the existing history texts were removed because they were said to incorporate a Western rather than Indian outlook (Upadhyay, 2001). In their place came text books that many 'secularist' historians claimed presented a particularly chauvinistic view of history complete with 'facts' that had already been discredited or had no basis in historical evidence (see, for example, Panikkar, 2004; Thapar, 2004). While there is some debate as to the charges of chauvinism (Rosser, 2003), the new textbooks did contain inaccuracies (Panikkar, 2004; Thapar, 2004; Wahi, 2003). Historical facts continued to be presented as incontrovertible so there was no room to challenge the misrepresentations of any groups nor to discuss anything in the Hindu tradition that might need to be challenged, for example the caste system (Rathnam, 2000).

While promotion of equality was still a goal of education, it was now seen in terms of a separate but equal kind of philosophy. Unlike the rationale of the previous era in the Hindutva version of citizenship, social identities based on caste and gender, in particular, were meant to be preserved with each group finding its place in the society as a whole; nothing would be done to acknowledge or dismantle the existing hierarchies. National identity would be based on a unifying Hindu identity; those who were outside of this identity would remain outsiders. Despite a formal acknowledgement of the value of all religions those that were seen as belonging to the Hindu fold (i.e. Jainism, Sikhism, Buddhism) were given more respect than those that were seen as foreign, especially Islam (see, for example, Bhattacharya, 2002). This brief period of time made citizenship education a topic of much public concern and discussion and opened the way for a new and promising era of reform.

NEW REFORMS: RADICAL POSSIBILITIES

The Congress Party won the federal election in May 2004 and NCERT almost immediately initiated a curriculum review process involving a open and transparent process to revise the National Curriculum Framework. A national steering committee was established involving prominent scholars, educators, and representatives of non-governmental organizations with interests in education and 21 national focus groups that also included scholars, educators, policy developers, activists, non-governmental organization representatives, and parents. Meetings and consultations were also held with state-level policy developers and rural teachers. Background papers were developed that became the foundation for the National Curriculum Framework, 2005.

While the Minister's statement asked NCERT to review the curriculum in light of the report of the Yash Pal Commission (Professor Yash Pal was appointed chair of the national steering committee), which highlighted the ways in which schooling had become increasingly competitive and alienating for students, the context of the review was obviously greater. In response to the Hindu nationalist agenda of its predecessor, the new government pledged to 'take immediate steps to reverse the trend of communalisation of education that had set in in the past five years' (Government of India, 2004). The discussions related to NCFSE, 2000 had brought to the fore concerns over both the status of social sciences in general, and citizenship education in particular. Finally, educators and activists paid attention to the methods that were used to teach about citizenship (Kumar, 1999; Nussbaum, 2005).

NCF 2005 articulates one of its key goals as '[b]uilding a citizenry committed to democratic practices, values, sensitivity towards gender justice, problems faced by the Scheduled Castes and the Scheduled Tribes, needs of the disabled, and capacities to participate in economic and political processes' (NCERT, 2005:126). In order to accomplish this it sets out a new approach to teaching the social sciences. Civics will be recast as political science to make a definitive break with its colonial past. Social sciences will be focused on conceptual understanding rather than rote memorization and a new pedagogical approach will be developed based on activities that will help students build the capacity and skills to think critically about social reality.

Since the NCF 2005 was released specific syllabi and new textbooks have been written and made available to teachers. The new syllabi for both elementary and secondary social sciences stress the need to actively engage students in learning processes (NCERT, 2006a, 2006b). The new textbooks do this by using a variety of methods including fiction, cartoons, and insert boxes with specific examples or activities. While the new textbooks do have a discernable leftist bent, in general they present information in ways that encourages students to question it rather than accept it at face value. The Class 11 textbook on the constitution, for example, encourages students to consider different opinions or rights and to develop their own position. Unlike earlier civics curricula, the new political science texts give emphasis to citizens' rights and the duties of government in addition to the duties of citizens.

BUILDING TOWARD A RADICAL FUTURE

The NCF 2005 and its associated textbooks continue the post-independence tradition of valuing diversity, promoting national identity, and advocating socially just change but they do so in way that creates space for an education for radical democracy based in both European and Indian tradition. Specifically the curricula and textbooks take up four key principles that were part of the development of the Constitution of India: rights, representation, selfhood, and ahimsa. A short discussion of each of these principles and how they are linked to the NCF 2005 will provide some insights into how the radical potential of the new curriculum might be achieved.

Rights

Under British rule the people of India were subjects; the struggle for independence was a struggle to become citizens (Beteille, 2005). While the newly independent country worked to define individual rights it also had to acknowledge the rights of minoritized and disadvantaged groups. At the same time the constitution 'made ample provisions for the rights of individuals as citizens of a kind that did not exist under British rule' (Beteille, 2005). This was done through the enunciation of fundamental rights, which applied to all citizens, and directive principles, which 'are intended to ensure "distributive justice" for removal of inequalities and disabilities and to achieve a fair division of wealth amongst the members of the society' (National Commission to Review the Working of the Constitution, 2002, point 3.25.3). Since the constitution came into effect both the political and legal systems have been sites for ongoing debates on how to reconcile the competing sets of rights.

Not surprisingly, the rights discourse in education appears primarily in reference to the constitution. The Fundamental Rights and Directive Principles contain specific references to the education of minorities groups. In the primary and secondary education systems this has led to the development of special programmes for the designated groups. In the post-secondary system it has led to a series of reservations of seats for dalit and adivasi students. While the special programs have generally caused little controversy, the reservations have been met with protests from non-dalit and non-adivasi students concerned that they are being unfairly denied their right to an education (Kumar, 1992; Wood, 1987). The new textbooks approach this issue in variety of ways that would allow students to engage with it from an early age. In Class 6, for example, students engage with material designed to make them think about structural inequality, with particular reference to dalits, adivasis, women and persons with disabilities. In Class 7, students discuss the reality of inequality in the daily lives of dalits and women as well as the concept of treating people with dignity. By class 11, they are engaging with case studies that challenge them to apply constitutional principles to addressing complex situations. This process has the potential to both sensitize the students to the issues faced by marginalized groups as well as to provide them opportunities to engage with the Constitution and Human Rights legislation.

Representation

The principle of representation follows directly from the work of Dr. B. R. Ambedkar, a legal scholar and leader of the dalit community who became the Minister of Law in the first post-independence cabinet in India. In this position he was responsible for overseeing the development of the constitution. Ambedkar believed that the essence of a democracy was representation, which he defined as 'transmit[ting] the force of individual opinion and preference into public action' (cited in Rodrigues, 2005). He also believed that members of marginalized groups could not adequately be represented by dominant group members because dominant groups would have no understanding of the beliefs and goals of the marginalized. He envisaged using representation as a way of establishing what he called 'social presence'. He argued that one of the reasons for the gulf between dominant and minoritized groups in society was that minoritized groups had had no social presence, that is, they had not been part of the public life of the nation. Joint participation in public life, he believed, would create shared bonds and common understandings that would ultimately lead to a strong and unified community built on principles of justice.

In education documents the discourse of representation is visible primarily through statements on promoting mutual understanding as in the National Policy of Education (1986), which states, '[s]teps will also be taken to foster among students an understanding of the diverse cultural and social systems of the people living in different parts of the country' (point 3.7). The National Curriculum Framework, 2005 extends the notion of representation by 'proposing the study of the social sciences from the perspective of marginalised groups. Gender justice and a sensitivity towards issues related to SC and ST communities and minority sensibilities must inform all sectors of the social sciences.' (NCERT, 2005: ix). The textbooks use stories, first person accounts, and a variety of activities to assist students at all levels to view the world from the perspective of minorities groups.

Selfhood

The principal of selfhood also traces its roots to Ambedkar. Ambedkar argued that it was not enough to enshrine rights and insist on representation. He posited that not only could social exclusion 'greatly impair the growth of the human person and communities' (Rodrigues, 2005), but, as in the case of the dalits, extended exclusion denies personhood to the members of the group. Individuals are dehumanized in their own minds as much as in the minds of dominant group members. Justice and equality could only be built if members of minoritized groups were given ways to reclaim their personhood.

Selfhood is most evident in statements addressing the empowerment of particular groups, such as girls and women 'by ensuring that children from different social and economic backgrounds with variations in physical, psychological and intellectual characteristics are able to learn and achieve success in school' (NCERT, 2005: 5).

From this perspective, active citizenship requires active and on-going attention to differences at both the group and individual level. It also requires different approaches to the instruction of children from marginalized backgrounds. While selfhood is not evident in the existing textbooks it is an area that can be developed by thinking about how the texts might be used with students from minoritized backgrounds.

Ahimsa

The concept of ahimsa was central to Mahatma Gandhi's understanding of peace. The idea of ahimsa has existed since at least the 6th century BCE as part of Hindu, Jain, and Buddhist philosophical traditions. While Gandhi and others have translated it into English as nonviolence I find this translation inadequate because, as Christopher Chapple has noted: 'In western cultures, nonviolence usually denotes passive, non-resistant civil disobedience, pacifism, and conscientious objection to war. ... In India, nonviolence ... is a personal commitment to respect life in its myriad forms. (Chapple, 1993: xiii). A commitment to ahimsa, thus, requires an appreciation of common humanity and the connection between all living things. It simultaneously requires a recognition that the common 'life force' is expressed in the world in myriad ways and that our task as individuals and members of communities is to understand, accept, and support the diversity around us. This simultaneous insistence on one and many requires the rejection of the 'either /or' way in which we usually frame the world in favour of an approach that considers 'each and'. While this discourse has been present in India for centuries, it has not been directly linked to education and diversity until recently.

The National Curriculum Framework, 2005 invokes both ahimsa and Gandhi to argue that the fundamental purpose of education is to create a just and peaceful society: 'Mahatma Gandhi had visualised education as a means of awakening the nation's conscience to injustice, violence and inequality entrenched in the social order.' (NCERT, 2005: 3). The National Curriculum Framework, 2005 proposes that the educational enterprise be guided by a value framework built on the notions of peace and ahimsa. A background paper to the National Curriculum Framework document notes that:

> Currently, the enterprise of education is driven by Market forces. Education for peace is not allergic to the Market. But it does not recognize the Market as the purpose of education. The Market is only a part of our life-world. Education for peace is education for life, and not merely training for a livelihood. Equipping individuals with the values, skills and attitudes they need to be wholesome persons who live in harmony with others and are responsible citizens is the goal of education for peace (Focus Group on Education for peace, 2005: 6).

Within the logic of ahimsa, education emphasizes 'the self-reliance and dignity of the individual, which would form the basis of social relations characterised by non-violence within and across society' (NCERT, 2005: 3). As a comprehensive approach to education, education for peace would emphasize:

> (a) peace-orienting individuals through education (b) nurturing in students the social skills and outlook needed to live together in harmony (c) reinforcing social justice, as envisaged in the Constitution (d) the need and duty to propagate the secular culture (e) education as a catalyst for activating a democratic culture (f) the scope for promoting national integration through education and (g) education for peace as a lifestyle movement (Focus Group on Education for peace, 2005: 5).

While the NCF 2005 proposes using this as the values framework for all education, it is not clear there this has been translated to the textbooks or how it will find its way to the classroom. An education developed from this values base has the potential to create citizens who are engaged, vigilant, and compassionate. It remains to be seen if this ideal can find its way into Indian schools.

CONCLUDING REMARKS

For the past century and a half regardless of the perspective of the ruling parties, Indian students have been subjected to a weak program of citizenship education. From the time of independence there has been a concern among educators and activists that the children of the elite would be disconnected from social reality of the majority of their compatriots. Given that the children of the elite were also cast in the role of future leaders, this was one issue that fed into citizenship education policy development. Recently, there has been a great concern that these prospective leaders are completely disengaged from political and civic activities (Nayar, 2004). The long established practice of rote learning and testing regimes has meant that all social science instruction has come in the form of facts to memorize. This coupled with the low status of social science subjects has meant that the lofty ideals of the leaders have never been translated into appropriate curriculum and methods to develop an aware and active citizenry. Ironically, it was the assault on the seemingly sacrosanct value of secularism that has spurred educators and policy developers to embark on a new era in citizenship education. The new approach incorporates active learning and a base of principles drawn from India's political and spiritual heritage. Perhaps this is the formula that will reawaken the civic spirit of the educated classes.

REFERENCES

Bajpai, R. (2002) Minority Rights in the Indian Constituent Assembly Debates,

1946–1949, Working Paper Number 30, *QEH Working Paper Series*, Oxford: Wolfson College.

Banaji, S. (2005) Portrait of an Indian education. *Changing English*, 12 (2): 157–166.

Beteille, A. (2005) Matters of Right and Policy. *Seminar Magazine Web Edition*, 549. Retrieved from http://www.india-seminar.com/semframe.htm July 20, 2006.

Beteille, A. (1998) The conflict of norms and values in contemporary Indian society. In Pierre L. Berger, (ed.) *The limits of social cohesion. Conflict and mediation in pluralist societies*. Boulder, Colorado: Westview Press. pp. 265–92.

Bhargava, R. (2004) India's model: faith, secularism, and democracy, *Open Democracy*.Retrieved March 12 2006 from www.openDemocracy.net.

Bhattacharyya, H. (2003) Multiculturalism in Contemporary India, *International Journal on Multicultural Societies*, 5 (2): 148–161.

Bhattacharya, S. (2002) NCERT has corrected the approach towards the teaching of civilization, Excerpts from an interview of Dr. Murli Manohar Joshi, HRD Minister, *The Indian Express*, January 29, 2002.

Chapple, C.K. (1993) *Nonviolence to animals, earth, and self in Asian traditions*. Albany, NY: SUNY Press.

Education Commission (1966) *Report of the Education Commission 1964–1966. Education and National Development*. Delhi: Government of India.

Focus Group on Education for Peace (2005) *Engaging The Essence Of Education – A Position Paper On Education For Peace*. New Delhi: NCERT.

Ganguly, S. (1999) Explaining India's transition to democracy. In L. Anderson, (ed.) *Transitions to democracy*. New York: Columbia University Press.

Glover, W.J. (2005) Sentiment in Colonial India, *The Journal of Asian Studies*, 64 (3): 539–66.

Government of India (2004) *Report of Panel Of Historians*. New Delhi: Ministry of Human Resources Development.

Government of India (1986) National Policy on Education. New Delhi: Ministry of Human Resources Development. Retrieved January 12 2007 from http://education.nic.in/cd50years/g/T/49

Government of India (n.d., a) Education Commissions And Committees In Retrospect. Retrieved May 10, 2007 from http://education.nic.in/cd50years/g/W/16/0W160301.htm

Government of India (n.d., b) Memorandum On Item 18: Measures For Emotional Integration-Pledge To Be Taken By All The Students. Retrieved May 10, 2007 from http://education.nic.in/cd50years/g/12/1K/121K0M01.htm

Government of India (n.d., c). National Commission for Backward Classes, Guidelines for Consideration of requests for Inclusion and complaints of under Inclusion in the central list of OBCs Retrieved March 6, 2007 from http://ncbc.nic.in/html/guideline.htm

Gupta, B.B. (1977) *The seven freedoms*. New Delhi: Ashish Publishing House.

Hardgrave, R.L. (1997) Dilemmas of democracy in India. In S.N. Sridhar and N.K. Mattoo, (eds.) *Ananya. A portrait of India*. Queens, NY: Association of Indians In America. pp. 329–346.

Kumar, D. (1992) The Affirmative Action Debate in India. *Asian Survey* 32 (3): 290–302.

Kumar, K. (1999) Democracy without democrats? *Seminar Magazine*. Retrieved July 12, 2006 from http://www.india-seminar.com/1999/481/481%20kumar.htm

Kumar, K. (1998) Origins of India's 'Textbook Culture', *Comparative Education Review*, 32 (4): pp. 452–464.

Lall, M. (2005) *The Challenges for India's Education System*. Asia Programme Briefing Paper 05/03. London: Chatham House.

Minute by the Honourable T.B. Macaulay, dated the 2nd February 1835. Retrieved January 12, 2007 from http://www.mssu.edu/projectsouthasia/history/primarydocs/education/Macaulay001.htm

National Commission to Review the Working of the Constitution, (2002) Report of the National Commission to Review the Working of the Constitution. Retrieved June 13, 2006 from http://lawmin.nic.in/ncrwc/finalreport/volume1.htm

Nayar, U.S. (2004) Education For Social Transformation: A Collective Step Forward, *Education for Social Transformation*, 50 (1): 9–14.

NCERT (2006a) Syllabus, Volume I, Elementary Level. New Delhi: NCERT.

NCERT (2006b) Syllabus, Volume II, Secondary and Higher Secondary Levels. New Delhi: NCERT.

NCERT (2005) *National Curriculum Framework 2005*. Delhi: NCERT.

NCERT (1999) *India: Education policies and curriculum at the upper primary and secondary education levels*. Country report to UNESCO. Delhi: NCERT.

NCERT National Focus Group on Indian Languages (2005) *Position paper*. Delhi: NCERT.

Nussbaum, M. (2005) *Education and Democratic Citizenship: Beyond the Textbook Controversy*, A Ravinder Kumar Memorial Lecture Delivered at Jamia Milia University, New Delhi, January 17, 2005.

Palshikar, S. (2006) The Promise of Democracy: 'Democracy' in the Pre-independence India. Paper prepared for the Project on State of Democracy in South Asia as part of the Qualitative Assessment of Democracy Lokniti (Programme of Comparative Democracy). Delhi: Centre for the Study of Developing Societies, 11 pp.

Panikkar, K.N. (2004) History Textbooks in India: Narratives of Religious Nationalism. Retrieved from www.sacw.net/India_History , June 5, 2007.

Panikkar, K.N. (1999) Secular and Democratic Education, *Social Scientist*, 27 (9/10): 70–75.

Parliamentary Committee On HRD (1999) 81st Report On Value – Based Education. Delhi: Government of India.

Rajput, J.S. (2001) Towards good citizenship. The Hindu Online, January 23, 2001. Retrieved January 12, 2007 from www.hindu.com/thehindu/edu/2003/01/21/stories/2003012100130200.htm

Rathnam, A. (2000) Common curriculum for a democracy? *Seminar Magazine Web Edition*, no.493. Retrieved July 20 2006 from http://www.india-seminar.com/2000/493/493%20aruna%20rathnam.htm

Registrar General and Census Commissioner, India, '2001 Census, Retrieved February13, 2007 from www.censusindia.net.

Rodrigues, V. (2005) Ambedkar on Preferential Treatment. *Seminar Magazine Web Edition*, 549. Retrieved July 20, 2006 from http://www.india-seminar.com/semframe.htm

Rosser, Y.C. (2003) *Curriculum as Destiny: Forging National Identity in India, Pakistan, and Bangladesh*. Doctoral dissertation. Austin, TX: University of Texas at Austin.

Sadler, M.E. (1907) Indian Education Report, Vol. 5, No. 11. Retrieved June 12, 2007 from www.chaf.lib.latrobe.edu.au/dcd

Saigol, R. (2000) *Symbolic Violence: Curriculum, Pedagogy and Society*. Lahore: SAHE.

Subramaniam, C.N. (n.d.) NCERT's National Curriculum Framework: A Review. Retrieved February 12, 2007 from http://www.revolutionarydemocracy.org/rdv9n2/ncert.htm

Thapar, R. (2004) The Future Of The Indian Past. Seventh D. T. Lakdawala Memorial Lecture delivered at FICCI Auditorium, New Delhi on 21 February 2004, organised by the Institute of Social Sciences.

The National Commission For Schedule Caste And Schedule Tribes (1997) Final Report. New Delhi: National Integration Commission. Retrieved June 13, 2006 from http://www.education.nic.in/cd50years/g/S/I6

Wahi, T. (2003) Text-Books, Politics and the Practice of History. Retrieved April 1,2007 from http://www.revolutionarydemocracy.org/rdv9n2/textbook.htm

Wood, J.R. (1987) Reservations in Doubt: The Backlash Against Affirmative Action in Gujarat, India. *Pacific Affairs*, 60 (3): 408–430.

Yadav, R.K. (1974) Problems of National Identity in Indian Education, *Comparative Education*, 10 (3): 201–209.

14

Citizenship Education in Israel: A contested Terrain

Orit Ichilov

INTRODUCTION

The purpose of this chapter is to provide an over view of how young people are prepared for citizenship in Israel, of the forces involved in shaping the political world of Israeli youngsters, and of the outcomes of citizenship education.

Civic knowledge is gained from a great variety of sources (Niemi and Junn, 1998; Torney-Purta et al., 2001). My point of departure is that the nature and content of educational influences concerning citizenship are structured by the various social contexts to which youngsters belong both inside and outside schools. This means that individual behaviors and attitudes are seen as partially contingent upon those of other individuals. Thus, civic orientations and knowledge of individual students are to be understood within the larger social aggregates of which they are part. In other words the education of future citizens is greatly sensitive to the macro-political cultures of nations and the micro-political culture of schools within these nations (Mintrop, 2002). To comprehend the enormity of the task of preparing young people to become citizens in Israel, a deeply divided society, the major features of both Israeli society and the schools must be considered.

I will start by briefly discussing issues concerning consensus and unity in multicultural societies, and go on to analyze the characteristics of the national and religious rifts within Israeli society. The structure of the Israeli educational system will be described next. This will be followed by an historical account tracing the evolution of citizenship education from the pre-state period (Yishuv) until recently.

PLURALISM AND UNITY IN DIVIDED SOCIETIES

To put the Israeli rifts in a broader context I will begin by discussing issues related to pluralism and unity within multiethnic societies. It is generally agreed that pluralism must fit within a certain kind of overarching unity, and certain ultimate values must be shared if the diversity in a democratic society is to be contained democratically (Janowitz, 1983; Etzioni, 1992; Ichilov, 2003b; Ichilov et al., 2005). Achieving a shared concept of citizenship that would bridge over ethnic, national, and socioeconomic rifts is considered vital for the functioning of democracies because it 'helps to tame the divisive passions of other identities' (Heater, 1990: 184).

Citizenship education in western democracies aims at creating community cohesion by inculcating simultaneously particularistic identities and values, such as patriotism and national pride, and universalistic and shared democratic codes such as tolerance and respect for a variety of civil liberties. It seems, however, that traditional visions of citizenship and citizenship education are being contested. There has been a growing awareness of the potential tensions between cultural, national, and social, heterogeneity and the virtues and practices of democratic citizenship and national unity (Kymlicka, 1991; Kymlicka and Norman, 2000).

The unifying effect of citizenship was traditionally founded on a shared collective memory, cultural togetherness and nationality and the collaborative sense of purpose in fraternity. These elements which bind people together with a common identity of citizenship have been eroding over the last decades, due to global changes, including multiculturalism, i.e., the growing ethnic, national, and cultural heterogeneity within existing societies. To be sure, pluralistic societies have existed throughout history and are not a novelty. Multiculturalism represents a new way of thinking about and coping with cultural pluralism and minority rights (Kymlicka, 1995; Ichilov, 2003b, 2004). Current multiculturalism endorses social visions that do not necessarily value unity and cohesion. While some contemporary political philosophers believe that the status of minorities can be resolved by supplementing individual rights with special collective rights (Taylor, 1994; Kymlicka, 1995), others have been suspicious of appeals for unity. 'Good citizenship', for example, is seen as a demand that minorities should quietly learn to play by

the majority's rules, and acculturate to majority culture (Kanpol and McLaren, 1995; McLaren, 1997). It is, therefore, argued that the call for unity should be replaced by the empowerment of minorities that are 'produced' within Western forms of hegemony, to enable them to dismantle their ideological scaffolding and develop strategies and practices of resistance (Kanpol and McLaren, 1995; McLaren, 1997). Young (1990) contests any attempt to bring multiplicity and heterogeneity into unity, arguing that such attempts entail a denial of difference and are, therefore, inherently oppressive. She advocates instead social life based on openness to unassimilated otherness, the 'being together' of strangers.

The ideas of community cohesion and unity are not necessarily as accepted and appealing as they probably were. Consequently, citizenship and citizenship education become contested terrains, with competing visions of the essence of social life in multicultural societies (Giroux, 1983). Educating the younger generation for citizenship in multicultural and especially in deeply divided societies is increasingly becoming a sensitive and difficult task (Byrne, 1997; Ichilov, 2004).

ISRAEL: A DEEPLY DIVIDED SOCIETY

Israel, as its Declaration of Independence states, was established in 1948 as a Jewish nation-state and a democracy. Politics in Israel is highly ideological. It concerns the identity of the State, not merely the size of slices of the social pie to be allocated to one group or another. A major attribute of Israeli society is the wide and deep rifts between religious and secular groups, between Israeli Arabs and Jews, between the political left and right, and between the rich and the poor, between newly arrived immigrants and veteran Israelis. These divides, that often intersect and overlap, represent contesting visions of Israel as a Jewish-democratic state and profoundly shape Israel's political culture. Israeli multiculturalism is reshaping collective identities and represents a continuous debate over the meaning of 'Israeliness,' 'Jewishness,' the rules of the game, and the criteria for distribution and redistribution of common goods (Kimmerling, 2001). Israeli society has become so radicalized over the years that it is more difficult than ever to arrive at a broad consensus on political and territorial issues, social issues, and issues related to state and religion (Cohen and Don Yehiya, 1986; Eisenstadt, 1989; Kimmerling, 1989; Arian, 1990; Ezioni-Halevy, 1993; Ichilov, 2003, 2004).

In this section I propose to briefly outline two major rifts that may affect perceptions of both citizenship and citizenship education – the national divide between Israeli Palestinian Arabs and Israeli Jews, and the religious rifts among Israeli Jews. These divides differ from one another. A distinction can be made between contested and uncontested polities (Merelman, 1990). Uncontested regimes exist where 'the majority of the population consents to a single political authority within a single defined territory where the legitimacy of the regime is unchallenged' (Merelman, 1990: 47). A contested regime represents a situation where competing pretenders to authority defy the legitimacy of a polity to exist, and seek to radically change the rules of the game. Disagreements and conflicts may arise within uncontested regimes as well. However, the basic foundations of the regime are not disputed. Western democratic regimes are typically 'uncontested', and the pursuit of conflicting views and interests usually proceeds without wide defiance of the legitimacy of the foundations of democracy itself. I will demonstrate that Israeli Palestinian Arabs contest the legitimacy of Israel to exist as a Jewish-democratic state, and wish to radically transform it. The religious divide does not challenge the legitimacy of Israel to exist. Religiously observant Jews mainly seek to make religious practices, such as the observance of the Shabbat, more visible in the public space.

The national divide: Israeli Palestinian-Arabs and Israeli Jews

Israel is the only country in the Middle East where Arabs are a minority, constituting about 18 per cent of the entire Israeli population. The presence of a large Arab minority within a Jewish state creates a sensitive situation for both Jews and Arabs inside and outside of Israel. Israeli Palestinian Arabs find it difficult to form allegiance with the Jewish state.[1]

As an illustration, they do not celebrate May 14 as Israel's 'Independence Day', and instead commemorate it as a day of Nakkba, i.e., their 'national disaster'. Since the 1967 Six Day War, Israeli Palestinian Arabs have undergone a radicalization process that involves the strengthening of the Palestinian national identity, and a concomitant weakening of the Israeli civic identity (Rekhess, 1976, 1989; Landau, 1993; Zureik, 1993a,b; Rouhana, 1997). The radicalization process stems from multiple sources, including the unresolved Palestinian-Israeli and Arab-Israeli conflicts; Palestinian Arabs' desire for cultural and political autonomy, Palestinian nationalism; Islamic fundamentalism; and large-scale socioeconomic inequalities and discriminatory policies and practices against Arabs (Rekhess, 1989; Smooha, 1989, 1985, 1984; Levin-Epstein and Semyonov, 1993; Jarbi and Levi, 2000; Kimmerling, 2001).

Survey findings among Israeli Palestinian Arabs reveal that already in 1984, prior to the 1987 Palestinian uprising (Intifada), 50 per cent of Israeli Palestinian Arab respondents recognized unconditionally the right of Israel to exist, 21 per cent categorically rejected this right, and 29 per cent expressed 'reservations'. Similarly, 64 per cent agreed that Zionism is a racist movement, about 64 per cent agreed that the Law of Return, which acknowledges the right of all Jews to return to their ancestral homeland, should be repealed, and about 47 per cent doubted that 'Arabs can be equal citizens in Israel as a Jewish-Zionist state and can identify themselves with the state' (Smooha, 1984).

Most Israeli Palestinian Arabs subscribe to the Palestinian national narrative, perceiving themselves as the descendents of the ancient people that inhabited the region in Biblical times (e.g., the Canaanites, Edomites, and Philistines) (Sakran, 1976). They claim to be the indigenous people that were displaced and occupied by the Israelites in ancient times, and by those who maintain to be their descendents – Zionist Jews – in recent years (Lewis, 1975). Recent surveys reveal the overwhelming primacy and salience of the Arab and Palestinian identities among Israeli Arabs, a tendency that was significantly greater among Muslim Arabs as compared with Christian Arabs. The Israeli Islamic Movement – based on revivalism of strict Islamic codes of religious observance and conduct as well as on political militancy – also has gained a stronghold as a form of collective identity among wide segments of the Israeli Arab population (Rouhana, 1997; Lissak, 2000). Surveys also reveal that about 63 per cent of the Jewish respondents doubt the loyalty of Arabs to the state of Israel, and expect that once a Palestinian State is founded the Arabs main allegiance will be with that state (Barda, 2002a, 2002b).

The optimal model for Arab integration into Israeli society was considered by both Jews and Arabs to be cultural pluralism, which encouraged the creation of ethnic enclaves, allowing minorities to preserve their culture while permitting their partial or full participation in the affairs of the larger community. However, this model of integration is no longer desirable for Israeli Palestinian Arabs.

Recently, two documents have been issued calling on Israel to stop defining itself as a Jewish state, recognize the Israeli –Palestinian Arabs as an indigenous group with collective rights, and replacing the current regime with consociational democracy. 'The Future Vision of the Palestinian Arabs in Israel' was published in December 2006 under the auspices of the National Committee of Mayors of Arab Municipalities in Israel, which represents the country's 1.3 million Arab citizens. A second report was published by the Legal Center for Arab Minority Rights in Israel (Adalah, 2007) in February 2007, drafting a constitution that clearly seeks to eradicate the existence of Israel as a Jewish state (The National Committee of Mayors of Arab Municipalities in Israel, 2006; Adalah, 2007) The document 'The Future Vision for the Israeli Palestinian Arabs' supports the establishment of a Palestinian state alongside Israel, a solution that is widely accepted by the Israeli Jewish population. However, the establishment of a Palestinian state does not fully satisfy the national aspirations of the Israeli Palestinian-Arabs, who demand in addition the transformation of Israel from a Jewish state into a bi-national state – an Israeli Jewish majority and Palestinian Israeli minority. It is recommended that consociational democracy will replace the present regime, with each group having the right to veto decisions made by the other (The National Committee of Mayors of Arab Municipalities in Israel, 2006). This arrangement is expected to inspire Arabs and Jews to reach consensus instead of being at a constant deadlock created by mutual veto. Consociationalism has always been controversial, but is recommended by some scholars as means to achieve stable democracy in highly segmented societies (notably: Lijphart, 1968, 1969). The draft of 'The Democratic Constitution' proposes the abolition of the Law of Return, and all the Jewish symbols of the state. Israel is to be transformed from a Jewish Democratic state, as stated in its Declaration of Independence, into a bi-lingual and multi-cultural state. The Jewish majority will be allowed to exist as a cultural entity operating Hebrew schools and cultivating a Hebrew culture (Adalah, 2007). It seems unlikely, however, that Israeli Jews will agree to a plan that denies Jews a national home in their ancestral homeland.

Under these circumstances, it seems impossible to create a shared civic identity between Israeli Palestinian Arabs and Israeli Jewish citizens. Situations of 'contested regimes' often result in prolonged low-intensity conflicts, or in full-fledged wars.

Northern Ireland, the Basque region of Spain, the Kurds in Iraq, and the Palestinian uprisings, provide examples of contexts where the legitimacy of a ruling regime has been challenged. When class and ideological or religious differences coincide with ethnic cleavages, severe conflicts will often appear (Williams, 1994). Some scholars claim that Israel can continue to be a Jewish democratic state just as France can be French and democratic, and that even politically and religiously Islamic fundamentalists seek to be integrated into Israeli society (Smooha, 1990, 1993; Smooha and Gharem, 1998). Others are skeptical about the feasibility of containing the national rifts within the Israeli multiethnic democracy (Peled, 1992; Zureik, 1993a, 1993b; Yiftachel, 1992; Shafir, 1989).

The religious divide

A major rift within the Jewish population of Israel concerns the place of religion in the public sphere, as well as the diverse perceptions of Judaism and of being Jewish. An official separation of state and religion does not exist in Israel. However, Judaism did not become a state church or a formal state religion. The religious authorities and courts of the three religions (Jewish, Christian, Muslim) are financially supported through the Ministry of Religion and are exclusively empowered to deal with matters of personal status and family law in their respective religious communities (Sharot, 1990). Nevertheless, Orthodox Judaism may be considered the 'official' religion of the Israeli Jewish population. It has a monopoly over all matters related to the personal status of individuals, such as marriage, divorce, and burial services. Orthodox Judaism serves as gatekeeper, determining peoples' Jewishness according to Jewish religious law (Halacha). This definition excludes many immigrants from being recognized as Jews, because of mixed marriages. Religious movements similar to the Reform and Conservative movements in the US operate in Israel but are not officially recognized.

Over the years the rift between the religious and secular interpretations of what Judaism is and the vision of Israel as a Jewish nation-state has grown deeper. There are several variants of religiously observant communities in Israel, notably national-religious and ultra-orthodox ones. While national orthodox Jews combine Zionism and Jewish religious observance, most ultra-orthodox communities are anti-Zionist and consider as heresy the rebuilding of Israel prior to the arrival of the Messiah. Non-orthodox Jews ascribe the Jewishness of Israel mainly to national and cultural attributes, and are alienated by the attempts of religious parties to enforce Jewish religious laws and traditions in public life (Deshen, 1978, 1982, 1995).

The religious dimension overlaps to some extent with political and ideological controversies within Israeli society. Since the Six Day War, and Israeli occupation of Judea and Samaria (the West Bank) which forms the heart of the biblical land of Israel, religious Jews became religiously and politically radicalized, and came to play central role in political movements and parties on the right side of the Israeli political map. Many settlements on the West Bank and the Gaza Strip[2] were founded by religious nationalist groups, who form the spearhead of opposition to territorial concessions and the evacuation of settlements as part of a peace treaty with the Palestinian Authority (Don-Yehiya, 1994).

REPRODUCING THE RIFTS: THE FRAGMENTED EDUCATIONAL SYSTEM

The very structure of the Israeli educational system creates in schools distinct ideological and educational climates. Three types of school sub-systems exist within the Israeli state education system: Arab state schools, Hebrew religious state schools, and Hebrew regular (i.e., non-religious) state schools. The type of school that students attend is of central importance because these schools cater to distinct sectors within Israeli society (Ichilov, 2004, 2007). Non-religious Jewish students form the majority and attend mainly regular (non religious) state schools. Originating from a great variety of socioeconomic and ethnic backgrounds, students' families share religiously non-observant life styles, and ascribe the Jewishness of Israel mainly to national and cultural, rather than theocratic attributes (Ichilov, 2004). Religious state schools serve primarily Zionist orthodox Jews. As was mentioned earlier, the religious dimension overlaps to some extent with political and ideological controversies within Israeli society. Research findings reveal that religious education at both the high school level, and in higher education religious institutions (Yeshivot Leumiot) produce the next generations of religiously and politically radicalized individuals (Bar-Lev and Kedem, 1992; Don-Yehiya, 1994).

Arab state schools serve Israeli Palestinian Arab students. The state-mandated curricula are frequently depicted as characterized by '... the absence of any reference to Palestinian identity in history, literature, and social studies. Instead the curriculum offers a detailed Zionist narrative of history ...' (Rouhana, 1997: 86). The present state curriculum, however, compared to earlier versions, reflects some movement toward the inclusion of Arab and Palestinian identities (Al-Haj, 1993, 1995).

Education is a contested terrain that both reflects existing rifts and reproduces them. Attempts to universally reinforce a core national curriculum, especially concerning cultural and national heritage, have not been successful. Ultra orthodox schools, that receive state funding but are outside the state education system, reject attempts to impose upon them the teaching of Zionist heritage and democracy. Israeli Palestinian Arabs decline to implement curricular materials developed by the Ministry of Education concerning Israeli heritage and identity. Recently, the Ministry of Education commissioned a curricular committee chaired by an Israeli Palestinian-Arab, Dr. Kassem Darawsha, to replace an existing programme

entitled '100 Zionist related concepts' with a new programme '100 concepts concerning heritage, society and democracy' for Arab state schools. Realizing that arriving at a common list of concepts for all state schools is highly unlikely, the Ministry issued three different lists of concepts, for Jews, Arabs and Druze (a small national and religious minority). The new lexicon for Arabs was heavily criticized by Israeli Palestinian Arabs. It was described as an attempt to present an orientalist-folkloristic image of Arab heritage, detached from Palestinian and Arab traditions and identity. The Ministry was accused of having a hidden agenda attempting to disconnect Israeli Palestinian Arabs from their land and heritage. An alternative list of concepts was developed and publicly introduced in 2005. The preparation of the curricular materials and programs was a joint effort of a number of Israeli Palestinian Arab organizations, and was supported by the Arab Supreme Follow-Up Committee. It was published, widely distributed, and put to use in Arab schools (http://business.smn.co.il/news; http://www.yneu.co.il; http://www.haaretz.co.il/itemNo=659103; http://news.walla.co.il/?w=//820310).

Existing rifts are clearly carried over from the students' families and communities into the schools and are reflected in students' and teachers' attitudes (Ichilov, 2000, 2003, 2004, 2005, 2007). Students in Arab and in Hebrew religious schools seem to be more politicized than students in regular (non-religious) Hebrew state schools. They were, for example, more supportive than students in regular state school of the use of military power to retrieve occupied territories. Arab students were willing to engage in militant and illegal protest activities, as well as in legal active citizenship practices. The alienation of Arab students manifests itself in their being less supportive and proud of Israel in comparison with students in Hebrew schools. Religious school students, in contrast, are most patriotic (Ichilov, 2005). In addition, Arab and religious school students participate more intensively than regular state school students in out-of-school organizations.

Teachers act as socialization agents that reinforce and transmit school attitudes and perceptions that are prevalent in the community to which they belong (Ichilov, 2002). Research evidence reveals that Arab teachers attached lower importance than teachers in Hebrew schools to classroom discussions of patriotism and national symbols, and to issues that are of greater concern for the Jewish population of Israel, such as global anti-Semitism. Arab teachers assigned greater importance to discussing views that challenge the Zionist historical narrative. Teachers in religious state schools were most supportive of discussing patriotism and the national symbols of Israel, and least supportive of discussing the peace process, and Arab-Jewish relations in Israel (Ichilov, 2002). It is reasonable to assume that teachers may interpret events and curricular materials in the classroom based on their ideological stance. This, in turn, would create differential climates of opinion in Hebrew and Arab schools, and in religious and non-religious Hebrew state schools. It seems reasonable to assume that by virtue of interacting with teachers and classmates, students encounter mainly political ideas that are prevalent in their families and communities, thus reproducing the rifts from one generation to the next. This would be especially true in Arab and Hebrew religious state schools.

CITIZENSHIP EDUCATION: HISTORICAL MILESTONES

Democratic societies assign schools a prominent role in the development of citizenship virtues, values, and skills (Converse, 1972; Niemi and Junn, 1998). Is this true of divided societies as well? Can the education of citizens restrain the fervor of contesting visions and encourage democratic deliberation among the diverse groups within Israeli society?

Let's examine the major phases that the education for citizenship has gone through from the pre-state period until recently.

Particularistic and universalistic components in citizenship education

Israel, as stated in its Declaration of Independence was established as a Jewish-democratic state, a state that attempts to promote simultaneously Jewish nationalism and democracy. However citizenship education preceded the establishment of the state and was entitled education for Zionist citizenship. The debate that is still relevant today, concerning the emphasis that should be given to national and universalistic values, and the recognition that these two sets of values may be at odds with one another, preceded the founding of the State. During the pre-state (Yishuv) period, this duality was viewed as an abnormality caused by Diaspora life. Jews who wished to be socially accepted and integrated, especially those who were part of the Enlightenment Movement in Europe, were compelled to separate their Jewish and more general identities. A leading theme of the Enlightenment was 'be a Jew at home, and be a person in the public place'. Zionism sought to do away with this split identity, and educate a person and a Jew as a unified identity. However, given the emphasis during the Yishuv period on the revival of national life, the resurrection of Hebrew and the renewal of the use of the Hebrew calendar, clear precedence was given to national values. The aims of education for Zionist citizenship were to instill in the younger generation a strong loyalty to the ideas of national rebuilding and the redemption of the land. The ideal was to produce 'pioneers' dedicated to the cause of erecting the foundations of the future state, who are willing to postpone the fulfillment of their personal wishes and give priority to collective goals. Zionist education permeated all school subjects, and the entire web of school-life became a passing parade of national symbols and an identification rite

(Ben-Yehuda, 1949; Ichilov, 1993; Ichilov et al., 2005). Educators were nonetheless aware of the dangers entailed in emotion-based education and attempts were made 'not to bring into the schools the emotionalism of propaganda, but vital national emotions, to stay away from the sensational character of propaganda, and stress instead emotional maturity through education' (Bistritzki, 1948: 25).

Re-socialization of adult immigrants also became a major task of the educational system (Zameret, 1997). About half of the immigrants came from Europe having survived the Holocaust and war, and half were refugees from Muslim countries in the Middle East and North Africa. Immigrants arrived mainly from non-democratic countries, and countries in which Jews had at best limited citizenship rights. They, therefore, lacked the experience of participatory citizenship in a democracy. Special adult education programs were employed to teach new immigrants Hebrew and to prepare them for becoming citizens in a democracy.

With the establishment of the state, special relations developed between the schools and the Israeli Defense Forces (IDF). The first Israeli chief of staff, Igael Yadin, believed that a most important educational objective is to raise conscientious Zionist soldiers, i.e., soldiers with a sense of mission, knowing what they are defending and what they are fighting for, should another war break. Educators stressed, nonetheless, the anti-militaristic spirit of education: 'from the dawn of childhood youngsters embroider their role as pioneers ... Hebrew youth should never regard the army as an adventurous cult, sharpening its swords ... our army is an army of defense and fulfillment of Zionism' (cited in: Ichilov, 1993: 83). In later years, pre-military training (GADNA) was offered in high schools. Overall, the schools played a key role in inculcating the view that military service is an integral and central component of citizenship.

Civic education focused on the structural and legal aspects of state institutions. The emotional emphasis that was dominant during the Yishuv period became marginal and cognitive components took precedence. Citizenship education came to rely largely on concepts rooted in the social sciences. In the curriculum the obligations of citizens were stressed while hardly any attention was given to citizens' rights and to human rights and children's rights. These trends remained dominant well into the 1980s.

During the 1980s the Ministry of Education was alerted to the need to foster democratic education in the schools. A series of studies examining students' knowledge and perceptions of democracy revealed great ignorance and intolerance especially among vocational program students (Notably, Zemach and Zin, 1987). A policy directive issued in 1985 assigns unprecedented importance to the universalistic aspects of citizenship while allotting national values a much more minor role (Ministry of Education, Culture, and Sports, 1985). Educators were instructed to teach students that when faced with dilemmas emanating from a clash between national and universalistic values 'citizenship rights that are derived from fundamental democratic principles and procedures should gain precedence [over national values] and provide behavioral guidance' (Ministry of Education, Culture, and Sports, 1985: 4). This policy represents a total reversal of the preeminence of Zionist values during the Yishuv period and first years of statehood. Each year, the Ministry of Education announces a central theme that should be embodied in and articulated through diverse educational activities in the schools. To enforce the new policy, the central theme for the academic years 1986 and 1987 was education for democracy.

REBALANCING THE PARTICULARISTIC AND UNIVERSALISTIC ELEMENTS OF CITIZENSHIP

Developments from the 1990s on, that inspired a more balanced emphasis on national and democratic values, and a much greater attention to civil and human rights, will be discussed in this section.

Two committees[3] were especially instrumental in setting a new agenda for citizenship education. The committee for the examination of Judaic studies in Hebrew state schools, was appointed in 1991, and was given a broad mandate to examine any aspect that could promote Judaic education in schools (Ministry of Education, Culture, and Sports, 1994). A steering committee appointed in 1995 was commissioned to 'develop a comprehensive program for the inculcation of citizenship as a common value and behavioral framework for all Israeli citizens' (Ministry of Education, 1996: 5).

The Ministry of Education adopted the recommendations of both committees, and established a special division in charge of implementing them in schools. The desire was to integrate the particularistic and universalistic aspects of citizenship into a coherent curriculum: to foster youngsters' knowledge and awareness of the cultural and spiritual values inherent in their Jewish heritage and to demonstrate how this heritage supports a democratic culture.

The Judaic studies committee submitted its recommendations in 1994. The major recommendation was to intensify the study of Jewish heritage in Hebrew state schools from a pluralistic point of view:

> Hebrew state schools should focus on the development of a plurality of options for Jewish Israeli cultural existence that is independent of Jewish religious law [Halacha], and that builds on attachment to the history and creation of the Jewish people using a critical, pluralistic, and innovative perspectives (Ministry of Education, Culture and Sports, 1994:5).

However, the committee's recommendations have hardly been implemented mainly for lack of resources and the shortage in educators capable of teaching Jewish traditions from a pluralistic and critical perspective (Resh and Ben-Avot, 1998).

The steering committee on education for democracy was commissioned to provide detailed recommendations concerning the contents of civic education such as the values, knowledge and competencies that students should acquire at each stage of their educational career, the pedagogical practices that should be employed, and the organizational frameworks and tools for implementing and evaluating the new citizenship education programme.

A report was submitted to the Ministry of Education in February 1996 (Ministry of Education, 1996). The recommendations included the need to create a strong universalistic civic identity that would provide a common basis for allegiance, solidarity and consensus; stressing the necessity of achieving a civilized public discourse, based on tolerance, attentiveness to other views and willingness to settle conflicts through negotiation. The curriculum should promote the understanding of the foundations of Israel as both a Jewish state and a democracy. Citizenship obligations and civic and human rights, as well as principles, processes and institutions of democratic regimes must be articulated in schools. Students should acquire the ability to consider the overall complexity of issues and to assess the merits and drawbacks of various solutions; ability to offer well-founded and constructive criticism; and to have discourse with those who agree with and those who are opposed to one's own views. It was recommended that a great variety of teaching methods, such as discussion of controversial issues and simulations and role-play, would be employed to engage students. The achievement of these objectives must be given high priority, and the teaching of civics must begin in the lower grades of elementary school, and be consecutively included in the curriculum of all school grades. Recently, curricular materials were developed for elementary school students in grades two to four.

A significant event that inspired discourse on the place of civic and human rights in education was the signing (in 1990) and ratification (in 1991) by Israel of the United Nations Convention on The Rights of the Child.

The Convention advances the view that children bear inherent rights that should be respected and implemented within various social frameworks, including schools. These rights clearly include citizenship rights, such as freedom of thought, conscience and religion (Article 14), freedom of association and freedom of peaceful assembly (Article 15). Each child should have the right 'to freedom of expression: this right should include freedom to seek, receive and impart information and ideas of all kinds, regardless of frontiers, either orally or in print, in the form of art, or through any other media of the child's choice' (Article 13, Clause 1) (Convention on the Rights of the Child, 1989). In 2001 the Students' Rights Law was legislated, implementing many of the principles of the UN Convention on the Rights of the Child within Israeli schools, and advancing a democratic school climate. The Ministry of Justice appointed a committee to implement the Convention in Israeli legislation pertaining to the various spheres of children's life. A subcommittee on education was subsequently formed to implement the principles of the Convention in educational legislation.[4] The recommendations of the subcommittee on education were submitted in 2003, but thus far have not been implemented (Ministry of Justice, 2003).

The Oslo Accords and the peace process between Israel and the Palestinian Authority that lasted until the outbreak of violence (the so called second Intifada of 2000) inspired the introduction of peace education in schools. The central theme for the academic year 1994–1995 was dedicated to 'the peace process'. To help educators implement the message of peace, the Ministry of Education circulated a catalogue containing hundreds of ideas and programs illustrating the idea of peace to children K-12 (Firer, 1995).

Civics as a school subject

The recommendation of the Kremnizer Committee to offer civics classes consecutively throughout the entire process of schooling has not been implemented. At the elementary school level (Grades 1–6) civics is not studied. However, some aspects of citizenship are taught in Grades 2–4 through a school subject entitled 'Homeland and Society'. Recently, a civics unit was added to this school subject, including the development of curricular materials. For the junior high school level (Grades 7–9) a civics curriculum together with instructional materials have been prepared. Yet, civics is not an obligatory part of the curriculum, and the decision concerning civic instruction is left to school principals. It is estimated that civics is taught in only about one third of the junior high schools, at the 7th or 8th grades, one hour per week. Consequently, many students reach high school without previously studying civics. Civics is a compulsory school subject at the high school level, and a matriculation examination in civics is obligatory for all students at either the 11th or 12th grade. That is usually taught or accelerated during the year in which students take the matriculation examination. A recent study revealed the marginality of civics as a school subject, especially within Arab schools. Three weekly hours are dedicated to the teaching of civics. Regular state schools intensify the study of civics in the grade in which students take the matriculation examinations more than Arab and religious state schools (Ichilov, 2000).

Civics as a school subject was introduced in vocational schools only in 1990. Until then, civics formed a section within the study of history of the Jewish people and the state of Israel, a school subject that was not universally taught. Consequently, only a few vocational school students had a chance to have a glimpse at civics. However, differential curriculum and curricular materials were developed for academic and vocational high schools. Consequently, students are guided into dissimilar citizenship roles. Academic school students are expected to acquire the capacity to perceive citizenship issues through a broad, interdisciplinary, and multifaceted prism. Students in vocational schools, in contrast, are initiated into an unsophisticated and uncritical pattern of citizenship (Ichilov, 2002).

Qualified civic education teachers are in short supply and they often lack subject-specific preparation. Civics has been taught by history and social sciences teachers. Recently, teacher training in civics and the acquisition of a teaching certificate in civics became possible.

The neglect of civics as a school subject is manifested in the results of the matriculation examinations. The scores achieved in civics have been in recent years the lowest of all other school subjects in the humanities and social sciences. A recent study revealed that overall students in Hebrew schools did better on a knowledge test about democracy than students in Arab schools, and Hebrew state school students did slightly better than both religious state school and Arab school students (Ichilov, 2000, 2007). An international comparison of knowledge of democracy scores in 14 countries revealed no statistically significant differences between the mean score of Israeli 11th graders and the international mean (Amadeo et al., 2002: 57). Thus, on the average, Israeli youth did not do worse then their counterparts in other countries.

Attempts at bridging the rifts: Curricular and extracurricular programs

Until 1994 there was no common civics curriculum for Arab and Hebrew state schools and only partial overlap existed. The Ministry of Education was determined to formulate a common core curriculum for all state high schools: Arab, regular state schools, and religious state schools (Ministry of Education, Culture and Sports, 1994a). The supreme goal of the unified curriculum was:

> To inculcate a common Israeli civic identity, together with the development of distinct national identities, and to impart to students the values of pluralism and tolerance, educate students to

> accept the diversity that exists within Israeli society, and to respect those who are different from oneself

and to help students become 'autonomous and conscious citizens, capable of critical thinking, of analyzing, evaluating, and forming an independent opinion, playing by the rules of democracy, and being 'immune' to demagogical influences' (Ministry of Education, 2001: 10).

The core curriculum should, thus, provide Arab and Jewish students alike with an opportunity for:

> A thorough examination of the values on which Israel and its government are founded, given that Israel is simultaneously a Jewish and democratic state. The analysis should reveal, on the one hand, how the Jewish and democratic components are connected, and on the other, the fact that tensions may arise between them. Examination of the social reality in Israel should be related to these two sets of values (Ministry of Education, Culture, and Sports, 1994a: 6).

A textbook was developed in collaboration with Arab and Jewish educators, and the new curriculum was initially implemented on an experimental basis in some schools, and was nationally implemented in 2001 (Ministry of Education, 2000, 2001). Civics teachers participated in training programs that were specially designed to familiarize them with the new curriculum, textbook, and form of the civics matriculation examination. The new curriculum clearly addresses the dual nature of Israel as a Jewish and democratic state, and enables students to familiarize themselves with how 'others' perceive this duality and are affected by it.

Formal education and the instruction of civics are not the only activities related to citizenship education, and attempts to bridge existing gaps and rivalries. There is a wealth of activities, programs and instructional materials offered through the Youth and Society Division and the Unit for Democracy of the Ministry of Education. In addition, non-profit organizations, such as the Adam Institute, the Israeli Civil Rights Society, the Van Leer Institute, the Jewish-Zionist Institute, and the Rabin Center for Peace, produce instructional materials and operate programs within schools, such as encounters between Jewish and Arab youngsters, and religious and non-religious Jewish students. Some of the curricular materials that these organizations produce have been officially approved and adopted by the Ministry of Education. However, the extent to which schools make use of such programs remains unknown.

High schools offer a service-learning program entitled: 'personal commitment – community service'. The programme is implemented in 10th grade, in schools that choose to participate, and all students are required to be engaged. Participation in the program is noted in students' certificate of high school graduation. The Ministry of Education estimates that about 70,000 students in about 300 schools take part in the program. Preliminary findings reveal that although participation is compulsory, students expressed the view that partaking in the program is a worthwhile experience that benefits both themselves and the community (Ichilov, 2003). Many students declared that they would be willing to continue their community work on a voluntary basis.

CONCLUSION AND DISCUSSION

Reaching consensus regarding what the fundamental nature of Israeli society should be, and what binds citizens together, is an extremely difficult task. Given the deep and multifaceted nature of the national and religious rifts within Israeli society, the mission that schools are expected to accomplish via citizenship education seems almost unattainable. Civics is often not constituted by a formalized codified body of knowledge, but by a patchwork of isolated projects and programs, and is a marginal school subject (Ichilov, 2003; Mintrop, 2002; Schwille and Amadeo, 2002). Interactions with teachers and peers in Arab schools could make Arab students resentful or indifferent to the kind of

'civic knowledge' that schools are expected to impart (Ichilov, 2007). This situation is not unique to Israeli society alone. Many western societies are becoming increasingly multicultural. The fact that citizenship and multiculturalism could be forces that are pulling in diverse directions: unity vs. disunity is often neglected. Minorities that are unable or do not wish to be absorbed and integrated into mainstream society, could resent the type of 'civic knowledge' that represents the ideas of the dominant majority. Can educators make a difference in achieving some consensus and unity in multiethnic societies? There are no simple solutions. While it is imperative that leaders of both, minorities and the majority will act responsibly, and seek compromises that would not threaten the existence of any group, educators must not despair, and must not wait for politics to change. Educators must act as pioneers of peace and understanding, and do their utmost to inculcate among their students respect and tolerance for 'otherness'. This is especially vital where schools do not offer students an opportunity to study and interact with 'others'. Attempts to erect bridges promoting tolerance and understanding among groups must be intensified and educators must open wide horizons for their students instead of insulating them in their own enclaves.

NOTES

1 The national symbols of the State of Israel represent Jewish themes that are not an acceptable form of Israeli identity for the Israeli Palestinian Arab minority. The flag shows the Star of David, and the national emblem exhibits the Menorah of the Temple. The national anthem describes the yearnings of the Jews during two thousands years of exile to return to their homeland. Its last verse is 'to be an independent nation in our land, the land of Zion and Jerusalem'.

2 In the summer of 2005 Israel evacuated all Jewish settlements in the Gaza Strip and transferred control to the Palestinian Authority.

3 The first committee was headed by Professor Aliza Shenhar, and is better know as the Shenhar Committee. The second committee was headed by

Professor Mordachai Kremnizer, and is better known as the Kremnizer committee.

4 The Committee for the Implementation of the UN Convention on the Rights of the Child in Israeli Legislation was chaired by the district court judge Saviona Rotlevy. Professor Orit Ichilov was appointed chairperson of the subcommittee on education. The recommendations of the education subcommittee included amendments to the Student Rights Law, to more fully implement the principles stated in the Convention.

REFERENCES

Adalah, The Legal Center for Arab Minority Rights in Israel (February, 2007) *Draft: The Democratic Constitution*. http:// www.adalah. org/eng/democratic_constitution-e.pdf

Al-Haj, M. (2000) 'Identity and orientation among the Arabs in Israel: A situation of a dual periphery.' In Ruth Gavison and Dafna Hacker (eds.) *The Jewish-Arab Rift in Israel: A Reader* (In Hebrew). Jerusalem: The Israel Democracy Institute. pp. 13–33.

Al-Haj, M. (1995) *Education, Empowerment, and Control: The Case of the Arabs in Israel*. Albany: State University of New York Press.

Al-Haj, M. (1993) 'Education for democracy in Arab schools: Problems and challenges.' In O. Ichilov (ed.), *Citizenship Education in Democracy*. Ramat-Gan: Massada and Tel-Aviv University, School of Education, Sociology of Education and the Community Unit. pp. 23–43.

Amadeo, J-A., Torney-Purta, J., Lehmann, R., Husfeldt, V. and Roumiana, N (2002) *Civic Knowledge and Engagement: An IEA Study of Upper Secondary Students in Sixteen Countries*. Amsterdam: IEA.

Arian, A. (1990) *Politics and Regime in Israel*. Tel-Aviv: Zmora Bitan (in Hebrew).

Barda, M. (2002a) *Perceptions of Israeli Jews of the Identity and Loyalty to Israel Among Israeli Arabs*. Jerusalem: The Knesset, Center for Research and Information, (In Hebrew).

Barda, M. (2002b) *Perceptions of Arabs and Jews of the Identity and Loyalty to the State Among Israeli Arabs*. Jerusalem: The Knesset, Center for Research and Information (in Hebrew).

Bar-Lev, M. and Kedem, P. (1992) 'Political attitudes of national-religious youth in Israel.' In Mordechai Bar-Lev (ed.), *Religious Education and Religious Youth: Dilemmas and Tensions*. Tel-Aviv: Tel-Aviv University, School of Education and Massada Publishing House (in Hebrew). pp. 79–95.

Ben-Yehuda, B. (1949) *The Teachers' Movement for Zion and its Redemption*. Jerusalem: The Jewish National Fund (in Hebrew).

Bistritzki, N. (1948) 'Summary of 20 years to the Teachers' Movement for Zion and its Redemption.' *Shorashim*, 3: 25–30 (in Hebrew).

Byrne, S. (1997) *Growing Up in a Divided Society*. Madison, Teaneck, NJ: Fairleigh Dickinson University Press, Associated University Press.

Cohen, S.A. and Don Y. E. (1986) (eds.) *Conflict and Consensus in Jewish Political Life*. Ramat-Gan: Bar Ilan Univrsity Press.

Convention on the Rights of the Child, (1989) In Ian Brownlie (ed) (1992) *Basic Documents on Human Rights*. New York: Oxford University Press. pp. 241–259.

Converse, P.E. (1972) 'Change in the American electorate.' In Angus Campbell and Philip E. Converse (eds.) *The Human Meaning of Social Change*. New York: Russell Sage Foundation. pp. 263–337.

Deshen, S. (1995) 'Editorial introduction: The study of religion in Israeli social sciences.' In Shlomo Deshen, Charles Lieberman and Moshe Shokeid (eds), *Israeli Judaism*. New Brunswick, NJ: Transaction. pp. 1–19.

Deshen, S. (1982) 'Israel: Searching for identity.' In Carlo Caldarola (ed.), *Religion and Society in Asia and the Middle East*. Berlin: Mouton. pp. 85–118.

Deshen, S. (1978) 'Israeli Judaism: Introduction to major patterns.' *International Journal of Middle East Studies*, 9 (2): 141–169.

Don-Yehiya, E. (1994) 'The book and the sword: The nationalist yeshivot and political radicalism in Israel.' In Martin Marty and Scott Appleby (eds), *Accounting for Fundamentalism: The dynamic Character of Movements*. Chicago: Chicago University Press. pp. 264–302.

Eisenstadt, Samuel N. (1989) *The Changing Israeli Society*. Jerusalem: Magnes (in Hebrew).

Etzioni, A. (1992) 'On the place of virtues in pluralistic democracy'. In Gary Marks and Larry Diamond (eds.) *Reexamining Democracy*. Newbury Park: Sage. pp. 70–79.

Etzioni-Halevy, E. (1993) *The Elite Connection and Israeli Democracy*. Tel-Aviv: Sifriat Poalim (In Hebrew).

Firer, R. (1995) 'From peace making to tolerance building.' In Rafael Moses (ed.), *The Psychology of Peace and Conflict: The Israeli-Palestinian Experience*. Jerusalem: The Truman Institute for the Advancement of Peace. pp. 79–86.

Giroux, H.A. (1983) *Theory and Resistance in Education*. London: Heinemann Educational.

Heater, Derek B. (1990) *Citizenship: The Civic Ideal in World History*. London: Longman.

Ichilov, O. (2007) 'Civic Knowledge of High-School Students in Israel: Personal and Contextual Determinants.' *Political Psychology*, 28 (4): 417–441.

Ichilov, O. (2005) 'Pride in one's country and citizenship orientations in a divided society: The case of Israeli Palestinian-Arabs and orthodox and non-orthodox Jewish-Israeli youth'. *Comparative Education Review*, 49 (1): 44–61.

Ichilov, O., Salomon, G. and Inbar, D. (2005) 'Citizenship Education in Israel – A Jewish-Democratic State.' In Raphael Cohen-Almagor (ed.), *Israeli Institutions at the Crossroads*. London and New York: Routledge. pp. 29–50.

Ichilov, O. (2004) *Political Learning and Citizenship Education Under Conflict*. London and New York: Routledge.

Ichilov, O. (2003) 'Education and democratic citizenship in a changing world.' In David O. Sears, Leonie H and Robert L.J. (eds), *Oxford Handbook of Political Psychology*. New York: Oxford University Press. pp. 637–670.

Ichilov, O. (2003a) 'Service learning and education for democracy: The personal commitment project.' *Studies in Education*, 5 (2): 237–255. (In Hebrew).

Ichilov, O. (2003b) 'Teaching civics in a divided society: The case of Israel.' *International Studies in Sociology of Education*, 13 (3): 219–242.

Ichilov, O. (2002) 'Differentiated Civics Curriculum and Patterns of Citizenship Education: Vocational and Academic Programs in Israel.' In David Scott and Helen Lawson (eds), *Citizenship Education and the Curriculum*. Volume 3 in the International Perspectives on Curriculum Series. (Series editor: David Scott). Westport CT: Greenwood. pp. 81–111.

Ichilov, O. (2000) *Citizenhip Orientations of 11th Grade Students and Teachers in the Israeli Hebrew and Arab High Schools*. Israel's National Research Report, IEA Civic Education Study. Tel-Aviv: Tel-Aviv University, School of Education.

Ichilov, O. (1993) *Citizenship Education in Israel*. Tel-Aviv: Sifrriat Poalim (in Hebrew).

Janowitz, M. (1983) *The Reconstruction of Partiotism: Education for Civic Consciousness*. Chicago: The University of Chicago Press.

Jarbi, I. and Levi, G. (2000) *The Socio-Economic Rift in Israel*. Jerusalem: The Israeli Institute for Democracy. Position paper No. 21 (in Hebrew).

Kanpol, B.S. and McLaren, P. (eds) (1995) *Critical Multiculturalism: Uncommon Voices in a Common Struggle*. Westport, CT: Bergin & Garvey.

Kimmerling, B. (2001) *The Invention and Decline of Israeliness*. Berkely: University of California Press.

Kimmerling, B. (1989) *The Israeli State and Society*. Albany: University of New York Press.

Kymlicka, W. and Norman, W. (eds) (2000) *Citizenship in Diverse Societies*. New York: Oxford University Press.

Kymlicka, W. (1995) *Multicultural Citizenship: A Liberal Theory of Minority Rights*. Oxford: Oxford University Press.

Kymlicka, W. (1991) 'Liberalism and the politicization of ethnicity.' *Canadian Journal of Law and Jurisprudence*, IV (2): 239–256.

Landau, J.M. (1993) *The Arab Minority in Israel, 1967–1991: Political Aspects*. Oxford: Clarendon Press.

Levin-Epstein, N. and Semyonov, M. (1993) *The Arab Minority in Israel's Economy: Patterns of Ethnoc Inequality*. Boulder: Westview Press.

Lewis, B. (1975) *History: Remembered, Recovered, Invented*. Princeton: Princeton University Press.

Lijphart, A. (1969) 'Consociational democracy'. *World Politics*, 21 (2): 207–225.

Lijphart, A. (1968) *The Politics of Accommodation: Pluralism and Democracy in the Netherlands*. Berkley: University of California Press.

Lissak, M. (2000) 'Major rifts within Israeli society.' In *Pluralism in Israel: From Melting Pot to Salad Bowl*. Interim report. Jerusalem: Center for the Study of Social Policy. (In Hebrew) (www.csps.org.il). pp. 27–55.

McLaren, P. (1997) *Revolutionary Multiculturalism: Pedagogues of Dissent for the New Millennium*. Boulder, CO: Westview.

Merelman, R.M. (1990) 'The role of conflict in children's political learning.' In Orit Ichilov (ed.), *Political Socialization, Citizenship Education, and Democracy*. New York: Teachers College Press, Columbia University. pp. 47–67.

Ministry of Education, Curriculum Department (2001) *Leaflet for Civics Teachers No. 16*. [Teacher's guide for academic high schools]. Jerusalem: Ministry of Education. (In Hebrew).

Ministry of Education, Curriculum Department (2000) *To Be Citizens in Israel: A Jewish and Democratic State*. Jerusalem. (In Hebrew).

Ministry of Education and Culture (1996) *To Be Citizens: Education For All Israeli Students*. Jerusalem: Interim Report of the Steering Committee on Citizenship Education (in Hebrew).

Ministry of Education, Culture, and Sports, Curriculum Department (1994) *Nation and World – Jewish Culture in a Changing World*. Recommendations of the committee for the examination of Judaic education in Hebrew state schools. Jerusalem.

Ministry of Education, Culture, and Sports, Curriculum Department (1994a) *Citizenship: [Academic] High School Curriculum for Jewish (general and religious), Arab, and Druz Schools*. (First Edition). Jerusalem. (In Hebrew).

Ministry of Education, Curriculum Department (1990) *Citizenship: High School Curriculum for the Lower Vocational Tracks in General and Religious Jewish Technological High Schools*. Jerusalem. (In Hebrew).

Ministry of Education, Culture, and Sports (May, 1985) *Special Dispatch No. 5: Education for Democracy*. Jerusalem. (In Hebrew).

Ministry of Justice (2003) *The Committee for the Examination and Implementation in Legislation of the Fundamental Principles Concerning Children*. Report of the Subcommittee on Education.

Mintrop, H. (2002) 'Teachers and civic education instruction in cross-national comparisons.' In Stiner-Khamsi, Gitta, Torney-Purta, Judith and Schwille, Jack (Eds.) *New Paradigms and Recurring Paradoxes in Education for Citizenship: An International Comparison*. Amsterdam: JAI Press, Elsevier Science. pp. 61–85.

Niemi, R.G. and Junn, J. (1998) *Civic Education: What Makes Students Learn*. New Haven: Yale University Press.

Peled, Y. (1992) 'Ethnic democracy and the legal construction of citizenship.' *American Political Science Review*, 86 (4): 479–492.

Rekhess, E. (2003) 'Editor's Corner.' *Elections Update 2003*: 2 (In Hebrew).

Rekhess, E. (1989) 'Israeli Arabs and Arabs of the West Bank and the Gaza Strip: Political ties and national identification.' *Hamizrah Hehadash* (The New East), 32: 165–191.

Rekhess, E. (1976) *The Arabs in Israel after 1967: The Exacerbation of the Orientation of Problem*. Tel-Aviv: Tel-Aviv University, Shiloach Center (in Hebrew).

Resh, N. and Ben-Avot, A. (1998) *Judaic Studies in Hebrew Middle Schools in Israel: Evaluation of the Implementation of the Shenhar Report Recommendations*. Jerusalem: Hebrew University, School of Education.

Rouhana, N. (1997) *Palestinian Citizens in an Ethnic Jewish State*. New Haven: Yale University Press.

Sakran, F.C. (1976) *Palestine Still a Dilemma*. Washington, DC: American Council on the Middle East.

Schwille, J. and Amadeo, J-A. (2002) 'The paradoxical situation of civic education in schools: Ubiquitous and yet elusive.' In Steiner-Khamsi, Gitta, Torney-Purta, Judith and Schwille, Jack (eds) (2002) *New Paradigms and Recurring Paradoxes in Education for Citizenship: An International Comparison*. Amsterdam: JAI Press, Elsevier Science. pp. 105–137.

Shafir, G. (1989) *Land, Labor and the Origin of the Israeli-Palestinian Conflict*. Cambridge: Cambridge University Press.

Sharot, S. (1990) 'Israel: Sociological analyses of religion in the Jewish state' *Sociological Analysis*, 51 (supplement): 63–76.

Smooha, S. and Ghanem, A (1998) *Ethnic Religious and Political Islam Among the Arabs in Israel*. Haifa: University of Haifa. Working Paper No. 14.

Smooha, S. (1993) 'Social, ethnic and national rifts and Israeli democracy.' In U. Ram (ed.), *Israeli Society: Critical Perspectives*. Tel-Aviv: Breirot (in Hebrew). pp. 172–202.

Smooha, S. (1990) 'Minority status in an ethnic democracy: the status of the Arab minority in Israel.' *Ethnic and Racial Studies*, 13 (3): 389–413.

Smooha, S. (1989) *Arabs and Jews in Israel*. Boulder: Westview Press.

Smooha, S. (1985) 'Existing and alternative policy toward the Arabs in Israel.' In Ernest. Krauz (ed.), *Politics and Society in Israel Vol 2*. New Brunswick, NJ: Transaction. pp. 334–361.

Smooha, S. (1984) *The Orientation and Politicization of the Arab Minority in Israel*. Haifa: University of Haifa, Monograph Series on the Middle East No. 2.

Smooha, S. (1980) 'Control of minorities in Israel and Northern Ireland.' *Comparative Studies in Society and History*, 22 (2): 256–280.

Taylor, C. (1994) 'The politics of recognition.' In A. Gutmann (ed.), *Multiculturalism: Examining The Politics of Recognition*. Princeton: Princeton University Press. pp. 25–74.

The National Committee of Mayors of Arab Municipalities in Israel (2006) *The Future Vision of Palestinian Arabs in Israel*.http://roter.net/forum/gil/7158.shtml

Torney-Purta, J., Lehmann, R., Oswald, H. and Schulz, W. (2001) *Citizenship and Education in Twenty-Eight Countries: Civic Knowledge and Engagement at Age Fourteen*. Amsterdam: IEA.

Williams, M. Robin (1994) 'The sociology of ethnic conflicts: Comparative international perspectives.' *Annual Review of Sociology*, 20: 49–79.

Yiftachel, O. (1992) 'The concept of "ethnic democracy" and its applicability in the case of Israel' *Ethnic and Racial Studies* 15 (1): 125–136.

Young, Marion I. (1990) 'The ideal of community and the politics of difference.' In Linda, J. Nicholson (ed.) *Feminism/Postmodernism*. New York: Routledge. pp. 300–323.

Zameret, Z. (1997) *On a Narrow Bridge*. Sde-Boker: Center for the Heritage of Ben-Gurion, and Ben-Gurion University. (In Hebrew).

Zemach, M. and Zin, R. (1984) *Attitudes Concerning Democratic Values Among Israeli Youth*. Jerusalem: Dachaf Institute and Van Leer Institute (In Hebrew).

Zureik, E. (1993a) 'Prospects of the Palestinians in Israel: I.' *Journal of Palestine Studies*, 22 (2): 90–109.

Zureik, E. (1993b) 'Prospects of the Palestinians in Israel: II.' *Journal of Palestine Studies*, 22 (4): 73–93.

15

Citizenship Education in Japan

Lynne Parmenter, Mitsuharu Mizuyama and Kazuya Taniguchi

The purpose of this chapter is to give an overview of the development and current state of citizenship education in Japan. After a brief review of the history of citizenship education in Japan in the first section, citizenship education policy and curriculum are considered in some detail in the second and third sections. The fourth section deals with the everyday practice of citizenship education in Japanese schools, as opposed to explicit policy and curriculum, and the final section highlights a few of the main issues that face citizenship education in Japan.

A HISTORICAL OVERVIEW OF CITIZENSHIP AND CITIZENSHIP EDUCATION IN JAPAN

The beginning of the modern nation of Japan is generally dated to the Meiji Restoration of 1868, and education policy at a national level began to take effect shortly afterwards. This, then, is the beginning of widespread citizenship education in Japan. In the 1870s, 'modern' ideas from Europe and other parts of the world were imported by government officials and others, among them the notion of 'citizenship'. There are three main translations

used in Japanese. 'Shimin' means 'a sovereign of the nation' or 'a private citizen' in Japanese. According to Horio (1987), this term is based on the concept of 'education for individual freedom', and was not apparent in Japan in practice until after democratization in 1945. 'Koumin', on the other hand, means both 'citizenship based on natural law' and 'citizenship based on the Imperial Family-State', and is dated back to 1868 or 1920, depending on opinion. Another term, 'kokumin', meaning 'national citizen' was introduced to Japan by Yukichi Fukuzawa, a highly influential thinker and reformer of the Meiji Restoration who was also the first person to introduce the term 'shimin' to Japan as a translation of the terms 'citizen', 'citoyen' or 'Burger' (Yamaguchi, 2004).

Similarly, citizenship education in Japan since 1868 has gone under various names and has taken various forms, according to the government of the time. From the time of the issuance of the Imperial Rescript on Education in 1890, citizenship education increasingly became the vehicle for nationalist and patriotic education (Tipton, 2002), although there were interludes in the liberal Taisho period (1912–1926), when progressivism swept the country and French and German models of civic education, as well as innovative experiments in child-centred moral education, were introduced to schools.

The role of citizenship education in promoting patriotism continued through to the end of WWII in 1945. At the beginning of the American Occupation (1945–1952), the teaching of Japanese history and geography and of moral education was forbidden by the Occupation authorities, and a proposal by the Japanese government for a new civics curriculum was also refused in 1946. In 1947, when the first post-war Course of Study was published, a new social studies curriculum, based on an American model, was introduced (Dower, 1999). This formed the basis of modern citizenship education in Japan, with the curriculum being revised and updated every ten years or so from 1947 to the present. The next two sections will examine current policy and the present Course of Study in greater detail.

CITIZENSHIP EDUCATION POLICY

Citizenship education is the development of citizens who will form democratic societies in the future. However, democracy includes both direct democracy and indirect democracy, and citizenship can be liberal and civic republican, which means that it is difficult to propose an all or nothing ideal definition of the ideal citizen or ideal citizenship education. There is great diversity in citizenship education between countries and even historically within a single country, as is apparent from even the brief history of citizenship education in Japan provided above.

In Japan, at policy level, citizenship education is the province of two Ministries; the Ministry of Health, Labour and Welfare and the Ministry of Education, Culture, Science, Sports and Technology (hereafter abbreviated to Ministry of Education). Partly in response to the lack of effective coordination between these two Ministries, the government in 2003 published the 'Youth Development Policy Plan' (Cabinet, 2003), which has

become the basis for policy measures in various Ministries. This plan is the basic blueprint for citizenship education in Japan. The plan highlights four priority areas, which are

(1) support for social independence;
(2) support for youth in particular need;
(3) adoption of a view of youth as active members of society; and
(4) stimulation of a climate of free and open discussion in society.

Based on this one plan, the Ministry of Health, Labour and Welfare formulates and implements policies focusing on social security, while the Ministry of Education focuses on educational aspects. However, the arena of Ministry of Education undertakings is mainly schools, while the arena of Ministry of Health, Labour and Welfare undertakings is primarily outside schools, so the lack of coordination remains an issue. The result is that no integrated structure of citizenship education, encompassing both school and community, exists in Japan. In this section, discussion will be limited to citizenship education in schools, and thus to Ministry of Education policies and curriculum.

22 December 2006 was an epoch-making day in the history of education policy in Japan. It was the day when the 'Fundamental Law of Education', which had remained unchanged since its promulgation in 1947, was revised. Article 1 of the new Fundamental Law of Education remains unchanged, stating as the aim of education:

> Education shall aim at the full development of personality, striving for the rearing of people, sound in mind and body, who shall love truth and justice, esteem individual value, respect labor, have a deep sense of responsibility, and be imbued with an independent spirit, as builders of the peaceful state and society.

This aim is obviously close in spirit to Crick's 'social and moral responsibility' strand (QCA, 1998) and is deeply connected with citizenship education. However, in the revised version, Article 2 (aims of education) goes further, stating that education should encourage 'public spirit, leading to independent participation in building society, together with the development of an attitude of wanting to contribute to its growth'.

In this way, the emphasis in the revised law, and in the debates and meetings that preceded it, is on 'public spirit', 'social and moral responsibility' and 'engagement in local communities', with no reference to 'political literacy'. This is reflected in the curriculum, to which we turn next.

CITIZENSHIP EDUCATION CURRICULUM

The curriculum being used in schools at the time of writing is based on the 'Course of Study' of 1998 and 1999. Courses of Study are published for elementary school (age 6–12), junior high school (12–15) and senior high school (15–18) respectively. The Courses of Study are revised approximately once a decade, and the revisions of laws and the Youth Development Plan mentioned above will be reflected in the next reforms, which are being formulated now and will be implemented in schools from 2010 or thereabouts. In this section, the focus will be on the current Courses of Study (Monbusho, 1998) for the junior high school stage, where citizenship is a particular issue. Discussion in this section will be organized under the categories of 'Social Studies as a subject', 'Other subjects' and 'Other areas of the curriculum'.

Social studies

In Japan, the subjects related to society (hereafter, social studies) taught in schools are 'Life Studies' in the first two years of elementary school, 'Social Studies' from the third year of elementary school through to the end of junior high school, and 'Geography/History' and 'Civics' in senior high school. In junior high school, Social Studies is divided into the three areas of geography, history and civics. The overall aim of Social Studies is as follows:

> From a broad perspective, to raise interest in society, to study [society] from various angles using various materials, to nurture understanding of and love for our country's land and history, and to cultivate the foundations of citizenship necessary to be a creator of a democratic and peaceful nation and society, while living in international society.

Social studies in Japan, based on the Course of Study, thus adopts the process of 'developing knowledge and understanding to develop attitudes and competence' (Katakami, 2000: 110). Using this methodology, students cultivate the foundations of citizenship by deepening their knowledge and understanding of basic human rights, democracy and international relations. However, there is criticism from those involved in social studies education about the connection between 'love for our country's land and history' and 'knowledge and understanding of our country's land and history' (Harada, 2004: 14).

The three areas of geography, history and civics each have four aims, the first dealing with the general aim of that area, the second and third dealing with specific aims of the area and the fourth dealing with skills and attitudes.

A particular feature of the geography area is that Japanese and world geography are treated more or less equally (Shibusawa, 2000: 22). The third aim, 'to examine comparisons and relations between the various large- and small-scale regions that make up Japan and the world', emphasizes Japan as part of a multi-layered structure of regions. In practice, however, the content section specifies 'Japan in comparison with the world', and the result is a dichotomization of Japan and the world, with little attempt to situate Japan in a multi-layered political or regional world structure.

In the history area, the first aim is 'to make [students] understand the main flow of history and features of each period of our country, against the background of world history'. In other words, the aim is to understand Japanese history, and world history is limited to a background role. The rationale for this is that the curriculum should be appropriate to students' developmental stage, but opinion is divided as to whether such Japan-centred education is appropriate to the junior high school stage (Mizoue, 2000: 5).

A further point of debate, as mentioned above, is the unclear link between love for our country's history and awareness as a national citizen in the aim 'to deepen love for our country's history and develop awareness as a national citizen' (Morimo, 2000: 100). History education in Japan is also well-known internationally for its promotion of a single, nationally centred view of history. Textbooks, which have to adhere to this version of history to be authorized for use in schools, have been the subject of debate throughout post-war history and are still the target of furious criticism from South Korea and China in particular (Ienaga, 2001; Barnard, 2003).

The civics area is central to citizenship, and is based on awareness of democracy and knowledge and understanding of human rights and the meaning and concepts of international relations. In this area, the following statement is made in reference to intelligent and active engagement in the 'public space' of citizenship:

> Making connections with the family and local community, make [students] realize that humans are essentially social beings, make [students] think about the relationship between the individual and society, the dignity of the individual in the contemporary family system, the intrinsic equality of the sexes, and make [them] realize the importance of conventions in social life, the significance keeping the conventions, and the responsibility of the individual.

The main focus here is the rules of social life and the aim is to make students aware of public space through these rules. However, students have no role in creating public affairs, which exist before they do, but are expected rather to understand them, not even going so far as to actively contribute.

The aim concerning skills and attitudes in the use of materials, which is common to all three areas, states that students should develop 'the skills and attitudes necessary to gather various relevant materials, select and analyse them from multiple perspectives, judge them impartially and present them appropriately'. However, most of these skills and attitudes are left ambiguous, with no concrete content.

Other subjects

Other subjects which deal in some way with citizenship are national language (Japanese), foreign language, music and art.

Japanese deals with the traditions and culture of Japan through the classics, literature and literary criticism. The guidelines for materials state that materials should 'serve to develop an attitude of respect for our country's traditions and culture' and 'serve to develop self-awareness as a Japanese person'. Materials that 'serve to deepen the cultivation of a spirit of international understanding and international harmony' are also recommended, but the definitions of international understanding and international harmony remain ambiguous, and there is a definite slant to patriotic content (Coulmas, 2002).

The subject 'foreign language' is, in practice, limited to English. Content is supposed to cover 'the daily life, customs, stories, geography and history and so on of the people of the world, with an emphasis on people who use English, and Japanese people', but 'the world' tends to equal the US to a large extent. The guidelines also specify that, in addition to learning English as a language, students should 'heighten their interest in culture' and 'deepen international understanding from a wide perspective', but again, the content of international understanding is vague and, as in Japanese, there is a leaning towards the further specification that, through English, students should 'heighten their self-awareness as Japanese people'.

In music, songs and works from countries other than Japan are introduced, and the selection is not limited to western music but extends to South American and Asian music.

On the other hand, it is specified that songs for choral singing should make students 'sense the beauty of our country's nature and four seasons' and 'taste the beauty inherent in our country's culture and the Japanese language', and such specifications are a deliberate move to form national identity.

Similarly, in art, the development of national identity is an issue, with one of the purposes of the subject specified to be 'to deepen understanding and love of Japanese art, culture and traditions'. One interesting point in the guidelines for art, however, is found in the materials section, where it is stated that 'in each year, works of children in Japan and abroad should be introduced, as should Asian cultural heritage'. This reference to Asian cultural heritage is notable as the only specific reference to Asia in such a context in the guidelines for all subjects, in contrast to the ubiquitous but ambiguous keyword, 'international understanding'.

Other areas of the curriculum

Moral education is an area of the curriculum that is supposed to transcend the timetable and be inherent in all education. The overall aim for moral education is thus:

'Through all school activities, to cultivate morality in the form of moral sentiments, powers of judgement and the motivation and attitudes to put these into practice'.

One class a week is also set aside specifically for moral education, and the aims here include the development of 'moral values' and 'moral practice', showing an extremely strong emphasis on the development of 'social and moral responsibility'.

Moral education is split into the three sections of 'aspects mainly to do with the self', 'aspects mainly to do with other people' and 'aspects mainly to do with the group and society'. Much of the content of the latter two sections has direct links with citizenship education, covering objectives such as 'understanding the significance of the group', 'roles and responsibilities', 'rights and duties', 'public spirit and social solidarity', 'creating a better school ethos', 'international perspectives' and so on. At the same time, many of these objectives are premised on explicitly stated values and ethics such as 'keeping laws and rules', 'respect for parents and grandparents', 'respect for teachers and school staff', 'self-awareness as a Japanese person and patriotic spirit' and so on.

Special Activities is another area of the curriculum, the aim of which is as follows:

To aim for holistic development and the expansion of individuality through desirable group activities, to develop an independent, practical attitude of wanting to build a better life as a member of the group and of society, to deepen self-awareness of living as a human being and to cultivate the ability of self-fulfilment.

Special Activities is the only area of the curriculum in Japan where students learn through experience and activities. In its emphasis on learning through group experience and activities, it has much in common with the 'active learning' promoted in citizenship education. The three areas of Special Activities are 'class activities', 'student council activities' and 'school events', and reference is also made to the necessity to work in collaboration with families and community members. Through the group activities of Special Activities, therefore, active 'social and moral responsibility' and 'contribution to the local community' are accorded a place in the school curriculum. However, as the specific content of Special Activities is left to the class or school, the range of activities tends to be wide, and there is no guarantee that students will gain a satisfactory level of political literacy through involvement.

Integrated Learning, like moral education and Special Activities, is not considered to be a subject, which means that teachers do not need to have any specific qualifications to teach it. The content of Integrated Learning is supposed to be adapted to each local community, school and students, and should be based on students' interests, and be wide-ranging and integrated. The four themes suggested as examples for Integrated Learning are international understanding, information technology, the environment and health and welfare. Taking cross-curricular themes such as these, the aims of Integrated Learning are for students to develop problem-solving skills, learn how to learn, be able to integrate and apply the knowledge they have learned in various subjects and develop the 'power of living'. In its concern with local and global issues and its focus on practical skills, Integrated Learning has potential as a place for citizenship education, although the actual practice varies from school to school (Mizuyama, 2000: 121).

EVERYDAY PRACTICE OF CITIZENSHIP EDUCATION IN SCHOOLS IN JAPAN

In addition to the formal curriculum described in the third section, the everyday practice of schools – the daily routines, familiar practices, shared events and common activities – is an essential element of citizenship education, not only reinforcing what is taught in the formal curriculum, but also providing a place for students to 'do' citizenship in their own community (Huddleston and Kerr, 2006: 81). In the case of Japan, these routines, practices and activities are shared to a great extent regardless of location or level of schooling. Whether they are 6 years old or 18 years old, the vast majority of students in Japan engage in school cleaning every day. Whether they live in Hokkaido in the north or Okinawa in the south, most students not only learn the same curriculum, but also engage in the same routines of morning and afternoon meetings. Whether they live in a village of 200 people or a city of over 2 million people, almost all students share the same annual events, from Sports Day to Culture Festival. Although there are obviously differences between individuals, schools and regions, therefore, it is possible to highlight some patterns of everyday practice relevant to citizenship education which would be recognizable

to the majority of people who have experienced school in Japan (Sugimoto, 2003: 132).

What children in Japan are doing on a daily basis from the time they start school at 6 is similar to what is identified in the National Curriculum for England and Wales Key Stages 3 and 4 as skills of participation and responsible action:

(a) understanding, empathy and advocacy;
(b) negotiation, decision-making and participation; and
(c) reflection.

This is not labelled citizenship education in Japan, but rather is the taken-for-granted culture of school. Just a few examples in each of the above categories will be given to illustrate the point.

In terms of school and class organization, children are organized into fixed mixed-ability workgroups (*han* in Japanese) within mixed-ability homeroom classes. Lewis (1995) describes in detail how, in most classes in most schools, teachers work extremely hard to ensure that everyone is included, and that children themselves learn to accept each other, and to accommodate classmates whose personalities, opinions and abilities may be very different from their own. Students take turns at being the head of the *han*, and in this position are required to summarize and present the opinions of their group members to the rest of the class on numerous occasions every week in lessons and other class activities. As this is a very common technique, students have frequent opportunities to think about, explain and evaluate views that are not their own. Similarly, children develop skills of empathy, explanation and advocacy through peer mediation, which is usually developed in kindergarten, where children from the age of 3 or 4 are encouraged to listen to and understand both sides of an argument before resolving the issue.

Children also have myriad opportunities for negotiating, deciding and participating responsibly in the class and school community (Parmenter, 2004: 89). In the classroom, daily duty rotas are ubiquitous, and the student on duty is usually expected to lead the morning and afternoon meetings as well as perform a range of other tasks. All schools have Student Councils, as mentioned in the section on Special Activities above, and all students are members. Each class usually elects one or two representatives to the Student Council main committee. Not all Student Councils are very active, but many are, and the head committee has real power to instigate activities and involve the whole school in projects which could range from cleaning up the local river to leading a town project to send aid to children in another country. Furthermore, all students from the upper years of elementary school are usually members of a school committee. The work of these committees is essential to the running of the school, as few staff apart from teachers are employed in Japanese schools. Care of the school grounds and pets, broadcasting, production of school newspapers, health promotion, library management, Student Council election management and general school life and rules management are all the responsibility of committees of students. Usually a teacher is allocated to be responsible for each committee, but in general the teacher performs an advisory role, and students are highly independent in setting goals and working towards them. A similar set-up is found in extra-curricular clubs, which are usually run by older students under the (less or more involved) supervision of a teacher. Teachers also encourage students to take the lead in planning and implementing school events, so that it is common for 6th grade elementary school students (11–12 year olds), as the senior students of the school, to organize most details of the School Sports Day, their class or school trip or their graduation ceremony. Beyond school, students are also encouraged to participate in the community, through volunteer activities and work experience, although such activities are still school-based rather than community-based.

Finally, it would probably be no understatement to say that the third element, reflection, is a tour de force of the Japanese education system. Reflection, known as *hansei*, is a built-in component of most educational activity in Japan (Lewis, 1995: 170), and by the age of 10 or 11, most students in Japan are experts at identifying weak points in their own individual or group activities, as well as specifying measures for improvement and new aims. On the other hand, they are neither expected nor encouraged to be critical of other individuals, and evaluation in this case (which is also very frequent) focuses on identifying the positive aspects or good points of the person's work, presentation or abilities.

In such ways, all students are actively involved in various roles in the daily life of the school, and also in its wellbeing as a community. As de Weerd et al., (2005: 16) point out, participation is central to active citizenship, and they specifically identify 'opportunities to participate in and have an influence on school' and 'opportunities to participate in the community through school' as relevant indicators for citizenship education. Students in Japan invariably have such opportunities, although they may have little choice in whether or not to take them; participation is expected rather than offered.

ISSUES IN CITIZENSHIP EDUCATION

As elsewhere, citizenship education in Japan is not perfect, and the aim of this section is to highlight four specific areas to which more attention could be paid in discussions of citizenship education in Japan.

Limited spheres

One feature of education policy and curriculum in Japan is that it allows very little room for identities or citizenship beyond the nation. In every country, of course, education is the main vehicle for preparing the future generation of national citizens to be able to contribute to the national welfare, and developing a strong sense of national identity is an important part of this endeavour. In Japan, however, such national aspects tend to be emphasized to the extent that any other territorial spheres of belonging or activity are discouraged (McVeigh, 2004). Historically, this entailed the prioritization of the national above the sub-national: standard Japanese over regional dialects, national knowledge over local knowledge and so on (Oguma, 2002). Now, it requires the prioritization of the national above the trans-national (Asia) and global. The lacuna vis-à-vis Asia is particularly striking (Parmenter, 2006), but at the global scale, too, despite all the rhetoric about Japan's place in the world and the need to develop people who can function in international society, the clearly stated aim of educational policy is to develop 'Japanese citizens who can live in a international society', which is very different from the aim of developing global citizens. This situation seems unlikely to change in the next decade.

Assumptions of homogeneity

A further assumption of education policy in Japan, although not explicitly stated as such, is that students in Japanese state schools are homogenously Japanese. This assumption is becoming increasingly divorced from reality as the numbers of foreign children and bicultural children (children with one foreign parent who will usually have Japanese nationality) are rising year by year (Murphy-Shigematsu, 2004). In schools in some areas now, up to one third of the students may be foreign or have a foreign parent, but no allowance is made in education policy for these children, and the vast majority of them are not even recognized by the Ministry of Education, which only publishes statistics on the number of children who need Japanese language education (i.e. the small minority of recent immigrant children, just over 20,000 in 2005 (Monbukagakusho, 2006)). What this underlying assumption of homogeneity

means is that diversity, tolerance and multicultural citizenship (Kymlicka, 1996) are non-issues in citizenship education policy in Japan, because 'officially' no such situation exists. As Murphy-Shigematsu (2006: 76) points out, 'Japan's progression towards diversity is powerful and irreversible', but acceptance of this notion will involve fundamental, radical psychological change among ordinary people. It remains to be seen how far reality has to depart from the assumptions of education policy before the assumptions become untenable, but in many schools already, it is individual teachers, students and parents who are left trying to bridge the gap (Okano and Tsuchiya, 1999; Ota, 2000).

The school's responsibility

A slightly different issue is the degree of responsibility left to the school in education for citizenship. For most students, schools are the site not only of academic learning, but also of extra-curricular activities and community participation. It is extremely common for junior and senior high school students (and virtually obligatory for teachers) to be at school after classes finish till 5.30 pm or so, at weekends and in holidays for various activities, usually club activity practice. Most students, as a result, have little direct involvement in society outside school. For most students, this high level of engagement in the school community is a positive thing, but for the significant number of school refusers (2.73 per cent of junior high school students in 2004), it means the loss not only of education about citizenship but also the loss of the only (in most cases) site of education for citizenship.

The question of active citizenship

In most European-centred discourse, it seems that an essential feature of education for active citizenship, although often not explicitly stated, is the volition of the students involved.

In Japan, a different philosophy holds, one that states that all students are equally responsible for their own community (the school) and that all should, therefore, be involved in its running and welfare. Students therefore have no choice as to whether they participate in Student Councils or not, for example, and even volunteer activities are usually compulsory! For some people, this degree of coercion may seem to contradict the fundamental principles of active citizenship. The counter-argument would be that students learn by doing, and all students should be provided equal chances to 'do' citizenship, and that it is illogical to say that the theoretical parts of citizenship (learning about society, government, democracy etc.) should be compulsory for all whereas the practical parts (engaging in the school community) should be optional. In fact, in Japan, as mentioned in Section 3, most of what is labelled education for citizenship in England and Wales and other countries is just seen as school life in Japan, and participation is rarely interpreted as coercion. This issue of student volition in active citizenship is one which could benefit from further research.

CONCLUSION

In this chapter, we have tried to show how citizenship education as conceptualized in many other parts of the world is practiced as taken-for-granted school life in Japan. Even though much of what we have described in this chapter is not referred to as citizenship education in Japan, it does reflect quite accurately, for example, Crick's three strands of citizenship education (social and moral responsibility, community involvement, political literacy) and four elements (key concepts, knowledge and understanding, values and dispositions, skills and aptitudes) (QCA, 1998). As in other countries, citizenship education in Japan has its strong and weak points, which we have highlighted throughout the chapter.

The weak points, or issues, were already summarized in the fifth section, so we will finish by listing the strong points of citizenship education in Japan:

(1) The firm establishment (post-war) of schools as micro-communities of learning about, for and through democracy, peace and freedom, and the commitment of many teachers to these ideals.
(2) The prevalence throughout school curriculum and life of possibilities for the acquisition and practice of all the above strands and elements, with the partial exception of political literacy.
(3) The generally positive school ethos and positive attitudes to school and learning, which facilitate citizenship education.

In conclusion, it is clear that effective citizenship education involves much more than explicit curriculum and policy. In Japan, at least, beliefs about education and human relations, attitudes to learning, school ethos, entrenched practices and societal context all play as great, if not greater, roles in students' experience of citizenship education.

REFERENCES

Barnard, C. (2003) *Language, Ideology, and Japanese History Textbooks*. London: RoutledgeCurzon.

Coulmas, F. (2002) Language Policy in Modern Japanese Education. In James Tollefson (ed.) *Language Policies in Education*. Mahwah, NJ: Lawrence Erlbaum Associates. pp. 203–223.

De Weerd, M., Gemmeke, M., Rigter J. and van Rij, C. (2005) *Indicators for monitoring active citizenship and citizenship education: final report*. http://ec.europa.eu/ education/ doc/reports/doc/citizenship.pdf (accessed 21 February 2007).

Dower, J. (1999) *Embracing Defeat*. New York: W.W. Norton.

Harada, T. (2004) Knowledge and Understanding of Our Country's Land and History, Social Studies, 534, Tokyo Meiji Tosho, 13–15. [in Japanese].

Horio, T. (1987) *The Imperial Nation and Education*. Tokyo: Aoki Publishing.

Huddleston, T. and Kerr, D. (eds) (2006) *Making Sense of Citizenship: A Continuing Professional Development Handbook*. London: Hodder Murray.

Ienaga, S. (2001) *Japan's Past, Japan's Future: One Historian's Odyssey*. Lanham: Rowman & Littlefield.

Katakami, S. (2000) The Aim of Social Studies, In Moriwake, T, and Katakami, S. (eds) *The Basic Knowledge of Three Hundred Important Words of Social Studies*. Tokyo: Meiji Tosho, p. 110 [in Japanese].

Kymlicka, W. (1996) *Multicultural Citizenship*. Oxford: Oxford University Press.

Lewis, C. (1995) *Educating Hearts and Minds*. Cambridge: Cambridge University Press.

McVeigh, B. (2004) *Nationalisms of Japan*. Lanham: Rowman & Littlefield.

Mizoue, Y. (2000) An Argument on Social Studies Education, In The Association for The Education of Social Recognition (ed.) *Social Studies Education in Junior High Schools (Revised Version)*. Tokyo: Gakujyutsu Tosho, pp.1–5. [in Japanese].

Mizuyama M. (2000) How to Learn Social Studies and Integrated Learning? In Takayama, H. et al. (ed.) *Integrated Learning and Social Studies in Junior High Schools*. Tokyo: Nihon Bunkyo Shuppan, pp. 116–121 [in Japanese].

Monbukagakusho [Ministry of Education] (2006) *Report on the situation of foreign children who need Japanese language instruction* http://www.mext.go.jp/b_menu/toukei/001/index32.htm (accessed 22 February 2007) [in Japanese].

Monbukagakusho [Ministry of Education] (undated) The situation regarding various problems in student guidance: summary http://www.mext.go.jp/b_menu/houdou/17/09/05092704.htm (accessed 22 February 2007) [in Japanese].

Monbusho (1998) *Course of Study for Junior High School*. Tokyo: Monbusho [in Japanese].

Morimo, T. (2000) Patoriotism, In Moriwake et al. (ed.) *The Basic Knowledge of Three Hundred Important Words of Social Studies*. Tokyo: Meiji Tosho, p. 100 [in Japanese].

Murphy-Shigematsu, S. (2004) Expanding the Borders of the Nation: Ethnic Diversity and Citizenship Education in Japan. In James Banks (ed.) *Diversity and Citizenship Education*. San Francisco: Jossey-Bass. pp. 303–332.

Murphy-Shigematsu, S. (2006) Diverse Forms of Minority National Identities in Japan's Multicultural Society. In Soo Im Lee, Stephen Murphy-Shigematsu and Harumi Befu *Japan's Diversity Dilemmas*. New York: iUniverse. pp.75–99.

Okano, K. and Tsuchiya, M. (1999) *Education in Contemporary Japan*. Cambridge: Cambridge University Press.

Oguma, E. (2002) *A Genealogy of Japanese Self-Images*. Melbourne: Trans Pacific Press.

Ota, H. (2000) *Newcomer Children in Japanese Public Schools*. Tokyo: Kokusai Shoin [in Japanese].

Qualifications and Curriculum Authority (1998), *Education for citizenship and the teaching of democracy in schools – Final report of the Advisory Group on Citizenship* QCA.

Shibusawa, H. (2000) The Purport and Essentials of Revision on Social studies in Junior High Schools, In Shibusawa et al.(ed.), *Development on The Course of Study in Junior High Schools*. Tokyo: Meiji Tosho, pp. 15–24 [in Japanese].

Sugimoto, Y. (2003) *An Introduction to Japanese Society (2nd edition)*. Cambridge: Cambridge University Press.

Tipton, E. (2002) *Modern Japan: A Social and Political History*. London: Routledge

Yamaguchi, Y. (2004) *Civil Society: Historical Inheritance and New Developments*. Tokyo: Yuhikaku [in Japanese].

Youth Development Promotion Committeee (2003) Youth Development Policy Plan. http://www8.cao.go.jp/youth/suisin/yhonbu/taikou.pdf (accessed 20 February 2007) [in Japanese].

16

Citizenship Education in Malawi: Prospects for Global Citizenship

Joseph Jinja Divala and Penny Enslin

Citizenship education in developed countries receives increasing attention in the international literature, as well as public and private funding for both policy and programme development. But less is known about the state of citizenship education in developing countries – especially those recently described as home to the 'bottom billion' of the world's population (Collier, 2007). In this chapter we explore the example of Malawi, mindful that while it illustrates the challenges of citizenship education in Africa it cannot be taken as representative of other African societies. Instead we take it to exemplify some of the challenges African and other developing countries face in educating their members as citizens in a globalizing world.

A small, landlocked country in the south eastern part of Africa, Malawi shares boundaries with Zambia, Tanzania and Mozambique. Malawi's projected population for 2006 was 12.3 million (National Statistical Office, 2006: 1). 88 per cent of Malawi's population lives in rural areas and 12 per cent live in urban areas (National Statistical Office, 2006: 18). 62 per cent of the population lives below the poverty line with 17 per cent of the

population regarded as ultra poor (National Statistical Office, 2006: 84). Additional statistics reported in 2006 (National Statistical Office, 2006: 37) indicate that literacy levels have risen to 66 per cent from the 59.2 per cent reported in 2002 (UNDP, 2002: 1).

Net enrolment in primary schooling rose from 48 per cent to 95 per cent between 1991 and 2005. While these increases are clearly positive, it is noteworthy that they represent a percentage decrease across enrolments from 1999 (free compulsory primary education was introduced in 1994). Statistics from that year show an overall enrolment in primary schooling of 26.3 per cent. Some caution is indicated with these figures though as there is a repeat rate of 20 per cent that inflates these numbers which include many over-age pupils. However, current (2005) net enrolment percentages in primary schooling indicate that Malawi fares well on a regional (sub-Saharan Africa) comparison being 25 per cent above the regional percentage for overall enrolment. Even accounting for caution, Malawi's primary schooling enrolments are still comparatively high for the region and come close to the goal of primary education for all, at least in terms of initial enrolment. However, statistics for 2004 indicate that only 42 per cent of those enrolled in school remain until grade 5 with 57 per cent of children remaining in primary school education until the last grade.

Enrolment in secondary school provides less cause for optimism with percentages for net enrolment rates again dipping from 1999 to 2002 and decreasing still further from 2002 to 2005. That said, although net enrolment percentages are unavailable, the gross enrolment rate percentages (the number of pupils enrolled in a given level of education regardless of age expressed as a percentage of the population in the theoretical age group for that level of education) increased between 1991 and 1999 from 8 per cent to 37 per cent. In 1999 the net enrolment rate of young people in secondary schooling was 29 per cent and in 2005 it was 24 per cent.

EDUCATION FOR GLOBAL CITIZENSHIP

Against this background, how has Malawi fared in addressing the task of citizenship education since independence in 1964? The challenges of citizenship education must be understood in context, always mindful of Kymlicka and Norman's question (1994): what is it to belong to a particular society, and what kind of life is it possible to live in this form of society? Yet this starting point inevitably runs the risk of confining us to the context of the nation state and conceptions of citizenship education increasingly understood to be too restrictively focused within its confines. Recent developments in the international literature on citizenship and citizenship education show a marked shift to reflection on the significance of globalization and its implications for understandings of citizenship and citizenship education that engage with the global as well as the local and the national. While the implications of

this shift are still being debated, we propose to explore some of these implications in the context of a critical assessment of citizenship education in Malawi since independence in 1964.

Historically the nation state has been the context in which the education of citizens has been both conceptualized and delivered. But the weakening of the nation state requires a new framework for citizenship education that responds to globalization (see for example Davies et al., 2005). Sharing the view that as a result of globalization we need to refocus the debate on citizenship education, Osler and Starkey (2005) argue that people need to be given the chance to acquire an understanding of the ways in which their own lives and those of others are linked – globally and locally – as well as a capacity to contribute to shaping the future they have in common with others across the globe. So, they also claim, a consensus is emerging that education for national citizenship is not an adequate response to globalization. Citizenship education needs to be underpinned by a more inclusive and global perspective in which a commitment to rights is followed through, including through recognition of citizenship rights to, in and through education. Osler and Starkey argue for cosmopolitan citizenship and propose that it requires an understanding of human rights and a global awareness and a recognition of common humanity across diverse cultures and contexts that reflects solidarity with those whose human rights have been denied. Learning cosmopolitan citizenship so understood should provide opportunities for effective agency in collaboration with others in acting to make a difference. In this way, '... education for cosmopolitan citizenship enables young people to perceive themselves as citizens with rights and responsibilities locally, nationally and globally' (Osler and Starkey, 2005: 93). In this recasting of the relationship between citizenship and community, Osler and Starkey argue that citizenship is practised both within communities and between communities. In this global political community boundaries are fluid, allowing a range of identities, including those within communities.

A set of criteria for a post-national conception of citizenship education thus begins to emerge. We discern the following, distinguishing between the first pair of features as pertinent to acquiring a capacity for global citizenship, and the second pair as highlighting access to resources for global citizenship education.

1. Knowledge and understanding of the global context and of globalization itself.
2. A shift in identity to a sense of belonging that transcends national boundaries to include a global community.
3. A capacity and resources for active citizenship that reaches beyond national boundaries.
4. Global access to global citizenship education for all.

Lest these criteria appear naïve, they require some qualification. We take it that such conceptions of global or cosmopolitan citizenship do not imply any dismissal of local and national contexts for citizenship, but rather that citizenship and education for its exercise are interpreted as appropriate to a variety of contexts which would complement each other. The case has now been made that to educate pupils as citizen actors located in a political relationship solely with the government of a nation state would mislead them about the world in which they now live. It is one thing to make this case about wealthy developed countries, which is the focus of much critique of current practice. Such arguments take on a more problematic twist in the case of children who are 'citizens' of failed states, or when applied to developing countries with weak governments and civil societies, and with fragile democratic structures. We take it that young citizens of Malawi fall within the latter category.

Before turning to examine citizenship education in Malawi from the perspective of the demands of citizenship education for a globalized world, we need to meet a further possible objection to our line of argument. This objection might start with the premise that globalization

… is a way of superimposing the values, aspirations, tastes, standards and colours of the powerful and strong communities on poor, weak and vulnerable communities of the world. It is a negation of the values of traditional African society especially as they relate to the extended family system (Avoseh, 2001: 484).

So Avoseh, reflecting on examples from a selection of West African traditional societies, concludes that, for Africa, citizenship education demands the retrieval and defence of African traditions of active citizenship within the local community as extended family, with its values of empathy, harmony and eschewal of individual self-interest. Such responses to globalization and its destructive effects on the African continent are understandable, but nonetheless problematic. Another take on the issue is offered by Preece and Mosweunyaneb (2006), whose research reports on the impact of globalization on the changing citizenship values of young adults in Botswana. The authors argue that youth citizenship in a country like Botswana can both build on indigenous value systems and recognize that citizens of such countries need to be active players in a wider world. Such participation would ensure a shift from young citizens as passive recipients, with globalization regarded as something done to African societies rather than a process in which people might contribute equally and actively to its development. Strengthened civil society organizations could enable young citizens to acquire the capacity to contribute to change, including change effected by globalization. Having a voice in such processes could be promoted by building on those discursive African traditions of community consultation and consensual decision-making (Preece and Moseunyaneb, 2006) thereby, for example, widening participation beyond the dominant role of older men.

Those skeptical of calls for global citizenship education could draw encouragement from the work of authors like Dryzek (2006) who defends transnational discursive democracy as the most viable path to deliberative global politics. In doing so he offers a new, wider dimension to supplement the already considerable attention given to deliberative democracy in debates about citizenship education (see for example Enslin et al., 2001; Divala, 2007) which attempt to accommodate active citizenship in a framework of communicative competence. Dryzek defends discursive transnational democracy as a process of democratization, which is neither electoral nor institutionalized, but is exercised in a decentralized global public sphere, for example in the anticorporate globalization discourse and environmental organizations – which do not require formal international institutions.

Notwithstanding Dryzek's skeptical view of the potential of cosmopolitan or global identities, for our purposes a positive implication of his defence of global discursive democracy is that it offers a means for the extension of African deliberative traditions beyond local communities to a wider discursive network. Furthermore, if successful, such a discourse could allow African citizens to contribute perspectives that bring traditional values to the wider global community and so could ameliorate the destructive dimensions of globalization. Taking on these potential contributions to a global community sets an ambitious educational agenda for global citizenship that should meet the four criteria sketched above, for new global identities and for global knowledge and understanding. And for developing countries like Malawi, these demands ought to extend accordingly to develop capacity and resources for global citizenship and provision of wider access to those by ensuring provision of education for global citizenship. While education for global citizenship presents new imperatives, it is worth noting that a post-national approach to citizenship education still retains some features in common with education for citizenship within the nation state, particularly those forms of citizenship education that have emphasized a capacity for active engagement, which for deliberative theorists is

exemplified in transnational as well as national communicative action.

CITIZENSHIP EDUCATION IN MALAWI: 1964–1992/3

The project of citizenship education in Malawi after the re-introduction of multiparty politics in 1993 must be understood in its historical context. Our analysis starts with the post-independence period (1964–1992/3) because of its influence on the period of multi-party rule after 1994. The need to look back is consistent with our second feature of post-national conceptions of citizenship education, namely that there requires a shift in identity to a sense of belonging that transcends national boundaries in order to identify in a global community. Additionally, if our third criterion for active global citizenship: 'a capacity and resources for active citizenship that reaches beyond national boundaries' and our fourth, 'global access to global citizenship education for all' are to be met then an understanding of Malawi's position on the trajectory from national to global, passive to active, disengaged to engaged will be useful.

Under colonial British rule, until independence in 1964, political elites including traditional leaders tended to ally themselves with the colonial government, but the masses had little share of power or its benefits. While some members of the political elite became allies in the colonial government, the local people did not have the opportunity to define political values and policies. Malawi's patterns of traditional life dominated forms of leadership and organization. Members of the ruling family exercised full citizenship rights, while the remaining members of society were subjects to the chief and the royal family. Access to fully engaged active citizenship was far from equal or inclusive.

After 1964, following Hastings Banda's ascent to, first, Prime Minister then President for life, his Malawi Congress Party established itself as the only legal political party. Under these conditions, education for citizenship was offered through officially controlled and structured courses in primary schools known as 'civics', built around and aimed at promoting the national values of Unity, Loyalty, Discipline and Obedience. These values, known as the Four Cornerstones and the foundation of the nation (Kasambara, 1998: 240–243), were supplemented in civics classes by issues of public awareness about the constitution of the republic, the different parts and functions of government, duties and responsibilities of a good citizen in relation to the party dictates and differences between local government and central government (Kasambara, 1998: 239). Other fora for citizenship education included the various mechanisms put in place by the ruling system. Attendance at political rallies was mandatory. The state-owned broadcaster, then the only radio in the country, also played a major role. The forced purchase of party cards became the sole condition for entrance to markets, hospitals, classrooms and bus stages. The Malawi Young Pioneers (MYP), a paramilitary wing of the ruling party, acted as watchdogs for the system. There was no distinction between the ruling party and the government. In general, the form of citizenship education that was promoted amounted to glorification of the 'heroism' of the president and a systematic attempt to uncompromisingly rally the nation behind the four national values noted above. Deviation from this dominant doctrine was tantamount to treason. Additionally, Kasambara (1998) argues that there was a concerted effort to keep the masses ignorant of extensive and active political awareness and participation and to make them feel this was their best possible world, which needed their support. Any opposition to this ideological hegemony could result in death. The president apparently endorsed such practices, and was reported to have commented that, '... to those who oppose us, accidents will happen ...' (Ross, 1996: 17), after the death of a political opponent.

Whilst the ideal of unity was used to promote a sense of nationhood among the diverse tribes of Malawi, by the same token political difference was perceived as 'dissidence', a threat to nationhood and unity itself. Loyalty and obedience were interpreted as complementary virtues with any critical examination of the operations of the party and government considered beyond the range of accepted political behaviour. The theme of unity served to evoke sentiments of developing the nation into a single family, like the extended family in the traditional system. Unity was understood as unanimity of views and perspectives on all political issues. Unity also became a symbol for maintaining a hierarchical order and due 'respect' for the status quo in society with difference regarded as a threat to national unity, an act of sedition. The ideal of loyalty was used to demand allegiance to the dictates of the single political party system.

The four cornerstones virtually became the centre of all citizenship education in Malawi for 30 years, from 1964 to 1993; and they permeated all aspects of life in the nation. As a result, citizens mostly kept their political views to themselves and attended mandatory political rallies to please the authorities and keep out of trouble. Imprisonment without trial, political detentions and loss of property were some of the punishments meted on those who dared oppose the system. Accordingly, the school curriculum and its daily activities were heavily screened and censored by the state. Between 1964 and 1993, citizenship programmes in schools and in public fora were exclusively centralized. In recounting forms of citizenship education in the first period, Kasambara, states:

> Primary schools had a subject known as civics, giving deliberately unspecific view of government, while the Malawi Young Pioneers visited villages to impose physical and agricultural training on adults. As with much else that took place in public, the glorification of the country's Life President was an integral part of this activity. (Kasambara, 1998 cited by Englund, 2004: 5–6)

In this period, education courses such as civics were narrowly focused and certainly did not encourage discussion of current political issues.

CITIZENSHIP EDUCATION IN MALAWI SINCE 1993

It is clear, then, that active citizenship for the masses was not encouraged in post-independence Malawi and therefore unsurprising that, at the inception of a multi-party system of government in 1993, citizens were ill prepared and ill informed to actively and effectively participate in a new democratic process. The need for a new approach to democratic citizenship and citizenship education in Malawi became apparent in 1992 when the system was changing from a single party system of government to a multi-party system. New forms of citizenship education emerged as a result of the campaign for democracy and a multi-party system of government. These mainly took the form of adult education that was directly linked to voter education. Education for democracy in schools can be considered to have taken place only on an ad hoc basis between 1994 and 1999. The National Education curriculum for schools officially introduced Education for Democracy through the teaching of Social Studies, which started in 1999 with selected pilot schools.

Now citizenship education in Malawi was supposed to mark a shift from a patriotic emphasis on knowing one's obligations and duties within the framework of strong political hegemony, to recognition and understanding of difference in politics and the cultivation of democratic citizenship virtues, duties and obligations. In principle, there did begin a shift to a sense of belonging potentially transcending national boundaries, with access to active citizenship education for all. Against a background of concern with human rights violations, unrest and dissent with the status quo, a human rights approach to citizenship education became attractive.

Early initiatives assumed, however, that this task could rest on a simple comparison between the merits of multi-party government over a single party system. This observation is confirmed by the approach taken in the Junior Certificate Social Studies curriculum (Mtunda and Namate, 2002: 83). This approach resulted in citizenship education being equated with voter education in relation to the upcoming referendum of 1993 and the general elections of 1994.

In the period of the transition to multi-party rule, two sets of key players were influential in citizenship education programmes. The national Department of Education and the national broadcaster, the Malawi Broadcasting Cooperation (MBC), were officially mandated to impart civic education. The two continued to promote the single party ideal because of the control the single party system had of these national institutions on the one hand, and also because the old curriculum framed by the single party system was still in use. They tended to emphasize the purported advantages of single party politics such as its ability to unite diverse groups and the importance of maintaining law and order in the state, whose orderliness would supposedly create better prospects for development. This imparted a form of citizenship education that was centrally geared to protecting the system of the day.

On the other hand, the pressure groups who later became parties, and other non-governmental organizations (NGOs),[1] concentrated on teaching the people the '... reasons for the referendum; what citizens were expected to do on voting day; their duty as citizens in taking part in the referendum ...' (Kasambara, 1998: 243). While they claimed neutrality, the efforts of these groups endeavoured to provide people with a choice that had long been denied. The Civil Liberties Committee (CILIC) and the Legal Resource Centre (LRC) promoted voter rights education, an emphasis that was to continue into the 1999 and 2004 elections. This form of citizenship education tends to assume that by voting citizens are ensuring a democratic regime that will protect and promote their rights. In the context of the preceding period of single party rule, the voter education approach was understandably intended to offset the legacy of elections as mere endorsement of pre-chosen candidates favourable to the ruling leadership. In the 1999 and 2004 elections, the orientation towards voter education as civic education did not change, partly confirming Kasambara's observation that there was a general failure on the part of government to embark on full-fledged citizenship education (1998: 251), as seen in the absence of appropriate school-based material for teaching democratic citizenship until 1999.

Several further problems have dogged Malawi's efforts towards educating for democratic citizenship. Most of the citizenship education efforts in Malawi for adults are ad hoc which is particularly problematic in a context where completion rates in primary and secondary schooling are low. The need for civic education has tended to be perceived as necessary only prior to elections and government does not seem to be prepared for systematic and sustained citizenship education (Kasambara: 1998). Apart from that, and the focus by civic education providers on far too few and too narrow topics, a national civic education curriculum was not in evidence until 1999.[2] Neither has there been a Malawi-specific reference book for use by stakeholders (Kamphambe Nkhoma, in Chirwa et al., 2004).

Having observed these general weaknesses in citizenship education initiatives so far, we turn now to critically examine the extent to which the programmes and materials that have become available reflect assumptions about democratic citizenship that are likely to foster active citizenship engagement in a global as well as a national context. This we do in relation to the themes of democracy and participation, human rights and freedom, and the interplay between development and democracy, as depicted in the citizenship education materials. The materials in question are those that the Department of Education has used in teacher training programmes, the Social Studies Curriculum in

primary and secondary schools, voter and civic education materials used by the National Initiative for Civic Education (NICE) and other groups, plus the newly introduced 'Democracy Consolidation' materials that can be used as a resource for both primary and secondary schools, as well as adult civic education or voter education.

Much attention has been given in citizenship education materials in Malawi to definition and characterization of 'democracy' (Cairns and Dambala, 1996; Chilambo, et al., 1999: 25; Fabiano and Maganga, 2002: 61; Mtunda and Namate, 2002: 83; Chirwa et al., 2004; Teacher Development Unit, undated). Such characterizations range from terminological definitions of rights and duties of citizens in a nation to functions of an elected government. Descriptions of the electoral system reflect the assumption that people choose who is to lead them and the leaders have to follow the wishes of the electorate. At the same time, the idea of citizen power is also a frequent theme. This 'power' is described in terms of the capacity of citizens to participate in '... civic affairs of one's community ...' (Teacher Development Unit [TDU]: 870); the people's rights to political activity; power to decide how and who is to govern them (TDU: 990; Malawi Government (undated): 11). Nevertheless, recognition that power rests with the participation of all citizens in the political life of the nation to make decisions, to formulate laws and also wield the power to administer programmes for the good of the community (TDU: 990–1) appears to reside ultimately in the ability of citizens to choose representatives. The materials also indicate, crucially, that once government is in power it can only be challenged in the next election polls, since the consent of the people '... is expressed through ... periodic elections ...' (Chirwa et al., 2004: 56). These materials also promote the assumption that the will of the people is known and carried out through the government. General elections and referenda are regarded as the definitive forms of this expression. Direct ways for expression of the people's will include demonstrations, boycotts, strikes or petitions

(Chirwa et al., 2004: 45). Chirwa et al. suggest that such direct means of participation are rare, placing as they would the democratic system under threat. In practice, direct forms of participation such as demonstrations, boycotts or mass action have often been barred by the Malawi Police. This leaves people with periodic and mainly electoral participation as their only option, reflecting a democratic process in which they continue to play the part of spectators rather than political actors, surrendering their will and power to a government that acts on their behalf.

Democratic participation is described as a citizen's right and duty. It is defined in terms of standing for election, debating issues, attending civic meetings, being members of organizations, paying taxes and protesting (TDU), and these are stated as obligations in a democratic society (Cairns and Dambula, 1996). On closer examination this right to participation falls well short of delivering our conception of active citizenship. The central framework of participation conceives of citizens as those acted upon and the political leaders as the actors. Proper participation by citizens involves the ability to control abuse of power by leaders; to take part in elections; to inform their leaders about their problems and to make sure leaders respond to these problems (Cairns and Dambula, 1996). This conception of participation does not consider the representative and the represented as equals who share the capacity to set the agenda, interrogate, and arrive at agreed solutions together. Rights such as expression and the press, of association, and of access to information are understood as pre-requisites to participation (Chirwa et al., 2004). Yet, the terms 'participation' and 'consultation' are also used interchangeably (Chirwa et al., 2004: 110) without acknowledgement that consultation can take highly non-participatory forms.

Meaningful participation by the Malawian citizenry is considered to take place in the affairs of their government through the cabinet, the judiciary and the legislature (Chirwa et al., 2004). References to citizen participation in formulating policies such as Vision 2020, the Poverty Alleviation Programme, the Malawi Poverty Reduction Strategy and others (Chirwa et al., 2004: 112), as the citizenship education manual would have us believe, are unconvincing. Ironically, although it is suggested that people were consulted, the same handbook has argued that consultation lacks the essence of democratic participation (Chirwa et.al, 2004:110). The fact that people were consulted through surveys does not constitute a sufficient condition for democratic participation.

The way power is conceived and exercised by those in leadership positions in Malawi overshadows the importance of citizen participation. For instance, a political party is defined as '... a group of people who are willing to assume power and to govern the nation ...' (Public Affairs Committee [PAC], undated: 12). This view further depicts the relationship between the parties and the people before any general election as essentially one in which the parties hold meetings and present themselves to the people to explain how they will govern the nation once in power. The citizens, on the other hand, are the ones who '... listen and then, in the general election, choose the party which will govern them ...' (PAC: 12). The citizens' responsibilities are reduced to registration, checking the voters' roll, gathering enough information on parties and candidates, respecting the rights of other voters, voting, accepting the results and desisting from fraud (Chirwa et al., 2004). Noticeably missing from such conceptualizations are questions of citizen participation in the process of party policy development and the selection of candidates for elections. The citizenship education materials are also silent on whether people and parties who stand for election should subject their manifestos to continuous public scrutiny and debate.

Although the citizenship education programmes and materials pay attention to human rights and freedoms, these too are presented in ways that are unlikely to foster active citizenship. Instead, freedom is conceived as '... the ability to make choices or do things without being worried or stopped by others as one creates the political, social or economic space *between oneself and others ...*' (Chirwa et. al, 2004: 90, our emphasis). Political freedoms are, therefore, characterized by the ability to hold and discuss one's views, to associate with others and to exercise freedom of movement. On the other hand, economic freedoms are marked by the ability to own and use property, to work in the absence of forced labour, whereas social freedoms are about equality and non-interference in individual privacy and dignity (2004: 91). These conceptions of freedom are formal, private or individually orientated. It is not clear if such individual freedoms take their social positioning seriously in terms of engaging the individual holder of the freedoms in interaction for some common or societal good. For instance, despite the recognition that levels of education are generally low, especially among females in Malawi, and that women have reduced access to schools and other formal educational institutions, the handbook still maintains that everyone has a right to education irrespective of these differential circumstances. There is no mention that unequal access to schooling denies the right to education. In this regard, a conception of active citizenship would require strong recognition of the differential circumstances people are born into, even in poor rural societies; where women and children need special attention for them to realize their freedoms and rights to education, for instance. Such recognition would in turn demand attention to traditional Malawian cultural practices that ascribe to women and children lesser forms of dignity, status and personhood than men. Similarly, while it is common knowledge that conditions of schooling in rural and urban areas are not the same, a formal recognition of the right to education puts every school going person on an equal footing with another. It assumes that differences and fundamental

gaps do not exist between different categories of people to an extent that these would affect educational goals. Therefore, no effort is made to acknowledge differences in social, cultural and economic positions and how these affect the teaching of human rights, let alone how rights are ascribed to the different categories of people in question. As a result, the approach produces different interpretations of human rights and freedom because of the influence of access and exposure.

Depiction of the state as protector and provider is further reflected in the concept of development that is promoted in citizenship education in Malawi, which is largely leader-driven, assuming that it is leadership that determines the nature and pace of development. The second stage of citizenship education, according to NICE, concentrates on HIV/AIDS, environment, gender, health, youth empowerment and poverty and food security. Yet the approach is consistently inclined to divorce development from politics (see also Englund, 2004). Such tendencies demand a proper re-conceptualization of the relationship between development and democracy.

There is some emerging evidence of a more thoroughly democratic conception of the relationship between democracy, human rights and development (Chirwa et al, 2004). For instance, one's rights include '... the right to be a central subject of development; the right to participate in development; the right to fair distribution of development benefits and the right to development itself ...' (Chirwa et al., 2004: 117). Yet this depiction of development is tempered when the right to achieve and live to one's potential is cast as an individual's own prerogative (Chirwa et al., 2004). Hence development is understood to lean heavily on formal concepts and formal recognition of human rights.

Development is commonly depicted as coming from poverty alleviation programmes, the investment of financial and technical resources and the proper utilization of natural resources. Most such programmes target the economic upliftment of citizens rather than holistic human development, reflecting the assumption that increased participation of citizens in the economic activities of the country would lead to their development (Chirwa et al., 2004). The Malawi Social Action Fund (MASAF), for instance, is said to provide direct employment and food safety nets, and to enable government to monitor levels of poverty (Chirwa et al., 2004: 241). In MASAF Phases 1 and 2, citizens had a say only in terms of indicating what needed to be constructed in their area.[3] The programme recruited village volunteers to work on the project for a daily wage, under the authority of the district coordinator, with the village committees ensuring that there were enough people working on the project. Project formulation and management has been carried out by elite members and the impoverished are expected to participate so that they sustain themselves. The narrow conception of citizenship reflected in such initiatives is likely to promote passive citizenship rather than contributing to fostering a culture of active democratic participation.

Nevertheless, in spite of this general trend, in some cases the citizenship education materials come to terms with a perspective on development that is people-centred, measuring development in terms of promoting and protecting the dignity and value of people: 'Human rights are central to the promotion of development that focuses on people because the rights empower people not only to satisfy their basic needs but also to realise their full potential as human beings' (Chirwa et al., 2004: 324). Chirwa et al., (2004: 324) argue that a 'person who has a right has the legal power to compel the relevant duty-bearer to deliver services or goods to which the right-holder is entitled'. This promising starting point requires further development so that people actively and continuously demand that their government provides necessary conditions through which they could direct their own development.

While most of the initiatives we have discussed above would probably be regarded as adult civic education undertaken to prepare

for general elections in Malawi, we suggest that a comparable approach is now being followed in primary and secondary schools, where citizenship education has developed more slowly and more recently. For instance, lessons on teaching democracy in primary schools are only considered in Standard Six, Unit 6 Lesson 4 (Chilambo et al., 1999: 25). This lesson discusses democratic leadership and processes by way of comparison to dictatorial forms of leadership. In this regard, the lesson teaches that it is government through the leaders which initiates the process of development. In one example of what democratic leadership means, it is stated:

> If for instance, the government wanted to construct a new borehole in your village, your chief would first of all ask the villagers to say where they think would be the best location for it. The chief would then advise government to locate the borehole where many people in the village prefer (Chilambo et al., 1999: 25).

In the secondary school the topic of democracy appears once in the first two years. At this level pupils are given a series of definitions of democracy both as a representative system and also as government of the people, by the people and for the people (Mtunda and Namate, 2002: 83). At Senior Certificate Level democracy is taught under 'systems of government' (Fabiano and Maganga, 2002: 61), which concentrates on representative democracy, citizen rights, free elections, judicial systems and other aspects of constitutional democracy (Fabiano and Maganga, 2002: 61). These features of the formal school curriculum mirror the predominant tendency in adult or informal education to discourage active citizenship. They are also matched by a school ethos which, while reflecting a traditional emphasis on community values, is nonetheless one in which authority is still exercised by teachers over pupils in a way that is not encouraging of egalitarian and democratic values and a strong student voice in the running of the school such as in participatory student government.

FROM NATIONAL TO GLOBAL CITIZENSHIP

Our analysis of citizenship education in Malawi has shown that, since independence, initiatives and materials, and the assumptions on which they have been based, have been heavily focused on consolidation of the nation state. During the period of one party rule, opportunities to exercise and to learn democratic citizenship fell woefully short of the standards of active, democratic citizenship.

In the ensuing phase after the reintroduction of multi-party democracy in 1993, programmes were not only ad hoc but also lacking a systematic national strategy, until the introduction of Social Studies in the national school curriculum in 1999. Alongside a preoccupation with the more modest demands of voter education, materials have been inclined to offer definitions of the meaning of key concepts like democracy, as well as accounts of freedom, rights and development. These features have suggested modest gestures towards formal recognition of human rights and have emphasized information given and received. Political power is assumed to be most appropriately delegated by citizens to their representatives, with limited opportunities for expression of dissent. Yet our analysis has also indicated the potential for further development of materials and their underpinning assumptions and for a more expansive participatory vision to emerge. Ultimately, read in context, we should not be surprised if citizenship education in post-independence and emergent democracies is initially preoccupied with consolidation and state building, especially in an ethnically diverse post-colonial population.

Turning from the local to the global context, it is clear that thus far citizenship education in Malawi, in the knowledge and understanding offered and the citizen identity it proffers has been premised on and appropriate to national citizenship rather than to global citizenship education. That the education for national citizenship provided has, so far, been disinclined to encourage active citizenship and assertive deliberative politics, threatens to exacerbate inequalities between its citizens and those of states now able to build global perspectives onto established national programmes for citizenship education. In relation to our second pair of features of the global citizenship now called for in recent debate on citizenship education, features that recognize the implications and challenges of globalization, the implications for citizens of countries like Malawi are profound. For if playing an equal role in the shaping of a shared global future in a global community is to be a possibility for its citizens, as it promises to become for citizens of developed societies with globally focused and well resourced citizenship education programmes, then the radical implications of Osler and Starkey's vision of the right to education as well as rights through education starts to become apparent.

The mutually interdependent goals of the active and the global in the acquisition of citizenship are now recognized in citizenship education. Potentially, however, this is likely to pertain only to those already enjoying active engagement with political processes in developed parts of the world. Until those in countries such as Malawi can enjoy access to and resources for active citizenship, they will be denied opportunities to assert their rights and voice for social justice in the world community of citizens. Indeed, until active citizenship is truly global then there will be no world community of citizens.

NOTES

1 The NGOs involved, although not at the same time, were Public Affairs Committee (PAC), Malawi Law Society (MLS), Legal Resource Centre (LRC), Civil Liberties Committee (CILIC), National Initiative for Civic Education (NICE). The prominent pressure groups that turned into parties were United Democratic Front (UDF) and Alliance for Democracy (AFORD), among others.

2 Mbewe, Mastone, personal communication, August 2007.

3 There is an indication that MASAF Phase III has taken a different approach by locating all the

processes from project proposal to implementation in the local people themselves (Liwonde, MASAF Official, 10-01-05). Efforts to source official documents on this shift proved futile.

REFERENCES

Avoseh, M.B.M. (2001) 'Learning to be active citizens: lessons of traditional Africa for lifelong learning' *International Journal of Lifelong Education*, 20 (6): 479–486.

Cairns, J.L. and Dambula, G.S. (1996) *Gwira Mpini Kwacha: Civic Education to Build Local Democracy – A Trainers Manual*. Balaka and Lilongwe: Montfort Missionaries and Public Affairs Committee.

Chilambo, M.N., Hara U.J., Liwewe, A.S., Maganga, J.C., Namate T.F., Sefu, E.L. and Tembo E.H. (1999) *Malawi Junior Certificate Social Studies Curriculum*. Domasi: Malawi Institute of Education.

Chirwa, C., Kanyongolo, E. and Kayambazinthu, E. (2004) *Building an Informed Nation: A Handbook for Civic Education and Human Rights in Malawi*. Blantyre: Montfort Press.

Collier, P. (2007) *The Bottom Billion: Why the Poorest Countries are Failing and What Can Be Done About It*. New York and Oxford: Oxford University Press.

Davies, I., Evans, M., Reid, A. (2005) 'Globalising Citizenship Education? A critique of "global education" and "citizenship education," *British Journal of Educational Studies*, 53 (1): 66–89.

Divala, J.J. (2007) 'Malawi's approach to democracy: implications for the teaching of democratic citizenship' *Citizenship Teaching and Learning*, 3 (1): 32–44.

Dryzek, J. (2006) *Deliberative Global Politics: Discourse and Democracy in a Divided World*. Cambridge: Polity.

Englund, H. (2004) 'Transnational governance and the participation of youth: the contribution of civic education to disempowerment in Malawi' *Centre for Civic Society Research Report. No.13* (Durban – South Africa).

Enslin, P., Pendlebury, S. and Tjiattas, M. (2001) 'Deliberative democracy, diversity and the challenges of citizenship education' *Journal of Philosophy of Education*, 35 (1): 431–440.

Fabiano, M. and Maganga, J. (2002) *Malawi Senior Certificate Social Studies*. Blantyre: MacMillan Malawi Limited.

Faiti, D. (1999) *GTZ-Democracy: History, Objectives and Vision of National Initiative for Civic Education (NICE) in Malawi*. Lilongwe: NICE.

Kasambara, R. (1998) Citizenship education in Malawi since 1992: an appraisal. In Ross, Kenneth and Phiri, Kings (eds) *Democratization in Malawi: A stocktaking*. Blantyre: Christian Literature Association in Malawi (CLAIM).

Kymlicka, W. and Norman, W. (1994) 'Return of the citizen: a survey of recent work on citizenship theory' *Ethics*, 104 (2): 352–381.

Malawi Government (undated) *Community Civic Educators' Voter Handbook*. Lilongwe: Government Print.

Mtunda, S.T. and Namate T.F. (2002) *Malawi Junior Certificate Social Studies*. Limbe: Dzuka Publishing Company.

National Statistics Office (2001) *Malawi National Statistics for 1999*. Zomba: National Statistics Office.

National Statistical Office (2006) *Malawi Multiple Indicators Cluster Survey*. Zomba: National Statistics Office. Available at: www.nso.malawi.net. Accessed: 29 July 2007.

Osler, A. and Starkey, H. (2005) *Changing Citizenship: Democracy and Inclusion in Education*. Maidenhead and New York: Open University Press.

Preece, J. and Mosweunyaneb, D. (2006) 'What citizenship responsibility means to Botswana's young adults; implications for adult education' *Compare,* 36 (1): 5–21.

Public Affairs Committee (PAC) (undated) *Public Affairs Committee Document on General Elections in Malawi*. Lilongwe: PAC.

Ross, K. (1996) The transformation of power in Malawi 1992–94: the role of the Christian churches. In Ross, Kenneth (ed.) *God, People and Power in Malawi*. Blantyre: Christian Literature In Malawi (CLAIM).

Teacher Development Unit (TDU) (undated) *Student Teacher Handbook 3*. Domasi: Malawi Institute of Education.

United Nations Development Programme (UNDP) (2002) *Millennium Development Goals: Malawi 2002 Report*. Available at http://www.undp.org.mw/reports/mdg2002.pdf

17

The Changing Face of Citizenship Education in Pakistan

Bernadette L. Dean

INTRODUCTION

One of the most important goals of education is the preparation of young people for their role as citizens. This chapter examines the discourse on citizenship and citizenship education in Pakistan within the wider social, political, cultural and educational context. It shows how the changing socio-political context has given rise to different conceptions of citizenship and citizenship education and argues for a citizenship education programme that will help realize the vision of creating a democratic society.

The chapter consists of four sections. Section one provides a brief background of Pakistan focusing on some of the key socio-political issues of particular relevance to citizenship and citizenship education such as the nature of the state, the political system and the position of women. A brief description of the system of education is also provided as background. Section two reviews Pakistan's education policies to demonstrate the changing conception of citizenship and citizenship education and its implications

for Pakistan. Section three focuses on the practice of citizenship education in Pakistani schools. Finally, suggestions for improving policy and practice are made in section four.

BACKGROUND OF PAKISTAN

The socio-political context

Pakistan was created in 1947 in the aftermath of WWII when the colonial empires were collapsing and the struggles of the colonized for freedom were becoming more urgent. In the Indian sub-continent, the struggle for freedom took an unexpected turn when the Muslims of India decided they did not want a change of rulers but a right to determine their own future (Ziring, 1997). The political leaders decided that Pakistan would be a secular state. Addressing the first constituent assembly on 11 August, 1947 Jinnah, the founder of Pakistan said: 'We are starting with the fundamental principle that we are all citizens and equal citizens of one state ... You may belong to any religion, caste or creed – that has nothing to do with the business of the state' (quoted in Rashid, 1985: 81).

However, soon after Jinnah's death in 1948, a struggle began between those who envisioned Pakistan as a secular state and those who believed it should be an Islamic theocratic state since independence was achieved on the basis of religion. This issue about the nature of the state still persists and is reflected in the education system especially citizenship education.

Pakistan's political history has been consistently unstable and uncannily repetitive oscillating between ten years of democracy followed by ten years of military dictatorship. In Pakistan, democracy has been reduced to the participation of people in choosing their representatives in elections while the other key aspects active participation of the people, accommodation of conflicting interests and the rule of law have been ignored. Military dictatorships have sought legitimacy through holding elections and declaring Pakistan to be a democracy. This has blurred the distinction between dictatorship and democracy, and created a tension about the form of government for Pakistan and the role of citizens.

Pakistan is among a few countries in the world where the proportion of men exceeds that of women as such it is a male-dominated society. Women have constantly struggled to improve their status. In 1961, their struggle resulted in legislation that eliminated child marriages, restricted polygamy and curtailed a man's (and increased a woman's) right to divorce. The 1973 constitution recognized men and women as equal citizens, repudiated discrimination on the basis of sex and provided for affirmative action by the state to ensure the full participation of women in all spheres of life. However, in 1977, the Islamization policy of General Zia-ul-Haq reversed these gains by rescinding women's rights, enacting discriminatory laws and promoting retrogressive attitudes through what some describe as a fundamentalist interpretation of the *Qur'an* and *Shari'ah*. These measures

were actively opposed by women's rights advocacy groups. Women's groups have continued to advocate for equality with little success as their efforts are on the one hand opposed by ethnic, regional or religious groups ready to use violence in pursuit of their goals and on the other hand by the lack of commitment of the state (Shaheed, 2002).

One right women in Pakistan have always had is the right to vote and contest elections but their political participation has been limited and political representation is almost entirely dependent on affirmative action provisions. Little was done to educate women for active participation in the political sphere so that affirmative action is still required.

The educational context

Pakistan does not have free, compulsory and universal education although it is a constitutional right. There are three education systems: the religious madrassas, the Matriculation and the Cambridge systems. The great majority of students attend Matriculation schools run by both the government and private sector. The Federal Ministry of Education is responsible for developing the national curriculum, syllabi and prescribing the content of the textbooks used in the Matriculation system. The low status of teachers is reflected in the short duration (one year) and poor quality of teacher training provided in government colleges of education which continues to perpetuate the notion that teacher's are skilled workers rather than professionals.

The education system of Pakistan suffers from a crisis of quantity, quality and relevance. No government has given the education sector the attention it requires. Pakistan has a population of 160 million of which 39 million are children of school attendance age (5–14). 20 million are between the ages of 5–9 and 19 million between the ages of 10–14 (Federal Bureau of Statistics, 2005a). Of the 20 million children between the ages of 5–9, 8 million are not enrolled in school. Of the 12 million enrolled 50 per cent drop out by class 5. Of the 19 million children between the ages of 10–14, 15 million are enrolled in secondary school. The overall gender parity index is 0.76 (Federal Bureau of Statistics, 2005b).

Teaching and learning in Pakistani classrooms is simply the transmission of textbook facts which students must memorize in order to pass examinations. School graduates are good at 'parroting' what they learn rather than thinking and reasoning for themselves. Every education policy and every book written on education in Pakistan laments the declining quality and relevance of education to the lives of Pakistanis and to Pakistani, society, observing that it does not prepare students well for higher education, employability or citizenship (Dean, 2000, 2005; Hayes, 1987; Hoodbhoy, 1998; Ministry of Education, 1998; Saigol, 1994; Warwick and Reimers, 1995).

THE CHANGING CONCEPTION OF CITIZENSHIP AND CITIZENSHIP EDUCATION

With each distinct political transition in Pakistan a new education policy was developed. A review of these policies indicates three distinct phases.

- Phase one: the search for indigenous democracy covers the period from the creation of Pakistan in 1947 to the end of the Z.A. Bhutto government in 1977.
- Phase two: the Islamization phase covers the period from 1977 to 1999.
- Phase three: a struggle for democracy began in 1999 and continues to-date.

The following section reviews each phase to identify how the education policies addressed the issues identified in section one, the role envisaged for citizens and the nature of citizenship education.

Phase 1: The search for indigenous democracy (1947–1977)

After independence in 1947, Pakistan faced multifarious problems. While dealing with them, the government recognized the need to address long term objectives of national development, one of which was the restructuring and reorientation of the colonial education system to make it more suitable 'to the genius of our people, consonant with our history and culture and having regard for [the] modern conditions' (Jinnah's message to the first education conference, Ministry of Interior (Education Division), 1947: 5).

Fazlur Rehman, the then Education Minister in his inaugural address to the education conference proposed that the education system of Pakistan be designed to build a 'modern democratic state based on Islamic principles' in which all members of the body politic, 'no matter what political, religious or provincial label' they possessed, were citizens of the state. According to the Minister, democracy required the education of all citizens in 'body, mind and character' to live a good life themselves and improve the lives of others. Thus, he believed education must include a vocational, a socio-political and a spiritual element. The socio-political element entailed 'training for citizenship' because

> The possession of a vote by a person ignorant of the privileges and responsibilities of citizenship ... is responsible for endless corruption and political instability. Our education must ...[teach] the fundamental maxim of democracy, that the price of liberty is eternal vigilance and it must aim at cultivating the civil virtues of discipline, integrity, and unselfish public service (p. 8)

The conference recognized illiteracy as a constraint to the creation of a democratic society and resolved that the state provide free, universal and compulsory basic education to facilitate adult literacy. It also resolved that education would be guided by the principles of Islam: 'universal brotherhood of man [sic], social democracy and social justice' (p. 3). However, by not elaborating on these principles they left them open to varying interpretations.

In 1958, the Martial Law Government of Ayub Khan appointed the Sharif Commission to evolve a national education system which would 'better reflect our spiritual, moral and cultural values' (Ministry of Education, 1958: 1) and assist in national development. The commission decided that education should serve the creation of a progressive and democratic society and identified three limitations to achieving this goal: 'the lack of national unity; the failure to make economic progress and create a social welfare state; and the attitudes of passivity, indiscipline and non-acceptance of public authority' (Ministry of Education, 1959: 11).

The commission recognized the importance of education for all citizens noting that: 'Such universal education is normally a concomitant of parliamentary democracy. A democracy requires that its citizens can distinguish between the claims of rival political parties, can interpret news intelligently and critically, and are willing to serve on local bodies, committees and councils' (p. 169).

However, instead of providing for universal, free, compulsory primary education, the commission focused on developing quality education at the tertiary level believing higher education would result in economic development and benefits accruing would 'trickle down' to the poor. To promote national unity and develop civic attitudes the commission proposed citizenship and character education. The aim of the former was to prepare knowledgeable and loyal citizens and of the latter to develop in young people the values of truth, justice, honesty and integrity.

In 1971, soon after the secession of East Pakistan (now Bangladesh) Zulfiqar Ali Bhutto, the President of Pakistan announced the New Education Policy 1972–1980. Having lost half the country and facing separatist movements in two of the four provinces that now constitute Pakistan the aims of education were to build national cohesion by promoting social and cultural harmony, achieve social justice and increase the participation of people in decision-making (Ministry of Education, 1972). The aim was to be achieved through three strategies: nationalization of schools to provide free and universal school education and a comprehensive adult education programme; the inclusion of Pakistan studies as a compulsory subject in schools and universities and mobilization of people for participation in development of the country. The aims of the education policy and the strategies to realize them demonstrate a socialist ideology.

The different ideological perceptions of each government were reflected in the education policies and influenced the conception of citizenship and citizenship education. The education policies also reflected alternate understandings of citizenship as active and passive. However, all three policies show a search for an indigenous form of democracy.

Phase 2: The Islamization phase

In 1977, the Z.A. Bhutto government was overthrown in a military coup by General Zia-ul-Haq. The Martial Law Government of Zia-ul-Haq announced a new National Education policy in 1979 which radically changed the direction of the education system.

The main aim of the policy was the Islamization of education and the development of Pakistan as an Islamic theocratic state. It sought to achieve this aim by developing in 'the people of Pakistan in general and students in particular a deep and abiding loyalty to Islam and Pakistan'; inculcate[ing] in accordance with the Quran and Sunnah, the character, conduct and motivation expected of a true Muslim and producing citizens 'fully conversant with the Pakistan movement, its ideological foundations, its history and culture so that they feel proud of their heritage and display firm faith in the future of the country as an Islamic state' (Ministry of Education, 1979: 1–2). Thus in the implementation of the plan the 'highest priority' was given to the revision of curricula so as to ensure that 'Islamic ideology permeates the thinking of the younger generation', and society is refashioned according to Islamic tenets (p. 2). Keeping in view that many young people do not attend school and there is a large uneducated adult population, a chapter entitled, 'Education of the Citizen' was added to the policy. The purpose of this addition was to 'impart the teachings of Islam', to the uneducated masses to prepare them for 'a clean, purposeful and productive life' (p.30). In keeping with the government's interpretation of Islam separate 'institutions' and 'curricula' were prepared for female education related to the traditional role assigned to women in Islamic society (p. 3).

For the first time in Pakistan the education policy defined citizenship in exclusionary terms. In viewing Pakistan and Islam as synonymous, the policy excluded non-Muslims from being Pakistani citizens, and women from equal citizenship by educating them for a different role. Furthermore, the aims of education came to resemble the aims of Islamic education and the task of citizenship education became the development of citizens as true practising Muslims 'reflecting in this respect a very narrow view held by a minority among Muslims that all education be that of Islamiat' (Nayyar and Salim, 2004: ii).

The 1992–2002 and 1998–2010 education policies announced by the Nawaz Sharif government in its first and second terms in office continued to stress the Islamization of Education begun in 1977. However, the policies also emphasized the need to produce a scientific and technologically educated workforce for an increasingly globalized economy. The 1992–2002 policy suggested that education 'should enable the students to understand the message of the Holy Quran, imbibe the spirit of Islam, and appreciate its worldview in the context of new scientific and technological advancements' (p. 2). The 1998–2010 policy sought to continue, to build 'a sound Islamic society' by educating 'the

future generation of Pakistan as true practising Muslims' and 'attract[ing] the educated youth to the world of work ... so that they may become productive and useful citizens and contribute positively as members of the society' (p. 5–6).

The 1992–2002 and 1998–2010 policies continued to view Pakistan as an Islamic state and define citizenship in exclusionary terms. Unlike the 1977 education policy, only non-Muslims are excluded from Pakistani citizenship, men and women being seen as equal citizens because there were no separate provisions for women. The role of citizens is to 'contribute to the social and economic development of the country and the Ummah' (p.11).[1] The policies recognized the need for citizenship education but suggest one that differs from the West, in that its aims must be both spiritual and materialistic: the creation of true practising Muslims and skilled worker citizens so as to promote the economic development of the country.

Phase 3: A struggle for democracy

In 1999, General Pervez Musharraf usurped power from Nawaz Sharif in a military coup. He promised to work towards national integrity, a buoyant economy and the establishment of 'true democracy'. However, it was only in 2006 that a move was made to reflect this in the education policy and curriculum. In keeping with democratic principles a very participatory process was used to develop a new education policy. The White Paper developed as a result of the deliberations, criticizes the vision statements of previous education policies for reflecting the 'dominant political paradigm and compulsions of the day' (Aly, 2007: 2) and articulates a new vision for education. It states

Recognizing education as the right of the citizens, it is the aim of the state of Pakistan to provide equal and ample opportunity to all its citizens to realize their full potential as individuals and citizens through an education that enriches the individual with value/skills preparing him/her for life, livelihood and nation building (p. 4).

To realize this vision the education policy seeks to develop highly knowledgeable, creative and confident individuals, with advanced reasoning and problem-solving skills, committed to democratic values and human rights and who will use their knowledge and skills to engage in activities aimed at promoting the common good.

The White Paper defines Pakistan as a democratic society in which all citizens are equal, where citizens are respectful of different beliefs and opinions and are committed to the cause of democracy. Ironically, the White Paper developed under a military dictatorship is by far the most explicit document with respect to citizenship education. Recognizing that the best place to develop a commitment to democracy is in schools it calls for schools to become places where democracy is lived so that students develop democratic ideas and beliefs and commit to leading democratic lives. It is to be seen if this vision is retained in the final policy.

SECTION 3: THE PRACTICE OF CITIZENSHIP EDUCATION

In Pakistan, the goal of the Social Studies/ Pakistan Studies is citizenship education (Ministry of Education, 1973). Citizenship concepts are also included in Urdu, English, Islamiat and Civics (an elective in grades 9–12). With the exception of English all are considered unimportant subjects. Thus, citizenship education gets little attention in schools. In this section I will discuss the practice of citizenship education in Pakistani schools. I will first discuss the inputs, that is, the curriculum and textbooks and teacher education. I will then focus on the process of teaching and learning in schools. Finally, I will suggest the kind of citizen being developed.

The curriculum and textbooks

Policy directions for education are translated into a national curriculum. Since 1977, the aims and objectives of education have been directed towards ensuring that the message of the Holy Quran is disseminated; true practicing Muslims are developed; Islamic ideology is accepted as the basis for Pakistan and foundation of national unity; knowledge that conforms to the moral, social and political framework of Islam is acquired; and Islamic, moral and civic values inculcated (Ministry of Education, 1979). Since 1998, two more aims have been added: preparing youth for the 'world of work', and 'the pursuit of professional and specialized education'. (Ministry of Education, 1998: 41). The aims of education are translated into a conceptual framework. The conceptual framework suggests the topics of study to be included and the perspective from which they have to be studied.

For social studies the aims of education are translated into nine social studies objectives. Of the nine objectives five are directed towards the development of true practising Muslims, three to the acquisition of knowledge about Pakistan and the world and one to promoting the values of co-existence and interdependence (Ministry of Education, 2002: 6). Thus from the large body of useful social studies instructional content a narrow body of content is selected a significant portion of which is about Islam and Muslims. Instead of developing conceptual understanding, the curriculum focuses on providing factual information chosen to serve ideological ends (Nayyar and Salim, 2004). A number of Islamic, moral and civic values are included in the curriculum. The curriculum seeks to inculcate these values rather than have students identify, develop and apply them in solving-problems and making-decisions.

The curriculum is translated into textbooks. To ensure textbooks adhere to the conceptual framework of the national curriculum, the curriculum provides instructions for textbook writers, and textbooks must be approved by the Ministry of Education for use in schools. There have been numerous critiques of the content of social studies textbooks (Ahmad, 2004; Ali, 1986; Aziz, 1992; Dean, 2000, 2005; Future Youth Group, 2003; Nayyar and Salim, 2004; Rehman, 1999; Saigol, 1993, 1994). These critiques have noted that the textbooks of social studies/Pakistan studies, are filled with facts which are selective, biased and distorted and which are carefully woven into narratives that provide a particular view of the struggle for, creation, existence and nature of the Pakistan nation.

Let us take a brief look at what the social studies textbooks teach with regard to citizenship education. This review of the textbooks will focus on how concepts related to the socio-political issues (discussed in section one) are represented in the textbooks through both inclusions and exclusions.

The textbooks repeatedly define national identity in a manner that excludes non-Muslims. National identity is defined in relation to the 'other' (India and Hindu). Descriptions of Pakistan's disputes with India, depict India as hostile and aggressive and Pakistan as seeking friendship and peace. Hindus are depicted as cruel and unjust whereas Muslims are shown as honest and virtuous (Dean, 2005). Since 1979, the idea of Pakistan as an Islamic state rather than a Muslim majority country and Pakistani citizens as Muslims has been developed (Nayyar, 2004). Further, patriotism has been equated with Islamic zeal. In doing this textbooks ignore the religious diversity of Pakistan, 'encourage prejudice, bigotry and discrimination towards fellow citizens', and renders suspect the patriotism and faith of opposing voices (Nayyar and Salim, 2004).

Textbooks provide a simplistic definition of democracy 'democracy means rule by the people' and go on to explain the need for electing representatives to rule since with such a large population all the people cannot rule. The textbooks do not discuss military dictatorship, but subtly promote a militarized state (Aziz, 1992; Nayyar and Salim, 2004;

Saigol, 1994) by creating enemies and promoting hatred towards them, glorifying war and the use of force, discussing specific battles and glorious victories and eulogizing military heroes. The textbooks also present factual descriptions of the structure and functions of the government and state institutions. The absence of the institution of the military from this description is noteworthy. Also absent are civil society institutions involved in development and rights based work so important to democracy. The texts thus uncritically promote government agency and ignore the vital role of citizen agency (Dean, 2005).

The world constructed by the textbook is one of gender apartheid. The world is divided into two spheres, the public and the private sphere. The public sphere, the sphere of political, economic and social activity is the domain of men. The private sphere of the home is the domain of women. Here the main role of women is that of mother and homemaker whose task it is to cook, clean and care for the children (Dean, 2007). Since social studies texts mostly deal with the public sphere women are absent. When they are included they are usually portrayed in care giving roles: teacher, nurse, social worker. The textbooks foster gender stereotypes, entrench biases against women and denigrate and relegate them to a secondary status. In so doing they enhance the status of men and perpetuate patriarchy.

The curriculum and textbook content are contrary to the requirements of democratic citizenship education. Examinations are based on the textbook and comprise low order questions which require students to restate the facts given in the textbook, thus ensuring students learn the given text with its factual distortions and omissions, narrow interpretations and encouragement of hostility towards others (Dean, 2005).

Teacher training

The teacher is the key to the provision of quality citizenship education. Only an extremely small number of teachers receive any training in citizenship education. Moreover, research (Bregman and Mohammad, 1998; Kizilbash, 1998; Warwick and Reimers, 1995) shows that the quality of teacher training is generally so poor that it has no effect on the education provided to children. Most teachers have poor content knowledge, use the algorithm of read-explain-question to teach every lesson, manage their classrooms in an authoritarian manner and use assessment strategies that test recall of textbook facts.

THE PROCESS OF CITIZENSHIP EDUCATION IN SCHOOLS

To become effective citizens, young people must learn a body of knowledge; develop relevant skills, values and dispositions and obtain a first-hand experience of citizenship through participation in student councils, active engagement in community service and involvement in social action that seeks to precipitate social change (Apple, 1999; Kahne and Westheimer, 1996; Kerr, 2003; Wade and Saxe, 1996). This chapter now turns to discuss the provision of citizenship education in Pakistani schools.

The school building and management

In Pakistan, the school premises are important to citizenship education. Lack of physical infrastructure and resources can have negative consequences for citizenship education. Lack of a boundary wall and toilet facilities make parents reluctant to send girls to school for fear of their safety and girls reluctant to continue their schooling. Girls are thus denied their right to education and to the empowerment required to claim other rights. On the other hand, some communities have built and resourced schools themselves – an important expression of citizenship.

Most Pakistani schools are organized hierarchically and managed in a highly authoritarian style. Decision-making power flows from the top down. In 2001 the government devolved decision-making power to the school community by establishing School Management Committees (SMCs) comprising of citizens from the community and teachers of the school. The aims and objectives of the SMCs are to: increase enrollment and retention of students, especially girls; improve academic performance; generate and manage funds and prepare and implement a school development plan (Education Department, 2001). While the potential for citizenship practice exists, unfortunately in most cases the SMCs exist only in name or serve only as fundraising bodies.

Citizenship education in and outside the classroom

An overwhelming majority of schools begin the day with an assembly. Standing in straight lines students recite verses from the Holy Qur'an and/or a prayer followed by singing the national anthem. Oftentimes, the assembly is also used to teach students the importance of punctuality, being neat and clean and praying regularly.

In most classrooms students sit two to three to a bench in rows facing the teacher. In many classrooms there is a raised platform for the teacher's desk and chair. The spatial distance between the teacher and students and the elevated position of the teacher serves to establish his/her authority.

For most teachers, the objective of teaching is to complete the prescribed textbook and ensure students' learn it so that they are successful in the examination. The authority of the teacher and the textbook is reinforced by the use of the lecture method in which teachers 'deposit' textbook facts into students (Freire, 1970) and by teachers maintaining strict discipline in the class. Students are not allowed to ask questions, present ideas or speak to each other. Students who do, are scolded, deprived of rewards and occasionally beaten. Following the lecture, teachers have students answer questions that require regurgitation of textbook facts. Most teachers teach as described below:

> When I first started teaching social studies I did not think of social studies as having any purpose except to teach the textbook and get students to learn to answer questions for tests and exams. I did not plan any lessons. ... I taught as I had been taught. For example, when teaching the topic 'The Universe' I would define the solar system, tell them how many planets there were, their distance from the sun, explain the solar and lunar eclipse and so on. When we finished the chapter I would have them answer the questions at the end of the chapter and do the fill in the blanks. Most of the time I lectured. I used to try and learn all the subject matter so I could talk for 40 minutes. There was no room for discussion. I never used to interact with the students in class ... (Dean, 2000: 158–9).

There is no room for students to be critical or to conduct any independent inquiries on issues. Even if a teacher were to independently supplement the curriculum with activities, student would still be tested on the factual material in the textbook. Much time is spent on tests and examinations in Pakistani schools. The high stake value of, end-of-the-year and school leaving examinations have resulted in teaching and learning being geared solely towards helping students memorize facts to pass the examinations.

While students acquire some citizenship knowledge in the classroom they are socialized into being obedient to and accepting of what the authority (teacher and textbook) says as true; attitudes not at all conducive to democratic citizenship.

Co-curricular activities also provide opportunities for citizenship education. In Pakistan, most schools generally celebrate national and international days and Muslim religious festivals and have students participate in inter-school competitions such as science fairs, debates and sports. The potential for citizenship education is limited because preparation for these events are not a regular feature of teaching and learning and only a few able students are chosen to participate. A few schools organize Girl Guides/Boy Scouts (government schools), student councils and community service (private schools). Becoming a Girl Guide or a Boy Scout provides students with opportunities to learn to help each other, solve daily life problems and learn about Pakistan while student councils and community service offer opportunities to develop leadership and problem-solving skills and greater understanding of school and community life. A minority of private schools also have students participate in human rights or environmental education programmes designed by non-governmental organizations (NGOs) whereas others use information and communication technologies to connect Pakistani students with students in other parts of the world to develop intercultural understanding. Greater benefits would accrue if there is better preparation for and reflection on these activities.

The student-citizen

Pakistani educators are scathing in their criticism of teaching and learning in Pakistani schools because the schools are not conducive to learning in general and democratic citizenship education in particular. Kizilbash (1986) claims that, 'The existing teaching practice is contributing to the socialization of obedient, passive citizens who lack critical thinking, questioning, decision-making and problem-solving skills, who are closed-minded followers rather than responsible and independent citizens'. Aziz (1992) agrees with Kizilbash stating, 'In Pakistan the textbook of social studies is the only instrument of imparting education on all levels because the teacher(s) do not teach ... but repeat what it contains and the student is encouraged or simply ordered to memorize its contents' (p. 1). He further observes that the teaching of social studies produces millions of educated slaves, not responsible citizens. Yet others (Dean, 2000, 2005; Hoodbhoy, 1998; Nayyar and Salim, 2004; Saigol, 1994) criticize the education system for preparing Pakistani children only to regurgitate what is written in Pakistani textbooks rather than to think, to obey authority rather than question and reason for themselves. The State of Education in Pakistan report prepared by the Social Policy and Development Centre for the year 2002–2003 states, 'Instead of being able to acknowledge diversity in points of views, they (students) are likely to look at the world in oversimplified, uncritical, "black and white" and "us versus them" terms and develop single dimensional, exclusivist mindsets' (p. 168).

POLICY AND PRACTICE IMPLICATIONS

Pakistan is making efforts to strengthen democracy. Devolution of power to districts, reserved seats for women at the local and national level, an active judiciary, greater freedom of information, education of voters in preparation for general elections in 2008 bode well for citizenship education. However, strong pressure continues to be exerted to convert Pakistan into an Islamic theocratic state, and there is strong resistance to devolution of power and to work being done to promote gender equality by individuals and groups who want to perpetuate their power and influence.

A key strategy aimed at institutionalizing democracy is a change in the education system through the development of a new education policy. A new education policy is being developed. The White Paper has envisioned a goal of education as the preparation of citizens for a democratic society. The policy recognizes the importance of schools for promoting democratic citizenship education but does not make a strong enough case for it. The policy also suggests quality improvements such as improved curricula, the use of multiple textbooks, better pre-service and continuing in-service teacher education and an improved examination system. These should serve citizenship education, albeit indirectly. At the time of writing this chapter a new curriculum is

being developed. This curriculum must be designed to address the limitations research has shown exist in the previous ones. It is imperative that textbooks content be factually correct and unbiased, include substantial knowledge about democracy, citizenship rights and responsibilities and socio-political issues, foster inquiry, critical thinking and decision-making, promote values of social justice, equality and diversity and encourage informed and responsible actions to address problems and issues in the society.

Essential to effective implementation of the curriculum is the education of teachers. Some teacher education institutions are leading the way by preparing teachers to educate for citizenship. In these programmes teachers develop understanding of key concepts, learn to use active participatory pedagogies such as inquiry, discussion and cooperative learning and the way to organize school councils and community service learning projects. However, there remains an urgent need for quality teacher education on a mass scale.

The possibilities of pedagogy are often limited 'by the examination system which serves as the penultimate tool of control over teaching and learning' (Saigol, 2004: 13). Recognizing this, the government has permitted the setting up of the first private examination board by the Aga Khan University. The examination board will assess student learning outcomes delineated in the curriculum rather that textbook content as has been the common practice. The direction it has set is being followed by some government examination boards.

It is important to recognize that citizenship education in Pakistan is not taking place in a democratic society. Therefore, schools and classrooms must reflect the kind of society to be created (Apple and Beane, 1995, 1999). In schools students should be given the opportunity not only to learn about but to experience democracy. School councils, school clubs, community service and other forms of student involvement that genuinely engage student in problem-solving and decision-making must be structured into school life.

Schools could both draw on and support the efforts of civil society organizations to provide the opportunities for young people to experience and work towards creating a democratic society.

NOTES

1 There is in the Qur'an a chronological development of the meaning of *ummah* from generic application to religious communities to a more focused reference to the Muslim community. The *ummahs* establishment as a community with political authority and autonomy, as well as religious and social characteristics, was in Medina. Colonialism's challenge instigated a great renewal of *ummah* awareness among Muslims, and a variety of discourses on the political as well as other meanings of the concept of *ummah* abounds today.

REFERENCES

Ahmad, I. (2004) Islam, Democracy and Citizenship Education: An Examination of the Social Studies Curriculum in Pakistan. *Current Issues in Comparative Education*, Teacher College Columbia University, 7 (1): 39–50

Ali, M. (1986) *Tareekh Aur Agahi (History and Awareness)*. Lahore, Pakistan: Urdu Art Press.

Aly, Javed H. (2007) *A White Paper on Education in Pakistan*. Islamabad: Government of Pakistan.

Apple, Michael W. (1999) *Power, Meaning and identity: Essays in Critical Educational Studies*. New York: Peter Lang.

Apple, Michael W. and Beane, James A. (1999) *Democratic Schools:Lesson from the Chalk Face*. Buckingham: Open University Press.

Apple, M.W. and Beane, J.A. (1995) *Democratic Schools*. Alexandria, Virginia: Association for Supervision and Curriculum Development.

Aziz, K.K. (1992) *The Murder of the History of Pakistan*. Lahore: Vanguard.

Bregman, J. and Mohammad, N. (1998) Primary and Secondary Education – Structural Issues. In Hoodbhoy, P. (ed.) *Education and the State: Fifty Years of Pakistan*. Karachi: Oxford University Press.

Dean, B.L. (2007) Creating Gender Apartheid: A Critical Study of an English Language Pakistani Textbook. In Rashida, Q. and Rarieya, J. (eds) *Gender and Education in Pakistan*. Karachi: Oxford University Press.

Dean, Bernadette L. (2005) Citizenship Education in Pakistani Schools: Problems and Possibilities. *International Journal of Citizenship and Teacher Education*. 1 (2): pp. 1–20.

Dean, Bernadette L. (2000) *Islam, Democracy and Social Studies Education: A Quest for Possibilities*. Unpublished doctoral dissertation: University of Alberta, Canada.

Education Department (2001) *School Management Committee*. Karachi: Government of Sindh.

Federal Bureau of Statistics (2005a) Demographic Survey, 2005. Islamabad: Federal Bureau of Statistics.

Federal Bureau of Statistics (2005b) National Education Census, 2005. Islamabad: Federal Bureau of Statistic.

Freire, P. (1970) *Pedagogy of the Oppressed*. New York: The Seabury Press.

Future Youth Group (2003) *Ideas on Democracy, Freedom and Peace in Textbooks*. Islamabad: Liberal Youth Forum.

Hayes, L.D. (1987) *The Crisis of Education in Pakistan*. Lahore: Vanguard Books Ltd.

Hoodbhoy, Pervez (1998) *Education and the State: Fifty Years of Pakistan*. Karachi: Oxford University Press.

Kerr, D. (2003) Citizenship: Local, National and International. In Gearon L. (ed.) *Learning to Teach Citizenship in the Secondary School*. London: Routledge Falmer.

Kahne, J. and Westheimer, J. (1996) In the Service of What? The Politics of Service Learning. *Phi Delta Kappan*, 77 (9): 593–599.

Kizilbash, H.H. (1998) Teaching Teachers to Teach. *Education and the State: Fifty Years of Pakistan*. Karachi: Oxford University Press. pp. 102–135.

Kizilbash, H.H. (1986) *Pakistan's Curriculum Jungle: An Analysis of the SAHE Consultation on the Undergraduate Curriculum in Pakistan*. Lahore: SAHE Publication.

Ministry of the Interior (Education Division) (1947) *Proceedings of the Pakistan Educational Conference*. Islamabad: Government of

Pakistan, Ministry of the Interior (Education Division).

Ministry of Education (1959) *Report of the Commission of National Education.* Islamabad: Government of Pakistan, Ministry of Education.

Ministry of Education (1972) *The New Education Policy 1972-1980*. Islamabad: Government of Pakistan, Ministry of Education.

Ministry of Education (1979) *National Education Policy and Implementation Programme*. Islamabad: Government of Pakistan, Ministry of Education.

Ministry of Education (1998) *National Education Policy 'IQRA' 1998–2010*. Islamabad: Government of Pakistan, Ministry of Education.

Ministry of Education (1992) *National Education Policy 1992–2002*. Islamabad: Government of Pakistan, Ministry of Education.

Ministry of Education (1973*) Elementary Social Studies Curriculum for Classes I–V*. Islamabad: Government of Pakistan, Ministry of Education.

Ministry of Education (2002) *Social Studies Curriculum for Classes 1–V*. Islamabad: Government of Pakistan, Ministry of Education.

Nayyar, A.H. (2004) Insensitivity to the Religions Diversity of the Nation. *The Subtle Subversion: The State of Curricula and Textbooks in Pakistan*. Islamabad: Sustainable Development Policy Institute.

Nayyar, A.H. and Salim, Ahmad (2004) *The Subtle Subversion: The State of Curricula and Textbooks in Pakistan*. Islamabad: Sustainable Development Policy Institute.

Rehman, T. (1999) Teaching Ideology and Textbooks. *Daily Dawn*. Karachi, September 27, 1999.

Rashid, A. (1985) Pakistan: The Ideological Dimension. In Mohammad Asghar Khan (ed.) *Islam, Politics and the State: The Pakistan Experience*. London: Zed Books. pp. 69–89.

Saigol, R. (2004) Concept Paper. *A paper presented at UNESCO Workshop on Gender and Curriculum Reform*, Islamabad, Pakistan 22–23 November 2004.

Saigol, R. (1994) *Locating the Self*. Lahore: ASR.

Saigol, R. (1993) *Education: Critical Perspectives*. Lahore: Progressive Publishers.

Shaheed, F. (2002) *Imagined Citizenship: Women, State & Politics in Pakistan*. Lahore: Shirkatgah Women's Resource Centre.

Social Policy and Development Centre (2003) *Social Development in Pakistan 2002-2003: The State of Education*. Available on http://www.spdc-pak.com/publications/pub disp.asp?id=anr5 retrieved on June 15, 2006.

Wade, R.C., and Saxe, D.W. (1996) Community Service-Learning in the Social Studies: Historical Roots, Empirical Evidence, Critical Issues. *Theory and Research in Social Education*, 24 (4): 331–359.

Warwick, D.P. and Reimers, F. (1995) *Hope or Despair? Learning in Pakistan's Primary Schools*. Westport CT: Praeger.

Ziring, L. (1997) *Pakistan in the Twentieth Century: A Political History*. Karachi: Oxford University Press.

18

From Subjects to Citizens: Citizenship Education in Palestine

Fouad Moughrabi

In a survey of work on citizenship theory, Kymlicka and Norman (1994) note, 'the concept of citizenship seems to integrate the demands of justice and community membership' (p. 352). The authors argue, along with John Rawls (1971) that the health and stability of a modern democratic polity depend upon 'the qualities and attitudes of its citizens' (p. 352). They then provide a list of such attributes of citizens that include a

sense of identity and how they view potentially competing forms of national, regional, ethnic, or religious identities; their ability to tolerate and work together with others who are different from themselves; their desire to participate in the political process in order to promote the public good and hold political authorities accountable; their willingness to show self-restraint and exercise political responsibility in their economic demands and in personal choices which affect their health and the environment (p. 353).

Kymlicka and Norman assume that citizenship education usually occurs in the con text of a sovereign state which can initiate policies designed to foster such values among its citizens. However, what happens to citizenship education when there is no independent and sovereign state? Who shoulders the

responsibility of educating the youth? Is it the family, the media or non-governmental organizations (NGOs)? And who then decides what qualities and attitudes need to be promoted?

This chapter will deal with citizenship education among the Palestinians in the West Bank and the Gaza Strip who have lived since June 1967 under an Israeli military occupation. Following the signing of the 1993 Oslo Accords, the Palestinians have been given partial autonomy and were permitted to set up a political authority whose power is nonetheless totally circumscribed by an Israeli military occupation. On the symbolic level, there is a façade of a political system, established as a result of the 1993 Oslo Accords, with the full regalia of a passport, a flag, a national anthem, an executive, a legislature and a court system. On a more basic level, none of this amounts to much: the passport still has to be approved by the Israeli military; the executive and the legislature have few real powers and the court system barely functions. Ironically, Palestinian Independence Day is celebrated every year on 22 November in a surreal manner that evokes what people aspire to rather than what they already have. In other words, the Palestinian people live in a legal grey zone under a political authority that is constantly waiting to become a state.

After a brief historical overview that helps situate the issue of citizenship education in Palestine, I will closely examine the formal text(s) and see how they are mediated to students, teachers and the general public. I will also take a look at the alternative text of everyday life where other forces are at play and where daily influences often shape perceptions and outlook in a much more decisive manner. In the end I will try to answer a fundamental question about what kind of education for citizenship is under way: is it to educate citizens for a new, emerging and independent state of Palestine at peace with its neighbors, or to educate citizens for a unitary state for all of its people within the borders of historic Palestine or for that matter, to educate citizens for a state in a condition of perpetual conflict.

THE POLITICAL AND SOCIAL CONTEXT

Following the 5 June 1967 war, the Palestinian territories of the West Bank and the Gaza Strip have been subjected to a protracted and harsh occupation by the Israeli military. The effects of this occupation on Palestinian society have been devastating. The statistics can only tell part of the story: more than half a million out of a population of approximately 3.5 million Palestinians have spent time in jail. As of June 2007, according to B'tselem (2007), the Israeli Information Center for Human rights in the Occupied Territories, there are 10,367 Palestinian prisoners held by Israel. Many of these prisoners are routinely tortured. Between 1987 and 2005, 1,115 Palestinian homes were totally demolished by the Israeli army and 64 were partially demolished. Furthermore, between September 2000 when

the Al-Aqsa Intifada broke out and the end of May 2007, 4,058 Palestinians were killed by the Israeli security services of whom 834 are considered minors (under the age of 12). The Palestinian Red Crescent Society (PRCS, 2007) reports that 4,486 Palestinians were killed during this period and 31,403 were injured, of whom 8,311 by live ammunition and 6,916 by rubber coated steel bullets while the rest were injured by tear gas and other methods.

Freedom of movement for the Palestinian population is highly restricted by an array of mechanisms that include 43 permanent checkpoints within the West Bank (UNOCHA, 2007). Palestinians wanting to cross encounter long delays and can only move about with special permits. There are 35 Israeli imposed checkpoints that regulate traffic between the West Bank and Israel proper and 73 gates in the separation barrier, also known as the apartheid wall, only 38 of which are for Palestinians while the others are for use by Jewish settlers who live in illegally established settlements within the occupied territories. Flying checkpoints often appear for a few hours and impose further restrictions on freedom of movement. In the city of Hebron there are 15 checkpoints that separate areas inhabited by Palestinians and areas occupied by Jewish settlers. Finally, 41 sections of roads in the West Bank are not open to Palestinian traffic while Israeli settlers are allowed to travel on them freely (UNOCHA, 2007).

There are no serious long-term studies of the deep wounds inflicted on Palestinian society by the Israeli occupation. What we have are scattered reports issued by various organizations. Perhaps the most instructive are those provided by the Gaza Community Mental Health Program, which is directed by Dr. Eyad Sarraj, a well-known Palestinian psychiatrist. In a recent report, entitled 'The Psychosocial causes for the Palestinian Factional War', Dr. Sarraj (2007) points out that torture victims in turn become victimizers creating a 'cycle of internal violence'. He also notes that many Palestinian children had been subjected to severe traumatic experiences during the First Intifada (1988–1993) including 'beating, bone-breaking, injury, tear gas and acts of killing' (p. 2). Additionally, many children were subjected to the excruciating experience of seeing their fathers beaten helpless by Israeli soldiers without being able to resist. The young men who pursue revenge and killing and who at times seek their own death are the same children who had cherished dreams of a better life only to see them fade away at the moment they saw their own fathers humiliated by the Israeli soldier. 'No wonder, then, that the Palestinian child will see his model in that Israeli soldier and that his language will be the language of force and his toys the toys of weapons and death' (p. 2). Brute force rather than morality emerges as the example to follow.

Dr Sarraj and his colleagues (Sarraj and Qouta, 2007) chronicle the striking increase in the phenomenon of post-traumatic stress disorder (PTSD) among Palestinian children, especially since the outbreak of the second Intifada in 2000. A research project on 944 Palestinian children in Gaza reveals a high level of PTSD:

> more than half of the children suffered from severe levels of PTSD. The percentage corresponds with the levels of PTSD among the Cambodian, South American and Bosnia-Herzegovina refugee children fleeing atrocities in their home countries. The level of PTSD was considerably higher than was reported among the Lebanese and Israeli children (22 per cent), but lower than was reported among Iraqi children (84 per cent).

Such are the levels of despair among children that, according to a research project conducted by the Gaza Community Mental Health Program, some 34 per cent of boys between the ages of 12 and 14 in the Gaza Strip say that the 'best thing to do in life is to die as a martyr' (p. 15).

Politically speaking, as things now stand in the summer of 2007, there does not appear to be any hope on the horizon. The prospect of a two state solution where an independent Palestinian state is established alongside Israel has now receded. Despite rhetorical support for it among the major powers, it is highly unlikely that Israel will be pressured to end its occupation and negotiate the emergence of an independent Palestinian state. Economically, the levels of poverty in the West Bank and the Gaza Strip have become similar to the kind of absolute poverty one sees in Sub-Saharan Africa. Socially, Palestinian society is beginning to show signs of falling apart on the inside, reflecting the stresses and strains that are typical of other defeated societies. This includes significant increase in family violence, rates of divorce, crime and drug addiction among the youth (Sarraj, 2007).

THE EDUCATIONAL CONTEXT

A sense of guarded optimism prevailed in the early years following the signing of the 1993 Oslo Accords, the withdrawal of the Israeli army from the major Palestinian cities and the establishment of the Palestinian Authority. Palestinians, by and large, welcomed the opportunity to produce their own textbooks. Many exiles were allowed entry by the Israeli authorities and some Diaspora Palestinians relocated in order to invest in what they saw as a possible new Palestinian state. For all practical purposes, it appeared that a major project in nation building was well on its way.

In the Palestinian case, the educational system was seen as the most critical component of this project in nation building and a primary vehicle in trying to shape new attitudes among citizens. In its five-year (2000–2005) development plan for general education, the Palestinian Ministry of Education (MOEHE, 2005) outlined the following five core principles:

- education as a human right, whereby all children between the ages of six and sixteen have the right to free basic education;
- education as the basis for citizenship whereby, along with family and community, the school

becomes the main instrument for forming Palestinian citizens through a unified curriculum;
• education as a tool for social and economic development;
• education as the basis for the promotion of values and democracy; and
• education as a continuous, renewable and participatory process.

Education is one of the areas allocated to the Palestinian Authority under the system of limited autonomy granted by the Oslo Accords, signed in a grand ceremony in the Rose Garden of the White House. A public school system is in place throughout the West Bank and the Gaza Strip. A unified curriculum has been adopted and implemented since 1994 and, by now, all twelve grades have new textbooks created by the new Palestinian Curriculum Center. In addition, there is a school system, from grade 1 through 8, administered and financed by the United Nations Relief and Works Agency (UNRWA) for Palestinian refugees. This school system also uses the new textbooks as do the few private schools.

By 2006, according to the Palestinian Central Bureau of Statistics (PCBS, 2006) there were 3,212 schools and kindergartens attended by 1,144,631 students out of a total population of nearly 3.8 million people. In the West Bank and Gaza Strip there were 43,924 school teachers including 28,230 in the West Bank and 15,694 in the Gaza Strip. In addition, there are eleven universities and nine colleges offering BA degrees, with 3,688 teachers and 113,417 students. The student body is split almost evenly between males and females. In other words, the new political system had access to a substantial pool of future citizens and a significant opportunity to mould their attitudes and perceptions.

The literacy rate is 92.9 per cent among individuals aged 15 years and older in the Palestinian Territory. The rate is higher among males (96.9 per cent) than among females (88.9 per cent).

The Palestinian educational system comprises a compulsory basic cycle covering grades 1 through 10. In secondary school, students enroll in one of three streams: scientific, literary or vocational. For the years 2004–05, 28 per cent of students enrolled in the scientific stream (51 per cent male and 49 per cent female); 69 per cent of students enrolled in the literary stream (45 per cent male and 55 per cent female) and only 3 per cent enrolled in the vocational stream (71 per cent male and 29 per cent female.

According to a World Bank Report (2006), repetition rates are low by regional standards standing at 1.1 per cent at government schools, 2.4 per cent at UNRWA schools and 0.4 per cent at private schools. Similarly, dropout rates stood at 0.8 per cent for government schools, 0.5 per cent for UNRWA schools and 0.2 per cent for private schools for the years 2004–05. The dropout rates are higher at the secondary school level standing at 2.9 per cent for males and 3.8 per cent for females in the West Bank and 1.9 per cent for males and 3.4 per cent for females in the Gaza Strip. More recent figures would probably show a higher dropout rate given the economic collapse of the Palestinian economy following the imposition of sanctions resulting from the victory of Hamas in the 2006 elections.

A total of 46, 424 students sat for the Tawjihi (Matriculation) exam (literary stream) in 2005, and 14,546 sat for the scientific stream while 1960 sat for the vocational stream. The pass rate was 64.08 per cent for the literary stream, 86.90 per cent for the scientific stream and 69.60 per cent for the vocational stream. No break downs by gender are available. In its review of these results over ten years, the World Bank Report (2006) notes that the evolution of Tawjihi results clearly describes a process of democratization of secondary education in Palestine.

The World Bank (2006) further notes that

the key accomplishment in the development of education in Palestine in this last five year period has been the construction of a national curriculum, followed by the editing and distribution of textbooks and the delivery of targeted in-service training to all teachers for curriculum implementation (p. 25).

The World Bank report also states that 'a national school curriculum is a central institution for nation building and citizenship formation' (p.25). It then lists a number of significant innovations that include the following: the first Arab country to teach English from the first grade; technology is introduced in the fifth grade all the way to the tenth as a compulsory subject. In grades 11 and 12, this subject is called information technology; home economics, environment and health are introduced in grades 7–10 as electives; a current issues class is offered in grades 11 and 12; civics is offered in grades 1 through 8; national education (a basic social science course) is also offered in grades 1–8 and history of Palestine as well as general history classes are offered in the secondary cycle. For the World Bank, all of this represents a fairly impressive achievement in spite of the harsh conditions imposed on them by the Israeli occupation.

One of the key priorities of the five-year plan (2000–2005) developed by the Palestinian Ministry of Education has been the introduction of information technology in Palestinian schools. According to the World Bank report (2006), 50 per cent of primary and secondary schools now have a computer laboratory, while a total of 70 schools have internet connection (p. 28). These numbers are probably much higher by now as a result of the launching in 2005 of the Palestinian Education Initiative, sponsored by the Ministry of Education, the private sector and major international corporations such as Microsoft, Dell and Cisco Systems. The main purpose of this initiative is to promote the use of information technology in schools in order to equip graduates with the needed skills for the new service economy.

THE FORMAL SYSTEM

Beginning in 1994, when it assumed control of the educational system in the West Bank and Gaza Strip, the new Palestinian Authority launched a textbook project designed to produce a unified school curriculum. Before that time, the West Bank schools used a Jordanian curriculum while schools in the Gaza Strip used an Egyptian one. This reflected the fact that these two regions were under Jordanian and Egyptian control prior to falling under Israeli control in June 1967. The Israeli occupation authorities decided to maintain this arrangement while imposing a regime of censorship that was aimed at eliminating any references to Palestinian national identity. During that period, even exhibiting the colors of the Palestinian flag was forbidden. Consequently, when the Palestinians were finally able to produce their own textbooks, starting in 1994, the process was met with great public approval and a sense of national pride.

With this new curriculum (Curriculum Center, 2002), the Palestinians hoped to reaffirm their own identity. New history texts were introduced where Palestinian school children were able, for the first time, to learn about their own history (Curriculum Center, 2005). At the same time, new texts in civic education were produced running from the first to the eighth grade.

Perhaps more than any other textbooks, the Palestinian texts have been subjected to numerous content analysis attempts by various groups in order to examine whether they incite anti-Israeli sentiment as alleged by some extreme right wing Israeli groups. One of the most thorough analyses was carried out by the German Georg Eckert Institute for International Textbook Research (Pingel, 2004) which examined textbooks on language, religious education, history and civics education. The authors conclude that the overall orientation of the curriculum is peaceful in spite of the harsh and violent realities in which schools operate. The study also finds that there is no open incitement to hatred or violence and that religious and political tolerance is emphasized in a good number of textbooks and in multiple contexts (Moughrabi, 2001; Brown, 2003).

Instead of doing a thorough content analysis of all civics textbooks which, in any case, is beyond the scope of this chapter, I shall limit myself to an examination of the prototypical eighth grade textbook on civic education produced by the Palestinian Ministry of Education (MOEHE, 2005) for 14-year-old children. A very important reason is that this age group constitutes nearly 46 per cent of the total population in the West Bank and Gaza Strip (Omari and Duraidi, 2007). Additionally, this is perhaps the most critical period because it comes at a point just prior to the transition to the secondary school cycle and represents the point where many young Palestinians begin to be active in political issues.

In the following descriptive analysis of this text I aim to convey a flavor of the work, its organization and the way it treats varied issues. The book is divided into four units. The first deals with the family and contains the following sections: the family as a microcosm of society; the responsibilities of the members of the family; the health of the family and the family and its members.

The narrative begins by describing the evolution of the family as it shrinks from a rural to an urban setting, from an extended one to a nuclear one. While the Palestinian family continues to be patriarchal, the fact that more women have entered the labor force has, nonetheless, brought about an increase in the contribution of the mother in the decision-making process.

The text then moves on to describe the need to promote democracy within the family as a way of strengthening social solidarity and deepening the sense of responsibility among its members to each other.

The second chapter deals with the responsibilities of the members of the family. Here, a new theme is introduced: the Palestinian family now includes a mother who works outside the home and who is also a care giver; therefore, she participates more in the decisions-making process within the family. Other themes include: the problems and difficulties associated with early marriage; the need to carry out medical exams before marriage in order to avoid various genetic problems that may emerge later. In a society where marriage among close relatives is still frequent, this becomes extremely important.

An entire section is devoted to procreation and fertility. A table is presented that includes the total population figures for developed and developing countries, in addition to infant mortality rates, fertility rates and longevity rates. The same figures are given for Palestine where a startling fertility rate of 6.4 per cent is given. The rate of population growth is then discussed as an issue of public and national concern rather than simply a personal choice. It is described as imposing health hardships on the mother, economic difficulties on the family and obstacles to national growth and development. The text does not shy away from asking students to discuss what religion has to say on these issues.

The second unit deals with the law and clearly spells out that no one should be above the law. A picture on page 17 shows a young woman addressing an oversized man who sits atop a bundle of posters that include things like elections, political parties, workers rights, children's rights and freedom of assembly. In the caption, the young woman tells the man to get down from on high. The bulk of the unit talks about the importance of the law, the need to fight against any kind of discrimination on the basis of color, religion, ethnicity, social class and so on. In another chapter, students are asked to identify the name of the person who represents their district in the legislative assembly, how to contact that person and how to invite that person to come to the school to describe the process of making laws. Some excerpts from the Basic Law (still a draft of a constitution) are then presented to illustrate basic freedoms, rights and responsibilities of citizens.

A chapter in the third unit deals with freedom of expression and the need to respect other peoples' opinions. Students are asked to draw a cartoon to illustrate freedom of expression. In one of the activities, some students are said to have written some nasty comments about one of their classmates on the wall of the school. The question to discuss is whether this can be considered within the range of freedom of expression.

The fourth unit talks about family safety and well being and emphasizes the need to renounce violence, to know one's rights, to express one's objections and to improve one's condition. The text talks about conditions that may provoke violence and lists various forms of violence including physical, verbal and psychological as well as social violence that results in denial of the right to education, to basic health care or to work. The victims of violence are said to include children, women and people with special needs.

I have presented these units and chapters in some detail in order to show that the authors make a serious effort at dealing with a variety of issues. Furthermore, the text does not shy away from examining controversial issues and it actually tries to deal with them in a clever and stimulating way.

TEACHING PALESTINIAN HISTORY

Palestinian students now have an occasion to learn about their own history by reading textbooks written by Palestinians. The question is what will Palestinian students actually learn about their own history and how. A comprehensive analysis of all history texts produced by the Ministry of Education is beyond the scope of this chapter. However, I will review the eleventh grade text on Palestinian history (MOE, 2005) and closely examine some of the basic units that it tries to cover.

The text is divided into two volumes and follows a fairly straightforward chronology. Volume 1 covers the following: the history of Palestine from ancient times to the end of the Mameluke period, circa 1516 A.D.; Palestine during the Ottoman period until the end of the nineteenth century and foreign penetration in Palestine from the end of the nineteenth century until the eve of the establishment of the British Mandate in 1920. Volume 2 examines the period of the British Mandate over Palestine from 1920 until 1948; the history of Palestine between 1948 and 1967 and the contemporary history of Palestine from 1967 until 2005.

A student who carefully reads these two volumes is likely to emerge with a very limited kind of knowledge of Palestinian history. This student may be able to recognize major events and some major characters but is unlikely to understand why events occurred. The text offers a quick, almost journalistic rendition of major events, juxtaposed together without any kind of logic. Students are expected to memorize these disjointed fragments and to answer questions that require recall of facts.

I will offer two specific examples. In the first, consider how the text covers a very important moment in contemporary Palestinian history, namely, the Arab rebellion of 1936. The text begins with a brief description of the call for a general strike by the Palestinians on the 20 April 1936 in order to pressure the British Mandate authorities to do the following: put an end to large scale and illegal Jewish immigration; to put an end to the transfer of Arab land to the Jews and to establish a representative national government that is accountable to an elected legislature. The population responded to the call for a general strike which lasted until October 12 1936. To my knowledge, this is the longest known strike in recorded history, lasting some 175 days, a fact that the text fails to mention.

The text goes on to say that the British adopted various oppressive measures to end the strike, without mentioning what kinds of measures and without giving any details about the numbers of Palestinians killed and wounded in the process. We are then told that, having failed, the British resorted to diplomatic maneuvers where they sought the help of compliant Arab governments to try to convince the Palestinians to end their strike.

The British then dispatched a royal commission to look into the causes of the rebellion. The Peel Commission recommended the partition of Palestine into a Jewish state and an Arab state with the Holy places to remain under British jurisdiction. The Palestinians refused this recommendation but the text does not explain why. The British then convened a conference in London attended by Jewish, Arab and Palestinian leaders. The text goes on to say that the conference failed because the British continued to side with the Jews. However, the British, we are then told, were obliged to find a way to pacify the Arabs for fear the latter would fight against them during the upcoming Second World War. They produced a White Paper in 1939 in which they made some vague promises to the Palestinians. This was promptly rejected by both the Jews and the Arabs for different reasons that again the text fails to explain.

Here is how Rashid Khalidi (1997), a well-known Palestinian historian, describes what occurred during that fateful period in Palestinian history. Khalidi shows how the general strike was followed by a three-year military uprising, in the course of which 'the British briefly lost control of much of the country, including cities like Jerusalem and Nablus' (p. 189). They then launched 'a massive campaign of repression by tens of thousands of troops and numerous squadrons of aircraft' (189–90) before they were able to restore order.

As a result, Khalidi points out that the 'Arab economy of Palestine was devastated by years of strikes, boycotts and British reprisals, and the fighting forces suffered casualties – 5,000 killed and 10,000 wounded – that were proportionately huge in an Arab population of about one million' (p. 190). The Arab leadership was shattered and divided by differences over tactics, with many leaders exiled and some fleeing the country, never to return. The net result, according to Khalidi, 'was that the Palestinians entered World War II in effect headless, without even the semblance of a unified leadership' (p. 190). Khalidi concludes that the crippling defeat the Palestinians had suffered in 1936–1939 was one of the main reasons why they were unable to confront the even more serious

challenges a few years later in 1947–1949. At that time, the Jewish forces launched an all out assault designed to establish a Jewish state that ultimately resulted in the dismemberment of Palestine and the forced evacuation of most of its inhabitants from their homes.

Here is another example of poor treatment of a searing moment in contemporary Palestinian history, namely, the massacres of unarmed Palestinian civilians in the refugee camps of Sabra and Chatila in Lebanon that occurred September 16–18, 1982 during the Israeli invasion of Lebanon.

The text offers only the following paragraph to describe the event:

> Following the departure of the Palestinian resistance from Lebanon, Lebanese Phalangist groups entered the Palestinian refugee camps of Sabra and Chatila aided by Israeli troops which controlled the entrances and exits of the camps. They committed a massacre, considered one of the most despicable in human history, for three consecutive days 16, 17, 18 September 1982, causing the death of nearly 3,500 Palestinian and Lebanese civilians (MOE, 2005).

There is absolutely no mention of some very significant facts: the record of the Israeli commission of inquiry which, at the time, found Ariel Sharon 'indirectly' responsible for the massacres; the fact that Ambassador Philip Habib, the US envoy at the time, had guaranteed, on behalf of the US government, that the Palestinian refugee camps would be protected after the PLO evacuates Lebanon. There is also no mention of eyewitness accounts written by various people including the famous Israeli journalist Amnon Kapeliouk (1984), one of the first to enter the camps after the massacre and someone who had written a critical book about the subject.

This is not the only massacre that receives little attention. The text makes only fleeting references on page 38 of volume 2 about massacres committed by Zionist forces in 1948 in Deir Yassin, Tantura, Lod and others despite the overabundance of archival studies by revisionist Israeli historians such as Ilan Pappe (2006), Benny Morris (1989), Simha Flapan (1988) and Avi Shlaim (2001). The accounts written by these historians firmly negate the Israeli claim that the refugees had left their homes at the instigation of the invading Arab armies. Instead, their research in the Zionist archives shows that the Palestinians were driven out through a premeditated policy of ethnic cleansing (Pappe, 2007).

I have heard, on various occasions, Palestinian educators complain that younger generations of Palestinians know very little of their own history. I am unaware that any serious studies have been conducted to find out if this is truly the case. However, one can safely assume that with a depoliticized media, inadequate school textbooks and minimal effort to communicate through oral history, most Palestinian youth probably do have limited knowledge of their own history.

A PEDAGOGY OF CITIZENSHIP EDUCATION

We have here a combination of a legal definition of citizenship as well as a politically specific definition that emerges out of a special set of historical experiences. Thus, according to the Palestinian Authority eleventh grade history book, a Palestinian is said to be a person who is descendant of fathers or forefathers who had lived in Palestine before 1998. This person enjoys all the basic rights of a citizen in a democratic state that is a parliamentary republic governed by the rule of law and has all the obligations of citizenship. What is distinctive here is the enumeration of a number of specific rights including the right to education, to work and to health care. Furthermore, this person has the right not to be deported from his/her homeland and not to be tortured. There is also special emphasis on the need to protect the rights of minorities and to ensure social justice. Finally, there is a clear statement that every Palestinian refugee who had been forced to leave his/her home has the basic right to return to his/her homeland.

All of the above is fine except that the state does not exist. It is a state in the making and its actualization is contingent on so many variables that are way beyond the control of the average citizen. All the rights enumerated are ones that Palestinians, in reality, aspire to because, so far, they are subject to the whims of the Israeli occupation authorities who can suspend them as they see fit. Furthermore, even in areas where the Palestinian authority has jurisdiction, the gap between norms and reality is quite large: violations of basic human rights are common and there is a perception out there that corruption runs rampant within the Palestinian political system.

Perhaps more striking is the juxtaposition of a set of universal norms and values within the context of an educational system that remains quite authoritarian and highly centralized. The question is how does one teach democracy in a non-democratic school system where students are mere receptacles of knowledge and not active participants in their own education. For example, consider the following scenes: a teacher stands in front of the classroom to talk about freedom of expression and promptly says that no one can speak without prior permission ... raise your hand and wait for permission before you speak. The student is likely to learn more about authority than about freedom of expression. Or, imagine the school principal holding a stick, and sometimes a whip in one hand and a notebook in the other where he records the violations of the teachers. How can a teacher instruct their students about rights when they have none? Notions of citizenship, human rights and democracy are offered as abstract ideas and are totally removed from their social, historical and political context.

The Palestinians went to the polls in January 2006 and voted in what international observers ascertained was a free and fair election to choose members of a legislative assembly. Hamas surprised everyone and won the majority of seats defeating Fatah, the ruling party. The US government along with the EU and Israel refused to endorse the results of this election. They decided to impose sanctions on the new Palestinian government choosing instead to work with president Mahmood Abbas from Fatah.

Teachers and civil servants went for months without receiving any salary. The bureaucracy came to a standstill and, as a result, the economy declined even more than it had during the years of the Intifada.

The Palestinian population enthusiastically participated in the election, seeing it as an affirmation of their right to self-determination. The voter turnout was quite high. The question, therefore, is what effect will the decision to abort this experiment in democracy have on the population? How can Palestinian teachers seriously talk about the value of democracy and citizen participation when the great and democratic powers simply dismiss it with impunity?

An interesting experiment in teaching democracy in a non-conventional manner was conducted by a leading educator from Birzeit University who adopted a case-based approach. Dr. Maher Hashweh (2004) worked with a number of school teachers in the West Bank who developed a number of cases and tried to teach them to their students. The author reports that some learning did in fact occur both among the teachers and the students including a better appreciation of the importance of democracy, citizenship and human rights. One student is reported to have said: 'How can I learn about democracy while I live with a father who denies me the right to choose my partner and forces me to live in the prison of tradition and custom' (p. 267). The author notes that some of the students associate democracy with freedom, a perspective that can obviously be built upon. However, according to him, they need to be taught that there is a need to create a balance between absolute freedom and social responsibility.

By and large, the students repeated the common clichés about democracy education that circulate within society namely, that notions of democracy and human rights are somehow idealistic in contrast to the oppressive conditions that people live under; or that learning about mathematics and science should take precedence over learning about democracy; or that politicians will do what they have to do while ordinary people have no way of changing this.

Overall, the results, as reported by the principal author himself, were modest. One possible reason may well be the artificial construction of the cases used which meant that they did not reflect real live situations that students and teachers could relate to. In general, however, talking about democracy in a hypothetical situation such as this occurs in the context of a situation where the student and the teacher live in a non-democratic household, attend a non-democratic school, within a non-democratic society where corruption and nepotism are the rule and where there is a lack of law and order.

The Palestinian educational system has opened up new avenues for learning and teaching through the Internet. As mentioned earlier, the Ministry's five-year plan (2000–2005) placed heavy emphasis on information technology and introduced computer labs and internet access in many schools. The PCBS (2005) reports that 56.8 per cent of youth between the ages of 10 and 24 in the West Bank and 45 per cent in Gaza now use the computer on a regular basis. No appreciable differences exist between male and female. Khoury-Machool (2007) reports that 'there has been a sharp increase in the number of Palestinian Internet users-especially youth-through connectivity at home, schools, universities and youth centers' (p. 17). The author further concludes, 'the Internet now acts as a new medium between teachers, students and their peers, as well as a tool for intense politicization and peaceful cyber-resistance in the public sphere' (pp. 17–18).

Palestinians are now by far the largest group of users of the internet in the Arab World. Restrictions imposed by the Israeli occupation on Palestinian freedom of movement have forced Palestinian youth to rely increasingly on the internet as a key instrument that enables them to connect with each other. When schools and universities are closed, teachers connect with their students through the internet. A fairly active non-formal educational system has also emerged as numerous non-governmental organizations organize activities to teach young people how to use the new technology.

According to Khoury-Machool (2007), the introduction of ICT and its use by Palestinian youths has created the following new opportunities: to engage in alternative virtual gatherings on the Net in the absence of physical gatherings; to communicate with other Palestinians both within the occupied territories and in the Palestinian Diaspora; to participate along with others in shaping and popularizing a Palestinian narrative and in the formation of a new political culture of active and peaceful resistance.

CONCLUSION

The principal aim of citizenship education in Palestine has been to prepare young people to live and function as citizens in a democratic state that was supposed to emerge at the end of the transitional period following the 1993 Oslo Agreements. The Palestinian Authority made a very serious effort, however flawed at times, to actually produce texts and materials that would enable students to learn about citizenship. Charges by extremist Israeli groups that the Palestinian texts actually incite anti-Israeli hatred among Palestinian children have been proven false. In an earlier work (Moughrabi, 2001), I showed how key sections were mistranslated and how evidence was at times fabricated. Unfortunately, despite convincing evidence to the contrary, (Brown, 2003) leading American politicians such as Senator Hillary Clinton were all too willing to lend their support to these false charges.

The new Palestinian state has not materialized. Instead, political conditions deteriorated drastically with the outbreak of the Second Palestinian Uprising and Israel's massive military response to try to quell it. At the moment of this writing, events have led to a splintering of Palestinian reality with Hamas in control of the Gaza Strip

and Fatah in control of the West Bank. The future appears to be uncertain in spite of some lukewarm efforts at international diplomacy launched by the US and some Arab governments. The uncertainty and confusion have magnified generalized feelings of despair among the Palestinian population. Furthermore, the sanctions imposed by the US and the EU on the democratically elected government that resulted in the victory of Hamas have led to a new phenomenon of absolute poverty among the population. More important, however, are the long-term effects on the Palestinian population that result from the sabotage by the international community of the democratic experiment that the population had freely engaged during the 2006 elections for a legislative assembly.

There is not much evidence that the current maneuvering by the US government and Israel, working with Palestinian President Abbas, will work to undermine the democratically elected government. Mark Perry (2007) of the international Conflicts Forum argues convincingly that the ruling party is in shambles and will not be able to mount a counteroffensive largely because it is now seen as a collaborationist government. Increasingly, therefore, Hamas appears to represent the mainstream. Therefore, no radical changes in civics education are likely to take place with Hamas in power. The new government knows that Palestinian society values education and most people fully expect that the emphasis on quality education will continue.

Many Israeli, Palestinian and foreign analysts (Tilley, 2005; Abunimah, 2006; Reinhart, 2006) are now highly skeptical that a two state solution of the Israeli-Palestinian conflict is feasible any more. The massive buildup of illegal Jewish settlement on confiscated Arab lands in the Palestinian territories that Israel occupied in June 1967, along with an elaborate system of roads designed for use by Jews only have created what many are now calling an apartheid system (Carter, 2006), similar to the one that existed in South Africa.

It is difficult to see what kind of citizenship education might develop among the Palestinians if the prospect of an independent state is finally removed from the realm of possibility. However, regardless of which solution or which scenario ultimately emerges, one thing is certain. The overall political situation greatly influences the kind of citizenship education that a society will undertake.

Nevertheless, a society will continue to socialize its youth in values and attitudes that are needed in the contemporary world even in the absence of a state. Interestingly, most professional middle class Palestinians tend to prepare their young to function as global citizens who can live and function in Europe and in the US with remarkable ease. Usually fluent in English, they attend prestigious American and European universities and often excel, enabling the Palestinians to have one of the highest numbers (40 out of every 1,000) of university graduates in the modern world.

If a political settlement is produced and if hope begins to appear on the horizon, people will adjust and begin to prepare themselves and their children to live and function in the new reality. At the moment, it is difficult to see any such hope. It is far more realistic to assume that a long period of perpetual conflict will prevail in the region and that people will simply try to find creative ways to survive.

What kind of research is needed? In my opinion, more than simply doing content analysis of textbooks, it is far more important to carry out ethnographic research to see how Palestinian teachers actually mediate texts to their students, what materials they use, how much they rely on official texts as opposed to oral history and how they try to deal with the contradictions in their society – talking about democracy as it is being sabotaged by their own political representatives and by the great democracies in the world.

REFERENCES

Abunimah, Ali (2006) *One Country: A Bold Proposal to End the Israeli-Palestinian Impasse*. New York: Metropolitan Books.

Brown, N. (2003) *Palestinian Politics after the Oslo Accords*. Berkeley: University of California Press.

B'tselem: The Israeli Information Center for Human Rights in the Occupied Territories (2007), 'Statistics on prisoners and detainees.' Retrieved 28 June 2007 from http://www.btselem.org

Carter, J. (2006) *Palestine: Peace not Apartheid*. New York: Simon and Schuster.

Curriculum Center (2002) *Civic Education for Eighth Grade*. Ramallah: Palestinian Authority Ministry of Education.

Curriculum Center (2005) *Modern History of Palestine for Grade 11*. Ramallah: Palestinian Authority Ministry of Education.

Flapan, S. (1988) *The Birth of Israel: Myths and Realities*. New York: Pantheon.

Hashweh, M. (2004) *Democracy Education: A Case-Based Approach*. Ramallah, Muwatin: The Palestinian Institute for the Study of Democracy.

Kapeliouk, A. (1984) *Inquiry into a Massacre*. Boston: Association of Arab-American University Graduates.

Khalidi, R. (1997) *Palestinian Identity*. New York: Columbia University Press.

Khoury-Machool, M. (2007) 'Palestinian youth and political activism: the emerging internet culture and new modes of resistance,' *Policy Futures in Education*, 3 (1): 17–36.

Kymlicka, W. and Norman, W. (1994) 'Return of the citizen: a survey of recent work on citizenship theory,' *Ethics*, 104 (2): 352–381.

Ministry of Education (2005) *Five Year Educational Development Plan 2000–2005*. Ramallah: Palestinian Authority.

Morris, B. (1989) *The Birth of the Palestinian Refugee Problem, 1947–1949*. New York: Cambridge University Press.

Moughrabi, F. (2001) 'The politics of Palestinian textbooks,' *Journal of Palestine Studies*, 31 (1): 5–19.

Omari, M. and Duraidi, M. (2005) 'Characteristics of youth (10–24) in the palestinian territory,' Palestinian Central Bureau of Statistics. Retrieved 28 June 3007 from http://www.pcbs.org

Palestinian Central Bureau of Statistics (2006). 'Educational Statistics.' Retrieved 30 June 2007 from http:// www.pcbs.gov.ps

Palestine Red Crescent Society (2007) 'Crisis tables. Retrieved 28 June 2007 from http://www.palestinercs.org.

Pappe, I. (2006) *A History of Modern Palestine: One Land, Two Peoples*. London: Cambridge University Press.

Pappe, I. (2007) *The Ethnic Cleansing of Palestine*. London: Oneworld Publications.

Perry, M. (2007) 'Why oblivion looms for Abbas.' Retrieved 2 August 2007 from http://www.tonykaron.com/2007/07.

Pingel, F. (2003) *Contested Past, Disputed Present: Curricula and Teaching in Israeli and Palestinian Schools*. Hanover: Georg Eckert Institute.

Rawls, J. (1971) *A Theory of Justice*. London: Oxford University Press.

Reinhart, T. (2006) *The Road to Nowhere: Israel/Palestine since 2003*. London: Verso Books.

Sarraj, E. (2007) 'The psychological causes for the palestinian factional war,' Gaza Community Mental Health Program.

Retrieved 28 June 2007 from: http://www.gcmph.net

Sarraj, E. and Qouta, S. (2007) 'Disaster and mental health: the palestinian experience,' Gaza Community Mental Health Program. Retrieved 28 June 2007 from: http://www.gcmph.net.

Shlaim, A. (2001) *The Iron Wall: Israel and the Arab World*. New York: Norton and Co.

Tilley, V. (2005) *The One State Solution: A Breakthrough for Peace in the Israeli-Palestinian Conflict*. Ann Arbor: University of Michigan Press.

United Nations Office for the Coordination of Humanitarian Affairs (2007), 'Closures and checkpoints. retrieved 30 June 2007 from http://www.ochaopt.org/documents.

World Bank (2006) West Bank and Gaza: education sector analysis. Washington, D.C.: World Bank Group.

19

Citizenship Education in the United Kingdom

David Kerr, Alan Smith and Christine Twine

INTRODUCTION

The United Kingdom (UK) is not one but four countries: England, Northern Ireland, Scotland and Wales. Writing a chapter on citizenship education in the UK is, therefore, challenging. While the last decade has seen a resurgence of interest in citizenship education and its inclusion as a priority in education policy-making and practice in all four countries, there remains considerable divergence in philosophy, approach and intent. Though the overall aims for citizenship education are similar, the policies and practices being developed in England, Northern Ireland, Scotland and Wales are distinctive, and increasingly diverse, influenced by the history, culture and education context of each country.

This chapter explores the reasons for these similarities and differences and provides a flavour of the variety of policy and practice in the UK. Following this short introduction, the overall context for policy and practice in the UK is outlined. There is then a description of the history and specific context of citizenship education for each country – England, Northern Ireland, Scotland and Wales.

The chapter concludes with the key challenges facing the development of citizenship education in the UK, now and in the future.

SETTING THE CONTEXT

Within the UK the current resurgence of interest in citizenship education can be traced to the election of the Labour government in 1997. The new government arrived armed with policies focused on citizenship. The emphasis on collective 'civic responsibility' was an antidote to the individualist 'civic obligation' promoted by the outgoing Conservative government (MacGregor, 1990). Central to this emphasis has been an explicit move, through education policy, to introduce children and young people, from an early age, to the habits and practices of citizenship, through the promotion of citizenship education in schools. The result is that

- In England, Citizenship was introduced as a new statutory subject in schools in 2002.
- In Northern Ireland, Local and Global Citizenship is a new statutory subject in schools from 2007.

- In Scotland, Values and Citizenship is one of the five National Priorities in Education.
- In Wales, Citizenship is part of the statutory provision for Personal and Social Education (PSE).

This push on citizenship through education has taken place within a broader policy emphasis on the promotion of civil renewal with the goal of shared identity through strengthened communities. There is considerable activity in UK countries to maximise the contribution of citizenship education to civil renewal in a lifelong learning context.

Meanwhile, the emphasis on strengthened communities responding to local needs has been accompanied at national level in the UK by a process of devolution. This has seen the establishment of new legislative Assemblies in Northern Ireland, Scotland and Wales with elected representatives and powers to make decisions concerning policy areas, such as education. Such steps have given rise to renewed debate on issues related to nationality, identity and citizenship, and how these can be addressed through citizenship education, in each of the countries of the UK.

However, citizenship education developments within the UK have not taken place as a linear policy process. They have been influenced by the need to respond to broader societal events, in particular, the London bombings of July 2005, and the shock realisation that they were carried out by British born and educated citizens, and the influx of migrant workers from Europe into the UK. These developments have caused the government to re-adjust its initial approach to citizenship education and place increased emphasis on its contribution in building community cohesion and strengthening shared identity. There is a growing concern in the UK and across the four countries, to understand how a sense of citizenship can be effectively maintained within a context of increasing social, cultural and political diversity.

The chapter now goes on to set out the history and specific context of citizenship education developments in each of the four UK countries.

CITIZENSHIP EDUCATION IN ENGLAND

The history of past approaches to citizenship education in England reveals that there is no tradition of explicit citizenship education in schools (Crick, 2000; Heater, 2001). The new Labour government changed that. It championed citizenship as 'civic morality': individuals taking up their civic responsibilities in partnership with the state, what is referred to as the 'Third Way'. A particular trigger for renewed interest in citizenship education in England is its potential as an antidote to growing signs of alienation and cynicism among young people about civil and public life and participation – which has been termed a 'democratic deficit' (Jowell and Park, 1998).

The government, with all-party support, in 1997, established an Advisory Group on *Education for Citizenship and the Teaching of Democracy in Schools* chaired by Professor (now Sir) Bernard Crick (Kerr, 1999; Crick, 2000). The Crick Group was asked to set out the aims and purposes of citizenship education and a framework for how it could be successfully delivered, within and outside schools.

The Crick Group defined 'effective education for citizenship' as comprising three separate but interrelated strands (Advisory Group, 1998: 11–13) namely:

- social and moral responsibility;
- community involvement; and
- political literacy: '... pupils learning about, and how to make themselves effective in, public life through knowledge, skills and values'.

The Crick Group's final report contained a bold statement that the central aim of strengthening citizenship education is to effect:

> no less than a change in the political culture of this country both nationally and locally: for people to think of themselves as active citizens, willing, able and equipped to have an influence in public life and with the critical capacities to weigh evidence before speaking and acting ... (Advisory Group, 1998: 7).

The Group's report was accepted and, following the revision of the national curriculum, the historic decision was taken to introduce citizenship education as an explicit part of the school curriculum from September 2002 (QCA, 1999). Citizenship is now part of a non-statutory framework for personal, social and health education (PSHE) and citizenship for pupils aged 5–11 and a new statutory foundation subject for students aged 11–16.

The Citizenship programme of study has three interrelated elements:

- knowledge and understanding about becoming informed citizens;
- developing skills of enquiry and approach; and
- developing skills of participation and responsible action.

The programme differs from those in other national curriculum subjects in being deliberately 'light touch'. It sets out a barebones but rigorous framework for what is to be taught and learnt but then leaves it up to the professional judgement of those in schools – leaders, co-ordinators and teachers – working in partnership with local communities, to decide how best to approach the framework.

The current historic developments in citizenship education in England are not without their critics. In particular, there has been dissent from those on the political Right who argue that citizenship education is best learnt, if at all, outside school (Tooley, 2000) and those who argue that Crick Group was not bold enough in its prescription to schools (Faulks, 2006). A number of others, though supportive of the introduction of citizenship education, have drawn attention to the deficiencies of the Crick Report in its handling of particular issues, such as race (Hall, 2000; Osler, 2000) and gender (Arnot and Dillabough, 2000). There has also been concern about the considerable practical challenges that need to be overcome if citizenship education is to be effectively developed in schools (McLaughlin, 2000; Frazer, 2000; Potter, 2002).

The policy process has moved on considerably since 2002. It has been marked by a fresh emphasis on getting people (including children and young people) to influence and inform the decisions that are taken in relation to the institutions (such as schools) in the communities in which they live. The launch of the Children Bill (GB, 2004), in particular, seeks to put children and families at the heart of policy with services built around those who use them (such as children) rather than those who deliver them. This push is mirrored in policy for citizenship education which, since 2002, has widened beyond schools to encompass other education and training phases and the wider community. For example, following the second Crick Report (FEFC, 2000) a series of pilot development projects was started in 2001 to explore what an entitlement to citizenship education might look like in the 16–19 age group education and training. A 16–19 citizenship programme is now being rolled out nationally. Meanwhile, the Home Office launched a major policy initiative around the concept of civil renewal (Blunkett, 2003).

These are still early days for citizenship education in England and policy-makers and support agencies have been working hard to meet the considerable development needs of schools and teachers. There has been a particular focus on: drawing up more detailed advice and guidance for schools on assessment, self-evaluation and inspection, including new GCSE and AS level qualifications (Huddleston and Kerr, 2006; Breslin and Dufour, 2007); encouraging the growth of professional and training networks, such as the Association for Citizenship Teaching (ACT) and Citized teacher education network; providing more access to training through a national CPD programme and setting up a stronger research and evidence base through the DCSF funded Citizenship Education Longitudinal Study.

The growing evidence base for citizenship in schools confirms the difficulties in surmounting the practical challenges that were identified when citizenship was introduced in 2002 (Kerr et al., 2007, 2004; Kerr, 2005; Gearon, 2003; Deakin-Crick et al., 2004).

It reveals: the existence of an implementation gap between the vision of the Crick Group and the ability of schools to understand and implement it (OFSTED, 2005, 2006); acceptance that provision is uneven, patchy and evolving with differing types of school approaches to citizenship emerging (Cleaver et al., 2005; Ireland et al., 2006) and the identification of a number of key challenges that remain to be tackled if citizenship education provision is to become more visible, coherent and effective, particularly in relation to teacher training, assessment and the promotion of active citizenship and pupil voice.

Most recently, the connection between citizenship education and civil renewal and, in particular community cohesion, has been made more explicit in a series of policy documents most notably: the *Diversity and Citizenship: Curriculum Review* (DfES, 2007; Maylor et al., 2007); the report of the Commission on Integration and Cohesion (2007) and *Guidance* [for schools] *on the Duty to Promote Community Cohesion* (DCSF, 2007). This connection has been formalised in the new National Curriculum to be introduced by schools in September 2008.

The new curriculum has three overarching aims, one of which is that is should enable all young people to become 'responsible citizens who make a positive contribution to society' (QCA, 2007a). The original Citizenship programme of study has been considerably revised (QCA, 2007b). The main revisions are a greater emphasis on the development of concepts, such as democracy and justice and rights and responsibilities and, more significantly, the addition of a new strand entitled *Identities and diversity: living together in the UK*, which involves students:

- appreciating that identities are complex, can change over time and are informed by different understandings of what it means to be a citizen in the UK;
- exploring the diverse national, regional, ethnic and religious cultures, groups and communities in the UK and the connections between them;
- considering the interconnections between the UK and the rest of Europe and the wider world; and

- exploring community cohesion and the different forces that bring about change in communities over time (QCA, 2007b).

It is this latter strand which considerably alters the focus of the citizenship curriculum and makes explicit its role in educating for community cohesion as recommended by the *Diversity and Citizenship: Curriculum Review* (DfES, 2007). Quite how schools will respond to this revised focus remains to be seen.

LOCAL AND GLOBAL CITIZENSHIP IN NORTHERN IRELAND

When the island of Ireland was partitioned in 1921, six counties in the north remained part of the United Kingdom of Great Britain and Northern Ireland, while the rest of the island became independent. Deep political, religious and cultural differences within Northern Ireland, between the majority population, who wished to remain British, and the minority population, who wished to be part of an independent Ireland, led to discrimination and economic and social inequalities, resulting in the Civil Rights movement of the 1960s and eventually to the outbreak of what has been termed 'The Troubles'.

As a result of a 30-year period of extreme violence and sectarian murder from the late 1960s to the late 1990s, more than 3,300 were killed in Northern Ireland. In 1998, a political agreement brokered by both the British and Irish governments recognised 'the birthright of all the people of Northern Ireland to identify themselves and be accepted as Irish or British, or both'. Power-sharing arrangements were put in place, which have led to the establishment of a new, devolved Northern Ireland Assembly in 2007.

A narrow concept of citizenship based on national identity is problematic in a divided society such as Northern Ireland. For example, a survey of 14–18-year-olds (Smyth and Scott, 2000) suggests that identity politics are deeply ingrained, with young people defining themselves as either Irish (42 per cent), British (23 per cent) or Northern Irish (18 per cent).

Since there is no consensus on nationality in Northern Ireland, or indeed the legitimacy of the state itself, the concept of citizenship remains problematic and contested. Any citizenship education curriculum must, therefore, go beyond simple 'patriotic' models that require uncritical loyalty to the nation state. One of the greatest challenges for citizenship education in Northern Ireland is whether or not it is possible to develop a concept of citizenship that is based on common rights and responsibilities rather than notions of national identity (Smith, 2003).

To address this issue, the Northern Ireland programme of Local and Global Citizenship takes an enquiry-based approach to exploring four core areas (Diversity and Inclusion; Equality and Justice; Human Rights and Social Responsibilities and Democracy and Active Participation). Young people are required to investigate these concepts through relevant local and global issues using case studies and resource materials that encourage 'active learning' (enquiry, information management, problem-solving and decision-making) and engagement with controversial and practical issues (for example, how to achieve a policing service that has the confidence of all sections of society). The programme also encourages exploration of what it means to be a citizen within a wider context, considering, for example, the increasing impacts of globalisation.

A similar form of citizenship education is being developed within non-formal education, through youth and community education programmes. With a view to not overburdening primary schools, citizenship is combined with health education within the Learning Area entitled 'Personal Development and Mutual Understanding'. Like Local and Global Citizenship, the programme encourages children to develop knowledge and understanding of the challenges and opportunities they may encounter in an increasingly diverse contemporary society; the skills, attitudes and values necessary for independent living, informed decision-making and responsible action and an understanding of their role in working for a more inclusive, just and democratic society.

Over the last five years, significant progress has been made in preparing schools for the statutory implementation of citizenship from September 2007. At post primary level, schools from all sectors have opted into a professional development programme that has provided seven in-service days for up to five teachers from each school. Civil society, the media and voluntary organisations have developed resources to support this area of the curriculum. Universities and Colleges of Education have also adapted their initial teacher education courses to include the preparation of student teachers for Local and Global Citizenship.

Apart from a Citizenship option within an optional GCSE entitled Learning for Life and Work, decisions about how Local and Global Citizenship will be assessed from age 4–14 have yet to be resolved. However, if we accept that 'what is assessed is what is valued' then citizenship requires some kind of an assessment profile. It will be important to ensure, therefore, that any mechanisms for the assessment of citizenship are informed by the values which underpin the concept itself, that is, that assessment of citizenship is to some extent active and democratic; that the issues explored are relevant to young people and the method of assessment involves the demonstration of skills as well as attitudes and dispositions associated with this area of learning.

An evaluation of the introduction of Local and Global Citizenship at Key Stage 3 commissioned by the curriculum authorities (CCEA) and undertaken by the UNESCO Centre at the University of Ulster is nearing completion. Spanning the preparatory four-year period from 2003 to 2007, it focuses on three levels of analysis: the impact of citizenship education on pupils and schools, the provision of in-service training programmes to teachers and the introduction of citizenship education into initial teacher education.

Initial findings from a pupil perspective suggest that young people have responded positively to active methodologies that have had a beneficial impact on their confidence, participation and relationships within schools, although less so on their civic and political engagement. There is consensus also that citizenship seems to have raised pupil expectations of democracy in schools and their awareness of the limitations of existing practice. Interestingly, while pupils' prefer to study local issues such as 'sectarianism' and 'conflict resolution' these are the least frequently addressed topics, while global issues to do with 'racism' and 'the environment' are the most common topics of study. The findings have also highlighted the critical role of the teacher, which raises questions about the values-base with which teachers enter their profession and the preparation they receive to teach sensitive and controversial issues.

EDUCATION FOR CITIZENSHIP IN SCOTLAND

Historically, Scotland has been ahead of other UK countries in addressing citizenship education in the curriculum. The introduction of Modern Studies, as a subject in 1962, has provided schools with opportunities to cover topical social and political issues and develop the political literacy of students (Maitles, 1999). The existence of Modern Studies has meant an evolution in approaches to citizenship education. There has been neither the need nor the inclination in Scotland for radical intervention and review in this area.

The current Scottish framework for education for citizenship is a case in point. It was established in *Education for Citizenship in Scotland: A Paper for Discussion and Development*, published in 2002 (LTS, 2002) following the outcome of a Review Group chaired by Professor Pamela Munn and a large-scale public consultation. The report provides a framework for the review and

development of education for citizenship for young people age 3–18. The framework is based on a definition of citizenship as the exercise of rights and responsibilities within communities, both of place and of interest. The aim of education for citizenship is described as the development of capability for thoughtful and responsible participation in political, economic, social and cultural life. The report argues that this aim cannot be encompassed within a single subject, whether an existing one or a new subject labelled 'citizenship education'. Rather, it calls on schools and early education settings to develop education for citizenship through four distinct contexts:

- opportunities for young people to participate in decision-making;
- learning and teaching in specific subjects;
- whole school and cross-curricular learning experiences; and
- opportunities for learning experiences in the community.

The Review Group concluded that the curricular requirements of education for citizenship could be achieved without any new subject by encouraging teachers to make more explicit the citizenship dimensions of existing subjects, such as Modern Studies.

Education for citizenship developments in Scotland have also emphasised the need for complementary whole school and cross-curricular activities, encouraging participatory approaches to decision-making and to learning and teaching and a wide range of community-based activities, including global citizenship, alongside work in subjects (LTS, 2007a, 2007b).

The 2002 framework has only advisory status and following its publication there has been a recognition that further strategies are required in order to make it realisable. Various initiatives from the Scottish Executive Education Department, supported by Her Majesty's Inspectorate of Education (HMIe) have attempted to provide these. An early supportive measure was the identification, in 2002, of Values and Citizenship as one of the five statutory National Priorities for Education. Since 2000 it has been the responsibility of all local authorities to formulate plans and gather evidence about the National Priorities. However, identification of meaningful measures for education for citizenship has proved problematic, and strategies around National Priorities have been superseded by developments related to *A Curriculum for Excellence* (HMI, 2003).

A Curriculum for Excellence (SEED, 2004) was published in November 2004, and now provides the overall framework for curriculum development in Scotland. It sets out a framework of values (wisdom, justice, compassion and integrity, as inscribed on the Scottish Mace), purposes (including producing responsible citizens, confident individuals and effective contributors) and principles (such as, challenge and enjoyment, breadth, personalisation and relevance) against which the curriculum is to be measured, and provides a template for a phased process of reform. Work is proceeding on a review of subjects and curricular areas 3–15, with various models under discussion of the way cross-cutting themes, like citizenship can permeate the subject framework. The last HMI report on education for citizenship (HMI, 2006) has been influential in this respect. The report points to many strengths in the system, but also to gains which may be planned for through *A Curriculum for Excellence*. It calls for closer consideration of the key role of schools in encouraging responsible personal and social values, and more systematic curriculum planning to ensure that education for citizenship is securely embedded.

In many respects *Curriculum for Excellence* is taking forward the ambition of the 2002 *Education for Citizenship in Scotland* framework. However, it remains to be seen how successfully the participatory approaches of education for citizenship, its promotion of controversial issues and its impetus towards community-based activities will be retained and embedded in wider national developments. For the time being

education for citizenship developments continue, in parallel, to monitor, inform and complement *A Curriculum for Excellence*.

CITIZENSHIP THROUGH PERSONAL AND SOCIAL EDUCATION IN WALES

The approach to citizenship education in Wales has long been marked by a national distinctiveness when set against the other UK countries. The hallmark, as in Scotland, has been evolution and revision, but with a particular emphasis on building consensus in educational policy-making in this area through partnership at all levels of society. Influenced by cultural and historical traditions, and facilitated by size of the country, the focus of citizenship education in Wales has been on its contribution, as part of a holistic approach, to strengthening community and celebrating Welsh culture. There has been much less emphasis on civic society and formal participation and much greater concentration on civil society and the roles and responsibilities of individuals in relation to their local and national communities. This has led to the promotion of citizenship through the community component of Personal and Social Education (PSE) rather than as a specific, separate subject or cross-curricular theme.

In the 1990s citizenship education was pursued through the theme of 'Community Understanding' as part of PSE in primary and secondary schools (CCW, 1991). By 2000, following devolution, the new Welsh Assembly published of a framework for PSE 5 to 16 (ACCAC, 2000). Personal and Social Education delivery was described as being around 10 aspects: social, community, physical, sexual, emotional, spiritual, moral, vocational, learning and environmental. The goal of PSE was defined as preparing learners to be personally and socially effective by providing learning experiences in which they could develop and apply skills, explore personal attitudes and values, and acquire appropriate knowledge and understanding. Specific aims included promoting self-respect, respect for others and for diversity, empowering learners to participate in their schools and communities as active responsible citizens and fostering positive attitudes and behaviour towards the environment and the principles of sustainable development locally, nationally and globally.

Three years later, in 2003, the Assembly declared that PSE was to become a statutory part of the 'basic curriculum' in Wales. Personal and Social Education was one of seven common requirements that schools should provide opportunities, where appropriate for pupil to develop and apply (ACCAC, 2003). These requirements were not separate subjects but cross-cutting themes that had to be delivered through subjects and across the whole curriculum. To support the introduction of statutory PSE, and a further sign of consensus policy-making, an 'All Wales PSE Network Group' was established. The Group included representatives from the Welsh Assembly, local authorities, voluntary sector organisations, youth agencies, as well as teachers. It was tasked with disseminating good practice in PSE, making links between formal and informal sectors and working with the Welsh Assembly on further developing a strategy for PSE in Wales. The Group's endeavours resulted in the publication of guidance on PSE to schools and local authorities.

Since 2003, the onus has been on providing further support and guidance to the promotion of particular aspects of PSE in schools and other sectors. A number of streams of development work have been successfully initiated. They include: the publication of a teaching pack for use in secondary schools; an action plan for embedding Education for Sustainable Development and Global Citizenship in all sectors of education (Welsh Assembly, 2005) and strengthening assessment through a GCSE Short Course in PSE and the piloting of a Welsh Baccalaureate that provides opportunities for active participation. The Welsh Assembly has also worked

tirelessly to promote the 'participation agenda' alongside PSE developments in order to increase the opportunities for all children and young people to have a say in the institutions (such as schools) and communities in which they are involved. To this end, and uniquely in the UK, school councils have been made statutory in all Welsh schools since 2006 with supporting training materials, youth forums have been set up across Wales and Funky Dragon, a Children and Young People's Assembly for Wales, has been established to provide a forum through which young people can voice their views on important issues direct to the Assembly.

Currently, the Welsh Assembly has initiated a wide-ranging review of the whole of the Welsh Curriculum, including the existing PSE framework, with a view to the introduction of a new curriculum in September 2008. The new curriculum will place more emphasis on skills development rather than knowledge acquisition and on young people receiving an education that is more relevant to their current and future lives.

A PSE working group is currently considering how the PSE framework should be adapted to reflect developments both in Welsh policy and wider societal issues. Specific elements of the framework which are under review include young peoples' entitlements, rights and responsibilities, pupil participation in decision-making, community participation and values education. Plans have already been announced to rationalise the 10 aspects of the existing framework into 5 key themes:

- health and emotional well-being;
- moral and spiritual development;
- active citizenship;
- sustainable development and global citizenship; and
- preparing for lifelong learning.

Further guidance will be published to support the implementation of the new PSE framework. The work underlines how the distinctive Welsh approach to citizenship, around community and culture, remains very much alive.

KEY CHALLENGES

The individual country descriptions highlight the many key challenges facing the development of citizenship education in the UK, now and in the future. The focus in this concluding section is on challenges across the UK as a whole. Available space means the identification of one key challenge concerning theory, policy, practice and research. The key challenge for:

- **theory** remains to provide a common, overarching working definition of citizenship education – what it is and what it is for – that is usable in all UK countries. This will not be easy but is essential in order to provide greater underpinning of evolving policy and practice;
- **policy** is to work through the tensions and contradictions inherent in where the power to make and enforce policy in this area lies. The current situation can best be described as one of 'policy busyness' at all levels, national, regional, local and school. The central Labour government, nationally devolved Assemblies in Belfast, Edinburgh and Cardiff, local authorities and schools all stake a claim to shape policy for citizenship education. The concern is that, with country and locally determined policies taking increasing precedence, the UK component of citizenship education and, in particular, the opportunity for young people to learn about the history and culture of all UK countries and the new devolved civic and political UK institutions will be neglected. That would be a missed opportunity;
- **practice** is to ensure the coherence and long-term sustainability of citizenship education in and beyond schools, by continuing to improve the quality of teaching, training, assessment and active citizenship opportunities, and demonstrating the relevance of citizenship education to a world class, modern education and training system; and
- **research** is to provide evidence-based advocacy for this area through the evaluation of citizenship education programmes and the sharing of outcomes within and across UK countries. The Citizenship Education Longitudinal Study

in England and the evaluation of Local and Global Citizenship in Northern Ireland will be important in this respect. England and Northern Ireland have also agreed to participate in the new IEA International Civic and Citizenship Education Study (ICCS) allowing the opportunity for national and international comparisons to be made.

Though citizenship education has made considerable strides in the UK over the past decade, in terms of policy development and evolving practice, it is still too early to make any assessment of its real impact and outcomes in England, Northern Ireland, Scotland and Wales. Indeed, with the Prime Minister, Gordon Brown, recently announcing potential constitutional reform, consideration of dropping the voting age to 16 and the setting up of a Commission to review young people's engagement and improve citizenship education as part of measures to 'give new life to the very idea of citizenship itself' (Brown, 2007), it is clear that developments in the UK still have some way to run in the coming years.

REFERENCES

Advisory Group on Education and Citizenship and the Teaching of Democracy in Schools (1998) *Education for Citizenship and the Teaching of Democracy in Schools* (Crick Report). London: QCA.

Advisory Council for Learning and Teaching in Scotland (2002) *Education for Citizenship in Scotland: A Paper for Discussion and Development*. Edinburgh: LTS.

Arnot, M. and Dillabough J.-A. (2001). *Challenging Democracy: International Perspectives on Gender, Education and Citizenship*. London: Routledge.

Blunkett, D. (2003) *Civil Renewal: A New Agenda*. London: CSV/Home Office.

Breslin, T. and Dufour, B. (eds) (2007) *Developing Citizens: A Comprehensive Introduction to Effective Citizenship Education in the Secondary School*. London: Hodder Murray.

Brown, G. (2007) Constitutional Reform Statement to Parliament, 3 July. Available:

http://www.pm.gov.uk/output/Page12274. asp Accessed: 7/07/07.

Cleaver, E., Ireland, E. Kerr, D. and Lopes, J. (2005) *Listening to Young People: Citizenship Education in England. Citizenship Education Longitudinal Study Third Annual Report.* (DfES Research Report 626). London: DfES.

Commission on Integration and Cohesion (2007) *Our Shared Future.* London: Department for Communities and Local Government.

Crick, B. (2000) *Essays on Citizenship.* London: Continuum.

Curriculum Council for Wales (1991) *Community Understanding, Advisory Paper 11.* Cardiff: CCW.

Deakin Crick, R., Coates, M., Taylor, M. and Ritchie, S. (2004) *A Systematic Review of the Impact of Citizenship Education on the Provision of Schooling.* London: EPPI – Centre, University of London.

Department for Children, Schools and Families (2007) *Guidance on the Duty to Promote Community Cohesion.* London: DCSF.

Department for Education and Skills (2007) *Diversity and Citizenship: Curriculum Review.*(Ajegbo Review) London: DfES.

Faulks, K. (2006) 'Education for citizenship in England's secondary schools: a critique of current principle and practice', *Journal of Education Policy*, 21 (1): 59–74.

Frazer, E. (2000) 'Citizenship education: anti-political culture and political education in Britain', *Political Studies*, 48: 88–103.

Further Education Funding Council (2000) *Citizenship for 16–19 Year Olds in Education and Training: Report of the Advisory Group to the Secretary of State for Education and Employment.* Coventry: FEFC.

Gearon, L. (2003) *How Do We Learn to Become Good Citizens? A Professional User Review of UK Research Undertaken for the British Educational Research Association.* Nottingham: BERA.

Great Britain Parliament House of Commons (2004) *The Children Bill.* London: The Stationery Office.

Hall, S. (2000) 'Multi-cultural citizens, mono-cultural citizenship?' In N. Pearce and J. Hallgarten (eds) *Tomorrow's Citizens. Critical Debates in Citizenship and Education.* London: IPPR.

Heater, D. (2001) *History of Citizenship.* Leicester: Allandale Online Publishing.

Her Majesty's Inspectorate of Education (2003) *How Good is Our School? Education for Citizenship,* Glasgow: HMIe.

Her Majesty's Inspectorate of Education (2006) *Education for Citizenship: A Portrait of Current Practice in Scottish Schools and Pre-school Centres,* Glasgow: HMIe.

Huddleston, T. and Kerr, D. (eds) (2006) *Making Sense of Citizenship: A Continuing Professional Development Handbook.* London: Hodder Murray.

Ireland, E., Kerr, D., Lopes, J. and Nelson, J. with Cleaver, E. (2006) *Active Citizenship and Young People: Opportunities, Experiences and Challenges in and Beyond School, Citizenship Education Longitudinal Study: Fourth Annual Report.* (DfES Research Report 732). London: DfES.

Jowell, R. and Park, A. (1998) *Young People, Politics and Citizenship: A Disengaged Generation?* London: Citizenship Foundation.

Kerr, D. (2005) 'Citizenship education in England – listening to young people: new insights from the Citizenship Education Longitudinal Study', *International Journal of Citizenship and Teacher Education*, 1 (1): 74–93.

Kerr, D. (1999) *Re-examining Citizenship Education: The Case of England.* Slough: NFER.

Kerr, D., Ireland, E., Lopes, J. and Craig, R. with Cleaver, E. (2004) *Making Citizenship Real. Citizenship Education Longitudinal Study Second Annual Report. First Longitudinal Survey* (DfES Research Report 531). London: DfES.

Kerr, D., Lopes, J., Nelson, J., White, K., Cleaver, E. and Benton, T. (2007) *Vision versus Pragmatism: Citizenship in the Secondary School Curriculum in England.* (DfES Research Report 845). London: DfES.

Learning and Teaching Scotland (2007a) *The Global Dimension in the Curriculum: Educating the Global Citizen.* Glasgow: LT Scotland.

Learning and Teaching Scotland (2007b) *Participation and Learning.* Glasgow: LT Scotland in association with Save the Children Scotland.

MacGregor, J. (1990) 'Helping today's children become tomorrow's citizens.' Speech at the Consultative Conference on Citizenship, Northampton, 16 February.

Maitles, H. (1999) Modern Studies Education. In T.G.K. Bryce and W. M. Humes (eds)

Scottish Education. Edinburgh: Edinburgh University Press.

Maylor, U. and Read, B. with Mendick, H., Ross, A. and Rollock, N. (2007) *Diversity and Citizenship in the Curriculum: Research Review*. (DfES Research Report 819). London: DfES.

McLaughlin, T.H. (2000) 'Citizenship education in England: Crick Report and beyond', *Journal of Philosophy of Education*, 34 (4): 541–70.

Office for Standards in Education (2005) *Citizenship in Secondary Schools: Evidence from OFSTED Inspections (2003/04)*. HMI Report 2335. London: OFSTED.

Office for Standards in Education (2006) *Towards Consensus?: Citizenship in Secondary Schools*. HMI Report 2666. London: OFSTED.

Osler, A. (2000) 'The Crick Report: difference, equality and racial justice', *The Curriculum Journal*, 11 (1): 25–37.

Potter, J. (2002) *Active Citizenship in Schools: A Good-Practice Guide to Developing a Whole-School Policy*. London: Kogan Page.

Qualifications and Curriculum Authority (1999) *Citizenship: Key Stages 3–4*. London: DFEE/QCA.

Qualifications and Curriculum Authority (2007a) *New Secondary Curriculum*. Available: http://www.qca.org.uk/qca_11717. aspx.Accessed: 17/08/07.

Qualifications and Curriculum Authority (2007b) Citizenship Programme of Study: Key Stage 4. Available: http://www.qca.org. uk/libraryAssets/media/Citizenship_KS4_ PoS.pdf Accessed: 17/08/07

Qualifications and Curriculum Authority for Wales (2000) *Personal and Social Education Framework*. Cardiff: ACCAC.

Qualifications and Curriculum Authority for Wales (2003) *Personal and Social Education Framework: Key Stages 1 to 4*. Cardiff: ACCAC.

Scottish Executive Education Department (2004) *A Curriculum for Excellence: The Curriculum Review Group*. Edinburgh: SEED.

Smith, A. (2003) 'Citizenship Education in Northern Ireland: beyond national identity?' *Cambridge Journal of Education*, 33 (1): 15–31.

Smyth, M. and Scott, A. (2000) *The Youthquest 2000 Survey*. INCORE, University of Ulster.

Tooley, J. (2000) *Reclaiming Education*. London: Cassell.

Welsh Assembly (2005) *Consultation Document on Education for Sustainable Development – A Strategy for Wales*. Cardiff: Welsh Assembly.

20

Education for Citizenship and Democracy in the United States

Carole L. Hahn

At the beginning of the twenty-first century, there is much interest in the US in the topic of education for citizenship and democracy. Numerous authors express dismay about declining levels of youth political engagement as reflected in voting rates and interest in following public issues; they wonder how to build on young people's preference for volunteering and community service activities to encourage deeper forms of civic engagement (Carnegie and CIRCLE, 2003; National Conference on Citizenship, 2006; Zukin et al., 2006).[1] These concerns have led to numerous local, state, and national initiatives to stimulate participatory citizenship in young people.

In exploring the topic of education for citizenship and democracy in the US, several contextual factors should be kept in mind. First, there is little agreement about the most appropriate definition of citizenship education. Broadly conceived, civic or citizenship education includes all of the ways in which young people come to think of themselves as citizens of local and cultural communities, the nation, and global society. It includes young people's socialization in the family,

experiences in schools and in out-of-school programs, numerous non-formal face-to-face interactions with members of their communities, and influences from the broader society. In the US there are hundreds of organizations from the Girl Scouts to professional organizations, such as the American Bar Association (lawyers) and the National Council for Social Studies (social studies educators), that sponsor programs to prepare youth for their citizenship role. People who think of themselves as civic educators and scholars who study citizenship education focus on different dimensions of the arenas in which citizenship education takes place, in particular the home, school, and out-of-school sites. In this chapter, I focus on the role of the school in citizenship education.

A second contextual factor to keep in mind is that citizenship education has a long history in the US. Since the founding of the country numerous scholars, policy makers, and citizens have written about the importance of educating young people for their role as citizens in a democracy. Yet, despite widespread agreement that schools should play a central role in such preparation, there have always been debates about how best to do that, with various camps advocating different approaches. In this chapter I briefly touch on the history of citizenship education and describe some of the traditions that have endured and are still shaping practice.

A third factor to consider in examining citizenship education in the US is that the educational system is decentralized; policies and practices are not uniform across the 50 states and 15,000 school districts. They vary from one state to the next and from one school district to the next, as well as among schools within districts and classrooms within a school. Nevertheless, there are forces that contribute to similarities across jurisdictions and it is possible to gain insights to prevailing policies and practices by examining available research. I draw on that research to describe trends in curriculum and instruction.

I begin this chapter by describing some of the history and different approaches to civic education. Next I describe the curriculum in civic education, both what is intended in official curriculum documents and what is widely implemented in schools. I discuss research on the effects of specially designed civic education programs and other instructional practices that have been associated with positive student outcomes. Finally, I discuss several promising lines of inquiry for future scholarship.

HISTORIES AND APPROACHES

Ever since Presidents Washington and Jefferson wrote about the importance of education to the preparation of citizens in the eighteenth century, Americans have placed a high priority on citizenship education (Carnegie and CIRCLE, 2003; Reuben, 2005). As mass public schooling spread in the nineteenth century, educators and the public expected the school as a whole, and the subject of social studies in particular, to prepare democratic citizens. The National Council for the Social Studies (NCSS), the professional association for social studies teachers, defines social studies as 'the integrated study of the social sciences and humanities to promote civic competence' and emphasizes that 'the primary purpose of social studies is to help young people develop the ability to make informed and reasoned decisions for the public good as citizens of a culturally diverse, democratic society in an interdependent world' (NCSS, 1994: 3). Whether individuals think of themselves as social studies teachers who teach history, civics, or an integrated subject called 'social studies' or whether they identify as history or civics/government teachers, it is clear that in the US the field of social studies is central to citizenship education for democracy.

Reflecting the long history of education for democratic citizenship, numerous scholars have contributed to an extensive historiography of social studies and citizenship education (Butts, 1980; Crocco and Davis, 1999, 2002; Evans, 2004; Hertzberg, 1981; Jenness, 1990; Lyberger, 1991; Reuben, 2005; Warren and Patrick, 2006; Woyshner, 2006; Woyshner et al., 2004). Woyshner (2006) identified two recurrent interpretative frameworks that have dominated historical analyses: the Progressive Era origins of social studies and civic education and a continuing struggle between the subjects of history and social studies. In the first framework, scholars attribute the key ideas about education for citizenship contained in the reports of the 1910–16 committees of the National Education Association (NEA) to Progressive ideology. The NEA committees recommended courses in community civics, Problems of Democracy, and modern history as elements of a social studies curriculum. In the second framework, scholars depict a continuing struggle from the 1890s to the present between groups advocating for social studies or for history as the best subject to prepare citizens. Recent scholars have added to the historical work by researching the histories of citizenship education for groups that were left out of the earlier histories of the field, such as women and girls; African-Americans,

Latina/os, and Asian-Americans; and gay, lesbian, bisexual, and transgendered (GLBT) individuals (Dilworth, 2006; Grimes, 2007; Ladson-Billings, 2004; Pak, 2000; Woyshner et al., 2004).

Although there has been widespread agreement that a primary purpose of schools in the US is to prepare citizens, there has never been agreement as to the best way to do that. Diverse approaches have been proposed over the years, with four approaches frequently cited in the social studies literature: citizenship transmission; social science; reflective inquiry; and informed social criticism (Nelson, 2001). Parker (1996a) categorized alternative approaches to citizenship education as traditional, progressive, and advanced. Traditionalists emphasize content knowledge (history and civics) and commitments to core democratic ideals. Progressives emphasize preparation for participatory aspects of democracy (deliberation and action). Parker argued that both of these views are inadequate because they approach unity and difference as requiring assimilation. He proposed an 'advanced' conception of democratic citizenship education that combines attention to the tensions inherent in a culturally plural democracy with participation. Extending such a view, proponents of multicultural and global approaches to citizenship education moved from the margins to the center of civic education discourse in the 1990s (Anderson, 1979; Banks, 1997; Banks et al., 2005). Additionally, Westheimer and Kahne (2004) proposed a typology for categorizing citizen education programs that is widely cited and has been used in evaluating some programs (Kahne et al., 2002). Differing programs emphasize preparing young people to be good citizens who are personally responsible, participatory or justice-oriented.[2]

Abowitz and Harnish (2006) identified several discourses of citizenship with correspondingly distinct approaches to citizenship education. They used discourse analysis to examine state curriculum documents and curricular materials produced by diverse organizations. They found that

Enlightenment-inspired citizenship discourses of civic republicanism and liberalism dominated the elementary and secondary curriculum and policy documents. Civic republicans, according to Abowitz and Harnish (2006), bemoan the level of students' civic knowledge and emphasize the importance of transmitting the heritage of US democracy. Civic republicans emphasize unity, consensus, and responsibility to society. The researchers found that this discourse was particularly evident in state curriculum standards and materials produced by some of the more politically conservative nonprofit organizations such as the Veterans of Foreign Wars and the Fordham Foundation. Further, they found that after September 11, 2001 the civic republicans emphasized patriotism. Abowitz and Harnish (2006) found evidence of political liberal discourse in the writings of some well-known civic educators who emphasize rights, reasoning, and deliberation. The researchers found examples of liberal discourse: in Parker's (2003) writing; in the document *The Civic Mission of the Schools* (Carnegie and CIRCLE, 2003); and in the NCSS journal, *Social Education*, following the terrorist attacks on September 11, 2001. They also found liberal discourse in the Kettering Foundation's *National Issues Forum* (NIF) materials that are used to teach students and adults how to deliberate about public problems and in some of the Center for Civic Education's (CCE) student materials.

Other researchers used the civic republican and liberal categories as well as communitarianism in conducting a content analysis of the *National Standards in Civics and Government* (Gonzales et al., 2001). They found that concepts associated with liberalism far outnumbered concepts associated with civic republicanism or communitarianism in the standards. Rights were mentioned twice as much as duties and responsibilities and there was little attention to participation. Thus, the voluntary national standards seemed to be sending one message (rights based) that was consistent with programs such as those sponsored by CCE and NIF, but some state standards and materials produced by conservative organizations sent another (civic republican) message. Turning from research on the history of citizenship education in the US and varied traditions that vie for attention, I next discuss the research on the intended and implemented curricula in schools across the country.

THE CURRICULUM

Standards

There is no national curriculum in the US. Rather, each state and school district sets the requirements within its jurisdiction. Nevertheless, in the 1990s Congress funded the development of voluntary national curriculum standards in civics and government (Center for Civic Education, 1994), history (National Center for History in the Schools, 1996), and geography (Geography Education Standards Project, 1994). Additionally, NCSS (1994) developed curriculum standards for social studies and the National Council on Economic Education (NCEE) (1997) developed voluntary standards in economics. All of these standards documents were rooted in the goal of preparing citizens of a democracy. Subsequent to the publication of the national documents, most states and many school districts wrote their own curriculum standards, sometimes referencing the national ones. In an age of accountability, many states also developed assessments to determine the extent to which students were attaining competencies specified in their standards. The Education Commission of the States' Center for Learning and Citizenship monitors state policies. According to their database in Spring 2007, all 50 states required their students to take a course in civics/government or at least to be taught material in civics and government (CIRCLE, 2007b); 21 states required students to take examinations in civics or social studies.

Assessments of student knowledge

The primary indicators of what students in the US are taught and learn in the area of civic education come from the National Assessment of Educational Progress (NAEP), referred to as 'the nations report card'.[3] NAEP assesses nationally representative samples of students at Grades 4, 8, and 12, when students are approximately ages 9, 13, and 17. Assessments in social studies, civics/government, history, and to a lesser extent, geography, provide information about 'typical' students' levels of achievement in civic education. Consistently, over the years students' civic knowledge scores tend to correlate with family income and parental education; White and Asian students tend to score higher than African-American and Hispanic students (NCES 1999, 2007; Niemi and Junn, 1998). In past years boys tended to have higher civic knowledge scores than girls, but that is no longer the case; there were no significant gender differences in achievement on the 1998 and 2006 civics assessments (NCES, 1999, 2007).

Another source of information about student knowledge, as well as school curriculum and classroom instruction, is the two-phased Civic Education (CivEd) Study of the International Association for the Evaluation of Educational Achievement (IEA). The US was one of 30 countries that participated in the study. In Phase 1, researchers in the US reviewed prior research, surveyed the 50 states, analyzed textbooks, and conducted focus groups with teachers and students in various locations across the country to develop a case study of civic education (Hahn, 1999, 2002). The purpose of the case study was to ascertain what young people were likely to learn in three domains:

1) democracy, political institutions, and rights and responsibilities of citizens;
2) national identity; and
3) social cohesion and diversity.

In Phase 2 of the IEA study tests and surveys were administered to a nationally representative sample of ninth graders – approximately 14 years old – and to teachers of civic-related subjects and administrators in the sampled schools (Baldi et al., 2001; Torney-Purta et al., 2001). The IEA study reinforced NAEP findings with respect to student knowledge by socio-economic level, race/ethnicity, and gender (Baldi, et al., 2001). Importantly, the IEA study provided much information about how 14-year-old students acquire their civic education.

Early experiences

Most children learn about civic ideals through elementary grade social studies lessons and celebrations of national holidays such as the 4 July, Thanksgiving, Martin Luther King Jr.'s birthday, and Presidents' Day. The flag is displayed in front of most schools and in many classrooms. The national anthem is often played at high school sports events and at 'pep rallies'. A morning flag salute accompanying a recitation of the pledge of allegiance to the flag are customary in many elementary and middle schools, as well as some high schools, although this is not a universal practice (Hahn, 1999, 2002).[4]

Courses

At the time of the IEA study, students in about one-third of the states had a course in civics in Grade 8 or 9, with most states requiring such a course later in high school (Hahn, 1999, 2002). In addition, most students learn about democracy, political institutions, and rights and responsibilities of citizens, as well as about the history of political institutions in US history and state history courses in Grades 5 to 9 (and later in high school). In NAEP assessments, as well as in the IEA study, more than 70 per cent of students in Grades 8 and 9 said they studied the US Constitution and Congress over the previous year; that compared to fewer than

half who said they studied about other countries' governments and international organizations (Baldi et al., 2001; NCES 1999, 2007).

Importantly, students who studied social studies every day had higher scores on the IEA civic knowledge test than students with less frequent instruction (Baldi et al., 2001). Students who reported studying topics like the Constitution had higher civic knowledge scores than those who did not study those topics, and the benefit of this instruction was especially pronounced for Hispanic students (Torney-Purta and Barber, 2004; Torney-Purta et al., 2006). Furthermore, civic knowledge was associated with students' expectation of voting as adults (Torney-Purta et al., 2001). In a longitudinal study of a nationally representative sample of students, researchers found that civic knowledge scores of twelfth-graders were statistically significant predictors of young adults' actual voting eight years after high school (Hart et al., 2007).

In several studies researchers found that students who took courses in civics/government or other social sciences had higher levels of civic knowledge than students without such instruction, although the relationship between knowledge and simply taking a course tends to be weak (Hart et al., 2007; Niemi and Junn, 1998). The way in which courses are taught seems to be of greater importance, as I discuss later. Nevertheless, the fact that courses have some effect on civic knowledge is noteworthy.

Additionally, in yet another study of a nationally representative sample, 48 per cent of high school students reported that their interest in politics and national issues increased as a result of taking courses in government and politics; that compared to 40 per cent who said the courses had no impact on their interest and only 8 per cent who said that their interest decreased (Zukin et al., 2006).

Textbooks

To ascertain the content of the intended curriculum, in Phase 1 of the CivEd study researchers examined widely used textbooks for Grades 7 through 9 civics and US history courses; they found that the different books covered almost identical topics, in the same sequence and conveyed similar messages (Avery and Simmons, 2000/2001). The civics books emphasized the structure and function of national, state, and local levels of government. They began with a discussion of representative democracy and presented the US Constitution as the foundation of government. They followed the same sequence in discussing the three branches of government: Legislative, Executive, and Judicial. The US history books followed a chronological narrative of US history, beginning with English antecedents, colonial history, and the American Revolution and proceeding through the westward movement, the Civil War, and industrialization to the Progressive Era, two World Wars, and the Civil Rights movement.

Individual rights played a prominent role in all of the textbooks; references to citizens' duties or responsibilities were far less frequent (Avery and Simmons, 2000/2001). All of the books that were examined depicted the country as a 'nation of immigrants'. The history books all contained discussions of slavery, the Civil War, Reconstruction, segregation, and the Civil Rights movement, as well as women's suffrage and immigration at different periods in history. The books told a story of expanding rights through the struggles of individuals and social movements. However, despite a concerted effort by publishers since the 1970s to give more attention to minorities and women than they had in the past, the books that were published in the 1990s still included many fewer women than men, and very few Hispanics and Asian-Americans (Avery and Simmons, 2000/2001).

Student views

In focus group interviews held in different parts of the country, 14-year-old students and middle and high school social studies teachers reported that the topics presented in the textbooks were the ones covered in classes (Hahn, 1999, 2002). With respect to teaching about social cohesion and diversity, students reported studying about slavery, the oppression of Native Americans, the internment of Japanese-Americans in World War II, and the women's suffrage and Civil Rights movements. They were knowledgeable about past injustices and about citizens who fought for 'equality and justice for all'.

Interestingly, as students recounted the narrative of the nation's history they often used terms such as 'we,' 'us,' and 'our' (Hahn, 1999, 2002). This tendency toward identifying with the national narrative (even when students' own ancestors were not part of the dominant group) was also found by other researchers (Barton and Levstik, 1998). Overall, unlike adults who fiercely debated whether the national unity or cultural diversity approach to citizenship education was preferable, the young people in the focus groups and in Barton and Levstik's (1998) study seemed to feel that diversity and unity existed simultaneously in their country. Other researchers, however, found that some samples of African-American students identified with a counter narrative of oppression (Epstein, 2000; Ladson-Billings, 2004) and some students said they had few opportunities to explore issues of diversity (Kahne et al., 2000).

Overall, the IEA study, as well as several other studies, reveals that many of the civic topics young people study in school are quite similar and that, for the most part, such content is presented as uncontested and non-controversial. The IEA study seems to indicate that many students receive a mixed message, reflecting some civic republican elements (unity out of diversity, consensus) and some liberal (rights-centered) elements. That is not to say, however, that students everywhere receive the same education for citizenship. Indeed, there is much variety in the ways in which citizenship education is delivered, as can be seen in the next section.

CLASSROOM- AND SCHOOL-BASED INSTRUCTIONAL ACTIVITIES

From the IEA CivEd and other studies, it appears that classes differ widely with regard to variety in instructional activities (Hahn, 1998, 1999, 2002; Rubin, 2007). Some teachers use many activities, and others very few. 'Most students seem to be in classes that fall between the two extremes, with frequent teacher talk and student recitation related to the textbook and, periodically, a simulation, written project, or discussion of a current issue' (Hahn, 1999: 87). Although most students report reading from the textbook and filling out worksheets, close to 75 per cent of students say they write reports, watch videos, and discuss current events in their social studies classes (Baldi et al., 2001; NCES, 1999, 2007). About one third of students in Grades 8 and 12 report participating in role-playing exercises and mock (simulated) trials (NCES, 2007). IEA focus group teachers and students reported widespread use of simulations, such as of historic events like the Constitutional Convention.

Issues discussion

One instructional activity that has received much attention from researchers is discussion of controversial issues. Many civic educators emphasize that in a democracy students need practice in deliberating about public issues (Evans and Saxe, 1996; Hahn, 1996a; Ochoa-Becker, 2007; Parker, 1996b, 2006). Furthermore, there is considerable evidence from samples of students in the US that students are more likely to develop civic/political knowledge, political interest, political efficacy, and a sense of civic duty if they experience such discussions in their high school classes (Ehman, 1980; Hahn, 1996a, 1998; Niemi and Junn, 1998).

In the IEA study an open climate for discussion was related to both civic knowledge and expectations of voting for the US sample (Campbell, 2005; Torney-Purta et al., 2001). Further, young people who debated issues in class are more likely to be civically and politically engaged in terms of following political news most of the time, being involved in organizations outside of school, having signed a petition, participated in a boycott, attended community meetings, and raised money for a charity (Zukin et al., 2006).

In a Chicago study which controlled for student prior beliefs and demographic variables, the researchers used a measure they called classroom civic learning activities, which included learning about problems in society, learning about current events, studying issues about which one cares, as well as experiencing an open climate for discussion. The researchers found, using a regression analysis, the impact of classroom civic learning opportunities overall on civic commitments was sizeable. When the researchers disaggregated the various learning opportunities, being required by teachers to keep up with politics and government and learning about ways to improve one's community were 'particularly consequential' (Kahne and Sporte, 2007: 19). Studying topics I care about, meeting civic role models, and open classroom discussions, were also important, but in descending order of magnitude.

Unfortunately, the evidence indicates that most students are encouraged to speak and express their views on non-controversial topics; many rarely examine issues about which citizens disagree (Baldi et al., 2001; Zukin et al., 2006: 143). It is not unusual for teachers and students to claim that they participated in class 'discussions' that followed a persistent pattern: the teacher asks a question to which he or she knows the answer, the student responds, and the teacher reinforces the correct answer or corrects an incorrect one, then moves on to the next question (Blankenship, 1990; Kahne et al., 2000). Further, there is some evidence that students in urban schools serving low-income minority students may have less opportunity than students in suburban schools to deliberate about public issues as will be discussed later.

Special civic education programs

Evaluators of a number of carefully developed civic education programs that are widely used across the country have found that students who participate in particular programs that engage them in explorations of public issues benefit in a variety of ways. When program participants were compared to similar groups of students who did not participate in the programs, participants tended to show increased knowledge, a greater tendency to follow the news and discuss political issues with family and peers, increased political interest and efficacy, increased desire to participate in civic life, and greater commitments to participatory citizenship and justice-oriented citizenship (Bennett and Soule, 2005; Broudy, 1994; Kahne et al., 2002; Leming, 1993; McDevitt and Chaffee, 1998, 2000; McDevitt and Kiousis, 2006; Peng, 2000; Vontz et al., 2000).[5]

Extra-curricular activities

In addition to providing civic experiences within classrooms, schools offer diverse opportunities for students to learn democratic citizenship (Hahn, 1999, 2002). Middle and high school students elect leaders in the band, on sports teams, and in clubs, as well as to membership on student councils. Many schools hold mock elections to correspond with state and national elections. Some schools sponsor mock trial programs, supported by their state bar association. Whereas these activities are designed to teach knowledge, skills, and attitudes for participatory democratic citizenship, others are designed to teach students to be law-abiding citizens and/or to work to improve their communities. In some elementary and middle schools students are given citizenship grades for good behavior or are selected to be Citizen of the Month. Some middle schools sponsor programs in conflict resolution and peer mediation.

In some schools students participate in state and nationally sponsored experiential programs, while in other schools, few such programs are offered. For example, in the CivEd study, school administrators in 11 per cent of schools reported that their school sponsored no civic-related programs, while others reported that they had several programs (Baldi et al., 2001). Furthermore within a single school some students participate in many activities while others participate in none. In the focus groups, students said that they learned much about democracy and about social cohesion and diversity from participating in extra-curricular activities, such as team sports and band (Hahn, 1999, 2002). Consistent with those claims, ninth graders who participated in extra-curricular activities scored higher on the IEA civic knowledge test than students without such participation (Baldi et al., 2001).

Importantly, participation in extra-curricular activities in high school was associated with higher rates of volunteering and voting in presidential elections eight years after high school graduation (Hart et al., 2007). Instrumental types of activities that support the school community, such as student government, working on school publications and participating in service activities, had a stronger relationship with adult volunteering than did expressive activities, such as participating in the band or sports; the specific type of activity did not affect voting. Earlier researchers found that women who were active in high school activities were the most likely to become members of and leaders in community organizations as adults up to 14 years after finishing high school (Damico et al., 1998). Being a leader in high school, such as a student council officer or newspaper editor, in particular, increased the likelihood of women's later civic activism.

Service learning

One type of co-curricular or extra-curricular activity that has become quite prevalent in US schools is service learning, whereby students do volunteer work in the community. Indeed, on the IEA CivEd questionnaires, 50 per cent of US 14-year-olds reported that they had participated in activities to help in the community, through school or religious or other organizations. Additionally, 24 per cent of school administrators reported that their school offered some form of service learning (Baldi et al., 2001).

Researchers have concluded that service-learning programs have positive effects on civic-political outcomes when students engage in problem solving about community problems to accompany their voluntary work (Billig et al., 2005; Torney-Purta et al., 2007). Additionally, programs are effective if they last at least a semester, are linked to curriculum standards, involve close contact with those served, and provide challenging reflection opportunities (Billig et al., 2005). Students who engage in civic-political action (working to influence policies or to get someone elected to office) score higher than students in other types of service learning projects on measures of civic knowledge and civic dispositions.

In the study of Chicago high school students, which controlled for student prior attitudes and a variety of demographic and contextual variables, the impact of experiencing service learning on civic commitments was sizeable (Kahne and Sporte, 2007). That is, students who participated in service learning were more likely than peers who did not participate in service learning to agree that in the next three years they expected to be involved in improving their community and being active in community issues is their responsibility. Importantly, in another large-scale longitudinal study, high school community service, regardless of whether it was required or voluntary, predicted adult voting and volunteering, after controlling for other relevant demographic variables (Hart et al., 2007).

Several researchers found that female students in the US tend to engage in community service activities more than do their male counterparts and the gender differences

continue into young adulthood (Chapin, 2001; Jenkins, 2005; Marcelo et al., 2007; Zukin et al., 2006).

Community variation

In the IEA study, focus-group teachers in several urban schools said that it was difficult to teach about democracy and speaking one's opinion when the atmosphere of the school worked against that. They explained that in many classes in their school, students were expected to be quiet, listen and take notes in their seats, rather than to participate in discussions. School policies emphasized order in the halls and on the school grounds (Hahn, 1999, 2002). There is an accumulating body of evidence that extends this point, demonstrating that schools serving students from different social and economic subcultures provide very different contexts for learning citizenship. In a number of case studies, researchers found that students in diverse communities, including a Midwestern rural community, a Northeastern urban working class community, a Southeastern suburban community, several Southwestern rural communities with substantial numbers of Native American students, and a Mexican-American community in Texas, have very different experiences of learning citizenship (Conover and Searing, 2000; Hart and Atkins, 2002; Martin and Chiodo, 2007; Rubin, 2007). Students in one working class urban community and Mexican-American students in another community participated in fewer extra-curricular and out-of-school groups and experienced less discussion of political issues in school than did students in predominantly White rural and suburban communities studied. Reinforcing findings from the IEA focus groups, researchers found that students in the urban communities studied were the least likely of the groups to report frequent in-class discussions about political issues or to experience a variety of instructional activities in which they learned to practice democratic citizenship (Conover and

Searing, 2000; Rubin, 2007). Students in the rural communities were most likely to think of a citizen as someone who is a member of a community and a good citizen as someone who helps others in the community; students in the suburban, urban, and immigrant (Mexican-American) communities were more likely to think of a citizen as a person with rights and duties (Conover and Searing, 2000; Martin and Chiodo, 2007). Students in the different communities also had differing conceptions of civic duties. As researchers study experiences of students in differing contexts, they are revealing the importance of understanding socio-cultural context and civic learning.

FUTURE SCHOLARSHIP

Many researchers are currently exploring different aspects of education for citizenship and democracy in the US. Amid such activity several lines of inquiry appear to be particularly promising. For example, increasing numbers of scholars are gathering qualitative data in purposefully selected classes and schools to gain insight into how students experience civic education in particular contexts. Some of these studies focus on school-based instruction (Alviar-Martin, 2008; Hahn, 1991, 1996b; Hess, 2002; Marri, 2005; Niemi and Niemi, 2007; Pace, 2008; Rubin, 2007). Others investigate young people's learning about the civic and political arena in after-school programs and service-learning programs sponsored by school and non-school organizations (Bixby, 2008; Westheimer and Kahne, 2004). In all of these studies, researchers emphasize that civic-political learning occurs through social interaction and that parents, teachers, and community leaders can foster civic-political engagement by planning for deliberation about issues through interaction across difference (racially, ethnically, and by viewpoint). Through cross-case analyses, scholars will continue to learn how educators who use

diverse sites as laboratories for democracy effectively prepare young people for citizenship in a multicultural democracy. These qualitative studies also reveal challenges to effective citizenship education in particular settings.

Quantitative studies of student knowledge, skills, and attitudes enable researchers to compare samples across time and space. Using nationally representative samples, NAEP assessments provide valuable information about variables associated with student knowledge and the 1999 IEA study provides information about student attitudes. Researchers conducting secondary analyses using these large data sets are revealing insights about student, class/school, and country level variables that are important to civic learning (Torney-Purta et al., 2007; Torney-Purta et al., 2006; Torney-Purta and Richardson, 2004). Researchers working with purposefully selected samples can use the instruments developed and validated in these large-scale studies (See Flanagan et al., 2007; Homana et al., 2006) in combination with rich qualitative data about particular contexts.

In recent years, most of the research on education for citizenship in the US focuses on middle and high school students and schools (exceptions are Angell, 2004; Ochoa-Becker et al., 2001). Studies are needed of how younger children make meaning of the civic-political world and how educators can create environments that are conducive to learning democracy.

Although scholars acknowledge that one's standpoint by gender, race/ethnicity, socio-economic status, and sexual orientation can affect how one sees oneself as a citizen in a democracy, empirical studies of how young people make meaning of the civic-political arena in light of their identity markers are not yet available. For example, Gay-Straight Alliances in some public schools are sites for civic education as gay and straight students work together for civic and political rights of LGBT individuals (Russell, 2002). A few scholars have begun to study the civic education experiences of immigrant and refugee youth. Womanist scholars emphasize that race, class, and gender intersect, for example, when African American (or Latina or White) women from middle and low-income families have both similar and differing experiences from one another; scholars do not yet know how such similarities and differences effect youth becoming citizens. Hopefully, in the near future researchers will provide new insights about citizenship education from such diverse viewpoints.

Many scholars recommend that citizenship education in the twenty-first century should address the reality that citizenship is complex, multileveled, flexible, and fluid. However, there is to date little empirical research in that vein. A few researchers have begun to focus on how students come to think of themselves as simultaneously citizens of cultural and local communities, as well as national and global communities (Alviar-Martin, 2008, Myers, 2006). We can expect to see more case studies along this line in the future.

There is considerable research from both qualitative and quantitative studies that underline the importance of issues investigation and discussion, and the need to connect service learning to investigation of related policy issues. However, this research tends to focus on young people at one point in their lives, or to be cross sectional in design. Longitudinal studies are much needed to complement the few that exist.

One of the most promising lines of research is reflected in this Handbook. Researchers from diverse civic-political cultures are increasingly looking at the experiences of youth in the US along with those of samples socialized in other national contexts. As a result scholars are beginning to learn much about the importance of the socio-cultural context of civic and political learning globally.

NOTES

1 There was a steady decline in youth voting rates from the 1970s through the 1990s; however, in 1992, 2004, 2006, and 2008, the numbers of 18–29 year-olds voting increased (CIRCLE, 2007a; The National Conference on Citizenship, 2006; Marcelo et al., 2007). In addition to considering voting rates, researchers note that the youngest cohort of voters (the generation born after 1976) express less interest in following political issues or engaging in traditional forms of political activity than did earlier cohorts at their age (Campbell, 2005; Zukin et al., 2006). However, they participate in civic activities, such as volunteering, raising money for charities, and boycotting or buycotting at rates comparable to older generations.

2 Westheimer and Kahne (2004) argued that programs such as character education and many service-learning programs were based on conceptions of good citizens as individuals who work hard, pay taxes, obey laws, recycle, and volunteer to help the unfortunate. Because those traits could be valued in authoritarian as well as democratic regimes, the researchers decided not to study such programs, instead focusing on programs that were rooted in democratic conceptions of citizenship.

3 There are no national examinations that report individual student knowledge. However, approximately half of the states require that students pass a state social studies test that includes civic knowledge items to graduate from high school. Most assessment is done by individual class teachers who assess students for their understanding of a unit of instruction or a chapter in the textbook. The tests are often of a multiple-choice format with a few essay items. Some teachers use performance or authentic assessments, such as writing a persuasive letter to an official or to a newspaper.

4 Though required by many state laws, a flag salute is irregularly enforced and it has been challenged in courts, particularly, the 'under God' phrase.

5 The programs that are widely used across the country for which there are published evaluation reports are: *Kids Voting, USA*; *We the People: Project Citizen* and *We The People: The Citizen and the Constitution* from the Center for Civic Education; Kettering's *National Issues Forum*; and *City Works* from the Constitutional Rights Foundation.

REFERENCES

Alviar-Martin, T. (2008) *Seeking Cosmopolitan Citizenship: A Comparative Case Study of Two International Schools*. PhD dissertation, Emory University, Atlanta, USA.

Anderson, L. (1979) *Schooling and Citizenship in a Global Age*. Bloomington, IN: Social Studies Development Center, Indiana University.

Angell, A. (2004) 'Making Peace in Elementary Classrooms: A Case for Class Meetings', *Theory and Research in Social Education*, 32 (1): 98–104.

Avery, P.G. and Simmons, A.M. (2000/2001) 'Civic Life as Conveyed in U.S. Civics and History Textbooks', *International Journal of Social Education*, 15 (2): 105–130.

Baldi, S., Perie, M., Skidmore, D., Greenberg, E. and Hahn, C. (2001) *What Democracy Means to Ninth-graders: US Results from the International IEA Civic Education Study*. Washington, D.C.: National Center for Education Statistics, U.S. Department of Education.

Banks, J.A. (1997) *Educating Citizens in a Multicultural Society*. New York: Teachers' College Press.

Banks, J.A., Banks, C., Cortes, C., Hahn, C., Merryfield, M., Moodley, K., Murphy-Shigamatsu, S., Osler, A., Park, C. and Parker, W.C. (2005) *Democracy and Diversity: Principles and Concepts for Educating Citizens in a Global Age*. Seattle, WA: Center for Multicultural Education, University of Washington.

Barton, K. and Levstik, L. (1998) 'It Wasn't a Good Part of History: National Identity and Students', Explanations of Historical Significance. *Teachers' College Record*, 99 (3): 478–513.

Bennett, S.F. and Soule, S. (2005, April) *We The People: The Citizen and the Constitution: 2005 National Finalists' Knowledge of and Support For American Democratic Institutions and Processes*. Calabasas, CA: Center for Civic Education. Accessed at www.civiced.org on June 1, 2007.

Blankenship, G. (1990) 'Classroom Climate, Global Knowledge, Global Attitudes, Political Attitudes', *Theory and Research in Social Education*, 18(4): 363–386.

Billig, S., Root, S. and Jesse, D. (2005) *The Impact of Participation in Service-Learning on High School Students' Civic Engagement*. CIRCLE Working Paper 33. Accessed at www.civicyouth.org on June 9, 2007.

Bixby, J. (2008) 'Working for Obama', in Janet S. Bixby and Judith L. Pace (ed.) (2008), *Educating Democratic Citizens in Troubled Times: Qualitative Studies of Current Efforts*.

Albany, New York: State University of New York Press.

Blankenship, G. (1990) 'Classroom Climate, Global Knowledge, Global Attitudes, Political Attitudes', *Theory and Research in Social Education*, 18 (4): 363–386.

Broudy, R.A. (1994) *Secondary Education and Political Attitudes: Examining the Effects on Political Tolerance of the We the People ... Curriculum*. Calabasas: Center for Civic Education.

Butts, R.F. (1980) *The Revival of Civic Learning: A Rationale for Citizenship Education in American Schools*. Bloomington, IN: Phi Delta Kappan Foundation.

Campbell, D.E. (2005, February) *Voice in the Classroom: How an Open Classroom Environment Facilitates Adolescents' Civic Development*. CIRCLE Working Paper 28. Accessed at www.civicyouth.org on June 9. 2007.

Carnegie Corporation of New York and CIRCLE: The Center for Information & Research on Civic Learning & Engagement (2003) *The Civic Mission of Schools*. New York: Author.

Center for Civic Education (1994) *National Standards for Civics and Government*. Calabasas, CA: Author.

Chapin, J.R. (2001) 'From Eighth Grade Social Studies to Young Adulthood Voting and Community Service: National Education Longitudinal Study of 1988 Eighth Graders', *The International Social Studies Forum*, 1 (1): 33–44.

CIRCLE (2007a, January) 'Youth Turnout Increases for Second Election in a Row'. *Around the CIRCLE: Research and Practice*. Accessed at www.civicyouth.org/?m=200701 on February 22, 2008.

CIRCLE (2007b, April) 'Four Years after the Civic Mission of Schools Report'. Around the CIRCLE: Research and Practice. Accessed at www.civicyouth.org/?p=116 on February 22, 2008.

Conover, P.J. and Searing, D. (2000) 'A Political Socialization Perspective', in L. M. McDonnell, P.M. Timpane and R. Benjamin (eds), *Rediscoverying the Democratic Purposes of Education*. Lawrence, KS: University Press of Kansas. pp. 91–124.

Crocco, M.S. and Davis, O.L. (eds) (1999) *Bending the Future to Their Will: Civic*

Women, Social Education, and Democracy. Lanham, MD: Rowman & Littlefield.

Crocco, M.S. and Davis, O.L. (eds) (2002) *Building a Legacy: Women in Social Education 1784–1984.* Silver Spring, MD: National Council for the Social Studies.

Damico, A., Damico, S. and Conway, M. (1998) 'The Democratic Education of Women: High School and Beyond', *Women and Politics*, 19 (1): 1–31.

Dilworth, P.P. (2006) 'Widening the Circle: African American Perspectives on Moral and Civic Learning', in Donald Warren and John J. Patrick (eds), *Civic and Moral Learning in American Schools.* New York: Palgrave Macmillan. pp. 103–118.

Ehman, L. (1980) 'The American School and the Political Socialization Process', *Review of Educational Research*, 50 (1): 99–119.

Epstein, T. (2000) 'Adolescents' Perspectives on Racial Diversity in US History: Case Studies from an Urban Classroom', *American Educational Research Journal*, 37 (1): 185–214.

Evans, R. (2004) *The Social Studies Wars: What Should We Teach the Children?* New York: Teachers' College Press.

Evans, R. and David W.S. (eds) *The Handbook on Teaching Social Issues.* Washington, D.C.: National Council for the Social Studies.

Flanagan, C., Syvertsen, A. and Stout, M. (2007) *Civic Measurement Models: Tapping Adolescents' Civic Engagement.* CIRCLE Working Paper 55. Accessed at civic.youth.org/research/products/working_papers.htm on June 1, 2007.

Geography Education Standards Project (1994) *Geography for Life: National Geography Standards, 1994.* Washington, D.C.: National Geographic Research and Exploration.

Gonzales, M., Reidel, E., Avery, P. and Sullivan, J. (2001) 'Rights and Obligations in Civic Education: A Content Analysis of the National Standards for Civics and Government', *Theory and Research in Social Education*, 29 (1): 109–128.

Grimes, P. (2007) 'Teaching Democracy before Brown: Civic Education in Georgia's African American Schools 1930–1954', *Theory and Research in Social Education*, 35 (1): 9–31.

Hahn, C.L. (1991) *Classroom Climate: Complementary Roles of Qualitative and Quantitative Research.* Paper presented at the annual meeting of the College and University Faculty Assembly of the National Council for the Social Studies. Washington, D.C.

Hahn, C.L. (1996a) 'Research on Issues-Centered Social Studies', in Ronald Evans and David Warren Saxe (ed), *Handbook on Teaching Social Issues.* Washington, D.C.: National Council for the Social Studies. pp. 25–41.

Hahn, C.L. (1996b) 'Gender and Political Learning', *Theory and Research in Social Education*, 24 (1): 8–35.

Hahn, C.L. (1998) *Becoming Political: Comparative Perspectives on Citizenship Education.* Albany, NY: State University of New York Press.

Hahn, C.L. (1999) 'Challenges to Civic Education in the United States', in Judith Torney-Purta, John Schwille and JoAnn Amadeo (eds), *Civic Education Across Countries: Twenty Four National Case Studies from the IEA Civic Education Project.* Amsterdam: The International Association for the Evaluation of Educational Achievement. ED 431 705. pp. 583–607.

Hahn, C.L. (2002) 'Education for democratic citizenship: One nation's story', in Walter Parker (ed.), *Education for Democracy: Contexts, Curricula, Assessments.* Greenwich, CT: Information Age Publishing. pp. 63–92.

Hart, D. and Atkins, R. (2002) 'Civic Competence in Urban Youth', *Applied Developmental Science*, 6 (4): 227–236.

Hart, D., Donnelly, T.M., Youniss, J. and Atkins, R. (2007) 'High School Community Service as a Predictor of Adult Voting and Volunteering', *American Educational Research Journal*, 44 (1): 197–219.

Hertzberg, H. (1981) *Social Studies Reform 1880–1980: A Report of Project SPAN.* Boulder, Colorado: Social Science Education Consortium.

Hess, D. (2002) 'How High School Students Experience and Learn from the Discussion of Controversial Public Issues', *Journal of Curriculum and Supervision*, 17 (4): 283–314.

Homana, G., Barber, C. and Torney-Purta, J. (2006) *School Citizenship Education Climate Assessment.* National Center for Learning and Citizenship. Accessed at www.ecs.org./qna on September 2, 2007.

Jenkins, K. (2005, June) *Gender and Civic Engagement: Secondary Analysis of Survey Data*. CIRCLE: The Center for Information and Research on Civic Learning & Engagement. Accessed on at www.civicyouth.org January 10, 2007.

Jenness, D. (1990) *Making Sense of Social Studies*. New York: MacMillan.

Kahne, J., Chi, B. and Middaugh, E. (2002, August) *City Works Evaluation Summary*. Accessed at www.crf-org on June 1, 2007.

Kahne, J., Rodriquez, M., Smith, B. and Thiede, K. (2000) 'Developing Citizens for Democracy', *Theory and Research in Social Education*, 28 (3): 311–338.

Kahne, J. and Sporte, S. (2007, April) *Developing Citizens: A Longitudinal Study of School, Family, and Community Influences on Students' Commitments to Civic Participation*. A paper presented at the annual meeting of the American Educational Research Association, Chicago.

Knight, A.K. and Harnish, J. (2006) 'Contemporary Discourses of Citizenship', *Review of Educational Research*, 76 (4): 653–690.

Ladson-Billings, G. (2004) 'Culture Versus Citizenship: The Challenge of Racialized Citizenship in the United States', in James A. Banks (ed.), *Diversity and Citizenship Education: Global Perspectives*. San Francisco: Jossey-Bass. pp. 99–126.

Leming, R.S. (1993) *An Evaluation of the Instructional Effects of the We the People ... The Citizen and the Constitution Program Using 'With Liberty and Justice for All*, Bloomington, IN: Social Studies Development Center.

Lyberger, M.B. (1991) 'The Historiography of Social Studies: Retrospect, Circumspect, and Prospect', in James P. Shaver (ed.), *Handbook of Research on Social Studies Teaching and Learning*. New York: MacMillan. pp. 3–15.

Marcelo, K., Lopez, M.H. and Kirby, E.H. (2007, March) *Civic Engagement Among Young Men and Women*. CIRCLE: The Center for Information and Research on Civic Learning & Engagement. Accessed on from www.civicyouth.org April 2, 2007.

Marri, A.R. (2005) 'Building a Framework for Classroom-based Multicultural Democratic Education: Learning from Three Skilled Teachers', *Teachers College Record*, 107 (5): 1036–1059

Martin, L.A. and Chiodo, J.J. (2007) 'Good Citizenship: What Students in Rural Schools Have to Say about It', *Theory and Research in Social Education*, 35 (1), 112–134.

McDevitt, M. and Chafee, S.H. (1998) 'Second Chance Political Socialization: 'Trickle up' Effects of Children on Parents', in Thomas J. Johnson, Carol E. Hays, and Scott P. Hays (eds), *Engaging the Public: How Government and the Media can Reinvigorate American Democracy*. Lanham, MD: Rowman and Littlefield. pp. 57–66.

McDevitt, M. and Chafee, S.H. (2000) 'Closing Gaps in Political Communication and Knowledge Effects of a School Intervention', *Communication Research*, 27 (3), 259–292.

McDevitt, M. and Kiousis, S. (2006, August) *Experiments in Political Socialization: Kids Voting USA as a Model for Civic Education Reform*. CIRCLE Working Paper 49. Accessed at www.civicyouth.org on January 21, 2007.

Myers, J.P. (2006) Rethinking the Social Studies Curriculum in the Context of Globalization: Education for Global Citizenship in the U.S.', *Theory and Research in Social Education*, 34 (3): 370–394.

National Center for Education Statistics (1999) *NAEP 1998: Civics Report Card for the Nation*. Washington, D.C.: National Center for Education Statistics, U. S. Department of Education. ED 435–583.

National Center for Education Statistics (2007) *The Nation's Report Card: Civics 2006*. Accessed at http://nces.ed.gov/nationsreportcard on June 5, 2007.

National Center for History in the Schools (1996) *National Standards for History: Basic edition*. Los Angeles, CA: University of California, Author.

National Conference on Citizenship, with CIRCLE and Saguaro Seminar (2006) *America's Civic Health Index: Broken Engagement*. College Park, MD: CIRCLE.

National Council for the Social Studies (1994) *Expectations of Excellence: Curriculum Standards for Social Studies*. Washington D.C.: Author.

National Council on Economic Education (1997) *Voluntary National Content Standards in Economics*. New York: Author.

Nelson, J. (2001) 'Defining Social Studies', in William B. Stanley (ed.), *Critical Issues in Social Studies Research for the 21st Century*. Greenwich, CT: Information Age Publishing. pp. 15–38.

Niemi, R.G. and Junn, J. (1998) *Civic Education: What Makes Students Learn*. New Haven: Yale University Press.

Niemi, N.S. and Niemi, R.G. (2007) 'Partisanship, Participation, and Political Trust as Taught (or Not) in High School History and Government Classes', *Theory and Research in Social Education*, 35 (1): 32–61.

Ochoa-Becker, A.S. (2007) *Democratic Education for Social Studies: An Issues-Centered Decision Making Curriculum*. 2nd edn. Greenwich, CT: Information Age Publishing (1st edn, 1988 by Shirley Engle and Anna S. Ochoa).

Ochoa-Becker, A.S., Morton, M., Autry, M., Johnstad, S. and Merrill, D. (2001) 'A Search for Decision Making in Three Elementary Classrooms', *Theory and Research in Social Education*, 29 (2): 261–289.

Pace, J.L. (2008) 'In a Civics Class', in Janet S. Bixby and Judith L. Pace (eds), *Educating Democratic Citizens in Troubled Times: Qualitative Studies of Current Efforts*. Albany, New York: State University of New York Press.

Pak, Y.K. (2000) 'Citizenship Education in the Seattle Schools on the Eve of the Japanese American Incarceration', *Theory and Research in Social Education*, 28 (3): 339–358.

Parker, W.C. (1996a) 'Advanced' Ideas about Democracy: Toward a Pluralist Conception of Citizen Education', *Teachers College Record*, 98 (1): 104–125.

Parker, W.C. (1996b) *Educating the Democratic Mind*. Albany, NY: State University of New York Press.

Parker, W.C. (2003) *Teaching Democracy: Unity and Diversity in Public Life*. New York: Teachers' College Press.

Parker, W.C. (2006, November) 'Public Discourses in Schools: Purposes, Problems, Possibilities', *Educational Researcher*, 35 (8). 11–18.

Peng, I. (2000) 'Effects of Public Deliberation on High School Students: Bridging the Disconnection Between Young People and Public Life', in Shielah Mann and John J.

Patrick (eds), *Education for Civic Engagement in Democracy*. Bloomington IN: ERIC Clearinghouse for Social Studies/Social Science. pp. 73–85.

Reuben, J.A. (2005) 'Patriotic Purposes: Public Schools and the Education of Citizens', in Susan Fuhrman and Marvin Lazerson (eds), *The Public Schools*. Oxford: Oxford University Press. pp. 1–24.

Rubin, B.C. (2007) 'Laboratories of Democracy: A Situated Perspective on Learning Social Studies in Detracked Classrooms', *Theory and Research in Social Education*, 35 (1): 62–95.

Russell, S.T. (2002) 'Queer in America: Citizenship for Sexual Minority Youth', *Applied Developmental Science*, 6 (4): 258–263.

Torney-Purta, J., Amadeo, J.A. and Richardson, W. (2007) 'Civic Service among Youth in Chile, Denmark, England, and the United States', in A.M. McBride and M. Sherraden (eds), *Civic Service Worldwide: Impacts and Inquiry*. New York: M. E. Sharpe. pp. 95–132.

Torney-Purta, J. and Barber, C. (2004) *Strengths and Weaknesses in US Students' Knowledge and Skills: Analysis from the IEA Civic Education Study*. CIRCLE Fact Sheet Accessed on at www.civicyouth. org August 1, 2005.

Torney-Purta, J., Barber, C. and Wilkenfeld, B. (2006) 'Differences in the Civic Knowledge and Attitudes of US Adolescents by Immigrant Status and Hispanic Background', *Prospects: A UNESCO Journal*, 36 (4): 343–354.

Torney-Purta, J., Lehmann, R., Oswald, H. and Schulz, W. (2001) *Citizenship and Education in Twenty Eight Countries: Civic Knowledge and Engagement at Age Fourteen*. Amsterdam: The International Association for the Evaluation of Educational Achievement.

Torney-Purta, J. and Richardson, W.K. (2004) 'Anticipated Political Engagemen among Adolescents in Australia, England, Norway, and the United States', in J. Demaine (ed.), *Citizenship and Political Education Today*. London: Palgrave/Macmillan. pp. 41–58.

Vontz, T.S., Metcalf, K.K. and Patrick, J.J. (2000) *Project Citizen and the Civic Development of Adolescent Students in Indiana, Latvia, and Lithuania*. Bloomington,

IN: ERIC Clearinghouse for Social Studies/ Social Science Education.

Warren, D. and Patrick, J.J. (eds) (2006) *Civic and Moral Learning in America*. New York: Palgrave Macmillan.

Westheimer, J. and Kahne, J. (2004) 'What Kind of Citizen? The Politics of Educating for Democracy', *American Educational Research Journal*, 41 (2): 237–269.

Woyshner, C. (2006) 'Notes Toward a Historiography of the Social Studies: Recent Scholarship and Future Directions',

in Keith C. Barton (ed.), *Research Methods in Social Studies Education*. Greenwich, CT: Information Age Publishing. pp. 11–38.

Woyshner, C., Watras, J. and Crocco, M.S. (2004) (eds) *Social Education in the Twentieth Century: Curriculum and Context for Citizenship*. New York: Peter Lang.

Zukin, C., Keeter, S., Andolina, M., Jenkins, K., Delli, C. and Michael, X. (2006) *A New Engagement?: Political Participation, Civic Life, and the Changing American Citizen*. Oxford, UK: Oxford University Press.

Key Perspectives

21

Key Perspectives, Traditions and Disciplines: Overview

Elizabeth Frazer

INTRODUCTION

When we talk about 'perspectives, traditions and disciplines' in relation to citizenship and education we can be thinking about one or two analytically distinct levels of analysis. First, and most obviously there are 'philosophies', 'ideologies', or bodies of thinking about education and citizenship. Examples are the political philosophy and ethics connected with the classical Greek polis life; republican thought as that developed in England, France and North America; Confucian philosophy; liberalism in all its varieties; social democracy; various forms of conservatism; Islamic theology and ethics. All of these and numerous others offer positive prescriptions regarding the conduct of government, social life and education. In some cases we find definite debates or prescriptions regarding 'citizenship' as such and in others we find, rather, cognate ideas and concepts, which might be used, nevertheless, as resources for thinking about citizenship now (Heater, 1990, 2004, 2006; Parry, 1999, 2003).

Second, distinct from these bodies of thought, but interacting and overlapping with them in complex ways, there are what we can loosely call political and citizenship education regimes and cultures. In historically specific contexts, there are distinct public or governmental policies, and distinct political and educational institutions and offices. We can typify more or less democratic or authoritarian, more or less liberal or conservative, states and societies. These societies will be characterized by specific patterns and levels of political participation and citizen activity. Typologies constructed from these and other variables can then help us analyze and understand specific cases, such as imperial Britain, post-World War II Japan or twenty-first century South Africa (Hanagan, 1997; Mann, 1987; Roche, 1987; Turner, 1990).

In addition to this two-fold distinction we find somewhat diverse preoccupations and problematics between academic disciplines and approaches. When historians, sociologists and political economists analyze citizenship and education regimes they tend to ask about the material and related conditions that explain certain institutions and cultures of citizenship, or their absence (Mann, 1987; Turner, 1990). Sociologists and psychologists enquire into the conditions at the level of the individual and group that explain such political cultural variables as the distribution and structure of attitudes and opinions, patterns and levels of participation and the effects of education (Emler, 2002; Emler and Frazer, 1999). A good deal of political and educational philosophy is focused on normative questions about the justification of citizenship and citizenship education (Brighouse, 1998; Callan, 1994, 1996, 1997, 2000; Galston, 1991; Gutmann, 1987; Kymlicka, 2003; Macedo, 2000). It is important to note, though, that a distinct division of labour between normative and explanatory theorists does not mean that the two enterprises are wholly disconnected from each other. Normative theory contributes established categories and distinctions to social science; normative theory itself must be based on some descriptive theory of how the world works; and, of course, normative theories influence the formation of policy and the construction of institutions (Frazer and Emler, 1997; Frazer, 2000).

At some times, and in some intellectual perspectives, citizenship as such is a prominent category in mundane and philosophical thinking, or a preoccupation for public policy or in political struggle. At other times, it is recessive, eclipsed by other categories and preoccupations. At the beginning of the twenty-first century, undoubtedly, we have a resurgence of citizenship thinking, and a focus on it in governmental and public policy, in political efforts and in philosophical and ethical reasoning. By contrast, it was relatively recessive in the twentieth century (Lister, 2003; Roche, 1987). It was criticized by Marxism, the dominant political philosophy of the left, and marginalized in liberalism. In social democratic states it was 'settled' in a distinctive and limited way, focused on the rights of the educational and welfare state. It was eclipsed in capitalist and planned economies alike, and suppressed by authoritarian state governments. Numerous factors explain its resurgence both in intellectual thinking and in practical politics and policy. Intellectual crises in the polar framework of Marxism and liberalism was both in part prompted and responded to by the critical stances of anarchism, feminism and communitarianism, and new ideas of citizenship

crystallized in the course of those encounters. The distinct policy crises of welfare states, liberal markets and planned economies, were responded to, in part, by diverse ideals of citizenship. The values and strategies of non-governmental organizations, new social movements and urban campaigns, in the context of state transformation and globalized economic relationships, were also citizen focused.

Two points are important here: First, we are the inheritors of a plurality of competing and contradictory philosophical ideals and political models of citizenship. These inherited ideals are now resources for thinking into the future, and there is a plurality of ideas of what the future should and might be. Our world is characterized by a number of profound disagreements. There is disagreement, for example, about the nature and values of political power, and hence the value of citizenship as such, as opposed to personal, 'private' values of cultural membership and economic force (Callan, 1997; Galston, 1991; Macedo, 1990). There is disagreement about the proper role of religion in public life and in personal ethics, with some arguing that polities and public discussions must consist in part of an encounter and argument between diverse religious viewpoints and claims, while others argue that when we enter public forums we should leave religion, along with other features of our personal, social and private identities behind (Rawls, 1993; Walzer, 2005). There is deep disagreement about the value of equality, and, if we do value equality, how to realize it in structures of difference and exclusion like that of sex and, indeed, nationality (Arnot, 2003; Yuval-Davis, 1991, 1997). In particular, it is problematic how political equality coexists with social and economic inequalities. For some thinkers, participation in public life must be the strategy of choice for claims making groups; for critics, this call is vacuous if there is not equal resourcefulness (Arnot, 2003; Dietz, 1992).

In addition to these disagreements, there is deep uncertainty about the future shape and boundaries of political formations. Citizenship is a political relationship with fellow citizens and common governing structures. This has taken various forms: city state, empire, nation state, but also federations and associations of various sorts, such as the British Commonwealth, and the European Union. More complex political structures mean more complex patterns of allegiance and membership. Added to this is the fact of the diverse and even crosscutting allegiances and memberships of a mobile world of migration. There is no simple answer to the question, now, about which political authority secures rights for any specific person; or in what political offices citizens participate. Normatively, it has at various times been assumed that some critical level of cultural assimilation is a precondition for the full enjoyment of citizenship rights and the full discharge of citizenship obligations. This assumption – if indeed it is one – is challenged in the changing world of political power, economic and material flows, and cultural transformations (Castles, 2005; Leca, 1992; Soysal, 1994).

Second, there is distinct uncertainty about education in its broadest sense. Philosophy of education focuses on the nature of the ideally educated subject, and on the process by which that ideal subject can be educated, and there are disagreements on both these fronts (Curren, 2007; Dewey, 2004 fp 1916; Oakeshott, 1956; Parry, 1999, 2003). The nature and extent of the autonomy of an educated person, their relationship with tradition and with social formations, is controversial. There is disagreement about the relationships between education, socialization and training. There is disagreement about what states may properly require in the way of education of individuals, and about the relative weights of family, cultural and religious associations and organizations, private and public schools, and the state, in the process of the education of children, young people and adults. Theologians articulate specifically religiously prescribed criteria for desired educational processes and outcomes.

There are also disagreements about how education actually works – to what extent cognitive changes, positional and network effects, or social experiences are causally connected with educational outcomes, such as increased participation, more tolerant attitudes or material success (Emler and Frazer, 1999; Nie et al., 1996; Niemi and Junn, 1998). Children do learn basic cognitive skills like reading, writing, calculating, memorizing, abstract reasoning, motor skills and so on. There are recognized roles for more or less professionalized teachers to coordinate and monitor this process of learning. But societies also ask for children to know history, or understand science and technology, or be sexually or emotionally literate; to be good parents, managers of money, to organize social events like meetings, to be team players and to develop capacities for leadership. Societies want children, variously, to inhabit exaggerated sex roles, or be autonomous judges of what is right and what is good. There are political, and historically situated disagreements about what all children should know and be; what children differentiated by sex or status should differently know and be; and what capacities it is important for some 'and only some' to have. In all of this there is profound uncertainty about the possibilities and limits of formal schooling – can schools really be expected to teach cooking, religion, parenting, sexual ethics and hygiene, sport and citizenship? Societies value such social skills as team cooperation, diligence, leadership, organizational capacity, turn taking, responsibility and managerial capability. But it is unclear how much explicit attention to these, rather than concentrating on the teaching of languages, mathematics, humanities and technology, actually retard rather than promote those effects. What are the effects of scaling up – trying to teach to large groups what can be taught to small groups? Trying to teach to all what is definitely teachable to some? All of these considerations are relevant to the broad question and project of citizenship education.

NORMATIVE MODELS OF CITIZENSHIP

The enquiry into what citizenship ought to be, and the more general enquiry into the ideal of social and political relationships, individual conduct, state action and so on, frequently proceeds in the context of argument between rival ideological accounts (Freeden, 1996). Diverse theologies dominate in certain societies and states, and people and governments have recourse to them in practical reasoning about how individuals should conduct themselves, how children should be socialized and educated. Enquiry into the nature of citizenship, for example, in Muslim societies and states, is linked with questions about the religious and philosophical tenets of Islam and what they imply for the conduct of the individual vis. a vis. government, the permissible or prescribed governmental institutions, the nature of public life and so on (Moussalli, 2001; Marfleet, 1998). This is similar for the explicitly Christian, church organized, states of Europe. But 'secularism' is equally influential. From the time of the religious wars in Europe, the claims of secularism and humanism were that they could enable people of various religions to coexist in a state which counted them as equal with each other, in which no one is favoured in the public sphere. Of course, this question of the role of religion in public life is not settled.

There are also rather imperfect mappings between types of state and society, and philosophical and ethical systems of thought. Confucianism is an obvious example – it deeply structures mundane cultures of kinship, neighbourhood and wider social relations, and is articulated by elites, and reflected in laws and administrative arrangements (Bell, 2000; O'Dwyer, 2003). Liberals in competition with republicans in political philosophy, can gesture to historical examples of types of state, society and government. Islamic thinkers envision a genuinely Islamic state and society; or consider the structures that are necessary to enable Muslims to live a good Muslim life in secular societies. Conservatives disagree with socialists about how government should be conducted.

But it is important to emphasize that any analysis of 'isms' runs into the problem of complexity. To take one example, liberalism can be analyzed temporally as having eighteenth, nineteenth, twentieth and now a twenty-first century variant. It simultaneously can have adherents who veer nearer to conservatism on the right wing, and those who veer to socialism on the left. Over a life time, of course, great liberal thinkers, like Mill, or Rawls, will propose distinctively diverse solutions to the problems they are wrestling with – now more, now less redistributive, or participatory. Liberalism can also coherently be said to have a US, British, French or German etc. variant – a tradition of thinking, in a natural language, connected to a particular nation state, and with all the cultural, historical and social influences that that entails (Bellamy, 1992).

Proto liberal thought in the seventeenth and eighteenth centuries and developing liberal thought in the nineteenth century were premised on the idea of a particular kind of state, and a particular kind of relationship between government and people. Rights, formal equality, the priority of liberty for the individual, the rule of law – these were all congruent with a broadly capitalist nation state. Later the claims of individuals to a more just egalitarianism, and the needs of and for autonomous individuals, led on the one hand to claims for social liberalism and a particular kind of feminism and on the other, and connectedly, to coherent normative claims for a welfare state. This then put into train, in some settings anyway, processes of bureaucratization which could be understood to be antithetical to the very citizenship that was at stake, and hence a new round of citizenship claims, counterclaims, debates and enquiries is necessitated.

For all the significant systems of thought which envision or partially construct state and social institutions, a similar story can be told. There are changing emphases, the ebb and flow of influential interpretations. Ideas are in a dialectical relationship with material constraints, problems and opportunities. Importantly, ideas are resources for claims, and for criticism.

CITIZENSHIP EDUCATION REGIMES AND CULTURES

Perhaps the major question at this level of analysis is how and why 'citizenship', or its absence, comes to be institutionalized in specific historical and political settings. Under what conditions do governments and states come to treat some proportion of people as 'citizens' or anything like it? Under what conditions do people think of themselves as 'citizens', and make demands for social and political arrangements which enable them to act as such? People are not only citizens – they also have a religious identity, are consumers, employers and cultural members. Under what conditions do individuals elevate citizenship to a central aspect of their lives and identities, and under what conditions does citizen action and interaction play a significantly shaping part in the culture and fabric of society? Under what conditions do formal public educational institutions come to think of themselves as having the function of educating citizens?

Political economists and historians explore the material factors which bring ordinary people into direct relationship with government and state agencies, and then construct this direct relationship as that of citizen. We have examples of 'citizenship' from historical settings distant from our own – ancient and medieval city states, early modern and medieval towns and cities – and these continue to inform our normative ideals of what citizenship might and ought to be. But the emergence and development of citizenship as that is relevant for contemporary political conflict, public policy and social relations is seen above all in the context of 'modernization' and development. According to accounts inspired by the political economy of Smith, Marx, de Toqueville and Weber, developing forms of taxation, changing organization of conscription, governmentally imposed and enforced standards of language, hygiene and, of course, schooling, are historical processes that profoundly change structures of authority.

Theoretically, within this historical and political enquiry there is controversy about the extent to which 'citizenship' is a genuinely popular achievement, or the extent to which it is a 'ruling class strategy' (Mann, 1987; Turner, 1990).

Citizenship as achievement

The first story focuses on people's claims to participation in the structures that govern them, and on the campaigns and efforts that are engaged in order to win changes in governing arrangements. Citizenship is fought for, it is a prize worth having, and citizens should care about what happens to it in relation to other social roles and institutions. Of course, such claims can be couched in the context of a range of values. In republican city traditions, in processes associated with medieval Europe, the claims of autonomous cities, self-governing entities with rights over markets, property, the organization of production, are pressed against the prerogatives of traditional or aspiring sovereign power. 'Property' and the demand that there should be no taxation without representation has carried political and social change forward in contexts like that of the English and American revolutionary settings. Alternatively, revolutionaries and progressives can proclaim 'liberty, equality and fraternity' for and between individuals, as in the French revolution. In the twentieth century, people have made citizenship claims to fair and dignified treatment by welfare state and educational agencies. In all these contexts, citizenship is a contested category. And we must not overlook revolutionary and reformist contexts in which it has no place, or in which it is a focus for attack, as in anti-bourgeois revolutions and campaigns.

In the context of this kind of account of the development of citizenship, the role of education is central. In revolutionary contexts, theorists focus on the role of parties and social organizations as places where people can learn the skills and modes of conduct necessary for political action, where they can learn about power structures and their history, and come to new understandings of the future. When suffrage and other political rights, and welfare rights, are won, there is the need to educate ordinary people for political power. Citizenship involves exercising powers, claiming benefits, negotiating with public authority, indeed asserting public authority oneself in certain situations. People with their most ordinary faculties have a capacity for all of this, but there is a question how that capacity is to be developed into real capability. So we need to be socialized appropriately, to be trained, to have opportunities for practice, to be able to reflect on our performance and understand where we are going wrong and right – to be educated politically. For all of this, people need to practise citizenship conduct in a variety of settings – their ordinary social and intimate networks, in formal associations like clubs, parties, membership networks, as well as in the public settings of state and society.

The role of schools is contested. In some revolutionary thought they are distrusted as inevitably reactionary; in other strands the use of school power to detach children from their families has been emphasized (Parry, 2003). Schools are a key site for associational life, for encountering strangers. Schools, in some sense, model the wider society and state (Levinson, 1997). They are places where, in order to learn maths, language, science and art, we have to work with others, interact with strangers and friends, be put into positions of leader or be led, accept authority and challenge it. Here, just as we gain the experience, understanding and skills that are necessary for adult life in society, economy and culture, so we learn what we need to participate in the polity – in the competition for governing power, in the debates and contestations over policy, in the selection of governors. And at some times, in some places, citizenship is part of schools' explicit or formal curriculum.

Citizenship as governing strategy

The second story about citizenship focuses on the problem that ruling classes face in dealing with discontent – claims, fights – from populations who live in cities and towns and villages, have to work, must be educated. On this kind of account rights and privileges, the recognition of certain kinds of equality, liberties – especially but not only suffrage – are a way that modern states have of maintaining people's loyalty and, in particular, maintaining social order. Critical historical accounts emphasize in particular that in conceding citizenship states are pre-empting and preventing more thoroughgoing social revolution. Citizenship, on this account, takes the state and the ruling regime, especially in its economic and military aspects, as given, and incorporates individuals more firmly into it (Mann, 1987).

Citizenship education in schools, and via other organizations that are firmly on the side of the state, whether these are state sponsored 'associations' or ruling class institutions, such as certain churches, military outreach organizations and so on, then can be seen as the strategy for instilling the right kind of values and conduct in order to achieve an orderly population. On this account, rights and suffrage have as their quid pro quo certain kinds of law abiding and responsible conduct; the duty of military service can be presented as a citizenship duty. Just as education in school will focus on the dominant language, the level of education and skills training that is necessary for the dominant economic demands of work and the professions, so it will focus on instilling the appropriate kind of knowledge, conduct and character, as that is understood by the government and ruling elites, for citizenship in the state.

Critical theories of citizenship

These two stories each have their place in scholarly accounts of citizenship. Broadly speaking, social scientists are disinclined to accept the categories of everyday life at face value (Roche, 1987). The idea that citizenship is just a ruling class strategy trades on the thought that people might experience themselves as citizens, and yet not be, really. The experience of power and freedom, for instance, can disguise true powerlessness. A weaker version of this thought is that it can be relatively cheap to concede the rights and freedoms of public life, providing those head off more costly demands for real freedom, or human emancipation.

Marx markedly distinguishes between human emancipation and political or any other partial, emancipation. Religious emancipation, for example, is premised on the idea that people can be bought off with freedom in the public realm, in the political state, while they 'or at least the poorer, the proletarian, among them' are still enslaved effectively in the economy. For Marx, the identity of 'citizen' always relies on a splitting of the individual into 'public' and 'private' and this is alienating, to say the least, consistent with real slavery, at worst (Marx, 1975, 1897). If we take this view of the state's investment in making people into citizens, then, we can conclude that ethically and humanly speaking citizenship is a sham. Instead of rejecting citizenship altogether, others think in terms rather of full as opposed to unsatisfactory and insufficient partial citizenship. Marshall's story about Britain is that civil and political rights have to be, and were, completed with the social rights of proper recognition of human dignity and the provision of material needs in welfare state institutions (Marshall, 1950, 1981).

As critics of Marshall point out, if he intended this account of the development of citizenship to be generalizable beyond the case of Britain, he was mistaken (Roche, 1987; Turner, 1990). In the history of Imperial Prussia and later united Germany, for example, developments were in a different order. A 'welfare state' – social citizenship – went hand in hand with the development of industry and of state infrastructure. This was continuous with older occupational privileges. But political citizenship – extended let alone universal suffrage, effective parliamentarianism, freedom of association and speech, a free press – were intolerable to the sovereign and the government. Insofar as they were conceded bit by bit, they were 'sham', as Max Weber protests. The case of Germany is relevant in some respects to the recent history of authoritarian states (Thompson, 2000). Importantly too, not least of Weber's complaints about parliament, legislation and representation in Germany was that the people as a whole, and those people who might aspire to positions of political leadership, completely lacked political education (Weber, 1994/1918).

Weber accounts for the development of modern states under the historical conditions of rationalization and secularization. He traces changing and successive forms of state, society and economy whereby political, economic, religious and social power evolve into the specific form of bureaucratized government of mass populations. Weber can see two ways that such formations might be 'managed'. One is the authoritarian use of police power, and the bureaucratization of poverty – giving legal power to capitalists, or to the managers of state run economic enterprises. The other is the assignation of rights and freedoms to individuals, the recognition that individuals are equals. Both of these ways are possible. One, of course, is ethically defensible while the other is not. Perhaps more importantly, the second way, of individual rights and freedoms, with the recognition of equality and autonomy, especially in universal suffrage, the civil liberties necessary for the formation of associations and parties, the institutionalization of effective parliamentarianism with legislators and representatives capable of truly holding executives to account really does, in some sense, reflect, or is congruent with, the modern state form. For, in this state form individuals as such come into a direct relationship with state power – we individually pay taxes for instance.

Individuals are held responsible for their actions, legally – that is, they are presumed to be autonomous (Weber 1994/1906).

Weber's account of the possibility of modern citizenship takes account both of the logic governing state institutions and actions, and the claims of ordinary people who struggle for advantage vis. a vis. competing classes. In this case the competing classes are working people in competition with capitalists. But the approach could be extended to frame study of the struggles of migrating groups, or people who hold passports that keep them relatively immobile. In this account the logic of values, as we might put it, is prominent. An aspect of the story of the emergence and development of citizenship in modern states focuses on the evolution of values and their instantiation in political and social life. The claims to justice in social arrangements, and of autonomy for individuals conduce to the development of social and political arrangements which recognize human equality, that institutionalize people's opposition to rule, that recognize rights. But, that these values are immanent, as it were, in modern state, supra-state and social structures does not mean that they will be recognized or institutionalized. And even if they are recognized and institutionalized, that is not sufficient for them to be fully realized. A condition of their realization lies in the daily conduct of people's lives, their patterns of action and interaction, as well as in laws and formal structures of power. The same point applies to those arguments which find consultation, diversity and other citizenship values in Islamic thought, or find rights and democratic values in Confucianism (Moussalli, 2003; O'Dwyer, 2003). It applies to the critique of international human rights discourse. This kind of critique, whether directed at institutions, or at more abstract and theoretical bodies of thought, of course begs what we might call the cultural question. How, under what conditions, can political democratic and citizenship values be prominent in the life of society and governing structures?

This question is complicated, too, by uncertainty about and changes in the actual and ideal forms of governing structure. Societies are heterogeneous with regards to religion and culture. Migration patterns mean that networks of allegiance are complex. People are subject to the claims of 'governing institutions' beyond the state they actually live in – countries of origin and destination, supra-national organizations like the International Court of Human Rights. According to some lines of thought this means new fractures between rights and obligations, and new hierarchies of citizenship (Castles, 2005; Leca, 1992).

CONCLUSION

Emphasis on changes in the concept, theory and institutionalization of citizenship over time, or from the context of democratic and broadly liberal, to authoritarian and conservative states, or from the context of relatively securely bounded sovereign nation states to an era of fragmented power, resource flows, and boundary contests, can generate scepticism about the extent to which, in talking of citizenship in all these different contexts, we are actually talking about the same thing. It might be thought that any study of republicanisms past, or the social democratic and liberal perspective of T.H. Marshall's analysis of citizenship and welfare states, is of no more than purely historical interest. By contrast, I believe that wide ranging study of how citizenship has been conceptualized, how it has been institutionalized, and competing theories of the conditions and consequences of its realization are of substantial interest. This is because in whatever context we study citizenship we are studying a political status in the context of other statuses. The citizen of a medieval town with aspirations to autonomy was also a merchant or an artisan or both, also a member of a kinship network, also the participant in a culture and a religion, oppressed by some forms of power and liberated by others. In thinking about citizenship we think about how political power is arranged.

Citizenship is frequently defined quite vaguely as 'a status bestowed on those who are full members of a community' (Marshall, 1950: Lister, 2003). But of course, it's not just any community. There is, to be sure, an extended sense in which we say of some member of a sports club, or a workplace, that they are 'a good citizen' meaning that they take care of the collective and public aspects of the life of the club, contribute to the common good, take responsibility and so on. In saying this, we are attributing to the club, or the workplace, the characteristics of a 'community' or site of shared goods. But the primary meaning of 'citizenship' does pertain to a political formation. Insofar as states, empires, commonwealths and the like are communities it is because political power is relatively concentrated, and political offices, institutions, authority structures, are common. And citizens enjoy a membership that exceeds that of visitors, denizens, incoming migrants and numerous other statuses. Citizens not only have rights and protections that others do not have, they also have a share in the political processes by which it is decided what rights and protections they, and others, should have. Citizenship is not the only status that brings this political power, of course – economic, religious and other social interests and pressures on governing institutions can come from actors in different roles. And, as this political power is a power to exclude, or to ignore, other moral claims, it must also be constrained morally.

This is why the competing theoretical understandings of the conditions of citizenship, the factors – material, economic, educational, psychological, sociological, cultural – that enable or disable its realization that are discussed here are so important.

REFERENCES

Arnot, M. (2003) 'Citizenship, Education and Gender.' In A. Lockyer, B. Crick, and J. Annette (eds) *Education for Democratic Citizenship.* Aldershot: Ashgate. pp. 103–119.

Bell, D.A. (2000) *East Meets West: Human Rights and Democracy in East Asia.* Princeton NJ: Princeton University Press.

Bellamy, R. (1992) *Liberalism and Modern Society.* Cambridge: Polity Press.

Brighouse, H. (1998) 'Civic Education and Liberal Legitimacy.' *Ethics*, 108 (4):719–745.

Callan, E. (1994) 'Beyond Sentimental Civic Education.' *American Journal of Education,* 102 (2): 190–221.

Callan, E. (1996) 'Political Liberalism and Political Education.' *Review of Politics*, 58 (1): 5–53.

Callan, E. (1997) *Creating Citizens: Political Education and Liberal Democracy.* Oxford: Clarendon Press.

Callan, E. (2000) 'Liberal Legitimacy, Justice, and Civic Education.' *Ethics*, 111 (1): 141–155.

Castles, S. (2005) 'Nation and Empire: Hierarchies of Citizenship in the New Global Order.' *International Politics,* 42 (2): 203–224.

Curren, R. (2007) *Philosophy of Education: An Anthology.* Malden MA.: Blackwell Publishers.

Dewey, J. (2004 fp 1916) *Democracy and Education.* Mineola NY.: Dover Publications.

Dietz, M.G. (1992) 'Context is All: Feminism and Theories of Citizenship.' In C. Mouffe (ed.) *Dimensions of Radical Democracy.* London: Verso.

Emler, N. and Frazer, E. (1999) 'Politics: The Education Effect.' *Oxford Review of Education*, 25 (1–2): 251–273.

Emler, N. (2002) 'Morality and Political Orientations: An Analysis of Their Relationship.' *European Review of Social Psychology,* 13: 259–291.

Frazer, E. (2000) 'Citizenship Education: Anti-Political Culture and Political Education in Britain.' *Political Studies*, 48: 88–103.

Frazer, E. and Nicholas E. (1997) 'Participation and Citizenship: A New Agenda for Youth Politics Research.' In J. Bynner, L. Chisholm, and A. Furlong (eds) *Youth, Citizenship and Social Change in a European Context.* Aldershot: Ashgate. pp. 171–195.

Freeden, M (1996) *Ideologies and Political Theory: A Conceptual Approach.* Oxford: Clarendon Press.

Galston, W. (1991) *Liberal Purposes.* Cambridge: Cambridge University Press.

Gutmann, A. (1987) *Democratic Education.* Princeton NJ: Princeton University Press.

Freeden, M. (1996) *Ideologies and Political Theory: A Conceptual Approach*. Oxford: Clarendon Press.

Hanagan, M. (1997) 'Introduction to Special Issue on "Recasting Citizenship"', *Theory and Society*, 26 (4).

Heater, D. (2006) *Citizenship in Britain: A History*. Edinburgh: Edinburgh University Press.

Heater, D. (2004) *A History of Education for Citizenship*. London: Routledge Falmer.

Heater, D. (1990) *Citizenship: The Civic Ideal in World History, Politics and Education*. London: Longman.

Kymlicka, W. (2003) 'Two Dilemmas of Citizenship Education in Pluralist Societies.' In A. Lockyer, B. Crick, and J. Annette (eds) *Education for Democratic Citizenship: Issues of Theory and Practice*. Aldershot: Ashgate. pp. 47–63.

Leca, J. (1992) 'Questions on Citizenship.' In C. Mouffe (ed.) *Dimensions of Radical Democracy: Pluralism, Citizenship, Community*. London: Verso. pp. 17–32.

Levinson, M. (1997) 'Liberalism versus Democracy? Schooling Private Citizens in the Public Square.' *British Journal of Political Science* 27 (3): 333–360.

Lister, R. (2003) *Citizenship: Feminist Perspectives*. 2nd edn (1st edn 1997). Basingstoke: Macmillan.

Macedo, S. (1990) *Liberal Virtues: Citizenship, Virtue and Community in Liberal Constitutionalism*. Oxford: Clarendon Press.

Macedo, S. (2000) *Diversity and Distrust: Civic Education in a Multicultural Society*. Cambridge Mass: Harvard University Press.

Mann, M. (1987) 'Ruling Class Strategies and Citizenship.' *Sociology*, 21 (3): 339–354.

Marfleet, P. (1998) 'Islamist Political Thought.' In A. Lent (ed.) *New Political Thought: An Introduction*. London: Lawrence and Wishart. pp. 89–111.

Marshall, T.H. (1950) *Citizenship and Social Class, and Other Essays*. Cambridge: Cambridge University Press.

Marshall, T.H. (1981) *The Right to Welfare and Other Essays*. London: Heinemann Educational Books.

Marx, K. (1975 fp 1843) 'On the Jewish Question.' In L. Colletti (ed.) *Early Writings*. Harmondsworth: Penguin. pp. 211–242.

Marx, K. (1897 fp German 1852) *The Eighteenth Brumaire of Louis Bonaparte*: Kessinger Publishing.

Moussalli, A.S. (2001) *The Islamic Quest for Democracy, Pluralism and Human Rights*. Gainesville: University Press of Florida.

Moussalli, A.S. (2003) 'Islamic Democracy and Pluralism.' In O. Safi (ed.) *Progressive Muslims on Justice, Gender and Pluralism*. Oxford: Oneworld Publications. pp. 286–305.

Nie, N.H., Junn, J. and Stehlik-Barry, Kenneth (1996) *Education and Democratic Citizenship in America*. Chicago: University of Chicago Press.

Niemi, R.G. and Junn, J. (1998) *Civic Education: What Makes Students Learn*. New Haven: Yale University Press.

Oakeshott, M. (1956) 'Political Education.' In P. Laslett (ed.) *Philosophy, Politics and Society*, vol. Series 1, *Philosophy, Politics and Society*. Oxford: Blackwell. pp. 1–21. (Also in Michael Oakeshott, *Rationalism in Politics and Other Essays* edited by T. Fuller, new edition Indianopolis: Liberty Fund, 1991.)

O'Dwyer, S. (2003) 'Democracy and Confucian Values.' *Philosophy East and West*, 53 (1): 39–63.

Parry, G. (1999) 'Constructive and Reconstructive Political Education.' *Oxford Review of Education*, 25 (1–2): 247–71.

Parry, G. (2003) 'Citizenship Education: Reproductive and Remedial.' In A. Lockyer, B. Crick, and J. Annette (eds) *Education for Democratic Citizenship: Issues of Theory and Practice*. Aldershot: Ashgate.

Rawls, J. (1993) *Political Liberalism, John Dewey Essays in Philosophy;* New York: Columbia University Press.

Roche, M. (1987) 'Citizenship, Social Theory and Change.' *Theory and Society*, 16 (3): 363–399.

Smith, A. (1974, fp 1776) *The Wealth of Nations*. Harmondsworth: Penguin.

Soysal, Y.N. (1997) 'Changing Parameters of Citizenship and Claims-Making: Organised Islam in European Public Spheres.' *Theory and Society*, 26 (4): 509–527.

Soysal, Y.N. (1994) *Limits of Citizenship: Migrants and PostNational Membership in Europe*. Chicago: Chicago University Press.

Thompson, M.R. (2000) 'The Survival of "Asian Values" as "Zivilisationskritik".' *Theory and Society*, 29 (5): 651–686.

22

Religion, Citizenship and Hope: Civic Virtues and Education about Muslim Traditions

Farid Panjwani

Bernard Crick's observation that 'nearly everywhere that there is citizenship education in schools ... some historical contingent sense of crisis has been the trigger' (Crick, 1999: 338) is certainly true in the case of Britain.[1] While there were many 'triggers' for the recent focus on return of England citizenship education, immigration and more specifically the concern about some of the tensions generated by the intersection of national and religious identities of immigrants are among the more important ones. Within these particular triggers, the issue can be narrowed further. Although the tensions between demands of modern secular citizenship and obligations of faith can be noted from India to America, spanning almost all major world religions, none is more likely to be noticed and discussed than those involving Muslims.[2] In this context, the chapter is concerned with the following question: what role can education for citizenship play in minimizing any possible tensions between national and religious – particularly Muslim – identities? Three nexuses

of citizenship education and Muslim traditions are suggested. These include the possibility of exploring religious symbols as a source of social criticism, challenging the moralization of politics through a closer association of citizenship education and social justice and revisiting approaches to the internal diversity among Muslims. The justification for these suggestions lies in the perspective on the recent history that has led to the emergence of Islam as a political identity competing with citizenry role. It is thus important to first present this perspective before outlining the suggestions.

Some three decades ago, the question about citizenship education's interaction with religious heritage would have seemed strange at best and outlandish at worst. Citizenship was expected to extract individuals from narrow religious and communal allegiances, not seek ways of negotiating with them. However, over the course of the last four decades, several theoretical and practical shifts have made this question possible and, to many, necessary.

Turner, B. (1990) 'Outline of a Theory of Citizenship.' *Sociology*, 24 (2): 189–217.

Walzer, M. (2005) *Politics and Passion: Towards a More Egalitarian Liberalism*. New Haven: Yale University Press.

Weber, M. (1994 fp German 1906) 'On the Situation of Constitutional Democracy in Russia.' In P. Lassman and R. Speirs (eds) *Weber Political Writings*. Cambridge: Cambridge University Press. pp. 29–74.

Weber, M. (1994 fp German 1917) 'Suffrage and Democracy in Germany.' In P. Lassman and R. Speirs (eds) *Weber Political Writings*. Cambridge: Cambridge University Press. pp. 80–129.

Weber, M. (1994 fp German 1918) 'Parliament and Government in Germany under a New Political Order: Towards a Political Critique of Officialdom and the Party System.' In P. Lassman and R. Speirs (eds) *Weber Political Writings*. Cambridge: Cambridge University Press.

Yuval-Davis, N. (1991) 'The Citizenship Debate: Women, Ethnic Processes and the State.' *Feminist Review*, 39:58–68.

Yuval-Davis, N. (1997) 'Women, Citizenship and Difference.' *Feminist Review*, 57: 4–27.

Thus, if the question about citizenship education and religious tradition needs to be answered in any meaningful manner, the effort should take account of the broader historical context of this change. The first part of the chapter will thus be an attempt to understand how Islam emerged to be a competitive source of political identity for a number of Muslims. Drawing upon this context, the second part of the chapter will make some specific recommendations for dovetailing the religious traditions of Islam and education for citizenship to promote the aim of creating a socially cohesive society which respects its plural nature.

RELIGION AND CITIZENSHIP: A CONTEST FOR HOPE IN SOME MUSLIM CONTEXTS

At the outset it needs to be noted that the vast majority of Muslims do not feel any conflict between their religion and nationality.[3] Still, in the last three decades increasing numbers have felt so; Allah and constitution, Ummah[4] and nation have competed. The understanding of Islam that sees it as a political ideology capable of resolving modern problems and thus supporting political and social activism has been called 'Islamism' or 'political Islam' (Clawson, 1999; Esposito and Tamimi, 2002; Hamzeh and Dekmejian, 1996; Mirsepassi-Ashtiani, 1994; Nasr, 2003).

Several explanations have been put forward to account for the rise of this understanding of Islam. Broadly, these can be put into two groups. There are essentialist theories stressing a historical pedigree of the current discourse by interpreting it as a continuation of a struggle that 'began with the advent of Islam' (Huntington, 1996; Lewis, 2004; Pipes, 1995). Then there are contextual theories arguing for the novelty, that is modernity, and the modern origins of the phenomenon by tracing its genesis back to contemporary socio-political developments, particularly the failure of the secular modernization project (Ayubi, 1980; Roy, 2004; Woltering, 2002).

The main methodological assumption in the historical pedigree camp is that the Muslim world is 'dominated by a set of relatively enduring and unchanging processes and meanings, to be understood through the texts of Islam itself and the language it generated' (Halliday, 1995: 401). There is some validity to this assumption. Islamic foundational texts continue to have relevance and impact in Muslim societies and the Islamist discourse refers to the Qur'anic verses and concepts in its justification of Jihad and martyrdom (Euben, 2002; Ansari, forthcoming 2008). The book *Ma'arka* (the Battle), for example, encourages young Muslims to participate in armed struggle by invoking Qur'anic verses and examples from the early history of Muslims (Azhar, 2001).[5] Yet, to say that this means that these texts have enduring and unchanging meaning is to miss the insight of hermeneutics that texts, particularly religious texts, are open to interpretation and reinterpretation and, in fact, their power to inspire generations after generations lies in this fertility. The interpretations of religious texts are always shaped by the social and cultural contexts of the reader/community. What the Qur'an – or for that matter any scripture – says cannot be separated from what believers *say* it says.

Thus, if religious traditions, including Islam, are internally diverse and hermeneutically open-ended, it becomes legitimate to ask why certain interpretations become dominant at particular times and to particular people? Lewis (1990) may be right in saying that many Muslims 'are beginning to return' (p. 49) to some classical Islamic views, the question is why are they doing so an at this point of time? This sociological question is often asked in the essentialized approaches. This is where lies the strength of those who look to socio-political contexts for the emergence of political Islam. Keddie, for instance, identifies eight factors put forward by scholars (Keddie, 1998), which range from demography to failed modernization. These factors provide the socio-political context within which certain interpretations of the Qur'anic verses become attractive.

Keddie, for instance, identified eight socio-economic factors – uneven distribution of the benefits of capitalistic growth, global economic slowdown, increasing migration, changing family structures, growth in secular state power, education and urban growth, cultural homogenization and population growth – which she believed contributed to the emergence of the 'New Religious Politics' (Keddie, 1998). For those taking a sociological stance on Islamism, such factors provide the context within which certain extremist interpretations of religious scriptures become attractive. Thus, neither the enduring meanings approach nor the socio-political approaches are sufficient in themselves to explain the rise of the Islamist discourse. Instead of either/or, insights from both sides of the debate are needed. It is proposed that the processes that led to making religious identity a competitor to citizenship identity in many Muslim contexts simultaneously involved the failure of the promises of modernization and accompanying citizenship rights and participation, and the resulting stepping in of the religious discourse to fill in the void, to provide a new source of hope.

The next section briefly traces these developments both in the Muslim majority contexts and in Britain. In this regard, distinction must be made between the genesis of the Islamist movements and their later transformations, with the Afghan War as the fulcrum of this shift.

Genesis of Islamist discourse

Citizenship is potentially emancipatory. Over the last century, its egalitarian promise was fulfilled for many religious and racial groups in the Western context, as 'becoming a citizen' meant for them 'a libratory dismantling of hitherto existing structures of oppression, which were replaced by more egalitarian and inclusive structures' (Roy, 2005: 3). This promise of democratic citizenship impressed many in the former colonies of European powers. Nehru and Jinnah,

for instance, fighting on the opposite poles of the Indian freedom movement, were both inspired by such an outlook.

In the post-colonial context, a wave of popular movements across many Muslim countries brought secular nationalist governments into power. In various forms, these governments attempted modernization/ secularization which implied, among other things, minimizing the role of religion in governance. Alongside this there was the expectation of self-determination, implicit in the very argument for decolonization, and economic prosperity. Secularization, self-determination and economic prosperity thus intertwined and became the test for the success or failure of the new states.

Self-determination or democratization was the first of these tests in which the new states failed. In varying degrees, leaders of the secular nationalist governments missed out on democracy, resulting in one-party rule or in some case outright civilian or military dictatorship.[6] The democratic deficit was followed in many countries by economic downturns, in some earlier than in others. Even the oil rich countries suffered economic downturns after the oil prices slump.

Countries that emerged as the intellectual hub of Islamic revival – Egypt and Pakistan, in particular – saw a destructive double failure, political and economical. As states failed to deliver economic and democratic promise, the third element, secularization, also lost credibility (Butko, 2004; Keddie, 1998; Mirsepassi-Ashtiani, 1994).

It was in the above context that Muslim societies' need for 'authenticity' (to be its own self) and 'effectiveness' (to be able to manage its own resources) were increasingly articulated by religious groups through a vocabulary that was drawn from traditional religious sources albeit reinterpreted to meet the needs of modern times.

Thus it should not be surprising to observe people resorting to Islam as a result of what they would consider the failure of other options. On one level they may turn to Islam as a refuge that provides emotional peace and comfort ... At another level,

Islam may become the spearhead for socio-political resistance (Ayubi, 1980: 488).

The traditional religious concepts were widely understood in the Muslim societies. The success of the writers such as Mawdudi lay in their ability to re-interpret some of these concepts into a modern dictum.

> The advocates of a return to Islam have been able to make religious values, however rigid, seem relevant to modern society. They have been able to bridge traditional and modern segments of society. ... They have both articulated the manner in which these symbols should serve political ends and convinced large number of citizens that 'Islamization' is a necessary and beneficial process (Nasr, 2003: 70).

By successfully re-interpreting traditional concepts the Islamist discourse was able to give the masses both the assurance of tradition and hope for the resolution of modern problems such as unemployment, lack of social services, police state, corruption and cultural imperialism etc. Thus, as a cure for disunity among Muslims, Islam was offered as a unifying force; the sense of degradation generated by the present conditions was alleviated by an appeal to a 'golden age' of Muslim past; and instead of socio-political and economic analysis of the crisis of the developing world, concepts, metaphors and symbols of Islam were offered. Islamic symbols thus became the way to articulate socio-political demands and resist real or perceived hegemony.[7]

The early Islamists operated mainly within national frontiers, though cross-national influences were also present. They sought an Islamic state and a society with Islam as its ideology. Violence was rarely their tool. Pakistan's Jama'at Islami, the Turkish Refah Party and most of the groups in the Egyptian Muslim Brotherhood are examples of early Islamists (Roy, 1999).

The Afghan War and transformations in Islamists' discourse

Perhaps the single most important element in the emergence of newer, radical Islamist movements was the Afghan War of the 1980s in which the Islamists were patronized by the US as well as countries such as Saudi Arabia, Kuwait and Pakistan. After the Soviets invaded Afghanistan in 1979, Muslim scholars from around the world called for Jihad (Denoeux, 2002; Sivan, 2003; Wiktorowicz and Kaltner, 2003). The military support to Afghan warriors was underpinned by a powerful network of recruitment and educational infrastructure. At the end of the Cold War, the liberal capitalists were not the only ones who felt triumphant. The Jihadi Islamist stance also felt victorious. At the same time it felt abandoned by its former patrons as the US support for the Jihad waned after the soviet withdrawal (Ahmad, 2003). This potent mix of triumph and abandonment ultimately boomeranged on the earlier supporters of the Afghan Jihad (Denoeux, 2002; Roy, 2004). Unlike a professional army, there were no barracks for these *mujahidins* to return; many sought new avenues for military Jihad. Chechnya, Bosnia, Kashmir and other places became attractive and the Jihadi movement soon acquired a trans-national character, associated most forcefully with Al-Qaeda. What distinguished these new radical movements most from the older Islamists was their approval of violence as a legitimate tool to bring political change (Denoeux, 2002; Sivan, 2003).

This move was supported theoretically as the ideas of Mawdudi, considered as the spiritual fore-father of Islamist movement and went through a transformation in the hands of people such as Sayyed Qutb, Mohammed al-Faraj, Abdullah Azzam, Abd al-Salam Faraj, Omar Abdul Rahman, Umar Abu Qatada, Maulana Masood Azhar and Ayman al-Zawahiri (Azhar, 2001; Haqqani, 2002; Mamdani, 2005; Wiktorowicz, 2001; Wiktorowicz and Kaltner, 2003). In the process, detailed internal debates took place among the Islamists with regard to the place of violence in the achievement of their goals. In this regard, the interpretation of modern history as a history of Muslim grievances was a key theoretical cornerstone. A good example of the internal debate among the Islamists of various kinds is provided in a statement released by the Al-Qaeda in April 2002 in which it sought to provide theological justifications for the September 11, 2001 killings (MEPC, 2002; Wiktorowicz and Kaltner, 2003).

While some were turning to a violent struggle, in the crucible of Afghan War and other military conflicts involving Muslims the vast majority of Islamists continued to adhere to peaceful approaches. In the late 1990s even some of those who had earlier taken up violence, revoked it and started to participate in the civic process. In Egypt, for example, these 'reformed' Islamists called themselves 'New Islamists'(Baker, 2003). Instead of challenging the government, they opted for social and cultural change at the grassroots as the way to transform society.

Consequently today's Islamist movements are a mix of those continuing the peaceful agendas of the 1970s and 1980s and those that are very different, yet not unrelated, from their pioneers; those seeking change through political and negotiated means and those willing to adopt violence. It is thus important to be attentive to the various 'Shades of Islamism'.[8]

As noted above, despite growth, the Islamists remained a minority. The vast majority of Muslims adhered to very different understandings of Islam. In fact, some of them consciously sought to counter the growth of the Islamists. Sufi reaction is one example of the rejection of political Islam from within (Hamzeh and Dekmejian, 1996). So are the varied progressive responses by scholars who have sought to question the ideology, use of history and the interpretation of the Qur'an employed in political Islam (Safi, 2003; Wolfe, 2002).

CITIZENSHIP AND RELIGIOUS IDENTITY IN BRITISH MUSLIM CONTEXT

In replying to a question about the causes of Islamism, Graham Fuller mentioned poor social and economic conditions, incompetence and corruption of regimes, authoritarianism and close affiliation with the Western powers. In response, Daniel Pipes retorted, 'I wonder. Do all these reasons you just gave apply to the United States? Clearly not – and yet Islamists dominate American Muslim institutions, publications, and mosques' (Clawson, 1999). He could have added Europe as well. After all, Muslims in the West hardly face the socio-economic struggles, political injustices and undemocratic regimes that the Muslim majority context faces.

Yet the connection between Islamism in the west and the human condition in the developing countries cannot be severed completely. A vast majority of Muslims who arrive in the UK do so to 'escape poverty and, sometimes persecution for the promise of a better life for their children' (Alsayyad and Castells, 2002: 1). As far as Britain is concerned, the identification with the host countries, and consequently the meaning of citizenship, varies significantly between those who came in search of better prospects and those who started life here – between the first and the subsequent generations.[9]

The first generation continued to hold the 'myth of return' and at the same time felt indebted to Britain for their quality of life which in most cases was relatively better. Further, in the 1960s when the first wave of migrants came, Islamism was barely in its initial phase and hope for social and economic progress was still attached to secular ideologies.[10]

The second and subsequent generations, however, took their citizenship to be ascribed and grew up without the feeling of indebtedness to the host society. Without the comfort of the 'myth of return', difficulties in integration were having far deeper impact on the second generation than they had on their parents (Hussain and Bagguley, 2005). There were no mitigating factors helping them deal with the double threat of alienation. On the one hand was the inter-generational alienation within the communities and families as tensions developed between the values of the first and second generation. On the other hand, there was the societal alienation because of the sections of the British society which were refusing to adjust to the changed multicultural contours of society (Hussain and Bagguley, 2005).

The research evidence points to the ubiquity of the second generations' struggle to mediate across two cultures (Bhatti, 1999; Abbas, 2007) and a gradual increase of the place of religion in their lives. But the consequence of cultural straddling and 'heightened salience' of Islam varied enormously. While many managed to find creative ways of calibrating and capitalizing on their diverse cultural resources, others found themselves in a precarious position of not fitting in and thus became susceptible to a variety of harmful influences. Current scholarship on Muslims in Europe seems to be divided with regard to its prognosis precisely along these lines; the accommodists who see that political and civic engagement of those who have integrated well will lead to strong social cohesion (Klausen, 2005; Soysal, 1994) and the alarmists who stress the growing radicalization of youth and their aim to transform Europe to Eurabia (Ye-or, 2005).

There are thus two challenges to conventional secular citizenship that have emerged from within Muslim contexts in the UK. The first is from those Muslims who are seeking to 'accommodate the universalism of citizenship claims with the particularism of their ethnic identities' (Hussain and Bagguley, 2005: 415) by engaging in a political process from within the democratic system. They are seeking to challenge the prevailing construction of Britishness forcing rethinking of the accepted models of citizenship, religion and public space and the very idea of the secular (Klausen, 2005; Modood, 1994; Werbner, 2000). Their demands, the so called 'test cases' (Waardenburg, 1988) are not the reflection of divided loyalties but of an empowered citizenship albeit with values and world views significantly different from those held in Britain for some decades (Werbner, 2000).[11]

It is important here to note that these Muslims are not only seeking recognition within wider societal polity. They are also seeking a new personal space in their own communities. For example, the traditional attitude to marriage – arranged and within the community – has been challenged by many young people by marrying by their own choice and from outside the community structure. They have justified their act by appealing to Islamic allegiance beyond race and ethnicity. Undoubtedly, the fact that these young people are seeking personal choice in their marital decisions is a reflection of their imbibing of Western ideals of autonomous individual. Yet, the language in which it is put is not Kantian but Qur'anic (Schmidt, 2004). It is among these relatively well-adjusted Muslims that one finds explorations in the arts – particularly in music – as well as in economics and other areas, seeking integration of traditional Islamic norms and modern Western approaches.

The second challenge is from those who have found integration very difficult against the backdrop of economic deprivation and potentially hostile elements within the majority culture (Peach, 2006; Abbas, 2007, Ansari forthcoming 2008). It is to these young people that political Islam becomes very attractive, particularly as they move into universities and thus away from the eyes of their families and community. Present research on how the movement from rootless to radicalism takes place is not substantial and in need of more empirical input. Ansari notes that "it has not been possible so far to construct a picture that convincingly models the process nor the cohorts that represents this form of extremist Islamism, since evidence suggests that those joining these Islamists organisations come from a wide range of culture, nationalities, class, ideologies and occupations" (Ansari, 2007). Still, from what we know so far the extremist outcome seems to be a product of factors both internal and external to Britain and that while it may have become potent in the last decade or so, it is a product of issues that have a longer history.

For instance, in a discerning – an article in *Prospect*, Shiv Malik has sought to provide some useful insights into the path towards militancy. He investigated the social and psychological dynamics that turned Mohammad Sidique Khan into the mastermind of the 7/7 London bombings. His analysis, supported by some other research, shows that a combination of factors to do with identity, intergenerational gap, lack of 'felt equality', experience of racism, Islamophobia and economic deprivation, all provide internal factors leading to psychological alienation from the mainstream society (Malik, 2007).

All of the above noted internal factors came together at a time when another development – this time external – was also taking place and without its influence the growth of political Islam among young British Muslims cannot be explained. Dislocation and anger among young males growing up as ethnic minorities may be commonplace but what tipped the balance was the linking of these factors with the rise of global political Islam that provided projected identity, existential meaning and a cause to fight for 'one's brothers'. The internal factors were necessary but not sufficient to ignite extremism, but the external factors also did not become attractive in a vacuum.

As we noted above, after the Afghan War the Islamist movements acquired a global dimension. For young people like Khan the tension between being British and being a Pakistani gets dissolved through the Islamist teaching of allegiance to an idealized, universal Islam. Having had little or no systematic education about Muslim history in their upbringing, such young people fill their knowledge vacuum with the images of a mythical past, monolithic and selective interpretations of the Qur'anic verses, portrayal of injustices and sufferings of millions of Muslims across the world and a belief in an exclusivist superiority of Islam. Echoing Nasr (quoted above), Ansari observes that the attraction of organizations such as Hizb ut Tahrir and al-Muhajiroun resides in the manner in which these groups "have

articulated issues that others have tried to avoid, and the fact that they have done so in a language that is accessible and comprehensible to many Muslims growing up in a highly urban and pluralistic British society" (Ansari, 2007). Politicized interpretation of Muslim identity in one stroke provides a language to articulate disquiet with racism, communal authority and nationalism. For many, this power of Islamism has outflanked that of traditional, rural Islam of the earlier generation (Yaqoob, 2007).

CITIZENSHIP EDUCATION AND RELIGIOUS HERITAGE: THE CASE OF MUSLIMS

The above survey points to Crick's notion of 'sense of crisis' which served as an important trigger for citizenship education. At the same time, it also points to the limitations on expectations from education for citizenship, since the possibility of resolution of many of the challenges created by the crisis lie outside of school. In fact, some of the ongoing national and international policies and social practices are continuing to have an impact almost contrary to that expected of schools in general and citizenship education in particular.[12] Yet, with cognizance of these limitations at least three nexuses of citizenship education and Muslim religious tradition can be put forward.

CONNECTED CRITICS: ACKNOWLEDGING THE ROLE OF RELIGIOUSLY INSPIRED SOCIAL CRITICISM

Citizenship requires, for its own health, that citizens are able and willing to engage in social critique. The comforts of passive citizenship enjoyed by many in twentieth century Western Europe became possible only because of the active citizenship practiced by the generations preceding them and continued by individuals and movements today. A key ingredient of active citizenship is the civic virtue of social criticism. Following Walzer, social criticism can be defined as a social activity in which individual members of a society speak in public to other members who join in the speaking and whose speech constitutes a collective reflection upon the conditions of collective life (Walzer, 1985).

As implied in the above survey, the language of secular citizenship discourse can no longer be thought of as the only way in which people can be galvanized to engage in this critique in the pursuit of their rights. Many religions, particularly Islam, now have the vocabulary to critique contemporary structures. Thus, citizenship education needs to take account of the power of religions to act as social critiques and, at the same time, help students learn to transform it into democratic forms of protest, criticism and negotiation.

In the modern context generally, religions themselves have been the subject of critique. There is much weight in such criticism and no religion seeking adherence in the modern world can ignore them. At the same time, it is now important to recognize that religions can have the power to inspire critique and protest. Religions are Janus-faced: they can mask exploitative structures but they also contain ideals with which such structures can be challenged. Recognition of social criticism inspired by the ethical ideals acquired from religions should be made part of political literacy. Citizenship education can capitalize on this potential of religion by introducing students both to the fact that religions can provide values by which policies and actions can be evaluated and the need for articulating this evaluation through the democratic process. By way of illustration, the following sub-section provides a brief survey of the tradition of social critique in Muslim history.

Peaceful social criticism in Muslim history

Islam, like many other religions, emerged with a critical stance towards the then prevailing conditions, both religious and socio-economic. The Makkan opponents of the Prophet were criticized for their blind imitation of their forefathers (Qur'an 26: 69–89) and were urged to take care of those on the margins of society – the orphans, widows and travellers (Qur'an 2: 177; 16: 90; 9: 34). A general command for enjoining the good and forbidding the evil (Qur'an 3: 104) was supported by the sayings of the Prophet.[13] The concern for caring for the destitute is very strong and even a slight neglect is not accepted (Qur'an 80: 1-12).[14]

From such beginnings, there evolved early on in the Muslim history a strong sense of justice. In the beginning when the rulers governed more like the 'first among equals' than a monarch, it was possible even for the ordinary Muslims to question the ruler if there were any doubtful dealings. By the time the Umayyad dynasty (661–749 CE) was ruling, such straight forward accountability was no longer possible. Still, there emerged a group of loosely connected individuals who showed practical but peaceful concern about the social conditions of their time and sought to hold the ruling elite accountable to their privileged roles. The letters of al-Hasan al-Basri (d. 728) to Umayyad caliphs were an early example of this tradition of outspoken criticism of social conditions of his time.

In the Muslim imagination, the good ruler was deeply committed to providing justice and removing sources of misery. Stories of rulers who went on nocturnal rounds of their cities in disguise to apprise themselves of the conditions of their subjects spread. Such expectation of a humane rule was captured in literature such as the 'Mirrors of Princes' and other art forms. For example, a Mughal miniature of the Emperor Jahangir showed him shooting an 'effigy of poverty'. The text in the painting ascribes Jahangir with the ambition of envisioning a world without poverty.[15]

Another expression of the desire for social justice was the widespread belief in the coming of a Mahdi. Many subjugated individuals and communities believed in the idea of mahdi, a saviour who would come in not so distant future to fill the world with justice.

Massignon is right in claiming that belief in Mahdi 'is an expression of the profound aspiration for social justice that ferments in every human community, especially religious community' (Massignon, 1982: 297).

In the modern period the spirit of social criticism from within Muslim tradition continued. From the poetry of Nazir Akbarabadi (1735–1830) in India to the social critique of religious leaders in Syria in the late nineteenth century, to the Gayo Islamic verses in Sumatra in the mid-twentieth century, there are many examples of this (Bowen, 1993; Commins, 1993).

There were phases in the Muslim history when this spirit of religious social criticism declined as a compromise emerged between the political powers and religious scholars. Thus, during the late Abbasid period the dominant political theory was quietist and urged people to accept even a corrupt caliph instead of questioning his deeds (Brown, 2000).

Thus, throughout Muslim history one finds a continuous, though with different intensities, strand of social criticism inspired, at least in part, by the Islamic scriptures. Sometimes it was in the form of an explicit challenge and at other times there was only a muted concern. Thus, through most of the Muslim history one finds a strand of social criticism, sometimes as an explicit challenge and at other times as a mild concern.

When students would learn about religion's potential to inspire protest in an educational setting rather than in a polemical setting, it can help them understand that people of faith can function as 'connected critics' (Walzer, 1985) – critics who are committed to the norms of democracy but also can 'appeal to transcendent ideals to critique current practice' (Thiemann, 2000: 85).

CITIZENSHIP, EMANCIPATION AND SOCIAL JUSTICE: RECLAIMING THE HOPE

Many Muslims today, both in majority and minority contexts, are extremely concerned about issues of social justice and equality. Social cohesion without social justice is not possible. If after 50 years of substantial migration, Muslims in Britain still feel a huge deficit of 'felt equality,' urgency of taking account of this cannot be overestimated. While there are limits to what school education can do to bring about social justice and 'felt equality', it can certainly provide students with opportunities to discuss these matters. Citizenship education thus needs to continue to concern itself with social justice, inequality and power.[16]

As we noted above, in many Muslim contexts, the language of religion has replaced the language of social analysis. In Britain watershed events such as the Rushdie Affair have strengthened categories such as Muslim and Islam as units of analysis, marginalizing understanding of the discourse in terms of race, gender and class. This process was facilitated by the media as well as government's policies of approaching Muslims as a community, seeking and nurturing unrepresentative community leaders and spokespersons (Allievi, 2006). The more children grow up accepting religion as their primary identity the more they are likely to understand the challenges they face in religious and moral terms rather than social and political terms. Citizenship education can help reverse this trend of the 'moralization of politics' (Mirza et al., 2007). By engaging students in the analysis of social issues in the language of social sciences, they can be prepared to withstand attempts to couch these issues in exclusively religious terms. Learning the role of social policy, decisions about resource allocation and role of politics in the creation, sustenance and change of social conditions can help students appreciate the role of human agency.

Students should become aware of the contemporary challenges in the developing countries. Much of the appeal of trans-national Islamist discourse lies in its being the first to make young Muslims aware of the crises in different parts of the world in which Muslims are involved, thus initiating them into the 'imagined community' of global Muslims. While to Huntington these crisis may be the evidence of Islam's 'bloody borders' (Huntington, 1993), to some Muslims these are the testimony of the West having blood on its hands. Education for citizenship needs to take up the challenge of introducing students to these conflicts in a manner that brings out the fact that these are not exclusively or even primarily religious conflicts but of social, economic and political nature.

DECONSTRUCTING ESSENTIALIZED ISLAM AND MONOLITHIC MUSLIM COMMUNITY

Many 'young Muslims relate that their studies (of Islam) began when they realized that they were in need of a firm knowledge of their religion' (Schmidt, 2004: 35). Where this search leads them depends substantially upon how it is fulfilled. Unsatisfied with the way Islam is articulated by the imported mosque imams in a language that the young barely understand, some are attracted by the sophisticated manner in which Islam is portrayed by the Islamists (Khatib, 2003) – a divinely ordained complete blueprint of life of supposedly unchanging values and practices which once produced an almost perfect brilliant civilization and can do so again if given a chance.

In place of this, students need to be acquainted with the actual developments in the Muslim history: the fact of continued interpretation and re-interpretation of foundational text; the contested and historical nature of norms, practices and institutions; and the rich diversity of opinions on any given matter. Students with such historical and interpretive understanding of their faith are far more likely to resist seduction of a simplistic presentation of a vast and complex phase of human history.

Essentialized understanding of Islam gets challenged when one looks at the internal diversity, both historical and contemporary, within the Muslim tradition. It is not sufficient to discuss that there are Muslims from many different cultures in Britain.

A deeper level of diversity needs to be brought out. When we learn about the debates between *Qadariya* and *Jabriya,* between *Ash'ariya* and *Mu'tazila,* different doctrinal positions of the *Shi'as, Sunnis* and *Kharijites*, varying interpretations of the same Qur'anic verses, diversity in ritual practices and so on, it becomes apparent that religious traditions are interpretive. In this regard, it may help if students are introduced to the works of Muslims scholars who are engaged in re-interpreting Islamic symbols to connect them with progressive ideas. Even if the actual thinking process involved in these efforts may be difficult to grasp by the young students, familiarity with names and basic ideas of scholars will at least ensure that students are aware of the existence of alternate discourses about democracy, gender, civil society, individual freedom and reason. It may assist them realize that religions are like a living metaphor, which continues to defy attempts to exhaust its interpretative possibilities.

CONCLUSION

It can be argued that while Islam never lost its power to bestow existential meaning, orient values and provide social symbols, many Muslims have turned to it as a solution to modern problems only after being disillusioned with other contenders–nationalism, capitalism and socialism in particular. It is not a coincidence that the word *adl*, justice, figures in the names of many Islamic parties across the Muslim world. Generally speaking, in the Western world citizenship has been an empowering idea. It has also been an expanding idea, covering increasing number of groups. The question is, will it be able to redefine itself to become inclusive of Muslim aspirations, at least those that do not go against the ideals of a pluralistic, peaceful co-existence. Citizenship education while being aware of its limitations, can play an important role in answering this question positively by providing a safe environment in which students can take a critical stance towards tradition, both of Muslims and of British society.

NOTES

1 I would like to thank Dr. Dina Kiwan for commenting upon an earlier draft of this Chapter.

2 The sentiments behind W W Hunter's essay, written in 1870, 'Our Indian Musalman: are they bound in conscience to rebel against the Queen?' have remained alive for some.

3 A recent research indicating this fact for British Muslims is published in Policy Exchange's report 'Living Apart Together: British Muslims & the Paradox of Multi-culturalism' (Mirza, et al., 2007).

4 Generally translated as community of believers.

5 For all the verses and examples quoted in such writings there is an alternative peaceful interpretation found in the writings of other Muslims. For example, while Azhar takes the true meaning of Jihad to be a physical struggle, others see it as a spiritual endeavour.

6 The role of the Western governments in supporting dictatorial regimes in the Third World countries is a moot point. In the Muslim contexts, the support of the CIA in overthrowing of Mossadeq in 1953 is widely quoted as an example of such support (Gasiorowski, 2000).

7 Frantz Fanon had noted this fusion of resistance and Islamic symbols way back in 1960s: '… the veil becomes a symbol of resistance as long as resistance isn't organized. Clinging to that tradition was the only way they could say no to France and its cultural hegemony' Fanon (1980).

8 In this regard, see a very useful issue of ISIM Review entitled 'Shades of Islamism', Autumn 2006.

9 Several recent findings, including those presented in the report 'Living Apart Together' provide useful data that indicates the differences in attitude towards religion, citizenship and violence between Muslims of older and younger age groups.

10 "In the 1960s, Muslims immigrants were largely involved in secular political movements that spoke to their ethnic and national concerns … or specific problems encountered by immigrants in the UK." (Mirza et al., 2007: 22).

11 In fact, as shown by studies on migrants groups in the US, religion has played positive role in helping communities integrate in the civil society processes (Kastoryano, 2004).

12 In this context, an ongoing debate is about the impact of some features of current British foreign policy.

13 For example: 'If you see something wrong, change it with your hands; if you do not have strength enough to do so, speak against it; if you do not have strength enough to do so, at least condemn it in your heart and that would be the lowest stage of faith' (*Sahih Muslim,* Book I, Number 0079).

14 In these verses a person is criticized for failing to pay attention to a poor blind person who had come to him. The person instead continued to converse with a group of rich Makkan merchants. The precise identity of the person has been a subject of debate among scholars and some commentators (for example, Ibn Kathir) have taken him to be the Prophet himself.

15 'Emperor Jahangir (reigned 1605–1627) Triumphing Over Poverty' by artist Abu'l Hasan, circa 1620–1625 (Los Angeles County Museum of Arts).

16 A positive development in this regard is the recently published Ajegbo Report which makes identity and social justice central in citizenship education.

REFERENCES

Abbas, T. (2007) 'A theory of Islamic political radicalism in Britain: sociology, theology and international political economy'. *Contemporary Islam,* 1 (2): 109–122.

Ahmad, I. (2003) *Confronting Empire: Interviews with David Barsamian.* Lahore: Vanguard.

Allievi, S. (2006) 'How and Why "Immigrants" Became "Muslims".' *ISIM Review,* Autumn (18): 37.

Alsayyad, N., and Castells, M. (2002) 'Introduction: Islam and the Changing Identity of Europe.' In N. Alsayyad and M. Castells (eds), *Muslim Europe or Euro-Islam.* Lanham: Lexington Books.

Ansari, H. (2007) *What is Islamism in Britain? A Historical Exploration.* Paper given at the Religious Studies Research Seminar, University of Cape Town, March 2007.

Anasari, H. (forthcoming, 2008) 'Sucide Bombings' or 'Martyrdom Operations'? British Muslim Understandings of Jihad and Terrorism. In C.A. Lewis, M.B. Roggers, R. Amlot, K.M. Loewenthal, M. Cinnirella, & H. Ansari (eds.), *Aspects of Terrorism and Marytyrdom: Dying for good, Dying for God* (Volume 1). Lewiston, New York: Edwin Melleen Press.

Ayubi, N. (1980) 'The Political Revival of Islam: The Case of Egypt.' *International Journal of Middle East Studies*, 12 (4): 481–499.

Azhar, M.M. (2001) *Ma'arka*. Karachi: Idara Al-Khair.

Baker, W.R. (2003) *Islam without Fear: Egypt and the New Islamists*. Cambridge, MA.: Harvard University Press.

Bhatti, G. (1999) *Asian Children at Home and School*. London: Routledge.

Bowen, J.R. (1993) 'A Modernist Muslim Poetic: Irony and Social Critique in Gayo Islamic Verse.' *The Journal of Asian Studies*, 52 (3): 629–646.

Brown, C. (2000) *Religion and State: The Muslim Approach to Politics*. New York: Columbia University Press.

Butko, T. (2004) 'Revelation or Revolution: A Gramscian Approach to the Rise of Political Islam.' *British Journal of Middle Eastern Studies*, 31 (1): 41–62.

Clawson, P. (1999) 'Is Islamism a Threat? A Debate.' *Middle East Quarterly,* I (4).

Commins, D. (1993) 'Social Criticism and Reformist Ulama of Damascus.' *Studia Islamica*, 78: 169–180.

Crick, B. (1999) 'The Presuppositions of Citizenship Education.' *Journal of Philosophy of Education*, 33 (3): 337–352.

Denoeux, G. (2002) 'The Forgotten Swamp: Navigating Political Islam.' *Middle East Policy*, IX (2): 56–81.

Esposito, J. and Tamimi, A. (eds) (2002) *Islam and Secularism in the Middle East*. London: Hurst & Company.

Fanon, F. (1980) *A Dying Colonialism,* trans. Charles Lam Markmann. New York: Grove Press.

Gasiorowski, M.J. (2000) *The CIA Looks Back at the 1953 Coup in Iran. Middle East Report* (216): 4–5.

Grillo, R. (2004) 'Islam and Transnationalism.' *Journal of Ethnic and Migration Studies*, 30 (5): 861–878.

Halliday, F. (1995) 'Review Article: The Politics of "Islam" – A Second Look.' *British Journal of Political Science*, 25 (3): 399–417.

Hamzeh, N. and Dekmejian, H. (1996) 'A Sufi Response to Political Islamism: Al-Ahbash of Lebanon.' *International Journal of Middle East Studies*, 28 (2): 217–229.

Haqqani, H. (2002) 'The Gospel of Jihad.' *Foreign Policy* (132): 72–74.

Huntington, S. (1993) The Clash of Civilizations? *Foreign Affairs, Summer* 72(3): 21–49.

Huntington, S. (1996) *The Clash of Civilizations and the Making of a New World Order*. New York: Simon and Schuster.

Hussain, Y. and Bagguley, P. (2005) 'Citizenship, Ethnicity and Identity: British Pakistanis after the 2001 "Riots".' *Sociology*, 39 (3): 407–425.

Keddie, N. (1998) 'The New Religious Politics: Where, When, and Why Do "Fundamentalisms" Appear?' *Comparative Studies in Society and History*, 40 (4): 696–723.

Khatib, L. (2003) 'Communicating Islamic Fundamentalism as Global Citizenship.' *Journal of Communication Inquiry*, 27 (4): 389–409.

Klausen, J. (2005) *The Islamic Challenge: Politics and Religion in Western Europe*. Oxford: Oxford University Press.

Lewis, B. (1990) 'The Roots of Muslim rage.' *Atlantic Monthly*, 266 (3): 47–56.

Lewis, B. (2004) *The Crisis of Islam: Holy War and Unholy Terror*. London: Phoenix.

Malik, S. (2007) 'My Brother the Bomber.' *Prospect*, June(135).

Mamdani, M. (2005) 'Whither Political Islam?' *Foreign Affairs, January/February*.

Massignon, L. (1982) *The Passion of al-Hallaj: Mystic and Martyr of Islam* (H. Mason, Trans. Vol. 1) Princeton: Princeton University Press.

MEPC (2002) *A statement from qaidat al-jihad regarding the mandates of the heroes and the legality of the operations in New York and Washington*. Retrieved July 25, 2007, from http://www.mepc.org/journal_vol10/0306_alqaeda.asp

Mirsepassi-Ashtiani, A. (1994) 'The Crisis of Secular Politics and the Rise of Political Islam in Iran.' *Social Text,* 38 (Spring): 51–84.

Mirza, M., Senthikumaran, A., Ja'far, Z. (2007) *Living Apart Together: British Muslims and the Paradox of multiculturalism*. London Policy Exchange.

Modood, T. (1994) Establishment, Multiculturism and British Citizenship. *The Political Quarterly*.

Nasr, V. (2003) 'Lessons from the Muslim world.' *Daedalus,* (Summer) 132 (3): 67–72.

Peach, C. (2006) 'Muslims in the 2001 census of England and Wales: Gender and economic disadvantage. *Ethnic and Racial Studies.* 29 (4): 629–655.

Pipes, D. (1995) 'There are No Moderates: Dealing with Fundamentalist Islam.' *National Interest,* (Fall).

Roy, A. (2005) *Gendered Citizenship: Historical and Cultural Explorations.* New Delhi: Orient Longmann.

Roy, O. (1999) 'Changing Patterns among Radical Islamic Movements.' *The Brown Journal of World Affairs,* VI(1): 109–120.

Roy, O. (2004) *Globalized Islam.* New York: Columbia University Press.

Safi, O. (ed.) (2003) *Progressive Muslims: On Justice, Gender and Pluralism* Oxford: Oneworld.

Schmidt, G. (2004) 'Islamic Identity Formation among Young Muslims: The Case of Denmark, Sweden and the United States.' *Journal of Muslim Minority Affairs,* 24 (1): 31–45.

Sivan, E. (2003) 'The Clash within Islam.' *Survival,* 45 (1): 25–44.

Soysal, Y.N. (1994) *Limits of Citizenship: Migrants and Postnational Membership in Europe.* Chicago: University of Chicago.

Thiemann, R. (2000) 'Public Religion: Bane or Blessing for Democracy?' In N. Rosenblum (ed.), *Obligations of Citizenship and Demands.* New Jersey: Princeton University Press.

Waardenburg, J. (1988) 'Institutionalization of Islam in the Netherlands, 1961–1986'. In T. Gerhom and Y. G. Lithman (eds), *The New Islamic Presence in Western Europe.* London: Mansell Publishing Ltd. pp. 8–31.

Walzer, M. (1985) *Interpretation and social criticism.* Retrieved April 25, 2007, from http://www.tannerlectures.utah.edu/lectures/walzer88.pdf

Werbner, P. (2000) 'Divided Loyalties, Empowered Citizenship? Muslims in Britain.' *Citizenship Studies,* 4 (3): 307–324.

Wiktorowicz, Q. (2001) 'The New Global Threat: Transnational Salafis and Jihad.' *Middle East Policy,* VIII (4): 18–38.

Wiktorowicz, Q. and Kaltner, J. (2003) 'Killing in the Name of Islam: Al-Qaeda's Justification for September 11.' *Middle East Policy,* X (2): 76–92.

Wolfe, M. (ed.) (2002) *Taking Back Islam: American Muslims Reclaim Their Faith.* New York: Rodale Press.

Woltering, R. (2002) 'The Roots of Islamist Popularity.' *Third World Quarterly,* 23 (6): 1133–1143.

Yaqoob, S. (2007) 'British Islamic political radicalism.' In T. Abbas (ed.), *Islamic political radicalism: A European perspective.* Edinburgh: Edinburgh University Press.

Ye-or, B. (2005) *Eurabia: The Euro-Arab Axis.* Madison, NJ: Fairleight Dickinson University Press.

23

Christianity, Citizenship and Democracy

James Arthur

INTRODUCTION

In Britain there is little attention given in modern educational discourses to religion and its role in shaping meanings of citizenship. In part this is due to the fact that many of the organizations that seek to promote a discourse on citizenship education are secular bodies who present issues of religious identity and faith in the language of community, equality, diversity and values. This language does not fully recognize the significance of faith and belief for notions of active citizenship or do justice to religious motivations and traditions. Such organizations also fail to take seriously the world revitalization of the main religious faiths and the forceful reappearance of religious issues in public affairs (see Kepel, 1994). Modern European notions of citizenship, whether liberal, communitarian or civic republican, are almost wholly founded on secular constructs. Many modern political scientists and educationalists therefore portray Christianity as a force that hindered the progress of citizenship. As Bryan Turner (2007: 259) says, there is an assumption that the rise of secular citizenship requires the erosion of the authority of institutional religion. These observations minimize the importance of religion in the political context denying religion a legitimate role. Consequently, accounts of citizenship in educational studies generally omit positive references to religion.

Many of the works of Dawn Oliver, Derek Heater (1994, 2004) and Bernard Crick (2000) make no reference to the Judaeo-Christian tradition in what they believe to be the foundations of Western citizenship. Crick makes his position explicit when he declared at a British Humanist Association conference at the University of London in October 2006 that 'Citizenship is secular, on historical and philosophical grounds'. Even when explicit reference is made to religion it is generally negative (see Held, 1996 1997). Why do these authors begin with an exclusive and elitist idea of citizenship in the classical period and ignore the relevance of Christianity for the subsequent development of notions of citizenship? With this lack of historical treatment, together with the underlying secular assumptions behind such an absence, it is not surprising that religious faith and citizenship are not seen as complementary.

I would argue that modern citizenship educators have a myopic vision of the historical origins of contemporary ideas of education for citizenship. In this paper I focus mainly on Christianity's relationship with citizenship and argue that the idea of citizenship endured and developed within the European context partly because of Christianity. I argue that there is a connection between Christianity and our modern ideas of active citizenship. Citizenship can only be defined as having a secular legal status if it is interpreted in a narrow way – as consisting of certain rights, duties and privileges such as the right to own land, to hold public office, to vote, to pay taxes and to serve on a jury. However, citizenship that encourages active public engagement and responsibility in a democracy *cannot* be a wholly secular concept, for it involves social attachments and allegiances which must in turn, for some, involve religious motivations. We need to ask again where does citizenship come from? What, if anything, does it have to do with religious faith? Can citizenship education be addressed independently of religion? Is citizenship stronger when the citizen is religious?

Those who adopt liberal secular positions generally argue that religion and politics are two distinct activities and that religion has little contribution to make to citizenship. Consequently, they advocate that those who have religious beliefs should keep them private and that they should not allow their religious beliefs to shape their conduct or judgements as citizens engaged in the public realm. It follows, from this line, that citizenship is a political and secular legal status and religious people should therefore 'bracket' out their religious beliefs if they want to participate in society's political order. John Rawls (1997: 781) has asked the question 'How is it possible for those of faith, as well as the non-religious, to endorse a secular regime even when their comprehensive doctrines may not prosper under it, and indeed may decline'. He answers that religious people should only argue for particular policies or laws by providing secular reasons

for them and Robert Audi (2005: 217) has gone even further by advocating the 'principle of secular jurisdiction' in which a religious person should exclusively think in secular terms when they vote in democratic elections. This is a secular definition of the role of religion in political life and it has many critics. If accepted as a principle it would entail that each religious tradition would have to accept a restrictive definition of the use of reason in order to participate in political associations. A person of faith would therefore presumably have to think in two different realms – the secular and the religious, which are somehow unconnected in their minds. Jurgen Habermas (2006) believes that this mental dualism would be impossible for any human being and that it denotes a 'narrow secular consciousness'. It is simply a secularization of the notion of citizenship that has much influenced the majority of those who write on citizenship education.

RELIGION AND CITIZENSHIP

The idea of citizenship holds a prominent place in the history of European political thought. Education for citizenship is a more recent development in UK schools and is both ideologically ambiguous and politically contentious. The relationship between religion, specifically Christianity, and notions of citizenship has also been historically problematic, indeed, it has been characterized as 'very complex, confusing and changing' (Niebuhr, 1952: 1). There is no doubt that religion is and has been a key factor in determining someone's character, moral norms, idea of duty and has provided many with a sense of national identity. Religion is not simply concerned with abstract ideas, but is also concerned with action and participation in the public realm – religion presupposes behaviour. It can be a powerful determinant factor in shaping a nation's politics and religious beliefs have significant public consequences. Organized religion can also be an agent of political change. Religious traditions embody a set of values that are far greater in intensity and meaning, or in the language of political philosophy, far thicker, than the promotion of citizenship education. Of course, the situation in regard to citizenship education and religion differs in many countries with a sizeable Christian population.

We are well acquainted with the idea that the practice of political citizenship originated in ancient Greece, but are perhaps less aware that biblical religion also had an important influence on the development of the meaning of citizenship in Europe. The citizen in Greek City-States was someone who had a voice in shaping the political life of the community, especially in making its laws through a deliberative process. In ancient Greece, religion and the State were coterminous, there were many Gods associated with most of these City-States and civic duty became nearly identical with religious obligation. The temple was also the civic centre, priests were public officials and religious festivals were public events, meaning that participation in the religious community was an essential aspect of citizenship. The secular and the religious were clearly inter-twined – civic buildings were even graced with statues of the Gods, altars and shrines. It is important to note however, that most people in the *polis* did not enjoy citizenship, which was an exclusive status reserved for the few. Citizens gained this status by virtue of their education, gender, family, wealth or leadership prowess. Citizenship meant having the responsibility and privileges of membership in the political community, but this smaller political community of citizens was an integral subset of the larger religious community (see Mickalson, 2005: 160; Carteledge, 1999; Zaidman and Pantel, 1992: 92).

In contrast, the Jewish people in Israel structured themselves not as a City-State but as the covenanted people of God, living under a legal order handed down by God to a nation made up of many family clans. All Jews were members of God's people and the community of which they were a part was more profound and historically far-reaching

than a Greek City-State. This produced a larger conception of human society than the Greek City-Sate. The Jewish tradition was based on the idea that all are equal in the eyes of God and the covenant was handed down from parent to child. The Jewish tradition emphasized family, friendships, charity, voluntary associations and traditions that together made up and formed the basis of civil society. Members of this society were linked by a bond of kinship which obliged its members not only to love their neighbour, but also to love and respect the stranger. Indeed, love could not be translated in civic and constitutional terms for this duty to love is laid upon human beings by religious commitment in a manner which cannot be articulated as constitutive of the state or as a matter of public policy. Love was seen as primary whilst laws, rights and contractual obligations were secondary. The idea of covenant meant that all were obliged to help each other beyond the letter of the law and loyalty and fidelity were emphasized. This is the tradition into which Jesus began his teaching and it was the achievement of Christianity to combine these two primary influences of ancient Greece and ancient Israel. This Judeo-Christian synthesis understood that a moral relationship exists between human beings that is more fundamental than one that is contractual. The combination of both the political order (institutions, States, governments and political systems) and the social order (family, friendships and voluntary associations) inevitably resulted in tensions as one order tended to be predominant at any given time. However, the social order was held together by bonds of free kinship whilst the political order was ultimately held together by the threat of force.

A *universal* idea of membership and belonging, so important to notions of citizenship, were concepts that developed early in Christian thought and from this it followed that all Christians are moral equals, at least theoretically, and consequently enjoyed equality in a form of world citizenship as baptized Christians. This universalistic thinking laid the important ideological foundations for a definition of citizenship not based on blood or kinship. There were clearly several important religious and political developments between the fall of the Roman Empire and the sixteenth century that inevitably influenced understandings of citizenship. Christianity looked towards the next life, offering its adherents the possibility of eternal or divine citizenship. Consequently, civic citizenship was not initially seen as an absolutely essential part of the good life for the early Church.

AUGUSTINE AND AQUINAS

This developing theological theory of citizenship in two realms made explicit the important connection between civic citizenship and divine citizenship. An important principle of this developing Christian notion was St. Augustine's conception of the world, in his *City of God*, as divided into the metaphors of the City of God and the City of Man. Two contrasted forms of citizenship were presented – spiritual citizenship and profane citizenship. The State, however Christian it may appear, can only be a community of saints and sinners because the City of Man, Augustine wrote, is flawed as a result of wars and corruption. The City of Man is a passing Kingdom, offering only a temporary and secondary level of citizenship, whilst the City of God is eternal and provides the Christian with primary anticipatory citizenship.

This perception of the world as being divided into the secular realm (government of temporal affairs) and the spiritual realm (government of men's souls) became a keynote of European culture. There was certainly conflict and tension between the political and religious authorities, but it was a time in which the political community was religious and the religious community political. In a sense everything was conceived as religious in the dominant worldview of the period and the personnel who ran the political community was practically the same

as those who ran the religious community. There was no conception of the secular as somehow divorced from religion. Augustine believed that his two cities were distinct but not separate, Christians had a stake in the earthly City and politics and religion necessarily overlapped. Augustine discusses the ideal secular State by emphasizing that the City of God exists within the City of Man, within separate individuals or in communities of believers so that it was possible to see within the City of Man an image of the City of God. So whilst the ultimate citizenship is in the next world Christians should not withdraw from the City of Man, but ought rather to work within it. They had to engage in the political community, not because politics is ultimate, but because Christians are commended to love both God and their neighbour – in other words they had important responsibilities to both Cities. Augustine presented a case for Christian citizenship which entailed that you could be a good Roman citizen as well as a good Christian by working for the good of society. So whilst for Augustine civic citizenship is a subordinate end, it is ordered to a higher end, but this did not mean that this subordinate end could not be pursued, in fact it was unavoidable. He raised the classic notion of civic citizenship to the level of a religious duty and admonished Christians to assume the obligations of civic citizenship. Christians were to give themselves completely in two directions: the 'upward' (vertical relationship with God) and the 'forward' (horizontal relationship with their neighbour) and each direction should not hinder the other, but on the contrary further it. Augustine had effectively invented the concept of the secular. Christianity therefore did not disable civic virtues, but provided a force to realize these virtues through public engagement. This developed, by the thirteenth century, into a strong tradition which positively affirmed human community. This teaching has been of the utmost importance in the history of Europe for it leaves to the Church or the individual's conscience the final judgement about whether obedience to the

State is spiritually and morally acceptable. In short, Christianity provided its members with the criteria to assist them as citizens in judging whether secular orders are permissible.

Whilst Augustine spoke of the theological foundations of citizenship Thomas Aquinas thought of citizenship as a natural aspect of human life in his *Summa Theologiae*. Aquinas believed that human beings were by nature social and political animals and that since all things natural are part of God's creation, so is the political order which is both natural and sacred. Aquinas believed that civil government was a positive force for the promotion of man's welfare. Therefore it is a mistake, he believed, to approach the issue of Christianity and public life as if they were two realms that we have to relate to each other. According to Aquinas and Augustine the public realm for the conduct of one's civic citizenship was already related to faith because it was created by God. Consequently, in addition to loving God, a person needs to feed their children and build for them a safe community and these activities do not direct them away from God, but rather, as Aquinas insists, points them to God.

Commenting on Aristotle's *Politics* (ST: Q105 reply to objection 2) Aquinas provides a definition of citizenship which he divides into two kinds: 'simple' and 'restricted'. The 'simple' citizenship is the full exercise of political rights whilst 'restricted' citizenship denoted *membership* of a community which involved certain rights and social obligations. The 'restricted' citizenship includes almost all the population residing in the territory of the City or State including women and children. It is an 'anagraphical' citizenship defined on a simple territorial basis. Simple citizenship is attributed by the City or State whilst 'restricted' citizenship is a more inclusive form of belonging conferred on the basis of residence and the minimal territorial unit which attributed it was the parish and the parish priest through compulsory baptism. It was a notion of citizenship that was bestowed only on Christians, based on their confessional status, and conveyed on them from a source lying outside of the material world. Records of baptism in the parish register ante-dated civil administration and conferred a form of citizenship in Christendom–the Catholic Church was the universal community in Europe at this time and Christendom was not simply a religious community, but also a coherent political entity which pre-dated the emergence of nation-States. Aquinas saw each sphere of human activity as enjoying its own autonomy. In matters regarding civic goods he said it was better to obey the secular authority even when it was controlled by non-Christians. Aquinas also believed that the common good was more important than the private good, he would not have distinguished between the individual and the community.

CIVIC SOCIETY AND THE GROWTH OF THE SECULAR

When civic society recovered its strength with its ability to look for appropriate political forms one model of political association that was available to Europeans was the City. The City represented a public space where citizens deliberated and decided their common affairs – the word citizen applied to all who lived in towns. However, political citizenship was held by a minority and was generally only inherited, but it could be granted to individuals. By the later Middle Ages, guild membership and citizenship had become fused together. Citizenship in the modern sense began to emerge with the creation of these independent cities in medieval Europe. At the Reformation a series of Protestant City-States were founded by the Swiss reformers, such as Calvin, Zwingli and Beza, based on what they personally thought to be the ideas contained in Augustine's *City of God*. They saw the Church as simply one institution among the organizing forces of society which God had ordained. Christian duty was seen in the wider context of civic citizenship. It was the evolution of Cities along the lines of State formation that gave citizenship in Europe its full institutionalized and formalized character and that eventually made nationality a key component of citizenship. Protestant ideas, some would say Protestant theories of citizenship, tended to conflate the Christian community with the surrounding culture and the emerging idea of the nation began to displace the Catholic Church and secure for itself the primary identity and allegiance of the people within its territory. It was thus the Reformation that aided the rise of the modern nation-State by separating out the heavenly kingdom from the earthly. Consequently, the European idea of the City or State became dependent on territorial jurisdiction and reliance on *ius sanguinis* as the determinant of citizenship. The Catholic Church saw the City or State as a society of individuals and what defined the nature of that society was its goal, its end or its ultimate good. A symbiotic relationship existed between religious and civic identity, principally through baptism. This medieval inheritance began to gradually separate out the powers of the State and Church, but the secular and religious were still understood as being directed by God. Nevertheless, religious criteria gradually ceased to be the chief means to regulate society and so religion and secular power began to disengage from each other.

CITIZENSHIP EDUCATION AND CHRISTIANITY

Today, citizenship education programmes are being introduced at a time of uncertainty and doubt within European societies. They are often ill-defined because citizenship itself is contested and their content in schools is often reduced to a basic language of rights. The outcomes of teaching based on this kind of content inevitably change according to circumstances. These citizenship education courses are based on a worldview of humanity as a market-place of autonomous and competing individuals; some would say 'consumerist unbelievers'. Such programmes

of citizenship education may refer to ideas of community involvement, solidarity, belonging and other forms of fraternity, grounded in a discourse of freedom and equality, a combination which form the basis of an understanding of a rights-orientated model of citizenship, but this fails to describe the richness of human cooperation and obligation. It fails to persuade people that they ought to trust and love each other. This secular worldview fails to provide adequate descriptions that are compelling for people to be moved to action, indeed, it fails to reach the heart. The idea that we are all, more or less, becoming modern and that as we become modern we will become more alike, and at the same time more homogenous and more reasonable, is a product of the secularization of citizenship. This secularization fails to recognize that, at the very least, echoes of their religious heritage continue to resonate with citizens and are often responsible for the way they demonstrate such qualities as altruism, compassion and love of their neighbour. In this context there appears to be a dual calling of citizenship and faith within the competing obligations among those who profess a religious faith. What is needed is a language of participatory citizenship that can be shared by those with faith and those with none. This cannot be done by ignoring religion.

If we understand citizenship as a legal status within a particular territory in which the State enforces legal requirements and bestows entitlement to certain services and basic rights then this 'minimal' or 'formal' citizenship may be seen as a secular construct. The responsibilities of this kind of citizenship for promoting the common good are minimal as it can simply be understood at the level of passive membership of a community. However, if we expand this definition to include the public practice-engagement of the responsible citizens and seek to promote this through citizenship education then we are promoting a 'maximal' or 'substantive' definition of active citizenship which makes it more problematic to recognize as a wholly secular conception. Such a conception of citizenship, especially republican notions of citizenship, have regard for the quality of an individual's response to membership in a community and understand the citizen as a political being who should not only act, but should desire to act and be disposed to act, in a way that fosters and maintains the main goals of the community. The State, in this conception of citizenship, adopts a formative educative role in seeking to produce a certain type of citizen with particular standards of conduct. It speaks of a citizen having certain kinds of virtues – citizens who are publicly spirited, who can discuss, cooperate and compromise with each other and above all can trust one another and undertake public responsibilities when called upon. This kind of citizenship is not simply about status, but involves an individual's deepest feelings and motivations.

The State therefore is not neutral for it extends itself into more profound areas of moral and social meaning. As William Galston (2002: 17) says:

> The more demanding the conception of citizenship, the more intrusive the public policies needed to promote it … the more our conception of the good citizen requires the sacrifice of private attachments to the common good, the more vigorously the state must act (as Sparta did) to weaken those attachments in favour of devotion to the public sphere.

The State moves from the regulation of public life (paying taxes, regulating voting, obeying the law etc.) to the regulation of private life (the way in which citizens interact with themselves, expressing views and associating with others of their own choice etc). The justification for this more expansive formative role for the State is to create a society which holds certain core values dear and to use the law to educate people to transform the culture of citizenship to make it more active, open, tolerant and inclusive. In so doing the State runs the danger of weakening civil society for by deliberately and publicly identifying what it considers to be worthwhile for citizens and then using legislation and regulations to support and promote these understandings – such as promoting responsibility through parenting classes or

through discouraging anti-social behaviour by means of exclusion orders, the State is defining citizenship more expansively and may clash with religious notions of what it means to be human and a good citizen.

Such a formative role for the State moves beyond simple citizen participation and sees its purpose as forming the moral character of its citizens (see Michael Sandel, *Democracy's Discontent*). If therefore behaving and acting like a citizen involves acquiring a range of dispositions and virtues, through a form of citizenship education, which help us to actively seek justice and promote human rights then the more we ask of the citizen the more religion impacts on the exercise of their citizenship. In this understanding of citizenship, the Church and State may be separate, but religion and politics are not. The later involve broader and deeper ideas of understanding citizenship, but it need not be seen as a kind of secular 'civil religion' where religious values and beliefs are secularized. Weithman (2002), drawing on empirical research, has shown how Christianity functions in politics and how Christians contribute to democracy by being good democratic citizens. Weithman argues that religion enriches political debate and aids political participation through developing political skills, especially among the poor and minorities. Christianity can certainly motivate people to get involved in their communities and many Christian values are compatible with the secular values of the liberal State. It could even be said that in the very identity and virtues of the Christian there is a stress on citizen action. Christianity can and does provide the motivational force for much active citizenship in practice. However, should the State celebrate one set of values over another whilst assuming the rhetoric and symbols of the neutral public sphere? Citizenship education is not a wholly secular process for it must also address and understand the significance of religious beliefs for an individual citizen's participation in society. As Brian Gates (2006: 589) says: '… citizenship depends upon beliefs and values, and these are both religious and moral. Therefore, citizenship education which pays scant attention to the process and content of both moral and religious believing is likely to stumble, for therein lie the springs of active participation'.

Nevertheless, there is a growing feeling within religious communities that the value of their particular worldview goes unrecognized in secular societies. There is a dominant view that only a secular State, in which public decision-making processes are based exclusively on secular arguments, is compatible with the principles of a liberal European democracy. This is simply a form of secularism: an ideology which seeks to exclude the influence of religion. Christianity makes the distinction between political rule and social life, with the latter counterbalancing the former. Many States make no such distinction. Jurgen Habermas (2006: 17) has commented that,

> As long as secular citizens are convinced that religious traditions and religious communities are to a certain extent archaic relics of pre-modern societies that continue to exist in the present … religion no longer has any intrinsic justification to exist … In the secularist reading, we can envisage that, in the long run, religious views will inevitably melt under the sun of scientific criticism and that religious communities will not be able to withstand the pressures of some unstoppable cultural and social modernization.

Habermas believes that those who adopt such a view of religion cannot take religion seriously in the public realm and are guilty of adopting a 'narrow secularist consciousness'. Habermas recognizes that the restrictions that Rawls (1997) and Audi (2005) would place on the role of religion in public discourse would not work in practice because they place an intolerable psychological burden on religious citizens. The separation of the private sphere from the public sphere or the separation of knowing and doing is not tenable. Whilst Habermas (1984 and 1987) had previously dismissed religious traditions from a role in politics, he is now more open and even suggests that secular minded citizens should adopt a more self-critical attitude towards the limits of secular rationality and be more open to the power of religious reasons.

CONCLUSION

From the beginning of the Church's history its mission in the world has included a political dimension, but one understood through the eyes of theology. From Constantine and on through the Middle Ages, Christendom had simultaneously an ecclesial and a political form, since religion was interconnected with secular government in complex ways. Both aspects were continually woven into each other and tensions and struggles inevitably arose. However, these two aspects began to separate at the Reformation as the temporal power of the Catholic Church was challenged by nation-States which demanded total loyalty from their citizens. The Catholic Church considered humanity to be flawed and thus in need of governance, whilst the enlightenment thinkers thought humanity to be perfectible and therefore in need of political liberation. It is therefore ironic that secular authorities continue to advance into every aspect of people's lives in modern States blurring the distinction between the political and social orders. Christianity also had a positive functional significance for democracy and for the obligations of citizenship by providing virtues for the advancement of social justice, for the welfare of citizens and for the idea of the individual who can criticize and dissent within the secular public realm.

It is constitutionally recognized within most European States today that citizenship is not dependent on adherence to any religion and therefore that religion is not a constitutive element of citizenship. Consequently, citizenship education tends to relegate and bracket off as private all connections with religion. The invention of the modern nation-State has resulted in authority being located in a single institution and within its own territorial borders such authority is often viewed as unlimited. Yet this does not recognize the contribution Christianity has made to our contemporary notions and exercise of citizenship. In the Catholic Christian tradition, responsible citizenship is a virtue; participation in the political process is a moral duty.

Christian citizens, therefore, have a duty to persuade, not to coerce and should not impose dogma on others, but rather educate other citizens about legitimate moral considerations that permeate public policy issues. Even if it is accepted that citizenship is a secular legal status it cannot be easily assumed that all citizens will therefore adopt views in the public realm that are impartial and by which particular interests and differences are transcended.

In conclusion, Rowan Williams (2005) has argued that the Christian heritage teaches that political power is always provisional and impermanent. As he says:

> Western modernity and liberalism are at risk when they refuse to recognize that they are the way they are because of the presence in their midst of that partner and critic which speaks of 'alternative citizenship' – the Christian community ... the distinctively European style of political argument and debate is made possible by the Church's persistent witness to the fact that states do not have ultimate religious claims on their citizens.

He warns that if States do not recognize this 'dual citizenship' they eventually stumble towards either totalitarianism or theocracy. This is a serious challenge to Western culture and the supremacy of secular politics.

REFERENCES

Augustine, *City of God* (Penguin Classics) (1984) David Knowles (ed.), and Henry Bettenson (Translator) London: Penguin.

Aristotle, *The Politics* (Penguin Classics) (1981) Trevor J. Saunders (ed.), T.A. Sinclair (Translator), London: Penguin.

Audi, R. (2005) 'Moral Foundations of liberal Democracy, Secular Reasons, and liberal Neutrality Towards the Good', *Notre Dame Journal of Law, Ethics and Public Policy*, 19 (1): 197–218.

Blythe, J.M. (1986) 'The Mixed Constitution and the Distinction between Regal and Political Power in the Work of Thomas Aquinas', *Journal of Historical Ideas* 47 (4): 547–565.

Carteledge, P.A. (ed.) (1999) *Religion of the Ancient Greeks*. Cambridge: Cambridge University Press.

Crick, B. (2000) *Essays on Citizenship*. London: Continuum.

Galston, W.A. (2002) *Liberal Pluralism: The Implications of Value Pluralism for Political Theory and Practice*. Cambridge: Cambridge University Press.

Gates, B. (2006) 'Religion as Cuckoo or Crucible: Beliefs and Believing as Vital for Citizenship and Citizenship Education', *Journal of Moral Education*, 35 (4): 571–594.

Habermas, J. (1984 and 1987) *The Theory of Communicative Action*, Vols. 1 and 2. Boston: Beacon Press.

Habermas, J. (2006) 'Religion in the Public Sphere', *European Journal of Philosophy*, 14 (1): 1–25.

Heater, D. (2004) *A History of Education for Citizenship*. London: Routledge.

Heater, D. and Oliver, D. (1994) *The Foundations of Citizenship*. New York and London: Harvester Wheatsheaf.

Held, D. (1996) *Models of Democracy*, 2nd Edition. Cambridge: Polity Press.

Held, D. (1997) 'Democracy: From City-States to a Cosmopolitan Order', in R. Goodin, and P. Pettit (eds) *Contemporary Political Philosophy: An Anthology*. Oxford: Blackwell. pp. 78–102.

Kepel, G. (1994) *The Revenge of God: The Resurgence of Islam, Christianity and Judaism in the Modern World*. Oxford: Clarendon Press.

Mickalson, J.D. (2005) *Ancient Greek Religion*. Oxford: Blackwell.

Niebuhr, H.R. (1952) *Christ and Culture*. London: Faber.

Rawls, John (1997) 'The Idea of Public Reason Revisited', *The University of Chicago Law Review*, 64 (3): 765–807.

Sandel, M.J. (1996) *Democracy's Discontent: America in Search of a Public Philosophy*. Cambridge, MA. and London: Belknap Press of Harvard University Press.

Turner, B. (2007) 'Religion and Politics', in E. F. Isin and B. Turner, (eds) *Handbook of Citizenship Studies*. London: Sage.

Weithman, P.J. (2002) *Religion and the Obligation of Citizenship*. Cambridge: Cambridge University Press.

Williams, R. (2005) Religion, culture, diversity and tolerance – shaping the new Europe, address to the European Policy Centre, Brussels, 7th November 2005.

Zaidman, L.B. and Pantel, P.S. (1992) *Religion in the Ancient Greek City*. Cambridge: Cambridge University Press.

24

Feminism and Gender in Education for Citizenship and Democracy

Jane Bernard-Powers

Contemporary press is a rich source of information on the breadth and diversity of gender issues in citizenship and education. For example the summer of 2007 yielded the following reports: the election of India's first female president, Pratibha Patil (Wax, 2007: A14); political activism in defense of a jihadist movement by young women from the Jamia Hafsa Islamic School for girls in Islamabad, Pakistan (Sengupta, 2007: A3); attempts to stop the selective abortion of girls in India, (India Tries to Stop Sex-Selective Abortions, 2007: 6) and the banning of female genital mutilation performed on Muslim and Christian girls (Egypt: All Female Cutting Banned, 2007: A12). These phenomena are representative of the uneven and variegated terrain of citizenship issues that are shaped by gender in contemporary international contexts.

In the global context gendered citizenship issues and perspectives encompass and influence social, economic and political institutions, policies and practices. Some of the issues identified in various media,

include; religious expression, freedom from violence, economic opportunities, community development, access to education, suffrage, the right to pursue public office and leadership and international protocols for asylum. Moreover, as has been noted elsewhere in this volume, gender is only one aspect of historic identities. Race, ethnicity, class, sexual preference and historic identities that assume meaning in variable local, national and international communities where women live alongside and/or separate from men are equally important. While much of the early work (1970–1985) on international gender issues was predicated on the notion that 'sisterhood is global,' the variance between the political, social and economic circumstances of women are vast and significant and they create complexity in the discussion of gender and feminism in relation to democracy, citizenship and education (Morgan, 1984).

There are fundamental assumptions this chapter is based on. One is that citizenship is broadly construed to mean formal and informal relationships between individuals, families, local communities, the state and transnational organizations. The second is that this discussion of citizenship and gender, assumes that identities such as ethnicity, social class, emigration status, religious affiliations and sexual orientation are dynamic elements in interdependent systems where power and resources are unevenly distributed. Gender does not function in social isolation: it is shaped by multiple identities in specific historic, political and economic contexts. The third is that while gender is ubiquitous, the relevance of gendered phenomena fluctuates based on the reality of shifting contexts and the expression of gender phenomena in specific practices (Thorne, 1997: 5).

This chapter on gender, feminism and citizenship, considers the history of feminism related to citizenship, but is primarily focused on contemporary issues. While feminist perspectives on rights, status and the interests of women can be traced to the first wave of feminism in late-nineteenth century Europe, and the US (1850–1920) (Offen, 1992: 72), it is the past 32 years that have rendered issues of gender, feminism and citizenship visible to scholars, educators, international agencies and sundry communities around the globe.

The four world conferences on women of the twentieth century provided a medium for developing visibility and activist networks. 1975 was a significant year for women globally: the United Nations Assembly proclaimed that year to be 'International Women's Year' and the UN sponsored the first international conference on women. 1985, the year of the Third United Nations World Conference on Women held in Nairobi, Kenya, was a watershed year for the mobilization and organization of the modern feminist movement and it set the stage for Beijing (Moghadam, 2005: 1). The Fourth World Conference on Women, held in Beijing, China in 1995, built on the platform of action developed in Nairobi and produced a series of goals, that were incorporated into the Millennium Development Goals, adopted by UN Member States in 2000 (United Nations

Development Fund for Women (UNIFEM), 2002: Preface).

In addition to the development of goals, assessments and networks, a resurgence of feminist scholarship that began in conference settings such as 'Women, Citizenship and Difference' held in 1996 at the University of Greenwich in London, has resulted in the publication of journal articles, books and edited collections that have extended the conversation and the feminist critiques (Yuval-Davis and Webner, 1999: xi).

Collaborative work between the scholarly communities of citizenship, feminist citizenship and citizenship education, however, is less evident and potentially very significant. As other contributors to this volume have indicated, the scholarship, government policy development and curricula program development in citizenship education has been a growing enterprise. Globalization with all its antecedent and effects is a theme in this developing domain. This focus on gender and feminism related to citizenship and citizenship education is a welcome and somewhat compensatory phenomena (Arnot and Dillabough, 2000; Bernard-Powers, 1996: 289; Foster, 2000).

The following chapter addresses key gender and feminist issues in education for citizenship and democracy. It is based on UN publications, scholarship on feminism and citizenship, and the nascent but growing body of work that links feminism, citizenship and education for citizenship in schools. Gender, feminism and citizenship are considered in two topical sections, a) feminist perspectives on citizenship issues and transnational networking, and b) connections between feminism and schooling for citizenship including research on gender and political learning and concerns 'about the boys.'

The domains of scholarship here are uneven in breadth and depth. There is more written about feminism, gender and citizenship, than is written about gender, feminism and citizenship education. This phenomenon suggests the need for more research, writing and articulation between scholars and practitioners.

FEMINIST PERSPECTIVES ON CITIZENSHIP

Turning first to definitions, feminism is a concept that has been in popular use for several decades and is defined in *The Glossary of Feminist Theory* as support and advocacy for the rights of women (Andermahr et al., 2000: 93). Historian Karen Offen defines feminism as a '... concept that involves both an ideology and movement for socio-political change' that is predicated on male privilege and female subordination in any given society' (Offen, 1992: 83). The term feminist 'implies the identification of women as systematically oppressed; the belief that gender relations are neither inscribed in natural differences between the sexes, nor immutable; and a political commitment to their transformation (Andermahr et al., 2000: 93).

A recent addition to the definitional process that emerged from postmodernism challenges the notion of an essential feminist perspective asserting that there are multiple feminisms. For example, there is Marxist feminism, lesbian feminism, bourgeois feminism and womanist or 'black and women of color feminism' (Voet, 1998: 25). There are also 'universalist feminisms' which focus on the idea that '... women are biologically and culturally equal to men,' but have been denied equality; separatist feminisms that characterize women as equal to but different from men, and 'particularist' which focus on the differences between women and the differences between women and men (Stone, 1994: 6).

The second wave of feminism emerged in the 1960s and along with calls for equity and rights, scholarship, applications to practice and theories expanded at a remarkable rate. At the same time the concept of gender developed into questions of origins and meanings with implications for social,

economic and political life. Is gender a function of biology or is it a socio-cultural construct? Herein, gender, refers to differences between males and females that are a function of both biology and socio-cultural constructs (Andermahr: 2000: 104).

A final addition to this definitional field is the query/commentary of Catherine A. MacKinnon, feminist political theorist, who summarized a discussion of feminism as follows. 'To answer an equally old question, or rather to question an equally old reality- what explains the inequality of women to men? Or, how does gender become domination and domination become sex? Or what is male power? -Feminism needs to create an entirely new account of the political world' (MacKinnon, 1989: 125).

Feminist inquiry and critique provide the method and ideas for understanding gender regimes, gender inequality and gender injustice, and for intervening in the material practices, and policies that sustain gender inequities. This section of the chapter provides feminist reflections and critiques of ideas about citizenship.

FOUNDATIONAL PERSPECTIVES/DUALISMS AND DEBATES

A central question of the feminist debate is, do woman claim solidarity across religion, class, race, sexuality and international communities? Karen Offen, an American feminist historian, asserts that, 'Without the category women, the feminist project founders' (1990: 14). Rian Voet (1998) addresses the question in *Feminism and Citizenship*, which provides an extensive analysis of feminist's writing and thinking about the problems and prospects of social-liberal citizenship (1998: 10.) She writes that from a social-liberal perspective, citizenship is universal and equal, it is available to adults who inhabit the territory of the state, and '... it guarantees civil, political and social rights in return for equal duties' (1998: 10). But essentially citizenship is based on specified rights, necessary for individual freedom, and specific duties, the balance of which are enacted in the public sphere, rather than the private sphere of family, community and religious sites. This definitive focus on rights enacted in the public sphere evolved into one of the essential feminist debates: do we take the woman out of citizen or do we define citizenship as woman-centered?

Analyses of the fact of women's desire for equal and full participation in both historical and contemporary settings evolved into the 'equality difference' debate. Is the feminist project for gender justice predicated on the achievement of equal rights identical to those that are held by men, or does the female identity, individually and collectively influence the definition of citizenship? In other words, should women work for respect by being like men, or by aiming at respect for women's difference (Voet, 1998: 24)? Feminists on both sides of the Atlantic and in South America positioned themselves around the apparent dualism in the first wave of feminism, 1850–1920 (Offen, 1992: 72) and the binary constructions and concepts became the catalyst for contemporary feminist discussions beginning in the 1970s.

For advocates of the rights position, personal independence and autonomy were important and equality under the laws and political system meant minimizing the significance of social roles, sex-linked qualities and child-care responsibilities. This reliance on the 'equality' part of the duality propels the seeker of rights into the public realm. The individual (woman) is the key unit in this political schema and conception of citizenship, (Offen, 1992: 76) and the site of activity is the public domain or sphere. Political action by women for the right to vote was significant in the UK and the US beginning in the mid-nineteenth century, however, campaigns in both countries and in Australia, Denmark, Finland, Norway and the USSR were not generally successful until the first two decades of the twentieth century (Boulding: 1976, 681–682).

On the other hand, the advocates of difference predicated their political strategy on the formal acknowledgement of the differences between men and women. Women differed fundamentally from men in their procreative functions and domestic responsibilities feminists argued. The celebration of motherhood and the distinctions between women and men in nature and in social roles were critical to the conception of citizen. Moreover the importance of women's responsibilities was the basis for a citizenship status equal to men's (Offen, 1992: 76). In a sense this conception of citizenship, based on maternity, provided a rationale for the elevation of the private sphere (household) to a position of equality with the public sphere. The maternal feminists essentially '... re-imagined citizenship and the public sphere to encompass 'feminine values' (Yuval-Davis and Webner, 1999: 7). Parenthetically the concept of maternity or 'Mutterschutz' can be traced to first wave feminists in northern Europe (Boulding, 1976: 681).

Voet established three umbrella categories that encapsulate the feminist work on citizenship, humanist, woman-centered and deconstructionist. Humanists focus on equal rights and duties for all and eschew the category, woman. They assert that 'women should simply be offered the same opportunities as men' (Voet, 1998: 26). Susan Moller Okin's work on *Justice, Gender and the Family* is representative of this category. Okin argues that the family is the seat of education for justice and that males and females should be equally responsible for the family and the education of the next generation. Work both paid and unpaid should be shared equally by men and women. 'A just future would be one without gender' (Okin, 1989: 171).

In contrast to the humanist perspective, a woman-centered perspective can be summarized as: 'Let us try to become included as woman citizens and ... change the concept of citizenship' (Voet, 1998: 29). The work of Carole Pateman is representative of this woman-centered perspective on citizenship. Pateman has argued that masculine dominance based on notions of rationality and autonomy is the problem because citizenship has been constructed in the male image and women were excluded (Pateman, 1992: 19). Pateman asserts that citizenship must be predicated on the assumption that women are mothers and that 'motherhood and citizenship remain intimately linked' (Pateman, 1992: 29). Patriarchy must give way to social and political equality between men and women, with motherhood as a key feature (Pateman, 1992: 29). Sexual difference has to 'cease to be the difference between freedom and subordination' (Pateman, 1992: 28). Nel Noddings has also contributed to the notion of woman-centered citizenship, with her work on the ethic of care that would optimally become the basis for values in the public sphere and for all citizens (Noddings, 1984, 1992).

Deconstructionist feminism is the third category and its contribution is to introduce the phenomenon of plurality in politics and society. Deconstructionists, according to Voet, are skeptical of a rights-based tradition, exemplified by social-liberal theories of citizenship and they deny the viability of citizenship based on motherhood (Voet, 1998: 29). Plurality means that the multiple identities of citizens must be kept in focus to define citizen status, and that the dominance of any one aspect of identity over another is not productive. A working class woman, who was also a Black woman, for example, would have to choose between the competing identities. A more ideal state would be having citizens who may or may not be women, acknowledge the 'multiplicity of their oppressed subject status' (Yeatman, 1997). Womanism, a concept identified by writer Alice Walker that refers to Black Feminism, (Walker, 1984) along with other particular feminisms referred to earlier in this document would also fit under this general deconstructionist category.

The consideration of feminist ideas about citizenship as here discussed is informative of the general outlines of historical and contemporary thinking. The categories provide a framework for understanding essential differences between feminists' ideas. However, it is important to keep in mind the categories can obscure the commonalities. Or in other words the ideas overlap more than is evident in the descriptions and labels (Voet, 1998: 26). Moreover, the outlining of positions invites the question: who and what lies in the shadows of these notions of citizenship for women? What is not addressed?

CONTEXTUALIZING GENDER AND CITIZENSHIP

One of the powerful and persuasive critiques of Western feminism voiced in the early 1980s was that the discussion of rights and entitlements and the conceptualizations of women's needs were narrow and parochial. It was the (preparatory work for the) UN 1985 Third World Conference on women, held in Nairobi, and the concurrent NGO forum that contributed to a shift in the focus of feminism. The 'Forward Looking Strategies' a plan of action for 1986–2000, and the international networking that developed in Nairobi were significant indicators of this shift to a more international and inclusive focus. The Fourth World Conference on Women in Beijing and a host of international UN conferences in the 1990s on the environment, human rights, population and women, helped to diversify the goals of feminism and gender justice for women, which 'implies full citizenship for women.'

Research on multiculturalisms and deconstructionist critiques of binary categories were also helpful in broadening academics' and activists' understanding of women's agendas, as indicated in the characterization of deconstructionist-feminism referred to earlier in this chapter. The importance of plurality and the significance of context were articulated by Will Kymlicka who argues for the 'multicultural accommodation in governance' (Goetz, 2007: 38). Kymlicka asserts that, 'Cultural membership provides us with an intelligible context of choice and a secure sense of identity and belonging, that we call upon in confronting questions and personal values and projects' (Kymlicka, 1995). This is essentially an argument for paying attention to the notion of rights, but only in terms of local contexts where the individuals and communities negotiate.

A publication of the International Development Fund for Research, entitled *Gender Justice, Citizenship and Development* (Mukhopadhyay and Singh, 2007) has addressed the significance of context for understanding women's rights and entitlements. Anne Marie Goetz identifies a set of 'wicked problems' (Roberts, 2004) that thwart gender justice, arguing that in many non-Western societies the mechanisms that under gird Western democracies have not developed. In her words, '... the struggles against feudalism did not pre-date the formation of modern states. Such struggles have been inhibited or forestalled by the imposition of Western notions of citizenship that presume the struggles have already taken place' (Goetz, 2007: 36). The consequence of this phenomena is that the 'concept of citizenship as a set of contractual relationships between the individual and the state is '... often overridden by the notion of the person as nestled in a relationships of kinship and community' (Joseph, 2002: 37). What actually exists are two forms of obligation, one being contractual arrangements with the economy or state and the other through one's social, kinship and community network. In general, it is in women's interest to acknowledge and develop their relationships with the traditional community in order to access rights, which means that their chances of realizing gender justice may be fragile (Goetz, 2007: 40).

While context implicates strategies in both Western industrialized countries and in developing countries, Goetz and her colleagues have addressed contexts where formal law has less relevance than informal, traditional relations. Strategies recommended for gender justice and citizenship in developing countries include:

1. Engaging in a positive way the existing legal worlds of women. In the words of Goetz, '... The emphasis is on identifying and building upon those aspects of customary law and practice that accord women rights over resources. For example, working with a tribal of elders in Bangladeshi villages to resolve traditional disputes, and resolving land rights issues in Kenya for women who have been displaced.

2. 'Interpreting customary law on the basis of international human rights.' The feminist human rights lawyer from Iran, Shirin Ebadi, winner of the 2003 Nobel Peace prize is cited here as an example of this kind of action. Ebadi used her legal expertise to sort out and propose revisions to Islamic jurisprudence that supports women. With acumen and patience she has exposed contradictions in the law and appealed to some of the more progressive clerics and lawmakers.

3. Taking collective action to support claims for citizenship rights. The example of collective action provided involved a workers rights organization in Rajasthan, India. The 'informal union' has been protesting about the underpayment of salaries to women by project overseers and public officials who shorted the wages of women who worked on drought relief public works programs. A tenacious information campaign involving public hearings resulted in a state wide policy guaranteeing access to official documents that could be used for redress of grievances (Goetz, 2007: 42–44).

To sum up this section on context, referring to the observations of Maitrayee Mukhopadhyay, the feminist projects in developing countries and areas means that; 'context-specific negotiation and translation' must take place to benefit different groups of women; that recognizing differences between groups of women is critical, and the goal of equality remains equally critical; and that feminism rejects cultural practices that subjugate women and deny them entitlements (Mukhopaddhyay and singh, 2007: 279, 281).

GLOBALIZATION AND TRANSNATIONAL NETWORKING

Globalization and the development of transnational networks were two related phenomena with implications for feminism and citizenship which developed in the 1980s. Globalization refers to the development of linkages and connections, which transcend the nation state, including the development of multinational corporations, transnational ownership of capital and the erosion of local controls and worker protections (Andermahr et al., 2000: 108). Transnational networks were a reaction to the forces of globalism and fundamentalism that emerged in the 1980s.

The distinction many feminists make between international feminism and global or transnational feminism is that international feminism developed in the context of the first wave of feminism in the early twentieth century when women's organizations such as the Women's International League for Peace and Freedom, the YWCA, the International Council of Women, and the socialist womens' movement and anti-colonial national liberation movements emerged to address issues that women shared in common (Tohidi, 2005: 3). Globalization as a feminist issue grew out of concerns about male biases in projects of nationalism, development and modernization that compromise women's rights and women's opportunities, concerns about ecological issues that impact women's lives, and confrontations with religious politics, especially Islamic fundamentalism (Tohidi, 2005: 4). Global mass culture, the diminishing power of the nation state and national borders, the new liberal economic policies, especially the decline of the welfare state, the emergence and expansion of communication technology, the internet in particular and the UN regional, national and world conferences on women all paved the way to the emergence of transnational feminism (Tohidi, 2005: 4).

Globalization has led to an increase in international forums, which in turn has had some positive effect on women's status internationally. One effect is the phenomenal development of Transnational Feminist Networks (TFNs) that provide education, support and action in a variety of domains that influence the quality of life for female citizens. These domains include women's human rights, peace and conflict resolution, reproductive health and rights, and critique's of economic policy. Valentine Moghadam's book entitled *Globalizing Women, Trans-national Feminist Networks*, provides extensive detail and case studies of the work that TFNs have done on behalf of women (Moghadam, 2005). The work includes, first, creating, activating and joining global networks and coalitions such as the Coalition to End The Third World Debt, and the Women's International Coalition for Economic Justice; second, engaging multi-lateral and intergovernmental political arenas such as departments of the UN and the World Bank's External Consultative Group to influence policy, by attending conferences, generating back ground papers and reports, and lobbying delegates and third, the lobbying and agitating within states to create visibility and awareness of women as participants in the international arena (Moghadam, 2005: 15). Examples of the latter include Women Living Under Muslim Laws (WLUML) organizing protests against patriarchal laws. In Pakistan and Nigeria WLUML branches have protested the Islamization of laws (Moghadam, 2005: 14).

While the global women's movement benefited from the UN conferences, on women and related topics, noted earlier in this chapter, the movement has also benefited from continued follow through with actions that support gender equality. The strategies adopted in Nairobi (1985) and Beijing (1995) informed the writing of the Millennium Development Goals and the Millennium Declaration. The declaration states that leaders pledge to 'promote gender equality and the empowerment of women as effective ways to combat poverty, hunger and disease and to stimulate development that is truly sustainable' (UNIFEM, 2002: 2).

It is axiomatic that the realization of goals will depend on resources to track data on progress and to develop programs—some of which are supported by TFNs. The ambitious agenda, with time lines is daunting, especially for areas of the world that are at war and are economically debilitated, such as Sub-Saharan Africa, the Middle East and South Asia. Nonetheless the publication, *Progress of the World's Women*, 2002, reported that on Goal Three, which is directed at promoting gender equality and women's empowerment, there was marked progress in women's share of seats in parliaments, and women's enrolment in school has increased in some countries (UNIFEM, 2002: 12–13). Although progress depends on finite resources, the establishment of goals and targets that speak to the most critical issues for women as citizens and members of communities represents a positive step forward. Moreover, as the first paragraph of this chapter indicates, the work of change agents and citizen activists is making a difference for women in many nations and states.

GENDER, FEMINISM AND CITIZENSHIP EDUCATION

This section of the chapter on schooling and the development of gendered citizens is predicated on the notion that there is a nascent dialogue between the three groups involved, feminist political theorists, education feminists and citizenship education theorists. In their edited collection, *Challenging Democracy*, Arnot and Dillabough observe that gender issues in education have not been linked to theoretical questions about female citizenship. More pointedly they suggest that feminist educational work has not been perceived as relevant to the work of feminist political theory (Arnot and Dillabough, 2000: 21). Voet, author of *Feminism and Citizenship*, has argued that citizenship theorists in education

dismiss or ignore feminist concerns because they have little to do with matters of citizenship. Clearly this emerging conversation is a challenge.

An additional challenge is the paradoxical nature of citizenship education. The goal of educating young people to assume their roles as active citizens, or socializing children for their support for the nation state is explicit in many countries, but the form is highly variable. It can be a formal part of the course structure, a semester course in government for example, it may be a cross-curricular theme or embedded in a course involving personal values and decision-making or it may be thematically integrated into social sciences courses. The paradox in citizenship education is that with highly variable approaches to citizenship education, that take place informally (in cafeterias, hallways, sports centers, parking lots, websites, television, film, religious organizations, neighborhood and families) there is significant learning about what it means to be an active citizen that takes place. There is a powerful, site variable, dynamic and difficult to define citizenship education curriculum that develops, in addition to or in spite of school curricula. The elusiveness and variability makes it difficult to generalize about gender, ethnicity, context and other significant variables. The following section is challenged by a limited amount of available data and variability of contexts.

This section of the chapter connects themes from the first section to relevant issues in education and schooling. The connections between ideas from feminist scholars on citizenship and feminist educationists are explored, research on the development of political knowledge is discussed, some observations about masculinity studies are considered, and the issues that are germane to education, gender and citizenship in the Millennium Development Goals are briefly addressed.

The gendering of school curricula was both common and contested practice at the turn of the nineteenth century in the US and in the UK and the preparation for same or separate spheres was part of a wider conversation referred to as the 'woman question.' With the second wave of feminism that developed on both sides of the Atlantic in the early 1970s, the gendering of education and the differences in opportunities provided for males and females, were drawn out of the shadows into the light. Feminist educators lobbied for changes in classroom practices, curriculum including gender fair history and extra-curricular activities such as sports, in the hope that it would transform gender roles in the short term and society in the long term. Title IX of the Education Amendments (1972) in the US, the Sex Discrimination Act of 1975 in the UK and the more recent Australian report, *The National Policy for the Education of Girls in Australian Schools* (1987) are representative of government responses to gender inequities that provided some support for aspects of gender discrimination in schools, but not for others (AAUW, 1999: 6–7; Arnot et al., 1999: 4, 40; Kenway and Willis, 1990: 5–6).

Themes

The foundational issue of the early work on gender discrimination in schooling, beginning in the 1970s was bias and the essential argument, incorporated into the title of a monograph in the US, was that girls were being short changed in multiple aspects of schooling. The claims developed in the UK, in the US, Australia, New Zealand and European countries such as Denmark, France, Germany and Portugal focused on a host of issues related to curricula, affirmative action policies, career issues, teacher education and development, classroom interaction and school site leadership. (Whyte et al., 1985: xxi–xxiii) By 1994 the field of gender studies in education had expanded considerably, a community of education feminists from many parts of the globe, had gathered under organizational umbrellas to articulate and interrogate various feminisms, and the themes of identity, difference, equality, public and private had

been identified. (Bailey, 2002: xxi–xxiii; Stone, 1994: 1–7) As Susan Bailey observes, 'Then, as now, the questions centered on whether the education of girls and boys should be separate and different, separate but the same, together and the same, or together but different' (Bailey, 2002: xxiii).

Gender and feminisms in citizenship education

For most teachers classroom practice and curricula concerns such as standards, bench marks and key targets, student relationships, linguistic diversities, inadequate resources, managerial competence and in some parts of the world, the absence of classrooms and texts, and presence of violence constitute the fabric of their professional lives. In citizenship education, textbooks, tests of student knowledge and student self-reporting are important data sources where gender is concerned.

Textbooks, which represented a starting point in understanding gender in civic learning, have been analyzed extensively in the US and elsewhere. Early analyses of textbooks in the US (1969–1971) were based on comparisons of women and men, girls and boys in indices, photos and text. Two studies in particular, one of texts for children aged 6–9, a second of history texts for young adolescents and a third of civics and government texts found that women were virtually absent from texts and when they were included their contributions or roles were distorted (Frisof, 1969: 303; MacLeod and Silverman, 1973; Trecker, 1971: 249–261).

More recently Obdura (1991) analyzed textbooks used in Kenya focusing on the portrayal of girls and women. Her findings in this very useful and unusual study were that the civics/history textbooks, generally excluded females from the curriculum content, both undermining the genuine activities of females and failing to meet the objectives set forth by the state curricula documents. When women were included they were pictured in the domestic sphere in helping roles

(Obura, 1991: 109–110). Finally a study conducted in 2000–2001 in the US of civics textbooks for grades 7 to 9 (11–15 year olds) found that there were 258 mentions of women and 1,899 of men collectively (Avery and Simmons, 2000/2001:105–130, 122–123). The lessons of curricula media are that women do not belong in public spaces and in leadership positions; they belong in the private sphere in sustaining roles. While this is only one small aspect of citizenship education it is nonetheless part of systemic portrayal of gender that reinforces or reproduces inequity. Textbooks represent official school documents and they are part of the academic and educational discourses that undermine gender equity and gender justice possibilities.

It is important to note that content analyses of textbooks used today would optimally include measures for the diverse identities of students. It is a concern of feminist citizenship educators that the relationship between the abstract discourse of civic education and the material circumstances of schools including students is distant. Students are diverse in terms of sexual orientation and preference, language, ethnicities, immigration status, ability and socio-economic circumstance. Standards of quality for textbooks and the research into them necessarily must consider the diverse identities of students as well as the philosophic perspectives that are sub-text in civics and history books. Willinsky's book, *Learning to Divide the World, Education at Empires End*, and Musgrave's study of textbooks used in Australian schools between 1895 and 1965, underscore the significance of biases toward the patriarchal and Eurocentric legacies that essentially leave out women and non-white people (Musgrave, 1994: 11–18; Willinksy, 1998: 249).

Comparisons of gender differences in knowledge and attitude have been a standard aspect of gender research since the early 1970s and they continue to be an important source of data on citizenship education in part because of the paucity of other data. In early periods, in the US – 1970s and 1980s

– girls did less well than boys on tests of civic knowledge (Hahn, 1996, 1998; Torney-Purta, 1984). Critiques of this early work found that the measures of and definitions of citizenship were narrow. (Hahn, 1996: 11). Parenthetically, these early comparisons reflected a conservative view of gender. More recent research by the National Assessment of Educational Progress and the 1999 IEA project in 28 countries, found no significant gender difference in civic knowledge, but gender differences in many civic attitudes, and a substantial understanding of the concept 'gender discrimination' for students in the United States (Hahn et al., 2007: 338; Kennedy, 2006).

Hahn's 1998 study of political learning in five countries, the US, UK, Denmark, Germany and Netherlands, was designed to inquire beyond political knowledge into attitudes, behaviors and contexts for males and females using qualitative as well as quantitative data. The concern that is expressed by Hahn in the summary of her findings is that there is variable support expressed for women as candidates, and the hope is for substantially more attention to be paid to support for women as political leaders. The other significant point is that in her observations of classes and discussions with students, neither the manifestation of gender discrimination in politics, nor the remedies that have been proposed and acted on were evident in classroom discussions (Hahn, 1998: 128). The substantial networking among women activists, written about by Moghadam, is not evident to young women in their classrooms (Moghadam, 2005: 205).

Studies that involve multiple data sources, including interviewing, and that are done across period of time are difficult to accomplish without substantial support. Yet as Hahn's work in this study indicates, they are necessary for gathering nuanced data that does not in itself reproduce gender inequities. It is a strength of this study that multiple contexts were used in the development of understanding about the nature of gender in different nation states.

There is also a sub-textual message that emerges from this important study which is that schools and formal curricula are not the source of learning about citizenship for students. The culture, internet and popular media are primary sources and thus media literacy, broadly construed might be an important place to initiate reform.

Foster, in her essay entitled, 'Is female educational "success" destabilizing the male-learner citizen' makes a substantial contribution to the topic (Foster, 2000: 203–215). A central idea in this essay on gender in Australian citizenship education reforms is that women have been marginalized in the curriculum, even though the rhetoric of reform included specific references to young women. A second major concern is that by addressing women's issues or the needs of girls in schools and policies, the issues are isolated from the real curricula, which incidentally serves the interests of boys and men. A third and important point she makes is that the issue now known as, 'what about the boys?' has distracted educators, parents and de-railed gender justice and citizenship education initiatives.

The 'boy problem' in US education that surfaced in the popular media in the mid-1990s was not new. The issue dates back to the early twentieth century, when educators and researchers marshaled evidence that boys did not do as well in school as girls, that the 'hand minded' boys, many of whom were immigrants, needed incentives to stay in school, and that a masculine tone in schools would mitigate the feminizing influence of women teachers (Tyack and Hansot, 1990: 66). The latter day pioneers in this burgeoning field, were British and Australian researchers who created the field of studies known as masculinity studies and who raised important questions about a phenomena that had been basically invisible. Connell, who is a senior researcher and sage in this area, has identified some key ideas about the field. The first is that there are multiple masculinities that are developed and functioning – there is no one concept of masculinity even though

stereotypes might be imagined. The second is that there are hierarchies and power differences among the masculinities. Sporting heroes and sport life cultures are viewed as the anti-thesis of gay mens' subcultures and life styles. The hierarchy therein can be laced with homophobic violence. The third point is that there are constructed masculinities that are associated with institutions and organizations. Transnational feminists have identified the image of the transnational corporate magnate, who moves money and resources around the world. Gendered body images, the dynamic nature of imaging and the internal complexity of contradiction of images are additional points (Connell, 2000: 10–14).

Relative to citizenship education, it seems axiomatic that in order to appreciate the issues and opportunities of reformed curricula and instruction, gender justice must be conceptualized and operationalized with both males and females at 'the table' in reality and metaphorically. Apart from the somewhat hysterical tone that popular authors and media have adapted, with the sub-text that woman and girls have created the 'boy problem,' the questions about masculinity and the development of critical perspectives have the potential to move 'the feminist project' along and address the needs of an increasingly mobile and diverse student population (Hightower, 2003: 471–498).

CONCLUSION

The articulation of issues and sharing of resources between education feminists and activists, citizenship theorists and citizenship educators has the potential to move gender and feminism out of the margins and into the 'texts' of the field. Gender issues on the global stage, related to citizenship, are a source of deep concern for women and men, children and families. Conflicts that ultimately result in human rights violations, displacement of populations, enhanced poverty and loss of life are the reality in many areas of the world.

Specifically related to education and the Millennium Development Goals (MDG), access to schools, literacy rates, training for jobs and freedom from sexual harassment while at schools are major issues. Including such issues in the curricula of civic education would represent an important step in reform.

Achieving specific goals such as those stipulated in the MDG documents is a work in progress and the results have been disappointing in some countries. While the UN is an organization that at times seems beleaguered, it is a beacon of hope and source of change. Along with UNESCO it is major participant in international program development and in specific has offered institutional support to issues that involve women and girls in particular and humans generally. The development along with the dissemination of information about programs and initiatives is another potential source of change.

Stromquist in her review of global gender equity (2007), identified programs and initiative that are situated in particular cultural, social, economic and political contexts.

Taiwan developed a Gender Equity Act in 2004, which addresses education needs from kindergarten through the university level. The United Girls Education Initiative (UNGEI) working with UNICEF has identified promising strategies that are being implemented and assessed in a small group of developing countries. 'These included such things as reducing distance between home and school; school expansion in Egypt, India, Indonesia; serving hard-to-reach outlying groups in Bangladesh, Burkina Faso, and India; developing leadership skill for girls in South Africa and Uganda' (Stromquist, 2007: 39). Strengthening education through programs for young women developed and supported by TFM's is a critical source of reform for citizenship education that represents attention to context.

Curriculum change accomplished through collaboration is one of the most important recommendations to be made here. Extrapolating from specific recommendations in 'Gender Equity in Social Studies,' authors recommend that '... social studies educators ensure that substantial attention is devoted to gender in curriculum in order to present an accurate view of gendered human experience' (Hahn et al., 2007: 350–351). This includes classroom interactions and curricula materials such as history texts. Authors also recommend that the notion of gender include men and boys, women and girls and transgender individuals.

Substantial attention needs to be paid to the intersection of gender with race, class, ethnicity and sexual orientation, and community contexts in curricula materials. Teachers need feedback and evaluation of their teaching relative to gender equity and justice, along with teacher friendly development. Continued research on gender, feminism and citizenship education that is both qualitative and quantitative is critical.

We can better understand and more effectively teach gender and feminism in citizenship education with a collaboratively developed agenda on the table. Moreover the future of this field depends on garnering international support from groups with resources, changing curricula media, expanding the definition of gender to include women and men and deepening our understanding of the diversity that geographic contexts require.

REFERENCES

American Association of University Women (1999) *Gender Gaps, Where Schools Still Fail Our Children*. New York: Marlow & Company.

Andermahr, S., Lovell, T. and Wolkowitz, C. (eds) (2000) *Glossary of Feminist Theory*. New York: Oxford University Press.

Arnot, M., David, M. and Weiner, G. (1999) *Closing the Gender Gap*. Cambridge: Polity Press.

Arnot, M. and Dillabough, J-A. (eds) (2000) 'Introduction'. In *Challenging Democracy, International Perspectives on Gender, Education and Citizenship*. London: Routledge/ Falmer. pp. 1–18.

Avery, P.G. and Simmons, A.M. (2000/2001) 'Civic life as conveyed in U.S. civics and history textbooks.' *Interna-tional Journal of Social Education* 15 (2): pp. 105–130, 122–123.

Bailey, S. (ed.) (2002) *Gender in Education*. New York: Jossey Bass.

Bernard-Powers, J. (1996) 'The woman question in citizenship education.' In Walter Parker (ed.) *Educating the Democratic Mind*. Albany: SUNY. pp. 287–108.

Bock, G. and James, Susan (eds) (1992) *Beyond Equality and Difference: Citizenship*. New York: Routledge.

Boulding, E. (1976) *The Underside of History*. Boulder: Westview Press.

Brooks, A. (2000) 'Citizenship, Identity and social justice: the intersection of feminist and post-colonial discourses.' In Madeleine Arnot and Jo-Anne Dillabough, (eds) *Challenging Democracy, International Perspectives on Gender, Education and Citizenship*. London: Routledge/ Falmer. pp. 41–57.

Connell, R.W. (2000) *The Men and the Boys*. Berkeley, CA.: University of California Press.

Dillabough, J-A. and Arnot, M. (2000) 'Citizenship, identity and social justice: the intersection of feminist and post-colonial discourses.' In Madeleine Arnot and Jo-Anne Dillabough, (eds) *Challenging Democracy, International Perspectives on Gender, Education and Citizenship*. London: Routledge/Falmer. pp. 41–57.

Dubois, E. (2005 18, May) Introductory Remarks. Transnational Feminism: A Range of Disciplinary Perspectives, a roundtable held and the University of California Los Angeles.

Egypt: All Female Cutting Banned (2007) *New York Times*, p. A12.

Foster, V. (2000) 'Is female "success" destablilizing the male learner-citizen?' In M. Arnot and J-A. Dillabough, (eds) *Challenging Democracy, International Perspectives on Gender, Education and Citizenship*. London: Routledge/ Falmer. pp. 203–215.

Frisof, J.K. (1969) 'Textbooks and Channeling.' In Diane Gersoni-Stavn, (1974)(ed.) *Sexism and Youth*. New York: R.R. Bowker.

Goetz, A.M. (2007) 'Gender, justice, citizenship and entitlements: core concepts, central debates'. In M. Mukhopadhyay, and N. Singh, (eds.) *Gender, Justice,*

Citizenship, Development. Ottawa: Zubaan—International Development Research Centre. pp. 15–57.

Hahn, C.L. (1998) *Becoming Political, Comparative Perspectives on Citizenship Education*. Albany: State University of New York.

Hahn, C.L., Bernard-Powers, J., Crocco, M., Woysher, C. (2007) 'Gender equity in social studies.' In Klein, Sue (ed) *Achieving Gender Equity Through Education*. Mahwah: Earlbaum. pp. 335–339.

Hightower, M. W. (2003) 'The "Boy Turn" in research on gender and education.' *Review of Educational Research* 73 (4): 471–498.

India Tries to Stop Sex-Selective Abortions (2007) *New York Times*, 15–7, p. 6.

Joseph, S. (2002) *Gender and Citizenship in the Arab World*. Amman:UNDP Development Forum.

Kennedy, K. (ed.) (1997) *Citizenship Education and the Modern State*. London: Falmer.

Kennedy, K. (2006) 'The Gendered Nature of Students'Attitudes to Minority Groups: Implications for Teacher Education.' *Citizenship Teaching and Learning* 2(1): pp. 55–65.

Kenway, J. and Willis, S. (1990) 'Self-esteem and the schooling of girls: An introduction.' In Kenway, J. and Willis, S. (eds) *Hearts and Minds, Self-Esteem and the Schooling of Girls*. London: Falmer Press. pp. 5–6.

Kymlicka, W. (1995) *The Rights of Minority Cultures*. Oxford: Oxford University Press.

Macleod, F.S. and Silverman, S.T. (1973) *You Won't Do: What Textbooks on US Government Teach High School Girls*. Pittsburg: Know, Inc.

MacKinnon, C. (1989) *Toward a Feminist Theory of the State*. Cambridge: Harvard University Press.

Moghadam, V. M. (2005) *Globalizing Women, Transnational Feminist Networks*. New York: Oxford University Press.

Morgan, R. (ed.) (1984) *Sisterhood Is Global: The International Women's Movement Anthology*. New York: Doubleday.

Mukhopadhyay, M. and Singh, N. (eds) (2007) *Gender, Justice, Citizenship, and Development*. Ottawa: Zubaan–International Development Research Centre.

Musgrave, P. (1994) 'How should we make Australians?' *Curriculum Perspectives* 14 (3): 11–18.

Noddings, N. (1984) *Caring. A Feminine Approach to Ethics and Moral Education*. Berkeley: University of California.

Noddings, N. (1992) 'Social studies and feminism.' *Theory and Research in Social Education* 20 (3): 230–241.

Obura, A.P. (1991) *Changing Images: Portrayal of Girls and Women in Kenyan Textbooks*. Nairobi: ACTS Press.

Offen, K. (1990) 'Feminism and sexual difference'. In Rhode, Deborah L. (ed.) *Theoretical Perspectives on Sexual Difference*. New Haven:Yale University Press. pp. 13–20.

Offen, K. (1992) 'Defining feminism: a comparative historical approach.' In Bock, G. and James, S. (eds) *Beyond Equality and Difference, Citizenship, Feminist Politics, Female Subjectivity*. New York: Routledge. pp. 13–20.

Okin, S.M. (1989) *Gender, Justice and the Family*. New York: Basic Books.

Pateman, C. (1992) 'Equality, difference, subordination: the politics of motherhood and women's citizenship.' In Bock, G. and James, S. (eds) *Beyond Equality and Differ-ence, Citizenship, Feminist Politics, Female Subjectivity*. New York: Routledge. pp. 17–31.

Pourzand, N. (1999) 'Female education and citizenship in Afghanistan: a turbulent relationship.' In N.W. Yuval-Davis, Pnina (ed.) *Women, Citizenship and Difference*. Bloomington: Indiana University Press. pp. 87–99.

Roberts, N.C. (2001) Coping with wicked problems: the case of Afghanistan. In L. Jones, J. Guthrie, & P. Steane (Eds.) Learning from International Public Management Reform (Vol.2, pp. 353–375). Amsterdam: JAI Press.

Sengupta, S. (24 July, 2007) 'Red mosque school fueled islamic fire in young women.' *New York Times*. New York: A3.

State Commission (1987) 'The National Policy for the Education of Girls in Australian Schools', Canberra, Australian Government Publishing Service.

Stone, L. (ed.) (1994) 'Introduction.' *The Education Feminism Reader* London: Routledge. pp. 1–13.

Stromquist, N. (2007) 'Gender equity in education globally.' In Klein, S. (ed.) *Achieving Gender Equity Through Education*.Mahway: Earlbaum. pp. 33–42.

Teese, R., Davies, M., Charlton, M. and Polesel, J. (1995) 'Who wins at school? Boys and girls in Australian secondary education, Department of Education Policy and Management, University of Melbourne.' In Arnot, Madeleine, David, Miriam and Weiner, Gaby (1999) *Closing the Gender Gap*. Cambridge: Polity Press. pp. 28–29.

Thorne, B. (1997*) Gender Play, Girls and Boys in School*. New Brunswick: Rutgers University Press.

Tohidi, N. (18 May, 2005) 'Remarks' Transnational Feminism: A Range of Disciplinary Perspectives,' a roundtable held and the University of California Los Angeles.

Torney-Purta, J.V., Oppenheim, A.N. and Farnen, R.F. (1975) *Civic Education in Ten Countries: An Empirical Study*. New York: Wiley, cited in Hahn, C. (1996) 'Gender and political attitudes.'

Torney-Purta, J. (1984) Political socialization and policy: The U.S. in a cross-national context. In H. Stevenson & R. Siegel, (Eds.) Child Development Research and Social Policy (pp. 471–524) Chicago: University of Chicago Press.

Torney-Purta, J. Lehmann, R. Oswald, H. and Schulz, W. (2001) *Citizenship and education in twenty eight countries: Civic knowledge and engagement at age fourteen*. Amersterdam: The International Association for the Evaluation of Educational Achievement.

Trecker, J.L. (1971) 'Women in U.S. history high school textbooks.' *Social Education*. 35 (3): pp. 248–260.

Tyack, D. and Hansot, E. (1990) *Learning Together, A History of Coeducation in American Public Schools*. New Haven: Yale University Press; New York: Russell Sage Foundation.

United Nations Development Fund for Women, (2002) *Progress of the world's women, Gender Equality and the Millenium Development Goals*. New York.

Voet, R. (1998) 'Feminism and Citizenship' In Bock, G. and James, S. (eds) *Beyond Equality & Difference, citizenship, feminist politics, female subjectivity*. New York: Routledge.

Walker, A. (1984) *In Search of Ours Mother's Garden*. London: The Women's Press.

Wax, E. (2007) Politician's elect India's first female president. *Washington Post/Reprint in San Francisco Chronicle*. San Francisco, CA: A14.

Werbner, P. (1999) 'Political Motherhood and the Feminisation of Citizenship: Women's Activisms and the Transformation of the Public Sphere' in Yuval-David, N. and Webner, P. (eds) *Women, Citizenship and Difference*. Bloomington: Indiana University Press.

Willinsky, J. (1998) *Learning to Divide the World, Education at Empire's End*.Minneapolis: University of Minnesota Press.

Whyte, J., Deem, R., Kant, L. and Cruickshan, M. (1985) *Girl Friendly Schooling*. London: Routledge.

Yeatman, A. (1996) 'Democratic theory and the subject of citizenship' Culture and Citizenship Conference, 30 September– 2 October.

Yeatman, A. (1995) 'Interlocking oppressions', in B. Caine and R. Pringle (eds.) Transitions: new Australian feminisism, N.S.W.: Allen and Unwin cited in Brooks, Anne (2000) Citizenship, Identity and social justice: the intersection of feminist and post-colonial discourses Arnot, Madeleine, & Dillabough, Jo-Anne (ed) (2000) Challenging Democracy, International Perspectives on Gender, Education and Citizenship. London, Routledge: Falmer, p. 44.

Yuval-David, N. and Webner, P. (1999) 'Women and the New Discourse of Citizenship.' In Yuval-David, N. and Webner, P. (eds) *Women, Citizenship and Difference*. Bloomington: Indiana University Press.

25

Antiracism

Hugh Starkey

INTRODUCTION: EDUCATION FOR CITIZENSHIP AND DEMOCRACY IS NECESSARILY ANTIRACIST

Any educational programme associated with citizenship and democracy is required to be intrinsically antiracist. Racism is a barrier to citizenship and is the antithesis of democracy. A racist perspective denies the fundamental claims of democracy and human rights. Both democracy and human rights depend on an understanding and agreement that all human beings are entitled to equal respect for their dignity and equal rights. Racism is a set of beliefs and practices, explicit or unwitting, premised on the greater entitlement of one group to both respect and rights. Racism therefore undermines the very basis of democracy and human rights. Its antidote is antiracism.

Democracy is a world view as much as a form of governance. It is a project usually embodied in a set of institutions and an explicit commitment to strengthen human rights. A healthy culture of democracy requires that its institutions constantly enhance their democratic credentials and seek to become more inclusive. This implies that those working in and with institutions,

including schools, should be alert to the limitations of democracy and the barriers faced by citizens who are entitled to participate but who may face discrimination. One major barrier to participation and equality that exists in societies across the world is racism.

Antiracism is a position and perspective that seeks to preserve, protect and promote democracy. A minimal definition of antiracism is that: 'It refers to those forms of thought and practice that seek to confront, eradicate and/or ameliorate racism. Antiracism implies the ability to identify a phenomenon – racism – and to do something about it' (Bonnett, 2000: 4).

An antiracist perspective within education for democracy and citizenship consequently needs to develop understandings of

- why racism is so inimical to democracy and human rights;
- different and mutating forms of racism and their consequences; and
- strategies for opposing racism.

This agenda may appear to be common sense and uncontroversial. It is founded on the entirely logical argument that if racism is an ideology or a practice or a phenomenon that corrodes or denies democracy and human rights, then supporters of democracy and human rights must, of course, attempt to understand it and oppose it.

The fact remains that antiracism is a term that it has become difficult to use rhetorically. It is often perceived as a controversial topic to be treated with extreme caution. Those who may be disinclined to address racism in citizenship education have found support from one extremely eminent promoter of citizenship education in the UK. Bernard Crick has criticized antiracism as a pedagogical strategy, arguing instead for 'indirect approaches'. Given the immense prestige he has deservedly enjoyed, such opinions may often be accepted without question.

I will argue that what Crick warns against is a pedagogical model that, if it has ever existed, is far from anything that I or colleagues involved in teacher education or inspection would ever recommend as good practice in citizenship education. We can agree that discussions of racism require great sensitivity on the part of the teacher. However, Crick bases his conclusion on a parody of a lesson. He argues that: 'explicit attacks on racism or teaching anti-racism full frontal can prove inflammatory – just what the racist white lads will look forward to in classroom discussion, or disruption' (Crick, 2000: 134).

This statement reinforces discourses from sections of the popular press that also use parody to discredit antiracism. The teacher, faced with a class containing 'racist white lads', is depicted as launching into 'explicit attacks on racism'. There is no indication of context. Perhaps it is a response to a racist incident. Given the military connotations of the word 'attacks' the class members may well see this as a threat and respond defensively. Crick evokes a second 'inflammatory' teaching strategy namely 'teaching antiracism full frontal'. The expression is sometimes related to 'nudity' though also to military assault. If the citizenship lesson is one in which the teacher combines race and sex in a macho battle with 'the racist white lads', clearly the whole enterprise is discredited. However, such naïve approaches to antiracism are

not inevitable. It is perfectly possible to develop other pedagogical models that enable teachers to address racism explicitly.

The Swedish education authorities do not share Crick's reservations. In guidance to schools they insist that: 'In interpersonal relations there should be no distinction between the worth of different groups of people and attitudes which deny this principle – such as *Nazism, racism, sexism, and the glorification of violence – shall be actively brought out into the open and combatted'* (Government of Sweden, 2001: 36, our emphasis in Osler and Starkey 2002: 156).

It is certainly the case, as I will suggest in the following sections, that if schools as organizations and institutions fail to address racism explicitly, they will be part of the problem rather than part of the solution.

However, challenging racism may well involve challenging structures and practices that are in place for apparently benign reasons. For Gillborn: 'simply asserting our anti-racist intentions means nothing if we leave unchanged the dominant systems of testing, the curriculum, teacher education, and punitive inspection regimes that penalize schools serving working-class and minoritised communities' (2006: 15).

An antiracist perspective is one that understands and looks out for differential or discriminatory outcomes as a result of apparently even-handed policies. The political task of trying to change such policies is one with which teachers, heads, parents and unions should engage.

RACISM AS A BARRIER TO CITIZENSHIP

Citizenship as a concept is a nexus of understandings involving, amongst other disciplines, politics, sociology, law, philosophy, social psychology and international relations. Education for citizenship requires a definition of 'citizenship' that accommodates these different understandings and that is also accessible to teachers and learners who do not necessarily have a strong background in any of those disciplines. Citizenship as a *status*, a *feeling* and a *practice* has been proposed as meeting this need for a concise and accessible definition (Osler and Starkey, 2005). I will expand on this definition, in order to show how racism is a barrier to accessing citizenship in each of the three dimensions.

Citizenship is perhaps most often understood as *status*. Almost all of the world's inhabitants are legally citizens of a state. Nationals of a state are citizens with an internationally accepted legal status that gives them some rights and perhaps some duties that may be no more than the requirement to sit on a jury if chosen. Citizenship, in this sense, is co-terminus with nationality. It describes the relationship of the individual to the State. In principle the State protects citizens through laws and policing. It provides some collective benefits such as security, a system of justice, education, health care and transport infrastructure.

As a concept, citizenship has a long and complex history and set of meanings. Since the formation of nation-states in the nineteenth and twentieth centuries, citizenship has effectively been nationalized. Citizenship as nationality is a very unequal status. States with high levels of income from taxation and natural resources provide considerable benefits, whilst poorer states struggle to provide even basic services and education.

Xenophobic political groups and parties play on nationalistic feelings, strengthening and focusing a division between citizens and foreigners. Such discourses are based on a claim that the status and privileges attached to national citizenship should be restricted, particularly through immigration laws. It has proved very hard for even the most liberal and egalitarian democracies to avoid racist effects of immigration policies.

Citizenship is a *feeling* of belonging to a community of citizens. Experience of discrimination undermines a sense of belonging. There is no lack of descriptions of the kinds of barriers to citizenship that minorities

encounter, as in the following example from the UK. The quotation is from a writer who had lived for many years in Britain and had made a notable contribution to literature and education. Nevertheless he concluded that:

> In spite of … any feeling I might entertain towards Britain and the British, I – like all other colored persons in Britain – am considered an 'immigrant' … (a) condition in which we have no real hope of ever enjoying the desired transition to full responsible citizenship (Braithwaite, 1967, quoted in Fryer, 1984: 382).

Although the quotation refers to the mid-twentieth century, the situation in which black and minority citizens may be perceived as migrants by members of dominant communities persists into the twenty-first century. Thirty years after the previous quotation was written, the presenter of the 1997 Reith Lectures, a prestigious annual series broadcast by the BBC (in the UK), provided numerous examples of the same phenomenon and confided that:

> the great philosophically-inspiring quandary of my life is that despite the multiculturalism of my heritage and the profundity of my commitment to the notion of the 'us'-ness of us all, I have little room but to negotiate most of my daily lived encounters as one of 'them' (Williams, 1997: 11).

Formal and informal barriers to full citizenship have also been well documented in the case of the US. James Banks notes that black Americans have encountered three consecutive problems, the first of which was legal exclusion, finally overcome during the civil rights struggle of the 1950s and 1960s. However, even when formal equality was achieved:

> they were often denied educational experiences that would enable them to attain the cultural and language characteristics needed to function effectively in the mainstream society. Third, they were often denied the opportunity to fully participate in mainstream society even when they attained these characteristics because of … discrimination (Banks, 1997: xi).

Access to citizenship requires more than a legal status, though this is an essential first step. As Banks later observed: 'A citizen's racial, cultural, language, and religious characteristics often significantly influence whether she is viewed as a citizen within her society' (Banks, 2004: 5).

It is clear that the attitudes and behaviour of majority groups may be determining in enabling minorities to feel included. Access to citizenship therefore requires a commitment by the State to ensuring that the education of all its citizens includes an understanding of the principles of democracy and human rights and an uncompromising challenge to racism in all its forms.

Citizenship is also defined in terms of *practice* associated with democracy and with human rights. Individuals can practice citizenship as holders of human rights, working individually, perhaps, but usually with others to change the way things are. It is this awareness of a capacity to influence the world, sometimes referred to as a sense of agency that leads citizens to exert themselves on behalf of others. A racist perspective would encourage action to favour one group over another. Such discrimination is by definition profoundly undemocratic.

CITIZENSHIP IN DEMOCRACY DEPENDS ON RIGHTS AND FUNDAMENTAL FREEDOMS

Rights are the essential starting point for citizenship. Rights provide the possibility to practice citizenship and to feel a sense of belonging. Whether defined in terms of national laws or whether the reference is to universal human rights the very basis of rights in democratic contexts is that they are available to all. National rights are granted to national citizens and usually to other inhabitants of the territory of a state, irrespective of their nationality. Human rights may be claimed by any human being without exception.

As I noted in the previous section, citizenship in the US is associated with civil rights and constitutional rights. In Europe the underlying principle of citizenship is more likely to be defined as human rights and fundamental freedoms. Human rights emerged from struggle against Nazism; civil rights from struggle against racial discrimination. In other words opposition to racism led to the construction of legal systems for the protection of citizens from racial discrimination.

The major European institutions, the Council of Europe (founded in 1949), the European Community (founded in 1957), the European Court of Human Rights and the European Parliament are all explicitly committed to democracy, human rights and the rule of law. These institutions underpin a European culture based on an ambition to achieve peace and stability in a continent that suffered two horrendous wars in the first half of the twentieth century.

The European movement that gave impetus to the creation of these institutions can be traced back to resistance to fascist and Nazi attempts to achieve dominance over Europe in the 1930s and 1940s. Given that the Nazi ideology was founded on racism and a denial of the essential equality of human beings, its opponents are, by definition, committed to the promotion of antiracism and race equality. In this the United Nations and the Council of Europe share the same ideals.

The founding principles of the Council of Europe are both regional and universal, as are those of the European Community and European Union. Both the Council of Europe and the European Community are profoundly committed to antiracism. Racism is seen as being based on principles entirely antithetical to European and international values of human rights, dignity and equality. Racism is therefore not only undemocratic, but is, in its essence the enemy of democracy. It threatens the stability of individual states and of the continent as a whole.

As we have previously noted, within the discourse on education for citizenship there is a tendency to categorize an increasingly diverse school population, and minority students in particular, as problematic. The characterization of multicultural societies as problematic is precisely the terrain on which xenophobic political parties have chosen to operate. Far right and populist politicians spuriously link multiculturalism to crime, insecurity and loss of national identity. Such discourses are profoundly antidemocratic as they deny the basic tenets of liberal democracy, namely equality of rights and respect for human dignity (Osler, 2000; Osler and Starkey, 2000, 2001; Starkey, 2000).

At an international and inter-governmental level in Europe, the rhetoric of opposition to racism is robust and consistent. There can be hardly any doubt that the principles of antiracism are promoted as fundamental to European policies. Whether this rhetoric translates into policies at national and local levels is unclear, but the principles are repeated and individual ministers hesitate to challenge them in international meetings.

As an example, in 1997, the Council of Europe launched the Education for Democratic Citizenship (EDC) programme aiming to promote best practice and develop new models for citizenship education and also to be 'instrumental in the fight against violence, xenophobia, racism, aggressive nationalism and intolerance' (Council of Europe, 2000a: 5).

The Council of Europe, working with the European Commission, convened a number of preparatory meetings before the 2001 UN World Conference Against Racism. The governments of the member states of the Council of Europe made a formal declaration that makes a strong if implicit case for antiracism as an essential element of democracy:

> Racism and racial discrimination are serious violations of human rights in the contemporary world and must be combated by all lawful means; Racism, racial discrimination, xenophobia and related intolerance threaten democratic societies and their fundamental values; Stability and peace in Europe and throughout the world can only be built on tolerance and respect for diversity (Council of Europe, 2000b).

Two years later, reviewing their programme of education for democratic citizenship, the Committee of Ministers provided specific guidance for EDC that explicitly support antiracist approaches: 'it would be appropriate to implement educational approaches and teaching methods which aim at learning to live together in a democratic society, and at combating aggressive nationalism, racism and intolerance and eliminate violence and extremist thinking and behaviour' (Council of Europe, 2002).

The World Conference Against Racism, held in Durban in 2001 was the site of competing definitions of racism and attempts to gain the attention of the world's media by groups from around the world who identified their struggle as essentially a demand for non-discrimination on grounds of race (Bhavnani et al., 2005). The contribution of the European Commission was significant in calling for an educational approach to the fight against racism.

> The fight against racism is now firmly rooted in European law. Specific reference to the fight against racism is contained in the Treaty establishing the European Community ...
>
> We know though, that there are many areas of discrimination that cannot be tackled by law. Practical action is needed to reach out to people and to help change the underlying prejudices that fuel racist attitudes and behaviour. Education is called to play a fundamental role in this endeavour (Diamantopoulou, 2001).

This is a key analysis, confirming that legislation, whilst important, needs to be accompanied by an educational programme designed to create a climate of human rights. By promoting equality, strengthening democracy and encouraging respect for human dignity, education can play a key role in overcoming the conditions in which racism flourishes. Ensuring that these values and dispositions are at the forefront of the public conscience requires that they permeate the whole education process. In other words, it is vital that antiracism be mainstreamed.

In fact the European Commission published a report *Mainstreaming the Fight Against Racism* (European Commission, 1999) which drew together various previous initiatives and highlighted how Community policies and programmes can contribute to the fight against racism. It suggested two main means by which racism can be challenged: first, by presenting diversity in a positive light; and second, by creating favourable conditions for a multicultural society. Both these proposals anticipate an educational response (Osler and Starkey, 2002, 2005).

RECOGNIZING RACISMS

Translating the rhetoric of policy and pronouncement into realities in schools requires, amongst other things an analysis of the kinds of racism that are of most relevance to the lives of all members of the school community. It is not just young people who are subject to racism. Teachers too are significantly affected within schools and in the wider society (Maylor et al., 2006; Osler, 2006).

Antiracism is a perspective that ensures that racism is identified in whatever form it occurs and that racism is confronted. Racism is often understood as blatant discrimination as enacted in the laws of Nazi Germany, apartheid South Africa and certain states in the US prior to the civil rights movement. Alternatively it is brutal street racism involving murderous attacks that demands attention. In fact racism also operates in very subtle ways and it is useful for teachers and young people to be able to recognize some of the main forms this takes.

I will now consider three forms of racism, that overlap and interact, but for which there is considerable evidence from personal testimonies. Further evidence of racism is based on quantifiable measures and statistics. In the following section I will examine in turn everyday racism (Essed, 1991), institutional racism (Carmichael and Hamilton, 1968; Macpherson, 1999) and colourblind racism (Ouseley, 1982 cited in Braham et al., 1992; Bonilla-Silva, 2006).

Everyday racism

Philomena Essed developed her theory from her experiences as a Dutch-Surinamese social scientist asking questions of migrants about their experiences of living in the Netherlands. Her research 'makes visible black women's knowledge and understanding of racism, where that knowledge comes from and how it is used in everyday life in order to identify even hidden and subtle forms of racism' (Essed, 2002: 462). The theory she derives is based on the fact that since she finds 'systematic, recurrent, familiar practices' (2002: 177) it is possible to generalize. In particular everyday racism creates structures of racial and ethnic inequality and serves to manage or break opposition.

In line with Essed's methodology, stories are a source of evidence of everyday racism. Research on the experiences of minority ethnic pupils in mainly white schools in England provides a rich source of such stories (Cline et al., 2002).

For instance Ming-Chen, a Chinese boy in Year 9 told how he had been subjected to repeated name-calling on his way home from school, providing examples of the names – *Chinky*, *check eyes*, *four eyes*. He was finally provoked into retaliating and whilst the incident was reported and there was no further trouble for a while, a few months later the racist insults started again. Ming-chen reported that: 'He followed me home, spitting, standing in front of the house, shouting and jeering, spitting and stuff like this, and then he started being racist again ...' and even when this incident had been dealt with 'he still keeps giving me dirty looks ... he hangs around outside my house all the time, on the bike' (Cline et al., 2002: 77).

Racist name-calling amongst young people in schools is very widely reported and it seems likely that it is experienced as everyday racism by many young people, particularly minorities. In Essed's terms it serves to create ethnic inequality, by identifying the target person as not one of us.

The young people interviewed by Cline and colleagues often reported that teachers rarely took such incidents as seriously as they and their parents felt they warranted. A lesson for teachers wanting to take an antiracist perspective must be that it is important to listen to young people. Since this corresponds with agendas on participation that derive from the United Nations Convention on the Rights of the Child (CRC), citizenship education would appear to be well placed to foster opportunities for both public and private expressions of experiences of racism.

Teachers in the same research reported, however, that when they contacted parents of students who had been behaving inappropriately to ethnic minorities, the parents were not always supportive of the school. Antiracism may also need to address attitudes prevalent in the community.

Rebecca Raby undertook research in schools near Toronto, Canada and listened to the stories of majority children as well as minorities. One student, Janelle, reported on the kind of behaviour she witnessed recurrently at her school:

> Somalian girls who have the wraps all around their faces. In summertime ... it's a religion and people know this, but just to be noticed or have someone trying to be popular they'll be making fun of them or asking stupid questions like 'Aren't you hot? Are you a Ninja?' (Raby, 2004: 367).

Janelle did not have the vocabulary to describe the headscarves worn by the 'Somalian girls'. She recognizes that the questions posed are designed to 'make fun' in other words to belittle the target in order to gain popularity with other students by creating an in-group and an out-group. The teasing installs a barrier to equal participation as the message is given out that students in hijab are not going to be included in friendship groups.

As the title of Raby's paper indicates, there was a broad denial that exchanges such as the one above are racist. However, a further quote from Janelle reveals the kind of racist discourses that circulate amongst the majority population students: 'I think that if she was probably lighter, everybody would have accepted her, things like that cuz' no one really said anything that shows racism, they were just "oh my god did you see how dark that girl is?" kind of thing ...' (Raby, 2004: 371).

This example suggests that the everyday behaviour and conversation of majority students may be deeply impregnated with racial awareness and stereotyping. An antiracist approach must provide opportunities to help students and teachers become aware of the power and effect of such discourses.

Everyday racism also affects school leaders. Audrey Osler interviewed black headteachers and senior administrators (Osler, 1997). A black secondary headteacher, Frank, confided that:

> There is a demand that the black community expect of you, you have got to be absolutely perfect ... At the same time, the white communities out there are watching you make one error and they will shoot you down and they will get you. So I am in a no-win situation (Osler, 2006: 139).

The everyday experience of this headteacher is that individuals and groups in the dominant community judge his performance more harshly than they would a white head. He is perceived to be someone who does not have a right to his post and who is expected constantly to prove that he is capable.

Institutional racism

For a brief moment in British history, between 1999 and 2000 it became acceptable across the political and social spectrum to discuss racism and antiracism. The trigger for this unique opportunity was the publication by the British government of a report into the police investigation of the murder allegedly by racist white youths of London teenager Stephen Lawrence. The report chronicled and analyzed in minute detail the embarrassingly ineffective police investigation and the failure to bring the perpetrators to justice, in spite of overwhelming evidence.

The *Stephen Lawrence Inquiry* (Macpherson, 1999) recognized that there was system or institutional racism within the police service and by extension and explicitly also in other institutions in British society including housing, social services and education.

Drawing on a concept from the work of Carmichael and Hamilton (1968) in the US, the report, in a now classic definition characterized institutional racism as:

> The collective failure of an organization to provide an appropriate and professional service to people because of their colour, culture, or ethnic origin. It can be detected in processes, attitudes and behaviour which amount to discrimination through unwitting prejudice, ignorance, thoughtlessness and racist stereotyping which disadvantage minority ethnic people. It persists because of the failure of the organization openly and adequately to recognize and address its existence and causes by policy, example and leadership. Without recognition and action to eliminate such racism, it can prevail as part of the ethos or culture of the organization. It is a corrosive disease. (Macpherson, 1999: para. 6.34)

In presenting the government's response, the Home Secretary of the time acknowledged the extent of institutional racism in Britain.

> Any long-established, white dominated organization is liable to have procedures, practices and a culture which tend to exclude or disadvantage non-white people. The police service in this respect is little different from other parts of the criminal justice system, or from government departments ... and many other institutions (Jack Straw, Hansard (House of Commons) 24 February 1999: column 391).

Although it is possible that institutional racism may permeate the education service and unconsciously perpetuate racist mentalities, the *Stephen Lawrence Inquiry* report recognized education as being perhaps part of the problem but also having the potential to be part of the solution. It recommended that schools play a key role in enabling the development of greater racial justice. Of the report's 70 recommendations, three address education. As well as proposing amendments to the national curriculum so that schools might more effectively value cultural diversity and

prevent racism, the Inquiry recommended that local education authorities (LEAs) and school governors take a lead in ensuring that racist incidents be recorded and reported. It recommended that schools monitor exclusions by ethnicity and that the school inspection agency, OFSTED, be given a lead role in monitoring how schools are addressing and preventing racism.

The Government's response to the *Stephen Lawrence Inquiry's* recommendations (Home Office, 1999) accepted these recommendations in principle and also identified citizenship education as a key means by which schools would address and prevent racism and encourage young people to value cultural diversity.

The lead ministry in following up the recommendations of the *Stephen Lawrence Inquiry* was the Home Office and a number of ministers from that department made powerful statements in favour of antiracism during the year 2000. However, despite the acceptance of the need for schools to prevent and address racism through their curriculum and ethos, education ministers avoided making positive statements on the role of schools in challenging racism in society and declined to acknowledge the existence of institutional racism in the education service.

The importance of the acceptance of institutional racism is that it is not enough for institutions to be well intentioned; they should be accountable for the outcomes they produce. There are now very well documented and measured inequalities of outcome from the British education system. These are comprehensively reviewed by Stevens (2007). These include disproportionate representation of certain minorities in those excluded from school for disciplinary reasons; lower expectations of exam success and lower accession rates to higher education.

Colourblind racism

In an apparently laudable attempt to be even handed and not to favour individuals or groups, it would appear that many teachers profess to ignore or not to notice outward and visible signs of ethnicity or religion. Indeed the whole basis of the French Republic, is to define ethnic and religious identities as irrelevant to the public sphere, including education. This can be presented as an antiracist stance. As Sarah Pearce puts this perspective: 'unlike racists, we don't judge people on the basis of the colour of their skin' (Pearce, 2005: 41).

Apart from the fact that this may be an example of 'the majoritarian privilege of never noticing oneself' (Williams 1997: 5), such a perspective can be part of a culture that can leave the effects of institutional racism untouched. The report *The Future of Multi-Ethnic Britain* noted that:

> (Since) citizens have differing needs, equal treatment requires full account to be taken of their differences. When equality ignores relevant differences and insists on uniformity of treatment, it leads to injustice and inequality; when differences ignore the demands of equality, they result in discrimination. ... (Runnymede Trust, 2000: ix).

This was taken up by Chris Gaine who explains that: '(n)oticing race is not racist because to do so recognizes that race has effects on people's lives ... Indeed it is racist *not* to notice race when it may be relevant, such as in cases of name-calling or in monitoring' (Gaine, 2005: 173).

Colourblind racism has been theorized by Bonilla-Silva (2006) on the basis of qualitative research with white college students. He identified four frames that can be used to categorize types of colourblind racism. The first is the liberal frame. This can be illustrated by the example of the French Republic above. Abstract philosophical concepts associated with liberalism such as equal opportunities, and freedom of choice are used to justify structures that appear to be founded on principles of human rights and equality, but that nonetheless produce inequalities. The second frame is referred to as naturalization and it is used to explain phenomena such as segregation. For instance it is seen as natural for ethnic minorities or dominant populations

to want to live in proximity. A third frame is that of cultural racism. Here people produce cultural arguments to explain disadvantage. For example, it may be claimed that certain communities lack experience of democracy or that they are poor because they have large families. A fourth frame is minimization of racism. Proponents argue that name-calling does no harm or that discrimination is less widespread than previously. Bonilla-Silva notes that these frames are used in combinations as people think through their positions and try to find explanations and justifications.

These frames are all susceptible to illustration from the research literature. A fine example of colourblind minimization is captured by Cline et al. in an interview with a headteacher who says: '... all the children are treated the same and I think the fact that they are ethnic minorities doesn't make any difference for me because the children all integrate and mix in' (Cline et al., 2002: 80).

Audrey Osler provides an example of a cultural response to the acknowledgement of racism amongst staff. A head she interviewed confided that 'some of our staff do have a racist approach'. Her solution was:

> being very supportive when students want to have an Eid party or, you know, when groups of students want to do something very much, making sure that they are respected and valued for doing it. ... you give that leadership and then that should percolate down (Osler, 2006: 137).

Here the racism is minimized and the provision of cultural opportunities linked to religion provided as a substitute for addressing the real issue.

A cultural colourblind frame was seen in the example of teasing Somali girls wearing headscarves. The teasers denied their behaviour was racist, but they were picking on a cultural feature of the girls' appearance and denigrating it. The outcome was discrimination in that the Somalis were excluded from friendship groups.

The next section of this chapter will explore some of the interdependent and interwoven antiracist perspectives identified in the literature.

STRATEGIES FOR CONFRONTING RACISM

With an awareness of contemporary, every-day and subtle forms of racism, it is possible to devise antiracist strategies for teachers, schools and education authorities. A good place to start for teachers of citizenship is to provide safe opportunities to discuss the issues of racism. Clearly the 'full-frontal' attack parodied by Crick is not appropriate, but strategies that develop a sense of psychological security and a climate of respectfulness can enable such discussions to take place without harm (Carter and Osler, 2000).

A second strategy is being prepared to put antiracism at the centre of citizenship education not see it as peripheral or the concern just of minorities. This requires being prepared to speak about, though not preach about racism. For many teachers this will require some courage, but Sarah Pearce testifies to ways in which this inhibition can be overcome 'It was only when I saw that by remaining silent I was actually supporting the continued presence of racist attitudes in the classroom, that I slowly gathered the courage to act' (Pearce, 2005: 125).

As the British government's review of citizenship education in the context of diversity discovered, the fact that the demographic composition of the school is diverse does not in itself provide education for diversity or a commitment to antiracism: 'we found evidence that, although in multiethnic schools teachers asserted that education for diversity is second nature to them, in practice this is not always the case' (DFES, 2007).

In fact the report suggests that it is important to secure a whole-school commitment to citizenship education for a diverse society: 'no curriculum change will work properly unless it is reinforced by the day-to-day routines of the school and its ethos – one which constantly combats both personal and institutional racism and religious intolerance, celebrates diversity and practises inclusion' (DFES, 2007).

As a minimum, schools can ensure legal policy responses are in place and taken seriously and owned. For example in order to enable British schools to implement the Race Relations (Amendment) Act, the Commission for Racial Equality issued schools with guidance on the duty to promote race equality (Commission for Racial Equality, 2002). The duty requires public authorities, including schools to:

- eliminate unlawful racial discrimination;
- promote equality of opportunity; and
- promote good relations between people of different racial groups.

The guidance covers issues such as admissions policies and the collection and analysis of data by ethnic group. Schools are expected to set targets for improving the performance of underachieving groups. It stresses that the policy must be applied irrespective of the number of ethnic minority children in the school:

> Race equality is important, even if there is nobody from an ethnic minority group in your school or local community. Education plays a vital role in influencing young people, because the views and attitudes they form as pupils or students will probably stay with them for the rest of their lives. Also, racist acts (such as handing out racist literature) can happen in schools with no pupils from ethnic minorities (Commission for Racial Equality, 2002: 7).

The legislation requires schools to prepare a written statement of policy for promoting race equality. The code of practice provides an example of how one school set about drafting and using such a statement. All members of the school community, including parents and pupils had opportunities to be involved. The draft policy was discussed in citizenship lessons and the pupil council was given responsibility, along with the school governors and the school's senior management, for monitoring the implementation of the policy.

The code of practice recognizes the importance of the school having a clear statement of values and the need for staff training in the implications of such a values statement for their teaching and for the procedures and ethos of the school. The opportunity provided by citizenship education to engage pupils in dialogue about the race equality policy and the values of the school is also clearly signalled.

More recently local authorities in Britain have been required to draw up a Children and Young People's Plan. The Ajegbo review highlights this as an opportunity to promote social cohesion, antiracism and education for diversity. It cites the example of Hampshire local authority where elected members and officers took a lead to encourage: 'education for diversity and citizenship, and a zero tolerance of racism, which has set the tone for a positive, inclusive culture. This has resulted in the active promotion of the UN Convention on the Rights of the Child' (UNCRC) (DFES, 2007).

Other research previously cited identified an individual school where a deputy headteacher is specifically responsible for antiracism. Whenever there is an incident a procedure is invoked that involves:

- interviews with both pupils and witnesses to ascertain what happened as well as possible;
- information to both sets of parents who have to be kept informed;
- advice and counselling to either or both parties as seems possible;
- other action, such as punishment of perpetrator (ranging from detention to exclusion) and informing other agencies; and
- a careful log of each step (Cline et al., 2002: 81).

I have highlighted the rhetorical support for antiracism provided by governments and their ministers when operating in intergovernmental organizations such as the United Nations and the Council of Europe. Policies at these levels rarely seem to be echoed in speeches or actions at national level. This provides an opportunity for citizens and citizenship educators to highlight the gap between such rhetoric and reality and campaign for change.

If citizenship educators are reluctant to engage with antiracism it may be because of a lack of concepts and a language with which to discuss racism and its effects. One thing that citizenship educators can do to overcome this lacuna is to study the literatures on racism and antiracism and familiarize themselves with concepts such as those introduced in this chapter. Being able to identify everyday racism, institutional racism or colourblind racism may help teachers to discuss these issues with students and with colleagues.

Finally, there are many practical steps that schools can take to confront racism. There are many examples of good practice available and many initiatives taken by local authorities and school boards. By adopting standard procedures such as recording and reporting racist incidents, schools can help to develop antiracist reflexes and cultures. In the end it is antiracist cultures even more than antiracist laws that protect minorities and enhance democracy.

CONCLUSION

This chapter has argued the case for antiracism to be central to education for democracy and citizenship. Such an argument should be redundant, but there has been relatively little development of support for antiracism within teacher education in the context of citizenship. In fact it has previously been presented as rather sensitive, counterproductive or controversial and thus best left to indirect approaches.

REFERENCES

Banks, J.A. (1997) *Educating Citizens in a Multicultural Society*. New York: London, Teachers College Press.

Banks, J.A. (Ed.) (2004) *Diversity and Citizenship Education: Global Perspectives*. San Francisco, CA.: Jossey-Bass.

Bhavnani, R., Mirza, H. and Meetoo, V. (2005) *Tackling the Roots of Racism: Lessons for Success*. Bristol: Policy Press.

Bonnett, A. (2000) *Anti-Racism*. London: Routledge.

Bonilla-Silva, E. (2006) *Racism without Racists: Color-Blind Racism and the Persistence of Racial Inequality in the United States.* Oxford: Rowman & Littlefield.

Braham, P., Rattansi, A. and Skellington, R. (1992) *Racism and Antiracism: Inequalities, Opportunities and Policies.* London: Sage.

Carmichael, S. and Hamilton, C. (1968) *Black Power: The Politics of Liberation in America.* London: Jonathan Cape.

Carter, C. and Osler, A. (2000) 'Human rights, identities and conflict management: a study of school culture as experienced through classroom relationships,' *Cambridge Journal of Education*, 30 (3): 335–356.

Cline, T., de Abreu, G., Fihosy, C., Gray, H., Lambert, H. and Neale, J. (2002) *Minority Ethnic Pupils in Mainly White Schools (Research Report No 365).* London: Department for Education and Skills.

Commission for Racial Equality, (2002). *The Duty to Promote Race Equality: Guidance for Schools.* London, CRE.

Council of Europe (2000a) *Project on 'Education for Democratic Citizenship': Resolution Adopted by the Council of Europe Ministers of Education at Their 20th Session, Cracow, Poland 15–17 October 2000.* Strasbourg: Council of Europe.

Council of Europe (2000b) *Political Declaration Adopted by Ministers of Council of Europe Member States on Friday 13 October 2000 at the Concluding Session of the European Conference Against Racism.* Strasbourg: Council of Europe.

Council of Europe (2002) *Recommendation Rec (2002)12 of the Committee of Ministers to Member States on Education for Democratic Citizenship.* Strasbourg: Council of Europe.

Crick, B. (2000) *Essays on Citizenship.* London: Continuum.

Department for Education and Skills (2007) Diversity and Citizenship: curriculum review (Ajegbo review). London: DfES.

Diamantopoulou, A. (2001) *Address of European Commissioner Responsible for Employment and Social Affairs to Plenary Session of the World Conference Against Racism, Durban, 2 September.* Brussels: European Commission.

Essed, P. (1991) *Understanding Every-day Racism: An Interdisciplinary Theory.* London: Sage.

European Commission (1999) *Mainstreaming the Fight Against Racism: Commission Report on the Implementation of the Action Plan Against Racism.* Brussels: European Commission.

Fryer, P. (1984) *Staying Power: The History of Black People in Britain.* London: Pluto.

Gaine, C. (2005) *We're all White, Thanks: the Persisting Myth about 'White' Schools.* Stoke-on-Trent: Trentham.

Home Office (1999) *Stephen Lawrence Inquiry: Home Secretary's Action Plan.* London: Home Office.

Macpherson, W. (1999) *The Stephen Lawrence Inquiry.* London: The Stationery Office.

Maylor, U., Ross, A., Rollock, N. and Williams, K. (2006) *Black Teachers in London: A Report for the Mayor of London.* London: Greater London Assembly.

Osler, A. (1997) *The Education and Careers of Black Teachers.* Buckingham: Open University Press.

Osler, A. (ed.) (2000) *Citizenship and Democracy in School: Diversity, Identity, Equality.* Stoke on Trent: Trentham Books.

Osler, A. (2006) 'Changing leadership in contexts of diversity: visibility, invisibility and democratic ideals,' *Policy Futures in Education*, 4 (3): 128–144.

Osler, A. and Starkey, H. (2000) Citizenship, Human Rights and Cultural Diversity, in: Audrey Osler (ed.) *Citizenship and Democracy in Schools: Diversity, Identity, Equality.* Stoke-on-Trent: Trentham.

Osler, A. and Starkey, H. (2001) 'Citizenship education and national identities in France and England: inclusive or exclusive?', *Oxford Review of Education*, 27 (2): 287–305.

Osler, A. and Starkey, H. (2002) 'Education for citizenship: mainstreaming the fight against racism?,' *European Journal of Education*, 37 (2): 143–159.

Osler, A. and Starkey, H. (2005), *Changing Citizenship: Democracy and Inclusion in Education.* Maidenhead: Open University Press.

Ouseley, H. (1982) *The System.* London: Runnymede Trust.

Runnymede Trust (2000) *The Future of Multi-Ethnic Britain. The Parekh Report.* London: The Runnymede Trust.

Pearce, S. (2005) *You Wouldn't Understand: White Teachers in Multiethnic Classrooms*. Stoke-on-Trent: Trentham.

Raby, R. (2004) '"There's no racism at my school, it's just joking around": ramifications for anti-racist education', *Race Ethnicity and Education*, 7 (4): 367–383.

Starkey, H. (2000) 'Citizenship education in France and Britain: evolving theories and practices', *Curriculum Journal*, 11 (1): 39–54.

Stevens, P. (2007) 'researching race/ethnicity and educational inequality in English secondary schools: a critical review of the research literature between 1980 and 2005', *Review of Educational Research*, 77 (2): 147–185.

Williams, P. (1997) *Seeing a Colour-Blind Future: The Paradox of Race*. London: Virago.

26

Sustainable Development

John Huckle

'The ultimate goal of education for sustainable development is to empower people with the perspectives, knowledge, and skills for helping them live in peaceful sustainable societies' (UNESCO, 2001: 1).

There is now a growing consensus that twenty-first century civilization is on a path that is not sustainable. Dominant forms of political economy are failing to conserve ecological resources and services, guarantee economic stability, reduce social inequality; maintain cultural diversity, and protect people's physical and mental health. We face related crises of ecological, economic, social, cultural, and personal sustainability, yet the means are available to set civilization on a more sustainable path. Adopting more sustainable forms of political economy involves the establishment of new forms of global governance guided by new forms of citizenship. Education that features such citizenships should lie at the heart of initiatives linked to the UN's Decade of Education for Sustainable Development (DESD) that runs from 2005 to 2014.

This chapter seeks to clarify the new kinds of governance and citizenship that may be necessary to set civilization on a more sustainable path and how these might be developed through citizenship education as

part of the DESD. It begins with considerations of philosophy and ethics.

PHILOSOPHICAL AND ETHICAL FOUNDATIONS

Central to the perspectives that ESD should develop is what Hartmann (1998) terms a social-ecological theory of reality and the values that stem from it. Rather than regarding nature and society as separate realms (modern dualism), we should acknowledge that reality is always the product of both ecological (bio-physical) and social relations and processes. The phenomena of global warming illustrates how the relations between objects in the bio-physical and social worlds enable ecological and social processes, how these processes affect one another constantly, and how our understanding of such phenomena can never be entirely neutral or objective because it is always partly a product of those social or power relations it needs to explain. The politics of sustainability is about the relations that humans are in with other human and non-human agents, how we understand these relations, and what we can do to ensure that they are more sustainable.

Hartmann argues that for a society to be sustainable (capable of evolving indefinitely alongside the rest of nature) three sets of relations have to be maintained:

1. Social relations amongst humans based on mutual respect and tolerance. These require equitable access to basic needs, freedom of thought and expression, and democratic forms of decision making and governance in all spheres of life including that of economic production and distribution.
2. Environmental relations between humans and their bio-physical environment that ensure the survival and well-being of other species (biodiversity) and their continued evolution alongside people.
3. Ecological relations between organisms (including humans) and their environment that ensure similar environmental conditions and opportunities (climate, water availability, soil fertility, radioactivity levels, etc.) to those that have prevailed throughout most of human history.

The question then arises, what form of ethics, politics, and governance should regulate social and environmental relations and their impact on ecological relations?

As regards ethics, a socio-ecological theory or reality, based in dialectical materialism (Harvey, 1996) or the new physical and life sciences and systems theory (Capra, 2003), recognizes that people are part of ecological relations (members of a biological species, dependent on ecological resources and services to supply their needs), yet partly independent of such relations as part of social relations (they have powers of language and technology that enable them to transform their own nature and that which surrounds them). In finding sustainable ways to live they have to balance ecology and society centred values or an ecocentric perspective that finds intrinsic values in the non-human world, with an anthropocentric or technocentric perspective that suggests the only value of this world lies in its usefulness to people.

In seeking sustainability we should be guided by a weak anthropocentrism. This maintains that while humans are the only source of value, they are not the only bearers of value. In addition to valuing or caring for present and future generations of people, we should value and care for the rest of nature by recognising its ecological, scientific, aesthetic, and spiritual value alongside its economic value, and acknowledging its right to exist. In other words, we should balance our rights to self-determination and development, with responsibilities towards the rest of the human and biotic community.

The ethics of weak anthropocentrism are reflected in the Earth Charter (ECI, 2007) that sets out fundamental principles for sustainable development. Part of the unfinished business of the 1992 Rio Earth Summit, the final version, approved in 2000, is essentially a people's treaty shaped by a global dialogue that involved both experts and representatives of civil society. Its preamble suggests that 'we must decide to live with a sense of universal responsibility, identifying ourselves with the whole Earth community as well as with our local communities. We are at once citizens of different nations and of one world in which the local and global are linked. Everyone shares responsibility for the present and future well-being of the human family and the larger living world'. The charter's vision recognizes that environmental protection, human rights, equitable human development, and peace are interdependent and indivisible, and its sixteen principles are grouped into four sections (respect and care for the community of life; ecological integrity; social and economic justice; and democracy, non-violence, and peace). Principle 13 suggests that the world community should 'strengthen democratic institutions at all levels, and provide transparency and accountability in governance, inclusive participation in decision making and access to justice'. Principle 14 advocates ESD as part of formal education and life-long learning.

In 2003 UNESCO affirmed member states' intention to use the Earth Charter as an educational tool for implementing the DESD.

SOCIAL THEORY, POLITICS, AND GOVERNANCE

Values reflect and shape ongoing social development and debates surrounding sustainability should be guided by social theory. This now seeks to integrate nature and the environment into its concerns (Barry, 2000, Sutton, 2004) and suggests that the world is undergoing fundamental change that goes to the heart of the individual-society relationship on which the concept of citizenship is founded. Following a crisis of profitability at the end of the 'post-war boom' powerful economic and political elites restructured political economies in ways that intensified globalization, environmental degradation, and social inequalities. This change is variously interpreted as, for example, a shift from Fordist to Post-Fordist modes of regulation (Lipietz, 1992); from modernity to post-modernity (Crook et al., 1992); or from scarcity to risk society (Beck, 1992). Its significance lies first in the ways it has further compromised the competence, form, autonomy, and legitimacy of the nation state as the prime container of political community and citizenship. The urgency of global issues, together with the growth of global networks of power and international political institutions and agencies, has prompted renewed attention to global models of democracy and citizenship, while the rise of movements and nationalisms from below, has prompted experiments with forms of direct or deliberative democracy encouraged by governments adopting new consultation procedures to improve their standing with citizens (Held et al., 2000).

Second, global change challenges the existential foundations of people's lives and brings new status and class divisions along with new interests and insecurities. In the advanced industrial economies, the old politics of production and class has been largely replaced by the new politics of consumption and identity. Consumer capitalism offers a vast array of cultural products and encourages individuals to use these to create

meaning and organise and monitor their own multiple identities and life narratives. Epistemological uncertainty may result in hedonism, or refuge in old and new fundamentalisms, but it can also prompt a new sensitivity to difference and subjectivity; scepticism towards grand narratives and universal truths; and a constructive postmodernism that seeks to acknowledge and correct the mistakes of modern development. This involves a reassessment of industrialism, liberalism and Marxism; a wider definition of politics; and the design and implementation of new forms of democracy and citizenship that can foster sustainable development.

Constructive postmodernism recognizes that government, in the form of the constitution, law and state policies, can act as protector and trustee of collective reason, but that self-managing citizens must increasingly act themselves in responsible and enlightened ways that express solidarity with others. Sustainability requires the extension of both legal and practical notions of citizenship: a restructuring of the state and international political institutions to facilitate new legal rights and responsibilities (environmental citizenship), and the strengthening and democratisation of civil society to foster moral responsibility and more sustainable ways of living (ecological citizenship). The Real World coalition of UK environment and development NGOs is one advocate of such improved governance (Christie and Warburton, 2001).

GREEN POLITICAL THEORY AND THE POLITICS OF SUSTAINABLE DEVELOPMENT

The green movement and green politics reflect the theory and practice of these new kinds of citizenship (Barry, 1998). Greens work 'in and against' the state urging it to meet new demands based in ethics, and 'beyond and around' the state by using international forums, treaties, and conventions to establish new environmental rights and responsibilities across borders. International NGOs shadow international governmental agencies, organise social forums offering alternative agendas alongside international summits (Hubbard and Miller, 2005), and use the new communication technologies to sustain virtual communities of active global citizens. As regards practical citizenship, greens seek to rescue society from the instrumental reason that dominates markets and states by fostering civil society and a public sphere in which ecological and social issues can be debated and self-managing sustainable communities can take root. Appropriate technologies, economic localisation, and deliberative democracy are key elements of green alternatives (Woodin and Lucas, 2004) with localisation or decentralisation encouraging both greater self-sufficiency and more deliberative decision-making (Baber and Bartlett, 2005). Encouraging dialogue and discussion, as part of community decision making, has moralising and pedagogical effects, and is a key element of social learning for sustainability.

Having suggested that greens are in the vanguard of new forms of governance, citizenship, and community development, it should be acknowledged that both liberals and Marxists now advocate variants of sustainable development. Liberals are reformist, strongly anthropocentric, and believe that such development does not require a radical restructuring of capitalist social relations. Economic growth can be balanced with environmental protection and social justice using existing and new forms of technology and global governance (Turner, 2001). Sometimes termed ecological modernization or the greening of capitalism, this liberal view is dominant within the international community and is reflected in Agenda 21, the agenda for sustainable development produced by the 1992 Earth Summit.

Marxists reject capitalism with a green face suggesting that market-based environmental policies do little to counter the anti-ecological characteristics of capital. While sceptical of the utopianism in much early green political theory, they now acknowledge the environmental crisis (the second contradiction of capitalism (Merchant, 1994)) but remind greens of the continuing significance of class struggle (Burkett, 2003), imperialism (Harvey, 2003), and state regulation and planning (Dickenson, 2003). Dresner (2006) argues that the language of sustainability returns us to many of the unfashionable ideas about fairness, solidarity, and the conscious regulation of social development that were associated with socialism in the past. Post-industrial socialists have updated these ideas with new concepts of welfare and citizenship.

UNESCO suggests that ESD should develop knowledge and understanding of the social, economic, and environmental dimensions of sustainable development. Addressing the social dimension clearly involves citizenship education as it seeks 'an understanding of social institutions and their role in change and development, as well as the democratic and participatory systems which give opportunity for the expression of opinion, the selection of governments, the forging of consensus and the resolution of differences' (Pigozzi, 2005: 2).

LIBERAL ENVIRONMENTAL CITIZENSHIP

Environmental citizenship (refers to) the way in which the environment-citizenship relationship can be regarded from a liberal point of view … this is a citizenship that deals in the currency of environmental rights, that is conducted exclusively in the public sphere, whose principal virtues are the liberal ones of reasonableness and a willingness to accept the force of better argument and procedural legitimacy, and whose remit is bounded political configurations modelled on the nation-state. For the most rough-and-ready purposes, it can be taken that environmental citizenship here refers to attempts to extend the discourse and practice of rights-claiming into the environmental context (Dobson, 2003: 89).

While liberal democracy is not the dominant form of government in the world, it is dominant in those advanced industrial states that cause most of the environmental degradation. Sustainable development may be pursued using existing and additional human rights, contained in state constitutions and international instruments (Alder and Wilkinson, 1999; Elliott, 2004). These should include substantive rights to life, to those basic needs that support it, and to a liveable and sustainable environment, together with procedural rights, such as the right of access to environmental information. Rights and associated laws that govern environmental management and land use planning are particularly significant, with activists in the environmental justice movement seeking to use and extend these in ways that protect the health, livelihoods, and amenities of disadvantaged communities.

In outlining a conception of environmental citizenship that is developed from an immanent critique of contemporary liberalism, Bell (2005) suggests that liberalism should abandon its conception of the environment as property and adopt a conception of the environment as provider of basic human needs and a subject about which there is reasonable disagreement. Such a concept reflects ethical principles of inter and intra-generational justice, subjects environmental decisions to democratic procedural principles, requires state policies to reflect conceptions of sustainable development that gain support in politically just debates, and thereby constrains rather than rejects capitalism. It leads Bell to suggest that environmental citizens do not have a duty to protect nature, wilderness, or 'green spaces' (particular conceptions of environment), nor do they have a duty to make lifestyle choices that promote global environmental justice (a negation of personal rights). They may however adopt private environmental duties (such as recycling) as a way of promoting change in policy and law and/or as citizens' duties to be exercised alongside legal duties.

POST-COSMOPOLITAN ECOLOGICAL CITIZENSHIP

Ecological citizenship deals in the currency of non-contractual responsibility. It inhabits the private as well as the public sphere, it refers to the source rather than the nature of responsibility to determine what count as citizenship virtues, it works with the language of virtue, and it is explicitly non-territorial (Dobson, 2003: 89).

Dobson starts his discussion of citizenship and the environment by noting that asymmetrical nature of globalization. Local acts with global consequences produce communities of obligation that are primarily communities of injustice. Cheap food in European supermarkets, for example, is often the result of exploited labour and land in Africa, and British consumers therefore have non-reciprocal duties to African farmers that should be discharged through redistributive acts.

Advocates of cosmopolitan citizenship, such as Held (1995), focus on the human community and suggest that uncoerced dialogue and greater democracy will allow the realization of universal values, such as those expressed in the Earth Charter. Dobson maintains that they focus on the wrong kind of community (the human community rather than communities of obligation), the wrong mode of operation (impartiality rather than partiality), and the wrong political objective (more dialogue and democracy rather than more justice and democracy). Rather than a thin and non-material account of the ties that bind members of the cosmopolitan community (common humanity and a commitment to dialogue), Dobson offers a thickly material account linked to the production and reproduction of daily life in an unequal and globalising world. This prompts him to canvass the emergence of post-cosmopolitan citizenship, alongside liberal and civic-republican forms.

Table 26.1   Three types of citizenship (Dobson, 2003: 39)

Liberal	Civic-republican	Post-cosmopolitan
Rights/entitlements (contractual)	Duties/responsibilities (contractual)	Duties/responsibilities (non-contractual)
Public sphere	Public sphere	Public and private spheres
Virtue-free	'Masculine' virtue	'Feminine' virtue
Territorial (discriminatory)	Territorial (discriminatory)	Non-territorial (non-discriminatory)

In comparing citizenship in its liberal, civic-republican, and post-cosmopolitan forms, Dobson focuses on four dimensions (rights/responsibilities, public/private, virtue/non-virtue, and territorial/non-territorial), see Table 26.1. It is the fact that citizens of globalizing nations are 'always already' acting on others that requires post-cosmopolitan citizenship to acknowledge non-reciprocal, non-contractual and unilateral duties. Since acts in the private sphere impact upon people and environments at a distance (have public implications), this sphere is properly a site for politics and the exercise of post-cosmopolitan citizenship. Such citizenship focuses on horizontal citizen-citizen relations rather than vertical citizen-state relations, and is committed to such 'feminine' virtues as care and compassion. It is non-territorial in that it spans borders and is associated with a global civil society as exemplified by the anti-globalization movement.

Ecological citizenship is a specifically ecological form of post-cosmopolitan citizenship. It recognizes that as members of global society we are 'always already' obligated to others at a distance, a concept best expressed in the notion of ecological footprints. Such a footprint is a measure of the total amount of ecologically productive land and water supporting one's lifestyle, and for the more affluent members of global society, much of this land and water is located far from their place of residence (Wackernagel and Rees, 1996). As we consume more, our ecological footprints grow, and we are obligated to more strangers across space and time (to those at a distance and to those not yet born). The community of ecological citizenship is created by our material activities and obligates us to protect a healthy, complex, and autonomously functioning ecological system for the benefit of present and future generations. Such obligation is encouraged by adopting a weak anthropocentrism as outlined above.

Ecological citizenship has international and intergenerational dimensions and its responsibilities are asymmetrical, falling on globalising rather than globalized individuals. Ecological citizens will want to ensure that their ecological footprints do not compromise or foreclose options for present and future generations and will be prepared to reduce them without expecting others to follow their example. Obligation ends when ecological space (resources and services) is fairly distributed but such fairness may require the righting of historical wrongs. Virtues normally associated with the private sphere, such as care and compassion, help ecological citizens meet their responsibilities, and this sphere will increasingly become a site of citizenship as they realize that by reducing household consumption they can reduce their ecological footprints. Such politicisation of the private sphere is a challenge for liberals since it questions personal choice and subjects the idea of the 'good life' to political scrutiny.

Valencia Saiz (2005) suggests that a blind spot in Dobson's work is his apparent insistence on the efficacy of individual political agency. He fails to address the conditions under which environmental or ecological citizenship can be engendered or the political economy of such citizenships. This is the theme of post-industrial socialism.

POST-INDUSTRIAL SOCIALIST CITIZENSHIP

A theory of post-industrial socialist citizenship (PISC) builds on the ideas of Gorz and Habermas (Goldblatt, 1996). Gorz focuses on the potential of new technologies to free citizens from work so that they can devote the time saved to self- and community development. Habermas writes of the colonization of the lifeworld, or the way in which the instrumental rationality of the economy and state invades everyday life, and argues that if citizens are to extend their autonomy, there needs to be a vibrant civil society or public sphere governed by communicative rationality or deliberative democracy.

PISC (Little, 1998) involves reduced working hours for those in paid employment to provide a more equitable distribution of work. At the same time all have an obligation to make some contribution to the wealth and well-being of society in return for a guaranteed social wage (a new economic right). This new right would increase the prospects of realising equal citizenship, but PISC also requires the redefinition of civil rights to promote autonomy, and of political rights to ensure participation. Rights to self-determination would emphasize positive freedoms, rather than the negative freedoms of liberal democracy, encourage a civil rather than national definition of citizenship, and counter alienation from politics. Political rights would provide citizens with an equal chance to influence the decisions affecting their lives and shift the balance from representative to more deliberative or direct forms of democracy. A universal requirement to contribute to social wealth would value much of the current unpaid work (such as that of carers) that is involved in the maintenance and reproduction of everyday life.

The relevance of PISC for sustainable development lies in its potential to free citizens from the treadmill of capitalist production and consumption and foster diverse green political economies. People would have the time and encouragement to act as environmental and ecological citizens by developing local economic trading schemes (LETSystems, 2007), participating in deliberative environmental management and planning, and building social capital (Smith, 2005), In these and other ways they would learn their way to sustainability.

CITIZENSHIP EDUCATION FOR SUSTAINABLE DEVELOPMENT

The DESD website suggests that education is the primary agent of transformation towards sustainable development since it can foster the required values, behaviour, and lifestyles. It recognizes however that there can be no universal model of ESD. Each country has to define its own priorities and actions, with goals, emphases, and processes that are locally defined to meet local conditions. As quality education ESD supports a rights-based approach, develops the learner's competence as a community member and global citizen (as well as an individual and family member), upholds and conveys the principles of a sustainable world as outlined in the Earth Charter is locally relevant and culturally appropriate, and conserves indigenous and traditional knowledge.

UNESCO publishes a booklet on the international implementation of the Decade (UNESCO, 2006) and reports on progress to date (for example UNESCO, 2007), while the DESD website provides access to developments around the world. SDELG (2005) provides a survey of ESD in 11 countries that suggests that there is a great deal of good practice but also a need to appreciate and signpost the embryonic and fragile nature of much ESD. It is most securely established within the curricula of formal education in those countries where it has government support and regional strategies, such as that of

UNECE (2005), are significant in prompting action by member states.

ESD has emerged since the 1992 Rio Earth Summit as a synthesis of environmental and development education. UNESCO has acknowledges the central roles of citizenship education and political literacy in ESD and the consequences that follow from this.

> ... a curriculum reoriented towards sustainability would place the notion of citizenship among its primary objectives. This would require a revision of many existing curricula and the development of objectives and content themes, and teaching, learning and assessment processes that emphasize moral virtues, ethical motivation and ability to work with others to help build a sustainable future. Viewing education for sustainability as a contribution to a politically literate society is central to the reformulation of education and calls for a 'new generation' of theorizing and practice in education and a rethinking of many familiar approaches, including within environmental education (Unesco, 1997, paras 67 and 68).

Something of what this new theorizing and practice may mean for citizenship education will now be outlined by reference to some of the key features of ESD as quality education listed on the DESD site.

ESD IS INTERDISCIPLINARY AND HOLISTIC (LEARNING FOR SUSTAINABLE DEVELOPMENT SHOULD BE EMBEDDED IN THE WHOLE CURRICULUM, NOT TAUGHT AS A SEPARATE SUBJECT)

Mention has already been made of a socio-ecological theory of reality and the need to see the world as a complex of inter-related ecological, environmental, and social relations and processes. Modern academic divisions of labour separate the natural and social sciences and humanities, divorce academic knowledge from people's everyday knowledge, and so prevent learners from developing a comprehensive understanding of their place in the world (Dickens, 1996). The primacy of ecology and nature study in much environmental education should be challenged and more attention given to the economic, political, and cultural structures and processes that cause social injustice and foster unsustainable practices. The curriculum *What We Consume* that I developed for WWF-UK in the mid to late 1980s (Huckle, 1988) was an early attempt to redesign environmental education as ESD using the Programme for Political Education's framework for political literacy (Crick and Porter, 1978), and a concept of citizenship education that embraces governance within the ecological, economic, political, social, and cultural domains, at all scales from the local to the global (Lynch, 1992). Experiential classroom activities focused on the political economy of goods students consumed; set out sustainable alternatives; and allowed critical consideration of environmental, ecological, and post-industrial socialist citizenship.

Clearly environmental citizenship education should develop propositional and procedural knowledge of environmental rights and the roles played by laws, regulations, tax and fiscal policies, and other instruments in shaping sustainable development. Students might for example study local planning issues, ecological tax reform via national budgets, and the introduction of a carbon trading scheme within the European Union. They might focus on the performance of corporations and NGOs as environmental citizens, examining for example the corporate social responsibility claims of a supermarket chain, and an NGO campaign to protect local farmers from land seizures linked to increased demand for bio-fuels. Such lessons require teachers to integrate citizenship education with other subjects (geography, science, technology, media studies, etc.) and by revealing the ecological footprints of the rich, lead to considerations of ecological citizenship. Encouraged to think and act, both globally and locally, students may revise their identities as they adopt more sustainable ways of living.

ESD IS VALUES-DRIVEN: SHARING THE VALUES AND PRINCIPLES UNDERPINNING SUSTAINABLE DEVELOPMENT

The Earth Charter guidebook for teachers (ECIIS, 2005) provides advice on introducing Earth Charter principles across the curriculum and is supported by a book of essays examining the principles (Corcoran et al., 2005). Moral and social responsibility, partly developed through moral and values education, is a key outcome of ESD, but there is political debate on whether or not the state should promote such principles through education.

Political liberalism maintains that the state should not intentionally promote any comprehensive religious, philosophical, or ethical doctrines. It deliberately avoids taking a stand on the purposes of human life or what constitutes our well being. Instead it aims to find principles of justice for a society that can be accepted by people with radically different metaphysical and ethical commitments. Bell (2004) draws on Rawl's concept of justice to suggest that sustainability is an anthropocentric concept arrived at through informed democratic deliberation of what is necessary for all (current and future) members of society to have a decent standard of life through social co-operation. Citizenship education should therefore promote political virtues (reasonableness; a sense of fairness, a spirit of compromise and a readiness to meet others halfway) designed to ensure intra-generational justice, and sustainability virtues (essentially the duty of the current generation to maintain the 'circumstances of justice' for future generations) designed to ensure inter-generational justice. The curriculum 'should aim to promote a positive attitude towards 'sustainability' and a basic understanding of the environmental and social science frameworks that citizens need to participate in "sustainability" decisions' (Bell, 2004: 47). It should not however promote particular green ideals or forms of sustainable development that are properly

matters of personal and collective choice. These might be aspects of the permissible curriculum (as they are in some national curricula) if the demos so decides, but schools that then promote green ideals should pay proper respect to the political liberal's concern for freedom. The school's environmental ethic is not the only environmental ethic that can be held in society, and education about some competing green ideals (and non-green or anti-green ideas) should also be part of the curriculum.

Dobson (2003) also considers whether a liberal education system can cope with the value-laden nature of sustainability questions, and concludes that liberalism's normative neutrality commits it to providing the 'mental and material wherewithal' for choosing from a wide range of options concerning the good life. Realism requires the teaching of some determinate habits, practices, and values and 'the appropriate liberal commitment is not to offer some determinate account of it (sustainability), but to ensure the conditions within which the widest range of opportunities for thinking and living sustainability are authentically available' (p. 198). Liberal ESD is more likely to fail by omission rather than indoctrination, and liberal education systems can teach citizenship ESD provided that they embrace the full implications of the indeterminate and contested nature of sustainable development, and develop students' reasoning ability through exposure to real examples of partiality and commitment.

Marxists question the neutrality of liberal states and consider their education systems to be principally concerned with the reproduction of unsustainable social and environmental relations. Education as praxis involves ideology critique and seeks, through reflection and action on lived realities, to bring students to a critical awareness of the limited nature of current forms of democracy and citizenship and the potential of radical alternatives such as those offered by post-industrial socialism. Building on the ideas of Freire, Capra and others, Gadotti (1996; Antunes and Gadotti, 2005) associates ESD with eco-pedagogy, a utopian project to change current social and environmental relations that emerged from the Rio Global Forum in 1992.

ESD INVOLVES CRITICAL THINKING AND PROBLEM SOLVING: LEADING TO CONFIDENCE IN ADDRESSING THE DILEMMAS AND CHALLENGES OF SUSTAINABLE DEVELOPMENT

Habermas' theory of knowledge constitutive interests suggests that ESD can be theorized and practiced as environmental science and management; values and behaviour change; or socially critical education (Huckle, 2006). Radicals acknowledge the conservative and idealist nature of the first two forms and draw on critical social theory of the environment and education to theorize the third. *What We Consume* is one example of such ESD. Another is UNESCO's multi-media teacher education program *Teaching and Learning for a Sustainable Future* (UNESCO, 2007) which contains a unit on citizenship education.

ESD that uses critical or eco-pedagogy claims to develop critical thinking and problem solving in democratic ways, but Gough and Scott (2006) suggest that it is prescriptive and manipulative. It is too ready to prescribe educational outcomes from a flawed understanding of the relations between the environment, citizenship and learning, and shape learners to behaviours designed to support the policy choices of others. It roots thinking about the future in what we know (or think we know) in the present, whereas a desirable ESD would acknowledge the uncertainty of many knowledge claims regarding sustainable development; the unpredictable ways in which society and nature co-evolve; and the need for learning characterized by open-endedness, negotiation, and the juxtapositioning of competing perspectives. These are characteristics that socially critical ESD already claims to possess and the debate is likely to continue.

MULTI-METHOD: WORD, ART, DRAMA, DEBATE

Bonnett (2004) argues that sustainability should be taught as a frame of mind or sensitivity to the multiple meanings of nature and the numerous ways in which it is valuable to human civilization. Art, literature, music, and film can all help teachers to develop sustainability as a frame of mind and prompt debate about the kinds of political economy and citizenship that would allow it to find expression in the real world.

Gilbert (1996) suggests that the political economy of culture and the environment should be incorporated into citizenship education. The power of cultural expression is increasingly available to youth, through such media as video and the internet, and plays an important role in their understanding of self and others. Along with the identity and lifestyle politics of environmentalism, it is a means whereby young people experiment with identity and life narratives, develop a sense of agency, and come to act out social alternatives. The sales of texts like *No Logo* (Klein, 2000) suggest that students can be motivated towards politics and citizenship education, but the starting points should be identity and lifestyle, rather than formal notions of the ideal citizen. Kenway and Bullen (2001) and Quart (2003) raise related issues in the context of consumerism.

LOCALLY RELEVANT: ADDRESSING LOCAL AS WELL AS GLOBAL ISSUES, AND USING THE LANGUAGE(S) WHICH LEARNERS MOST COMMONLY USE

Clearly citizenship ESD should be practiced in and beyond educational institutions that are seeking to be more sustainable. There are growing international movements of sustainable schools (Henderson and Tilbury, 2004) and universities (Corcoran and Wals, 2004) and as these green the curriculum, campus and community, there are opportunities for pupils and students to participate in decisions, learn through active citizenship or community involvement (Hart, 1996, Adams and Ingham, 1998), and thereby develop action competence (Carlsson and Jensen, 2006).

Environmental management, participatory planning, corporate social responsibility, urban greening, rural development, and ethical consumerism, are examples of contexts in which individuals can learn their way to sustainability alongside businesses, governments, and civil society organisations. There is an emerging literature on social learning for sustainability: 'the learning that takes place when divergent interests, norms, values, and constructions of reality meet in an environment that is conducive to learning' (Wals, 2007: 18). Wals' text outlines principles, perspectives and praxis from across the world while Keen et al. (2005) draw on Australian experience.

There is much in these volumes to support this chapter's argument that 'new generation' theorizing and practice in citizenship ESD is well established and that it is possible to teach activist and duty-based forms of citizenship linked to visions of more just, sustainable, and democratic futures.

REFERENCES

Adams, E. and Ingham, S. (1998) *Changing Places: Children's Participation in Environmental Planning*. London: The Children's Society.

Alder, J. and Wilkinson, D. (1999) *Environmental Law and Ethics*. Basingstoke: MacMillan.

Antunes, A. and Gadotti, M. (2005) 'Ecopedagogy as the Appropriate Pedagogy to the Earth Charter Process' in P. B. Corcoran, M. Vilela and A. Roerink (eds.) *The Earth Charter In Action*. Amsterdam: KIT Publishers. pp. 135–137.

Baber, W.F. and Bartlett, R.V. (2005) *Deliberative Environmental Politics: Democracy and Ecological Rationality*. London: MIT Press.

Barry, J. (1998) 'Green Political Thought', in A. Lent (ed.), *New Political Thought: An Introduction*. London: Lawrence & Wishart. pp. 184–200.

Barry, J. (2000) *Environment and Social Theory*. London: Routledge.

Beck, U. (1992) *Risk Society*. London: Sage Publications.

Bell, D. (2004) 'Creating Green Citizens? Political Liberalism and Environmental Education', *Journal of Philosophy of Education*, 38 (1): 37–53.

Bell, D. (2005) 'Liberal Environmental Citizenship', *Environmental Politics*, 14 (2): 179–194.

Bonnett, M. (2004) *Retrieving Nature: Education in a Post-Humanist Age*. Oxford: Blackwell.

Burkett, P. (2003) 'Capitalism, Nature and Class Struggle', in A. Saad-Filho (ed.), *Anti-Capitalism: A Marxist Introduction*. London: Pluto.

Capra, F. (2003) *The Hidden Connections: A Science for Sustainable Living*. London: Harper Collins.

Carlsson, M. and Jensen, B. (2006) 'Encouraging Environmental Citizenship: The Roles and Challenges for Schools', in A. Dobson and D. Bell (eds.) *Environmental Citizenship*. London: MIT Press. pp. 237–261.

Christie, I. and Warburton, D. (2001) *From Here to Sustainability: Politics in the Real World*. London: Earthscan.

Corcoran, P.B., Vilela, M. and Roerink, A. (eds.) (2005) *The Earth Charter In Action*. Amsterdam: KIT Publishers.

Corcoran, P.B. and Wals, A.E.J. (eds.) (2004) *Higher Education and the Challenge of Sustainability*. Dordrecht: Kluwer Academic Publishers.

Crick, B. and Porter, A. (eds.) (1978) *Political Education and Political Literacy*. London: Longman.

Crook, S., Pakulski, J. and Waters, M. (1992) *Postmodernization: Change in Advanced Society*. London: Sage Publications.

Dickens, P. (1996) *Reconstructing Nature, Alienation, Emancipation and the Division of Labour*. London: Routledge.

Dickenson, P. (2003) *Planning Green Growth, a socialist contribution to the debate on environmental sustainability*. London: CWI Publications and Socialist Books.

Dobson, A. (2003) *Citizenship and the Environment*. Oxford: Oxford University Press.

Dobson, A. and Bell, D. (eds.) (2006) *Environmental Citizenship*. London: MIT Press.

Dresner, S. (2006) *The Principles of Sustainability*. London: Earthscan.

Elliott, L. (2004) *The Global Politics of the Environment*. Basingstoke: Macmillan Press.

ECI (Earth Charter Initiative) (2007) *The Earth Charter. http://www.earthcharter.org/innerpg.cfm?id_menu=19*

ECIIS (Earth Charter International Initiative Secretariat) (2005) *Bringing Sustainability into the Classroom: An Earth Charter Guidebook for Teachers*.

Gadotti, M. (1996) *Pedagogy of Praxis: A Dialectical Philosophy of Education*. New York: State University of New York Press.

Goldblatt, D. (1996) *Social Theory and the Environment*. Cambridge: Polity Press.

Gilbert, R. (1996) 'Identity, Culture and Environment: Education for Citizenship in the Twenty-First Century', in J. Demaine and H. Entwistle (eds). *Beyond Communitarianism: Citizenship, Politics and Education*. New York: St Martins Press.

Gough, S. and Scott, W. (2006) 'Promoting Environmental Citizenship through Learning: Toward a Theory of Change', in A. Dobson and D. Bell (eds), *Environmental Citizenship*. London: MIT Press.

Hart, R. (1996) *Children's Participation: The Theory and Practice of Involving Young Citizens in Community Development and Environmental Care*. London: Earthscan.

Hartmann, F. (1998) 'Towards a social ecological politics of sustainability', in R. Keil, D. Bell, P. Pentz and L. Fawcett (eds.), *Political Ecology: Global and Local*, London: Routledge.

Harvey, D. (2003) *The New Imperialism*. Oxford: Oxford University Press.

Harvey, D. (1996) *Justice, Nature and the Geography of Difference*. Oxford: Blackwell.

Held, D. (1995) *Democracy and the Global Order: From the Modern State to Cosmopolitan Governance*. Cambridge: Polity Press.

Held, D., McGrew, A., Goldblatt, D. and Perraton, J. (2000) *Global Transformations: Politics, Economics and Culture*. Cambridge: Polity Press.

Henderson, K. and Tilbury, D. (2004) *Whole-School Approaches to Sustainability: An International Review of Sustainable School Programs*. Sydney: ARIES.

Hubbard, G. and Miller, D. (eds.) (2005) *Arguments Against G8*. London: Pluto Press.

Huckle, J. (1998) *Teachers Handbook* (for the What We Consume module of the Global Environmental Education Programme). Richmond: WWF & Richmond Publishing Company.

Huckle, J. (2006) *Education for Sustainable Development: A Briefing Paper for the Training and Development Agency for Schools*. http://www.ttrb.ac.uk/Browse2.aspx?anchorId=14633&selectedId=14634

Keen, M., Brown, V.A. and Dyball, R. (eds.) (2005) *Social Learning in Environmental Management: Towards a Sustainable Future*. London: Earthscan.

Kenway, J. and Bullen, E. (2001) *Consuming Children: Education, Entertainment, Advertising*. Milton Keynes: Open University Press.

Klein, N. (2000) *No Logo*. London: Flamingo.

LETSystems (2007) http://www.gmlets.u-net.com/

Little, A. (1998) *Post-industrial Socialism: Towards a new politics of welfare*. London: Routledge.

Lipietz, A. (1992) *Towards a New Economic Order: Postfordism, Ecology and Democracy*. Cambridge: Polity Press.

Lynch, J. (1992) *Education for Citizenship in a Multi-Cultural Society*, London: Cassell.

Merchant, C. (ed.) (1994) *Key Concepts in Critical Theory: Ecology*. New Jersey: Humanities Press.

Pigozzi, J. (2005) 'Sustainable Development through Education', keynote address to UK Launch Conference of DESD, London. http://www.unesco.org.uk/UserFiles/File/DESD/ConferenceReport_MaryJoyPigozzi3.pdf

Quart, A. (2003) *Branded: The Buying and Selling of Teenagers*. London: Arrow.

SDELG (Sustainable Development Education Liaison Group) (2005) *Sustainable Development Education: an international study*. Glasgow: Learning and Teaching Scotland. http://www.ltscotland.org.uk/sustainabledevelopment/images/SDELG%20international_tcm4-306104.pdf

Smith, G. (2005) 'Green Citizenship and the Social Economy', *Environmental Politics*, 14 (2): 27–289.

Sutton, P.W. (2004) *Nature, Environment and Society*. Basingstoke: Palgrave Macmillan.

Turner, A. (2001) *Just Capital: The Liberal Economy*. Basingstoke, Macmillan.

UNECE (United Nations Economic Commission for Europe) (2005) *UNECE Strategy for Education for Sustainable Development*.

http://www.unece.org/env/esd/Strategy&Framework.htm

UNESCO (1997) *Educating for a Sustainable Future: A Transdisciplinary Vision for Concerted Action*. http://www.unesco.org/education/tlsf/TLSF/theme_a/mod01/uncom01t05s01.htm

UNESCO (2001) *The Luneburg Declaration on Higher Education for Sustainable Development*. http://portal.unesco.org/education/en/file_download.php/a5bdee5aa9f89937b3e55a0157e195e6LuneburgDeclaration.pdf

UNESCO (2006) *Promotion of a Global Partnership for the UN Decade of Education for Sustainable Development: The International Implementation Scheme for the Decade in brief*. http://unesdoc.unesco.org/images/0014/001 473/147361E.pdf

UNESCO (2007) *Highlights on DESD Progress to Date*. http://www.environment.gov.au/education/publications/undesd-progress.html

UNESCO (2007) *Teaching and learning for a sustainable future*.http://www.unesco.org/education/tlsf/

Valencia S.A. (2005) 'Globalization, Cosmopolitanism and Ecological Citizenship', *Environmental Politics*, 14 (2): 163–178.

Wals. A.E.J. (ed.) (2007) *Social Learning: Towards a Sustainable World*. Wageningen: Wageningen Academic Publishers.

Wackernagel, M. and Rees, W. (1996) *Our Ecological Footprint: Reducing Human Impact on the Earth*. Gabriola Island: New Society Publishers.

Woodin, M. and Lucas, C. (2004) *Green Alternative to Globalization: A Manifesto*. London: Pluto Press.

27

History

Keith C. Barton and Linda S. Levstik

Whether history education can, or should, contribute to citizenship is a controversial matter. Some educators argue passionately that history is the chief means of developing an informed citizenry, and they justify the subject's inclusion in schools by pointing to its benefits for civic knowledge and participation. Others maintain that using history in this way distorts the nature of the academic discipline; any civic benefits of studying history, they insist, should be incidental ones rather than the result of direct planning. Proponents of each position, however, tend to conflate differing elements of citizenship and history, and in particular to mix together aspects of liberal and republican perspectives.

Our purpose in this chapter is not to revisit these debates but to clarify and evaluate arguments for history's contribution to citizenship. We do this first by distinguishing among three separate claims about what the subject is meant to develop – that is, the aspects of citizenship that are thought to result from historical study. In addition, to the extent possible, we evaluate these claims on the basis of empirical evidence of students' historical understanding. This allows us not only to warn against unrealistic faith in the benefits of historical study but to suggest ways in which the curriculum may need to be reconceptualized in order to better meet the citizenship expectations placed on it.

DEVELOPING KNOWLEDGE AND SKILLS

In liberal democracies, individuals are invested with the responsibility to make choices that affect their own welfare and that of others, including actions that directly influence public policy, such as voting, joining political groups, and attempting to persuade others. Citizen actions that may lie outside institutionalized politics – such as efforts within schools, unions, neighborhoods, and the like – also depend on choices made by individuals. A principal assumption of this form of government is that citizens will ground their choices in knowledge and in reasoned consideration of evidence (Audigier, 2000; Dewey, 1910; Engle and Ochoa, 1988). This requires both an understanding of human society and a mastery of certain skills, such as the ability to locate, evaluate, and synthesize information. Formal education is widely believed to play a crucial role in developing the knowledge and skills necessary for this kind of informed and effective citizenry, and history is often credited with four distinct contributions to that effort.

History's most frequently defended contribution to liberal democracy lies in its ability to provide citizens with an understanding of people and society (McNeill, 1989; Stearns, 1998). In this view, citizens use history the way scientists use laboratories: Through learning about historical events, they can better understand relationships among elements of the social world, as well as how changes in those relationships come about and how developments in one area may have consequences for another. Equipped with such knowledge, citizens would be better able to make reasonable decisions about which current policies they wish to support. The complexity and concreteness of historical experience, from this perspective, provides a basis for choices that would be less well-informed if citizens were limited only to their knowledge of the contemporary world. A second aspect of history considered especially important for citizenship involves tracing the origins of current issues (Becker, 1913; Marwick, 1970; McNeill, 1989). Political affairs, ethnic relations, social attitudes, and economic patterns all have evolved over time, and an understanding of their historical development should help citizens clarify how they can preserve or challenge various elements of the world they have inherited.

Not only scholars but students themselves frequently point to these aspects of history as a reason for the subject's importance: They expect to learn how the world got to be the way it is, and they expect to generalize beyond particular circumstances in order to make more informed decisions in the present and future (Barton, 2001b; Barton and McCully, 2006; VanSledright, 1997). However, although individuals may indeed look to the past as a way of making decisions, there is little evidence that history education leads to better-informed decisions on any widespread basis, or that public policy is effectively informed by historical knowledge. Why, then, does knowledge of history fail to lead to the benefits for citizenship that are so often claimed for it?

One answer is that the knowledge gained from history is so complicated, and so open to interpretation, that it can provide little direct guidance for contemporary policy (Commager, 1965; Lee, 1984). That argument injects an appropriate note of caution into predictions that sometimes veer toward wild optimism, and it warns against expectations that increasing the amount of history in schools will have an immediate payoff for democratic action. Yet the claim that history cannot guide decision-making is ultimately a nihilistic one, and it can lead to the conclusion that there is no reason to teach the subject except for personal fulfilment or the training of professional historians. A more productive approach might be to ask whether the current structure of the history curriculum stands in the way of developing insights that are useful to current affairs, and if so, how it might be revised.

Teaching history as a chronological narrative may be the chief barrier to facilitating knowledge that would inform understanding of the contemporary world. Simply exposing students to a chronological narrative, no matter how well taught, will not necessarily result in concepts that generalize to the modern world. If students are expected to understand broad patterns – such as how nations justify warfare, how groups mobilize for social change, or how population growth affects the environment – then instruction may need to be organized around such persistent issues (Saye and Brush, 2005), with examples from different eras and regions grouped together, rather than spread out over many years of instruction in hopes that students eventually will induce the overarching themes. Similarly, if the purpose of studying history is to understand the origins of the present, more explicit links between past and present may need to be made. This might take the form of reverse chronology, in which students begin with a contemporary issue and trace its historical roots (Misco and Patterson, in press), or it may involve frequent comparisons of past and present so that students see connections between the two (Arthur et al., 2001). Simply teaching students about events that are relevant to the present, however, without ever directly mentioning that relevance, may not be effective.

Similar issues arise with the citizenship skills that are most often associated with history. The first of these is the ability to make reasoned judgments. Citizens in a democracy must consider claims and evidence from multiple sources, none of them complete or inherently authoritative. This kind of interpretive process is also at the core of history, because all historical knowledge consists of conclusions developed from evidence that is partial, incomplete, and sometimes contradictory. If students learn to evaluate and draw conclusions from historical sources, they should be able to transfer this skill to the information and arguments that they face in the contemporary world (Kownslar, 1974; VanSledright, 2002b). In addition, developing reasoned judgment depends on understanding how personal and societal values influence public action, how the values of groups and individuals differ, and how democratic discourse can be used to negotiate the conflicts that arise from these differences. Because history is replete with events that illustrate conflicting values, the subject is often considered particularly useful in developing students' ability to consider the value dimensions of public issues (e.g., Oliver and Shaver, 1966).

A related skill involves understanding how actions are situated in broader societal contexts. In order to understand historical events, it is necessary to see how values, attitudes, beliefs, and institutional structures influenced the actions of people in the past, and how such factors differed from those today. A major emphasis of history educators in recent decades has been to include such consideration of context in the curriculum – an approach variously known as empathy, perspective taking, or perspective recognition.

The same skill is necessary for democratic citizenship, particularly in pluralist societies. In order to communicate with fellow citizens, it is necessary to understand how their backgrounds influence their perspective; without such understanding, differences of opinion may be mistaken for ignorance, malevolence, or lack of intelligence. By learning to contextualize the differing perspectives of people in the past, students should be better able to do the same with regard to contemporary differences and thus to more effectively engage in the discourses of democratic life (Barton and Levstik, 2004).

There is increasing evidence that both elementary and secondary school students can evaluate evidence and contextualize historical perspectives, particularly when they receive sustained classroom practice in doing so (Barton, 2008). Transferring these skills to current problems, however, is not quite so straightforward, and students may fail to apply what they have learned when considering issues outside the classroom (Levin, 1972). Students who can analyze the partiality of historical sources on relatively uncontroversial topics, for example, may not do the same when confronted with sources related to issues that have strong contemporary relevance (Austin et al., 1987), and they may even draw conclusions about historical sources based, in part, on the extent to which they perceive them as being on the same 'side' as present-day social identifications (Pollack and Kolikant, 2007; VanSledright, 2002a). Similarly, students who can recognize and contextualize the perspectives of historical actors may retreat from the suggestion that they do so for groups who are closer in time and space, and whose views on important current issues conflict with their own (Levstik, 2001; McCully et al., 2002). Transfer of skills is always a difficult educational endeavor, and it depends in part on the extent to which students are alerted to the circumstances under which such transfer is expected (Bransford et al., 1999). Analysis of historical evidence, for example, may not enhance students' ability to analyze contemporary sources unless they are given the chance to connect the two settings. Similarly, learning about differences in historical perspectives may not help students deal with contemporary differences if the curriculum never addresses current issues. As with historical knowledge, the benefits of historical skills for decision-making may not accrue unless connections are made between past and present.

DEVELOPING COMMITMENT

An enduring perspective, sometimes referred to as 'civic republicanism', holds that citizenship depends on certain commitments on the part of individuals, and that education's primary task is to develop such commitments – variously known as values, virtues, morals, dispositions, or character traits. The roots of this perspective usually are traced to the classical tradition of Greece and Rome, where scholars and orators insisted that citizenship required the cultivation of 'civic virtue', most notably a commitment to public duty and affairs of state (Oliver and Heater, 1994), but this view also resembles classical Confucianism, which assumed that proper ordering of the state and society depended on attitudes such as respect, concern, duty, and loyalty (Ketcham, 2004).

These classical traditions have continued to prove appealing, and in recent years a number of authors have argued that liberal views of citizenship – in which conceptions of what is good or right compete in an impartial and impersonal public sphere – have eroded civic virtue, to the detriment of society as a whole, and that the renewal of citizenship depends on re-establishing a widely shared commitment to certain values (e.g., Oldfield, 1990; White, 1996). Although political conservatives have been in the forefront of advocating a return to shared values, those on the opposite end of the political spectrum also hope that schools will develop students' dedication to given causes, such as ending oppression, celebrating pluralism, or protecting

the environment. Even procedural theories of citizenship require that individuals be committed to certain features of public life, such as tolerance, impartiality, and respect for others (Macedo, 1991).

There are three principal ways in which history is sometimes thought to develop the commitments necessary for citizenship. The first is by providing models of civic virtue, especially in the form of biographies of prominent individuals from the past. Through these stories, students are expected to both understand and adopt character traits such as respect or honesty. In many nations, such inspirational role models have long been a feature of the history curriculum, particularly at the primary level. A revival of this approach has been recommended by more recent commentators, particularly advocates of 'character education' (e.g., Lickona, 1991).

This approach is generally a didactic one, as students are told specifically what traits are embodied by historical figures, and little room is left for interpretation or ambiguity. Because of the need for moral clarity in such stories, advocates of this approach tend to be less concerned with the completeness of the historical record than with the ability of a given story to illustrate desired values, and they can be highly selective in their representations of historical figures in order to accomplish this purpose. Yet despite the directness and simplicity of this approach, and despite its intuitive appeal for many educators, there is no evidence that it develops desired character traits in students. Like many educational strategies, its popularity depends more on its intuitive appeal – particularly for those who prefer an authoritarian style of teaching – than on systematic empirical support.

A different method of developing commitment is taken by an approach usually referred to as 'values analysis'. The purpose of this approach is to help students use empirical data, systematic investigation, and rational discussion to deal with values dilemmas, by engaging them in a process whereby they clarify the nature of public issues, develop definitions of the values involved, consider the actions and consequences that would follow from those values, and test their conclusions against evidence (Superka et al., 1976). Applied to history, this approach involves students in analyzing concrete historical circumstances and making judgments about which values were reflected in those events, how people might have acted had they adhered to different values (or had their values and actions been more closely aligned), and whether the consequence of their actions – or the likely consequences of alternative actions – were desirable (Lockwood and Harris, 1985; Schultz et al., 2001).

When values analysis aims only at enabling students to examine current social issues more carefully (e.g., Oliver and Shaver, 1966), it represents an example of citizenship-related knowledge and skills developed in a historical context, as described in the previous section. However, some proponents of this approach aim for more than that: They assume that not only should students be able to analyze values such as liberty, equality, or tolerance, but that by developing expertise in their analysis, students will also become committed to those values and will therefore act in more socially responsible ways. There is, however, limited empirical evidence that by analyzing values in the past, students' own values will change in predictable ways. Holocaust education, for example, is associated with only small and uneven changes in civic attitudes or racism (Cowan and Maitles, 2007; Schultz et al., 2001), and it is not clear to what extent even those changes are related to the values dimension of historical study. Yet there is some evidence that students who study value-laden topics such as the Holocaust think of themselves as more tolerant toward differences and more sympathetic toward the oppressed, even when their knowledge of specific historical events is not very nuanced or complete (Carrington and Short, 1997; Schweber, 2004). At this point it is premature to conclude that analysis of values in historical contexts directly leads students to adopt

(or reject) given values, but such an approach at least provides a forum in which students can engage in such discussions. This is a critical practice for those who believe that public discourse can lead to enhanced concern for the common good (e.g., Barton and Levstik, 2004), and the field would benefit immeasurably from research into the conditions under which approaches such as historically-grounded values analysis might promote changes in students' attitudes, as well as into the obstacles to such changes.

A final approach has received less explicit justification, but it may be the most common means by which educators aim to develop commitment through historical study. In this approach, historical events are assumed to have such clear and obvious meanings that they cannot help but lead to certain commitments on the part of students. Students' attention is not explicitly drawn to any particular set of values, but it is assumed that by carefully selecting the topics students are exposed to, as well as by emplotting them in particular ways (i.e., representing a historical episode as a triumph or a tragedy), students will nonetheless develop the desired commitments. One example of this approach is found in a common perspective on teaching about the Holocaust: Many educators assume that the meaning of this event is so self-evident that upon learning about it, students will necessarily become more committed to tolerance, diversity, or the dignity of life – regardless of how (or whether) the moral dimensions of the topic are represented in class (Schweber, 2004). Similarly, a prominent curriculum for civics in the United States assumes that studying the history of US constitutional democracy will foster a 'freely given, reasoned commitment' to the values and principles necessary to preserve that system (Quigley and Bahmueller, 1991: 14). Alternatively, educators may assume that the *method* of study will lead to certain commitments, particularly to procedural values such as comparing multiple perspectives or evaluating evidence. If students are consistently asked to consider differing perspectives in their history classes, for example, then it is hoped that they will recognize the value of doing so in all contexts – even if they are never explicitly encouraged to adopt this as a generalized commitment. The appeal of this implicit approach is that teachers need not state their own convictions nor engage students in any explicit consideration of values, particularly with regard to potentially controversial topics.

Research, however, does not provide support for the inductive approach as an effective means of developing commitment. Its most notable drawback is that students' pre-existing ways of interpreting the world – such as narrative frameworks grounded in political or religious beliefs – may lead them to draw different conclusions from historical study than educators expect. Students who study the Holocaust, for example, may interpret it as a narrative of religious redemption and thus implicitly or explicitly blame its victims (Schweber, 2004; Spector, 2007). Similarly, those who study US slavery may see it primarily as a humanitarian issue rather than a political one and thus fail to see the contemporary implications that their teachers expect (Wills, 1996). In addition, although exposing students to a limited range of stories about the past may channel their interpretations in particular ways (Barton and Levstik, 1998), this does not mean that they become committed to those interpretations; that is, they may 'master' a story (of national struggle, for example) without accepting the commitments that the story implies (Wertsch, 2002). They may even use the elements of officially sanctioned historical narratives as a way of criticizing the value commitments that underlie such narratives (Wertsch, 1998). And although students' perspectives may be complicated by engaging them in procedures that contrast with their experiences outside school (such as considering multiple perspectives), this strategy does not completely overshadow the commitments they develop elsewhere (Barton and McCully, 2005, 2006).

DEVELOPING LOYALTY

In the classical republican tradition, one of the commitments required for citizenship is loyalty to the polity. With the rise of the nation-state as the dominant form of political organization in the nineteenth century, history became a particularly important way of developing the 'imagined communities' around which such loyalties revolve (Anderson, 1991; Hobsbawm, 1994), and this effort often involved the 'invention' of traditions that explained and justified national achievements and aspirations (Hobsbawm and Ranger, 1983). Combined with the extension of public educational systems and compulsory schooling in many nations in the late nineteenth and early twentieth centuries, school history – and particularly the content of the textbooks used there – become important vehicles for developing national loyalty, and in many nations this importance has continued through to the present (Foster and Crawford, 2006; Moreau, 2003).

School history is commonly used to develop national loyalty in three ways. The first is simply through the choice of topics: In many countries, the chief content of the curriculum involves the history of the nation, and students are expected to recognize that this focus represents the group with which they should identify. Although this expectation may seem unremarkable, its significance becomes clear in situations where national identities are contested. Changes in the Taiwanese history curriculum in the 1990s were controversial, for example, because they involved devoting greater attention to the island's unique past rather than presenting it chiefly in terms of the history of China as a whole; this was perceived as sending a clear message that students should identify with Taiwan as an independent political entity (Liu et al., 2005).

In addition, in many countries the history curriculum specifically focuses on national *origins*, in hopes that a common set of founding events (or people) will inspire a shared sense of the past. This seems particularly important when a politically defined nation comprises several languages, ethnicities, or religions. The imagined descendents of 'explorers' or 'settlers', for instance, may recall their forebears for having braved the wilderness, discovered new worlds, and founded new countries. In other cases, a national story of colonial subjugation met by resistance, struggle, and sacrifice may provide a shared sense of history for diverse ethnic groups. As with stories of civic virtue, tales of founders and origins are likely to be highly selective (or even mythical), because their purpose is establish a common origin rather than to explore the complexity of historical developments.

Finally, national narratives often glorify a country's past. Students' willingness to identify with the nation and its founders is presumably enhanced when purported ancestors and their achievements can be presented in a way that inspires pride, and so the national histories taught to young people typically emphasize positive accomplishments and either ignore or downplay darker episodes in the past. Stories of military conflict, for example, may extol the justness of one country's reasons for war and the bravery of its people, while others are demonized as oppressive or aggressive, and its soldiers as either brutal or cowardly. When dealing with events that are less overtly conflictual, a nation's history is often portrayed in upbeat and optimistic ways. US textbooks, for example, tell a story of social and material progress in which historical 'problems' – such as the treatment of native peoples or the rights of women and minorities – largely have been solved (Loewen, 1995). Such narratives are assumed to inspire such a degree of appreciation that citizens cohere as a unified people, come to cherish their mutual affiliation, and exhibit loyalty to the nation that embodies such a past.

There is evidence from the US that history education can, to some extent, successfully achieve such objectives. Young people there use history as a way of establishing a community of identification, and they find significance in historical events that revolve around the origins of the nation (Barton, 2001b; Barton and Levstik, 1998). Moreover, they interpret US history primarily in terms of an overarching narrative of increasing freedom and social and material progress, and they consider the country uniquely good and just; they have few tools for making sense of deviations from this pattern, even when they recognize that not all historical events can be so neatly categorized (Barton, 2001a; Barton and Levstik, 1998; Wertsch, 1998). Although students from some religious and ethnic groups may find this narrative less convincing or salient (Mosborg, 2002; Epstein, 2000), many of its key features nonetheless are shared widely among students from varied backgrounds (An, 2007; Terzian and Yeager, 2007).

If national stability, cohesiveness, and survival depend on the willingness of group members to carry on what they perceive as an important legacy, then historical narratives may well be necessary to support valuable forms of political life (Barton and Levstik, 2004). However, national narratives also pose significant dangers, due primarily to their exclusiveness (Smith, 2003). The first danger is that a nation's history may exclude the experiences of much of the population that lives within its boundaries. A variety of vernacular histories are preserved in ethnic, religious, linguistic, or other sub-national communities (Bodnar, 1992; Grever, 2006; Huata, 1998; Seixas, 1993), and if not recognized in the 'official' histories that usually form the basis of the curriculum, these groups may fail to develop the very loyalty that schools purport to establish – ultimately leading to the marginalization, disaffection, or even armed conflict that are evident in so many countries today. In addition, when national histories are constructed around male-dominated forms of political organization and discourse, they promote a gendered form of civic identity that may misrepresent the needs and experiences of most women and many men (Arnot, 1997).

A second danger involves exclusion of those outside national boundaries. Historical grievances have long been used to justify warfare against other countries or discrimination against their citizens. Indeed, national loyalties can justify some of the worst horrors imaginable – torture, enslavement, and wholesale slaughter – and history educators have long recognized this problem (e.g., Salmon, 1899). By the middle of the twentieth century, two devastating world wars led the newly formed United Nations to sponsor attempts to reduce the amount of national prejudice found in European textbooks (Lauwerys, 1953). The use of school history (and specifically of textbooks) to present exclusive versions of the national past, however, remains an ongoing controversy in many nations.

Those concerned with history education have addressed these problems in widely varied ways. Perhaps the most common response to the issue of internal diversity has been to advocate national histories that are more inclusive of diverse experiences and do not privilege those who have traditionally wielded social and political power. Some historians, politicians, and educators, however, have argued that schools should present an even more celebratory and less ambiguous narrative of national unity, because they fear that recognition of the divergent experiences, multiple perspectives, and unique histories of specific groups would lead to the 'disuniting' of an otherwise cohesive nation (e.g., Granatstein, 1998; Schlesinger, 1992). Still others disavow the use of history to promote national identity altogether; they argue that the curriculum should focus on the development of historical understanding without regard to the identity of students (e.g., Shemilt, 2006).

Ignoring multiple experiences and issues of identity, however, ultimately may be self-defeating. Fears of disunity are based on the premise that current political systems already command the loyalty of diverse citizens (Banks, 1993) – a dubious proposition given that extensive internal strife exists in many nations despite the presence of an officially sanctioned unifying narrative. Certainly school history cannot be counted on to single-handedly create identification, for when the curriculum differs significantly from the beliefs and experiences people develop outside school, they may reject, in whole or in part, the stories they have learned there (Wertsch, 2002). But ignoring identity may be just as unwise. In Northern Ireland, where there is no attempt to create shared identity through the history curriculum, many students in adolescence nonetheless turn to sources outside school for their historical perspectives, and these sources promote sectarian identities rather than common ones (Barton and McCully, 2005). Rather than severing the link between history and identity, then, schools may simply be leaving students susceptible to forces that have their own agendas and that are willing to provide a sense of identity in order to pursue divisive goals.

To address the second problem of national history – the danger of excluding or demonizing those outside national borders – some have argued for developing pan-national identities, and this has been apparent in discussions of how history could be used to develop European identity, a project closely linked to promotion of European citizenship (Arthur et al., 2001; Macdonald and Fausser, 2000; Philippou, 2005). Sometimes, this approach has involved the same strategies found in older, nationalist histories (van der Leeuw-Roord, 2000): focusing on a single geopolitical entity through, for example, developing a common European history textbook (Kroeger, 2007); emphasizing shared ethno-cultural origins; and telling a celebratory story that revolves around qualities presented as uniquely European, such as progress, reason, tolerance, and democracy (Hansen, 2004; von Borries, 2000). Using these strategies to develop a pan-national identity, however, hardly avoids the problems found in single-nation histories. Focusing on European political history excludes the legacy of many of the immigrants who reside there today, and constructing European identity around ethno-cultural origins marginalizes numerous European minorities and even entire countries (Hansen, 2004). Furthermore, telling a celebratory story of reason and progress in this day and age is likely to strain the limits of both academic and public credulity, as well as to set up unproductive and indefensible distinctions between Europe and the rest of the world (von Borries, 2000).

Potentially an even more inclusive approach involves helping students develop a cosmopolitan identity, one in which they see themselves as having obligations toward people throughout the world, regardless of differences in background, behavior, or values (Appiah, 2006). A global history, in which national and sub-national experiences are studied in the context of worldwide patterns, might be one way of developing this kind of cosmopolitan identity (Bender, 2006). Such cosmopolitanism would not replace forms of identity grounded in nationality, religion, ethnicity, and so on; rather, it would become one of the array of identities that people already hold (Smith, 2003). There is evidence that the curriculum in Ghana, for example, does help students there develop multiple allegiances – ethnic, national, and pan-African (Levstik and Groth, 2005).

Whether the Ghanaian experience could be duplicated in other settings, or whether it could be extended to include identification with all of humanity, remains to be seen. In order to fully address the problem of exclusivity, no pattern of historical development can be privileged, but it is difficult to imagine how all experiences could be accommodated within a single narrative, particularly in a format that could be taught meaningfully to young people in schools. Moreover, the only intellectually and socially defensible historical narratives (at national, transnational, or global levels) would be those that problematize ideas of development, present multiple perspectives on the nature of progress and decline, admit of both achievements and disasters in human civilization, and represent identity as socially constructed (von Borries, 2000; Barton and Levstik, 2004; Philippou, 2005). Such narratives could certainly lead to more nuanced and complete historical understanding and inform students' decision-making

as citizens – but whether they would lead to a sense of identity that encourages loyalty to all the world's inhabitants is unknown.

CONCLUSIONS

In order to encourage a more productive discussion of history's potential contribution to citizenship, educators will have to demonstrate conceptual clarity with regard to both the aspects of citizenship they hope to develop and the means by which the history curriculum might be oriented toward accomplishing such goals. They should also be modest in claims about the portion of civic knowledge and attitudes that can realistically be attributed to history education as opposed to other influences, and they will certainly need a more extensive research base to test assertions about history's benefits for citizenship. Current research suggests caution: As currently taught, history may develop students' loyalty to the nation (in some contexts, at least), but whether it enables students to bring knowledge and skills to bear on decisions related to public policy, or whether it leads to other commitments necessary for democratic life, are more doubtful. This is not to say that a transformed history curriculum could not develop such traits and capacities, and we have argued elsewhere that it could and should do so (Barton and Levstik, 2004). This transformation, however, would require considerable development and experimentation, as well as a principled evaluation of its impact. This would be a formidable but potentially rewarding endeavor.

REFERENCES

An, S. (2007) 'Korean-American adolescents' perspectives on U.S. history', paper presented at the annual meeting of the American Educational Research Association, Chicago.

Anderson, B. (1991) *Imagined Communities*. London: Verso.

Appiah, K.A. (2006) *Cosmopolitanism: Ethics in a World of Strangers*. New York: W. W. Norton.

Arnot, M. (1997) '"Gendered citizenry": New feminist perspectives on education and citizenship', *British Educational Research Journal*, 23 (3): 275–95.

Arthur, J., Davies, I., Wrenn, A., Haydn, T., and Kerr, D. (2001). *Citizenship through History Teaching*. New York: Routledge Falmer.

Audigier, F. (2000) *Basic Concepts and Core Competences of Education for Democratic Citizenship*. Strasbourg: Council of Europe.

Austin, R., Rae, G., and Hodgkinson, K. (1987) 'Children's evaluation of evidence on neutral and sensitive topics', *Teaching History*, 49: 8–10.

Banks, J. (1993) 'Multicultural education: Development, dimensions, and challenges', *Phi Delta Kappan*, 75 (1): 22–28.

Barton, K.C. (2008) 'Students' ideas about history', in Linda S. Levstik and Cynthia A. Tyson (eds), *Handbook of Research on Social Studies*. New York: Routledge.

Barton, K.C. (2001a) 'A sociocultural perspective on children's understanding of historical change: Comparative findings from Northern Ireland and the United States', *American Educational Research Journal*, 38 (4): 881–913.

Barton, K.C. (2001b) '"You'd be wanting to know about the past": Social contexts of children's historical understanding in Northern Ireland and the United States', *Comparative Education*, 37 (1): 89–106.

Barton, K.C., and Levstik, L.S. (2004) *Teaching History for the Common Good*. New York: Routledge.

Barton, K.C., and Levstik, L.S. (1998) '"It wasn't a good part of history": Ambiguity and identity in middle grade students' judgments of historical significance', *Teachers College Record*, 99 (3): 478–513.

Barton, K.C., and McCully, A.W. (2005) 'History, identity, and the school curriculum in Northern Ireland: An empirical study of secondary students' ideas and perspectives', *Journal of Curriculum Studies*, 37 (1): 85–116.

Barton, K.C., and McCully, A.W. (2006) 'Secondary students' perspectives on school and community history in Northern Ireland', paper presented at the European Social Science History Conference, Amsterdam.

Becker, C. (1913) 'Some aspects of the influence of social problems and ideas upon the study and writing of history', *American Journal of Sociology*, 18 (5): 641–675.

Bender, T. (2006) *A Nation among Nations: America's Place in World History*. New York: Hill and Wang.

Bodnar, J. (1992) *Remaking America: Public Memory, Commemoration, and Patriotism in the Twentieth Century*. Princeton, NJ: Princeton University Press.

Bransford, J.D., Brown, A.L., and Cocking, R.R. (eds) (1999) *How People Learn: Brain, Mind, Experience, and School*. Washington, DC: National Academy.

Carrington, B. and Short, G. (1997) 'Holocaust education, anti-racism and citizenship', *Educational Review*, 49 (3): 271–283.

Commager, H.S. (1965) *The Nature and Study of History*. Columbus, OH: Charles E. Merrill.

Cowan, P. and Maitles, H. (2007) 'Does addressing prejudice and discrimination through Holocaust education produce better citizens?', *Educational Review*, 59 (20): 115–130.

Dewey, J. (1910) *How We Think*. Boston: D. C. Heath.

Engle, S.H. and Ochoa, A.S. (1988) *Education for Democratic Citizenship: Decision Making in the Social Studies*. New York: Teachers College Press.

Epstein, T. (2000) 'Adolescents' perspectives on racial diversity in U.S. history: Case studies from an urban classroom', *American Educational Research Journal*, 37 (1): 185–214.

Foster, S.J. and Crawford, K.A. (eds) (2006) *What Shall We Tell the Children? International Perspectives on School History Textbooks*. Greenwich, CT: Information Age Publishing.

Granatstein, J.L. (1998) *Who Killed Canadian History?* Toronto: HarperCollins.

Grever, M. (2006) 'Nationale identiteit en historisch besef. De'risico's van een canon in de postmoderne samenleving', *Tijdschrift voor geschiedenis* 119 (2): 160–177.

Hansen, P. (2004) 'In the name of Europe', *Race and Class*, 45 (3): 49–62.

Hobsbawm, E.J. (1994) *Nations and Nationalism since 1780: Programme, Myth, Reality*. 3rd edn. Cambridge: Cambridge University Press (1st edn, 1990).

Hobsbawm, Eric J., and Ranger, T. (eds.) (1983) *The Invention of Tradition*. New York: Cambridge University Press.

Huata, D.A. (1998) 'First things first', In Witi Ihimaera (ed.), *Growing up Maori*. Auckland, New Zealand: Tandem. pp. 141–152.

Kownslar, A.O. (1974) 'Is history relevant?', in A. O. Kownslar (ed.), *Teaching American History: The Quest for Relevancy*. Washington, DC: National Council for the Social Studies. pp. 3–15.

Ketcham, R.L. (2004) *The Idea of Democracy in the Modern Era*. Lawrence, KS: University Press of Kansas.

Kroeger, A. (2007) 'Germany seeks joint history book', BBC News. Retrieved April 23, 2007 from http://news.bbc.co.uk/2/hi/europe/6411047.stm

Lauwerys, J.A. (1953) *History Textbooks and International Understanding*. Paris: United Nations Educational, Scientific and Cultural Organization.

Lee, P.J. (1984) 'Why learn history?', In Alaric K. Dickinson, Peter J. Lee, and Peter J. Rogers (eds.), *Learning History*. London: Heinemann Educational. pp. 1–19.

Levin, M.A. (1972) 'Teaching public issues: Some evaluation data from the Harvard Project', *Social Education*, 36 (8): 883–889

Levstik, L.S. (2001) 'Crossing the empty spaces: Perspective taking in New Zealand adolescents' understanding of national history', in O.L. Davis, Jr., Elizabeth A. Yeager, and Stuart J. Foster (eds.), *Historical Empathy and Perspective-taking in the Social Studies*. Lanhan, MD: Rowman and Littlefield. pp. 69–96.

Levstik, L.S. and Groth, J. (2005) '"Ruled by our own people": Ghanaian adolescents' conceptions of citizenship', *Teachers College Record*, 107 (4): 563–586.

Lickona, T. (1991) *Educating for Character: How our Schools Can Teach Respect and Responsibility*. New York: Bantam.

Liu, M-H., Hung, L-C., and Vickers, E. (2005) 'Identity issues in Taiwan's history curriculum', In Edward Vickers and Alisa Jones (eds.), *History Education and National Identity in East Asia*. New York: Routledge. pp. 101–132.

Lockwood, A.L., and Harris, D.E. (1985) *Reasoning with Democratic Values: Ethical Problems in United States History*. Instructor's Manual. New York: Teachers College Press.

Loewen, J.W. (1995) *Lies My Teacher Told Me: Everything Your American History Textbook Got Wrong*. New York: New Press.

Macdonald, S. and Fausser, K. (2000) 'Toward European historical consciousness: An introduction', in Sharon Macdoald (ed.), *Approaches to European Historical Consciousness: Reflections and Provocations*. Hamburg, Germany: Körber-Stiftung. pp. 9–40.

Macedo, S. (1991) *Liberal Virtues: Citizenship, Virtue, and Community in Liberal Constitutionalism*. New York: Oxford University Press.

Marwick, A. (1970) *The Nature of History*. London: Macmillan.

McCully, A., Pilgrim, N., Sutherland, A., and McMinn, T. (2002) '"Don't worry, Mr. Trimble, we can handle it": Balancing the rational and emotional in the teaching of contentious topics', *Teaching History*, 106: 6–12.

McNeill, W.H. (1989) 'How history helps us to understand current affairs', in P. Gagnon and The Bradley Commission on History in Schools (eds.), *Historical Literacy: The Case for History in American Education*. Boston: Houghton Mifflin. pp. 157–169.

Misco, T. and Patterson, N. (in press). An old fad of great promise: Reverse chronology history teaching. *Journal of Social Studies Research*.

Moreau, J. (2003) *Schoolbook Nation: Conflicts over American History Textbooks from the Civil War to the Present*. Ann Arbor, MI: University of Michigan Press.

Mosborg, S. (2002) 'Speaking of history: How adolescents use their knowledge of history in reading the daily news', *Cognition and Instruction*, 20 (3): 323–358.

Oldfield, A. (1990) *Citizenship and Community: Civic Republicanism and the Modern World*. New York: Routledge.

Oliver, D. and Heater, D. (1994) *The Foundations of Citizenship*. New York: Harvester Wheatsheaf.

Oliver, D.W., and Shaver, J.P. (1966) *Teaching Public Issues in the High School*. Boston: Houghton Mifflin.

Philippou, S. (2005) 'The "problem" of the European dimension in education: A principled reconstruction of the Greek Cypriot curriculum', *European Educational Research Journal*, 4 (4): 343–367.

Pollack, S. and Kolikant, Y. (2007) 'The asymmetrical influence of identity: A triad encounter of Israeli Jews, Arabs, and historical text', paper presented at the annual meeting of the American Educational Research Association, Chicago.

Quigley, C.N., and Bahmueller, C.F. (1991) *CIVITAS: A Framework for Civic Education*. Calabasas, CA: Center for Civic Education.

Salmon, L.M. (1899) 'Appendix II: Study of history below the secondary school', in American Historical Association, *The Study of History in Schools: Report to the American Historical Association by the Committee of Seven*. New York: Macmillan.

Saye, J.W. and Brush, T. (2005) 'The persistent issues in history network: Using technology to support historical inquiry and civic reasoning', *Social Education*, 69 (4): 168–171.

Schlesinger, A.M. (1992) *The Disuniting of America*. New York: Norton.

Schultz, L.H., Barr, D.J., and Selman, R.L. (2001) 'The value of a developmental approach to evaluating character development programmes: An out-come study of Facing History and Ourselves', *Journal of Moral Education*, 30 (1): 3–27.

Schweber, S. (2004) *Making Sense of the Holocaust: Lessons from Classroom Practice*. New York: Teachers College Press.

Seixas, P. (1993) 'Historical understanding among adolescents in a multicultural setting', *Curriculum Inquiry*, 23 (3): 301–327.

Shemilt, D. (2006) 'The future of the past: How adolescents make sense of past, present and future', paper presented at the National History Standards Conference, University of Utrecht, The Netherlands.

Smith, R. (2003) *Stories of People-hood: The Politics and Morals of Political Membership*. New York: Cambridge University Press.

Spector, K. (2007) 'God on the gallows: Reading the Holocaust through narratives of redemption', *Research in the Teaching of English*. 42(1): 7–55.

Stearns, P. (1998) 'Why study history?', American Historical Association. Accessed April 18, 2007, from http://historians.org/pubs/Free/WhyStudyHistory.htm

Superka, D.P., Ahrens, C., Hedstrom, J.E., Ford, L.J., and Johnson, Patricia L. (1976) *Values Education Sourcebook, Materials Analyses, and an Annotated Bibliography*. Boulder, Co, Social Science Education Consortium.

Terzian, S., and Yeager, E.A. (2007) '"That's when we became a nation": Urban Latino adolescents and the designation of historical significance', *Urban Education*, 42 (1): 52–81.

van der Leeuw-Roord, J. (2000) 'Working with history – developing European historical consciousness' in Sharon Macdoald (ed.), *Approaches to European Historical Conscious-ness: Reflections and Provocations*. Hamburg, Germany: Körber-Stiftung. pp. 114–124.

VanSledright, B.A. (2002a). 'Fifth graders investigating history in the classroom: Results from a researcher-practitioner design experiment', *Elementary School Journal*, 103 (2): 131–160.

VanSledright, B. (2002b) *In Search of America's Past: Learning to Read History in Elementary School*. New York: Teachers College Press.

VanSledright, B.A. (1997) 'And Santayana lives on: Students' views on the purposes for studying American history', *Journal of Curriculum Studies*, 29 (5): 529–557.

von Borries, B. (2000) 'Narrating European history', in Sharon Macdonald (ed.), *Approaches to European Historical Consciousness: Reflections and Provocations*. Hamburg, Germany: Körber-Stiftung. pp. 152–162.

Wertsch, J.V. (1998) *Mind as Action*. New York: Cambridge University Press.

Wertsch, J.V. (2002) *Voices of Collective Remembering*. New York: Cambridge University Press.

White, P. (1996) *Civic Virtues and Public Schooling: Educating Citizens for a Democratic Society*. New York: Teachers College Press.

Wills, J.A. (1996) 'Who needs multicultural education? White students, U. S. history, and the construction of a usable past', *Anthropology and Education Quarterly*, 27 (3): 365–389.

28

Literacy

Bethan Marshall

In December 2006, the Home Office announced that people wishing to have residency in the UK had to take a test in the English language. This was a reinforcement of the exam already in place for those wishing to gain British nationality. That there was a need for individuals to become conversant with the English language was seen by many as a necessary tool in their integration into the country. It made them more employable and allowed them to take a more active part in society. But the need for English language as a means of citizenship is a far more complex instrument than that.

In his *Notes Towards a Definition of Culture*, TS Eliot wrote that education was,

A subject which cannot be discussed in a void: our questions raise other questions, social, economic, financial, political. And the bearings are on more ultimate problems than even these: to know what we want in education we must know what we want in general, we must derive our theory of education from our theory of life (1948).

Eliot's attempt to define the culture in which he lived was to the right of centre but the dilemma he identified – that our view of education begs other questions – remains pertinent to an understanding of what it means to be a citizen. Perhaps the most obvious concern of English in the curriculum

is that of our contribution to the economy of the country. How that is realized, however, depends largely on your view of what English means. In his introduction to the National Literacy Strategy, David Blunkett, the then Secretary of State for Education, claimed that, 'All our children deserve to leave school equipped to enter a fulfilling adult life. If children do not master the basic skills of literacy and numeracy they will be seriously disadvantaged later' (DfEE, 1998).

Blunkett's view was that literacy in general, not English in particular, is a basic standard that all must attain: failure to do so will lead to damage in adult life. Both the New Labour government and the Tories before them agreed that these standards were to be measured by national curriculum levels – a level 4 for 11-year-olds and a level 5 for pupils of f14. New Labour announced that 80 per cent of children at 11 were expected to get a level 4, a target that they have almost achieved – 79 per cent achieving level 4 or above.

But there are some who disagree with this 'basic' view of literacy. Henrietta Dombey, for example, is clear about the effects high scores in the national tests at 11 are meant to secure: 'It seems that higher scores on literacy and numeracy for the country's

11-year-olds are expected to reverse the tide of economic decline, unemployment and national uncertainty' (Dombey, 1998: 128). Yet central to Dombey's argument is that the National Literacy Strategy (NLS), as it is currently framed, has, as its view of what it means to be literate, something which is a definable product, something that can be articulated and written down (Marshall, 1999). Such a definition, for Dombey, limits what can be understood by the term literacy, seeing it as a much more nebulous, unquantifiable substance that is difficult to pin down.

Gunther Kress goes one stage further:

> The question I am posing is simply this: in relation to the economic and social futures such as these, what is the English curriculum doing? ... If jobs are moveable with the speed of global fiscal markets, then certain requirements of a fundamental kind follow the kind of person whom we are preparing for that world. Somehow they will have to be prepared not just to cope, but to control their circumstances (Kress, 1995: 18).

For Kress it is impossible to consider what English, and its related subject, literacy, have to do without contemplating the world in which they have to operate. He sees our economic future as dependent on fast capitalism, and the need to have agency in a world that changes almost every time we look at it.

> If we represent literacy, in the curriculum, as a matter of fixed, immutable rules, we encourage a different attitude to the one suggested by a representation of literacy as a set of resources shaped by society and constantly reshaped by each individual reader and writer. The former encourages an acceptance of what is; a certain attitude to authority; a limitation accepted and internalised by the individual. The latter encourages curiosity about how things have come to be as they are; a certain attitude to individual responsibility and agency; and an internalisation of the individual as active, creative and expansive (Kress, 1995: 75).

Literacy, then is less fixed and more fluid. While the NLS and now the primary strategy sets out all that is to be taught in the subject as unquestionable Kress argues that his approach brings a greater flexibility of mind – encouraging 'curiosity' and a sense of

'agency' in the process. Essential to his point of view is that world of literacy changes and is in constant flux. Teacher and student encounter this world together.

Though her conclusions may not be as extreme as Kress, the economist Diane Coyle has fears about concentrating too much on the nuts and bolts of the literacy curriculum. 'Although literacy and numeracy are essential of course – making it tricky to argue with the official Gradgrinds focused on achieving higher standards in this small area of necessary skill set – the real need is a robust need to think independently' (Coyle, 2001: 48).

Her anxiety appears to be, rather as Kress's is, that children need to think for themselves. The dominance of an official strategy might make it less likely for them to do this. Alan Greenspan, former chair of the US Federal Reserve, shares her worries. In a commencement day speech, for Harvard Business School, he commented:

> Skill has taken on a much broader meaning than it had only a decade ago. Today's workers must be prepared along many dimensions – not only with technical know-how but also with the ability to create, analyse and transform information and with the capacity to interact effectively with others. Moreover, they must recognize that the skills they develop today will likely not last a lifetime (Greenspan, 2000).

Like Kress and Coyle he believes that workers in the future will not only have to face the fact that the what they have learned today may not prepare them for tomorrow but that they will need to be creative to survive.

Such a world is very different from the 'basics' that Blunkett and others feel is necessary for 'a fulfilling adult life'. And it is different, too, from the way in which some people originally thought about English. While standards of written and spoken English are now taken for granted, in whatever form, it was not always the case. As education was beginning to take hold in the late-eighteenth and early-nineteenth centuries the role of reading and writing and its necessity, or otherwise, was keenly taking place. In his book, Richardson, looking at the Romantics and education, found that for some the ability to read and write had subversive qualities.

Citing Thomas Peacock's satire *Nightmare Abbey* he writes, ' How can we be cheerful when we are surrounded by a reading public, that is grown to wise for its betters?' (Peacock, cited in Richardson, 2004: 1), to indicate how some had come to feel about a growingly literate population. While for others it was 'It was a levelling revolution' (Gaskell, cited in Richardson, 2004: 1). Gaskell, who was writing in the Victorian period, again parodied the reaction to an increased ability to read in *Lady Ludlow*, 'If our lower orders have these "edge-tools" give them, we shall have terrible scenes of the French revolution acted all over England' (Gaskell, cited in Richardson, 2004: 1). 'Edge tools' was the ability to read and with it came the fear that the 'lower orders' would read revolutionary tracts that would make them restless. Such a philosophy now seems hopelessly out of date but it had sufficient currency to make it an idea worth satirising.

A century later, however, George Sampson was arguing the opposite: English was necessary to keep the working, middle and even the upper class content: 'There is no class in the country that does not need a full education in English. Possibly a common basis for education might do much to mitigate the class antagonism' (Sampson, 1921). Indeed he went on to say that education in English might be the answer to stop revolution. With the Russian Revolution at the forefront of his mind he wrote: 'Deny to working class children any common share in the immaterial and presently they will grow into the men who demand with menaces a communism of the material' (Sampson, 1921).

While his views may seem somewhat conservative in tone, fearing communism, there is an equal opportunities element as well. For Sampson, English was the subject above all that united the nation and ourselves. The Newbolt Report, which came out in the same year, and to which Sampson contributed, wrote,

In its full sense connotes not merely acquaintance with a certain number of terms, or the power of spelling these terms correctly and arranging them without gross mistakes. It connotes the discovery of the world by the first and most direct way open to us, and the discovery of ourselves in our native environment … For the writing of English is essentially an art, and the effect of English literature, in education, is the effect of art upon the development of the human character (Departmental Committee of the Board of Education (Newbolt Report), ch.1, para 14: 20).

This view of English, as that of an art, owes much to the poet and school's inspector Matthew Arnold, who was one of the first to argue for the inclusion of English in the curriculum. He believed that the subject brought a humanising, almost spiritual effect into education. In *Culture and Anarchy*, written in 1869, he observed,

Faith in machinery is, I said our besetting danger; often in machinery most absurdly disproportioned to the end which this machinery, if it is to do any good at all, is to serve; but always in machinery, as if it had a value in and for itself (Arnold, 1948: 48).

For Arnold, the arts, and English in particular, lay opposed to machinery that he felt was so prevalent in society. Teach children the power of language and the possibility of creativity and culture would be forthcoming. By the time George Sampson was writing, fifty years later, Arnold's ideas had been taken even further. Sampson did not believe in vocational education at all: 'the purpose of education, (is) not to prepare children for (sic) their occupations, but to prepare children against (sic) their occupations (Sampson, 1952: 11). His views were echoed by Leavis, who started writing on the English curriculum around ten years later. Indeed there is evidence to suggest that until at least ten years ago many English teachers placed preparation for the workforce at the bottom of their list of priorities. Andrew Goodwyn surveyed English teachers on the chair of the first national curriculum for English in 1989, Brian Cox's, five views of English – literary heritage, personal growth, cultural analysis cross-curricular and adult needs. He found that adult needs came last (Goodwyn, 1992).

Mere teaching to prepare for jobs, then, had little support but the idea of being literate to enable one to take a full part in society had a slightly different reading. Freire and Macedo, pioneers in the critical literacy movement, believed that, 'Literacy becomes a meaningful construct to the degree that it is viewed as a set of practices and functions to either empower or disempower people. In the larger sense, literacy must be analysed according to whether it promotes democratic and emancipatory changes' (Freire and Macedo, 1987: 41).

Their belief in ensuring all were critically literate separated them for a liberal arts view such as that held by Matthew Arnold and his later followers. For Arnold liberation came for an individual, for Freire it was for all. Critical literacy meant seeing your place in society and critiquing it for the benefit of yourself and of others. The unit of analysis had become social rather than focusing on the concerns of the individual. It was this that was to bring about the democratic shift in society. As Aronowitz and Giroux wrote,

> Critical literacy responds to the cultural capital of a specific group or class and looks to ways in which it can be confirmed, and also at the ways in which the dominant society disconfirms students by either ignoring or denigrating the knowledge and experiences that characterise their everyday lives. The unit of analysis is social and the key concern is not individual interests but with the individual and collective empowerment (Aronowitz and Giroux, cited in Ball et al., 1990: 61).

Critical literacy does not always have to have such a radical agenda. Richard Hoggart, writing in *Literacy is Not Enough*, turned his attention to the so-called mass producers or persuaders of society. His desire was to educate people to read beneath the lines of their persuasion by making them critically literate and thus function as citizens in a democracy.

> The level of literacy we now accept for the bulk of the population, of literacy unrelated to the way language is misused in this kind of society, ensures that literacy becomes simply a way of further subordinating great numbers of people. We make them literate enough to be conned by the mass

persuaders ... The second slogan has to be 'Critical Literacy for All'. Critical Literacy means ... teaching about the difficulties, challenges and benefits of living in an open society which aims to be a true democracy (Hoggart, 1998: 60).

This wish to create citizens who think and question what they are being given does not have whole-hearted support, however. For some this amounts to the overthrowing of an order that had much in common with the characters fear in *Nightmare Abbey* or *Lady Ludlow*, albeit a literate one. 'The overthrow of grammar coincided with the acceptance of the equivalent of creative writing in social behaviour. As nice points of grammar were mockingly dismissed as pedantic and irrelevant, so was punctiliousness in such matters as honesty, responsibility, property, gratitude, apology and so on' (Rae, cited in Graddol et al., 1991: 52).

Grammar is united with honesty and responsibility but also with property as if there is a fear that a split verb will induce theft. But it is not with grammar in particular that worries everyone. It is with the broader issues of what English means and its attendant culture that concern writers like Melanie Phillips. Writing just over ten years ago the columnist observed,

> English, after all is the subject at the heart of our definition of our national cultural identity. Since English teachers are the chief custodians of that identity we should not be surprised to find that revolutionaries intent on using the subject to transform society have gained a powerful foothold, attempting to redefine the very meaning of reading itself (Phillips, 1997: 69).

Her concerns find their antithesis in the critic Edward Said. In *Culture and Imperialism* he wrote, 'In time, culture comes to be associated, often aggressively, with the nation or the state; this differentiates 'us' from 'them', almost always with some degree of xenophobia' (1993: xiii). Phillips belief in a 'national cultural identity' of which English teachers are 'the chief custodians' evokes Said's picture of an 'us' differentiating itself very strongly from 'them'. And for Said, xenophobia was never far behind.

Said's view of criticism of culture as a kind of handed down wisdom has echoes in the writing of the American, John Dewey. Dewey was in a way the father of democratic thinking, pedagogy and education, writing a book called *Democracy and Education* in 1916. But by the thirties his central thesis had been challenged by those who attempted either to follow him or who those violently disagreed with his philosophy. Attempting to set the record straight he wrote *Experience and Education* in which he defined what he meant by progressive and traditional teaching.

The young for future responsibilities and for success in life, by means of acquisition of the organised bodies of information and prepared forms of skill which comprehend the material instruction. Since the subject matter as well as standards of proper conduct are handed down from the past, the attitude of the pupils must, upon the whole, be one of docility, receptivity, and obedience (Dewey, 1966: 18).

For Dewey traditional education meant a certain passivity was built in to the reception of information on the part of the child and for him this was not truly educational. Pupils, he believed, should have the opportunity to think and challenge ideas. He went on to write,

Just because traditional education was a matter of routine in which plans and programs were handed down from the past, it does not follow that progressive education is a matter of planless improvisation ... Revolt against the kind of organisation characteristic of the traditional school constitutes a demand for high organisation based upon ideas (Dewey, 1966: 28–9).

Teachers, then, were asked to build in opportunities for pupils to discuss and debate, to disagree. This was education and democracy; it is what citizenship meant. The purpose of the teacher was to 'demand for high organization based upon ideas'. Such a view of citizenship, of engaging with the society in which you are a part, is central to a certain view of literature. Christopher Hitchens, writing about Thomas Paine, identified, it thus,

Paine belongs to that strain of oratory, pamphleteering, and prose that runs through Milton, Bunyan, Burns and Blake and which nourished

what the common folk like to call the Liberty Tree. This stream as chartered by EP Thompson and others often flows underground for long periods. In England it disappeared for a long time (Hitchens, 1988: 16).

In identifying such writers Hitchens was calling upon a tradition that was dissenting in its methodology but essentially literary in kind. Writing was to be connected to an understanding of liberty. The 'Dissenters' were originally a group of people who did not sign the Act of Uniformity, an act which would have bound them to the Church of England, in the mid seventeenth century. Later, around the turn of the nineteenth century, through writers such as Hazlitt, it became more secularised in its thinking. But, until the mid nineteenth century it meant that certain children could not be educated in schools, which were part of, or had connections with the Anglican church. As a result advocates of Dissent established schools of their own, known as Dissenting Academies, and these broke away from the mainstream of education. While religious in origin these academies were rational in their approach. Andrew Motion, writing about the school which Keats attended, commented that it was, 'distinctly progressive' (Motion, 1998: 22) adding that other Dissenting academies were 'defiantly forward looking ... they explored rational teaching methods that emphasised the value of doubt and questioning' (Motion, 1998: 24). Most notably these schools educated their pupils in English and not in the classics. Part of their rational was to create a citizenship of the future and in particular they did so by teaching their pupils literature. The Dissenters' believed that all were equal in the sight of God, and this meant that they believed in social equality and justice also. In turn it led to support for the common man, a belief in his rights as a citizen, and, by association, the English vernacular. Language was power.

William Enfield, a prominent exponent of the Dissenting tradition, taught in the Warrington Academy, along with another radical thinker Joseph Priestley. In 1774 he published what might be called one of the first English text books in schools: *The Speaker: or miscellaneous pieces selected from the best English writers, and disposed under the proper heads, with a view to facilitate the improvement of youth in reading and speaking* (Enfield, 1774). As the lengthy title suggests, this was essentially an anthology of writing, unusually for the time, organised under thematic headings such as Narrative Pieces, Didactic Pieces, Argumentative Pieces etc. Again, as the title makes clear, the aim was both to improve the elocution of pupils as well as to extend their thinking through encounters with good writing. Enfield did not confine his efforts to producing text books and was a regular contributor to the *Monthly Magazine* under the pseudonym The Enquirer. One of his essays 'The Enquirer On Verse and Poetry' (Enfield, 1796) is said to have influenced Wordsworth's 'Preface to the Lyrical Ballads', which also celebrated the vernacular tongue.

The egalitarian streak within the Warrington Academy did not fully extend to girls but the daughter of another member of staff, John Aiken, did attend and was inspired to produce a similar anthology for girls. Anna Laetitia Barbour published *The Female Speaker* in 1816. Some years earlier Wollstonecraft had also published *The Female Reader*. In her preface she explains her debt to Enfield and while much of her justification for the volume may seem slightly conservative or modest for such a proto feminist nevertheless the link between thought, literature and its role in education is evident. For her thinking is more important than perfect elocution which 'may teach young people what to say; but will probably will prevent them ever learning to think.' (Wollstonecraft, 2003). For Wollstonecraft education was the key to empowerment.

The belief that literature had the power to alter opinion, however, was not confined to the Dissenters. As literature, and in particular novels, became popular so the thought that might educate the readers also gained currency. And it is this last that has made the teaching of English so vital to arguments over citizenship. For writers create and mould the world into their way of thinking. Jane Austen, for example, writing at the time of the dissenting academies, and while certainly no dissenter herself, saw reading in way that was similar in kind, if not in substance, to Mary Wollstonecraft. She saw the dangers of books as well as their advantages. Writing *Northanger Abbey* she ironically observed of her heroine Catherine, 'From fifteen to seventeen she was in training to be a heroine; she read all such books as heroines must read to supply their memories with those quotations which are so serviceable and so soothing in the vicissitudes of their eventful lives'.

It took Henry Tilney, the male protagonist of the novel, to point out the alarming shortcomings of such an approach. Gripped with the idea that Tilney's mother had been brutally murdered at Northanger Abbey it was Henry who appealed to Catherine Morland's sense of the reasonable.

> 'Consult your own understanding, your own sense of the probable, your own observation of what is passing around you …' Catherine was completely awakened. Henry's address, short as it had been had more thoroughly opened her eyes to the extravagance of her late fancies than all their several disappointments had done.

In his request he asks that Catherine should pay heed, in some senses to her role as a citizen. She is to consult her 'own understanding' and 'sense of the probable' and observe what goes on around her and by this means work out what has actually been going on rather than trust in the 'fancies' that have plagued her for so long. In so doing he asks the reader to draw a similar conclusion. Jane Austen requires a similar fate for all her heroes and heroines and in so doing set a precedent for how her novels and those like them were to be read. The main character learns how, or teaches others, the right way to think and in so doing provides answers as to how we should behave.

Children's novels have adopted similar plot devices where the central character must discover a truth about himself or those around him. If we just look at the blurbs on the back of such books we find that many of them show the story as a path to enlightenment. In David Sachar's *Holes* the main character has to 'dig up the truth', which is both a pun on the main activity in the book, digging holes, and a pointer to the need to discover why they are involved in such an apparently pointless activity. In *Feather Boy*, 'To get to the truth, Robert must learn what it really means to fly and in Michael Morpurgo's *Kensuke Kingdom* the novel is described as 'A beautifully written account of a boy's voyage of discovery'. Each is written with the hint that they will discover what it means to be human.

While this takes the discussion of citizenship further than might have originally been intended it is, to an extent, what novels, plays and poetry are for. They are an author's attempt to show what living in a world of their creation is like. The disagreements arise over what we as readers make of them. Citizenship in English, then, has to be a negotiated curriculum, less about the apparent facts of literacy and more about how writers make sense of what life is like for them.

REFERENCES

Arnold, M. (1948) *Culture and Anarchy*, J. Dover Wilson (ed). Cambridge: Cambridge University Press.

Austen, J. (1972) *Northanger Abbey*, London: Oxford University Press. pp. 5–6 and 212.

Ball, S.J. Kenny, A. and Gardiner, D. (1990) Literacy Policy and the Teaching of English. In I. Goodson and P. Medway (eds) *Bringing English to Order*, London: Falmer.

Coyle, D. (2001) How Not to Educate the Information Workforce. *Critical Quarterly*, 43 (1): 46–58.

DfEE (1998) *The National Literacy Strategy*, London: HMSO.

DfEE (2001) *Framework for Teaching English: Years 7, 8 and 9*, London: HMSO.

Departmental Committtee of the Board of Education (1921) *The Teaching of English in England: Being the report of the departmental committee appointed by the president of the board of education to inquire into the position of English in the educational system of England* (The Newbolt Report), London: HMSO.

Dewey, J. (1916) *Democracy and Education*. New York: Macmillan.

Dewey, J. (1966) *Experience and Education*. London: Collier Books.

Dombey (1998) Changing Literacy in the Early Years of School. In B. Cox (ed.) *Literacy Is Not Enough: Essays on the Importance of Reading*. Manchester: Manchester University Press.

Eliot, T.S. (1975) Notes Towards a Definition of Culture. In F. Kermode (ed.) *Selected Prose of TS Eliot,* London: Faber and Faber.

Freire, P. and Macedo, D. (1987) *Literacy: Reading the Word and the World*. London: Routledge.

Graddol, D., Maybin J., Mercer, N. and Swann, J. (eds) (1991) *Talk and Learning 5–16: An inservice pack on the oracy for teachers*. Milton Keynes: Open University Press.

Greenspan, A. (19 Oct. 1999)\ http://www.bog.frb.fed.us./BoardDocs/Speeches

Goodwyn, A. (1992) English Teachers and the Cox Models. *English and Education*, 26 (3): 4–11.

Hitchens, C. (1988) *Prepared for the Worst: Selected Essays and Minority Reports*. London: Chatto and Windus.

Hoggart, R. (1998) Critical Literacy and Creative Reading. In B. Cox (ed.) *Literacy Is Not Enough: Essays on the importance of reading*. Manchester: Manchester University Press.

Kress, G. (1995) *Writing the Future: English and the Making of a Culture of Innovation*. Sheffield: NATE Papers in Education.

Marshall, B. (1998) What They Should Be Learning and How They Should Be Taught. *English in Education*, 32 (1): 4–9.

Motion, A. (1998) *Keats*. London: Faber and Faber.

Phillips, M. (1997) *All Must have Prizes*. London: Little, Brown and Co.

Said, E. (1993) *Culture and Imperialism*. London: Chatto and Windus.

Richardson, A. (2004) *Literature, Education and Romanticism: Reading as Social Practice 178–1832*. Cambridge: Cambridge University Press.

Sampson, G. (1952) *English for the English*. Cambridge: Cambridge University Press.

Characterizations and Forms

29

Political Literacy

Ian Davies

INTRODUCTION

In 1969, Bernard Crick, referring to the introducing of politics in schools argued: 'Since it cannot be avoided, it had better be faced. Since it should not be avoided, quite a lot of care and time should be given to it. And since it is an interesting subject, it should be taught in an interesting manner' (Crick, 1969: cited in Crick, 2000: 5).

The influential essay from which the above quotation is taken contains many significant ideas. Some of those ideas were discussed in the collection of work edited by Crick and Porter (1978) on *Political Education and Political Literacy* and the whole piece was reprinted with a very brief foreword in a collection on citizenship edited by Crick in the year 2000 (Crick, 2000). This brief historical reference illustrates some of the roots of citizenship education, the stamina of its current proponents and the subtleties of its changing nature. Whereas in 1969 the emphasis was placed on 'the teaching of politics' things had changed by the mid-to-late 1970s in favour of 'political education and political literacy' and in the early twenty-first century to 'citizenship education' with the last, according to Crick, being

'a creative synthesis of politics and social studies' (2000: 13). Within significant variation across curriculum initiatives the political root remains constant. But the variation that is noticeable in England is even more apparent when cross-country analysis is undertaken. In order not to attempt too much – from the work of the US-based American Political Science Association, the German political education initiatives after World War II, the distinctively less obviously politically inspired Japanese approaches and the tradition in communist countries of Marxist-Leninist inspired teaching – this chapter focuses on England.

Asserting the importance of politics in schools is, of course, not a simple business and does not in itself provide an educational justification. Crick and others went some way towards a very useful indication of what should be taught and learned and suggested something of an elaboration for how teachers, students and others should or could act. In this chapter, I attempt to discuss some of the key issues that relate to political literacy with a principal – but not exclusive – focus on how things have developed in England since the 1970s. This involves a brief elaboration of the nature of what is proposed as 'politics' and a discussion of its connection with education and/or what has been termed 'political literacy'. Following that initial discussion I will use three sections in this chapter to discuss what Crick suggested in the above quotation as key issues. I will discuss the nature of politics, agreeing with Crick that it is unavoidable; I will explore the nature of the care that might be needed when thinking about a programme of political education that aims at the achievement of political literacy and I will suggest ways to teach and learn that are interesting and educationally valid.

'SINCE [POLITICS] CANNOT BE AVOIDED IT HAD BETTER BE FACED'

It is probably not possible to argue that programmes of political education that lead to people becoming more politically literate are necessary. No school subject could make such a claim convincingly. But education is widely regarded as being something that we can justifiably aim to compel people to have, and the political is always present in education. There are at least two ways in which the inescapable nature of politics can be discussed: as a philosophical account that suggests that politics and education are so intertwined that distinctions cannot easily be made and as an interpretation of contemporary society and the opportunities it affords people that suggests that there is a very strong desire for people to learn about the political and to practise political literacy.

The first and more fundamental position is nicely elaborated by Frazer (1999). She suggests several ideas beginning by reference to the work of Gutman (1989) and others with the notion that 'education *is* political' (p. 12). She suggests that education as a public or merit good supplied largely by government or others who are subject to political pressures and are operating at least at the rhetorical level for the supposed purpose of benefiting all demonstrates an activity that is inherently political. Of course, there are distinctions about the nature of those politics. Harber (1991), for example, discusses the distinctions between political indoctrination, socialization and education. Others have noted differences between political education and the schooling that is intended to lead to political education. We might want to reflect on whether the power to govern is understood and demonstrated explicitly or implicitly; whether politics is exercised democratically or in other ways and, whether and, if so to what extent, we might want to divide 'personal politics' that may relate to, for example, aspects of feminism from other perhaps more 'public politics' that focus on constitutions and institutions. But the point made here is simply that whatever understanding of politics we have it will always be present in educational contexts.

If philosophically a case can be made for seeing politics and education as occupying pretty much the same ground it is necessary to move to an elaboration of the second means by which that link can be demonstrated. Some interpret contemporary society in order to suggest that a case can be made to explain the emergence of relatively recent attempts to promote political literacy. Broadly, there are four reasons that are normally offered in England for this development. First, the extension of the franchise by lowering of the age of majority in many countries to 18 means that school students could vote. The connection between education and the franchise had been made in the nineteenth century very clearly by, for example, Robert Lowe who had claimed following the 1867 Reform Act that it was 'necessary to educate our future masters' and the argument was made more precisely about the need for political education in the UK in 1970 following the lowering of the age at which people could vote to 18. Second, research, especially in the field of political socialization, meant that long-established notions about the inappropriateness of politics for young people were challenged with increasing frequency from the 1960s. Politics had been thought of as something of which children were ignorant, it being too complex and too sensitive for anything but the possibility of carefully handled interventions in the privacy of one's own home. Political socialization research (e.g. Dawson et al., 1977) and especially that which focused directly on children (e.g. Jahoda, 1963; Greenstein, 1965; Connell, 1971) as well as explorations of the political nature of textbooks (e.g. Gilbert, 1984) meant that there was some acceptance of the need for political education to be undertaken more explicitly. Third, key policy makers took note of research that claimed young people were experiencing or expressing widespread distancing from the political process. In some studies this was expressed in terms of lack of knowledge and understanding (e.g. Stradling, 1977) while other work relates to data on voter turnout and a possible increase in micro (privately oriented action such as insisting on better health care for one's own family) and a possible decline in macro (public oriented action such as trade unionism) participation (Whiteley, no date). Whatever data sets are used policy makers have, especially at points of perceived crisis, been keen to 'edge young people away from the margins of politics into the mainstream' (Stradling, 1987: 3). Even when there have been few concerns about extremism policy makers have wanted to move young people away from common practices that may be perceived as being insufficiently focused on responsibilities associated with civic republican conceptions of society (Bottery, 1999). Finally, and hinted at in the last point, is the notion that participation is seen – in a democracy and perhaps particularly when communitarian notions are expressed – as a good thing and should be promoted through educational programmes. The democratization of educational structures with encouragement and expectation that people would access schools with due consideration of social justice (Chitty and Benn, 1996) and participate actively in their own governance in line with notions of communitarianism espoused in America (e.g. Etzioni), the UK (e.g. Giddens, 1997) and elsewhere meant that some form of political education would be seen as desirable.

'SINCE IT SHOULD NOT BE AVOIDED, QUITE A LOT OF CARE AND TIME SHOULD BE GIVEN TO IT'

Crick is arguing for care to be given to political education. I intend in this part of the chapter to refer to two key issues: the opposition (in practice and explicitly argued) to paying any attention to it and, the meaning of political education that Crick is claiming should be prioritized.

Many, including Heater (1977), Brennan (1980) and Batho (1990), have referred to the neglect of and active opposition to political education in England. Apart from teaching high-status academic students about constitutions and institutions and teaching low-status students a form of civics that emphasized the virtues of adherence to rules very little was done explicitly prior to the 1970s. Exceptions such as fundamentally significant pieces of work (e.g. Dewey, 1916/1966), relevant research and development (e.g. Oliver and Shaver, 1966) and key organizations such as the Council for Education in World Citizenship (Heater, 1983) did not disguise the overall picture of neglect. There was an attempt (led by Crick) in 1970s to promote political education through the Programme of Political Education (PPE). The influence enjoyed by the PPE, however, was short lived. During the 1980s and 1990s, political education and political literacy were largely ignored in the face of competing approaches. Three notions seemed particularly effective in reducing the emphasis that had been placed on political literacy. Firstly, some preferred to use single issues (e.g. environmental education) to educate young people about contemporary society. Secondly, holistic perspectives (e.g. global education) were favoured by some as a means of concentrating, largely, on the affective. Thirdly, forms of citizenship education were promoted that had more to do with instructing young people to meet their 'voluntary obligations' (Hurd, 1988). This latter negative approach occurred at a time when it was perceived unjustly that the welfare state could no longer be afforded and the crime rate had reached crisis point.

The lack of a tradition in political education except at short-lived crisis points (Gollancz and Somervell, 1914; Stewart, 1938) suggests that it will not be easy to secure current initiatives and does not inspire optimism for the future. There is no obvious career path for political education teachers with, until very recently, an almost complete lack of specialist professional training or education for teachers and now only relatively few opportunities (see House of Commons Select Committee report 2007). The continued use of non-specialists within schools (which has some limited benefits) ultimately serves only to raise problems. Citizenship education (of which political education is a key aspect) is seen both as something that has high significance (indeed it may, for some, be the essence of good education) but low status. When these factors are considered alongside the uncertainty about the meaning of citizenship (Davies et al., 1999) it seems that the challenge to develop a professional and explicit form of political education for all will not easily be overcome.

These challenges seem particularly significant in light of recent developments in England. It needs to be emphasized that the carrot (or stick) of the Crick report that emphasized political literacy has not been strengthened in the subject order provided as part of the National Curriculum (QCA/DfEE, 2000). Although there are elements that many see as relating directly to political understanding it is perhaps still a matter of interpretation in order to see political literacy as being a requirement. Crick's (2000) elision (see above) in seeing citizenship education as merely a simple conjunction of politics and social studies is politically shrewd at a time when communtarianism was high on the political agenda; an entirely reasonable conception given his particular

understanding of politics; a means by which professionals could begin to develop fundamental ideas in interesting ways but in the context of the controversial and contested area of social studies education staffed by teachers battered through increasingly strident forms of centralization was merely another layer of confusion that would lead to further neglect of the political.

But I now need to turn to a discussion of the form of political education that could be proposed. Crick (1978) insisted that 'underlying any theory of political education and any ideal of political literacy, there must be a theory of politics' (p. 38).

Politics can be variously characterized (see Cloonan and Davies, 1998) and some possibilities are shown below:

- Contents: For some, politics is seen, variously, as a study of key circumstances (constitutional structures or events).
- Substantive concepts: This characterization allows for an exploration of more than 'mere' content. The meaning of phenomena such as war, revolution monarchy are investigated in order to give a much greater explicit emphasis on conceptual underpinning as opposed to a narrow concentration on events or issues.
- Perspectives: The essential nature of interpretation is acknowledged by all political scientists, although it is usually those who adopt Marxist or feminist, or postmodernist perspectives who are seen as being more explicitly committed to this emphasis. This particular focus can also include those who adopt particular approaches to the study of politics favouring, perhaps, political philosophy over the claims of other work (e.g. Horton, 1984).
- Action: This area is often rather hopelessly entangled with certain perspectives. There are those who seek to make the link between study and action in their role as public intellectuals (Goodson, 1997) with the work of Edward Said often referred to as one way of bridging the academic and 'real' world of politics.

Politics is thus a complex field that is open to varied interpretation and there have been claims for each of the above as the means by which education (about and through politics) can be developed. During the 1970s, when

Crick was spearheading the first real attempt in England to promote political education for majority school populations, he insisted that:

Our theory of politics is much broader than many conventional views of politics – broader in two ways:

- It stresses that politics is inevitably concerned with conflicts of interest and ideals, so an understanding of politics must begin with an understanding of the conflicts that there are and of the reasons and interests of the contestants: it cannot be content with preconceptions of constitutional order or of a necessary consensus. A politically literate person will not hope to resolve all such differences, or difficulties at once; but he (sic) perceives their very existence as politics.
- It stresses the differential distribution of power there is in any society and the differential access to resources. Hence we are concentrating on a whole dimension of human experience which we characterise as *political* (Crick, 1978: 38).

Crick's approach as outlined in the quotation above has enjoyed remarkable longevity at least in terms of the rhetoric employed by educationalists and others (notwithstanding a hiatus experienced in the 1980s and 1990s). The following two quotations show this continuity:

A politically literate person will know what the main political disputes are clearly about; what beliefs the main contestants have of them; how they are likely to affect him, and he (sic) will have a predisposition to try to do something about it in a manner at once effective and respectful of the sincerity of others. (Crick, 1978: 33).

Pupils learning about and how to make themselves effective in public life though knowledge, skills and values – what can be called 'political literacy', seeking for a term that is wider than political knowledge alone. The term 'public life' is used in its broadest sense to encompass realistic knowledge of and preparation for conflict resolution and decision-making related to the main economic and social problems of the day, including each individual's expectations of and preparation for the world of employment, and discussion of the allocation of public resources and the rationale of taxation. Such preparations are needed whether these occur in locally, nationally or internationally concerned organisations or at any level of society from formal political institutions to informal groups, both at local or national level (QCA/DfEE, 1998: 13).

Thus it is necessary to recognise three important factors about the way that political literacy is currently officially characterized, at least in England. Firstly, that a compound of knowledge, skills and procedural values is needed with the latter to include such areas as respect for truth and reasoning and toleration as opposed to substantive values which meant that pupils would be told what to think about particular issues. Secondly, that Crick's wider definition of politics would mean that knowledge of Whitehall and town halls is insufficient but that the politics of everyday life would be worthy of study. Finally, that 'the ultimate test of political literacy lies in creating a proclivity to action not in achieving more theoretical analysis' (Crick and Lister, 1978: 41).

'SINCE IT IS AN INTERESTING SUBJECT, IT SHOULD BE TAUGHT IN AN INTERESTING MANNER'

It is unsurprising that surveys suggest that not all the activities of members of parliament and civil servants are the stuff that excites young people but key ideas about politics and the decisions taken by politicians are of great interest (e.g. Haste – 2005). If this were not true then it would be hard to explain why young people express interest in green issues and social justice, join organizations such as Amnesty International and express an intention to vote. However, I suggest that Crick's argument for politics to be taught in an interesting way is necessary but not sufficient. Politics has to connect with young people: it must be taught and learned in ways that are congruent with the essential nature of political education in order to have a reasonable chance of helping people becoming politically literate. I argue in this section of the chapter on the basis of research (e.g. Davies et al., 2002; Davies and Thorpe, 2003) and direct professional experience that there is a way to develop this level of interest. In doing so I agree with Huddleston and Rowe (2001) who argue:

> What is needed at this point in the development of political literacy is a practical rationale and a clearly-articulated pedagogy. This will enable schools and teachers to plan political literacy teaching in an organised and systematic way – a conceptual framework which will, among other things enable teachers to make rational decisions on how they can: translate learning outcomes into specific learning objectives; select and structure lesson materials in terms of the principles such as 'breadth and balance', 'coherence', etc.; match their teaching to pupils' learning characteristics; choose and implement appropriate teaching methodologies; introduce controversial issues in a way which is balanced, fair and objective.

Those authors argued for teachers

> to induct pupils into the language, concepts, forms of argument and skills required to think and talk about life from a political point of view, emphasising both process and product. Factual knowledge is important but is made subservient to other aspects that are centrally important to political literacy (Huddleston and Rowe, 2001).

By implication several possible approaches to teaching and learning are unlikely in themselves to be successful in the achievement of politically literate young people. Civics (i.e. the didactic transmission of factual information about constitutions and institutions) may be boring and, worse, mislead young people to think that political decisions are made in line with stated constitutional arrangements and not, as is much more likely, as a result of a complex set of interlocking factors. An exclusively issues-based approach may, without great care, lead to students feeling confused and powerless faced by a bewildering succession of disconnected insuperable problems. The 'constitutional classroom' (Reid and Whittingham, 1984) in which democracy is practised by young people may be seen as relevant to broad conceptions of political understanding and activity but is unlikely to be realistic in most schools and suffers from the inappropriate conflation that an authoritative teacher is always prone to authoritarianism. A narrowly academic programme that encourages discussion of the concepts of high Politics and the production of elegantly expressed essays may be useful for intellectual development but will not be suitable for all and tends not to allow for the development of political skills. Programmes in which the 'personal' is seen as precisely the same as the 'political' are likely not to be effective for the achievement of political literacy if links with public contexts and concepts are not made. Action-related educational programmes will not be useful if they are developed as programmes of service learning that emphasise volunteering and other sorts of community involvement within or beyond schools without critical political understanding. Action by young people that is directed towards substantive political goals identified by a teacher would be open to the charge of attempted indoctrination and would pay insufficient attention to the development of better understanding and enhanced skills. Emphases on developing political education through longer established school subjects (such as, for example, history or science) are likely to lead principally to the achievement of better understanding of the 'carrier' subject and neglect political learning.

Of course many of the above approaches can, when used in conjunction with the approach I am suggesting, be valuable. But if with so many ways of promoting political education rejected it is necessary to turn to an elaboration of the conceptually based and practically realized approach that I am suggesting. I argue for an approach that is based around procedural (or second order) concepts with teachers and students discussing the meaning of political matters and looking for ways of involvement that are directly targeted on enhanced learning. Procedural concepts are distinct from substantive concepts (such as government or war) that relate more narrowly to the study of particular issues. I suggest that teachers may go beyond asking students to memorise details of specific cases, and also to go further than to have students consider the nature of the contexts and substantive concepts which may relate to a number of cases. The ambitious position would be to assert that by identifying procedural concepts it would be possible to invite students not just to think *about* political aspects of citizenship but to think (and learn to think and act better) *as* politicized citizens. Teachers and others, we hope, would be encouraged, when using procedural concepts, to identify more clearly what students need to do and how they should think in order to demonstrate effective learning.

This should not be too ambitious an aim. It is an approach which has its pedagogical origins in Bruner's work on social education. Bruner suggested that curriculum development lies in the identification of the key concepts which structure thinking about particular areas of social life. Developments in other subject areas (e.g. science education Newton et al., 1999; Osborne et al., 2001; and history education, Lee et al., 1996) suggest that the determination to get students involved in active debate is now commonly regarded as being highly appropriate for developing skilful performance. In areas that are more obviously related to political understanding there is a similar level of support for this approach. Hahn (1996) in a review of research on issues-centred social studies argues for many of the central ideas and practices promoted by the project (also see Hahn 1998). The IEA Civic Education Project (see the work in England by Kerr et al., 2001) found that 'schools that model democratic practices are most effective in promoting civic knowledge and engagement' (p. 5). Research by Hughes et al., (n.d) into the nature of students' understanding of political concepts shows that there is potential in this approach.

It is problematic to be able to state with any certainty the precise procedural concepts that could form the basis of a political literacy programme but perhaps as a starting point I could highlight the following:

- rationality grounded in a critical appreciation of social and political realities;
- toleration within the context of a pluralistic democracy; and

- participation arising from an acceptance of one's social and political responsibilities and appreciation of one's own rights and entitlements.

This is, however, a very provisional list. It is, of course, necessary to relate these procedural concepts to substantive concepts of politics otherwise it would be possible for school students to explain and tolerate and participate in any lesson or activity in the school or community. A few words are needed to clarify what is meant by these procedural concepts. Perhaps the most straightforward is rationality. Teachers routinely expect and require students to comprehend, analyze, synthesize, judge, evaluate. If these skills were to be developed through a study of political events and issues and highlighting political concepts then a good deal would be achieved. Toleration is potentially more challenging. It may be controversial for some to assert that young people should do more than understand toleration but rather that they should *be* tolerant. Some might feel that this would require indoctrinating children into the existing norms of a liberal society and in so doing be accused, at the very least, of condescension as others' ways of life are 'merely' tolerated. And yet, I am arguing, following Crick (2000: 134–136),

it is necessary to make judgements unless we are to accept everything. We should not be ashamed of toleration as a prime value of freedom and civilization. Total acceptance would be the end of what we all are, significant differences as well as rights and humanity in common. We should be far more conscious of being a multicultural society and a multinational state. To demand full acceptance rather than toleration is to demand assimilation rather than integration, a single common culture rather than what we have long had, a pluralistic society. The practices of a common citizenship hold together real differences of national, religious and ethnic identities to the mutual advantage of minorities and majorities alike (p. 135–6).

But what does this means in classrooms? What do teachers need to think about and practise? First, what is the statement or action that has been developed by a learner? This might lead us to an initial consideration of toleration in trying to determine whether a person has said something that is genuinely tolerant. Second, the way in which toleration is constructed may tell us about toleration itself. It may be possible, for example, that people are prepared to be differentially tolerant. A discussion about gay rights might bring one sort of response; a conversation about immigration might result in something very different. If those differences have occurred what is the reason for them? Third, what does, it seem that the pupil intended by making the statement or action? Similar statements can be made which have very different meanings. Fourth, what does it tell us about toleration if there are unintended negative outcomes? We will need to ask ourselves if toleration is essentially concerned with an outcome or merely with the thinking or feelings that led to a particular statement or action.

Participation is similarly challenging but necessary as political literacy is, as Crick argued some time ago, about developing a proclivity to action. There are a number of issues that need to be considered before one can be sure that participation is occurring in a way that is meaningful and appropriate for political literacy. Teachers should resist becoming involved in a drive to demand particular forms of participation such as increasing voter turnout. There is currently a lack of consensus around the question of whether we are experiencing a *generational* decline in voting turnout (i.e. we do not know if young people who are currently less likely to vote than others will retain that practice into later life). A decision not to vote may be taken after a serious consideration of the policies offered by a range of political parties. A considered decision to stay at home and not vote may be a better example of participation than the exercise of a simple cross on a ballot paper every 4 or 5 years. Perhaps instead the context, purpose and effectiveness of participation should be considered.

Teachers can take action to promote political literacy through an exploration of rationality, toleration and participation by engaging with learners in particular ways.

The shapes of lessons should be congruent with their aims: if students are to learn through discussion then, obviously, there should be opportunities for that sort of engagement. Teachers should focus students' minds on key issues and manage those discussions, helping students to justify their arguments. Further, teachers and students should explicitly reflect on what they are doing when they are felt to be producing good work. Through various projects I have seen teachers work with skill in promoting different sorts of dialogue or discourse: contextualizing matters so that learners can understand the nature of the issue or event that is being discussed; encouraging the making of judgements; justifying or elaborating on those decisions or points of view; persuading others of what they believe; and talking about their own talk, identifying what they are doing well and what could be developed further.

It is very important for teachers to work towards a clearer understanding of what sort of responses are to be valued. It is vital to encourage discussions that are relatively open-ended but unless we have some idea about what counts as good work. A great deal more work with young people will be required before there can be any confidence about the ways in which we discuss how political literacy can be demonstrated. But, very generally, there seem to be two main types of student response: the procedural and the substantive (Harris, 1996). Each of the two types of response themselves might have two components (open-mindedness and support mobilisation; and, knowledge and understanding) i.e.:

Procedural matters		Substantive matters	
Open mindedness	Support mobilization	Knowledge	Understanding

It seems likely that for students to achieve high quality work not only would they have to perform well in both general areas but they would need to understand the links between them. In other words neither a very general ability to argue nor an isolated academic political understanding would be sufficient. It may be possible to develop in the future a model for encouraging high quality teaching and learning that relies on a form of interactive development and allows students to realise explicitly what they are learning. Discussions could be developed in which teachers consciously promote both parts of the framework. Furthermore, each of the various sub categories displayed in the table may only be meaningful if they are seen as being closely related. For example, open-mindedness is certainly not a separate feature from support mobilization.

The procedural, generally, may include a number of factors that include knowledge, dispositions and skills. Linguistic and presentational skills will be very relevant. Students should know how to use appropriate body language, tone and volume of voice and vocabulary. These skills should be used in relation to certain dispositions. Students should be willing to listen to others and they should be aware of the ways of speaking and acting that are acceptable in discussion between mutually respecting individuals and groups. It is certainly not suggested that students should be drilled into mechanistic performance that emerges from narrow behaviourist conception of the nature of debate.

Open-mindedness is essential if one is to avoid the possibility that discussions are undertaken only for the purpose of ramming home one's own views dogmatically. The latter might be politically effective in certain situations but it is at times not evidence of an intelligent or democratic form of interaction.

Open-mindedness, however, needs to be developed in a particular way so that it can be the basis for a robust and appropriate discourse. As argued above, certain boundaries need to be in place. Thinking the unthinkable would not extend to certain types of thought or action that are clearly harmful to oneself or others. Furthermore, certain strategies can be used to allow a thoughtful exploration.

The ability to use a variety of question types is important as well as the willingness and skill to have undertaken appropriate preparation so as to know what specific questions can be posed.

The mobilization of support is complementary to an open-minded approach. Students are more likely to be able to attract support if they have been able to enquire and understand others' positions. A number of techniques can be used towards that goal. The use of persuasive language suited to particular audiences would clearly be necessary. The section of this chapter about persuasive discourse is particularly relevant here.

With certain caveats (respecting others, searching for truth, using logical reasoning, seeking to persuade rather than provoke further opposition, etc.), it may be necessary for students to learn, positively and constructively, how to challenge others' views. Searching for inconsistencies, a judicious use of analogies and the use of vocabulary in which one's own position is described positively are also likely to be effective in discussion. When used carefully and infrequently interruption is a skill that can be used to great effect either to prevent another person continuing to contribute what is felt to be or to divert the discussion into safer territory. It could also be possible to learn to display the sort of body language that suits one's purpose. The appearance of not listening as well as seeming to be totally engaged can be used for a variety of purposes. Many examples of student interruptions have been observed in classrooms. The nature and extent of this sort of interaction seems to require further investigation.

The other area that I am suggesting might require further attention relates to the substance of their arguments. There are perhaps two key considerations: are they able to show that they can use the sorts of contextual information about an issue that will help their case; and, can they display an appropriate level of broader, usually conceptual, understanding? The two areas are related although it seems from the lessons that I have observed that far less attention is given towards the amount and type of information that students hold. Simply, students are currently not expected by teachers to display a great deal of factual knowledge.

The lack of emphasis on knowledge exclusively in the form of information seems, generally, to be sensible and necessary. However, we should be careful that we are not imperceptibly moving towards a situation in which it is more difficult to insist upon evidence based arguments, that inaccuracies can go unchecked and that politics is seen, when presented in the form of imaginary scenarios, to be irrelevant to 'real life'. More work may be needed on the ways in which evidence is used during discussions to develop or refute arguments. The already large literature (e.g. Parker, 2006) on discussion will need to be added to.

What then should be considered as the sorts of understandings that are achieved by students? Work is developing on the sorts of responses that may be expected and encouraged from students (e.g. QCA, 2006) within classrooms and important work awaits researchers and teachers as they seek to develop understandings about political literacy in a wide variety of contexts.

But, simply and positively, I am arguing for learners to be given an opportunity to understand and become involved politically. An argument for purposeful discussion is not a very controversial position

There is support from related fields. There is already a massive literature associated with discussion, discourse, argument and argumentation (e.g. see Andrews, 1995; Andrews and Mitchell, 2001). Some of this literature emerges from the US based NCSS (National Council of Social Studies), work in Canada (e.g. Tinsdale et al., 2000) and publications such as the *Journal of Language and Social Psychology*. It includes explicit reference to the links between argumentation and democracy, descriptions of the essential elements of an argument, suggestions for teaching methods and issues that are relevant to assessment. The techniques and methods of debate and discussion are already made plain in that literature. What is needed is for that advice to be brought to bear upon political matters. In doing so it might be possible both to make clearer the sorts of teaching methods that can be used when political literacy is on the agenda but also to explain the sort of responses that teachers need to look for when working with young people.

CONCLUSION

Political literacy is perhaps one of the most challenging of all the aspects of citizenship education. Can we, in the real world of schools, expect models of progression in political literacy to be established in lessons that occur infrequently, often under another heading (e.g. 'civics', 'personal and social education' 'history') and staffed by teachers whose own subject knowledge might be insecure? Will teachers manage to achieve an appropriate balance between allowing and encouraging student contributions and leading learners to a realisation of what they should be doing? Will an attempt to achieve clarity about the nature of political literacy lead to inappropriate limits on discussion and action?

REFERENCES

Batho, G. (1990) The history of the teaching of civics and citizenship in English schools. *The Curriculum Journal*, 1: 91–100.

Bottery, M. (1999) Getting the balance right: duty as a core ethic in the life of the school. *Oxford Review of Education*, 25 (3): 369–386.

Brennan, T. (1981) *Political Education and Democracy*. Cambridge: Cambridge University Press.

Chitty, C. and Benn, C. (1996) *Thirty Years On: Is Comprehensive Education Alive and Well or Struggling to Survive?* London: David Fulton.

Connell, R.W. (1971) *The Child's Construction of Politics*. London: Melbourne University Press.

Crick, B. (2000) *Essays on Citizenship*. London: Continuum.

Crick, B. and Heater, D. (1977) *Essays on Political Education*. Lewes: The Falmer Press.

Crick, B. and Porter, A. (1978) *Political Education and Political Literacy*. London: Longman.

Davies, I., Hogarth, S., Huddleston, T. and Rowe, D. (2002) Political literacy: an essential part of citizenship education. *The School Field*, 13 (3/4): 133–148.

Davies, I. and Thorpe, T. (2003) Thinking and acting as citizens, in A. Ross and C. Roland-levy (eds.) *Political Learning and Citizenship in Europe*. Stoke on Trent: Trentham Books.

Dawson, R.E., Prewitt, K., and Dawson, K.S. (1977) *Political Socialization*. Boston, MA.: Little Brown.

Dewey, J. (1916/1966) *Democracy and Education*. London: Macmillan Free Press.

Frazer, E. (1999) Introduction: the idea of political education. *Oxford Review of Education*, 25 (1&2): 5–22.

Gilbert., R. (1984) *The Impotent Image: Reflections of Ideology in the School Curriculum*. London: Falmer Press.

Greenstein, F. (1965) *Children and Politics*. London: Yale University Press.

Gutman, A. (1989) Undemocratic education, in N. Rosenblum (ed.) *Liberalism and the Modern Life*. Cambridge, MA: Harvard University Press.

Hahn, C.L. (1996) Research on Issues-Centered Social Studies, in R. W. Evans and D. Warren Saxe (eds.) *Handbook on Teaching Social Issues*. NCSS Bulletin 93. NCSS, Washington.

Hahn, C.L. (1998) *Becoming Political: Comparative Perspectives on Citizenship Education*. New York: SUNY.

Haste, H. (2005) My Voice, My Vote, My Community: A Study Of Young People's Civic Action and Inaction. Nestle Social Research Programme and ESRC. http:www.spreckley.co.uk/nestle/my-voice-my-vote.pdf Accessed 3 March 2006.

Heater, D.B. (ed.) (1969) *The Teaching of Politics*. London: Methuen.

Heater, D. (1977) Political education in England: the official attitude, in B. Crick and D. Heater *Essays on Political Education*. Lewes: The Falmer Press.

Heater, D. (1983) *Education through Peace: The Work of the Council for Education in World Citizenship*. Lewes: Falmer Press.

Huddleston, T. and Rowe, D. (2001) Political literacy in secondary schools: process or product? Paper presented to the Diverse Citizenships? Conference, University of North London, March.

Hughes, A., Bourgeois, K., Corbett, B., Hillman, B., and Long, N. (n.d) *Children's Understanding of the Concept of Dissent: mapping prior knowledge*. Unpublished paper, University of New Brunswick, Canada.

Jahoda, G. (1963) The development of children's ideas about country and nationality. *British Journal of Educational Psychology*, 33: 143–153.

Kerr, D., Lines, A., Blenkinsop, S., and Schagen, I. (2001) *Citizenship and Education at Age 14. A Summary of the International Findings and Preliminary Results for England*. Slough: NFER/DfEE.

Lee, P., Ashby, R., and Dickinson, A. (1996) Progression in children's ideas about history, in M. Hughes (ed.) *Progression in Learning*. BERA Dialogues 11. Clevedon: Multilingual Matters.

Newton, P., Driver, R., and Osborne, J. (1999) The place of argumentation in the pedagogy of school science. *International Journal of Science Education*, 21 (5): 553–576.

Oliver, D.W. and Shaver, J.P. (1966) *Teaching Public Issues in the High School*. Boston, MA: Houghton Mifflin.

Osborne, J.F., Erdunan, S., Simon, S., and Monk, M. (2001) Enhancing the quality of argument in school science. *School Science Review,* 82 (301): 63–70.

Parker, W. (2006) Public Discourses in schools: purposes, problems, possibilities. *Educational Researcher*, 35 (8): 11–18.

Reid, A. and Whittingham, B. (1984) The constitutional classroom: a political education for democracy. *Teaching Politics*, 13 (3): 307–330.

Stradling, R. (1977) *The Political Awareness of the School Leaver*. London: Hansard Society.

Stradling, R. (1987) Political education and politicization in Britain: a ten year retrospective, paper presented at the international round table conference of the research committee on political education of the International Political Science Association, Ostkolleg der Bundeszentrale for Politische Bildung, Koln, March 9–13.

Whiteley, P. (no date) *A Health Check for British Democracy: What do we Know about Participation and Its Effects in Britain?* Swindon, Economic and Social Research Council.

30

Community Involvement, Civic Engagement and Service Learning

John Annette

To what extent should citizenship education be based on a more 'political' or civic republican conception of citizenship as compared to a liberal individualist conception, which emphasizes individual rights, or a communitarian conception, which emphasizes moral and social responsibility. In what ways are young people finding new ways to engage in civic participation? To what extent does a curricular practice like service learning as part of citizenship education enable students to become democratic citizens? These are some of the questions I would like to explore in this chapter.

CITIZENSHIP EDUCATION AND THE CONCEPT OF CITIZENSHIP, EVERYDAY POLITICS AND CIVIC ENGAGEMENT

It could be argued that the conception of citizenship underlying the UK curriculum is a civic republican one which emphasizes democratic political participation. This reflects the influence of Sir Bernard Crick and the former cabinet minister David Blunkett. One of the key challenges facing civil renewal and the introduction of citizenship education in the UK is the question about whether and in what respects citizenship is 'British'. Elizabeth Frazer has written about the 'British exceptionalism' towards discussing citizenship (Frazer, 1999a) and David Miller has written that

> citizenship – except in the formal passport-holding sense – is not a widely understood idea in Britain. People do not have a clear idea of what it means to be a citizen....Citizenship is not a concept that has played a central role in our political tradition (Miller, 2000: 26).

The question concerning to what extent British people are familiar or comfortable with the concept of citizenship raises questions about the extent to which the political language of citizenship and civic republicanism can increasingly be seen as a tradition of 'British' political thought which can provide the basis for a transformation of the more dominant liberal individualist political traditions.

In the UK, the current 'New Labour' government has espoused a programme of civil renewal that links the public, private and voluntary and community sectors to work for the common good. This is informed by a set of beliefs and values involving faith traditions, ethical socialism, communitarianism and more recently civic republicanism.

According to the then, Home Secretary, David Blunkett,

> The 'civic republican' tradition of democratic thought has always been an important influence for me... This tradition offers us a substantive account of the importance of community, in which duty and civic virtues play a strong and formative role. As such, it a tradition of thinking which rejects unfettered individualism and criticises the elevation of individual entitlements above the common values needed to sustain worthwhile and purposeful lives. We do not enter life unencumbered by any community commitments, and we cannot live in isolation from others (Blunkett, 2003: 19).

It is this civic republican conception of politics which I would argue animates key aspects of New Labour's policies from citizenship education to its strategy towards revitalising local communities.

Richard Dagger in his influential study of civic education argues that a civic republican conception of citizenship can reconcile both liberal individuality and the cultivation of civic virtue and responsibility. He writes that,

> There is too much of value in the idea of rights – an idea rooted in firm and widespread convictions about human dignity and equality – to forsake it. The task, instead, is to find a way of strengthening the appeal of duty, community and related concepts while preserving the appeal of rights (Dagger, 1997:58 and cf. Maynor, 2003)

The creation of a shared political identity underlying citizenship should also allow for multiple political identities based on gender, race, ethnicity, social exclusion and so on. It may be that the civic republican politics of contestability, as recently argued for by Philip Pettit (Pettit, 1997), may provide a more pluralist basis for citizenship in contemporary Britain than traditional republican politics. Equally, recent theorists of liberal democracy like Eamonn Callan also argue that an education for citizenship must hold fast to a constitutive ideal of liberal democracy while allowing for religious and cultural pluralism (Callan, 1997). A more differentiated but universal concept of citizenship (Lister, 2003), which encourages civic virtue and participation while maintaining individual liberty and allows for cultural difference,

will create a way of understanding citizenship that is appropriate for an education for citizenship and democracy.

It could be argued that the establishment of an education for citizenship is based more on a communitarian concern for moral and political socialization then promoting civic engagement. Following Elizabeth Frazer's distinction between a 'philosophical communitarianism' and a 'political communitarianism' (Frazer, 1999b), Adrian Little raises some important questions about the apolitical conception of community in communitarianism. He writes that,

> As such, the sphere of community is one of contestation and conflict as much as it is one of agreement. Thus, essentially, it is deeply political. Where orthodox communitarians see politics as something to be overcome to the greatest possible extent, radicals argue that the downward devolution of power will entail more politics rather than less (Little, 2002: 154).

Both Little and Frazer in their studies of the political communitarianism consider the revival of civic republicanism as emerging from the debate between liberal and communitarian conceptions of the politics of community. In civic republicanism (cf. Oldfield, 1990; Petitt, 1997 and Maynor, 2003) freedom consists of active self-government and liberty rests not simply in negative liberty but in active participation in a political community.

In the US it is also reflected in the writings of Benjamin Barber, Michael Sandel and William Galston which have been promoting a civic republican conception of citizenship (Barber, 1984; Sandel, 1996; Galston, 2001). According to Barber,' the fundamental problem facing civil society is the challenge of providing citizens with 'the literacy required to live in a civil society, the competence to participate in democratic communities, the ability to think critically and act deliberately in a pluralist world, the empathy that permits us to hear and thus accommodate others, all involve skills that must be acquired.' (Barber, 1992) Joseph Kahne and Joel Westheimer recommend a model of citizenship education based on the principles of social justice and Harry Boyte advocates a model based on the concept of 'public work' (Kahne and Westheimer, 2003; Boyte, 2004). This debate about what is an appropriate model of citizenship education for citizenship education raises questions about the need for students to move beyond an individualistic conception of citizenship and a consumer model of citizenship and develop a model of 'civic republican' democratic citizenship education

This reconsideration of the concept of citizenship and citizenship education should also be informed by the recent work on the 'politics of everyday life' which can broaden our understanding of what 'the political' could mean in the lives of students (Crick, 2005; Bentley, 2005; Boyte, 2004; Ginsbourg, 2005; Stoker, 2006). We need to have more research into how young people understand the 'political' as it relates to their everyday concerns in their communities as compared to the more formal political sphere of voting, political parties and holding public office. This broader conception of the political reflects the decline of formal political participation and lack of trust in formal politics at a time when there is evidence of continuing forms of civic engagement which may escape the radar of Robert Putnam's research into social capital. (cf. Sirianni and Friedland, 2004 and Power Inquiry, 2006) This also reflects the important distinction that should be made between volunteering which lead to active citizenship and a more political form of civic engagement in community which can lead to democratic citizenship.

In the US and now in the UK, academics are beginning to view service learning or community based learning as an important part of an education for active citizenship which I would argue can be based on either a more communitarian conception of citizenship (volunteering or community service) or a more 'political or civic republican conception of citizenship (civic engagement and formal political participation).

CIVIL/CIVIC RENEWAL AND *ACTIVE* CITIZENSHIP

David Blunkett in his Edith Kahn Memorial Lecture and various publications and speeches called for a new *civic renewal*, or *civic engagement* which emphasizes new forms and levels of community involvement in local and regional governance. This new democratic politics, which would include referendums, consultative activities, and deliberative participation, has found support from organizations as diverse as the Local Government Association and the prominent think tank IPPR (IPPR, 2004). One outcome of this shift in thinking, which might be termed a switch from *government* to *governance*, is the obligation upon local authorities to establish Local Strategic Partnerships, a duty arising from the Local Government Act 2000. These partnerships seek to involve local communities in the development of Community Strategies. In 2000, the UK Government established a Civil Renewal Unit, which is now called the Community Empowerment Unit, which has piloted an 'Active Learning Citizenship' programme through which it is intended that adult learners will develop the capacity to engage in deliberative democracy at a local level.

In the US, this civic renewal movement has led commentators to challenge the assumption of Robert Putnam and others that there has been a fundamental decline in social capital and civic participation. Carmen Sirianni and Lewis Friedland have mapped out the different dimensions of this movement. While recognizing the decline of more traditional forms of civic engagement and political participation, like membership of formal organizations, voting and membership of political parties, they argue that there are new and changing forms of civic renewal and call for greater and more creative forms of civic engagement. (Sirianni and Friedland, 2004; 2005) Internationally, there is evidence of new global networks emerging which promote these new forms of civic engagement and deliberative democracy (Fung and Wright, 2003).

There is growing research which shows that young people are developing new forms of civic engagement, including wide ranging social networking and e-civic participation. Based on the National Youth Civic Engagement Index Project funded by the Pew Charitable Trust from 2001 to 2005, Cliff Zukin and colleagues have developed a national telephone survey of 3,200 respondents of four generational cohorts. They find that the younger cohort, the 'DotNets', engage in volunteering and community problem-solving activities but lag behind in electoral activities. They then analyse the implications of these findings for future civic participation in the US. This research is important not only for distinguishing between civic and electoral forms of civic activity but also for taking into account life cycle and generational differences. (Zukin et al., 2006) More recently, Peter Levine sees the new forms of youth civic engagement as part of a wider civic renewal movement in the US and argues that school based service learning that is based on community based problem solving and political engagement is an important part of this movement (Levine, 2007). It is interesting to compare these findings with the work of the Youth Electoral Study (YES) Project based in the University of Sydney, which has examined the decline of youth voting and the changing forms of youth participation in Australia. (cf. http://civics.edfac.usyd.edu.au/projects.shtml and Print and Coleman, 2003; Print, 2007) In the UK recent qualitative research studies have considered some of the new forms of civic engagement among young people (cf. Lister et al., 2003 and Weller, 2007).

ACTIVE CITIZENSHIP, CITIZENSHIP EDUCATION AND CIVIC RENEWAL

Given the introduction of the new Citizenship curriculum in England and other developments in the rest of the UK (Advisory Group, 1998; Annette, 2003) and following the subsequent publication of the report of Sir Bernard Crick's second Advisory Group which examined Citizenship provision for 16–19-year-olds in education and training (Advisory Group, 2000), opportunities to develop new models of Citizenship learning across the developing 14–19 phase and into adult education are now emerging. In the US, there is a growing concern about the political disengagement of young people and academics are being to ask what model of citizenship education can lead to the development of active citizenship (Battistoni, 2002; Levine, 2007).

Crick's second report viewed citizenship less as a 'subject' for the classroom and more as a life skill for the maturing student, arguing that all young adults should have an entitlement to citizenship education based on participation and that they should all have the opportunity to have this participation academically recognized. As a result, September 2001 saw the launch of a developmental programme of pilot projects centrally coordinated by the new Learning and Skills Development Agency (LSDA) and managed locally by groups as diverse as Education Business Partnerships, LEAs, LSCs and the Citizenship Foundation. Following the successful completion of the Post-16 Citizenship Development Programme, the Quality Improvement Agency (QIA) has commissioned the Learning and Skills Network (LSN) to manage a new support programme for post-16 citizenship. The programme's central aim is to disseminate as widely as possible, and build on, outcomes from the development programme in order to mainstream citizenship provision in post-16 education and training.

Citizenship's place in the National Curriculum, the publication of this second report and the associated pilot programme (and, more recently, the issuing of Crick's third report into the educational needs of newcomers to Britain during 2003) together provide the basis for establishing citizenship education as a key component within not just schooling but within ongoing (or 'lifelong') learning provision. Especially, beyond the school the focus is likely to be on active citizenship, civil renewal and regeneration. Indeed, the third Crick report expressly, if controversially, links adult learning, volunteering, community involvement and the process of becoming a UK citizen.

Given the introduction of the new Citizenship curriculum in England and other developments in the rest of the UK (Annette, 2003) and following the subsequent publication of the report of Sir Bernard Crick's second Advisory Group which examined Citizenship provision for 16–19-year-olds in education and training (Advisory Group, 2000), opportunities to develop new models of Citizenship learning across the developing 14–19 phase and into adult education are now emerging. In the US, there is a growing concern about the political disengagement of young people, and academics are being to ask what model of citizenship underlies the development of citizenship education (Battistoni, 2002; Crick, 2002; Colby et al., 2003).

'POLITICS' AND COMMUNITY INVOLVEMENT: THE CASE FOR SERVICE LEARNING

Crick's three strands of citizenship (social and moral responsibility, political literacy and community involvement) are interwoven into a set of knowledge and skills within the national curriculum that has subsequently emerged. I remain concerned, though, that the interpretation of 'community involvement' that underpins the citizenship curriculum will involve a conception of the community that sees it simply as a place or neighbourhood where students are merely 'active': doing good rather than political action. That is, the new curriculum will result in forms of volunteering that will fail to challenge the students to think and act 'politically': volunteering *without* Service Learning. (cf. Crick, 2002: 115).

In contemporary political thinking, the concept of community has become both philosophically and 'politically' significant. Community has also become increasingly the focus of government policy in the UK and the US. From the 'Third-Way' communitarianism of New Labour or the New Democrats, to the emergence of communitarian-based 'Compassionate Conservatism', the idea of community is now seen as a key to rethinking the relationship between civil society and the state. Government social policy concerning neighbourhood renewal and urban renaissance stresses the role of citizens in inner city areas in designing and rebuilding their communities (Sirianni and Friedland, 2002; Taylor, 2003).

Linked to this challenge is the perceived sense of the loss of community in contemporary British society. This lost sense of community also underlies the idea of social capital, which has recently been popularized by Robert Putnam in his study of the decline of civic engagement and social capital in the US (Putnam, 2000). The concept of social capital has provided a theoretical basis for understanding the importance of community, which according to the neo-Tocquevillian analysis of Robert Putnam and his colleagues has important consequences for citizenship and political participation. While Putnam and others have analysed the decline of traditional volunteering in the US it is interesting to note that in the UK there has been a much smaller decline (Hall, 2002).

In contemporary sociological theory, there has been a renewed interest in the idea of community (Bauman, 2000; Delanty, 2003). The concept of community is an elastic concept which allows for an enormous range of meanings. From virtual communities to imaginary communities there are conceptual understandings of community to be found in a wide range of traditions of thought and academic disciplines. I would argue that there are at least four main ways of conceptualizing community. (There are a number of contemporary writers who offer alternative ways of representing the varying understandings of the meaning of community (cf. Delanty, 2003; Frazer, 1999a, 1999b; Nash, 2002 and Taylor, 2003)). The first is to consider community descriptively as a place or neighbourhood. The second is to talk of community as a normative ideal linked to respect, solidarity and inclusion, which can be found in the now well-established debate between liberalism and its communitarian critics (Mulhall and Swift, 1996). The third way of understanding community is based on the construction of cultural identities and can be found in communities of 'interest'. This conception is based on a politics of identity and recognition of difference. The fourth way is to consider community as a political ideal which is linked to participation, involvement and citizenship, especially on the level of the community.

It is the case, of course, that these conceptual understandings of community are often elided and combined to produce hybrid conceptualizations of contemporary community. Thus a political understanding of community may be based in a specific neighbourhood where there are public places and may include a variety of communities of identity or interest. It is also the case that political communitarianism can be understood through the analysis of the politics of community in terms of liberalism, communitarianism or civic republicanism. Advocates of both communitarianism and civic republicanism have recently begun to revive the idea of a civic service linked to the ideal of service to the local community. In Britain, a number of authors have argued for a national voluntary Citizen's Service initiative and more recently in the US there has been a renewed interest in establish a form of national service, which would build on the success of the Americorps programme of the Corporation for National Service (Dionne et al., 2003). Susan Stroud, based on her previous work for the Ford Foundation, has also been exploring this theme internationally (cf. www.icip.org).

CITIZENSHIP EDUCATION, ACTIVE CITIZENSHIP AND SERVICE LEARNING

So, what is the link between citizenship education and service learning? And what role might service learning play in delivering the objectives of citizenship education? As readers will be aware, Crick's first and seminal report, *Education for Citizenship and the Teaching of Democracy in Schools* (DfEE, 1998), resulted in the addition of Citizenship to the National Curriculum. This report also recognised the importance of active learning in the community, learning that is, by definition, *experiential* in nature.

This pedagogy of experiential learning is based on the learning cycle of David Kolb and is now beginning to establish itself in schools, colleges and in higher education and in professional development and training programmes. As a form of learning it is based not just on experience but on a *structured learning experience* with *measurable learning outcomes*. A key element of Kolb's model is that learning emerges from the structured reflection of the learner. Thus, as applied to citizenship education, the student learns not just through, for instance, volunteering or civic engagement but through their reflections on this. Thus, Carnegie Ypi, CSV Education for Citizenship, Continyou, Changemakers, the Citizenship Foundation, Envision and other voluntary sector organizations have highlighted the importance of encouraging the development of, for example, citizenship education through reflective service learning. In the US one important leader in this area is Terry Pickeral who is the director of the National Center for Learning and Citizenship which provides leadership in the Compact for Learning and Citizenship, a national organization of chief state schools officers and district superintendents committed to integrating service-learning into K-12 schools. The center has led on the 'Policy and Practice Demonstration Project', which is part of the W.K. Kellogg-funded 'Learning In Deed' national service-learning initiative and the Ford Foundation-funded 'Every Student A Citizen' initiative which focuses on citizenship education and service-learning. Many schools in the UK and the US now provide school students with the opportunity to engage in this kind of Service Learning (to use the prevalent US terminology) or 'active learning in the community', 'community based learning for active citizenship', as UK based programmes frame such activity (Wade, 1997 and for the UK cf. Annette, 2000; Potter, 2006). A key challenge facing such programmes is to go beyond traditional volunteering and doing good works and link the service learning with political knowledge, skills and understanding.

While there has been a tradition of community-based internship and experiential education since the 1960s, the new emphasis in the US since the early 1990s has been on the link between Citizenship Education and Service Learning (Rimmerman, 1997; Battistoni, 2002). There is also an increasing emphasis on the need for Service Learning programmes to meet the needs of local community partners (Cruz and Giles, 2000). Thus, Service Learning helps to build a type of 'bridging as well as bonding social capital' (cf. Putnam, 2000) *and* may also develop the capacity building for democratic citizenship within civil society. (Annette, 1999; Kahne and Westheimer, 2000, 2003) An important research question that needs to be examined, albeit one beyond the reach of this chapter, is: 'what are the necessary elements of a service learning programme which can build not only social capital but also active citizenship?' (Eyler and Giles, 1999; Billig, 2000; Kahne and Westheimer, 2000, 2003; Annette, 2003, and forthcoming).

ACTIVE CITIZENSHIP, SERVICE LEARNING AND THE DELIVERY OF THE NATIONAL CURRICULUM

In UK schools, the problem for teachers is to integrate citizenship education, including the opportunity to engage in service learning, into a national curriculum, which many view as already overcrowded. And the service learning element poses an additional burden: providing the opportunity for students to participate in service learning requires strong partnerships with local community-based organizations, businesses and service providers *and* timetable flexibility. Nonetheless, it is important if Crick's ambitions are to be fulfilled:

> We aim at no less than a change in the political culture of this country both nationally and locally: for people to think of themselves as active citizens, willing, able and equipped to have an influence in public life and with the critical capacities to weigh evidence before speaking and acting; to build on and to extend radically to young people the best in existing traditions of community involvement and public service, and to make them individually confident in finding new forms of involvement and action among themselves (DfES, 1998: 7 and cf. Crick 2000b and 2002).

The vision of Crick's advisory group Report is a formidable one and there are, of course, many challenges to be faced if it is to be realized. Terence McLoughlin, among others, has raised a number of issues arising from the Advisory Group's report (McLaughlin, 2000 and cf. Osler, 2000). Here I want to build on these and encourage further debate and discussion about how citizenship education through service learning might help to bring about the more participative democratic political culture that Crick seeks.

SERVICE LEARNING AND POLITICAL AWARENESS: THE EVIDENCE

Until recently, there has been relatively little empirical research in the UK into citizenship and citizenship education beyond some pioneering studies of youth political socialization. Ivor Crewe and his colleagues noted that much of the debate about Citizenship is 'conducted in what is virtually an empirical void' (Crewe et al., 1997) There has been more recently an increasing amount of research into citizenship education and its learning outcomes internationally. In the UK, there have been a number of small-scale studies since 1998 and more recently the eight-year *Citizenship Education Longitudinal Study* has been launched. Outlined elsewhere in this text, the study has been commissioned by the Department for Education and Skills and is being carried out by David Kerr and colleagues at the National Foundation for Educational Research (NFER) (Kerr et al., 1997, 2003; and subsequent research reports). This will, for the first time in the UK, provide a comprehensive understanding of the outcomes of Citizenship Education as a compulsory core National Curriculum subject at Key Stages 3 and 4 and it will complement the Post-16 Citizenship Education Survey that is also being funded by DfES and undertaken by NFER. There are a number of contextual factors raised in the first report of the longitudinal study, and in other research. Critically, these focus on the competing definitions of Citizenship with which practitioners contend, the lack of a coherent vision for Citizenship Education but here and elsewhere there are also concerns about the 'definitions, purposes and outcomes' of Citizenship Education, particularly given the competing claims for emphasizing 'equality, identity and diversity', global citizenship, etc.

Although research into Citizenship Education in the UK remains in its infancy, there is an extensive range of research studies in the US into the learning outcomes of Service Learning programmes for students in both secondary schools and higher education (for example, Billig, 2000; Furco, 2002 and Melchoir and Bayliss, 2003; Ehrlich et al., 2007). What is especially interesting about this research is the almost universal finding that Service Learning, where volunteering is part of a formal Citizenship curriculum, is more effective in its link with 'Citizenship' outcomes then with 'Community Service' or volunteering itself. That is, it serves to develop just the type of political awareness and literacy that Crick and his colleagues intended the new UK curriculum to do: A service learning, which builds citizenship *knowledge* and develops citizenship *skills* which can lead to active citizenship and civic renewal.

Recent research by Joseph Kahne and Susan Sporte (Kahne and Sporte, 2007) is based on the study of 3,805 students from 47 high schools in Chicago and examines the impact of a variety of curricular and extra-curricular activities on students' commitment to civic participation. Following on from the IEA civic Education Study of 14-year-olds in 28 countries in 1999 (Torney-Purta, 2002) they find that certain curricular features are associated with particular civic outcomes. They note that,

> While taking a government course may not make much difference, we find that particular pedagogical and curricular experiences in high school can meaningfully influence students commitments to civic participation. Specifically, social learning opportunities that focus on civic and political issues and ways to act (eg. Undertaking service learning projects, following current events, discussing problems in the community and ways to respond, providing students with a class room in which open dialog around controversial issues is common and where students study topics that matter to them, as well as exposure to civic role models) appear to be a highly efficacious means of fostering commitments to civic participation. In fact, the effect size of service learning opportunities and the overall measure of civic learning opportunities is larger than the size of any factors in this study. (Kahne and Sporte, 2007, p. 23).

In another recent research study, Daniel Hart and colleagues (Hart et al., 2007) note that,

> The most striking finding to emerge from our analyses is that high school community service predicted adult volunteering and voting, after controlling for other relevant predictors and demographic variables....Our results strongly suggest that civic participation in adulthood can be increased through community service participation in adolescence, a conclusion contrary to claims by some that service detracts from political involvement (Hart et al., 2007: 213).

The authors also note that an important part of such a service learning experience, along with a deeper civic identity, is the experience of developing and using civic skills (cf. Kirlin, 2003). Project 540 was a network of 270 high schools that enabled school wide deliberation and action about issues that students chose. Data from a research survey indicates that the students who participated in Project 540 had a more positive commitment to deliberative democracy, civic action and a greater sense of political efficacy. (Project 540 and Battistoni, forthcoming) This raises questions about the importance of the theory of deliberative democracy for citizenship education and highlights important issues about the need to enable inclusive voices and to develop the civic skills of civic listening and inter-cultural understanding. It also challenges citizenship educators to learn from the innovations of the practice of deliberative democracy and to apply them to the curricular practice of an education for democratic citizenship. Not all research findings, however, find service learning as clear-cut predictor of adult civic participation and Billig et al., (2005) find that only 'high-quality' service learning experiences have significantly different civic outcomes then social studies classes. We need more research into the outcomes of different types of service learning that range from community service to more 'politically' based service learning.

These research findings and the evidence of new kinds of youth civic participation raise the issue of how we develop through community involvement, especially on the local level, a more deliberative and democratic politics that can also provide a more active and political framework for enriching citizenship education. Thus, learning about citizenship through active community involvement should, at least in part, be based on the pedagogy of overtly reflective experiential service learning linked to models of public problem solving or more deliberative democracy. There are now an increasing number of academics who are exploring how the theory and practice of deliberative democracy can be provide an effective way of providing learning for democratic citizenship (Eslin et al., 2001; Gastil and Levine, 2005). Here, the key to success is to be found in asking how community based or focused learning experiences can best be structured to challenge students to become

'political' such that they become more aware of the political significance of civic engagement in local communities.

ACKNOWLEDGEMENTS

I would like to thank Carole Hahn for her advice in revising this chapter with all its limitations despite her good efforts.

REFERENCES

Advisory Group on Citizenship (Crick 1), (1998) *Education for Citizenship and the Teaching for Democracy in Schools*. Available at www.dfes.gov.uk/citizenship

Advisory Group on Citizenship (Crick 2), (2000) *Citizenship for 16–19 Year Olds in Education and Training*, Further Education Funding Council. Available at www.dfes.gov.uk/citizenship

Annette, J. (2000) 'Education for Citizenship, Civic Participation and Experiential Service Learning in the Community,' in R. Gardner et al., (eds), *Education for Citizenship*. London: Continuum.

Annette, J. (2003) 'Community and Citizenship Education' in Andrew Lockyer, Bernard Crick and John Annette, (eds), *Education for Democratic Citizenship*. Aldershot: Ashgate.

Annette, J. (forthcoming) 'Where's the Citizenship in Service Learning?'

Barber, B. (1984) *Strong Democracy*. University of California Press.

Barber, B. (1992) *An Aristocracy of Everyone*. Oxford: Oxford University Press.

Battistoni, R. (2002) *Civic Engagement Across the Curriculum*. Campus Compact.

Battistoni, R. (forthcoming) 'Democracy's Practice Ground: The Role of School Governance in Citizenship Education,' in Janet Bixby and Judith Pace (eds) *Educating Democratic Citizens in Troubled Times: Qualitative Studies of Current Efforts*. SUNY Press.

Bauman, Z. (2000) *Community*. Polity Press.

Bentley, T. (2005) *Everyday Democracy*. Demos.

Billig, S.H. (2000) 'Research on K–12 school-based service-learning: The evidence builds.' *Phi Delta Kappan*, (81) 9: 658–664.

Billig, S., Root, S. and Jesse, D. (2005). The impact of participation in service learning on high school students civic engagement. CIRCLE working paper 33. Available www.civicyouth.org.

Blunkett, D. (2003) Civil Renewal – a new agenda, (Edith Kahn Memorial Lecture), CSV.

Boyte, H. (2004) *Everyday Politics: Reconnecting Citizens and Public Life*. University of Pennslyvania Press.

Colby, A. et al. (2003) *Educating Citizens, The Carnegie Foundation for the Advancement of Teaching*. Jossey-Bass.

Crewe, I., Searing, D. and Conover, P. (1997) *Citizenship and Civic Education*. London: Citizenship Foundation.

Crick, B. (2005) *In Defence of Politics*. 5th edition, Continuum.

Crick, B. (2002) *Democracy*. Oxford: Oxford University Press.

Cruz, N. and Dwight G., Jr. (2000) 'Where's the Community in Service-Learning Research?', *Michigan Journal of Community Service Learning*, 7: 28–34.

Dagger, R. (1997) *Civic Virtues: Rights, Citizenship and Republican Liberalism*. Oxford: Oxford University Press.

Delanty, G. (2003) *Community*, Routledge.

Dionne, EJ, Jr, et al. (eds) (2003) *United We Serve: National Service and the Future of Citizenship*. Brookings Institute Press.

Eslin, P., Pendlebury, S. and Tjiattas, M. (2001) 'Deliberative Democracy, Diversity and the Challenges of Citizenship Education,' *Journal of the Philosophy of Education*, 35 (1): 116–124.

Eyler, J., and Dwight G., Jr. (1999) *Where's the Learning in Service Leaning?*, San Francisco: Jossey-Bass.

Frazer, E. (1999a) 'Introduction: The idea of political education', *Oxford Review of Education*, 25 (1–2): 5–22.

Frazer, E. (1999b) *The Problems of Communitarian Politics*. Oxford: Oxford University Press.

Archon, F. and Wright, E.O. (eds) (2003) *Deepening Democracy*. London: Verso.

Furco, A. (2002) Is service-learning really better than community service? A study of high school service. In A. Furco and S. H.

Billig (eds), *Advances in service-learning research: Vol.1. Service-learning: The essence of the pedagogy*. Greenwich, CT: Information Age. pp. 23–50.

Galston, W. (2004) 'Civic Education and Political Participation. PS: Political Science and Politics, April.

Ginsbourg, P. (2005) *The Politics of Everyday Life*. Yale.

Hall, P. (2002) 'The Role of Government and the Distribution of Social Capital', in Robert Putnam (ed.) *Democracies in Flux*. Oxford: Oxford University Press.

Hart, D., Donnelly, T., Youniss, J. and Atkins, R. (2007) 'High School Community Service as a Predictor of Adult Voting and Volunteering,' *American Educational Research Journal*, (44) 1: 197–219.

IPPR (2004) *The Lonely Citizen*. IPPR.

Kahne, J. and Westheimer, J. (2000) 'Service-Learning and Citizenship: Directions for Research', *Michigan Journal of Community Service Learning*, Special Issue: 42–51.

Kahne, J. and Westheimer, J. (eds) (2003) 'Special Section on Education, Democracy and Civic Engagement, *Phi Delta Kappen*, 85 (1): 9–14.

Kahne, J. and Susan S. (2007) 'Developing citizens: A Longitudional Study of School, Family and Community Influences on Students' Commitment to Civic Participation,' unpublished paper.

Kerr, D. (1977, rev. ed. 1999) *Citizenship Education Revisited-National Case Study-England*, National Foundation for Educational Research (NFER).

Kerr, D. et al. (2003) Citizenship Education Longitudinal Study: First Cross-Sectional Survey 2001–2002, National Foundation for Educational Research.

Kirlin, M. (2003) The role of civic skills in fostering civic engagement, CIRCLE Research Paper, www.civicyouth.org

Kolb, D. (1998) *Experiential Learning*, Eaglewood Cliffs, NJ: Prentice Hall.

Little, A. (2002) *The Politics of Community*. Edinburgh University Press.

Levine, P. (2007) *The future of democracy: Developing the Next Generation of American Citizens*. Tufts Univertsity Press.

Lister, R., Smith, N., Middleton, S. and Cox, L. (2003) 'Young People Talk about Citizenship: Empirical Perspectives on Theoretical and

Political Debates,' *Citizenship Studies*, 7 (2): 235–253.

McLaughlin, T. (2000)'Citizenship Education in England: The Crick Report and Beyond' *Journal of Philosophy of Education*, 34 (4): 541–570.

Maynor, J. (2003) *Republicanism in the Modern World*. Polity Press.

Melchoir, A. and Ballis, L. (2002) 'Impact of Service Learning on Civic Attitudes and Behaviours of Middle and High School Youth: Findings from Three National Evaluations,' in A.Furco and S.Billig (eds) *Advances in Service Learning Research*. Information Age Publishing.

Miller, D. (2000) 'Citizenship: what does it mean and why is it important?,' in N.Pearce and J.Hallgarten (eds) *Tomorrow's Citizens: Critical Debates in Citizenship and Education*. London: IPPR.

Mulhall, S. and Swift, A. (1996) *Liberalism and Communitarianism*, 2nd edn. Oxford: Blackwell.

Nash, V. (2002) *Reclaiming Community*. London: IPPR.

Oldfield, A. (1990) *Citizenship and Community*. Routledge.

Osler, A. (2000) 'The Crick Report: Difference, Equality and Racial Justice,' *The Curriculum Journal*, 11 (1): 25–37.

Petit, P. (1997) *Republicanism: A Theory of Freedom and Government*. Oxford: Oxford University Press.

Potter, J. (2006) *Active Citizenship in Schools*. Kogan Page.

Print, M. and Coleman, D. (2003) Towards understanding social capital and citizenship education. *Cambridge Journal of Education*, 33 (1): 123–149.

Print, M. (2007) Citizenship Education and Youth Participation in Democracy, *British Journal of Educational Studies*, 55(3).

Project 540, Students turning into Citizens: Lessons Learned from Project 540, Providence College, 2004.

Putnam, R.D. (2000) *Bowling Alone in America*. New York: Simon and Schuster.

Rimmerman, C. (1997) *The New Citizenship*. New York: Westview Press.

Sandel, M. (1996) *Democracy's Discontent*. Harvard University Press.

Sirianni, C. and Friedland, L. (2004) *Civic Innovation in America: Community Empowerment, Public Policy, and the Movement for Civic Renewal*. University of California Press.

Sirianni, C., and Friedland, L. (2005) *The Civic Renewal Movement*. The Kettering Foundation, 2nd edn.

Stoker, G. (2006) *Why Politics Matters?: Making Democracy Work*. Palgrave.

Taylor, M. (2003) *Public Policy in the Community*. Palgrave.

Torney-Purta, J. (2002) 'The School's Role in Developing Civic Engagement: A study of Adolescents in Twenty-Eight countries,' *Applied Developmental Science*, 6 (4):

Wade, R. (ed.) (1997) *Community Service-Learning*. SUNY Press.

Weller, S. (2007) *Teenagers' citizenship*. Routledge.

Zukin, C., Scott, K., Molly, A., Krista, J. and Michael, X.D.C. (2006) *A New Engagement?: Political Participation, Civic Life and the Changing American Citizen*. New York: Oxford University Press.

31

Educating for Civic Character

Marvin W. Berkowitz, Wolfgang Althof, and Scott Jones

In this handbook, citizenship education is discussed from a variety of perspectives. The current chapter examines the relationship of character education and citizenship education and will focus on what we call educating for civic character. The widely read consensus paper 'The civic mission of the school', as well as many other documents (e.g. Patrick and Vontz, 2001), describe civic knowledge, skills (competencies), and dispositions (attitudes) as the three core dimensions of citizenship and hence as the focal targets of citizenship education. In Chapter 29 of this handbook, Ian Davies discusses issues related to the first of this triumvirate, namely civic knowledge and civic-political literacy. While an important topic, it will not be the focus here. Rather we will look mainly at the third component, civic dispositions, but will also touch upon civic skills as they relate to what we term *civic character*.

In this chapter, we will first offer some terminological clarification. Then we will give an introduction to the concept of character and the field of character education. We will not provide a parallel discussion of the concept of citizenship and the field of citizenship education, because this volume more than adequately addresses that in many chapters.

We have also done so elsewhere (Althof and Berkowitz, 2006). Following this, we will discuss some historical and more recent approaches to integrate moral character and democratic citizenship, and, in doing so, explore the potential of integrating elements from both domains in educating democratic and responsible citizens. Finally, we will address some contemporary challenges to the integration of character education and citizenship education.

We understand *dispositions* to be enduring tendencies to act in certain ways. As Flanagan et al. (2007) have argued, 'For democracy to work, society has to nurture certain key dispositions in the people' (p. 422). The concept has considerable overlap with concepts such as character, personality, traits, and virtues. A moral disposition is a sort of 'moral inertia.' It means a person has a tendency to continue to move in a certain trajectory of direction (e.g. to continue to be honest in most circumstances). Nevertheless, for a disposition to be fully effective, it requires the capacity to act in those ways; that is for a disposition to lead to consistent behaviour, one often requires certain behavioural competencies (that is the *skills* in the knowledge/skills/dispositions trilogy). Ideally it leads to a sense of trust in one's ability to act according to one's moral dispositions (a sense of moral self-efficacy). It is worth noting the parallel to political efficacy (Bandura, 1997), that is, a sense of one's ability to influence the functioning of a government (Flanagan et al., 2007). It is also worth noting that the very concept of a stable personality or dispositions (character traits) is not without controversy (see, e.g. Doris, 2002).

Both character education and citizenship education are fields that are awash in alternative terminology, depending on disciplines and ideologies of authors. We will call the set of psychological characteristics that motivate and enable an individual to act as a moral or pro-social agent 'character', and the educational strategies designed to promote the development of such characteristics as 'character education.' We will call the effective, appropriate participation in the democratic public sphere 'citizenship', and will use the term 'civic' as the corresponding adjective for the noun 'citizenship.' Hence, 'civic character' refers to the part of character that has to do with democratic functioning (note that we have chosen to focus on democratic citizenship, but recognize that one can be a citizen in a non-democratic society as well; it is simply not our interest). We consider the terms *civic* and *citizenship* to be interchangeable in meaning.

OVERVIEW OF CHARACTER AND CHARACTER EDUCATION

The field of character education, albeit under different names and ideologies, dates back at least to classic Greek times in Western society. There was a peak period for it under the name character education from the late nineteenth century until World War II in the US. It largely disappeared under that name however until the 1980s and its current resurgence began in the early 1990s. Regardless, the project of socializing youth in schools is millennia old. It has almost always been understood that the primary socialization of youth occurs in the family, but that schooling is a major contributor to this project which is necessary for societal survival, especially in a democracy. In fact, the founders of American democracy emphasized and elaborated upon this point repeatedly (Pangle and Pangle, 2000).

As noted above, character is the set of psychological characteristics that motivate and enable an individual to act as a moral or pro-social agent, or, as Berkowitz and Bier (2005a) have stated, 'the composite of those psychological characteristics that impact the child's capacity and tendency to be an effective moral agent; i.e., to be socially and personally responsible, ethical, and self-managed' (p. 1). Character education therefore is school-based attempts to foster the

Table 31.1 Eleven principles of effective character education (Character Education Partnership)

1.	Promotes core ethical values as the basis of good character.
2.	Defines 'character' comprehensively to include thinking, feeling, and behavior.
3.	Uses a comprehensive, intentional, proactive, and effective approach to character development.
4.	Creates a caring school community.
5.	Provides students with opportunities for moral action.
6.	Includes a meaningful and challenging academic curriculum that respects all learners, develops their character, and helps them to succeed.
7.	Strives to foster students' self-motivation.
8.	Engages the school staff as a learning and moral community that shares responsibility for character education and attempts to adhere to the same core values that guide the education of students.
9.	Fosters shared moral leadership and long-range support of the character education initiative.
10.	Engages families and community members as partners in the character-building effort.
11.	Evaluates the character of the school, the school staff's functioning as character educators, and the extent to which students manifest good character.

development of that set of psychological characteristics, that is character. The Character Education Partnership (www.character.org) has identified *Eleven Principles of Effective Character Education* (Lickona et al., 2003); see Table 31.1. The principles collectively define character education as comprehensive school reform that is democratic, empowering, and based on intrinsic moral motivation.

Character education is a difficult field to define, largely because it is so broad that it includes a wide range of perspectives, theories, and methods. The Character Education Partnership has attempted to be a 'big tent' organization (and has largely succeeded in that goal); hence, it encompasses fairly didactic and even authoritarian examples on one end of the spectrum and highly egalitarian, progressive, and developmental examples on the other end. Some examples rely heavily on teaching *about* virtues and character, others on relatively behaviouristic shaping of behaviours and virtues, yet others on creating school and classroom climates of democratic empowerment, and so on. Clearly, if one takes the CEP *Eleven Principles* (Table 31.1) as the blueprint, some of these are more representative of what they define as effective character education. Ultimately, character education is that which effectively promotes the development of character in students. For this reason, Berkowitz and Bier (2005a) reviewed the existing research literature to ascertain what is empirically known about the impact of school-based interventions on student character development. In a review of 69 research studies of 33 character education programs, they concluded that character education positively impacts a wide range of student character outcomes, plus academic achievement (cf. Benninga et al., 2003). Furthermore, effective character education programs tended to share certain features. They incorporated various peer interactive strategies (e.g. class meetings, moral discussions, cooperative learning, peer mentoring). They included substantial professional development for the implementing educators. They

intentionally trained social-emotional competencies (e.g., anger management, peer conflict resolution). Parents and other community members were incorporated as audience, clients, and/or partners (cf. Berkowitz and Bier, 2005b). Character education was integrated into the academic curriculum. Effective programs employed approximately eight different strategies and the most effective programs employed nearly 11 different strategies.

Other research has demonstrated that effective character education depends upon the development of a safe, pro-social, caring school and classroom climate (Benninga et al., 2003; Berkowitz and Bier, 2005c; Solomon et al., 2001) and a related network of positive interpersonal relationships (Howes and Ritchie, 2002; Watson, 2003), including the adult culture of the school (Bryk and Schneider, 2002). Clearly, research suggests that character education is multifaceted, including didactic, social-learning, sociological, and constructivist methods. This should not be surprising given the complexity of human development in general and the multivariate nature of moral psychological development in particular (Berkowitz, 1997).

DEFINING CIVIC CHARACTER

We have argued for the centrality of civic character for democratic society (Althof and Berkowitz, 2006). As the Center for Civic Education has suggested in their National Standards for Civics and Government,

> the goal of education in civics and government is informed, responsible participation in political life by competent citizens committed to the fundamental values and principles of American constitutional democracy. Their effective and responsible participation requires the acquisition of a body of knowledge and of intellectual and participatory skills. Effective and responsible participation also is furthered by development of certain dispositions or traits of character that enhance the individual's capacity to participate in

the political process and contribute to the healthy functioning of the political system and improvement of society (1994: 1).

But what exactly is civic character? What comprises the set of dispositions and skills necessary for functioning effectively and ethically in a democratic society? Under different but often overlapping terms, it is defined as follows. According to the National Council for the Social Studies (1997), *civic virtue* refers 'to what Alexis de Tocqueville called "habits of the heart," that is, a commitment to democratic principles and values that manifests itself in the everyday lives of citizens. A focus on knowledge and skills alone is insufficient for the task of civic education. Civic education must also foster civic character in citizens.' Oakes et al. (2000) report on schools that adopted a middle grades reform program known as *Turning Points: Preparing American Youth for the 21st Century*. A major focus of the reform program was to entice educators and policy makers toward developing a positive *civic virtue*, which they defined as the development of 'policies and practices that characterize the public good as embodied in a citizenry that can come together across differences and solve common problems in a democratic sphere' (p. 569), but admittedly they had trouble reaching consensus on the 'common, public good.' In elaborating on a position paper, *Pathways to civic character*, jointly issued by the Association for Supervision and Curriculum Development (http://www.ascd.org), in partnership with the First Amendment Center (http://www.firstamendmentcenter.org) and the Character Education Partnership (http://www.character.org), Boston (2005) describes *civic character* as 'responsible moral action that serves the common good' (p. 5) and suggests that any reform program that attempts to develop that end should be included under the umbrella term of civic character. He specifically identifies character education, civic (citizenship) education, service learning and social and emotional learning as programs that develop the civic

character of students by fostering 'the knowledge, skills, virtues and commitment necessary for engaged and responsible citizenship' (p. 31).

We therefore define civic character as the set of dispositions and skills that motivate and enable an individual to effectively and responsibly participate in the public sphere in order to serve the common good.

THE ROLE OF CHARACTER AND CIVIC EDUCATION IN A DEMOCRACY

This still leaves open the question of how democratic forms of government interface with the character of their citizens. How critical is the nature of civic character? What is the role of government in its formation and sustenance? The role of government in educating citizens for democracy traces its development back to the first western democracy, Athens. However, Plato (1945) believed that the citizens were not capable and were too engrossed in their own personal obsessions with material greed, a sentiment echoed by Alexis de Tocqueville (1831/2001) and the American founders (Pangle and Pangle, 2000). In order to protect the citizens from themselves, the state should focus on the education of those who could overcome this obsession and rule through the reason and moral characte these 'philosopher-kings' developed in the schools. Contrary to Plato's elitist solution, the founders of the American democracy believed in the power of education to counter such hedonistic tendencies, along with the checks and balances of the democratic political structure. This perspective was originally posited by Plato's most famous student. Unlike his mentor, Aristotle (1962; Krout, 2002) did not believe the average person to be incapable of developing the skills necessary to participate in the Athenian democracy. Instead, he believed people had a political nature that drove them to shared ownership in the state. Because of this, Aristotle believed the state had the responsibility to educate people in public schools so that the citizenry would have the proper communitarian spirit, reason and habits necessary to act in a virtuous manner.

These two philosophies have dominated Western thought as it pertains to citizenship education. The impact of Plato is seen in the philosophies of Machiavelli (1513/1980; de Alvarez, 1999) and Hobbes (1651/1982). Machiavelli did not concern himself with the moral character of the state ruler nor its citizenry. Instead, whatever was necessary to strengthen the state was the correct course of action. Hobbes believed humanity to be naturally corrupt and, therefore, in need to be forced into actions that help strengthen the community. In such communities, education is only needed for those who will govern.

The philosophers of Enlightenment contrasted with these thoughts. Both Locke (2003) and Rousseau (1762/1968) developed the idea that human beings are good by nature. In the *Two Treatises of (Civil) Government* (1689; in Locke, 2003), Locke develops a theory of natural law and natural rights (life, liberty and property) that allows him to distinguish between legitimate and illegitimate, tyrannical government. For Locke and for Rousseau, the citizen will only turn to corruption because the greater society threatens these natural rights. In order to protect themselves from government encroachment of their rights, citizens must participate in the society and in the various levels of government. Rousseau warns that once civic participation declines, the ability to defend against abuses of the natural rights by government declines as well. Once there is no participation, there is no just government. The leaders of the first experiment in liberal democracy believed that education was the key to guaranteeing the success of a society built around the principles of limited government (Pangle and Pangle, 2000). George Washington, Benjamin Franklin, Thomas Jefferson, and many others claimed that if America was to survive, it needed to develop public schools that would teach students how to be democratic citizens with proper dispositions and participatory skills. An enlightened citizenry is indispensable for the proper functioning of a republic. Self-government is not possible unless the citizens are educated sufficiently to enable them to exercise oversight; which, on the other hand, implies that suitable education can develop the potential in all citizens to be part of the 'aristocracy of virtue and talent' that Thomas Jefferson envisioned instead of an aristocracy of wealth leading the republic.

Alexis de Tocqueville (1831/2001) observed in the early part of the nineteenth century that American democracy had grown strong because of its citizens' intense participation in matters of the government. The ideas of educating for democratic citizenship and participation have remained strong in America. Dewey (1916/2004) emphasized the role of schools in developing citizens that have the proper democratic dispositions and participatory skills necessary to act for the common good (also see Boyte, 2003). Many contemporary authors claim that education in general and citizenship or democratic education in particular is an essentially moral enterprise (e.g. Blades and Richardson, 2006; Gutmann, 2000; Haydon, 1999; Kerr, 1997; Rowe, 1992). In *The Morality of Democratic Citizenship*, Butts (1988), for example, gives a noted listing of core values of democracy, many of which have a clear moral connotation, including justice, equality, truth, freedom, diversity, and human rights. These values are at the core of what Butts calls 'education for civic virtue' (2006: 14). Emphasizing the moral foundations of democratic societies, Bull (2006) states, 'Civic education is certainly a kind of moral education in that it promotes and supports a public morality, that is, the agreements about the principles governing citizens' relationships and obligations to one another' (p. 26).

In many Asian countries, the concepts of citizenship education and moral education are culturally intertwined (Lee et al., 2004). Individual character development – as expressed in self-awareness, self-cultivation, and the ability to maintain harmonious relations, 'both in terms of relations with the universe, and relations with one another in society' (Lee, 2004, p. 280) – is strongly emphasized; however, the individual and the collectivity, are considered to be interdependent and mutually reinforcing. The resulting understanding of citizenship education is less concerned with politics and more focused on issues of morality, or, as Kennedy and Fairbrother (2004) state, 'Asian citizenship education is characterized more by conceptions of moral virtues and personal values than by civic and public values' (p. 294). In a recent account of trends in curriculum development in Asia and the Pacific, W.O. Lee (2006) summarizes, 'the general picture I can draw is a common emphasis on culture, a common understanding that civics and moral education is a twin relationship, [and] a common expectation of the development of social responsibility to be supported by healthy and positive values' (p. 13).

Certainly, basic concepts of character and citizenship differ by culture. However, a strong focus on the moral dimension of citizenship, and, hence, a strong relation of civic and moral character, is clearly not specific to a certain region. Comparative analyses of teacher perceptions regarding the priorities in citizenship education show that a strong emphasis on the social and moral qualities of citizenship is very common throughout the nations studied (for example, Davies et al., 2004; Lee and Fouts, 2005). This concurs with a trend in the US to combine or even integrate character and citizenship education in curricular frameworks, mission statements and educational practice (Althof and Berkowitz, 2006).

As will be detailed below, we are not arguing for a reduction of one to the other. When citizenship only is 'seen in terms of being a good person' (Davies et al., 2004: 371) and narrowed down to responsible behaviour in the immediate personal domain, it becomes depoliticised; the resulting practice of

citizenship education 'might not help us to achieve more critical and political notions of society' (Davies et al., 2004: 373; also see Westheimer and Kahne, 2004). The fact that education for global citizenship (e.g., Blades and Richardson, 2006; Osler and Vincent, 2002) apparently is not advocated strongly by the average teacher does not prove its irrelevance in times of economic and cultural globalisation. Lee (2005) gives a speculative yet convincing explanation of teachers' priorities:

> The teachers are the ones who are facing their students every day. They have to deal with behavioural problems. They have to cultivate a sense of responsibility and moral concepts to develop good citizens among students. That is, caring about the social, moral and duty dimensions of good citizens is, as a matter of fact, the day-to-day concerns and the here-and-now job of the teachers' (p. 255).

However, there can be no doubt that any liberal democracy calls for citizens who are civically minded and skilled as well as morally responsible. Colby et al. (2003) emphasize

> that many core democratic principles, including tolerance and respect, impartiality, and concern for both the rights of the individual and the welfare of the group, are grounded in moral principles. (...) The problems that confront civically engaged citizens always include strong moral themes. (...) No issue involving these themes can be adequately resolved without a consideration of moral questions and values. A person can become civically and politically active without good judgment and a strong moral compass, but it is hardly wise to promote that kind of involvement (p. 15).

Civic responsibility calls for moral responsibility. Morality lies at the heart of civic character, and education for civic character necessarily has to address issues of morality (e.g., Youniss and Yates, 1999). Democracy relies on certain procedural rules and political institutions but it cannot flourish if its citizens do not hold moral and civic values, and manifest certain personal virtues – that is, display democratic or civic character. Both moral or character education and citizenship education are central to the development of the civic character of citizens that is foundational to a democracy.

A SYNTHESIS

Clearly, the concepts of moral and civic character overlap significantly. Much of what we call civic character is the same as much of what we more generically call character. Lickona and Davidson (2005) suggested that character education should focus on both, the moral psychology of individuals (moral character) and the characteristics of their nature that support effective performance, in moral endeavours as well as in other forms of achievement, such as academics and politics (performance character). The Character Education Partnership (www.character.org), the national character education professional organization, has recently redefined character to include both aspects, having in the past focused much more heavily on the moral side of character.

When one defines character as purely moral characteristics, then it is clear that civic character only partially overlaps with moral character, for civic character necessarily includes competencies and propensities toward democratic forms of communication, persistence in advocacy and seeking quality relevant information for making civic decisions, etc. However, when one broadens the definition of character to include both moral and performance character, then most (if not all) of civic characters can be subsumed under the more generic concept of character.

When one moves from the definition of character to the school-based formation of character (character education), again the overlap is substantial but not absolute. We have strongly argued for the necessity of character (and character education) for a democratic society (Althof and Berkowitz, 2006; Berkowitz, 2000). This is essentially the argument for schools to be involved in the civic part of character that is necessary for the optimal functioning of a democratic political system and broader society. If a democratic society is to thrive, its citizens must both be virtuous and have the civic character that motivates and enables them to engage in the democratic process. The

methods and pedagogy of character education and civic education again overlap, by necessity, as their outcome goals (civic character, moral and performance character) overlap so strongly. In one of the more ambitious forms of character education, Kohlberg (Power et al., 1989) relied heavily on civic processes as he created democratic high schools in the second half of the twentieth century, in this case with the goal of promoting individual moral development along with a just school community.

Acquiring virtues such as personal and social responsibility, tolerance, or respect necessitates interpersonal experience and reflection. Traits of fairness, honesty, courage, and integrity do not develop in a social solitude. Civic skills such as public speaking, problem solving, and consensus building require practice. Schools can provide manifold opportunities of practice by not only providing instruction but also creating a school climate of care and recognition, by involving students in meaningful discussions and by encouraging student participation in community-building activities, including school governance. There are clear differences however. In both character and citizenship, the tripartite concepts of behaviour/cognition/affect are acknowledged. We have been focusing on the affective and behavioural aspects in this discussion. Certainly, in the classroom, all three components must be addressed. A core part of the cognitive side is knowledge. Knowledge necessary for citizenship is not isomorphic with the knowledge base for morality. For example, democratic citizenship requires education in civics, including facts about the form and functioning of the government. These topics are not central to moral formation (although teaching history, law, and government may provide opportunities to explore a multiplicity of issues of morality in public life, particularly at the higher grades).

Overall, education and development are quite robust. That which counts as good education (e.g., Marzano, 2003) overlaps with what counts as effective character education

(Beland, 2003; Berkowitz and Bier, 2005a) and effective civic education (e.g. Flanagan et al., 2007). Teacher-student relationships and school climate are at the heart of academic, moral, and civic education. Nonetheless, style and emphasis may make a large difference across these three interrelated goals of education. For example, Flanagan et al. report that civic commitments and a belief in a just society were greater if teachers were seen as fair to and respectful of students. Democratically run classrooms tend to promote the motivation to engage in public life and a belief in the efficacy of doing so. Such a democratic, challenging, and caring environment tends to be at the heart of both character and civic education, just as it is at the heart of parenting for moral character (Berkowitz and Grych, 1998). But not all effective education has to follow the same formula. Academic achievement can occur in more hierarchical classrooms as long as teachers use effective instructional strategies, manage behaviour effectively, and design effective curricula (Marzano, 2003). In other words, democratic empowerment of students may be more central to character and civic education than to academic achievement; however, research shows that effective character education also promotes academic achievement (Benninga et al., 2003; Berkowitz and Bier, 2005). Clearly, more work is needed to understand the complex relationships between school characteristics that promote the development of character, citizenship, and academic success.

CHALLENGES TO THE INTEGRATION OF CHARACTER AND CIVIC EDUCATION

At the Center for Character and Citizenship in St. Louis, we see a large overlap and potential synergy between character education and citizenship education. However, we have also encountered much resistance when one of the two camps attempts to penetrate the other. One source of such friction is simply territoriality. Experts are often protective of their circumscribed domains of expertise. Consequently, they become overly wedded to terminology and labels. It is more important, however, to remember that the child is not segmented along academic lines. It is in everyone's interest to put Humpty Dumpty back together again after the parochial academics have disassembled him. A child's morality is highly integrated with the child's civic character. To ignore this is to ignore human nature. After all, it is a whole person standing in the voting booth or honestly filing her taxes, not just the civic or moral part of the person.

A second source of friction between character and civic education is prejudice and stereotyping. Character education has a negative connotation to many outside its sphere of influence. Interestingly it is somewhat of a projective test as those on the more liberal progressive side perceive it threateningly as a tool of conservative, often religious, indoctrination while those on the conservative traditionalist side often see it as a form of liberal secular humanism. In fact, character education is very hard to pin down as it is such a 'big tent' field that it includes both of those extremes and many more perspectives and approaches that fall between them. This is in fact a persistent problem in generating acceptance of character education from those outside the field. Character education has grown to such a degree that it includes a startling range of perspectives, ideologies, and methods. We hope it is clear that we take a decidedly progressive and developmental perspective on the promotion of moral character in schools. It is this perspective that resonates so strongly with civic education as we have demonstrated. Some, however, reject the relevance of character education because they focus on more authoritarian and indoctrinative strands, and at times strands that are largely 'straw men' and do not actually exist or are so rare as to be largely irrelevant to academic discourse. In fact, this has become a common theme in the critiques of character education. Many distinguished scholars have criticized character education by focusing on the narrow traditionalist side of character education (e.g. Kohn, 1993; Noddings, 2002; Westheimer and Kahne, 2004). We do not consider this form of discourse very helpful as it reifies the skewed notion of character education as solely or largely a behaviouristic, indoctrinative, and authoritarian enterprise and it makes the integration of related fields such as character and citizenship education more difficult to accomplish.

A third source of friction comes from differences due to the academic discipline of the proponent. For instance, much of civic education is informed by political scientists and historians. Frequently they emphasize civic knowledge as the core of civic education. Psychologists however tend to emphasize civic skills and dispositions. Given that many character educators are psychologists and few are historians or political scientists, this divide is not uncommon. Of course, as noted above, it requires all three components (political knowledge, intellectual and participatory skills, and civic dispositions) to form the goals of a complete civic education.

What is needed is a more interdisciplinary and integrative perspective on what needs to be developed in children for them to become effective, pro-social, participatory citizens of a democracy and what schools can most effectively do to realize that. Integrating character education and civic education is one step toward such a comprehensive and effective approach.

REFERENCES

Althof, W., and Berkowitz, M.W. (2006). Moral education and character education: Their relationship and their roles in citizenship education. *Journal of Moral Education*, 35 (4): 495–518.

Alvarez, L.P.S., de (1999) *The Machiavellian enterprise: A commentary on the Prince*. DeKalb, IL: Northern Illinois University Press.

Aristotle (1962) *The Politics*. Baltimore, MD: Penguin Books.

Bandura, A. (1997) *Self-Efficacy: The Exercise of Control*. New York: Freeman.

Beland, K. (2003) *Eleven Principles Sourcebook: How to Achieve Quality Character Education in K-12 Schools*. Washington, DC: Character Education Partnership.

Benninga, J.S., Berkowitz, M.W., Kuehn, P., and Smith, K. (2003) The relationship of character education implementation and academic achievement in elementary schools. *Journal of Research in Character Education*, 1 (1): 19–32.

Berkowitz, M.W. (1997). The complete moral person: Anatomy and formation. In J.M. Dubois (ed.), *Moral Issues in Psychology: Personalist Contributions to Selected Problems*. Lanham, MD: University Press of America. pp.11–41.

Berkowitz, M.W. (2000) Civics and moral education. In B. Moon, S. Brown and M. Ben-Peretz (eds.), *Routledge International Companion to Education*. New York: Routledge. pp. 897–909.

Berkowitz, M.W., and Bier, M.C. (2005a) *What Works in Character Education*. Washington DC: Character Education Partnership.

Berkowitz, M.W., and Bier, M.C. (2005b). Character education: Parents as partners. *Educational Leadership*, 63 (1): 64–69.

Berkowitz, M.W. and Bier, M.C. (2005c). The interpersonal roots of character education. In D.K. Lapsley and F.C. Power (eds.), *Character Psychology and Character Education*. Notre Dame, IN: University of Notre Dame Press. pp. 268–285.

Berkowitz, M.W., and Grych, J. (1998) Fostering goodness: Teaching parents to facilitate children's moral development. *Journal of Moral Education*, 27 (3): 371–391.

Blades, D.W. and Richardson, G.H. (2006) Restarting the interrupted discourse of the public good: Global citizenship education as moral imperative, In G.H. Richardson and D.W. Blades (eds) *Troubling the Canon of Citizenship Education*. New York: Peter Lang. pp. 115–123.

Boston, B.O. (2005) *Restoring the Balance Between Academics and Civic Engagement*. Washington DC: American Youth Policy Forum.

Bryk, A.S. and Schneider, B. (2002). *Trust in Schools: A Core Resource for Improvement*. New York: Russell Sage Foundation.

Bull, B.L. (2006) Can civic and moral education be distinguished? In D. Warren and J.J. Patrick (eds) *Civic and Moral Learning in America*. New York: Palgrave Macmillan. pp. 21–31.

Boyte, H.C. (2003) A different kind of politics. John Dewey and the meaning of citizenship in the 21st century. *The Good Society*, 12 (2): 1–15.

Butts, R.F. (1988) *The Morality of Democratic Citizenship: Goals for Civic Education in the Republic's Third Century*. Calabasas, CA: Center for Civic Education.

Butts, R.F. (2006) The politics of civic and moral education. In D. Warren and J.J. Patrick (eds) *Civic and Moral Learning in America*. New York: Palgrave Macmillan. pp. 7–19.

Center for Civic Education (1994) *National Standards for Civics and Government*. Calabasas, CA: Center for Civic Education (2nd ed. 2003).

Colby, A., Ehrlich, T., Beaumont, E. and Stephens, J. (2003) *Educating Citizens. Preparing America's Undergraduates for Lives of Moral and Civic Responsibility*. San Francisco: Jossey-Bass.

Davies, I., Fülöp, M., Hutchings, M., Ross, A., and Berkics, M. (2004) Citizenship and enterprise: issues from an investigation of teachers' perceptions in England and Hungary. *Comparative Education*, 40 (3): 363–384.

Dewey, J. (1916/2004) *Democracy and Education*. New York: Kensinger Publishing.

Doris, J.M. (2002) *Lack of character: Personality and Moral Behavior*. New York: Cambridge University Press.

Flanagan, C.A., Cumsille, P., Gill, S., and Gallay, L.S. (2007) School and community climates and civic commitments: Patterns for ethnic minority and majority students. *Journal of Educational Psychology*, 99 (2): 421–431.

Gutmann, A. (2000) Why should schools care about civic education? In: L.M. McDonnell, P.M. Timpane and R. Benjamin (eds) *Rediscovering the Democratic Purposes of Education*. Lawrence, KA: University Press of Kansas. pp. 73–90.

Haydon, G. (1999) The moral agenda of citizenship education. *The School Field*, 10 (3/4): 47–54.

Hobbes, T. (1651/1982) *Leviathan*. Edited with notes by C.B. MacPherson, New York: Penguin Classics.

Howes, C., and Ritchie, S. (2002) *A Matter of Trust: Connecting Teachers and Learners in the Early Childhood Classroom*. New York: Teachers College Press.

Kerr, D. (1997) *Toward a Democratic Rhetoric of Schooling* In J.I. Goodlad and T.J. McMannon (eds), *The public Purpose of Education and Schooling*. San Fransisco: Jossey-Bass pp. 73–83.

Kennedy, K.J., and Fairbrother, G.P. (2004) Asian perspectives on citizenship education in review: Postcolonial constructions or precolonial values? In W.O. Lee, D.L. Grossman, K.J. Kennedy and G.P. Fairbrother (eds), *Citizenship Education in Asia and the Pacific. Concepts and Issues*. Hong Kong: The University of Hong Kong, Comparative Education Research Centre. pp. 289–301.

Kohn, A. (1993) *Punished by Rewards: The Trouble with Gold Stars, Incentive Plans, A's, Praise and Other Bribes*. New York: Houghton Mifflin.

Krout, R. (2002) *Aristotle: Political Philosophy*. New York: Oxford University Press.

Lee, W.O. (2004) Concepts and Issues of Asian Citizenship: Spirituality, Harmony and Individuality. In W.O. Lee, D.L. Grossman, K.J. Kennedy & G.P. Fairbrother (eds), *Citizenship education in Asia and the Pacific. Concepts and issues*. Hong Kong: The University of Hong Kong, Comparative Education Research Centre. pp. 277–288.

Lee, W.O. (2005) Cross-national comparisons and conclusions: Teachers' perceptions towards social citizenship. In W.O. Lee and J.T. Fouts (eds.), *Education for Social Citizenship. Perceptions of Teachers in the USA, Australia, England, Russia and China*. Hong Kong: Hong Kong University Press. pp. 249–262.

Lee, W.O. (2006) *Tensions and contentions in the development of citizenship curriculum in Asian countries*. Paper presented at the CITIZED International Conference, Oriel College, Oxford, 25–27 July 2006.

Lee, W.O., Grossman, D.L., Kennedy, K.J., and Fairbrother, G.P., (eds) (2004) *Citizenship Education in Asia and the Pacific. Concepts and issues*. Hong Kong: University of Hong

Kong, Comparative Education Research Centre.

Lee, W.O., and Fouts, J.T. (eds) (2005) *Education for Social Citizenship. Perceptions of Teachers in the USA, Australia, England, Russia and China*. Hong Kong: Hong Kong University Press.

Lickona, T. and Davidson, M. (2005) *Smart and Good High Schools: Integrating Excellence and Ethics for Success in School, Work, and Beyond*. Cortland, N.Y.: Center for the 4th and 5th Rs (Respect & Responsibility), and Washington DC: Character Education Partnership.

Lickona, T., Schaps, E., and Lewis, C. (2003) *Eleven Principles of Effective Character Education*. Washington, DC: Character Education Partnership.

Locke, J. (2003) *Political Writings*. Edited by D. Wootton. Indianapolis, IN: Hackett.

Machiavelli, N. (1513/1980) *The Prince*. Translated with notes by L.P. de Alvarez. Irving, TX: University of Dallas Press.

Marzano, R.J. (2003). *What Works in Schools: Translating Research into Action*. Alexandria, VA: Association for Supervision and Curriculum Development (ASCD).

National Council for the Social Studies (1997). *Fostering Civic Virtue: Character Education and the Social Studies*. Silver Spring, MD: NCSS. Accessed on 15 May 2007 at http://www.socialstudies.org/positions/character/.

Noddings, N. (2002) *Educating Moral People: A Caring Alternative to Character Education*. New York, New York: NY: Teachers College Press.

Oakes, J., K.H. Quartz, S. Ryan, and M. Lipton (2000) Becoming good American schools: the struggle for civic virtue in education reform [Carnegie Council report]. *Phi Delta Kappan*, 81 (8): 568–75.

Osler, A. and Vincent, K. (2002) *Citizenship and the Challenge of Global Education*. Stoke. on-Trent, UK, and Sterling, VA: Trentham Books.

Pangle, L.S. and Pangle, T.L. (2000). What the American founders have to teach us about schooling for democratic citizenship. In L.M. McDonnell, P.M. Timpane, and R. Benjamin (eds.) *Rediscovering the Democratic Purposes of Education*. Lawrence, KS: University Press of Kansas. pp. 21–46.

Patrick, J.J. and Vontz, T.S. (2001) Components of education for democratic citizenship in the preparation of social studies teachers. In J.J. Patrick and R.S. Leming (eds), *Civic Learning in Teacher Education. Vol. 1: Principles and Practices of Democracy in the Education of Social Studies Teachers*. Bloomington, IN: ERIC Clearinghouse for Social Studies. pp. 39–63.

Plato (1945) *The Republic*. Translated with notes by F.M. Cornford. (1945) New York: Oxford University Press.

Power, F.C., Higgins, A., and Kohlberg, L. (1989) *Lawrence Kohlberg's Approach to Moral Education*. New York, NY: Cambridge University Press.

Rousseau, J.J. (1762/1968) *The Social Contract*. Translated and introduced by M. Cranston. New York: Penguin Classics.

Rowe, D. (1992) The citizen as a moral agent: The development of a continuous and progressive citizenship curriculum. *Curriculum*, 1(3): 178–187.

Solomon, D., Watson, M.S. and Battistich, V.A. (2001) Teaching and Schooling Effects on Moral/Prosocial Development. In V. Richardson (Ed.), *Handbook of Research on Teaching* (4th ed., pp. 566–603). Washington, DC: American Educational Research Association.

Tocqueville A., de (1831/2001). *Democracy in America*. Edited and abridged by R.D. Heffner. New York: Signet Classics.

Watson, M. (2003) *Learning to Trust*. San Francisco: Jossey-Bass.

Westheimer, J. and Kahne, J. (2004) What kind of citizen? The politics of educating for democracy. *American Educational Research Journal*, 41 (2): 237–269.

Youniss, J. and Yates, M. (1999) Youth service and moral-civic identity: A case for everyday morality. *Educational Psychology Review*, 11 (4): 361–376.

32

Democratic Schools: Towards a Definition

Bernard Trafford

This analysis of school democracy, extensively rooted in UK-based research but drawing also on experience from Europe and across the globe, is obliged to begin by attempting a definition. Can a school be democratic? Some would assert that it cannot. In general, schools operate within a fairly rigid command structure. However heads/principals may choose to run their institutions, above them will be a hierarchy of governance and government which almost inevitably imposes a traditional line of authority and accountability. Indeed, heads have such considerable positional power because they are appointed by that hierarchy, however much consultation may have been involved in the process. Similar pressures operate on others: teachers in many countries feel beleaguered by the requirements of government-enforced examination and programmes of study. Thus Huddleston (2007: 6) finds in a survey of European member states:

> The idea of school democracy does not as yet have universal acceptance within the teaching profession (Rowe 2003) and the ethos in schools in a number of countries is still often dominated by authoritarian power structures (Birzea et al 2004: 39). Opportunities for student participation are often perceived to be constrained by the requirements of nationally or regionally prescribed curricula and testing regimes and by the need that teachers and school leaders feel to moderate their principles in the light of parental and other external expectations.

Similarly, although Torney-Purta et al. (2001: 5) see the argument being won for the 'effectiveness of an open and participatory climate in promoting civic knowledge and engagement', they find that such an approach is 'by no means the norm in most countries.' Moreover, if externally imposed constraints provide a measure of justification for the perpetuation of autocratic leadership styles, Hahn (1984) identifies what she describes as 'self-righteous authoritarianism': those who work in schools will recognize that trait as far from being limited to the American setting of Hahn's study. Indeed, Huddleston adds as a European footnote: 'The All-European Study reported that in the Eastern and South-Eastern European regions the democratic school is 'not yet the prevalent model ... the dominant model continues to be an authoritarian-type governance and a rigid institutional background' (Birzea et al., 2004: 39).

So can this kind of organization have any hope of giving rise to democratic practice within individual institutions? In practice, and despite this widespread and persistent authoritarian tradition in schooling, schools do indeed function well as democracies, frequently in a highly developed state. As long ago as 1989, Polan (1989: 29) was describing school as the 'inevitable democracy': 'Despite impressions to the contrary, schools amount to some of the most advanced formal social institutions … in terms of democracy, debate and participation.'

Certainly there is no simple definition of a democratic school, though a good starting point is Watts (1977: 129), writing about his experience of running a school that was – in UK education terms – democratic during the 1970s: '… a formal school in which teachers and school students have been able to enjoy an increase in dignity which results from their sense of determining, to a large extent, the conditions under which they work and grow.'

If they are involved in determining the conditions under which they work and grow, teachers and students are inevitably participating in the democracy as it develops in the school. Huddleston (2007: 6) finds that definitions of student involvement vary as widely as do the styles and practices that are broadly described as democratic:

> Whereas some understand it simply to refer to the work of student representative bodies – such as school councils or pupil parliaments – others define it more widely to encompass all aspects of school life and decision-making where students may make a contribution, informally through individual negotiation as well as formally through purposely-created structures and mechanisms.

The present author's own experience of developing democracy in a school used as a working definition of democracy in schools:

> … a considerable degree of consultation, a right for individuals to speak their minds, whether or not they agree with the official or majority line of the school, and […] an implication that the rights of the individual will be enshrined while at the same time being balanced with the needs of the community as a whole (Trafford, 1993).

Since then it has seemed necessary to add to that definition the expectation of active participation by all those involved. But each time that definition is revisited, it seems essential to add still more elements. The 1993 definition refers to the implication of the rights of the individual, but what about the fundamental respect and dignity of each? And respect and dignity in turn imply a requirement for tolerance and mutual support. The definition keeps growing and becoming more sophisticated (Trafford, 2003: 28).

Watts (1989: 26–27) returns to the search for a definition: 'If democracy in school is about anything, it is not so much about power … as the free exchange of ideas. Without that open, continuous debate, power-sharing is pointless.' The democratic view, therefore, is less concerned with deciding where (or in whom) power resides and more interested in creating a climate in which all those involved can genuinely participate. Participation, of course, lies at the heart of democracy, so the school that claims to be democratic will do more than simply operate an open and consultative management style with regard to teachers. It implies of necessity that all the stakeholders are involved, and have a voice: a fundamental principle of democratic schooling must be, therefore, that pupils have the right to have their views heard and taken into account, a right both enshrined in principle and encouraged in practice. Holdsworth (1999), writing in Australia, employs the analogy of a tripod to outline his view of participation. The three essential and balanced legs are:

- Student representation on school decision-making bodies;
- Student-run organizational structures; and
- Participatory approaches within the curriculum and classroom.

These accord with Huddleston's recommendations (2007: 28–29).

Harber (1995: 9) approaches the question from a different angle, identifying the atmosphere in which education *for* democracy may satisfactorily take place:

> Tolerance of diversity and mutual respect between individuals and groups, a respect for evidence in forming opinions, a willingness to be open to the possibility of changing one's mind in the light of

such evidence, the possession of a critical stance towards political information and regarding all people as having equal social and political rights as human beings. In other words there is, or should be in a democracy, an emphasis on reason, open-mindedness and fairness. These are some of the values that education for democracy must foster ...

These values echo those of the American National Council for Social Studies' 1979 position statement on democratization of schools:

> ... the school should be a micro-society and should reflect what is happening in the real world. Schools, like society, have a system of justice and notions of equity ... Students need to feel a part of the system of justice, and they need to tackle the problems within the school setting in order to gain experience in the agony and frustration of democratic decision making (in Hepburn, 1984: x).

These are values to which many schools would lay claim, whatever their *modus operandi* from day to day, and raise the question of *why* schools should be democratic: this will be considered after the following section.

LIMITATIONS OF THIS ANALYSIS

This chapter deals with democratic schools but recognizes that, for the most part, it will be describing features of schools operating within a state/government-run system and developing and promoting democratic practice and ideals within the limitations of that system. There are globally a very few, invariably small schools which are genuinely democratic in both foundation and practice. The website of the International Democratic Education Network (www.idenetwork.org), which mounts an annual global conference of its members, lists over 200 schools 'offering democratic education in more than 30 countries, working with over 40,000 students.'

Principal among such schools, as identified by Hannam (2000), are The Forsoksgymnaset in Oslo (FGO), Norway; Sands School, Ashburton, Devon, England; The Democratic School of Hadera, Israel; Sudbury Valley School, Framingham, Massachusetts.

(To these one might add such examples as Booroobin Sudbury Democratic Centre of Learning, Australia, and Naestved Fri Skole, Denmark.) Probably the most influential of these, and the one most frequently copied, is Sudbury Valley School. Hannam (2000) describes its democratic structure, drawing heavily on the school's website:

> It has a totally democratic structure not unlike Hadera's on which it has had a considerable influence. All students and staff (though not parents) are members of the school Assembly, which resembles a traditional New England Town Meeting. The Assembly has an elected chairperson, always a student, and deals with most of the school's decision-making including the creation of the many school laws. Attendance is not compulsory. Teachers are appointed by the Assembly and it also reviews and renews their contracts annually. Most teacher contracts are renewed but even the most long-serving staff have no security of tenure beyond their annual contracts.

Space does not permit further consideration of this important minority of schools. Similarly it is beyond the scope of this chapter to consider the 'free school' or libertarian tradition. Libertarians (who seek free, not strictly democratic, education) believe that 'education has to be freed from the authority of the teacher as well as from the state', (Shotton, 1993: 9–11). Shotton gives a full account of the growth and, in general, the ultimate demise of that libertarian view of schooling to which tradition, rather than the democratic, A.S. Neill's (1990) famous Summerhill really belongs. However, Neill's writings and the work of the democratic and free schools mentioned above have exerted a powerful, yet impossible to measure, influence on many Western educators who have felt encouraged and challenged by them to make their own schools very much more democratic than they would otherwise have been.

WHY DEMOCRATIC SCHOOLS?

Democratic education is on the agenda. Global concern with the development of the democratic citizens of tomorrow from the children of today is leading many countries to look again at their systems of schooling, regarding them as the chief – indeed, to a large extent the only hopeful – setting in which the next adult generation can learn and experience the meaning of democratic citizenship. The Council of Europe, for example, designated 2005 as its Year of Education for Democratic Citizenship (EDC). Writing for the Council, Liègeois (2007: 91) describes EDC as:

> a set of practices and activities designed to prepare people to live in a democratic society by ensuring that they actively exercise their rights and responsibilities. It includes human rights education, civic education and intercultural education. EDC is very closely linked to the idea of participation, since no one can pass on democratic citizenship without practising it.

She quotes (Liègeois, 2007: 90) the 20th Session of the Standing Conference of European Ministers of Education (Krakow, Poland, 2000) as agreeing that EDC 'promotes and is promoted by [...] a whole-school approach, in terms of school ethos, learning and teaching methods and the participation of pupils, students, educational staff and parents in decision-making and, as far as possible, in determining the formal and informal curriculum.'

Significantly, Liègeois is writing in an appendix to one of four volumes which comprise a Council of Europe-published Toolkit for EDC, circulated across its 46 member states, reflecting the importance the Council attaches to this agenda. This is not surprising given the disparate nature of the Council's membership. Some countries are old, established democracies with school systems that enjoy advanced democratic structures Scandinavia comes immediately to mind – while others are still fledgling democracies where racial and other tensions create problems in schools as in every other aspect of their societies. In such settings, the development of a universal appreciation of democracy becomes an imperative.

Notwithstanding the extent to which authoritarian governance structures prevail even now, schooling is seen as both the appropriate place and a convenient one in which to provide young people with genuinely democratic experience. It is a not a new view, and the literature tends to share it unanimously. In *School and Democracy* (1916) John Dewey was urging: '... a [democratic] society must have a type of education which gives individuals a personal interest in social relationships and control, and the habits of mind which secure social changes without introducing disorder ...' (Dewey, 1916: 99).

He went on to lament the fact that schools at that time were so inimical to such an education. In his vision (expressed originally in a still earlier lecture):

> When the school introduces and trains each child of society into membership within ... a little community, saturating him with the spirit of service, and providing him with the instruments of effective self-direction, we shall have the deepest and best guaranty of a larger society which is worthy, lovely and harmonious (Dewey, 1990: 20).

The 1979 American NCSS position statement was mentioned above: earlier than that, a study of the political attitudes of elementary school children in eight cities and four regions of the US identified the school as 'the most important and effective instrument of political socialization in the United States', (Hess and Torney 1967: 101, quoted in Hepburn 1984: 6). With such a powerful national train of thought, it is scarcely surprising that a recent US grouping of some 100 schools called *First Amendment Schools* directly links schooling with the development of democratic skills and ideals. Their vision statement (available at www.firstamendmentschools.org) describes schools as 'laboratories of democratic freedom'. The practice of democracy within school life is seen as an imperative so that 'students confront the challenge of self-government, including the difficult task of balancing a commitment to individual rights with a concern for the common good'. The schools are described as modelling the Constitution of US.

Belief in the ability and power of schools to develop the citizens of tomorrow is not confined to America. In their study of citizenship and education in 28 European countries, Torney-Porta et al. (2001: 4) are emphatic: schools, that model democratic practice are most effective in promoting civic knowledge and engagement. The argument is persuasive: indeed, politically it is arguably won. Democracy is regarded as a 'good thing', desirable as both process and outcome. However, Huddleston (2007: 6–7) warns that a lack of clarity about both purposes and means with regard to democracy in schools means that neither in approach nor in measures of success is there any consistency or coherence. Nor is there much recognition in the literature of the fact that different theoretical emphases, while positive towards the general idea of student participation, might sometimes conflict in practice (2007: 10).

FEATURES OF A DEMOCRATIC SCHOOL

What is most distinctive – and, indeed, most immediately noticeable – about a democratic school is the feel of it, as Harber describes above. Education in democracy is thus, inevitably, education for democracy – and vice versa. The two develop together. Democratic structures (such as school councils) will not flourish in an undemocratic climate: but their presence helps to transform the climate into a democratic one. Like Harber et al., Inman and Burke (2002: 30) list among the core values that characterize a democratic school 'co-operation, mutual respect, autonomy, justice, and commitment to diversity and equity.'

Huddleston (2007: 11) identifies significant factors in Europe, features which are held in common throughout the literature:

- students' level of confidence in the value of participation and sense of 'empowerment' in their schools;
- the existence of student representative structures, such as school councils or pupil parliaments;

- opportunities for students to be respected for their contribution to solving school problems;
- extent to which the school environment models democratic principles or fosters participation practices;
- links between participation and explicit teaching about democratic practice;
- an open classroom climate for discussion; and
- links with the wider community and participatory organizations beyond the school.

The most significant individual features of schools which are demonstrably – or palpably democratic – are considered below.

Ethos

The 'feel', the way people live their lives within the institution, is the direct result of the ethos, something which in a democratic school will be carefully nurtured. Radz (1984: 73) terms this the 'climate', commenting that those who spend time in schools can attest to its impact on 'how they feel, how they perform, and how they grow as individuals.' Inman and Burke (2002: 48) describe what this democratic ethos feels like in day-to-day life:

> … we were stuck by the openness and warmth that we were routinely shown by staff and students. Visitors were clearly not a threat to adults or students. The staffroom was striking – noisy and vibrant, with much talk and laughter. There was a confidence in the atmosphere that was impossible not to feel, though difficult to describe.

They received comments (2002: 49) about the ethos from year 11 students along these lines:

> 'It's not like a prison'
> 'I think they give you independence'
> 'You're heard'
> 'They give you freedom'
> 'They care about you'
> 'I think why the school is so good is because the students are so friendly to each other. They really are.'

They continue:

> From the observations and interviews we observed an underlying culture of respect and equality between members of the school community.

We observed a politeness and respect in the manner that staff talked to students. We saw staff opening doors for students and vice-versa as a matter of routine practice. The corridors were largely free of stress and tension but rather were spaces where people engaged in communication (2002: 49).

It is important to stress that, in those schools where democracy has really taken root, it is not in the formal structures that the change is most felt. Harber (1989: 55) finds that, at Countesthorpe School: 'The day-to-day democratic 'feel' comes less through its formal structures than through the informal democracy that characterises contacts in the classroom. The atmosphere is relaxed, friendly, non-authoritarian, and pupils' opinions matter.' At the heart of a democratic school ethos, it is clear that there lies deep respect between everyone in the school, teachers, students, other staff, and indeed all others (not least parents) who become involved in the school atmosphere. Which comes first? Is the ethos democratic because the relationships are so good, or are the relationships so good because it is democratic?

Inman and Burke (2002: 49) see 'treating pupils with respect' as a vital element in this democratic ethos. Like so much of the living reality of democracy in a school, respect given and respect received create a virtuous circle. The more it is given, the more it is returned. If teachers set examples of politeness, of opening doors, or of picking up litter, pupils develop similar behaviours: far better than screaming at them for being slovenly! If children are treated as intelligent beings capable of developing and exchanging ideas, they respond in kind.

The School (or Student) Council

It is arguably impossible to imagine a democratic school that does not have at its heart some kind of formal democratic structure such as a school council. Of course, a very small school (such as one of those listed by Hannam, above, perhaps) might simply gather all its pupils together in one place rather as the ancient Athenian Demos met when important decisions had to be taken. The rest need to create a democratically elected representative council. There are nowadays numerous countries that legislate to require that students have a democratic voice in their schools (Scandinavian countries come to mind, as do Slovenia, the Czech Republic, Spain and, part of the UK, Wales). Legislation does not, of course, ensure that representation is of good quality, so those countries continue to work on their school or youth democracy and surveys and comparisons of practice and experience of necessity continue across continents.

> Democratic schools require school structures in which pupils are consulted and given opportunities to experience responsibility. In theory then, school councils would seem to be an essential feature of a school that promotes active citizenship. School councils have the capacity to send powerful messages to all pupils about the possibilities of participation and about their value and worth within the institution and beyond. Moreover School Councils at their best will raise fundamental questions for those who control and manage the school as to the nature of the institution they wish to promote (Inman and Burke, 2002: 29).

It is not easily demonstrable whether the presence of a council creates and promotes the democratic ethos or vice versa. Davies (1998: 36) has no doubts: 'What has become clear is that for a school council or other system of representation to work it must be embedded in a total ethos of democracy, equity, and concern for pupil and staff welfare and performance.' The mere existence of an effective school or student council makes a statement about the school and its attitude to its students. The principle of open management and the right of children to express their views and concerns, while respecting the rights of others not to be damaged by such expression, are both enshrined and made real by the presence of an active council. The right to a voice in the way the school operates is shown to be real for staff and students, and thus begins to permeate the fabric of school life. The presence of a school council further emphasizes the right of anyone, staff or student, to talk to anyone about what is worrying them, rather than being sent through 'proper channels' – which, even if they exist, can too easily seem to a worried individual like being fobbed off.

It goes without saying, perhaps, that the student representatives in a truly democratic school council are democratically elected: a school that cannot resist nominating students who it feels are 'suitable' has already left the democratic path. Holdsworth (1999) is emphatic that students who have been otherwise excluded from success and value be included – without being stigmatized by being included on some kind of special programme.

School councils take a variety of forms. Some will bring representatives of the student body together in a forum with other stakeholders. The commoner, and probably more successful, model sees a council consisting solely of students: this student council may well in turn send delegates to other groups within the management or governance structure (but note the observations below about effective as opposed to tokenistic school councils).

Reservations about the effectiveness of some school councils demonstrate to Inman and Burke (2002: 6) the council's dependence for success on the existence of a wider democratic setting. Moreover, the school council itself creates and strengthens that democratic framework and promotes engagement:

> ... technical weaknesses in the structure, form and scope of councils [...] are often symbolic of wider whole school weaknesses in relation to pupil participation and engagement. The [...] literature on democratic schools would suggest that there is a dynamic interplay between effective school councils and democratic schools. School councils flourish most effectively in the context of a wider democratic ethos and structure, but they also play a significant role in promoting and sustaining that democracy.

However, inefficiencies in the functioning of the school council, notwithstanding the support of the school, can undermine it. In a newsletter for Australian school councils (generally termed there Student Representative Councils), Holdsworth

(2007) is blunt. His article, entitled 'Don't do it ... manage it', advises elected student officers to avoid the trap of trying to do everything for the student body themselves, urging them instead to get organized and operate effective delegation and reporting systems.

This is crucial. Communication is a key challenge. So while it is comparatively easy to design a council, it will only be effective if all the links work smoothly. A typical school council structure will have individual classes electing representatives to a larger forum (council, assembly or parliament are the names commonly used to describe this major body). Frequently this full assembly is seen as being too large to be efficient in making decisions or taking action. Accordingly task-groups may be set up to deal with specific issues, or that large body will elect some kind of smaller executive group. In theory that is a sensible structure: but in a busy school where students find themselves, after all, for only a few hours each day, communication from the executive, though the assembly and back to the grass roots in the class, is often poor.

For those reasons, schools sometimes decide that it is impossible to bring representatives from all the year-groups together into a single forum, so classes simply send delegates to meetings for that year-group alone, or for a section of the school. Efficiency may increase, but one powerful component of school democracy, in which older students listen and accord respect to younger and vice versa, has been lost.

Some schools place particular value on the full assembly as a visible symbol of democracy: others choose the efficiency of smaller meetings. There is no one correct model, and all stand or fall by the effectiveness of representation, of action taken, and of two-way communication between grass roots and representatives. Huddleston (2007: 20) identifies this feature as an imperative emerging from a Slovenian study:

> ... the most effective forms of representative structures will be those that maximize the number of students who have the opportunity to represent their peers. One way of achieving this is through

multi-levelled structures ... We should look in general towards the development of in-school structures and procedures that encourage more 'grass-roots' participation by students – such as class councils, or by better use of existing structures – such as the regular 'tutor periods' built into the school day in countries like England and Spain.

So how should we recognise an effectively functioning school council? Inman and Burke (2002: 7) list characteristics shared by the school councils in their case study schools: these are very close to characteristics identified throughout the literature.

- Meetings are timetabled into lesson times.
- The council is whole-school rather than being class or year-based.
- There are explicit representation and reporting mechanisms.
- Meetings run formally with agendas and minutes.
- The council has a formal constitution.
- The council is formally consulted about major policy decisions.
- The scope of the agenda can be determined by pupils as well as staff.
- The council is under the direct oversight of the head teacher.

For the school council to be effective, then, it has to be an integral part of the school. Something that is missing from the list above is the sense and collective understanding of a clear purpose. What is the council there for? Many UK schools are nowadays seeing the value of involving the student body in school improvement and issues of teaching and learning (though this involves some dangers with regard to manipulation of the student voice for managerial purposes: see following sections). In other schools, the expectation may be only that students will organize their own activities and events, leaving teachers to do what is seen as their exclusive, professional job. Flexibility is a democratic virtue – but lack of clear expectations and boundaries can cause great frustration.

The literature is full of examples of loss of confidence in the school council as a result of its coming up against insuperable barriers so that belief and trust are lost. Conversely, Boomer (1992: 14) values obstacles as providing opportunities for negotiation: 'Negotiation also means making explicit, and then confronting, the constraints of the learning context and the non-negotiable requirements that apply.' To achieve Boomer's aim in that context requires courage and confidence on the part of school leaders, teachers and students: issues of leadership are dealt with below.

The school has to value its council as both a practical and a symbolic demonstration of respect for the pupil voice. If the school has a philosophy of engaging with its students, harnessing their energy and enthusiasm, and giving children responsibility for their lives and learning, the school council will be in harmony with the school ethos. The more the students are given opportunities to demonstrate how much their participation can contribute to the well-being and development of the school, the more that democratic engagement will strengthen the school ethos. Thus a virtuous circle is created.

Student leadership of school activities

Torney-Purta et al. (2001: 5) found that across Europe: 'Students prefer to belong to organizations in which they can work with peers and see results from their efforts. Such organizations can have positive effects on civic knowledge, attitudes and future engagement by giving students opportunities for participation in settings that matter to them.' This reflects the experience of all who chart democratic growth in schools. Much of Holdsworth's work and publishing in Australia is concerned with young people's participation in, and above all leadership of, community-based activity. America's First Amendment Schools promote what they term community engagement, describing opportunities to 'translate civic education into community engagement', (website:www.firstamendmentschools.org). Within a democratic climate, young people are quick to join or even set up activities, and to make them work, rather than waiting for teachers to organize it. Thus both the breadth and the quality of such activities grow.

Leadership and management in democratic schools

Inman and Burke (2002: 35) are unequivocal about the kind of leadership that must inevitably be present in a democratic school. Their interviewees identify the following as characteristics of leaders of democratic schools:

- The ability to take risks, to be able to live with uncertainty
- The ability to facilitate others to take leadership and power
- Visionary
- Has a commitment to the good of children
- Values staff as well as children
- Is outward looking, involving the school community in the wider communities and welcoming external projects into the school
- Is able to admit to mistakes, is self-reflective and analytical
- Is inclusive

Their findings echo Hannam's (2001) research:

> It is evident that the vision and commitment of the headteacher and other key senior and middle managers is crucial to the process and that this vision is usually most effective when formulated in collectively developed policy that is consistently documented and against which progress is evaluated.

It is hard to picture a democratic school where the tone is not set by those in leadership roles: or where the management of (and by) the staff is not as open and democratic as that of the pupils. Indeed, one comes across words such as 'courageous' and 'strong' connected with democratic leadership styles. As Radz (1984: 69) observes wryly, to be a relaxed, open, and secure school principal (the desired qualities) is no easy task: 'know thyself', he advises (p. 75).

Other features of democratic schools

Ethos, the free sharing of information and ideas, the involvement of all stakeholders as far as possible in analysis and review, in identifying problems and planning and implementing solutions, the formal structure of a school (or student) council, community engagement and leadership that allows and encourages it all to happen: these are the outstanding characteristics of a democratic school. Other features are also likely to be present. Briefly these might include:

- a constant process of self-review and improvement within those democratic structures;
- regular/routine use of democratic techniques (such as Circle Time) as learning and pastoral/social strategies in the classroom, often feeding (from class council through year council) to the over-arching school council;
- a student-run school newspaper (or, increasingly, a digital equivalent);
- student-run peer support/counselling and mediation;
- increased levels of inclusion;
- reduced feelings of alienation, tension and conflict;
- increased engagement in the community;
- effective and readily supported discipline structures (with significant student input); and
- students involved in teacher appointment procedures.

SCHOOL DEMOCRACY AND SCHOOL EFFECTIVENESS

As the body of research into democratic schools grows, it is becoming increasingly evident that the growth of democracy in a school is a powerful force to school improvement. Indeed, it would not be unreasonable to assert that democratic schools are more effective schools.

> A democratically structured and functioning school will not only promote EDC [Education for Democratic Citizenship] and prepare students to take their place in society as engaged democratic citizens: it will also become a happier, more creative

and more effective institution. The value that is added is immense: the research evidence of this is growing in volume all the time. So this […] does not simply describe a mission to do something morally right: starting down the democratic path is also a pragmatic step towards making schooling a more pleasant and productive process (Bäckman and Trafford, 2007: 6).

In 2001, the UK government commissioned a study of 12 secondary schools that described themselves as 'student participative', to find out whether, in those that were already 'taking seriously the "participation and responsible action" elements of the Citizenship order', there had been an improvement in 'attainment across the full range of GCSE results' (Hannam, 2001: 10). Hannam found that the 12 schools did indeed produce 'higher than expected levels of attainment at GCSE' (p. 63). He also made an explicit link between the warmer, more relaxed teacher-student relationship which comes with democracy and the resulting improvement in academic (and other) standards. One reason for this is that young people *believe* that they can achieve improvement, for themselves or for their institution, though usually for both, as Torney-Purta et al. (2001: 5) find in their European study.

When informal school relationships match those represented by the formal structures, a school may be seen to be operating consistently. When these circumstances prevail the experience of researchers is that discipline and the students' sense of responsibility are high. Ashworth (1995: 44), reporting the views of headteachers gleaned from a survey, indicates that:

Discipline improved when school structures worked towards students taking personal responsibility. Students became more caring towards each other, for the school environment and for the decisions they made. Motivation in lessons improved as did students' commitment, pride and enthusiasm for their school work … Overall, school life became more pleasant because students worked harder and behaved better. In addition, school management benefitted from students' ideas and some head teachers described how a sense of community had grown in their schools. They wrote about shared values, common understanding and increased dialogue between staff and students.

In the same way, America's First Amendment Schools talk about ensuring that everyone is given a meaningful voice is shaping the life of the school, so that 'all have a real stake in creating and sustaining safe and caring learning communities', (website: www.firstamendmentschools.org).

It is clear that, whenever students are involved in the discussion and formulation of school rules, the rules tend to be better kept and communication in the school is improved. Harber (1995: 11) observes, 'There is an increased sense of responsibility […] staff and students have more control over their own organization […] overcoming the "them and us" alienation in most schools'. Davies (1998) reaches similar conclusions in her research on the links between school councils and reduced levels of school exclusions. She finds that when students felt they are listened to, where they have a stake in the whole education process, they are less likely to suffer feelings of alienation, to play truant or to be excluded.

A democratic school constantly reminds everyone (teachers, other staff, parents, and students) that it is there for the benefit of the students. This tends to result in increased student motivation But democratic schooling is not merely about 'being nice to children': it is about a carefully judged, empowering ethos in which young people are given responsibility and are able to make the most of it. Unsurprisingly, then, in a school that has generated a democratic ethos:

- Relationships are better between students and teachers
- Young people are willing to take and exercise responsibility
- Standards of attainment rise
- Discipline is improved
- Alienation is reduced
- Truancy and exclusions are reduced
- Inclusion is increased
- Motivation is increased
- Confidence and self-esteem are raised
- Challenge is readily accepted
- High expectations are the norm
- Schools become more effective

(Trafford, 2005: 60–61)

By every measure, it seems, democratized schools become more effective. And they are pleasanter to work in, too, for students and staff alike.

CURRENT DEVELOPMENTS IN THE UK

Democratic schools contribute to the agenda currently being pursued by numerous governments to promote the values and practice of participation and citizenship among young people. A foreword written by the UK's Minister for School Standards, Lord Adonis, to guidance on making school councils more effective (Trafford, 2006) both outlines that political thrust and links its implementation to the establishment of effective democratic and participatory structures in schools:

> I strongly support the principle of ensuring that our children and young people participate more effectively in democratic processes. The introduction of citizenship as a statutory subject in secondary schools in September 2002, the Education Act 2002 and subsequent guidance to local authorities and schools has opened the way for much greater pupil participation. As a result, the number of school councils has increased substantially and the benefits to school ethos and achievement are clear. Pupils now have a real opportunity to impact on the way their school is run …
>
> Whilst many schools already have good practice in this area, the [UK] government is actively encouraging the spread of best practice so that school councils are truly democratic and the pupil body is given real power and responsibility.

In response to the citizenship imperative, UK schools are routinely embracing, for example, school councils as a means both of demonstrating their commitment to student participation and of providing opportunities for their students actively to engage. Moreover student voice, the term now most commonly used in this context and regarded during the 1990s as a strange and possibly dangerous fringe activity, is now widely accepted as a major contributor to school improvement: its historic proponents have moved from being seen as eccentrics almost to guru status. Accordingly, as the involvement of student voice more closely in matters of teaching and learning, and even of teacher performance, is increasingly covered in the educational press, so schools become readier to push back what were previously insuperable barriers. Thus it is now common (though not yet uncontentious) in the UK to see panels of pupils taking part in the selection and appointment of teachers, and there is a growing willingness to consult pupils about which teaching styles suit or appeal to them, and which do not.

An important action three-year research project came to completion in 2007, reported by a team from the University of Birmingham (Davies and Yamashita, 2007). School Councils UK's London Secondary School Councils Action Research Project (LSSCARP) followed in detail the development of democracy in several London secondary schools: naturally it was more successful in some schools than in others. LSSCARP breaks new ground in its coverage of how some schools brought pupils deeply into the observation, evaluation and planning of teaching and learning. Pupils were trained as observers and, in negotiation with the teacher, would record either the teacher's strategies or pupil reactions, discussing them in detail afterwards. A significant part of the action research project involved monitoring the training given by the School Councils UK project manager in these new approaches to both students and teachers in the project schools and tracking and analyzing the outcomes. Poor behaviour is acknowledged to be an intransigent problem in many London schools, and LSSCARP records how pupils were involved in behaviour panels, not only in the planning and implementation of rules but also in interventions and consultations in cases of bad behaviour.

How unusual it is even now to see students involved in planning curricula or even monitoring teaching and learning can be judged by comparing this with other experiences. Describing a school that had already travelled a long way down the democratic path in 1984, Grundfest et al. (1984: 99–100) describe a sticking point when students undertook an evaluation of teachers. By this stage of development most teachers accepted it, but a few were nonetheless outraged. More recently, Huddleston (2007: 15) reports experience of venturing into this territory in Czech Republic:

> [The researchers] said that involving students in curriculum or teaching and learning methods is 'the hardest challenge of democratic practice in Czech schools.' ... The students ... interviewed felt there was very little opportunity for them to influence curriculum content or learning methods. A number said that trying to do so was often a 'bad experience', that 'no one listens to what they say' and that 'the reaction of the teacher is negative'. So they 'start to be passive and don't think that they could influence anything at all'.

This remains a difficult area, though the LSSCARP research illustrates some signs of change. In Australia, though Holdsworth (1999) espouses involving students in teaching or tutoring other students, and in preparing curricular material, he does not venture into the territory of watching or evaluating the work of teachers. An anecdote from LSSCARP illustrates how defensive teachers remain, even to the point of absurdity. A teacher, when asked to become involved in using students as observers of teaching strategies, exclaimed, 'I'm not having pupils watching me teach!'

CONCLUSION

Some dangers

The lessons drawn from the UK LSSCARP research will prove to be important in the coming years, as more and more schools become aware of and seek to harness the power and energy inherent in the student voice. Even where pupils' active engagement is not sought, schools are making increasing use of questionnaires, surveys and focus groups. So much are schools concentrating on gaining student views on an ever-wider range of issues that there is a danger that they

may neglect the truly democratic structures such as school councils. It is commonplace to read, in guidance on implementation of a new educational initiative, that the views of the school council might be sought – or even that the council might be 'tasked' with carrying out some research in school. This risks a directive approach where the school hands out jobs to students through their democratic structure, which must in time become very much less of a representative voice. Curiously, this could well bring about the sort of pseudo-democracy observed back in the 1980s. Ball (1987: 9) for example, though dealing with the consultation of teachers rather than pupils, notes that:

> At times schools *are* run as though they were participative and democratic: there are staff meetings, committees and discussion days in which teachers are invited to make policy decisions.... at other times they are bureaucratic and oligarchic, decisions being made with little or no teacher involvement or consultation, by the head and/or senior management team.

Meighan (1986: 26) similarly observes that consulting pupils and using only some of their responses 'can become a means of coaxing them into niches of society rather than ordering them.' Persuasive voices can indeed be a threat to democratic freedoms and may often possess a veneer of openness and dialogue which masquerade as true participation:

> Many of us who enjoy teaching and who get on well with their students may feel that we know that they are thinking and what is important to them. My experience suggests that from informal chats one derives only a piecemeal impression of what really matters to children at school (Trafford, 1994).

Critical discourse at the heart of democratic schools

Critical dialogue lies (or should lie) at the heart of school democracy, not mere surveys of views or expressions of preferences, nor indeed observation or critiques of provision, though all these may contribute to the democratic life of the school. There are so many pitfalls for schools that attempt to develop democratic practice that the only way safely to avoid most of them is to ensure that the participants, teachers and pupils, are encouraged to engage in genuine critical discourse, and to be unafraid to air conflict when it emerges.

> A major part of empowering students is the matter of giving individuals courage, or what might often be described as self-confidence. It is self-confident individuals – who can see themselves critically and assess realistically their strengths and weaknesses in relation to others – who will be able to assess risks, to try original ideas, to overcome the fear of failure and so on. Empowering students is not so much concerned with neutralising their dissent as allowing them to feel able to explore, to experiment, to learn to argue and to negotiate within the sheltered environment of the classroom, the peer group, the School Council: this learning will prepare them to do likewise – and better – in the larger, less protected world outside school, (Trafford, 1993: 14).

Excessive emphasis on gathering student opinions for management purposes may lead some schools to forget that the effective structures they are using emerged from genuinely democratic growth, not from questionnaires or focus groups. It will be necessary to ensure that true empowerment remains at the heart of democratic schools if they are to continue the meteoric development that they have enjoyed over the past decade or two.

REFERENCES

Ashworth, L. (1995) *Children's Voices in School Matters: A Report of an ACE Survey into School Democracy*. London: Advisory Centre for Education.

Bäckman, E. and Trafford, B. (2007) *Democratic Governance of Schools*. Strasbourg: Council of Europe Publishing.

Ball, S.J. (1987) *The Micropolitics of the School: Towards a Theory of School Organisation*. London: Methuen/Routledge.

Birzea, C., Kerr, D., Mikkelsen, R., Froumin, I., Losito, B., Pol, M. and Sardoc, M. (2004) *All-European Study on Education for Democratic Citizenship Policies*. Strasbourg: Council of Europe.

Boomer, G. (1992) 'Negotiating the curriculum', in Boomer, G, Lester, N, Onore, C and Cook, J (eds) (1992) *Negotiating the Curriculum: Educating for the 21st Century*. London: The Falmer Press.

Boomer, G., Lester, N., Onore, C. and Cook, J. (eds) (1992) *Negotiating the Curriculum: Educating for the 21st Century*. London: The Falmer Press.

Davies, L. (1998) *School Councils and Pupil Exclusions*. Birmingham, Centre for International Education and Research, University of Birmingham (published by School Councils UK. Available www.school-councils.org

Davies, L. and Yamashita, H. (2007) *School Councils and School Improvement: The London Secondary School Councils Action Research Project*. London: School Councils UK. Available www.schoolcouncils.org

Dewey, J. (1916) *Democracy and Education*. New York: The Free Press.

Dewey, J. (1990) *The School and Society* and *the Child and the Curriculum*, new edition. London: The University of Chicago Press.

Grundfest S.E. and Jenisch, D. (1984) 'It all fits together: a case study of citizenship experiences in Upper Valley High School' in Hepburn, M (ed) *Democratic Education in Schools and Classrooms*. Washington DC, National Council for the Social Studies Bulletin No. 70.

Hahn, C. (1984) 'Foreword' in Hepburn, M (ed) (1984) *Democratic Education in Schools and Classrooms*. Washington DC, National Council for the Social Studies Bulletin No. 70.

Hannam, D. (2000) *In this life we want nothing but the facts sir, nothing but the facts. A Democratic Response*. Keynote speech given at annual conference of Elevorganisjonen I Norge (Norwegian school students organisation), March 2000, Sandefjord, Norway. Available on-line at www.forsok.vgs.no/Hannam.htm (full text) and www.forsok.vgs.no/d-schools.htm (appendix)

Hannam, D. (2001) *A Pilot Study to Evaluate the Impact of the Student Participation Aspects of the Citizenship Order on Standards of Education in Secondary Schools*. London: Community Service Volunteers (CSV). Available

Harber, C. (1989) 'Political education and democratic practice', in Harber, C and Meighan, R (eds) *The Democratic School*. Ticknall: Education Now Books.

Harber, C. (ed.) (1995) *Developing Democratic Education*. Ticknall: Education Now Books.

Harber, C. and Meighan, R. (eds) (1989) *The Democratic School*. Ticknall: Education Now Books.

Hepburn, M. (ed) (1984) *Democratic Education in Schools and Classrooms*. Washington DC: National Council for the Social Studies Bulletin No. 70.

Hess, R. and Torney, J. (1967) *The Development of Political Attitudes in Children*. Chicago: Aldine Publishing Co.

Holdsworth, R. (1999) *Thirty-Three Curriculum Approaches: Enhancing Effective Student Participation*. Melbourne: Connect No.116, April 1999.

Holdsworth, R. (2007) *Don't do it ... manage it*. Melbourne: Connect No.163, February 2007.

Huddleston, T. (2007) *From Student Voice to Shared Responsibility: Effective Practice in Democratic School Governance in European Schools*. London: Citizenship Foundation.

Inman, S. and Burke, H. (2002) *Schools Councils: An Apprenticeship in Democracy?* London: Association of Teachers and Lecturers (ATL).

Liègeois, D. (2007) in Bäckman, E and Trafford, B *Democratic Governance of Schools*. Strasbourg: Council of Europe Publishing.

Meighan, R. (1986) *A Sociology of Educating*. London: Cassell.

Neill, AS. (1990) *Summerhill*. new edition. London: Penguin Books.

Polan, A. (1989) 'School: the inevitable democracy?', in Harber, C and Meighan, R (eds) *The Democratic School*. Ticknall: Education Now Books.

Radz, M. (1984) 'The school society: practical suggestions for promoting a democratic school climate', in Hepburn, M (ed.) *Democratic education in schools and classrooms*. Washington DC: National Council for the Social Studies Bulletin No. 70.

Rowe, D. (2003) *The Business of School Councils: An Investigation Into Democracy in Schools*. second edition. London: Citizenship Foundation.

Shotton, J. (1993) *No Master High or Low: Libertarian Education and Schooling in Britain 1890–1990*. Bristol : Libertarian Education

Torney-Purta, J., Lehmann, R., Oswald, H. and Schulz, W. (2001) *Citizenship and Education in Twenty-Eight Countries. Executive Summary*. Amsterdam: International Association for the Evaluation of Educational Achievement (IEA).

Trafford, B. (1993) *Sharing Power in Schools: Raising Standards*. Ticknall: Education Now Books.

Trafford, B. (1994) 'Sharing Power with students: one school's experience', *Citizenship*. 4 (1): 10–12.

Trafford, B. (2003) *School Councils, School Democracy, School Improvement: Why, What, How*. Leicester: Secondary Heads Association.

Trafford, B. (2005) 'School democracy and school improvement', in *Learning for Democracy*, 1 (1):

Trafford, B. (2006) *Raising the Student Voice: A Framework for Effective School Councils*. Leicester: Association of School and College Leaders.

Watts, J. (ed.) (1977) *The Countesthorpe Experience*. London: Allen and Unwin.

Watts, J. (1989) 'Up to a point', in Harber, C and Meighan, R (eds) (1989) *The Democratic School*. Ticknall: Education Now Books.

33

Multicultural Citizenship Education

Paulette Patterson Dilworth

Multicultural citizenship education has been theorized as a transformative education reform effort that seeks to help students from diverse ethnic, racial, and cultural backgrounds experience academic success while developing multicultural civic competence (Freire, 1994). As an educational reform movement, multicultural citizenship education aims to prepare young people with the knowledge and skills necessary for learning, living, and working in a pluralistic democratic society. Education scholars and researchers have written extensively about the benefits of multicultural education for teachers and students. However, it appears that research on students' perspectives of what they learn *about* and *with* multicultural content has not kept pace with the philosophical and theoretical progress in the field. Much of the empirical research on multicultural citizenship education tends to focus on teachers, teaching, and teacher preparation. In education research, few studies exist to explain the ways in which students express their views about what they learn from multicultural content or to clarify students' perspectives on the professed benefits of multicultural citizenship education.

In this chapter, I explore the ways in which young people in the US experience multicultural citizenship education in their social studies classes. I begin with a synthesis of research on content, pedagogy, and classroom climate in diverse classrooms. I then use data collected from interviews with students in two social studies teachers' classes to showcase students' perspectives on their experiences with multicultural content, pedagogical practices, and classroom climate. I conclude by discussing the implications for practice focusing on teachers and teacher education, especially the knowledge and dispositions needed to work effectively with students who are diverse in terms of race, class, and culture.

THE ROLE OF MULTICULTURAL CITIZENSHIP EDUCATION

The research upon which the study builds comprises three distinct but related bodies of literature: citizenship education, multicultural education, and social studies. Drawing on those three literatures, prior research focusing on curriculum content, culturally relevant pedagogy, and classroom climate will be discussed and findings about students' views from one study will be presented.

MULTICULTURAL CITIZENSHIP EDUCATION IN SOCIAL STUDIES

In the US, a primary mission of social studies is to prepare young people for their role as future citizens in a democratic pluralistic society. Multicultural citizenship education refers to a communal task in which students and teachers are challenged to critically examine curriculum content, themselves, and others through different and multiple perspectives (Dilworth, 2004). Broadly defined, multicultural citizenship education is about helping students to acquire the knowledge, skills, and values appropriate to life in an increasingly ethnic diverse global nation-state (Banks, 1997). In this view, multicultural citizenship education redefines traditional notions of citizenship and what it means to be a citizen by moving beyond conventional approaches and definitions such as voting, paying taxes, and obeying the law. Multicultural citizenship education is also concerned with community building through dialogue and deliberation to resolve controversial political issues and social tensions (Marri, 2005). Thus, it seems reasonable to imagine social studies classrooms as ideal sites to advance democratic ideals that are rooted in principles of equality, justice, and liberty. Today, most educators agree that developing multicultural civic competence is integral to education for a diverse citizenry and to the mission of public schools. The preparation of all students for multicultural citizenship includes attention to content for multicultural civic competence and the application of knowledge and skills for 'associated living' (Dewey, 1916).

MULTICULTURAL CIVIC COMPETENCE: KNOWLEDGE, SKILLS, AND DISPOSITIONS

Despite variation in approaches to civic education in the US, a recurrent theme among many scholars is the importance of deliberating about and respecting the nation's social and political history emerging from documents such as the Declaration of Independence, the Bill of Rights, and the Constitution by focusing on principles of liberty, equality, and justice as the guiding vision for democratic life (Patrick, 1999). Other advocates promote developing the capacity and ability of students to think critically (Engle and Ochoa, 1988) to engage with others to deliberate controversial political issues (Hahn, 1991; Hess, 2001), and when necessary to engage in social action to challenge authority and injustice to make society more just (Banks, 1997).

These approaches are not 'mutually exclusive' and to some degree they all advance important knowledge and skills for citizenship. Today, young people will need to move beyond a prescribed set of knowledge and skills. They need participation and social action skills to monitor and influence civic life, including the ability to work well with diverse groups of people. Multicultural civic competence includes personal and intercultural communication skills; knowledge of cultural, social, and political systems; and the ability to critically think about civic and political life among and between diverse groups. Social studies and civic education researchers continue to debate the efficacy of civics education classes in schools to truly increase students' civic competence. Some civic education scholars advocate including civic knowledge, skills, and dispositions as necessary components of citizenship education curriculum.

Multicultural civic competence includes the capacity to analyze and understand the world from multiple historical, social, and political perspectives. Moreover, it recognizes the need for individual and group action to foster and extend equality, justice, and civil rights to others (Banks and Banks, 1997; Bennett, 2006).

Although education scholars and researchers have given much attention to debating about what core civic knowledge and skills should be taught only a few empirical studies have focused on perspectives of students' understanding of diversity and multicultural citizenship education (Cornbleth, 2002, 2003). If multicultural citizenship education is to live up to its promise, the gulf between what content is prescribed and what students ultimately experience must be examined and understood.

For decades educators have been concerned with developing tolerance for diversity. During the 1940s and 1950s, national education organizations such as the Progressive Education Association, the National Council for the Social Studies, and the American Council on Education actively supported school efforts to foster positive intergroup relations (Banks, 1991). Individual scholars suggested that social studies was the subject that offered promise for teaching cross-cultural understanding (Taba, 1955). However, since the 1950s, US schools have made little progress toward implementing programs to address intergroup relations (Banks, 1994) and few researchers have conducted studies of practice.

Although not dealing with ethnic, racial, or gender differences, a few studies have explored the potential of the civic education curriculum to develop in students a willingness to grant rights to people with diverse beliefs. For example, researchers investigated the extent to which adolescents were willing to extend basic human rights to their least-liked sociopolitical groups (Avery, 1992). In this study, adolescents completed questionnaires that measured political tolerance and they were interviewed about their attitudes toward rights for groups they disliked such as the Ku Klux Klan, Neo Nazis, feminists, skinheads, and fundamentalists. Interview results suggested that adolescents

identified as tolerant or intolerant differ in their conceptualizations about dissent and dissenters. Those findings illustrate how in various ways students do possess opinions about diverse groups and the way students view and respond to those groups may influence their attitudes toward citizens' rights in a democracy.

For a variety of reasons, intergroup relations and prejudice reduction programs were never fully integrated into the social studies curriculum in the US (Banks, 1994). Such programs were often superficially treated as part of a special holiday, month, or ritualized exercise. Race, ethnicity, gender, disability, sexual orientation, religion, and social class make intergroup relations complex and complicate the process of teaching about and for a diverse society.

MULTICULTURAL PEDAGOGY

Researchers have explored how core values of the dominant culture represented in schools are often at odds with the way members of a particular group interpret and respond to them (Anyon, 1979; Banks and Banks, 1997; Irvine, 1990; Noddings, 1992). The complexity of characteristics students bring to the classroom challenges teachers to discover ways to help students navigate the home-community-school divide. Multicultural pedagogy is a way of addressing those challenges.

Irvine (1990) advanced the idea of 'cultural synchronization' to characterize the interpersonal nature of the relationship that must exist between the teacher and African American students to facilitate learning. Ladson-Billings (1995) defined 'culturally relevant pedagogy' as a deliberate attempt by teachers to use student culture to transcend the negative effects of the dominant culture while empowering students intellectually, socially, and emotionally. Culturally responsive pedagogy as a concept shares many of the same characteristics as multicultural education.

Banks (1997) defined 'equity pedagogy' as a process by which teachers modify their teaching in ways that facilitate the academic achievement of all students from diverse cultures, races, and genders. Other scholars have advanced similar approaches (Giroux, 1993; Neito, 1994; Sleeter and Grant, 1993). Although these models are not the same, researchers advocating their use agree that teachers must acquire knowledge of the cultures represented in their classroom. Advocates of culturally sensitive models contend that teachers must then translate this knowledge into instructional practice in order to maximize learning opportunities for culturally diverse learners.

Although not using the term 'culturally relevant pedagogy,' several researchers have addressed pedagogy and student diversity in civic education. For example, Bickmore (1993) illustrated the extent to which differing teaching styles contribute to different outcomes for some students. Bickmore studied two social studies teachers' classes in urban school districts populated by ethnically and economically diverse students. The teachers followed the same district guidelines for the course world studies, but they made different choices regarding how to involve their diverse students in classroom instruction. In one class, the students 'learned inclusion' by analyzing teacher-interpreted information about diverse cultures and ideologies. In contrast, the students in the other class were 'included in the learning' by examining conflicting viewpoints related to course topics. The differing ways in which Bickmore's teachers implemented the same curricular guidelines reflected their own interpretations of what is essential to citizenship education. One teacher taught about her interpretation of global cultural diversity while the other teacher engaged her students in the democratic process. However, the first teacher's students learned about inclusion rather than seeing themselves as included in the democratic process.

Merryfield (1992) examined the influence of student characteristics on teacher decision making in middle and high school social studies classes. Although Merryfield focused on global education, her findings have implications for teaching with multicultural content. Merryfield found that the teachers she studied selected content to capitalize on their students' diverse cultural backgrounds. For example, one teacher planned activities to confront stereotypes by paying attention to the insensitivity her students displayed in the classroom. Merryfield's findings indicate that what students learn from multicultural pedagogy is connected, at least in part, to the makeup of the student population.

Hollingsworth et al. (1995) investigated literacy and social studies instruction. Although the focus was primarily on literacy, their attention to concepts such as democracy, equity, power, society, and wealth is insightful for multicultural civic education. The students in an urban eighth-grade world history class had African American, Caucasian, Latino, and Native American backgrounds. In this study, the action researchers sought ways to help students negotiate the literacies of home, school, and community to learn mainstream concepts in social studies. The researchers concluded that by using multiple literacy sources, students' understanding of the concepts of power, equity, wealth, society, and democracy improved. They created what Delpit (1988) refers to as opportunities that acknowledge discourse patterns, interactional styles, and spoken and written language codes, which can contribute to minority student learning.

In general, researchers note that teachers' response to student diversity, such as gender, race, and social class are important to student outcomes. Another researcher investigated the sociocultural context of cooperative learning in a multicultural seventh grade social studies classroom (Santora, 1999). Although the teacher said she desired to create a democratic learning environment, her practice conflicted with her stated goal, pointing to the importance of teacher knowledge about students' cultures and how they make use of that knowledge.

These four qualitative case studies (Bickmore, 1993; Hollingsworth et al., 1995; Merryfield, 1998; Santora, 1999) highlight important considerations about teachers' pedagogy and student characteristics. Although the central focus of these studies was not multicultural civic education per se, the interest in understanding how teachers make connections with students of diverse backgrounds is relevant. It appears that when teachers focus on multicultural content and deliberately connect content or pedagogy to student diversity, student learning or inclusion may be enhanced.

CLASSROOM CLIMATE

Some social studies research that focuses on classroom environments and climates that support controversial issues discussion points to lines of inquiry that are relevant to multicultural citizenship education. In reviewing research on classroom climate in secondary social studies, Harwood (1991) noted that students' perceptions of their teachers' behavior was important. The difference in the relationship between classroom climate variables and student outcomes was distinguished by the students' ethnicity.

In middle and high school classrooms with diverse students, it is likely that the ways in which students respond to instruction with multicultural content may be related to their perceptions of factors related to the classroom management environment. Teaching with multicultural content often requires the introduction of controversial themes and topics which teachers might perceive as creating management problems.

Ehman (1980) defined classroom climate as 'the intersection of teacher behavior and classroom curriculum factors' (p. 108). In the social studies literature, 'classroom climate' is concerned primarily with democratic discourse in the classroom, focusing on the extent to which controversial issues are discussed and the extent to which students feel comfortable expressing different views (See Hess, this volume). Classroom climate has been examined in another body of research that is relevant to the implemented curriculum in social studies. A consistent finding across studies is that open classroom climates encourage student expression of different perspectives, and are more likely to result in students developing more participatory citizenship attitudes than closed classroom climates (Hahn, 1991).

There is some indication that students from different groups may be affected differently by classroom climate. For example, in a quantitative and observational study Ehman (1980) found that classroom climate had differential effects for White and African American students in his study. Open classroom climates increased African American students' political interest and desire to participate in civic activities, but had no effect on White students.

Harwood (1991) also used qualitative and quantitative methods to investigate the impact of classroom climate upon the development of urban high school students' political attitudes in multicultural settings. All of the students in the open climate classrooms Harwood studied were African Americans, while in the closed climate classrooms there was a mix of African American, Asian, Caucasian, and Hispanic students. The students who perceived their classes recalled more discussion and interaction than did their peers. In contrast, students who perceived their classes as closed reported more instances of worksheets and individual seat work. Additionally, many of the students reported that the media, their parents, and their own political experiences were important influences on their attitudes toward politics.

The findings from research reviewed in this section suggest that a variety of factors may influence the instructional choices teachers make related to pedagogy and multicultural content integration in the social studies in general. Such factors include teachers' conceptions and approach to theorizing about curriculum and instruction, teachers' response to the diverse characteristics students bring to the classroom, and factors related to controversial issues discussion and classroom climate. It is possible that, due to the controversial nature of certain multicultural content, teachers will implement it differently than other aspects of the social studies or citizenship curriculum.

The research reviewed for this chapter suggests that content, pedagogy, and classroom climate are associated with complex outcomes for multicultural citizenship education. At the same time, scholars acknowledge that, because of changing demographics, multicultural perspectives are necessary for teaching and learning. Unfortunately, beyond concluding that some groups of students score higher than others on various measures, researchers have given scant attention to multicultural content and its relationship to pedagogy, classroom climate, and student outcomes in citizenship education. In the next section, I discuss one study that explored how students perceived those variables.

A STUDY OF MULTICULTURAL CITIZENSHIP EDUCATION

In culturally, ethnically, and linguistically diverse urban schools what do students perceive they are learning about multicultural citizenship education? That question is the focus of my study, which was part of a larger case study that also examined teacher perspectives, classroom observations, and a student survey. I purposefully selected schools with diverse student populations and within those schools, two teachers were nominated as strong multicultural social studies teachers. For the aspect of the study reported here, I then asked the teachers to nominate students from their classes that represented differing abilities to participate in focus group interviews. The resulting sample of students that I interviewed contained three male and eight female students; five 8th graders and six 11th graders; four African American, three white; two Latino, and one Asian, and one multiracial student (For a full description of methods of data collection and analysis, see Dilworth, 2004).

The research setting

The two schools that were the sites for this study are located in an urban school district in a southeastern state. The schools, Pierson High School and Ashton Middle School (pseudonyms) are affected by cultural, political, and social diversity in the community. Both schools are well regarded by parents, students, community leaders, and district administrators.

The two teachers who were the focus of case studies in the larger study (Dilworth, 2004) were well regarded by their colleagues, district staff, students, and parents. Troy Kirby teaches 11th grade US history at Pierson and Keith Berry teaches 8th grade State history at Ashton (teacher and student names are pseudonyms). Both teachers were considered to be veterans, having taught about 20 years each, and both hoped their students would gain valuable knowledge and skills relating to multicultural citizenship education. Indeed, observations of the two teachers' classes confirmed that they both had clear academic goals for teaching with multicultural content.

Students' views about teaching and learning multicultural citizenship

For the most part, Mr. Kirby and Mr. Berry were well regarded by their students. According to the students I interviewed, both teachers demonstrated a great deal of caring for and commitment to the personal and academic success of their students. In turn, students viewed the teachers as among the 'best' in their schools. Interestingly, the lived experiences of both teachers predisposed them to being multi-cultural civic educators. The manner in which the teachers created open class-room climates was important to promoting students' positive perceptions of their teaching and learning experiences. Also, because both teachers were so well regarded by their students, at times, it was difficult to separate climate factors from their indi-vidual teaching styles. In the sections that follow, I provide examples to illustrate what was learned from students about their experiences with multicultural citizenship education.

Multicultural content

Students were asked to share their percep-tions about what they learned about and their attitudes toward multicultural content in their classes. Although some students expressed disinterest in many of the topics covered, most of the students thought the discussions about multicultural content were very inter-esting and that they learned a great deal from those lessons. All of the students said they learned about the Civil Rights Movement, immigration, women's rights, discrimination, and cultural differences. Typical of their comments were these:

> We are covering everything from when people founded the U.S., people that came before, people from Europe. We talked about Native Americans, the people who were here first. We talked about the people coming here from Europe like Columbus and then Ponce de León. And then how the English came to Virginia (Carlos, Mexican American male).

> We are studying the immigrants coming over from Europe. We have moved through the Civil War and Reconstruction Era. Lately, we have been talking about Black Codes and Jim Crow laws and all the discrimination that happened in the late 1800s and early 1900s (Sharon, white female).

> We just finished studying the women's movement and I like to study what happened to the people during the wars. I think the reasons for the Civil War were interesting. Everyone wanted power. I like the human aspect of the whole thing (Evelyn, African American female).

> In the Progressivism topic we learned about civil rights and how some presidents had a part in it. In the last couple of classes we talked about Woodrow Wilson and Roosevelt (Shawn, African American male).

The students in Mr. Kirby's classes were precise in describing the topics they under-stood as multicultural content. Consistently, students made reference to details about events and concepts like discrimination, slav-ery, immigration, and political movements. Two students identified multicultural content by describing historical events they viewed as specific to their heritage. A Spanish-speaking student, Carlos, described what he considered to be multicultural content specific to a Mexican heritage:

> We talked about Native Americans and how they were forced to give up their land to the Europeans. We've talked about the Spanish exploration and Ponce de León. I guess I think about the cultural clashes more than anything else. I enjoyed talking about the cultural clashes. They define me a lot.

An African American female explained her understanding of multicultural content by describing events leading to the Civil War, making connections to content that she thought defined her heritage:

> When we covered the Civil War, we talked about the slavery of Black people. We looked at slavery and the reasons why the people from the North and people from the South could not get rid of slavery without a war. We also talked about the Emancipation Proclamation and how some people think that Abraham Lincoln agreed to abolish slavery. I think he did it [signed the Proclamation] because he was trying to hold the country together. We talked about the reasons for the Civil War a lot. I like the discussion we have about Black history and they are always interesting to me.

In addition to describing the multicultural content covered in their classes, students were unanimous in their perceptions of what they learned about these topics. Students expressed agreement about the manner in which they were able to openly discuss their views about the topics in class. Almost all the students said that they learned more about multicultural issues when they had the opportunity to go beyond what was presented in the textbook.

Several students credited their teachers with 'knowing a lot about the different topics and people' covered in their classes. These students also expressed positive views about the ways in which Mr. Berry and Mr. Kirby set the tone for class discussions.

> One topic I remember is the civil rights movement. We've talked about people like Martin Luther King, Jr. and Rosa Parks and Black people's struggle for equal rights. We have studied the women's rights movement and how women in [the state] were a part of the fight for better opportunities for women (Shelby, African American female).

> I liked the lessons we had on Native Americans. Mr. Berry knows a lot about the history of Native Americans. So when we were covering them he told us some interesting stories about their religion and how they were really the first people to live in our state. Some of them, like the Woodland Indians were real creative (Martha White Female).

> The most important thing I remember that we talked about was the civil rights movement. Mr. Berry helped us to see that people were really divided about equal rights for Blacks and for women. I remember once we had a very heated discussion about civil rights and students in my class were angry. Some of the Black students were very upset because some White students didn't get it that racism is still around us (Jason, African American male).

> I think we've talked about a lot of different people. We just finished discussing W. E. B. DuBois and Booker T. Washington. We had to compare their beliefs about equality (Tosha, African American female).

The students in Mr. Berry's classes agreed that Mr. Berry shared a great deal of information about multicultural topics that was not covered in their textbook. All the students who were interviewed said that they appreciated the opportunity to learn about cultural differences.

Students were asked to share an example of a time where they were able to use what they learned with multicultural content outside the classroom. Helena stated that discussing controversial issues was a good learning experience for her and she was able to diffuse an argument between several of her friends using what she learned in Mr. Kirby's class. She also wanted her friends to understand how men and women may have different perspectives about some issues.

Students clearly understood that multicultural content was included in their social studies lessons. During the interviews, students tended to describe particular events and concepts by elaborating on the contributions made by various ethnic groups.

Classroom climate and culturally relevant pedagogy

The effects of classroom climate on students' attitudes were felt almost immediately upon entering the classrooms. In each teacher's classes students exhibited positive behavior and refrained from engaging in disruptive actions. Both teachers attempted to make their classroom a thoughtful place by demonstrating through their actions that they valued and welcomed students' originality and differences of opinion. The students in Mr. Kirby's classes seemed to develop a trust in his teaching and they believed that Mr. Kirby respected them and cared about their success. Carlos, a Spanish-speaking student, appreciated his teacher's ability to listen:

> Mr. Kirby listens to students and he doesn't just say what he feels. He listens to us, and he pushes us to think about the issues and to question other people's ideas. At times, he will make you think about how other people feel. It makes you think about a lot of different things.

A White female was the most outspoken of the six students I interviewed from Mr. Kirby's classes. Sharon, who described herself as having attention deficit disorder, indicated that at times she felt her learning disability caused some students to react negatively to her comments when she participated in class discussions. Yet she said that she was comfortable with the fact that some students reacted to her in this manner, crediting Mr. Kirby with creating an atmosphere that was supportive of her and other students who might be intimidated by the intensity of the discussions. In commenting on how she perceived Mr. Kirby's actions she said:

> Sometimes Mr. Kirby forces us to participate. Because we are graded on our participation I guess

that's a good thing for him to do. He will sit there and let people talk and if other students are quiet. He will call on them. Like, Jack what is your view on this topic? What do you think about what Sharon just said? Or the statement that Clare made, do you agree with her? He will ask you questions to make you think.

Sharon was sensitive to the fact that some students did not participate because they were not comfortable speaking out in class. She thought that Mr. Kirby expressed a great deal of concern for the well being of all students.

Another student added that she thought that the classroom climate was open because of Mr. Kirby's respect for them. Evelyn, an African American female, said that Mr. Kirby was 'much better' than other social studies teachers she had encountered:

Mr. Kirby lets us know his limits. But he also respects us. In his class we can relate to his jokes. Mr. Kirby is a teacher that you can have a good relationship with but not necessarily disrespectful. I like the fact that we can talk to him about anything. I talked to him about some problems I had in another teacher's class. He was very concerned and was willing to help me clear up the misunderstanding with the teacher. Sometimes he jokes about things and plays with us about the topics. I like the way he keeps the class straight and people respect him. We can't do that with some teachers.

Other students thought that Mr. Kirby's approach was exceptional when they compared his teaching style to other social studies teachers. The students thought that Mr. Kirby's style of interacting with them was friendly and respectful. All of the students described experiences that drew on their knowledge of what they viewed as good and bad experiences in the classroom. Helena, who stated that her mother is Korean and her father is Black, was impressed by Mr. Kirby's knowledge of history. She thought that Mr. Kirby was a unique teacher and described her perceptions of him by stating:

Mr. Kirby has the tendency to make you feel like you can speak whatever is on your mind. There are a lot of students in our class who don't bite their tongues. They say a lot of things that may offend people sometimes but Mr. Kirby allows it to open our minds. He lets us speak whatever we want to say, even if its going to offend some people. But he

also brings us to the light and lets you know that what you're saying is not right. But he does it with a lot of care and respect. It's really hard to describe how he does it.

At times, Helena was very animated in expressing her views about the classroom climate. At one point when I asked her to describe the classroom atmosphere when controversial issues were being discussed she stated: 'We get live.' I asked her to explain, she said that everybody wants to participate, especially if they disagree with a statement or comments.

Overall, students' perceptions about the classroom climate were very positive. Students expressed positive views about the multicultural content, and Mr. Kirby's use of discussion to facilitate student participation. When students were asked to make suggestions for Mr. Kirby to improve his teaching some students thought he was doing a good job. Some students said that they would like to have the opportunity to do more projects. Shawn, an African American male, said that Mr. Kirby should 'slow down on the teaching,' that in covering some multicultural content they moved through the topics too fast. He also thought that including more information about culture might help some of the Asian students participate in the discussions.

The students who were interviewed from Mr. Berry's classes viewed Mr. Berry as a 'very good' teacher. They thought that Mr. Berry was exceptional in allowing students to express their opinion about issues. In describing the class discussions when they focused on multicultural content, Shelby an African American female said:

Everyday we have discussions about any and everything. It doesn't have to be just history. Sometimes we talk about discrimination and racism and one topic leads to another. Sometimes we get off the subject, but Mr. Berry has a way of showing us how things connect to what we are covering in the book. Mr. Berry really gets into the discussion with us and I like that he does.

Another student said that she thought Mr. Berry did a good job of showing them how to be considerate of the opinions expressed by other students. When asked to describe what Mr. Berry does that makes students feel comfortable expressing their opinion, Martha, a white female stated:

> I think because he just lets them talk. I guess he sees that some things are really heated issues and by some students saying what they have to say and get it off their chest is going to help them out in the long run. So he just kind of sits back and makes sure that nobody gets too loud or says anything inappropriate and lets everybody talk.

Overall, the students in Mr. Berry's classes perceptions of the classroom climate were positive. Although several students thought that Mr. Berry's classes were very structured, they seemed to appreciate his orderly approach to instruction. The students' were unanimous in their agreement that Mr. Berry held high expectations for their performance in his classes.

CONCLUSIONS

This chapter focused on understanding how students in culturally, ethnically, and linguistically diverse urban middle and high schools perceive their experiences with multicultural citizenship education in their social studies classes. Researchers have shown that many students are alienated, uninvolved, and discouraged by schools and social studies classes (Bickmore, 1993; Fine, 1993; Hollingsworth et al., 1995). However, in this study, students expressed appreciation for the multicultural content covered in their social studies classes. Importantly, the manner in which the two teachers implemented content, pedagogy, and classroom climate supported students' affirmative perceptions of teaching and learning. Further, students who perceived that their teachers respected and cared about their opinions were engaged in learning about multicultural content.

Fine (1993) found that although controversial political issues might be perceived as problematic in the classroom, students are able to handle controversy and related activities and discussions can be constructive. The results in this study support Fine's findings that students can be flexible and handle disagreement. Students are very aware of political controversy in the larger society and appreciate the opportunity to openly express their views in the classroom. A final finding is that teachers who are sensitive to the diverse characteristics of learners are more likely to encourage student engagement.

During their interviews students confirmed a clear understanding that their teachers were interested in helping students develop knowledge about the multicultural nature of national history. Some students made the connection that at the same time, the teachers hoped that by including multicultural content in history lessons students would be able to make connections to their own lives.

The student interviews were useful for understanding how students experienced their teachers' pedagogical practices. For the students in this study, it appears that the teachers played an important role in making the difference. Mr. Kirby and Mr. Berry both worked out interesting ways to engage their students with multicultural content.

Although the teachers in this study attempted to balance the emotional and cognitive components of the learning process they were often challenged by the presence of diversity in their classes. For example, both teachers indicated that the presence of some non-English speaking students created a pedagogical dilemma. In particular, both teachers noted the presence of several Asian and Hispanic students in their classes and their efforts to overcome the language barrier.

The themes of incorporating personal experience in the classroom, culturally responsive pedagogy, and taking a critical stance to knowledge emerged from the qualitative findings of this study. Student perspectives on the teachers' practice depicted them helping their students develop a multicultural understanding of history. The teachers hoped that by using a variety of approaches to teaching with multicultural content students would become engaged in the learning process. For these teachers it was important to place their students' daily lives at the center of their teaching. In doing so, the teachers hoped that students would connect their personal lives to what they learned about history.

In this study the teachers used a variety of instructional methods that included lectures, whole class discussion, small groups, simulations, current events, and individual projects. The teachers viewed these methods of instruction as the safest and most respectful approach to engage students with multicultural content. These veteran teachers attempted to be reflective in their practice and their use of multicultural content. Both teachers recognized and acknowledged that the presence of diverse students in their classes required they make use of culturally responsive pedagogical strategies.

The teachers attempted to draw from the concrete and personal experiences of their students as the basis for imparting knowledge about multicultural content. Both teachers attempted to use sufficient time to help students process sources of contradiction and confusion emerging from students' personal experiences and multicultural content. As veteran teachers, Mr. Kirby and Mr. Berry made explicit use of their personal experiences to explain complex aspects of particular topics and themes. For example, when teaching about issues relating to social justice, both teachers relied on their personal knowledge and experiences to explain and clarify particular aspects of the topic.

During their interviews students were asked to explain how their teachers' practice affected how they participated in class. Observations of the two teachers' classes, interviews with students, and results from a student questionnaire confirmed that the two teachers attempted to foster open climates to support discussions of controversial issues. Across the two cases, classroom climate appears to be the most powerful determinant of students' positive perceptions about their classroom experiences in general. Students

shared positive comments about what occurred in their social studies classes. Interestingly, students were unanimous in their agreement that although they often had heated discussions related to some multicultural topics they were comfortable with the controversy.

Students were also asked to describe what they liked and disliked most about the class activities. In general, most students who were interviewed gave positive responses to those questions. However, female students were more communicative in their responses than male students. Throughout the two months of observations, in both teachers' classes, female students were more communicative than male students. During classroom observations, female students tended to dominate class discussions. However, male and female students appeared to be equally communicative during discussions about some controversial issues. For example, during a discussion about the civil rights movement and women's rights, male and female students participated equally. During their interviews, female students were also able to provide greater details about their perceptions of specific teaching behaviors. For example, several female students said they liked the open discussions that occurred in their classes. During the interviews, two male students tended to perceive that not all students have an equal chance to express their opinion about other cultures and groups. During their interviews, two male middle school students said that in their classes female students tended to dominate the class discussions. Observations of Mr. Berry's classes revealed that male students seemed to accept what the teacher did as a matter of routine whereas female students were more likely to raise questions.

In general, the students' responses in this study support the findings of previous studies that students who perceive their classroom climate as open have positive attitudes about their learning experiences. For the students in this study, the manner in which the teachers created open classroom climates fostered meaningful learning experiences. Both teachers who participated in the case studies had developed distinctive teaching styles, and those teaching styles helped to shape students positive perceptions of the classroom climate. For the students in this study, the manner in which the teachers created open classroom climates fostered powerful learning experiences. As noted earlier, both teachers attempted to establish a classroom climate in which students felt comfortable expressing their views.

Implications for practice

Realizing that this study focused on only two teachers' classes in one school district on one country, it is important to replicate this study to determine if similar results would be found elsewhere. If replications yield similar findings then there are several implications for practice. The findings of this study support earlier research that suggests open classroom climates foster students' positive attitudes about their experiences. There are implications for social studies teacher educators, curriculum supervisors, and professional development staff who are interested in improving the effectiveness of citizenship education.

Helping students become effective multicultural citizens is a challenge because of the increasing changes occurring in our global society. Multicultural education advocates stress the importance of teachers helping students develop multicultural knowledge and understanding as essential to effective citizenship participation. The findings from the case studies suggest that more work is needed to bridge the gap between multicultural theory and classroom practice. Social studies and citizenship teacher education and professional development programs must begin to recognize and address the gap between multicultural theory and practice. Teacher education and professional development programs could benefit from a more expanded view of multicultural education to help preserve and in-service teachers develop transformative and social action approaches to teaching.

The implications of the case examples focusing on student perspectives stress the important role of teachers in fostering a classroom climate that supports academic engagement for all students. Students enrolled in the case study teachers' classes are in some ways fortunate. They have the good fortune to be taught by teachers who believe that multicultural content is important to teaching and learning. It appears that those students are able to have meaningful discussions about multicultural issues in classrooms that welcome and value their opinion. More important, the teachers included multicultural content as the basis for helping students develop a multicultural perspective about the history of their communities, state, and nation. It can be concluded from the case studies of the two teachers that their success is due in part to their attitude and their beliefs about teaching and the importance of integrating multicultural content in the social studies curriculum. Some educators advocate selecting pre-service teachers who have the prior experience and attitudes necessary to teach in multicultural classrooms. Other educators believe that teachers can develop the open and responsive temperament needed to be effective with all students. Teacher education programs need to consider the personal qualities of students preparing to teach in multicultural classrooms. Professional development programs need to consider the personal qualities of in-service teachers and develop ways to help them foster responsive attitudes in multicultural classrooms. Teacher preparation programs and in-service professional development programs need to give more attention to helping teachers understand the factors that support open classroom climates with diverse students.

Civic educators and researchers continue to stress the importance of students attaining multicultural civic competence to help foster the capacity of young people to become effective citizens in pluralistic democratic societies. Embedded within this expectation is the desire to have social studies/citizenship teachers who have a deep understanding of the relationship between diversity and democracy. Collaborative efforts between social studies researchers, teacher educators, curriculum supervisors, and teachers may begin the process leading to the implementation of a multicultural citizenship education curriculum that is effective for all students.

REFERENCES

Anyon, J. (1979) 'Education, Social Structure, and the Power of Individuals', *Theory and Research in Social Education*, 7 (1): 40–55.

Avery, P.G. (1992) 'Adolescents, Civic Tolerance, and Human Rights', *Social Education*, 52 (?): 534–537.

Banks, J.A., and Banks, C.A. (eds.) (1997) *Multicultural Education* (3rd ed.). Boston: Allyn & Bacon.

Banks, J.A. (1997) *Educating Citizens in a Multicultural Society*. New York: Teachers College Press.

Bennett, C.A. (2006) *Comprehensive Multicultural Education: Theory and Practice* (6th ed.). New York: Allyn and Bacon.

Bickmore, K. (1993) 'Learning Inclusion\Inclusion in Learning: Citizenship Education for a Pluralistic Society', *Theory and Research in Social Education*, 21 (4): 341–384.

Cornbleth, C. (2003) *Hearing America's Youth: Social Identities in Uncertain Times*. New York: Peter Lang.

Cornbleth, C. (2002) 'Images of America: What youth DO know about the United States', *American Educational Research Journal*, 39 (2): 519–552.

Delpit, L. (1988) 'The Silenced Dialogue: Power and Pedagogy in Educating Other People's Children', *Harvard Educational Review*, 58 (3): 280–298.

Dewey, J. (1916) *Democracy and Education: An Introduction to the Philosophy of Education*. New York: Macmillan Company.

Dilworth, P.P. (2004) 'Multicultural Citizenship Education: Case Studies from Social Studies Classrooms', *Theory and Research in Social Education*, 32 (2): 153–186.

Ehman, L.H. (1980) 'Change in High School Students' Political Attitudes as a Function of Social Studies Classroom Climate', *American Educational Research Journal*, 17 (2): 253–265.

Engle, S.H. and Ochoa, A.S. (1988) *Education for Democratic Citizenship: Decision Making in the Social Studies*. New York: Teachers College Press.

Freire, P. (1994) *Pedagogy of Hope*. New York: Continuum Publishing.

Gay, G. (1997) 'The Relationship Between Multicultural Education and Democratic Education', *Social Studies*, 88 (1): 5–11.

Giroux, H.A. (1993) *Living Dangerously: Multiculturalism and the Politics of Difference*. New York: Peter Lang Publishing.

Hahn, C.L. (1991) 'Controversial Issues in Social Studies', in James P. Shaver (ed.), *Handbook of Research on Social Studies Teaching and Learning*. New York: Macmillan. pp. 45–64.

Harwood, A.M. (1991) *Social Studies Classroom Climates and Students' Political Attitudes: Views from Three High School Civics Classes*. Unpublished doctoral dissertation, Emory University, Atlanta, Georgia.

Hess, D. (2001) 'Teaching to Public Controversy in a Democracy', in James J. Patrick and Robert S. Leming (eds.) *Principles and Practices of Democracy in the Education of Social Studies Teachers*. Bloomington, IN: ERIC Clearinghouse for Social Studies/Social Science, Education. pp. 87–109.

Hollingsworth, S., Gallego, M., and Standerford, N.S. (1995) 'Integrative Social Studies for Urban Middle Schools: A Case for Multiple Literacies', *Theory and Research in Social Education*, 23 (3): 204–233.

Irvine, J.J. (1990) *Black Students and School Failure*. Westport, CT: Greenwood Press.

Ladson-Billings, G. (1995) 'But that's Good Teaching! The Case for Culturally Relevant Pedagogy', *Theory Into Practice*, 34 (3): 159–165.

Marri, A. (2005) Building a Framework for Classroom-based Multicultural Democratic Education (CMDE): Learning from three skilled teachers. *Teachers College Record*, 107 (5):1036–1059.

Merryfield, M. (1998) 'Pedagogy for Global Perspectives in Education: Studies of Teachers' Thinking and Practice', *Theory and Research in Social Education*, 26 (3): 342–379.

Neito, S. (1994) 'Moving Beyond Tolerance in Multicultural Education', *Multicultural Education*, 1 (4): 9–12.

Noddings, N. (1992) 'Social Studies and Feminism', *Theory and Research in Social Education*, 20 (3): 230–241.

Patrick, J.J. (1999) 'Concepts at the Core of Education for Democratic Citizenship', in C.F. Bahmueller and John J. Patrick (eds.), *Principles and Practices of Education for Democratic Citizenship*. Bloomington, IN: ERIC Clearinghouse for Social Studies/Social Science, Education. pp. 1–40.

Sleeter, C.E. and Grant, C.A. (1993) *Making Choices for Multicultural Education: Five Approaches to Race, Class, and Gender* (2nd edn). New York: Merrill.

Taba, H. (1955) *Curriculum Intergroup Relations: Case studies in Instruction*. Washington, DC: American Council on Education.

34

Peace and Conflict Education

Kathy Bickmore

All education regulated by nation-states is, in one sense, education for some kind of 'peace.' In the liberal 'social contract' tradition, the purpose of any government is to protect citizens from violence, as a prerequisite for their individual pursuit of well-being (Henderson, 2006). Collectively, citizens (defense, security) serve as justification for – and (through taxation) funders of – military spending and deployment (Franklin, 2006a). Governments have had a monopoly on the legitimate use of force in order to serve as security guarantors. Further, governments since the nineteenth century have had a virtual monopoly on 'legitimate education' (Gellner, cited in Tawil and Harley, 2004), used to create and maintain a sense of shared national identity and social cohesion among their citizens. Thus citizenship education has always had ramifications for peace and conflict, both domestic and international. This chapter does not ask *whether* citizenship education should include peace and conflict education. Rather, it examines *how* implicit and explicit citizenship education in schools already does teach about peace and conflict, and *what kinds* of citizenship education about peace and conflict would be most fruitful for developing and sustaining inclusively pluralistic, democratic peace.

CONTEXTS FOR LEARNING CONFLICT AND VIOLENCE

The broad social and technological changes of postmodern globalization have influenced the quality and quantity of naturally-occurring social interaction among young citizen peers, especially in the relatively affluent West (Franklin, 2006b). For example, instant mass communication and homogenized popular culture, wide use of personal computers, and the increasingly prespecified curricula of public schools have all tended to reduce the time most young people spend interacting with one another, face to face, in unprogrammed and unmonitored ways. Many social learning and engagement opportunities that, in the past, might have occurred implicitly in the lives of young people, are now absent (or damaging) in the social fabric. Further, mass communications have made the resource gap between rich and poor, and the associated 'ingenuity gaps,' appallingly obvious to those experiencing relative deprivation, thereby exacerbating global conflict and violence (Homer-Dixon, 2000). Thus the burgeoning interest in social skills, conflict resolution and peacemaking, and tolerance as part of citizenship education is both understandable and paradoxical.

Public schools face demands for short-term safety and accountability (achieved through control), and at the same time for longer-term sustainable and democratic security (achieved through empowerment of communication among diverse citizens, community-building, and learning constructive conflict management). Understandably, schools tend to be pre-occupied with order and control – often to the detriment of students' learning. Highly controlled school and classroom environments tend to reduce diverse students' opportunities to practice self-direction and social conflict management (Schimmel, 1997; Tjosvold, 1995). Many schools have moved to fill this gap, through infusion of explicit conflict- and peace-related lessons and through facilitation of interactive, student-centred activity structures in classrooms.

Public schools are natural arenas for conflict. They may attract contestation and attack because they represent the government, for example in Sudan, Bosnia-Herzegovina, and Colombia (Williams, 2004). Selections and silences in curriculum content, evaluations, or language of instruction often foster or reproduce destructive social conflict. For example, students in the Turkish and Greek sectors of Cyprus are each taught national chauvinist and exclusionary historical narratives about the other side (Harber, 2004). Further, schools may implicitly or explicitly condone violent behaviour, such as sexual imposition or homophobic harassment, among students and/or educators (Bickmore, 2002). For example, one study reports that 20 per cent of school-aged girls in the US report having been sexually abused, and 80 per cent report having been sexually harassed, many of them in school (Sadker, 1999: 24). Another study reports an almost overwhelming climate of sexual violence in schools in some parts of Africa (Leach, 2003). While disruptive school violence garners substantial attention, the 'quiet' dropouts resulting from sexual imposition persist with barely a ripple.

The visible tip of the social conflict iceberg is direct, physical violence – interpersonal,

intercommunal, and international. Most armed conflicts in this century occur within states, between so-called 'ethnic' identity groups (Ware et al., 2005). Rape and other gender-based violence increase in contexts of war, but virtually never disappear even from otherwise peaceful contexts (Davies, 2004). This subjugation of half the human race is still remarkably invisible, condoned in popular culture and ignored by many peace activists and citizenship educators, among others. Yet as feminist theory has made clear, sexual domination is inextricable from patterns of personal and social violence: '... if we can't stop rape in one fraternity house on one campus, there is not even a glimmer of hope for global peace' (Johnson, 1987: 243–244). Caprioli (2000), for example, demonstrates a clear correlation between nation-states' military involvement and domestic gender equality. Gender-based violence, and the hierarchy of domination it supports, highlights the complex linkage between interpersonal behaviour and large-scale social patterns and institutions.

Physical violence is itself a threat to democracy, and also a visible clue that there is something further wrong underneath, causing and reinforcing this violence. Norwegian peace studies scholar Johan Galtung (1969) defines inequitable social structures that reproduce harms such as poverty and marginalization, and cause much physical violence, as 'structural violence.' The embedded systems of norms and beliefs, including sexism, that accept and normalize such subjugation and violence are 'cultural violence' (Galtung, 1996). Marc Howard Ross (1993) has studied these 'two faces of conflict' in many different cultures, finding that both tangible interests (fulfilled or impeded by social structures and institutions) and psychocultural beliefs (fears, interpretations, and narratives) contribute to escalation of conflicts, threats, and violence.

Galtung further distinguishes 'negative peace' (absence of physical violence) from 'positive peace' (presence of institutions and relationships to redress structural and cultural violence and handle conflicts nonviolently). *Peacekeeping* can create negative peace temporarily by controlling violence, but it does not resolve the problems causing the violence. Due to an emphasis on peacekeeping control, schools are generally safer from physical violence than the communities surrounding them (Akiba et al., 2003). However, their major contribution is not as fortresses, but as social and educational centers that address (or uncritically reinforce) the problems that underlie such violence. Positive peace, in contrast, is a complex, long-range goal that implies resourcefulness. It requires both *peacemaking* (negotiation and problem-solving to identify creative, mutually acceptable resolutions to conflicts) and *peacebuilding* (long-term development of complex social institutions for overcoming exploitation and dehumanization). Negative and positive peace have ramifications for learning: '[Escalated, violent] conflict tends to reduce people's willingness to learn, as well as what might be called agency – the capacity of individuals, families, communities and systems to care for themselves. Conflict tends to reduce openness to new ideas ...' (Williams, 2004: 478). Consequently, schools can attract both direct and systemic violence, which can impede democratic learning, inclusion, and citizen agency.

At the same time, there remains across the world a widely shared hopefulness that, despite or because of the above challenges, schools also can be part of the solution, a crucial component of building equitable, sustainable peace (Nkomo et al., 2007; Tawil and Harley, 2004). Education can help citizens become aware of the nature and extent of particular social conflicts and their negative consequences especially for weaker parties, and can develop skills, efficacy, and understanding of alternative possibilities for change (Curle et al., 1974). Such peace and conflict education is an essential part of critical and active approaches to citizenship education. Schools are one major locus for citizenship learning about conflict and peace. There is no neutral space: Schools conduct this peace and conflict education in the context of the structural and physical violence that surrounds and infiltrates them.

IMPLICIT PEACE AND CONFLICT LEARNING: ANTI-VIOLENCE INITIATIVES

Young people learn citizen behaviour by witnessing and participating in the ways conflict and violence are handled in schools, communities, and popular media. Youth violence rates are actually stable or slightly decreasing, at least in Canada and the US (Doob and Cesaroni, 2004). Nonetheless, there is widespread coverage and fear about youth violence, resulting in increasingly punitive *responses* to youth infractions. In the US, increasing numbers of nonviolent and first-time offender youth are routed into the adult punishment system and incarcerated; this was also true in Canada, until the 2003 Youth Criminal Justice Act. Severe punishments are imposed, inside and outside schools, for defiance, drug, or property offenses, *not* necessarily for violence (re: schools, see Bickmore, 2004).

Students in the same school may have very different conflict learning experiences. Poor and visible minority males are often most harshly and disproportionately punished (Adams, 2000; Jull, 2000; McCadden, 1998; Verdugo, 2002). Meanwhile, bias-based and gender-based aggression are often ignored by typical school conflict management practices (Bergsgaard, 1997; Conrad, 2006; Gewertz, 2006; Mishna et al., 2005).

Strict anti-violence policies, sometimes called 'zero tolerance,' are implemented in a wide range of ways (Dunbar and Villarrue, 2004). When school discipline emphasizes restriction, punishment, and exclusion of certain students (complicated by racism and other bias), these policies can damage relationships and destroy the human rights climate for learning (Noguera, 1995; Osler and Starkey, 1998). In contrast, where standards for nonviolent behaviour are communicated clearly and implemented equitably through a broad repertoire of restorative conflict management practices, strict consequences for serious violent behaviour may form a defensible part of an effective anti-violence system (Claassen and Claassen, 2004; Skiba et al., 2004). Clearly, students would have different opportunities to learn and practice citizenship in an equitable, nonviolent climate than in a repressive, violent one.

Rigorous meta-analyses of anti-violence initiatives substantiate the effectiveness of explicit programs of instruction and practice that facilitate young people's development of social and cognitive competence, respect and tolerance across differences, inclusion of marginalized students, and opportunities to build engagement and strong relationships (Catalano et al., 2002; Erickson and McGuire, 2004; Hazler and Carney, 2002; Scheckner et al., 2002). Programs emphasizing peer-oriented conflict resolution appear to be at least as effective as other kinds of violence prevention (Skiba, 2000). While well-implemented, high-quality programming with the above characteristics is reliably effective, many violence prevention initiatives actually implemented are of lower quality and/or not fully sustained (e.g. Crosse et al., 2002). Thus there are demonstrative, effective ways of improving negative peace in schools, which would teach implicitly about conflict management and establish climates for learning: however, what is typically implemented in schools does not approach that standard.

TOWARD POSITIVE PEACE: PEACEMAKING AND EDUCATIONAL INITIATIVES

Learning may be facilitated in every phase of the conflict cycle, to radically reduce the need for punitive security interventions:

- *Before* harm is done, through implementing fair classroom and school management practices, developing inclusive community relationships,

and teaching conflict management and anti-discriminatory concepts and skills;
- *During* interventions to handle conflicts that emerge, through modeling and guiding thoughtful, respectful, and equitable dialogic conflict resolution processes; and
- *After* harm is done, through restorative justice practices to repair relationships and resolve problems causing conflict, and re-establishing cross-cutting social ties.

Social and political problems, controversies and sensitive issues, as well as interpersonal disputes and intergroup frictions, can be addressed in ways that offer (or deny) constructive guided opportunities to learn.

In general terms, educational initiatives called 'conflict resolution' or social-emotional learning have emphasized interpersonal conflicts and communication, while initiatives called 'peace education' or global education have emphasized citizen engagement with social and political issues on a societal and/or transnational scale (Deutsch, 2001; Harris and Morrison, 2003; Iram, 2003; Salomon and Nevo, 2002). Many initiatives blend elements of each. It is not surprising that interpersonal conflict resolution initiatives (which tend to avoid confronting controversial issues, and to reinforce the governability of students) often have received more support from school and district administrations. However, both streams of work have had evident influence on mandated curriculum guidelines in many jurisdictions (Bickmore, 2005), and also on many international aid initiatives in war-torn regions (e.g. Bretherton et al., 2003; UNICEF, 2002).

The most widely researched type of conflict resolution education initiative is peer mediation, which includes actual intervention to manage conflicts as well as development of awareness and skills through guided practice (Association for Conflict Resolution, 2006). Here, tangible responsibility for negotiating their own concerns with peers is delegated to students. Peer mediation programs may operate in the co-curriculum or in regular classrooms. Most school-based mediation programs use a 'cadre' approach to peer mediation: A small group of students are trained to work as a peer leadership team, and provide the mediation service in their own schools. Less frequently, some programs train whole classes to handle conflict and to take turns acting as mediators. Teams of peer mediators that represent diverse social, cultural, and gender identities and achievement levels improve the sustainability and effectiveness of mediation programs as compared to more elite student teams (Bickmore, 2001; Day-Vines et al., 1996). Such youth leadership approaches to peer mediation have spread widely, because they involve low cost and require minimal organizational change. However, they can be difficult to sustain in the context of curriculum standardization and budget cuts. Adequately implemented peer mediation programs have clear positive effects, including reducing destructive aggressive behaviour and developing both mediators' and participants' reasoning, social skills, and openness to handle conflict constructively (Bickmore, 2002; Burrell et al., 2003; Cunningham, 1998; Harris, 2005; Heydenberk and Heydenberk, 2005; Jones, 2004).

Like peer mediation, dialogic group problem-solving such as class meetings, conferencing, and other circle processes constitute both interventions to resolve or mitigate particular conflicts, and at the same time arenas for developing participants' awareness and capacity to recognize and resist victimization (Angell, 2004; Palazzo and Hosea, 2004). Such 'restorative' and 'transformative' justice processes for conflict management involving youth are an effective alternative to punitive court-based systems in Australia, New Zealand, Canada and the US (Braithwaite, 2001; Consadine, 1999). Further, these circles facilitate citizen engagement and learning, '[enabling] the wider community to participate in denouncing crime, supporting victims, and building true solutions' that address underlying causes of crime (Morris, 2000: 254). Carefully constructed circle processes, conducted by skilled facilitators, are more capable than peer mediation to handle complex, power-imbalanced, and inter-group conflicts and aggression (also Pranis et al., 2003). Whether restrictive and punitive, or dialogic and restorative, the ways conflict and aggression are handled inevitably teach witnesses and participants about expected and possible citizen roles.

VALUES IN CONFLICT AND PEACE EDUCATION

Education about conflict and peace inevitably embeds values. Some interpersonally oriented conflict resolution education programs have been criticized because, like punishment approaches, they may implicitly locate the problem of conflict and violence in the individual students who get into disputes, rather than in social institutions, youth-adult relations, or structural injustice (Devine, 1996; Gadlin, 1994). Similarly, some internationally funded peace education initiatives may uncritically assume the superiority of Western cultural norms, ignore problems of power and justice, and treat individual learners as if they have a deficit (Bush and Saltarelli, 2000; Lederach, 1995). Other conflict resolution and peace education programs, however, do embody a more critical approach, including at their core anti-bias education and attention to power, justice, and social responsibility (e.g. Brenes-Castro, 2004; Prutzman and Johnson, 1997).

Some peace education initiatives, including the international *Hague Agenda for Peace and Justice for the 21st Century* (1999), emphasize the inculcation of core values such as nonviolence, tolerance, human rights, and environmental sustainability to develop a 'culture of peace' (Burns and Aspeslagh, 1996; Toh, 2002). Highlighting women's roles in many societies, American scholar Betty Reardon (1996) demonstrates that peaceful, nurturing behaviour occurs as naturally among humans as does aggression, and argues that positive peacebuilding requires people to develop love for the 'other.' Others argue that too much value consensus would stifle diversity and democracy: 'Indoctrination in the name of god, country, and goodness may simply be replaced by talk of the right way to make peace and build justice ... and expand creative forms of dispute resolution' (Fisk, 2000: 181).

Further, teaching values directly actually may not effectively facilitate the learning and enactment of those values. Based on a review of research on anti-bias workshops and other social learning studies, McCauley (2002) argues that 'feet first' education (practising small changes in behaviour) is more likely to change hearts and minds, than is 'head first' education (teaching values and attitudes) likely to change behaviour. For example, people may unlearn racism by finding themselves participating constructively in de-segregated situations where there is institutional support for non-discrimination – 'head' following 'feet,' rather than the other way around.

Richard Merelman's (1990) review of research in political socialization suggests how such values might be learned differently, through implicit modeling and practice, in different kinds of social environments. In contexts of escalated inter-group conflict such as revolution or civil war, where a large proportion of people contest the legitimacy of the existing government, children grow up and learn in the context of highly visible value conflicts. Here, they may develop little fear of conflict and some understanding of how conflicts work, although they may need to learn how to rehumanize and communicate across differences. In contrast, in relatively uncontested regimes where the stability of the existing government is not particularly threatened, value conflicts and their roots in inter-group relations are less visible and more marginalized. In these situations, young people may have little experience with recognizing alternate viewpoints, and may learn to view conflict as abnormal and dissenters as bad. Here, they may need

explicit education to learn to handle uncertainty and conflict. Further, children growing up in different social identity positions, such as female and male or rich and poor, may glean from their environments – and consequently need from their schooling – different values and understandings for handling conflict and making peace. In any case, peace and conflict education is value-laden, although these values may be relatively visible (because contested) or hidden (assumed).

DIVERSE TYPES OF PEACE AND CONFLICT EDUCATION

Some peace and conflict education initiatives emphasize curriculum content, such as re-thinking historical narratives, understanding patterns of injustice such as anti-racism, engagement with global issues, and building competence with a range of 'peace tools' (Alger, 1995) that can be used at interpersonal and/or international levels. Others emphasize pedagogical process and patterns of social interaction such as desegregation, intercultural education, dialogue, and inclusive discussion.

People's thinking and feeling about conflict is often shaped by stories; the re-telling and re-invention of those narratives can be a powerful element of conflict reproduction or conflict transformation and reconciliation (Funk and Said, 2004; also Ross, 1993). History education in schools is often hotly contested because this is where those narratives are most visible, and regulated by the nation-state. For example, analyses of various Israeli history textbooks have found more open and complex perspectives in recent editions, but with the mainstream Zionist narrative still organizing most texts, leaving little space for meaningfully considering Palestinian narratives (Al-Haj, 2005; Firer, 2002). Similarly, Sri Lanka, Rwanda, and Cyprus have endured raging debates over history curriculum, and some pilot initiatives for change (Hadjipavlou, 2002;

Obura, 2003; Perera et al., 2004; Rutayisire et al., 2004).

The challenges of addressing conflict through history education are especially acute when that history includes serious injustice, human rights violation, or genocide within the 'same' nation. Yet again there is widespread belief in the possibility of facilitating redress of injustice and reconciliation through history-linked citizenship curricula (Mátrai, 2002). Many educators agree that 'the battle against racism and hate propaganda will ultimately be won through increased efforts to incorporate multicultural, anti-racist, and human rights education in our schools' (Mock, 2000: 471). Mock and others advocate Holocaust education, referring primarily to the Nazi attempt to exterminate the Jews in Europe, usually including comparison and contrast with other human rights crises and genocides and current issues, as an ideal opportunity for such learning (also Cowan and Maitles, 1999; Riley and Totten, 2002). For example in one study, the 10-week course Facing History and Ourselves yielded greater pre- to post-course gains in relationship maturity, and reduction in racist attitudes and in reported fighting behaviour, relative to comparison classes (Schultz et al., 2001). In that study, the average positive impact of the course was significantly greater for girls than for boys: the interactions between gender identity and conflict behaviour, including racist attitudes and physical violence, deserve further study. In addition to being taken up in different ways by diverse students, Holocaust histories – and presumably other conflict narratives – may be presented in ways that offer widely different perspectives on the human actions and responsibilities contributing to the escalation of violence, and the lessons to be derived (Schweber, 2006).

A widely practised and widely studied form of peace education that includes attention to historical narratives, designed to reduce prejudice in social conflict situations, is the inter-group 'contact' dialogue approach. Inter-group contact encounters take many forms, but generally bring together individuals from two or more adversary groups, face-to-face, for facilitated sharing, cooperative activity, and dialogue about the participants' understandings of the current and historical conflict between their groups. Contact groups are typically small, non-formal, and voluntary, primarily attracting participants who are already open to peacebuilding. Although such programs therefore affect fewer people than would broad public schooling reforms, contact program participants often report profound, life-changing personal impacts. However, inter-group contact and other anti-bias education are by no means guaranteed to reduce enmity. Gordon Allport's 1954 'contact hypothesis' and subsequent scholarship have articulated certain conditions under which inter-group contact would be likely to reduce prejudice and increase openness to the other side's perspectives: process and participant selection designed to equalize status between the groups, close and prolonged contact, cross-group cooperation toward common goals, and institutional environments that support such cooperation and prejudice reduction (cited in Tal-Or et al., 2002; Stephan, 1999). Unfortunately, these conditions are often not met in many actual, implemented programs. As in other anti-bias and peace education around the world, such prejudice reduction initiatives are often marginal efforts of short duration, undertaken without much social-institutional support for status equalization or behaviour change.

A great deal of inter-group contact education research and practice has been conducted in Israel and Palestine and in Northern Ireland, although such initiatives increasingly exist in other places, such as Project DiaCom in Bosnia-Herzegovina (Farnam, 2001). An emergent alternative to the inter-group contact approach is a 'single identity' or 'common identity' approach, which attempts to reduce the reliance on 'bipolar' adversary identities through de-categorization (helping participants to view people as individuals rather than as merely 'one of them') and by instilling superordinate shared identities that cross-cut the adversary identities (Church et al., 2004). Nation-state-sponsored programs often frame these superordinate identities as national identities.

Such initiatives are sometimes connected with local-global and pluralistically oriented state-sponsored citizenship education initiatives. An example is the Speak Your Piece pilot project, conducted under the auspices of the required Education for Mutual Understanding curriculum in Northern Ireland (Arlow, 2004; McCully et al., 1999; Smith, 2003). This program employed youth worker facilitators, television programs, teaching conflict resolution skills, and class discussion – mostly in identity (segregated home school) groups, but also including some opportunity for positive contact with the 'other,' directly, and via computer conferencing. The leaders/researchers in that project believed they were fairly successful in facilitating open, forthright, and inclusive dialogue on controversial issues, to 'generate respect for the right to express points of view and to show sensitivity to personal biographies' (McCully et al., 1999: 126).

Even when integrated with long-term school programs, contact dialogue initiatives have been criticized for their usually short duration, the individualistic psychological assumptions on which they are based, their essentialized and monological notions of identity and culture, and their inadequate approaches to inequality and power (Bekerman, 2007). Bekerman argues for more critical and nuanced approaches to conscientization and identity and, consistent with McCauley's theory, for connection of new knowledge to social activity including political and practical action. Recent initiatives to establish integrated schools that facilitate ongoing transformative learning begin to demonstrate the possibilities as well as difficulties of teaching justice, inter-group understanding, and positive peace, implicitly as well as explicitly, through shared, daily experiences and struggles over time (Bekerman and Horenczyk, 2004; McGlynn and Bekerman, 2006).

Compatible with the analysis of Bekerman and colleagues, comparative international work by Helen Haste (2004) and Gita Steiner-Khamsi (2003) argues that citizenship education of and about visible minority populations has often relied on simplistic assumptions about identity and bipolar intergroup differences, whereas instead it needs to speak to complex, multipolar identities; language and cultural context relative power and status, economic distribution and political action for problem-solving. Global education scholars, similarly, highlight the value of critical thinking opportunities, multiple and fluid layers of identity, and development of agency to address local and global conflicts (Hicks, 2003; McIntosh, 2005; Merryfield and Subedi, 2001; Parker, 2004). McKenzie (2006), for example, affirms the importance of agency, 'the ongoing process of (un)making ourselves through explorations of our positioning within [multiple and contrasting] discourse,' in transnational citizen engagement. Haste (2004) explains that a person is motivated to engage in action when their sense of self defines them as a holder of particular beliefs and/or a member of a certain group, in relation to particular social conflicts. Thus efficacious citizen learning is closely associated with recognition of complex and overlapping individual differences, and with opportunities to engage in making sense of, and doing something about, social and political conflicts.

Based on qualitative data from the IEA Civic Education Study (Torney-Purta et al., 1999), Hungarian scholar Zsusza Mátrai (2002) shows how some school systems, such as in Greece, Hong Kong, and Hungary, emphasize unidimensional nationalist identities in ways that deny or avoid conflictual questions of social diversity, leaving students unprepared to handle the challenges of identity-group conflict. Other school systems, such as in Germany, explicitly attempt to teach inter-group solidarity by addressing problems of identity conflict and intolerance, such as those arising in Nazism and the Holocaust. Israeli scholar Hillel Wahrman

(2003) uses analysis of three Israeli civics textbooks to illustrate the ramifications of this silencing or confronting of painful conflicts for peace education. It is easy to understand how people in power, seeking nation-state stability, often would choose to silence classroom discussion of intractable conflicts. However, young people would still learn elsewhere about those axes of dehumanization. Wahrman argues that, despite the inevitable risks, questions of identity and identity conflict should be discussed explicitly in relation to democratic politics, to encourage student engagement. This coincides with international research findings that open, facilitated discussion of meaningful and controversial public issues (conflicts) in classrooms is an effective way to develop skills, awareness, relationships and inclination to participate in democracy (Hess and Posselt, 2002; Hahn, 1998; Torney-Purta et al., 2001).

Curriculum always teaches implicitly – by the way it embodies assumptions and structures interaction – as well as explicitly through textbooks and lesson content. Clearly, an implicit curriculum of superiority-inferiority, enemy images, and status competition can exacerbate social conflict and structural violence (Bush and Saltarelli, 2000; Davies, 2004). In contrast, schools and classrooms that emphasize inclusive and democratic dialogue processes, such as student governance and well-structured cooperative learning, can help to build healthy and equitable relationships and to reduce violence (Aronson, 2000; Bickmore 1999; Romo, 1997). There are countless ways to infuse conflict awareness and skill-building opportunities in pedagogical processes, with or without addressing controversial issues. For example, drama-based lessons, often integrated with other curriculum, may help young participants to develop understandings of conflict and a sense of efficacy in addressing it, without prescribing any particular approach to resolution (O'Toole and Burton, 2005). Ongoing opportunities for inclusive, critical inquiry dialogue about controversial

and sensitive issues may develop students' engagement in schools and communities, respect for alternative points of view, and sensitivity to matters of discrimination and equity (Otoya-Knapp, 2004).

Campaigns to empower poor and marginalized people, through a dialogic learning process Brazilian scholar Paulo Freire (1970) called 'conscientization,' have been mounted in contexts such as revolutionary Cuba, Nicaragua, and Guinea-Bissau. In practice, the stresses of ongoing violence, resource scarcity, and insufficient teacher training tended to reduce the capacity of some of these literacy campaigns to successfully implement dialogue-based learning (Arnove, 1999: 148–149; Spring, 2006). Thus educational initiatives may help to alleviate some elements of social conflict and structural violence such as marginalization, while at the same time they may reinforce other aspects of the power structure by promoting acceptance of the current government.

Inclusive, participant-centred pedagogies create democratic space for disagreement, dissent, and inclusion of previously silenced voices, thus for constructive and educative attention to conflicts. The *theory* of peace and conflict education embraces such long-range, dialogic, culturally appropriate and locally grounded curriculum and pedagogies. However, the funded and implemented *practices* often tend to distill prevailing practices into relatively narrow, short-term packages, developed in isolation from local cultures and curricula, that avoid confronting the controversies of asymmetrical power, masculine domination, and inter-group divisions (Davies 2004; Weinstein et al., 2007). Based on his years of conflict resolution facilitation and training in Latin America and many other violence-torn contexts, John Paul Lederach (1995) argues that top-down 'prescriptive' conflict management training, rooted in the individualistic and rationalistic cultures of the privileged world, is often inappropriate and ineffective in cross-cultural contexts, and leaves little space for agency by participants. Lederach advocates more 'elicitive' training methods, designed to derive and give voice to the implicit knowledge rooted in each culture's experiences, stories and proverbs. As with any human endeavor, the intended value dimensions of peace and conflict education may not match the value-laden consequences of implemented initiatives.

There is no reason to assume that dialogic, elicitive pedagogies are unworkable, foreign, or culturally inappropriate in resource-poor or so-called Third World contexts – in fact, the hierarchical teacher-centred pattern of globalized Western formal education may represent a much greater contrast to many indigenous learning traditions. Mark Ginsburg and colleagues review a range of prior research demonstrating that, while challenges such as resource scarcity, minimal teacher preparation, and centralized short-answer examinations do impede student-centred pedagogies around the world, 'it is possible to overcome each of the various challenges with some teachers in some settings' (2006: 7), drawing on local traditions.

DISCUSSION: IMPLEMENTING PEACE AND CONFLICT EDUCATION

This chapter has discussed the ways peace and conflict education takes place in schools, through modeling and practice in the management of conflict and aggression, and explicitly in the content and pedagogies of various educational activities. Because real life is full of conflicts large and small, there are myriad opportunities for constructive conflict learning embedded in all facets of the schooling experience. Building positive peace, like democracy, is a complex system, not a simple or static destination. Conflict continues, and peacebuilding means preparing to meet that conflict equitably and openly, as an opportunity for learning and social development.

The persistent problem of gender-based repression and violence demonstrates that even the goal of negative peace – safe spaces without violence – continues to be elusive, even in supposedly peaceful contexts. Because schools generally put considerable energy into control and discipline, those domains of schooling consume substantial resources, and embody unsolved problems. Thus these areas of activity are ripe for transformation – from anti-democratic control, toward institutionalized educative systems for democratic peacemaking and peacebuilding such as peer mediation, peacemaking circle conferences, and anti-bias dialogue.

Meanwhile, in the explicit work of classrooms, infusion of constructive peacebuilding education requires rethinking curriculum content such as the treatment of history and the silencing of sensitive conflicts. Equally essential is to transform pedagogies away from competitive individualism, toward inclusive cooperation and open conversation about meaningful issues. In this sense, explicit lessons about conflict and peace are a case of, or space for, educational democratization.

Access to resources for education in general, as well as for peace and conflict citizenship education in particular, makes sustainable peacebuilding possible. Children learn what their societies and governments value by observing where tangible resources are allocated. In many school systems today, resources allocated for competitive assessment, regulation, and punishment far outweigh those for proactive relationship-building and problem solving learning activities of any kind.

Teachers need both expertise and confidence, to effectively encourage and guide student participation in conflict and peace education. A two-year study in the UK highlights this challenge: researchers interviewed students ages 8–11 and 13–16, teachers, and others about their perceived needs for teaching and learning about global issues. Even during the part of the research project when UK involvement in the Iraq war was not quite such a burning, front-page issue, the students overwhelmingly brought up (unprompted) their interest in learning about and discussing much more specific information, including multiple perspectives, about current issues, especially issues of war and peace. In direct contrast to what their teachers thought about needing to protect them from frightening information, even the youngest children were already well aware of the war from news and community sources, and expressed specific questions and opinions about the political issues involved. Their teachers, on the other hand, considered global citizenship education in general, and open discussion about controversial current war events in particular, to be 'their least confident area of teaching' (Yamashita, 2006: 32). Teachers felt that they needed considerably more prior knowledge in order to handle such issues, and were afraid they might be seen as indoctrinating, whereas students just wanted opportunities to learn and discuss these matters together openly. A US study in three high schools, similarly, found that open discussions of controversial and sensitive issues were extremely rare, yet these were described by students as their most meaningful educational experiences (Simon, 2001).

To facilitate democratic learning that does not silence conflict, in the context of student diversity and globalization, requires more substantive knowledge, as well as more pedagogical facilitation skills and more comfort with difference, openness, and uncertainty, than to teach fragmented, neutralized information. Yet many of today's teachers had little opportunity to gain the confidence or skills for handling such complex social, political, and moral subject matter, when they were students or even in typical teacher education (Boler and Zembylas, 2003; Tupper, 2005). It is clear from the research cited above that education addressing peace and conflict, and giving students opportunities to participate actively in deliberation, peacemaking, and peacebuilding, is what engages students in school. Further, it is clear that such engagement in school expands opportunities and inclinations for engagement in political society. Democracy's

fragility is evident around the world, as it depends on the engagement of citizens who have been increasingly disengaged from traditional institutions of conflict management through governance (Osler and Starkey, 2006). Thus it seems well past time to refocus resources and energies on improving engagement in constructive conflict learning, to make peacebuilding a full and effective part of citizenship education.

REFERENCES

Adams, A.T. (2000) The Status of School Discipline and Violence. *Annals of the American Political Science and Sociology Society* 567: 140–155.

Akiba, M., LeTendre, G., Baker, D. and Goesling B. (2003) Student Victimization: National and School System Effects on School Violence in 37 Nations. *American Educational Research Journal* 39 (4): 829–853.

Al-Haj, M. (2005) National Ethos, Multicultural Education, and the New History Textbooks in Israel. *Curriculum Inquiry* 35 (1): 47–71.

Alger, C. (1995) Building Peace: A Global Learning Process. In M. Merryfield and R. Remy (eds) *Teaching about International Conflict and Peace*. Albany: SUNY Press.

Angell, A. (2004) Making Peace in Elementary Classrooms: A Case for Class Meetings. *Theory and Research in Social Education* 32 (1): 98–104.

Arlow, M. (2004) Citizenship Education in a Divided Society: The Case of Northern Ireland. In S. Tawil and A. Harley (eds) *Education, Conflict and Social Cohesion*. Geneva: UNESCO/ International Bureau of Education. pp. 255–314.

Arnove, R. (1999) Reframing Comparative Education: The Dialectic of the Global and the Local. In R. Arnove and C. Torres (eds) *Comparative Education: The Dialectic of the Global and the Local*. Lanham, MD: Rowman & Littlefield. pp. 1–23.

Aronson, E. (2000) *Nobody Left to Hate: Teaching Compassion after Columbine*. New York: Worth Publishers.

Association for Conflict Resolution (2006). *Recommended Standards for School-based*

Peer Mediation Programs. Washington, DC: Association for Conflict Resolution, Education Section.

Bekerman, Z. (2007) Rethinking Intergroup Encounters: Rescuing Praxis from Theory, Activity from Education, and Peace/Co-existence from Identity and Culture. *Journal of Peace Education* 4 (1): 21–37.

Bekerman, Z. and Horenczyk, G. (2004) Arab-Jewish Bilingual Co-education in Israel: A Long-term Approach to Intergroup Conflict Resolution. *Journal of Social Issues* 60 (2): 389–404.

Bergsgaard, M. (1997) Gender Issues in the Implementation and Evaluation of a Violence-Prevention Curriculum. *Canadian Journal of Education* 22 (1): 33–45.

Bickmore, K. (1999) Teaching Conflict and Conflict Resolution in School: (Extra-) Curricular Considerations. In A. Raviv, L. Oppenheimer and D. Bar-Tal (eds) *How Children Understand War and Peace*. San Francisco: Jossey-Bass. pp. 233–259.

Bickmore, K. (2001) Student Conflict Resolution, Power 'Sharing' in Schools, and Citizenship Education. *Curriculum Inquiry* 31 (2): 137–162.

Bickmore, K. (2002) How Might Social Education Resist (Hetero)sexism? Facing the Impact of Gender and Sexual Ideology on Citizenship. *Theory and Research in Social Education* 30 (2): 198–216.

Bickmore, K. (2002) Peer Mediation Training and Program Implementation in Elementary Schools: Research Results. *Conflict Resolution Quarterly* 19 (4): 137–160.

Bickmore, K. (2004) Discipline for Democracy? School Districts' Management of Conflict and Social Exclusion. *Theory and Research in Social Education* 32 (1): 75–97.

Bickmore, K. (2005) Foundations for Peacebuilding and Discursive Peacekeeping: Infusion and Exclusion of Conflict in Canadian Public School Curricula. *Journal of Peace Education* 2 (2): 161–181.

Boler, M. and Zembylas, M. (2003) Discomforting Truths: The Emotional Terrain of Understanding Difference. In P. Trifonas (ed.) *Pedagogies of Difference: Rethinking Education for Social Change*. Halifax: Fernwood. pp. 110–136.

Braithwaite, J. (2001) Youth Development Circles. *Oxford Review of Education* 27 (2): 239–252.

Brenes-Castro, A. (2004) An Integrated Model of Peace Education. In A. Wenden (ed.) *Educating for a Culture of Social and Ecological Peace*. New York: SUNY Press. pp. 111–140.

Bretherton, D., Weston, J. and Zbar, V. (2003) Peace Education in a Post-conflict Environment: The Case of Sierra Leone. *Prospects* 33 (2): 219–230.

Burns, R.J. and Aspeslagh, R. (1996) *Three Decades of Peace Education around the World: An Anthology*. New York: Garland Publishing.

Burrell, N., Zirbel, C. and Mike, A. (2003) Evaluating Peer Mediation Outcomes in Educational Settings: A Meta-analytic Review. *Conflict Resolution Quarterly* 21 (1): 7–26.

Bush, K. and Saltarelli, D. (2000) *The Two Faces of Education in Ethnic Conflict: Towards a Peacebuilding Education for Children*. Florence, IT: UNICEF Innocenti Research Centre.

Caprioli, M. (2000) Gendered Conflict. *Journal of Peace Research* 37 (1): 51–68.

Catalano, R., Berglund, L.M., Ryan, J., Lonczak, H. and Hawkins, J.D. (2002) Positive Youth Development in the United States: Research Findings on Evaluations of Positive Youth Development Programs. *Prevention and Treatment* 5: article 15. Available www.psycinfo.com/psycarticles/2002-14078-001.html.

Church, C., Visser, A. and Shepherd, L.J. (2004) A Path to Peace or Persistence? The 'Single Identity' Approach to Conflict Resolution in Northern Ireland. *Conflict Resolution Quarterly* 21 (3): 273–293.

Claassen, R. and Claassen, R. (2004) Creating a Restorative Discipline System: Restorative justice in schools. *The Fourth R* (Winter): 9–12.

Conflict Resolution, Association for (2006) *Recommended Standards for School-based Peer Mediation Programs*. Washington, DC: Association for Conflict Resolution Education Section.

Conrad, R. (2006) Report: School System still Failing Black Kids. *The Halifax Chronicle-Herald*: Available http://www.herald.ns.ca/Metro/499603.html.

Consadine, J. (1999) *Restorative Justice: Healing the Effects of Crime [2nd edition]*. Lyttelton, New Zealand: Ploughshares Press.

Cowan, P. and H. Maitles (1999) Teaching the Holocaust in Primary Schools in Scotland: Modes, Methodology and Content. *Educational Review* 51 (3): 263–271.

Crosse, S., Burr, M., Cantor, D., Hagen, C. and Hantman, I. (2002) *Wide Scope, Questionable Quality: Drug and Violence Prevention Efforts in American Schools.* Rockville, MD: Westat (in affiliation with Gottfredson Associates).

Cunningham, C. (1998) The Effects of Primary Division, Student-mediated Conflict Resolution Programs on Playground aggression. *Journal of Child Psychology and Psychiatry* 39 (5): 653–662.

Curle, A., Freire, P. and Galtung, J. (1974) What can Education Contribute towards Peace and Social Justice? Curle, Freire, Galtung panel. In M. Haavelsrud (ed.) *Education for Peace: Reflection and Action.* Keele, UK: University of Keele. pp. 64–97.

Davies, L. (2004) *Education and Conflict: Complexity and Chaos.* London: Routledge/Falmer.

Day-Vines, N., Day-Hairston, B. Carruthers, W. Wall, J. and Lupton-Smith, H. (1996) Conflict resolution: The Value of Diversity in the Recruitment, Selection, and Training of Peer Mediators. *School Counselor* 43 (May): 392–410.

Deutsch, M. (2001) *Practitioner Assessment of Conflict Resolution Programs.* ERIC Digest #163. Available www.ed.gov/databases/ERIC Digests/ed451277.html

Devine, J. (1996) Violence: The Latest Curricular Specialty. In J. Devine (ed.) *Maximum Security: The Culture of Violence in Inner-City Schools.* Chicago: University of Chicago Press. pp. 161–177.

Doob, A. and Cesaroni, C. (2004) *Responding to Youth Crime in Canada.* Toronto: University of Toronto Press.

Dunbar, C. and Villarruel, F. (2004) What a Difference the Community Makes: Zero Tolerance Policy Interpretation and Implementation. *Equity and Excellence in Education* 37 (4): 351–359.

Erickson, C. and McGuire M. (2004) Constructing Nonviolent Cultures in Schools: The State of the Science. *Children and Schools* 26 (2): 102–116.

Farnam, A. (2001) *The Hard Work of Getting Along: Muslim and Serb Teachers Sit Down Together to Confront the Divisive Legacy of War* (August 14). Christian Science Monitor [downloaded November 18 2001]. Available www.csmonitor.com/2001/0814/p13s1-leca.html

Firer, R. (2002) The Gordian Knot between Peace Education and War Education. In G. Salomon and B. Nevo (eds) *Peace Education: The Concept, Principles, and Practices around the World.* Mahwah, NJ: Lawrence Erlbaum Associates. pp. 55–61.

Fisk, L. (2000) Shaping Visionaries: Nurturing Peace through Education. In L. Fisk and J. Schellenberg (eds) *Patterns Conflict, Paths to Peace.* Peterborough, ON: Broadview Press. pp. 159–193.

Franklin, U. (2006a) What of the Citizen? In *The Ursula Franklin Reader: Pacifism as a Map.* Toronto: Between the Lines. pp. 87–99.

Franklin, U. (2006b) Personally happy and publicly useful. In *The Ursula Franklin Reader: Pacifism as a Map.* Toronto: Between the Lines. pp. 353–363.

Freire, P. (1970) *Pedagogy of the Oppressed.* New York: Seabury Press.

Funk, N., and Said, A.A. (2004) Islam and the West: Narratives of Conflict and Conflict Transformation. *International Journal of Peace Studies* 9 (1): 1–28.

Gadlin, H. (1994) Conflict Resolution, Cultural Differences, and the Culture of Racism. *Negotiation Journal* (10): 33–47.

Galtung, J. (1969) Violence, peace, and peace research. *Journal of Peace Research* 6 (3): 167–192.

Galtung, J. (1996) *Peace By Peaceful Means: Peace and Conflict, Development, and Civilization.* London: Sage Publications & International Peace Research Assn.

Gewertz, C. (2006) Reactions to School Climate Vary by Students' Races. *Education Week* (April 5): 5 and 16.

Ginsburg, Mark, and AIR American Institutes for Research (2006) *Challenges to Promoting Active-Learning, Student-Centered Pedagogies.* Washington, DC: USAID and Educational Quality Improvement Program.

Hadjipavlou, M. (2002) Cyprus: A Partnership between Conflict Resolution and Peace Education. In G. Salomon and B. Nevo (eds) *Peace Education: The Concept, Principles, & Practices around the World.* Mahwah, NJ: Lawrence Erlbaum Associates. pp. 193–208.

Hague-Appeal (1999) The Hague Agenda for Peace and Justice for the 21st Century. Geneva: UNESCO, UN ref A/54/98 www.haguepeace.org.

Hahn, C. (1998) *Becoming Political: Comparative Perspectives on Citizenship Education*. Albany: State University of New York Press.

Harber, C. (2004) *Schooling as Violence: How Schools Harm Pupils and Societies*. London: Routledge.

Harper, T. (2007) Youth Crime and Punishment. *Toronto Star*, March 25, p. A11.

Harris, I.M. and Morrison, M. (2003) *Peace Education (2nd edition)*. Jefferson, NC: McFarland.

Harris, R. (2005) Unlocking the Learning Potential in Peer Mediation: An Evaluation of Peer Mediator Modeling and Disputant Learning. *Conflict Resolution Quarterly* 23 (2): 141–164.

Haste, H. (2004) Constructing the citizen. *Political Psychology* 25 (3): 413–439.

Hazler, R., and Carney, J.L. (2002) Empowering Peers to Prevent Youth Violence. *Journal of Humanistic Counseling, Education and Development* 41 (2): 129–149.

Henderson, G. (2006) The Public and Peace: The Consequences for Citizenship of the Democratic Peace Literature. *International Studies Review* 8 (2): 199–224.

Hess, D. and Posselt, J. (2002) How High School Students Experience and Learn from the Discussion of Controversial Public Issues. *Journal of Curriculum and Supervision* 17 (4): 283–314.

Heydenberk, R. and Heydenberk, W. (2005) Increasing Meta-cognitive Competence through Conflict Resolution. *Education and Urban Society* 37 (4): 431–452.

Hicks, D. (2003) Thirty Ysears of Global Education: A Reminder of Key Principles and Precedents. *Educational Review* 55 (3): 265–275.

Homer-Dixon, T. (2000) *The Ingenuity Gap*. Toronto: Alfred Knopf.

Iram, Y. (ed.) (2003) *Education of Minorities and Peace Education in Pluralistic Societies*. Westport, CT: Praeger.

Johnson, S. (1987) *Going Out of Our Minds: The Metaphysics of Liberation*. Freedom, California: The Crossing Press.

Jones, T. (2004) Conflict Resolution Education: The Field, the Findings, and the Future. *Conflict Resolution Quarterly* 22 (1–2): 233–267.

Jull, S. (2000) Youth Violence, Schools and the Management Question: A Discussion of Zero Tolerance and Equity in Public Schooling. *Canadian Journal of Educational Administration and Policy* (17). Available www.umanitoba.ca/publications/cjeap

Leach, F. (2003) *Gender Violence in Schools: What is it and Why Does it Happen?* Gender Violence in Schools Newsletter no 1. Available www.id21.org/education/gender _violence/index.html

Lederach, J.P. (1995) *Preparing for Peace: Conflict Transformation across Cultures*. Syracuse: Syracuse University Press.

Mátrai, Z. (2002) National Identity Conflicts and Civic Education: A Comparison of Five Countries. In G. Steiner-Khamsi, J. Torney-Purta and J. Schwille (eds) *New Paradigms and Recurring Paradoxes in Education for Citizenship: An International Comparison*. Amsterdam: JAI/ Elsevier Science. pp. 85–104.

McCadden, B.M. (1998) Why is Michael always Geting Timed Out? Race, Class and Disciplining other People's Children. In R.E. Butchart and B. McEwan (eds) *Classroom Discipline in American schools: Problems and Possibilities for Democratic Education*. Albany: State University of New York Press. pp. 109–134.

McCauley, C. (2002) Head First versus Feet First in Peace Education. In G. Salomon and B. Nevo (eds) *Peace Education: The Concept, Principles, and Practices around the World*. Mahwah, NJ: Lawrence Erlbaum Associates. pp. 247–258.

McCully, A., O'Doherty, M. and Smyth, P. (1999) The Speak Your Piece Project: Exploring Controversial Issues in Northern Ireland. In L. Forcey and I. Harris (eds) *Peacebuilding for Adolescents*. New York: Peter Lang. pp. 119–138.

McGlynn, C. and Bekerman, Z. (2006) The Challenges of Initiatives for Catholic-Protestant and Palestinian-Jewish Integrated Education in Northern Ireland and Israel. Paper read at American Educational Research Association, April 7–11, at San Francisco, CA.

McIntosh, P. (2005) Gender Perspectives on Educating for Global Citizenship. In N. Noddings (ed.) *Educating Citizens for Global Awareness*. New York: Teachers' College Press. pp. 22–39.

McKenzie, M. (2006) Three Portraits of Resistance: The (Un)making of Canadian Students. *Canadian Journal of Education* 29 (1): 199–222.

Merelman, R. (1990) The Role of Conflict in Children's Political Learning. In O. Ichilov (ed.) *Political Socialization, Citizenship Education, and Democracy*. New York: Teachers College Press pp. 47–65.

Merryfield, M. and Subedi, B. (2001) Decolonizing the Mind for World-centered Global Education. In E. W. Ross (ed.) *The Social Studies Curriculum: Purposes, Problems and Possibilities [revised edn]*. Albany: SUNY Press. pp. 277–290.

Mishna, F., Scarcello, I., Pepler, D. and Wiener, J. (2005) Teachers' Understanding of Bullying. *Canadian Journal of Education* 28 (4): 718–738.

Mock, K. (2000). Holocaust and Hope: Holocaust Education in the Context of Anti-racist Education in Canada. In F.C. Decoste and B. Schwarz (eds) *The Holocaust's Ghost: Writings on Art, Politics, Law and Education*. Edmonton: University of Alberta Press. pp. 465–482.

Morris, R. (2000). *Stories of Transformative Justice*. Toronto: Canadian Scholars Press.

Nkomo, M., Weber, E. and Malada, B. (2007) Sustaining Peace through School and Civil Society: Mortar, bricks and human agency. *Journal of Peace Education* 4 (1): 95–108.

Noguera, P. (1995) Preventing and Producing Violence: A Critical Analysis of Responses to School Violence. *Harvard Educational Review* 65 (2): 189–212.

O'Toole, J. and Burton, B.(2005) Acting against conflict and bullying. The Brisbane DRACON project 1996–2004 – emergent findings and outcomes. *Research in Drama Education* 10 (3): 269–283.

Obura, A. (2003) Never Again: Educational Reconstruction in Rwanda. Paris: UNESCO International Institute for Educational Planning <www.unesco.org/iiep>.

Osler, A. and Starkey, H. (1998) Children's Rights and Citizenship: Some Implications for the Management of Schools. *International Journal of Children's Rights* 6 (3): 313–333.

Osler, A. and Starkey, H. (2006) Education for democratic citizenship: A review of research, policy and practice 1995–2005. *Research Papers in Education* 21 (4): 433–466.

Otoya-Knapp, K. (2004) When Central City high school students speak: Doing critical inquiry for democracy. *Urban Education* 39 (2): 149–171.

Palazzo, D. and Hosea, B. (2004) Restorative justice in schools: A review of history and current practices. *The Fourth R* (Winter): 1 and 7–8.

Parker, W. (2004) Diversity, globalization, and democratic education: Curriculum possibilities. In J. Banks (ed.) *Diversity and Citizenship Education: Global Perspectives*. San Francisco: Jossey-Bass/ Wiley. pp. 433–458.

Perera, L., Wijetunge, S. and Balasooriya, A.S. (2004) Education reform and political violence in Sri Lanka. In S. Tawil and A. Harley (eds) *Education, Conflict and Social Cohesion*. Geneva: UNESCO/ International Bureau of Education. pp. 375–433.

Pranis, K., Stuart, B. and Wedge, M. (2003) *Peacemaking Circles: From Crime to Community*. St. Paul, MN: Living Justice Press.

Prutzman, P. and Johnson, J. (1997) Bias awareness and multiple perspectives: Essential aspects of conflict resolution. *Theory Into Practice* 36 (1): 26–31.

Reardon, B. (1996) Militarism and sexism: Influences on education for war. In R. Burns and R. Aspeslagh (eds) *Three Decades of Peace Education around the World: An Anthology*. New York: Garland. pp. 143–160.

Riley, K. and Totten, S. (2002) Understanding matters: Holocaust curricula and the social studies classroom. *Theory and Research in Social Education* 30 (4): 541–562.

Romo, H. (2006) *Improving Ethnic and Racial Relations in Schools: ERIC digest* [report]. ERIC Clearinghouse on Rural Education and Small Schools 1997 [download May 7 2006].

Ross, M. (1993) *The Culture of Conflict*. New Haven, CT: Yale University Press.

Rutayisire, R., Kabano, J. and Rubagiza, J. (2004) Redefining Rwanda's future: The role of curriculum in social reconstruction.

In S. Tawil and A. Harley (ed.) *Education, Conflict & Social Cohesion*. Geneva: UNESCO/ International Bureau of Education. pp. 315–374.

Sadker, D. (1999) Gender equity: Still knocking at the classroom door. *Educational Leadership* 56 (7): 22–26.

Salomon, G. and B. Nevo, eds. (2002) *Peace Education: The Concept, Principles, and Practices around the World*. Mahwah, NJ: Lawrence Erlbaum Associates.

Scheckner, S., Rollin, S., Kaiser-Ulrey, C. and Wagner, R. (2002) School violence in children and adolescents: A meta-analysis of the effectiveness of current interventions. *Journal of School Violence* 1 (2): 5–32.

Schimmel, D. (1997) Traditional rule-making and the subversion of citizenship education. *Social Education* 61 (2): 70–74.

Schultz, L., Barr, D. and Selman, R. (2001) The value of a developmental approach to evaluating character development programs: An outcome study of facing history and ourselves. *Journal of Moral Education* 30 (1): 3–27.

Schweber, S. (2006) 'Breaking Down Barriers' or 'Building Strong Christians': Two Treatments of Holocaust History. *Theory and Research in Social Education* 34 (1): 41–50.

Simon, K. (2001) *Moral Questions in the Classroom*. New Haven: Yale University Press.

Skiba, R. (2000) *Violence Prevention and Conflict Resolution Curricula: What Works in Preventing School Violence*. Bloomington, IN: Indiana University.

Skiba, R.M. Karega Rausch, and Shana Ritter (2004) Discipline is always teaching: Effective alternatives. *Education Policy Briefs* 2 (1 and 3).

Smith, A. (2003) Citizenship education in N. Ireland: Beyond national identity? *Cambridge Journal of Education* 33 (1): 15–31.

Spring, J. (2006) *Pedagogies of Globalization: The Rise of the Educational Security State*. Mahwah, NJ: Lawrence Erlbaum Associates.

Steiner-Khamsi, G. (2003) Cultural Recognition or Social Redistribution: Predicaments of Minority Education. In Y. Iram and H. Wahrman (eds) *Education of Minorities and Peace Education in Pluralistic Societies*. Westport, CT: Praeger Publishers. pp. 15–28.

Stephan, W. (1999) *Reducing Prejudice and Stereotyping in Schools*. New York: Teachers College Press.

Tal-Or, N., Boninger, D. and Gleicher, F. (2002) Understanding the Conditions Necessary for Intergroup Contact to Reduce Prejudice. In G. Salomon and B. Nevo (eds) *Peace Education: The Concept, Principles, and Practices around the World*. Mahwah, NJ: Lawrence Earlbaum Associates. pp. 89–107.

Tawil, S. and Harley, A. (eds.) (2004) *Education, Conflict and Social Cohesion*. Geneva: UNESCO/ International Bureau of Education.

Tjosvold, D. 1995 [orig.1980]. Control, Conflict, and Collaboration in the Classroom. In L. Roberts and R. Clifton (eds) *Crosscurrents: Contemporary Canadian Educational Issues*. Toronto: Nelson Canada. pp. 456–481.

Toh, S. (2002) Peace building and peace education: Local experiences, global reflections. *Prospects* 32 (1): 87–93.

Torney-Purta, J., Lehmann, R., Oswald, H. and Schultz, W. (2001) *Citizenship and Education in 28 Countries: Civic Knowledge and Engagement at Age 14*. Amsterdam: IEA (International Assn. for the Evaluation of Educational Achievement).

Torney-Purta, J., Schwille, J. and Amadeo, J.A. (1999) *Civic Education across Countries: 24 National Case Studis from the IEA Civic Education Project*. Amsterdam: International Association for the Evaluation of Educational Achievement.

Tupper, J. (2005) Social studies teachers speak up! Uncovering the (im)possibilities of citizenship. Paper read at American Educational Research Association, April, at Montreal.

UNICEF (2002) *Children affected by armed conflict: UNICEF actions* [download January 2002]. Availablewww.unicef.org/ emerg/files/AffectedbyArmedConflict.pdf

Verdugo, R. (2002) Race-ethnicity, social class, and zero tolerance policies: The cultural and structural wars. *Education and Urban Society* 35 (1): 50–75.

Wahrman, H. (2003) Is Silencing Conflicts a Peace Education Strategy? The Case of the 'Jewish State' Topic in Israeli Civics Textbooks. In Y. Iram and H. Wahrman (eds) *Education of Minorities and Peace Education in Pluralistic Societies*. Westport, CT: Praeger Publishers. pp. 229–254.

Ware, H., Greener, P., Iribarnegaray, D., Jenkins, B., Lautensach, S., Matthews, D., Makuwira, J., and Spence, R. (2005) *The No-Nonsense Guide to Conflict and Peace*. Oxford, UK and Toronto: New Internationalist Publications/ Between the Lines.

Weinstein, H.M., Freedman, S.W. and Holly Hughson (2007) School Voices: Challenges Facing Education Systems after Identity Based Conflict. *Education, Citizenship and Social Justice* 2 (1): 41–71.

Williams, J. (2004) Civil Conflict, Education, and the Work of Schools: Twelve Propositions. *Conflict Resolution Quarterly* 21 (4): 471–481.

Yamashita, H. (2006) Global Citizenship Education and War: The Needs of Teachers and Learners. *Educational Review* 58 (1): 27–39.

35

Human Rights Education: The Foundation of Education for Democratic Citizenship in our Global Age[1]

Audrey Osler

INTRODUCTION

This chapter examines human rights education (HRE) as a right for all, and considers some of the reasons why this right is yet to be fully realized, several decades after the Universal Declaration of Human Rights 1948 (UDHR) was adopted by the General Assembly of the United Nations. I argue that the human rights project is a cosmopolitan one and that effective education for our global age requires a cosmopolitan vision, based on a shared understanding of human rights. I discuss some of the problems that exist in realising HRE programmes in schools in a range of national contexts and consider the strengths and limitations of education for democratic citizenship (EDC) as a vehicle for teaching and learning about human rights.

HUMAN RIGHTS EDUCATION: A UNIVERSAL RIGHT

Following the adoption of the UDHR on 10 December, 1948, the UN General Assembly called upon all UN member-states to publicise the text of the UDHR and 'to cause it to be disseminated, displayed, read and expounded principally in schools and other educational institutions, without distinction based on the political status of countries or territories' (UN, 1948). From its very beginnings those who drafted the UNHR envisaged that it would be made available to young people and that it would be found on school notice boards and in classrooms. Thus, from the earliest stage of the human rights project, member-states of the United Nations made a moral commitment to HRE for all.

The UDHR (Article 26:1) confirms that: 'Everyone has the right to education.

Education shall be free, at least in the elementary and fundamental stages.' The right to education is clearly defined to include the right to human rights education:

> Education shall be directed to the full development of the human personality and to the *strengthening of respect for human rights and fundamental freedoms*. It shall promote understanding, tolerance and friendship among all nations, racial or religious groups, and shall further the activities of the United Nations for the maintenance of peace (UDHR, Article 26: 2, my emphasis).

The right to HRE has later been repeatedly confirmed in binding legislation, as for example, in Article 13 of the International Covenant on Social and Cultural Rights 1966 (UN, 1966). Particularly helpful to educators are the detailed provisions of the binding Convention on the Rights of the Child (CRC), relating to the quality of education and the entitlement to HRE:

> 1. States Parties agree that the education of the child shall be directed to:
>
>   (a) The development of the child's personality, talents, and mental and physical abilities to their fullest potential;
>   (b) The development of respect for human rights and fundamental freedoms, and for the principles enshrined in the Charter of the United Nations;
>   (c) The development of respect for the child's parents, his or her own cultural identity, language and values, for the national values of the country in which the child is living, the country from which he or she may originate, and for civilizations different from his or her own;
>   (d) The preparation of the child for responsible life in a free society, in the spirit of understanding, peace, tolerance, equality of sexes, and friendship among all peoples, ethnic, national and religious groups and persons of indigenous origin; and
>   (e) The development of respect for the natural environment (UN, CRC, Article 29, 1989).

This implies not only the right *to* education, but rights *in* education and rights *through* education (Verhellen, 2000). All children, whether or not they hold citizenship rights, are equally entitled to quality education which enables them to achieve their 'fullest potential'. The principle of

non-discrimination implies that the nation-state has taken adequate steps to prevent school dropout and to address problems such as truancy and exclusion from school. So, for example, evidence of differential exclusion rates between children from different ethnic groups (Osler and Hill, 1999; Osler and Vincent, 2003) and differentials in examination outcomes between these groups (Tikly et al., 2005) are key human rights issues relating to the right *to* education.

School exclusion also undermines rights *through* education, that is to say, it threatens access to an education in human rights. Rights in education include the right of the student to participate and to be consulted in school decision-making processes, which imply the introduction of democratic structures and basic legal provisions to guarantee learner participation (Osler and Vincent, 2002). The development of EDC within curricular frameworks provides an opportunity for the development of HRE or rights through education, but such initiatives need to be matched by policy developments and legal safeguards which also protect children's right *to* education and rights *in* education. These safeguards are critical when considering the needs of specific groups of children, such as those with disabilities or from minority groups, who in many contexts experience some difficulties in accessing these rights on the basis of equality.

COSMOPOLITANISM AND CITIZENSHIP

The human rights project is a cosmopolitan one, requiring us to acknowledge, and where appropriate, to defend, the dignity and rights of our fellow human beings across the globe, who are characterized as members of the same 'human family'. This is made explicit in the opening sentence of the preamble of the Universal Declaration of Human Rights: '... recognition of the inherent dignity and of the inalienable rights of all members of the

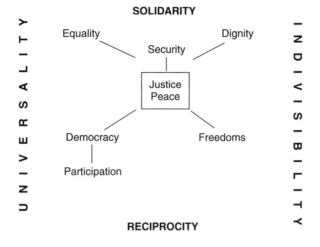

Figure 35.1 The basic concepts of human rights (from Starkey, 1992)

human family is the foundation of justice and peace in the world' (UN, 1948).

Starkey (1992) has helpfully encompassed this cosmopolitan vision diagrammatically, enabling us to see the relationship between the goal of justice and peace in the world, and key human rights concepts. Drawing on the UDHR, he reminds us that the realisation of justice and peace is at the heart of the human rights project and that this is closely linked to issues of security, both personal and global. All human beings are entitled to equal dignity and to equality of rights. Human rights can only be fully realized when individuals have an opportunity to participate in decision-making, and this implies democracy.

The concept of universality is central; rights belong to all members of the human family. Rights are indivisible; they come as a package, they are not offered as a menu, from which individuals or governments can select. This is not to deny that there may often be tensions between competing rights, such as freedom of opinion and expression on the one hand, and the right to a fair and public hearing by an independent tribunal, in the case of a criminal charge, on the other. This means the freedom of the press is not

limitless, and newspapers do not have the right, for example, to publish material which might prejudice a fair trial.

Rights demand human solidarity; something which is at the heart of cosmopolitanism. We need to be willing to recognise and defend the rights of strangers, including people with different cultures and belief systems from our own. Finally, there is the key concept of reciprocity. My rights cannot be secured unless you are prepared to defend them, and vice versa. This means inherent in the concept of human rights is the notion of responsibility. We all have a responsibility to protect the rights of others.

In our globalized world, our lives are interconnected with those of strangers in distant places. Our actions and behaviours, and the decisions of the government we elect will have an impact, not only on our own lives, but also on theirs. Our local communities are increasingly diverse, and we live alongside people with many different belief systems. Cosmopolitanism requires us to engage with difference, rather than create the illusion that it is possible to live parallel lives. Appiah (2006: 71) characterizes this day-to-day process of living together with people holding different values and beliefs as a pragmatic one: 'We can live together without agreeing on what the values are that make it good to live together, we can agree about what to do in most cases, without agreeing about why it is right'. Human rights provide us with some broad principles within which we can work and engage with each other and which we can apply in our efforts to resolve problems when we cannot easily agree what to do.

Living within a plural society, we are making assessments of other cultures and beliefs all the time, whether we acknowledge this or not. Human rights provide us with some broad principles which allow us to examine cultural practices and values, including our own. They help us develop skills of intercultural evaluation (Hall, 2000; Parekh, 2000) and to avoid cultural relativism, a position where anything goes or anything can be accepted, simply because it is 'part of someone's culture'. All cultures are in a process of change. Cultures are not separate, but interrelated, borrowing from each other. Educators need to help their students develop skills of intercultural evaluation, based on human rights principles. Part of this process is a process of self-evaluation and self-reflection. As Figueroa (2000) argues: 'Pluralism does not mean a radical relativism. That would be self-defeating. One must stand somewhere. It is not possible to stand nowhere. But neither is an attempt to stand everywhere tenable'.

Within our schools and local communities, not all individuals will be citizens, but all are holders of human rights. Across Europe, all individuals living within each nation-state can seek redress under the European Convention on Human Rights if they believe their rights have been infringed, whether or not they are citizens of the country in which they are living. Although governments have a responsibility for protecting human rights, human rights are not dependent in this respect on citizenship rights.

In practice, some citizens find it difficult to access their rights. The struggle for citizenship is an on going one, rather than something which is complete. Some groups

of citizens who seek to belong may nevertheless be excluded. In the 1960s E. R. Braithwaite, the author of the novel *To Sir, With Love*, summed up the kinds of contradictions which a citizen may feel:

> In spite of my years of residence in Britain, any service I might render the community in times of war or peace, any contribution I might make or wish to make, or any feeling I might entertain towards Britain and the British, I – like all other colored persons in Britain - am considered an 'immigrant'. Although this term indicates that we have secured entry into Britain, it describes a continuing condition in which we have no real hope of ever enjoying the desired transition to full responsible citizenship (Braithwaite, 1967, quoted in Fryer, 1984: 382).

Braithwaite reminds us that for some citizens, even the choice to identify with the nation can be denied. Citizenship as feeling is often considered to be a question of identity. But the choice to identify with a particular group can be denied by an excluding society. Braithwaite's observation, that 'full responsible citizenship' was denied to black settlers, still has some resonance today for particular groups. Many British citizens continue today to be viewed by others as outsiders, as can be observed in more recent debates about the allegiance of British Muslims (Richardson, 1997; 2004; Jawad and Benn, 2003).

Formal and informal barriers to full citizenship on the basis of gender and/or ethnicity continue to exist in many societies. They have been well documented in the case of the US:

> Becoming citizens of the [American] commonwealth has been much more difficult for ethnic groups of color and for women from all racial, ethnic and cultural groups than for mainstream males. Groups of color have experienced three major problems in becoming citizens of the United States. First, they were denied citizenship by laws. Second, when legal barriers to citizenship were eliminated, they were often denied educational experiences that would enable them to attain the cultural and language characteristics needed to function effectively in the mainstream society. Third, they were often denied the opportunity to fully participate in mainstream society even when they attained these characteristics because of ... discrimination (Banks, 1997: xi).

At the climax of the civil rights struggle in the US, Malcolm X claimed: 'We can never get civil rights in America until our human rights are first restored. We will never be recognised as citizens there until we are first recognised as humans' (Malcolm, 1964). Recognition of citizenship rights may first require recognition of our common humanity. Although in 1954 the Supreme Court had ruled in the pivotal *Brown v. Board of Education* that segregated schools were unconstitutional, a decade later racial segregation remained an everyday reality for American citizens in the Southern states. In July 1964, just a few weeks before Malcolm X made this statement, the Civil Rights Act was passed, which enforced the constitutional right to vote, and prohibited discrimination in public facilities, in government, and in employment. It became illegal, and therefore punishable, to continue to enforce segregation in schools, housing or in employment. The struggle for formal equality was not immediately realized, as it took some years before the powers to enforce all aspects of the new law were strengthened.

Malcolm X's statement reminds us that citizenship, and education for democratic citizenship, must be premised on recognition of our shared humanity. In those places in the US where African Americans experienced overt and structural discrimination, recognition of shared humanity required not only legal provisions, but also, over a longer period, a cultural and emotional shift; it required a recognition among individuals in white communities that civil rights imply more than a formal legal equality. This cultural and emotional shift demands the recognition that fellow citizens, regardless of ethnicity, gender, culture, sexuality, religious or political belief, or any other difference, are also human beings, capable of feeling as we do.

Our commonality is important. It extends beyond national boundaries and requires us to acknowledge a shared heritage with those we live alongside who do not share our citizenship, and to strangers in distant places. Human rights are universal and all human beings, regardless of their behaviour or even their commitment to human rights, have an equal entitlement to these rights. During 1964, Malcolm X travelled extensively in Africa and the Middle East and these travels seem to have opened his mind to a new cosmopolitan vision. He began to situate the struggles of African Americans within the broader international struggle for the realization of human rights for all.

As I have argued elsewhere (Osler, 2005a), programmes of education for democratic citizenship in multicultural societies require teachers and students to face some of the contradictions and tensions of citizenship. While citizenship can be conceived as inclusive, it is also used to exclude. The inclusive side of citizenship refers to universal human rights. All are included in this definition of a community of citizens. The challenge is to develop citizenship education programmes which build upon this inclusive and cosmopolitan vision of citizenship.

INTERNATIONAL AND NATIONAL COMMITMENTS TO HUMAN RIGHTS EDUCATION

At the United Nations World Conference on Human Rights, held in Vienna in June 1993, representatives of 171 states adopted by consensus the *Vienna Declaration and Programme of Action* (UN, 1993) a common plan for the strengthening of human rights around the world. Over 800 non-governmental organizations (NGOs) were represented at the conference, two thirds of whom were working at grass roots level to protect human rights. The Vienna Conference thus reaffirmed the universality of human rights, recognised not only by governments, but also by the wider global community.

The *Vienna Declaration and Programme of Action* reminds us that education is at the heart of the human rights project:

> States are duty-bound, as stipulated in the Universal Declaration of Human Rights and the

International Covenant on Economic, Social and Cultural Rights and in other international human rights instruments, to ensure that *education is aimed at strengthening the respect of human rights and fundamental freedoms*. The World Conference on Human Rights emphasizes the importance of incorporating the subject of human rights education programmes and calls upon States to do so. Education should promote understanding, tolerance, peace and friendly relations between the nations and all racial or religious groups and encourage the development of United Nations activities in pursuance of these objectives. Therefore, *education on human rights ... should be integrated in the education policies* at the national as well as international levels (UN, 1993: section 1: Para 33, my emphasis).

The then United Nations Secretary-General Boutros Boutros-Ghali, in a message to the World Conference, told delegates that not only had they strengthened and renewed the international community's commitment to the promotion and protection of human rights but had forged 'a new vision for global action for human rights into the next century'(OHCHR, 1993). At the centre of this new vision is the duty of governments 'to ensure that education is aimed at strengthening the respect of human rights and fundamental freedoms' (UN, 1993) and the expectation that HRE be integrated into national education policies.

Following a proposal at the World Conference, the United Nations Decade for Human Rights Education (1995–2004) was proclaimed by the UN General Assembly (UN, 1994). During the decade, we saw progress in the global development of HRE, although it remains a long way from being at the heart of educational planning across the globe. Recognising this, on 10 December, 2004, the UN General Assembly proclaimed the World Programme for Human Rights Education (2005–ongoing) (UN, 2004) to advance the implementation of HRE programmes in all sectors. The first phase of the World Programme (2005–2007) focused specifically on primary and secondary schools, with a specific plan of action to support this sector.

CHALLENGES AND PROGRESS IN IMPLEMENTING HRE

Although a number of governments have now made substantial commitments to HRE, the task of implementing HRE into the school curriculum is one fraught with challenges. An examination of the situation in South Africa illustrates some of the difficulties that may be encountered in seeking to implement HRE policies, even when there is goodwill and relatively strong political commitment to the project.

Post-apartheid South Africa is widely recognised as having one of the most progressive constitutions in the world, designed to support 'a society based on democratic values, social justice and fundamental human rights'. The advancement of human rights and freedoms is one of the founding provisions of the Republic of South Africa, as spelt out in the constitution, yet incorporating human rights education into the school curriculum has not been a straightforward or simple procedure. Rather than introduce a new curriculum subject labelled HRE or even civics, the education authorities have sought to integrate HRE and awareness of social justice into established curriculum areas. The curriculum statement for grades 1–9 states:

> The curriculum can play a vital role in creating awareness of the relationship between human rights, a healthy environment, social justice and inclusivity. In some countries this is done through subjects such as civics. The Revised National Curriculum Statement has tried to ensure that all learning Area Statements reflect the principles and practices of social justice, respect for the environment and human rights as defined in the Constitution. In particular, the curriculum attempts to be sensitive to issues of poverty, inequality, race, gender, age, disability, and such challenges as HIV/AIDS (quoted in Keet and Carrim, 2006).

Despite the central and symbolic place which HRE has been assigned in the South African curriculum, and goodwill among curriculum planners, the challenges of developing appropriate HRE curricula which allow learners to understand and explore the relationship between human rights and the specific social justice issues facing their own communities and the nation as a whole have proved considerable. Keet and Carrim (2006) argue that the absence of a coherent implementation strategy and consequent decontextualized and ahistorical approaches to HRE have meant that learners in South African schools have not been able to access their entitlement. Efforts to infuse HRE into conventional subject disciplines have been further hindered by the complex processes of curricular reform which have been enacted in the post-apartheid era. Thus, an education in human rights, which is every young person's entitlement under the Convention on the Rights of the Child (UN, 1989) and which, addresses children's specific social and cultural needs, and is 'sensitive to issues of poverty, inequality, race, gender, age, disability, and such challenges as HIV/AIDS, has not yet been made available to all South African learners as a right.

Notwithstanding the often complex challenges of introducing HRE, a number of governments have made significant steps forward in enabling learners to access their right to HRE. Sometimes these commitments have come about, at least in part, as the result of efforts by NGOs and committed individuals who have formed partnerships and lobbied for change. For example, in Taiwan in 1998 a group of political scientists and educators from Soochow University and Taipei Teachers' College organized a workshop to raise awareness of human rights education among teachers and teacher educators. They invited a number of international guests to speak. By 2004, following a change of government in 2000 which ended one-party rule in Taiwan, HRE was incorporated into the formal school curriculum. In April of that year, the group of Taiwanese educators and activists hosted a number of conferences across the country to publicize local and international initiatives in HRE (Osler, 2005b). Their intention was to gain the support of school principals and politicians in implementing

HRE as a newly recognised subject in the Taiwanese school curriculum. Not only did they invite their international guests back to participate and share in their success, but they also arranged a meeting between these guests and the minister of education. Having worked to get HRE onto the formal curriculum, the next stage was to lobby government for support and training so that teachers and school leaders will be in a position to implement HRE in Taiwanese schools.

In Britain, the Education in Human Rights Network (EIHRN) was set up in 1986 to disseminate the work of the Council of Europe in the field of human rights education, in the absence of government efforts to promote HRE. A small group of educators working in teacher education and in NGOs met twice a year to share good practice and to build up support for this work. They began by organizing a human rights fair and followed this with a series of conferences and other activities over a period of some 15 years.

In 1998, again following a change of government, draft proposals were published to introduce citizenship education to schools in England. There was no mention of human rights in the draft report. EIHRN lobbied the Chair of the government-appointed working group, Bernard Crick, responsible for drafting the report. We invited him to a conference on Human Rights and Democracy in Schools, where we argued that human rights principles should underpin the citizenship curriculum. At the same time the UK Economic and Social Research Council (ESRC) sponsored a series of seminars at which scholars and other interested parties, including members of the EIHRN, were able to explore in greater depth the significance of HRE for UK schools. Following this process of lobbying, the final report of the citizenship working group, while not placing human rights at the heart of the new proposals for citizenship education in England, acknowledged that students should learn about key human rights documents (Osler, 2000a).

CITIZENSHIP EDUCATION, DIVERSITY AND SHARED VALUES

Over the past decade, there has been a considerable growth in interest in education for democratic citizenship (EDC) from both nation-states and from a range of international organizations, including UNESCO, the Council of Europe, and the Organization for Economic Cooperation and Development (OECD). A review of research literature and official policy documents has identified six key contextual factors which go some way to explaining this growth in interest, namely: concern about global injustice and inequality (linked, since 2001, to concerns about global security and terrorism); processes of globalization and migration and their impact on local communities and schools, concerns about levels of civic and political engagement, a perceived youth deficit, the end of the cold war, and anti-democratic and racist movements (Osler and Starkey, 2006).

Following the work of the Council of Europe, there is a growing recognition of human rights as the underpinning principles of EDC at the level of the nation-state. Human rights were identified as one of four key principles (along with diversity and unity, global inter-connectedness and experience and participation) which an international consensus panel convened at the University of Washington's Center for Multicultural Education argued should underpin citizenship education programmes in contexts of diversity and in our global age (Banks et al., 2005). Human rights principles tend to be explicit in the EDC programmes of newly democratized states, such as those of Latin America and of Eastern and Central Europe and (as our recent European Commission-funded transnational research project INTERACT indicates) in countries such as Spain and Portugal, which experienced a period of dictatorship during the latter half of the twentieth century (Osler and Starkey, undated).

However, not all countries make explicit the values base underpinning EDC. Britain, for example, with a long and unbroken history of democracy, does not acknowledge human rights as the values base for citizenship education within the National Curriculum for England. Indeed, recent media debates have tended to focus on the need to emphasize British values and Britishness as part of the preparation of young people for living together in a society characterized by ethnic diversity. These debates have been particularly strong following the terrorist bombings of London on 7 July 2005. In December 2006, the then Prime Minister Tony Blair identified British values as 'belief in democracy, the rule of law, tolerance, equal treatment for all' (Blair, 2006). Earlier the same year Gordon Brown gave a widely reported speech on 'The future of Britishness' in which he listed shared British values as 'liberty, responsibility fairness'. Citizens of other nations might well ask, as have many British citizens, what is peculiarly British about these values? They are in keeping with international human rights principles and might be the expressed values of any modern democracy.

The processes of introducing and implementing citizenship education into the National Curriculum for England provide us with an interesting case study of how EDC may neglect the specific needs and interest of minorities. My own analysis of the Crick Report on EDC in England, *Education for Citizenship and the teaching of democracy in Schools* (QCA, 1998) suggests that the images and understandings of multiculturalism within the this official document are problematic and that the ways in which it deals with questions of difference, equality and justice are inadequate (Osler, 2000b). A key aim of any programme of citizenship must be to enable young people to understand the barriers to citizenship, including that of racism, and equip them with the skills to challenge and overcome such barriers.

Yet the Crick report adopts terminology which reflects a lack of familiarity with the everyday realities of multicultural Britain. For example, it refers to the 'homelands of our minority communities' (QCA, 1998: 30), a phrase which is not only patronizing in tone but which effectively serves to question and even undermine the Britishness of students of colour and their right to identify with Britain as their home country.[2] Hybrid and multiple identities mean that many students at school in England, and not just those from visible minority communities, are able to identify with a number of places, including Britain, but also their locality and often other countries with which their families have a direct link (Osler and Starkey, 2003 and 2005).

The language of the Crick report also reveals some negative stereotyping of minority communities within Britain. For example, it states: 'Majorities must respect, understand and tolerate minorities and minorities must learn to respect the laws, codes and conventions as much as the majority – not because it is useful to do so, but because this process helps foster common citizenship (QCA, 1998: 3.16: 17–18).

According to those who drafted the report, one of the keys to a successful multicultural society is tolerance. But this tolerance is seen as a one-way process; majority society's norms are left unquestioned. There is no recognition that minorities are also exercising tolerance in living alongside a supposedly homogeneous majority. The behaviours, cultures and values of this majority community are taken as standard. This is not a model of multiculturalism where we all learn to live together and in which these processes of learning are seen as enriching, but one in which difference remains problematic, even as it is tolerated. Tolerance, by all parties, may be an essential first step towards the development of a multicultural society and the development of a multicultural form of citizenship, but it is unlikely to be a sufficient requirement. It needs to be balanced by guarantees of equality of rights, and the absence of discrimination not just at the level of interpersonal relationships but also within the structures of government at national, local and community levels, in the workplace and in key services such as housing and health.

The second part of the above quotation from the Crick Report also presents some difficulties. Minorities are asked to 'learn and respect the laws codes and conventions' of British society. It is not clear whether minorities are perceived to have cultures and values at odds with the laws and conventions or whether they have not yet been socialized into these conventions, perhaps because they are recent migrants. Or maybe those who drafted the report are aware of statistical or other evidence which suggests that individuals from minority communities break the law more often than do individuals from majority communities? However we seek to explain these references to 'minorities', it is apparent that, from the perspective of those drafting the report, minorities are seen as 'other' and that these minorities suffer from a deficit.

Bernard Crick has defended the report against criticisms that it fails to address racism as a barrier to citizenship, arguing that explicitly anti-racist approaches are likely to be 'inflammatory – just what the racist white lads will look forward to in a classroom discussion' (Crick, 2000). Crick wishes to promote free and equal citizenship, yet it is not clear how this will be achieved if we are unable to engage directly with racism as a barrier to equal citizenship, examine ways in which it serves to deny citizenship, and identify strategies for overcoming it (see also Starkey, this volume).

In 2006, the government ordered a review which set out to examine ways in which diversity might be addressed within the citizenship curriculum and to consider the role of British history in teaching for citizenship. Although official recognition of the need to develop citizenship for diversity is to be welcomed, the report of the review team led by Sir Keith Ajegbo (DfES, 2007) appears to look back to a notion of multiculturalism from the 1980s which overlooks structural inequality and instead lays emphasis on 'celebration' of different identities. It notes the legal obligations of schools to address race equality but does not discuss human rights or engage with a practical or theoretical framework in which racism is acknowledged and challenged as a barrier to full and free citizenship (Osler, 2008).

Thus government support for EDC does not necessarily mean that the needs of minorities will be met or that students from all backgrounds will be provided with skills to challenge the inequalities and discrimination which hinder the full citizenship and participation of many from minority communities.

SOME CHALLENGES FACING HUMAN RIGHTS EDUCATORS

The Council of Europe has not always distinguished between education for democratic citizenship and human rights education; the unspoken assumption is that they cover the same core ground and both are concerned with strengthening human rights and democracy. Yet, in practice, programmes of EDC and HRE may differ considerably in the ways in which they characterize the relationship between the individual and the nation-state. It is this issue which I believe needs to be addressed if EDC is to be an effective vehicle for human rights education. I have already discussed how EDC may fail to address the needs of learners from minority groups on the basis of equality, and how it is not guaranteed that such programmes will necessarily prioritize the dismantling of barriers to full citizenship for minority citizens – something which I would argue is a key responsibility of all, regardless of whether they are themselves from a minority group or from the mainstream.

One serious limitation of citizenship education programmes as a vehicle for HRE is that they do not generally encourage learners to be critical of government. National programmes of citizenship education may have, as one of their goals, the encouragement of allegiance to the nation-state and a sense of patriotism. Our research suggests that teachers in England may feel uncomfortable with

such an approach, and may wish to avoid reference to national symbols, such as the national anthem or the flag. Nevertheless, regardless of national contexts teachers need to remember that:

> Patriotism is a double edged sword ... The accusation of 'unpatriotic behavior' can intimidate teachers and students into self-censorship. They may bow to conformist pressure from powerful media, clergymen and the government as to what is legitimate and what is out of bounds.
>
> ... To guard against abuses of patriotism, teachers should emphasize critical patriotism. This approach eschews the irrational 'My country, right or wrong!' Critical patriotism encourages reasoned loyalty; pride in the 'rights' of the nation alongside a commitment to correct its 'wrongs' (Banks et al., 2005).

Our research suggests that in France, programmes of civic education are more likely to encourage this critical assessment of certain aspects of national policy. For example, civics courses address the right of workers to strike and to take action against policies of which they disapprove. By contrast, it is inconceivable that learners in England would be presented with an official programme of study in which the right to strike would be emphasized (Osler and Starkey, 2001). One analysis of the citizenship education initiative in England, based on interviews with the Crick committee, examines how efforts to erase politics from policy-making risks placing citizenship education policy beyond political critique (Pykett, 2007). In such a climate, and where the major research funding into citizenship learning in schools is, in fact, an assessment of policy implementation or identification of best practices, measured against criteria in official documents, there is a danger that more critical analyses and alternative ways of knowing are lost. Effectively, citizenship education is in danger of being depoliticized. Teacher compliance may be given greater weight than critical thinking by both teachers and learners.

One key difference between HRE programmes and citizenship education is that effective human rights education necessarily requires learners to be made aware of the need to hold governments to account. Governments are responsible for securing our human rights. While we may only be able to claim our rights if others are prepared to defend them, we should not see human rights as an exclusive contract between individuals. Some HRE programmes in schools might be criticized for placing too much emphasis on the responsibilities we owe to each other (horizontal ties) and insufficient attention to the responsibilities which nation-states have towards their citizens and towards others living under their jurisdiction. So, for example, a programme which encourages young people to address bullying, stressing the need of young people to look after each other's interests, is emphasizing the horizontal obligations of citizens to defend each others' rights. If the programme fails to explain how specific forms of bullying are abuses of human rights and how the law has been developed to protect the individual from such abuse; how teachers, schools and other agencies have specific legal duties to protect young people from racist, sexist or homophobic bullying; and that failure to protect young people leaves authorities open to processes of legal redress; such a programme would be ignoring the duties of the nation-state to protect and guarantee rights.

As we have seen, governments have an obligation to ensure that the promotion of human rights is a key educational goal, with the requirement that HRE be integrated into national education policies. Across Europe, it would appear that the most common response among governments to ensuring that HRE is a part of the formal school curriculum is to integrate human rights into the citizenship curriculum. Yet:

> Spending an occasional hour or two on the subject of children's rights in schools would clearly fall short of the obligation States Parties have taken upon themselves. Essentially, there has to be a shift in fundamental attitudes on respect for children's rights. Theoretical teaching on the values of human rights and democracy serves little purpose if these values are not also put into practice (Verhellen, 2000: 42).

I have sought to demonstrate that HRE is not an alternative to civics, social studies, religious education, moral education or education for democratic citizenship. Nation-states have made a commitment to integrating HRE into their education policies. If EDC is to be the vehicle for HRE then human rights, or children's rights, cannot simply be another topic within an overcrowded citizenship education programme. Human rights principles need to underpin both the content and the practice of citizenship teaching and learning. They also need to be reflected in the leadership practices and day-to-day management of the school.

As the quote from Malcolm X, discussed above, reminds us, citizenship and education for democratic citizenship must be premised on recognition of our shared humanity. This implies a cosmopolitan approach in which EDC is extended so that learners are able to imagine an interconnected world, in which they recognise their common interests and interdependence with others, in their local communities, the nation and internationally. It requires recognition of the strengths of cosmopolitan and diverse communities as an asset to democracy, as practiced at local and national levels. It is through engaging with difference at these levels that democratic practices will be strengthened and renewed. After all, it is difficult to see the point of practising democracy and democratic dialogue if we all agree, and have no differences to resolve. The human rights project is a cosmopolitan one, in which nationality and citizenship are not privileged over our common humanity. This vision of our shared humanity and of our interdependent world is at the heart of the theory of education for cosmopolitan citizenship which we have been developing (Osler and Vincent, 2002; Osler and Starkey, 2003: 2005). Education for cosmopolitan citizenship, which is underpinned by human rights and emphasizes our shared humanity, is a potentially powerful framework enabling governments to meet their obligations in promoting human rights as a key educational goal.

NOTES

1 This chapter draws on material first published as Osler, A. (2008) 'Human rights education and education for democratic citizenship', in: C. Mahler., A. Mihr and R. Toivanen (eds.) *The United Nations Decade for Human Rights Education and the Inclusion of National Minorities*. Frankfurt: Peter Lang Verlag. My thanks to the editors for allowing me to re-use this material in this chapter.

2 Interestingly, research which included interviews with members of the Crick committee revealed a desire among those involved to play down the political implications and assumptions of the report, with one member even denying the use of this phrase 'homelands of our minority communities' (Pykett, 2007).

REFERENCES

Appiah, K.A. (2006) *Cosmopolitanism: Ethics in a World of Strangers*. New York: W.W. Norton.

Banks, J. (1997) *Educating Citizens in a Multicultural Society*. New York: Teachers College Press.

Banks, J.A., Banks, C.A. McGee, Cortes, C., Hahn, C.L., Merryfield, M., Moodley, K., Murphy-Shigematsu, S., Osler, A., Park, C. and Parker, W.C. (2005) *Democracy and Diversity: Principles and Concepts for Educating Citizens in a Global Age*. Seattle, WA: Center for Multicultural Education, University of Washington.

Blair, T. (2006) 'Our nation's future: multiculturalism and integration', speech given at 10 Downing Street, 8 December 2006. Availablehttp://www.number10.gov.uk/output/Page10563.asp Accessed 3 August 2007.

Brown, G. (2006) 'Who do we want to be? The future of Britishness' speech given to the Fabian Society, 16 January 2006. Available http://fabians.org.uk/events/new-year-conference-06/brown-britishness/speech Accessed 3 August 2007.

Crick, B. (2000) 'Friendly arguments', in: *Essays on Citizenship*. London: Continuum.

Department for Education and Skills (DfES) (2007) Curriculum *Review: Diversity and Citizenship (Ajegbo Report)* PPSLS/D35/0107/14. London: DfES.

Figueroa, P. (2000) Citizenship education for a plural society, in A. Osler (ed.) *Citizenship and Democracy in Schools: Diversity, Identity, Equality*. Stoke-on-Trent, UK and Sterling, VA: Trentham.

Fryer, P. (1984) *Staying Power: The History of Black People in Britain*. London and Sydney: Pluto Press.

Hall, S. (2000) 'Multicultural citizens: monocultural citizenship', in: N. Pearce and J. Hallgarten (eds) *Tomorrow's Citizens: Critical Debates in Citizenship and Education*. London: Institute for Public Policy Research.

Hwang K-K. (2001) 'Introducing human rights education in the Confucian society of Taiwan: its implications for ethical leadership in education', *International Journal of Leadership in Education*, 4 (1): 321–332.

Jawad, H. and Benn, T. (2003) (eds) *Muslim Women in the United Kingdom and Beyond: Experiences and Images*. Leiden: Brill.

Keet, A. and Carrim, N. (2006) 'Human rights education and curricular reform in South Africa', *Journal of Social Science Education*, 2006, 1. On-line journal: Available http://www.jsse.org/2006-1/keet_carrim_s-africa.htm

Malcolm, X. (1964) 'Racism: the cancer that is Destroying America,' Egyptian Gazette, 25 August. Available http://www.cmgworld-wide.com/historic/malcolm/about/quotes_articles.htm Accessed 7 August 2007.

Office of the High Commissioner for Human Rights (OHCHR) (1993) World Conference on Human Rights 14-25 June, Vienna, Austria. Available http://www.unhchr.ch/html/menu5/wchr.htm Accessed 1 August 2007.

Osler, A. (ed.) (2000a) *Citizenship and Democracy in Schools: Diversity, Identity, Equality.* Stoke-on-Trent, UK and Sterling, VA: Trentham.

Osler, A. (2000b) 'The Crick report: difference, equality and racial justice', *The Curriculum Journal*, 11 (1): 25–37.

Osler, A. (2005a) 'Looking to the future: democracy, diversity and citizenship education', in A. Osler (ed.) *Teachers, Human Rights and Diversity: Educating Citizens in Multicultural Societies*. Stoke-on-Trent, UK and Sterling, VA: Trentham.

Osler, A. (2005b) 'Preface', in A. Osler (ed.) *Teachers, Human Rights and*

Diversity: Educating Citizens in Multicultural Societies. Stoke-on-Trent, UK and Sterling, VA: Trentham.

Osler, A. (2008) 'Citizenship education and the Ajegbo report: re-imagining a cosmopolitan nation', *London Review of Education*, 6(1): 9–23.

Osler, A. and Hill, J. (1999) 'Exclusion from school and racial equality: an examination of government proposals in the light of recent research evidence', *Cambridge Journal of Education*, 29 (1): 33–62.

Osler, A. and Starkey, H. (2001) 'Citizenship education and national identities in France and England: inclusive or exclusive?', *Oxford Review of Education*, 27 (2): 287–305.

Osler, A. and Starkey, H. (2003) 'Learning for cosmopolitan citizenship: theoretical debates and young people's experiences', *Educational Review*, 55 (3): 243–254.

Osler, A. and Starkey, H. (2005) *Changing Citizenship: Democracy and Inclusion in Education.* Maidenhead: Open University Press.

Osler, A. and Starkey, H. (2006) 'Education for democratic citizenship: a review of research, policy and practice 1995-2005', *Research Papers in Education*, 21 (4): 433–466.

Osler, A. and Starkey, H. (undated) INTERACT: Intercultural Active Citizenship http://www.education.leeds.ac.uk/research/cchre/projects.php?project=66&page=1

Osler, A. and Vincent, K. (2002) *Citizenship and the Challenge of Global Education.* Stoke-on-Trent, UK and Sterling, VA: Trentham.

Osler, A. and Vincent, K. (2003) *Girls and Exclusion: Re-thinking the Agenda.* London: RoutledgeFalmer.

Qualifications and Curriculum Authority (QCA) (1998) *Education for Citizenship and the Teaching of Democracy in Schools* (Crick Report). London: QCA.

Parekh, B. (2000) *Rethinking Multiculturalism: Cultural Diversity and Political Theory.* London: Macmillan.

Pykett, J. (2007) 'Making citizens governable? The Crick report as governmental technology', *Journal of Education Policy,* 22 (3): 310–319.

Republic of South Africa, Preamble to the Constitution of South Africahttp://www.southafrica.info/ess_info/sa_glance/constitution/constitution.htmAccessed 8 August 2007.

Richardson, R. (1997) *Islamophobia: A Challenge for Us All.* London: Runnymede Trust.

Richardson, R. (ed.) (2004) *Islamophobia: Issues, Challenges and Action.* Stoke-on-Trent: Trentham with the Uniting Britain Trust, London.

Starkey, H. (1992) 'Teaching for social responsibility', in: J. Lynch, C. Modgil, and S. Modgil (eds.) *Cultural Diversity and the Schools: Human Rights, Education and Global Responsibility.* Volume 4. London: Falmer.

Tikly, L., Osler, A. and Hill, J. (2006) 'The ethnic minority achievement grant: a critical analysis', *Journal of Education Policy,* 20 (3): 283–312.

United Nations (1948) Universal Declaration of Human Rights, adopted by General Assembly resolution 217 A (III) of 10December,1948.http://www.un.org/Overview/rights.html Accessed 9 August, 2007.

United Nations (1966) International Covenant on Economic, Social and Cultural Rights, adopted by General Assembly resolution 2200A (XXI) of 16 December 1966 http://www.unhchr.ch/html/menu3/b/a_cescr.htm Accessed 1 August, 2007.

United Nations (1989) UN Convention on the Rights of the Child, adopted and opened for signature, ratification and accession by General Assembly resolution 44/25 of 20 November 1989 http://www.unhchr.ch/html/menu3/b/k2crc.htm Accessed 10 August, 2007.

United Nations (1993) *Vienna Declaration and Programme of Action.* World Conference on Human Rights 14-25 June. A/CONF.157/23 12 July. http://www.unhchr.ch/huridocda/huridoca.nsf/(Symbol)/A.CONF.157.23.En

United Nations (1994) General Assembly Resolution, 49/184, 23 December.

United Nations (2004) General Assembly Resolution, 59/113, 10 December.. http://daccessdds.un.org/doc/UNDOC/GEN/N04/483/04/PDF/N0448304.pdf?Open Element Accessed 31 July, 2007

Verhellen, E. (2000) 'Children's rights and education', in: A. Osler (ed.) *Citizenship and Democracy in Schools: Diversity, Identity, Equality.* Stoke-on-Trent, UK and Sterling, VA: Trentham.

36

Global Education

Graham Pike

THE HISTORICAL CONTEXT

Since the late 1960s, global education has developed as a curriculum reform movement that attempts to respond to the increasing interdependence and rapid change that characterizes the contemporary world. Beginning in the developed world, notably in the US and the UK (where the term 'world studies' was initially preferred), the ideas and practice of global education, in various formats and guises, have gradually spread around the globe and can be found in at least 38 countries on six continents (Tye, 1999). The roots of global education in Europe can be traced back to the interwar movements of the 1920s that sought to use formal education as a vehicle to promote a more sustained peace and, post-1945, flourished under the banner of 'education for international understanding' (Fujikane, 2003; Heater, 1980; Richardson, 1996). During the Cold War era, seminal work in the US by Lee Anderson (1979), James Becker (1979) and Robert Hanvey (1975) sought to expand the Eurocentric social studies curriculum by infusing perspectives from other world regions and promoting understanding of global systems (Merryfield, 2001). In the final quarter of the twentieth century, the rationale for incorporating a global perspective in the curriculum shifted as the multiple and inexorable impacts of globalization became more starkly apparent (Anderson, 1990). During the same period, students' apparent lack of knowledge about global issues and world geography, and their concomitant lack of preparedness to face the realities of an interdependent global system, began to cause alarm among educators in Western nations, particularly in the US (Merryfield, 1991; Torney, 1977).

Throughout its short history, global education has been characterized – and, some would argue, troubled – by the search for a single, widely accepted definition that encompasses its diverse content, pedagogy and philosophical positions. As will be explored in this chapter, the wide range of ideological and pedagogical assumptions to be found in the host of educational initiatives that shelter under the umbrella of 'global education' renders an agreed and succinct definition unlikely. Popkewitz (1980: 304) contends that the term global education operates more as an educational slogan, a label that creates a 'unity of feeling and spirit about the tasks to be confronted in schooling'. To add to the confusion, global education is regarded by some as an overarching concept that provides unity and coherence to several related fields, including development education, environmental education, human rights education and peace education (Greig et al., 1987; Heater, 1980; Tye, 1999). Some clarity is provided by the various conceptual frameworks that are frequently cited in the literature, including those of Case (1993), Hanvey (1975), Kniep (1986), Merryfield (1995, 2001), and Pike and Selby (1995, 1999). From among these frameworks, it is possible to discern some common threads that are likely to be found in the conceptual make-up of most theoretical articulations of global education. These are:

- global connections and interdependence;
- global systems;
- global issues and problems;
- cross-cultural understanding;
- human beliefs and values; and
- awareness of choices for the future.

In practice, global education in the classroom may not feature all of the threads found in proponents' theoretical models. Pike (2000b: 65) found several common ideas explored by teachers in Canada, United States and United Kingdom.

- *Interdependence* of all people within the global system, often expressed in terms of the connections between students in one country with people and environments in other parts of the world.
- *Connectedness*, in a wider sense, sometimes formulated in terms of the shared universal attributes of humankind, at other times applied to real or desired links between areas of knowledge, curriculum subjects, aspects of schooling or humans and their environments.
- *A global perspective*, generally interpreted to mean the provision of insights, ideas and information that enable students to look beyond the confines of local and national boundaries in their thinking and aspirations.
- *Multiple perspectives*: a belief in the educative value of considering differing views on any issue before reaching a judgment.

The characterization given above could be regarded as the relatively non-controversial face of global education, an eminently justifiable infusion of a broad set of ideas that emanates from global educators' beliefs about the world and about schools' responsibilities in preparing students for global realities. Beneath this bland visage, however, lie variations of global education, in both theory and practice, that span a spectrum of ideological positions and which, in some cases, have given rise to considerable controversy (Hicks, 2003; Lamy, 1990; Schukar, 1993). Central to the more contentious manifestations is a critique, at times explicit, of the role of schooling in the promotion of nationalism or in supporting the institutions of, and values ascribed to, the nation state (Pike, 2000b; Richardson, 1979; Tye, 1999). Robin Richardson (1979), an early pioneer of world studies in the UK, threw down the gauntlet in constructing 'a map of the field', on which he plotted various curriculum initiatives in UK and the USA. His 'map' suggests that global educators are rooted in divergent educational and political philosophies. This insightful analysis reveals an ideological schism in global education that remains to this day.

Toh (1993: 9) explores the schism in depth in his description of two 'paradigms of global literacy' which, he suggests, characterize different practices in global education. The 'liberal technocratic paradigm', most likely to be found within schools in Canada and elsewhere, promotes relatively superficial understanding of other cultures, an uncritical and self-centred acceptance of the nature of interdependence and a belief in progress through unbridled economic growth (10–11). The alternative 'transformative paradigm' emphasizes ethical concern for victims of injustice, equitable sharing and sustainability of global resources, social and political activism, and a critical and empowering pedagogy (12–15). Likewise, O'Sullivan (1999) identifies 'global economic competitiveness' and 'global interdependence' paradigms of global education with similar, though not identical, features. These two models, which I shall term conservative and reformative, highlight distinct differences in the political underpinning and the pedagogical practice of global education and the role that schools play in the preparation of the next generation.

FROM NEO-LIBERALISM TO NEO-NATIONALISM

The more radical manifestations of global education, especially those which encouraged critical thinking on social issues and questioned the school's role in promoting nationalism, were already under attack from the political and religious right wing (Cunningham, 1986; Kjos, 1990; Scruton, 1985) by the time neo-liberal policies began to influence educational decision-making in many developed countries in the 1980s. The influential report, *A Nation at Risk: The Imperative for Educational Reform,* delivered by the US National Commission on Excellence in Education in 1983, was soon followed by key reports in Canada and by the unveiling of the 1988 Education Reform Act in United Kingdom. The major thrust of these initiatives was a move away from the 'ethical liberalism' (Manzer, 1994) of the post-war years towards requiring school curricula to focus principally on developing the knowledge and skills required for global competitiveness, based on a perception that schools were failing to adequately prepare students for ensuring their nation's success in the rapidly expanding global economy (Mitchell, 2003). The key impacts of these school reform movements have been similar: standardization of curriculum; increased measurement of student achievement and, consequently, a narrowing of what is taught to that which can be most effectively measured and holding teachers and schools accountable for the performance of their students. The net effect on the tenuous progress of global education, the pedagogical outcomes of which were not well-researched or documented (Merryfield, 1998) as well as being very difficult

to measure, was quickly revealed in its marginalization within revised curriculum frameworks and in a decline in grassroots activities due to cuts in government funding (Gaudelli, 2003; Hicks, 2003; Mundy, 2007; Pike, 2000a).

It is somewhat ironic, given their impact on global education, that neo-liberal educational reforms were instituted largely as a response to a recognition of the increasing impact of globalization. On the face of it, globalization would seem to suggest that schools should distance themselves from their traditional role in developing citizens who are loyal only to the nation state (Green, 1990) and favour the creation of multiple identities and allegiances, some of which cross national boundaries. However, as Bottery (2006) points out, it is economic globalization that sets the context in which other forms of globalization operate, and a critical need in the 'knowledge economy' is control of access to knowledge. The desire to 'manage' knowledge, so that intelligence, innovation and creativity can be better packaged to the benefit of business and industry, lead to the standardization, measurement and accountability reforms noted above, in an attempt to better understand what students – the future workforce – know and need to know. On top of this, international reports on measures of student achievement, such as the Programme for International Student Assessment (PISA) conducted by the Organisation for Economic Co-operation and Development (OECD), began to highlight the relative success of its members' youth in reading, mathematics and science, thereby increasing the focus on these curriculum areas in many nations. Thus, the educational response to globalization has been the emergence of what might be termed 'neo-nationalism', in which a nation's children are subjected to an increasingly narrow, controlled and standardized curriculum in order, it is believed, to better serve national interests in the global economy and to be seen to compete more effectively with students from other nations.

Even when viewed from within the conservative paradigm of global education, the neo-liberal education agenda would seem to be seriously flawed. First, as indicated above, it is predicated on the traditional model of schooling serving the national interest, with a particular emphasis on the national economy, in an era in which the distinction between national and global interests is increasingly blurred. It is, in essence, based on pre-globalization thinking, a view of the world emanating from the time when economies were more tightly tied to nations. With transnational corporations able and willing to seek skilled employees from every part of the globe, the idea of preparing a nation's children for making a contribution exclusively to their own country's economy is quickly becoming outdated (Zhao, 2007). Second, the neo-liberal agenda responds to one critical need of the knowledge economy – standardization and predictability in the management of knowledge – but fails dismally to answer another: the need for creativity and flexibility (Bottery, 2006; Zhao, 2007). As Yong Zhao argues in his critique of the US 'No Child Left Behind' policy:

> To remain competitive, a nation must cultivate new industries and its businesses must innovate. As traditional industries move to other countries, those jobs get outsourced. Instead of trying to keep them, the United States should consider creating new ones, which demands different talents and intelligences (Zhao, 2007, 10).

For Zhao, the eventual impact of the concerted attempt to increase test scores in mathematics, reading and science will be to 'kill the most important and sought-after commodity in the twenty-first century – creativity' (p. 5). In giving priority to curriculum outcomes that can be more easily measured, and to those subjects which feature in international comparisons of achievement, there is less room in the curriculum for creativity and critical thinking, and for subjects – such as the arts – that foster alternative visions of reality.

From a reformative global education standpoint, those alternative visions are critical (Davies, 2005, 2006). The neo-liberal education agenda is based on a premise that better performance in the 'basic' subjects of mathematics, reading and science will raise educational standards and, ipso facto, produce citizens better able to contribute to human advancement. Furthermore, it is assumed that enhanced competition between countries (and between schools and communities in those nations that have established 'league tables') will produce better results. Yet, the 'basic' subjects are those that have been at the heart of the school curriculum for a century or more and which, it could be argued, have given rise not only to considerable scientific and technological progress but also to environmental and social problems of great magnitude. It is interesting to note that some teachers in Finland, the country that has performed best overall in PISA tests, have recently expressed the need for more understanding of world cultures as the foreign-born school population rises (Tuomi, 2004). Davies (2005) argues that the increased emphasis on standardization and competitiveness in schools is directly linked to a worldwide breakdown in social cohesion and suggests that an 'alternative' PISA research program is needed to track schools' achievements in democracy and peace. Central to the arguments of the reformative global educators is the belief that solutions to prevailing social and global problems, which are infinitely complex and interdependent, are unlikely to be found within the confines of a few 'basic' disciplines, even if studied in more depth and in school environments where competition, measurement and accountability are enforced. Rather, it is argued, solutions will emerge from collaborative learning ventures that encourage the creative interplay of insights from several disciplines and lead to the development of new knowledge that is provisional and unpredictable (Selby, 1999).

Perhaps the most telling critique of neo-nationalism in schools comes from students themselves. Not only are young people in many countries concerned, and interested in learning more, about world events and global issues (Holden and Hicks, 2007; One World Alliance, 2006; War Child Canada, 2006; Yamashita, 2006), they are also breaking free from the shackles of nationalism through their own actions and relationships (Careless, 2004). The instantaneous global reach of communications technology has shattered the national boundaries that used to determine and contain their friendships, while the increasing cosmopolitanism of urban centres is continuously recreating the world within their home communities. Mitchell and Parker (2008) argue that social scientists' dichotomizations of national and global are outdated and inadequate for understanding the shifting allegiances of young people who, because they were born into an interconnected world, already imagine the world in global terms. Teenagers, they suggest, have developed 'an increased spatial and temporal flexibility of multiple allegiances' (p. 8) which allows them to move their affinities and loyalties back and forth quite readily from local to global scales. Patriotism, though undoubtedly strong in the United States after September 11, 2001, appears to have 'a 'shelf-life' of emotive energy for many young people' (p. 23), for whom patriotic allegiance is linked to the actions of humans in particular situations, rather than in specific nations. The phenomenon of 'blogging', growing at a staggering rate, allows concerned citizens to read first-hand reports from war zones and other real-life contexts inaccessible to mainstream media and affords bloggers the opportunity to participate actively in global dialogues (Lewis, 2007). The extent to which open access to global information creates new understanding is less clear. Merryfield's (2007) study of American teachers' use of web-based materials to teach about the world found a very strong preference for American websites, even though sites from other countries were highly recommended and easily accessible.

THE METAMORPHOSES OF GLOBAL EDUCATION

The flexibility and multiplicity of allegiances in the contemporary world is central to the emergence of new forms of global education that are oriented around changing perceptions of the concepts of identity, loyalty and citizenship. Given the struggles for legitimacy and dwindling resources faced by global educators as neo-liberalism took hold in public education, it is not surprising that they should seek alliances with other curriculum reform movements that enjoy more mainstream support. In US, especially, the experiences of immigrants have brought global education and multicultural education closer together, based on the premise that greater understanding of the perspectives of ethnic and marginalized groups within the nation will afford insights into, and greater comfort with, ideas and practices in other parts of the world (Banks, 2001; Banks et al., 2005). Additionally, the hybrid identities and multiple allegiances fostered by immigration challenge 'the imperial habit of defining culture by national boundaries' (Merryfield, 2001) and critique 'the Eurocentric, Cold War framework' of global education that divides the world into 'us' and 'them', with an assumed superiority of Western viewpoints.

Another emergent form of global education is linked to the renewed interest in citizenship education, as explored in this volume. The idea of global or world citizenship is not new, dating back to the Stoic ideal of cosmopolitanism, though it did not find a robust foothold in public education until after World War II (Heater, 2004). Even then, world citizenship was not often mentioned as a key concept in the global education literature, though it may have been implied, and – with the notable exception of the long-established Council for Education in World Citizenship in London – it rarely featured in the titles of organizations, projects or resources. 'Global citizenship education' or 'education for global citizenship' are terms now commonly found within the literature, especially in UK where Hicks (2003: 265) notes a 'resurgence of interest' in global education fuelled by funding from the Department for International Development and the emergence of citizenship education as a key element of the National Curriculum. In US, Martha Nussbaum's (1996) celebrated essay on cosmopolitanism continues to attract considerable attention from philosophers and educators (Dower, 2003; Mitchell and Parker, 2008) and Nel Noddings (2005) joins other notable American educators in her volume that advocates for global citizenship education. Interest in the concept is also emerging in other countries (Evans and Reynolds, 2004; Lee and Leung, 2006; Mundy, 2007; Pike, 2008; Richardson et al., 2003).

What is meant by global citizenship education is subject, not surprisingly, to debate. Davies (2006) introduces several interpretations through offering different permutations of global + citizenship + education; Davies et al. (2005) point to significant differences between citizenship education and global education but propose a substantive fusion of the two; Andrzejewski and Alessio (1999) suggest that citizenship education should not only be viewed in a global context but should also develop the knowledge and skills for social and environmental justice. Several writers focus on the multiple dimensions of citizenship in their rationale for a global conception. Heater (2004) proposes a 'cube of citizenship' that illustrates the interplay of three dimensions: elements of citizenship, geographical levels and education; Selby (1994) highlights the 'plural and parallel' allegiances of the global citizen; Cogan and Derricott (1998) propose four dimensions of 'multidimensional citizenship': person, social, spatial and temporal. Dower (2003) explores the many tensions in the idea of global citizenship from ethical and political viewpoints and Pike (in press) relates these dilemmas to the educational context. Whereas the confusion around the definition of global education focused principally upon its breadth and scope as an educational movement, the challenge for global citizenship education appears to lie more in the interpretation of, and justification for, its central concept.

The principles and strands of global education are clearly evident in those models of global citizenship education that identify its key components. Oxfam's (2006) 'Curriculum for Global Citizenship' echoes in many ways the earlier world studies/global education models developed in the United Kingdom, both in the choice of topics for study and in its insistence that education for global citizenship comprises knowledge, skills and attitudes that can be addressed at all levels of schooling. Cogan and Derricott's (1998) dimensions of 'multidimensional citizenship' present a conceptual model that is strikingly similar to Pike and Selby's (1988, 1995) four dimensions of global education. In Gaudelli's (2003) 'five critical dimensions of global citizenship'– population movement, economics, rights and responsibilities, cultural diversity, and contact – can be seen most of the key topics and ideas proposed by the pioneers of global education in the US. Similar, too, is the advocacy for a certain pedagogical style that considers the transmission mode as inadequate and argues for active student involvement in the learning process. Evans and Reynolds' (2004) handbook for teachers is replete with active learning ideas and practices for exploring global citizenship; Cogan and Derricott (1998) propose a 'deliberation-based curriculum', a structured process of collaborative discussion and decision-making around a set of core ethical questions; Griffith's (1998) construct of global citizenship is deeply imbued with a pedagogy of 'independent learning' which encourages students to initiate their own collaborative research projects on real social issues in the community.

As Ibrahim (2005: 182) suggests, 'citizenship education provides a vehicle through which global citizenship can become an entitlement for all pupils within a learning framework that is based on human rights, social justice and democratic participation'. Global citizenship education borrows substantially from global education, but locates itself around a core concept, the promotion of global civic consciousness, that has found increasing – though still contested – public acceptance due to recent political events and growing awareness of global interconnectedness (Fujikane, 2003). While it mirrors much of the substance of its predecessor, global citizenship education would appear to have a subtle, yet distinct anthropocentric bias. Perhaps because it draws from citizenship education as well as from global education, democracy, peace and human rights are the conceptual tools with which global citizenship education is most frequently crafted; elements of a global consciousness rooted in an environmental ethic have less prominence. Whereas environmental issues were a cornerstone of the broader global education models (Greig et al., 1987; Hicks, 2003), these are now given more attention under the banner of 'education for sustainable development' (see Huckle, in this volume). In this context, it is interesting to note that UNESCO, the United Nations body that was given the responsibility of promoting world citizenship after World War II (Heater, 2004), has chosen to pursue this goal through a major initiative to reorient education to address sustainable development (Pigozzi, 2006; UNESCO, 2005). Although there are obvious overlaps with global citizenship education, the conceptual triad at the heart of education for sustainable development – economy, environment and society – draws more from the development/environment/ social justice strands of global education and, thus, focuses more on social and political structures than on personal identity and loyalty. That said, given the fluid and emergent nature of these new developments, it is entirely possible to find characterizations and models of both that bear a strong resemblance to each other.

SOME CHALLENGES ON THE ROAD AHEAD

It is unclear whether global education, as a conception or as a title, is giving way to these newer incarnations, as it would appear from the recent literature, or whether it will be retained as a generic term that broadly describes any attempt to infuse a global perspective in education. The US National Council for the Social Studies, perhaps the first national curriculum organization to endorse global education in 1982, reaffirmed its commitment in 2004 in a position statement that – to add to the confusion – also supports the 'complementary approach' of 'international education', defined as 'the in-depth study of a specific area or region of the world to develop knowledge and understanding of another culture' (NCSS, 2004: 293). Certainly, education for global citizenship and education for sustainable development have the advantage of featuring, in their titles, the key concept upon which they are based, however contested the definition and legitimacy of that concept may be. This may help to overcome one of the difficulties encountered by global education practitioners, that of explaining what it encompasses (Pike, 1997; Mundy, 2007). More important than its nomenclature, however, is the possibility, both exciting and discomforting, that global education (which I shall use henceforth in its generic sense) may yet find a substantive niche in the neo-liberal education agenda.

One of the factors in the resurgence of global education is, unquestionably, the interest of students in world events. Blanket television coverage of the September 11 attacks in the US, and of the subsequent invasion of Iraq and acts of terrorism around the world, have resulted in bewilderment among young people and a yearning to understand what is happening and why it involves people in their own countries (Davies, 2005; Yamashita, 2006). While students report that war and conflict is the global issue they learn most about in school, much of the curriculum focus is historical and television and parents provide most of their information on contemporary conflicts (Holden and Hicks, 2007; War Child Canada, 2006; Yamashita, 2006). Other global issues that young people want to know more about include environmental destruction, HIV/AIDS, famine and human rights abuses (Davies, 2006; Our World Alliance, 2006; War Child Canada, 2006). According to national opinion polls, two-thirds of Canadians aged 15 to 24 claim to follow global issues in the news to some degree (War Child Canada, 2006), while eight out of ten 11–16-year-olds in the United Kingdom feel it is important to learn about global issues in school in order to make better choices for the future (Hicks, 2003).

Unfortunately, students' desire to know more about global issues is often thwarted by teachers' lack of knowledge or confidence in these topics (Andrzejewski and Alessio, 1999; Holden and Hicks, 2007; Yamashita, 2006). Reasons for their insufficient preparedness to teach global issues include the omission of any relevant instruction in their own undergraduate and teacher education programmes, a lack of exposure to or direct experience in other cultures or countries and a concern about how to address such complex and controversial issues in ways that will not overwhelm children or cause them distress. Even among teachers who wish to include discussion of contemporary global issues in their classrooms, there are fears about stepping outside the boundaries of the prescribed curriculum and of being accused of taking a partisan position on a sensitive issue. Despite official government support in some countries for teaching global issues as part of the mandate for citizenship education, teachers feel restricted by a lack of clear guidance and by the prevailing neo-liberal discourse in education which does not give a high priority to global education (Davies, 2006; Mundy, 2007; Schweisfurth, 2006; Yamashita, 2006).

Teachers' lack of preparedness in global education has clear implications for teacher education programmes which, with some notable exceptions, are found to be deficient in this regard in most countries (Tye, 1999). However, teacher education itself is subject to constraints and pressures that emanate from the responsibilities – often legislated – of teacher educators to adequately prepare their students to teach the existing curriculum. Even in institutions where global education is integral to the teacher preparation program (Merryfield, 1997; Pike, 2000c; Steiner, 1996; Schweisfurth, 2006), a fine line has to be walked between the desire to broaden the thinking and experience of students and the need to fully orient them to the narrower realities of schools and curricula. Teacher education is also influenced by the availability of relevant research: although empirical research on global education is growing, the dearth of a substantive body of widely known research does not help in the debates that inevitably take place among teachers and academics concerning a justification for its place in the curriculum. Davies (2005: 370) makes a strong plea for comparative educators to participate in 'interruptive democracy', to establish a comparative and international education research agenda which will challenge educational policies and practices that sustain neo-liberal thinking and will show how schools can teach for active citizenship, peace and democracy. Others suggest a less combative approach that focuses on exploring the effectiveness of global education pedagogy in meeting its desired goals; Tye (1999) argues that, while more research is needed, global educators tend to ignore the relevant research that is available and would support their cause.

The search for legitimacy has been at the heart of the global education movement since its inception. The early years were marked by attempts to define the scope of global education and to carve out a niche in the contested territory of social and political reforms to the curriculum. As conservative and neo-liberal forces took control of educational policy-making, global education was increasingly marginalized and existed principally at the grassroots level in the classrooms of the many teachers around the world who had been inspired by the resources and workshops through which the pioneers had successfully promoted their vision. There are now signs, particularly in the current discourse on education's role in addressing the concepts of global citizenship and sustainable development, of a larger public appetite for some form of global education, perhaps as a strand within a broader curriculum initiative such as citizenship education. As Davies et al. (2005) argue, there is merit in blending the pedagogical expertise and grassroots popularity of global education with the greater academic coherence of, and political support for, citizenship education in a new form of education for global citizenship that will help students understand better their rights and responsibilities as citizens in the era of globalization. However, a critical question remains: What form of education for global citizenship is most appropriate for that task?

It would appear that the schism between two conflicting paradigms of global education, alluded to in Robin Richardson's 'map of the field' in the 1970s, remains though, arguably, there is more overlap between conservative and reformative visions in the stated rationale for global education. A lead article in a recent edition of *Time* magazine critiques the neo-liberal fixation with competency in the basic skills as aiming too low, suggesting that success in the global economy demands not only high level expertise in traditional academic disciplines but also in 'twenty-first century skills'. These are defined as: 'knowing more about the world', 'thinking outside the box,' 'becoming smarter about new sources of information' and 'developing good people skills' (Wallis and Steptoe, 2006: 34–5). Many of the attributes of the 'global economic competitiveness model' of global education are lauded in this article but so too are approaches, such as student investigations of the environmental impact of consumer products, that would not be out of place in more radical models. Likewise, Zhao's (2007) damning critique of the

'No Child Left Behind' policy draws on both economic arguments and on the need for twenty-first century citizens to negotiate cultural difference and manage multiple identities. However, neither of these articles – aimed at public and general education audiences – advocates a critical social justice perspective, as advanced by Toh (1993), nor offers a critique of imperialism as recommended by Merryfield (2001), in the conception of global education they proffer.

When a leading international news magazine promotes global education, in whatever form, it suggests a shift in the prevailing public mood. Academic debates about the ideological underpinnings of various models should – and no doubt will – continue, but the critical and urgent need is to establish more widespread acceptance for at least some of global education's goals. Where such acceptance appears to exist, as important, and just as challenging, is to increase understanding of the contradictions and tensions there may be between these goals and the prevailing norms and practices of the education system (Davies, 2005; Mundy, 2007). There are risks in this strategy, of course. Current interest in the global competitiveness model could usher in reforms such as more foreign language learning, interdisciplinary teaching, intercultural understanding programmes and school exchanges without seriously challenging the basic tenets of neo-nationalism. Certainly, it seems unlikely that this model would embrace a critical social justice perspective to any significant degree. However, if global educators wish to have more impact on public education than has been enjoyed heretofore, they would do well to understand the process of educational change. As Tye (1999) notes, there exists a substantial body of literature on effective educational change that is highly relevant for global educators and its insights can be employed to their benefit. Two of Fullan's (1993: 21–2) 'eight basic lessons of the new paradigm of change' are particularly pertinent here: 'neither centralization nor decentralization works' and 'every person is a change agent'. A combination of grassroots enthusiasm, which global education appears to enjoy, and consensual support among policy makers, which – though limited – seems to be growing, is required to implement and sustain change. Furthermore, it is individuals working together who bring about lasting change, not systems. The global education literature suggests that both students and teachers desire changes that are in line with its key principles and, with some loosening of the policy constraints that currently inhibit implementation, interesting things could occur.

The model of global education that emerges, and where it is located on Richardson's 'map of the field', will probably depend – as it has in the past – on an interplay of forces from within and outside education. As global events and trends unfold, the urgency of finding solutions to challenges such as climate change, international and inter-group conflict, poverty and enforced migration may well strike a chord in public consciousness that leads to demands for more critical and more effective global education. Perhaps less debatable is the potential impact of an increasingly globally aware younger generation with personal connections that span the globe and allegiances that are tied as much to universal values as they are to national identities. Whether or not these mega trends coalesce, the task for global educators will be to continue to challenge narrow and outdated thinking in public education to ensure that it responds appropriately in undertaking its responsibility for nurturing active and critical global citizens.

NOTE

The author would like to acknowledge Maryam Wagner's assistance in preparing this chapter and to thank Deborah Hutton and Merry Merryfield for their insights into recent developments in the US.

REFERENCES

Anderson, L.F. (1979) *Schooling for Citizenship in a Global Age: An Exploration of the Meaning and Significance of Global Education.* Bloomington, IN: Social Studies Development Center.

Anderson, L.F. (1990) 'A rationale for global education', in Kenneth A. Tye (ed.), *Global Education. From Thought to Action.* Alexandria, VA: Association for Supervision and Curriculum Development. pp. 13–34.

Andrzejewski, J. and Alessio, J. (1999) 'Education for global citizenship and social responsibility', John Dewey Project of Progressive Education, University of Vermont. Retrieved from www.uvm.edu/~dewey/monographs/glomono.html

Banks, J.A. (2001) *Cultural Diversity and Education.* 4th edn. Boston, MA: Allyn and Bacon.

Banks, J.A., Banks, C.A. McGhee, C., Carlos. E., Hahn, C.L., Merryfield, M.M., Moodley, K.A., Murphy-Shigematsu, S., Osler, A., Park, C. and Parker, W.C. (2005) *Democracy and Diversity: Principles and Concepts for Educating Citizens in a Global World.* University of Washington.

Becker, J. (1979) *Schooling for a Global Age.* New York: McGraw Hill.

Bottery, M. (2006) 'Education and globalization: redefining the role of the educational professional', *Educational review,* 58 (1): 95–113.

Careless, J. (2004) 'Global education outside the classroom', *Education Canada,* 44 (2): 38.

Case, R. (1993) 'Key elements of a global perspective', *Social Education,* 57 (6): 318–325.

Cogan, J.J. and Derricott, R. (1998) *Citizenship for the 21st* Century. An *International Perspective on Education.* London: Kogan Page.

Cunningham, G.L. (1986) *Blowing the Whistle on Global Education.* Denver, CO: Region VIII Office, United States Department of Education.

Davies, I., Evans, M. and Reid, A. (2005) 'Globalising citizenship education? A critique of 'global education' and 'citizenship education', *British Journal of Educational Studies,* 53 (1): 66–89.

Davies, L. (2005) 'Schools and war: Urgent agendas for comparative and international education', *Compare,* 35 (4): 357–371.

Davies, L. (2006) 'Global citizenship: Abstraction or framework for action?', *Educational Review,* 58 (1): 5–25.

Dower, N. (2003) *An Introduction to Global Citizenship.* Edinburgh: Edinburgh University Press.

Evans, M. and Reynolds, C. (2004) *Educating for Global Citizenship in a Changing World.* Toronto: Ontario Institute for Studies in Education.

Fujikane, H. (2003) 'Approaches to global education in the United States, the United Kingdom and Japan', *International Review of Education,* 49 (1–2): 133–152.

Fullan, M. (1993) *Change Forces. Probing the Depths of Education Reform.* London: Falmer Press.

Gaudelli, W. (2003). *World Class. Teaching and Learning in Global Times.* Mahwah, NJ: Lawrence Erlbaum Associates.

Green, A. (1990) *Education and State Formation: The Rise of Educational Systems in England, France and the USA.* New York: St. Martin's Press.

Greig, S., Pike, G. and Selby, D. (1987) *Earthrights. Education as if the Planet Really Mattered.* Godalming: World Wildlife Fund/Kogan Page.

Griffith, R. (1998) *Educational Citizenship and Independent Learning.* London: Jessica Kingsley Publishers.

Hanvey, R.G. (1975) *An Attainable Global Perspective.* New York: Center for War/Peace Studies.

Heater, D. (1980) *World Studies. Education for International Understanding in Britain.* London: Harrap.

Heater, D. (2004) *Citizenship. The Civic Ideal in World History, Politics and Education.* 3rd edn. Manchester: Manchester University Press.

Hicks, D. (2003) 'Thirty years of global education: A reminder of key principles and precedents', *Educational Review,* 55 (3): 265–275.

Holden, C., and Hicks, D. (2007) 'Making global connections: The knowledge, understanding and motivation of trainee teachers', *Teaching and Teacher Education,* 23 (1): 13–23.

Ibrahim, T. (2005) 'Global citizenship education: Mainstreaming the curriculum?, *Cambridge Journal of Education,* 35 (2): 177–194.

Kjos, B. (1990) *Your Child and the New Age.* Wheaton, IL: Victor Books.

Kniep, W.M. (1986) 'Defining a global education by its content', *Social Education,* 50 (6): 437–466.

Lamy, S.L. (1990) 'Global education: A conflict of images', in Kenneth A. Tye (ed.) *Global Education. From Thought to Action.* Alexandria, VA: Association for Supervision and Curriculum Development. pp. 49–63.

Lee, W.O. and Leung, S.W. (2006) 'Global citizenship education in Hong Kong and Shanghai secondary schools: Ideas, realities and expectations', *Citizenship Teaching and Learning,* 2 (2): 68–84.

Lewis, G. (2007) 'Blogging democracy: The contribution of political blogs to democracy', Winning essay in *The Dalton Camp Award 2007.* Toronto: Friends of Canadian Broadcasting, 8–14.

Manzer, R. (1994) *Public Schools and Political Ideas: Canadian Educational Policy in Historical Perspective.* Toronto: University of Toronto Press.

Merryfield, M.M. (1991) 'Preparing American secondary social studies teachers to teach with a global perspective: A status report', *Journal of Teacher Education,* 42 (1): 11–20.

Merryfield, M.M. (1997) 'A framework for teacher education in global perspectives', in Merryfield, M.M, Jarchow, E. & Pickert, S. *Preparing Teachers to Teach Global Perspectives. A Handbook for Teacher Educators.* Thousand Oaks, CA: Corwin Press. pp. 1–24.

Merryfield, M.M. (1998) 'Pedagogy for global perspectives in education: Studies of teachers' thinking and practice, *Theory and Research in Social Education,* 26 (3): 342–379.

Merryfield, M.M. (2001) 'Moving the center of global education: From imperial world views that divide the world to double consciousness, contrapuntal pedagogy, hybridity and cross-cultural competence', in William B. Stanley (ed.), *Critical Issues in Social Studies Research.* Greenwich, Conn: Information Age Publishing. 179–208.

Merryfield, M.M. (2007) 'The web and teachers' decision-making in global education', *Theory and Research in Social Education,* 35(2): pp. 256–275.

Mitchell, K. (2003) 'Educating the national citizen in neoliberal times: From the multicultural self to the strategic cosmopolitan', *Transactions of the Institute of British Geographers,* 28 (4): 387–403.

Mitchell, K. and Parker, W. (2008) 'I pledge allegiance to … Flexible citizenship and shifting scales of belonging', *Teachers College Record* 110 (4), 2008.

Mundy, K. (2007) *Charting Global Education in Canada's Elementary Schools.* Toronto: UNICEF Canada.

NCSS (2004) 'Preparing citizens for a global community. A position statement of the National Council for the Social Studies', *Social Education,* 68 (4): 293.

Noddings, N. (2005) *Educating Citizens for Global Awareness.* New York: Teachers College Press.

Nussbaum, M. (1996) 'Patriotism and cosmopolitanism', in Cohen, J. (ed.) *For Love of Country: Debating the Limits of Patriotism.* Boston: Beacon Books. pp. 3–17.

One World Alliance (2006) 'World Youth Identity and Citizenship Survey'. Retrieved from www.ourworldgce.net.

O'Sullivan, B. (1999) 'Global change and educational reform in Ontario and Canada', *Canadian Journal of Education,* 24 (3): 311–325.

Oxfam (2006) *Education for Global Citizenship. A Guide for Schools.* Oxfam GB.

Pigozzi, M.J. (2006) 'A UNESCO view of global citizenship education', *Educational Review,* 58 (1): 1–4.

Pike, G. (1997) 'The meaning of global education: From proponents' visions to practitioners' perceptions'. PhD dissertation, University of York, UK.

Pike, G. (2000a) 'A tapestry in the making. The strands of global education', in Goldstein, Tara and Selby, David, *Waeving Connections. Educating for Peace, Social and Environmental Justice.* Toronto: Sumach Press. pp. 218–241.

Pike, G. (2000b) 'Global education and national identity: In pursuit of meaning', *Theory into Practice,* 39 (2): 64–73.

Pike, G. (2000c) 'Preparing teachers for global citizenship: The impact of the specialization in international education', *Exceptionality Education Canada,* 10 (1 and 2): 95–106.

Pike, G. (in press) 'Reconstructing the legend: Educating for global citizenship', in Abdi, A. and Schultz, L. (eds.) *Educating for Human Rights and Global Citizenship.* Albany: SUNY Press.

Pike, G. and Selby, D. (1988) *Global Teacher, Global Learner.* London: Hodder & Stoughton.

Pike, G. and Selby, D. (1995) *Reconnecting. From National to Global Curriculum.* Godalming: World Wide Fund for Nature UK.

Pike, G. and Selby, D. (1999) *In the Global Classroom 1.* Toronto: Pippin Publishing.

Popkewitz, T.S. (1980) 'Global education as a slogan system', *Curriculum Inquiry,* 10 (3): 303–316.

Richardson, R. (1979) 'World studies in the 1970s: A review of progress and unresolved tensions', *World Studies Journal,* 1 (1): 5–15.

Richardson, R. (1996) 'The terrestrial teacher', in Steiner, Miriam (ed.), *Developing the Global Teacher. Theory and Practice in Initial Teacher Education.* Stoke-on-Trent: Trentham Books. pp. 3–10.

Richardson, G., Blades, D., Kumano, Y. and Karaki, K. (2003) 'Fostering a global imaginary: the possibilities and paradoxes of Japanese and Canadian students' perceptions of the responsibilities of world citizenship', *Policy Futures in Education,* IX (2): 402–420.

Schukar, R. (1993) 'Controversy in global education: Lessons for teacher educators', *Theory into Practice,* 32 (1): 52–57.

Schweisfurth, M. (2006) 'Education for global citizenship: Teacher agency and curricular structure in Ontario schools', *Educational Review,* 58 (1): 41–50.

Scruton, R. (1985) *World Studies: Education or Indoctrination?* London: Institute for Defence and Strategic Studies.

Selby, David (1994) 'Kaleidoscopic mindset. New meanings within citizenship education', *Global Education,* 2: 20–31.

Selby, D. (1999) 'Global education: Towards a quantum model of environmental education', *Canadian Journal of Environmental Education,* 4: 125–141.

Steiner, M. (ed.) (1996) *Developing the Global Teacher.* Stoke-on-Trent: Trentham Books.

Toh, S.-H. (1993) 'Bringing the world into the classroom. Global literacy and a question of paradigms', *Global Education,* 1 (1): 9–17.

Torney, J. (1977) 'The international knowledge and awareness of adolescents in nine countries', *International Journal of Political Education,* 1: 3–19.

Tuomi, M.T. (2004) 'Planning teachers' professional development for global education', *Intercultural Education,* 15 (3): 295–306.

Tye, K.A. (1999) *Global Education. A Worldwide Movement.* Orange, CA: Interdependence Press.

UNESCO (2005) *Guidelines and Recommendations for Reorienting Teacher Education to Address Sustainability.* Paris: UNESCO.

Wallis, C. and Steptoe, S. (2006) 'How to bring US schools out of the 20th century', *Time,* 168 (25): 32–38.

War Child Canada (2006) *The War Child Canada Youth Opinion Poll.* Toronto: War Child Canada.

Yamashita, H. (2006) 'Global citizenship education and war: the needs of teachers and learners', *Educational Review,* 58 (1): 27–39.

Zhao, Y. (2007) 'Education in the flat world: Implications of globalization on education', *Edge,* 2 (4): 3–19.

Pedagogy

37

The Citizenship Curriculum: Ideology, Content and Organization

Kerry J. Kennedy

INTRODUCTION

Citizenship education can be found as a component of the school curriculum in most nations but the priority afforded it in curriculum terms varies from nation to nation and even within nations. Thus in the US, jurisdictional authority rests with the thousands of school districts while in Australia it rests with the eight sub-national authorities that have responsibility for education. In the European Union a similar situation exists so that attempts to educate for 'European citizenship', while initiated by the European Commission, inevitably rely for successful implementation on the member states. It is only where there are unitary systems of government such as England, France, New Zealand and the People's Republic of China that uniform citizenship education curriculum can be developed. Despite this potential for variability in curriculum terms, it is now not unusual to measure student understanding of civic and citizenship concepts. This has been done in countries like the United

States (Lutkus et al., 1999) and Australia (Ministerial Advisory Council on Education, Employment, Training and Youth Affairs, 2006) and internationally through the IEA Civic Education Study (Torney-Purta et al., 2001) and the proposed International Civic and Citizenship Education Study (ACER et al., n.d.). These studies may or may not be curriculum related yet they often provide content frameworks which can be a 'substitute' for the actual curriculum.

This potential for variability in the citizenship curriculum will be the focus of this chapter as will attempts to standardize it through testing regimes. The chapter will consider how different jurisdictions both within and across national boundaries seek to shape citizenship education for young people through the school curriculum. In particular, it will examine:

- ideological conceptions of the citizenship curriculum and their implications for practice;
- citizenship education as a component of the school curriculum: Content and frameworks
- curriculum organization for citizenship education.

IDEOLOGICAL CONCEPTIONS OF THE CITIZENSHIP CURRICULUM

The school curriculum is a social construct representing what any society believes to be important knowledge, skills and values for young people (Brady and Kennedy, 2007). In terms of the citizenship curriculum, this means knowledge skills and values that can contribute towards the development of citizens who, in the future, will accept their responsibilities as citizens and exercise their rights in such a way as to contribute to the nation-state in useful and productive ways. There is always an expectation in the citizenship curriculum, even when future citizens are expected to be critical and active in relation to their citizenship rights and responsibilities, that the basic values of the existing political system will be maintained. This expectation is as true in the US as it is in the People's Republic of China. It is because of such an expectation that ideology of one kind or another is the real driver of the citizenship curriculum. Ideology helps to account for the content and substance that makes up the curriculum across different national jurisdictions.

Ideology is not always immediately apparent in citizenship curriculum documents. It can be easily overlooked without a deeper examination of the theory behind the recommended practice. In order to demonstrate this point, the role of ideology in the citizenship curriculum in three countries will be examined. The purpose is twofold: to demonstrate the relationship between ideology and the citizenship curriculum and to show how different ideologies construct the citizenship curriculum differently. The argument of this section is that while all nation states promote a citizenship curriculum, its function, purpose and content will be largely determined by the ideology that drives it.

In the Australian context, Howard and Patten (2006: 1) have identified multiple conceptions of citizenship embedded in older forms of citizenship education as well as in more recent initiatives. They argued that the current government has been attracted to neo-liberal conceptions of citizenship where the focus is on electoral democracy, the development of the self-regulating individual in a civil society that encourages participation in the market economy and voluntary associations and a conception of rights that highlights political rights. This view of citizenship is opposed to what they call a 'radical democratic' view. Such a view also supports electoral democracy, but does not confine political participation to it, social decision making that takes into account the benefits for all citizens rather than relying on individual interests, a civil society that is a political means of influencing governments and a focus on political, social and cultural rights. These views – neo-liberal and radical democratic – represent conflicting conceptions of democracy and citizenship. A citizenship curriculum can be designed to reflect either view, but the resulting curricula will be different.

Thus Australian citizenship curriculum designers face a choice, that Howard and Patten (2006: 472) argue needs to be well informed and in so arguing they make their own values very clear:

> In sum, the Australian case exemplifies the notion that new civics education initiatives that are not strongly and explicitly committed to radical democracy are vulnerable to being pulled in the direction of powerful neo-liberal political discourses and governing practices. The recent explicit moves to introduce universal values into the Australian civics curriculum provide the clearest example of the vulnerability of new civics initiatives to ascendant neo-liberal discourses.

In England there is a somewhat different although not unrelated set of underlying assumptions for the citizenship curriculum. The aim of the proposed new statutory Citizenship curriculum represented (Crick, 2003: 17):

> ... no less than a change in the political culture of this country both nationally and locally: for people to think for themselves as active citizens, willing, able and equipped to have an influence in public life and with critical capacities to weight evidence before speaking and acting; to build on and extend

radically to young people the best in existing traditions of community involvement and public service, and to make them individually confident in finding new forms of involvement and action among themselves

Lockyer (2003: 2) identified the ideological tensions in the new citizenship curriculum as 'the compromise to be sought, or the balance to be struck, between liberalism and civic republicanism'. In the simplest terms this can be characterized as the tension between individual rights and collective responsibility. A citizenship premised on individual rights gives priority to the interests of individuals rather than the interests of larger groups to which individuals belong. Freedom in all spheres of activity is the catch cry of liberal citizenship. On the other hand, civic republicanism is based on the assumption that individuals come together around common purposes, common values and a common good. The responsibility of citizenship, therefore, is to contribute actively to the 'common-wealth' and to recognize at times that individual interests might need to be subjugated to a higher common good.

The tension between individual rights and collective responsibility can be compared in some ways to Howard and Patten's (2006) neo-liberalism and radical democracy. The former represents the revival of a liberal ethic to match the focus of market economics, the dominant international economic discourse. Neo-liberalism seeks to abolish all restraints on freedom – economic, social and political – so that individuals are free to pursue their own self interests. Radical democracy, however, does not equate directly with civic republicanism. While radical democracy highlights collective responsibility over individual interests, there is also a certain element of liberalism in radical democracy, especially in relation to political, social and cultural rights. This is not just a theoretical issue – the nature of freedom and its role in the citizenship curriculum has become a contested issue in recent times. The following example from the England demonstrates this.

The Minister who commissioned the Report on Citizenship Education, David Blunkett, articulated a view of freedom that is both complex and enlightening:

> In addressing the issues of liberty, security and justice, it is essential to consider what sort of freedom we are trying to achieve. My belief is that we need to strive for freedom in its widest form—not just freedom from interference, but freedom for people to engage in providing solutions for themselves, their families and their communities. As the Ancient Greeks would have it, the freedom to contribute to the Polis.
>
> Quite simply, I am interested in freedom from external interference, physical protection, the protection of civil liberties, but I am also interested in the positive freedom to get involved in formal politics, and, importantly, in the development of civil society. These types of freedom are, of course, complementary. Participation as active citizens and engagement in the democratic process are crucial to the very survival of a pluralistic, civilised and free society (Blunkett, 2004: 78).

In the first paragraph of this statement, excerpted from a paper on 'The new politics of insecurity' Blunkett delivered to an international seminar on European social democracy, he reveals all too clearly his preference for a classical, republican conception of freedom ('freedom for people to engage in providing solutions for themselves') rather than a traditionally liberal concept of freedom ('freedom from interference'). This was an important public statement on the issue of security in the context of a post-9/11 world. As Blunkett asserted, 'all of us agree to forego some of our personal sovereignty and to combine our individualism in order to achieve common goals' (pp. 79–80).

This latter statement well represents civic republicanism, but it does not represent radical democracy. Thus in the Australian and UK cases there is a continuum between neo-liberal and liberal conceptions of citizenship on one end and radical democratic and civic republican conceptions on the other end. Each conception will translate into a quite different curriculum with different values, different emphases and different priorities.

The final case comes from the People's Republic of China (PRC) whose citizenship education programmes have attracted a good deal of scholarly attention in recent times (Zhong and Lee, 2008; Cheung and Pan, 2006; Law, 2006). The reason for including this example here is to highlight the fact that citizenship education is a priority for all nation states – both democratic and non-democratic. Yet the case of China also shows how competing ideological conceptions of citizenship within the authoritarian state leads to changing emphases in the citizenship curriculum. Law (2006: 601), for example, described the changes that have taken place in redefining citizenship in China:

> The framework for the PRC's socialist citizenship has gradually shifted from an exclusive to an accommodative orientation ... the new framework comprises five interrelated elements: a wider opening of the nation to the world, use of the market for economic reform, reinstatement of the law, reintroduction of Chinese virtues, and repositioning of the CPC [Chinese Communist Party].

Law (2006: 607) goes on to show how each of these elements has influenced the opening up of the citizenship curriculum to meet new needs in the light of new ideological orientations. Yet he also makes the point that such changes share a common purpose, 'to initiate students into a set of sociopolitical skills, values, and behaviors that the CPC deems acceptable'.

Across three different countries, therefore, it is ideology that constructs the underpinnings of the citizenship curriculum. In liberal democratic countries there can be competing ideologies and their influence will depend on the vicissitudes of electoral politics with the legitimacy of particular ideologies tested within the framework of the rule of law. In authoritarian countries, on the other hand, while ideological conceptions can change, their purpose is to support the state apparatus. Despite these fundamental differences between liberal democratic and authoritarian political systems, Law's (2006: 619) description of citizenship applies across political boundaries:

> Citizenship is not just a social construct and social practice, but a process in which different players,

with various memberships, concerns, priorities, and criteria, select which qualities and contents should be highlighted. Citizenship as a sociopolitical selection from a multilevel polity is competitive among different players.

It follows from this, that the citizenship curriculum as a reflection of the a nation's requirements of its young people as citizens, will reflect current values and priorities that are subject to change and revision depending on the salience of particular ideologies. Such a curriculum is never value free or neutral: it will always reflect current conceptions of the 'good citizen' as the ends towards which the curriculum is directed.

CONTENT FOR THE CITIZENSHIP CURRICULUM

Country reports from the IEA Civic Education Study (Torney-Purta et al., 2001: 162, 166) made the point 'that civic education content is often less codified and less formalized compared to other subjects' and this was 'related to the uncertainty in conceptualizing civic education knowledge due to the amalgamated disciplinary base of the subject and teachers' varied subject matter backgrounds'. A similar view was expressed in relation to civics and citizenship education in Australia at a time when a national assessment was being planned (Ministerial Council on Education, Employment, Training and Youth Affairs, 2006):

> At the time of the assessment, civics and citizenship was not a key learning area in any Australian jurisdiction. The delivery of instruction in civics and citizenship was fragmented and marked by a lack of formality. The definitions associated with certain key concepts were not generally agreed across the jurisdictions, nor was their appearance in formal curriculum documents universal. The year levels at which some treatment of these concepts and knowledge was to be undertaken, how much time was to be spent on the teaching of civics and citizenship and within which key learning areas have been matters for debate during recent developments (Ministerial Council on Education, Employment, Training and Youth Affairs, 2006: 3).

Thus unlike school subjects such as Mathematics and Science, there is little agreement about what is essential civic knowledge and skills, the best time to teach it and what should be the expected outcomes at different points in time. Different frameworks have been used in different contexts to try and provide a common approach within countries and sometimes *across* countries. These frameworks can reflect either curriculum or assessment priorities and are indicators of what is regarded as important civic learning for students. A number of these frameworks used in different jurisdictions and for different purposes are shown in Table 37.1.

Three of these frameworks were developed as part of citizenship assessment projects rather than as attempts to define the content of the citizenship curriculum. The European Union survey (European Commission, 2005) was more specifically curriculum oriented attempting to assess the common elements in citizenship curriculum from thirty European countries. The domains used in this survey seem to have been adopted from England's Citizenship curriculum (Crick, 2003: 19) where the emphasis is on 'active citizenship', that is also a European priority. Yet the European domains also represent generic curriculum organizers focusing on knowledge (political literacy), skills (participation) and values (attitudes/values) thus highlighting the multidimensional nature of citizenship education. Yet the survey did not find any consistency across countries in the weight attached to the three domains and at times (e.g. in the cases of Germany and Finland) the

weights were reversed with Germany giving more weight to Political Literacy while Finland gave more weight to values and participation (European Commission, 2005: 25). There is thus a great deal of space for variation of content in citizenship education even with common domain descriptors.

The first assessment framework for citizenship education is shown in Table 37.1. Ministerial Council for Education, Employment, Training and Youth Affairs (2006) provides another perspective on identifying the knowledge, skills and values students at different ages are expected to possess. Testing of any kind requires assessment items that contribute to an understanding of learning in identified domains of knowledge, attitudes or skills. Very often these items can be based on the curriculum taken to be the specified domain of knowledge for a particular school subject. Yet where there is no common curriculum – as was the case with citizenship education in Australia referred to earlier – assessment domains as shown in Table 37.1 can be specified drawing on items that can assess student progress in learning. Assessment domains, therefore, are perhaps better understood as learning domains representing what it is expected that students should know and be able to do.

On a comparative basis, the Australian learning domains shown in Table 37.1 are similar to the three curriculum domains used in the European survey: the Australian 'Civics' domain corresponds to the European 'Political literacy' domain and the 'Citizenship' domain corresponds to the European 'values'

Table 37.1 Selected approaches to identifying content for citizenship education

Jurisdiction/purpose	Domains			
Australia: national civics and citizenship sample assessment, 2004[1]	Civics: knowledge and understanding of civic institutions & processes	Citizenship: dispositions and skills for participation		
European Union survey of citizenship education[2]	Political literacy	Attitudes/values	Active participation	
Second IEA Civic Education Study[3]	Democracy/citizenship	National identity/ international relations	Social cohesion/ diversity	
International Civic and Citizenship Education Study[4]	Civic society & systems	Civic principles	Civic participation	Civic identities

and 'participation' domains. Thus curriculum and assessment frameworks can play complementary roles: the former outlines what is expected to be taught while the latter highlights what it is expected students have learnt. Normally, it would be expected that there will be a relationship between what is taught and what is learnt. The purpose of assessment is to provide an indication of what students know or understand at a particular point in time. It should be expected that what students know is, in part at least, related to what has been taught. The absence of an explicit curriculum framework, however, is not a barrier to defining citizenship content. The assessment development processes itself, in terms of defining explicit domains and constituent items, becomes a surrogate for the curriculum because it necessarily makes assumptions about what students know and are able to do.

At another level, the assessment frameworks used internationally (Torney-Purta, et al., 2001; ACER et al., n.d.) provide another approach to identifying citizenship content. Given that such frameworks need to cater for student leaning across different countries, specific civic knowledge reflected in a curriculum domain like 'Political literacy' or even a national assessment domain such as 'Civics: knowledge and understanding of civic institutions and processes' is not appropriate. Thus the assessment frameworks for international assessments of civics and citizenship tend to be conceptually driven more than they are for local assessments or for local curriculum. It is also clear that over a ten year period (the time between the second IEA Civic Education Study and the International Civic and Citizenship Education Study), concepts underpinning the area underwent change and refinement. The proposed assessment domains for the current study ('Civic society and principles', 'Civic principles', 'Civic participation' and 'Civic identities') can be taken to represent the latest thinking about civics and citizenship education content. While these particular domains will be used to select items for the

study, they could equally well be used to develop a school curriculum. In this sense, curriculum and assessment can inform each other in the search for defining content, identifying conceptual frameworks and in making explicit what students ought to know and be able to do in the area of civics and citizenship.

ORGANIZING THE CITIZENSHIP CURRICULUM

The recognition of ideological influences and the selection of specific content (including knowledge, skills and values) represent two important processes that help to delineate the citizenship curriculum. The content included in the curriculum in either democratic or authoritarian societies will be determined by these two processes. Yet as important as these are, they are not the only processes that need to be considered in forming the citizenship curriculum. There is also the issue of how to insert 'Citizenship' alongside standard school subjects such as Mother-tongue Language, Mathematics and Science so that it can take its place as a body of valued content in the education of young people. The following paragraphs will explore this issue.

In general terms, different components of the school curriculum can be organized in different ways and reflect different emphases across jurisdictions, depending largely on history and local preference. The second IEA Civic Education Study (Torney-Purta et al., 2001) reported on teachers' preferred mode of curriculum organization for civic education and recently a study supported by the European Commission (2005) identified different ways in which the citizenship curriculum is currently organized across thirty countries that were surveyed. Table 37.2 draws on these different sources to show the options that are available for the organization of the citizenship curriculum.

While all countries in the European Union appear to value citizenship education, there is

Table 37.2 Approaches to organizing the citizenship curriculum

	Citizenship curriculum			
	Optional		Compulsory	
Primary	Single subject (e.g. citizenship education)	Taught through other subjects (e.g. History/Geography)	Integrated across all subjects	Extra curricular activity

no agreement on how best to deliver it (European Commission, 2005: 91). In general, it seems that at the primary level there is a preference for integrated or cross curriculum delivery while in the secondary, the general preference is for citizenship as a single subject. Yet there are exceptions to these generalizations and in some countries multiple forms of delivery are used. There is little evidence about the effectiveness of different kinds of delivery either in terms of student learning or status within the school curriculum. Nevertheless there are some clear preferences expressed in terms of teacher choices.

In the second IEA Civic Education Study (Torney-Purta et al., 2001: 167–168) teachers were asked to rate the extent to which they agreed with different organizational options for the citizenship curriculum. The results indicated that overall, the strongest support was for the integration of citizenship into social science subjects although it cannot be claimed it was universal. There was some strong support, particularly in Eastern European countries, for Citizenship as a single subject. On the other hand, there was least support for extracurricular activities as a form of curriculum organization to deliver the Citizenship curriculum. At the same time teachers in individual countries such as Switzerland and Germany registered some strong support for this form of curriculum organization and Hong Kong, Italy and the Russian Federation indicated a medium level of support.

The specific form the citizenship curriculum might take – specific subject, integrated with social science subjects, integrated across all subjects or as an extra-curricular activity – has implications for other curriculum related issues such as whether the citizenship curriculum is

optional or compulsory and the amount of time allocated to it. The compulsory/optional nature of citizenship is an important policy decision in all countries because it signals the value placed on this component of the school curriculum. From the major reviews of civics and citizenship education (European Commission, 2005; Torney-Purta, et al., 2001) it does seem that most countries do include citizenship as part of the school curriculum and some have developed policy mechanisms to monitor its effectiveness. These mechanisms will be discussed in the conclusion to this chapter, but before doing that, an important issue to raise is the relationship between the compulsory nature of citizenship in the school curriculum and the time allocated to it. This relationship can be problematic in light of the specific organizational form adopted to deliver the citizenship curriculum.

The issue of time allocation is important because the more time that is available for the citizenship curriculum, the greater will be the coverage and, hopefully, the greater will be student engagement with the subject matter. It is at this point that the organizational form of the citizenship curriculum is salient. It is much easier, for example, at least in a structural sense, to allocate time to citizenship when it is a compulsory single subject. It is much more difficult to allocate a specific amount of time when citizenship is mandated as an integrated curriculum theme. In the European surveyed referred to in Table 37.2, it was not possible for national jurisdictions to indicate how much time was allocated to citizenship when it was integrated into other school subjects (European Commission, 2005: 20). The integration model for citizenship requires a great deal of flexibility because it is embedded in broader curriculum objectives that themselves demand time. Any citizenship theme or specific content, therefore, has to compete with other objectives for a limited amount of curriculum space. Success in this context will depend entirely on teacher professional judgment with the potential for considerable implementation variation across classrooms and schools. This means that a favoured form of curriculum organization for the citizenship curriculum, its integration into other social science subjects, can be problematic in guaranteeing the delivery of specific content to all students.

CONCLUSION

The citizenship curriculum, while valued at different levels, also raises a number of issues. First, there is a lack of agreement on the specific content that should be included. This chapter has tried to show how there does appear to be a convergence on this issue related to curriculum organizers such as 'Political literacy', 'Participation' and 'Values and attitudes'. Yet there are also competing models for organizing what might be referred to as 'citizenship content' and as often as not these appear as assessment models rather than curriculum models. As shown throughout the chapter, these models are not always in opposition, but it is a distinctive characteristic of citizenship as a component of the school curriculum that its content is often defined implicitly as part of a program of assessment.

Second, the issue of defining citizenship content is also related to the organizational form it often takes in the school curriculum. When it is an integrated cross curriculum theme, either with specific reference to the social science or in relation to all subjects, then citizenship content depends on the curriculum specifications for the official subject or subjects in which it is meant to be embedded. What is more, as shown previously, there is no way of monitoring how much time is devoted to citizenship as a cross curriculum theme. This is perhaps an issue more in the primary school where the integrated approach appears to be preferred, but it is an important point if it is seen that citizenship knowledge, skills and values should be developed across time and in an incremental fashion. Integrated approaches to citizenship could only do this if they are accompanied by a clear specification of student learning outcomes at different stages of schooling.

Third, it might seem to follow from this, that the organization of the citizenship curriculum as a separate school subject is the optimal approach for ensuring curriculum coverage and providing access to all students. This form of organization is already a feature of many secondary schools both in Europe and Asia. As such, it has implications for well entrenched subjects such a mother-tongue language, Mathematics and Science in the context of the limited amount of available for the entire school curriculum. In addition to the time issue there is also the issue of identifying distinctive citizenship content that does not overlap with other subjects. Torney-Purta, et al. (2001: 163), for example, identified national history, constitution and political systems, citizen and human rights, international organizations and relations, economic and welfare, media, environmental issues and civic virtues as possible areas for citizenship content. Many of these would also be covered in other areas of the school curriculum and thus the appeal of integrated approaches to citizenship curriculum. If citizenship is to be a separate subject, then an important issue would be to reconcile these overlaps to develop distinctive content directed at citizenship development.

Fourth, the difficulties for the citizenship curriculum outlined above seem to be inconsistent with the importance of the area in the thinking of politicians and the community. The induction of young people into a community's civic values is a universal process yet in many jurisdictions the curriculum means for doing do not deliver unequivocal outcomes. It is perhaps for this reason that governments have resorted to assessment and testing programs in citizenship as a policy mechanism to try and ensure a basic level of civic knowledge for young people. Yet this can be a problematic strategy where the curriculum foundations have not been adequately laid. An important issue facing policy makers in the future will be to align curriculum and assessment regimes so that what is tested is part of students' curriculum experiences and performance can be related to what has been taught. The clear specification of the citizenship curriculum, therefore, and its adoption into an organizational form that gives it a valued place in the school curriculum remains a key challenge for the future.

NOTES

1 Ministerial Council for Education, Employment, Training and Youth Affairs (2006).
2 European Commission (2005)
3 Torney-Purta et al. (2001)
4 ACER. (nd)

REFERENCES

ACER et al. (n.d.) *The International Civics and Citizenship Education Study (ICCS) – Information Brochure*. Retrieved 29 April 2007. Available http://iccs.acer.edu.au/uploads/File/ICCS%20Information%20Brochure(1).pdf

Blunkett, D. (2004) 'The place of security in progressive politics', in Policy Network (ed.), *Where Now for European Social Democracy?* London: Policy Network. pp. 75–84. Retrieved 22 April 2007. Available http://www.progressivegovernance.net/uploadedFiles/Publications/Publications/WhereNowForSocialDemocracy.pdf

Brady, L. and Kennedy, K. (2007) *Curriculum Construction*. 3rd edn. Sydney: Pearson Education.

Cheung, K.W. and Pan, S.Y. (2006) 'Transition of moral education in China: Towards regulated individualism', *Citizenship and Teaching*, 2 (2): 37–50.

Crick, B. (2003) 'The English Citizenship Order 1999: Context, content and presuppositions', in A. Lockyer, B. Crick and J. Annette (eds), *Education for Democratic Citizenship – Issues of Theory and Practice*. Aldershot, England: Ashgate Publishing Limited. pp. 15–29.

European Commission (2005) *Citizenship Education at School in Europe*. Brussels: Eurydice European Unit. Retrieved 29 April 2007. Available http://www.eurydice.org/ressources/eurydice/pdf/0_integral/055EN.pdf.

Howard, C. and Patten, S. (2006) 'Valuing civics: Political commitment and the new citizenship education in Australia', *Canadian Journal of Education*, 29 (2): 454–475.

Law, W.W. (2006) 'Citizenship, citizenship education, and the state in China in a global age', *Cambridge Journal of Education*, 36 (4): 597–628.

Lockyer, A. (2003) 'Introduction and review', in A. Lockyer, B.Crick and J. Annette (eds), *Education for Democratic Citizenship – Issues of Theory and Practice*. Aldershot, England: Ashgate Publishing Limited. pp. 1–15.

Lutkus, A., Weiss, A., Campbell, J., Mazzeo, J., and Lazer, S. (1999) *NAEP Civics Report Card to the Nation. U.S. Department of Education (Office of Educational Research and Improvement)*. Washington, DC: National Center for Education Statistics.

Ministerial Council on Education, Employment, Training and Youth Affairs. (2006) *National Assessment Program – Years 6 and 10 Civics and Citizenship Report 2004*. Melbourne: Curriculum Corporation. Retrieved 18 February 2007. Available http://www.mceetya.edu.au/mceetya/default.asp?id=17149.

Torney-Purta, J., Lehmann, R., Oswald, H., and Schulz, W. (2001) *Citizenship and education in twenty-eight countries: Civic knowledge and engagement at age fourteen*. Amsterdam: IEA.

Zhong, M. and Lee, W.O. (2008) 'Citizenship curriculum in China: A changing discourse in democracy and psychological health', in D. Grossman, W.O. Lee and K. Kennedy (eds), *Citizenship Curriculum in Asia and the Pacific*. New York and Amsterdam: Comparative Education Research Centre and Springer. pp. 61–74.

38

Organizing a Curriculum for Active Citizenship Education

Alistair Ross

CURRICULUM CONSIDERATIONS

Heater and Oliver (1994) set challenging goals for the outcomes of citizenship education. Our pupils should be able to:

- actively practise 'civic virtue and good citizenship';
- enjoy – but not exploit – civil and political rights;
- contribute to and receive social and economic benefits;
- not discriminate against others;
- experience non-exclusive multiple citizenship; and
- teach citizenship to others.

(derived from 1994: 6)

In considering what we should include in the citizenship curriculum, and how we should organize and order this into a coherent and logical structure that will achieve these outcomes, we might turn to a pioneer writer on citizenship, Aristotle, on the purposes of education:

> In modern times there are opposing views about the tasks to be set, for there are no generally accepted assumptions about what the young should learn, either for their own virtue or for the best life; nor is it yet clear whether their education ought to be conducted with more concern for the intellect than for the character or soul...It is by no means certain whether training should be directed at things useful in life, or at those most conducive to virtue, or at exceptional accomplishments. (Aristotle, 1962).

This chapter makes the basic assumption that citizenship education must be for all pupils, and it is intended to make all of them aware of citizenship as 'a thing useful for life', and its practice 'conducive to virtue'. It follows that we are not concerned – as we may be in many other aspects of the curriculum – in grading or ranking pupils as more or less successful citizens, although Jerome, later in this volume, makes an argument for this. The exigencies of contemporary society mean that we cannot afford a single 'failed citizen', and that all must succeed. 'Exceptional accomplishments' in citizenship will be necessary for some, but not all, members of society, but education toward such contributions lies beyond the consideration of core citizenship education for all.

This is not, however, to therefore argue that we need not plan a curriculum that progresses pupils through different levels of skill and understanding, that hones and refines sensibilities and feelings through sequences of learning activities, nor that we need not assess and evaluate progression. Responsible teaching requires all of these aspects to be considered, but with the goal of ensuring that all acquire the competences of citizenship, rather than of distinguishing between democratic sheep and uncivic goats. 'Democratic sheep' may be tautologous; but non-citizens, or even poorly skilled citizens, are a danger.

Citizenship is the relationship between the individual and society, between the self and others. The curriculum must reflect this: it must help the individual understand both their own identity and the nature of society, and, most importantly, how to manage the complex relationship of rights and responsibilities that exist between the two. Audiger's observation, already quoted in this volume, underlines the magnitude and scope of this: 'Since the citizen is an informed and responsible person, capable of taking part in public debate and making choices, nothing of what is human should be unfamiliar to him (sic), nothing of what is experienced in society should be foreign to democratic citizenship' (1998: 13). This opens the way for a vast range of exhilarating and stimulating work, drawing from the whole canvas on contemporary political and social debate. In one sense, the content of the citizenship curriculum is straightforward, based on the social and political debates of the day. What is critical however, and the major thrust of this chapter, are the conditions and means by which these issues are debated, argued, analysed and acted upon by pupils. How do we order this into some kind of coherent development? How do we ensure that pupils make progress in the broadening and enhancement of the skills, their values and moral susceptibilities?

This chapter addresses these questions, within the following framework. The goal is the development of the citizen: while many politicians would settle for a passive citizen (who votes, subscribes to the state obeys the law), many others – including perhaps most teachers – would hope to empower active citizens, who critically engage with and seek to affect the course of social events. This critical distinction being active citizenship and passive citizenship will be analysed, particularly in terms of its implications for curriculum planning.

This leads into a discussion of the key elements within a citizenship curriculum, and in particular the use of categories such as values and attitudes, skills and competences, knowledge and understanding and creativity and enterprise to analyse this. The significance of these categories varies in planning progression, attainment and differentiation, particularly in terms of encouraging active, as opposed to passive, citizenship.

The two significant core concerns of citizenship education are those of identities (Isin and Wood, 1999) and of rights (Osler, in this volume). Each in turn can be related to key values, skills and knowledge in active citizenship education.

This chapter then turns to some core principles of curriculum design in this area. Reviewing critical studies of the practice of citizenship curriculum design, various key elements are identified that inform approaches to progression and differentiation. These include dialogic methods, based on values approach, set in an ethos of the whole school; radical reordering of traditional teacher-learner relationships to be based on respect for learners, and the empowering of experiences. Two critical strategies emerge: the imperative of a whole school approach to determining values, structures, planning and attitudes towards pupils' identities and rights (expanded in part by Evans, later in this volume) and the need for a radical classroom dialogic, based on relationships and respect for learner (addressed more fully by Amory and Hess later in this volume).

EDUCATION FOR ACTIVE AND PASSIVE CITIZENSHIP

A considerable literature has developed on 'the democratic deficit' in a number of countries in the world (see, e.g. Verdun, 1998; Moravsci, 2004; Avbelj, 2005; Mitchell, 2005; Hirschhorn, 2006). In many democratic states, the level of participation in elections appears to be falling from election to election, and it is claimed that the percentage of young people voting also tends to be less than that of older people. On the other hand, many in the citizenship education movement, and others, would also aspire to educational processes that empowered active citizens – individuals who will critically engage with, and seek to affect the course of, social events. Active citizenship is, very broadly, about doing things, while passive citizenship is generally seen as related simply to status, to the act of being. The distinction between active and passive citizenship has been particularly debated over the past five to six years (Ireland et al., 2006; Nelson and Kerr, 2006), and though there is no international consensus, the model suggested by Kennedy (2006) may be helpful.

He distinguishes four forms or levels of activity in citizenship. Conventional political activity – the level at which those concerned with the democratic deficit would have us act – is engaging in voting, in belonging to a political party and in standing for office. The first of these, though an activity, is of course a minimalist action, but these kinds of traditional conformity are nevertheless participation, and participation with a view to changing civic society.

The second form of activity lies in social movements, in being involved with voluntary activities – either working as a volunteer with agencies or collecting money on their behalf. This form of participation in civil society (as opposed to the former civic action) is essentially conformist and ameliorative in nature: it is action to repair rather than to address causes, or even to acknowledge possible causes. These, and the previous conventional form, constitute what is sometimes derided as the 'voting and volunteering' approach to citizenship education.

The third form consists of action for social change, when the individual is involved in activities that aim to change political and social policies. This would range from such activities as letter writing and signing petitions to working with pressure groups and participating in demonstrations, pressure groups and other ways of trying to influence decision making. This form would also have various illegal variants, such as taking part in occupations, writing graffiti and other forms of civil disobedience. Common to both legal and non-legal forms of activity is a conflictual model of civic and civil change.

The fourth active form is of enterprise citizenship, an essentially individualist model of citizenship action, in which the individual engages in such self-regulating activities as achieving financial independence, becoming a self-directed learner, being a problem solver and developing entrepreneurial ideas. This is very much an economic model of citizenship activity, and individualistic in its range.

These four forms in no sense comprise a hierarchy or sequential form of development – the individual does not need to progress through one form to achieve the next. Any curriculum should see these as concurrent activities to be encouraged, at any age or stage of development.

Kennedy also distinguished two forms of passive citizenship. The first of these is concerned with national identity, where the individual understands and values the nation's history, and the symbolic and iconic forms of the nation – in its institutions, the flag, the anthem and the political offices. This kind of passive citizenship is commonly taught through transmission models of education; through civic education and the hidden curriculum of unspoken mores, structures and assumptions.

A second and variant form of passive citizenship is seen in patriotism, a more extreme national identity that includes military service and unconditional support for one's country against any claims of other countries. This form of passive citizenship would inculcate values of loyalty and unswerving obedience, and stress the value of social stability and hard work.

But these distinctions are not necessarily clear-cut, and Nelson and Kerr's analysis (2006) demonstrates that there are strong cultural variations in what might be considered as appropriate forms of 'active' citizenship. In some countries, it is clearly considered that many of the attributes characterized above as forms of passive attributes concerned with accepting status are elements of active citizenship that are to be encouraged and developed. This may depend on the particular historical development and configuration of the state: in some countries (perhaps particularly in Europe), there is a greater perception that citizenship and national identity may now be seen as social constructs, and that active citizenship may embrace a diverse range of relevant political scenarios in which to be a 'politically active citizen'. The idea of multiple citizenship has been possible for the past half century, and ideas about nested citizenship were developed in Heater, 1990; European Union, 1992, 1993; and the Council of Europe, 2002.

These variant forms of citizenship all imply a much greater sense of activity than passive citizenship, or even of conventional active political behaviour. Thus Davies and Issitt (2005), for example, suggest that aspects of the global citizenship education programme might usefully be incorporated into citizenship education, as separation appears to constrain both movements. Active citizenship, it is now being suggested, moves necessarily beyond the confines of the nation state.

Differentiating citizenship education into active and passive is not uncontroversial. The development of citizenship as a simple passive identity has led to some issues as individuals are formally incorporated as citizens in France, for example (Sutherland, 2002), while others (Mannitz, 2004) identify parallel issues of identity and civic belonging amongst young people from non-German heritages in Germany.

KEY ELEMENTS

What are the key elements or components of an active citizenship education programme, and how might these be differentiated within the curriculum? Can they be ordered into

some form of progression? There is an emerging consensus in the US and the UK (Crick and Lister, 1979; Crick, 1998; Kerr and Ireland, 2004; Cleaver and Nelson, 2006) that three major elements can be distinguished in any effective citizenship education programme: values and dispositions, skills and competences and knowledge and understanding.

First, and perhaps fundamental, is the identification and demonstration of certain values and dispositions, though the precise identification of these values, and the extent to which they agreed to be universalistic (or even universalistic in contemporary times) is not unanimous. These key values might, for example, include the upholding of human rights (though, as will be discussed below, the conception of the extent of these rights continue to develop); ideas of social responsibility and obligations towards others, particularly in relation to equity, diversity and minorities; certain legal values, particularly those concerning the rule of law, democratic processes and various (contested) notions of freedom and humanistic values of tolerance and empathy for others. This list may appear at first sight to be relatively uncontentious: a survey by Kidder (in Sutherland, 2002) suggested that people from all across the world, when asked to identify their core moral values, would all agree on the same five ideas – honesty, respect, responsibility, fairness and compassion – but these words may have subtly different meanings or even less than subtle differences in different cultural contexts and societies.

Crick and Porter (1978) and Crick and Lister (1979), in their pioneering works on political literacy in the 1970s (described in Clarke, 2007) had a somewhat more critical edge on these values: they argue for attitudes of scepticism to be tempered with self-awareness, self-criticism and an awareness of consequence. They also qualified the conception of tolerance of the substantive values of others (religious, ethical political doctrines) with the need to maintain particular procedural values necessary to freedom – respect for truth and reasoning, open-mindedness and willingness to compromise. Toleration, they argued, was not just accepting difference, but welcoming diversity, though not exploitation, racism or the suppression of opinion. Memorably, having an open mind did not mean having an empty mind.

Planning how to locate these values within the curriculum raises particular issues. These values cannot be introduced sequentially: there is no natural sequence of progression, though we know that young children do have political knowledge and beliefs (Greenstein, 1965; Hess and Torney, 1967; Connell, 1971). I would argue that they need to be adopted in their entirety by every learning institution, and to inform the fundamental ethos of the institution. While the language used to articulate them will develop, the principles behind such a value as respect for individual rights, the rule of law or acceptance of diversity should be as absolute and as manifest in the pre-school as they are in the university.

Thus Russell (2002), for example, describes the theme of 'fairness' as central to the talk of seven- and eight-year-olds, and of eleven- and twelve-year-olds. They begin their discussions with broad definitions and refine these through interaction with others. 'Fair' is first defined as quantitative equity, and then expanded by the age of eleven to include forgiveness and reciprocity. As utilitarianism and deductive reasoning grow, girls tend to see fairness in terms of awareness of the needs of others and sharing, while boys move from fairness being keeping to the rules towards taking equity into account and accommodating individual difference. All the children in his study suggested doing what is 'right', even if this conflicted with authority.

But the ubiquity of these values does not imply that planning is not required: on the contrary, to articulate and live these values requires whole school planning of an exceptionally high order, moving from the didactic to the dialogic, so that all members of a school community understand and subscribe to them, a constant programme of induction, so that new members of the school community (students, teachers and all non-teaching staff) are introduced to the practice of these values, and a continuing programme of self-critical questioning, to ensure the maintenance and possible extension of these values.

The second group of key elements comprise the skills and competences necessary to be a citizen. These include the skills of enquiry, of rationally seeking to establish processes, causes and the bases for action; sophisticated skills of communication, which include being able to consider and respond to the views of others, being able to persuade, and being capable of being persuaded; skills of participation, which include an understanding of group dynamics and of how to contribute to the social development of civic action and skills of social action.

These competencies also need to be planned as part of the curriculum. While again they need to be seen as all being in place throughout any educational institution, it is here possible to consider and plan the progressive development of each of these skills. Communication skills, for example, will be developed through increasing levels of sophistication in listening and responding to others. This again raises important and fundamental questions for a school's learning style: teachers will need to model how to question, listen and respond in ways that are very different from traditional didactic models of teaching, dominated by simplistic models of transmission (Galton et al., 1980). To develop skills of communication in citizenship may require remodelling pedagogic styles in all subject areas, because switching from transmission-based teaching in mathematics to dialogic teaching in citizenship will be confusing and counterproductive for the learner.

Both these groups of key elements – values and skills – are necessary for active citizenship, as described in the preceding section. The third group, of knowledge and understanding, are necessary for passive citizenship, but also underpin active engagement. These include both a conceptual understanding of key concepts of politics and society, but also knowledge of particular institutions and their procedures, local, national and international.

It can be argued that an understanding of the underlying principles of the role of the law; of the nature of representative democracy; the powers of and restraints on government and some awareness of the premises of the economy, society and the environment are necessary for the educated citizen.

It is perhaps easier to use terms such as progression and differentiation in terms of knowledge and understanding. One can expect an increase in the depth of sophistication in the use of these conceptual terms over the educational cycle, and that some will develop a greater ability to discuss and articulate them. Schools could be reasonably expected to provide a schema for the introduction, development and assessment of these elements. Therein lies a particular danger. Because it is these items that can be classified and assessed, while skills and values are far less susceptible to assessment (and, it has been argued above, should not be introduced sequentially, but all of a piece), any emphasis on the measurement and categorisation of citizenship education might distort the curriculum to overemphasize these elements. Their assessment would enable a categorisation of 'success', of individual pupils, teachers and schools, that would measure only a fraction of what needs to be accomplished in citizenship education, and would moreover be an assessment based on the one element alone that could lead to passive citizenship. Values, skills and knowledge are necessary factors for active citizenship (ineluctable, difficult to measure and imprecise though this may be); knowledge alone is sufficient for passive citizenship (though it may be efficiently and accurately assessed).

CORE CONCERNS: IDENTITIES AND RIGHTS

Two concerns are currently critical to education for active citizenship: the encouragement of pupils to understand and articulate their various identities and the focus on the development and extension of human rights (Ross, 2007). The first gives the individual the security and authority to act with others and to understand and articulate values and dispositions to others; the second provides an essential forum for activity and the location to hone and practice the skills and competences necessary for participation and change. This section considers how each of these can be incorporated into curriculum design.

Several recent reports suggest that individuals do not have singular identities, but a repertoire of different identities: the individual uses these, individually or in combination, contingently on where they are, whom they are with, and the particular social setting in which they find themselves (Hall, 1996; 1997). Amaryta Sen has attacked 'the fallacy of ... forcing people into boxes of singular identity. This attempts to understand human beings not as persons with diverse identities but predominantly as members of one particular social group or community' (Sen, 2006: 176). Gundara cites examples of young people's multiple identities, arguing that they contribute to meeting the challenge of how 'experimental democratic education can guarantee social integration in highly differentiated contexts' (Gundara, 2006: 25). Some of these identities are related to geographic location (often nested one within another), other identities could be seen as membership of a group, and yet others are relationships (such as friend or parent).

Identities are thus contingent. The identity or group of identities selected for presentation is a response to the group(s) that constitute the audience, to the location of the encounter, and to the history and events that preceded it. This is challenged by Brubaker and Cooper (2000), who argue that identity should be used only in its 'strong' meaning, representing a long-lasting notion of the self, linked to a strong sense of national identity. But Hall does not argue that all identities are constantly in flux: people generally maintain a fairly constant repertoire of identities, each more or less in a particular set of social contexts. The individual has one self, expressed through different identities and in relationship to others: they are constructed in social contexts and would be meaningless if divorced from social settings.

Jamieson (2002, 2005) uses a social constructionist position to argue that some of these identities are more likely to be 'primary' identities than others, and there are conditions in which some supranational identities (such as European) are more likely to be primary than local identities. The categorization of groups and identities is not necessarily always deep and fundamental – putting oneself into a group does not wholly align oneself with all others in the group. In many cases, feeling a sense of identity with others may be rather transient.

The processes of schooling often include children creating categories for groups of their peers who become 'the other'. Such distinctions have been observed as based on ethnicity and race (Archer, 2003), gender (Hey, 1997) class and sexuality (Mac An Ghaill, 1994). Mannitz describes adolescents of migrant descent in contemporary European schools (London, Berlin, Amsterdam and Paris) as not just understanding such civil conventions but 'As well as becoming German, French, Dutch of British, these young people have apparently adopted types of globally marketed youth culture' (Mannitz, 2004: 308).

Widdicombe and Woofitt (1995) point out that for young people social shaping is not always profound: individual adolescents often resisted being categorized, asserting that, far from being distinct members of particular youth subcultures, they saw themselves as 'normal' and as individuals, and their badges of youth identities were heuristic and casual. Identities are thus not always primary, and recognising this can be useful in considering multiple nested identities related to place and territory.

This is to argue that young people will be developing these identities, adding to their repertoire, from a very early age: and these have an implication for their sense of to whom they 'belong', and hence for their conception of civic identity (Osler and Starkey 2003). For, as W. J. M. Mackenzie argued (1978), we can in the broader sense be citizens of several 'places' – of the planet, of the city, or of a range of 'places' in between. Three particular definitions of citizenship are of relevance at this point: the work of Marshall (1950), Vasak (1979) and Urry (1995).

Marshall suggested that citizenship is essentially about the establishment and the exercise of rights. Citizenship is a process of belonging to a political entity that gives its members the protection of particular rights. He proposed three stages in the development of the rights of citizenship – citizenship gave civil rights in the eighteenth century, political rights in the nineteenth century and social rights in the twentieth century. The Czech-French jurist Karel Vasak proposed (1979/1982) dividing human rights into three generations. The first of these concern liberty, and are civil and political in nature, protecting the individual from the state: they broadly summate Marshall's first two waves of rights. Second-generation human rights concern equality, and are essentially social, economic and cultural in nature. They should lead to different citizens having equal conditions and treatment, the right to work and to be employed and thus the ability to support a family. This range of rights is equivalent to Marshall's third wave of rights. Third-generation rights concern fraternity and solidarity, and focus on the rights an individual has as a claim upon society. Generally, this third generation has not yet been addressed in any binding human rights agreement, and the new categories of rights suggested by John Urry (1995) identifies some specifics within this third generation: he suggests cultural citizenship (a culture's right to preserve its identity) (Turner, 1993), minority citizenship (a minority's rights to residence and equivalent rights to the majority) (Yuval-Davis, 1997), ecological citizenship (the right to a sustainable environment) (van Steenbergen, 1994), cosmopolitan citizenship (the rights to relate to other cultures and societies) (Held, 1995), consumer citizenship (rights of access to goods, services and information) (Urry, 1995) and mobility citizenship (the rights of visitors and tourists) (Urry, 1990).

The importance of these newer rights is that they give opportunities for young people to actively work and achieve in citizenship activities, rather than simply passively learn about (or be taught about) rights won long ago. In the post-national model of society and education suggested by Davies et al. (2005; also Davies, 2006) there is an emphasis on the external focus, on extra-national perspectives and identities and on the civic inclusion of the historically excluded.

PRINCIPLES FOR DESIGNING THE CITIZENSHIP CURRICULUM

The argument of this chapter has so far identified learning for active citizenship; the need to address values, skills and understanding; and issues of identity and rights as at the heart of a citizenship education programme. How do we combine these into a realistic curricular programme for a school or other educational institution? To offer some suggestions, I now draw extensively on the very useful analysis undertaken by Deakin Crick and her colleagues (2004) in a meta-review of recent research of the practice of citizenship education.

These analyses of the citizenship curriculum suggest certain four key areas for the planning and delivery of effective learning. These constitute a package – they are closely related to each other and interdependent, not a 'shopping list' from which a selection might be made. They are facilitating classroom discourse and a dialogic pedagogy in the classroom; a concomitant valuing and respect for the student and their experiences, as a partner in citizenship learning; a coherent and radical construction of the school as a democratic institution that accords genuine

rights and responsibilities to all its members and finally a structure to support teachers and other staff to engage in these processes.

Deakin Crick's first set of principles suggest that the quality of dialogue and discourse is central: this is essential in pupils identifying shared values and rights, and in constructing concepts of justice and equality. Higher order critical and creative thinking skills depend on the processes of learning, the quality of pupil-teacher and pupil-pupil relationships and on the dialogue associated with these relationships. Such a facilitative and conversational pedagogy will require a reordering of the traditional power and authority structures of the school, and necessitate an inclusive and respectful quality to teacher pupil relationships.

This leads to a second group of principles: the empowerment of the pupil voice, and the space and opportunity for them to articulate and construct meaning of their life experiences and identities. The use of pupils' contextual knowledge in a problem-solving context will, it is argued, lead to citizenship engagement and action. The classroom and school need to make opportunities to engage with the values embedded in all subjects, across the curriculum, but that also demonstrably linked to pupils' lives and personal narratives.

This in turn implies the whole school adopting a strategy that defines itself as exemplifying, in all its practices, community values that define it as a democratic and respectful institution. Such a strategy not only requires powerful leadership, but needs to involve every member of the school community. Educational establishments need structures that allow participation and democratic processes to be at the core, and this in turn puts particular demands on the skills and attitudes of all members of the community, pupils and staff: citizenship education is not a bolt-on activity to be transmitted by a small group of staff in isolation from the rest of the school. The student voice needs not merely to be listened to, but to be trusted and honoured.

Finally, such transformations require the establishment of support for teachers and other school staff to develop their professional skills to accomplish these classroom and whole school transformations.

A WHOLE SCHOOL ETHOS

There have been a number of attempts to classify how schools have approached the organization of citizenship education. One of the largest studies, undertaken by the UK's National Foundation for Educational Research (NFER), is a longitudinal study (still in progress) of how English secondary schools have implemented the new national curriculum subject (see, for example, Ireland et al., 2006). This offers a largely descriptive model of the extent of school engagement with the subject, classifying schools in four types: progressive (high involvement, specific citizenship education), focused (low involvement, specific citizenship education), implicit (high involvement, implicit citizenship) and minimalist (low involvement and implicit citizenship). This does not really help us understand what kind of school ethos is necessary for effective learning, and why. More helpful is McGettrick (2002), who identifies three broad approaches in teachers' practice: the transmission approach (a focus on knowledge and content, a traditional instructional style and an inflexible programme design); the process approach (centred on the context of schooling and its organisation, characterized by developmental teaching and flexible programme design) and – McGettrick's preference – professional transformational (teachers become reprofessionalized as facilitators for transforming society as the primary agent of social change in the community).

This approach is articulated most clearly in the case study of a school in England by Deakin Crick (2002). She described how a carefully planned whole school intervention in the structuring and delivery of spiritual, moral and cultural education was able to change the way pupils saw and articulated the core values of school. These values were not transmitted in the conventional manner through distinct lessons, but were introduced to underpin all school approach to teaching and learning. All teachers were involved in the identification of nine core values (such as valuing oneself and others, justice, forgiveness, truth and trust), and all agreed to their implementation. Curriculum planning followed from this, and Deacon Crick tracked how they were introduced over two terms. She identifies that in addition to this 'whole school, whole person' approach, the quality of student thinking and talking in the classroom was critical, and that the value of quality discourse could not be understated.

Most schools are less committed to such a root-and-branch revision. A study described by Leighton (2004) found many teachers assumed that they were already naturally democratic: they fell into a syllogistic trap that 'democracy is good, we are democratic, therefore we are good', without considering what was meant by democratic in the practice of the school. Consequently there was often a contradictions between the stated ethos of a school and its practices: he noted that this disjuncture, clearly identified by students, did 'not appear to depress or alienate the young so much as disinterest them' (p. 179).

There are examples of less radical whole school approaches than that described by Deakin Crick. For example, Sliwka (2006) describes very substantial deliberative projects in some German secondary schools, involving whole schools considering an issue over several non-consecutive days with the participation of politicians and others. More common is the introduction of schools councils. These can provide valuable lessons in different systems of voting (the author recalls exploring various forms of alternative voting patterns with ten-year-olds as they elected two classroom representatives, in which we managed to demons-trate the different results between first-past the vote systems and alternative transferable voting: this lead to an exploration of constituencies and gerrymandering). The evidence of their effectiveness in bringing about active citizenship is mixed. A study by Flecknoe (2002) found that pupils appreciated how councils enabled pupils to be listened to, which lead to an increase in self-confidence, in decision-making abilities, cooperation and in conflict resolution. But both pupils and staff needed to be supported concurrently in developing skills, and that to be successful democratic participation had to centre around real topics rather than peripheral issues.

These caveats were largely repeated in a wider study of schools councils in England by Taylor (2002). Secondary schools found more difficulties in initiating effective councils, partly from the nature of the schools themselves, and partly because of practical issues. There was a tendency to exclude younger pupils from participation, in both primary and secondary schools, and the focus of much discussion was on the improvement of school facilities (the playground, buildings and catering), on the organization of the school day organisation and on fundraising. There was little discussion of the curriculum and teaching styles, nor of issues such as consistency in school discipline, where inconsistencies in approach have been noted by Gillborn (1992) to be critical in developing racialized patterns of behaviour. Two-thirds of secondary teachers thought that councils were not worthwhile.

THE CLASSROOM DIALOGIC

Schools as institutions need to become infused with democratic processes: this is equally true of classrooms. The second set of features identified in Deacon Crick's analysis concern the introduction of dialogic processes of teaching and learning. Traditional models of teaching as a transmission process, where the knowledge accumulated by the teacher in transmitted to the learner necessitate both a hierarchical power relationship, itself inimical to 'democratic' processes and a denial of the identity and experience of the learner, whose previous understandings of and encounters with social life are overwritten by the teacher's narrative.

Introducing student's experience as valid data for learning requires a form of dialogue between pupils and teacher, that acknowledges a partnership in exploring ideas. The questioning style of teachers – often designed to elicit from the student a repetition of the knowledge the teacher already possesses (Galton et al., 1980; Delamont, 1986; Wragg and Brown, 2001). Asking questions that are genuinely open-ended, to which the teacher doesn't know the answer, and where the teacher accepts the response as supplying genuine fresh knowledge that will contribute to the development of the classroom discourse, is relatively uncommon, and can be as confusing for the student as it is a disconcerting role-shift for the teacher.

The content of what is discussed may in some ways make a transition to this form of discourse easier. Talking about identities – who do you feel you are, in this particular context – is, for example, an area in which it is very evident to questioner and respondent alike that the terms of the reply are the property of the respondent. There's no question that the answer given is 'correct'. The other suggested focus for the context of citizenship – the development of human rights – is equally an area in which divergences of views and opinions may be anticipated. Osler and Starkey (2003) show how such conversations about multiple identities and loyalties can identify and extend conceptions of citizenship. Carter and Osler (2000) explore how human rights discussions were used to create positive interpersonal relationships and a culture consistent with human rights in classroom conversations with 14–15-year-old boys. They suggested a fundamental development in classroom culture was needed to move from a collection of atomised individuals who lack the means to build relationships between members, towards the progressive establishment of democratic methods, so students and staff have time to work with them. In the traditional classroom, they reported, many students expressed the view that discussing human rights displayed weakness and need, and was 'unmasculine'. Rigid classroom approaches were antipathetic to the development of a school community, and rigid discipline reduces positive relationships.

Similar outcomes in secondary education were reported in a small-scale study of a theatre-in-education project by Day (2002). A focus on moral dilemmas allowed the students to move from particularistic data towards generalized principles. Building on students' own experiences of and familiarity with refugees and the homeless became possible because new interactive rules were introduced, different from the normal classroom approach: these allowed a new dialogic to emerge within which students participated as adults, and teachers as learners.

In primary schools, Holden (2000) described situations in which teachers had no policy for moral and social education, though they would describe such an ethos seen as being paramount. But she observed that talk was used to develop moral and social development, and that children demonstrated a complex understanding of social relationships and morals from early age. But citizenship education opportunities were missed by teachers, including opportunities of discussing rights and responsibilities beyond the school, democratic processes, rights and values, participation by pupils in debate and agenda setting. Clare et al. (1996) show how teachers can develop conversational styles of discourse, particularly in identifying moral dilemmas in literature. They describe nine-year-old children initiating discussion of the values implicit in stories. However, this was not simply a consequence of reading the stories: the teacher had first to create situations of cognitive dissonance, focusing developmentally appropriate questions and helping pupils work on them through interactive discussion. The teacher needed to be able to recognize appropriate dilemmas, and then to present them within a facilitative pedagogy.

A dialogic classroom requires the development of a particular set of skills. Teachers need to manage discussions so that their students learn the skills of turn-taking, and of building on each others' experiences, points of view and arguments. Skills of decision-making, and of accepting the consequences of one's decisions, can be initiated at a very young age, and then refined and differentiated over time. A wide series of procedural values and rules need to inform such a classroom: the need to listen to others as well as to articulate one's own views, and to synthesis shared positions from these; the need to tolerate the substantive values of other and a fundamental respect for truth and inquiry.

This remodelling of classroom interaction allows the valuing, understanding and acknowledgement of different experiences and points of view, and, it has been argued here, is necessary to meet the requirements of citizenship. We might conclude by turning to a pioneer writer on education, Aristotle, on the meaning of being a good citizen:

> ... it is not possible to be a good ruler without first having been ruled. Not that good ruling and good obedience are the same virtue – only that the good citizen must have the knowledge and ability both to rule and be ruled. That is what we mean by the virtue of a citizen – understanding the governing of free men from both points of view (Aristotle, 1962).

REFERENCES

Archer, L. (2003) *'Race' Masculinity and Schooling: Muslim Boys and Education*. Buckingham: Open University Press.

Aristotle (1962) *The Politics* (trans. T.A. Sinclair). Harmondsworth: Penguin.

Audigier, F. (1998) *Basic concepts and core competencies for education for democratic citizenship* (Project 'Education for Democratic Citizenship'). Strasbourg: Council for Cultural Co-operation. DGIV/EDU/CIT (2000) 23.

Avbelj, M. (2005) 'Can the New European Constitution Remedy the EU 'Democratic Deficit'?', *EUMAP On-line journal*. Available http://hdl.handle.net/1814/4166.

Brubaker, R. and Cooper, F. (2000) 'Beyond identity', *Theory and Society*, 29 (1): 1–47.

Carter, C. and Osler, A. (2000) 'Human Rights, Identities and Conflict Management: A study of school culture as experienced through classroom relationships'. *Cambridge Journal of Education*, 30 (3): 335–356.

Clare, L., Gallimore, R. and Patthey-Chavez, G. (1996) 'Using Moral Dilemmas in Children's Literature as a Vehicle for Moral Education and Teaching Reading Comprehension', *Journal of Moral Education*, 25 (3): 325–341.

Clarke, S. (2007) 'The Trajectory of "Political Education"' in English Schools: The Rise and Fall of Two Initiatives', *Citizenship Teaching and Learning*, 3 (1): 3–16.

Cleaver, E. and Nelson, J. (2006) 'Active Citizenship: From Policy to Practice', *Education Journal*, 98: 34–37.

Connell, R. W. (1971) *The Child's Construction of Politics*. Melbourne: Melbourne University Press.

Council of Europe (2002) *What is Education for Democratic Citizenship – Concepts and Practice*. Available http://www.coe.int.

Crick, B. (1998) *Education for Citizenship and the Teaching of Democracy in Schools* [Report of the Advisory Group on Education for Citizenship]. London: Qualifications and Curriculum Authority.

Crick, B, and Lister, I. (1979) Political Literacy: The Centrality of the Concept. *International Journal of Political Education*, 1 (1).

Crick, B. and Porter, A. (1978). *Political Education and Political Literacy*, London: Longman.

Davies, I. and Issitt, J. (2005) 'Reflections on Citizenship Education in Australia, Canada and England', *Comparative Education*, 41 (4): 389–410.

Davies, I. Evans, M. and Reid, A. (2005) Globalising Citizenship Education? A Critique of 'Global Education' and 'Citizenship Education', *British Journal of Educational Studies*, 53 (1): 66–89.

Davies, L. (2006) 'Global Citizenship: Abstraction or Framework for Action?', *Educational Review*, 58 (1): 5–25.

Day, L. (2002) '"Putting Yourself in Other People's Shoes": The Use of Forum Theatre to Explore Refugee and Homeless Issues in School'. *Journal of Moral Education*, 31 (1): 21–34.

Deakin Crick, R. (2002) *Transforming Visions, Managing Values in Schools: A Case Study.* Bristol: Middlesex University Press.

Deakin Crick, R., Coates, M., Taylor, M. and Ritchie, S. (2004) *A Systematic Review of the Impact of Citizenship Education on the Provision of Schooling*. London: EPPI-Centre.

Delamont, S. (1986) *Inside the Secondary Classroom*. London: Routledge and Kegan Paul.

European Union (1992) *Treaty on European Union*, Maastricht. *Official Journal* C 191, 29 July 1992.

European Union (1993) *Green Paper on the European Dimension in Education*, 29 September 1993. COM (93) 457 final, 29 September 1993.

Flecknoe, M. (2002) 'Democracy, Citizenship and School Improvement: What Can One School Tell Us?', *School Leadership and Management*, 22 (4): 421–437.

Galton, M., Simon, B. and Croll, P. (1980) *Inside the Primary Classroom*. London: Routledge and Kegan Paul.

Gillborn, D. (1992) 'Citizenship, "Race" and the Hidden Curriculum', *International Studies in the Sociology of Education*, 2 (1): 57–73.

Greenstein, F. (1965) *Children and Politics*. New Haven, MA.: Yale University Press.

Gundara, J. (2006) 'The Sacred and the Secular: Multiple Citizenship and Education'. In J. Sprogøe and T. Winther-Jensen T (eds) *Identity, Education and Citizenship and Multiple Interrelations*. Frankfurt am Main: Peter Lang.

Hall, S. (1996) Introduction: Who Needs Identity? In S. Hall and P. du Gay (eds) *Questions of Cultural Identity.* London: Sage.

Hall, S. (1997) Representation, Meaning and Language: The Spectacle of the 'Other'. In S. Hall (ed) *Representation: Cultural Representations and Signifying Practices*. London: Sage.

Heater, D. (1990) *Citizenship*. London: Longmans.

Heater, D. and Oliver, D. (1994) *The Foundations of Citizenship*. Hemel Hempstead, Harvester Wheatsheaf.

Held, D. (1995) *Democracy and the Global Order.* Cambridge: Polity Press.

Hess, R.D. and Torney, J.V. (1967) *The Development of Political Attitudes in Children*. Chicago IL: Aldine.

Hey, V. (1997) *The Company She Keeps: An Ethnography of Girls' Friendship*. Buckingham: Open University Press.

Hirschhorn, J. (2006) *Delusional Democracy: Fixing the Republic Without Overthrowing the Government*. Monroe, Maine: Common Courage Press.

Holden, C. (2000) Ready for Citizenship? A Case Study of Approaches to Social and Moral Education in Two Contrasting Primary schools in the UK', *The School Field: International Journal of Theory and Research in Education*, 11 (1): 117–130.

Ireland, E., Kerr, F., Lopes, J. and Nelson, J. (2006) *Active Citizenship and Young people: Opportunities, Experiences and Challenges in and beyond School. Citizenship Education Longitudinal Study: Fourth Annual report*. London: Department for Education and Skills.

Isin, E. and Wood, P. (1999) *Citizenship and Identity*. London : Sage.

Jamieson, L. (2002) Theorising Identity, Nationality and Citizenship: Implications for European Citizenship Identity. *Sociológia*, 34 (6): 507–532.

Jamieson, L. (2005) SERD-2000-00260 *Final Report: Orientations of Young Men and Women to Citizenship and European Identity*. Available http://www.socresonline.org.uk/10/3/grundy.html.

Kenendy, J.K. (2006) 'Towards a conceptual framework for understanding Active and passive Citizenship'. Unpublished, quoted in Nelson, J. and Kerr, D., 2006.

Kerr, D. and Ireland, E. (2004) 'Making Citizenship Education Real', *Education Journal*, 78: 25–27.

Kidder, R. (2002) 'The strength to care', *Times Educational Supplement, Scotland*. 12 April 2002: 21.

Leighton, R. (2004) 'The Nature of Citizenship Education Provision: An Initial Study', *Curriculum Journal*, 15 (2): 167–181.

Mac an Ghaill, M. (1994) *The Making of Men: Masculinities, Sexualities and Schooling*. Buckingham: Open University Press.

Mackenzie, W.J.M. (1978) *Political Identity*. Harmondsworth: Penguin.

Mannitz, S. (2004) Pupils' Negotiations of Cultural Difference: Identity Management and Discursive Assimilation. In W. Schiffauer, G. Baumann, R., Kastoryano and D. Vertyovec (eds) *Civic Enculturation: Nation-State, School and Ethnic Difference in the Netherlands, Britain, Germany and France*. New York: Berghahn Books.

Marshall, T.H. (1950) Citizenship *and Social Class and Other Essays*. Cambridge: Cambridge University Press.

McGettrick, B. (2002) *Emerging Conceptions of Scholarship, Service and Teaching*. Toronto: Canadian Society for the Study of Education.

Mitchell, J. (2005) 'The European Union's 'Democratic Deficit': Bridging the Gap between Citizens and EU Institutions', *EUMAP On-line journal*, 2005/03/10. Available www.eumap.org/journal/features/2005/demodef/mitchell/

Moravsci, K.A. (2004) 'Is There a Democratic Deficit in World Politics? A Framework for Analysis', *Government and Opposition*, 39 (2): 336–363.

Nelson, J. and Kerr, D. (2006) *Active Citizenship in INCA countries: Definitions, Policies, Practices and Outcomes: Final Report*. London: Qualification and Curriculum Authority.

Osler, A. and Starkey, H. (2003) 'Learning for Cosmopolitan Citizenship: Theoretical Debates and Young People's Experiences', *Educational Review*, 55 (3): 243–255.

Prior, W. (2006) 'Civics and Citizenship Education', *Ethos*, 14 (3): 6–7.

Ross, A. (2007) 'Multiple Identities and Education for Active Citizenship', *British Journal of Educational Studies*, 55 (3): 286–303.

Russell, J. (2002) 'Moral Consciousness in a Community of Inquiry.' *Journal of Moral Education*, 31 (2): 142–153.

Sen, A. (2006) *Identity and Violence: The Illusion of Destiny*. London: Allen Lane.

Sliwka, A. (2006) 'Controversial Issues in German Secondary Schools: The deliberation project', paper presented at the Second International CitizED conference, Oxford, July 2006. Available http://www.citized.info/pdf/ejournal/conf_2006/013.pdf.

Sutherland, M. (2002) 'Educating Citizens in Europe', *European Education*, 34 (3): 77.

Taylor, M. (2002) *Schools Councils: Their Role in Citizenship and Personal and Social Education*. Slough: National Foundation for Educational Research.

Turner, B. (1993) Contemporary Problems in the Theory of Citizenship. In B. Turner, *Citizenship and Social Theory*. London: Sage.

Urry, J. (1990) *The Tourist Gaze*. London: Sage.

Urry, J. (1995) *Consuming Places*. London: Routledge.

van Steenbergen, B. (1994) Towards a Global Ecological Condition of Citizenship. In B. van Steenberg (ed) *The Condition of Citizenship*. London: Sage.

Vasak, K. (1979/1982) 'For the Third Generation of Human Rights: The Rights of Solidarity (International Institute of Human Rights, Strasbourg, July 1979), cited in P. Alston, A Third Generation of Solidarity Rights: Progressive Development Zor Obfuscation of International Human Rights Law? (1982)', *Netherlands International Law Review*, 29: 307.

Verdun, A. (1998) 'The Institutional Design of EMU: A Democratic Deficit?', *Journal of Public Policy*, 18 (2): 107–132.

Widdicombe, S. and Woofitt. R. (1995) *The Language of Youth Subcultures: Social Identity in Action*. Hemel Hempstead: Harvester.

Wragg, E. and Brown, G. (2001) *Questioning in the Secondary School*. London: Routledege Falmer.

Yuval-Davis, N. (1997) *National Spaces and Collective Identities: Border, Boundaries, Citizenship and Gender Relations* (Inaugural Lecture, University of Greenwich).

39

Discussion of Controversial Issues as a Form and Goal of Democratic Education

Diana Hess and Patricia G. Avery

In democratic societies, discussion in schools is viewed as a critical component of citizenship education. This should not be surprising given both the theoretical and practical links between discussion and democracy and the tremendous growth of democracy in the past 20 years. A larger percentage of the world's people live in democratic nations now than during any previous time in history (Puddington, 2007).

Support for engaging young people in classroom discussions as part of democratic education comes from various quarters. The governments of France, Northern Ireland, and Britain, for example, have adopted formal curriculum documents that promote discussions of political issues in schools. Teachers and students from many democratic nations report their affinity for discussion (Hahn, 1998; Yamashita, 2006). Political theorists advocate discussion as a vital component of democratic living (Gutmann, 1999). Civic education researchers laud discussion about authentic political issues as a key component of the pathway toward greater political

knowledge and participation (Torney-Purta et al., 2001). Discussion is thus advanced as both a pedagogical form in and of itself and as a critical part of democratic education (Parker and Hess, 2001).

Discussions in democratic societies are markers of what Dahl calls 'intrinsic equality' – the fundamental assumption that the good of every human being is intrinsically equal to that of any other (1998: 65). The ideal egalitarian discussion supports the validity of intrinsic equality by implying, at least symbolically, that all members of a community are political equals, equally well qualified to participate in discussion and hence to participate in decisions.

Our purpose in this chapter is to describe what is both fairly well understood and less well understood about the use of discussion in classroom-based democratic education. In doing so, we hope to illuminate the core beliefs, contradictions, and debates in the field. The literature on this topic constitutes a vast territory that we negotiate with four questions as our guide.

- For what reasons is discussion in democratic education advocated?
- What is the prevalence of discussion in democratic education?
- What do teachers who are good at using discussion do, and for what reasons?
- And, how do students experience and learn from discussion, and what influences those effects?

We conclude by suggesting avenues for future research that would advance our understanding of the role discussion can play in democratic education.

RATIONALES FOR DISCUSSION

Much of the advocacy for discussion in democratic education is rooted in the belief that for a healthy democracy to exist, political discussion among citizens is public, robust, and ongoing. Mansbridge posits that, 'Democracy involves public discussion of common problems, not just silent counting of individual hands' (1991: 122). Those who hold this conception of democracy advance the inclusion of controversial issues in the school curriculum to prepare young people to participate fully and competently in a form of political engagement that is authentic to the world outside the classroom. However, there is evidence that in many democratic nations, few people actually engage in much political discussion. In a study of adults in six communities in Britain and the US, Conover et al. (2002) found that 30 per cent of the sample in the US and 50 per cent in Britain are 'silent citizen.' That is, a large percentage of each nation's respondents discuss issues in private only. Virtually no one discussed in public only, and a mere 18 per cent of US citizens and 9 per cent of British citizens reported speaking in both contexts. Further, Conover et al. suggested that these discussions are often marred by inequality and a lack of analysis and critique. Ironically, students who act as 'silent citizens' rather than vocal participants in class discussions could

be considered more 'authentic' to what adults typically do.

Other rationales for issues discussions promote them as *vehicles* for a host of outcomes, some of which are explicitly connected to democratic education. Examples include the expectation that via issues discussions students will develop an understanding and commitment to democratic values, such as tolerance, equality, and diversity (Oliver and Shaver, 1966); become comfortable with the nature and ubiquity of conflict about issues in the world outside of school (Hibbing and Theiss-Morse, 2002); enhance their sense of political efficacy (Gimpel et al., 2003); increase their interest in engaging in public life (Zukin et al., 2006); and learn how to break down historic divides in a community or nation and forge bonds between groups of people in a society who are markedly different from one another (McCully, 2006). Issues discussions are also advocated for reasons traditionally associated with schooling outcomes writ large, such as learning important content (Harris, 1996), improving critical thinking, or building more sophisticated interpersonal skills (Johnson and Johnson, 1995).

To date, however, we do not have a clear understanding of what students *do* learn from controversial issues discussions and why. Although there is some empirical evidence to support the use of discussions for specific outcomes, it is difficult to draw generalizations. Hahn (1996) argues that one of the central problems with researching what students learn from issues discussions is that there are so many different approaches, and virtually all of them are embedded within a course of study. A second problem is that it is highly unusual to find schools in any nation that have infused controversial issues discussions into the curricula in a systematic way. Consequently, researchers often study the effects of one course that includes some attention to controversial issues discussions and find, not surprisingly, that even exceptionally well-taught courses do not result in significant gains on measurable outcomes (Hahn and Tocci, 1990; Hess and Posselt, 2002).

Third, there is a contradiction between what teachers and students report with respect to the prevalence of issues discussions in schools and what researchers observe in classrooms.

THE PREVALENCE OF CONTROVERSIAL ISSUES DISCUSSIONS

In the 1999 International Association for the Evaluation of Educational Achievement (IEA) Civic Education Study, items such as 'teachers encourage us to discuss political or social issues about which people have different opinions' were included as part of an open classroom climate construct. This scale measures the 'extent to which students experience their classrooms as places to investigate issues and explore their opinions and those of their peers' (Torney-Purta et al., 2001: 137). The researchers report that an open classroom climate for discussion is an especially significant predictor of civic knowledge and political engagement (2001: 155).

Although there was variance within and across nations with respect to the number of students who assessed their classrooms as open, the overwhelming majority of students gave positive responses to each of the six items. For example, when asked whether students 'feel free to disagree openly with their teachers about issues,' 67 per cent said that was 'sometimes' or 'often' the case (2001: 207).

Teachers in many nations also report democratic education programs that are rich with controversial issues discussions, especially as compared to the past. In Britain, 58 per cent of teachers in one recent large study reported that 'exploring, discussing and debating issues' occurred often in their classes. Just two years earlier, only 47 per cent indicated that was the case (Kerr et al., 2007: 59).

What is perplexing to many researchers is that observational studies report virtually no classroom discussion. For example, Nystrand and his colleagues analyzed discourse in 106 middle and high school social studies classes in the US, reporting that 'despite considerable lip service among teachers to "discussion", we found little discussion in any classes' (Nystrand et al., 2003: 178). Kahne and his colleagues (2000) describe similar findings in their analysis of observers' reports of 135 middle and high school social studies classes, in Chicago. In over 80 per cent of the classes there was no mention of a social problem, and even when problems were mentioned, there was rarely any discussion of possible solutions or connections to contemporary life.

What accounts for the difference between what students report occurs in their classes and what researchers observe? Researchers report that students and teachers alike tend to conflate classroom talk with discussion (Hess and Ganzler, 2007; Larson, 1997). Additionally, Richardson (2006) finds that the majority of students do not make a distinction between a controversial issue and a current event, and that discussion is defined broadly to include any talk with a teacher (171, 173–174).

In a study involving 941 students and 34 teachers in 20 high schools, researchers report that discussions of issues are not necessary in order for students to label their classroom climate as open (Hess, 2007; Hess and Ganzler, 2007). In one classroom dominated by teacher lecture, the students reported an open classroom climate on the same items used on the IEA Civic Education survey. Thus, these items may not be a proxy for issues discussions per se. Instead, students may be communicating that they are in classrooms with at least some modicum of a democratic ethos with some student talk and references to issues.

The implications of this possibility are potentially far-reaching because many of the effects reported to stem from controversial issues discussions are based on students' assessment of whether they are in an open classroom climate (i.e. one that includes issues discussions). It may be that while controversial issues discussions do matter in terms of democratic outcomes, students' sense that they are in a classroom where they can speak and their opinions are respected also matters. Researchers, however, may not be distinguishing between students who are in issues-rich discussion classes and those who are simply in classes with student talk and tangential attention to issues. This raises the possibility that in classes that include more genuine issues discussions, the effects associated with the rationales for issues discussions, such as increased tolerance, political knowledge, and political interest, may be stronger than in those classes students perceive as simply open according to the 'open' classroom climate scale. We will not know until we are better able to discriminate between the two types of classes.

TEACHER PRACTICE

The issues discussion approach is clearly supported by many teachers, and this support is growing. Rich case study literature shows that teachers in many nations infuse their courses with issues discussions (Hahn, 1998; McCully, 2006). This is surprising given that many teachers report receiving little or no instruction in how to facilitate such discussions in their teacher education programs or professional development activities (Oulton et al., 2004).

One factor that influences whether controversial issues discussions will be used by teachers is the characteristic of their students. Notwithstanding evidence that young children can participate well in issues discussions (Angell, 2004; Paley, 1992), it is more common for teachers of older students to use issues in their classes (Oulton et al., 2004).

There also appears to be an inverse relationship between the degree of racial and ethnic diversity that exists within a class and the teacher's willingness to infuse controversial issues discussions into the curricula (Campbell, 2007). Conover and Searing (2000) found that students in immigrant and urban communities were significantly less likely to engage in political discussions in school (34 and 25 per cent respectively) than were rural (68 per cent) and suburban (50 per cent) students. This is a particularly troubling finding because it suggests that for at least some teachers, a diverse group of students in the same class may be seen as a barrier to deliberation. Conversely, political theorists conceptualize diversity as a deliberative asset, and schools as a particularly powerful place for issues discussions. Gutmann advocated the use of discussions in schools because 'schools have a much greater capacity than most parents and voluntary associations for teaching children to reason out loud about disagreements that arise in democratic politics...' (1999: 58). Schools' greater capacity is embodied in the fact that they almost always contain more diversity than one would expect to find in the other private and public spaces that young people inhabit.

Teachers who are skillful in facilitating high quality discussions of controversial issues report some similarities in both their practice and in the challenging pedagogical issues they confront (Cotton, 2006; Hess; 2002). Skillful practitioners carefully select issues of genuine controversy, prepare students for discussions, and attend to creating and maintaining norms that are designed to promote a discussion-friendly environment. Experienced discussion teachers also tend to assume that students need to be taught discussion skills, instead of assuming that students come into their classes with their skills already developed (Hess and Posselt, 2002).

Skillful discussion teachers tend to have sophisticated concepts of discussion that they try to make concrete for their students, often by teaching them specific models of discussion (Rossi, 1995). Discussion models, such as the Public Issues Approach, work to ensure that discussion is not a shouting match or a lecture punctuated by occasional teacher questions or student comments.

The use of controversial issues discussions requires teachers to take a position (implicitly or explicitly) on a number of pedagogical issues, two of which are particularly significant. The first is determining what criteria should be used to decide whether a topic is genuinely an issue, or a question for which there is a right answer. The second is whether a teacher should disclose her personal views on the controversial issues students discuss.

CONTROVERSY ABOUT DEFINING CONTROVERSY

Hand argues that there is quite a bit of agreement in the educational literature about what it means for a topic to be considered controversial:

> To teach something as controversial is to present it as a matter on which different views are or could be held, and to expound those different views as impartially as possible. It is to acknowledge and explore various possible answers to a question without endorsing any of them. The intended outcome of such teaching is, at least, that pupils should understand a range of views on a topic and arguments in their support, and at most, that they should hold and be able to defend considered views of their own; it is emphatically *not* that they should come to share the view favoured by the teacher (forthcoming: 1).

The problem with this definition, as Hand rightly points out, is that it rests on a presumption that there is agreement about whether the different views held are normatively consistent with the larger purposes of education. In some cases, that agreement actually does exist. For example, it is generally not controversial in democratic societies for teachers to believe that young people should learn that racism is wrong. If the question of whether racism is wrong is advanced in school, it is taught with an answer. Hand labels this 'teaching as settled' as opposed to the 'teaching as controversial.'

Hand points out that there seems to be a conflation in many teaching guides between topics that should be taught as settled versus those that are more appropriately dealt with as controversial. He notes that controversial issues teaching resources published by generally well-regarded organizations (such as Oxfam) state that bullying, racism, and prejudice are examples of controversial issues even though evidence suggests that normative agreement exists that all three topics should be presented as settled. There is no serious discussion among educators, for example, about whether bullying in schools is good or bad. This is not to suggest that there are not legitimate controversial issues related to settled topics (such as what kind of government policy, if any, should be enacted to combat the effects of racism). But often there is little differentiation between problems that require attention (e.g. prejudice) and issues that are controversial. Hand suggests that the way to solve this problem is to be much more explicit about what criteria determine whether an issue is controversial or settled.

The more challenging problem for teachers arises when there really is disagreement about whether a question should be presented as settled or controversial. Issues are not controversial by nature, but are socially constructed in ways that cause them to be more or less controversial. This is why it is common for issues that are considered well settled in one nation (or even part of a nation) to be controversial in others. The question of whether evolution or other ideas about the origin of life should be taught in schools is a matter of bitter controversy in some parts of the US, but does not generate the same level of controversy in much of Europe.

Over time issues also 'tip' from controversial to settled, and vice versa. Much controversy arises from disagreements about whether a teacher has made the right decision about which side of the 'tip' to promote (Hess, 2004). For example, at one time the question of whether suffrage should be extended to women was quite controversial in many democratic nations, and now it is settled in most nations. Although it would not be controversial in many nations for teachers now to teach about women's suffrage as a settled matter, imagine what it was like for teachers when society was 'tipping' from viewing this issue as controversial to one that was settled.

What is unclear is what causes schools to lead or follow during the tipping process. In some cases, disputes about settled versus controversial are curricular 'canaries in the mine,' whose purpose is to provide early warning to society that an issue is ready to tip from being considered a matter of legitimate controversy to a settled question or vice versa. In other cases, schools follow society and change the curriculum to reflect the consensus that has emerged about what was once a controversial issue.

It is often teachers who make the decision about whether an issue should be presented as settled or controversial. Hess (2002) asked US middle and high school teachers to analyze a list of topics that sparked controversy in society (such as abortion and gay rights), and found significant disagreement about whether some topics are legitimate matters of controversy. One teacher characterized gay rights issues not as controversial, but as human rights issues for which there were answers he wanted his students to understand and believe. This suggests that a threshold criterion teachers use to select issues is based on their personal views of whether they think the issue is legitimately in the public square.

Considerable evidence also indicates that many teachers, especially those with less experience, will not select issues that may be upsetting to the community or to students, or are simply deemed 'too hot to handle.' Phillips (1997) found that teachers were unwilling to include abortion in the curriculum; they were also reluctant to include issues about pornography or creationism in fear of community reprisals. Another frequently cited reason for keeping an issue out of the curriculum is that the discussion of it may be particularly upsetting to some students. One teacher refused to include issues about gay rights in her classes because she feared students may not talk about them with sensitivity, and that gay students in her class may feel uncomfortable (Hess, 2002).

TEACHER DISCLOSURE

Teachers must make a decision about whether to disclose their own views on issues to their students. Until recently, there was a dearth of research that probed how teachers make sense of this critical question.

Miller-Lane and his colleagues (2006) interviewed four middle and eight high school social studies teachers in a rural county located in the northeastern US to understand how teachers' perceptions of community norms influence their decisions about disclosure. The teachers were presented with Kelly's (1986) framework of four different stances that could be taken on the disclosure issue, ranging from *committed partiality* in which the teacher fosters discussion, is committed to disclosing, and encourages students to do the same, to *neutral impartiality* in which the teacher fosters discussion, but is committed to not disclosing his or her personal views to students. All but 3 of the 12 teachers rejected disclosure of their position in favor of the role of an impartial facilitator. All of the middle school teachers supported this position, and five of the eight high school teachers agreed. Those teachers who rejected disclosure did so because they were concerned that the tolerant environment they were trying to create in their classrooms did not exist in the larger community. Conversely, two of the three teachers who chose disclosure did so because they enjoyed the 'give and take of a genuine argument and stressed that they tried to foster disagreement with understanding that their opinion was one of many in the class' (Miller-Lane et al., 2006: 38).

McCully (2006) investigated how teachers and youth workers in Northern Ireland dealt with disclosure when facilitating discussions among young people about sensitive issues related to 'the Troubles.' Only 1 of the 20 educators chose not to disclose his/her personal views to young people during discussions (and that one person was not from Northern Ireland). McCully reported that the 'consensus was that, as products of a divided society, neutrality was impossible' (2006: 62).

Cotton's study (2006) of three experienced teachers delivering an A-level geography course in Britain makes clear that even when teachers advocate a position of balance and neutrality with respect to their own views during controversial issues discussions, their viewpoints had a much greater impact than they intended or realized. Using elaborate discourse analysis of transcripts from controversial issues discussions, Cotton found that there were times when the teachers' intent appeared to be primarily one of persuasion. Through the content of their questions and by control of students' turns in discussions, the teachers were implicitly, but clearly 'disclosing' their views.

In a recent study of six high school government courses in upstate New York, Niemi and Niemi (2007) report that while five teachers did not explicitly share their opinions on controversial issues (including voting preferences), they are hardly neutral or silent in their views of the political system and politicians. Teachers regularly made derogatory remarks about political leaders (in one especially stunning example the superintendent of the school districts pokes his head into the classroom and asks, 'Are you talking about Hilary Rotten Clinton?'), and communicated impoverished views of how individuals can or should participate politically. Niemi and Niemi express concern that this form of 'teacher disclosure' is anti-thetical to the goals of democratic education:

> But the extent to which teachers made derogatory comments about the knowledge and ability of ordinary citizens, about political leaders, about governmental institutions, and about political processes (campaigns, law-making) was at times overwhelming. That a presidential debate made you 'dumber,' that Kermit the Frog was the best candidate, that our 'wonderful' Congress was 'idiotic,' and so on, hardly suggest healthy, serious-minded criticism. That teachers and even a superintendent resorted to name-calling is even more indicative of a degree of cynicism greater than one might wish for among those teaching about democratic governance (2007: 56).

There is clearly a lively debate about teacher disclosure. However, it seems wise for teachers to make their decision about disclosure carefully, and to analyze the implicit messages they are communicating to their students.

THE EFFECTS OF CONTROVERSIAL ISSUES DISCUSSIONS

Research on the development of democratic values provides strong support for the inclusion of controversial issues in democratic education. The strongest line of research in this area involves the relationship between issues discussions and the development of tolerance, as examined in a study of 338 middle and high school students (Avery et al., 1992). Defining tolerance as 'the willingness to extend civil liberties to groups with whom one disagrees,' researchers worked with a group of teachers to develop a four-week unit focusing on controversial issues related to freedom of expression. Using a quasi-experimental design with control and experimental classes, the researchers find that participation in the curriculum causes most students to move from mild intolerance to mild tolerance, regardless of their previous achievement levels in schools, their gender, or their socio-economic status. However, for 22 students who demonstrated low levels of self-esteem and high levels of authoritarianism, the curriculum actually causes them to become less tolerant.

It is reasonable to expect high quality issues discussion to cause students to build content understanding. However, it is difficult to design studies to assess what impact issues discussions have on students' content knowledge because the content students might learn varies with each issue. Some researchers try to avoid the problem by developing content-related outcomes that might be achieved regardless of the content of the issues students discuss. Johnston et al. (1994) implemented a study that compares high school students who learned about the background of an issue and then discussed it in classrooms with teachers trained in the public issues approach against high school students who were exposed to the same background but did not discuss the issue. The background was delivered via a Channel One news program that focused on differing views on a public issue. Students in the experimental group scored higher on a current events test and showed more improvement in their ability to analyze public issues discussions. However, their discussion skills did not improve relative to the control group.

Kahne and his colleagues (2006) use a quasi-experimental design to assess the effects of a government class curriculum that includes learning about problems in the community, how local government works to address these problems, and issues the students find personally relevant. Personal relevance was the strongest predictor of civic outcomes with significant relationships to all outcomes they measured, including various civic norms, knowledge of social networks and trust. Students were much more likely to say that they know who to contact if they have concerns about their community, know what resources are available to help them with a community project, and know how to work effectively with organizations in their community when they were in classes that included a focus on issues that the students considered personally relevant to their lives (Kahne et al., 2006: 14).

Participation in issues discussions can influence students' actual civic and political engagement. A quasi-experimental longitudinal study of the impact of Kids Voting USA, an interactive curriculum that includes classroom discussions of controversial issues (McDevitt and Kiousis, 2006), shows students who participated in the curriculum were much more likely to engage in acts associated with deliberative democracy than students without such exposure. Three curricular components were found to have a dramatic influence on the long-term civic development of young people: frequent classroom discussions of election

issues, teacher encouragement for expressing opinions, and student participation in get-out-the –vote drives (p. 3). The study shows the positive effect of the curriculum on outcomes such as political knowledge, issues discussions with friends and family, volunteering, and some forms of conventional and unconventional political activism.

To summarize, there is evidence that participating in controversial issues discussions can build pro-democratic values, enhance content understanding, and cause students to engage more in the political world. However, much more research is needed to understand the causal pathways between issues discussions and these outcomes.

HOW STUDENTS EXPERIENCE CONTROVERSIAL ISSUES DISCUSSIONS

Most students in issues-rich classes have positive attitudes toward discussion. In a study of deliberations in secondary classrooms across six countries – Azerbaijan, Czech Republic, Estonia, Lithuania, Russia and the US – 89 per cent of the 2,060 students responding to a questionnaire indicated that they enjoy participating in the deliberations (Avery et al., 2007). In focus groups, students described what they like about the deliberations: the opportunity to express their opinions; to hear other perspectives; and to learn about authentic, 'real' issues were among the reasons most often mentioned. The students, who learned a model of deliberation called Structured Academic Controversy (Johnson and Johnson, 1995), appreciated the structured format of the process because it gave everyone a chance to speak. Many students offered accounts of other teachers attempting discussions that ended in 'yelling matches' among a group of students. Students often reported that the deliberations are significantly different from what they experience in other classes. A Czech student stated that '[the deliberations are] very different from everything...in other classes, we are only supposed to speak when we are asked and otherwise, we listen' (Avery et al., 2007: 32).

There were modest differences in students' reactions to the deliberations by country, underscoring the significance of context. The Azeri students were most likely to mention that they had increased their knowledge of democratic principles and norms, while students in the US were particularly likely to state that the deliberation process helped them to develop the type of positive attitudes and behaviors that would stimulate more civil (as opposed to uncivil) conversations about public issues. The students may be responding to what they perceive to be weaknesses in their own democracies.

Still, across six countries with different histories, cultures, and norms, students responded very positively to classroom discussions about public issues. Other researchers also report that discussions are highly engaging to students (Hess and Posselt, 2002; Hess and Ganzler, 2007). The high level of student involvement generated by issues discussion may account, in part, for the pathway that exists from discussion to political participation.

However, it is also important to recognize that classrooms are complicated social spaces experienced differentially by students, based on a range of factors, including a student's affective views toward schools, previous academic performance, race, class, religion, gender, and so on. (Homana and Barber, 2007; Torney-Purta et al., forthcoming). Rossi (1995) reports that some of the students in a controversial issues course found it engaging and relevant, while others thought it was dull. Similarly, Hess and Posselt (2002) found that for students who were wary of their peers' judgment, especially from classmates they perceived as popular and powerful, controversial issues discussions provoked anxiety and anger. Hemmings' study of discussions in two high school classes (2000) illustrates how sociocultural divisions within each class influence how and why students participate. She found that there were deep divisions based on race and class that were masked by students' displays of tolerance.

Hemmings' finding raises a troubling challenge for teachers who want to include controversial issues discussions in their courses. Much of the theory supporting issues discussions is based on the idea that it is important to see diversity as a deliberative strength (Parker, 2003). Issues discussions are much more likely to be an asset in a multicultural society if the classroom represents that diversity rather than reifying divisions based on race, class, religion, and so on. But just as diversity can be a deliberative strength, it can also re-inscribe social divisions if students feel they are being silenced or do not want to voice opinions that differ from the majority. Moreover, there is evidence that diversity heightens teachers' fears about using controversial issues (Campbell, 2007).

For some teachers, the challenge is not how to deal with diversity, but how to use issues discussions well in groups in which people are quite similar. In an essay about the use of issues discussions in Northern Ireland, Barton and McCully (2007) point out that in classes that are homogenous on the dimension that matters the most (religion), there are differences in students' views that can be activated in discussion to good effect. In particular, they advocate exposing students to divergent perspectives *within* their own religious and political traditions.

In one study of US high school students in ideologically diverse classes, Hess and Ganzler (2007) found that students begin to see political conflict as a normal and necessary part of democracy if the teachers purposely activate the students' awareness of the diversity in their midst via issues discussions.

Students experience controversial issues discussions in different ways. However, the fact that students' participation in controversial issues discussions are typically public makes it important to create a classroom environment that is interpreted by students as welcoming, or these discussions instead may reify some of the inequalities that exist in the deliberative world outside of school.

CONCLUSION

Issues discussions in democratic education are advocated for a plethora of reasons, some better supported by research than others. It is clear that most young people have an affinity for this form of democratic education. It is also evident that participation in issues discussions has some powerful effects on what students learn. But among the challenges faced by democratic educators who value discussion are their desires to simultaneously forge classroom community while nurturing controversy, to develop students' commitments to particular values while respecting their rights to hold ideas that are not shared, and to encourage the expression of political 'voice' without coercively demanding participation.

There are also barriers that prevent many teachers from engaging their students in genuine issues discussions. Teachers often fear a community backlash if they include issues that are too controversial, especially when the controversy is about whether the issue should be taught as settled or open. Many teachers recognize that they have had inadequate preparation to use this sophisticated and challenging form of pedagogy, and they often lack the necessary support from colleagues and school administrators to try to implement issues discussions.

There is much we have yet to learn. First, while the correlational evidence strongly suggests that there is a relationship between issues discussions and many democratic outcomes, we do not understand the causal pathways. For example, what accounts for the apparent link between issues discussions and political and civic engagement? Do students become more interested in learning about the political world? Research demonstrates a positive link between knowledge and political engagement, so perhaps issues discussion leads to more knowledge about politics, which

in turn, leads to engagement. We also need to understand the impact of teachers' pedagogical decisions with regard to controversial issues discussions. For example, although many students, teachers, parents, and community members have strong views on the teacher disclosure issue, we do not understand how disclosure or non-disclosure affects what and how students learn in the classroom.

Research is also needed into the disparate opportunities young people have to participate in discussions about public issues in their schools. Although it is apparent that few students overall experience significant issues discussions in school, urban immigrant, lower socioeconomic status, and minority students are especially unlikely to have opportunities to engage in these discussions. Thus, the students who tend to have the least political and social capital are also the ones least likely to be served by schools in developing that capital through issues discussions. We need to have a better understanding of why this happens, but more important, what types of pedagogical supports teachers need in order to engage these students in issues discussions that are meaningful and relevant to them.

Finally, we need to develop a better conceptual map of the ways in which various contexts matter. In this chapter, we mentioned several ways in which national, school, and classroom contexts shape content, teaching, and learning. We need to develop a fuller understanding of these contexts. Cross-national comparisons are potentially a fruitful means of exploring these contexts.

Most teachers, students, theorists, and researchers believe that issues discussions hold an important place in the education of young people. As both a form and goal of democratic education, issues discussions are one means of creating a more enlightened and engaged citizenry. We know much about how skilled teachers use issues discussions in their classrooms, and how such discussions benefit young people. Unfortunately, we also know that in-depth issues discussions are not commonplace. Such a state fails our youth, and ultimately, our democracies.

The authors thank Alison Turner, Simone Schweber, Sohyun An, and Shannon Murto for their very helpful assistance in the preparation of this chapter.

REFERENCES

Angell, A. (2004) 'Making Peace in Elementary Classrooms: A Case for Class Meetings', *Theory and Research in Social Education*, 32 (1): 98–104.

Avery, P.G., Bird, K., Johnstone, S., Sullivan, J. and Thalhammer, K. (1992) 'Exploring Political Tolerance with Adolescents', *Theory and Research in Social Education*, 20 (4): 386–420.

Avery, P.G., Simmons, A. and Freeman, C. (2007) *The Deliberating in a Democracy (DID) Project Evaluation Report: Year 3*. Available http://www.deliberating.org/

Barton, K. and McCully, A. (2007) 'Teaching Controversial Issues…Where Controversial Issues Really Matter', *Teaching History*, 127: 13–19.

Campbell, D.E. (2007) 'Sticking Together: Classroom Diversity and Civic Education', *American Politics Research*, 35 (1): 57–78.

Conover, P. and Searing, D. (2000) 'A Political Socialization Perspective', in McDonnell, Lorraine, Timpane, Michael and Benjamin, Roger (eds.), *Rediscovering the Democratic Purposes of Education*. Lawrence, Kansas: University of Kansas Press. pp. 91–126.

Conover, P.J., Searing, D.D. and Crewe, Ivor M. (2002) 'The Deliberation Potential of Political Discussion', *British Journal of Political Science*, 32 (1): 21–62.

Cotton, D. (2006) 'Teaching Controversial Environmental Issues: Neutrality and Balance in the Reality of the Classroom', *Educational Research*, 48 (2): 223–241.

Dahl, R.A. (1998) *On Democracy*. New Haven, CT: Yale University Press.

Gimpel, J., Lay, C. and Schuknecht, J. (2003) *Cultivating Democracy: Civic Environments and Political Socialization in America*. Washington, DC: Brookings Institution Press.

Gutmann, A. (1999) *Democratic Education*. 2nd edn. Princeton: Princeton University Press.

Hahn, C.L. (1996) 'Research on Issues-Centered Social Studies', in Evans, Ronald and Saxe, David (eds.), *Handbook on Teaching Social Issues*. Washington, DC: National Council for the Social Studies. pp. 26–39.

Hahn, C.L. (1998) *Becoming Political: Comparative Perspectives on Citizenship Education*. Albany: State University of New York Press.

Hahn, C.L. and Tocci, C. (1990) 'Classroom Climate and Controversial Issues Discussions: A Five Nation Study', *Theory and Research in Social Education*, 18 (4): 344–362.

Hand, M. (forthcoming) 'What Should We Teach as Controversial? A Defense of the Epistemic Criterion', *Educational Theory*.

Harris, D. (1996) 'Assessing Discussion of Public Issues: A Scoring Guide', in Evans Ronald and Saxe, David (eds.), *Handbook on Teaching Social Issues*. Washington, DC: National Council for the Social Studies. pp. 288–297.

Hemmings, A. (2000) 'High School Democratic Dialogues: Possibilities for Praxis', *American Educational Research Journal*, 3 (1): 67–91.

Hess, D. (2002) 'Teaching Controversial Public Issue Discussions: Learning from Skilled Teachers', *Theory and Research in Social Education*, 3 (1): 10–41.

Hess, D. (2004) 'Controversies about Controversial Issues in Democratic Education', *PS: Political Science and Politics*, 37 (2): 253–255.

Hess, D. (2007) 'What Students Think about Whether Their Teachers Should Disclose Their Views on Political Issues during Classroom Discussions,' paper presented at the Annual Meeting of the College and University Faculty Association of the National Council for the Social Studies, San Diego, CA.

Hess, D. and Ganzler, L. (2007) 'Patriotism and Ideological Diversity in the Classroom', in Westheimer, Joel (ed.), *Pledging Allegiance: The Politics of Patriotism in America's Schools*. New York: Teachers College Press. pp. 131–138.

Hess, D. and Posselt, J. (2002) 'How High School Students Experience and Learn from the Discussion of Controversial Public Issues', *Journal of Curriculum and Supervision*, 17 (4): 283–314.

Hibbing, J. and Theiss-Morse, E. (2002) *Stealth Democracy: America's Beliefs About How Government Should Work*. New York: Cambridge University Press.

Homana, G. and Barber, C. (2007) 'School Climate for Citizenship Education: A Comparative Study of England and the United States', paper presented at the 51st Comparative and International Education Society Annual Conference, Baltimore, MD.

Johnson, D. and Johnson, R. (1995) *Creative Controversy: Intellectual Conflict in the Classroom*. 3rd edn. Edina, MN: Interaction.

Johnston, J., Anderman, E., Milne, L., Klenck, L. and Harris, D. (1994) 'Improving Civic Discourse in the Classroom: Taking the Measure of Channel One', *Research Report 4*. Ann Arbor, MI: Institute for Social Research, University of Michigan.

Kahne, J., Chi, B., and Middaugh, E. (2006) 'Building Social Capital for Civic and Political Engagement: The Potential of High School Civics Courses', *Canadian Journal of Education*, 29 (2): 387–409.

Kahne, J., Rodriguez, M., Smith, B.A. and Thiede, K. (2000) 'Developing Citizens for Democracy? Assessing Opportunities to Learn in Chicago's Social Studies Classrooms', *Theory and Research in Social Education*, 28 (3): 311–338.

Kelly, T.E. (1986) 'Discussing Controversial Issues: Four Perspectives on the Teacher's Role', *Theory and Research in Social Education*, 14 (2): 113–138.

Kerr, D., Lopes, J., Nelson, J., White, K., Cleaver, E. and Benton, T. (2007) *Vision versus Pragmatism: Citizenship in the Secondary School Curriculum in England' Citizenship Education Longitudinal Study: Fifth Annual Report*. Research Report 845: National Foundation for Educational Research.

Larson, B.E. (1997) 'Social Studies Teachers' Conceptions of Discussion. A Grounded Theory Study', *Theory and Research in Social Education*, 25 (2): 113–136.

Mansbridge, J. (1991) 'Democracy, Deliberation, and the Experience of Women', in Murchland, Bernard (ed.), *Higher Education and the Practice of Democratic Politics: A Political Education Reader*. Dayton: Kettering Foundation. pp. 122–135. (Eric Document 350909).

McCully, A. (2006) 'Practitioner Perceptions of Their Role in Facilitating the Handling of Controversial Issues in Contested Societies: A Northern Irish Experience', *Educational Review*, 58 (1): 51–65.

McDevitt, M. and Kiousis, S. (2006) *Experiments in Political Socialization: Kids Voting USA as a Model for Civic Education Reform*. CIRCLE Working Paper 49. Available www.civicyouth.org.

Miller-Lane, J., Denton, E. and May, A. (2006) 'Social Studies Teachers' Views on Committed Impartiality and Discussion', *Social Studies Research and Practice*, 1 (1): 30–44.

Niemi, N. and Niemi, R. (2007) 'Partisanship, Participation, and Political Trust as Taught (or not) in High School History and Civic Classes', *Theory and Research in Social Education*, 35 (1): 32–61.

Nystrand, M., Wu, L., Gamoran, A., Zeiser, S. and Long, D. (2003) 'Questions in Time: Investigating the Structure and Dynamics of Unfolding Classroom Discourse', *Discourse Processes*, 35 (2): 135–198.

Oliver, D. and Shaver, J. (1966) *Teaching Public Issues in the High School*. Logan: Utah State University Press.

Oulton, C., Day, V., Dillon, J. and Grace, M. (2004) 'Controversial Issues: Teachers' Attitudes and Practices in the Context of Citizenship Education', *Oxford Review of Education*, 30 (4): 489–507.

Paley, V. (1992) *You Can't Say You Can't Play*. Cambridge, MA: Harvard University Press.

Parker, W.C. and Hess, D. (2001) 'Teaching With and for Discussion', *Teacher and Teacher Education*, 17 (3): 273–289.

Parker, W.C. (2003) *Teaching Democracy: Unity and Diversity in Public Life*. New York: Teacher's College Press.

Phillips, J. (1997) 'Florida Teachers' Attitudes toward the Study of Controversial Issues in Public High School Social Studies Classrooms'. PhD dissertation, The Florida State University. Retrieved on August 3, 2006, from ProQuest Digital Dissertations database. (Publication No. AAT9813696).

Puddington, A. (2007) 'Freedom in the World 2007: Freedom Stagnation Amid Pushback Against Democracy', Accessed at www.freedomhouse.org on July 29, 2007.

Richardson, W. (2006) 'Combining Cognitive Interviews and Social Science Surveys: Strengthening Interpretation and Design', in Barton, Keith (ed.), *Research Methods in Social Studies Education: Contemporary Issues and Perspectives*. Greenwich: Information Age Publishing, Inc. pp. 159–181.

Rossi, J. (1995) 'In-depth Study in an Issues-Orientated Social Studies Classroom. *Theory and Research in Social Education*, 23 (2): 88–120.

Torney-Purta, J., Lehmann, R., Oswald, H. and Schultz, W. (2001) *Citizenship and Education in Twenty-eight Countries: Civic Knowledge and Engagement at Age Fourteen*. Amsterdam: International Association for the Evaluation of Educational Achievement.

Torney-Purta, J., Wilkenfeld, B. and Barber, C. (forthcoming) 'How Adolescents in Twenty-Seven Countries Understand, Support, and Practice Human Rights', *Journal of Social Issues*.

Yamashita, H. (2006) 'Global Citizenship Education and War: The Needs of Teachers and Learners', *Educational Review*, 58 (1): 27–39.

Zukin, C., Keeter, S., Andolina, M., Jenkins, K. and Delli C.M.X. (2006) *A New Engagement?: Political Participation, Civic Life, and the Changing American Citizen*. Oxford, UK: Oxford University Press.

40

Citizenship Education, Pedagogy, and School Contexts

Mark Evans

Many educationalists maintain that schools play and ought to play a critical role in nurturing and even transforming democratic citizenship learning. Schools provide fertile grounds for investigating civic living, where the diverse dimensions of democratic citizenship can be explored, nurtured, and experienced. They offer conditions where understandings of key concepts, issues, and processes of informed democratic citizenship can be developed; where conflicting beliefs and perspectives within local, national, and global contexts can be examined and analyzed; where notions of civic membership and identity, inclusion and exclusion, moral purpose and legal responsibility can be explored; and where basic capacities of civic literacy and participation can be practiced and reflected upon.

During the past century a number of curriculum initiatives and research studies have been undertaken to better understand the democratic intent and practices of schools in different parts of the world. More recently, attention to the role that pedagogy plays in fostering democratic citizenship has been a central focus of these

efforts as evidence mounts that teachers' pedagogy is one of the most important factors affecting student learning (Darling-Hammond, 1998; Fullan et al., 2006; Joyce et al., 2000). This chapter focuses on five broad themes:

- changing understandings of pedagogy;
- understandings of democratic citizenship pedagogy in school contexts and 'fitness of purpose';
- the multidimensional nature of democratic citizenship pedagogy in school contexts today;
- connections between curriculum policy orientations and pedagogical experiences; and
- a brief discussion of some of the persisting challenges and issues.

Note that a complete understanding of citizenship education pedagogy is complicated by the absence of a general theory of pedagogy and a certain patchiness of data on this subject (Osborne, 1996; Nelson and Kerr, 2007) and what is provided in this chapter is, at best, a representation of some of the evolving and prevailing perspectives and practices.[1]

CHANGING UNDERSTANDINGS OF PEDAGOGY

Watkins and Mortimore (1999: 3–8) suggest that understandings of pedagogy have moved through at least four distinct phases in recent decades.

1. A focus on different styles of teaching (e.g. authoritarian/ democratic, traditional/progressive, teacher-centered/student centered).
2. A focus on the contexts of teaching (e.g. inner city; rural).
3. A focus on the qualities of an effective teacher and the intricate processes of teaching, in relation to various theories of cognition and meta-cognition.
4. And more recently, an emerging focus on an integrated conception of pedagogy that attends to technical competencies of teaching in relationship to critical knowledge bases and contextual forces.[2]

These more recent understandings of pedagogy are more attentive to and differentiated by the relationship among its many elements: the teacher, details of context, content, the view of learning, age and stage of learner, purposes and so on. These elements are reflective of a more deeply integrated conception of pedagogy. Turner-Bisset (2001: 7), for example, argues that although earlier studies of the qualities and processes of effective pedagogy were helpful, they were in many ways illustrative of 'tip of the iceberg' approaches and lacked attention to varying dimensions of knowledge required for effective teaching. Referring back to Shulman's work (1986, 1987) and to types of research on pedagogy that have occurred since that time, she advocates a conception of pedagogy that recognizes the technical competenices of teaching and the wide range of interrelated knowledge bases required to inform and guide wise pedagogical decisions and effective teaching practices.

Recent understandings of pedagogical practice are more focused on 'fitness of purpose', that is, the alignment among desired learning outcomes, the learning experiences designed by the teacher to achieve those outcomes, appropriate types of assessment for particular forms of learning, learner capabilities, and contextual circumstances (Hunter, 1982; Mortimore, 1999). Certain pedagogical practices are better suited to achieve particular learning goals while other, less-suited practices may obstruct the intended learning. Methods that encourage the development of capacities for critical enquiry (e.g. jurisprudential inquiry, group investigation), for example, or the development of capacities for collaboration (e.g. cooperative learning structures like think-pair-share, group investigation) are more appropriate because they are viewed as being better suited to achieve certain goals of learning.

Another important facet of these shifting understandings of pedagogy is a growing acknowledgement that enacted forms of pedagogy, often connected to curriculum policy, communicate different messages that are *not* politically neutral (Apple and Beane, 1995; Freire, 1970; Ross, 2000). Curriculum theorists appropriately point out that particular curriculum perspectives and practices indeed privilege particular learning goals. Eisner (1985), for example, has identified five basic orientations to the curriculum: development of cognitive processes, academic rationalism, personal relevance, social adaptation and social reconstruction, and curriculum as technology. Miller (1996, 2007) identifies three broad orientations, transmission, transactional, and transformational. Ross (2000) refers to three distinct approaches within the context of citizenship education: content-driven, objectives-driven, and process-driven curricula. Westheimer and Kahne (2004) identify three conceptions of the 'good' citizen – personally responsible, participatory, and justice-oriented – that call attention to a range of ideas often represented in school curricula in relation to citizenship education. Each of these distinctive orientations influence decisions about pedagogical experience and convey important messages about which forms of learning will be given priority and which ones will be ignored or silenced (e.g. notions about power and authority, issues of equity and diversity, work and learning). In this next section, a brief overview of developing under-standings of pedagogy for democratic citizen-ship in school contexts is explored.

DEMOCRATIC CITIZENSHIP PEDAGOGY AND 'FITNESS OF PURPOSE'

Pedagogical practices that aim to nurture a particular vision of civic engagement have been evident in different parts of the world throughout history. From early Islamic and Buddhist teachings to the times of the Greeks and Romans, a rich tradition of educational practice has been advocated to achieve cer-tain civic aspirations through education.

This past century, understandings of peda-gogical practice in relation to democratic cit-izenship education in school contexts have been given particular attention and developed steadily. From Harold Rugg's early work in the 1920s (Nelson, 1977) on 'problem clari-fication and problem solving' to Lynn Davies (2006) current pedagogical work on 'con-flict, global citizenship, and social justice', there has been significant attention to 'fitness of purpose,' that is classroom and school-based pedagogical practices that address shifting and expanding goals of citizenship education and that focus on particular aspects of democratic citizenship learning. Studies of pedagogical practice in relation to demo-cratic civic understanding, have been proba-bly 'more common than on any other general teaching method as far as educational litera-ture is concerned.'[3] A few examples are pro-vided below.

Perhaps best known is Dewey's (1916) pioneering work that emphasized the impor-tance of enquiry and a focus on real civic problems and issues, as important pedagogical practices to be foregrounded in any democratic citizenship curricula. Dewey emphasized the importance of social learning and the habits of reasoning as critical elements of citizenship learning and encourage classroom and school-wide practices (e.g. group investigation) that would nurture these aspects of learning within the context of real civic issues and problems.

A focus on classroom and school-wide practices that explicitly encourage planned and deliberate attention to knowledge acqui-sition, conceptual understanding, and higher order thinking has gained special considera-tion throughout this past century. Bloom's ideas (1956, 1971) in relation to higher-order thinking, and grounded in behavioural under-standings of learning have been evident in classroom questioning process and discus-sions. Hunter's attention to mastery teaching (1976, 1982) and Rosenshine's work (1985) on direct instruction offered different ideas for classroom practice for improving student learning and supporting notions of informed citizenship.

Building on this base pedagogical practices infusing deepened understandings of 'think-ing' and 'skills of enquiry' into the curricula received explicit attention in the second half of the century. Taba's (1967) attention to the development of understanding about the processes and skills of enquiry, Hunt and Metcalf's (1955) issue-centered pedagogical approaches, Engle's (1960) focus on decision-making, Oliver and Shaver's (1966/1974) work on the use of the jurisprudential frame-work to teach about controversial public issues, and Newmann et al.'s (1977) peda-gogical work on the development of skills in citizen action and public affairs, and Case and Daniels's work on critical challenges have been critical to the development of the citizenship education pedagogy landscape and have been reflective of the widening and deep-ening understandings of a 'thinking' citizen. At the same time as a heightened focus was placed on enhancing critical thinking in the curricula, the exploration of beliefs, values, and morals that underpin civic decisions and action emerged as principles of psychology, philosophy, and sociology were considered. Kohlberg's moral reasoning project (1976), and Nel Noddings' work on feminist approaches to ethic and moral education (1984), for example, aimed at developing students' sense of fairness and 'purposeful' citizenship by bringing them into intimate dialogue on matters of civic living.

As understandings of citizenship education continued to expand during the 1980s, 1990s, and into the twenty-first century, attention to citizenship education pedagogy in relation to conflict and cooperation, equity, diversity and social justice, political participation and service learning, and global citizenship became more apparent, prompting further study and debate about appropriate and effective pedagogical practice in school contexts in relation to these newly emerging and shifting conceptual emphases. Work focusing on pedagogies related to diversity and citizenship education (Banks, 2004; Stevick and Levinson, 2007), conflict, cooperation, and controversy in relation to civic literacy (Bickmore, 2001; Evans and Saxe, 1996), decision-making and deliberation (Parker, 1996), political participation and service learning practices (Avery, 1997; Annette, 2005), and the global dimension of citizenship (Merryfield, 1998; Pike and Selby, 2000; Holden and Hicks, 2007) added to the growing range of pedagogical practices associated with democratic citizenship education.

Today, recent curriculum reform initiatives in different parts of the world have prompted continued attention to various aspects of citizenship education pedagogy. Classroom and school-wide pedagogies continue to be developed and studied, with increasing attention to 'fitness of purpose' and the range of different interconnected elements (e.g. details of context, view of learning, age and stage of learner, purposes, etc) that influence pedagogical decisions and practices. Educators wishing to explore and integrate new understandings of citizenship into classroom and school-wide approaches and practices are finding a rich array of performance-based classroom and school-wide ideas and activities to inform and guide their pedagogical practice, both locally and internationally.[4] Multiple approaches are being used in classrooms and across schools to assist young people in learning about the principles and practices of citizenship.

Case studies, the infusion of substantive and procedural concepts, mock elections, public issue research projects, model town councils, school councils, peer mediation programs, peace-building programs, special commemorative days (e.g. United Nations Day), community participation and service activities, public information exhibits, peer mentoring and conflict resolution programs, online international linkages, and youth forums are examples of practices being used to nurture the more comprehensive goals now associated with citizenship education. A cursory examination of these practices reveals the emergence of a range of activities and strategies that have the potential to attend to deepened conceptual understanding, substantive public issue investigation (from the local to the global), critical judgment and communication, personal and interpersonal understanding, provision for community involvement and political participation, and authenticity – a focus on real-life themes, contexts, and performances. At the same time, there is increasing attention to the democratic culture of schools through the development of 'professional learning communities' and 'communities of practice' built around the ongoing study and support of teaching and learning in relation to citizenship education. A variety of longer-term research initiatives are also underway that focus on comparative aspects of citizenship education pedagogy within and across different cultural contexts.

CURRICULUM ORIENTATIONS AND PEDAGOGICAL EXPERIENCES

Similarly, there has been increased consideration of broad curriculum orientations evident in curriculum policy documents in distinctive contexts (e.g. provincial, national) the goals of citizenship learning that are given priority, and the implications for pedagogical practice. Different curriculum and pedagogical orientations have been evident in the evolution of citizenship education in different contexts, from the local to the global, usually illuminating distinctive contextually rooted perspectives and priorities (Sim and Print, 2005; Dean, 2005; Ikeno, 2005; Lee and Leung, 2006).

For the purposes of this chapter, I refer to Miller's 'transmission – transactional – transformational' framework (2007) to illuminate the relationship between curriculum orientations and the kinds of learning experiences that are given priority, three broad, interconnected orientations are suggested below. It should be emphasized that these perspectives are neither exclusive nor exhaustive and that there are strong interconnections among them. Rather these general orientations provide one way of understanding the connection between curriculum policy goals and pedagogical experiences that appear to present themselves on the citizenship education landscape, in perhaps idiosyncratic and interesting ways.

The 'transmission' orientation

The 'transmission' or 'content-driven' orientation is often associated with a functionalist perspective that involves developing or reproducing a reflection of existing societal patterns (Ross, 2001: 5). Core knowledge and skills are 'seen as fixed rather than as a process' (Miller, 1996: 6) and to be passed on from one generation to the next generation. Curriculum is viewed in terms of a fairly limited number of academic subject-based disciplines delivered by the teacher, with the requisite expert knowledge, to the student, often represented as the 'passive' recipient (Miller, 1996). The classroom-learning environment is viewed primarily as a location where important content is transmitted from the teacher to the student. Classroom resources (e.g. texts, videos) are selected and provided by the teacher for purposes of conveying information. Rules for class behaviour are usually top-down and desks are often organized in rows to ensure that the teacher can directly address students, and that interruptions by other class members can be minimalized.

Classroom space (e.g. bulletin boards) is organized by the teacher and most often conveys important course content. Teaching practices often associated with this orientation have as their aim the mastery of content and basic skills. Teaching activities and strategies that transmit information or basic skills (e.g. mini-lectures, reading or viewing for content, copying notes, practice and drill skill activities) are highlighted. Assessment practices primarily aim to assess knowledge acquisition and/or skill development. Content quizzes and other types of short answer tests (e.g. multiple choice, completion tests) are supported.

The 'transactional' orientation

The 'transactional' orientation, or what some refer to as 'instrumentalist', stresses individual development within the context of social and economic need. This orientation, attends to 'objectives that meet specific needs for competencies – of society, of the economy, of the individual – are specified in advance, and a curriculum is drawn up to achieve these objectives. Abilities and capabilities necessary to meet the needs of contemporary life are specified and used to justify the collection of subjects that constitute the curriculum' (Ross, 2001: 8). Unlike the 'transmission' orientation, which views knowledge as something that is largely fixed, the 'transactional' orientation reflects 'utilitarian' tendencies and views knowledge as something that is changing and can be manipulated. Learning goals are achieved through dialogue, problem-solving activities, or some other form of enquiry. The classroom environment is viewed primarily as a location where problems can be discussed and enquiries carried out between the teacher and the students. Classroom resources are located and selected by the student, with the assistance of the teacher within the context of the specified objectives of the curriculum. Rules for class are usually worked out between the teacher and the students and desks are often organized in small groupings to encourage interaction and dialogue. Classroom space is organized by the teacher and the students and most often displays their work. Teaching activities and strategies, often associated with this orientation, have as their aim the development of problem-solving, decision-making, and/or enquiry skills. Independent and group enquiry projects, case study/decision-making approaches, and moral dilemmas of real-life issues are some of the teaching practices connected to this orientation. Assessment practices tend to aim to assess the application of cognitive skill processes (e.g. processes involved in carrying out an investigation, resolving a conflict). Evaluation of students' work usually looks at various steps applied in the process and the actual product. Criteria-referenced essay answer and performance-based assessments (e.g. checklists, rating-scales, rubrics) are reflective of practices linked with this orientation.

The 'transformative' orientation

The 'transformative' orientation is often associated with more 'reform' and 'liberative' perspectives. This orientation focuses the development of the whole person and emphasizes personal and social connectivity, not a reduced set of core knowledge or thinking skill intentions (Miller, 1996). Learning in this orientation, according to Miller (1996: 4), integrates 'skills that promote personal and social transformation', 'a vision of social change that leads to harmony with the environment', and acknowledges 'a spiritual dimension to the environment'. Political and social change and improvement are advocated in this orientation and it is believed that students ought to be made aware of the political, cultural, historical, and social aspects of their society and of themselves as active and responsible participants in it (Pratt, 1994). Students and teachers are actively engaged in all phases of learning, knowledge is constructed through varying forms of dialectic and collaborative enquiry. The classroom-learning environment is viewed as a location to meet

and discuss ongoing enquiries. Classroom resources are located and selected primarily by students, with the assistance of the teacher, for purposes of working through a particular enquiry or problem related to the curriculum. Rules for class behaviour are worked out mutually and desks are often organized in pods or small groups in order that students can learn collaboratively with their peers. Moving beyond the classroom walls into the broader school and local community contexts is encouraged. Classroom space (e.g. bulletin boards) is organized by the students and often represents work from their investigations. The teacher's role is largely one of guide and facilitator. Teaching activities and strategies that encourage students to critically enquire into various social and political themes and issues and use their findings to bring about personal and/or social change are encouraged. Assessment practices aim to assess personal growth and integration and social awareness. Opportunities for self-evaluation and reflective journals and portfolios are advocated.

An understanding of these varying curriculum orientations have been helpful in the analysis of curriculum goals and practices in particular contexts in relation to citizenship education. That said, a blend of curriculum orientations is found in most classrooms.

A MULTIFACED YET UNCERTAIN PRACTICE

The extent to which particular pedagogies or more broadly based curriculum/pedagogical orientations receive widespread application in classrooms and schools is less certain and this situation mitigated by a scarcity of research about how teachers educate for democratic citizenship. Studies that explore citizenship education pedagogy are rare and only a few national and international studies (e.g. Hahn, 1998; Kerr et al., 2003; Nelson, and Kerr, 2006; Torney-Purta et al., 1999) exist that provide guidance in this area.

Existing studies reveal wide-ranging practices that are both eclectic, contextually distinctive, and cut across various curricular orientations (e.g. transmission, transactional, and transformational). More significantly perhaps, they reveal varying levels of support for certain curricular purposes and policy goals but that this support tends to diminish as purposes are translated into practice. A considerable gap appears to exist between the theoretical and/or policy aims for citizenship and the actual practice exhibited in schools. Davies (2000: 93) has astutely observed that in the English context, for example, 'there has been something of a confusing and confused situation. It seems as there has never been a point at which an initiative in this field has been simultaneously successfully and clearly articulated by academics and teachers and legitimated by central and or local government or professional bodies.' Davies' observation connects to with other contexts as well. A rather limited research base exists on citizenship education pedagogy and what is being practised in the name of democratic citizenship education in the classrooms and across schools in most countries remains uncertain.

Hahn's study (1998) of citizenship education in five countries (Denmark, England, German, the Netherlands, and the US), undertaken from 1985 to the mid-1990s describes the varied political contexts in which youth are being politically socialized. Of particular interest is her focus on the role of schooling in this process in the five distinctive national contexts. Her study reveals many shared experiences but also the considerable differences in the ways that youth are prepared to participate as democratic citizens. In relation to pedagogical practice, Hahn notes the use of similar didactic practices in the classrooms across the countries to encourage democratic understanding and participation. She is also quick to point out many important differences. She notes, for example, widespread student involvement in decision-making in issues of group or public importance in Danish schools in contrast to the English

context where decision-making takes on a more personal and ethical path. Hahn also notes that these differences may be attributed to a range of additional elements including age, academic track, gender, and so on. At the same time, Hahn points out, however, that much more could be done in the classroom and across schools to further enhance civic participation.

The *Civic Education Study*, under the leadership of Torney-Purta et al. (1999) and organizational umbrella of The International Association for the Evaluation of Educational Achievement (IEA), involved a major multinational study (approximately 24 countries) of civic education since 1993, provided some helpful findings. The first phase of the study, for example, examined what students are expected to learn about their nation and citizenship and is summarised in *Civic Education Across Countries: Twenty-four National Case Studies from the IEA Civic Education Project* (1999). It provided many interesting insights about learning goals and pedagogical practices associated with citizenship education. In relation to pedagogical practice, almost all of the authors of the 24 case study chapters expressed the belief that 'civic education' ought to be cross disciplinary, participatory, interactive, related to life, conducted in a non-authoritarian environment, cognizant of the challenges of societal diversity, and co-constructed by schools, parents, and the community. Yet, it was clearly reiterated that there remains a widely perceived gap between the goals for democracy expressed in the curriculum and the reality presented by societies and their schools (Hahn, 1998 and Torney-Purta 1999: 425).

The *Citizenship Education Thematic Studies* undertaken in 1999 and 2006 as part of the International Review of Curriculum and Assessment Frameworks (IRCAF) Project (2) revealed similar concerns. The IRCAF Project involved an international review of curriculum and assessment frameworks in 16 countries and was managed by NFER for the Qualifications and Curriculum Authority (QCA). These studies, involving

16 and 14 countries respectively, aimed to provide: descriptions of practice in the countries concerned, consideration of contextual factors, and an analysis of fundamental issues. The first study (2000: 1, 2) combined material from the IRCAF Project, specific enquiries about citizenship education addressed in the 16 countries, discussion at the invitational seminar on Citizenship Education, held in London, in January 1999, and published sources such as the National Case Study chapters from Phase 1 of the IEA Citizen Education Study. Both studies reveal that while teaching practices have moved in many countries away from narrow, knowledge-based approaches to citizenship education to broader approaches. A substantial variety of approaches exist from school to school and classroom to classroom yet a continuing gap between the rhetoric of policy and the reality of practice remains evident. The second study (Nelson and Kerr, 2006) which focused on 'active citizenship', revealed continuing concerns. 'At this stage', the report (vi.) reads, 'understanding of the effectiveness of different approaches to the learning and teaching of citizenship is somewhat scant and requires further investigation.'

In England, the *Citizenship Education Longitudinal Study* (Kerr et al., 2003; Kerr, 2006), initiated by The Department of Education and Skills (DfES) and commissioned by the National Foundation for Educational Research (NFER) to study citizenship in schools in England over eight periods has reported similar concerns. The initial report revealed a general lack of effective pedagogical practice in schools in England in relation to the introduction of citizenship education as a mandatory part of the National Curriculum in 2002, that

teacher-led approaches to citizenship-related topics were predominant in the classroom, with more participatory, active approaches much less commonly used. Teachers relied on their own ands media sources in their planning for citizenship education and had little or no experience of assessing student outcomes. Just over four-fifths of teachers (83%) and just under four fifths of college tutors

(79%) said that they did not assess students in citizenship education (Kerr et al., 2003: vii).

More recent reports from the longitudinal study reveal improvements but also suggest the need to reduce the gap that exists between the policy aims for citizenship and the actual practice exhibited in schools.

These studies suggest that citizenship education pedagogy in school contexts take a variety of distinctive forms. Different practices are used to nurture and assess learning and to shape aspects of the classroom and school learning environment, reflecting varying purposes and perspectives. Yet, these studies also reflect a considerable gap among theory, policy, and practice. They suggest an overemphasis on teacher-directed practices that emphasize knowledge acquisition and skill development and less evidence of the use of more effective classroom-based teaching practices like enquiry-based research assignments, deliberation about public issues, student publications in local newspapers about different civic questions offered in Hahn's pedagogical 'wish list' (Hahn, 1998: 245, 246).

PERSISTING CHALLENGES

The effective application of different pedagogical practices in classrooms and across schools is complicated by many factors. In this section, three persisting challenges will be considered: conceptual ambiguity, pedagogical complexity and professional learning, and contextual pressures.

Conceptual ambiguity

Increasingly sophisticated, and sometimes conflicting, conceptions of citizenship and citizenship education have led to a certain level of conceptual ambiguity. Dominant views of citizenship – the civic republican (responsibilities-based) and the liberal (rights-based) – offer varied understandings of citizenship education (Heater, 2000) whereas other perspectives (e.g. communitarian, social democratic, multiculturalist, post-national) further complicate the situation (Davies, 1999; Kerr et al., 2003; Shafir, 1998). Although these contrasting conceptions are instructive in providing deepened conceptual understanding to inform citizenship education curriculum, inherent ambiguities become more evident in terms of conceptual understanding (e.g. individualist vs. collectivist, political rights vs. social rights, local vs. global). This situation poses significant uncertainty for educators trying to determine which learning goals ought to be to nurtured and how it ought to be represented in school curricula in meaningful ways. McLaughlin (1992), for example, believes that this situation has led to 'minimalist' interpretations of citizenship being encouraged. Heater (2000: 175), in contrast, worries that certain perspectives offer little more than the indoctrination of youth to the purposes of the state.

Pedagogical complexity and the challenges of professional learning support

As conceptions of citizenship gain increased sophistication, pedagogical practices required to nurture the diverse and interconnected learning intentions are also becoming more complex. Research on pedagogical practice in recent years, as mentioned earlier, is suggesting the need for a more sophisticated conceptual understanding of pedagogy, one that attends to the technical competencies in relation to critical knowledge bases and contextual forces that ought to inform this practice. Current studies portray a rather uncertain picture of teachers' pedagogical practice. Although a diverse range of classroom and school-wide practices is evident, the emphasis on transmission-orientated practices and there is less attention on those practices in which beliefs, values, and notions of social justice and/or participating

in civic life are emphasized. This situation is further complicated by the challenge of appropriate professional learning provision. Teachers often find themselves overloaded and without adequate support and anticipating anticipate much serious engagement in curriculum and pedagogical reform of this type is difficult. 'A number of countries commented on the inadequacy of the preparation of teachers to handle citizenship education in the school curriculum' (Kerr 2000: 7).[5]

Contextual pressures

Schools are viewed as locations where democratic citizenship learning can be nurtured and practiced. That said, the stated goals and ethos of schools often conflict with the expected goals and practices of the citizenship education curriculum. Schools are essentially hierarchical organizations, ones that are neither able to, nor necessarily intend to, fully nurture the understandings, capacities or values associated with democratic citizenship (Joyce et al., 2000; Torney, 1974). Schools tend to reinforce norms of hierarchical control, and in doing so, undermine the impact of certain types of curricular reform. Schools, historically, have emphasized obedience and conformity for most students and have used schooling as a form of social control (Osborne, 1991). To this end, the citizenship education agenda finds itself part of an overloaded and competing educational agenda that is often overshadowed by an increasing emphasis on other valued educational goals like employability skills and/or preparing students to work in a global economy (Dechaur, 2007; Osborne, 2000). Contextual pressures beyond the school further complicate matters. Teachers and school systems are subject to pressures of rapid change and increasing levels of accountability, often with low status. Students' interest in civic matters, as Hahn (1998) noted in her five nation study, are influenced by a range of factors (e.g. country, age, media, academic track, gender). Educational communities find themselves acting in complex ways, best explained at least in part by the realities and tensions they have to deal with each day.

CONCLUSION

The purpose of this chapter was to stimulate thinking about democratic citizenship education pedagogy in school contexts. Changing notions of pedagogy, the gradual expansion of classroom and school-based pedagogical practices, the multidimensional nature of democratic citizenship pedagogy in school contexts today, connections between curriculum orientations and pedagogical practice, and a brief discussion of some persisting challenges that relate to the application of different pedagogical practices in classrooms and across schools have been considered. Below are a few concluding reflections that perhaps suggest a way forward.

Evidence reports that a teacher's pedagogy is one of the most important factors in determining student learning. 'Teachers who know a lot about teaching and learning and who work in environments that allow them to know students', according to Darling-Hammond (1998: 7–8) 'are the critical elements of successful learning.' Careful attention and action to enhance the critical role of pedagogy in relation to student learning within the context of citizenship education needs to be ongoing. Simply put, pedagogy matters.

Understandings of pedagogy for democratic citizenship continue to expand and become increasingly sophisticated. Conceptual understanding, fitness of purpose, contextual relevance, and a growing awareness that enacted forms of pedagogy communicate different messages that are *not* politically neutral are considerations being given particular attention in the development of understandings of pedagogy. Yet, clearly an uncertain – and unhelpful - gap exists between rhetoric and practice. It is apparent that more attention to those 'transformative' pedagogical practices is needed if some of the more sophisticated goals now associated with democratic

citizenship education are to be addressed in meaningful ways.

Little evidence of professional learning programs exists to support citizenship education pedagogy. Ongoing comprehensive professional learning programs – both preservice and inservice – are required that focus on student learning and pedagogy in relation to citizenship education. Given the recent concern for and sophistication of this curriculum area, attention to professional development, in particular, is critical and needs to be carefully considered. Increased support for effective professional communities and networks that cultivate both practitioner learning and study in relation to democratic citizenship education is needed.

Considerable disparity exists between democratic values and classroom and school-wide practices in most schools. Attention needs to be directed to those factors within and beyond the schooling context that impede the implementation of the goals of democratic citizenship education. Likewise, there needs to be action take to respond to the contextual differences and cultural appropriateness and relevance of particular pedagogical approaches. Action is needed to support professional learning about what we know already about how to educate for citizenship. Continued study is needed that explores and documents how students, teachers, schools, and communities are reshaping citizenship education learning opportunities and how such reforms are benefiting student learning.

NOTES

1 This situation is supported by Bruner's (1982) long-standing claim about the absence of a general theory of pedagogy and the need for more guidance in this area. Anderson (2002: 22) wrote that the study of pedagogy can be 'empirically elusive'. Turner-Bisset (2001: 1) suggested that the study of pedagogy presents a 'paradigm problem'.

2 Understandings of pedagogy have also been linked to what might be referred to as the 'hidden curriculum'. For the purposes of this chapter, the deliberate aspect of pedagogy is the focus. This is not to diminish the importance of the hidden curriculum

and the pedagogical implications, but rather to clarify this chapter's central intent.

3 *Models of Teaching* (Joyce and Weil, with Calhoun, 2000) is perhaps the most illustrative of this focus on pedaogical practices and is studied widely. It provides a helpful framework for thinking about pedagogical approaches and practices in more holistic and integrated ways, rather than seeing pedagogy as simply a collection of isolated activities. Joyce, Weil, and Calhoun identify four broad schools of thought evident in the literature: the social family, the information-processing family, the personal family, and the behaviourial systems family.

4 In Canada, for example, Case's Critical Challenges Across the Curriculum Series, the Canadian International Development Agency's (CIDA) Global Classroom Initiative, and the Library of Parliament's Teachers' Institute on Parliamentary Democracy are providing helpful ideas for analysing and designing effective instruction, with the underlying intent to encourage young Canadians to become informed and involved citizens. The development of instructional resources like Historica's *YouthLinks,* UNICEF Canada's *Global Schoolhouse,* CIDA's *Youth Zone, Citizenship: issues and action,* Kielburgers' *Take action: a guide to active citizenship, and* Classroom Connections *Cultivating a culture of peace in the 21st century* are illustrative. In England, the Citizenship Foundation, for example, has developed a range of activity-based teaching ideas and source materials that have been piloted in schools. Newly established associations like citizED and the Association for Citizenship Teaching (ACT) provide professional support, knowledge and good practice, skills and resources for the teaching and learning of Citizenship in schools. Pedagogical resource support is undergoing significant development. The Hansard Society's resources on parliamentary democracy, OXFAM's Cool Planet website, the British Youth Council's peer education and youth councils materials, The Young Citizen's Passport, The Changemakers' initiative, and The Institute for Citizenship's Activate Series are reflective of the significant pedagogical work underway.

5 In England, in particular, there has been a variety of professional learning activities initiated to encourage the growth of professional 'communities of practice". New one year initial teacher preparation courses have been set up under the auspices of the TTA (Teacher Training Agency), funding for the Advanced Skills Teacher (AST) professional learning support, and the establishment of the itt citizED (Initial Teacher Training for Citizenship Education and funded by the Teacher Training Agency) network are examples of curricular and pedagogical support. The itt citizED network provides various forms of pedagogical support through its website, newsletters, conferences, and commissioned research. The National Foundation for Educational Research's (NFER) longitudinal study of citizenship education over 8 years is an example. International research support is also evident through organizations like the International Association for Citizenship, Social and Economics Education (IACSEE) which provides professional learning support and a research journal that informs educators about relevant developments in citizenship education, largely from a European perspective.

REFERENCES

Anderson, S. (2002) Teachers talk about instruction, *Orbit,* 32 (4): 22–26.

Annette, J. (2005) Character, civic renewal and service learning for democratic citizenship in higher education, *British Journal of Educational Studies,* 53 (3): 326–340.

Apple, M. (1971) The hidden curriculum and the nature of conflict. *Interchange,* 2 (4): 27–40.

Apple, M. and Beane, J. (eds) (1995) *Democratic Schools.* Alexandria, Association for Supervision and Curriculum Development. (ASCD).

Avery, P. (1997) *The future of political participation in civic education.* Minnesota: Social Science Education Consortium.

Banks, J.A. (ed.) (2004) *Diversity and Citizenship Education.* San Francisco: Jossey-Bass.

Bennett, B., Anderson, S.E., and Evans, M. (1997) Towards an integrative theory of instructional expertise: Understanding teachers' instructional repertoires. Paper presented at the Annual Meeting of the American Educational Research Association, Chicago, United States, April 17–21.

Bennett, B. and Rolheiser, C. (2001) *Beyond Monet: The Artful Science of Instructional Integration.* Toronto: Bookation.

Beyer, L. (ed.) (1996) *Creating Democratic Classrooms: The struggle to integrate theory and practice.* New York: Teachers' College Press.

Bickmore, K. (2001) Student conflict resolution, power 'sharing' in schools, and citizenship education, *Curriculum Inquiry,* 31 (2): 137–162.

Bloom B. (1956) *Taxonomy of Educational Objectives, Handbook I: The Cognitive Domain.* New York: David McKay.

Bloom, B. (1971) Mastery learning. In J. Block (ed.) *Mastery learning: Theory and Practice.* New York: Holt, Rinehart, and Winston.

Bruner, J. (1982) *Towards a Theory of Instruction.* London, UK: Harvard University Press.

Case, R. and Daniels, L. (2003) *Introduction to the CT2 [Critical Thinking Consortium]: Conceptions of critical thinking.* Available https://public.sd38.bc.ca/RTRWeb/PDFdocuments/CCIntro.pdf, 1.

Claire, H. and Holden, C. (2007) *The Challenge of Teaching Controversial Issues.* Stoke-on-Trent: Trentham Books.

Darling-Hammond, L. (1998) Teachers and teaching: Testing hypotheses from a National Commission Report, *Educational Researcher,* 27 (1): 5–15.

Davies, I. (1999) What has happened in the teaching of politics in schools in England during the last three decades, and why? *Oxford Review of Education,* 25 (1/2): 125–140.

Davies, I., Gregory, I. and Riley, S. (1999) *Good Citizenship and Educational Provision.* London: Falmer Press.

Davies, L. (1999) Comparing definitions of democracy in education, *Compare,* 29 (2): 127–140.

Davies, L. (2006) Global citizenship: Abstraction or framework for action. *Educational Review,* 58 (1): 5–25.

Dean, B. (2005) Citizenship education in Pakistani schools: Problems and possibilities. *Citizenship Teaching and Learning,* 1 (2): 35–55.

Dewey, J. (1916) *Democracy and Education. An introduction to the philosophy of education* (1966 edn.). New York: Free Press.

Dreeban, R. (1968) *On What is Learned in School.* Reading: Addison-Wesley.

Eisner, E.W. (1985) *Educational Imagination: On the design and evaluation of school programs,* 2nd edn. New York: Macmillan Publishing Company.

Engle, S. (1960) Decision making. *Social Education,* 24 (7): 301–306.

Evans, M. and Hundey, I. (2000) Educating for citizenship in Canada: New meanings in a changing world. In T. Goldstein and D. Selby (eds) *Weaving Connections: Educating for Peace, Social and Environmental Justice.* Toronto: Sumach Press. pp. 120–145.

Evans, M. and Hundey, I. (2004) Instructional approaches in Social Studies education: From 'what to teach' to 'how to teach'. In A. Sears and I. Wright (eds), *Challenges and Prospects for Canadian Social Studies.* Vancouver: Pacific Education Press. pp. 218–235.

Evans, R. and Saxe, D.W. (eds) (1996) *Handbook on Teaching Social Issues.* Washington: National Council for the Social Studies.

Freire, P. (1970) *Pedagogy of the Oppressed.* New York: Continuum Publishing Company.

Fullan, M. Hill, P. and Crevola, C. (2006) *Breakthrough.* London: Sage Publications.

Hahn, C. (1998) B*ecoming Political: Comparative Perspectives on Citizenship Education.* Albany: State University of New York Press.

Hallam, S. and Ireson, J. (1999) Pedagogy in the secondary school. In P. Mortimore (ed.) *Understanding Pedagogy and its Impact on Learning.* London: Paul Chapman. pp. 68–97.

Heater, D. (2000) *What is Citizenship?* Cambridge: Polity Press.

Hébert, Y. and Sears, A. (2001) Citizenship Education, Canadian Education Association. Available http://www.cea-ace.ca/foo.cfm?subsection=edu&page=sto.

Hill, G. (2002) *Reflecting on professional practice with a cracked mirror: Productive pedagogy experiences.* Available www.aare.edu.au/02pap/hil02657.htm.

Holden, C. and Hicks, D. (2007) *Teaching the Global Dimension: Key Principles and Effective Practice.* London: Routledge.

Hunt, M. and Metcalf (1955) *Teaching High School Social Studies: Problems in Reflective Thinking and Social Understanding.* New York: Harper and Row.

Hunter, M. (1976) *Improved Instruction: Take 10 Staff Meetings as Directed.* California: TIP Publications.

Hunter, M. (1982) *Mastery Teaching.* California: TIP Publications.

Ichilov, O. (1998) Patterns of citizenship in a changing world. In Ichilov, O. (ed.) (1998) *Citizenship and Citizenship Education in a Changing World.* London: The Woburn Press. pp. 11–27.

Ikeno, N. (2005) Citizenship education in Japan after World War II. *Citizenship Teaching and Learning,* 1 (2): 93–98.

Joyce, B. and Weil, M. with Calhoun, E. (2000) *Models of Teaching,* 6th edn. Boston: Allyn and Bacon.

Kerr, D. (2006) *Active citizenship in INCA countries: Definitions, policies, practices and outcomes* (Final Report). National Foundation for Educational Research/ Qualifications and Curriculum Authority (England), International Review of Curriculum and Assessment Frameworks (INCA).

Kerr, D. (2000) Citizenship education: An international comparison across 16 countries. Paper presented at the Annual conference of the American Educational Research Association, New Orleans, USA, 26–29 April.

Kerr, D., Cleaver, E., Ireland, E. and Blenkinsop S. (2003) *Citizenship Educational Longitudinal Study First Cross-Sectional Survey 2001-2002* (Research Report 416 for the Department for Education and Skills). London: DfES.

Kohlberg, L. (1976) The cognitive developmental approach to moral education. In D. Purpel and K. Ryan (eds) *Moral Education...It Comes with the Territory*. Berkeley: McCutchan.

Kymlicka, W. (1995) Multicultural citizenship. In G. Shafir (ed.) (1998) *The Citizenship Debates*. Minneapolis: University of Minnesota Press. pp. 167–188.

Lee, W.O. and Leung S.W. (2006) Global citizenship education in Hong Kong and Shanghai secondary schools. Ideals, realities, and expectations. *Citizenship Teaching and Learning*, 2 (2): 68–84.

Marzano, R. (1992) *A Different Kind of Classroom: Teaching with Dimensions of Learning*. Alexandria, VA: ASCD.

Marzano, R. with Pickering, D., Arredondo, D., Blackburn, G., Brandt, R., Moffett, C., Paynter, D., Pollock, J., and Whisler, J. (1997) *Dimensions of Learning: Teacher's Manual, 2nd Ed* Alexandria: ASCD and Mid-continent Regional Educational Laboratory.

Merryfield, M. (1998) Pedagogy for global perspectives in education: Studies of teachers' thinking and practice, *Theory and Research in Social Education*, 26 (3): 342–378.

Miller, J. (1996, 2007) *The Holistic Curriculum* 2nd edn. Toronto: OISE Press.

Mortimore, P. (ed.) (1999) *Understanding Pedagogy and its Impact on Learning*. London: Paul Chapman.

National Foundation for Educational Research (England) (NFER) (2003) *The Citizenship Education Longitudinal Study*. Available www.nfer.ac.uk/research/citlong.asp

Nelson, J. and Kerr, D. (2006) *Active citizenship in INCA countries: Definitions, policies, practices and outcomes* (Final Report).

National Foundation for Educational Research/ Qualifications and Curriculum Authority (England) International Review of Curriculum and Assessment Frameworks (INCA).

Nelson, M. (1977) The development of the Rugg Social Studies Program. *Theory and Research in Social Education,* 5 (3): 64–83.

New South Wales Department of Education and Training (Australia) (NSW) (2003) *Productive pedagogy.* Available www.det.nsw.edu.au/inform/yr2002/mar/pedagogy.htm, 4

Newmann, F., Bertocci, T.A., and Landness, R.M. (1977) *Skills in Citizen Action*. University of Wisconsin Publications.

Newmann, F. and Wehlage, G. (1993) Standards for authentic instruction, *Educational Leadership*, 50 (7): 8–12.

Noddings, N. (1984) *Caring: A Feminine Approach to Ethics and Moral Education*. Berkeley: University of California Press.

Oliver, D. and Shaver, J. (1966/1974) *Teaching Public Issues in the High School*. Boston: Houghton Mifflin.

Osborne, K. (1996) Education is the best national insurance: Citizenship education in Canadian schools, past and present, *Canadian and International Education*, 25 (2): 33–58.

Osborne, K. (1999) *Education: A Guide to the Canadian School Debate or Who Wants What and Why?* Toronto: Penguin.

Osborne, K. (2001) Democracy, democratic citizenship, and education. In J.P. Portelli and R.P. Solomon (eds) *The Erosion of Democracy in Education*. Calgary: Detselig Enterprises. pp. 29–61.

Osler, A. and Starkey, H. (2000) Citizenship, human rights and cultural diversity. In Osler, A. (ed.) *Citizenship and Democracy in Schools: Diversity, Identity, Equality*. Stoke on Trent: Trentham Books. pp. 13–27.

Parker, W. (ed.) (1996) *Educating the Democratic Mind*. Albany: State University of New York Press.

Pike, G. and Selby, D. (2000) *In the Global Classroom 2*. Toronto: Pippin.

Rosenshine, B. (1985) Direct instruction. In T. Husen and T. Postlewaite (eds) *International Encyclopedia of Education*, Oxford: Pergamon Press. Vol. 3, 1395–1400.

Ross, A. (2000) *Curriculum: Construction and Critique*. London: Falmer Press.

Sears, A. (2004) In search of good citizens: citizenship education and social studies in Canada. In A. Sears and I. Wright (eds) *Challenges and Prospects in Canadian Social Studies*. Vancouver: Pacific Education Press. pp. 90–106.

Shafir, G. (ed.) (1998) *The Citizenship Debates*. Minneapolis: University of Minnesota Press.

Shulman, L. (1986) Those who understand: knowledge growth in teaching, *Educational Researcher,* 15 (2): 4–14.

Shulman, L. (1987) Knowledge and teaching: Foundations of the new reform, *Harvard Educational Review,* 57 (1): 1–22.

Sim, J.B.Y. and Print, M. (2005) Citizenship education and social studies in Singapore: A national agenda. *Citizenship Teaching and Learning*, 1 (1): 58–73.

Sorensen, K. (1996) Creating a democratic classroom: Empowering students within and outside classroom walls. In L. Beyer (ed.) *Creating Democratic Classrooms: The Struggle to Integrate Theory and Practice*. New York: Teachers' College Press. pp. 87–105.

Stevick, D. and Levinson, B. (2007) *Reimagining Civic Education: How Diverse Societies form Democratic Citizens*. Lanham: Rowman and Littlefield.

Taba, H. (1967) *Teachers' Handbook for Elementary School Social Studies*. Reading: Addison-Wesley.

Torney-Purta, J., Schwille, J., and Amadeo, J. (eds) (1999) *Civic Education Across Countries: Twenty-four National Case Studies from the IEA Civic Education Project*. Amsterdam: International Association for the Evaluation of Educational Achievement (IEA).

Turner-Bisset, R. (2001) *Expert Teaching: Knowledge and Pedagogy to Lead the Profession*. London: David Fulton Publishers.

Watkins, C. and Mortimore, P. (1999) Pedagogy: What do we know? In Mortimore, P. (ed.) *Understanding Pedagogy and Its Impact on Learning*. London: Paul Chapman Publishing. pp. 1–19.

Westheimer and Kahne (2004) What kind of citizen? The politics of educating for democracy. *American Educational Research Journal*, 42 (2): 237–269.

41

A Justice-Oriented Citizenship Education: Making Community Curricular

Lew Zipin and Alan Reid

CITIZENSHIP EDUCATION, DEMOCRACY AND COMMUNITY

The concept of community has been a constant presence in formal citizenship education programs; yet its meaning and connection to curriculum tend to be assumed. This taken-for-grantedness masks a number of significant ideological assumptions, not least of which are the views of democracy and citizenship upon which school and classroom practice are based. Despite these silences, it is possible to discern some dominant models. In this chapter, we describe and critique two mainstream curricular approaches to linking citizenship education and community, arguing that they are based on, and serve to reinforce, thin conceptions of democracy. We then propose an alternative approach, and draw upon a research project in which we have been involved to explore problems and possibilities of connecting community and curriculum differently: to *make the community curricular*, thereby promoting more socially just education.

The personally responsible citizen

One dominant conception of democracy assumes an individualistic society with a competitive market economy, minimal state intervention and a citizenry whose prime political activity is to choose from options presented by an elite political leadership (Carr and Hartnett, 1996). Democracy is thus an aggregation of individual citizen preferences in choosing public officials and policies (Young, 2002). The good citizen therefore is one who votes at election times, pays taxes, obeys laws and voluntarily undertakes good community works. Westheimer and Kahne (2004) describe this idealized version as the *personally responsible citizen*. Citizenship education's task is to prepare good citizens by developing knowledge about the political system and the role they will play in the future. It involves learning *for* democracy.

In this conception, community is understood as locations outside the school – most often official agencies – to be plundered for curriculum contents and activities. For example, students may learn about structures and functions of different government levels, visiting Parliament and courts, interviewing local dignitaries and engaging in volunteer service activities; or official agents might visit the school to work with students. Community is thus an *object* of study and a resource that supplements the official curriculum.

The participatory citizen

In a more progressive but still mainstream conception, democracy is a form of social life constituted by values of 'positive' freedom and political equality. From this perspective, democracy only flourishes in a society of informed and active citizens who are involved in political debate and public decision-making on equal terms, with minimal bureaucratic control. The good citizen actively participates in civic affairs at local, state and national levels. Westheimer and Kahne (2004) describe this idealized version as a *participatory citizen*. Citizenship education's task is to develop both knowledge needed to participate judiciously in political processes, and skills and dispositions to do so actively and productively. It involves learning *through* democracy.

In this conception, community is seen as an arena for civic engagement where young people learn democracy by participation in local activities, issues and debates. For example, students might identify a local environmental issue, investigate its causes and develop a case to put to the local council or state government for change. Community is still something to be acted upon – a place where future citizens undertake an *active* apprenticeship in democracy.

Whilst the *active* dimension of the participatory model suggests a stronger democracy than the *passivity* of the personally responsible model, it still constructs 'community' as a site for pre-given ways of learning how to act in society. In relation to curriculum, local community thus effectively remains an object

of study – wherein 'participative' citizens lack agency to (re)shape contexts in which their citizenship is enacted – rather than spaces for participatory (re)*making* of social life through curriculum activity. Both models short-change the potential of community not simply as sites for learning but also for creating more robust participatory democracy in education and society.

A critique of the dominant models of citizenship education

Our critique entails three major concerns. First, these approaches sit squarely within dominant and discriminatory curriculum grammars (Tyack and Tobin, 1994). In assuming learners as blank slates to be inscribed by formal education processes, these models reify official knowledges that encode the cultural capital of power elite groups – which 'less advantaged' learners are seen to 'lack' – over experiences and knowledges that such students gain in their lives beyond school. A *deficit* view of non-elite students and their communities is thus projected, while ignoring learning *assets* in their lifeworlds.

A second and associated point is that both approaches imply acceptance of status quo social structures. The participatory citizen model might tinker at the edges of societal change, but broadly takes for granted current social, political and cultural arrangements, and thus the inequalities of recognition and distribution inhering within them. This is a far cry from what Westheimer and Kahne (2004) call the *justice-oriented citizen*, engaged in challenging social inequalities.

Finally, we concur with Biesta (2007) that both approaches are instrumentalist and individualistic. They are instrumentalist in conceiving education as the major social mechanism for producing the democratic person, thus placing an unrealistic burden on schooling. They are individualistic in their focus on developing a pre-specified set of knowledge, skills and dispositions for individualised citizens, assumed to need the same citizenship capabilities, disregarding cultural differences.

What is the alternative? In our view, a rejuvenated and socially just citizenship education must be based on more expansive views of democracy, citizenship and community. We are committed to what Young (2002) calls a *deliberative* model of democracy. This involves active discussion of problems, conflicts and claims of need or interest where, through open and public dialogue, proposals and arguments are tested and challenged: a 'process in which a large collective discusses problems such as those that they face together, and tries to arrive peaceably at solutions in whose implementation everyone will cooperate' (Young, 2002: 28). This model, Young maintains, entails key normative ideals for the relationships and dispositions of democratic deliberators: inclusion, equality, reasonableness and publicity.

A deliberative model of democratic decision-making – which, on a respectful and non-dominating basis, includes and accords due agency to all who might significantly be affected by problems under discussion – is more apt to result in socially just decisions. Deliberative democratic processes, argues Young, rely on 'institutional conditions for promoting self-development and self-determination' (2002: 33) – two ideals that encourage people collectively to counter unequal social relations by pursuing more just arrangements.

Such a model calls up Deweyian conceptions of democratic subjectivity as more than 'individual' in being constituted through participatory social relations. We share this orientation but observe that, in *education*, Dewey is often invoked on behalf of projects still premised on 'producing' democratic citizens defined by certain capacities and attributes that they receive without dialectically remaking. In our view, this lapses into mainstream individualistic conceptions of education for citizenship. By contrast, our view of

the politics of subjectivity accords with that of Biesta (2007) who, following Arendt (1958), proposes that the quality of human interaction, rather than particular characteristics possessed by individuals, constructs democratic subjectivity. In this conception, say Lawy and Biesta (2006), citizenship is '... an inclusive and a relational concept which is necessarily located in a distinctive socio-economic, political and cultural milieu' (p. 46). They propose the idea of citizenship-as-practice:

> Instead of seeing citizenship as the outcome of a learning trajectory, citizenship-as-practice suggests that young people learn to be citizens as a consequence of their participation in the actual practices that make up their lives. From the point of view of democratic citizenship their lives comprise a complex mix of democratic and non-democratic practices that are never ideal ... *Citizenship-as-practice enables an understanding of the dynamics of citizenship learning that is related to the real lives of the young people.* (Lawy and Biesta, 2006: 45, emphasis added)

Such a view challenges how 'community' has been mobilised in the two mainstream approaches to citizenship education and argues for a significant re-conceptualization, which we will call: *making the community curricular.*[1] It is based on a view that moves well beyond approaches positing community as a resource for the official curriculum or as something mainly to be accepted, and to lesser degrees 'fixed', by 'active' citizens who apply sets of skills and understandings which citizenship education programs presume and transmit. It is an approach that respects communities whilst recognizing that they are not perfect democratic arenas. Correlatively, a conception of citizenship-as-practice mobilises active engagement in (re)making communities, which are not marginal but central to curriculum work in and for democracy.

In the next section, we begin to ground our idea of 'making the community curricular' and to explore its implications for a more socially just and participatory citizenship education that brings community life into, rather than bracketing it from, curriculum.

A JUSTICE ORIENTATION TO COMMUNITY, DEMOCRACY AND PARTICIPATORY CITIZENSHIP: MAKING COMMUNITY CURRICULAR

As should be clear, our critiques of mainstream approaches to citizenship education do not de-emphasize 'participation' but promote fuller and stronger participatory citizenship in democratic communities, as suggested in different ways by Barber (1984), Habermas (1990), Fraser (1997) and others. Whether democratic or not, we conceive communities as internally complex, dynamic and shared social spaces, continually under construction by diverse agents who inhabit them. In democratic communities, those diverse agents share equivalent agency to shape their self-governing discourses, norms, practices and relations through knowledge-constructing communicative interactions.

Indeed, we view current social spaces – and particularly institutional spaces such as schools – as transected by historically sedimented social structures of unequal power relations that prevent equivalent agency among culturally diverse peoples. To be socially just, then, communities need ongoing capacity to reconstruct communicative processes in the direction of more egalitarian social relations across – and sustaining – cultural differences. Balancing the sometimes contradictory but dually compelling ethical principles of (1) redistributing more equally the means – material, social, political and cultural – of agency to influence change and (2) recognizing diverse cultural claims is a crucial challenge for building strongly democratic institutions in globalizing times (Benhabib, 2002; Fraser, 2003).

As microcosmic community spaces that work to re-make society, democratic classrooms would foster capacities to contest institutional mechanisms that privilege more powerful social-cultural groups and so reinforce unequal schooling experiences and outcomes. A major challenge is to cease giving primary curriculum place to power-elite

cultural capital (Bourdieu and Passeron, 1990), instead incorporating diverse cultural knowledges and dispositions. Correlatively, educators would abandon transmissionary modes of pedagogy in which they position themselves as monological imparters to learners, assumed as 'receptive vessels' (Freire, 1996), filling presumed 'deficits' in knowledge and skills that 'count'. Rather, educators would pursue an 'unsilenced dialogue' (Delpit, 1995), positioning themselves to learn *from* students about their cultural assets for learning – their lifeworld 'funds of knowledge' (Moll et al., 1992; Gonzalez et al., 2005) – which could be incorporated in more relevant and thus engaging curriculum.

Increased learning engagement is thus built through curriculum that connects classroom learning community to lived cultural communities that learners inhabit outside school. This is a key sense of 'making the community curricular': taking learners' community lives *into* curriculum. Another key sense, in reverse direction, is to re-*make* communities through curriculum work in which students create new knowledge about, and for, their locales. In this way, learners *give back to*, and so revitalize, their local communities. Such curricular (re)making of community is a proactive civics: a participation in (re)building civil society, constituting a far more engaged civics education than that which mines community locations for contents to plug into official curricula that covertly privilege the cultural modes of power-elite social groups.

The root (or 'radical') democratization that takes non-elite community cultures seriously (not 'tokenistically') within curriculum goes against deeply systemic grains of power asymmetry. While there have been notable successes (e.g. Wigginton, 1986; Meier, 2002), they stand as exceptional cases, without precipitating broad systemic reform. Even the most favorable contexts for root curricular democracy encounter systemic obstacles and problematic tensions, calling for ethical courage, conceptual clarity and pragmatic readiness to experiment. In what follows, we first draw on literatures to outline a general rationale and approach for pursuing a 'making community curricular' approach (hereafter referred to as MCC) to facing deeply problematic tensions in pursuit of social-educational justice. We then look more finely at the pragmatic complexities of negotiating systemic obstacles, drawing on the illustrative case of an action research project in which, with colleagues, we sought to put this MCC approach to work.

DESIGNING ASSET-ORIENTED CURRICULUM: PUTTING LIFEWORLD FUNDS OF KNOWLEDGE TO USE

A deep problematic for all efforts to build curriculum that justly values the cultures of diverse learners, and not just power-elite culture, is the ethical warrant – in societies structured by contests to accumulate capital – to re-distribute the cultural capital needed to 'win' in school to learners who do not inherit it from their families. Our MCC approach embraces Delpit's (1995) argument for a two-way approach to 'doing justice' when educating 'other people's children' (those from less powerful social positions, and so 'other' to the 'culture of power'). On the one hand, we need to redistribute the codes of elite cultural capital, making them explicit and practicable through pedagogic scaffolding techniques. On the other hand, we need to embed such efforts within curricula that recognize, valorize and make use of home and community knowledges of those we teach.

Redistributing power-elite cultural capital is crucial to combating differential effects in which the less powerful are tracked downward through 'community-based' curricula alone, while the elite march upward along paths of 'academic' distinction (Bernstein, 1990). Chances at mainstream academic success matter for accessing trajectories beyond poverty, ill health and more. Yet the recognition impulse is even more vital, both for broader ethical purposes of keeping diverse

cultures alive, and for pedagogical purposes of engaging 'other people's children' through familiar social-cultural resonances. After all, if students are not meaningfully engaged they are not really 'there' in teaching-and-learning interactions; and curriculum based primarily on power-elite cultural capital, no matter how well we make it explicit and practicable, tends to alienate learners from 'other' cultures.

Thin democratic efforts toward multicultural recognition of other cultures tend to treat them as tokenistic add-ons with secondary capital value (as when the learning of other cultures is touted as 'valuable in a global knowledge economy'). This relegates 'other cultures' to weaker value relative to dominant curricular 'standards', which does nothing to challenge the win-lose logic that converts culture into capital. We argue that cultural knowledge loses its use value – and therefore its vital use for creating engaged learning – when traded as a commodity for 'profit' in education 'markets'. For example, when power-elite literacy modes become the coin of the realm to win in school, their prime value becomes the power they accumulate to exchange in order to accumulate yet more advantage. To thus convert cultural literacies to exchange values abstracts them from their use values for making communicative meaning in contexts of lived relevance. When schools operate as high stakes markets of cultural competition, the vitalities of cultural practices among people in diverse local communities are sadly diminished in relation to 'gold standards' of restricted exchange value.

In pursuing vital learning engagement, MCC seeks to attenuate the culture-as-capital logic that privileges power-elite ways of knowing. MCC instead embraces the culture-as-use logic in the concept of community funds of knowledge offered by Moll, Gonzalez and associates (Moll et al., 1992; Gonzalez et al., 2005). Moll et al. (1992) define 'funds of knowledge' as 'historically accumulated and culturally developed bodies of knowledge and skills' (p. 133) of significant use as 'household and other community resources' (p. 132). When curriculum builds around knowledge and skills thus put to use in the fuller lives of learners beyond school, 'we can organize classroom instruction that far exceeds in quality the rote-like instruction that ... children commonly encounter in schools', argue Moll et al. (p. 132), thus 'transforming students' diversities into pedagogical assets' (Moll and Gonzalez, 1997, p. 88). This asset orientation inverts the typical deficit view in which schools see non-elite families and communities 'as places from which children must be saved or rescued, rather than places that, in addition to problems (as in all communities) contain valuable knowledge and experiences that can foster ... educational development' (Moll and Gonzalez, 1997: 98).

The democratic importance of 'turning around' (Comber and Kamler, 2005) from a deficit to an asset view of the cultural knowledges and learning potentials of 'less advantaged' students is accented in Thomson's (2002) concept of virtual school bags. This metaphor signifies what Bourdieu (1977) calls *habitus*: the subjective embodiment of cultural ways of knowing that infuse practices of intimate social habitats, especially in early childhood. The contents of virtual school bags are thus acquired at a deeply internalized level, as more-or-less subconscious dispositions for perceiving and acting as a self in relation to others in social contexts. As put by Thomson and Hall (2007: 2–3):

> [C]hildren come to school with virtual school bags ... [filled with home and community] knowledges, experiences and dispositions. However, school only draws on the contents of some children's school bags ... [that] match those required in the game of education. Children who already 'know' and can 'do' school are thus advantaged in the classroom right from the outset while those ... [not showing] the required ways of speaking, acting and knowing start at a disadvantage. Through the selective practices of pedagogy, the gap grows between ... [those of different] class, [cultural] heritage and gender.

In hidden curricula of early schooling, 'other people's children' thus pick up messages that cultural ways of knowing in their 'school bags' – vital to their family/community-based identities – are gravely 'deficient' and should stay zipped up for the duration of their school years. To design curricula that welcome these ways of knowing out of the bag and into classroom use – as assets for learning – is thus an act of radical democracy: it gets to the root of participatory democracy as a governance mode that accords equivalent agency to diverse learners. As Thomson and Hall (2007) say, it challenges 'what counts as important knowledge so that the dominant forms of knowledge are de-centered and more inclusive models of knowing – and being – are allowed for and taught to all' (p. 3).

A view of diverse cultural knowledges as funds for learning, based on use-values in people's lives, thus interrupts the mainstream educational 'game' that selects for elite cultural capital. While accepting a pragmatic need, in societies structured by a capital accumulation logic, to redistribute 'winning' cultural modalities to learners from less powerful families, it gives curricular pride of place to use values wherein all have agency to (re)make community more democratically. It stimulates qualitative and ethical shifts in both educators' and learners' senses of what knowledge, and what knowledge-transacting relations, have teaching-and-learning 'value': not the exchange-value power of restricted cultural knowledge, enacting relations structured by competition to accumulate capital; but the use-value agency of people to create egalitarian and inclusive – that is democratic – curriculum and society that puts their richly diverse cultural learning assets to use.

Shifting from a deficit/exchange-value to an asset/use-value approach to curriculum entails a participatory democratic concept of 'culture' as open to change through the agency of social groups to (re)make their knowledge, practices and relations. Emphasis is on 'the everyday lived experiences of students and their families' (Moll and Gonzalez, 1997: 90): i.e. on culture as lived process, not static products or artifacts. This dynamic and internally variegated sense of lived culture troubles holistic reifications such as 'the culture' of a class, ethnic group or even local community. Such reductions conceal diversity in and across communities sharing a geographic locale or school; and they fail to indicate where culture is vitally lived by particular learners. Our MCC approach thus favors the phenomenological concept of lifeworlds, signifying multiple spaces of concretely lived and experienced embodiment – in homes, peer groups, sports fields and so on. It understands intimate lifeworlds, not more generalized 'community', as the loci wherein students use and re-make knowledge funds around which they build significant identities. MCC thus seeks to negotiate curriculum units in which learners' lifeworlds are the starting point for student engagement with, and research of, funds of knowledge.

However, we have so far addressed MCC in the direction of taking lifeworld funds of knowledge into curriculum. A concept of community gathers renewed importance in the reverse direction, as a locus of giving back. It is also where possibilities and problematics for rich civics education were highlighted in an action research project with a MCC design: Redesigning Pedagogies in the North (RPiN).[2]

POSSIBILITIES AND PROBLEMATICS FOR A RICH COMMUNITY-BUILDING CIVICS

A three-year project with middle-years focus, RPiN is located in the South Australian city of Adelaide's northern suburbs, among the most 'disadvantaged' regions in Australia. Alienated by mainstream curricula, secondary students typically leave school early or barely graduate, with uncertain future trajectories (Smyth et al., 2000). Mobilizing MCC approach, RPiN pursued curriculum and pedagogy that both *engages* students and *enables academic success* by: (1) building rigorous curriculum

units around culturally resonant funds of knowledge from students' local lifeworlds and (2) pedagogic scaffolding of such 'curricula of engagement' into connection with learning the cultural capitals needed for mainstream academic success.

The 13 University and 32 teacher researchers (from 10 secondary schools) met in periodic roundtables to plan and evaluate project work. Early roundtables involved study of literatures, and exercises to develop ethnographic imagination about students' local lives, informed by classroom activities in which students taught about their lifeworlds: for example, by selecting and explaining cultural artifacts that carry significant identity resonances in their lives outside school. In the next stage, teachers designed and ran curriculum units – negotiated with students – that sought to make meaningful connections with students' localities of place: in effect putting them to work as researchers of their own lifeworlds. This was followed by analysis and reflection – looking for cultural funds of knowledge with potentials to revitalize school curricula – and then redesign of curriculum units for a second action research cycle.

Focus on lifeworlds as sources for curriculum can tap into deep dispositional *ways* of knowing – culture as vital processes – within students' virtual school bags. However, such focus on proximate sites of immediate life may conceal how students' lives connect to wider social worlds. Indeed, a number of RPiN teachers portrayed their early teen students as not yet 'of age' for curricular extension into wider social ambits. This was partly fed by initial student tendencies to resist invitations to do curricular work in settings beyond school. In our analysis, students who accumulate experiences of 'losing' in school contests have formed habits of reactive distrust toward institutionally offered 'alternatives', opting for devils they know such as dull worksheets, around which they have built coping strategies to avoid humiliations, rather than promises of new angels that may be devils in disguise. However, some RPiN teachers read student resistance to indicate lack of mature readiness for curricular work in community sites.

Thus, in the first RPiN round, some curriculum units that teachers 'negotiated' with students stayed within peer/school perimeters. Others ventured into wider social orbits as community-lite, for example, interviewing local police officials about crime statistics for a mathematics unit. Curricular links primarily with official infrastructure tend not to tap into issues of deep identity resonance in students' lives. As such, they lapse into taking 'community' as resource for bits of knowledge that insert into official curriculum, rather than revitalizing curriculum through funds-of-knowledge infusions carrying meaningful use values. Nor do they offer opportunities for a civics that develops critical insights about, and imagination/action toward re-building, local community.

The RPiN project sought learning connected both to deeper ways of knowing in student's lifeworlds, and to civic-social engagement. A problematic, then, was how to cut through synergies of student and teacher habit to negotiate 'safe' rather than expansionary work. Between the first and second rounds of curriculum units, Shirley Brice Heath, well-known ethnographer of working class and African American 'ways with words' (1983), visited our University. Some of the RPiN team talked with her about our concerns over thin curriculum units. Heath suggested three methodological rules for stronger connection to 'the social'. One was for teachers, in negotiating units with students, to persist in making meaningful connection to wider social contexts a 'must'. Second, in attending to student body languages and energies during such negotiations, teachers' ethnographic imaginations should be alert for vital hooks: local themes/issues that actually resonate within identity.

Heath's third suggestion was an assessment approach that attached performative expectations to curriculum units: students should present their learning to audiences in some form – installations, live exhibitions, and so on – with each student having responsibility to fulfill roles and meet deadlines on which all collectively depended for performance success. This offers an antidote to teacher tendencies to allow 'individual choice' (understood as 'student centered') projects that do not converge toward collective learning community. Performance events also can be civic occasions for offering fruits of student learning about the locale back to people of the locale.

However, this runs into the problematic of whether/how an audience represents 'the local community': that is, *who* is meant by 'the community'. Typical attendees are peers, parents and people with whom students interfaced in their projects – an apt audience for students of a given classroom; however, those students do not constitute a homogenous socio-economic or ethnic entity but a diverse multiplicity of communities. The problem of constructing a 'community' audience is accentuated by de-industrialization and demographic shift toward diverse and fluid local populations. Thomson (2002), in her book on the challenges for 'doing justice' in schools of this 'rustbelt' region, chronicles how, in a 1940s/1950s national context of post-war industrial boom, northern Adelaide's regional infrastructure was planned as a settlement of (white) blue collar workers for local factories. However, as factories downsized and closed since the 1980s, an un(der)employed 'working class without work' (Weis, 1990) emerged (now in its fourth generation in some northern Adelaide pockets), joined by poor Aboriginal and immigrant groups drawn to affordable housing (an effect of the lack of adequate paid work).

This mosaic mode of local 'community', demographically mixed and fluid, is uneven across the region, with pockets more and less poor, more and less mixed. This is so for regional schools as well. An educational civics for re-making local community needs to promote critical understanding of local, national and global histories in relation to current social-cultural groups and how they each inhabit the locale. And it needs to foster re-imaginings of local community through curricular work that creates new knowledge and builds local resources and infrastructure. Such projects need to be of feasible local scope, while comprehending forces and complexities of local-national-global interface (Appadurai, 1996). We suggest that, curricularly and extra-curricularly (extending beyond a 'school subject' basis), schools can act as democratic sites of public sphere dialogue that bring students, teachers and diverse adults of the locale into communicative interactions to understand and work across – while respecting and sustaining – social-cultural differences.

RPiN further encountered how poverty-area mosaic communities can be abject communities in crucial emotional registers (Worsham, 2001). This, too, should not be ignored in making community curricular. We are wary to contribute to negative stereotypes of the sort that populist media coverage of such locales often constructs. Yet classroom discussions and student curriculum work registered what we'll call 'dark shades of place', indicating drugs and violence in families and neighborhoods, but more significantly student savvy about intricate structural dimensions of their locales. With literate articulation that surprised their teachers (compared to 'usual' work), students explained social dynamics and microtextures of local neighborhoods, including how 'safeties' and 'dangers' vary according to complex factors. Both teacher and university researchers felt mixes of excitement and fear – linked to institutional and legal concerns, and larger ethical questions – in contemplating ways and degrees for letting such 'dark' lifeworld knowledge into the light of classroom discourse. Yet if students show acute literacy around such aspects of their lifeworlds, then we need to take up the problematic of how 'dark shade' knowledge might have curricular use as funds – that is assets – for learning. Gonzalez et al. (2005) frame the dilemma: 'On the one hand ... [we need] to

present ... [a positive] perception of the neighborhoods based on ... an asset orientation. On the other hand, it is important for both instructors and students to address the difficult structural issues found in these neighborhoods' (p. 196).

In the literature are examples of curriculum that takes up dark dimensions of place in age-appropriate ways with good learning effect. Jones (2004) reports on literacy work in which year 1 students spoke/drew/wrote stories of feelings about family/community members in prison for violent acts, after this aspect of their lives leaked into classroom dialogue that began as a unit on 'peer bullying'. Comber et al. (2001) tell of similar work in which year 3 students registered experiences of 'urban renewal' that threatened to remove their families from the area. Along with processing feelings, and countering negative stereotypes by understanding issues structurally, this critical literacy work gave back to community politically through letter-writing to local government about lived effects of urban renewal. As an example from the RPiN projects, an art teacher, having heard her year 8/9 students talk of violent incidents and relations in their locales, negotiated a curriculum unit in which student groups created clay animation stories of such experiences, with the agreed stipulation to narrate not just problems but solutions with an imagined 'politics' of local implementation.

FURTHER DIRECTIONS

A community-re-making civics could take such initiatives further into politically proactive dimensions. Extending from student presentations of work, schools could host public discussion in which students, teachers and local citizens develop critical and imaginative ways to contend with raised issues. Of course, institutional forces may inhibit this, which would in turn need public critical diagnosis. A challenge for teachers in 'disadvantaged' areas is that many neither live in the area nor hail from similar contexts. It then becomes crucial to learn how to listen to, and deeply hear, local students and adults (Delpit, 1995), with ethnographic imaginations attuned for textures of local knowledge carrying implications for social-change politics that could be taken up in curriculum.

A rich civics that makes community curricular in dialectical directions – taking local community in; and giving back to the socio-political life of school locales – requires clarity, courage and methodologies for raising consciousness about local issues in relation to wider structural contexts, and for addressing issues in ways that seek socially just change (Freire, 1996; Shor, 1992). Such efforts (a) enable critical appreciation of local complexities, avoiding simplistic negative stereotypes and (b) galvanize imagination and ethical impulse to engage local community life proactively. A community-making civics based on strong democratic participation calls for both critical and utopian agency: for seeing things 'as they are' and enacting 'resources of hope' (Apple and Beane, 1995).

We have argued for a vitalized concept of community, and its centrality to citizenship education that enacts and builds strong participatory democracy. We have also discussed problematics – emerging in an action research project – that present both challenges and possibilities for making community curricular. We've lacked textual space to talk about further barriers inhering in school worlds-such as workloads, staffing, resources and other mechanisms – which vary across differently situated schools in systemic ways that sustain elite advantages. These, too, need investigation, since the challenge of transferring a vitally engaging depth, and wide community breadth, of knowledge funds from lifeworlds into school-worlds is not simply a matter of discovering them and then changing curriculum accordingly. Serious efforts at socially just curriculum re-design run up against barriers and complexities that must

be negotiated with pragmatic wisdom and with ethical-political commitment to participatory engagement and achievable life chances for 'other people's children' through schooling.

ACKNOWLEDGEMENT

We thank our RPiN teacher co-researchers, industry partners and university colleagues: Andrew Bills, Kathy Brady, Marie Brennan, Barbara Comber, Phillip Cormack, Robert Hattam, David Lloyd, Bill Lucas, Faye McCallum, Philippa Milroy, Helen Nixon, Kathy Paige, Brenton Prosser, John Walsh, and PhD student Sam Sellar.

NOTES

1 We are indebted to our colleagues Rob Hattam and Sam Sellar for conversations on the concept of 'making community curricular'.

2 Redesigning Pedagogies in the North (RPiN), led by a research team from the University of South Australia, is partly funded by the Australian Research Council as a 'Linkage' project (LP0454869) with industry partners: (1) the Northern Adelaide Secondary School Principals' Network; (2) the Social Inclusion Unit of the government of the state of South Australian; and (3) the South Australia branch of the Australian Education Union. The project operated from 2005–2007.

REFERENCES

Appadurai, A. (1996) *Modernity at Large: Cultural Dimensions of Globalization*, Minneapolis: University of Minnesota Press.

Apple, M. and Beane, J. (eds) (1995) *Democratic Schools*, Alexandria, VA: Association for Supervision and Curriculum Development.

Arendt, H. (1958) *The Human Condition*, Chicago: The University of Chicago Press.

Barber, B. (1984) *Strong Cemocracy: Participatory Politics for a New Age*, Berkeley: University of California Press.

Benhabib, S. (2002) *The Claims of Culture: Equality and Diversity in the Global Era*, Princeton, NJ: Princeton University Press.

Bernstein, B. (1990) *The Structuring of Pedagogic Discourse: Volume IV Class, Codes and Control*, London and New York: Routledge.

Biesta, G. (2007) 'Education and the democratic person: Towards a political conception of democratic education', *Teachers College Record*, 109 (3): 740–769.

Bourdieu, P. (1977) *Outline of a Theory of Practice*, New York: Cambridge University Press.

Bourdieu, P. and Passeron, J.-C. (1990) *Reproduction in Education, Society and Culture*. London: Sage.

Carr, W. and Hartnett, A. (1996) *Education and the Struggle for Democracy*, Buckingham: Open University Press.

Comber, B. and Kamler, B., (eds) (2005) *Turn-around Pedagogies: Literacy Interventions for At Risk Students*, Newtown: PETA Press.

Comber, B., Thomson, P. and Wells, M. (2001) 'Critical literacy finds a 'place': Writing and social action in a neighborhood school', *Elementary School Journal*, 101(4): 451–464.

Delpit, L. (1995) *Other People's Children: Cultural Conflict in the Classroom*, New York: The New Press.

Fraser, N. (1997) *Justice Interruptus: Critical Reflections on the 'Postsocialist' Condition*, New York: Routledge.

Fraser, N. (2003) 'Social justice in the age of identity politics: Redistribution, recognition and participation', in Fraser, N. and Honneth, A. (eds) *Redistribution or Recognition: A Political-Philosophical Exchange*, New York: Verso. pp. 7–109.

Freire, P. (1996) *Pedagogy of the Oppressed*, London: Penguin.

Gonzalez, N., Moll, L. and Amanti, C. (eds) (2005) *Funds of Knowledge: Theorizing Practices in Households and Classrooms*, Mahwah, NJ: Lawrence Erlbaum and Associates.

Habermas, J. (1990) *Moral Consciousness and Communicative Action*, Cambridge, MA: MIT Press.

Heath, S.B. (1983) *Ways with Words: Language, Life, and Work in Communities and Classrooms*, New York: Cambridge University Press.

Jones, S. (2004) 'Living poverty and literacy learning: Sanctioning topics of students' lives', *Language Arts*, 81 (6): 461–469.

Lawy, R. and Biesta, G. (2006) 'Citizenship-as-practice: The educational implications of an inclusive and relational understanding of citizenship', *British Journal of Educational Studies*, 54 (1): 34–50.

Meier, D. (2002) *The Power of Their Ideas: Lessons for America from a Small School in Harlem*, Boston: Beacon Press.

Moll, L. and Gonzalez, N. (1997) 'Teachers as social scientists: Learning about culture from household research', in P. M. Hall (ed.), *Race, Ethnicity and Multiculturalism: Missouri Symposium on Research and Educational Policy*, Vol. 1. New York: Garland. pp. 89–114.

Moll, L., Amanti, C., Neffe, D. and Gonzalez, N. (1992) 'Funds of knowledge for teaching: Using a qualitative approach to connect homes and classrooms', *Theory into Practice*, 32 (2): 132–141.

Shor, I. (1992) *Empowering Education: Critical Teaching for Social Change*, Chicago: University of Chicago Press.

Smyth, J., Hattam, R., Edwards, J., Cannon, J., Wilson, N. and Wurst, S. (2000) *Listen to Me I'm Leaving: Early School Leaving in South Australian Secondary Schools*, Adelaide: Flinders Institute for the Study of Teaching.

Thomson, P. (2002) *Schooling the Rustbelt Kids: Making the Difference in Changing Times*, Crows Nest, NSW: Allen & Unwin.

Thomson, P. and Hall, C. 'Opportunities missed and/or thwarted? 'Funds of knowledge' meet the English national curriculum', paper presented at the American Educational Research Association Annual Conference, Chicago, Illinois, April 2007.

Tyack, D. and Tobin, W. (1994) 'The grammar of schooling: Why has it been so hard to change?' *American Educational Research Journal*, 31 (3): 453–480.

Weis, L. (1990) *Working Class without Work: High School Students in a De-industrializing Economy*, New York: Routledge.

Westheimer, J. and Kahne, J. (2004) 'What kind of citizen? The politics of educating for democracy', *American Educational Research Journal*, 44 (2): 237–269.

Wigginton, E. (1986) *Sometimes a Shining Moment: The Foxfire Experience*, Garden City, New York: Anchor Press/Doubleday.

Worsham, L. (2001) 'Going postal: Pedagogic violence and the schooling of emotion', in Giroux, H. and Myrsiades, H. A. (eds) *Beyond the Corporate University: Culture and Pedagogy in the New Millennium*, Oxford: Rowman & Littlefield Publishers, Inc.

Young, I. M. (2002) *Inclusion and Democracy*, Oxford: Oxford University Press.

42

Assessing Citizenship Education

Lee Jerome

'In examinations, the foolish ask questions the wise cannot answer.'

Oscar Wilde

In one noted citizenship school in south-east London, teachers wrote a case study detailing their success implementing the new national curriculum. At the end of that case study, they identified areas for future work: 'One major challenge for the school is to develop a viable framework for assessing citizenship education and planning for development, coherence and continuity in pupils' learning experiences across the key stages' (Douglas and Hudson, 2003: 206).

They also acknowledged that an even more challenging task lay ahead in creating a set of indicators by which they might judge 'the success and quality of citizenship education in the formal curriculum, in the school's culture and ethos and in its interaction with the community.' It is surprising in some ways that a subject could be implemented successfully in a school whilst clarity about these important issues remains outstanding. However, it also is a reflection of how difficult it is to achieve such clarity in citizenship education. In response to this challenge, some citizenship teachers in England, as elsewhere, have avoided doing too much in the area of assessment, trusting somehow

that good teaching will have the hoped-for effect. On the other hand, a variety of elaborate mechanisms for testing and measuring citizenship has been developed around the world, and we shall consider some of these below. I leave it to the reader to decide to what extent the examiners have avoided Wilde's wry warning.

This chapter aims to explore these issues through addressing three questions.

(1) Should we assess citizenship education at all?
(2) What should we assess in citizenship education?
(3) How could we assess citizenship education?

SHOULD WE ASSESS CITIZENSHIP EDUCATION AT ALL?

Several authors have expressed concerns about the role of assessment in citizenship education (Turnbull, 2002; Breslin, 2006; Halstead and Pike, 2006). Turnbull argues that the contested nature of key concepts such as citizenship and democracy makes it difficult to ensure assessment can be objective. Breslin observes that assessing citizenship 'seems to go against the grain of what active, effective citizenship is' (Breslin, 2006: 321). Kerr has countered these concerns by stressing that teachers are 'not assessing the development of a young person as a "citizen" per se, but rather the quality of their learning related to citizenship education' (Kerr, 2002). Nevertheless the question for some remains, are we trying to measure the unmeasurable (Inman et al., 1998)?

This latter area is the major concern of Halstead and Pike (2006: 151), who wonder about the state's right to promote and assess certain values, especially if these are different from those held by a child's family. This echoes the earlier warning from Arthur and Wright (2001) who pointed out the possible risks of teachers engaging in superficial and misguided assessment tasks which might indirectly focus on beliefs and attitudes (which may stem from the family or cultural group) as opposed to an individual's learning and progress.

Halstead and Pike (2006: 152) make a separate point when they argue that 'summative, external government-controlled assessment of citizenship, used to wield power over children and teachers, may not be entirely congruent with many of the aims and principles of the citizenship curriculum.' Following Foucault, they argue that examinations operate as examples of disciplinary power, which sort young people into hierarchies, organised around the concept of the norm (Schrag, 1999 quoted in Halstead and Pike, 2006: 154). They go on to urge us to consider:

> ... if there is an inherent tension between the individual's right to liberty and the practice of assessment which limits the individual's liberty by pronouncing judgements about him or her. Assessment in citizenship that marks out success and failure and discriminates between them may be inappropriate for a subject which seeks to promote inclusion (Halstead and Pike, 2006: 153).

Whilst there is obviously a tension in summative assessment and the aims of citizenship education, it does seem to push the point too far to claim that summative assessment is in and of itself an infringement of young people's liberty. Liberty must include the opportunity to fail or succeed, so I do not see that this line of argument can be sustained. However, leading on from the findings of the

Assessment Reform Group (2002), which details the negative effects of high stakes testing, it seems that the problem is likely to lie in the unintended consequences of summative assessment strategies. They are likely to have a negative impact on some students' life chances and subsequent behaviour as citizens because a decreased sense of engagement with the life of the school and a low sense of self-efficacy are not strong foundations for nurturing engaged and effective citizens. Whilst the correct response to Halstead and Pike's analysis would entail the rejection of summative assessment, this second position encourages teachers to engage with student-centred approaches to teaching which focus on the learner and their understanding of the learning, rather than the teaching and the test (ARG, 2002: 8).

Despite these concerns the American Psychological Association (1997: 6–7) makes a general argument for assessment, which establishes four important purposes, all of which could be said to apply to citizenship education. First, learners who understand their current achievement are more likely to be able to plan ahead for further improvement. It seems unlikely that learning in citizenship should be substantially different to learning in any other area of school or through wider life experiences in this regard. Black et al. (2003: 53–57) indicate the problems and potential of this insight for teachers and argue that even summative assessment procedures can be used productively to feed back into effective learning strategies, if integrated into classroom activities.

Second, teachers who understand how their students are making progress over time (for example identifying areas of relative difficulty) can use this information to provide appropriate individual feedback to the learner or to make adjustments to the teaching overall. This is as important for citizenship teachers as for any other teacher and whilst one might readily imagine this in terms of the traditionally taught series of lessons looking at aspects of knowledge, it will also be helpful for teachers supervising students on more active projects. In the latter example, careful monitoring and intervention might be necessary to keep students on track. Here the teacher adopts what Dann (2002: 36) calls 'dynamic assessment' through which the teacher is able to gauge the level of support required by students to complete a complex task and use this to adjust subsequent support offered. Such an approach derives from an interpretation of the role of the teacher in Vygostky's zone of proximal development (Dann, 2002: 36).

Third, teams of teachers are able to compare results and discuss patterns of achievement with a view to developing collaborative strategies to improve practice or to adapt teaching schemes. This evaluative aspect of citizenship education assessment is important if citizenship teachers are to continue to develop their own practice and, in the current rhetoric of education policy, in order to demonstrate appropriate systems for quality assurance and accountability (Ball, 2007).

Fourth, learners who are encouraged to become actively involved in their own assessment are likely to gain a deeper insight into their own learning and the area in which they are learning. As the work of the Assessment Reform Group (ARG, 1999; Black and Wiliam, 1998; Black et al., 2002) has demonstrated, self-assessment is first and foremost a strategy for enabling students to take control of their learning and to work at a meta-cognitive level, it secures aims that 'cannot be achieved in any other way' (Black et al., 2002: 12).

This leads us back to the problem identified at the beginning of this chapter – what does progression look like and what standards should we be aiming for?

WHAT SHOULD WE ASSESS IN CITIZENSHIP EDUCATION?

'A criterion-referenced test is used to ascertain an individual's status with respect to a well-defined behavioural *domain*' (Popham, 1978 quoted in Black, 1998: 64).

Reflecting on the implications of Popham's definition, Black reminds us that tests are constructed by people who understand the domain and 'the outcome of the test will be interpreted as a measure of attainment in that domain' (Black, 1998: 64). Within domains, test constructors have to think about devising questions which make different levels of cognitive demand. Bloom's taxonomy represents one attempt to identify different levels of cognitive demand that might be tested by different types of questions aiming to elicit knowledge, comprehension, application, analysis, synthesis or evaluation. However, subsequent research has shown that this model does not always stand up to rigorous testing and that distinctions blur until there are just two broad categories: knowledge and higher order skills (Black, 1998: 65).

Perhaps the answer lies in exploring the nature of each domain in more detail? Quigley et al. (1995: 8) have argued that we need to reflect on the nature of citizenship in order to identify the relevant domains for assessment:

> Each subject matter field has its own cognitive strategies. Critical or higher order thinking skills therefore cannot be taught in isolation; knowledge of the content or subject matter of civics and government is necessary, for example, to cast an intelligent vote, to understand public issues or to join with others to solve problems.

Reflecting on the problem of finding reliable models of cognitive challenge or progression, Black emphasises that the construction of adequate tests within a specific domain is in part a philosophical investigation but also requires an empirical process. A philosophical dimension is inevitable because domains may be ideologically contested to some extent, however, a priori definitions are likely to run into problems when they are operationalized. This necessitates the empirical dimension, as test constructors are required to undertake an iterative procedure in which experts in the domain test out their hunches and see how students respond to specific types of question.

Ultimately, if we want to claim reliability, we need to be able to assume that 'the proportion of items in a sample a person gets correct is an estimate of the proportion he would get correct if he answered every item in the universe' (Wood, 1991 quoted in Black, 1998: 68). Black argues however, building on research undertaken by Lehman (1990), that the number of externally conducted tests that a student would need to undertake in order to generate a reliable generalization in a specific domain can be very high. Lehman's empirical research, for example, found that 13 different assignments were required to obtain a satisfactory measure of writing achievement.

This complexity is exacerbated by the fact that most school subjects include a variety of different skills elements. Hoffman acknowledges this when he describes the search for a single score representing overall achievement in each subject as 'irrational', even though it is clearly required by exam systems (1978 in Black, 1998: 71). This failure of national attainment measures to reflect evidence from research has led to some dissatisfaction among teachers, for example, Burnham and Brow (2004: 5) make an argument in relation to history assessment in the English national curriculum, that could be generalized to other subjects:

> Assessment is *for* learning. The level descriptors cannot get anywhere near achieving this. They do not define the changing ideas, patterns of reasoning and layers of knowledge that make up *progression* in historical learning, and they certainly do not offer guidance for designing the detailed *learning paths* that will secure such progression.

Many history teachers carry on regardless, but some history educators continue to develop their own alternative models of progression by studying the responses of young people to historical problems and abstracting models for use by teachers (Lee and Ashby, 2000). In relation to citizenship education in the English national curriculum, this work is less advanced but it has started in a small way. Davies (2003) is pursuing the history model explicitly by setting out to establish procedural concepts for citizenship, and Rowe (2005) has mirrored the empirical aspect of this work.

Rowe (2005) asked 13- and 14-year-old students to respond to a political problem – whether or not the local council should allow a quarry to expand. His analysis of students' responses enabled him to identify three facets of their thinking, around which we can begin to formulate ideas about progression. First, answers differed according to students' ability to conceptualise the problem in a simple way (e.g. focus on the loss of land that would result from the expansion of the quarry) or in a more complex manner (such answers drew on a range of schemas including the likely impact on the environment, the local economy, and the local residents). Second, some students merely stated solutions, whilst others considered alternative approaches and weighed them against one another. Third, answers differed in the extent to which students were able to engage in consequential (e.g. someone would be better off) or principled reasoning (drawing on concepts such as rights or a duty of care). Such research is useful in that it begins to develop models which teachers can use to clarify teaching objectives and against which they can assess students' work. They enable us to think more clearly about current levels of understanding and about possible next steps.

In this research, Rowe is clearly interested in exploring political literacy, as one aspect, or domain in citizenship education. The National Center for Learning and Citizenship (2007) has identified a set of domains and assessment tools linked to them. Here we identify four areas for brief consideration (a) knowledge, (b) debate and deliberation, (c) participation (d) attributes/the affective dimension.

The first domain identified in many studies and education projects relates to knowledge and understanding. Indeed a European survey of assessment practices discovered that several EU countries acknowledged that the full breadth of citizenship education is so difficult to assess reliably that they would only focus on assessing knowledge (Eurydice, 2005: 39). In considering subject knowledge, there can be a temptation to focus on easily assessable facts but Quigley et al. (1995: 8) argue that assessors need to develop a framework for assessment which 'measures not only what information or knowledge students have, but how well they understand it.'

In responding to Quigley's challenge the American *National Assessment of Educational Progress* (NAEP) programme for Civics defined the domain and achievement levels for civic knowledge (Cooper-Loomis and Bourque, 2001). Through consultation with expert groups these areas were further defined through three attainment level descriptors – basic, proficient and advanced. The exercise was repeated to define attainment levels for grades 4, 8 and 12. In grade 4, students described as being at the basic level 'should understand how national holidays and symbols such as the flag, the Statue of Liberty, and the Fourth of July reflect shared American values', whilst to be graded as proficient they 'should be able to explain the importance of shared values in American democracy, to identify ways in which citizens can participate in governing, and to understand that with rights come responsibilities' (Cooper-Loomis and Bourque, 2001: 7–8).

Vontz (1997) argues that such an approach embodies a broad consensus among American civics educators, and similar definitions of knowledge have been adopted elsewhere. In Australia, for example, the *National Assessment Program – Civics and Citizenship* (Curriculum Corporation, 2006) focused less on what it called 'iconic knowledge' (e.g. flags and national holidays), but argued that between years 6 and 10 students should progress from being able to 'recognise that Australia is a pluralist society' to being able to 'analyse how Australia's ethnic and cultural diversity contributes to Australian democracy, identity and social cohesion' (Curriculum Corporation, 2006: 97).

The limitations of such an approach to assessment are self-evident. The students are being assessed in relation to criteria, which are themselves political constructions. Surely one can legitimately discuss whether and to what extent cultural diversity contributes to cultural cohesion in Australia? Similarly, in order to be 'proficient' in the NAEP project,

American students must demonstrate their understanding of the importance of shared values, when that is itself clearly a contentious issue. It is possible to adopt a politically informed position, as does Appiah (2006: 71), that 'we can live together without agreeing on what the values are that make it good to live together; we can agree on what to do in most cases, without agreeing about why it is right.' According to these assessment criteria, Appiah fails to reach even the basic level for civics education in grade 4. This exemplifies Halstead and Pike's concern (see above) that citizenship education can become a vehicle for the attempted transmission of values, and therefore assessment becomes a means for checking the extent to which such transmission has occurred. This shows how even the apparently uncontroversial area of knowledge can become embroiled with the problems associated with moral education more broadly (Beck, 1998). This approach also sits uneasily within the tradition of citizenship education, which focuses on empowerment and critical thinking.

In relation to our second domain, Windsor Central School District teachers joined together to develop what they referred to as 'real world' assessment systems to assess debate and discussion, as a specific dimension to citizenship education. The approach they adopted replicated, albeit on a smaller scale, the NAECP methodology of consulting experts to set criteria (Summers, 1996: 3). For grades 3–5, groups of students are encouraged to debate a position related to a current unresolved problem, and teachers grade the students according to the following broad levels:

- emerging – students state the issue;
- functional – students state the issue and their position, and give minimal support for their position; and
- independent – students state the issue and provide substantial support with multiple examples using research.

Such basic models for assessment might be useful for working with very young children, who are learning the basics of debate and deliberation. At the other end of the spectrum, in terms of the expected level of sophistication of debate, are research tools such as the Discourse Quality Index (Steiner et al., 2004: 55–61), which has been designed to assess the extent to which contributions to parliamentary debates meet the criteria of Habermas' ideal speech act. In between these two extremes, there is a tradition of competitive debate, for example the World Schools Debating Championship (WSDC, undated), which includes marking criteria under the following broad headings: (a) content, (b) style and (c) strategy.

The Winona State University website (undated) provides examples of assessment rubrics from universities and school districts in the US. These varied examples build on the WSDC criteria and typically include grade descriptors based on some or all of the following criteria:

(1) quality of argument;
(2) use of relevant information;
(3) understanding of the topic;
(4) organization;
(5) presentation/style;
(6) rebuttal/response; and
(7) respect for the other team.

Such approaches are useful in schools because they clarify what success sounds like. This enables citizenship teachers to apply rigorous assessment, whilst also providing them with useful tools for planning and teaching.

The second skills area to have attracted much attention in citizenship education, and the third domain considered here, relates to students' active participation, and their ability to learn through such experience. In the US, much of the work in this area has been undertaken by educators involved in service learning programmes, although as Annette (1999: 96) points out there has been relatively little in this literature focusing on assessment. Whilst there are resources for assessing and evaluating such projects (see for example Service Learning's CART web resources) Moon (2004: 154–5) highlights the problem with defining assessment in this area when she urges teachers to think carefully about

whether the assessment will focus on the learning content of a project, or on the experiential learning process itself. In terms of citizenship, these two aspects are likely to fall into two domains, (a) knowledge and (b) skills/efficacy, although the two are obviously linked. Oates and Leavitt (2003) start from the assumption that service learning assessment should balance both and they offer three core questions as the basis for an assessment strategy:

(1) How has the course content strengthened the student's understanding of the service learning experience?
(2) How has the service learning experience affected the student's understanding of the course content?
(3) How has the student demonstrated, through reflection on his or her service learning, the ability to integrate theory and practice?

The connection between experience and learning is, as Dewey illustrated, far from straightforward (Dewey, 1938). Annette (1999) draws attention to the prevalence of Kolb's (1984) model of experiential learning in this area, for example in Dennison and Kirk's (1990) simplified model of *do – review – learn – apply*. The *learning* stage of this cycle requires specific activities, and Boud et al. (1985) provide one example of how to achieve this through three distinct stages. First, students must return to the experience in their mind and recall what happened. Second, they have to deal with their emotional response, and remove feelings that may obstruct clear thinking. Third, they should attempt to re-evaluate the experience by exploring their feelings, identifying key learning outcomes and testing their conclusions for consistency.

We have then several layers of outcomes that could be assessed. From a narrow knowledge perspective students may learn about specific public issues; from a political literacy perspective they may learn about civic participation and the range of actions available to citizens; from an interpersonal perspective they may learn about strategies for working with others and from an intrapersonal perspective they may also learn something about themselves, their own motivations and interests. Even when these reflective activities have been completed, the teacher or examiner may still need to make a formal judgement about the quality of the outcome, and this requirement will often narrow the range of perspectives which are taken into account. We have already seen that this causes unease among some teachers, who feel that it is more important that students participate and feel this was a positive experience, than it is for teachers to give specific grades (Breslin, 2006). However, in the short-course GCSE examinations available in England, such assessment is a formal requirement. The extract from a coursework mark scheme (below) illustrates the ways in which such outcomes could be assessed.

Finally, Deakin-Crick et al. (2005) draw our attention to the wider potential of citizenship education to lead to affective outcomes and therefore urge us to recognise that achievement 'may pertain to cognitive, personal, social, emotional or moral/political domains of human experience' (Deakin-Crick et al., 2005: 9). In a similar vein, the NAEP assessment framework (Cooper-Loomis and Bourque, 2001: 5) also included civic dispositions as one of the main areas to be tested and aimed to identify the extent to which

American students possessed the 'character traits necessary to preserve and improve the system of governance.' Deakin-Crick et al. (2005) do not go this far, but instead argue that a thorough assessment of the impact of citizenship education should include changes in self-concept and increased self-confidence (Deakin-Crick et al., 2005: 4). They draw on a model developed by Johnston (1996) to focus on three broad domains, which seem particularly appropriate to citizenship.

(1) Affective   –   I feel   –   Developing
(2) Cognitive   –   I know   –   Processing
(3) Conative   –   I act   –   Performing

For Deakin-Crick et al. (2005), the conclusion to be drawn from such a model is that citizenship learning tends towards high-level thinking skills and that efforts to delineate individual skills or subsections are not helpful.

In their review into the impact of citizenship education on learners, Deakin-Crick et al. (2005) identify a number of studies which appear to demonstrate a clear and measurable impact on the students. The range of indicators in these studies highlights the variety of ways in which citizenship education outcomes can be measured. Some studies focused on measurements of attitudes towards civic participation (Melchior, 1999), others attempted to measure students' reasoning about

Extract from Short Course GCSE Mark Scheme for Active Citizenship Coursework

Assessment objective 2: obtain, explain and interpret different kinds of information	Assessment objective 3: plan and evaluate the citizenship activities in which they have participated
9–10 marks	
• Detailed, structured in depth explanation of the activity	• Comprehensive demonstration of their learning from a range of experiences
• Background and context fully investigated and explained with reference to selected evidence and showing an appreciation of the complexity of issues	• An in depth reflection on and critical evaluation of experiences
• Detailed explanation of the impact of the activity on others using specific relevant examples from people they worked with	• Evaluation of the planning processes, and problem-solving strategies used with reference to specific examples
	• Evaluation of the contribution of others recognising their different perceptions
	• Examples of how they facilitated the participation of others
	• A clear reflection on how they might build upon the experience in future

(OCR, 2003)

human relationships (Beyer and Presseisen, 1995), whilst others focused on behavioural impacts, such as rates of absenteeism and referrals for misbehaviour (Garcia-Obregon et al., 2000). A similar range of diverse outcomes was reported by schools participating in an Australian review of values education (Curriculum Corporation, 2003), which focused on character education and moral reasoning approaches, which are obviously related to Deakin-Crick's affective dimension of citizenship. Schools reported on teacher and student views about the school atmosphere, feelings about whether people felt they were treated with respect and judgements about the quality of teacher-student relationships. Whilst many schools felt able to report positive outcomes, few were able to produce what might be seen as reliable assessment data, and the report concluded that very few research projects have been constructed in such a way that firm conclusions can be drawn from values education studies (Curriculum Corporation, 2003: 184–185).

HOW COULD WE ASSESS CITIZENSHIP EDUCATION?

Richardson (2006) found that many teachers were suspicious of assessment in citizenship, often through a fear that it tends to drive the curriculum. However, even in her small sample of schools, she discovered teachers were using a combination of formal examinations, class tests, extended writing, presentations, portfolios and peer assessment. In this final section, we will look briefly at some of this variety of approaches to assessing citizenship education.

The IEA Civics Education Study (Torney-Purta et al., 2001) provides an example of how tests might be constructed to include a variety of questions aiming to explore different aspects of students' understanding and skills development. These were carefully developed using a range of statistical tests to ensure

reliability; however, validity remains a perennial problem and a particular challenge for test writers is how to construct tests which actually measure citizenship understanding rather than merely reflect literacy levels. This is especially important given the frequency with which citizenship teachers ask students to locate information in newspaper sources or examine constitutional documents (Chall and Henry, 1991 quoted in Niklova and Lehman, 2003). The following examples provide an illustration of what such tests for 14-year-olds looked like.

Example of a question assessing content knowledge

In a democratic country (society) having many organizations for people to join is important because this provides:

(a) A group to defend members who are arrested
(b) Many sources of taxes for the government
(c) Opportunities to express different points of view
(d) A way for the government to tell the people about new laws

(Torney-Purta et al., 2001)

In responding to this question, rated as one of the easiest in the test, respondents needed to acknowledge the 'general role of institutional pluralism' in order to correctly identify answer (c) (Niklova and Lehman, 2003: 376).

Example of a question assessing interpretive skills

'We citizens have had enough!
A vote for the Silver Party means a vote for higher taxes
It means an end to economic growth and a waste of our economic resources
Vote instead for economic growth
Vote for more money left in everyone's wallet!
Let's not waste another 4 years! Vote for the Gold Party'

This is an election leaflet (political advertisement) which has probably been issued by:

(a) The Silver Party
(b) A party or group in opposition to (running against) the Silver Party
(c) A group which tries to be sure elections are fair
(d) The Silver Party and Gold Party together

(Torney-Purta et al., 2001)[1]

This question is again selected as one of the easiest examples and this was rated as being below average in terms of demand.

The correct answer, (b), was identified by 65 per cent of 14-year-olds on average, and by 75 per cent of English respondents (Kerr et al., 2002).

Of course, the problem with such questions is that it is impossible to know why a student chose an answer, and alongside the phenomenon of the 'educated guess', teachers also have to be aware that some students may select the right answer for entirely the wrong reasons (Black, 1998: 83). In addition, it is actually fairly time and resource consuming to construct and test the reliability of such tools, although this process may be aided by the National Center for Learning and Citizenship's web-based database (NCLC, 2007), which provides teachers and researchers with access to a variety of tried and tested questions linked to various domains. Nevertheless, there are issues with how such tests are administered, for example when used for evaluation purposes students may not perceive them as particularly important and not give them their full effort (Niemi, 2000), whereas when they are used as a high stakes tests, there is a temptation for teachers to teach to the test. Even if these problems are avoided, these responses can only really provide a snapshot of isolated elements of knowledge and do not help teachers assess the extent to which students understand complex concepts and connections and are able to use them in relevant contexts. For these reasons, other test items are designed to be open-ended and to provide students with an opportunity to develop their own response. These are inevitably harder to assess, and often require more subjective judgements, as students have more freedom to interpret the question in idiosyncratic ways but they do provide the opportunity to explore students' understanding in greater depth. Such open-ended tasks will obviously be useful for class teachers, trying to 'gain understanding of the child's understanding' (von Glaserfeld, 1989: 14) to inform their teaching strategies. They are also used in some of the larger national programmes discussed above, for example, in the Australian *National Assessment Program* the following question appeared:

Example of an open-ended question

'Jenny is walking along the street and has some rubbish to get rid of. She knows it is against the law to litter, but there are no bins around. She also knows it is very unlikely that she will get caught and get a fine.
In this situation, why is it *not* okay for Jenny to drop her rubbish on the ground?
Give what you think is the *most important* reason.'

(Curriculum Corporation, 2006: 27)

Advice to markers includes a brief set of level descriptors:

- Level 1 – response reiterates legal aspects
- Level 2 – response refers to environmental effect and shows greater complexity
- Level 3 – response refers to Jenny's sense of social responsibility.

Answers enabled the marker to infer (a) students' understanding of how internal ethical values influence behaviour and (b) their awareness of the impact of one's actions on others (Curriculum Corporation, 2006: 31–2). Even if one altered the question to allow students to say whether they thought it was or was not okay for Jenny to litter, the nature of the question still enables students to respond in ways which provide insight into the depth of their understanding of such issues. The marking levels identify similar features to those identified by Rowe (above), and the higher level mirrors Kohlberg's higher stages of moral reasoning (Kohlberg, 1969 in Halstead and Pike, 2006). This explicit focus on moral development calls into question the extent to which assessment in citizenship is similar to assessment in other subjects – is it appropriate, for example, to assign scores to these levels in the way that we might score a student's ability to use grammar conventions in English or their ability to solve algebra problems in mathematics?

We also need to be careful in the contruction of these assessment criteria that we do not end up focusing on what is easy to measure, and forget the aims of citizenship education.

Wrigley (2003: 41–2) is fearful that this process is already underway:

> Now that education for citizenship has been introduced, we will need to ensure that it isn't undermined by mindframes of accountability. Already multiple choice tests are being introduced by examination boards, which may serve to trivialise learning. Official guidelines to teachers classify three different levels of social understanding in the most absurd manner ... Issues such as poverty, racism, globalisation are marginalised, distorted and trivialised when treated this way.

Rather than the teacher having always to adopt the role of ultimate arbiter and grade-giver, the portfolio can provide a mechanism which starts with learner choice and encourages dialogue and discussion. Harrison goes so far as to claim that portfolios might help educators bridge the 'chasm between the liberal positions of our pedagogy and the coercive positions of our assessment' (Harrison, 2004 quoted in Halstead and Pike, 2006: 158). Klenowski (1996: 11) recognises this potential when she argues that the role of students' evaluation in the process of maintaining a portfolio would be difficult to achieve 'without corresponding changes to pedagogy and the curriculum.' Such changes include (a) a commitment to constructivist pedagogy with the teacher adopting the role of facilitator; (b) a recognition that learning is socially embedded and that much learning happens in collaboration with others; and (c) a commitment to help students become adept at self-management and self-regulation (Klenowski, 2002: 138). Klenowski herself discusses a range of examples where portfolio assessment has been developed in place of formal examinations, but still leading to vocational qualifications (Klenowski, 2002). However in England, there have been some concerns about the bureaucratic burden associated with such approaches. One might argue that this is because such programmes did not fully engage with the pedagogical challenges outlined above. In a more optimistic case study, Meier and Schwarz (1999) describe how one school has embedded portfolio pedagogy across the life of the school. All students present portfolios to a graduation committee and in order to use the portfolio to its full potential the school management has introduced smaller classes, teacher collaboration time, parental involvement, and curriculum flexibility all of which contribute to an ethos in which presenting one's portfolio is seen as a key moment in one's education.

CONCLUSION

We have seen that defining subject knowledge, which is often assumed to be the least complex area, can be contentious and that methods for testing it are often limited. It is not easy in practice to separate the domain of subject knowledge from the moral dimension to citizenship education. We have also seen how difficult it is to define skills separately from these other domains, for example, debate and argument are linked to subject knowledge and the ability to strike an appropriate attitude towards one's opponent, which might entail some degree of moral judgement. In active citizenship too this difficulty arises and there is no consensus about whether how to assess the experience for skills development, as distinct from the knowledge gained through the experience.

The diverse range of factors used to assess the outcomes of citizenship projects, especially active citizenship and service learning projects, is important in demonstrating the wide-ranging effects of citizenship education. It is also though a problem for assessment. Congruence between teaching objectives, learning activities and assessment criteria is a key element to constructing meaningful assessment opportunities and this is difficult when the assessment criteria are so broad. Webb (2006) draws our attention to the gap that often exists between the intended curriculum that teachers set out to teach, the enacted curriculum that students experience and the assessed curriculum, which is embodied in examinations and tests. The more teachers engage in a professional dialogue about the precise nature of the area or domain being taught, the more likely it will be that these three curricula will be aligned (SCASS, 2006). However, the examples considered in this chapter indicate that there is a need to analyse and define the domains of citizenship education more effectively, and to clearly distinguish between the types of outcomes teachers will be expected to measure and report.

In the meantime, there is still something to be said for the notion of teachers developing a clear vision of their subject and continuing to apply their craft knowledge to support students to make progress. Tolstoy (quoted in Schön, 1983: 66) wrote that:

> The best teacher will be he who has at his tongue's end the explanation of what is bothering the pupil. These explanations give the teacher the knowledge of the greatest possible number of methods, the ability of inventing new methods and, above all, not a blind adherence to one method but the conviction that all methods are one-sided, and that the best method would be the one which would answer best to all the possible difficulties incurred by a pupil, that is, not a method but an art and talent.

This process starts with what we would today call diagnostic assessment, but it reminds us that the diagnosis itself depends on the student, their needs and ways of understanding. Tests and formal strategies for assessment may have a part to play in this diagnosis, but so do listening, observing and reflecting. It is ultimately in this sense, in this creative response, that teachers will help their students make progress and grow as citizens, and along the way be successful in citizenship education.

NOTES

1 Many of the test items are now available at: www.wam.umd.edu/~iea

REFERENCES

American Psychological Association (1997) *Learner-Centred Psychological Principles: A Framework for School Reform and Redesign*. Available www.apa.org/ed/cpse/LCPP.pdf [Accessed on 17/5/07]

Appiah, K.A. (2006) *Cosmopolitanism: Ethics in a World of Strangers*. London: Allen Lane.

Arthur, J. and Wright, D. (2001) *Teaching Citizenship in the Secondary School*. London: David Fulton.

Assessment Reform Group (1999) *Assessment for Learning: Beyond the Black Box*. Cambridge: University of Cambridge School of Education.

Assessment Reform Group (2002) *Testing, Motivation and Learning*. Cambridge: University of Cambridge School of Education.

Ball, Stephen J. (2007) *Education plc: Understanding Private Sector Participation in Public Sector Education*. London: Routledge.

Beck, J. (1998) *Morality and Citizenship in Education*. London: Cassell.

Beyer, F.S. and Presseisen, B.Z. (1995) *Facing History and Ourselves: Initial Evaluation of an Inner-City Middle School Implementation*, Philadelphia, PA: Research for Better Schools Inc.

Black, P. (1998) *Testing: Friend or Foe? The Theory and Practice of Assessment and Testing*. London: Routledge.

Black, P. and Wiliam, D. (1998) *Inside the Black Box: Raising Standards Through Classroom Assessment*. London: King's College London School of Education.

Black, P., Harrison, C., Lee, C., Marshall, B. and Wiliam, D. (2002) *Working Inside the Black Box: Assessment for Learning in the Classroom*. London: King's College London Department of Education and Professional Studies.

Black, P., Harrison, C., Lee, C., Marshall, B. and Wiliam, D. (2003) *Assessment for Learning: Putting it into Practice*. Maidenhead: Open University Press.

Boud, D., Keogh, R. and Walker, D. (1985) 'Promoting Reflection in Learning: A Model' in David Boud, Rosemary Keogh and David Walker (eds) *Reflection: Turning Experience into Learning*. New York: Nicols Publishing.

Breslin, T. (2006) 'Calling Citizenship to Account: Issues of Assessment and Progression' in Tony Breslin and Barry DuFour (eds) *Developing Citizens*. London: Hodder Murray.

Burnham, S. and Brow, G. (2004) 'Assessment without level descriptions', *Teaching History*, 115: 5–15.

Chall, J.S. and Henry, D. (1991) 'Reading and Civic Literacy: Are We Literate Enough to Meet our Civic Responsibilities?' in Sandra Stotsky (ed.) *Connecting Civic Education and Language Education*. New York: Teachers College Press.

Cooper-Loomis, S. and Bourque, M.L. (eds) (2001) *National Assessment of Educational Progress Achievement Levels, 1992–1998 for Civics*. Washington DC: National Assessment Governing Body.

Curriculum Corporation (2003) *Values Education Study. Final report August 2003*. Carlton South Victoria: Curriculum Corporation.

Curriculum Corporation (2006) *National Assessment Program – Civics and Citizenship Years 6 and 10 Report 2004*. Carlton South Victoria: Ministerial Council on Education, Employment, Training and Youth Affairs.

Dann, R. (2002) *Promoting Assessment As Learning: Improving the Learning Process*. London: RoutledgeFalmer.

Davies, I. (2003) *Procedural Concepts and Citizenship Education: A Small Scale Study Undertaken with PGCE Students*. Available www.citized.info [Accessed on 17/5/07]

Deakin-Crick, R., Taylor, M., Tew, M., Samuel, E., Durant, K. and Ritchie, S. (2005) 'A systematic review of the impact of citizenship education on student learning and achievement', in *Research Evidence in Education Library*. London: EPPI Centre, Social Science Research Unit, Institute of Education.

Dennison, B. and Kirk, R. (1990) *Do, Review, Learn, Apply: A Simple Guide to Experiential Learning*. London: Blackwell.

Dewey, J. (1938) *Experience and Education*. New York, Macmillan.

Douglas, A. and Hudson, A. (2003) 'Establishing a community of practice for citizenship education at Deptford Green School', in Sally I., Martin B. and Miles T. (eds) *Enhancing Personal, Social and Health Education: Challenging Practice, Changing Worlds*. London: RoutledgeFalmer. pp. 186–214.

Eurydice (2005) *Citizenship Education at School in Europe*, Brussels: Eurydice European Unit. Available www.eurydice.org [accessed on 7/5/07]

Garcia-Obregon, Z., Trevino, J., Uribe-Moreno, S. and Zuniga, S. (2000) *The Effectiveness of a School Based Service Learning Program 'Community Connection' at a South Texas Middle School*. Texas: South Texas Research and Development Centre.

Halstead, J. Mark and Pike, M. (2006) *Citizenship and Moral Education: Values in Action*. London: Routledge.

Harrison, C. (2004) *Understanding Reading Development*. London: Sage/Paul Chapman.

Hoffman, B. (1978) *The Tyranny of Testing*. New York: Greenwood Press.

Inman, S., Buck, M. and Burke, H. (1998) *Assessing Personal and Social Development: Measuring the Unmeasurable?* London: Falmer Press,

Johnston, C. (1996) *Unlocking the Will to Learn*. Thousand Oaks, CA: Corwin Press.

Kerr, D. (2002) 'Assessment and evaluation in citizenship education', Paper presented at British Council Seminar in Beijing, China, July 2002, Slough: National Foundation for Educational Research.

Kerr, D., Lines, A., Blenkinsop, S. and Schagen, I. (2002) *England's Results from the IEA International Citizenship Education Study: What Citizenship and Education mean to 14 year olds*, Research Report 375, Slough: National Foundation for Educational Research,

Klenowski, V. (1996) 'Connecting assessment and learning', Paper presented at the British Educational Research Association Annual Conference, Lancaster University, 12–15 September.

Klenowski, V. (2002) *Developing Portfolios for Learning and Assessment: Processes and Principles*. London: RoutledgeFalmer.

Kohlberg, L. (1969) 'Stage and sequence: the cognitive developmental approach to socialisation', in David Gosling (ed.) *Handbook of Socialisation, Theory and Research*, Chicago: Rand McNally.

Kolb, D. (1984) *Experiential Learning*. London: Prentice Hall.

Lee, P. and Ashby, R. (2000) 'Progression in historical understanding among students ages 7–14', in Peter N. Stearns; Peter Seixas and Sam Wineburg (eds) *Knowing, Teaching and Learning History*. New York: New York University Press.

Lehman, R. H. (1990) 'Reliability and generalizability of ratings and compositions', *Studies in Educational Evaluation*, 16: 501–512.

Meier, D. and Schwarz, P. (1999) 'Central Park East Secondary School: The hard part is making it happen' in Michael W. Apple and James A. Beane (eds) *Democratic Schools: Lessons from the Chalkface*. Buckingham: Open University Press.

Melchior, A. (1999) *Summary Report: National Evaluation of Learn and Serve America*. Waltham, MA: Center for Human Resources, Brandeis University.

Moon, J. (2004) *A Handbook of Reflective and Experiential Learning*. London: RoutledgeFalmer.

National Center for Learning and Citizenship (2007) *Civic Assessment Resources*. Available www.ecs.org/qna [accessed 15/7/07]

Niemi, R.G. (2000) 'Invited commentary: uses and limitations of the NAEP 1998 civics assessment', *Education Statistics Quarterly*, 1 (4). Available http://nces.ed.gov/ programs/ quarterly/

Nikolova, R. and Lehman, R.H. (2003) 'On the dimensionality of the cognitive test used in the IEA civic education study: analyses and implication', *European Educational Research Journal*, 2 (3): 370–383.

Oates, K.K. and Leavitt, L.H. (2003) *Service Learning and Learning Communities: Tools for Integration and Assessment*. Washington DC: Association of American Colleges and Universities.

Oxford Cambridge and RSA Examinations (OCR) (2003) *GCSE Citizenship Studies: Short Course. Teacher Support: Coursework Guidance Booklet*. Available www.ocr.org.uk/ Data/publications/teacher_support_and_cou rsework_guidance/GCSE_(Shor5689.pdf [accessed 1/6/07]

Popham, J.W. (1978) *Criterion-referenced Measurement*. Eaglewood Cliffs, NJ: Prentice Hall.

Quigley, C.N., Branson, M.S. and Craig, E. (1995) *Issues Concerning a National Assessment of Civics. National Assessment of Educational Progress (NAEP)*. Washington DC: Center for Civic Education.

Richardson, M. (2006) '"You're a Grade 'A' Citizen," Teachers' and students' perceptions of assessing citizenship', *Reflecting Education*, 2 (2): 104–118.

Rowe, D. (2005) 'The development of political thinking in year 8 and 9 students: an English perspective', *International Journal of Citizenship and Teacher Education*, 1 (1): 97–110.

Schön, D.A. (1983) *The Reflective Practitioner*. Aldershot: Ashgate.

Schrag, F. (1999) 'Why Foucault Now?' *Journal of Curriculum Studies*, 31 (4): 375–83.

Service Learning (undated) *Compendium of Assessment and Research Tools (CART)*. Available http://servicelearning.org/ resources/ links_collection/index.php?popup_id=134 [accessed 19/6/07]

State Collaboration on Assessment and Student Standards (SCASS) (2006) *Aligning Assessment to Guide the Learning of All Students: Six Reports*. Washington DC: Council of Chief State School Officers.

Steiner, J., Bächtiger, A., Spörndli, M. and Steenbergen, M.R. (2004) *Deliberative Politics in Action: Analysing Parliamentary Discourse*. Cambridge: Cambridge University Press.

Summers, P. (1996) *Standards of Excellence: Toward Becoming a Successful Citizen*. New York: Windsor Central School District.

Tolstoy, L. (1967) 'On teaching the rudiments' in Leo Weiner (ed.) *Tolstoy on Education*. Chicago: University of Chicago Press.

Torney-Purta, J., Lehman, R., Oswald, H. and Shulz, W. (2001) *Citizenship and Education in Twenty-eight Countries: Civic Knowledge and Engagement at Age Fourteen*. Amsterdam: International Association for the Evaluation of Educational Achievement (IEA).

Turnbull, J. (2002) 'Values in educating for citizenship: sources, influence and assessment', *Pedagogy, Culture and Society*, 10 (1): 123–134.

Von Glaserfeld, E. (1989) 'Learning as a constructive activity', in Patricia Murphy and Bob Moon (eds) *Developments in Learning and Assessment*. London: Hodder and Stoughton.

Vontz, T.S. (1997) *Strict Scrutiny: An Analysis of National Standards in Civic Education through the Perspectives of Contemporary Theorists*. Indiana: Indiana University.

Webb, N.L. (2006) 'The Web alignment tool: development, refinement and dissemination', in SCASS *Aligning Assessment to Guide the Learning of All Students: Six Reports*.

Washington DC: Council of Chief State School Officers.

Winona State University (undated): www.winona.edu/AIR/rubrics.htm [accessed 15/7/07]

Wood, R. (1991) *Assessment and Testing*. Cambridge: Cambridge University Press.

World Schools Debating Championship (WSDC) (undated) www.schoolsdebate.com/guides.asp [accessed 15/7/07]

Wrigley, T. (2003) *Schools of Hope: A New Agenda for School Improvement*. Stroke on Trent: Trentham Books.

Index

Tables are given in italics